The Everyman Dictionary of
Religion and Philosophy

OTHER BOOKS BY
GEDDES MacGREGOR

Angels: Ministers of Grace
Apostles Extraordinary
Immortality and Human Destiny (ed.)
The Christening of Karma
Reincarnation as a Christian Hope
The Gospels as a Mandala of Wisdom
The Nicene Creed
Scotland Forever Home
Gnosis
Reincarnation in Christianity
He Who Let Us Be
The Rhythm of God
Philosophical Issues in Religous Thought
So Help Me God
A Literary History of the Bible
The Sense of Absence
God Beyond Doubt
The Hemlock and the Cross
The Coming Reformation
Introduction to Religious Philosophy
The Bible in the Making
Corpus Christi
The Thundering Scot
The Vatican Revolution
The Tichborne Impostor
From a Christian Ghetto
Les Frotières de la morale et de la religion
Christian Doubt
Aesthetic Experience in Religion

GEDDES MacGREGOR

The Everyman Dictionary of
Religion and Philosophy

J. M. Dent & Sons Ltd
LONDON

First published this edition 1990
Originally published in the United States by
Paragon House under the title
Dictionary of Religion and Philosophy, 1989

Copyright © by Geddes MacGregor

Printed in Great Britain by
Butler & Tanner Ltd, Frome and London for
J. M. Dent & Sons Ltd
91 Clapham High Street, London SW4 7TA

British Library Cataloguing in Publication Data
is available upon request

ISBN 0–460–87020–3

CONTENTS

CONTENTS

PREFACE

The primary focus of this dictionary is on religious studies. Since any serious study of religion entails some understanding of the philosophical implicates of religious beliefs and practices, many entries relate to philosophical issues and the thinkers who have addressed them, ranging from Plato and Kant to William James and Charles Peirce. While the entries and the bibliographies at the end of the book include a wide spectrum of religions associated with the Orient, such as the Hindu, Buddhist, Jain, Sikh, Zorōastrian, and Islamic traditions, an emphasis will be found on the Judeo-Christian tradition. This emphasis is warranted not only because it is the tradition that predominates in the West, to which most readers of the book are likely to belong, but also because many of us in the West often do not know our own tradition as well as do others looking at it from outside.

A dictionary such as this is a practical tool. It is designed for serious students, whether working for a university degree or simply enriching and enlarging their understanding of the intellectual and cultural worlds around them. It is the student's personal desk companion, a reliable and comprehensive source of information that will be consulted more than occasionally in academic and other intellectual pursuits. For a special project and more extensive research, the student may need to consult a multivolume encyclopedia far too expensive for the majority of individuals to acquire, such as *The Encyclopedia of Religion,* under the general editorship of Mircea Eliade, 17 vols. (New York: Macmillan, 1987). Highly specialized works may also be helpful for particular projects, such as *Harper's Dictionary of Hinduism* (New York: Harper & Row, 1977) and *The Oxford Dictionary of the Christian Church* (2nd edition), edited by F. L. Cross and E. A. Livingstone (Oxford: Oxford University Press, 1974, revised 1977).

While the entries include a large number that are philosophical rather than religious, these entries have mostly a direct bearing on the serious study of religious concerns, such as Meaning and

Truth, the Vienna Circle, Logical Fallacies, Spinoza, Mind-Body, and Monism.

Having conferred with experts in the writing of so many of the entries, my indebtedness to these is such that to list all would be tedious, while to mention some would be invidious. My gratitude to all who have listened to my inquiries and answered them so as to enhance this monograph of mine is none the less as profound as it will be enduring.

Although some entries are so obviously important that their inclusion is undebatable, the choice of others may seem arbitrary. The work is the result of a professional lifetime of the study of religion, which has shown me repeatedly that any compiler of a book of this kind must in some measure exercise personal judgment in what is included or excluded. By no means can the compiler expect that others will always agree with any such choice. No doubt my inclination has tended to be to emphasize what would have helped me most in my own beginnings in this very demanding field of study and what would have most helped the generations of students I have taught over the years. My hope is that the updated accumulation of my life's study compressed into a handy desk companion will so serve students that they will come to look upon it not merely as a tool but as a friend.

Geddes MacGregor

NOTE ON SANSKRIT
PRONUNCIATION

The phonetic value assigned here to transliterated Sanskrit vowels and consonants is approximate and for elementary purposes only.

a	as in	b*ut*	kh	as in	ba*ck h*ome
ā		*fa*ther	l		du*ll*
ai		*eye*	ḷ		*l*ength
au		pr*ou*d	m		*m*an
b		*b*oy	n		*n*othing
bh		a*bh*or	ñ		ti*n*ge
c		*ch*icken	o		*so*
ch		chur*ch-h*ouse	p		*p*an
d		*d*ie	ph		u*p-h*ill
dh		a*dh*esive	r		*r*ow
e		*ei*ght	s		*s*it
g		*g*ull	ś		ki*ss*
gh		do*g-h*ouse	ṣ		*s*ugar
h		*h*ip	t		*t*ip
i		h*i*p	th		ca*t-h*eaven
ī		d*ee*p	u		b*oo*k
j		*j*am	ū		r*u*le
jh		he*dge-h*og	v		*v*eer
k		*k*eep	y		*y*ell

Various exceptions and refinements are ignored here. They can be expressed by phonetic symbols used by the International Phonetic Association, as can the sounds and intonations of any language. What is provided here is merely a safeguard against gross mispronunciation. E.g., the Sanskrit word *karma* is pronounced more nearly *kurma* than *kahrma*, although when treated as an anglicized word it is of course pronounced accordingly: *kahrma*. Several terms such as *Upanishads* and *darshana* are so anglicized that they are both written and spoken according to English usage. Many terms, however, in the vocabulary of Hinduism have no anglicized forms and must therefore be pronounced according to Sanskrit rules. The same principle applies, of course, to temporary imports from other languages such as Latin, French, or German.

DICTIONARY OF
RELIGION
AND PHILOSOPHY

A

Aaron. Although Aaron comes down to us in Hebrew tradition as the brother of Moses and Miriam and being often associated with Moses (e.g., he accompanied Moses to the summit of Sinai [Exodus 24.1]), accounts about him vary. He and his sons are designated priests (Exodus 18.1 ff.) and he is installed among them as high priest (Leviticus 8.1–10.20); yet much obscurity attends his historical character and function. He is represented as important, but he is dwarfed by the figure of Moses, who is the undoubted leader of the Hebrew people. Since Moses, however, is less gifted as a speaker, Aaron (according to Exodus 4.14 and 7.1) is appointed to be his mouthpiece. Whatever the historical facts may be, he has come down in tradition as the symbol of the Hebrew priesthood, although it seems clear that before the construction of the Temple of Solomon and to some extent after that, the Israelites worshipped at various local sanctuaries, each served by its own hereditary priesthood. Rival claims emerged, however, from time to time (e.g., between Aaron and Levi), and the basis of these various claims is much wrapped in obscurity. Aaron died before the Israelites reached Canaan, and his priestly vestments were transferred to his son Eleazar.

Abailard, Peter. See **Abelard.**

Abba. This word is a form of the Aramaic *ab*, used as familiar speech by children, probably somewhat as "dada" is used in the English-speaking world. New Testament writers used it in some instances alongside the Greek, indicating its use in the Aramaic form by early Christians (e.g., Romans 8.15 and Galatians 4.6) following the usage attributed to Jesus himself in Mark 14.36. Its use plainly implies the closeness and intimacy of the relationship perceived between God and his children: in the Household of Faith, although God as Sovereign and Creator is unique and apart from all his creatures, he invites his creatures to address him with the loving intimacy of a little child lisping at his parent's knee.

Abbé. Nowadays the ordinary designation for any priest in French-speaking countries not a member of a religious order: *Monsieur l'abbé.* Originally it was used only of the abbot of a monastery and still is so used in designations such as *Le Très Révérend Père Abbé.*

Abbess. Title accorded to superiors of certain orders of nuns, notably Benedictines but also Franciscans and others. Benedictine abbesses are elected for life, wear the ring, and carry the staff. The title occurs in an inscription as early as 514.

Abbot, Ezra (1819–1884). American biblical scholar, Unitarian, born in Maine. In 1856 became assistant librarian at Harvard and in 1872 professor at the Harvard Divinity School.

Abbot, George (1562–1633). Archbishop of Canterbury, a Balliol man, he became, in 1597, Master of University College, Oxford and in 1600 Dean of Winchester. Sympathetic to the Puritan cause, he became Bishop of Lichfield in 1609, and in 1611 Archbishop of Canterbury. In hunting he accidentally shot a gamekeeper and was temporarily suspended as technically a "man of blood" and therefore unable to exercise ecclesiastical functions. James I signed a dispensation, and he resumed his functions. He crowned Charles I to whom, however, his opinions against the Divine Right of kings were unwelcome.

Abbreviator. An official at the Vatican at one time charged with the duty of preparing writs for the collation of church dignities. So named from the many abbreviations used in papal documents. The functions are nowadays performed by a group of protonotaries.

Abduction. In logic, two principal forms of logical reasoning have been recognized: see **Induction** and **Deduction**. Aristotle, however, used the term "abduction" in reference to types of deductive inference that do not provide the certain conclusion that is expected of a valid syllogism, although they yield what seems nevertheless a plausible argument. The American philosopher Charles Sanders Peirce (1839–1914) used the term specifically as one of three forms of logical inference, along with deduction and induction, although yielding only probability, not certainty. Example: Having observed a fact that seems to have gone unnoticed by everyone, so far as I can determine, I suggest a possible explanation that, if it were true, would make the observed fact a normally observable one. The suggested explanation may therefore be possibly correct. The value of such a procedure lies in the progress toward the discovery of novel truths that such disciplined speculation may expedite, while a certain conclusion is not yet obtainable.

Abel. According to Genesis, Abel was the second son of Adam and the brother of Cain who, out of envy, murdered him (Genesis 4.2 ff.). All indications point to a Mesopotamian origin for the story. In both Jewish and Christian tradition, as Cain became a symbol of evil, Abel became a symbol of righteous action. The story reflects the natural conflict that had given rise to a feud between the peasant class (represented by Cain) and that of the nomadic herdsmen (represented by Abel), and the nar-

rator plainly is supporting the latter and denigrating the former. The symbolism and imagery, although long forgotten, survived in the mind of the great Latin Father of the Christian Church, Augustine, who in his *De civitate Dei* (a classic work for medieval political theory on Church/State relationship in the West) employs them prominently: Cain comes to be the symbol of Babylon, Abel of Jerusalem in an emerging age in which Augustine saw Babylon (the State) as good (in the sense that it is better than anarchy) while Jerusalen (the Church) is better and must in the long run prevail over the State.

Abelard, Peter (1079–1142). The most important and probably the most influential Christian philosopher in the Middle Ages before Thomas Aquinas. Of Breton stock, he was born at Pallet, near Nantes, and studied under Roscelin, William of Champeaux, and Anselm of Laon. On the fashionable problem of the Universals he argued, on the one hand, against the extreme Realism of William of Champeaux and on the other, against the too simplistic Nominalism of Roscelin, holding instead a position for which he found support in Aristotle, that only individuals exist and that the *nomina* (names of things) are derived from them by a process of abstraction, so that the universal has only a logical function. In ethics he so emphasized intention that he practically ignored the distinction between good and evil acts in themselves.

His brilliant teaching career at Paris, where he had attracted vast audiences, ended in 1118 with the tragic outcome of his love affair with Héloise, the story of which is well known. For his teaching on the doctrine of the Trinity and other theological questions he was much persecuted by influential churchmen, notably by Bernard of Clairvaux. Yet he continued to exert great influence on both the philosophers and the theologians of his day.

His teaching included an opposition to the customary respect for authority as such. He taught that the individual thinker should be free to judge from evidence alone without dependence on what traditional authorities had said. Against the fashion of his day, he taught the importance of doubt, which leads to inquiry, through which one is led to truth. His contribution to medieval logic is of notable historical importance. His last years were spent at Cluny.

The wide spectrum of his intellectual interests is reflected in the range of his writings, which include: *Sic et Non* (Yes and No), 1122; *Theologia christiana*, 1124, *Theologia summi boni* (Theology of the Supreme Good), *c.* 1120; *Scito teipsum* (Know thyself), a work on ethics, various treatises on logic, several hymns, his *Historia calamitatum*, an account of his personal tribulations, and his letters to Héloise. His name Abailard is conventionally but less correctly spelled "Abelard".

Abelites. A small sect in north Africa, known to Augustine, by whose time it had ceased to exist. Members, while holding marriage to be obligatory, abstained from all sexual activity, each couple adopting a boy and a girl. They were so named after Abel, who according to Genesis was the son of Adam and Eve and according to tradition had become the symbol of purity and innocence in contradistinction to Cain.

Ābhāsvaras. In Sanskrit the term signifies "the Shining Ones." It is applied in Hinduism to a group of sixty-four deities attendant upon Śiva, who dwell in an ethereal dimension of being and preside over enlightenment. See **Śiva.**

Abhaya-Hasta. In both Hinduism and Buddhism the *abhaya* is a gesture of reassurance and encouragement performed (somewhat like the Christian priestly blessing) by raising the right hand (*hasta*) with palm extended toward the recipient.

Abhimantraṇa. A rite of consecration in Hinduism performed by the recitation of certain *mantras*. See **Mantra.**

Abiathar. After Saul's slaughter of the priests (I Samuel 22.9 ff.), he fled to David, taking the priestly oracle Urim and Thummim and using them in David's service. He figures along with Zadok as a priest in the service of David (I Samuel 23.6 ff; 30.7 ff.).

Abjuration, Oath of. An oath renouncing the Stuart dynasty, required of all taking public office in England. First proposed in 1690 although not mandatory till 1701. In 1778 it was required of all Roman Catholics. Abolished in 1858.

Ablutions. In the Mass, after Communion, the priest cleanses the chalice first with wine, then with water. The ceremony was introduced about the 10th c. and varies in detail according to the rite, e.g., in the Greek and Mozarabic rites it is performed privately after the Mass.

Abortion. The termination of a pregnancy before the fetus has reached viability, i.e., capacity for independent existence. When this occurs is medically disputable and laws fixing a date (e.g., twenty-four or twenty-eight weeks after the last menstrual period) vary. In medical usage, abortion may be (1) spontaneous (popularly called miscarriage), which occurs in about one pregnancy in five, or (2) induced by dilation of the cervix, drugs, or mechanical intervention. The ethics of induced abortion is highly controversial, with opinions ranging from (a) total opposition to induced abortion in all circumstances, based on the view that life begins at the moment of conception and that from there on the fetus has the same moral right to life as any other human being, to (b) a permissive stance based on the view that a woman has the same right over the fetus in her body, until it is viable, that she has over the rest of her own body. Between these extremes is a wide variety of opinions on the ethics of abortion, especially as it is affected by questions concerning the health, mental and physical, of mother or child. On the one hand one may point to cases of pregnancy resulting from, say, rape by a syphilitic lunatic or other unpromising circumstance likely to bring about much anguish and misery. On the other, one may show that the genetic result of any conception is never absolutely predictable and that some of the most unpromising pregnancies have resulted in offspring of the highest quality. Many of the greatest geniuses in human history, e.g., Leonardo da Vinci, have been illegitimate and therefore likely candidates for abortion, had the more "liberal" view prevailed. In Judaism, rabbinic opinion is generally against abortion but permits it if strong medical or social reasons warrant it. In Islam a similar moral tradition exists, with a perhaps more permissive interpretation tending to prevail. The Roman Catholic Church has traditionally opposed all induced abortion for whatever reason and the papal encyclical *Humae Vitae* (July 25, 1968) reasserted that position along with the prohibition of all "artificial" methods of birth control. Anglicans and other heirs of the Reformation, while emphasizing the moral tradition that upholds the sanctity of human life, would allow abortion in special cases. Abortion is universally condemned in Buddhism as fundamentally opposed to the principle of reverence for life. In other major religions it is generally looked upon with disapproval.

Abraham. Hebrew patriarch probably living about 1700 BCE. Venerated among Christians as well as Jews as an exemplar of the life of faith.

Abraham, Apocalypse of. An apocryphal writing, dating from probably the first century CE although the oldest extant text is Codex Sylvester, in Slavonic and dating from the 14th c., describes Abraham's conversion from idolatry (a legend based on Jewish tradition) and a series of visions culminating in the divine promise of deliverance of the elect. For English translation see G. H. Box, *The Apocalypse of Abraham.* London: S.P.C.K., 1918.

Abraham, Testament of. An apocryphal writing, possibly dating from the second century CE. and in widespread use in the Eastern Church in Greek and other languages from the fifth century CE. It describes how Abraham sees a vision of two roads, one to hell, the other to heaven. For English translation, see G. H. Box (London: S.P.C.K., 1927).

Absalom. Son of David and of Maacah, the daughter of Talmai, the king of Geshur (II Samuel 3.3). In revenge against his half-brother, Amnon, who had raped Absalom's full sister, Tamar, Absalom murdered Amnon (II Samuel 13.1 ff.) and then fled to Geshur. After many complex maneuvers, involving much duplicity, Absalom was defeated in a battle and fled from the scene on a mule, but his long hair, which he seems to have prized, became entangled in the branches of an oak. On his being discovered by one of David's soldiers who reported his discovery to Joab, the latter killed him, to the great grief of David, who deeply loved his son despite his transgressions and the political embarrassments he had brought to him (II Samuel 19.1 ff.).

Absolute. A term used by some philosophers to designate that which is independent of relation. Descartes, Fichte, Schelling, and Soloviev are among those who have used it, each in a way adapted to his own system. Nicholas of Cusa used it substantively to designate God, whom he accounted both the Absolute Maximum and the Absolute Minimum.

Absolute Idealism. The philosophical system of Hegel in which the whole of reality is conceived as the expression of an Idea that is independent of relation. Bradley, Bosanquet and McTaggart are among thinkers who represent this Hegelian influence in the English-speaking world.

Absolution. In the early Church absolution of repentant sinners was administered publicly after public performance of penance. The practice later gave way to private confession of sins to a priest who privately enjoined a penance to be performed and gave absolution in the name of God and the Church.

Abstinence. In contrast to fasting, which consists of denying oneself all food or allowing oneself very little food of any kind, abstinence is a penitential denial of certain kinds of food, e.g., flesh meat. The Christian Church abrogated in principle the dietary laws inherited from Judaism, but various forms of abstinence were practiced among Christians from early times. Clement of Alexandria and others mention as an established practice the abstinence from flesh meat on Fridays that became general in both East and West. Ancient religious Orders such as the Camaldolese, the Carthusians, and the Cistercians have traditionally abstained totally or almost totally from flesh meat, and in Eastern Orthodoxy the practice has been stricter and more extensive than in the West even for the faithful generally. The Reformers, however, renounced the practice. In Anglican tradition the practice of abstinence on Fridays has never been entirely lost and under Tractarian influence it has been strongly encouraged. Since the Second Vatican Council the Roman Catholic Church has de-emphasized the practice, which till then had been for centuries obligatory on all the faithful unless dispensed for special reasons.

Abstraction. From the Latin *abstrahere* (to draw from). In Aristotle, the process by which universal ideas are appropriated by the mind. The mind receives an image or sense datum of a substance and abstracts from that substance its form or essence. Example: Suppose that I have never before seen or heard of a lawnmower. On seeing one for the first time I may have difficulty in guessing what its purpose is. Then, on seeing it in action, my mind quickly perceives its function: I abstract from what I see the "form" or "essential nature" of lawnmowers. Locke, in the 17th c. used the term somewhat similarly: One observes various things and, noting the similarities and dissimilarities among them, draws out (abstracts) what is common to a group of them, e.g., chairs, all of which have, despite a wide variety in their appearance and structure, one common element—they are all designed for human beings to sit on. The term "abstraction" is also used in a specific technical sense in logic and in mathematics to designate that operation on a variable that produces a function.

Acacius of Caesarea. Early 4th c. Arian theologian. His extreme form of Arianism had a considerable following, and his followers had importance, although shortlived, as a theological school.

Academy. Platonic and Neoplatonic tradition has been much woven into Christian thought. The grove of olives in which Plato taught was called the Academy (*akadēmeia*). The work of the Academy (later known as the Old Academy) was continued under various leaders. In the 3rd c. BCE. Arcesilas of Pitanē, who introduced the skeptical doctrines traditionally called Pyrrhonism and engaged in controversy with the Stoics, was the founder of what has come to be known as the Second or Middle Academy. The skeptical attitude was further developed and a reconciliation with the Stoic school was effected in the first c. BCE. Antiochus of Ascalon, leader of the conciliatory movement, is the leading figure in the Second Academy. The Third Academy, whose principal figures are Carneades and Clitomachus, was more skeptical still and developed interest in probability theory. The School of Athens (*c.* 380–529 CE) is sometimes called the Fourth Academy. It was the most classical school of Neoplatonism. Related to this school was the Alexandrian School of Neoplatonism, which flourished from *c.* 430 CE to the Muslim conquest of Alexandria in 642. This school included many Christian members and others sympathetic to Christianity. These schools continued to exercise strong influence on Christian thought. The Florentine Academy, whose first head was Marsilio Ficino, was founded in the Quattrocento (15th c.) in the Platonic and Neoplatonic tradition, fostering a humanism that was deeply religious in spirit. In England the Cambridge Platonists in the 17th c. were, in their own way, in the same heritage.

Acarie, Madame (Barbe Jeanne Avrillot). See **Mary of the Incarnation**

Acceptants. Those who, in the Jansenist controversy, accepted the papal bull **Unigenitus** (1713).

Accident. A term used by Aristotle to designate a mode of being whose nature is to inhere in some other being, designated a substance; e.g., the greenness of foliage is said to be a mode of being inhering as "accident" in the "substance" of the foliage. The medieval thinkers, borrowing from Aristotle, developed, out of this distinction, a theory to explain the concept of Transubstantiation in the Eucharist: after the substance of the bread and wine has been changed into the Body and Blood of Christ, the accidents of the bread and wine remain (e.g., the whiteness of the bread, the redness of the wine, and the taste of both) although the substance has been changed. This doctrine of "accidents without a subject" came to be widely accepted in Catholic eucharistology, although never officially defined by the Church. The Reformers generally repudiated the notion and even the Council of Trent (1549–1560), instead of reasserting it, was content to make no mention of it, preferring to speak rather of the continuance of the *species* (kind) of bread and wine after their miraculous transformation into the Body and Blood of Christ.

Accidie. (Greek *akēdia*, "indifference") Term used in the Septuagint and later in a modified sense to signifiy the spiritual weariness or torpor that at times

especially affects monks and nuns. The standard remedy prescribed is perseverance in prayer.

Acoemetae. (Greek, *akoimētai* = the unsleeping ones) A group of Eastern Orthodox monks founded *c.* 400 devoted to poverty, missionary enterprise, and the singing of psalms perpetually in choir, which they achieved by relays changing guard. Eventually they embraced Nestorianism and suffered accordingly.

Acolyte. Traditionally, the highest of the four minor orders in the Roman Catholic Church. Their duties include lighting the candles, preparing the wine and water for Mass and assisting the celebrant, deacon, and subdeacon. In this sense we hear of them at Rome from about the middle of the third century. Today "altar boys" and other lay persons who assist the priest at Mass are commonly called "acolytes".

Acosmism. The term used by Hegel to designate the view that the only reality is God and that everything else in the universe is therefore unreal. It is doubtful whether any historically important philosophical view would strictly conform to that requirement.

Act. The term comes from the Latin *agere* (to do, to act) and corresponds to the Greek term *energeia*, which Aristotle contrasted with *dynamis* (act and potency respectively). The bulb I plant in the garden has the power to become a tulip and is in process of doing so. To the extent that it realizes itself by blooming into a tulip it is in *act*. Everything in the universe, however, is both in potency and in act; only God is simply *energeia*. The medieval schoolmen followed Aristotle closely here, calling God *actus purus* (pure act). Some modern philosophers have used the term "act" in other, non-traditional ways within their respective systems.

Acta Apostolicae Sedis. The official gazette of the Vatican, founded by Pius X in 1908 and first published in 1909.

Acta Sanctorum. An important series of lives of the saints begun by the Bollandists in the 17th century.

Action, Philosophy of. The philosophy of Maurice Blondel is sometimes so designated. See **Blondel, Maurice.**

Action Française. A French movement that began in 1898 and later became much associated with Charles Maurras, who, although not a believer in the Church's teaching, taught that France had a special duty to maintain Catholic culture and practice as expressions of the ancient Greco-Roman civilization. The Vatican at first looked with some sympathy on the movement, then wavered, and eventually forbade Catholics to participate in it. In the years before World War II, it was favored by the political right wing in France. Maurras was arrested and imprisoned for six years after the war and died in 1952.

Acton, John Emerich Edward Dalberg (Lord) (1834–1902). A learned Roman Catholic layman and friend of Döllinger. He opposed Ultramontanism, the *Syllabus Errorum* (1864), and papal Infallibility.

Acts, The Book of. Scholars almost universally recognize this book as a sequel to the Gospel according to Luke and dated probably between 70 and 85 CE. It emphasized the divine origin of the Church. It gives us probably the most intelligible and reliable picture available in the New Testament of early Christian life.

Acts of the Martyrs. Our knowledge of the martyrdoms of the early Christians in times of persecution depends on a variety of accounts varying in authenticity and dependability. Most reliable among them are actual court reports of the trials, of which only a few survive. (Notable among them is Cyprian's *Acta Proconsularia.*) Many other sources, however, exist. Eusebius of Caesarea produced a collection, now lost. A smaller collection, however, is extant in Syriac and also some fragments of it in Greek. The Acts of the Martyrs were collected and used liturgically from very early times.

Actus Purus. A Latin term meaning "pure actuality": a state attributed in medieval Christian philosophy to God alone. All other beings are in process of growth and therefore in a state of potentiality and incompleteness. This distinction was drawn from Aristotle.

Adalbert of Bremen (*c.* 1000–1072). German archbishop and missionary to the northern lands of Europe, which were about his time being christianized.

Adam. In Christian theology Adam has been taken both literally as "the first man" and figuratively as a symbol for unredeemed humanity. He appears in both creation stories in the Bible: Genesis 1.26–31 and 2.5–7. Paul (Romans 5.14 and I Corinthians 15.45) calls Christ the "second Adam" because he restored humankind to the righteous state that Adam was deemed to have lost. Traditionally, Adam in his original state before the Fall was in such perfect moral health that he lacked all evil desire and was endowed with immortality. Although Tatian and a few others held that he had been damned, Christian tradition, when it has taken Adam literally as "the first man," has generally taught that Christ rescued him from Limbo. The figurative understanding of Adam taken in the light of what we know of the evolutionary nature of the universe, is adumbrated in patrisotic thought, e.g., in Augustine's ingenious suggestion of an acronym in Adam's name: the four points of the compass (Anatole, Dysis, Arctos, Mesembria).

Adam, Karl (1876–1966). Roman Catholic theologian, born in Bavaria, ordained priest in 1900. Professor at Tübingen 1919–1949. Ecumenical in outlook yet orthodox in his teaching.

Adamantius. An early 4th c. Greek Christian writer whose work includes a controversial dialogue with Valentinus and other Gnostic writers.

Adamites. A small Christian sect whose followers recommended nudism as a means of return to the state of innocence originally enjoyed by Adam and Eve. They are mentioned by Epiphanius and Augustine. Whether they are to be identified with the Carpocratians, who recommended sexual promiscuity, is doubtful.

Adam Kadmon. In Cabbalistic thought (See **Cabbala**), the primordial human being, who was a hermaphrodite.

Adamnan (*c.* **625–704**). Elected Abbot of Iona in 679. Much respected in Scotland and Ireland for his scholarship and sanctity, he produced a life of Columba that is an important source for historians. He was canonized and his feast day is September 23.

Adam of Marsh. A 13th c. English Franciscan theologian. Regent of the Franciscan house of studies at Oxford from *c.* 1247. A close friend of Grosseteste, he exerted much political as well as scholarly influence, being now recognized as "the illustrious doctor of the Church" (*doctor illustris*).

Adam of St. Victor. A 12th c. Victorine, author of many well-known sequences.

Addai. Traditionally, the founder of the Church at Edessa and one of the seventy disciples of Jesus. He probably belonged, however, to a later date, e.g., the second century. The "Doctrine of Addai," a Syriac manuscript preserved in Leningrad, dates from *c.* 400 and described how Addai was sent to Edessa to convert King Abgar. The historicity of the story is much to be questioned.

Addai and Mari, Liturgy of. The liturgy probably composed *c.* 200 for the Syriac-speaking Church of Edessa and still the standard rite for Nestorians.

Adelard of Bath. An early 12th c. English philosopher. He defended Dem-

ocritus' theory of atoms and tried to reconcile the Platonic and the Aristotelian doctrines of the Universals.

Adequation. A term used in medieval philosophy in connection with the question of the nature of truth. Truth was said to be the *adequatio* of thought to thing, i.e., thought and thing are "made equal."

Adeste Fideles. Christmas hymn of unknown date and authorship; probably 17th or 18th c. and French or German authorship.

Adharma. That which is diametrically opposed to *dharma* (the right) and is personified in Indian thought as the wrong, the vicious, the unnatural, the evil. Adharma, when so personified, is related to various other evil personifications, such as Hiṁsā (violence), Māyā (deceit), and Dambha (hypocrisy).

Adherents. In the Scottish Kirk those who wish to be affiliated without becoming full communicants may be enrolled as adherents. In some areas, especially in the Highlands, a considerable percentage of the parishioners may feel their manner of life not blameless enough to warrant their being in full communion and so remain adherents.

Adhideha. In Indian thought, an embodiment finer than the human one, being the vesture of those who are temporarily in the spirit world (*pitṛoloka*) on their departure from earthly life pending their re-embodiment in a subsequent reincarnation.

Ad Hoc. This Latin phrase means literally "to this." Traditionally, the phrase is applied to a hypothesis that is not derivable from other phenomena or does not yield other verifiable consequences. The value of such a hypothesis is therefore much limited. The phrase is also very widely used in a general, non-philosophic sense to signify anything that refers to a particular purpose, e.g., an *ad hoc* meeting.

Adiophorists. In a 16th c. Lutheran controversy, some theologians (e.g., Melancthon) argued that, in the interests of peace, certain Catholic practices should be permitted to those who held to them, on the ground that they were matters of indifference (Greek *adiophora* = indifferent things) that did not radically affect the core of the Lutheran position. Flacius Illyricus, in 1549, opposed the Adiophorists. The controversy continued till 1577 when the Formula of Concord ruled that although in times of persecution no concessions ought to be permitted they could be made in other circumstances by individual churches, provided they did not entail what is expressly unscriptural. A further adiophorist controversy arose a century later between Pietists who opposed all secular pleasures such as dancing as sinful and orthodox Lutherans who accounted them matters of indifference.

Aditi. According to the Vedas, the goddess of space. She has affinities with the Greek concept *to apeiron,* for like this the term means literally "the unlimited." She comes to represent, therefore, the concept of heaven-and-earth in its boundlessness. She also stands for cosmic energy, and according to some Indian literature she has sons who represent specific aspects of nature, such as the sun and the moon, fire, wind, and water.

Admonition to Parliament. An English document issued anonymously in 1572 (probably attributable to two Puritan divines, John Field and Thomas Wilcox) opposing ecclesiastical and academic dignities and demanding an English Church without bishops, by whom it was opposed. It was defended by Thomas Cartright but suppressed by royal proclamation in 1573.

Adonai. One of the divine names used in the Hebrew Bible. It is used among Jews as a substitute for the name of God (the unutterable Tetragrammaton, Yahweh) and it also occurs in one of the

Greater Antiphons of the Christian Church, used on December 18 for the *Magnificat.*

Adoptianism. An important Christian heresy asserting that Jesus Christ was the Son of God only in the sense of his having been adopted as such, not as the Logos. It originated in Spain in the 8th c., possibly with the aim of making the Christian faith more acceptable to the Muslims. It was revived in modified forms in the 12th and later centuries and supported by some important medieval theologians, although generally condemned as heterodox. It represents the development of a tendency to be found in early christologies such as that of the Ebionites.

Adoption. In Hebrew law no provision seems to have been made for any formal procedure for adoption, although that of Moses by an Egyptian princess (Exodus 2.10) and that of Esther by her uncle Mordecai (Esther 2.7) are clear instances of the practice. The legal codes of Mesopotamia, by contrast, where adoption was a very common procedure, certainly provided for it, as is attested by the preservation of adoption contracts. The acceptance of non-Hebrew families into the Hebrew community, however, must have entailed some form of adoption, however informal. In the New Testament literature, Paul's use of the term "adoption" (*hyiothesia*) is derived from Roman law, in which (because of the absolute power of the father over his family, *patria potestas*), the adopted child's rights and duties in respect to his or her father had to be clearly established in law. So in Paul's imagery, the Christian is adopted in the Family of God, the Household of Faith, and is entitled to address God in the familiar form (see **Abba**) as a child of God.

Adoro Te Devote. Medieval hymn attributed, not without question, to Thomas Aquinas. It celebrates the presence of God hidden in the consecrated bread and wine of the Eucharist. For an important textual note see *The Oxford Book of Medieval Verse*, ed. F. J. E. Raby.

Adultery. In the Hebrew code of ethics, the wife was the property of her husband. By adultery was understood, therefore, sexual intercourse that violated the rights of a husband. A wife had no rights of this kind that could be violated. Unlawful intercourse between a married man and an unmarried woman was not such a violation of anyone's marital rights, although damages might be incurred. A betrothed girl, however, was treated for this purpose as a married woman, so that unlawful intercourse with her constituted adultery. The punishment for adultery was death by stoning of both parties (Ezekiel 16.40), and it would seem that the adulteress was stripped naked before the execution of the sentence. Adultery was much deplored in Hebrew writings and the apostasy from Yahweh is often called, by analogy, adultery. Jesus, following the Deuteronomic code, insisted that the desire to commit adultery is as evil as the act itself (Deuteronomy 5.18, 21 and Matthew 5.28).

Advent. The season of the Christian Year immediately preceding Christmas and having as its theme "waitingness" for the Coming of Christ. It begins, in the West, on the Sunday nearest November 30, which Sunday marks the beginning of the Christian Year. (In the East, Advent begins earlier.) The liturgical color is violet; but see **Gaudete.**

Advent Candle. The custom is observed in some churches and Christian homes of having a set of candles in the form of a wreath, the candles of which are lighted successively, one on the First Sunday of Advent and so on through the Advent season till all are lighted. The origin of the custom seems somewhat obscure, but it appears to be German and Lutheran and to date from only the 19th c. With the emergence of a German youth movement prior to World War I, it became popular in Ger-

many, presumably spreading thence to the United States, where it is now a fairly common practice. See **Hanukkah** for a comparable practice in Judaism.

Adventists. All who throughout Christian history have stressed the expectation of the Second Coming of Christ as imminent may be so called. In a narrower sense the term designates a movement having its origin in William Miller (1782–1849) who in 1831 began in the State of New York to predict the imminence of the Second Coming. The movement is nowadays represented chiefly by the Seventh-Day Adventists and some other bodies.

Advocatus Diaboli. In the lengthy process of officially recognizing anyone as a saint of the Roman Catholic Church, an official is appointed whose task is to examine reasons against such recognition. This official is called "promoter of the faith" (*promotor fidei*) and more popularly "the devil's advocate" (*advocatus diaboli*), a term now in general literary use to designate anyone arguing against any cause by picking flaws to evoke controversy and so bring out the whole truth.

Advowson. A legal term used in England to denote the right of appointing a cleric to a parish or other ecclesiastical benefice.

Aelfric (*c.* 955–*c.* 1020). Leader of the Benedictine revival in England. He provided the rural clergy with books in their native language and is an important figure in the literary as well as the ecclesiastical history of England.

Aelred (1109–1169). Abbot of Ríevaulx. Followed closely the tradition of spirituality taught by Bernard of Clairvaux and other Cistercians in continental Europe.

Aeneas of Gaza. Late 5th c. Christian philosopher, much influenced by Platonic and Neoplatonic teachings.

Aeon. The name given by some Gnostics (e.g., the Valentinians) to a category of beings lying between God and the world of matter, so forming a bridge between good and evil. Such entities might be regarded as semi-divine, for they emanated from God as sparks emanate from a fire.

Aer. Veil used in the Eastern Church to cover the chalice and paten during the liturgy.

Aerius. A 4th c. Christian writer who, according to Epiphanius held many heterodox opinions and denied any difference between the function of priests and bishops.

Aesthetics. Historically, the term "aesthetic" (from the Greek *aisthēsis*, sensation) was opposed to "noetic" (from the Greek *nōēsis*, intelligence or thought), and was used to designate the entire domain of the sensible. Baumgarten (1714–1762) was probably the first to use it in what is now its universally accepted sense (the philosophy of beauty), although his contribution to the subject was of comparatively little importance. Hegel used the term more specifically in relation to his theory of art and his influence no doubt fixed the usage that became universal in the 19th c. onward. Plato, following a general view among the ancients, saw art as mimesis, imitation. Aristotle slightly modified Plato's view on art, seeing it as the imitation not necessarily of a particular object but of a possible one. Plato, however, had distinguished art (for which he had a somewhat low opinion) from beauty, which he greatly admired, seeing it in proportion and in symmetry. Thomas Aquinas had a somewhat simplistic or at least undeveloped view of beauty as *id quod visum placet*, that which pleases the eye. Toward the end of the 19th c. writers began to talk of art as having value in its own right, in contrast to the view that had generally been taken that had given it a comparatively lowly place among the branches of philosophical inquiry. Croce was the first modern thinker to bring this Cinderella among the branches of philosophy into the limelight, by making it the groundwork of all the rest and therefore the one on which all others must depend. He did this in his first great work on the subject, his *Estetica*, which appeared in 1901. See **Croce, Benedetto**. Since then, aesthetics has become an important and recognized field in philosophy and has given rise to a wide variety of interpretations of the nature of beauty and of art.

Aetius. A fourth century Christian teacher who maintained an extreme form of Arianism.

Aeviternity. The medieval philosophers distinguished *aeternitas* from *aeviternitas*. *Aeviternitas* is an infinite temporal series—unending time; *aeternitas* is a nontemporal order transcending all temporal sequence—that is, eternity.

Affect. This term is used by Spinoza in designating the variety of feelings, drives, and aims by which we are motivated. These affects are internal and therefore permit some sort of self-determination.

Affective prayer. A mystical type of prayer in which one seeks to unite oneself to God by an act of the will rather than by intellectual, emotional, or other means.

Affinity. A term traditionally used in canon law and moral theology to designate certain relationships that create impediments to marriage.

Affirmation. Certain Christian bodies, notably the Quakers, have traditionally claimed that taking an oath can add nothing to the sincerity or the solemnity of a simple "yes" or "no". They have been for long widely permitted, in deference to their view on this matter, to make instead an affirmation or declaration, where otherwise an oath would be required.

Affirming the Antecedent/Consequent. For these technical terms in traditional logic, see **Syllogism.**

Affusion. Baptism by the pouring of water on the candidate's head rather than by immersion of the body.

Afghanistan, Buddhism in. Archaeological research has shown that a Buddhist culture flourished in the region now so designated before the decline of that culture about the 7th c. CE. It was finally displaced by Islam by the beginning of the 10th c.

A Fortiori. Latin phrase meaning "with greater force." It is used of a form of argument in which one compares two cases: one lesser in degree than the other. Example: If I can get a plant to grow in a poor soil that is not conducive to its growth, I may expect it to thrive even better in a more favorable soil, or at least as well.

Āgama. A name given in Mahayana Buddhism to certain collections of sacred scripture, notably to one of the three divisions of the Tripitaka that is known as the Sutta-Pitaka.

Agapē. Three terms are used in Greek to express love and friendship: (1) *erōs*, (2) *philia*, and (3) *agapē*. *Erōs*, which is used in classical Greek literature to express the idea of any kind of love or desire for a thing, the primeval force that draws one thing to another, came to be more and more associated with sexual desire. In Greek mythology Erōs came to be recognized as the son of Aphrodite, the goddess of love. The Romans identified him with Cupid and in Hellenistic times he had come to be associated with romantic love, often represented as a little winged archer who playfully shoots his arrows at both men and gods. *Philia* was used of friendly affection and the kindly disposition and loyalty that should accompany such friendship, distinguishing it from the passionate nature of *erōs*. *Agapē*, a term much used in the New

Testament, was probably coined by the biblical writers, partly to avoid the sexual connotations of *erōs* and partly to express a specific form of love that they held to be beyond both *erōs* and *philia:* a love that is rooted in and issues from God and is to be found specifically in the Christian community wherever this is in a state of spiritual health. It is represented as a selfless love that participates in the love that is at the source of all things in God himself. As such it inspires those who follow Christ to transmit the divine *agapē* to others: not only within the Household of Faith but to all our fellow creatures everywhere. The term is used only twice in the Synoptic Gospels (Matthew 24.12; Luke 11.42), but frequently in John and in the Pauline and Johannine letters, being most notably commended in I Corinthians 13 as greater than even faith and hope. The term *agapē* was translated into Latin as *caritas* and thence into English as "charity"; but since the latter term has acquired other connotations that would be misleading in English today, modern translations usually use the term "love".

The term *agapē* is also applied to the common meal that was apparently in use in the primitive Christian Church in association with the Eucharist. This agapē-feast is referred to in the New Testament itself (e.g., I Corinthians 11.17–34) and in some early Christian documents, notably the writings of Ignatius. It would seem that this agapē-feast came to be detached from the Eucharist by early in the third century.

Agapē and Reconciliation, Order of. This semi-monastic Anglican religious community was founded in 1972 by Father Cyril (Enrico) Molnar, who built consciously on the tradition of such a community that had been founded at Little Gidding, England, by Nicholas Ferrar (1592–1637). *See* **Little Gidding.** It is semi-monastic in the sense that it follows in principle a specific rule, laying special emphasis on the ideal of peace and non-resistance (to be practiced uncompromisingly) and with some Carthusian features. It accepts married couples as well as single men and single women, forming a sort of Christian ashram. It has associates and life-professed in fourteen countries and several priories, such as the Prince of Peace Priory at Chemainus, British Columbia. The concept of communities of this kind is not by any means novel. Saint Paulinus and his wife Saint Therasia founded such a community at Nola, Italy, and Saint Basil and Saint Macrina founded one at Tabernisi, Asia Minor. Both of these examples pertain to the 4th c. The Order is ecumenical, having within its membership not only Anglicans but some Orthodox, some Roman Catholics, and even some Protestant clergy and lay people.

Agatha. A female saint martyred in Sicily. Much venerated from at least the 5th c., she is commemorated in the Roman Mass. The dates of her life are, however, unknown.

Agatho (*c.* 577–681). Pope in the late 7th c. who in 680 held a council at Rome against the Monothelites.

Agde, Council of. A council held at Agde in the south of France in 506, dealing with clerical celibacy, church property, and other subjects.

Age, Canonical. A technical expression in Canon Law used especially in connection with the age requirement for ordination as deacon, priest, or bishop.

Aggiornamento. An Italian term much used in connection with the pontificate of Pope John XXIII to denote the fresh spirit that he sought to foster in the Church, entailing new ways of presenting the eternal truths enshrined in Christian doctrine and practice. The word implies "updating" or "renewal".

Agnellus of Pisa (*c.* 1194–1235). Founder of the English province of the Franciscan Order. He engaged Grosseteste to teach at Oxford.

Agnes. A female saint and martyr much venerated since the 4th c. but whose dates are unknown. A basilica was erected in Rome *c.* 350 to commemorate her. She is represented in iconography by a lamb, because of a confusion of her name with *agnus*, "lamb".

Agni. One of the most important Hindu gods. His cult dates back to Vedic times. He is the god of fire: a vital element in the sacrifices. He has eternal youth and is present in every god. His magical power drives away darkness and evil spirits.

Agnoetae. A Monophysite group founded by Themistius of Alexandria in the 6th c. They attributed ignorance to the humanity of Christ (Greek, *agnoeō*, "to be ignorant of"). They were declared heretical by Pope Gregory the Great.

Agnosticism. The origin of this term is generally ascribed to T. H. Huxley, who is said to have coined it while reading, as an undergraduate, about the Gnostics. They seemed to him to claim to know everything about the spiritual chemistry of the universe. By contrast, he felt that he could claim to know nothing about that or indeed about anything other than empirical phenomena. In a looser sense the term came to be used of any form of skepticism, such as from ancient times it had been commonly known as Pyrrhonism.

Agnus Dei. In the Roman liturgy, the phrase ("Lamb of God") is used in the Mass by the celebrant before the Kiss of Peace and the Communion. It has been in use since at least the 7th c., although the threefold form now familiar in Roman Catholic usage dates from only about the beginning of the 11th c. The phrase itself, however, is found in the *Gloria in excelsis* and is, of course, rooted in biblical texts such as John 1.29.

Agrapha. (Greek, meaning "not written"). Term used to designate sayings of Jesus not recorded in any of the four canonical Gospels but occurring in other early Christian literature and manuscript fragments.

Agricola, Johann (*c.* **1494–1566**). German Reformer, born in Eisleben. He studied under Luther at Wittenberg. For a time he supported Antinomianism but later recanted. He also tried unsuccessfully to conclude the controversy with the Adiophorists. He pioneered in collecting German proverbs.

Agrippa. Greek skeptical philosopher. The dates of his life are uncertain except that he must have lived later than Aenesimus who lived in the 1st. c. CE. Following Aenesimus and Pyrrho in the general form of his thought, Agrippa set forth five arguments in support of the skeptical approach in philosophy. Noting the general difficulty of establishing any criterion for knowing anything, he went on to point out that every proof requires premises; these in turn require proof, and so forth in an infinite regress; therefore we can be certain of nothing. The relativity of all data received by the human mind prevents our knowledge of what reality is: a child apprehends it in one way, a great sage in another; a mouse in one way, a man in another. Hypotheses are submitted for verification, but we can never be certain of any conclusion. Agrippa foresaw many of the problems that have troubled thinkers of later ages.

Agrippa von Nettesheim, Heinrich Cornelius (1486–1535). German scholar sympathetic to the Reformation but in some respects more conservative than Luther although in other respects much more skeptical.

Ahab. King of Israel from 869 to 850 BCE, he was married to Jezebel, daughter of the King of Tyre. He had four encounters with the prophet Elijah. Despite Ahab's military and political success, he ⌐h reviled in the Bible, e.g., ·   ⌐7 where he is

represented as questioning whether Israel should worship Yahweh or Baal.

Ahimsā. The term comes from the Sanskrit word *himsā* (violence, injury) and *a* (not); hence "non-violence". It is a central virtue in Hinduism and common to all its very diverse forms. In Vedic times, when there was little by way of moral or legal codes, warfare had been brutal, punishments cruel, and conduct generally ruthless. Not till the period of the Upanishads did an ethical conscious develop to produce a revulsion against unbridled bloodshed. Then *ahismā* acquired its central place in Hindu ethics. It was held to go hand in hand with truthfulness, gentility, love, modesty, and virtually every other aspect of the life of a good person. This teaching was especially promulgated by the Jains and, later on, by the Buddhists, but it remains central to the ethical teaching of all Hindu schools of thought. The ideal of ahimsā has been by no means always upheld in practice in modern India.

Aidan. A 7th c. monk of Iona; Bishop of Lindisfarne. Followed the practices of the Celtic Church.

Aisle. The word is from the French *aile*, "wing", and designates any area extending the nave or even the chancel or transept. Its common use to designate a passageway (e.g., "the bride walked up the aisle") is incorrect, while "center aisle" is self-contradictory.

Akhenaten. The Egyptian Pharoah Amenophis IV, who reigned *c.* 1367–1350 BCE. Rejecting the official state worship of Amen-Re, he introduced in its place the worhip of Aten (the sun's disc), which he elevated to the status of sole god, so that he may be said to have adumbrated the *concept* of monotheism, although only in an indirect way, for much had to be developed to reach the ethical monotheism taught by the Hebrew prophets. Changing his name to Akhenaten, he abolished the state priesthood and moved his capital to

Amarna. His queen, Nefertiti, shared in his religious outlook. The cult, however, was demolished after his death.

Akkadian. The eastern Semitic language that was spoken in Mesopotamia from *c.* 2000 to *c.* 500 is nowadays called by scholars Akkadian. It was written in cuneiform, as had been Sumerian, and it appeared in two dialects: Babylonian and Assyrian. Extensive literary remains in Akkadian have been discovered from about 1835 and provide invaluable information about the background of the Bible as well as on the linguistic ancestry of Hebrew. It is therefore an important tool for Old Testament scholars today.

Alacoque, Margaret Mary (1647–1690). Visitandine nun, foundress of the devotion to the Sacred Heart. In 1671 she entered the convent at Paray-le-Monial, France, of which she eventually became a superior. Devotion to the Sacred Heart had been fostered much earlier among the Carthusians and others, but it had never been a widespread cultus till through her visions (which were at first disparaged by her superiors) she won for it a prominent place in popular Catholic devotion. It was officially recognized as a liturgical observance in 1765.

Alain of Lille. 12th c. preacher and theologican. Studied and taught at Paris, then later moved to the south of France, where at that time the Albigensian movement, against which he preached, was dominant. Near the end of his life he entered the abbey of Citeaux, where he died.

Alapa. Till recently the bishop, in administering the Sacrament of Confirmation, gave candidates a slight slap on the cheek, generally taken to symbolize the spiritual warfare that lay ahead of them as soldiers of Christ. It was technically called *alapa*.

Alaric (*c.* 370–410). A Visigothic chief who served under Theodosius I. He later besieged and entered Rome on August 24, 410. This event was the immediate occasion of the writing of Augustine's *De Civitate Dei*, an extremely influential work recognizing that two "cities", symbolized by Babylon and Jerusalem: the former, the earthly power of Rome, is good, although the latter, the spiritual power of the Church, is better.

Alb. A white linen ankle length tunic with tight fitting sleeves, held at the waist by a white cord (girdle). Originally the under tunic worn in Graeco-Roman society, it eventually came to be regarded as part of the liturgical dress of the ministers at Mass.

Alban. First British martyr, he was a pagan of Verulanium, now St. Alban's, Hertfordshire, England, who was converted by a fugitive priest. He was martyred either in the persecution under Diocletian *c.* 303 or in that under Septimius Severus *c.* 209.

Albertus Magnus (*c.* 1200–1280). Born in Lauingen, near Ulm; philosopher and theologian. Entered the Dominican Order in 1222. Among his works, probably the most important are his commentaries on Aristotle. Although overshadowed by his illustrious student, Thomas Aquinas, his work is of great importance in the history of the development of medieval philosophy. Beatified 1622; canonized and proclaimed a doctor of the Church in 1931.

Albigenses. So powerful was the Albigensian movement that in some regions of Western Europe (notably in the south of France where it first appeared early in the 11th c.) it looked as though it might displace the Church. Although its adherents seem to have been in some respects in the tradition of the Manichees of the ancient world, no evidence exists to establish any direct lineage. Their teachings resembled, however, those of the Bogomils in Eastern Europe. They taught a form of Reincarnationism, rejected the sacraments of the

Church, interpreted the Bible allegorically and in a Docetist direction, were vegetarian.

They inculcated the ideal of an extreme rigorism in moral conduct. Since not all adherents could hope to conform to this ideal, two categories were recognized: (1) the *perfecti* who kept the moral precepts fully and (2) the believers who were not required to do so but who hoped at the approach of death to be received into full membership. Their savage persecution by the Church seemed only to foster their growth. The Church, after several unsuccessful attempts to cause them to give up their beliefs, resorted to force. Under Simon de Montfort a crusade was launched against them: in effect a genocidal campaign. Such Albigenses as were left were eventually demolished by the Inquisition under the Dominicans, so that the movement went underground leaving no visible trace. The cruel manner of their extirpation is one of the worst episodes in the history of the Church. The Albigenses were so named from the town of Albi in Southern France. They were also known as the Cathari or "pure ones."

Albinus. A 2nd c. Greek philosopher of the School of Gaius, associated with the Fourth Academy. He combined Platonic and Aristotelian thought with Stoicism, regarding knowledge as a means to religious insight.

Alcoholism. A serious and widespread condition in the United States and elsewhere, in which dependence on alcohol is such as to result in noticeable mental disturbance or interference with mental or physical health, interpersonal relations, and smooth social and economic functioning. It is more and more recognized as a malady probably involving certain genetic factors and body chemistry, nevertheless raising complex ethical questions for the victim, society and (in the case of Christians) the Church. Lack of adequate education concerning the risks and dangers attending the use of alcohol has often resulted in alcoholism among both the clergy and medical practitioners themselves, to say nothing of their failure to understand the problems of other victims. The perception of alcoholism as a disease by no means absolved the victim from the ethical responsibility of seeking to rectify his or her situation and of co-operating with those who are trying to help. The tragic consequences of driving an automobile while under the influence of alcohol are well known, and failure to appreciate the danger attending such conduct exhibits grievous moral irresponsibility. The alcoholic is not absolved from responsibility on the ground that he or she, at the time of an accident in which people were maimed or killed, was not responsible for the accident. Such a driver was responsible for getting into such a condition of irresponsibility and must be held accountable accordingly. Organizations such as "Mothers Against Drunk Driving" (MADD) are fully justified in upholding this salutary principle on behalf of victims of alcoholics' behavior.

"Alcoholics Anonymous" is an organization that has for long been remarkably successful in treating alcoholism with understanding and showing alcoholics how to face their condition and cope with the process of their recovery. (See also **Drug Dependence.**)

Alcuin (*c.* 715–804). English scholar, leader in the Carolingian Renaissance. Long connected with York, he became toward the end of his life Abbot of Tours, France. His interests included liturgical studies. In 1897 an Anglican society called the Alcuin Club was formed to promote such studies.

Aldrich, Henry (1647–1710). A learned and versatile English divine; as Dean of Christ Church, Oxford, he opposed the "High Church" party.

Aleander, Girolamo (1480–1542). Christian humanist; sought disciplinary reform in the Church but vigorously opposed Luther at the Diet of Worms.

Alesius, Alexander (1500–1565). Scottish divine and controversialist; influenced by the Lutheran teachings of Patrick Hamilton.

Alexander (died 328). Bishop of Alexandria from 313; excommunicated Arius.

Alexander, Samuel (1859–1938). British philosopher. Australian born, Oxford trained, he was Professor of Philosophy at Manchester University from 1893 to 1923. He expounded a philosophy of emergent evolution, in which the emergents have physical, chemical, physiological, and mental qualities, moving toward complexity and having within them a *nisus* (impetus or striving) toward higher and higher levels. A thing is a complexus of motions. Space-time, which is pure motion, is the source of existing things. Motion, however, is only one of a number of the properties (or, as he calls them, categories) of space-time. There are also the categories of substance, quantity, number, existence, universality, relation, and order.

In Alexander's system "God" is a term that can mean either (1) the entire space-time in *nisus*, i.e., evolving toward the next emergent, or (2) the transcendence that the next emergent has in relation to its predecessor. This transcendence he calls "deity": whatever lies ahead in the evolutionary process. The evolutionary process goes on infinitely. God, in Alexander's view, is not the source of all things as in Judaeo-Christian thought; rather, he is a part or aspect of the process. Among Alexander's writings, some of the most important are: *Space, Time, and Deity*, 2 vols. (1920), *Spinoza and Time* (1921), and *Beauty and Other Forms of Value* (1933).

Alexander II (died 1073). Elected pope in 1061; engaged in many disciplinary reforms, including the prohibition of simony and the enforcement of clerical celibacy.

Alexander III (died 1181). Elected pope in 1159; much encouraged scholarship; assembled the Third Lateran Council in 1179, which vested in the cardinals exclusive right of electing a pope by a two-thirds majority.

Alexander VI (1431–1503). A Spaniard by birth, Roderigo Borgia, he was elected pope in 1492, the year Columbus sailed. He divided the New World, when it was discovered, between Spain and Portugal. Notoriously immoral both in his personal life and in his public relationships, he obtained his election to the papacy by bribery, favored his bastard son Caesar, and excommunicated and brought about the torture and execution of Savonarola.

Alexander VII (1599–1667). Elected pope in 1655, he opposed Jansenism and supported the Jesuits.

Alexander VIII (1610–1691). Elected pope in 1689, he opposed Gallicanism and Jansenism.

Alexander of Hales (c. 1186–1245). English-born Franciscan scholar, he spent much of his life in Paris; pioneered in introducing the Franciscans to the life and work of the universities. Introduced Peter Lombard's *Sentences* into the theological curriculum of the university. He largely set the pattern for the scholastic method of stating and dealing with philosophical and theological problems by means of setting forth objections, answering them, solving the problem, and exhibiting justifications for the solution.

Alexandria. The importance of this Egyptian city in the ancient world cannot easily be exaggerated. Founded by Alexander the Great c. 332 BCE, it lay near the Canopic mouth of the Nile. It was the capital city of the Ptolemies and also of the Roman administration in Egypt. References to its magnificence, its parks and spacious avenues, abound in ancient literature and, with a population of possibly half a million, it ranked with Rome and Antioch as one of the three leading cities of the Roman Empire. It became the undisputed center of the intellectual life of the entire Hellenistic world. As such it attracted scholars from every part of the known world and in turn disseminated Hellenistic culture and learning to the ends of the earth. As naturally happens in such a cosmopolitan city, each of the various cultural and religious groups tended to establish its own identity within the mix. The Jews, for example, occupied one of five municipal districts, forming possibly the largest concentration of Jews anywhere in the ancient world and certainly one of the richest and most influential. It was here that the Old Testament was translated into Greek (see *Septuagint*), and it was here that Philo (30 BCE - 50 CE), a native of that city, sought to show that the teachings of Moses and the Hebrew prophets had anticipated the wisdom of the Greeks such as had been expressed in the writings of Plato and the Stoics. The city is mentioned in the New Testament (Acts 18.24) as the home of Paul's companion in his missionary endeavors and in other connections; yet we hear nothing of Paul's ever having visited Alexandria, despite his extensive missionary journeys and his knowledge of other leading cities of the Empire. Nor do we find any clear historical account of the first establishment of a Christian community there, although the Christian School at Alexandria had become famous by the end of the 2nd c. and was to become unrivalled even by Antioch as the center of Christian scholarship, the arena of theological controversy, and the focus of the development of Christian intellectual life. The libraries at Alexandria (the larger one in the Brucheum quarter and a smaller one in the Serapeum) were for long far famed as the greatest collection in the Hellenistic world. Writers in the ancient world give varying accounts of the holdings, but an estimate of half a million items would be reasonable.

Alexandrian School. In a general sense the term may be applied to any one of the several intellectual traditions associated with Alexandria between 310 BCE, when a school of philosophy was founded there by Ptolemy Soter along with a library that was to become famed throughout the entire known world, and 642 CE when Alexandria was captured by the Muslims. Alexandria became a focus for scholars of every sort, Neoplatonists, Jews, and Christians. Philo Judaeus, Clement, and Origen were among them. In specifically Christian usage, the term is applied to those Christian scholars and teachers in Alexandria, who from the 2nd c. onward developed a catechetical school there that addressed itself to the better educated and more cultured classes. The first known Christian teacher there was Pantaenus in the 2nd c. Clement and Origen were among its great Christian luminaries. Because of Origen's difficulties with his bishop, Demetrius, the school came more directly under episcopal control and although it continued to attract great scholars such as Theognostus and Didymus the Blind, it never again had such an intellectual giant as Origen. What gives this school its special interest is not only its interpretation of Christian faith in Platonic terms but its teaching it in conjunction with the best scientific thought and humane learning of the day.

Al-Farabi. See **Farabi, al-**.

Alfred the Great (849–899). English king from 871, who did much to promote both scholarship and ecclesiastical reform.

Al-Ghazzāli. See **Ghazzāli, al-**.

Alienation. This term is used in three radically different senses. (1) Marx used it in his *Economic and Philosophical Manuscripts of 1844* in reference to what he saw as the process by which man's inner nature becomes private property and so separates one man from another. (2) In existentialism, alienation is a term used to designate a fundamental aspect of human existence. (3) In modern Christian theology the term is widely used to designate the state of humanity in its resistance to God: Man is said to be alienated from his Creator by his rebellion against God that is traditionally called "sin."

Al-Kindi. See **Kindi, al-**.

Allah. The name given to God by Muslims. See **Islam**.

Allegorical Interpretation of Scripture. Figurative interpretations of the Bible do not necessarily exclude all connection with historical reality; on the contrary they are often seen as transcending it. The term "allegory" is used by Paul himself (Galatians 4.24) and the method, Philo tells us, was well recognized in rabbinical practice. Christian exegetes in the Alexandrian School used it extensively. Both Clement of Alexandria and Origen recognized levels of biblical interpretation, from the bare, "literal" one to a deeper, spiritual one, and in principle such a distinction continued to be recognized by exegetes in the West throughout the Middle Ages. Indeed, there was a medieval tendency to excessive and fanciful allegorization, which some, notably the Victorines, sought to check. A strictly "literal" interpretation of the Bible or indeed of any great literature, "sacred" or "secular", is obviously impossible. Parable, familiar in Gospel stories such as the Good Samaritan and the Prodigal Son, is a *form* of figurative interpretation apart from which the stories would be deprived of all but the most trivial meaning.

Alleluia. Ancient Hebrew liturgical exclamation, meaning "Praise ye the Lord." Adopted at an early date into the Christian liturgy, it is especially used at Mass as an expression of Eastertide joy.

All Saints' Day. An important Christian festal day, celebrated in the Western Church since the eighth century on November 1. The significance lies primarily in recognition of the unity of all Christians on both sides of the veil of death. See also **Communion of Saints, The.**

All Souls' Day. A day commemorating the souls of the faithful departed, observed on November 2.

Almsgiving. Importance is attached in almost all the major religions of the world to the giving of alms to the needy. It is traditionally recognized in Judaism and presupposed in the ethical teaching of Jesus. It is one of the Five Pillars of Islam where it is known as *Zakāt*. In the Hindu and Buddhist traditions it is likewise taken to be a virtue that acquires great merit for the one who practices it. Under Buddhist influence in China, belief in the merit of almsgiving grew rapidly not only among Buddhists there but among Taoists and Confucians. Buddhist influence in Japan similarly affected popular attitudes.

Alogi. A heretical group in Asia Minor who flourished *c*. 170. They opposed Montanism and, according to Epiphanius, denied the divinity of the Holy Spirit and of the Logos.

Aloysius Gonzaga (1568–1591). Roman Catholic saint and patron of youth. Having entered the Jesuit novitiate in 1584, he died in 1591 at the age of 23 after ministering to the plague-stricken at Rome. Canonized in 1726.

Alphonsus Liguori (1696–1787). Founder of the Redemptorist Order. As a moral theologian he developed Equiprobabilism. See **Probabilism**. Beatified 1816, canonized 1839.

Altar. The normal term, inherited from Hebrew usage, for the table that is the focus of worship. Used from very early times of the eucharistic table. The practice of celebrating Mass on the tombs of martyrs encouraged the use of stone rather than wood for the Christian altar. When Christianity had been established, under Constantine, as a permitted religion, the practice developed of enclosing under the altar a relic or relics of martyrs. Where there is more than one altar, the principal one is called the "High Altar". If there is more than one altar, one of them is usually the Lady Altar, dedicated to the Virgin Mary. For emergency purposes portable altars are permitted. Since the Second Vatican Council, the traditional place of the altar at the eastern end of the chancel, with the priest facing east, has been generally replaced by a free standing altar with the priest facing westward toward the congregation. The advantages of this change remain, however, highly controversial.

Altar Lights. See **Candles.**

Altizer, Thomas. See **Death of God Theology.**

Altruism. Term used by Auguste Comte to signify care for the interests of others over one's own.

Amalekites. A nomadic tribe mentioned in Genesis 14.7 and listed among the tribes cited in Esau's genealogy (Genesis 36.12). Amalek is said to have dwelt in the Negev (Numbers 13.29), and his city is mentioned in I Samuel 15.5. He seems to have been continually at war with the Israelites. The bitterness between the Amalekites and the Israelites seems to have been rooted in a very ancient feud.

Amalric. A 12th c. philosopher at Paris whose teachings, reflecting at some points the system of Erigena, were condemned by the Lateran Council, 1215.

Amana. A small Christian group, pietistic in spirit, that originated in Germany in 1714. In 1842 a large number of them emigrated to America and in 1855 settled in Iowa where they are still to be found. The quality of their produce is highly regarded.

Ambikā. An Indian mother goddess. She was formed out of the energies of all the other gods in order to overcome demons. She assumes various forms,

being associated with harvest and fall, the season at which she is to be propitiated, so that she may be discriminating in what she destroys. She is part of a general nature-worship, figuring also in Jain outlook and practice.

Ambo. In a Christian basilica the raised platform used for those parts of the liturgy that are specifically addressed to the people, such as the lessons and homily. There were often two: one on the Epistle (south) side and one on the Gospel (north) side. After the 14th c. the pulpit generally replaced them.

Ambrose (*c.* **339–397**). As Bishop of Milan he was a celebrated preacher who championed accepted orthodox positions against the Arians and others. Much admired by Augustine who attributed his own conversion in large part to Ambrose's preaching. One of the four Doctors of the Latin Church.

Ambrosian Rite. One of the few rites in the West (apart from the Roman) to have survived in the Roman Catholic Church, it is associated with Milan and is believed by some scholars to be older than the Roman rite although other scholars account it a development of the Roman rite. It exhibits interesting differences, e.g., the Offertory precedes the Creed and is accompanied by a procession. The chant has some Eastern characteristics.

Ambulatory. The space behind the apse in certain churches.

Amen. A Hebrew word in general use among both Jews and Christians at the end of prayers and other devotional utterances.

Amerindian Religions, Revitalization of. Attempts among Amerindian groups to recover their early religious practices and outlook are generally so designated. They are often syncretistic, drawing from the pan-Indian movement, and so do not always appeal to all groups, whose traditions and practices are very diverse. Some practices, however, are characteristic of most North American Indians, although variously interpreted, e.g., the "vision quest," usually associated with a rite of passage in which a young individual, usually male, is encouraged by the elders to set out to acquire spiritual power by encounter with a supernatural being. Ascetic practices are employed, e.g., fasting, purification in a "sweat lodge," and retirement to a remote place where he begs for a vision, usually granted by a "guardian spirit" who teaches the seeker a "spirit song" and empowers him to set forth as a shaman or medicine man, and bestows on him a physical symbol ("medicine bundle") of his status. The sacred pipe (calumet) may be associated with such initiation. It is a microcosmic symbol of the universe and the act of smoking it reaffirms the network of cosmic relations.

Ames, William (1576–1633). Calvinist moral theologian and controversialist; noted for his uncompromising distaste for Catholic usages; much revered by his Calvinist contemporaries.

Amiatinus, Codex. See **Codex Amiatinus.**

Amice. A linen cloth used with the alb as a neck covering. Some albs are equipped with a hood that makes the use of the amice unnecessary.

Amida. The Japanese name for Amitabha, a transcendental being in Mahayana Buddhism. His cult seems to antedate Nāgārjuna, i.e., about 100 CE. Known as the personification of mercy, compassion, and love, he became central in the Pure Land sects of Buddhism, both in China and Japan: Jodo and Shin. In popular devotion great importance has been attached to the physical utterance of his name.

Amish. The Anabaptists were much divided, with the Mennonites as the largest group of them to survive the persecutions they suffered in continental Europe. The Mennonites also, how-

ever, were divided. One branch, which took its name from that of the 17th c. Jacob Ammann, came to be known as the Amish. They sought to return to the strictest Mennonite ideals. They are to be found in considerable numbers in Pennsylvania.

Amitabha. See **Amida.**

Ammon. Early 4th c. Egyptian hermit.

Ammonites. An Aramaean tribe that settled on the upper Jabbok, probably somewhat earlier than the 12th c. BCE. They are represented in the Bible as descended from Lot (Genesis 19.38) and as having been already settled when the Israelites entered Canaan (Deuteronomy 2.19, 37), although this is historically doubtful. They appear as being at enmity with the Israelites, along with the Amalekites and the Moabites and were defeated by the tribes of Gilead. It was in the context of such enmities that Saul emerged as a great leader who defeated them. Among others they opposed the rebuilding of the walls of Jerusalem (Nehemiah 4.1). The name of the modern city of Amman, capital of Jordan, derives from Ammon.

Ammonius Saccas (c. 175–242 CE). Generally accounted the founder of Neoplatonism; much influenced Plotinus.

Amnon. The eldest son of David, he fell in love with Tamar, his half-sister, and raped her. See **Absalom.** Absalom slew him in revenge.

Amos. Hebrew prophet of the 8th c. BCE. Much emphasized the ethical demands of God. A herdsman of Tekoa, he was chronologically the first of the prophets in the Hebrew Scriptures.

Amsdorf, Nikolaus von (1483–1565). Lutheran theologian. Closely associated with Luther, he carried some of Luther's teachings to extremes, especially in the Synergist controversy in which he argued against "good works" so strongly that he alienated many

Lutherans from him. He also argued vehemently against the Adiophorists.

Amsterdam Assembly. An assembly of ecclesiastical leaders who met in 1948 in the Concertgebouw and formally constituted the World Council of Churches.

Amulets. Small religious objects worn to preserve the wearer from evil spirits, were much used in Egypt. Contrary, perhaps, to expectation, the Bible nowhere condemns their use and some have been found that archaeologists date from the Israelite period, although most are of pre-Israelite origin and principally of Egyptian provenance.

Anabaptists. The mainstream Reformation leaders, such as Luther, Calvin, and Zwingli were in many respects conservative in the sense that they sought to reform the Catholic Church's constitution and practice, not to instigate a revolt against it. A revolutionary wing, however, had another bent, seeking a much more radical surgery. They refused, for example, to recognize infant baptism, where it had taken place, and insisted on the "baptism of believers"; hence the nickname "anabaptists", which literally means "rebaptizers." They usually taught other revolutionary principles and practices such as nonresistance, common ownership of property, and in at least one case even a form of polygamy. A large variety of groups developed espousing Anabaptist views. These included the followers of Münzer who appeared in Wittenberg as early as 1521, the Swiss Brethern who came to Zürich teaching "believers' baptism", the Hutterites (led by Jacob Hutter), the Melchiorites (follwing Melchior Hoffmann), and the Mennonites. Anabaptists were bitterly persecuted by Catholics and Protestants in Europe and many fled to America.

Anagogical Interpretation. A type of allegorical reading of the Bible designed to lead the reader upward toward a spiritual, mystical understanding.

Analogia Entis. See **Analogy.**

Analogy. A method of predication whereby a concept derived from an object that is relatively well known is applied to one that is relatively unknown. The use of analogy in discourse about God presupposes that God, though largely inaccessible to us, is not wholly unknowable. While in human language nothing can be predicated of God univocally (that is on the assumption that there is an unqualified likeness between God and man), we need not say the predication must be completely equivocal (that is, on the assumption that there can be no similarity at all). For example, the kindness predicated of God cannot be by any means the same as the kindness predicated of human beings; nevertheless, it need not be so totally dissimilar as to make kindness wholly meaningless in human discourse. The basis of analogy lies in relationship, that is 4:6 as 26:39. The *analogia entis* (analogy of being) in medieval theology is based on the notion of such a relationship; we may say that God: his being as Man:his being.

Analysis, Philosophical. In the view of many 20th c. philosophers, the function of philosophy consists entirely or almost entirely in translating sentences that demand clarification of one sort or another into other sentences that clarify their meaning. The analytical process consists in resolving the original sentence in such a way as to exhibit and make intelligible its meaning. See also **Analytic/Synthetic.**

Analytical Judgment. Both Leibniz and Hume, each in his own very different way, had distinguished truths of reason (e.g., that A cannot be not-A) from truths of fact (e.g., that water boils at a certain temperature). Kant, accepting this basic distinction, developed it in a way that has affected philosophy ever since. He perceived and noted that a judgment or statement or proposition having the properties of necessity and universality may be called analytic, since the predicate of the judgment or statement or proposition is discoverable through analysis of the subject. Example: the fact that a triangle has three sides and three angles within it and that the sum of these angles is always equal to the sum of two right angles is a fact obtainable through an analysis of the term "triangle". Such predicates do not yield any knowledge not obtainable through such analysis of the subject. By contrast, if I say that this book is red or that it contains x number of pages, I am asserting what purports to be a fact that conveys knowledge not contained in the subject. The book might be blue, green, or any other color and it might have y pages or any other number. In the case of the triangle, however, everything we have predicated of it here can always be predicated of any triangle. Followers of the early 20th c. philosophical school called "logical empiricism" or "logical positivism" emphasized this distinction between "analytic" and "synthetic" propositions, making it very rigid. Quine and others, however, have argued against such rigidity in making the distinction, basic though it is.

Analytic/Synthetic. If the truth-value of a proposition depends only upon the cognitive meaning of the terms it contains (e.g., $2 + 2 + 5 = 9$ and "no bulls are pregnant"), the proposition is an analytic one. If it depends also on factual referents beyond itself (e.g., "some cats have no tails", "Mary has fractured her humerus", and "the velocity of light is 186,000 miles per second," it is synthetic. Kant laid the basis for the distinction. For him an analytic judgment is one in which the predicate concept is included within the subject concept, and so, since its sole criterion is the law of contradiction, it requires no verification by experience. By contrast, a synthetic judgment, having a predicate concept not included within the subject, depends on ground beyond itself.

Anamnesis. The term is a Greek one, meaning the recall of something to memory, e.g., in Plato, the recall of ideas known to the soul in past lives. In Christian liturgics the term is used to designate the reference in the Mass (usually following the Words of Institution) to the Passion, Resurrection, and Ascension of Christ.

Anaphora. The solemn and central part of the Mass, beginning with the Preface.

Anarchism. The term comes from the Greek words *an* (without) and *archos* (head). It came to be used in the 19th c., having been apparently employed first by Joseph Proudhon, then by Mikhail Bakunin. Although used in various ways, its basic significance is the notion of a politically non-organized society. Some (e.g., Bakunin) have contended for violent revolution as the means necessary to attain such a condition in society; others (e.g., Proudhon) have believed that as humanity develops morally and spiritually the various forms of government (democratic, oligarchic, monarchical, totalitarian, etc.) will become unnecessary and will gradually disappear. Tolstoy, a Russian thinker of considerable originality, advocated a form of non-violent resistance to state government that would eventually lead to its disappearance. Kropotkin argued similarly, although using different premises, that greater moral awareness would eventually lead to the abolition of government as an outmoded political phenomenon. The anarchist ideal generally assumes not only the moral perfectibility of man but its practical attainment within the foreseeable future. In the ancient world Confucius thought that if only human beings were sufficiently well educated they would need no political constraints. His experiments in political administration, for which he had been granted opportunity, provided no warrant for such optimism, notwithstanding that the ideal is, of course, a noble one.

Anārya. A name applied by the invading Aryans to the indigenous Indian tribes whom they subdued and also to foreigners generally, whom they deemed inferior.

Anastasius. 7th c. abbot of the monastery of St Catherine, Mount Sinai, and a vigorous champion of orthodoxy against the Monophysites.

Anath. A Canaanite goddess personifying sex. She was typically represented in nude form and she combined virginity with maternity. Her worship spread to Egypt. Only slight traces of it are found in the Old Testament.

Anathema. The term is rooted in the Hebrew Bible where it signifies the separation of anything as not for ordinary use. It came to have the more negative implication of cutting off as unfit for association with the community and it is in this sense that it occurs in Paul and in Christian practice generally, eventually having a close association with the formal process of excommunication.

Anaxagoras. (499–422 BCE). Greek philosopher who went to Athens and joined the circle of Pericles. Persecuted and imprisoned because his teaching that the sun and the moon are made of substance like the earth, which offended those who held to the popular belief that they were divinities, he escaped and fled back to his native Ionia. Having a mind of notable philosophical acumen, he anticipated many of the great philosophical problems that later thinkers had to confront. He conceived of the universe as composed of infinitely small "seeds" and saw mind (*nous*) as a collection of the tiniest and most pure of such "seeds" and the only ones that are self-moving. He saw *nous*, moreover, as the force that brings about all processes of change in the universe. His writings exist only in fragments.

Anaximander (610–547 BCE). Greek philosopher, born in Miletus. He used as a key concept that of *to apeiron* (the boundless), which is that which lies beyond all change and out of which all changes come. He saw in the operation of all things a law of balance or "justice", similar to the karmic principle in Indian thought. He saw space as associated in a special way with *to apeiron* and argued for a plurality of worlds. He is noted for his proposal that, since life has its origin in moisture, all living things have evolved from watery conditions and man himself from a kind of fish. See also **Evolution**.

Anaximenes (588–524 BCE). Greek philosopher, born in Miletus. He taught that all things have their origin and their destiny in air, which is the fundamental principle of the universe. By "air" he seems to have meant more than physical air; he saw it as a divine principle holding everything together. "When air is dilated so as to be rarer, it becomes fire; while winds, on the other hand, are condensed air." Stones are the most condensed of all. He believed the earth to be flat: "the form of the earth is like a table." He believed the world to be perishable but "infinite worlds exist in the infinite in every cycle."

Anchorite. A hermit, more especially one who is enclosed in his or her cell. In the later Middle Ages some parish churches had a cell for a resident anchorite.

Ancrene Riwele. An important medieval work central to the English tradition of Catholic spirituality. Composed *c.* 1200 for a group of female anchorites. The anonymous author shows learning and imagination in his writing of a work intended to guide its readers through the pitfalls of their very special way of life.

Andrew. Brother of the apostle Peter. The tradition that he was martyred by crucifixion on an X-shaped cross appears only very late (13th c.). An apocryphal book dating from the 3rd c. is known to have existed. A fragment of it has survived in its original form and a

Coptic translation of part of it survives. According to it, the apostle was imprisoned at Patras, but it does not mention the X-shaped cross. Since the 8th c. Andrew has been acknowledged as the patron of Scotland.

Andrewes, Lancelot (1555–1626). Bishop of Winchester; important and influential Anglican theologian, scholar, and preacher. He sought a theology based on authentic learning, free of the excesses of the Puritans and encouraged the use of Catholic language and ceremonial. His *Preces Privatae* is a great classic of Anglican devotional literature.

Andrew of Crete. (*c.* 660–740). Theologian and writer of homilies and hymns; born at Damascus.

Andrew of St. Victor. A 12th c. biblical exegete who insisted on a more literal interpretation of the Bible than was customary in the Middle Ages; Canon of St. Victor, Paris, and for some time abbot of a Victorine abbey in England. See **Hugh of St. Victor.**

Androgyn, The Myth of the. Among the most interesting of concepts in the history of religion is the notion that human sexual differentiation (maleness and femaleness) are the result of a division from a once-unified state. The motif is frequently encountered in Gnostic systems. Androgyny is not to be confused with hermaphroditism. The hermaphrodite has both male and female capacities and characteristics; the androgyn pertains to a state in which the differentiation has not emerged because the need for it has not arisen. Androgyny, according to the myth, is therefore a more perfect state than either that of the perfect man or the perfect woman, since it encompasses the perfections of each. The myth reflects not only a longing for and admiration of wholeness but also a disparagement of human sexuality as a fractured state. There may be echoes of the androgyn myth in some passages in the New Testament, e.g., (Mark 12.18–25) the response of Jesus

to the Sadducees who, not believing in resurrection, tried to trap him with a question that evoked from him the categorical statement that in the resurrected state there is to be no more marrying, for we are to be as the angels in heaven, i.e., not limited, as now we are, by our male or female sexuality. This does not mean that we are to be sexless; it means that the male-female polarity will have been transcended and we shall have been returned to our original, superior state: one of sexual wholeness.

The myth of the androgyn reappears, not unexpectedly, in Milton, whose angels seem to be androgynous: "all heart they live, all eye, all ear, all intellect, all sense" (*Paradise Lost*, vi, 350). Milton, who was extraordinarily learned, would be indubitably familiar with the myth of the androgyn as it appears in Gnostic literature. The Valentianian Gospel of Philip proclaims that when Eve was still "in Adam" death was unknown and that if he were to attain his former, his original self, death would end. Such is an expression of the androgynous ideal that presupposes our being in a state of brokenness, resulting in an insatiable longing of men and women for one another: a longing that at present cannot be fully overcome because it pertains to and is the inevitable consequence of our fractured sexual state. Neither marriage nor celibacy, neither heterosexuality nor homosexuality, which may all be seen as attempts to overcome or otherwise "cure" our fractured state, can achieve the wholeness they all seek, but which only the fulfilment of the androgynous ideal can actually achieve. The celibate life, with all its deprivation, may *symbolize* the androgynous ideal and point the way toward it; it cannot attain it any more than can the married state. According to the ancient myth of the androgyn, our human malaise springs not only from sexual apartness and loneliness but from an even deeper existential anguish: longing for the integrity of the androgyn.

Andronicus of Rhodes (1st c. BCE). He is said to have recovered the writings of Aristotle, which had been lost for many decades, and codified them. It was he who gave to one of Aristotle's writings that had been without a title the title "Metaphysics", seemingly meaning by that "the book that comes after the Physics" (i.e., in the order in which he had found the untitled work). Since the formerly untitled work deals with general philosophical principles, the term "Metaphysics" came to be used to designate that field of philosophical inquiry that deals with the most fundamental questions, which are often highly speculative ones yet at the same time often the most interesting and, some would contend, the most important.

Angel. From the Greek *aggelos,* a messenger. The Bible is saturated with references to angels, who are recognized in Judaism, Christianity, and Islam. Their existence was recognized by the early Christian Fathers, who generally attributed to them a rarefied or ethereal body. Dionysius, however, the "pseudo-Areopagite", who *c.* 500, developed an angelology that was to become normative for Christians throughout the Middle Ages, regarded angels as immaterial, and Thomas Aquinas and other medieval thinkers developed his views into a more systematic form. The Roman Catholic Church fully recognizes angels as an ontological reality, although in popular devotion their cult is subordinated to that of the saints.

With the recognition among educated Christians of the evolutionary character of the universe, including life, the possibility that angels may be interpreted as a more advanced stage in the evolutionary process and their identification, for example, with forms of extraterrestrial life, is not to be excluded.

According to the angelology of Dionysius, angels are arranged in three hierarchies, each containing three choirs: (1) Seraphim, Cherubim, Thrones; (2) Dominations, Virtues, Powers; (3) Principalities, Archangels, and Angels. Michael, although traditionally accounted "Prince of the Heavenly Hosts" is an archangel, as are Gabriel and Raphael.

Angela Merici (1474–1540). Foundress of the Ursulines. Canonized 1807.

Angela of Foligno (*c.* 1248–1309). Italian mystic; a married woman who after her husband's death became a Franciscan tertiary. Her visions were taken down from dictation by her confessor. She was beatified in 1693.

Angelus, The. The history of this widespread and popular Catholic devotion is obscure. It came into general use in the 17th c. in its present form throughout Western Europe, but forms of it were in use from the 13th c. It consists in the recital of three Ave Marias, each preceded by a versicle and response and the whole devotion concluded with a collect. The faithful are summoned to the devotion by a bell. The painting by Jean-François Millet (1814–1875), depicting a peasant couple standing with bowed heads in the fields in response to the Angelus bell is well known. The bell is rung thrice daily: morning, noon, and evening. The rhythm and brevity of the devotion contribute much to its beauty and charm.

Angelus Silesius (1624–1677). Mystical poet; convert from Lutheran to Roman Catholic faith; influenced by Eckhart; also engaged in controversy.

Anglicanism. The system of doctrine and practice upheld by those Christians who are in ecclesiastical communion with the ancient see of Canterbury. Anglicans are distinguished from Protestants by their claim to be in the apostolic succession of bishops as required for Catholic order, and from Roman Catholics by their claim to be also heirs of the Reformation. Many Anglicans see themselves today as having special affinities with Eastern Orthodoxy. The Anglican Communion comprises, besides the Church of England, various autonomous churches of which the Episcopal Church of the United States is an example. All recognize the spiritual leadership of the Archbishop of Canterbury. The traditional Anglican ethos encourages not only learning and piety but a deep reverence for Scripture and the early Christian councils and a high regard for Catholic tradition in general. Anglicans attach much importance to the Book of Common Prayer as an authoritative expression of doctrinal orthodoxy as well as a liturgical focus. For further reading, see BIBLIOGRAPHY: **Christian Thought and History.**

Anglo-Catholicism. That party in the Anglican Communion that emphasizes its historic continuity with the ancient and medieval Church, both in doctrine and in liturgical practice. Although the Latin term *Anglo-Catholicus* occurs in the 17th c., the use of the term "Anglo-Catholicism" came into general use only from 1838, when it seems first to have occurred. Like other ecclesiastical parties it often presents itself in narrow and uncritical forms; nevertheless, its influence on Anglican thought and practice is immense.

Angst. Kierkegaard used the term *Angest* (older Danish spelling) to express an agonizing premonition prompted by a sense of dread at being on the edge of an abyss of nothingness. The German equivalent is *Angst*, widely used in existentialist philosophy. Usually, translated *angoisse* in French, *agonía* in Spanish, it has no completely satisfactory English rendering.

Anima Christi. A medieval prayer, probably dating from the 14th c. and used especially in eucharistic devotion. It is prominently used in the Spiritual Exercises of Ignatius Loyola. The opening words in English are, "Soul of Christ, sanctify me."

Animism. A primitive form of religious development in which nature-spirits are worshipped. See **Dynamism.**

Anna. The name given in Hindu literature to food, considered in its sacramental aspect as manifesting the Supreme Essence and that which continuously transforms energies and conserves them.

Anne. The first mention of Anne as the name of the mother of the Virgin Mary seems to be in the Protevangelium of James, dating from the 2nd c. Devotion to her became extremely popular in the Middle Ages, being sometimes expressed in forms so extravagant as to include reference to her as "the Grandmother of God," which very properly of course evoked the strong opposition of the 16th c. Reformers.

Anno Domini. The traditional phrase used by Christians as a system of dating. The phrase means "in the year of the Lord" and was devised by Dionysius Exiguus in the early 6th c. (Judaism, Islam, and other religions have other conventions.) The basis for the dating is nowadays recognized as slightly wrong, since it is now known that the birth of Jesus must have occurred a few years earlier than traditionally calculated. Since scholarly enterprises are now conducted on inter-religious lines to a greater extent than formerly, modern scholars tend to adopt a convention more widely acceptable: instead of AD and BC (before Christ), they use CE (according to the Common Era) and BCE (before the Common Era) respectively.

Annunciation. This festal day (March 25), also known in England as "Lady Day", commemorates the announcing by the angel Gabriel to the Virgin Mary that she would be the Mother of Christ, as recorded in Luke 1.26–38. The first reference to its celebration in the West is in the Gelasian Sacramentary. From the 8th c. it has been universal.

Anointing. The ceremonial use of oil is widespread in the religions of the world, and the Hebrew Bible records the practice of the anointing of kings and priests. Anointing was used in New Testament times (e.g., James 5.14) in connection with healing and soon came to be used not only in Baptism and Ordination but in Unction and other sacramental practices and even in consecrating bells and other furnishing. It is prominently used in the Coronation of Christian kings, a practice that dates back to at least the 7th c.

Anomoeans. A name given to those who, in the 4th c., espoused a doctrine similar to that of the Arians. They held that Christ, although the complete expression of God's creative will, is unlike him in essence.

Anselm (*c.* **1033–1109**). Archbishop of Canterbury and very important figure in the history of philosophy and Christian theology. He attempted a more strictly intellectual defense of belief in the existence of God than had been generally undertaken before his time, expounding it in the *Monologion* and the *Proslogion*, a treatise in which he developed what is now known as the Ontological Argument. Although this argument was rejected by Thomas Aquinas (another form of it by Descartes was also later rejected by Kant), it is still not without its defenders today among philosophers and philosophical theologians. His *Cur Deus Homo*, a treatise on the Atonement, had immense influence on medieval thought on that subject.

Anselm of Laon (**died 1117**). Influential teacher who counted among his pupils William of Champeaux and Peter Abelard. Although traditionalist in outlook, he used new methods in expounding Scripture so as to open the way to theological discussion.

Ante-chapel. Some medieval college and other chapels were built with a truncated nave. Examples at Oxford would include those at Magdalen and New College.

Ante-Communion. A term used in Anglican tradition to designate that part of the eucharistic service, down to the "Prayer for the Church Militant," that precedes the more solemn part of the service. It corresponds to the part of the service in the early church that catechumens could attend, the rest being closed to all but the baptized.

Antependium. A cloth that hangs in front of the altar, varying in color according to the season of the Christian Year.

Anthropocentrism. The view that man is at the center of reality or at any rate must so regard himself. This view is in some respects adumbrated by the saying of Protagoras, in the 5th c. BCE, that "man is the measure of all things."

Anthropomorphism. In its crudest form, the representation of God iconographically in human terms, e.g., as a bearded old man. Anthropological language, however, is used in the Bible and other religious literature figuratively in phrases such as "the arms of God" and "the hand of God." In Christian theology, when personality and other such attributes are applied to God they are applied by way of exhibiting the claim that God includes values that we commonly call personal as well as those we regard as impersonal, yet recognizing that God is suprapersonal. Since we are human beings, our language about everything has built-in anthropomorphic tendencies.

Anthropopathism. A term coined by John Ruskin (1819–1900) to designate an outlook derived from what he called "the pathetic fallacy," e.g., the ascription to nature of human feelings or emotions such as tenderness or cruelty, gentleness or revenge.

Anthroposophy. A system evolved by Rudolf Steiner with features borrowed from theosophical tradition but putting man rather than God at the center of all things. Reincarnation and karma are included in its teachings.

Antiburgher. In the numerous schisms within the Scottish Kirk, a group that seceded from the Burgher group in 1747, denying that a Christian ought to take the "Burgess Oath." See **Burgher.**

Antichrist. In the New Testament, especially in the Apocalypse, a power is identified as at war with Christ. Although this power may be regarded as an evil principle at work in the universe, fancy has often seen it personified, e.g., in Nero and other notorious enemies of the Christian cause.

Antidoron. In the Eastern Church, the remainder of the loaves from which the eucharistic bread has been cut is distributed to the people in place of the consecrated bread. Originally intended as an alternative to the latter, a substitute for those who for one reason or another were not receiving the Sacrament, it is now often given to everybody present, whether they are communicating or not. The theory behind the practice is that, although not consecrated, it somehow mystically participates in some measure in the sanctity of the Eucharist itself, although fundamentally distinguished from the latter.

Antilegomena. Term used by Eusebius of Caesarea to designate books whose canonicity was disputed.

Antimension. A portable altar used in the Eastern Church, consisting of a cloth decorated and enclosing relics. Originally intended as a substitute for a regular, fixed altar, it is now used, along with the eileton, much as the corporal is used in the West.

Antinomianism. The view, denounced as heretical, that Christians, because of the grace they receive, are dispensed from the need to observe any law or ethical precept. The term, by extension, may be applied to the view or anyone who claims to be exempt from all law. Some Gnostic sects, for example, taught that there is such a sharp cleavage between matter and spirit that nothing done in the corporeal realm could make any difference in the spiritual one. The Nicolaitans, for instance, who are mentioned in the New Testament (Revelation 2.6 and 2.14f.) as a definable sect or group existing in New Testament times, are presented as urging a return to pagan practice in sexual and other matters on the supposition that they could affect only the body, not the spirit. Some extremists at the Reformation such as Johann Agricola (c. 1494–1566) and some groups of Anabaptists taught doctrines tending in this direction, claiming that they followed from Luther's teaching on justification by faith. Luther vigorously disowned them and denounced all such misunderstanding of his theological position. Antinomian views were widespread in Oliver Cromwell's England, although the extent of their incidence may have been exaggerated by his enemies. Sects advocating abundant engagement in sin in order to obtain proportionately great forgiveness (a notion akin to Antinomianiam) have existed in Russia and elsewhere.

Antinomy. In a general sense, the opposition of two contradictory conclusions. Kant used the term in a more special, technical sense to designate two opposing conclusions, each of which is deduced from apparently acceptable premises and by means of validly worked out inference. In the *Critique of Pure Reason* he gives four examples of this kind of antinomy.

Antioch, Council of (341). The first of several councils held in the 4th c. in attempts to modify acceptance of the principles enunciated at the Council of Nicaea.

Antiochene Tradition. The theology of the early Christian Church at Antioch tended to be historical and Aristotelian, in contrast to the Platonic tendencies of the Alexandrian tradition. The Antiochenes also tended to emphasize the humanity of Christ.

Antiochus. Ten kings of the Seleucid dynasty were so named and four of them are mentioned in the Bible: (1) Antiochus IV Epiphanes, King of Syria from 175 to 164 BCE; (2) Antiochus V Eupator, son of Antiochus IV and King of Syria from 164 to 162 BCE; (3) Antiochus VI Dionysos, who (being a minor) ruled under the regency of Tryphon from 145 to 142 BCE; and (4) Antiochus VII Sidetes, King of Syria from 139 to 129 BCE.

Antiphon. Originally a passage sung by two choirs alternately. In Western usage a passage, usually from the Bible, sung before and after a series of psalms sung as the mainstay of the Divine Office.

Antipope. Term used to designate a person claiming to be the rightful pope against one who claims to have been elected to the papal office. Some thirty-five antipopes have so claimed the papacy.

Antisthenes (*c.* **444–366** BCE). A Greek philosopher in the Socratic tradition, he was sometimes held to have been the founder of the Cynic school, rather than Diogenes, who seems to have been in fact its founder. Only fragments of the writings of Antisthenes are extant. He followed Socrates in various key points; e.g., that there are no gods such as can be expressed iconographically but only one God who cannot be so delineated. Like Socrates, he also perceived definition as one of the most important of philosophical activities. He used myth, as did Socrates, as a vital means of communication of philosophical concepts and arguments.

Antithesis. That which is placed in opposition to a given thesis. Kant used the term to designate the negative item in the antinomy. (See **Antinomy.**) Both Fichte and (very notably) Hegel used the term as part of a triad: thesis, antithesis, and synthesis. The synthesis gathers up and in some way resolves the opposition between thesis and antithesis.

Antonelli, Giacomo (1806–1876). Cardinal Secretary of State under Pius IX. He was influential in fostering the authoritarian tendencies of that pope, although he advised him against maintaining the doctrine of Infallibility during the Vatican Council. After 1870 he was sometimes called "the Red Pope." Although a cardinal, he had never been ordained priest and was widely regarded more as a shrewd politician than as a churchman.

Antonino (1389–1459). Dominican and Archbishop of Florence; founded the Convent of San Marco, Florence, and was much admired for his wisdom and rectitude. The practice of accepting interest for money lent was generally disapproved among Christians in the Middle Ages (hence the role of Jews as moneylenders) and Antonino was probably the first to recognize the rightness of receiving interest for money lent and was also in other ways ready to adapt to changing circumstances.

Antony of Egypt (died 356). Probably the most celebrated among the hermits of the ancient Church. At first a solitary, he came out to organize a community of men who sought to imitate him and on whom he exercised much influence.

Antony of Padua (1195–1231). Born in Lisbon he was at first received into the Order of Augustinian Canons but later became a Franciscan friar. His preaching at an ordination at Forli was so eloquent that his fame became widely known. He came to be acclaimed as the patron saint of the poor and eventually he has been popularly invoked for finding lost property: a reputation probably fostered by the story of a novice's having absconded with a psalter that Antony was using and who, receiving a divine warning, hastened to restore the book. He also protects pregnant women and all travelers. Money given in his name is widely known as "Saint Antony's bread."

Anurādhapura. The ancient capital of Sri Lanka until the 10th c. CE. Its great monastery was a stronghold of Theravada Buddhism from the 3rd c. CE. It is now a very notable repository of Buddhist culture and architecture.

Apathy. From the Greek *apatheia*, meaning "not-suffering". In the sense in which it was used by the Stoics, it refers to a state of mind in which one has complete serenity and peace. It has a counterpart among the Epicureans, which they emphasized under the name of *ataraxia*. The notion is very similar to the serenity that is so highly valued in Buddhist attitudes.

Apeiron. In Greek philosophy *to apeiron* means the boundless, the indeterminate, the infinite, the unlimited. See **Anaximander.**

Aphraates. Early 4th c. writer, first of the Syriac Church Fathers; known as "the Persian sage"; his works shed light on early Christianity in Persia.

Aphthartodocetae. A Monophysite group who taught that the earthly body of Christ was incorruptible (*aphthartos*) and immortal by nature. Their founder was Julian, Bishop of Halicarnassus, who died in the early 6th c.

Apocalypse. From the Greek word *apokalypsis*, meaning "revelation" or "unveiling." Apocalyptic literature is represented in the Old Testament by the Book of Daniel (156 BCE) and popular thereafter in both Jewish and early Christian literature, being represented in the New Testament by the Book of Revelation. It purports to exhibit truths generally unknown and to predict the turn of events leading to the end of the age. See **Apocalyptic.**

Apocalyptic. A literature that purports, through an unveiling of the meaning of present events, to exhibit the future. Apocalypse (Greek, *apokalypsis*) means "unveiling" or "revelation." Jewish apocalyptic literature, which dates from the beginning of the second century BCE to the end of the first century CE, has its origin in the growing conviction that the attainment of Jewish national aims was hopeless except through the intervention of God who, the apocalpytic writers believed, would destroy Israel's enemies and establish the messianic kingdom of God on the earth. Early Christian writers inherited the apocalyptic spirit, which appears in various places but notably in the book called the Revelation (or Apocalypse) of St. John the Divine. See **Apocalypse.**

Apocatastasis. Greek term meaning "complete restoration," used for the doctrine, held by Origen and others that all intelligent beings (angels, humans, devils) will ultimately be saved. It was opposed by Augustine and condemned by the Council of Constantinople in 543. It has been revived in modernized forms in more recent times, e.g., by Schleiermacher.

Apocrisiarius. Diplomatic representative of a patriarch; the title is sometimes used of other ecclesiastic officials of high rank.

Apocrypha. The Greek term *ta apokripha* means literally "the hidden things." Its technical use is attended by various ambiguities too complex to be fully treated here. Briefly, the term is used in two different senses: (a) Traditionally it is used of certain books (e.g., Wisdom, Tobit, Ecclesiasticus) not included in the text of the Hebrew Bible that was recognized at the Jewish Synod of Jamnia (*c.* C.E. 100) but nevertheless held in high esteem among both Jews and Christians, almost all of them being included in the Septuagint (q.v.). (b) Modern biblical scholars also use the term "apocryphal New Testament" to denote an early Christian literature which, though it may perhaps in some cases embody some elements of an authentic, trustworthy oral tradition, was excluded from the New Testament as received by the early Church. Such works were excluded because, for instance, they contain Gnostic or other interpretations deemed heretical or because the stories they recount of the life of Jesus are trivial and fanciful, having been obviously devised to meet a growing demand for details not provided in the accepted Gospel narratives.

Apodeipnon. In the Eastern Church the counterpart of Compline. The word means literally "after the evening meal."

Apollinarianism. A christological view taught by Apollinarius (*c.* 310–390) and condemned by the Church as heterodox. According to this teaching, in Christ the divinity and humanity are one and there could be no moral development in his life. The Logos replaced what to other men is the human spirit. The effect of this teaching is to attenuate the humanity of Christ.

Apollinarius, Claudius. A 2nd c. Christian apologist; Bishop of Hierapolis; author of a defense of Christianity that was presented to Marcus Aurelius.

Apollo. In Greek mythology, the son of Zeus and Leto. Eminent in the Greek pantheon, he came to be a symbol of all that is accounted manly, handsome, wise, and radiant.

Apollonian. Nietzsche contrasts two element that he sees in Greek tragedy: (1) the Apollonian, representing harmony and order; (2) the Dionysian, representing passion and emotion. This contrast between the rational and the nonrational elements in human experience is, of course, in one form or another, widely recognized in philosophy and literature.

Apollonius of Tyana (1st c. CE). Greek philosopher. A neo-Pythagorean (see **Pythagoras**), he founded a school at Ephesus in that tradition. He represented the Pythagorean tradition as teaching that there is one God above all other gods and beyond reason itself.

Apologia Pro Vita Sua (1864). The title of Newman's autobiography, an impor-

tant classic and source for the Tractarian Movement.

Apologists. Those early Christian writers who, mainly in the 2nd c., engaged in reasoned defenses of the Christian faith (e.g., Justin Martyr, Aristides, Theophilus) are so designated. Such a defense is technically known as an "apology" (*apologia*), and engagement in such exercises is "apologetics".

Apolysis. In the Eastern Church, a blessing at the end of the liturgy and other services.

Apolytikion. In the Eastern Church, the principal troparion of the day, sung at the end of Vespers and Orthros.

Apophthegmata Patrum. A 4th and 5th c. collection of sayings of the Egyptian monks.

Apostasy. Term designating total defection from Christian faith and practice. In the Roman Catholic Church it is also used in other, technical senses such as the desertion of a solemnly professed monk or nun.

A Posteriori. A term designating that kind of knowledge that issues from experience. See **A Priori.**

Apostle. Title given to the twelve principal disciples of Jesus, including Matthias who replaced Judas. In a more general sense, the term is also used of pioneering missionaries such as Patrick, "Apostle of Ireland."

Apostles' Creed. A brief statement of Christian faith, widely used in the West, of early origin but unknown date. First mentioned as such toward the end of the 4th c. by Ambrose, it was traditionally but erroneously by then attributed to the apostles.

Apostolic Canons. A series of eighty-five articles that form the concluding chapter of the Apostolic Constitutions, dating from the 4th c. They deal mainly with disciplinary questions concerning the duties and responsibilities of the clergy.

Apostolic Constitutions. A digest of ecclesiastical law dating from the 4th c.

Apostolic Delegate. An ecclesiastic appointed by the Holy See to keep the Vatican informed of ecclesiastical matters in the territory to which he has been assigned.

Apostolic Fathers. Those Fathers of the Church who lived immediately after the age of the apostles, e.g., Clement of Rome, Hermas, and Papias.

Apostolic See. Title claimed by the Roman Catholic Church for the See of Rome.

Apostolic Succession. A theory of how doctrinal orthodoxy and ecclesiastical order in the Church have been and must be safeguarded throughout the ages. Most commonly, the historic continuity of a line of bishops from apostolic times is held to provide the basis of the safeguard. Interpretation of how precisely the nature of the succession is to be understood varies, however, from crude formulations to qualified, intricate theological arguments. The concept is important in ecumenical discussions, since it is a controversial issue and a stumbling block to achieving the organic unity of the Christian Church.

Apostolic Tradition, The. A document attributed to Hippolytus, containing a detailed description of the practices of the Church in Rome in the early 3rd century. The principal source for the text is a Latin codex at Verona.

Apotheosis. A term meaning deification, the elevation of a mortal human being to that of a god or goddess. This practice, known in many religions, was conspicuous in the Roman Empire in which Christians were persecuted largely because of their refusal to acknowledge the divinity of the Emperor. In the medieval use of the term *divus*

(divine) as a title for the saints has been seen by some a tendency in the same direction, but Catholic theology expressly repudiates such a notion, insisting upon absolute distinction between God as Creator and his creatures, which is clearly enunciated in the Bible.

Appearance. A term used traditionally in philosophy to designate that which stands in contrast to reality. The notion that the world as we see it is totally or almost totally illusory (*māyā*) is to be found in Hindu and Buddhist thought, e.g., in Vedanta as represented by Shankara. In the West, Parmenides held such a view and Plato, while critical of Parmenides, taught a very modified form of it. In modern times Bradley held a view close to the Parmenidean one. That our grasp of reality is limited by our human condition is, of course, indisputable and well recognized in Christian thought.

Appellants. Those who, in the Jansonist controversy, appealed against the papal bull *Unigenitus* (1713).

Apperception. In Leibniz, while the term perception refers to our inner awareness of external things, apperception refers to our inner awareness of our inner state. In Kant, apperception denotes the unity of self-consciousness either in its transcendental or in its empirical form.

Appetites. Aristotle held that the dynamic part of human nature, the appetites of the soul, constitute its irrational aspect, which the development of the will must bring under control by subjecting the soul to reason. Thomas Aquinas took over this concept, developing it with some reference to the thought of John of Damascus. He also distinguished three kinds of appetite: the concupiscible, the irascible, and the rational.

Appian Way. The great road built by Appius Claudius Caecus in 312 BCE from Rome to the south, originally to

Capua and later to Brindisi. Paul, on his first journey to Rome, used it.

Appropriation. An important term in Kierkegaard's thought. He noted the limitations of "objective" methods (such as are used in the sciences and in much philosophical thought) and stressed the value of a subjective approach that he called "appropriation". One can appropriate the most fundamental and therefore the most important truths only by so "appropriating" them subjectively in personal relationship. He takes this to be preeminently the case in the individual's relationship with God. In this, his thought has affinities with that of Pascal, who distinguished the living God from the "God of the philosophers." See **Kierkegaard, Søren Aabye,** and **Pascal, Blaise.**

A Priori. Kant used the term *a priori* to designate all principles and judgments whose validity is not dependent in any way on sense impressions. Space, for instance, cannot be apprehended through the senses and being a necessary condition of experience it must be *a priori*. The opposite term is *a posteriori*: a term that logicians have applied to inductive reasoning (see **Induction and Deduction**) and in philosophy generally to the data of the mind that originate in the external world and are accepted as coming to it through the senses.

Apse. The eastern end of the chancel, generally circular, universal in basilican churches and derived from the old Roman style of public building, but sometimes adapted for use in other types of church architecture. The adjectival form is *apseidal*.

Aquila. Native of Sinope in Pontus who lived in the 2nd c. and translated the Old Testament into Greek, intending it to replace the Septuagint.

Aquileia. A village on the Adriatic coast for long the seat of a patriarchate. The 4th c. basilica, reconstructed in the eleventh century by the patriarch Poppo, contains some of the most remarkable mosaics in early Christian art.

Aquinas. See **Thomas Aquinas.**

A Quo. A phrase used by the medieval schoolmen to designate the principle or assumption or presupposition that is taken as the starting point of an argument, contradistinguished from the *ad quem,* its end or goal.

Arabic Versions. No known version of the New Testament in Arabic antedates the rise of Islam. The oldest surviving manuscript is an 8th c. translation from the important Syrian Peshitta.

Arahat. A Pali term applied to a Buddhist (usually a monk) who has attained the final stage in spiritual progress. It is also used of Mahāvira, founder of the Jain religion. The arahat is usually considered to be one who lives quietly in human society without taking any particular interest in it, but he can be a solitary.

Aramaeans. They first appear as a nomadic tribe in the Syrian desert. About the 12th c. BCE they began to settle in northern Syria. They developed a group of city states that flourished till they were absorbed by Assyrian conquests in the ninth and eighth centuries. Their relations with Israel were close and of great antiquity and they are often mentioned in the Old Testament. Aram is described (Genesis 10.22) as a son of Shem. See **Aramaic.**

Aramaic. In later Old Testament times Hebrew was becoming more and more a language for the learned and was being gradually displaced by Aramaic, a language that had for long been spoken by the Aramaeans in Syria and Mesopotamia. Some passages in the Old Testament (e.g., in Daniel and Ezra) are in Aramaic. Translations or paraphrases called Targums of the Hebrew Bible were made in Aramaic. Aramaic would be the customary language of Jesus and a few Aramaic words are found in the New Testament itself, e.g., *Talitha cumi* (Mark 5.41).

Ararat. The region in which the ark built by Noah is reported (Genesis 8.4) to have rested after the Flood. It is to be identified with Urartu, located in the mountains of Armenia near Lake Van.

Archbishop. Title given to bishops having jurisdiction over a province or group of Sees and sometimes to those whose See is a metropolitan or other important one.

Archdeacon. Clerical holder of an administrative office with duties delegated to him by the bishop, which usually include supervision of the clergy and care of ecclesiastical property.

Archelaus (5th c. BCE). Greek philosopher. A disciple of Anaxagoras, he taught that *nous* (mind) is separate from the rest of the universe and its principle of motion.

Arches, Court of. An ecclesiastical court to which appeals may sometimes be allowed from the diocesan courts of the Province of Canterbury. Before 1534, an appeal from the Court of Arches could be made only to the Pope; in that year an appeal could be made only to the Sovereign in Chancery. The entire appellate system was modified in 1965, however, by the Ecclesiastical Jurisdiction Measure.

Archetype. This term, which comes from the Greek *archē* (primal) and *typos* (figure, pattern) is used as a central concept in Plato's philosophy to designate the original forms of all things. Medieval Christian thought recognized this Platonic notion but placed the archetypes within the mind of God rather than as self-subsistent. In modern times, Jung has used the term extensively to designate the primordial forms of the collective unconscious.

Archimandrite. A title in use in the Eastern Church since the 4th c. It is used (a) for the head of a monastery, similar to the term "abbot" in the West, (b) the head of a group of monasteries; and (c) as a title of honor for any monk of the Eastern Orthodox Church.

Archpriest. A title used from the 5th c. for the senior priest of a city. In the Eastern Church nowadays it survives as a title of honor.

Arcosolium. A tomb excavated in the wall of the catacombs at Rome. The term is sometimes used of any sarcophagus.

Ardigo, Roberto (1828–1920). Italian philosopher who was in his day the leading figure among the Italian positivists against the school of neo-Idealism that was represented by men such as Croce and Gentile, which was influential about the turn of the century. His writings include *Psychology as a Positive Science, Empiricism and Science*, and *Philosophy and Positivism*. His collected works were published in twelve volumes (1882–1918).

Areopagite. Paul, in his speech on the Areopagus, refers to a certain Dionysius (Acts 17.34). In the Middle Ages, the mystical writer Dionysius, who flourished about 500 CE, was widely and erroneously identified with that much earlier one and on that account was accorded more authority than would otherwise have been given him. Scholars nowadays refer to the later Dionysius as Dionysius the Pseudo-Areopagite or as the Pseudo-Dionysius.

Arianism. The most widespread and important of the heterodox christological views in the early Church. The Arians denied the divinity of Christ, maintaining that he was not eternal but created by God for the creation of the world and is therefore a creature and therefore not divine. He is accorded the title "Son of God" by way of honor, not as asserting his divinity. This movement gave rise to groups holding such teachings in various forms. The Semi-Arians, for instance, regarded Christ as *homoiousios* (i.e., of similar *substance*) so as to distinguish him from the Father without so radically repudiating his divinity; but the victorious party in the Church, under Theodosius at the Council of Constantinople in 381, insisted that Christ was *homoousios* (i.e., of the same substance) as the Father and therefore equally divine. See also **Anomoeans,** the party that stressed the radical difference between the divinity of the Father and the non-divinity of the Son, and **Homoeans,** the party that avoided as far as possible any precise distinction by simply suggesting a certain similarity.

Ariminum and Seleucia, Synods of. Synods to which the Emperor Constantius summoned the bishops of both East and West in 359, in hope of settling the Arian controversy. Although the majority at the larger of the two synods (Ariminum) were on the anti-Arian side, that side did not succeed and no happy outcome ensued.

Aristides of Athens. A 2nd c. Christian apologist, who sought to defend the existence of God and argued that Christians had attained a fuller understanding of him than either pagans or Jews had achieved, and that Christians alone had learned how to love according to the highest biblical ideals.

Aristion. According to Papias, as reported by Eusebius, he was a primary authority in the first c. for the traditions about Jesus.

Aristo of Pella. A 2nd c. Christian apologist whose work Origen defended. Eusebius testifies that he wrote an account, no longer extant, of the destruction of Jerusalem under Hadrian.

Aristotle (384–322 BCE). Along with his teacher Plato, the most influential and important philosopher in the West, he immensely influenced the mould of Jewish and Islamic as well as of Christian thought. Although his system differed sharply from his master's in important respects, Plato's influence on him was very strong. In contrast to Plato, however, he taught that ideas exist only in the individual object, not in a world of Ideas beyond the world of sense. By a stroke of great philosophical genius, he provided the theory of a "first cause," God, who needs not to move in order to act, since he is able to draw everything to himself as a magnet draws nails. Although Aristotle did not attribute personality to God, his formulation of God proved to be eminently amenable to a Christian interpretation. So, despite the suspicion of Aristotle in the early centuries of the Christian Church, he eventually came to be held in enormously high repute among Christian thinkers. Translated into Arabic by Muslim and Jewish scholars, his thought was rediscovered by Christians in the 12th c. He was at first approached by Christian thinkers with caution, for they suspected him somewhat as 19th c. churchmen at first suspected scientists who talked of evolution as a basic principle in the universe. Thomas Aquinas and others in the 13th c. were able to show, however, his compatibility with Christian thought: a reconciliation of the science of their day, as represented by Aristotle, with their traditional forms of Christian faith.

Arius (*c.* 250–*c.* 336). Leader of the heterodox view called Arianism, which denied the divinity of Christ. He was probably a Libyan by birth and a pupil of Lucian of Antioch. See **Arianism**.

Arjuna. This hero in Indian lore appears in many diverse forms. He is probably a composite figure. In the ever-popular *Bhagavadgītā* he appears as a central figure, but he is found in so many other legends and in such various roles that it is difficult to attach him to any particular historic framework.

Ark. The Hebrew word *tēbāh*, meaning a chest or box is traditionally translated into English as "ark". It is used (Genesis 6.14ff.) of the vessel in which Noah is said to have escaped the Flood. Its size and arrangements are described in considerable detail. In the Babylonian Flood story the ark of Utnapishtim is likewise elaborately described. The Israelite story of the Flood bears striking resemblances to the Babylonian version from which it seems to have been derived. As described, the ark could not possibly have functioned as a river boat or seagoing vessel. The description would appear to have symbolic meaning of some kind.

The Ark of the Covenant, as described in Exodus 25.10ff., was made of acacia wood overlaid with gold inside and out, about 45 by 27 inches, surmounted by a gold plate overshadowed by two cherubim facing each other. It contained two stone tablets believed to go back to the time of Moses. When the Hebrews went through the desert it was carried ahead of the column (Numbers 10.33ff.) as it was carried in front of the army when they went into battle, e.g., in the battle against Ammon (II Samuel 11.11). It symbolized the presence of Yahweh. For a nomadic people it would have served originally as the equivalent of a temple: the meeting place of God and his people as well as the housing of his presence.

Arles. At least fifteen councils of the Church were held at Arles in France between 314 and 1275. The first summoned by Constantine to deal with the Donatist schism was especially important.

Armagh, The Book of. A most important codex on vellum, dating from the 8th or 9th c. and containing a collection of documents, some Irish, some Latin. Of considerable importance for Irish history, it is preserved at Trinity College, Dublin.

Armenian Christianity. Armenia was the first nation officially to embrace the Christian faith, having been converted by Gregory the Illuminator. Their doctrinal position today is similar to that of the Eastern Orthodox Church. They have two classes of priests: (1) "vardapets" who are celibate and from whom bishops are generally chosen, and (2) parish priests who are generally required to marry before ordination to the diaconate. They have been much influenced by Latin usage, for example, having adopted the Latin manner of making the sign of the cross.

Arminianism. The historically important theological position takes its name from Jacobus Arminius (Jakob Hermans), a Dutch Reformed theologian (1560–1609). The Arminian system, opposed to Calvinism, is set forth in the Remonstrance of 1610. Against the Calvinists who held that Christ died only for the elect (although in this they may have gone beyond Calvin himself), the Arminians taught that he died for all humanity. They emphasized the freedom of the will and rejected both the Supralapsarian and the Infralapsarian interpretations of divine predestination. The Synod of Dort (1618–1619) condemned Arminianism and for a time the Remonstrants, as the Arminian party in the Dutch Reformed Church was called, were persecuted. Only in 1795 did they attain complete toleration. Their influence throughout Protestantism, however, direct and indirect, was very notable. John Wesley, for example, taught an Arminian type of theology, and Methodism has tended on the whole toward an Arminian outlook, Calvinistic Methodism notwithstanding.

Arnauld, Antoine (1612–1694). French theologian, priest, and leader of the Jansenists; he engaged in controversy with both the Jesuits and the Calvinists, was supported in his opinions by Pascal and is the author of more than 300 works, including a major treatise against Calvinism. See **Arnauld, Jacqueline.**

Arnauld, Jacqueline Marie Angélique (1591–1661). Abbess of Port-Royal and sister of Antoine Arnauld, she was commonly known as Mère Angélique. Born in Paris, she became abbess of Port-Royal in 1602. In 1608 the preaching of a Capuchin friar so moved her that she introduced a series of disciplinary reforms at Port-Royal, which had been up to then, although reputable, somewhat easygoing. She imposed strict enclosure, silence, regularity in the recitation of the Divine Office, and insisted on the cultivation of the interior life of her nuns. The community prospered and grew. In 1630 her sister Agnes became abbess, and from about that time Angélique came much under the influence of Saint-Cyran and Port-Royal became a stronghold of Jansenism. See **Port-Royal** and **Arnauld, Antoine.**

Arndt, Johann (1555–1621). Lutheran theologian, follower of Melanchthon. Strongly Lutheran and inclined toward a Pietistic christology, he evoked Calvinist opposition.

Arnobius. An early 4th c. Christian apologist who included Lactantius among his disciples.

Arnobius. A 5th c. African monk who attacked Augustine's teachings on divine grace. He also opined that immortality is not a given condition of the human soul but one that must be won.

Arnold, Gottfried (1666–1714). German theological and devotional writer, whose somewhat eccentric teachings evoked opposition by the Lutheran Church. For example, he taught that before the fall the first man was androgynous and that Christ restored that androgynous nature to humanity.

Arnold, Matthew (1822–1888). English poet and critic, son of Thomas Arnold. Deploring both the moral irresponsibility he found in the English society of his day and the dogmatism he saw in the Church, which he saw as at odds with the scientific spirit and alien from the ethical aspect of religion that he took to be its essence. He defined religion as "morality touched with emotion." A man of spirituality and moral refinement, he exercised a profound influence on his educated contemporaries in Victorian England and left a permanent mark on religious attitudes in the English-speaking world.

Arnold, Thomas (1795–1842). As headmaster of Rugby School, England, he engaged in radical educational reforms with such success that his ideals and methods permanently transformed the education of upper middle-class children in England and prepared them in a unique way for an ethically motivated type of political leadership. Stressing the paramount importance of personal character, he developed a system of education based upon a deeply ethical and religious outlook. In religion he opposed dogmatism and especially opposed the Tractarians.

Arnold of Brescia. A 12th c. reforming churchman whose heterodox teachings led eventually to his excommunication in 1148 and his execution at Rome in 1155. His teaching included denunciation of the worldliness of the clergy and against their possession of material goods and their exercise of authority in political and other secular affairs. More specifically, he opposed the temporal dominion of the Pope. Against the traditional anti-Donatist view that the personal unworthiness of a priest did not affect the validity of the sacraments he administered, he held that it did diminish and could even destroy their value. He also taught that Christians, instead of confessing their sins to a priest, should confess them to one another.

Arrow Prayer. An extremely short form of prayer. A classic example is attributed to Jacob Astley as he went into battle at Edgehill: "O God, Thou knowest how busy I must be this day. If I forget Thee, do not Thou forget me."

Articles of Religion. In Anglican tradition, the theological position of the Church has tended to express itself in liturgy rather than in rigid doctrinal formulation; nevertheless theological guidelines have been set forth at various times under the heading of "articles." Examples include the Six Articles imposed on the Church in 1539, mainly against Reformation doctrines and maintaining Catholic doctrines and practices such as transubstantiation and the celibacy of the clergy; the Forty-Two Articles, issued in 1553 and requiring the subscription of clergy and others; and the Thirty-Nine Articles that, first issued in 1563, eventually became normative for the Anglican Communion. They are to be found in the Book of Common Prayer. Designed to avoid rigid, narrow doctrinal propositions, rather than to set forth creedal propositions, they allow for a variety of interpretations while nevertheless providing pointers to the direction of the Anglican understanding of Christian belief, especially in its steering of a middle course between what are regarded as the extravagances of Roman Catholic statements, on the one hand, and, on the other, Calvinistic and other formulations within the Reformation heritage.

Artificial Insemination. When a marriage is infertile and the couple desire children, they may resort to the now common medical practice of artificially (i.e., without coitus) introducing into the wife during the fertile period of her menstrual cycle the semen of either (a) the husband (AIH) or another donor (AID). AIH generally raises no serious ethical questions and is the course followed when the infertility is due to the husband's impotence. When, however, the infertility of the marriage is due to a more incapacitating defect in the husband, the couple may resort to AID, in which case ethical questions do arise, especially in respect of the divorce of the donor from all parental responsibility but also on account of the commercial nature of the transaction and the usual anonymity of the donor. Legal difficulties also arise, e.g., in respect to the child's legitimacy, which has been upheld in some States but denied in others. Moreover, the fact of AID is

generally concealed from the child, while in cases of adoption it is generally communicated. If AID is undertaken by the wife without the husband's full knowledge and consent, obvious ethical questions arise, both in respect of deception and in regard to the violation of the vows taken in Christian marriage. Otherwise, Christian attitude toward the practice, which is now well established socially and medically, must depend upon whether it is regarded as violating the sanctity of the marriage or not. In principle the practice would seem to be unobjectionable so long as deception or other independently unethical accompaniments are excluded.

Artophorion. In the Eastern Church, the tabernacle within which the eucharistic Sacrament is reserved.

Arundel, Thomas (1353–1414). Archbishop of Canterbury. He was a notable opponent of the Lollards, whom he much persecuted.

Aryan. This adjective is of uncertain origin, except that it seems originally to have been connected with land and its owners. The name *Ārya* is the name applied to the fair-skinned nomadic horse and cattle breeders occupying the plains of the region north of the Caucasus between the Black and the Caspian seas who about or soon after the year 2,000 BCE began a migration in several directions, some spreading into northern Europe, others into India and Iran. They were patriarchal in their organization of society and they worshipped male deities. Many words that are recognized in the West as of Graeco-Roman origin have a more ancient lineage in Aryan sources. Their eventual fusion with other peoples, notably in the Indus Valley, makes their disentanglement difficult, but they seem to have been proud warriors who claimed a right to be overlords of the land and to have been prototypes of those who in Vedic times were recognized as *rājanya* (kings or nobles). They were apparently fair-skinned and showed in some of their prayers great pride in this ethnic characteristic, beseeching the gods to save them from contamination through intermarriage with the indigenous population. In India this attitude has left a permanent mark on the general outlook that still attaches value to lightness of complexion, in both women and men.

The view that persons of Aryan race are innately superior to others, having greater intelligence, beauty, and capacity for culture has had a variety of exponents, perhaps most notable among whom is Arthur Gobineau (1816–1882), a French thinker and diplomat who introduced the notion into the philosophy of history. Among his writings are his *Essay on the Inequality of the Human Races*, 4 vols. (1853–55) and *The Religions and the Philosophies in Central Asia* (1865).

Asana. From the Sanskrit, meaning "sitting". The importance of posture for spiritual purification and progress is much emphasized in yogic and other types of Indian religious thought and practice. The concept has counterparts in the West, e.g., in Catholic ritual, in which posture has a significance comparable to that of speech and functions similarly, so that both minister to the completeness of liturgical expression and the beneficent effect on the development of the interior life.

Asanga. Indian Buddhist philosopher (4th c. CE), founder of the Yogācāra or Vijñāna-vāda school. He held that all phenomena are subjective and that the real is pure consciousness. We are surrounded by illusion, and only in fully perceiving and appropriating the truth of this can one attain pure consciousness, which takes one beyond both existence and non-existence. His thought has some resemblance to aspects of Manichaean and Neoplatonic philosophy. It is noteworthy that the region in which Asanga lived (Gandhāra) is one that had been subjected to strong influence from the Graeco-Roman world.

Asaph. A 6th c. Welsh saint.

Āsava. A Pali term, from the Sanskrit *āsrava*. In Buddhist thought it designates the "taints" that are regarded as intoxicating the mind and inhibiting spiritual evolution. They are: *kāmāsava* (sensuality), *bhav-ā* (desire to be reborn), *ditth-ā* (false doctrine), and *avijj-ā* (ignorance). See **Avidyā**.

Asbury, Francis (1745–1816). Along with Thomas Coke, one of the two first superintendents (bishops) of the Methodist Church in the United States.

Ascension. A major feast of the Christian Year, celebrating the close of the period of post-resurrection appearances of Christ. Only two New Testament texts represent it as suggesting an historical, empirically observed fact, and even these are notably restrained in their presentation of it (Luke 24.50f. and Acts 1.9f.). Other texts allude to it in theological terms and often obliquely, while the silence of other New Testament books is noteworthy. In Ephesians 4.8–10, the reference suggests to educated modern readers the entry into another dimension of being: a dimension "far above all heavens" and one in which he is able to "fill all things."

Ascesis. The term, from the Greek *askēsis*, which means literally "exercise" or "work", is used to signify the rigorous self-discipline and self-restraint that constitute an element in the practice of most, if not all, the great religions of the world. The verb *askein* (whence *askēsis*) is used by Paul (I Cor. 9.25) in a passage in which he compared the Christian's striving to that of an athlete in the games. Asceticism was a familiar notion among the Stoics and other ancient philosophical schools, being used to denote a set of practices believed to promote virtue and to curb vice. Buddhism has an elaborate set of ascetic rules for monks and others who wish to strive for perfection. In Christian thought, Origen and Clement of Alexandria developed the notion of ascetic discipline as a way of purging the soul of its earthly passions and attachments and preparing it for the pure contemplation of God. The ascetic ideal, already present in the Wisdom literature (e.g., Proverbs and Ecclesiastes) and characteristic of much New Testament teaching, was highly developed in the patristic and medieval periods, finding expression in the eremitical and monastic ways of life, which demand both external disciplines such as fasts and abstinences and great interior self-restraint. The ascetic way was chosen and stressed by those who, in later medieval times, wished to use it as a protest against the worldliness of many of the clergy. After the Reformation it reappeared in the Puritan movement, for example. Asceticism, however, was only one of three great influences in the medieval Christian outlook. There were two other important influences, one humanistic, the other mystical. These three elements have counterparts in most of the great religions of the world.

Ascetical Theology. That branch of theology that treats of normal or ordinary ways of attaining personal perfection in the practice of the Christian life, contradistinguished from Mystical Theology.

Asclepius of Alexandria (5th c. CE). Hellenic philosopher. He was a member of the Alexandrian school of Neoplatonism and had studied under Proclus and Ammonius of Alexandria. His writings include a commentary on Plato's *Timaeus*.

Aseitas. In medieval philosophy, this term (meaning "being for oneself") was applied to the Being of God, contrasted with the being of everything else, which take their being *ab alio*, i.e., they are dependent on God for their existence. The term is sometimes rendered in English as "aseity".

Asherah. In Ugaritic lore, she was the consort of El. In the Old Testament she is the consort of Baal and is frequently mentioned as a sort of cult-object, probably a stake of wood crudely carved

with the image of the goddess, functioning somewhat as a fertility goddess such as Ishtar and Astarte. See **Anath** and **Astarte**.

Ashkelon. One of the five cities of the Philistines, mentioned frequently both in Egyptian texts and in the Bible.

Ashram. An Indian term, derived from the Sanskrit and signifying a place of retreat, which may be either a hermitage or a colony of persons studying under a master of the spiritual life.

Ash Wednesday. The first day of Lent. For more than a thousand years it has been marked by the imposition of ashes on the foreheads of clergy and people to symbolize the penitential nature of the season. The words "memento mori" are used as a reminder of the brevity of human life: "Remember, man, that thou art dust and unto dust thou shalt return."

As If. The name given to a philosophical view developed by Hans Vaihinger. See **Vaihinger, Hans**.

Asmita. From the Sanskrit, meaning "I-am-ness". It is applied to the tendency to confuse the sensible or empirical self with the *puruṣa* or "true" self.

Aśoka. Ruler of the Mauryan empire of Northern India in the 3rd c. BCE. He became a Buddhist and is greatly venerated in Buddhist societies to this day.

Asperges. The ceremony of sprinkling holy water over the people at the beginning of the chief Sunday Mass. The term is from the first word of the verse of the *Miserere*, that is sung during the ceremony except at Eastertide when the *Vidi Aquam* replaces it. In the Roman Catholic Church this beautiful rite is no longer obligatory.

Aspersion. In the administration of Baptism the practice of merely sprinkling water on the head of the candidate, contradistinguished from pouring it (affusion). Although aspersion is the method widely used in some Christian denominations, affusion is the norm in the West wherever traditional Catholic practice is upheld. In the Eastern Churches, immersion and submersion are the methods used.

Assent. Newman recognized two ways of giving assent: (1) that which we give to a proposition, which he called "notional" and (2) that which we give to the reality to which the proposition refers, which he called "real" assent. In all matters pertaining to religious decision, notional assent is only the first step; it must be completed by real assent. See **Newman, John Henry.**

Assent. Anglican clergy are required at Ordination to the diaconate and priesthood to assent to the Book of Common Prayer and the Articles of Religion. By "assent" is understood a less formal and rigid adherence to such documents than would be intended by subscription. The distinction is highly significant, since the giving of assent, while it implies a promise not to teach anything radically opposed to the spirit of the documents, does not bind one in a legalistic way to the details of formal statements they may contain.

Assertion Sign. The mark ⊢, used by 20th c. logicians (e.g., Frege and Russell) to distinguish the mere stating of a proposition and the maintaining of its truth.

Assizes of Jerusalem. A series of lawbooks setting forth the customary law of the Latin Kingdom of Jerusalem, compiled from 1197 onwards and derived from the feudal customs of Western Europe at the time of the First Crusade.

Associations, Law of. A French law promulgated in 1901 forbidding the formation of any religious congregation in France without State authorization. It also required existing religious congregations to report details of their membership and activities to the State. When, in 1902, a further enactment forbade engagement in any form of educational activity, members of male congregations exiled themselves, while members of female ones generally formed themselves into nursing congregations. Such legislation eventually led, in 1905, to a radical break between Church and State.

Assumption of Mary. On November 1, 1950, Pope Pius XII, in an encyclical, *Munificentissimus Deus,* defined as *De fide* the doctrine that Mary had been corporeally assumed into heaven. This doctrine, unknown in the early Church, first appears in some late fourth century writings and in orthodox Christian circles not till two centuries later. The Eastern Church doctrine of the Koimesis is less rigidly understood. Anglicans, even those highly sympathetic to devotion to Mary, generally regard the action of Pius XII in this matter as reactionary and in the light of modern modes of conceptualization, a retrograde step.

Assumptionists. A religious congregation originating in France in 1843 for teaching and missionary work. It follows the Augustinian rule in a modified form.

Assyria. The city of Ashur, located on the right bank of the Tigris, between the upper and the lower Zab. Its name came to be given to the entire surrounding district and its people. It lay close to the Zagros mountains on the east and the Armenian mountains on the north. The Assyrians, as we hear of them in the Old Testament, were notorious for their rapacity and lust for conquest that carried them far beyond their original settlement. Originally, however, it seems likely that, lacking natural frontiers, they had had to struggle against being absorbed into larger empires and so acquired a taste for and skill in warfare. The Assyrian god was Ashur (identical with the name of the principal city), a warrior-like god symbolized as an archer within a winged disk. Assyria was a vital factor in Israel's history for at least two centuries. Assyrians excelled in art, especially sculpture and provided a channel for the spread of Babylonian culture. But above all they were a most formidable military power. Their empire eventually passed to the Babylonians and thence to the Persians and to Alexander. To the Hebrew people it represented the earthly power that stood as an obstacle to the attainment of the Kingdom of God, which at times it threatened to destroy.

Assyrian Christians. A group of Christians whose Patriarch lives in San Francisco and who have survived in the Middle East from early times. While denying that they have ever held to Nestorianism, they traditionally hold Nestorius in honor.

Astarte. One of the three fertility goddesses of the Canaanites. Similar to Anath, she was identified with the evening star. (See **Anath** and **Asherah**.) Figurines and other representations of her have been found at Israelite levels of occupation, showing that her cult persisted comparatively late in Hebrew history.

Asterius. A 4th c. Arian theologian.

Āstika. This term is used in Hinduism to signify that which is "orthodox" or "right teaching" understood as a recognition of the sacred writings as divinely inspired in such a way that even the sounds of the words are divine. It corresponds approximately to what in Judaism and Christianity would be regarded as "biblical literalism."

Astrology. Astrology seems to have originated in Mesopotamia in the 2nd millenium BCE, where it was used for State purposes as a means of providing omens to guide rulers in making their decisions. From *c.* the 5th c. BCE it developed there and then later in the Greek world into a system more akin to what it is today. It probably reached its definitive form *c.* 100 CE in the Roman Empire, further developing later still in Byzantium, Islam, and Western Eu-

rope. Historically, astrology had remarkable prestige at least down to the 18th c. CE, being linked to astronomy yet having a religious slant. Although popularly seen as an art claiming to predict future events and therefore implying a determinism that would exclude human freedom, astrology is not necessarily so interpreted. It can be understood, (as it is by many), rather as providing only an indicator of the cosmic forces at work at an individual's birth: his or her cosmic circumstances, which the individual must find the means of surmounting. No proponent of the view that human beings enjoy freedom of choice claims that the freedom is unlimited, i.e., entirely unfettered by circumstance; astrology, therefore, whatever value may be placed upon it, by no means necessarily encourages fatalism.

Astronomy. Astronomy is the oldest of the "natural" sciences and its success in antiquity is formidable and too little appreciated by most people today. Even the Babylonians and the Egyptians, who had been observing the heavens for thousands of years before the Greeks, had learned through calculations how to predict lunar eclipses and, although much less accurately, solar ones. The Pythagoreans, however, through astonishingly felicitous hypotheses, discovered as early as the end of the 5th c. BCE that the earth is approximately spherical. About a century later Eratosthenes calculated its diameter within about fifty miles of what is known today. So remarkable were the advances among the Greeks at this stage in antiquity that Aristarchus of Samos, who flourished about 270 BCE, worked out what was virtually the system developed 1800 years later by Copernicus, although unfortunately later on such authentic scientific progress declined and many fanciful notions prevailed. Astronomy, moreover, provided the ancients with a model of scientific method, including the careful use of observation and quantitative relations characteristic of the methods of the natural sciences.

Astruc, Jean (1684–1766). A French medical man who pioneered critical study of the Book of Genesis. By showing that in its present form it must have been the result of an editorial process, he adumbrated what later became a key principle in biblical studies.

Asuras. A term widely used in ancient India for demons. In Buddhism they are generally understood as a collective host hostile to all beneficent forces.

Athanasian Creed. A credal statement of disputable date composed in Latin but certainly not attributable to Athanasius with whose name it has been traditionally but erroneously connected. It cannot have been composed before *c.* the 5th c. It was in considerable use in the Church for many centuries, but because of its vehement anathemas and denunciatory clauses attempts were made in some branches of the Christian Church in the 19th c. to have it removed from use entirely. In the Anglican Churches, for example, its use has been restricted and in some of them abandoned, not through repudiation of its doctrine but rather from a distaste for its manner of expression. It expounds particularly the doctrine of the Trinity and of the Incarnation. Although not recognized as an official standard of faith in the Eastern Church, it has been used in a modified form in some Greek and Russian Churches. It is sometimes known as the "Quicunque Vult": the opening words of the original Latin form.

Athanasius (*c.* 296–373). Having been secretary to Alexander, Bishop of Alexandria, whom he attended at the Council of Nicaea in 325, he succeeded him in 328. He was the most vigorous opponent of Arianism and in various ways succeeded in defending what came to be accepted as orthodox Christianity.

Athanasius. A 10th c. monk of the Eastern Church who established the Lavra, which was to become the most famous of the monasteries on Mount Athos. He eventually became head of all the monastic houses on Athos.

Atheism. In the ancient world the term *atheos* or its equivalent was generally applied to anyone who expressed disbelief in the State gods. So Socrates was charged with disseminating atheism, although he was no doubt by modern reckoning a religious man. In Christian usage, the term came to be applied to anyone who in any way questions the existence of God or accounts the evidence for it insufficient. In the 19th c. the term "agnostic" came into use to designate the position of those who denied the sufficiency of the evidence for God's existence without their categorically denying it. This was the position of a large number of thoughtful people among the educated classes and by no means implied an irreligious spirit. The term "atheist" then came to be used almost only of those who claimed, rather, that God can be shown not to exist: a comparatively rare claim. In the 20th c., a fashionable stance among those analytical philosophers who have come to be known as "logical positivists" or "logical empiricists" is the denial that terms such as "God" can have any meaning, so that there can be no question of doubt, since doubt as to the truth of a proposition can arise only where it is intelligible. Such a position probably implies atheism in the modern sense as does also dogmatic Marxist teaching on the subject.

Athenagoras (2nd c. CE). Athenian Christian apologist who defended the Christian faith by philosophical, literary, and religious arguments. His defense was presented to Marcus Aurelius, in which he attacks the polytheistic attitudes and practices of popular religion and exhibits support for monotheism in the Greek thinkers and other writers of antiquity. His principal writings include *Apology; Embassy for the Christians;* and *On the Resurrection of the Dead.* He was profoundly influenced by Plato.

Athos. Mount Athos is the chief place of pilgrimage for Eastern Orthodox Christians and the traditional focus of the spirituality of that tradition. Founded more than a thousand years ago and known as *Athōs* or *ho hagios oros* ("the holy mountain"), it consists of some twenty monasteries and many smaller houses organized as a religious republic under the protection of Greece and situated on the northernmost of three peninsulas that project into the Aegean Sea from the coast of Macedonia. The monasteries, which contain many valuable manuscripts, icons, and other treasures, observe (except for the monastery of Vatopedi) the old Julian calendar, which runs thirteen days behind the Gregorian calendar of the West. The Athonite rule has from early times prohibited not only women but even female animals on Athos. Contrary to popular belief, the reason claimed for this prohibition is not so much misogyny as to discourage the monks from diverting their attention from the spiritual exercises proper to their vocation and into pursuits such as breeding live stock for food and profit, a practice widespread in monasteries in the Western Church and one that has often made such monastic institutions very wealthy.

Ātman. This Sanskrit term, of great importance in the history of religious ideas, is to be understood as signifying the life-principle. In later Indian thought it came to denote the "essential" self, contradistinguished from the empirical self. The *ātman* in this developed sense is not used as "soul" and "spirit" are used in the West. It is even more fundamental, for while the empirical self comes to be regarded as having several embodiments, some crasser than others, none is entirely imperishable as is the *ātman*, which lies at the core of them all. Originally the concept was attached to the cosmic principle, *brahman* and it has retained this in such a way that the individual *ātman* is to be understood as the *brahman* principle of the cosmos in immanent form. In simple language, it is an individual spark of the cosmic fire and therefore participates in its eternality and immortality.

Atomism. The view that the universe consists of a collection of building blocks or units (atoms) that together constitute it, each of which is indivisible, was propounded by thinkers in antiquity both in India and in Greece. It occurs, for instance, among Jain thinkers centuries before it was expounded by Democritus and his followers in Greece in the 5th c. BCE. In the 4th c. BCE, Epicurus developed the theory, which Heraclides refined by proposing that the atoms are not all of the same quality. In the 3rd c. BCE, Strato proposed the view that the atoms are infinitely divisible. The tradition was continued in the 1st c. BCE by Lucretius who, however, proposed the important and then novel view that the atoms possessed a power to swerve by their own volition and so to set up vortices and new worlds, i.e., he endowed them with a rudimentary form of free will. Atomism remained compatible with the cosmologies developed in Europe in the Renaissance and later. The corpuscular theory, for example, had its roots in it.

Atonement. In the Old Testament, the Hebrew word *kappēr*, which is rendered in English as "atonement" (*at-one-ment*), means etymologically to cover up or cloak an offending object in such a manner as to pave the way for reconciliation. The gold plate on the Ark of the Covenant (see *Ark*) was called *kappōret*, i.e., the place of atonement. The concept as found in the Old Testament is carried over into the New Testament with, however, some important changes of meaning, notably that the reconciliation is accomplished by God and the atonement by Christ, representing the whole of humankind.

The Day of Atonement, still observed as a most solemn day in modern Judaism, is mentioned in Leviticus and elsewhere, and the ritual attending it is described in detail in various passages of that book (e.g., Leviticus 16.1ff. and Numbers 29.7ff.). The blood of the victim of the animal sacrifice represents life and is the atoning agent.

Atrium. In the houses of ancient Rome the main court of the dwelling was so designated. Christians took over the term as the designation of the forecourt of a church, which often consisted of a quadrangle surrounded by a colonnade and having a fountain at the center. The atrium was connected to the church by a narthax.

Atterbury, Francis (1662–1732). Bishop of Rochester and a famous preacher of his day; banished from England for alleged complicity in a Jacobite plot.

Atto (c. 885–961). A learned canonist and theologian; Bishop of Vercelli.

Attribute. This term as it has come to be used in western thought, has its origin in Aristotle, who recognized the world as consisting of substances and their attributes: that which can be predicated of the substances. The medieval philosophers followed Aristotle with some slight modifications. In the mind-matter dualism developed by Descartes in the 17th c., thought and spatial extension constitute two different attributes of reality, each opposed to the other. Spinoza accepted that concept in principle but notably enlarged it by postulating that the attributes that Descartes had specified are the two known to us but that there is an infinite number of them. In theology in the Judaeo-Christian tradition, the term is much used in reference to what can be predicated of God, e.g., unity, simplicity, eternity, omnipotence, omniscience, and incorporeality.

Attrition. A technical term in Catholic theology, contradistinguished from contrition. Both entail sorrow for one's sin, but while contrition springs from a pure love of God, attrition arises merely from an inferior disposition such as self-hate or the fear of hell.

Auburn Declaration (1837). A statement by a group of American Presbyterians who were charged by another group with having departed from the strict traditional Calvinism and the standards of the Westminster Confession of Faith that was held to have embodied them. When, in 1868 the General Assembly had recognized the statement as containing what was deemed to be the fundamentals of the Calvinist position, the two groups were reunited in 1870.

Auctorem Fidei. The papal bull of 1794 that condemned many of the articles of the Synod of Pistoia (1786), which had urged various reforms in the Church.

Audiani. A 4th c. sect that opposed the worldliness of the clergy, broke from the Church, and then conducted missionary work in Scythia. They are named from their founder, Audius.

Audience, Papal. Three kinds of papal audience are granted: (1) public, at which large gatherings of visitors are received several times a week; (2) private; and (3) special, consisting of small groups of pilgrims or others (*udienza speciale*).

Audientes. In the early Church catechumens (those preparing for Baptism) were divided into two classes: (1) *audientes* (auditors) who had not yet committed themselves and *competentes*, those who sought instruction and admission to the Church.

Aufklärung. See **Enlightment**.

Augsburg Confession (1530). The Lutheran confession of faith drawn up by Melanchthon and approved by Luther. It consists of two parts: (1) twenty-one articles setting forth the fundamental Lutheran doctrines, and (2) seven articles reviewing the abuses of the medieval Church that called for rectification. Presented to the Emperor (Charles V) on June 30, 1530, it was intended as a moderate and irenic statement. Since it did not satisfy the

Roman Catholic theologians to whom it was sent, it went through various modifications over the course of many years. In 1548, after a doctrinal formula had been accepted as the provisional basis of a religious settlement between the two parties and after this had failed to achieve that goal, the Emperor had a formula prepared as a provisional basis pending the Council of Trent, which was about to be convened in 1549. The "Interim of Augsburg" as this formula was called compromised on some points such as the celibacy of the clergy, but it still did not succeed in its aims. In 1555 came a political settlement, the "Peace of Augsburg," recognizing the existence of both Lutheran and Catholic states in Germany, under the principle *cuius regio eius religio*. This meant that one should follow the religion of one's prince or else migrate to a principality in which the prince's religion coincided with one's own. The Augsburg Confession remains to this day the classic doctrinal formula for Lutherans.

Augustine (354–430). Recognized both in Catholic tradition and within the Reformation heritage as the Father of Western theology, apart from whom even the mold of Christian thought would not have been shaped as it is. Born at Tagaste, North Africa, of a pagan father who was a Roman citizen and of a Christian mother, he studied at Carthage, intending a career in law, but turned to literary activities. The reading of a work (now lost) by Cicero sparked in him a lively interest in philosophical questions and for nine years he espoused Manichaean principles, which eventually, however, failed to satisfy him. For a time he passed through a skeptical phase, then became interested in Neoplatonism, which deeply affected the turn of his mind ever afterwards and, through him, the cast of Western Christian thought. As a result of the preaching of Ambrose in Milan, he was attracted to Christianity and in 387 he was baptized, returning to his native Tagaste the following year where he es-

tablished a Christian community. In 391 he was ordained priest and in 396 became Bishop of Hippo. Against the Donatists, he developed the view that the validity of the Sacraments of the Church cannot be affected by the unworthiness of the priest who administers them. He saw the State as a great good, because it provided a basis of law and order and so promoted a civilized society; but he regarded it as nevertheless inferior to the Church to which eventually it must yield. In the controversy with Pelagius, he developed against the latter what were to become some of the most notable of the traditional Christian views, such as the concept of the Fall, Original Sin, Election, and Predestination. Among his writings, his *Confessions*, an autobiography, is probably the best known, being loved for its patent sincerity and candor and his passionate conviction of having been rescued, by the pure grace of God and in face of his total personal unworthiness, from perdition to everlasting acceptance by God. His other writings include his *De Civitate Dei* and his *De Trinitate*.

Augustine of Canterbury. A 7th c. missionary sent by Gregory the Great in 596 to England. He was consecrated Archbishop of Canterbury at Arles. His attempt to reconcile the ancient Celtic Church with Roman customs and practices was unsuccessful.

Augustinian Canons. An order of Canons Regular originating in the 11th c.

Augustinian Friars. The 13th c. saw the rise of various orders of friars such as the Dominicans and Franciscans. Among these were the Augustinians, technically called "hermits" (*eremiti*), founded in 1256. Luther belonged to a German congregation of this order.

Augustinian Rule. An early monastic rule traditionally but probably erroneously attributed to Augustine. Dating from the 6th c. or perhaps even earlier, it was revived by the Augustinian Canons and various other orders such as the Premonstratensians and the Dominicans.

Augustinus. The title of a treatise that came to be recognized as the classic exposition of Jansenist principle. It was the work of Jansen and published posthumously in 1640 at Louvain.

Aulén, Gustaf (1879–1977). Swedish Lutheran bishop and theologian, leader of a school that sought to look behind verbal formulations of Christian doctrine to truth underlying them. See Bernard Erling, "Gustaf Aulén: A Life Well Lived" in *Christian Century*, 95 (April 19, 1978), 422–424.

Aumbry. A recess in the wall of a church in which the reserved Sacrament is kept in some Anglican churches.

Aureole. In iconography the entire figure of a saint is sometimes surrounded by a golden background of light. It is to be distinguished from the halo or nimbus.

Auricular Confession. Confession of one's sins to God may be made in various ways, e.g., publicly as part of an act of public penance or privately and secretly to God. Auricular confession is confession made "into the ear" of a priest.

Aurobindo (1872–1950). Indian thinker. In expounding Advaita Vedanta, he maintained that Sankara had misinterpreted the Upanishads. He held that reality consists in a graded series, beginning in matter and culminating in Brahman, the nature of which is such as to necessitate his descent into the finite, which in turn is such as to necessitate its movement toward the infinite. Aurobindo's thought implies an evolutionism. Lower forms have a compulsion to evolve into higher forms. The process is accomplished by means of what he calls "internal yoga," involving a transformation of body, life, and mind. In his youth Aurobindo was involved in political agitation and imprisoned but soon devoted himself to philosophical writing and religious meditation. His ashram at Pondicherry commemorates his religious development and outlook. His writings include *The Life Divine* (2 vols., 1947), *The Synthesis of Yoga* (1948), and *The Supramental Manifestations upon Earth* (1952).

Austin, John (1911–1960). Oxford philosopher of language. He conducted extensive examination of the problems posed by language, distinguishing various forms, e.g., locutionary, illocutionary, and perlocutionary (i.e., performative utterances) language. The concept of performative utterance was important in various ways, not least for theologians in their treatment of the significance and role of ritual acts in liturgy. His writings include *Philosophical Papers* (1961); *Sense and Sensibilia* (1962); and *How to Do Things with Words* (1962).

Authenticity. This term has played an important role in modern existentialism. Jaspers held that the purpose of philosophy is to awaken people to the need to achieve authentic existence. Heidegger sought to specify the nature of authentic existence. In Spanish thought, Ortega held that the purpose of life lies in the attainment of authenticity. Among Christian theologians who have been influenced by modern existentialist thought, the concept has been much discussed in reference to its implications for Christian life and practice.

Authority. As a theological concept, authority is much misunderstood. In contrast to, say, political or military authority, which is vested with powers to secure obedience, if necessary, by force, authority in religion is a spiritually compelling person, book, or tradition that so fundamentally affects and influences us that we recognize in him or her or it a spiritual power which, in the Quaker phrase, "speaks to our condition" and to which therefore we look for guidance. It is contrasted with yet cannot be totally divorced from, our personal experience of spiritual realities. It arises from an unfolding to us ("revelation") of spiritual truth that we have found, for example, in a particular literature such as the Bible or in a particular teacher. For Christians, Jesus Christ is accepted as the supreme revelation of God to humankind.

Autocephalous Churches. A term used of national churches that are within the Eastern Orthodox Communion but are governed by their own synods and so have a very considerable autonomy. In the early Church some bishops were regarded as autocephalous in the sense of being independent of patriarchal or other superiors.

Auto-Da-Fé. In the Spanish Inquisition, those who had confessed to what was accounted heresy were dressed in a yellow penitential garb with a red cross front and back, called a *sanbenito* (being shaped like a Benedictine scapular). After Mass and Sermon, they were ceremonially handed over to the secular authorities for burning at the stake. The last instance of this barbaric procedure occurred at Seville in 1781.

Auxentius. A 4th c. Arian bishop, predecessor of Ambrose as Bishop of Milan.

Avancini, Nikola (1611–1686). A Jesuit theologian and devotional writer.

Avatāra. This Sanskrit term means literally "descent" and is frequently used of the manifestation of a deity. Although certain lists are to be found in Indian literature designating the gods who manifest themselves in human form, the concept is so pervasive that it has become what might be called a recognized principle. Any outstandingly holy man or great sage is readily regarded, in popular Hinduism at any rate, as a manifestation of deity. Any person of the caliber of an Albert Schweitzer or a Mother Teresa might be

so regarded, no less than may Gandhi and other exemplars of the same spirit within the Indian framework. In the Hindu context, therefore, the concept of such avatars of deity is not at all a counterpart to the Christian concept of Christ as God incarnate, although there are superficially common elements in the two notions.

Ave Maria. A traditional Catholic prayer based on the words attributed to the angel Gabriel (Luke 1.28). In its developed form it dates only from the 16th c., but the first half (the biblical words) devotionally at least as early as the 11th c.

Ave Maris Stella. A hymn to the Virgin Mary, dating from the 9th c. or perhaps even earlier.

Averroes (1126–1198). The Latin form of the name Ibn Rushd, an important and learned Muslim thinker whose commentaries on Aristotle caused him to become known as "The Commentator". His interpretation tended to be Neoplatonic. He saw God, the Prime Mover, as entirely separated from his creation. Providence, therefore, is ruled out, as was also personal immortality, for Averroes taught a monopsychism according to which the entire human race has only one intellect in which each individual merely participates, somewhat as swimmers participate in the ocean in which they swim. Averroes became known *c.* 1230 to Latin Christendom. Albert the Great and Roger Bacon were among those who took up his teachings. Some, notably Siger of Brabant, were teaching Averroistic doctrines at the Sorbonne that were clearly incompatible with the Christian faith as generally accepted. So it was that Thomas Aquinas perceived Averroism as a danger to Christian orthodoxy and sought to answer it. He especially attacked what he took to be a doctrine of "double truth" in Averroes, who is supposed to have propounded the view that there is one kind of truth such as we might call "religious" and another that we might call "scientific", which Thomas, insisting rightly that truth must be one, opposed. Thomas, however, may not have fully understood Averroes at this point. Averroism was forbidden at the Sorbonne after 1277, although so strong was its influence that in the great universities it continued to be taught from time to time in one form or another down to the Renaissance. A few years before Averroes' own death his teachings had been declared heretical for Muslims.

Avesta. The principal Scriptures of the Zoroastrian religion. (See **Zoroastrianism**). Traditionally, this literature is attributed to Zoroaster himself, i.e., revealed directly to him by God. In fact, only some seventeen hymns, the *Gathas,* are attributable to Zoroaster. Other parts of the Avesta antedate him, while others again postdate him by several centuries. The Avesta was for long considered too sacred to be committed to writing. It was transmitted orally, being memorized by the priestly class, until, in early Christian times, a special language was devised to conserve it in written form. After the rise of Islam the manuscripts were largely destroyed by successive invaders, so that only portions, liturgical in character, survived. These are still regularly used in Zoroastrian worship. Parsee scholars translated the literature into Sanskrit in the 12th c. CE. Subordinate to the Avesta are the translations with commentary made into various languages other than the specially devised one. This subordinate literature was known as the Zand (Zend); hence the popular, although somewhat misleading, name "Zend-avesta" widely given to the Zoroastrian Scriptures.

Ave Verum Corpus. A eucharistic hymn, medieval in origin.

Avicebron. The name commonly given to the 11th c. Spanish Jewish philosopher, Salomon ben Gabirol. Medieval Christian writers seem generally to have taken him to be a Muslim writer. He taught a form of pantheism with Aristotelian and Neoplatonic elements in it. One of his works was very popular in the Middle Ages in a Latin translation entitled *Fons Vitae,* ("The Fount of Life"), against which Thomas Aquinas wrote one of his *opuscula, De substantiis separatis.*

Avicenna (980–1037). A Muslim thinker whose work exerted considerable influence over some of the medieval Christian philosophers. Like other Arab thinkers in the heyday of Muslim thought, his work reflected both Aristotelian and Neoplatonic elements. He distinguished, in Aristotelian fashion, necessary being (God) from contingent being (the created world), but set between the two the world of ideas as a sort of divine blueprint for creation.

Avidyā. In Sanskrit, the lack of *vidyā* (true knowledge), i.e., ignorance. The upanishadic writers use the term, however, in a very complex way in their attempt to solve epistemological and metaphysical problems, including the virtually universal belief in spiritual evolution through a chain (*saṃsāra*) of embodiments governed by the karmic principle.

Avignon. This city in the south of France was from 1309 to 1377 the residence of the Popes and became in fact papal property in 1348, when Pope Clement VI purchased it from the Queen of Naples. This period of the residence of the popes at Avignon is called the Babylonian Captivity. Avignon had been in the 12th c. an important center of the Albigensian movement.

Axiology. Value theory. The term comes from the Greek *axios* (value) and *logos* (theory). Under whatever name, the discussion of values is of course as ancient as philosophical thought itself, but the term seems to have come into use about the beginning of the 20th c.

The term Value Theory is, however, more commonly used. That ethical and religious thought notably entail the discussion of values is self-evident.

Axiom. In traditional logic and mathematics, a proposition that, although not demonstrable, is taken to be so certain as to need no demonstration. It is distinguished from a postulate, which is the starting point of an inquiry that is neither a provisional assumption nor so certain that it can be taken as axiomatic. A hypothesis, by contrast, is an assertion capable of being verified or falsified.

Axum. The religious capital of Ethiopia, much revered in the Ethiopic Church as the place were Christianity was established in the 4th c.

Āyurveda. A body of ancient Indian literature comprising the corpus of Hindu medical lore from its early beginnings in magico-religious ideas to later perceptions based upon more scientific methods. The earlier outlook tended to regard disease as caused by evil deities or spirits and its cure to depend on the intervention of beneficent ones. Indications of a development toward a more scientific approach to the medical arts may be discerned as early as the 6th c. BCE, but the first successful attempt to distinguish between the old medical lore and methods based upon scientific observation and mathematical calculation may be seen in the text called the Caraka, which is possibly named after a court physician who flourished toward the end of the 1st c. CE. His original writings have been lost, but a redaction of it, dating possibly from the 9th c. CE has survived. In matters of medical concern, the Buddhist Scriptures generally follow the Āyurveda. Buddhists also generally follow the Hindu outlook on such matters in emphasizing the connection between the patient's mental condition and his or her disease. Included in the Āyurveda is a treatise on what would nowadays be called medical ethics.

B

Baal. A term found in most Semitic languages, signifying "possessor" or "owner", e.g., of a house or other property. As a title of divinity it signified the owner of a place or object. Baal worship was common in the dynamistic form of religion that persisted among the Hebrews even in biblical times and which their prophets denounced. The *baalim* or "high places" that were the center of Baal-worship were destroyed by Elijah and other leaders. So detested did the old Baal-worship become that later Jewish writers substituted the word Bosheth, meaning "shame", for the word Baal.

Baal Shem Tov. Name (meaning "The Good Master of God's Name") given to an 18th c. Jew who is generally regarded as the founder of Hasidism. (See **Hasidism.**) He was a kindly man who scorned the Talmudists for following the Law so literalistically that they thereby lost sight of God. He saw God in everyday life, in nature, and in every human situation. He believed strongly in prayer and practiced faith-healing. His real name seems to have been Israel of Moldavia.

Ba and Ka. The ancient Egyptians had a very strong belief in afterlife. Despite their enjoyment of the present life, they probably gave more thought to the afterlife than any other people on earth. The belief, focused at first on their kings, grew (with the breakdown of the authority of the pharoahs in the period about 2200 to 2000 BCE) that a blessed afterlife was attainable by all. They had two separate concepts of the soul.

One was the *ba*, iconographically shown as a human-headed bird situated somewhere in the thoracic cavity of the human body and which, at the last breath, flew from the body. It nevertheless loved the body and returned to it with longing and with undiminished appetite for food, drink, and other bodily needs. Hence the importance of preserving the body and providing food and drink in the tomb, along with an opening to allow the *ba* to gain access.

There was also, however, another soul: the *ka*, which may be understood as the mental aspect of the individual, usually represented by two outstretched arms or by an attendant figure formed as a sort of double of the original man or woman. The *ka* took up its abode in the statue of the deceased person. The *ka* had two aspects: (a) a lower one, the shadow that always accompanies a person walking in the sunshine, an aspect called the *khaibit*; (b) a higher one, which flew off to heaven in the form of a bird, the spirit or *ikhu*.

So important was mummification and the beliefs attached to it and to the afterlife that not only was the *ba* provided with such essentials as food and drink; the *ka* was provided with beds, chairs, and even sometimes with boats, carriages, combs, hairpins, and games for amusement.

Bab. From the Arabic, meaning "gate". In 1844 Mirza Ali Muhammad, proclaimed himself Bab-ud-Din ("gate of the faith") and his followers were called Babis. He was executed in 1850 for heresy. His followers eventually called themselves Bahais. See **Baha'i.**

Babel, Tower of. According to a biblical story (Genesis 11.1–9), a tower was built with the presumptuous intention of reaching heaven. God thwarted the builders by confusion in the languages they used. In the original text is a pun between the Hebrew verb *balal* (to confuse) and the noun *Babil* (Babylon). The Babylonians did build a temple-tower (ziggurat) to which no doubt the biblical story refers. The moral to be drawn is that God will punish the pride and arrogance of great unrighteous nations and exalt his own people, the righteous and humble.

Babylon. The name comes from the Akkadian *bab-ilu*, meaning probably "the gate of the gods." The city called Babylon lay on the left bank of the Eu-

phrates, not far south of modern Baghdad, near which the Euphrates and the Tigris meet. The region is a wide alluvial plain, enriched by the silt of the two rivers yet endangered by the floods that may occur. Even in prehistoric times, canals and reservoirs were constructed to mitigate this danger. The religion of Babylonia and Assyria was a syncretistic compound of both Sumerian and Semitic elements. It was polytheistic, with more than 3,000 names of deities, although some of these were attributed to the same god. The gods, usually portrayed in art by a horned cap, were typically represented in larger-than-life human form. They were divided into two groups, both immortal, the celestial deities (*Igigi*) and the terrestrial ones (*Anunnaki*). Among the chief deities were Anu (the god of the heavens), Enlil or Bel (the god of the upper air), and Ea, the god of the watery abyss. The astral triad consisted of Shamash (the sun), Sin (the moon), and Ishtar (the planet Venus). Babylonian civilization is historically important, although the extensive literature seems on the whole to be of little merit. The Babylonians borrowed the cuneiform writing from the Sumerians. The epic of Gilgamesh is of considerable interest to biblical students, providing a parallel to the story of the Flood.

Babylonian Captivity. The phrase is used by Christians in three senses: (1) the captivity of the Jews in Babylon to which they were deported in 597 and 586 BCE. When Cyrus captured Babylon in 538 BCE, they were permitted to return, although many did not do so till long afterwards. (2) Petrarch used the phrase in allusion to the exile of the papacy to Avignon from 1309 to 1377. (3) Luther used the phrase in a polemic against the corruption of the late medieval Church.

Bach, Johann Sebastian (1685–1750). German composer who from 1723 till his death was cantor at the Thomas school at Leipzig. Bach's church music, although long neglected after his death, was recognized by the 19th c. romantics, and its deeply religious spirit is now universally acclaimed.

Bacon, Francis (1561–1626). Lord Bacon, a distinguished jurist who, under James I, became Lord Chancellor of England. His deepest interest, however, was in philosophical questions. An empiricist, he held that by induction from experience man can discover the basic principles of all things. Among his most important works are his *The Advancement of Learning* (1605) and his *Novum Organum* (1620). He was a faithful English churchman and his essay on atheism, in which he says that atheism is "rather in the lip than in the heart of man," reflects the theological underpinnings of his thought.

Bacon, Roger (c. 1214–c. 1292). English Franciscan philosopher, influenced by Grosseteste, he was interested in mathematics and experimental science. He had a wide knowledge of works translated from Greek and Arabic sources. Pope Clement IV seems to have been impressed by what he had heard of his ideas and encouraged him to submit writings to him. Bacon did so, showing in his work (now known as the *Opus majus*) the importance of philosophy, the sciences, and linguistic studies for all theological pursuits and biblical studies. After Clement's death in 1268, he seems to have incurred the wrath of his Franciscan brethren. Although his originality as a thinker is not easy to assess, he does have a significant niche in the development of medieval thought.

Bagot, Richard (1782–1854). As Bishop of Oxford he was embroiled in the Tractarian controversies. While he appreciated Newman and other leaders of the movement and even sometimes defended them, he deplored the attitude of many of the followers who lacked the wisdom and discrimination of their leaders.

Baha'i. A religious movement initiated by Bahau'llah, a heretical Muslim who founded it in 1844. Bahaism teaches that since God's essence is beyond our comprehension (an orthodox doctrine in all the monotheistic religions), he can be known only through his manifestations, e.g., Moses, Jesus, Mohammed. These manifestations are one and when any one of them is outgrown a new one appears and so on in an infinite series. See also **Bab.**

Bain, Alexander (1818–1903). Scottish philosopher and one of the founders of modern psychology, he discarded the old "faculty psychology" and emphasized the importance of introspection. Writings include *The Senses and the Intellect* (1855) and *Logic, Deductive and Inductive* (1870).

Bainbridge, Christopher (c. 1464–1514). Archbishop of York and a cardinal. Entrusted by both Henry VIII and the Pope (Julius II) with important diplomatic missions. He was poisoned by one of his chaplains.

Baius, Michel (1513–1589). Flemish theologian whose system in some ways anticipated Jansenism. He incurred the displeasure of the Chancellor of the University of Louvain, where he taught, and of the Archbishop of Malines. In 1560, eighteen theological propositions of his were censured by the Sorbonne. He taught that original sin is a habitually corrupt desire transmitted genetically, not merely a lack of grace, and that the work of redemption is simply the recovery of our original innocence, enabling us to live truly moral lives by letting love rather than selfish interests rule our hearts.

Baker, Augustine (1575–1641). English Benedictine priest and mystical writer.

Bala. A Buddhist term from a Sanskrit word meaning "power". It occurs frequently in the Pali canon. The five chief moral powers are: faith (*saddhā*), energy (*viriya*), mindfulness (*sati*), concentration (*samādhi*), and wisdom (*paññā*). In Mahayana Buddhism there is a list of ten moral powers with which a bodhi-sattva is endowed, and others are mentioned occasionally.

Baldachino. Canopy covering an altar. The most famous is Bernini's over the high altar of St. Peter's, Rome. The oldest (9th c.) is at Ravenna.

Balfour, Arthur James (1848–1930). British philosopher and statesman. He sought to show that mankind's ultimate convictions rest on religious faith and that all human knowledge, philosophical and scientific, leave fundamental problems unsolved. Among his works are his Gifford Lectures: *Theism and Humanism* (1915) and *Theism and Thought* (1923).

Bali. A term applied to the offering of grain or rice to various divinities, as part of the daily household ritual duty of Hindus.

Ballerini, Pietro (1698–1769). Canonist and theologian. In moral theology he defended probabiliorism.

Balm of Gilead. This aromatic resin mentioned in Jeremiah 8.22 was probably obtained from the mastix tree, a bushy sort of evergreen that was indigenous to Palestine.

Balsamon, Theodore. 12th c. Greek canonist. Among his works is one of the principal collections of canon law in the East.

Baltimore, Councils of. A series of ten provincial councils (1829–1869) and three plenary councils (1852–1854) determined the ecclesiastical policy and discipline of the Roman Catholic Church in the U.S.A.

Bampton Lectures. Under an endowment created by the will of John Bampton, a canon of Salisbury, in the 18th c., a series of eight lectures is delivered, nowadays biennially, at St. Mary's Church, Oxford. The lecturers had to be priests of the Anglican Communion, but in 1952 another series was established under the same fund, for which

non-Anglican speakers could be elected. More recently the restriction has been abolished.

Banāras. One of the five sacred cities of India. Also called Vārāṇasī, its original name was Kāsī, the kingdom of a people so called in the late Vedic age. Banāras was a focal point in the history of north-eastern India, being notable from the 6th c. BCE. Its proximity to the Ganges enhanced its importance. The Buddha first expounded his doctrine there, and it is revered not only by Hindus and Buddhists but by Jains and others too.

Bancroft, Richard (1544–1610). Archbishop of Canterbury. He was an uncompromising foe of the Puritans and a vigorous defender of the divine origin of episcopacy.

Bañez, Domingo (1528–1604). Dominican theologian who taught at Salamanca and other Spanish universities. He followed the teachings of Thomas Aquinas closely and was the confessor of Teresa of Ávila.

Banners. Banners were used by kings in antiquity, and in the 6th c. Christians adapted them for processional and other use, employing crosses and red streamers as emblems of their faith.

Banns, Marriage. The practice of announcing forthcoming marriages is ancient, probably pre-Christian, but it came to be enjoined, e.g. by the Lateran Council, 1215.

Baptism. Traditionally, Baptism is, along with the Eucharist, one of the two most fundamental sacraments in Christian practice. Both Catholic and classic Reformation teaching (except for Zwingli) see it as the entry of the candidate into the Household of Faith that is the Church. On the Catholic view, preserved in Anglican tradition and usage, it is a visible sign and seal of the regeneration of the soul, conferring grace on those who receive it, putting no obstacle in the way. The pouring of water (affusion) on the candidate and the use of the Trinitarian formula are considered necessary for the validity of the sacrament. Other ceremonies may be added. Traditionally, Baptism is normally administered to infants, on whose behalf sponsors take the vows to renounce Satan and all his works.

The practice of infant baptism, although not specifically authorized in the New Testament, was general from early Christian times and is implied in certain New Testament passages, e.g., Matthew 19.14, Acts 16.33, and I Timothy 2.4. According to Augustine, Baptism administered by a heretical or schismatic minister is valid so long as it is administered according to the Catholic formula taken to be rooted in Scripture. When there is doubt concerning the validity, conditional baptism is administered in terms such as "If thou art not already baptized, I baptize thee in the Name of the Father, and of the Son, and of the Holy Spirit." In the Greek Church, baptismal candidates, infant or adult, are immersed; in the West affusion (pouring) is considered sufficient.

Among Baptists, the theory behind Baptism is radically different and implies the necessity of a personal affirmation and undertaking by the candidate, which excludes infants, since they cannot make such an affirmation or give such an undertaking. Theologically, this separates them from both Catholic and classic Reformation practice more than does immersion.

The origins of Christian Baptism are very complex and give rise to much theological and historical controversy.

Baptistery (also Baptistry). The part of the church (in Italian and other Mediterranean churches often a separate building) set apart for Baptism.

Baptist Missionary Society. See **Carey, William.**

Baptists. The Baptists constitute probably the largest denominational group in Protestantism today. Their roots go back to the early 17th c. and their distinctiveness consists in their (a) being a "gathered" fellowship of Christians and (b) recognizing as their pivot the practice of baptizing "conscious believers." Apart from these two common features, they may be Calvinistic, Arminian, or otherwise. They are strong on all five continents. Although they are often biblicist, they have produced some very notable scholars. Many famous preachers have been nurtured in Baptist principles. Their polity fosters a strong emphasis on the local church.

Barbarian. The term came from the Greek word *barbaros*, which means simply a non-Greek, i.e., one who does not speak Greek. It was originally used pejoratively or derisively, but by the time of the New Testament writers, it meant simply a non-Greek.

Barberini. From this Roman family came the holders of many high offices in the Church in Italy in the 17th c., including Pope Urban VIII (Maffeo Barberini) and Francesco, who built the Palazzo Barberini in Rome and founded the Barberini Library, which in 1902 passed to the Vatican. The family was of Tuscan descent.

Barclay, Robert (1648–90). Quaker apologist. Born at Gordonstown, Scotland and educated at the Scots College, Paris, as a Roman Catholic, he became a Quaker in 1667 and one of the most impressive defenders of the doctrine of the Inner Light and other Quaker teachings. After helping William Penn to found Pennsylvania, he later was appointed Governor of East New Jersey. His *Apology* is a Quaker classic.

Bar-Cochba. Leader of a Jewish rebellion in Palestine in 132 CE against Hadrian's attempt to rebuild the Temple at Jerusalem as a temple to Jupiter. He claimed to be the Messiah.

Bardenhewer, Otto (1851–1935). German patristic scholar whose *Geschichte der altkirchlichen Literatur* (various editions, 1902–1932) is a standard reference work in patristics.

Bar Jonas. This Aramaic name is applied in Matthew 16.17 to Peter. It means "son of Jonah."

Barley. Barley has been cultivated in the Near East from the Stone Age and was widely cultivated and used in Palestine, being frequently mentioned in the Bible. Barley bread was accounted inferior and was cheaper than wheat.

Barlow, Thomas (1607–1691). English churchman of Calvinistic views who was successively Librarian of the Bodleian Library, Provost of The Queen's College, Oxford, Lady Margaret Professor of Divinity, and Bishop of Lincoln.

Barlow, William (c. 1565–1613). Bishop of Lincoln and one of the translators of the King James Version, he supported Divine right and sought unsuccessfully to impose episcopacy on Scotland. His account of the Hampton Court Conference (1604) is important.

Barmen Declaration. In opposition to the tendencies of the German Church under Hitler, the Confessing Church, much under the influence of Karl Barth, met at Barmen in 1934, declaring its allegiance to God as revealed in Jesus Christ and renouncing all other political allegiance or theological tendency.

Barnabas. Early Christian of Jewish ancestry who introduced Paul to the apostles after his experience on the Damascus road.

Barnabas, Epistle of. A letter ascribed by Clement of Alexandria to the Christian apostle Barnabas, although modern scholars generally think this very unlikely. The letter, which is anti-Jewish in tone, is probably the work of a Christian of Alexandria writing toward the end of the first century.

Barnett, Samuel Augustus (1844–1913). Anglican priest and social reformer.

Baronius, Cesare (1538–1607). Church historian, Oratorian priest, cardinal, and Vatican librarian.

Baroque. That style of art and architecture that flourished in Italy in the 17th c. and spread through western Europe, especially Germany, Austria, France, and Spain. It was an attempt to enliven the severity of classical Renaissance styles. In a more general sense, the term is sometimes applied to any art form that seems too florid or fanciful.

Barrier Act. An act passed on January 8, 1697 by the General Assembly of the Scottish Kirk with the purpose of avoiding hasty legislation detrimental to the accepted doctrine and practice of the Kirk. It required that any proposal involving important constitutional change must be presented to the General Assembly and then passed down for the consideration of the various presbyteries and ultimately remitted to Assembly.

Barrow, Henry (c. 1550–1593). English Congregationalist divine. He was emphatically opposed to the Established Church of England and in the last years of his life was confined by order of John Whitgift, Archbishop of Canterbury.

Barrow, Isaac (1630–1677). Mathematician and Anglican divine.

Barsumas. Monophysite leader at the Council of Chalcedon, 451.

Barsumas. A 5th c. Nestorian bishop.

Barth, Karl (1886–1968). Swiss Protestant theologian. He sought to deliver the Church from what he accounted injurious influences of art, science, and especially politics, and secure a return to Reformation principles, notably an emphasis on the transcendence of God. Among his many works the *Kirchliche Dogmatik* is on the largest scale. His prophetic style was immensely influential, even on many who did not share all his theological stances. He has been indubitably one of the great forces in twentieth-century theological thought. See also **Barmen Declaration** and **Confessional Church.** Seeing God as wholly different from everything else, including human things, he decried all forms of theology that fail to emphasize that central opposition between God and the world. Human reason stands under the judgment of God and is confounded by grace and put to shame by faith as the response to revelation.

Bartholomaeans. A congregation of German secular priests founded in 1640 by Bartholomew Holtshauser. They spread through various countries in Europe and engaged in seminary education, but they eventually were extinguished in the early 19th c.

Bartholomew, Gospel of. An apocryphal Gospel, Gnostic in standpoint.

Bartholomew, Massacre of St. A massacre that occurred in France on the night of August 23, 1572, and days following, during which many (possibly 10,000) Huguenots were killed in Paris and other French cities. Catherine de Medici seems to have been the chief instigator.

Bartholomew of Pisa (*c.* **1260–1347**). Dominican theologian. His best known work is on moral theology: *Summa de casibus conscientiae.*

Bartholomites. A community of Armenian monks who settled in Genoa in 1307. A church dedicated to St. Bartholomew was built for them, and they flourished for some time. Eventually they were suppresed in 1650 by Pope Innocent X.

Bartolommeo, Fra (*c.* **1475–1517**). Florentine painter, friend of Raphael. In 1498 he entered the Dominican Order.

Barton, Elizabeth (*c.***1506–1534**). Known as "The Maid of Kent," she was a servant girl who claimed to make prophecies which in time became turned on Henry VIII for his proposal to divorce.

A confession of having feigned the trances during which her prophecies were uttered was extorted from her, and she was executed in 1534.

Basel, Confession of. A statement of doctrine used as the basis of the reform introduced at Basel, Switzerland, in 1534. It was a development of a shorter statement that had been proposed in 1531 by Oecolampadius. It represents an attempt at compromise between the Lutheran and the Zwinglian positions.

Basel, Council of. This great Church council was convened in 1431 by Pope Martin V to take up problems that had been left over at the Council of Constance, which had unanimously elected him to the papal office in 1417. It was a council that not only received the support of both the universities and the princes but also provided for a more democratic procedure that reduced the power of the bishops. It reaffirmed the decrees of the Council of Constance in respect to the superiority of a General Council over the papacy. Modern Roman Catholic canonists seek to reject its decisions either totally or partially on various technical grounds such as the lack of papal recognition of its acts. It is of key importance in the struggle between conciliarism and papalism in the Roman Catholic Church in the Middle Ages and down to the First Vatican Council, 1869–1870.

Basil, Liturgy of St. An ancient liturgy still used on certain days in the Eastern Orthodox Church.

Basil, Rule of St. The monastic rule that is generally followed in the Eastern Orthodox Church. It is named after Basil the Great who laid down its principles in the 4th. c., although its present form comes from a revision by Theodore of Studios. The spirit of the rule is to encourage a strict form of religious life in community without the extreme (not to say fanatical) severities practiced by the early Christian hermits. It provides for the education of children, from among whom could be drawn such as showed signs of vocation to the monastic life. As with the Benedictine rule in the West, emphasis was placed on hospitality toward the stranger and care for the poor. The text of the Basilian rule may be found in English translation by W. K. L. Clarke, *The Ascetic Works of Saint Basil* (1929).

Basilica. When, thanks to recognition by Constantine, Christians could feel free to worship openly without fear of persecution, they naturally took as a model for the places of worship that they built, the Roman basilica, a general public building used as a law court and for other secular purposes, although they sometimes introduced special features, e.g., from the chapels they had used in the catacombs. The typical pattern included an atrium leading to a narthex that led into the main building, which would have a nave with aisles and pillars supporting architraves or arches. At the east end would be an apse with an altar under a canopy and standing on a dais.

The term "basilica" in modern practice is applied as a term of honor or privilege to certain churches so designated by the Pope. The four chief ("major") basilicas are in Rome: St. John Lateran; St. Peter's; St. Paul's (*San Paulo fuori le mura*); and St. Mary's (*Santa Maria Maggiore*). In Rome and elsewhere are various other ("minor") basilicas, e.g., the Basilique du Sacré-Coeur in Montmartre, Paris.

Basilides. A 2nd c. Gnostic Christian theologian of the Alexandrian school. Because of misrepresentations by his contemporaries, his views, like those of other Gnostic Christians of his time, are not easy to specify accurately, but he probably taught a form of reincarnationism and may have had docetic tendencies, besides including the Platonic and Stoic elements common to the Alexandrian school.

Basil "the Great." A 4th c. theologian, one of the three Cappadocian Fathers.

An eloquent controversialist who combined qualities of personal holiness with business administration, he successfully opposed Arianism.

Basnage, Jacques (1653–1723). French Calvinist theologian and ecclesiastical historian. His writings include his *Histoire de la religion des églises réformées* (2 vols, 1690).

Batiffol, Pierre (1861–1929). Roman Catholic Church historian whose writings fostered critical, scholarly studies in France. He was associated with the Modernist movement and a work of his on the Eucharist was placed on the Index in 1911.

Bauer, Bruno (1809–1882). German theologian and biblical scholar who, adopting an even more extreme view than that of his contemporary D. F. Strauss, saw the origins of Christianity in Graeco-Roman thought. His views are now generally discarded as historically untenable.

Bäumer, Suitbert (1845–1894). Benedictine liturgical scholar.

Baumgarten, Alexander (1714–1762). German philosopher of considerable importance in the development of modern philosophy. From his work *Aesthetics* (1750) comes the modern use of the term to signify the philosophy of art and beauty rather than the then traditional sense of the term, which referred to *aesthēsis* as the area of sense perception in general, contradistinguished from *noesis*, the area of thought or intelligence.

Bautain, Louis (1796–1867). French thinker and priest who accepted Kant's objections to the possibility of rational arguments for the existence of God and held that God can be known only through faith and mystical insight. This view which came to be known as Fideism, was condemned by Gregory XVI in 1840. Bautain, like Galileo and others in similar circumstances, recanted.

Bayle, Pierre (1647–1706). French skeptical thinker whose principal work, *An Historical and Critical Dictionary* (1702), expressed his agnostic approach to religion and his defense of freedom in interpreting it. Critical of popular understanding of the Bible in his time, he anticipated in his own way the results of later biblical analysis. He also defended a naturalistic ethics, denying that Christianity as such has anything to add to the understanding of morality that reason can attain.

Bead. From the German *beten*, to pray. The word was used of a prayer before it was applied to the physical components of the rosary that provide a convenient means of counting one's prayers. The original meaning is preserved in the archaic word "bidding", traditionally used of the call to the people to offer prayers for specific intentions, e.g., "Pray for the peace of the world" and "Pray for the repose of the soul of Mary Smith."

Beadle. An officer in the Scottish Kirk whose functions include the care of the church building and sometimes other duties such as are performed in England by a verger.

Beaduin, Lambert (1873–1960). Belgian Benedictine liturgist. He was prominent in work for the unity of Christians.

Beard. While the Sumerians and the Egyptians seem to have been generally clean-shaven, the Semitic peoples generally wore a full beard. The Egyptians sometimes wore an artificial square, goatee type of beard for ceremonial purposes. By the time of Jesus, the Jews wore the full beard and seem to have attached importance to it, while the Greeks and Romans were usually clean-shaven.

In the Eastern Church the beard has been from the earliest times traditionally an indispensable mark of both monks and secular priests. In the West, at least since the 5th c., the practice of shaving the face clean became no less standard, becoming indeed an outward sign of the growing division between East and West. In the course of the centuries, however, when beards were normal for men generally, they became acceptable and even standard among the clergy. Even when beards were generally unfashionable they have been sanctioned for the mission field in those areas in which the beard is the expected accoutrement of a priest.

Beatification. A procedure through which a deceased individual is recognized, in the Roman Catholic Church, as worthy of public veneration. He or she is then accorded the title of Blessed. In the past it was customary for local bishops to grant this status to an individual within their own dioceses. It is generally taken as a step toward possible canonization afterwards. See **Canonization.**

Beatific Vision. In Christian theology, the final state of the redeemed is traditionally called the Beatific Vision, i.e., the state of the *beati*, the blessed ones. Its joy consists primarily in knowledge of God's essence. Some, including Thomas Aquinas, have held that a *foretaste* of this joy may be granted exceptionally on earth, e.g., in mystical experience.

Beating the Bounds of a Parish. In medieval England, before the development of cartography, the custom prevailed of annually processing round the parish boundaries, beating the bounds of the parish with rods by way of exhibiting them to parishioners, especially the young. The custom is ancient, going back to about the year 900. Although it has fallen into desuetude in most places, some parishes have revived it.

Beaton, David (*c.* 1494–1546). Cardinal Archbishop of St. Andrews and Primate of Scotland. He wielded enormous power in both Church and State, was much hated for his notoriously evil life. He encouraged the persecution of Protestants, notably the burning at the stake (in exceptionally cruel circumstances even for those days) of Patrick Hamilton, the first Scottish martyr for the Reformation cause to be burned in Scotland. He was assassinated in his own castle fortress at St. Andrews by John Leslie.

Beaulieu, Abbey of. Pronounced *byooly,* a Cistercian abbey in Hampshire, England, founded in 1204 by King John. Many parts of the building still stand.

Bec, Abbey of. Norman abbey lying between Rouen and Lisieux, France. Anselm and Lanfranc are among its many famous monks.

Becket, Thomas. 12th c. English churchman (son of Norman settlers), who became Archbishop of Canterbury in 1162. Intransigeant in his resolve to uphold the rights of the Church over the State, he incurred the wrath of the King, Henry II. Henry, in a fit of rage, encouraged four knights to go to Canterbury and wreak vengeance on him. He was assassinated in Canterbury Cathedral in the late afternoon of December 29, 1170: an act that drew widespread indignation throughout Western Europe. The literature on this notorious event is extensive and it has been dramatized by T. S. Eliot in *Murder in the Cathedral.*

Becoming. A traditional term in philosophy to designate process and change in contrast to changeless Being, both of which Plato recognized, the one in Heracleitus, the other in Parmenides. The concept occurs also in Hegel.

Becon, Thomas (*c.* 1511–1567). English churchman. He was a vigorous champion of the Reformation cause and wrote extensively in its defense.

Bed. In biblical times most people slept on the ground, on a mat or on straw, but rich people had beds, often somewhat like the modern daybed but sometimes, especially in royal palaces, highly ornate beds decorated with ivory, gold, and other precious materials.

Bede (*c.* 673–735). Historian and biblical scholar, known as "The Venerable Bede." He became much famed for his learning and some of his works are primary sources for English history. His bones were translated to Durham in the 11th c. where a memorial stone in the cathedral commemorates him. He is one of the greatest figures in English church history.

Beelzebul (Beelzebub). The precise significance of this name is somewhat obscure. In the Old Testatment, Beelzebub was the god of the Philistine city of Ekron. Jesus was charged by the Pharisees with acting under the authority of Beelzebub. "Beelzebul" is the form used in the best Greek manuscripts and modern scholars take it to be derived from the Ugaritic word *zbl,* meaning prince. The Ugaritic fertility god Aleyan Baal, is called "prince of the earth" or "lord of the earth." In the New Testament he seems to be identified as "the prince of this world" in opposition to the True God who is the source of all good.

Beghards. See **Beguines.**

Beguines. Communities of women developed in the Low Countries toward the end of the 12th c., whose organization grew out of a deeply mystical spirit that seems to have been indigenous to the southern regions there. Eventually taking a stable and organized form, in Flanders and in the Duchy of Brabant, they obtained papal approval in 1216. They took no vows and were free to marry and to have private property. Their male counterparts were called beghards. The houses were called beguinages. The character of their mystical life encouraged the development of an intense interiority that was hospitable to diverse elements that the movement eventually encompassed, e.g., elements that came to them from the north of France among women widowed in the Crusades and representing or echoing Byzantine features in their mystical approach. Louis IX founded a beguinage in Paris in 1264. They engaged in charitable work. Although ecclesiastically approved, their sympathies with certain heretical groups led to their being held suspect, and in 1311 the Council of Vienne condemned their teaching. They survived, however, a century of persecution. They still exist in much attenuated numbers, e.g., in Ghent, Lierre, and Herenthals. The old beguinages, grouped around a little church and enclosed by great walls with handsome entrances still exist in many Flemish towns, e.g., Antwerp and Bruges. The Beghards adopted a reform and were encouraged in 1321 by John XXII to continue, becoming extinct, however, at the French Revolution. See A. Mens, *Oorsprong en betekenis van de Nederlandse beguinen- en Begaardenbeweging.* Antwerp, Ed. Standard, 1947.

Behaviorism. A school of psychology representing a form of "materialistic" naturalism, related to certain forms of pragmatism. The school may be said to have J. B. Watson as its founder, whose work was continued by B. F. Skinner. Behaviorists seek to drop the traditional vocabulary of introspective techniques, which are of course essential to Christian and other religious understandings of the nature of man and the universe.

Being. Traditionally the most important philosophical category, the term is derived from the Greek *ontos;* hence the area of philosophy that deals with it is called ontology. In ancient and medieval thought it was a fundamental category. In Hegel it is the starting point of all the categories. Recognition of the importance of the term as pivotal to all serious philosophical discussion continues today and has been developed by Heidegger and many others.

Belgic Confession (1561). This confession was drawn up in French as a statement of the Flemish and Walloon Reformed Churches. Based on the Gallican Confession (1559), it attempted to mollify the State authorities. Adopted by a synod at Antwerp in 1566, it was a landmark in the acceptance of Calvinism in the Netherlands.

Belief. Philosophers generally regard belief as a weak form of knowledge. One may be said to believe in the truth of a proposition or statement when one acquiesces in it, even if the evidence is insufficient to justify a claim to knowledge. For example, one says "I believe it is going to rain" without any pretensions to meteorological expertise but merely from a general impression. One may also affirm a belief in someone's good character or in the likelihood of his succeeding in his work. So I may say "I believe that kangaroos exist but I do not believe in dragons." When, however, you ask me whether John Smith is to be trusted to do a certain job and I reply "Yes, I believe in him" or "No, I don't believe in him," I am not affirming or denying his existence, which I take for granted; I am stating my opinion about his competence or reliability. I may be said to be betting on him. My wager may be large or trivial. In the latter case, if Smith turns out to be unworthy of my trust I may shrug my shoulders and murmur "Well, that was my honest opinion, and I admit I was wrong"; but in the former case I may be shattered by his failure to meet my expectations or embarrassed by his exceeding them to such an extent as to warrant your charging me with a serious error in judgment.

In theological usage (e.g., in the historic creeds of the Church), the believer's conviction is so strong that he is willing to wager everything on the truth of what he affirms and to put his trust totally in the Being toward whom he expresses his belief. Such belief, far from excluding doubt, implies both doubt and the transcending of the doubt. Claim to *such* belief is claim to a *kind* of knowledge.

Bellarmine, Joseph (1542–1621). Jesuit controversialist and cardinal. He was canonized in 1930 and the following year named a Doctor of the Church.

Belloc, Joseph Hilaire Pierre (1870–1953). Roman Catholic writer. Educated at the Birmingham Oratory under Newman, he served for a year with the French artillery and then went to Balliol College, Oxford. He was elected to Parliament in 1906. Closely associated with Chesterton, he wrote extensively in a witty, journalistic style.

Bells. Bells for use in Christian worship are mentioned by Gregory of Tours in the 6th c. Used in Britain in the 6th and 7th c., they were in general use throughout the Christian Church by the 8th c. See **Campanile.**

Bema. The platform behind the iconostasis in Eastern Orthodox churches.

Benares. Anglicized form of Banāras, now known as Vārāṇasī. See **Vārāṇasī.**

Benedict (c. 480–c. 550). Born at Nursia and educated at Rome, he withdrew to a cave at Subiaco c. 500, where he lived as a hermit. As men sought his spiritual counsel, a community grew up around him, and he eventually moved to Monte Cassino with a small, well ordered community of monks. His sister Scholastica founded a community for women. Benedict, although he seems not to have intended to found an order, is generally regarded as the father of Western monasticism. See **Benedictine Order.**

Benedict, Rule of. The monastic rule drawn up by Benedict at Monte Cassino. It borrowed from the Basilian rule of the Eastern Church but was conceived on Roman lines, with the Roman genius for administrative common sense and moderation. In terms of its day, its provisions were humane. The chief work of the monks was to be the *opus Dei:* the singing of the Divine Office. The monks vowed not only poverty, chastity, and obedience, but *stabilitas,*

i.e., permanent attachment to the particular house to which they belonged. The abbot was to be elected by the monks and held office for life.

Benedict's rule was by no means universally followed by all Benedictine houses till several centuries after his death, but it remained a model and the ideal, and gradually its principles were adopted and its provisions followed by all houses within the Benedictine tradition, both of monks and of nuns. The Benedictine habit is black.

Benedict of Aniane (c. 750–821). French Benedictine abbot. Systematized discipline and practice in all the French monastic houses.

Benedictine Order. Although Benedict of Nursia (c. 480–c. 550) gathered a community of monks together, he cannot be said, strictly speaking to have founded the great Benedictine Order that bears his name. His Rule was not at first universally followed, but by the time of Charlemagne in the late 8th c. it had become general. Western monasticism looked more and more to Benedict as its progenitor. Various relaxations of his Rule were followed by attempts to recover its pristine austerities, even to exceed them. Several branches appeared as new orders around the 11th c., e.g., the Camaldolese, the Carthusians, and the Cistercians. Generally speaking, the Benedictine spirit favored a great deal of independence for each monastic house, so that only a loose sort of federation held them together, but in the 10th c. one branch of the Benedictines, the Cluniacs, developed a much more structured and organized system with central control by the abbots of Cluny. The Roman authorities of the Church repeatedly sought to impose more unity on the Benedictines to bring them in line with the way in which other great orders of the Church were organized, but the Benedictines succeeded in resisting such intrusions on their accustomed ways, preferring to achieve reform by a system of congregations according to which individual abbeys came under one or another of such organizational units, binding them together fraternally with a minimal sacrifice of the autonomy of each house.

The Benedictine spirit encouraged learning as well as spiritual contemplation. Members of Benedictine houses were essentially monks, although some would be also priests. Nowadays most are also priests. They have a special concern for liturgy, and certain abbeys, notably Solesmes, are famed for their erudition and expertise in the study and performance of the liturgy of the Church. Although the monastic spirit encourages the contemplative life, Benedictines nowadays engage in teaching, parochial, and other duties outside their houses. They take, however, a special vow of *stabilitas in loco*, i.e., they are attached to the particular abbey that is their home for life, wherever some of them may be sent. Benedictine nuns, some of whose convents are strictly enclosed (i.e., cloistered), also sometimes engage in "active" work such as teaching. Both monks and nuns wear black habits. Organizationally, Benedictine abbeys nowadays are grouped into congregations, and the congregations together form a Benedictine federation. Historically, the Benedictines and those other orders (e.g., Cistercians and Carthusians) that appeared as Benedictine offshoots, tended, because of their attachment to the land, to side with the landed Establishment in the countries in which respectively they were founded. This inevitably made them less internationally minded than the friars (Dominicans, Franciscans, and others) and clerics regular (e.g., Jesuits), who moved about in more military fashion as needed and who were therefore more readily geared to the service of the Papacy. Nevertheless, the Benedictines have played an enormously important role in the life of the Western Church: so much so that it is virtually impossible to dissociate them from the life of the Church from the dawn of the Middle Ages down to the present day.

Benediction. From the Latin *benedictio*, a blessing, the concept of asking and obtaining a blessing as a pronouncement of divine approval and favor goes back to Old Testament times. Blessings play a considerable role in Christian worship, Eastern Orthodox and Roman Catholic, Anglican and Reformed. Catholic practice has encouraged the blessing of objects as well as of people, e.g., churches, altars, vestments, rosaries. A formal benediction by the officiant at the end of the service is very general both in Protestant and in Catholic usage. See also **Berakah.**

The service called "Benediction", common in Roman Catholic churches (although much less emphasized since Vatican II) and encouraged in some Anglican dioceses, begins with the exposition of the Host in a monstrance, surrounded by lights and flowers. After traditional hymns have been sung and the Host censed, a priest raises the monstrance and makes the sign of the Cross with it over the people. This devotion has been widely popular since the 16th c.

Benefice. In ecclesiastical usage, a benefice consists of the emoluments of an office (e.g., the rectorship of a parish) and has been traditionally used to denote the office itself as in expressions such as "The young priest has obtained a benefice in another diocese." The term "beneficed clergy" traditionally refers to parochial clergy, contradistinguished from non-stipendiary clergy who receive no emoluments from the Church.

Beneke, Friedrich (1798–1854). German philosopher who opposed Hegel and claimed that all philosophy is rooted in psychological phenomena.

Bennett, William (1804–1886). Anglican priest whose strong Tractarian principles embroiled him in much controversy in mid-Victorian England.

Ben Sira. A name often applied to the book of Ecclesiasticus; also called the book of Sirach.

Benson, Edward White (1829–96). Archbishop of Canterbury.

Benson, Richard Meux (1824–1915). Founder of the Society of St. John the Evangelist, popularly known as the Cowley Fathers.

Benson, Robert Hugh (1871–1914). The youngest son of E. W. Benson, he was received into the Roman Catholic Church in 1903 and became a noted Roman Catholic apologist, through both his sermons and his novels.

Bentham, Jeremy (1748–1832). Important Oxford philosopher, founder of the Utilitarian school, he held that the end of every human being is the pursuit of pleasure and the avoidance of pain. From an ethical standpoint, the end of life is "the greatest good for the greatest number."

Berakah. A Jewish blessing, which may be said over a cup of wine and may possibly have been the model from which the Christian eucharistic prayer was derived.

Berdyaev, Nicolas (1874–1948). Russian Orthodox philosopher. Born in Kiev and educated at the University of Moscow, he established a school of philosophy first in Berlin, then in Paris. He taught that man, like God, is creative, that creation is *ex nihilo*, that human freedom consists in self-creation, that creation is ongoing, and that suffering and joy belong to both God and man. Among his works are *The Destiny of Man* (1931) and *Dream and Reality* (1951).

Berengar of Tours (c. 1010–1088). Early medieval theologian. His teaching on the Eucharist, although not fundamentally deviant from that of his contemporaries, evoked controversy. While insisting on the Real Presence of Christ in the Eucharist, he denied that any material change is needed to explain it, such as is implied in the doctrine of Transubstantiation, which relied on the logical categories of Aristotle. Many writings by his contemporaries were directed, however, against his position.

Bergson, Henri (1859–1941). An important French philosopher of Jewish descent, who lectured at the Collège de France from 1901 to 1921, he taught that the dynamic and static aspects of our experience have roots in the world, which temporally is fluid and dynamic but spatially is static. The temporal facet is identified with spiritual development and growth, the spatial with materiality. God works through the evolutionary process. He is the force (*élan vital*) behind that process. Evolution is purposive, and through it freedom is attained. The past continues to exist, being a dimension of the present, preserved in human beings as memory. Reason tends to look at things statically, intuition dynamically. Among his writings are: *Time and Free Will* (1889), *Matter and Memory* (1896), *Laughter* (1900), and *Creative Evolution* (1907).

Berkeley, George (1685–1753). Irish philosopher. He became Dean of Derry, Ireland, in 1724 and Bishop of Cloyne in 1734. Although in the British Empiricist tradition and, along with Locke and Hume, one of its three great exponents, his distinctive position represents a form of subjective idealism. Claiming that nothing material exists as such but only as mental construct, he called his position "Immaterialism". His teaching, plainly susceptible to much popular misunderstanding, is of great interest to Christian and other philosophers of religion, having immense importance in and relevance to modern philosophical and scientific thought that goes beyond mere positivism. His writings include *Treatise Concerning the Principles of Human Knowledge* (1710) and *Alciphron* (1733).

Bernadette (Marie Bernard Soubirous) (1844–1879). At the age of fourteen, she claimed to have received many visions of the Virgin Mary near Lourdes, the last on July 16, 1858, during which the Virgin identified herself as immaculately conceived. She was beatified in 1925 and canonized in 1933.

Bernardino of Siena (1380–1844). Franciscan reformer whose preaching was widely acclaimed, despite repeated accusations of heresy. He became, in 1438, Vicar General of the Friars of the Strict Observance.

Bernard of Chartres (c. 1080–c. 1130). Important formative influence on the school of Chartres. He held that ideas are eternally in the mind of God, although not co-eternal with God. His form of Christian Platonism much affected the development of the thought of the school of Chartres.

Bernard of Clairvaux (1090–1153). Cistercian abbot. An extremely conservative churchman who organized the Second Crusade, Bernard exercised much power in his time and used it in his opposition to Abelard and others whom he deemed heretical. Yet he had a very loving side to his nature, expressed in his mystical and other writings.

Bernard of Cluny. A 12th c. monk of Cluny and poet, noted for his long poem, *De contemptu mundi,* whence come many well-known hymns such as "Jerusalem the Golden."

Berne, The Theses of. A series of ten theological propositions drawn up in defense of a Zwinglian interpretation of Reformation doctrine. They formed part of a decree of 1528 that enforced Reformation teaching.

Bérulle, Pierre de (1575–1629). French cardinal. He established the reformed Carmelites in France and in 1611 founded the French Oratory. A skilled diplomat, he was very influential in Church and State. As a theologian he showed acute insight into problems relating to the nature of the relationship between the Church and Christ as the Incarnate Word.

Bessarion, John (1403–1472). Cardinal and scholar of great distinction. He sought to achieve union between the Eastern Church and Rome. His great library is conserved in the Marciana, Venice.

Bethlehem. The native city of David and the birthplace of Jesus. It contains the Church of the Holy Nativity built by Constantine in 330 on what was taken to be the site of the manger in which Jesus was born. Much of the original structure survives despite its rebuilding in the 6th c. by Justinian.

Beulah. A name sometimes applied to Palestine, signifying its restoration to Yahweh after the exile (Isaiah 62.4). The term means literally "married woman" and the underlying notion is that Palestine is now figuratively married to Yahweh.

Beuron Congregation. An important congregation of monks of the Benedictine Order. The mother house is in Hohenzollern, on the Upper Danube. The famous abbey of Maria Laach belongs to this congregation as formerly did Maredsous. The congregation is famous for its work in liturgical reform.

Beverley Minister. This parish church, one of the best examples of Gothic architecture in England, stands on the site of a Saxon church founded by St. John of Beverley in the early 8th c.

Beyschlag, Willibald (1823–1900). German Evangelical theologian. Professor of pastoral theology at Halle, he attacked the teachings of Strauss and others and in later years helped the cause of the Old Catholics.

Beza, Theodore (1519–1605). Calvinist theologian and biblical scholar. In 1548 he broke with the Roman Catholic Church and went to Geneva. Some of his theological writings express an exaggerated form of Calvinism. He defended the burning of Servetus. In 1565 he brought out what is the first critical edition of the Greek text of the New Testament.

Bezae, Codex. *See* **Codex Bezae Cantabrigiensis.**

Bhagavad-Gīta. Title of a philosophical poem in Book VI of the *Mahābharata*, which may date from the 6th c. BCE. The main theme of the poem is that salvation is achieved through the love of God, however it may be expressed. The ethical path of adherence to duty, although the highest of such expressions, is not the only one. All paths can lead to salvation. The poem is in the Bhakti tradition of Hinduism and has had considerable influence on many within the Christian tradition. The divine appears in two forms: Brahman (impersonal deity) and Krishna (personal incarnation of deity).

Bhakti. A school or way within the Hindu tradition. The term is derived from the Sanskrit root *bhaj* (to adore) and may be applied to any of the Hindu schools that emphasize personal devotional love and faith as the way to salvation, rather than karma, the path of works. It has been very popular in India, notably among devotees of Vishnu, and may be said to represent an emotional rather than an intellectual form of Hinduism. Its spirit has been seen by some as having an affinity to the spirit of certain forms of Protestant Christianity.

Bhaṭṭa. An honorific title prefixed or appended to the name of a learned brahmin.

Bhūtas. In Hinduism, malignant spirits, sometimes described as similar to the vampires of European folklore, but they appear under various guises. They blight crops, cause violent deaths, plague people for various reasons or none, and since they cast no shadow they are difficult to deal with. The frequent burning of turmeric does, however, deter them, for it seems to be almost the only thing they fear. They are also feared as spirits of the dead, much as are ghosts in Western lore.

Bhūti. From a term meaning "good fortune" or "well-being," it is a name given to the Hindu goddess Lakṣmī, who is the personification of prosperity. The term is also applied, however, to certain superhuman powers attained by the practice of austerity (*tapas*).

Biasca Sacramentary. The oldest surviving manuscript of the Ambrosian rite, it dates from the 10th c. and is preserved in the Ambrosiana Library in Milan.

Bible. As is suggested by the word itself (Greek *ta biblia*, the books), the Bible is not a book but a literature. Christians recognize both the Old Testament and the New Testament. The former is in Hebrew and consists of three parts: (1) Torah (Law), the first five books of the Old Testament; (2) Prophets; (3) Writings, which include books as diverse as the Psalms, Proverbs, Job, and Chronicles. For the convenience of Greek-speaking Jews, the Hebrew Bible was translated into Greek and the most influential version was the Septuagint (LXX), probably begun about the middle of the 3rd c. BCE but continued over a considerable period. It contains books (e.g., Wisdom, Tobit) not in the Hebrew Bible. About 100 CE the Jews repudiated these books, but the Christian Church, as soon as it had spread to the Gentile world, used and recognized the LXX as Scripture. The New Testament, written in Greek, did not entirely reach its present form till the 4th c. CE. It represented those early Christian writings that the Church especially recognized and revered. Many Latin versions were made, the most famous of which is the Vulgate. The work of Jerome, it became the official Bible of the Roman Catholic Church.

Although there were vernacular translations of the Bible in the Middle Ages (e.g., Wyclif's in English), the lack of printing made its dissemination in the language of the people difficult. Soon after the invention of printing by movable type in mid-15th c., however, translations of the Bible or parts of it appeared in various languages including German and English, before the Reformation was in full spate.

The English Bible has a special history, from the first printed New Testament (Tyndale's in 1525) to the present time, including the Great Bible (1539), the Geneva Bible (1560), the Bishops' Bible (1568), the Douai Bible (1609–1610), the King James Version (1611), the Revised Version (1881–1885), the American Standard Version (1901), the Revised Standard Version (1946–1957), the New English Bible (1961–1970), and the Jerusalem Bible (1966), besides a vast number of private translations. The Geneva Bible was the one favored by the English Puritans, and the copy actually carried on the *Mayflower* is preserved at Harvard. The King James Bible immensely influenced English speech and English literature.

Textual and literary analysis of the Bible, although it had some precursors, began in the 19th c. in scholarly circles and has enormously helped educated people to understand biblical thought. See also **Chapter and Verse**.

Biblicism. A term that may be used to designate the attitude of those who purport to read the Bible literalistically.

Biddle, John (1615–1662). Educated at Oxford, he wrote various tracts against the doctrine of the Trinity, was much persecuted and narrowly escaped sentence of death. He was several times imprisoned and finally died in prison. He helped to edit an edition of the Septuagint. He is generally considered the father of the Unitarian movement in England.

Biel, Gabriel (c. 1420–1495). Late scholastic philosopher, inclined to Nominalism.

Bigg, Charles (1840–1908). Church historian. Among his works is *The Christian Platonists of Alexandria*.

Bilney, Thomas (c. 1495–1531). English Protestant martyr. He apparently accepted traditional Catholic doctrine such as Transubstantiation but bitterly opposed other less central ones such as the use of relics and devotion to the saints. He was burnt at Norwich.

Bilocation. The miraculous presence of an individual in more than one place at the same time. Antony of Padua is one of the saints to whom this miracle has been attributed by Catholic piety.

Bination. The celebration by one priest of two or more Masses on the same day: a practice which, in the Roman Catholic Church, at one time required special dispensation. Today, dispensation is required to say three or more Masses on the same day.

Bioethics. The study of ethical problems arising from the interrelationship of medical and related technological advances, on the one hand, and, on the other, human rights, duties, and the future of humankind. Well-known examples include abortion, cloning, and euthanasia. A bibliography and guide to the growing literature on bioethics is published annually by the Center for Bioethics, Kennedy Institute, Georgetown University.

Biretta. The stiff, square hat worn by Roman Catholic and some Anglican priests. Its use by Roman Catholic priests was formerly very general. Traditionally, Anglicans use the Canterbury cap made of softer material, such as velvet cloth.

Birth Control. See **Contraception**.

Bishop. (From the Greek *episcopos*, superintendent). The early development of the office of bishop is controversial. At first *episcopos* and *presbyteros* seem to have been used interchangeably (e.g., Acts 20.17, 28), but the distinction was developed so that by mid-2nd c. it was clearly made. In Catholic tradition and practice, Eastern Orthodox, Roman Catholic, and Anglican, a threefold ministry is recognized: bishop, priest, and deacon. Whether the episcopate is a separate order or the plenitude of the priesthood has been, however, a much debated question. Thomas Aquinas argues impressively for the latter view. (*Summa Theologiae*, III suppl., qq. 34, 37, 40), although recognizing that for certain purposes the episcopate may be regarded as another order.

A bishop has both a sacramental and an administrative function. Traditionally he is also, at least in theory, *pastor pastorum*, a pastor to all the clergy of the diocese he serves. Many Anglican bishops in the past were notable scholars and some (e.g., Berkeley) even highly original thinkers, but today the office has become increasingly administrative in character. The mitre, which in the Eastern Church takes the form of a crown but in the West that of a shield with two fringed tapes behind, is the liturgical headdress of a bishop, who also carries a staff or crosier (in the East a cross between two serpents, in the West a stick in the form of a shepherd's crook) and other insignia. See also **Apostolic Succession.**

Black Friars. A popular name for the Dominicans, an order of friars who, over their white habit, wear a black mantle; hence the name.

Black Mass. This expression is used in two very distinct ways: (1) to designate a requiem mass, for which black vestments are traditionally used, and (2) in allusion to a blasphemous parody of the Mass as sometimes used in satanistic rituals and other perversions of Christian liturgy.

Black Rubric, The. In the Anglican Book of Common Prayer, 1552, a Declaration on Kneeling was printed at the end of the Communion Service. It was removed in the Book of 1559 but replaced in that of 1662. The purpose was not to deny the Real Presence of Christ in the Eucharist but to discourage vulgar notions about it such as had developed in the Middle Ages. The expression "Black Rubric" dates from the 19th c., when the practice of printing the rubrics in red was introduced. Since the Declaration was not really a rubric at all, it was printed in black.

Blake, William (1757-1827). English mystical poet and artist. A theosophical visionary whose teachings adumbrated in some ways Schweitzer's "reverence for life" principle. His works include *The Marriage of Heaven and Hell* (1793) and *Illustrations to the Book of Job* (1826).

Blasphemy. In the Levitical code, blasphemy, which consisted primarily in the use of language contemptuous of God but was applied to many crimes that were held to imply such contempt, was punishable by stoning. Many of the assertions made by Jesus respecting his power to forgive sins and to be the Messiah were taken by many to be blasphemous. More generally the term has come to be applied, both by Jews and Christians, to any disparagement, by word or act, of holy things.

Blass, Friedrich Wilhelm (1843-1907). German philologist and New Testament scholar.

Bleek, Friedrich (1793-1859). German New Testament scholar, professor at Bonn.

Blemmydes, Nicephorus (1197-1272). Greek theologian who participated in attempts to unite the Eastern and Western Church.

Blessed. See **Beatification.**

Blessing. See **Benediction** and **Berakah.**

Blik. A term used by R. M. Hare—presumably invented by him—to designate a life-stance, an attitude toward the universe or interpretation of the way things are. A *blik* does not have the logical function of an assertion, nor could it function as does an assertion or even a system of assertions. Hare contends, however, that because a *blik* expresses a fundamental attitude, having the right one is very important indeed; hence theological utterances that are *bliks* (e.g., "The souls of the righteous are in the hand of God") behave logically as do statements such as "The solar system will continue in its regular course tomorrow as it did yesterday." No facts or number of facts could "disprove" a category of thought so ultimate as is a *blik*.

Blondel, Maurice (1861–1949). French philosopher. A profoundly religious thinker closely associated with some of the leaders of the Modernist Movement, including von Hügel. His great work, *L'Action* (1893) was very influential on French religious thought. Its sequel, *La Pensée* (1934) is somewhat less impressive, but his writings, in which he follows a Platonic tradition rather than an Aristotelian and Thomist one, are of great importance for an understanding of the development of French religious thought.

Blount, Charles (1654–1693). Deist; author of *Anima Mundi* (1649), a discussion of immortality from a skeptical standpoint and of other works containing ideas sympathetic to Thomas Hobbes and expressing strongly anticlerical views.

Bloxam, John Rouse (1807–1891). Anglican ecclesiologist and pioneer in the ceremonial revival associated with the Tractarian Movement. Closely associated with his Oxford college (Magdalen) for much of his life, he served for some years as Newman's curate at Littlemore.

Blumhardt, Johann Christoph (1805–80). German evangelist. Having studied at Tübingen, he taught at Basel from 1830. When, in 1838, he became pastor of the church at Möttlingen in Würtemberg, he was soon acclaimed for his evangelical work, which sometimes included physical healing. From 1852, his work at Bad Boll, near Göppingen, made it an international center of Prot-estant missionary work. His theology reflected Pietistic influence. After his death, his work at Bad Boll was taken up by his son, Christoph Friedrich (1842–1919). He was among much else a pioneer in modern methods of spiritual healing.

Bobbio. An abbey founded by Columbanus in 612 in this little town forty miles north-east of Genoa contained a renowned collection of manuscripts, many of which dated before the year 1,000. This collection has been largely dispersed to great libraries such as the Vatican and the Ambrosiana (Milan). The Bobbio Missal, now in the Bibliothèque Nationale, Paris, contains important liturgical texts.

Bodha. In Hindu philosophy, "knowledge" or "understanding" as personified in a son of Buddhi (intellect), one of the daughters of Dakṣa.

Bodhidharma (c. 470–543 CE). An Indian Buddhist monk who went to China where he established the Ch'an school of Buddhism, which stresses meditation. In Japan it took the form of Zen. See **Zen**.

Bodhirukkha. The bodhi-tree under which the Buddha, according to tradition, received enlightenment. Various trees are held to have been planted from shoots of the original tree, for example the one at Anurādhapura in Sri Lanka.

Bodhisattva. In Buddhism (especially but not exclusively Mahayana), one who postpones the Buddhahood to which he or she is entitled in order to dally on earth to help others.

Bodhi-Tree. See **Bodhirukkha**.

Bodleian Library. The library of the University of Oxford and one of the seven libraries that may legally claim to be presented with a copy of every book published in the United Kingdom. Apart from its vast collection of books, many very rare, it contains thousands of important manuscripts. The oldest part of the Bodleian is Duke Humphrey's Library, housed over the Divinity School and dating from the 15th c. Each of the Oxford colleges has also its own library, which, especially in the larger ancient colleges, usually is extensive and contains many treasures.

Bodmer Papyri. A collection of manuscripts of extraordinary importance dating from at least the early 3rd to the 7th century CE, mostly Christian and including one of the Gospel according to John dating from *c* 200, almost complete. Most are on papyrus and all but one in codex form. The earlier manuscripts are in Greek, the later ones in Coptic.

Body of Christ. This term (Latin, *Corpus Christi*) is used by Christians in several senses: (1) The human body of Jesus, transformed at the Resurrection; (2) The eucharistic bread; (3) The Church as the community or People of God and the vehicle of God's redemptive activity on earth; (4) the name of a feast (Corpus Christi) held in the West since the 13th c. to honor the Blessed Sacrament.

Boehme, Jakob (1575–1624). German theosophist and mystic. Educated in the Lutheran tradition, he claimed to describe his personal mystical experiences. He ran into opposition by the Lutheran Church authorities. He borrowed much from Paracelsus. Although his language is not easy, his thought is important to mystically minded students of theosophy, and he has been highly influential on a remarkably important circle of writers, including Hegel and Schelling, Newton and the Cambridge Platonists.

Boethius, Ancius Manlatus Torquatus Severinus (*c.* 480–*c.* 524). Philosopher, friend and adviser of Theodoric. He is especially known for his *De Consolatione philosophiae* in which he describes, as a political prisoner, how the Lady Philos-

ophy visited him in prison. When he asked the old question, *unde malum* (whence comes evil?), she told him, in Stoic fashion, that evil hurts only bad men, because good men do not depend for their happiness on external circumstances such as we call evil. According to Boethius, the soul attains a vision of God through philosophical inquiry. Although he does not seem to expound specifically Christian teaching and scholars formerly questioned whether he was indeed to be accounted a Christian, certain treatises attributed to him that are plainly Christian are now generally regarded as authentically his.

Bogomils. A medieval sect in the Eastern Church, appearing in the Balkans in the 8th c., that questioned ecclesiastical authority. The Bogomils were accordingly declared heretical, being denounced *c.* 972. They reflected Manichaean teachings and took a Docetic view of Christ. In many ways their views adumbrated those of the Albigenses. They taught reincarnationism. The movement continued for several centuries despite brutal persecution. Bogomilism was even for a time the national religion of Hungary, although Catholicism was nominally restored in 1450.

Bohemian Brethren. These (later known as the Moravian Brethren or *Unitas Fratrum*) were a group of Utraquists who separated from the main body of the Utraquists in 1467. Like the Quakers of a later date, they refused to take oaths or engage in military service, renouncing the life of society for a life based on strict Christian discipline, separated from the world. They persisted through the Reformation despite persecution from both Catholic and Protestant sides and eventually joined the Herrnhuter, accepting an offer from Zinzendorf to do so in 1721. They had some affinities with the Waldensians and they much influenced the development of the earlier stages of Methodism.

Bollandists. Jesuit editors of the Acta Sanctorum, whose founder was J. van Bolland (1596–1665). The work was intended to be a critical edition of the lives of the saints.

Bolsec, Hieronymus Hermas (d. 1584). Reformation theologian, originally a Carmelite. Sought at first to follow Calvin's teaching but was disaffected from it and, after challenging it in Geneva in October 1551, he was handed over to the secular authorities and imprisoned. Eventually he returned to the Roman Catholic Church.

Bombastus von Hohenheim, Theosphrastus. See **Paracelsus.**

Bon. This term was applied to the officiants in the pre-Buddhist religion of Tibet. Later, all pre-Buddhist rites and beliefs were called Bon.

Bonaventure (c. **1217–74).** One of the three greatest of the 13th c. Latin schoolmen, he was Italian by birth and trained at the University of Paris. In c. 1243 he entered the Franciscan Order and studied theology under Alexander of Hales. In 1257 he was elected Minister General of the Order. Theologically he was more conservative than Thomas Aquinas or Duns Scotus, following the Augustinian tradition and giving less acknowledgment than did Thomas to the role of reason and human knowledge. His mystical theory of knowledge by illumination is expounded in his *Itinerarium*. Like Thomas, however, he denied that Mary was immaculately conceived. (See **Immaculate Conception.**) In 1273 he was elected Cardinal Bishop of Albano. The following year he died while the Council of Lyons was in session.

Bonhoeffer, Dietrich (1906–1945). Lutheran clergyman, much influenced by Barth. Trained at Tübingen and Berlin, he developed a strong interest in the ecumenical movement and an unbending opposition to the Nazi party and the "German Christians," eventually signing the Barmen Declaration in 1934. When World War II broke out he happened to be in the U.S. He returned to Germany and tried to engage in conciliation between Germany and Britain. In 1943 he was arrested, sent to Buchenwald, and in 1945 he was hanged by the Gestapo. In his writings he urged a radical reform of the church and a life of faith in which the Christian can dispense with traditional forms, when necessary, in the interest of authentic discipleship. He did not seek to depreciate either the individual or the community but saw revelation as divine disclosure to the Church through the preaching of the Word of God. He taught the need to reach spirituality by seeking to find it in the here-and-now.

His earlier works are on the nature of the Church: *Sanctorum Communio* (1930) and *Akt und Sein* (1931), translated under the title *Act and Being*. Important for an understanding of his later development are *Die Nachfolge* (1937) and his *Ethik* (1949) translated respectively as *The Cost of Discipleship* and *Ethics*. Probably his best known work is his *Widerstand und Ergebung* (1951), translated as *Letters and Papers from Prison*.

Boniface (680–754). Born in Devon, England, and originally called Wynfrith, he came to be known as the Apostle of Germany. After some success in missionary enterprises in Bavaria and elsewhere, he received the fullest support and authority from the Pope (Gregory II) to found a regular ecclesiastical organization in Germany and, later on, to carry out a reform of the entire Frankish Church. In 747 he became Archbishop of Mainz. He returned, however, to Frisia, which had been his first mission, and there he was martyred in 754. His name is much associated with the Roman Catholic Church in Germany. For example, the Boniface Society was founded in 1849 for the support of Roman Catholics living in predominantly Protestant regions of Germany.

Bonner, Edmund (*c.* 1500–1569). The last Bishop of London to die in communion with Rome. He refused, in 1559, to take the oath under the Act of Supremacy.

Bonosus. A fourth century bishop who denied the perpetual virginity of Mary. His teaching was condemned, but he refused to submit and founded a group called the Bonosians, which continued down to the 17th c.

Boodin, John Elof (1869–1950). Swedish-born American philosopher; disciple of Josiah Royce. He taught that creation is eternal and that evolution is spiritual as well as physical and biological.

Book of Common Prayer, The. The unity of the public worship of the Anglican Communion as well as its distinctiveness is determined largely through the Book of Common Prayer (BCP), which contains the liturgy for the Sacraments and other rites and offices of the Church. The Latin service books of the medieval Church had been complex, and in the 16th c. the need and desire for a simplification was felt. Thomas Cranmer and others compiled a single volume, simplifying the old usages and rendering the prayers into English. This liturgical reform was accomplished in a conservative, typically English fashion. Like the English of the King James Version of the Bible in the following century, the English of the BCP was dignified, traditional, and restrained, yet easily understood by ordinary people. Like the English Bible itself, it soon came to be much beloved. It has been a lasting influence on the English language, on the literature of the English-speaking peoples, and even on the mold of their thought and life. After some preliminary drafts and experimentation, Cranmer discussed the proposed BCP with a group of scholars in 1548, and the following year the English Parliament caused the "First Prayer Book of Edward VI" to be printed and its use enforced throughout England. This 1549 BCP reflected theological moderation: it was an attempt to conserve the traditional Catholic temper of medieval worship with the best in the fresh ideas that had been generated by the theological insights of the Reformers and the biblical Renaissance that they were achieving. As with most compromises, neither side was satisfied. Controversy ensued, modifications were made in further editions, concessions were made to the Puritan party, and at length was issued the 1662 BCP, which remained practically unchanged for three centuries, by which time the 1662 BCP, although hallowed by long use, had come to need revision. In Scotland and other parts of the British Commonwealth in which changes could be accomplished by the Church without parliamentary control, the BCP was revised and issued for use with fewer bureaucratic obstacles than in England, although seldom if ever without dissatisfaction on the part of one element of the Church or another. Nevertheless, the BCP continues to keep its central place in the life of the Anglican Communion as the basic document, after the Bible, in that branch of the Christian Church. The American BCP as issued in 1789 has undergone various revisions. The one currently authorized was issued in 1979.

Book of the Dead. In ancient Egyptian religion, a book of prayers, hymns, and other utterances designed to help the deceased person in the passage from this world to the next.

Booth, William (1829–1912). Founder of the Salvation Army. He became a Methodist and in 1844 experienced a conversion that led to his becoming two years later a revivalist preacher. In 1855 he married Catherine Mumford, who also attained fame as a preacher. Having become unacceptable to the Methodists by reason of what they accounted a histrionic style of preaching, he broke with them in 1861 and founded a movement of his own which developed into the Salvation Army. His emphasis was on a combination of evangelical, revivalistic preaching combined with a special concern for the social evils among the poor in Victorian England. His work spread quickly, however, to America, Australia, and continental Europe, where he spent much time and energy in organizing Salvationist work. In his latter years he received much encouragement from King Edward VII. With little or no theological training, he did not profess to conduct any sort of scholarly ministry, but his rescue work and his outstanding organizational gifts brought astonishing success to his movement even during his lifetime. On his death he was succeeded by his son, William Bramwell Booth (1865–1929). He insisted at an early date on the organization of his "army" along military lines with military ranks for his officers, regarding them as enlisted in the war against the Devil. His book, *In Darkest England and the Way Out* (1890), published in collaboration with W. T. Stead, is a classic in Christian social work.

Booths, Feast of. See **Tabernacles, The Feast of.**

Borborians. A Gnostic sect, libertine in outlook, which flourished from the 2nd through the 5th c.

Bordeaux Pilgrim, The. So far as is known, the first person to make a pilgrimage from Western Europe to the Holy Land did so in 333–334 CE and is so known to historians. He visited Constantinople en route and left a description of some of the places he visited in Palestine, preserved in an account, *Itinerarium Burdigalense.*

Borgia, Francis (1510–1572). Jesuit friend and adviser of Ignatius Loyola and Teresa of Ávila. Ordained a priest in 1551, he became in 1565 the third General of the Jesuit Order. Of noble birth he used his influence to obtain a favorable reception in France for the Jesuits.

Borrow, George (1803–1881). Writer and traveler. Author of *Lavengro* (1851), *The Romany Rye* (2 vols., 1857). Probably the most popular of his stories was *The Bible in Spain* (3 vols., 1843), written as a Bible Society agent.

Bosanquet, Bernard (1848–1923). British philosopher much indebted to Hegel, he expounded a system of Absolute Idealism, along with F. H. Bradley, that was distinctively English. Educated at Balliol College, Oxford, he became a Fellow of University College in 1870, where he remained for eleven years before going to London where he lived for the rest of his life privately, except for a period of five years (1903–1908) when he was professor of Moral Philosophy at the University of St. Andrews, Scotland. His philosophy was fundamentally a religious one, and his religious stance was pantheistic. Like Hegel, he tended to think of religion as a sort of "baby" philosophy.

Bosco, John (1815–1888). Founder of the Salesians. Claiming to have received a vision, at the age of nine, during his upbringing in and near Turin, and for many years later, he sought to win young boys to the Christian Way. His educational methods tended to stress a minimum of restraint along with a maximum of vigilance and much personal encouragement.

Bosio, Antonio (1576–1629). Italian pioneer in archaeology who was the first to perceive the importance of the discovery of a subterranean passage, a burial place, on the Via Salaria, Rome. He made extremely important discoveries published in 1632 in his *Roma sotterraneo.*

Bossey. An institute of the World Council of Churches, opened at the Château de Bossey, near Geneva, in 1946, chiefly through the munificence of John D. Rockefeller, Jr.

Bossuet, Jacques Bénigne (1627–1704). Famous preacher and Bishop of Meaux.

Trained at the College de Navarre, Paris, for the priesthood, he quickly attracted notice, even in his teens, for his oratorical gifts. From 1670 through 1681 he was tutor to the Dauphin. He was a moderate Gallican and zealous exponent of Catholic teaching. He was involved in an acrimonious controversy with Fénelon on the subject of mysticism and he secured the latter's condemnation in 1699. He was probably one of the greatest preachers in Christian history.

Bourdaloue, Louis (1632–1704). Jesuit preacher. He was noted for the lucidity and fine organization of his sermons, in which he sought to emphasize the moral implications of Christian faith. He delivered courses of sermons before Louis XIV. His preaching style was admired not least for the subtle insight he evinced toward the frailties of the human psyche.

Bousset, Wilhelm (1865–1920). New Testament scholar. His work exhibited the connection of early Christianity and Judaism with the Hellenistic religions. From 1916 he was professor at Giessen.

Boutroux, Emile (1845–1921). French philosopher, taught at the Sorbonne, influenced by Maine de Biran. Among his students were Bergson and Blondel.

Bowden, John William (1798–1844). Tractarian and close friend of Newman.

Bowing. The practice of bowing in church, on entering, before the Cross on the altar, at the name of Jesus, and on other occasions, is ancient, although the degree of antiquity is disputable. It is to be distinguished from Genuflection, a reverence for the Blessed Sacrament.

Bowne, Borden Parker (1845–1910). American philosopher of the Personalist school, he held that no form of impersonalistic thought can adequately treat the data of experience. Personality is the concept that best expresses the ultimate nature of reality.

Boy Bishop. A common custom in the Middle Ages, especially in England, consisted of the election on December 6 (St. Nicholas' Day) of a boy who, till December 28 (Holy Innocents' Day) would perform certain functions normally performed by bishops. The idea seems to have been to celebrate in a picturesque way the importance of children that is so much stressed in the Gospel reports of Jesus' attitude toward them.

Boyle, Robert (1627–1691). Commonly acclaimed as the father of modern chemistry. He was one of the founders of the Royal Society. He is important in the history of Christianity for his attempt to show how the new developments in the understanding of scientific method harmonized with Christian faith.

Bracketing. A term used by Husserl to denote the mental suspension of the presuppositions implicit in the sciences. By so eliminating such presuppositions one can see more clearly and in better perspective how things actually appear in human consciousness. Thus, one is able to describe and intuitively grasp kinds of experience in all their variety and in their pure subjectivity. See **Phenomenology** and **Husserl, Edmund**.

Bradford, John (c. 1510–1555). Protestant martyr. Born in Manchester, he studied law, which he abandoned for theology and in time gained the favor of Nicholas Ridley, Bishop of London. On the accession of Mary in 1553, however, he was imprisoned in the Tower. Eighteen months later he was tried, found steadfast in his Protestant views, and burnt at Smithfield on July 1, 1555.

Bradlaugh, Charles (1833–1891). Notable in his day as a lecturer, pamphleteer, and champion of atheism, he became, after many difficulties, a well-known lecturer and, from 1858 through 1890, President of the London Secular Society. He co-edited the *National Reformer* with Mrs. A. Besant. Elected to

Parliament, he refused to take the required oath in the prescribed form and was for some time excluded but eventually permitted to take his seat.

Bradley, Francis Herbert. (1846–1924). British philosopher, much influenced by Hegel. He was an exponent of Absolute Idealism and perhaps the most important British metaphysician of his time. While rejecting traditional theism with its implicates of selfhood, personhood, and personal immortality, he focused on the Absolute as the ultimate and, in the last resort, only reality. Among his many works, *Appearance and Reality* (1893) was probably the most influential. An Oxford man, he was from 1870 till his death a Fellow of Merton College.

Bradwardine, Thomas (*c*. 1290–1349). Theologian. Trained at Oxford he was successively a Fellow of Balliol and of Merton College. In 1349, he was consecrated Archbishop of Canterbury and died the same year of the plague. Noted for his erudition, he upheld the ontological argument and taught in the tradition of Augustine, Anselm, and Duns Scotus. Like Augustine he emphasized the importance of grace so that his teaching predisposed later thinkers to move in the direction of a predestinarian theology. He was also, in his day, a noted mathematician.

Brahe, Tycho (1546–1601). Danish astronomer. Educated at Copenhagen, Leipzig, Rostock, and Augsburg, he immensely improved the precision of astronomical observations in his time. See **Copernicus, Johann** and **Kepler, Nicolas.**

Brahmā. In late Vedic and subsequent Hindu literature, Brahmā is represented as the Creator of the universe, but this concept seems incompatible with the notion of a fundamental, eternal principle that is impersonal: *brahman*. ("Brahmā" is the masculine form of "brahman".) The concept of Brahmā is introduced in the upanishadic literature as a sort of mental personification of brahman apparently as a means of providing for a monotheistic dimension to the Hindu view of the universe. This move in turn produced the triadic concept of Brahmā, Viṣṇu, and Śiva, which are three aspects of Brahmā. Each member of the triad has its own devotees. In this system, so developed, Viṣṇu, the preserver, and Śiva, the destroyer, are opposed; Brahmā then has the function of synthesizing them. In some revivals of the primeval myths of Hindu lore, Brahmā becomes the creative instrument of the eternal brahman and is sometimes presented as androgynous. In such a model, Brahmā could be represented as dividing himself into male and female, while allowing for the retention of brahman as the eternal principle behind all things, grammatically neutral. See also **Brahman.**

Brahmagupta. A 7th c. CE Indian mathematician and astronomer. His calculation of the circumference of the earth seems to have been remarkably accurate for his time. He fostered an interest in mathematics that culminated in the 9th c. in the work of a Jain, Mahāvīra of Mysore.

Brahman. As a neuter noun, the term in Hindu philosophy may be rendered "universal, self-existing power." It stands for the notion of cosmic unity. At first a fairly simplistic notion, it gradually became part of a much more developed and complex system. See **Brahmā.**

Brahman. Originally (in the Vedas) a term identified with wind, breath (compare the Hebrew *ruach* and the Greek *pneuma*), it was developed in the Upanishads, where it became central, as that essentially pure, unchangeable and eternal Being, in which all things have their origin. It is especially fundamental to the Vedantist school of Hinduism.

Brāhman. As a masculine noun, highest of the four castes in the traditional division of Hindu society. He may be either a priest or a layman who is engaged in non-priestly functions. Traditionally, however, he is supposed to be able to repeat the Vedas, which he knows by heart. In modern times, those who are descended from families of the Brāhman class who would not or could not become priests and so engaged in secular occupations are generally called "brahmins".

Brāhmana. The term is used in two distinct senses: (a) A literature consisting of the elaboration of priestly ritualistic manuals. It varies very considerably in quality, much of it being somewhat dreary and prolix. It dates from roughly 800 to 600 BCE. (b) The name given to the priestly class, collectively, although in the course of Indian history it has come to be applied to priests individually. According to Vedic principles and practice, priests must be male. If, as occasionally happened, a priest delegated to his wife the performance of the priestly sacrifice, the gods were said to despise the offering.

Brahma-Sūtra. A summary of earlier attempts to interpret the upanishadic literature of India. (It is also known as the Vedānta-Sūtra.) It may be dated probably between 200 and 450 CE.

Brahmin. See **Brāhman.**

Branch Theory. A theory of the Church fostered by the English Tractarians, according to which the Church, although divided by internal schisms, maintains its essential unity like a tree that has several living branches. Each branch, so long as it holds the faith of the original, undivided Church and preserves the episcopal succession (see **Apostolic Succession**) is a part of the same living tree, drawing its sustenance from Christ. So, it is argued, the Eastern, Roman, and Anglican Churches are branches of the same living tree.

Brasses, Medieval. The practice of erecting monuments and sculptures in churches for the purpose of honoring notable personages tends, in time, to create disfiguring clutter. Indeed, three-dimensional art of any kind (such as is traditionally permitted in the Western although not in the Eastern Church) can have such a result. The practice of making an engraving on a flat brass panel representing the figure of the deceased and identifying it was seen to have many practical advantages as well as aesthetic ones. So from at least as early as the 13th c. this practice grew up in England, France, Germany, and elsewhere in Western Europe.

Bread, Eucharistic. Till about the year 1,000 CE, the use of leavened bread in the Eucharist was widespread, but in the West the use of unleavened bread had grown. The difference in usage became, after the Schism (1054), an outward sign of the cleavage. Unleavened bread is still generally used in the Roman Catholic Church. Anglican rubrics have generally and characteristically permitted either, although the use of unleavened bread is very widespread, while Eastern Orthodoxy insists on the use of leavened bread. Protestant Churches also generally use leavened bread.

Breeches Bible. Name popularly given by collectors and others to the Geneva Bible because (Genesis 3.7) where the King James Version reports that God made Adam and Eve aprons to cover their nakedness, the Geneva Bible has "breeches".

Bremond, Henri (1865–1933). Christian humanist. Entered the Jesuit Order in 1882, ordained priest 1892; left the Order in 1904 to have greater freedom in his writing, but encountered difficulties with the Church which was then in the midst of the Modernist controversy. His principal work is his *Histoire littéraire du sentiment religieux en France* (1913–1932), in 11 vols. plus an index (1936), which is a masterpiece of Christian spirituality. Bremond's sympathies were with what he called "devout humanism," i.e., a gentle, humane, intelligent understanding of Christian faith;

he disliked fanaticism in any form. His style is charming and his understanding of the French tradition of spirituality deeply penetrating. His little book, *Prière et poésie* (1926) exhibits his fine spiritual insight and sensitivity as well as his literary genius.

Brendan. A 5th c. Abbot of Clonfert, Galway, Ireland. According to a widespread medieval tradition, he visited islands in the north, presumably the Orkneys and the Hebrides. This legend is reported in the 11th c. "Navigation of Saint Brendan."

Brentano, Franz C. (1838–1917). Austrian philosopher. Ordained a Roman Catholic priest in 1864, he renounced the Church in 1873, while retaining a strong belief in both God and the Christian concept of the soul. He was especially influential on phenomenologists such as Husserl and Meinong. His aim was to produce a descriptive psychology without prior assumptions, such as would lead to a new way of classifying psychical phenomena. These he found to be characterized by what he called "intentional inexistence" requiring reference to a context. "Existence" is a "synsemantic" term expressive of our acceptance or rejection of things. Value judgments depend on internal evidence and can be objective. His principal writings include his *Psychology from an Empirical Standpoint* (1874) and his *On the Origin of Moral Knowledge* (1889).

Brenz, Johann (1499–1570). Lutheran Reformer. Born at Weilderstadt, he studied under Oecolampadius at Heidelberg and came under Luther's influence in 1518. Unlike Oecolampadius he upheld, with Luther, the doctrine of the Real Presence in the Eucharist. Although he opposed the Calvinists, theologically he was inclined to favor their views on Church Order.

Brest-Litovsk, Union of. In 1596, with the approval of Pope Clement VIII and Sigismund, King of Poland, a concordat was reached under which the Metropol-itan of Kiev, with the Ruthenian bishops and millions of Ruthenian Christians, all Eastern Orthodox, submitted to Rome while retaining permission to use their own Byzantine rite. Many Ruthenians later on, however, returned to Orthodoxy, and others adopted the Latin rite.

Brethren, The Lord's. Various references occur in the New Testament to the Lord's brethren (e.g., Mark 6.3; John 7.3; Acts 1.14; I Cor. 9.5). Those who do not insist on the "perpetual virginity of Mary" generally accept the men mentioned (James, Joseph, Simon, and Jude) to be children of Mary and Joseph born after Jesus. Jerome repudiated this view, however, holding that they were the sons of Mary, the mother of James and Joses (Mark 15.40), whom he identified with the Virgin Mary's sister. Others again (e.g., Epiphanius) have held that they were sons of Joseph by a former marriage: a view generally upheld in the Eastern Orthodox Church.

Brethren of the Common Life. An association formed in the 14th c. to promote deeper spirituality in the Church. Their founder, G. de Groote, a canon of Utrecht, imposed no vows on his followers, priests or laypeople. They founded very good schools available free. They did much to keep the Church's life from decay at a time of ecclesiastical corruption. They persisted till the 17th c..

Brethren of the Free Spirit. A term applied to various groups in the Middle Ages who thought and worked independently of the mainstream of the Church and often engaged in mystical forms of religion. There is no evidence that they had any formal organization.

Bretschneider, Karl Gottlieb (1776–1848). German theologian. In his *Probabilia* (1820) he anticipated later developments in the literary analysis of the New Testament, notably the distinction between John and the Synoptists. He founded the *Corpus Reformatorum*, an edition of the works of the Protestant Reformers.

Breviary. The breviary is a Roman Catholic liturgical book consisting of psalms, lessons, prayers, and hymns and constituting what is called the Divine Office (*divinum officium*) of the Church. It existed in some form before the time of Benedict, but he both prescribed its daily use for his monks and developed it by adding other elements such as canticles and responsories. The entire psalter was recited weekly and a large part of the Bible annually. Gradually various hagiographical elements were introduced, and by the time of the Council of Trent (1549–60) legendary stories had so proliferated that their abolition was ordered and from time to time other such purifications have been made. Traditionally, the cycle consisted of Mattins (the night office) and Lauds, Prime, Terce, Sext, None, Vespers, Compline (the day office), honoring the psalmist's cry (Ps. 119.164): "Seven times a day do I praise thee. . . . " The Second Vatican Council recommended a simplified and modernized breviary, which Pope Paul VI issued in 1971. All Roman Catholic priests and certain others are required to recite the breviary daily. The monastic breviary differs in some minor respects from that which is used by the clergy in general.

Bridges, Robert Seymour (1844–1930). British poet laureate from 1913. Educated at Eton and Oxford, he was much attracted in his youth to Anglo-Catholic ideals and practices, but in later life he tended to dismiss the dogmatic aspects of Church teaching while remaining profoundly Christian in spirit. His principal works are his *Testament of Beauty* (1929), in which he sought to overcome the barrier between scientific and religious thought, and *The Spirit of Man* (1915). He was one of the founders of the Society for Pure English.

Bridget (or Bride or Brigid). Early 6th c. Abbess of Kildare and (along with Saint Patrick) patron saint of Ireland. Historically obscure she has been and remains highly reverenced in Ireland and identified with the soul of that country.

Bridget of Sweden. A 14th c. foundress of the Bridgittine Order. Daughter of one of the richest families in Sweden, she married at the age of 13, had eight children, made a pilgrimage to Compostella with her husband, who died soon afterwards, so freeing Bridget to devote herself entirely to her religious aims. She founded her Order in 1346 and went to Rome in 1349, where she obtained confirmation of her Order by the Pope. She continued to reside in Rome till her death, being noted for revelations she was believed to have been given. She died in 1373 and was canonized in 1391. The Bridgittines, although bound by the customary vow of poverty, were permitted to have as many books as they wished. Originally it was intended that the Order should consist of men and women living in separate sections of the same monastery but worshipping in the same chapel: an arrangement that ceased during the 16th c. Some Bridgettine houses survive in Holland, Spain, Germany, and England. The Order is officially known as *Ordo Sanctissimi Salvatoris.*

Brief. A papal letter less formal than a Bull. See **Bull.**

Brightman, Edgar Sheffield (1884–1952). American philosopher of the Personalist school. Argued for a God of limited power who works on a "given". His writings include *The Problem of God* (1930) and *A Philosophy of Religion* (1940).

British Israelites. A group who have held that the British people are descended from the ten Israelite tribes taken into captivity in Assyria in 722–721 BCE. Proponents of this theory have often belonged to the military classes. It is entirely lacking in any scientific evidence and has no support from archaeologists or biblical scholars.

Broad Church. A term popularly used and fashionable in the second half of the 19th c. to denote those Anglicans who disliked dogmatic theological definition. It was used in opposition to both the "High" (Anglo-Catholic) and the "Low" (Evangelical) Church parties. Thomas Arnold was an influential representative of the kind of view favored by "Broad" churchmen. All three terms are inexact and should be avoided in serious discussion.

Brompton Oratory. An important Roman Catholic church in London, consecrated in 1884 and belonging to the Oratorians. The first Oratory in London was founded in 1849, largely through the work of Newman.

Brooks, Phillips (1835–1893). Noted American preacher, Anglican Bishop of Massachusetts, and author of the much loved Christmas carol, "O little town of Bethlehem."

Browne, George. Archbishop of Dublin from 1535. He helped to unite the Irish Church to the Church of England under the royal supremacy.

Browne, Robert (c. 1550–1633). English Puritan, generally regarded as the father of what came to be called Congregationalism. After establishing some independent parishes, for which he was imprisoned, he went to Holland where he wrote in support of the Congregationalist or Independent principle in church government. Having returned to England, he submitted to the English Church, but ministered for a while to an independent congregation. In 1591 he received Anglican Orders and obtained a benefice as Rector of Achurch, Northants, which he held till his death.

Browne, Sir Thomas (1605–1682). Author and medical practitioner who, after study and travel in France, Italy, and Holland, settled in 1637 at Norwich, where he remained till his death. His writings reflect not only immense learning but a delightful openness of mind and above all a unique combination of skepticism and faith. Although he shared some of the prejudices of his age and was in some way old-fashioned even in his day he had a breadth of outlook that is very refreshing. His best known work is his *Religio Medici* (1642), but among his other works his *Hydriotaphia* (1658), which is a learned treatise on burial customs in various parts of the world, is still fascinating reading.

Brownists. Name popularly given to the early followers of the English Congregationalist way.

Bruce, Alexander Balmain (1831–1899). Scottish theologian, appointed to a Free Church chair at Glasgow in 1875. Among his many writings *The Humiliation of Christ* is especially important in the history of the theories of proponents of Kenotic christology. Like other scholars of his age and circumstances, he was suspect by conservative churchmen for his use of the then new methods of biblical analysis, but he escaped the active persecution that befell others such as his Scottish contemporary Robertson Smith.

Brunner, Emil (1889–1966). Swiss theologian, he taught at Zürich and elsewhere. Like Barth, he opposed the secularistic tendencies of Protestant theology in his time, but unlike Barth he recognized that man may obtain a knowledge of God, however limited, through created things. He supported, therefore, the Thomist doctrine of analogy (*analogia entis*), which Barth repudiated. Like other Protestant theologians (e.g., Karl Heim and F. Gogarten), he was also influenced by Buber. *Der Mittler* (1927; tr., *The Mediator*, 1934) and *Das Gebot und die Ordnungen* (1932; tr. *The Divine Imperative*, 1937) are among his many works.

Bruno. A 10th c. Archbishop of Cologne, youngest son of the Emperor

Henry I. He exercised much influence on imperial policy, fostering peace within his domains and encouraging learning.

Bruno (*c.* 1032–1101). Founder of the Carthusian Order. In his early years of teaching at Reims he had among his pupils the future Pope Urban II. He became chancellor of his diocese and came into conflict with the Archbishop, a man of evil life. In 1084 he founded the Carthusian Order and was later (1090) summoned to Rome by the Pope (Urban II) to live in Italy, where he founded the monastery of La Torre in Calabria.

Bruno, Giordano (1548–1600). Italian thinker. He joined the Dominicans at Naples in 1562 but, on being censured for what were seen as heterodox opinions he fled in 1576 and wandered as a fugitive till his capture in 1592 by agents of the Inquisition, who secured his confinement in Rome till 1600, when, on February 17, he was burnt at the stake on the Campo dei Fiori. Bruno had adopted the Copernican theory in astronomy and had developed a metaphysical view of the universe that a later age would have called panentheistic. He expounded his views in two treatises, *De la Causa, Principio, ed Uno* and *De l'Infinito, Universo, e Mondi* (both 1584).

Brunschvicg, Léon (1869–1944). French philosopher. A Critical Idealist, he regarded reality as a function of thought. He saw human progress as moving toward spiritual values. His writings include *The Modality of Judgment* (1897); *Spinoza and His Contemporaries* (1923); *Philosophical Writings* (2 vols., 1951, 1954).

Bryennios, Philotheos (1833–1914). Born in Constantinople and trained in Ecclesiastical History at various German universities, he eventually became Metropolitan of Serrae, Macedonia, in 1875 and of Nicomedia in 1877. In 1873, while Director of the school in the Phanar at Constantinople, he dis-covered in the library of the hospice of the monastery of the Holy Sepulchre there an 11th c. manuscript containing early documents of the Christian Church, including the Didache, the Epistle of Barnabas, and two epistles of Clement to the Corinthians, all of paramount importance, but especially the Didache, which describes the conduct and practice of the early Christian community at a very early point in Christian history, possibly even the 1st c.

Buber, Martin (1878–1965). Jewish thinker, born in Vienna, he became active in the Zionist movement before taking his doctorate in Vienna in 1900. His religious studies led him to an interest in Hasidism. After various appointments including one at Frankfurt University where he taught Jewish theology and ethics, he left Germany in 1938 and became Professor of Sociology at the Hebrew University in Jerusalem. Among his many books, the small one entitled *Ich und Du* (1923; tr. *I and Thou*, 1937) gained great popularity and exercised an enormous influence throughout the Christian theological world as well as elsewhere. It exhibits the difference between a person-and-thing relationship and a person-and-person one, including a personal relationship with God.

Bucer, Martin (1491–1551). German Reformer. A Dominican friar, he obtained in 1521 papal dispensation from his vows. He had been in correspondence with Luther as early as 1518, soon after the latter's nailing of his famous 95 theses to the door of the Schlosskirche in Wittenberg. By 1523 he was openly supporting the Lutheran Reformation and was excommunicated by the Bishop of Speyer. As his views developed, especially on the Eucharist, he tended toward a position between that of Luther and that of Zwingli. After the latter's death in 1531, he became the leader of the Swiss Reformation. In 1549 he went to England where he became Regius Professor of Divinity at

Cambridge. Cranmer sought his counsel on various matters.

Buchman, Frank (1878–1961). Founder and leader of a movement later called variously "the Moral Rearmament Movement," "the Group Movement," "the Buchmanites," and, more commonly but very misleadingly, "the Oxford Group." An American Lutheran, he resigned his parish in 1908 and as a result of a conversion experience at the Keswick Convention later he began doing evangelistic work, first in the U.S. and then in India and China. He returned to England, visiting Cambridge and then Oxford, and here the group associated with his name seemed to take a more definite shape. He made a deep impression on many undergraduates wherever he went and gradually his work took him all over the world. He had no church organization or building but conducted the work largely at house parties and by personal contact, as the movement has continued to do its work.

Budde, Karl (1850–1935). German biblical scholar. As professor of Old Testament, first at Strassburg, then at Marburg, he was influential in developing the literary analysis of the Bible that has transformed biblical scholarship.

Buddha. The term means "an enlightened one" and is therefore not a name such as "Jesus" or "David" but a designation, as is also the name "Christ". Buddhism recognizes many buddhas, but the designation is given especially to Gautama (Gotama), whose dates are controversial but most modern scholars place him as living from c. the mid-seventh to the mid-sixth century BCE. He was a member of the Sakya tribe, who inhabited the foothills of the Himalayas. According to Buddhist tradition, he was born in a miraculous way. His mother, Mahā Māya, having at the time had no sexual relations with her husband, dreamed that the Buddha-to-be entered her womb in the form of a white elephant. The ensuing birth took

place in the Lumbini grove while she was traveling between Kapilavatthu and her parents' home. (This tradition has sometimes been embellished by stories of angels having sung at the birth.) Mahā Māya died seven days after the birth. Traditionally, Gautama is said to have been brought up in comfort and to have married and had a son; then at the age of twenty-nine he renounced his family and his way of life and resolved to live the life of an ascetic. For some years he lived such a life but was eventually led to see that it did not provide the final answer to his quest, which at length he found in meditation under the bodhi-tree. While some modern scholars have questioned the historicity of Gautama's existence, the more general opinion today is that, embellished by legend as the traditional accounts may be, an historical personage to whom may be attributed the foundation of the Buddhist religion did exist.

Buddhaghosa. A scholarly Theravada Buddhist monk who lived in Sri Lanka in the 4th to 5th c. CE. He is famed for his commentaries on the Pali canon of Buddhist scriptures, being regarded by Theravada Buddhists as their greatest interpreter. According to tradition he was born in India, of brahman caste, but nothing is known with certainty about his origin.

Buddhism and Christianity. While Buddhism and Christianity have many elements in common they have radically different ancestries: the former in Hinduism, the latter in Judaism. This results in a fundamental difference in outlook, despite the many similarities. Buddhism has two main branches, Hinayana (the "little vehicle") and Mahayana (the "great vehicle"). Hinayana, the older and stricter form, is itself divided into four schools, Therevada (the oldest), Sarvastivada, Sautrantika, and Vaibhasika, all similar in viewpoint. Mahayana, the form in which Buddhism has developed in China, Korea, and Japan, tends to envision progress toward a state of bliss or buddhahood: progress assisted by the bodhisattvas, who function somewhat as do angels of mercy in the Judeo-Christian tradition. Nevertheless, all forms of Buddhism, but especially Hinayana, tend to approach the problems of life psychologically with little interest in ontological questions and much more on the analysis and development of the psyche, although certain forms of Mahayana introduce elements that reflect ontological presuppositions. The characteristic direction of all Buddhist thought is toward enlightenment such as the Buddha (560–477 BCE) attained under the Bo tree. Historically Buddhism is *inter alia* a protest against the institutional aspects of its Hindu parent (e.g., caste), while it conserves much of the basic outlook of the great documents of Hinduism such as the Upanishads, including the concepts of karma and reincarnation. Such concepts have certainly played a greater part than is commonly supposed in the spiritual life of the West, but under the Christian banner they acquire in some respects a different significance.

Buddhist Councils. See **Councils, Buddhist.**

Bulgakov, Sergius (1871–1944). Russian Orthodox theologian. Influenced by Hegel he became a skeptic with inclinations to Marxism. Then, disillusioned, he gradually returned to the Orthodox Church, first as a layman, later as an ordained priest. Expelled after the Bolshevik Revolution, he became Dean of the Orthodox Theological Academy in Paris where he remained till his death. In theology he made much of the concept of Sophia or "Divine Wisdom," a concept that has deep roots in Russian Orthodoxy and contains an element of theosophical esotericism in it. His works include *Du Verbe incarné* (1943) and *The Wisdom of God* (1937).

Bull, George (1634–1710). Anglican theologian who defended ancient Catholic doctrine with much vigor. One of his

works *Judicium Ecclesiam Catholicae* (1694) was formally praised by the French clergy at a synod in 1700. Bull was consecrated Bishop of St. Davids, Wales, in 1705. Among his more popular works is *The Corruptions of the Church of Rome* (1705).

Bull. A papal document issued as a mandate of a more solemn kind than a brief. So called because, in earlier times, it was sealed with the Pope's own signet ring (*bulla*).

Bullinger, Johann Heinrich (1504–1575). Swiss Reformer. After the death of Zwingli in 1531, he succeeded him as chief pastor of Zürich. The Second Helvetic Confession was his work. Queen Elizabeth I sought his counsel.

Bultmann, Rudolf (1884–1976). New Testament scholar and theologian. After study at Marburg and elsewhere and various academic positions in German universities, he returned to Marburg in 1921 to a chair he held till his retirement in 1951. Of great importance in 20th c. Christian theology, he carried the methods of the Formgeschichte school to a methodological skepticism about the historicity of the Gospels. In his later work he engaged in a demythologizing of the entire Christian message, noting that many of the traditionally central doctrines presuppose outdated concepts such as a three-storied universe and contain plainly antiquated mythological elements. On the positive side, his work sought to emphasize faith and claimed to see the Cross at the center of Christianity; but he insisted that all attempts to work out a Christian theology today must include the reinterpretation along existentialist lines of the meaning of the *kerygma*.

Bunyan, John (1628–1688). Following his father's trade as a brazier, with little or no formal education, he acquired such a mastery of the English language, mainly through a reading of the Bible, that he eventually became the author of one of the greatest classics of English literature, *The Pilgrim's Progress.* Written probably during an imprisonment in 1676, it is notable for the clarity and simplicity of its style and as one of the greatest religious classics in the entire world. Received in 1653 into an Independent congregation at Bedford, he engaged in preaching and was frequently imprisoned between 1660 and 1672. Among his other works, his autobiography, *Grace Abounding to the Chief of Sinners* (1666) is one of the most moving documents of its kind in English literature.

Burckard, John. 15th c. liturgist. Appointed papal master of ceremonies in 1483, he amassed many benefices and in 1503 was created a cardinal. He was the first to provide detailed rubrics for the celebration of Mass and for other ceremonies.

Burgher. Among the various schisms that have divided Scottish Presbyterianism was one that occurred in 1733, when the first Secession took place on the question of State interference in church patronage. The Seceders believed it damaged orthodoxy of doctrine by depriving individual members of the Church of freedom to protest against what were held to be corrupting intrusions. In 1747, within this seceding body a further schism occurred between two splinter groups, the Burghers, who held that it was lawful for a Christian to take the civil Burgess Oath and the Antiburghers who held that it was unlawful to do so.

Burial. Although cremation is no longer forbidden in the Roman Catholic Church and is now widely accepted by many other Christians, burial is the traditional way for Christians to dispose of their dead. In the ancient Church, partly because of the association of cremation with the pagan custom and partly because of a literalistic understanding of the resurrection of the body, it was repugnant to followers of the Christian Way. The catacombs in Rome attest to the use of burial from earliest Christian times. Not till the 4th c. do we have clear information about the burial customs of Christians, and we know that at that time white, expressive of joy, was the color used by the people attending the burial service. (White is used in other cultures too, e.g., China.) From about the 8th c., however, black had become the customary color, presumably because, in a society in which Christianity was by then well established as part of the social structure, many lacked the lively faith that can confidently look to death as the gateway to life beyond. At any rate the Requiem service became, during the Middle Ages, more and more mournful. (See **Dirge.**) Prayers for the dead are traditional and universal except in certain Protestant circles where a strong opposition to the notion of an intermediate state (see **Purgatory**) lingers.

Buridan's Ass. Medieval philosophers discussed a case in which a donkey, set between two bundles of hay, precisely equal in every respect and equidistant from it, would have no motive to choose one over the other. Would not it die of starvation? The problem relates, of course, to the problem of determinism and free choice. The case in question was attributed (probably in error) to John Buridan, an early 14th c. schoolman.

Burke, Edmund (1729–1797). British statesman and philosopher. Born in Dublin and educated at Trinity College, Dublin. His work *On the Sublime and the Beautiful* (1756), in which he distinguished the two psychologically, was translated into German by Lessing and influenced Moses Mendelssohn. He recognized that both the American and the French Revolutions flowed from a conservative principle (the preservation of traditional rights and liberties); he approved of the American one on the ground that it had as its aim only this practical concern but disapproved of the French one because, in his view, it sought merely to destroy traditional institutions for nothing but a doctrinaire ideal.

Burkitt, Francis Crawford (1864–1935). Biblical and patristic scholar, from 1905 till his death professor of divinity at Cambridge. He had an unusual and original mind and made important discoveries, e.g., in the relation of the Old Syriac to the Peshitta versions of the New Testament and also in connection with the Syriac liturgies. *The Gospel and Its Transmission* (1906) and *Christian Beginnings* (1924) are among his writings.

Burney, Charles Fox (1868–1925). Biblical scholar, elected in 1914 Oriel professor at Oxford. His *Aramaic Origin of the Fourth Gospel* (1922) exhibited his insistence on the importance of Aramaic for an understanding of the Gospels.

Burning Bush. According to a biblical passage (Exodus 3.2–4), an angel appeared to Moses in a flame out of the middle of a bush that the flame did not consume. (Certain plants do give off a vapor ignitable at high temperatures and the ensuing sound could mimic the name of Moses in Hebrew, *Moshe*.) The Burning Bush is used by the Scottish Kirk as an emblem or logo, along with the words *Nec tamen consumebatur,* "Nevertheless it was not consumed."

Burrough, Edward (1634–1663). English Quaker, converted to that stance by his having heard George Fox preach in Westmorland in 1652, after which he became a staunch defender of the Quaker outlook, e.g., against John Bunyan, who attacked it and against the persecution of the Quakers by the New England Puritans. He was arrested in 1662, imprisoned in Newgate for holding a Quaker meet, which was at that time illegal, and he died in prison the following year.

Burse. A liturgical cover used since the 17th c. to hold the corporal, which was formerly kept in a bag or folded inside the Missal. The burse is carried on top of the chalice and paten.

Burton, Edward (1794–1836). Regius professor of divinity at Oxford from 1829. He compiled editions of various scholars' writings (e.g., George Bull and John Pearson) and was noted for the breadth and exactness of his scholarship.

Bushido. A Japanese term, from *bushi* (warrior) and *do* (path, principle). In this concept is celebrated both the chivalric ideal of the Confucian tradition and the role of the warrior in Zen Buddhism. The Bushido code had an occidental counterpart in the chivalric code of the knights of the military orders in medieval Europe. In Japan, however, the national religion of Shinto so exalted it that its practice by the samurai or military class of the feudal period of Japan commanded the widespread admiration of the general populace. Like much else of Confucian origin, it was not a code of fixed rules but rather a convention that dictated how people ought to behave; an unwritten law. Confucianism, however, provided only the ethical foundation for the bushido ideal. Shinto exhibited the patriotic application of the ideal as uncompromising loyalty and devotion to the nation. Zen further contributed a spirit of unquestioning obedience to superiors. A good knight carried two swords: one to fight the enemy, the other, a shorter one, to turn on himself in case of failure. The suicide that such failure entailed was a ceremonial one called *harakiri*: a disembowelment performed unemotionally, calmly, according to a recognized method. Women performed such suicide by cutting their jugular veins: a method called *jigai*. The underlying principle in such acts is that death is preferable to disgrace. Other elements in the bushido code are: loyalty, courage, justice, truthfulness, politeness, and a reticence that prohibits the display of personal feeling. Important as are all these ingredients in the bushido attitude, gratitude is the one upon which they all rest: gratitude to one's superior, to the Emperor, or to the nation.

Bushnell, Horace (1802–1876). American Congregationalist, born in Lichfield, Connecticut and associated with that region all his life, being a pioneer in New England of a movement to modify the doctrinal orthodoxy of his day. For example, he did not take the doctrine of the Trinity to express the real nature of God but only a way of showing how God may be apprehended by human beings. He sought to explain miracles in terms of the wonders of nature, in which he saw God as immanent. He no doubt exercised profound influence on the minds of thoughtful people in his day.

Butler, Alban (1710–1773). Educated at Douai and ordained a Roman Catholic priest in 1735. He laboriously collected hagiographical material and published the results in *The Lives of the Fathers, Martyrs, and other Principal Saints* (1756–1759), which, although it does not attempt to distinguish historical from legendary elements, is still a valuable scholarly tool for those working in this field.

Butler, Joseph (1692–1752). Bishop of Durham and author of the very celebrated *Analogy of Religion* (1736) in which he sought to argue, against the fashionable Deism of his day, that "Revealed Religion" and "Natural Religion" are not incompatible. Although he did not directly attack the Deists, this work was extremely influential in discrediting their position. Having been brought up as a Presbyterian, he entered Oriel College, Oxford, in 1714 and was ordained priest at Salisbury in 1718. His ethics, which have the supreme authority of conscience as their central theme, also reflect his powerful mind. His writings were prescribed during most of the 19th c. for candidates for Anglican ordination and did much to foster the scholarly tone and temper of the Anglican clergy of that age. Newman acknowledged a great debt to the work of Butler whose admirers have included men as diverse as Gladstone and A. E. Taylor. There is no question that he is one of the most illustrious exponents of natural theology in the history of the English Church.

Butler, Josephine Elizabeth (1828–1906). Christian social reformer, wife of George Butler, a Canon of Winchester. She was predominantly concerned with the suppression of the "white slave" traffic. A meeting she called in Geneva in 1875 resulted in the founding of the International Federation for the Abolition of the State Regulation of Vice. Her personal life, modeled on that of Catherine of Siena, was deeply prayerful and contemplative, hidden behind her active zeal in her social action. She has reported the story of her activities in her *Personal Reminiscences of a Great Crusade* (1896), published a few years after William Booth's *In Darkest England and the Way Out* and reflecting similar concerns.

Butterfield, William (1814–1900). English architect. Much influenced by the Tractarians, he designed many churches and cathedrals in England and abroad, including St. Augustine's College, Canterbury (1845), All Saints, Margaret Street, London (1859), and Keble College, Oxford (1870).

Byblos. A Phoenician city lying about twenty-five miles north of Beirut on the Mediterranean coast. According to tradition, Philo is supposed to have called it the oldest city in the world, founded by the god El, who walled it. Certainly it was the most important Phoenician city from earliest times to *c.* 1000 BCE. As a meeting place of various important cultural influences (Egyptian, Mesopotamian, and Mycenean), it evinced an interesting mix of culture and was an important center of commerce. Importing the Egyptian papyrus, which it sold throughout the entire Mediterranean region, it gave its own name to the Greek word for book (*biblos*) and thus to what today we call the Bible. The inhabitants of Byblos worshipped Baal, whom the Greeks called Adonis and whom the Egyptians identified with Osiris. Byblos is mentioned only a few times in the Bible, e.g., I Kings 5.32, where we read that carpenters and masons from Byblos helped to build Solomon's temple; but the city was of far greater importance than is suggested by a few such biblical references. It had been already of immense antiquity before the time of Moses. Parts of its temple were built in the 4th millennium BCE.

Bye Plot. Before the Gunpowder Plot (an attempt in 1605 to blow up the Houses of Parliament) an attempt had been made in 1603 to kidnap the new king, James I, and extort certain concessions from him, partly at least for the recusants, who were largely behind the attempt. This plot came to be known as the Bye Plot. Two Roman Catholic priests were among the perpetrators.

Byrd, William (*c.* **1543–1623**). English composer, appointed organist of Lincoln Cathedral in 1563 and then to the Chapel Royal in 1570, along with T. Tallis. A recusant, he experienced difficulties but seems to have continued as a practicing Roman Catholic while performing his duties in the Church of England. As a composer he immensely influenced English Church music.

C

Cabbala. The Jewish mystical or theosophical system that was developed during a period between the last centuries BCE and the 14th c. CE. It emphasizes notions that Jewish orthodoxy specifically rejects, e.g., a doctrine of emanations relating God to the world; a doctrine of the "spheres" (*sefiroth*), mediating between the infinite light and the created universe; a recognition of angels and other such beings who act as lines of communication between God and man; belief in a primordial forerunner of humanity who was androgynous, transcending the sexual dividedness of men and women; and a dualism such as is typical of many forms of Gnosticism. Among later exponents of the Cabbalistic tradition (the rabbinic Hebrew word

qabbālāh means "tradition") is Israel ben Eliezer, Ba'al Shem Tov (1700–1760), who founded the Hasidim, representing a movement in the Cabbalistic tradition that opposed the mainstream, which followed the Talmudic tradition. A Christian form of Cabbalism was developed in Renaissance times and expounded by Reuchlin (1455–1522) and Paracelsus (1493–1541). For a major reinterpretation of the Cabbalistic tradition, see Mosche Idel, *kabbalah* (1988).

Cabrol, Fernand (1855–1937). An important Benedictine liturgical scholar, trained at Solesmes, who became Abbot of Farnborough, England, in 1903.

Caecilian. A 4th c. Bishop of Carthage. In the Donatist controversy some questioned the validity of his consecration as bishop, on the ground that he had received his orders from a "traditor" and they consecrated another bishop in his place. See **Traditors.**

Caedmon. According to a legend, he was a laborer at the monastery of Whitby in the 7th c. and so shy that when songs were called for in the evening, he would rise from the table before his turn came, since he felt ashamed that he had no gift for song. Then one night, after he had fallen asleep on his straw, Christ appeared to him in a vision and encouraged him, saying, "Caedmon, sing *Me* something," whereupon Caedmon composed a verse consisting of a paraphrase of a biblical passage. It was later written down in Anglo-Saxon and is the first native growth English poetry. Bede provides virtually all the information we have about him.

Caesarea. Two cities so named must be distinguished. (1) A coastal city in Palestine north of Jaffa, built by Herod the Great and later renamed in honor of the Roman Emperor Augustus. This city became the capital of Palestine a few years BCE. In Christian times it became a seat of Christian learning and of a bishopric held by Eusebius, the most learned bishop of his time. Origen had made his home there from 231. (2) Caesarea Philippi, the scene of Peter's confession of faith in Christ as the Messiah, according to Mark 8.27 and Matthew 16.13. It was situated at the foot of Mount Hermon. Eusebius records that it was the home of the woman who touched the robe of Jesus (Matthew 9.20) and that in his day her house was shown to visitors.

Caesarean Text. Biblical scholars identify various families of texts of the Gospels such as the Neutral and the Western. A British scholar, B. H. Streeter identified one now known as the Caesarean, having been shown to have been the one used at Caesarea in Palestine in Origen's time there. (See **Caesarea.**) Kirsopp Lake and others, however, have questioned its existence as a distinct textual family.

Caesarius (c. 470–542). Archbishop of Arles from 502. He played a prominent part in the condemnation of Semi-Pelagianism at the Council of Orange in 529.

Caesaropapism. A term used to designate any system of government in which the State in the person of an absolute monarch has unlimited power over the Church, but most commonly applied to the form of government exercised by the Byzantine emperors over the Church.

Cahier, Charles (1807–1882). French Jesuit and archeologist. Born in Paris, he devoted his entire life to archeological studies. He wrote extensively on Christian art and archeology.

Caird, Edward (1835–1908). Scottish philosophical theologian, who in 1866 became professor at Glasgow University and in 1893 succeeded Jowett as Master of Balliol, Oxford. He represented the Neo–Hegelian school in British philosophy. Among his works are *The Evolution of Religion* (1893), *The Evolution of*

Theology in the Greek Philosophers (1904), and important studies of Kant.

Caird, John (1820–1898). Professor of Divinity in and Principal of the University of Glasgow. He was the elder brother of Edward Caird. Among his works, also in the Neo–Hegelian tradition, is *An Introduction to the Philosophy of Religion* (1880).

Caitanya. The founder of one of the four chief Vaiṣṇava sects in Hinduism, he was born in Bengal in 1485 CE, the son of an orthodox brahman father. His followers, who bestowed on him much *bhakti* (devotion), have held him to have been an incarnation of Kṛṣṇa and of Rādhā. In iconography he is represented as fairskinned, like Rādhā and unlike Kṛṣṇa. He is sometimes portrayed in female attire and is said to have believed himself to be Rādhā, Kṛṣṇa's beloved consort.

Caitya The caitya tree (*caitya-vṛkṣa*) was held in great veneration by Hindus, being believed to be the resort of devas and other such beings, so that it was forbidden to destroy even a leaf of this tree. Shrines and other buildings were constructed as memorials to a hero or leader or teacher and so designated. Their plan was similar to that of the early Christian basilica with a nave, two side aisles, and an apse. The practice was followed by the Jains and Buddhists.

Cajetan (1480–1547). Born at Vicenza and ordained priest at Rome in 1516, he founded the Theatines, a congregation of priests living in community and doing pastoral work. He was canonized in 1671.

Cajetan, Thomas de Vio (1469–1534). Born at Gaeta, he entered the Dominican Order in 1484, becoming General (1508–18), a cardinal (1517), and in 1519 Bishop of Gaeta. He was prominent in theological controversy, arguing with Luther in 1518 and opposing, in 1530, the divorce sought by Henry

VIII. His commentary on the *Summa Theologiae* of Thomas Aquinas, still a classic of late medieval scholasticism, fostered a revival of interest in the scholastic method and Thomistic thought.

Calatayud, Pedro de (1689–1773). Spanish Jesuit and spiritual writer. After a period of teaching he devoted himself to preaching and became much famed throughout Spain. On the expulsion of the Jesuits from Spain in 1767, he left it and died in Bologna.

Calced. See **Discalced**.

Calculus. (1) Any formal system for the solution of logical problems may be so designated. (2) The term is used also of (a) the procedures and definitions to be followed in determining the application of concepts, e.g., the calculus of probability and (b) the quantification of something, as in Bentham's utilitarian or hedonistic calculus, according to which one may claim to determine the greatest good for the greatest number.

Calderwood, David (1575–1650). Scottish ecclesiastical historian. Educated at the University of Edinburgh, he was ordained in 1604 and became a vigorous opponent of the attempted introduction of episcopacy to Scotland by James VI and I, who caused him to be imprisoned and then exiled. After James's death in 1625, he returned to Scotland. The General Assembly of the Kirk provided him with a handsome pension to write *The True History of the Church of Scotland* during his last years, which became his best work and one that is still an important source for Scottish ecclesiastical history.

Caldey. An island off the south coast of Wales that was the seat of a monastic foundation in the 5th c. In 1906 Aelred Carlyle (1874–1955) established an Anglican abbey on the ruins of the ancient buildings and in 1913 the majority of the monks submitted their allegiance to Rome, then leaving Caldey for their present house at Prinknash, near Gloucester, England. Caldey was taken over by Belgian Trappists. For further information see Peter Anson, *The Benedictines of Caldey* (1940).

Calendar, The Christian. The dating of the Christian era to begin with the birth of Christ was at the suggestion of Dionysius Exiguus in the 6th c. The calculation was from March 25 (supposed to be the date of the Annunciation) of year 1. When Jesus was born, the calendar in use had been the Julian, so called from its having been constructed by Julius Caesar in 46 BCE. It was not precisely correct, so that by the year 325 CE it was already five days out. By 1582, when Pope Gregory XIII reformed the calendar it was so much further out as to require the omission of ten days from that year to make up the difference. The rules for leap year were changed to prevent the occurrence of discrepancies in the future. The Gregorian Calendar, which also restored New Year's Day to January 1, was not universally adopted throughout Christendom. England did not adopt it till 1752 and some sections of the Eastern Orthodox Church still have not adopted it. The Jewish Passover, on which Easter had been modelled, was a movable feast according to the moon. Easter therefore became a movable feast with some Christian festivals moving according to the date of Easter and others fixed on specific dates annually. Sunday, the first day of the week, had been already a hebdomadal Christian festival in New Testament times. Wednesday and Friday soon afterwards came to be in one way or another marked as days of fasting.

Caliphate. When Muhammad died, the question of determining who should succeed him was predictably one that threatened to cause a schism in Islam. Should the succession be made on a hereditary basis or should the successor be chosen from among the Prophet's close associates? Fortunately, Abu Bakr, whom Muhammad had often designated to lead the prayers during his absence, was chosen to succeed him, so for a time, avoiding schism. The principle of succession remained, however, a debatable question. Three answers to it were given at various times: (1) the Companions (associates of the Prophet, the Muhajirin and the Ansar) assumed that the caliph should be drawn from their number by some form of election; (2) the Legitimists, a later group, contended for the hereditary principle, arguing that Muhammad's descendants, through his daughter Fatima and her husband 'Ali, should inherit the caliphate; and later still (3) the Unmayads, leaders of Muhammad's tribe, maintained that they had the right to determine the succession.

Abu Bakr and his three immediate successors put down opposition ruthlessly and consolidated their position by astounding conquests for Islam throughout the Byzantine world. The internal political strife continued to fester, however, even in the midst of the sweeping military victories and their consequent enrichment of the conquering tribes. The Unmayads eventually seized the caliphate in 661, ruling from Damascus over an Islamic empire that stretched from Spain to India. In 750 another group overthrew them and, removing their capital to Baghdad, ruled over the whole territory with the exception of Spain. Baghdad rose to great fame as a city of fabulous wealth and notable culture. It was in this period that the great caliph Harun al-Rashid (736–809) flourished. Soon, however, divisions developed and the Islamic empire was cut into rival states. Rival caliphates emerged. It looked as though the Shi'ite cause (the party of 'Ali) would triumph, but that hope was dashed with the murder of 'Ali and various events following it. The Ottoman Turks rose to power in Asia Minor, crossed the Bosphorus, taking Byzantium (Constantinople, now Istanbul) in 1453, and establishing the Ottoman Empire that stretched through the Danube to Vienna and through Palestine into Egypt. Although forced to retrench, it held a large area under its

control down to early in the 20th c. With Islam now irreparably divided as a political entity, the significance of the caliphate dwindled. The Ottoman caliphate was abolished in 1924.

Calixtines. See **Utraquists**

Callistus I. Early 3rd c. Bishop of Rome, for whom the catacombs of San Callisto on the Appian Way are named, because he had been in charge of them while in the service of his predecessor, Zephyrinus. An emancipated slave, he succeeded the latter *c.* 217. Hippolytus, his adversary, charged him with having too easy a policy in readmitting to the communion of the Church persons found guilty of adultery: a sin classed in the early Church with murder when committed by a baptized person.

Callistus II, Pope. Elected to the papacy at Cluny in 1119, he was engaged for long in the struggle between pope and emperor, which concluded with the Concordat of Worms in 1122, leading to the Lateran Council of 1123, at which decrees were issued concerning simony, clerical marriage, and the election of bishops. He died in 1124.

Callistus III, Pope (1378–1458). Elected pope in 1455, he organized a crusade against the Turks, although with scant success. He overturned the sentence of Jeanne d'Arc, declaring her innocent.

Calovius, Abraham (1612–86). Lutheran theologian, professor of theology at Wittenberg, he engaged in controversies, championing Lutheran orthodoxy over Pietism and Socinianism. His great work, *Systema locorum theologicorum*, in 12 volumes (1655–77) remains a standard source for Lutheran theology.

Calvin, John (1509–64). Religious reformer. Born at Noyon, Picardy, he studied theology at Paris and law at Orléans and at Bourges, where he became interested in Reformation ideas and embraced the Reformation cause. In 1535, because of the danger of persecution in France, he fled to Switzerland, where, at Basel, he resolved to spend the rest of his life in theological study. The following year, however, at the instigation of Farel, he joined the latter at Geneva to engage in the formal organization of a Reformed Church. In the same year he published the first edition of his *Institutes*, one of the greatest theological classics in the history of the Christian Church. (See **Institutes, The**) His demand that the citizens of Geneva accept the severe discipline he imposed for the fulfilment of this aim was predictably resisted at first, and by the end of 1538, Farel and he were expelled from Geneva and fled to Strassburg, where Calvin became minister of the French congregation there and lecturer in theology and engaged in vigorous theological controversy. In 1541 he was able to return to Geneva, where he proceeded to establish a theocratic society in which the pastors and other rulers of the Church exercised enormous powers over the citizenry, whose entire conduct was governed by ecclesiastical legislation along the lines of his interpretation of Reformation ideals. He was indubitably a man of great abilities and versatile talents whose clarity of French style gave his thought and his writings a sharpness that brought him wide and enduring fame even in circles hostile to his concept of ecclesiastical discipline and his narrow though brilliantly constructed theological system.

Calvinism. What is called Calvinism is a theological system having Calvin's *Institutes* as its focus but interpreted and developed by his followers, some of whom were more extreme than the founder himself. Although it has much in common with Lutheran teachings, such as an immense emphasis on the Bible as the supreme authority for Christians and on the exaltation of faith and the divine initiative in the process of human salvation, it has also notable features that have alienated Calvinism from the Lutheran tradition. Among these features are the predestination not only of the elect to salvation but of the non-elect to damnation ("double" predestination) and the notion that grace is irresistible. Since human beings, by reason of the corruption of their will that is a consequence of the Fall, have "no power of themselves to help themselves," and are therefore in bondage, they can be saved only by divine grace. Calvinism, so commendable in what it emphasizes (e.g., the sovereignty and unity of God, the splendor of divine grace, etc.), can degenerate, especially in the extreme forms in which some later exponents presented it, into a theology more akin to that of Islam than to traditional Christian doctrine as expounded by the early Fathers. No doubt, however, it was a vitally important corrective in Calvin's time and circumstances. Moreover, it has, if often indirectly, profoundly influenced even those elements of the Christian Church that have been traditionally hostile to Calvinist teaching and practice. It has affected, for instance, the Anglican, Baptist, and Methodist traditions, and perceptive Roman Catholic theologians have recognized its value, which may be deemed more noteworthy than its limitations. Its influence in the Reformation movement in France and Holland and Scotland has been overwhelming, and in various guises it has affected the complex American scene, where its effects may be detected often in unexpected quarters. Karl Barth, who stood firmly in the Calvinist tradition, did much to revive an appreciation of it among 20th c. theologians.

Camaldoli. An order of hermit monks founded by Romuald in the early 11th c. at Camaldoli, near Arezzo, Italy. Although a relatively small order, little known outside Italy, it has spread in recent years to the United States, where an important hermitage was founded in mid-20th c. at the Big Sur, California. Some Camaldoli live more in community, but the ideal more closely resembles the Carthusian model, which emphasizes solitariness. There are also Camoldolese nuns.

Cambridge Platonists. A group of English divines who flourished at Cambridge between 1633 and 1688. Philosophically minded, they advocated openness and tolerance, recognizing the value and importance of reason in religion, understanding reason in a manner dictated by the Neoplatonism that strongly affected their outlook. They included Cudworth and More. They exercised a very beneficial influence on English Christian thought, mediating between the extravagances of extremist parties in the Church.

Camelaucum. See **Tiara.**

Camerlengo. The office held by a cardinal charged with the administration of the financial affairs of the Vatican. During a vacancy in the papacy, he is in charge of the finances of the entire Roman Catholic Church. He is also in charge of the assembling of the cardinals.

Cameron, Richard. 17th c. Scottish leader of the Covenanters. A schoolmaster, he was converted to the cause of the Covenanters and became renowned for his eloquence in preaching.

Cameronians. A name given to those who followed the views and hopes preached by Richard Cameron, more particularly the "Reformed Presbyterians," who were dissatisfied with the Established Kirk as recognized in 1690 under William III.

Camisards. A group of Protestant extremists in the Cévennes, France, who, after Louix XIV had suppressed Protestantism, conducted a violent revolt in 1702. They fought fanatically, often conducting their attacks at night, and were cruelly suppressed in 1705. Some found refuge in England.

Campanella, Tommaso (1568–1639). Philosopher. He became a Dominican friar in 1582, but was soon suspected of heresy. In 1603 he was sentenced to life imprisonment but released six years later. Then in 1634, he fled to France where he remained for the rest of his life at the convent of St.-Honoré, Paris. He repudiated the Aristotelianism of his day. Holding that individual human consciousness is the mainspring of all philosophy and that the presence in it of the idea of God provides ground for belief in God's existence, he may be regarded as a forerunner of Descartes. A Platonist at heart, he sought to encourage the development of a society on the lines of Plato's *Republic*. His vision was of a society of philosopher-theologians corresponding to the "philosopher-kings" in Plato who would serve the Church and guide the State and its citizens. Among his works is his *Civitas Solis* (1623) in which he discusses such ideas.

Campanile. Although this name may be given to any tower or steeple containing bells, it specifically applies to the detached bell tower common in Italy such as is to be found at Ravenna, at the famous leaning tower of Pisa, at San Marco, Venice, and at many other Italian churches.

Campbell, Alexander (1788–1866). Founder of the Disciples of Christ. The son of a Scottish Presbyterian of the Secession group, he left Glasgow and went to the United States in 1809. Associating himself at first with the Baptists, he founded, in 1827, a congregation called the Disciples of Christ, seeking to achieve Christian unity on a biblical basis. See also **Disciples of Christ.**

Campbell, John McLeod (1800–1872). Scottish Presbyterian divine. Minister of the West Highland parish of Row (Rhu), Dumbartonshire, he found that his teachings evoked opposition as deviating from what was taken to be the Calvinistic norm, and in 1831 he was tried before the General Assembly, found guilty of heresy, and deposed. Better informed than many of his judges, he contended that he had been deposed groundlessly and continued his ministry to a congregation of his followers, never actually separating himself from the Established Kirk. Within his lifetime his book, *The Nature of the Atonement* (1856) expressing teachings that had been a main source of his adversaries' displeasure, became a standard theological work in Scotland, used by every one of its four divinity schools. Urged in his old age to be welcomed back to the Kirk, he declined on the ground that he had never left it. He taught that Christ died for all men, not for the elect only, and quoted patristic sources and even Calvin in support of his contention. For details of the trial see *A Full Report of the Proceedings in the General Assembly of the Church of Scotland in the Case of the Rev. John McLeod Campbell, Late Minister of Row.* (Greenock: R. B. Lusk, 1831.)

Campion, Edmund (1540–1581). English Jesuit martyr. Educated at Christ's Hospital, London and St. John's College, Oxford, he distinguished himself as an orator and as a leader. In 1571 he was received into the Roman Catholic Church, entered the Jesuit Order at Rome in 1573, and was ordained priest in 1578, and in 1580 he became part of the first Jesuit mission to England. Arrested the following year, he refused to return to the Church of England and, being charged with conspiracy against the Crown, he was tortured on the rack and executed at Tyburn on December 1, 1581. He was one of the forty martyrs canonized in 1970.

Camus, Albert (1913–1960). Born in Algiers and educated at the University of Algiers, he moved to Paris in 1940, where he became much involved in the French Resistance movement during World War II. The philosophy behind his novels shows many affinities with that of Sartre. He held human solidarity to be one of the supreme values of life. He opposed capital punishment and discountenanced suicide, contending that although (in common with the nihilistic existentialists generally) he held human life to be absurd, he argued that the adequate response to it is to live it out despite its absurdity. Apart from his novels, his principal writings include *The Myth of Sisyphus* (1942), *The Rebel* (1951), and *Reflections on Capital Punishment* (1960). The thought of Camus, like that of Sartre, has had much influence on 20th c. religious thought, notably in displaying individualism and freedom of the will as fundamental dimensions of human life. For an extensive bibliography, see *Camus: A Bibliography.* Madison, Wisconsin: The University of Wisconsin Press, 1968.

Canaanites. The region lying between Egypt and Syria in which the Israelites settled was called Canaan. The name is found in extrabiblical sources dating from the second century BCE. The terms Canaan and Canaanite are used somewhat vaguely, however, so that we do not know with precision the boundaries of the land so called nor can we always establish as exactly as one would wish the distinctive habitats of the people so designated, although they tended to favor the seashore as did the Amorites the mountains. It seems that the population of Palestine and southern Phoenicia in the second half of the second millennium BCE was Canaanite, but when precisely the Canaanites entered this region is obscure. After 2000 BCE invaders forced the Canaanites south and after the conquest of Palestine by the Egyptians in the 15th c., the Canaanites, now further weakened, were invaded by several peoples, including the Hebrews, the Philistines, and the Aramaeans. The Canaanites continued their own civilization in Phoenicia, but those in Israel were gradually absorbed. Both the Canaanites and the Israelites were Semitic peoples, but the biblical record leaves us in no doubt that the Hebrews despised the Canaanites and their religion. Nevertheless, the Canaanites exercised very considerable influence over the life, culture, and religion of the Hebrews. The fact that the designation "Canaanite" is often used in later Hebrew literature to allude to any trader or merchant suggests that they had become identified with the merchant class, hence presumably their preference for the coastal and other regions adapted to trading.

Caṇḍa. A being in Hindu mythology whose daughters form a class of female demons who must be exorcized from the household.

Caṇḍāla. In Hindu tradition, an outcaste belonging to the lowest of mixed ancestry, especially one born of a śūdra father and of a mother of the brahmin caste.

Candlemas. The name traditionally given to a feast commemorating the purification of Mary and the presentation of Jesus in the Temple, forty days after his birth, in accordance with Jewish law. It was kept at least in Jerusalem from the 4th c., in Constantinople, by order of Justinian from 542, then later in the West, where the blessing of the candles is performed on that day (February 2). After an antiphon, during which the candles the people hold are lighted, a procession is made into the church while a canticle such as the Nunc Dimittis is sung.

Candles. Candles were no doubt used from very early times for practical reasons, e.g., to enable the priest to read the book at the altar or elsewhere. They were used in procession as a mark of honor and then placed on the floor behind the altar. The first use of two candles flanking a cross on the altar is mentioned *c.* 1175 as the then prevailing custom at the papal chapel. There seems to be no clear evidence of any general custom of that kind before then. Gradually the practice of additional candles was developed, e.g., six at High Mass instead of two at Low Mass. Gradually, too, were developed elaborate interpretations of the symbolic significance of the candle, e.g., the light of Christ issuing from the body of the Virgin Mother. (Hugh of St. Victor, in typical medieval fashion, writes that "as wax is formed from the juice of spotless flowers in the virginal body of the bee, and this, made into a candle, surrounds the wick, and from the union of these two light is produced, so in like manner the Body of the Lord, taken from the spotless Virgin Mother and surrounding his glorious soul, when united to his divine nature, sheds its light over all creation.") In the West a large additional candle is blessed on Holy Saturday then carried by the deacon through the church and eventually placed on a large candlestick on the floor in the north of the sanctuary where it is lighted at all liturgical functions throughout Eastertide. Traditionally, many elaborate ceremonies were observed in connection with it, but these have been much modified in the Roman Catholic Church since 1969. The use of two candles to accompany the deacon at every High Mass to the place on the north side of the church where he is to sing the Gospel has also been deeply rooted in tradition. See also D. R. Dendy, *The Use of Lights in Christian Worship* (1959). The practice developed, moreover, of setting apart areas of the church in which candles may be lighted by individuals as offerings symbolic of their personal prayers. These are called "votive" candles.

Candra. In Hindu lore this name, derived from *ścandra* (radiant), is given to the moon, personified as a god.

Candrakānta. The moonstone, supposed in Hindu lore to be formed by the rays of the moon.

Canisius, Peter (1521–1597). Jesuit theologian. Zealous controversialist, he published his *Summa Doctrinae Christianae*, an exposition of Roman Catholic teaching in catechetical form, which has run into at least 130 editions. He was immensely successful in promoting the Roman Catholic cause in southern Germany and as Provincial of Upper Germany he founded colleges in Augsburg,

Innsbruck, and Munich. The Emperor Ferdinand offered him the bishopric of Vienna, which, however, the General of the Jesuits ordered him to decline. He was canonized in 1925.

Cano, Melchior (1509–1560). Dominican theologian. Having entered the Dominican Order in 1523, he studied at the University of Salamanca under F. Vitoria, to whose chair at Salamanca he eventually succeeded. He took part in the Council of Trent.

Canon. This term, which in Greek (*kanōn*) meant a straight rod, has come to have several distinct meanings in Christian usage. (1) By the biblical Canon is meant those books of Scripture that have been officially accepted by the Church as containing the "rule" or standard of Christian faith. This does not mean a denigration of the value of writings called apocryphal. (2) Ecclesiastical law is called "canon law" contradistinguished from "civil law." In the Roman Catholic Church, the body of canon law was published in 1582 by Pope Gregory XIII, known as the *Corpus Juris Canonici*. A more recent codification was promulgated under the same designation in 1917 under Benedict XV. (3) The Canon of the Mass is so called in contradistinction from the less solemn part of the Mass, e.g., the introductory part containing the various readings including Epistle and Gospel. The Canon of the Roman Mass is indubitably based on Greek models. It begins immediately after the Preface and the Sanctus, with the words "Te igitur." and contains the most solemn words, the words of Institution, the Anamnesis, the Epiclesis, and other prayers. In Anglican usage it is uttered audibly. In Roman Catholic usage it was said silently from *c.* 800 to 1967, when its audible recitation was authorized, as was also the use of the local vernacular rather than the traditional Latin. (4) In the Eastern Church a series of nine canticles (one of them normally omitted except in Lent) are sung, chiefly at the Orthros, and constitute the hymnological canon. (5) As an ecclesiastical title the term is used in various senses, e.g.: (a) Originally all clergy (other than members of the monastic orders and certain other special cases) who were officially attached to a diocese were so designated; (b) The term was later restricted to secular clergy serving a cathedral or collegiate church. (c) Such canons came to be called "secular" canons in contradistinction to "regular" canons such as the Premonstratensians and the Augustinian canons regular who follow a monastic rule with the customary monastic vows, although, unlike monks, they are primarily priests and only secondarily monks. (d) Corresponding to the canons regular are orders of canonesses regular, standing to canons regular as do nuns to monks. (e) Residentiary canons are part of the regular clerical structure of a cathedral church and bear certain responsibilities that may in some cases be specifically so designated, such as "canon sacrist" or "canon theologian." (f) Honorary canons, who are non-stipendiary, are so entitled *honoris causa* and normally have a stall assigned to them in the cathedral to which they are attached and may have certain other privileges and certain duties. (6) Clerics having special responsibilities in a cathedral, such as the singing of services in choir, are sometimes called minor canons. See also **Apostolic canons.**

Canonization. From very early Christian times holy men and women, more particularly martyrs, were venerated by the faithful. Bishops began to control such expressions of devotion to them. The fame of some such holy ones spread far beyond their own region and seemed to call for some sort of more general regulation by the Church, leading eventually to an official recognition by the Church that a particular person was to be regarded as deserving of public devotion. As this practice grew, an elaborate legal process was developed for giving such official recognition of a saint by the Church. In the early stages of that process a departed person is called "Servant of God" and is accorded the title of "Venerable". When certain conditions have been fulfilled (e.g., the attestation of four miracles attributable to the deceased person), he or she is pronounced "beatified", which in modern practice signifies that a restricted public devotion (e.g., within a certain region) may be accorded the person so recognized. In the course of the proceedings an official called the Promotor Fidei (popularly the Advocatus Diaboli or Devil's Advocate) is appointed to show whatever reasons can be adduced *against* the recognition that is proposed. The person beatified may be advanced to full sainthood and accorded the title of "saint", for which two additional miracles must be attested as well as the fulfilment of many other conditions. The final stage in the process is that official recognition of the person's merit and status as one of the saints of the Church whom the faithful may invoke in public worship. Mass may be offered publicly in his or her honor, and relics may be exhibited for public veneration. In Eastern Orthodoxy the proceeding is less formal, as indeed it was in earlier times in the Roman Catholic Church too. Since the claims of the Roman Catholic Church implied by canonization are by no means recognized by other Christians and since some branches of the Christian Church recognize certain persons' entitlement to be so designated while others do not, the modern scholarly practice of omitting the title may be regarded as wise. The treatise by Pope Benedict XIV, *De Servorum Dei Beatificatione et Beatorum Canonizatione* is the classical authority on Roman Catholic practice. See also E. W. Kemp, *Canonization and Authority in the Western Church* (1948). The article "Canonizzazione" in *Enciclopedia Cattolica* (Vatican City, 1949), Vol. III, pp.570–607, gives an authoritative account of the process of canonization in its various aspects and with pictorial representation.

Canon Law. By canon law the Western Church generally understands the collection of ecclesiastical laws gradually evolved over the centuries and eventually assembled as the *Codex Juris Canonici*. It consisted of the *Decretum* of Gratian, put together in the 12th c. by a Bolognese monk, Gratian, with various additions promulgated through the centuries down to modern times. The *corpus* of canon law had its beginnings early in the history of the Church and naturally some enactments were regarded as having universal authority (such as twenty canons promulgated at the Council of Nicaea in 325), while other canons were only of local significance and authority. Wherever any kind of religious organization exists, some form of legislation is required. Each of the various branches and sects of the Christian Church has its own rules which, whatever they may be called, function as what might be called canon law.

Canopy. An awning held over the Host when carried in procession and used also as a mark of honor to some high dignitaries of the Church.

Canterbury. When Augustine landed in Kent, England, in the summer of 597, under orders to organize the country in two provinces (eventually Canterbury and York), he established his first church (according to Bede an already existing Roman basilica) as the cathedral church. This church, destroyed by fire in 1067 and rebuilt in the Norman style, was again destroyed and rebuilt in the course of several centuries, eventually in the Perpendicular style. Canterbury, always pre-eminent in the English Church, has become the principal focus of the entire Anglican Communion in which the Archbishop of Canterbury (whose official title is that of "Primate of All England," while that of the Archbishop of York is "Primate of England") is accorded a primacy of honor. Only to that extent, however, does his position correspond in any way in Anglicanism to that of the papacy in the Roman Catholic Church.

Canticle. The term is applied to any song or prayer derived from the Bible other than from the Book of Psalms and used in public worship. Examples are the Magnificat, the Nunc Dimittis, and the Te Deum. The term is also used of a hymn composed by Francis of Assisi in celebration of the beauties of nature as manifestations of the divine glory: *canticum solis* or canticle of the sun.

Cantor. A singer who leads the liturgical music. On special occasions there may be four cantors, each wearing a cope. On ordinary occasions, the cantor will wear a surplice. Cantors need not be clerics. The cantor or cantors normally sit on the north side of the choir.

Capitalism. The name loosely given to any economic system in which the importance of capital is recognized. The classic expression of capitalism is found in *The Wealth of Nations* by Adam Smith (1723–1790), the Scottish economist and moralist, who expounded in that work on the thesis that if only a free market is unimpeded by excessive governmental interference, capital and labor would move from less profitable to more profitable enterprises and the interests of all would be thereby advanced. This aspect of Adam Smith's economic theory came to be associated with the phrase *laissez-faire*, used by the 18th-c. French school of economic theory headed by François Quesnay (1694–1774) and known as the Physiocrats. The phrase became international as the watchword of those who favored a minimum of government interference in economic affairs, believing such interference to create an enslaving stranglehold on society. The rise of individualism naturally tended to favor the development of the *laissez-faire* ideal in the economic workings of society. Comparatively few people favoring *laissez-faire* would seek to abolish government regulation totally; most would

be content with its elimination so far as practically expedient.

Capital Punishment. In Christian ethics the legitimacy and the propriety of death as a judicially administered punishment for grave crimes has given rise to very serious controversy. Before the 19th c., sentence of death was pronounced for a wide variety of kinds of crime. There can be no question that it has biblical warrant. Not only is this attested in many Old Testament passages (e.g., according to Leviticus 20.10 both parties to an adultery are to be put to death); Paul seems to recognize the rightness of such a punishment (e.g., Romans 13.1–5). In the 19th c., however, its use in civilized countries came to be usually limited to crimes regarded as particularly heinous, notably murder. Many Christians today regard it as a practice that might have been acceptable in bygone ages but must now be accounted a barbaric survival. Quakers regard it as immoral. Nevertheless, the Christian Church, even in face of a widespread opposition to it on the part of educated people, has reached no consensus on the subject. Moreover, it has not produced any clear, official demand by the Churches for its total abolition as intolerable to the Christian conscience, even though it has been abolished in many countries (e.g., in Britain since 1965). Its moral acceptability seems to be regarded as depending upon the quality of civilization that a society has reached and preserved. As a military punishment in time of war it is generally taken for granted. The situation is neither civilized nor peaceful when many thousands of murders, often abhorrently brutal, some capricious shootings at passing cars for "sport", are being committed in the large metropolitan areas of the United States and accepted widely as an unavoidable aspect of the scenery in a large modern society. The case for capital punishment in such circumstances was well put by Sir Ian Percival, a member of the British Parliament, who, speaking in favor of the restoration of it in Britain twenty-two years after its official abolition there, said: "There is no place for the death penalty in a civilized society . . . but first find your civilized society." Extreme pacifists, of course, would object to killing of any kind, even in defense of one's life or that of one's family, and either in time of war or in time of peace.

Capito, Wolfgang (1478–1541). Reformer, associated with Erasmus who participated in the leadership of the Reformation movement at Strassburg, favoring the use of persuasion rather than violence in its promotion.

Capitulum. From the Latin, meaning "little chapter." It is the name traditionally given to a short passage consisting of a verse or so of the Bible to be read in the various offices. (See **Breviary**.) In the new (1971) *Breviary* it is called the *lectio brevis*, "little reading."

Cappa. See **Cope**.

Cappadocian Fathers, The. Three great philosophical theologians of the 4th c. are so designated: Basil the Great; Gregory of Nazianzus; and Gregory of Nyssa. At the Council of Constantinople (381) they were prominent in securing the defeat of the Arian position. Their designation is due to their all having been born in Cappadocia.

Cappa Magna. A cloak used by cardinals, bishops, and other dignitaries in the Roman Catholic hierarchy. It is scarlet in the case of cardinals, violet in other cases. In use since *c.* 1500, it was till recently designed with a long train and was used for many occasions; both its form and the extent of its use have been now much modified.

Capuchins. Early in the history of the Franciscan Order a protest developed by those who felt the original ideals of the founder were being lost and who sought therefore to return to his spirit. (See **Observants**.) Among these was a group that became a separate branch of

the Order and adopted a distinctive cowl, modelled on that worn by Francis himself, and were discalced and bearded. Their rule, which dates from 1529, is traditionally accounted the most severe in the Franciscan family. They are noted for their missionary zeal and for the appeal of their preaching to the masses. See also **Franciscan Order** and **Conventuals**.

Carbonari. A secret society who, early in the 19th c., developed in France and Italy with the aim of securing political reform. They were anticlerical and sought emancipation from political and religious absolutism.

Cardinals. The title of cardinal was at first used in a more general sense and then restricted to the parish priests of Rome, the bishops of its suburbicarian dioceses, and the district deacons who, because of their administrative positions under the Pope, wielded much influence at Rome. This body of cardinals eventually formed a college which, when assembled in Consistory, acted as what might nowadays be called an advisory board to the Pope. During a papal vacancy they took over the government of the Church until a new pope was elected. The College of Cardinals, whose members are nominated by the Pope, is now an administrative body one of whose more conspicuous functions is the election of a successor when a pope dies. Their number, fixed at 70 by Pope Sixtus V in 1586, has now, since the pontificate of Pope John XXIII, no upper limit. Cardinals are of three ranks: cardinal bishops, cardinal priests, and cardinal deacons. Some reside in Rome; many, however, are archbishops and other churchmen with responsibilities that keep them most of the time geographically distant. Certain archbishops (e.g., of Paris, Westminster, New York, and Los Angeles) are usually created cardinals, but any priest may be for one reason or another so created. Until the reforms of the Roman Catholic Church instituted in 1969, the "red hat" (a flat, broad-brimmed red hat with 15 tassels) was conferred on each cardinal at the first public consistory after his appointment and placed, on his death, over his tomb. Nowadays he receives a red biretta, along with othe insignia such as the sapphire ring. The Pope may create a cardinal *in petto*, i.e., secretly ("in his heart"), which means that, although such action does not have any public effect at the time, it does afterwards if and when the creation is publicly announced, for then the cardinal's seniority dates from when the Pope originally and secretly determined the appointment. See also **Consistory.**

Cardinal Virtues. Those virtues on which all ethical conduct depends are traditionally so designated. Christian moralists took over the notion from Plato and Aristotle, recognizing four: prudence, temperance, fortitude, and justice. By "temperance" (*sōphrosynē*) the Greeks understood the notions of moderation and self-control, by the exercise of which one may attain a state of harmony and achieve the ability to distinguish good from evil, avoiding the latter and obtaining the former. To these the Christian writers added what have come to be called the "theological virtues": faith, hope, and love (see I Corinthians 13).

Carey, William (1761–1834). English Baptist missionary. A shoemaker by trade, he experienced a conversion that caused him to devote himself to evangelical work and preaching, which led to the foundling, on October 2, 1792, of the Baptist Missionary Society, whose work spread to India, China, Africa, and the West Indies and included a considerable impetus toward the abolition of slavery. Gifted in languages, he sailed for India in 1793 where he visited 200 villages and translated the New Testament (eventually, in 1809, the entire Bible) into Bengali. See also **Suttee.**

Carlile, Wilson (1847–1942). Anglican priest, founder of the Church Army, an organization modelled on the lines of the Salvation Army and dedicated to similar work but operating as an Anglican agency of lay workers within the structure of the Church of England. Carlile founded it in 1882, and it began its work in the London slums as an evangelical mission. Soon its work included social and moral welfare among the poor and has spread widely, ministering both in war and in peace.

Carlstadt (Andreas Bodenstein) (c. 1480–1541). German Reformer, so named from his birthplace. Having studied at Erfurt and Cologne, he taught at Wittenberg, where he championed Thomism. After a spiritual crisis, however, he turned in the direction of Reformation emphases and published theses in that vein in 1518. So extreme was he in his attacks on traditional usages that he evoked Luther's opposition to him as an embarrassment to the Reformation cause. His later years were spent in Switzerland where he held a professorial chair at Basel.

Carlyle, Thomas (1795–1881). Scottish essayist and historian. An opponent of formal creeds and other expressions of ecclesiastical structure, he was deeply religious, believing that the spiritual forces of humanity must unite against materialism. He had an extremely high regard for the importance of the individual and for human liberty. He thought that salvation is to be found through the rule of the strong just man, not by the rule of the mob. His style, denigrated by some critics, is unique and suited to the message that he sought to convey, in which moral strength is seen as the primary manifestation of true spirituality.

Carmelites. The Carmelite Order was founded *c.* 1154 in Palestine. The rule required severe asceticism, including total abstinence from flesh meat. Eventually the Order spread to Europe, where it was organized on the lines of the orders of friars (e.g., Dominicans and Franciscans) that were by then being founded and becoming very active. In

1452 a Carmelite Order for women was founded and quickly spread through much of Western Europe. By the 16th c., Carmelite practice had become considerably relaxed and reforms were undertaken, principally by Teresa of Avila and by John of the Cross. Those Carmelites who follow the reform are discalced, while those who follow the modified rule are calced. (See **Discalced**.) In medieval theological controversies, the Carmelites generally upheld the doctrine of the Immaculate Conception of Mary, which the Dominicans opposed. They cherished a legend that their Order is of far greater antiquity than its medieval founding, having had its roots in a prophetic lineage stemming from Elijah himself, in the 9th c. BCE. Carmelite friars wear a dark brown habit and scapular with a white mantle (hence the popular traditional name of "Whitefriars"). The nuns wear a black veil. Discalced Carmelites use the designation O.C.D. after names, while the Calced use O. Carm. The Carmelite Order received papal approbation in 1226. The convent and church of the Carmelites on Mount Carmel in Israel provides a focus for the Order.

Carol. Carols are traditionally distinguished from hymns by their being less formal and an essentially popular art form, although that distinction has largely broken down. Carols, however, do represent a religious development of what originally were simply songs accompanying a popular dance and having no religious significance.

Caroline Books, The. A treatise, *Libri Carolini*, compiled *c.* 790 by a theologian (probably Theodulf of Orléans) but attributed to Charlemagne, attacking both those who forbade the use of images entirely and those who gave them too much importance and honor. See **Iconoclastic Controversy.**

Caroline Divines, The. This slightly misleading term is used to designate those 17th c. Anglican divines who may be regarded as supportive of High Church views. It is not necessarily restricted to divines whose work was issued in the reign of either Charles I or Charles II.

Carolingian Revival. Charlemagne, who in 800 was crowned the first Emperor of the Holy Roman Empire, was a patron of art and learning. He established a school at his palace where members of his court and many others were introduced to the seven liberal arts. He encouraged literacy. Advised by Alcuin, Theodulf of Orléans, and others, Charlemagne developed schools attached to monasteries and cathedrals (e.g., at Tours and Orléans), which, elementary though they were, were foci for the scholars of the day and provided the roots out of which later on were to grow great universities such as Paris. When one reflects upon the intellectual barrenness of the earlier Middle Ages, this period may indeed be justly celebrated as the Carolingian revival or renaissance. See also **Liberal Arts, The Seven.**

Carpenter, Lant (1780–1840). Educated at the University of Glasgow, he entered the Unitarian ministry, in which he did much to foster the tolerant spirit that was to prevail in that denomination but had not been in his time so well developed. As a headmaster in Bristol he had among his pupils James Marineau, destined to become one of the most famous of Unitarian divines, and his sister Harriet. Carpenter's grandson, Joseph Estlin Carpenter (1844–1927), also became a very prominent figure in Unitarianism.

Carpzov, Johann Gottlob (1679–1767). Lutheran biblical scholar; professor of oriental languages at Leipzig.

Carroll, John (1715–1815). The first Roman Catholic bishop to serve in the United States. A native of Maryland, he entered the Jesuit Order in 1753 and was ordained priest in 1769. In 1774 he returned to Maryland as a missionary, was active in the movement toward independence from the British, and in 1776 he took part in Benjamin Franklin's embassy to Canada. In 1784 the Pope, partly through Franklin's influence, named him Superior of the Missions in the United States, making the Church in America independent of the Roman Catholic authorities (vicars-apostolic) in England. This led to his being consecrated in 1790 to the See of Baltimore and in 1808 he became archbishop.

Carstares, William (1649–1715). Scottish Presbyterian divine. Educated at the University of Edinburgh and later at Utrecht. While in Holland he met William of Orange who was seeking agents in Britain. He became a trusted adviser to William and was prominent in the political maneuvers leading to the Union of Parliaments in 1707. He was several times Moderator of the General Assembly of the Kirk.

Carta Caritatis. The constitution of the Cistercian Order, first presented to the Pope in 1119, is so called (a "charter of love") because of the skill with which it was drafted in such a way as to provide an efficient administration, yet with a sense of a large family consisting of independent houses that are nevertheless bound to one another in familial love.

Cartesianism. The rationalistic system of philosophy expounded by René Descartes. ("Cartesian" is the adjectival form of "Descartes.") The term is applied to those systems that used Cartesian methods and followed his aim of constructing all human knowledge on the basis of a rational, geometrical system that would explain all phenomena in terms of mathematical principles. See **Descartes, René.**

Carthage, Councils of. Church councils were held at Carthage from the middle of the 3rd c. to early in the 6th c. Under Cyprian, councils were held there in 251, 252, 254, 255, and 256. The earlier of these were concerned chiefly with how to deal with those

Christians who had lapsed during the great persecution under the Emperor Decius. (Many Christians failed to show the fortitude expected of them under torture.) The later among these councils were concerned with the rebaptism of heretics. Two more councils were held at Carthage in the 4th c. Under Aurelius many were held in the late 4th c. and early 5th c. An important one was held in 419 when the African Church vigorously resisted the claim of Rome to have jurisdiction over it. Finally, two councils were held, one in 525 and one in 534. The text of the canons of many of these councils are extant.

Carthusian Order. Founded in 1084 by Bruno at the Grande Chartreuse in what is now the Hautes Alpes, France, the Carthusians were from the first and have remained semi-eremitical, i.e., they live in separate cells or huts within the monastery. Their meals are brought to them by a lay brother who pushes them through a hatch with a brief word of Christian greeting. In their cells they have an altar, a desk, and perhaps a little work corner. They meet together only for the conventual Mass and on special occasions, although they do gather for recreation, such as a long walk together during which they engage in conversation, perhaps once a week. From the first they had lived a life of silence and total renunciation of the world. They had at first no rule, although gradually statutes were developed. It is perhaps the only Order that can claim, as it does, that it has been "never reformed because never deformed."

The Carthusian habit is white and worn with a white leather belt. There are also some houses of nuns living under virtually the same rule as the monks. The Prior of the Grande Chartreuse, the mother house, is elected by the monastic community there and administers the affairs of the Order, the government of which rests with him and with the General Chapter, which meets annually and consists of the priors of the various monasteries and certain others. Although the Carthusian Order is partly inspired by Benedictine monastic ideals, it has a unique spirit. No other ancient religious order in the West, with the exception of the Camaldoli, can be said to resemble it. The Order has numbered many famous mystics and has fostered many devotional practices.

Cartwright, Thomas (1535–1603). Probably the most learned and able among the 16th c. English Puritan divines. Educated at St. John's College, Cambridge, he eventually became Lady Margaret Professor of Divinity there in 1569 but was deprived the following year because of his outspoken criticism of the Church of England. After periods in Geneva he returned to England in 1585, where he suffered persecution again for his views and his propagation of Puritan ideas. On the accession of James in 1603, however, he drew up the Millenary Petition and was to have presented it at the Hampton Court Conference, but died before that could have been done.

Cārvāka. In Hinduism, one of the heterodox philosophical schools. It is of considerable antiquity: its teahings are represented in the *Bārhaspati Sūtra*, which may be dated *c.* 600 BCE. It seems to have arisen out of skepticism about the Vedic teachings. It taught that the universe emerged from a fortuitous concurrence of particles of matter. In ethical questions it is hedonistic, teaching that a good action is that which leads to happiness and a bad one that which leads to unhappiness.

Casal, Gaspar (*c.* 1510–1584). Portuguese theologian who took part in the Council of Trent.

Casaubon, Isaac (1559–1614). Classical scholar. Born in Geneva, he became professor of classical studies there. In 1599, Henry IV gave him a post in Paris. He disliked both Roman Catholic and Calvinistic theology, although prob-

ably the latter less than the former. When Henry died in 1610, Casaubon decided to go to England where James I gave him patronage. He edited editions of Suetonius, published a translation of the New Testament, and wrote in defense of the Anglican position. He was buried in Westminster Abbey.

Casel, Odo (1886–1948). Benedictine monk at Maria Laach, he wrote notable works on the Eucharist and other liturgical matters.

Cashel, Synod of. After the invasion of Ireland by Henry II, this synod was held (*c.* 1172) to complete the work of bringing the usages of the Celtic Church into line with Roman usages.

Cassander, Georg (1513–1566). Theologian. Born near Bruges, he studied at Louvain. He sought to reconcile the theological emphases of the Reformers with the Roman Catholic theology in which he had been trained. His principal work, published anonymously at Basel, is *De Officio Pii ac Publicae Tranquillitatis vere amantis Viri in hoc Religionis Dissidio* (1561). Working from a biblical and patristic foundation, he contended that the abuses in the Roman Catholic Church did not justify so drastic a step as the Reformation, while he recognized no less that the claims of the papacy were, to say the least, excessive. He also tried to read into certain of the Reformation documents an interpretation making them more amenable to Roman Catholic acceptance. As commonly happens to those who undertake such eirenic enterprises, he displeased both parties and when an edition of most of his works was published posthumously in 1616, it was placed on the Index the following year.

Cassian, John (*c.* 360–435). Details of the early life of this important figure in the early history of monasticism are somewhat shadowy, but it is clear that he studied monasticism in Egypt, being much influenced there by Evagrius Ponticus. About 415 he founded two monastic houses near Marseilles. His writings include his *Institutes*, which sets forth the general principles of the monastic life and what a monk must recognize as obstacles to the spiritual perfection that is his aim. He seems to have been among the first, if not the first, to teach a form of Semipelagianism.

Cassinese. A Benedictine Congregation, having its origin in Padua in 1409, with the aim of achieving certain reforms in the organization and administration of the Benedictine Order. See **Monte Cassino.**

Cassiodorus. A 6th c. monk and writer. Born of a noble family, he held various high offices of State. He succeeded in reconciling Theodoric, an Arian, with the Romans. Retiring from public office in 540, he became a monk, founding two monasteries. Having failed to establish a theological school at Rome on the lines of the great school at Alexandria, he tried to fulfill that aim in the monasteries he founded, establishing secular as well as Christian learning there and so promoting the great tradition of learning that was to be maintained during the intellectually dark centuries to come. His greatest achievement was his success in linking sacred and profane literature together in such a way as to cause the one to nourish and illumine the other. His *Institutions of Divine and Secular Literature* influenced the salutary tradition that was to develop in Christian scholarship in which humanism in the Socratic tradition might be seen not as the enemy of the Gospel but its ally. Augustine reflects this influence in his *De Doctrina Christiana* and it reappears at various points in the Middle Ages, e.g., strikingly in Dante and dramatically in the classical Renaissance.

Cassock. The ankle length dress worn by clergy in the West, corresponding to the "rason" used in the Eastern Church. It is normally black, although certain dignitaries may wear violet.

(The Pope wears a white cassock; cardinals wear red as do also, in England, royal chaplains.) The cassock is an adaptation of the normal secular dress (*the vestis talaris*) in use up to the 6th c., when shorter clothes for men came into vogue. Already in the late 6th c. the cassock was prescribed for the clergy, and it has remained the basic clerical dress to this day. Monks wear the habit of their order, which is similar in form but varies in color according to the Order. See **Habit.**

Caste. The concept of caste as a fundamental element in social structure is to be found in one way or another in all forms of human society. Plato expresses it as an ideal in his *Republic*, in which he envisions three classes or castes (philosophers, warriors, and artisans) reflecting the three modes of human existence. In India, however, the caste system was for many centuries developed into a very notable part of the structure of Indian society, being supported by the ancient Hindu scriptures, notably in the Laws of Manu, the chief ancient Hindu legal code. The four castes in traditional institutional Hinduism are: (1) the Brāhamaṇa (the priests and learned); (2) the *Kshatriya* (princes and warriors); the *Vaisya* (the merchant and professional class); and (4) the *Sudra* (farmers and other manual workers). Caste, however, although certainly a vital element in Indian society throughout the centuries, was not unchallenged. Buddhism, the most important offshoot of Hinduism, provided a way of salvation apart from the institutional system of caste, and the *bhakti* tradition, which has been very influential in Indian thought and practice for many centuries, has tended to minimize the significance of caste. In any case, the concept of caste operates differently from the way in which many in modern American society tend to imagine it. By no means does one necessarily spend one's life longing to have been born into a higher caste. In many cases this may happen and within the Hindu structure one would seek to live so as to have the karmic inheritance that would fulfil that hope in one's next incarnation. Many, however, are proud of the caste to which they belong and to which they feel immensely strong family ties, recognizing also that it is no shame to belong to, say, the farmer caste, for surely it is better to be a good farmer than a mediocre brahmin, or to be a competent carpenter rather than an incompetent historian. The case of the pariah or outcaste is another matter, akin to the question of slavery rather than to societal caste. Plato and Aristotle, in their political treatises, did not seriously address themselves to the ethics of slavery as a socially accepted institution of their time. See also **Slavery.**

Castel Gandolfo. Since the 17th c. the popes have had their summer residence in this little town about eighteen miles from Rome in the Alban Hills, where the heat is less oppressive at that season than in Rome. The papal palace and gardens are (under the Lateran Treaty) part of the area of the papal domains and therefore exempt from Italian jurisdiction.

Castello, Sebastian (1515–1563). Theologian and humanist. Born in Savoy, he met Calvin at Strassburg in 1540. Calvin influenced him to embrace the Reformation cause, but soon his humanistic and eirenic spirit evoked Calvin's hostility. He became professor of Greek at Basel in 1552. Among his works are translations of the Bible into Latin and into French and a posthumous treatise on predestination.

Casuistry. The notion (familiar in modern Christian ethics under names such as Situationism and Contextualism) that general ethical principles must be considered in their application to particular cases has a long history in Christian thought and practice. The term "casuistry" refers to such applications to "cases". From the 7th c., formal casuistry in the Church was developed and expressed in various manuals. In the 16th c., various rival forms of casuistry began to arise in the Roman Catholic Church. See **Probabilism, Probabiliorism,** and **Equiprobabilism.**

Caswall, Edward (1814–1878). An Oxford man, he was received into the Roman Catholic Church in 1847 and in 1850 joined the Oratorians under Newman. He is the author of many hymns.

Catacombs. This term was used for the cemetery of San Sebastiano as early as 354. By the 9th c. it was used widely of all early Christian subterranean burial places. Although such burial places were to be found in many other parts of Europe as well as in North Africa and Asia Minor, those at Rome, extending for hundreds of miles, are by far the most famous. Among the surviving ones (about forty of them) are those named for Saints Callistus, Sebastian, Domitilla, Agnes, Pancras, and Commodilla. They are passages with connecting chambers, typically arranged in two or four stories, one atop the other, with the bodies in niches in the walls. The bodies of some of the more prominent Christians were placed in sarcophagi. The paintings are of great historical and theological interest as not only the earliest examples of Christian art but as illustrating the views of Christians of the earliest period concerning the afterlife. Eucharistic services were held in the catacombs of Rome in commemoration of those who had suffered martyrdom. Neglected during the Middle Ages, they were rediscovered toward the end of the 16th c., and by the 19th c. important scientific research was being undertaken on them. One of the most important 19th c. studies is that by G. B. de Rossi, *Roma sotteranea cristiana* in 3 volumes (1864–77).

Catafalque. A term used for the coffin and its various accoutrements.

Catechesis. When catechumens were preparing for Baptism, they received instruction in the basic tenets of the

Christian faith and this instruction was called catechesis.

Catechism. A term used for manuals of Christian instruction intended for popular use. Little books of this kind existed in the Middle Ages to help the clergy in the instruction of children and others, often arranged in such a way as to help people to commit to memory the elements of Christian doctrine such as are set forth in the Beatitudes and lists such as the Seven Deadly Sins. The term, however, seems to have come into use about the beginning of the 16th c. The Reformation produced an avalanche of catechisms and the practice was followed by the Roman Catholic Church. These catechisms ranged from very elementary expositions to others that were more like sustained theological treatises. Catechisms are still used in many Christian denominations for the instruction of children.

Catechumens. Much importance was attached in the early Church to a period of probation and instruction before a convert was admitted to Baptism. During that period, candidates attended the services but were formally dismissed before the solemn part of the Eucharist was to begin. They were not only trained in the basic tenets of the Christian faith and the spiritual and ethical implications of embracing it but also subjected to close scrutiny till at length, at Easter, they were ready for Baptism. Such persons, during that preparatory period, were called catechumens. The concept, in abeyance for many centuries, was revived by the Roman Catholic Church in 1962, with a view more especially for application to the mission field. What is sometimes called the Mass of the Catechumens is the Proanaphora, being the introductory part of the Mass before the Anaphora and the part that in the early Church the catechumens were permitted to attend.

Categorical Imperative. Kant recognized a moral law that is absolute and the ultimate foundation of all ethical behavior. It is given to human reason and absolutely binding on every human being. It may be expressed in a maxim such as: "So act that you can will the principle of your action to be universally binding on the will of every other rational being." It is to be distinguished from what Kant recognized as a hypothetical imperative, conditional on a desire to possess a particular good, e.g., "If you wish for longevity, you should exercise your body and mind regularly and avoid stress and the ingestion of animal fat." Not only is such a moral imperative subject to change as new discoveries are made in medicine and psychology; it is in principle prudential and therefore not an absolute duty as is the categorical imperative. For study of this concept see H. J. Paton, *The Categorical Imperative* (1947).

Categories. In logic, a category may be considered as: (1) any class or type or genus that is set apart for conceptual analysis; (2) any basic notion, principle, idea, or concept within a philosophical system; and (3) one of the conceptual forms considered to be ultimate and by which knowledge is made possible. For example, Aristotle recognized the following: (substance (*ousia*), quantity (*poson*), quality (*poion*), place (*pou*), relation (*prosti*), time (*pote*), condition or state (*keisthai*), possession (*echein*), activity (*poiein*), and being affected (*paschein*). Beyond these are what might be called hyper-categories or meta-categories: concepts that pervade all categories: (1) being, (2) unity or oneness, (3) sameness or identity, and (4) otherness. Kant set forth a more elaborate set of categories in four groups, each divided into three and constituting what he called the categories of logic from which he deduced another set of twelve categories, which he called the categories of the understanding. All experience, Kant held, presupposes these categories and apart from them no knowledge is possible. They are categories of the mind, i.e., they do not classify reality as it is in itself, only reality as it is represented in the phenomena of the world of our experience. The philosophical procedure of thinking in terms of categories issues from Plato who, in the *Sophist* listed five: being, rest, motion, identity, and difference.

Category Mistake. A common error in logic, found not least in religious discourse. It consists of erroneously grouping unrelatable classes of meaning, resulting in meaningless utterances which, although they may be grammatically correct and analyzable, are semantically nonsensical, e.g., "Time rolls speedily on through the amber glory of divine eternity."

Catena. This term, from the Latin, meaning "chain", is used of biblical commentaries from the 5th c., when the practice grew of expounding chains of passages quoted or derived from earlier commentators.

Cathari. The name given in some regions of Europe to a very important medieval group known in France as the Albigenses. It has also sometimes been applied to the adherents of other movements in the history of Christianity that have held similar views and engaged in similar practices. See **Albigenses.**

Catharinus, Ambrosius (Lancelot Politi) (*c.* 1484–1553). Dominican theologian. Born at Siena, he entered the Dominican Order at the Convent of San Marco, Florence, in 1517, taking the name of Ambrosius Catharinus from two Sienese Dominican saints. An able theologian, he was given the task of combatting the doctrines of Luther that were appearing on the theological scene at that time. He proved too independent for his superiors' liking, however; e.g., he defended the doctrine of the Immaculate Conception of Mary, contrary to the then prevailing Dominican opinion against it. He also developed original ideas on various theological topics, e.g., on grace, predestination, and papal authority, that alienated him from

and alarmed many in his own Order. He took an important part, nevertheless, in the Council of Trent and became Archbishop of Conza.

Catharsis. From the Greek *katharsis*, meaning "purging" or "purification", which Aristotle considered the function of tragedy, through the reading or viewing of which the reader's or spectator's emotions are purged. The concept is important in the history of the philosophy of art as well as in the philosophical study of religion.

Cathedral. The church containing the *cathedra* (chair or throne) of the bishop of a diocese is so called. It is frequently a large and impressive building, such as Winchester, Durham, Reims, and Milan. The great ancient cathedrals usually have a complex history, and many of them are noted for elaborate musical and other programs. Neither architectural grandeur, however, nor indeed any other such claim to distinction or size is relevant to its status as a cathedral, which is constituted by the presence of the bishop's *cathedra*; e.g., in a new diocese having no cathedral, the bishop (at least in theory) may choose any church as the cathedral. In early times the position of the *cathedra* was behind the high altar, but the practice grew of having it at the side of the chancel, which has been the custom for many centuries. Since Vatican II a movement to return it to its earlier place behind the high altar has developed, despite the opinion of those liturgists who consider that position to impede the focus on the altar.

Catherine De' Medici. (1519–1589). Queen Consort of France. Related to Pope Clement VII, she married Henry, son of Francis I of France in 1533. In her later years she exerted much influence on French politics and at first sought to exercise a mediating policy between Catholics and Protestants, but later she vacillated and began to support the persecution of the Protestants, culminating in her active involvement in the Massacre of St. Bartholomew on August 23, 1572. See **Bartholomew, Massacre of St.**

Catherine of Alexandria. Veneration of a saint of this name is of very long standing but is supported almost entirely by legend. She was believed to have been martyred in Alexandria and is represented symbolically by a spiked wheel, known sometimes as a Catherine wheel.

Catherine of Genoa (1447–1510). One of the greatest of medieval Christian mystics. Caterinetta Fieschi, of a noble Ligurian family, was married at sixteen and ten years later experienced a profound religious conversion. She is one of the few married women to have been canonized. Her mystical teachings are to be found in her *Vita e dottrina* (1551). Her *Treatise on Purgatory* is especially interesting. For an important study of her life and work see Baron von Hügel, *The Mystical Element in Religion as studied in St. Catherine of Genoa and her Friends* (2 vols., 1908). For an English translation of her treatise on purgatory see C. Balfour and H. D. Irvine, *Treatise on Purgatory* (1946).

Catherine of Siena (14th c.) Caterina Benincassa from an early age in her life claimed to have received visions. She devoted herself to the service of the sick and the poor. Her sanctity of life attracted many followers. Her *Dialogo* exhibits the character of her spirituality. She was canonized in 1461.

Catholic. The Greek word from which this term is derived is *katholikos*, which means "universal" or "general". It is used at a very early point in Christian history to distinguish what is general or universal in the Church from what is merely local. In this sense the word "catholic" still functions in secular contexts. A fish might be called "catholic" from its being found in waters all over the world, not just in a particular region. Christian teaching came to be regarded as "catholic" or "heretical" according to whether it was deemed to be what would nowadays be accounted "mainstream" or otherwise. "Catholic" came to be synonymous, in this context, with "orthodox" as distinguished from "heterodox". When in 1054, the Great Schism between East and West divided the Christian Church, the East used the term "Orthodox" to describe itself, while the West used the term "Catholic". Since the Reformation, the Roman Catholic Church, at least in popular discourse, has tended to designate itself "the Catholic Church" and all other Christians "non-Catholics". Many bodies who share in the Reformation heritage are content with this popular usage, since they repudiate all connection with historic Christianity as developed through the ages; but others that claim to participate fully in the continuity of the Church from earliest times and to recognize themselves as part of the life of that Church find that popular usage unacceptable. Anglicans, for instance, although they recognize (except for extremist parties within the Anglican Communion) immense value and importance in the Reformation heritage, regard themselves as thoroughly within the life of the historic Church from its beginning as described in the Book of Acts to the present day, through all its vicissitudes, and would therefore (as would also Old Catholics) find the term "non-Catholic" as partisan a nickname as the term "Papist" that was formerly fashionable among Protestant polemicists.

Catholic Apostolic Church. Name assumed by followers of Edward Irving. See **Irving, Edward.**

Catholic Emancipation in Britain. See **Roman Catholic Relief Acts.**

Catholic Epistles. Certain of the letters in the New Testament are addressed to particular Christian communities (e.g., Romans and Ephesians); others (e.g., James, II Peter, I John, and Jude) are not. The latter group were called the Catholic Epistles because they were general rather than addressed to a particular community. See also **Catholic.**

Catholicos. This title is given to the Patriarchs of the Armenian and the Nestorian Churches and to the head of the Georgian Church.

Catholic University of America. Founded in 1889 at Washington, DC, as a center of secular and religious learning under the control of the Roman Catholic Church, it is governed by a board of trustees appointed by the Roman Catholic hierarchy. The Roman Catholic Archbishop of Washington is Chancellor *ex officio.*

Caton, William (1636–1665). Under the influence of George Fox, he became a Quaker preacher. His *Journal* (1689), which Fox edited, is a Quaker classic.

Causa Sui. The assertion that God makes everything can evoke the question "Who made God?" The question is not entirely simplistic, for although the original assertion purports to explain how the universe comes to be, it does not even claim to explain how God comes to be. One way of answering the question is to say that God is *causa sui,* i.e., that while everything else is caused by God, God himself is self-caused. As Thomas Aquinas perceived, however, God cannot be said to cause himself, for in order to do so he would first have to exist and if he first existed he would have no need to cause his existence. What is meant by saying that God is the first cause or prime mover (see **Cosmological Argument**) is to affirm, rather, that God is beyond causation as we know it. So God is more properly designated *He Who Is.*

Causation, Principle of Universal. The theory that every event has a cause, whether we can identify the cause or not. Hume sought to repudiate this traditionally accepted view by arguing that we perceive only "constant conjunction" or "regular succession" but no necessary connection between event and cause. We see the sun "rise" and have seen this happen every day throughout our lives, so we say it "must" rise tomorrow; but we ought strictly speaking to say, rather: "I have never seen it happen otherwise any day during the past forty years, so I fully expect to see it happen tomorrow." Kant, however, made causation one of the "categories of the understanding." See **Cosmological Argument**.

Caussin, Nicholas (1583–1651). Jesuit. Born at Troyes, he was chosen in 1637 by Richelieu to be confessor to Louis XIII, but incurred the anger of that extremely influential cardinal, who banished him from Paris to Quimper (Brittany) the same year. On the death of Richelieu on 1642, however, he was recalled to Paris, where eventually he died.

Caxton, William (*c.* 1422–1491). The first English printer. He learned the art of printing at Cologne.

Cayer, Pierre-Victor-Palma (1525–1610). French theologian. Born of a Roman Catholic family in Montrichard, he studied in Germany and returned to France as a Calvinist pastor at Montreuil-Bonnin. He later returned to the Roman Catholic Church, became professor of oriental languages at the College of Navarre in 1596 and was ordained to the priesthood in 1600. The Sorbonne censured some of his teachings, e.g., that the Pope's authority is no higher than that of the bishops.

Cecilia. According to an early tradition she lived during the 2nd or 3rd c. and was martyred. She is one of the most highly venerated among the early Roman Christian martyrs. Valerian, her husband, and Tibertius, her brother, were both also martyred. She is the patroness of ecclesiastical music.

Celebret. In the Roman Catholic Church, when a priest is traveling and wishes to say Mass in a locality where he is not known, he carries with him a certificate called a *celebret,* to introduce him to the local church authorities so that they may permit him to say Mass. The Latin term means "let him celebrate [Mass]."

Celestine I. Early 5th c. pope who engaged in efforts to stamp out Pelagianism and Semi-pelagianism. He also, at a synod in Rome in 430, condemned Nestorius.

Celestine III (1106–1198). A 12th c. pope, elected in 1191 at the age of eighty-four. At the Council of Sens in 1140, he had defended Abelard, and after becoming a cardinal in 1144 he showed himself tolerant by the standards of the day in his relations with both Church and State.

Celestine V (c. 1215–1296). Pope for only a few months during 1294, he had become a Benedictine at the age of 17, but had sought greater seclusion in a mountain in the Abruzzi where his fame as a man of deep spirituality and ascetic life attracted much attention. His election to the papacy was occasioned by the failure of the Conclave to agree upon a candidate, so that finally they turned to him. His reign was, however, as disastrous as it was brief. Politically inexperienced, he quickly lost the support of even those who had favored him and before the end of the year he was forced to abdicate. His successor, Boniface VIII, one of the most politically minded popes in the history of the papacy, abrogated all Celestine's acts and caused him to be imprisoned in the Castello di Fumone, where he died. He was the founder of the Celestine Order, a branch of the Benedictine Order, which after a period of much influence declined and finally became extinct in 1785.

Celestine Order. See **Celestine V.**

Celestius. A 5th c. Pelagian who, shocked at the low ethical standards in the Christian Church, emphasized human freedom and responsibility. His teachings were condemned at various councils as heretical.

Celibacy of the Clergy. The ideal of a life of total continence has been upheld in the Christian Church from early times, finding biblical authority in Paul and elsewhere and practical expression in the prestige accorded to the monastic way of life that entails perpetual chastity in the celibate state as one of the vows taken by monks and nuns. Nevertheless, the concept of the celibacy of priests not members of such a community under such vows was developed only gradually. At the Council of Nicaea in 325 a proposal was made to require priests to be celibate, but it was rejected, and the right of priests to marry was re-emphasized at the Council of Trullo in 692. In the Eastern Church the practice has remained unchanged: priests may marry before ordination but not afterwards, and if widowed they may not marry again. Bishops, however, must be celibate and are usually drawn from the monks. In the West, early in the 4th c., enactments were already being made to try to enforce celibacy on all priests. Such efforts were frequently made. The Second Lateran Council (1139) declared the ordination of married priests to be invalid as well as illegal. The Council of Trent (1545–1563) not only decreed against the marriage of clergy but in various ways instituted reforms to try to insure the implementation of the decrees of the Church on this subject. In practice, the concept had remained only an ideal, upheld by comparatively few priests, especially during certain periods in the Middle Ages such as the 10th c. and the 15th c. but to a great extent in other periods too. Concubinage among the clergy was extremely common and the laity more or less became accustomed to it. Some medieval advocates of clerical celibacy went so far as to assert that it was part of divine law. Thomas Aquinas, however, with characteristic perspicacity, held it to be merely a law of the Church (*Summa Theologiae* II–IIae, 88, 11), with the implication that it can be changed at any time by papal and/or conciliar authority. Nevertheless, it has remained the Law of the Church: a position specifically upheld by Pope Paul VI in his encyclical *Sacerdotalis Caelibatus* (1967) and also by his successor Pope John Paul II, in face of widespread demand within the Church for making it an option, not a requirement. The rule of celibacy, traditionally upheld as an ideal and a token of the priest's total dedication of his energies and powers to God and having also the practical advantage of relieving him of the financial and other burdens of raising a family, is now seen by many as having at best disadvantages, spiritual as well as practical, that outweigh its advantages, if it be not (as many would contend) fundamentally pernicious. Formidable arguments, many of them psychologically obvious, can be levelled against the concept; yet the *mystique* attached to the notion in the eyes of many, clerical and lay, fosters its maintenance as an integral part of ecclesiastical discipline in the Roman Catholic Church. Since 1549 the rule of celibacy has been abolished for Anglican clergy, leaving the Roman Catholic Church virtually alone in maintaining it. Anglicans as well as the Eastern Orthodox recognize, however, no less than the Roman Catholic Church, the place of monastic and other religious communities in the Church, with the customary vows proper to their special vocation.

Cell. The room assigned to a hermit or monk or nun is called a cell. Hermits and semi-hermits such as the Carthusians and the Camaldoli live each in a separate building. Some monks and nuns, e.g., the Trappists, so emphasize community that the members of the community live in dormitories. The assignment of a private room, very simply furnished, for each individual is increasingly common. The term "cell" was also sometimes used of small monastic houses that were dependencies of the mother house of the Order.

Cella. In early times a small cemetery chapel, designed for the commemoration of the departed, was called by this name.

Cellarer. In monastic communities in the Middle Ages the cellarer was an important official, charged not only with the cooking and serving of the community meals but usually also with the mundane business connected with running the house and dealing with outside tradesmen and others.

Celsus. An important 2nd c. pagan opponent of Christianity. His work *Alēthes logos* is the first literary attack on the Christian faith that has survived. It included a vigorous plea for greater political and religious tolerance in the Christian Church. The contents of his work has been reconstructed from Origen's reply, which includes the text of most of it.

Celtic Church. The Christian Church as it existed in the British Isles before continental influences (such as Augustine's mission to England from Rome in 596) affected it is called by this name. The Celtic Christians had customs and practices that caused them to resist as innovations those that such missionaries sought to impose. The Celtic Church in Scotland, for instance, was organized on monastic lines and used a date for Easter different from that in use in Rome. Although the cross was used extensively, the crucifix seems to have been unknown. Such differences persisted in Scotland till the coming of Queen Margaret in the 11th c.

Cemetery. The word is derived from the Greek word *koimētērion*, which means "sleeping place." Since it was used exclusively of Christian burial places, the name exhibits the primitive Christian attitude toward afterlife as entailing a period of resting or sleeping in expectation of the coming general resurrection.

Cenaculum, The. The "upper room" (Mark 14.15) in which the Last Supper took place and (Acts 1.13) the Holy Spirit descended on those present at Pentecost.

Cenobites. Monks living in community, contradistinguished from hermits.

Censures. Ecclesiastical punishments are technically so designated. They range from the mildest (e.g., an admonition) to the most extreme, i.e., excommunication. Others include deposition (the removal of a cleric from his standing as such in the Church), deprivation (removal of a cleric from a particular position in the Church) and interdict. See **Interdict.**

Cerdo. A 2nd c. Syrian Gnostic who taught that the God of the Old Testament is other than the God whom Jesus claimed as his Father. Marcion, who taught similar views, may have learned from him. See **Marcion** and **Gnosticism.**

Cere Cloth. A cloth treated with wax and laid directly on the altar to help to protect the linen cloths above it from staining.

Ceremonial and Ritual. In popular usage the two terms are used synonymously. Strictly, however, ceremonial consists of the formal actions that are part of the liturgy, e.g., the genuflections and the making of the sign of the cross. The form of words that accompany the ceremonial (e.g., the words used in the consecration of the elements in the Eucharist) constitute the ritual.

Cerinthus. Late 1st c. Gnostic who taught, as did some other Christian Gnostics that the universe was created by a Demiurge or angel, not by the Eternal One who transcends all material "stuff". He also taught that Jesus was not Deity incarnate but a man on whom a divine power descended during his teaching and healing ministry. According to Irenaeus, the Gospel of John was written to refute the teaching of Cerinthus. See **Gnosticism.**

Cerne, The Book of. A manuscript in the library of the University of Cambridge containing a collection of prayers, mostly Celtic in origin. The manuscript dates from the 9th c.

Certainty. When, in logic, an argument is valid, the conclusion is said to be certain, e.g., if $A = B$ and $B =$ bitumen, then $A =$ bitumen. The certainty consists, however, only in the validity of the argument that yields this conclusion; it does not by any means insure the truth of either the premise $A = B$ or the premise $B =$ bitumen. Such is mathematical certainty, e.g., if $2 + 2 = 4$, then $4 - 2 = 2$. One can never attain that *kind* of certainty concerning a proposition such as "Planet Earth will continue in its customary orbit tonight," even though the probability is overwhelmingly great; nor can one be certain *in that way* that no pigs can fly, although a flying species of pig would astonish everyone. The impossibility of certain knowledge other than the deductive kind indicated above has implications of the most fundamental kind in the philosophy of religion, not least in arguments for or against the existence of God. We may nevertheless have psychological certainty (some philosophers have preferred the name "certitude" for this) about many things. Believers and unbelievers alike may claim such certitude on the question of the existence of God, claiming that the view they respectively take is subjectively certain for them, being moreover confirmed in the experience of their lives. Such affirmations as they make on the basis of such "certitude" may be supported by various kinds of argument, although these cannot be expected to yield certainty such as is to be found in the proposition that the internal angles of a triangle $= 180°$. See **God.**

Cesarini, Julian (1398–1444). Of a noble Roman family, he served in diplomatic missions for the Curia and was created a cardinal in 1426. A friend of Nicholas of Cusa, he sought to adopt a conciliatory policy in dealing with forces accounted hostile to the interests of Rome, e.g., the Hussites. He was prominent in the negotiations to reunite Greek and Latin Christians. He was killed in a war with the Turks in which the Christians were thoroughly defeated.

Chaburah. A Jewish practice whereby a group of friends join together, e.g., on the evening before the Sabbath, partly to prepare for the proper observances, partly for friendly conversation. Jesus may have conducted such a gathering with his disciples on the night of the Last Supper. On this view (supported by the Gospel according to John) the Last Supper was not directly connected with the Passover meal (John 18.28)

Chad. 7th c. Northumbrian saint who studied under Aidan at Lindisfarne.

Chalcedon, Council of. This, the 4th Ecumenical Council of the Christian Church, held at Chalcedon in Asia Minor in 451, affirmed that the two natures of Christ, the human and the divine, are united unconfusedly (*asygchyntōs*), unchangeably (*atreptōs*), indivisibly (*adiaretōs*) and inseparably (*achōristōs*). This definition was aimed at rejecting both the views of Eutyches, on the one hand, and, on the other, those of Nestorius, by making explicit the concept that the divinity and humanity in Christ are to be equally recognized. He is both "True God" and "True Man" and neither one nature nor the other must be in any way underestimated. The consequences of this decree were accepted universally, at least in theory, except by those Churches that adhered (as some do to this day, e.g., the Ethiopic Church) to the Monophysite view that in Christ there is only one nature, the divine. An implicate of the Chalcedonian teaching on this subject is that the use of the term Theotokos of the Virgin Mary is fully justified and proper: she is the *bearer* of God. (See **Theotokos.**) The council also reaffirmed the decrees already made at Nicaea and at Constantinople. While such enactments have by no means excluded further christological controversy within the mainstream of the Church (nor were they intended to do so), they set a limit and gave direction to the lines on which further controversy would proceed.

Chalice. The name given to the cup used in the Eucharist for the wine that is consecrated. Early chalices were made of glass or whatever other material might have been available, but precious metals such as silver and gold became general by the 4th c., and the use of chalices of silver adorned with precious gems is mentioned by Augustine and others, although there was no absolute church rule on the subject. From the 9th c., however, the use of metal was required and only since 1969 has the Roman Catholic Church again permitted the use of chalices other than metal. In Anglican practice, chalices are always metal unless in very extraordinary circumstances. The veil, a square of material matching the eucharistic vestments is used to cover the chalice and paten during the Mass when not in use. This practice, although now virtually universal in Catholic usage (except for the Carthusians, who conserve several liturgical peculiarities of their own and other customs of the past), is comparatively modern. The sacred vessels were formerly covered with a folded white linen corporal: a practice commendable for its simplicity and reverence.

Challoner, Richard. (1691–1781). Roman Catholic devotional writer and bishop. He was the author of *The Garden of the Soul*, a devotional aid that was extremely popular among English Roman Catholics from the time of its publication in 1740 through the 19th c.

Chalmers, James (1841–1901). Congregationalist missionary-explorer. Of Scottish birth, he was trained for the ministry in England, which he left in 1866 to set sail for the New Hebrides. His entire life was spent in the mission field, principally in New Guinea. He was murdered while visiting an island on the south coast of Papua, while trying to establish peaceful relations with the tribesmen there.

Chalmers, Thomas (1780–1847). Perhaps the greatest figure in the history of the Scottish Kirk. He became professor of Moral Philosophy at the University of St. Andrews in 1823 and of theology at Edinburgh in 1828. Gifted in many directions, not least as an evangelical preacher but also as a mathematician, he led the movement against the appointment of ministers to parishes by the old system of patronage and for their election by the members of the respective parishes. This movement brought about, in 1843, the greatest of the schisms that for long divided the Kirk. See **Disruption, The.**

Chancel. That part of the church building set apart for the principal altar, the clergy, and choir, that lies to the east of the nave, being sometimes separated from the latter by a screen.

Chancellor. The chancellor of a diocese is an important official who works closely with the bishop in its administration, especially in judicial and legalistic matters. In the Roman Catholic Church he is always a priest; in the Anglican communion he is either a barrister or at least someone with legal knowledge and experience.

Chandas. The name (meaning "metre") given in Hindu practice to one of the six Vedāṅgas, which sets the rules for the precisely correct performance of sacrificial procedure, in which great importance is given to the use of the proper metre in chanting. Hindus traditionally attach enormous importance to metre. The efficacy of the ritual depends on several factors, of which the correctness of the metre used is one.

Chang Tsai (1020–1077). Neo-Confucian philosopher. The son of a magistrate, he became a magistrate in

1057 and in 1069 obtained a position in the imperial library. After exploring Buddhism and Taoism he returned to his native Confucianism. In his writings he emphasized the concept of yin-yang as representing fundamental aspects of the material force that preserves the balance and sustains the power in the universe. This force has various aspects or poles. He rejected the notions canvassed by Taoists and Buddhists in so far as they entailed a spiritual dimension of being, preferring to find the solution to all problems within the framework of a cosmos understood in Confucian terms, in which the principle of balance (the golden mean) is emphasized.

Channing, William Ellery (1780–1842). American Unitarian divine. Trained at Harvard, he ministered at Boston as a Congregationalist, but when Congregationalism was divided between conservatives and liberals he took the side of the latter and preached against many of the doctrines the conservatives accounted essential, including the Trinity and the total depravity of man. Although he was acclaimed, therefore, as a Unitarian, he disliked being identified with any particular denomination. His works, in 4 volumes, were published in Boston in 1841 and he is generally regarded as preeminent in the Unitarian tradition.

Chantry. A practice developed in the Middle Ages, which became very common in the later part of that period, of endowing a foundation for the erection of a small chapel and the support of a priest to provide for Masses in perpetuity to be said or sung for the repose of the soul of the founder and of the souls of those whom he nominated. (The priest would often act as local schoolmaster or undertake some other duties to eke out his living.) The chapel built for this purpose was called a chantry chapel and the priest a chantry priest. At the Reformation some two thousand such chantries were closed and the income applied to other purposes.

Chapel. The term is used in several senses but probably most often applied to any building other than a cathedral or parish church that is set aside for Christian worship. It is often but by no means necessarily small. Some college chapels are very large (e.g., Princeton University Chapel, whose extreme length is 249 feet, width over 61 feet, height over 78 feet) and some of the chapels at Oxford and Cambridge are both large and very beautiful (e.g., King's at Cambridge, which is one of the great architectural glories of England). The term is traditionally used, moreover, of Methodist and other non-Anglican churches in England and formerly of Roman Catholic churches there and is still often used in Ireland in that sense. Large churches often have many small chapels within them, notably the "Lady Chapel." When some parishioners in a church live far from it, another church may be built for their convenience if the situation warrants it, and such a church is called a chapel of ease. A chapel royal is a private chapel attached to a royal court. The Sainte-Chapelle in Paris is probably the most famous, historic, and beautiful of such chapels royal. In England there are several, such as Windsor, which are served by chaplains appointed by the Sovereign and exempt from episcopal jurisdiction.

Chaplet. See **Rosary.**

Chapman, John (1865–1933). Biblical scholar. Having entered the Benedictine Order in 1892, he became Prior of Downside in 1922 and Abbot in 1929. He sought to show the priority of Matthew among the synoptists, contrary to the general opinion of New Testament scholars, and in other writings upheld views contrary to the mainstream of scholarship in his day. His *Spiritual Letters* (1935) are an important contribution to the literature on Roman Catholic spirituality.

Chapter. In the early days of monasticism a section of the Rule of St. Benedict was read regularly to the assembled monks and was called a chapter. The term designates primarily the regular meeting of the monks held to receive spiritual admonitions from the abbot and to assist him in the conduct of the general administration of the house. The assemblies held at less frequent intervals for the entire Order are called general chapters. Cathedrals also have chapters, consisting of a body charged with running them: commonly the Dean or Provost of the cathedral and the canons. The building or room in which cathedral or monastic affairs are conducted is called the chapter house. Separate buildings for the purpose appeared in the 9th c.

Chapter and Verse. The division of the Bible into chapter and verse as we know it today is a useful convention unknown to the ancients or in the early Middle Ages. The division into chapters is a device attributed to Stephen Langton, Archbishop of Canterbury, and dates from only *c.* 1200. The division into verses was devised by Rabbi Nathan, who employed it for the Hebrew Bible in 1448. It was adopted in a Latin Bible printed in 1528, in which a similar method was used for the New Testament. Robert Estienne of Paris issued a Bible in 1555 in which the New Testament verses were differently arranged, but the principle was the same. The Geneva Bible, published in 1560 (see **Bible**) followed Estienne's arrangement which became the customary convention.

Character. The Sacraments of Baptism, Confirmation and Ordination are held to cause an indelible imprint on their recipients, according to traditional Catholic theology. This imprint is called a "character." The implication is that a priest, for example, remains forever a priest, however unworthy; indeed even in hell.

Chardon, Louis (c. 1596–1651). French Dominican mystic, author of *La Croix de Jésus* (1647).

Charisma. This Greek word (plural *charismata*) means a favor bestowed. It is traditionally rendered in English "grace" (from the Latin *gratia*). Paul lists various *charismata* that may be bestowed on Christians for the fulfilment of the various kinds of work that they may be called upon to do in their ministry (I Corinthians 12.8–11, 28). In 20th c. English, the word is often used in a general sense to designate a person who has magnetic personality and in Christian discourse today the adjective "charismatic" is commonly used to designate a person or group of persons whose outlook and practice in the Church emphasizes emotional spontaneity rather than the more formal type of life and worship that is traditional.

Charity. This word, from the Latin *caritas*, is the term used to translate the Greek word *agapē*, which is used by Paul and other New Testament writers to designate a selfless, disinterested love such as is bestowed on Christians through the action of the Holy Spirit. (See **Agapē**.) The word has acquired a different connotation in modern English, so that it is now usually translated "love" in order to avoid such misleading overtones.

Charlemagne (*c.* 742–814). "Charles the Great," the first emperor of the Holy Roman Empire. His enormous conquests through a large part of Western Europe, including much of Spain, brought at least a semblance of order to what for long had been territory beset with wars and lacking the conditions necessary for political stability and cultural development. He encouraged the reform of the Church, and his interest in theology was genuine, as was also his patronage of scholarship. His personal interest in arts and letters, usually in the strong men and military leaders of his day, did much to set the stage for the development of the painting, sculpture, poetry, literature, philosophy, and theology, that were to flourish in Western Europe in the later Middle Ages.

(See **Carolingian Revival.**) He also did more than did the popes of his time to bring about discipline and unity in the Church in the West. He was crowned as the first emperor of the Holy Roman Empire by Pope Leo III on Christmas day, 800, in the old St. Peter's, Rome. See **Holy Roman Empire.**

Charles I (1600–1649). In the decades preceding the accession of Charles I to the British throne, the Puritan party in the English Church had been strong, sometimes expressing itself in extreme forms alien to the English temper. There was nevertheless also a strong party among the clergy who favored a more traditionally Catholic stance and practice, which was moreover to the King's personal liking. He made William Laud, a vigorous champion of the latter party, Archbishop of Canterbury. Charles, however, was beset by many difficulties on all sides, and his policy of enforcing his own ecclesiastical preferences and of repressing opposition to them fostered a spirit of rebellion among those with Puritan beliefs or tendencies. Moreover, he unwisely inflamed the Scots (whose Kirk at the time had not been immutably opposed to some form of episcopacy as a form of ecclesiastical government) by an ostentatious insistence on Anglican ceremonial and, with even more predictable results, by a policy that would have brought a Scottish episcopate directly under the control of the King and the Archbishop of Canterbury. Charles was defeated in the Civil War that had broken out in England in 1642. His execution by the Army in 1649 was considered by his sympathizers to be such as to make him worthy to be hailed as a martyr. He was indeed a man of noble character, deep religious feeling, and personal courage, but he lacked prudence and political wisdom. See also **Eikōn Basilikē.**

Charles V (1500–1558). The grandson of Ferdinand and Isabella and the eldest son of Philip of Burgundy, he had become, by the time of his election as Emperor, easily the most powerful man in Europe. Nevertheless, the rise of the Reformation movement confronted him with serious difficulties in many parts of his dominions and while in some regions (such as Spain where the Roman Catholic Church dominated) his rule was dictatorial, in others his policy vacillated and he was forced to accept the principle imposed by the Diet of Augsburg: *cujus regio, ejus religio*. See **Augsburg Confession.**

Charles Borromeo (1538–1584). Born at Arona on Lake Maggiore, of noble parentage, he received his first benefice at the age of twelve. In 1560 he was created a cardinal and became Archbishop of Milan. At the Council of Trent he took a notable part.

Charterhouse. The monastery of Carthusians is so called in English. The name is inherited by one of the most famous schools in England, now located near Godalming (accented on the first syllable), Surrey. See **Carthusian Order** and **Grande Chartreuse, La.**

Chartres. Particularly famous in the earlier Middle Ages for its school and the many great names associated with it, e.g., Gilbert de la Porée, Fulbert, Bernard, and Thierry. The cathedral, begun in the 11th c. and dedicated in 1260, is one of the great architectural glories of Europe. Chartres was traditionally noted for its concern and respect for humane learning as well as for theology, and that tradition is reflected in the sculptures representing Mary as Wisdom or the Lady Philosophy with the Seven Liberal Arts. The magnificent glass is among the best in the world.

Chasidim. The name, meaning "godly," is applied to those conservative Jews who in the 2nd c. BCE sought to maintain what was distinctively Hebrew in the Jewish tradition, contradistinguished from the cosmopolitan Greek influences. The word is applied also to

a Jewish group that emerged in the 18th c. and has played an important part in mystical Jewish thought.

Chastity. One of the three vows taken by members of religious orders, congregations, and societies is that of "perpetual chastity," entailing the expectation of total, lifelong abstinence from all intentional sexual expression. The concept of chastity, however, as used in Christian discourse, has a wider and more positive connotation: that of a disposition and outlook rather than mere abstention from carnal, sexual activity. In this sense married persons no less than single ones may be chaste or unchaste. Chastity in this sense designates a state of mind in which the sexual desires that human beings share with other animals tend through habitual sublimation to be transformed into specifically human attitudes, desires, and concerns, such as are beyond the capacity of lower forms of mammalian life. Traditional Christian thought exalts chastity as a virtue that promotes the development of that inner awareness of a dimension of being beyond the one known directly through the five senses and so makes possible that life "in Christ" that is the Christian goal, which unchastity impedes.

Chasuble. The vestment used exclusively for the celebrant of Mass. It corresponds to the phelonion of the Eastern Orthodox Church. Originally a sort of cloak, with an aperture for the head, it was adapted for use at the altar and in the course of time came to take somewhat degraded forms, such as the "fiddleback" chasuble worn almost like a "sandwich board." Liturgical reforms have encouraged the more graceful form of chasuble sometimes called Gothic. Designed to give the celebrant the free use of his arms at the altar, it is a practical (and can be a beautiful) vestment.

Chateaubriand, François René, Vicomte de (1768–1848). French writer and diplomat. Born at St.-Malo in Britanny, he published several writings, including, in 1844, a life of De Rancé, but his most remarkable work is his *Génie du christianisme*, in which he defends the Christian faith as the catalyst of the uniquely rich cultural, artistic, and literary development of European civilization. He belongs to the Romantic movement of the early 19th c. that succeeded the rationalistic and materialistic preoccupations of the thought characteristic of the preceding century, the age of the *Aufklärung*.

Chaucer, Geoffrey (c. 1343–1400). Generally acknowledged as the greatest English poet before the age of Shakespeare, Chaucer (because of the satirical elements in the *Canterbury Tales*) has sometimes been taken to be of a disposition personally hostile to religion. It is more likely, however, that his anticlerical jibes in that great classic of English literature reflect, rather, the characteristic, general sentiment, and attitude of people in his time toward the Church: an attitude which from other sources is known to have been ready to ridicule its prevalent corruption.

Chemnitz, Martin (1522–1586). Lutheran divine. He defended the Lutheran Reformation and consolidated its teachings and practices after Luther's death. His works include his *Loci Communes* (1553) and his *Loci Theologici* (1591).

Cherubicon. A hymn sung in the Eastern Church at the Great Entrance.

Cherubim. The Bible gives this name, which is a Hebrew plural, to an order of angels who guard the Lord, e.g., Ezekiel 28.14. In Christian tradition they are accounted the second of the nine orders of angels, ranking immediately below the seraphim.

Chester Beatty Papyri. In 1931 Chester Beatty acquired a group of papyrus codices, including large portions of several books of the Bible and other literature, some dating from early in the 2nd c. and most of them at least a century

older than the oldest extant manuscripts of the Bible, which are on vellum. Most of Ezekiel is at Princeton University and thirty leaves of Paul are at the University of Michigan.

Chesterton, Gilbert Keith (1874–1936). Literary critic, essayist, poet, and satirist. A convert to the Roman Catholic Church, he defended its theology and practice by the use of his unique paradoxical style. He conveyed the notion, contrary to the fashion of men of letters of his day, that it is the opponents of Christian orthodoxy who are unimaginative, dull, and estranged from the vitality of the human spirit, while its champions are those who see reality with clarity and as the apostles of common sense. Such a theme he developed in *Heretics* (1905) and *Orthodoxy* (1908), but it runs through much of his writing on ostensibly profane subjects. He wrote on Dickens, Shaw, Stevenson, and other literary giants as readily as he did on Francis of Assisi. He wrote mysteries such as *The Man Who Knew Too Much* (1922) and a series of detective stores in which a seemingly simple, unostentatious priest is the perceptive sleuth. He was also a formidable polemical journalist ready to pillory whatever he took to be hypocrisy or cant in the Establishment. Yet he could be fair and judicial as a critic, as when he stated the case for Swinburne, a poet whose views on religion and life were diametrically opposed to his own. His poems alone reflect the spectrum of his talent. *The Secret People*, for instance, which encapsulates the history of England as seen through his eyes, captures the spirit of England with remarkable lyrical power, while his *The New Freethinker* mocks political ambition with robust vigor, as *A Ballade of an Anti-Puritan* ridicules the literary fashion of his age. It might well be argued, moreover, that his *Antichrist*, in which he mocks the hypocrisy of the future Lord Birkenhead, most famous counsel in England in his day, who had called the proposal to disestablish the Welsh

Church "a bill which has shocked the conscience of every Christian community in Europe," might be the most pungent religious satire in the English language. His *Autobiography* (1936) is historically valuable in providing a vivid picture of the literary, political, and religious scenario of his lifetime. Chesterton, a man of enormous bulk, was also an amusing wit who on one occasion in 1933 claimed to be the politest man in England, being the only one who could rise and offer his place to three ladies.

Chevetogne. A Benedictine community in Belgium founded with the aim of fostering closer relations between the Roman Catholic Church and Eastern Orthodoxy. It publishes a journal called *Irenikon*.

Chichele, Henry (*c.* 1362–1443). Archbishop of Canterbury and founder of All Souls College, Oxford.

Chichester. Ancient English city and a diocese that dates from the 7th c. Lancelot Andrewes was one of its bishops. The cathedral was built in the 12th c.—13th c. A Roman inscription called the "Pudens Stone" (found outside the Town Hall) records the gift of land for a pagan temple.

Chih-I (538–597). Chinese thinker and founder of the important T'ien T'ai school of Buddhism. Born at Chekiang, he was a prominent scholar of his time and much respected. He taught that existence is essentially mental, and that the physical phenomena that constitute what we think of as "real" are in fact illusory. Mind exists in and of itself and the enlightenment attained by those who achieved buddhahood consists in perceiving one's own unity with that mind.

Child Abuse. Reports of violence by parents against their own children have grown so much in recent times that they suggest a pathological condition in sections of modern society such as was absent in former times. No one doubts that child abuse has existed in the past to a greater extent than was reported or recognized; nevertheless, the surge in reported incidence and the horrible features of so many cases do suggest the development of a problem for the Christian moralist of an urgency and a dimension new to our age and that may have some relation to the character and the stress of modern life, particularly in metropolitan societies. Child abuse consists not only of the infliction of severe physical injury but also of any unreasonable deprivation, such as occurs by starvation or gross neglect. What precisely constitutes child abuse is not always easily determined. The law generally recognizes the principle of reasonableness in this as in other matters; i.e., it condones, for example, the infliction of physical punishment (spanking or some form of deprivation) such as is customary in the particular society. Child abuse, however, usually goes far beyond any such discipline and involves the infliction of cruelties such as burning or battering the child's body or causing emotional distress so severe that the child's mental balance is endangered. The Christian ethic although recognizing the right and duty of a parent to chastise a child, if only as a last resort (Proverbs 13.24), must recognize also the duty of all Christians to intervene where the cruel abuse of the parental relationship occurs. Doctors, social workers, and other professional people have plainly a special duty here. Child abuse often arises from psychological disturbances or weaknesses in the parents inflicting it, and doctors and others may have to face making difficult ethical decisions (e.g., to refrain from reporting a case to the police even when the law would seem to call for such action) with a view to averting even worse consequences for the child such as separating the child from his or her parents by having the latter sent to prison and so forcing the child into the care of a state agency or the like, when the rehabilitation of the parent would produce by far the better longterm result for the child. The overriding principle ought always to be the child's welfare and the rights of the child to be treated as an individual and not as a material possession. The importance that Christian faith places on the value of the individual makes this an especially vital concern for Christian judgment. The judgment that is required for such a decision is one that can spring only from a deep spirituality in the person making it.

Chiliasm. See **Millenarianism**, with which this term is synonymously used. It comes from the Greek *chilioi*, a thousand, referring to the thousand years of the reign of Christ before the end of the world.

Chillingworth, William (1602–1644). Anglican divine. So persuaded was he in his youth as a result of a controversy with the Jesuit John Fisher, that he was converted to the Roman Catholic Church and went to Douai in 1630 to study. He returned to England a year later, declaring himself for the Reformation cause. Denying that the Church is in any sense infallible, he emphasized the place of reason in religious inquiry and is famed for his statement that "the Bible only is the religion of Protestants."

Chimere. A sleeveless gown worn by Anglican bishops and by Oxford and Cambridge doctors in divinity.

Chisholm, Roderick M. (1916–   ). American philosopher. Born in North Attleboro, Massachusetts, he was trained at Harvard and taught at the University of Pennsylvania and at Brown. Starting from Brentano's concept of the "intentional inexistence" of the psychical, he maintained that sentences are intentional when they employ substantival expressions in such a way that neither the sentence nor its contradictory can be said to imply the existence or non-existence of that which the sentence predicates. Enabled thus to accept the notion of abstract entities, he

was critical of positivism and behaviorism for their failure to provide for the notion of intentionality that is central to his system. So he defended a realist position in epistemology against a phenomenalist one. His chief writings include *Perceiving* (1957), *Realism and the Background of Phenomenology* (1960), *Theory of Knowledge* (1966), *The Problem of the Criterion* (1973), and (with R. J. Swartz) *Empirical Knowledge* (1973).

Choice. A decision made among alternative possibilities. Choices may be judged good or bad, right or wrong; they are never true or false. The making of choices in a habitual pattern is generally held to tend the individual making them to develop a character according to the choices he habitually makes. Choices cannot be made accidentally; they imply awareness of alternatives, and they require intention, however minimal. The concept of choice is important in theology and the philosophy of religion, since many of the most basic affirmations in religious discourse presuppose authentic human decision: the exercise of choice. See **Freedom.**

Choir. Bodies of singers, men and boys, generally clerics in minor orders, were used in the liturgy as early as the 4th c. By the 6th c. the Schola Cantorum was functioning. Traditionally, cassock and surplice are worn by choristers. The term "choir" is also used to designate that part of the church building to the east of the nave that is set apart for the clergy and choir.

Choir Monks and Nuns. Those members of a religious Order whose functions include the daily recitation of the Divine Office in choir, contradistinguished from lay brothers and lay sisters who are so designated.

Chorepiscopus. In the early Church chorepiscopi, who were very common in the 4th c., especially in Asia Minor, were bishops in rural areas whose functions were in several ways much restricted. The chorepiscopus was in effect a sort of assisting bishop empowered to do only what the diocesan authorized him to do. The Council of Laodicaea in that century and further conciliar enactments forbade or discouraged the appointment of chorepiscopi. The term survives in the Eastern Orthodox Church as an honorary title sometimes used in the patriarchate of Antioch. They existed also in the West in the earlier Middle Ages, where, however, they had disappeared by c. 1200.

Chrism. The oil used in liturgical functions. See **Oils, Holy.** The small vessel used for storing the various holy oils is sometimes called a christmatory.

Christ. The Greek word *christos* means the "Anointed One." (See **Messiah.**) Its use by the disciples of Jesus after the Resurrection to designate their Master was no doubt a cause of their being commonly called "Christians." The name "Christian" was first used by non-followers, according to Acts 11.26, at Antioch, c. 40 CE. The term seems not to have been used by the followers themselves and was apparently used by others more as a nickname, as "Quaker" was used much later of members of the Society of Friends. It was then adopted eventually as a means of distinguishing members of the Church from those outside it. Christians did at a very early stage, however, refer to themselves as being "of the Way," the Way being of course the Way of salvation through the Risen Christ.

Christadelphians. This body, founded by John Thomas, an American, in mid-19th c., claims to have returned to the belief and practice of the primitive Christians. They are pacifist and teach that Christ will return to set up a theocracy throughout the earth, focused in Jerusalem. They teach spiritual rebirth through immersion and renounce the structure and many traditional doctrines, e.g., the Trinity.

Christian Science. This movement, founded by Mrs. Mary Baker Eddy (1821–1910), born in New Hampshire, teaches that mind is the only reality and that illness, pain, and death itself are the results of wrong thinking. Christian Scientists are opposed to the treatment of illness by the medical profession or by any means that fail to recognize the unreality of matter. The founder's book, *Science and Health* (1875), which was from the first highly successful, is the classic exposition of Christian Science teaching. The first 'Church of Christ, Scientist' was founded in Boston in 1879. The movement is now very widespread, especially in the English speaking world. Simple services are held, but the emphasis is on the reading of *Science and Health* and the application of its teaching to the healing of disease. Although the movement has something in common with spiritual healing as widely practiced by many Christians and others, its undergirding outlook on mind-body is generally accounted too simplistic.

Christian Socialism. The name given to a movement for social reform that was expounded by some leading English churchmen in the mid-19th c. in reaction to the tendency of the English Church of that time to ignore social problems. Maurice and Kingsley were among its leaders. It played some part in the development of the trade union movement.

Christian Year, The. This term is used of the liturgical year of the Church, which begins with the first Sunday in Advent. A collection of poems by John Keble, published in 1827, which had much vogue in the 19th c., bears this title.

Christina of Sweden, Queen (1626–1689). Having succeeded in infancy to the throne of Sweden, she was well educated in history and political theory as well as in philosophy and languages and eventually became a notable royal patron of learning and scholarship at home and abroad. She abdicated the Swedish throne in 1654 for several reasons, prominent among which was her interest in the Roman Catholic Church, into which she was received in November of the following year. She died at Rome, leaving a splendid collection of theological and other manuscripts, now in the Vatican Library. She also left some writings of her own, in admirable French. She was indubitably a remarkable woman of intellectual gifts that were widely acknowledged and were admired by many of the greatest men of her day, including men as diverse as Descartes and Milton.

Christmas. Along with Easter, Christmas is one of the two greatest festivals of the Christian Year. The date, December 25, seems not to have been specifically mentioned till the year 336 and was probably selected to supplant the *Natalis Solis Invicti,* an old Roman festival attended by much merrymaking, some of the spirit of which has been carried on to accompany the celebration of Christmas. The conventional date is almost, though not quite, universally accepted. (The Armenians used the date January 6.) The historic date of the birth of Jesus is unknown and was the subject of some speculation in the early Church.

Christology. The study of the nature and work of Jesus Christ. It is an important and highly controversial area of Christian theology, dealing with many widely divergent points of view, especially about the Incarnation and the divinity and humanity of Jesus. See **Incarnation, Kenosis, Monophysitism, Monothelitism,** and **Hypostatic Union.**

Christopher. The name given to a saint widely popular as patron and protector of travelers. Nothing is known of him historically and he probably never existed. A beautiful legend is attached to him, representing him as a very strong man who wished to serve someone stronger than himself but could never find one. He obtained employment in carrying people across a river and was so strong that he could carry any of

them, however weighty the burden. One day a little child asked to be ferried across. Christopher threw him on his shoulders and waded into the river only to discover that the child seemed to be so heavy that by the time Christopher reached the middle of the river he was so bent that he almost drowned and begged the child to help him, whereupon the child suddenly grew so light that Christopher was able to ford the rest of the river even more easily than was his usual habit. Then as he put the child down on the other side, he perceived that he had been carrying the Christ Child and with him the burden of the entire world, which had been taken away as soon as he had called for the child's help. In the Ambrosian rite of the Roman Catholic Church a feast is observed on January 7, called Christophoria, which commemorates the carrying of Christ during the return from Egypt (Matthew 2.21), but there is no evidence of any connection between this and the Christopher legend.

Chromatius. A late 4th c. scholar and Bishop of Aquileia in Northern Italy. He mediated between Jerome and Rufinus in a dispute over Origen and is one of the most learned Christians of his age.

Chrysogonus. This saint, whose name has been traditionally included in the Canon of the Roman Mass, is historically obscure. He was venerated at Rome, however, from at least the 5th c. According to legend, he became a victim of the persecution under Diocletian and was killed at Aquileia.

Chrysostom, John (*c.* 347–407). Patriarch of Constantinople and one of the most celebrated preachers of his time as well as one of the greatest of biblical expositors in the Christian Church, despite the literalistic tendencies in his exposition. His forthrightness and candor, combined with his irreproachable life and personal sanctity, inspired resentment among certain powerful people of his time, including Theophilus and the Empress Eudoxia. Most unjustly deposed from office in 404, he was (despite warm support from both the people of Constantinople and the Pope) banished and so ill treated that he died.

Chrystostom, Liturgy of St. The form of liturgy generally used in the Eastern Orthodox Church is so called although, at least in its present form, it is of much later date than Chrysostom. Its connection with him, if there be one at all, is obscure. The authorship of the prayer traditionally ascribed to him and used at the end of the Anglican service of Morning Prayer is unknown.

Chuang Tzu (4th c. BCE). Taoist philosopher who had considerable influence on the development of both Taoism and of Zen. He taught that all knowledge is relative in such a way that two apparently contradictory statements can both be true, since neither expresses the whole truth. He saw in nature a continuous flux within which, however, is a cosmic oneness. One achieves an understanding of all this by relating oneself to the Tao: a process that entails tranquillity of spirit that opens oneself to this oneness. The One, the Tao, had its origin in non-being. The One divides into yin and yang, producing all things through motion and rest. He who achieves relation to the Tao transcends the changing world by going beyond it to its inner principle.

Chu Hsi. (1130–1200). Confucian thinker. Born at Anhui, he spent his life mainly as a temple guardian, attaining great importance in Chinese and other oriental thought. His arrangement of the Confucian classics was used in the world-famous Chinese system of civil service examinations from 1313 till the beginning of the 20th c. According to Chu Hsi, a principle lies behind everything, the Great Ultimate. But a principle must be actualized, and this actualization requires, besides the indispensable principle, a material force, so

that there is both what in the language of Western thought might be called the universal and the particular. Chu Hsi also emphasized the ancient Confucian concept of *jen,* interpreting it in a novel way. In dealing with the problem of the One and the Many (historically a basic problem in both Eastern and Western thought), he used both the yin-yang principle and that of the Great Ultimate. The principle remains constant and is absolute; its manifestations are incalculable and relative. Since mind is directly related to the Great Ultimate, whole and physical objects are more indirectly related to it, mind is superior to the rest of nature. This view entails a very serious attention to the role of the human mind in achieving both its own clarity and the individual's proper ethical relation to other individuals.

Church. The Greek word *ekklēsia* (Latin *ecclesia*) was used in ordinary secular discourse of any assembly, chiefly of an assembly of self-governing citizens. It is used in the Septuagint of the assembly of Israel, i.e., the people of the covenant contradistinguished from foreigners. It is first used in a Christian sense in Acts 5.11. The term seems plainly to have been used at a very early date by Greek-speaking Christians. What the early Christians thought was the nature of the Church is less certain, but there is no doubt that the concept of a carefully organized and structured institution was developed soon and that the unity of the Church was accounted important. The Church, moreover, was soon seen to embrace both the faithful on earth and those who had gone beyond the veil of death and were conjoined in Christ with the visible Church. Any attempt to divide the Church was regarded as a grievous sin; hence the gravity with which the great schism between East and West in 1054 was regarded, with each side claiming to be the Church and holding the other to be in schism. The Reformation did not in the least diminish the importance of the concept of the Church. Nevertheless, in contrast to the traditional Roman Catholic view, which, acknowledging the Bible as having the highest authority among the documents available to the Church, claimed that it is within the custodianship of the Roman Catholic Church, which has the sole right to interpret it, the Reformation Fathers taught that the Church is under the authority of the Bible. Generally speaking, the Reformation was at least as much about the nature of the Church as it was about the Bible. The movement had come about partly as a biblical renaissance but even more as an attempt, when all else had failed after more than a century of effort on the part of the learned to bring about much needed reform in a more peaceable way, to purify the Church while preserving what was essential in its traditions and structure. Opinion varied, however, so that some of the forms that the Reformation took were more traditional and conservative, while others were much more revolutionary. The Lutheran form was in some respects much inclined to conservative attitudes. The English Reformation was such that while the Reformers' theological ideas much influenced the learned, the sense of the continuity of the *ecclesia anglicana* as the same institution before and after the Reformation was very strong in the English Church and prevailed despite the protests of the more extreme among the Puritan party. Nevertheless, the recognition that the "True Church," although reflected in some way in the visible Church on earth, is in the last resort invisible and "known only to God" is what has more than anything else been the dominant insight of the heirs of the Reformation and is now shared by some members of the Roman Catholic Church too.

Church Army. See **Carlile, Wilson.**

Church Union. An Anglican society for the purpose of promoting the ideals of the Anglo-Catholic party in the Church of England.

Church Unity Octave. See **Couturier, Paul.**

Churchwardens. In the Anglican communion a churchwarden is appointed by the rector or other incumbent and another by the parishioners. The duties include assisting the incumbent in promoting the spiritual welfare of the parish and in keeping the church property in good order.

Ciborium. A vessel, similar in shape to a chalice but with a lid. It is used to hold the consecrated hosts for the Eucharist.

Cicero, Marcus Tullius (106–43 BCE). Roman philosopher. Although his thought notably reflects Stoic influence, he made use of virtually all the great schools of Greek philosophy. He is noted for the exemplary grace and felicity of his literary style, which he used with much effect in urging a moderate view of everything, avoiding fanaticism of every kind. Likewise, he opposed revolutionary uprisings. Essentially a conservative politically, he sought a progressive development of society and deplored violence as self-defeating. Behind such views lay his profound belief in a divine Being at the heart of the universe, a Being who has established a natural law (see **Jus naturale**) that lies beneath and is the source of all good human ethics and legislation.

Cimabue. Late 13th c. Florentine painter. Dante in the *Purgatorio* attests his fame, which is such that a 16th c. Italian art historian credits him with having taught Giotto. Little, however, is known of his life. Among the paintings attributed to him are several at Assisi and a Madonna and Child in the Louvre.

Cincture. A white cord worn to gird the alb. The Latin word is *cingulum*. In English the word "girdle" is traditionally used for this liturgical article. It is one of the six eucharistic vestments.

The others are: chasuble, stole, maniple, amice, and alb.

Circumcision. The Torah or Law of Moses prescribes the circumcision of male children (Genesis 17.21; Exodus 12.48), and the practice was so identified with Judaism that the term even came to be used as a synonym for the Jewish people. (Paul so uses it in Romans 3.30 and elsewhere.) The practice, which consists of the removal of the foreskin, has been used from time immemorial in many parts of the world, e.g., among African tribes and in Asia, Australia, and elsewhere. The Jews, however, who perform it on the eighth day of life, invest it with special significance as a mark of their unique relation to God. The Christian Church was at first divided on whether Christians should follow the practice along with the rest of the requirements of the Law of Moses. Paul's view that it is optional for Christians and in any case useless except to the extent that it is accompanied by inner cleansing of the heart, prevailed, so that the practice was abandoned soon after Christianity had spread to the Gentile world. (An exception is the Ethiopic Church, where male infants are circumcised before they are baptized.) In Europe and Britain, outside of Jewry, tradition has been against circumcision, so that only a very small percentage of non-Jewish males are circumcised, while in the USA the practice is widespread. The reason usually adduced is a medical one: the operation is believed to make personal hygiene easier and thus reduce the incidence of penile cancer in later life and of cervical cancer in the wives of circumcised men. Evidence for this is by no means conclusive, however, since in some societies in which circumcision is not practiced the incidence of such forms of cancer are rarer than in societies that do practice it. Ethically, therefore, the practice would seem to be justified only for religious reasons or where special medical conditions warrant it.

Circumcision, Feast of the. The liturgical commemoration of the Circumcision of Jesus dates from the 6th c. It is held on January 1, except in the Armenian Church, which observes it on January 13. The date is conventional, but the Jewish custom was for the child to be circumcised on the eighth day after birth, and this was done in the case of Jesus, according to Luke 2.21.

Circumincession. See **Perichoresis,** also **Trinity.**

Cistercian Order. In 1098, Robert of Molesme with some others founded at Cîteaux, Burgundy, France, a monastic house in the Benedictine tradition but more rigorous and severe in its interpretation of Benedictine discipline than any other Benedictine house in existence at the time. In 1112, Bernard of Clairvaux became a novice there, eventually becoming its most notable member. So rapidly did the Order spread that within a century of its founding there were more than 500 of its abbeys scattered throughout Western Europe. The Cistercians emphasized manual labor as an important part of the daily round of work and prayer. The furnishings of the abbey and even the abbey church were to be austere and simple, reflecting the spirit of piety that gave the Order its character and appeal. The houses were built in secluded areas with land to develop, and soon the monks became famed for their farming skills and achievements, while at the same time being noted for their ideal of a life of constant prayer and adoration of God, whether laboring in the fields or singing the Office in choir. Although each abbey operated independently of the others, it was annually visited by the abbot of the mother house. The Cistercian spirit considerably influenced other Orders too, such as the Premonstratensians. By the 17th c., however, the Cistercians had for the most part lost their primitive fervor, although a considerable number of their houses, especially in France, continued to uphold the original ideals. These were called abbeys of the Strict Observance, contradistinguished from those of the Common Observance, which by that time had become far more numerous. The abbeys following the Strict Observance came to be influenced by the monks of the abbey of Notre-Dame de la Trappe, which by *c.* 1500 had fallen far from the Cistercian ideals but by the later part of the 17th c. had been drastically reformed by the remarkable abbot, Armand-Jean de Rancé, providing along with Cîteaux, a focus for Cistercians of the Strict Observance, now commonly called Trappists. See **Trappists**. See also **Rancé, Armand-Jean le Bouthillier de** and **Bernard of Clairvaux**. In contrast to the Benedictines, popularly called "the Black Monks" because their habit is entirely black, the Cistercians, whose habit is white, were traditionally known as "the White Monks."

Citta. This important term in Buddhist usage may be translated "consciousness" or "mind." In Mahāyāna Buddhism it is generally used as a synonym for *vijñāna*. It is believed to pertain to all entities superior to vegetable life. Every citta (i.e., every momentary state of consciousness) is characterized by pleasure, indifference, or pain, and gathers up karma.

Civiltà Cattolica. A periodical published by the Jesuits in Italy.

Clapham Sect. In the latter part of the 18th c., a small group of Anglican churchmen were so called because most of its members lived near Clapham. They represented the Evangelical party of the English Church and sought to stir the Church into action by urging the abolition of the slave trade and by encouraging missionary work abroad. Because they were for the most part men of position and wealth, they exerted considerable influence on popular opinion and on legislation.

Clapton Sect. A group of Anglican churchmen representing the party in the English Church popularly called "High Church" who met at Clapton, England, early in the 19th c., at the home of their leader, Joshua Watson.

Clare (1194–1253). Inspired by the preaching and teaching of Francis of Assisi, she renounced all her property and sought to join him at the Portiuncula. He set up a community of the women who wished to follow the Franciscan way, and Clare was installed as abbess in 1215. So by Francis and Clare was founded the Order of Poor Clares, following as closely as possible the rule of the Franciscan Order. (See **Poor Clares**.) She was canonized in 1255.

Clarke, Samuel (1675–1729). Anglican divine. Born at Norwich, England, and educated at Cambridge, he was influenced by Isaac Newton and, although to some extent critical of the Deism fashionable in his day, he leaned in that direction and toward Unitarian ideas. Appointed Rector of St. James's, Piccadilly, in 1709, he engaged in the controversies of his time, e.g., by his *Scripture-Doctrine of the Trinity* (1712). He corresponded with Leibniz on space and time.

Clarkson, Thomas (1760–1846). Educated at Cambridge, he made the abolition of the slave-traffic his life's work. With W. Wilberforce and some prominent Quakers, he formed a political lobby in 1787. In 1807 they achieved the abolition of the slave traffic and in 1833 the emancipation of the slaves. His writings include *History of the Rise, Progress, and Accomplishment of the African Slave Trade by the British Parliament* (2 vols., 1808). He did not confine his campaign to the British Empire. He sought to promote his cause in France and other European countries too, and his success in changing British legislation indubitably played an important part in the circumstances leading later to the constitutional amendment in the United States in 1865 that abolished slavery there. See **Slavery**.

Clauberg, Johannes (1622–1665). German Occasionalist and among the first to introduce the term "ontology" to the vocabulary of philosophy.

Claudel, Paul Louis Charles (1868–1955). Born at Villeneuve-sur-Fin, he underwent a religious conversion at the age of 18. He had a distinguished diplomatic career, eventually becoming French Ambassador to Japan in 1921. His plays and poems exhibit a profoundly sensitive understanding of the spiritual significance of Christian life and are of a quality unsurpassed in the Christian poetry and drama of his age. Among his plays are his *L'Annonce faite à Marie* (1912) and *Le Soulier de Satin* (1929). His poems include his *Un poète regarde la Croix* (1938).

Claudianus Mamertius. A 5th c. Christian philosopher. Born near Lyons, he was influenced, as had been Augustine, by Neoplatonism: an influence reflected in his *De Statu Animae* (467–472).

Claudius. Early 9th c. theologian and biblical commentator. Despite the originality of some of his views, accounted heretical by many of his contemporaries, he became Bishop of Turin.

Clausura. The cloister, i.e., that part of a monastery or convent from admission to which members of the opposite sex are excluded.

Clayton, John (1709–1773). One of the members of the Holy Club founded by the Wesleys.

Clement of Alexandria (*c.* 150–*c.* 215). Christian Gnostic philosopher and theologian. Born probably at Athens, he studied Christian theology and philosophy, was a student under Pantaenus at Alexandria whom he succeeded in 190. Clement was one of the greatest Christian theologians of his age. Deeply influenced by Gnosticism, he perceived the impoverishment of Christian thought by what he took to be the loss of its insights, which he tried to conserve in his own thinking as a Christian. His form of Christian Gnosticism is based upon a profound regard for the apostolic faith, which he regarded as an indispensable step on the way to the Christian illumination that brings authentic knowledge of God. He taught with Paul that God became man in the Person of Christ in order that man might attain immortality through him. He saw spiritual ignorance as a greater obstacle to full salvation than any moral transgression. He was among the first to see hope for all men and women, however depraved, and to recognize that human destiny may be attained in many different forms and in many degrees of blessedness. He was succeeded at Alexandria by the great Origen.

Clement of Rome. A 1st c. Bishop of Rome. It is possible, although no hard evidence is available, that he is the Clement to whom allusion is made in Philippians 4.3. The letter known as I Clement was written by him *c.* 96 in an attempt to bring back peace to the Church in Corinth, where strife had arisen. This letter was held in very high regard in the Church, and it is remarkable indeed that it was not eventually included in the New Testament canon as it has come down to us. For other letters and writings attributed to Clement of Rome, see **Clementine Literature, The.**

Clement VII, Pope (1478–1534). A cousin of Pope Leo X and the son of Giuliano de' Medici, he quickly attained eminence in the Church and in 1523 succeeded Hadrian VI in the papacy. His reign was marked by indecision and intrigue, as is suggested by his procrastination on the subject of divorce sought by Henry VIII from Catherine of Aragon. Worse still was his reluctance or inability to secure the kind of ecclesiastical reform within the Church that might have averted the need for the Protestant Reformation. He was nevertheless, as was the tradition of the Medici family, a great patron of art.

Clement XIV (1695–1774). The son of a surgeon near Rimini, he entered the Franciscan Order in 1723 and in 1769 was elected to the papacy after a controversial election, for the Bourbon courts seem to have been resolved to secure the election of a pope who would have the Jesuits suppressed. His reign was marked by a good deal of irresolution, but in 1773, by his Brief *Dominus ac Redemptor,* he did suppress that great Order, giving no reason other than that they had introduced controversy and disquiet into the Church and had evoked opposition. His action did nothing in the long run to enhance papal prestige.

Clementine Literature, The. Besides the authentic letter by Clement of Rome, known as I Clement, many writings were ascribed to him, which scholars generally regard as spurious. They contain much that is mere legend.

Clementines. A collection of decretals issued by Pope Clement V and containing such documents issued by various popes. They were eventually promulgated by Pope John XXII in 1317 and became part of canon law.

Clerical Disabilities Act. Clergy of the Church of England incur, by their clerical status, certain disabilities that other citizens may enjoy, e.g., they are ineligible for election to Parliament, and they cannot be admitted to the Bar. An Act of Parliament passed in 1870 enabled a cleric to renounce his clerical status through a carefully arranged procedure. Later legislation by the English Church made it possible for a clergyman who had so renounced his clerical status to recover it in certain cases.

Clerics Regular. Societies of priests living a disciplined life under the threefold vow of poverty, chastity, and obedience are so called in contradistinction to monks, canons regular, and friars. Monks are not necessarily priests and are attached to a particular house (abbey or other monastery) for life. Canons

regular, although primarily priests, live much like monks. Friars emerged in the thirteenth century with a more mobile structure that enabled them to go on short notice wherever they might be sent and with a more democratic constitution than that of the ancient monastic orders. Clerics regular take the same vows as monks and friars but are primarily priests. The most notable example is that of the Jesuits.

Clermont, Council of. This council had as its principal aim the planning of the First Crusade. It met in 1095 and, besides its primary purpose, it made certain reforms. It also made a pilgrimage to Jerusalem of such merit as to relieve the pilgrim of the necessity of doing any other penances.

Clifford, John (1836–1923). English Baptist who championed the cause of the laboring classes in England. He was theologically more open than was usual among Baptists of his generation in England. He became President of the Baptist World Alliance.

Clitheroe, Margaret (c. 1556–1586). English Roman Catholic martyr. A butcher's wife in York, she was arrested and charged with having harbored Roman Catholic priests. In order to avoid having her children forced to testify against her, she declined to plead, whereupon she was most cruelly tortured by having three hundredweights of stones pressed down on her. Before she died she is said to have uttered the Triune Name of God, crying out that she suffered for him. See the poem by Gerard Manley Hopkins, *Margaret Clitheroe.*

Cloister. See **Clausura.**

Clotilde, Queen (474–545). A Burgundian princess by birth, she married King Clovis of the Franks, whom she eventually converted to the Christian faith. After her husband's death she retired to the Abbey of St. Martin.

Cloud of Unknowing, The. See **Unknowing, The Cloud of.**

Clovis, King (*c.* **466–511**). After becoming King of the Salian Franks in 481, he conquered large areas, and after his conversion to Christianity he attacked Alaric, King of the Goths, who was an Arian, defeating him at Vouillé in 507. Extremely able and plainly ruthless, he did much to prepare the way for the founding of France as a nation.

Cluniac Order. The Abbey of Cluny had become, by the early 10th c., an exemplar of the great ideals of Benedict and, especially after Odo, its abbot during that time, it had become so admired that many monasteries in southern France and in Italy undertook reforms with Cluny as the model. Manual labor was 'diminished and greater emphasis was placed on liturgical splendor and personal spirituality. By the mid-12th c., there were some thousand Cluniac houses. Their aim was to return to the primitive ideas of Benedict as they interpreted them (in some respects in the opposite direction of the Cistercian interpretation), and they emphasized efficient organization and administration. At the zenith of their influence in the 12th c. they commanded widespread admiration among the parish clergy and others.

Coadjutor. The term is derived from the Latin *con* + *adjutare* (to help with). (Although the accent may be placed on either the second or third syllable, the second is to be preferred.) A bishop appointed to assist a diocesan bishop. In contrast to a suffragan, who has no implied right of succession, a coadjutor generally has that right or expectation.

Cocceius, Johannes (**1603–1669**). Dogmatic theologian. Of German birth, he studied in Holland and eventually became a theological professor at Leyden. Although nominally a Calvinist, he deviated from the strict Calvinist orthodoxy of his time, teaching a system that came to be known as *Föderaltheologie* and laid the ground for the development of Pietism. His writings include his *Summa doctrinae de Foedere et Testamento Dei* (1648).

Cochlaeus, Johann (**1479–1552**). German humanist, prominent in Reformation controversies. Having graduated at Cologne and at Ferrara, he was ordained priest at Rome. He became a canon of Mainz in 1526, later a canon of Meissen, and finally a canon of Breslau in 1539, where eventually he died. He was an extremely bitter critic of Luther and of the Reformation movement in general.

Codex Alexandrinus. One of the most important manuscripts of the Greek Bible, it dates from the early 5th c. and was the gift of Cyril Lukar to King James I, although the manuscript reached England only in 1627, after the King's death. In 1757 it came to the British Museum. It includes the first letter of Clement of Rome and also another attributed to him. Unfortunately, it came too late to England to be used by the panels of scholars who translated the Bible into the version done at the instigation of King James and published in 1611. Its origin is not clear, but it seems likely that it came from Mount Athos. The shorthand symbol for it used by biblical scholars is the letter A.

Codex Amiatinus. The oldest extant manuscript of the Vulgate Bible, it was written near Durham, England (either at Jarrow or Wearmouth) in the last decade of the 7th c. From sometime between 800 and 1000 it was in the monastery of Monte Amiata; hence its name. In 1752 it was passed to the Laurentian Library, Florence. This manuscript was actually used by the revisers of the Vulgate for the Sixtine edition published at Rome, 1590. It remains a primary instrument for the scholarly study of the Vulgate text.

Codex Bezae Cantabrigiensis. A 5th c. manuscript of the Gospels and the Book of Acts, belonging to the Western textual family, of which it is the principal representative. It was presented by T. Beza to the University of Cambridge (hence its name) in 1581. Its origin is obscure, except that it was almost certainly written in the West. That some of its variants suggest a *theologically* anti-Judaic tendency on the part of the scribe is argued by E. J. Epp, *The Theological Tendency of Codex Bezae Cantabrigiensis in Acts* (Cambridge U. P., 1966). Biblical scholars designate this codex by the symbol D. At the time of the copying of this codex, two other copies were made and fragments of one of these, discovered early in the 20th c., are preserved in the British Museum.

Codex Ephraemi. A 5th c. Greek manuscript of the Bible, which in the 12th c. was made into a palimpsest by superimposing on it some writings by Ephraem Syrus (hence its name), which had to be subsequently removed.The text is therefore not always entirely readable. It is nevertheless one of the most important among extant biblical manuscripts. Scholars designate it by the symbol E. It is the property of the Bibliothèque Nationale, Paris.

Codex Sinaiticus. A 4th c. manuscript of the Greek Bible and one of the most important of all biblical manuscripts, it was discovered in the 19th c. in the monastery of St. Catherine on Mount Sinai by Constantin Tischendorf, while he was rummaging in trash baskets there. The history of its discovery and subsequent adventures (a romantic one) is reported in detail in standard works on the transmission of the Bible. Eventually coming into the possession of the Russian Tsar, it passed at the Bolshevik Revolution of 1917 to the Soviet Government, which sold it to the British Museum for £100,000 (at that time only about half a million U.S. dollars). It contains, in addition to the Bible, all of the Epistle of Barnabas and some of Hermas. Along with the Codex Vaticanus, whose text of the New Testament

it closely resembles, it is the principal representative of the Neutral text. It is known to scholars by the symbol א (the letter Aleph in Hebrew).

Codex Vaticanus. A 4th c. manuscript of the Greek Bible, it is one of the greatest treasures of the Vatican Library, where (except for a brief period when it was taken by Napoleon as a prize of war, studied in Paris and then returned to the Vatican) it has been since at least 1475 and probably much earlier. Its origin is unknown, but most scholars argue for its having been written in Alexandria. It is known to scholars by the symbol B. It is along with Codex Sinaiticus, the principal representative of the Neutral text.

Coenobitic. This adjective is used to designate the life of a monk or nun who lives in community, in contrast to eremitic, used to describe that of a hermit or of a monk or nun whose life is to a large extent solitary rather than communal. Examples of the latter are the Camaldoli and the Carthusians.

Cogito Ergo Sum. From this axiom, which means "I am thinking, therefore I exist," Descartes developed his rationalistic system of explanation. In attempting to doubt my existence I fail at once in the enterprise, since my doubting proves my act of thinking to be in progress, and if I am thinking I must exist. I thereby establish myself as a *res cogitans*, a "thinking thing," a self. See **Descartes, René.**

Cognition. From the Latin *cognoscere*, "to know," this term means "the act of knowing."

Coke, Thomas (1747–1814). Along with Francis Asbury, one of the two first superintendents (bishops) of the Methodist Church in the United States.

Coleridge, Samuel Taylor (1772–1834). Poet and religious thinker. Born in Devon and educated at Cambridge, he met Wordsworth and in 1798 published, with him, the *Lyrical Ballads*, which include his poem *The Ancient Mariner.* Besides his literary gifts, he had a deeply religious sense. Having been in his youth inclined to Unitarianism, he became attracted to pantheistic philosophies such as those of Spinoza and Boehme. Goethe also appealed to him. He was affected by many diverse intellectual influences, including Schelling and Voltaire. Heterodox from almost any Christian standpoint of his day, he pleaded for an openness among Christians to every movement of the human spirit, humanistic and scientific.

Colet, John (*c.* **1467–1519**). Born in London, where his father had been Lord Mayor, he went to Paris in 1493 where, and in Italy, he studied law and learned Greek, becoming acquainted with Erasmus and with the teachings of Savonarola. In 1496, he returned to Oxford, was ordained, and began teaching there, using novel methods rather than the traditional scholastic ones, much impressing Erasmus when the latter visited him at Oxford in 1498. He became Dean of St. Paul's Cathedral, London, and re-founded St. Paul's School. The clergy of his time regarded him as a heretic, but he was never prosecuted. Thomas More was among his friends and he preached at Wolsey's installation as cardinal.

Coligny, Gaspard de Chatillon (1519–1572). Huguenot leader. Of very aristocratic ancestry, he was converted to Calvinism, secretly protected many of the Huguenots in France and, after the death of the Prince de Condé, he became the acknowledged leader of the movement. Catherine de' Medici tried to have him assassinated and, having failed, instigated the notorious Massacre of St. Bartholomew, in which he was killed.

Collation. Traditionally, on days of fasting, one full meal is allowed, called the *comestio*, and in the evening a light one, called a *collatio.*

Collect. A form of prayer developed in the earliest Latin Sacramentaries (the Leonine, Gelasian, and Gregorian) and used extensively in the West. The basic form of the collect, usually a crisply short and carefully structured prayer, consists of an invocation (e.g., "Almighty God" or "Eternal One"), followed by a brief petition, then concluding with words such as "through Christ our Lord" or an ascription of glory to the Triune God.

Collegiality. The term *collegium* (college) was used of bishops corporately by Cyprian in the 2nd c. The concept has been central in the "conciliarist," contradistinguished from the "papalist" party in the struggles between Pope and Council. According to the collegialist view of the episcopate, bishops constitute a body; they are not merely individuals. See **Vatican Council, The Second.**

Collegiate Church. A church that is endowed with a chapter consisting of a dean and a body of canons (e.g., Westminster Abbey), yet, not being the seat of a bishop, is not a cathedral.

Colletines. A branch of the Order of Poor Clares founded by Colette and now represented principally in France. Colette was canonized in 1807.

Collingwood, Robin George (1889–1943). Oxford philosopher, who in his later work saw religion, science, history, and philosophy, as each limited aspects of the truth. He saw philosophy as bringing to light the basic presuppositions of thought in this or that period of history. He was much influenced by Croce. His writings include *Speculum Mentis* (1924), *Essay on Philosophical Method* (1933), *An Essay on Metaphysics* (1940), and *The Idea of History* (1946).

Collins, Anthony (1676–1729). English Deist. Born in Middlesex and educated at Eton and Cambridge, he was a friend of John Locke and much influenced by him. He wrote extensively in vigorous protest against traditional doctrines of the Church such as the inspiration of the Bible and the immortality of the soul, expounding instead a radical freedom of thought governed only by the principle of reason. His chief work is *A Discourse of Freethinking* (1713).

Collyridians. A 4th c. sect said to have consisted principally of women and to have originated in Thrace. They are represented as worshipping the Virgin Mary, offering her *collyris* (cakes) in sacrifice, as had been a pagan custom honoring the goddess Ceres.

Cologne. The bishopric of Cologne was founded in the reign of Constantine in the 4th c., if not before it, and had become very important by the 12th c. The cathedral dates partly from the 13th c. Severely damaged in World War II, it has been restored.

Colombini, Giovanni. The 14th c. founder of the Gesuati, a congregation of laymen.

Colonna. A very important Roman family who, between the 12th c. and the 18th c., played a key role in European politics. Although vassals of the Pope, they sided in the Middle Ages with the Ghibelline (i.e., the Imperial) party. Vittoria (1490–1547), a member of this family and its most gifted daughter, was deeply interested in the reform of the Church. A patron of arts and letters, she was instrumental in attracting Michelangelo and other great artists.

Color, Liturgical. The use of colors proper to the season (e.g., violet for Lent, white for Christmas) has been by no means either uniform or universal. It seems to have arisen *c.* 1200 in the West, but the arrangement has varied considerably from place to place, so that what is now commonly regarded as traditional is a much more recent convention, and even that is not universal in the West, while in the East the choice is to a large extent arbitrary, although with a tendency to use bright colors for joyous occasions and others for penitential ones. In the Roman Catholic

Church, since Vatican II, a tendency has arisen to permit parishes to use for the greater festivals whatever are the best vestments they possess, irrespective of color.

Columba (*c.* 521–597). Celtic missionary. Of a noble Irish family, he was trained according to the standards of the day. He founded several monasteries in Ireland. In or about 563, he went to the small island of Iona where, with twelve companions, he established a monastic house to be used as headquarters for his missionary work throughout the neighboring regions. He converted both the king of the Picts and the king of the Scots to the Christian faith. See **Iona.**

Columbanus (*c.* 543–615). Missionary. Born in Ireland, he went to Gaul towards the end of the 6th c. and set up monasteries in the region of the Vosges, where the usages of the Celtic Church, to which he and his monks adhered, caused resentment. He insisted upon them, defending them before a Gallican synod in 603 and at Rome. When his monks were expelled from Burgundy because of the forthrightness of his rebukes of the royal court, they eventually settled in 612 at Bobbio, where their house acquired much repute as a center of learning. See **Bobbio.**

Comenius, Johann Amos (1592–1670). Pioneer in education. Born in Moravia and belonging to the Bohemian Brethren (Moravians), he studied theology at Herborn and Heidelberg, traveled in Holland and England, then became rector of a school. In 1621 he went to Poland where he taught at Lissa. Soon thereafter he became bishop of the Bohemian Brethren. His educational methods were in advance of their day and attracted much attention. He taught languages by conversation and even used pictures in some of his books for children, being probably the first to use this educational tool. In 1638 the Swedish Government invited him to draw up an educational program for its schools. He died in Amsterdam.

Commandments of the Church. The Roman Catholic Church claims the right to impose on all her faithful certain commandments beyond those listed in the Book of Exodus. The number of these commandments or precepts of the Church has varied through the centuries, but according to current practice four are recognized: (1) attendance at Mass on all Sundays and certain other days of the year; (2) observance of such days of fasting as the Church prescribes, which may vary from place to place; (3) making one's confession to a priest once a year at the least; and (4) receiving Holy Communion at least during the Easter season.

Commendam. According to an ancient custom, which led to great abuse in the Church, a benefice might be held *in commendam*, i.e., in trust on a temporary basis. The holder, who might be a layman, received the revenues, although if not a cleric he was barred from performing the duties attached to the benefice. Abuses developed as bishops and others held benefices *in commendam* in addition to their own.

Commodian. Christian Latin poet, probably of the 3rd c.

Common Order, The Book of. A form of liturgy drawn up by John Knox in 1556 for use in the Protestant congregation at Geneva and then appointed by the General Assembly of the Scottish Kirk in 1562 for use in Scotland. Revised in 1564, it continued in use in the Kirk till 1645, when it was replaced by the Westminster Directory. Neither of these was ever intended as a liturgy in the traditional sense but rather as a guide for the conduct of worship. Free prayer within the general parameters of the structure provided was encouraged and expected. These books have long been out of use and have been superseded in the 20th c. by a "Book of Common Order" authorized by the General Assembly of the Kirk for a sim-

ilar purpose, modernized in the sense of reflecting to some extent a somewhat more ecumenical rhythm and style.

Common Prayer, The Book of. See **Book of Common Prayer, The**.

Communicantes. The name given to a section of the Canon of the Roman Mass consisting of a prayer commemorating various saints including the Virgin Mary, Joseph, the Apostles, and several early martyrs.

Communicatio Idiomatum. This phrase (in Greek *antidosis tōn idiōmatōn*) expresses a christological notion proposed by Cyril of Alexandria and some other early Fathers, namely, that although the divine and the human natures of Christ are separate, the attributes of the one nature may be predicated of the other, since they are united in the Person of Christ. This notion, which was accepted as orthodox in the early Church, was developed in an innovative and exaggerated way by some of the Lutheran divines of the 17th c., when Lutheran scholasticism was at its height. They transformed what had been in the early Fathers a recognition of the claim of faith to grasp, through the mystery of the Risen Christ, both the divine and the human, into an elaborate and detailed theory of the mechanism by which this occurs. The result was a ponderous dogmatic structure that in the end lost hold of the simple but penetrating insight of the original idea.

Communion of Saints, The. By this phase is traditionally understood the concept (as theologically important as it is poetically beautiful) that the bond that binds Christians to one another is not confined to those on this side of the veil of death but extends to unite those on either side with the other. The Church consists not only of the Church Militant, as the Church here on earth is called, but also the Church Triumphant in heaven and the Church Expectant in the intermediate or purgatorial state. It includes also all creatures such as angels, as is recognized in the ancient words of the Preface to the Canon of the Mass in which the priest joins "with angels and archangels, and with all the company of heaven," in celebrating the Sacred Mysteries. Thus is recognized the interpenetration of two dimensions of being: a concept apart from which Christian theology cannot make sense from any point of view. (See also **All Saints' Day**.)

Communion Plate. This term is applied to the vessels (usually silver or silver gilt) used for the celebration of the Eucharist, especially when referring to collections of them, such as may be found in the treasury of an ancient abbey or church. The term also occurs in a special, narrow sense in Roman Catholic usage, to denote a small metal plate held under the communicant's chin.

Communion Table. A term preferred by some Protestants to the term "altar," because of the connotation of sacrifice implied in the use of the latter term.

Communion Tokens. Small metal pieces similar in appearance to coins but usually inscribed with a scriptural verse or image such as a chalice and used traditionally in the Scottish Kirk as warrants of the holder's admissibility to Communion. Nowadays, cards usually replace them and the older metal tokens relegated to museums, although the use of the latter may still survive in some remote areas in Scotland and in some Presbyterian churches elsewhere.

Communion Under Both Species. By this phrase is meant the administration of both the consecrated bread and the consecrated wine to the laity. This was a general practice till c. the 12th c., although not universal. The practice of intinction (i.e., the dipping of the bread into the wine) became very common from the 7th c., although from time to time forbidden. By the 13th c., however, the practice of administering the chalice to the laity had virtually vanished, evoking protest in some quarters. (See **Utraquists**.) At the Reformation in the 16th c., the subject became one of

the many that divided the Roman Catholic Church and those of the Reformation way. The latter insisted that Communion must be received under both species, while the Roman Catholic Church contended that Christ is received entire under either kind, and that therefore the administration to the laity of the Host alone is sufficient. Since 1969, however, that Church has provided for certain exceptions for which Communion under both species may be permitted. In the Eastern Orthodox Church the general practice is to administer under both species, but by intinction. In Anglican practice, communion is administered under both species, with intinction as optional. (See **Intinction**.) In Protestant usage, Communion under both species is universal.

Community of the Resurrection. An Anglican religious society founded at Oxford by Charles Gore in 1892. In 1898 it moved to Mirfield, Yorkshire, where it trains candidates for the priesthood. It was intended from the first to be a society for the deepening of the spiritual life of its members and for the revitalizing of the life of the Anglican Communion through the recovery of a deeper sense of its ancient Catholic heritage. The letters "C. R." are used to designate a member.

Comparative Religion. A term used to designate the study of the history, teachings, and practices of the religions of the world in relation to one another. Beyond a study of religious phenomena, which is important in itself, scholars in this field raise questions about the meaning of the doctrines taught by leaders of the religions of the world and about what precisely are differences among them. For example, one may ask questions such as, "If Christian doctrine is true, are the doctrines of other religions false?" and "Has the Christian doctrine of, say, grace a counterpart in, say, Mahāyāna Buddhism and, if so, what restriction if any, must be placed upon their being accounted synonymous?" Through studies of this kind scholars can understand better the riches of their own religious heritage, as, say, a New Yorker who leaves New York to travel the world may be able to understand and appreciate it better than can one who has never left it. (As Kipling asked, "What should they know of England who only England know?")

Compassion. In Hinayana Buddhism, compassion, though a very great virtue, was regarded as secondary to wisdom. In Mahāyāna, however, it is given equal place. Compassion is one of the four "illimitable" virtues. Exemplified *par excellence* in the buddhas and bodhisattvas, it ought to be acquired and practiced by all who aspire to a spiritual life.

Compline. The office recited or sung immediately before retiring for sleep. Although a similar office was used by monks in the East, Compline in the form traditional in the West has its origin in Benedict, who formalized it for the use of his monks. Its content has varied to some extent from age to age and place to place, but its focus has always been that of turning the soul to God as the final act of the day and so composing both soul and body for peaceful sleep by putting oneself entirely in the hands of God, whatever the night may bring.

Complutensian Polyglot. This edition of the Bible, begun in 1502 by the scholarly Spanish cardinal, Francisco Ximénes and edited by scholars at the University of Alcalá that he had founded. For the Old Testament, the Hebrew, Latin (Vulgate), Greek (Septuagint) are printed in parallel columns. The work was printed in six folio volumes and is bibliographically as well as otherwise of great importance. The designation comes from the Latin word (*Complutum*) for Alcalá.

Compostela. A Spanish city traditionally supposed to have been the burial place of the Apostle James. Toward the end of the 11th c. it became the focus of the movement against the Muslims in Spain and it has remained a place of pilgrimage. Santiago de Compostela, situated at the extreme north west of Spain, was famed for its scallops, and pilgrims there brought back scallop shells as souvenirs of their pilgrimage thither, through which association scallop shell became the symbol of Compostela. It is possible that there may be an echo of this association in the poem by Sir Walter Ralegh (Raleigh) (*c.* 1552–1618), entitled *The Pilgrimage*, which contains the lines: "Give me my scallop-shell of quiet,/My staff of faith to walk upon . . . /And thus I'll take my pilgrimage."

Comte, Auguste (1798–1857). Founder of Positivism, which he conceived as a "religion of humanity" to supersede Christianity and to focus on humanity as "the great Being" rather than God. He also sought to move the focus of attention from the state to society. He introduced an elaborate system of devotion, borrowed from Catholic practice, with priests, sacraments, and a calendar in which scientists and scholars would take the place traditionally assigned to saints canonized by the Church. He regarded the improvement of the status of women essential to the progress of society. His *Système de politique positive* appeared in 1822, followed in 1830–42 by his six-volume *Cours de la philosophie positive*.

Concelebration. In contrast to the celebration of the Eucharist by one priest, concelebration is the practice whereby several priests celebrate together. It may have been customary in the early Church, but in the West the practice of celebration by one priest had been general until Vatican II when, in 1963, concelebration became an authorized practice in the Roman Catholic Church and is now quite customary in monastic communities and wherever there are enough priests to make it practicable. It has become common among Anglicans also. In the East a form of concelebration has for long been practiced.

Conceptualism. Central among the controversies of the medieval schoolmen was the problem of the "universals." (See **Universals.**) Two extreme positions were held: realism and nominalism. The realists held that the universal (e.g., "humanity" as opposed to the individual human being, Mary or John) has some kind of reality independent of the mind. (This view had roots in the Platonic tradition.) The nominalists, by contrast, held that the universal is no more than a name, a mere sound used to designate the class of entities to which Mary and John belong, i.e., human beings. It has no existence in itself except as a designation, arbitrarily applied in the mental operation of cataloguing the entities it recognizes. Between these two extremes was a position that has been called "conceptualism," which did not go to either extreme. Nevertheless, there were so many shades both of nominalism and of realism that this middle position tended to be indistinguishable from very moderate forms of realism, on the one hand, and, on the other, from very moderate forms of nominalism.

Conciliarism. Two conflicting opinions were held by the medieval canonists and theologians concerning the locus of supreme authority in the Church. All were agreed that it is vested in Pope *and* Council, meaning by "Council" a General Council of all the bishops of the Church. But what if a pope and such a council were in irreconcilable conflict? Wherein would lie the ultimate authority? The question began to be seriously considered in the 13th c., by which time the papacy was beginning to make extravagant claims. The increase in such claims, the outbreak of the Great Schism in 1378, when rival claimants to the papacy appeared, and other circumstances, made the question no longer a theoretical one. The popes and their entourage predictably argued for the pa-

palist view that the supreme authority in the event of such difficulty resides in the Pope, but a very strong and growing conciliarist party supported by many learned champions, contended that it must in such a case reside in the General Council. Nevertheless, by the 15th c. the debate had, in effect, reached an impasse, and the failure of the conciliarists to achieve what they sought was indubitably a major factor in eventually bringing about the Reformation movement, which the success of conciliarism could have averted. The conciliarist view was still strong at the First Vatican Council, but through the extremely autocratic conduct of Pius IX the papalist view seemed to have won. (See **Vatican Council, The First** and **Gallicanism.**) At Vatican II, however, the collegial concept (see **Collegiality**) strengthened the conciliarist outlook within the Roman Catholic Church, although not to the point of diminishing the unique authority claimed by the papacy.

Conclave. From the Latin, "with a key," the term is used to designate any meeting of the cardinals for official business but more particularly that which is held in the closed apartment in which the College of Cardinals is secluded and locked up against all outside interference and influence during the process of a papal election. The custom dates from the 13th c., when a papal election had not been made during a period of three years. In 1271 this device was introduced to try to expedite the process. It has been followed ever since. The term is also used for the closed apartment itself.

Concomitance. The teaching that Christ is fully present in each of the consecrated species, i.e., in the Host and also in the Chalice. (See **Communion Under Both Species** and **Utraquists.**) It implies that the traditional Roman Catholic practice of administering only the Host to the laity and withholding the Chalice from them is justified.

Concord, The Formula of. This formula is of paramount importance for Lutherans, since it sums up with much precision the orthodox Lutheran stance. It deals with all the principal controversies current at the time. It was published, along with the Apostles', the Nicene, and the Athanasian Creeds, and various Lutheran confessional documents in 1580 as "The Book of Concord." This book, however, although widely supported among Lutherans, did not win universal acceptance among them or the status achieved by the Augsburg Confession. See **Augsburg Confession.**

Concordance. A reference work listing in alphabetical order all the words or principal words as they occur in a particular book or author (e.g., Dante or Shakespeare) with an indication of the passage in which each is found and the canto and line or chapter and verse for ready consultation by the reader. Biblical concordances existed in the Middle Ages, e.g., one for the Vulgate was compiled in 1230 by a team of Dominicans and toward the end of the 15th c. one for the Hebrew Bible was made and published at Venice in 1523. For the English Bible, the concordance compiled by Alexander Cruden in 1737 has remained, in its later editions, the best known and standard tool, as is, for the Greek New Testament, the Moulton-Geden.

Concordat. The agreement reached in July 1801 between Napoleon and Pope Pius VII led to the formal restoration of the Roman Catholic Church in France. The following year, however, the advantages that the Concordat had seemed to assure the Church were considerably diminished. See **Organic Articles, The.**

Concupiscence. By this term theologians in the West have traditionally expressed the human tendency to lust excessively after what are merely material ambitions and ends, investing them with an importance that only spiritual aims can merit. The preoccupation may take the form of power-mania or sex-mania or merely a fondness for sensual pleasure of any kind. Various views have been taken by theologians about its relation to Original Sin (e.g., whether it is a consequence of the latter or sin itself), but all agree that it is an impediment to spiritual development.

Condillac, Etienne (1715–1780). French philosopher. Born in Grenoble and educated at Saint-Sulpice and the Sorbonne, he was ordained priest but devoted his life to philosophical rather than theological pursuits. Largely influenced by Locke, he acquired much recognition in France in his lifetime, becoming tutor to the grandson of Louis XV. In 1768 he was elected to the French Academy. Against Descartes, the great luminary among French thinkers, he denied that there are any innate ideas and, like Locke, he held that all ideas begin in the experience of sensations. Nevertheless, the individual who has the experience makes judgments arising from it, so we must recognize the existence of what is traditionally called the soul. He attached much importance to the concept of habit. Through habit and association we attach signs to things and so gradually weave a network of signs such that our intellects can reason even when the individual things signified are absent. He distinguished three kinds of sign: (1) accidental, (2) natural, and (3) conventional. Conventional signs make possible the development of mathematics. Although one cannot know the external world but only the "private" world of one's own thoughts, one does become aware of one's own body, with its pleasant and unpleasant sensations, and so one comes to infer, from the pressure of external objects upon one's body, the existence of that world external to oneself. Condillac's writings include his *Essays on the Origin of the Human Understanding* (1746), *Treatise on Systems* (1749), *Treatise on Sensations* (1754) and *Course of Study for the Instruction of the Prince of Parma,* 13 volumes (1769–73).

He was one of the Encyclopedists. (See **Encyclopedists**.)

Conditional Immortality. See **Immortality, Conditional.**

Confessio Augustana. See **Augsburg Confession.**

Confession. In Christian usage this term has a variety of meanings. Most commonly it consists of an acknowledgement of sin, made either privately to God with or without the presence of a priest or publicly, either by an individual in presence of an entire congregation (a form of penance now very rare but formerly common both before and after the Reformation) or (most common of all) by a congregation who recite such an acknowledgement together as part of a liturgical service. The term is also used, however, of the profession or statement of faith made by a martyr or confessor, i.e., one who acknowledges his Christian faith in face of persecution. (See **Confessor**.) From this ancient usage springs that of calling the Creeds of the Church (more especially those made by Churches in the Reformation heritage) "confessions," e.g., the Augsburg Confession and the Westminster Confession of Faith. Technically, moreover, the term *confessio* (derived from such usage) is applied to the tomb of a confessor or to the structure connected with it.

Confessional Church. The group of German Evangelical Christians who, in the years immediately before and during the National Socialist regime in Germany, resisted the German Christian Church set up by the Nazis and sponsored by them. In opposition to the latter, Martin Niemöller led a movement out of which emerged the Confessional Church. It was much persecuted. After the defeat of Germany in World War II, the Evangelical Church of Germany was founded in 1948. The original need for the Confessional or Confessing Church (*Bekennende Kirche*) no longer existed, but the influence of its principles and its stance has permanently affected theological thought in Germany.

Confessio Scotica. See **Scots Confession.**

Confessor. This term is used in two entirely distinct senses: (1) a priest who hears confessions. (2) A person who confesses his or her Christian faith in face of persecution, torture, and possible martyrdom but who, although suffering (often cruel torture), is not actually martyred. Such a person is honored in the Church Calendar and commemorated in Mass as a confessor. Such confessors were very highly esteemed in the early Church as heroes of the faith.

Confirmation. Traditionally, Confirmation has been regarded as a sacrament (or at the least a sacramental rite) of the Church, whereby the recipient, having been baptized (usually in infancy, with a sponsor taking the baptismal vows on his or her behalf), now (having reached an age and condition of capacity to confess the Christian faith personally) takes responsibility for those baptismal vows. According to the general view, the Holy Spirit descends upon and strengthens the recipient in such a way as to fit him or her to be an efficient soldier for Christ in the Church Militant. Theologians find biblical authority for Confirmation in passages such as Acts 8.14–17, but the subject is one attended by great and complex difficulties and has been and still is the occasion of theological controversy.

Confiteor. A prayer in the form of an acknowledgement of one's sinfulness, used liturgically at the beginning of Mass and in the Office of Compline. It is also sometimes used as an introduction by the penitent in making his or her private Confession in the presence of a priest. The traditional form makes it first to God, then to the Virgin Mary, to Michael, to John the Baptist, to Peter, to Paul, each by name (sometimes also specifying other saints, such as the founder of the Order to which the supplicants may belong), to the entire company of all the saints, and to the persons present, including, at Mass, first the celebrant and then all others. It ends with the prayer that all these will intercede to God on behalf of the supplicant. This form has also been widely used in Anglo-Catholic practice. Since 1969 the Roman Catholic Church has modified the content of this traditional form of the prayer.

Confucius (551–479 BCE). Chinese philosopher who, as in many ways the Oriental counterpart of Socrates, has indirectly influenced much in modern Christian thought. He was probably the first professional teacher in Chinese history. His students went through a long training in all branches of the traditional learning of China. He was given some administrative positions in government, but he was not successful in such capacities, probably because of his excessive faith in the innate goodness of all men and his belief (similar to that of Socrates) that since ignorance is the only basic impediment to rational action, education is a political panacea. The Chinese educational system became, after his death, one of the greatest achievements of humankind. Once again reminiscent of the teaching of Socrates, Confucius regarded man as the most basic of all study, through which a harmonious society might be attained. Essentially a conservative, he saw consideration for others and propriety in social conduct as the way of good taste, called in Chinese *li*, to which, however, all art and literature (as we might say today the entire humanistic tradition) minister. Especially important is the relation between parents and children, masters and servants, entailing a deep respect for the elderly as one of the marks of a civilized man, a *chün-tzu*, i.e., a man of inwardly noble character and disposition, cultured and considerate. Confucius taught a standard similar to that implied in Kant's Categorical Imperative and in the teach-

ing of Jesus: "What you do not wish to be done to yourself, do not do to others." He showed little or no interest in speculation about the afterlife and to the extent that he talked of anything such as would be called in the West divine, what he envisioned was an ethical principle rather than a Being such as the biblical God. Confucian influence on China has been incalculably great, helping to make China into probably the greatest civilization on earth at a time when Europe (e.g., in the early Middle Ages) was a cultural desert and a political anarchy. Its influence seems to have remained in some respects ineradicable even in face of the 20th c. revolution.

Congé d'Élire. From the French, meaning "permission to elect," this phrase refers to the manner in which bishops in England are nominated and elected. In 1214, King John consented to the principle that the dean and chapter of a cathedral should elect but required that the permission of the Crown (the *congé d'élire*) must first be obtained, and that after the election the Crown's assent must be given in confirmation of the election. Such was the practice until 1534 when by statute the appointment of bishops was vested in the Crown. A *congé d'élire* was granted to the dean and chapter who were then required to elect the Crown's nominee. (See also **Praemunire.**) This has remained substantially the procedure for the appointment of bishops in the English Church.

Congregationalism. As an ecclesiastical polity and form of church government, Congregationalism represents the view that each congregation of Christians, gathered together for common worship and life, is independent of all ecclesiastical authority beyond itself. It is self-governing in all matters spiritual and temporal. It recognizes Jesus Christ as the only Head of the Church. In matters of doctrine and liturgy it inclines toward great openness. So, although historically it inherits certain models in both of these areas, it allows for wide variation, e.g., some Congregationalist churches have a formal, even an elaborate liturgy, although many have a very informal one. Doctrinally each congregation has its own tendency, guided (but only guided) by its minister, and each individual has the right and the duty to deviate from that tendency, although recognition of some general affirmation such as that "Jesus is Lord" is expected. Congregationalists have a long tradition of insistence on a "learned ministry" and have produced some of the best scholars in the Christian Church as well as a relatively high quality in the ministry as a whole. Congregationalism invokes the Reformation insistence on the "priesthood of all believers." Historically, it has its roots in the Puritan party of the English Church and in the work of those who followed the teachings of Robert Browne. (See *Browne, Robert.*) It played a most important part in the shaping of both the religious temper and the political concepts that eventually led to the way in which the United States developed. Although Congregationalists place so much emphasis on the independence of each congregation, there is a fraternal concern among congregations for each other's welfare within the Congregationalist Way.

Congregation Versus Order. (1) In the Roman Catholic Church a distinction is made between those religious societies whose members live under "simple" vows and those who take "solemn" vows. Members of the great ancient monastic Orders, such as the Benedictines and the Cistercians, and of the various Orders of friars, such as Dominicans and Franciscans, usually take "simple" vows for a period of some years, after which they take "solemn" vows for life. Many religious societies, however, both of men and of women, such as the Salesians and the Sisters of the Immaculate Heart of Mary, take only "simple" vows, in some such societies even only

temporary ones for a certain number of years and thereafter renewable for further periods. Their canonical status in the Church differs in various ways from that of the ancient Orders. The term "nun", for example, is strictly speaking applied only to women who are members of the Order, while members of a Congregation are properly called sisters, not nuns. (2) Groups of monastic houses within an ancient Order are called congregations, e.g., within the Benedictine Order the Cassinese.

Congruism. A doctrine much favored by the Molinists and more generally by the Jesuits to the effect that God gives grace to individuals for the performance of works such as he desires them to do, congruently with the circumstances that he sees will be most favorable to the performance. The doctrine was developed in an attempt to mediate between the extremes of Predestinarianism and human Freedom.

Connotation. In logic this term is treated as the correlative of denotation. See **Denotation and Connotation**.

Conrad of Gelnhausen. (*c.* 1320–1390). Conciliarist. His chief work is his *Epistola Concordiae* (1380). He advocated the calling of a General Council without papal convocation.

Conrad of Marburg (*c.* 1180–1233). Inquisitor. Under Pope Innocent III, he preached eloquently in favor of the Crusade. In 1231 Pope Gregory IX appointed him the first papal inquisitor with absolute authority in Germany over all heretics. Ruthless and sometimes arbitrary in his heresy hunting, especially of the Albigensians and the Waldensians, he was murdered on his return journey to Marburg in July 1233.

Consanguinity. Incestuous marriage is forbidden in the Bible (Leviticus 18). In canon law, certain degrees of blood relationship (consanguinity) constitute an impediment to marriage that makes it not only unlawful but invalid. See **Diriment Impediment.**

Conscience. Fundamentally the term (Latin *conscientia*) signified self-knowledge, self-awareness, consciousness, but in English it has come to have the more restrictive meaning of moral or ethical consciousness. (In French *conscience* still means "consciousness".) In medieval Western thought a distinction came to be made between what was called *synteresis* (a copyist's error in transcribing the Hellenistic Greek *syneidesis*), which was taken to mean the general knowledge of ethical principles, on the one hand, and the application, on the other hand, of such principles to particular cases, which latter was called *conscientia*. The notion of conscience as a guide to conduct is obviously fraught with danger, since so much depends on the sensitivity of the particular individual's conscience. Such is the frailty of men and women that they need their consciences to be both guided and trained. Nevertheless, only through one's conscience can one act authentically according to the ethical standard that one has learned to recognize.

Consecration. In Christian usage the term is employed in several distinct technical senses. (1) In the Mass or Eucharist the bread and wine are said to be consecrated as they become, through the liturgical action, in one sense or another the Body and Blood of Christ. (2) When one is made a bishop, he is said to be consecrated to that office in the Church and the ceremony of so making him a bishop is called consecration. (3) Churches and certain furnishing such as altars and Eucharistic vessels are not merely blessed or dedicated but consecrated; i.e., they are irrevocably set apart for sacred purposes and cannot thereafter be lawfully given or sold for profane ones.

Consistory. Originally the Roman Emperor administered justice from his seat in the imperial palace, with other members of the tribunal standing (*consistentes*) around him. In the Roman Catholic Church the term is used of any assembly of the cardinals convoked by the Pope and meeting in his presence. The term is also employed in Anglican practice of a bishop's court for the administration of ecclesiastical law in his diocese.

Constance, Council of (1414–1417). This General Council was held primarily to end the Great Schism, but it had also other subsidiary purposes. When it met, there were three claimants to the papacy: Gregory XII, Benedict XIII, and John XXIII. After many delays and highly complicated proceedings and events, a conclave met and in three days elected Oddo Colonna, who took the name of Martin V. Attempts were made though with scant success, to reform the Church. Most importantly, however, it asserted the authority of General Councils over that of the papacy.

Constantine. Having become senior ruler of the Roman Empire in 312, after a battle in which he had raised the *Labarum* standard as the champion of Christianity, he gave (whether by edict or more informally) toleration and special favor to Christianity as a *religio licita*, a permitted religion. His aim and his policy was to unite Church and State as closely as possible, so adumbrating the Byzantine theory of the Emperor's role as supreme ruler of Church and State. By moving the seat of the Empire from Rome to Byzantium, which he rebuilt and renamed "Constantinople" in 330, he broke continuity with the Roman Empire. While no doubt he was capable of only a limited appreciation of the nature of Christian faith and a meager understanding of what was involved in the theological controversies that he encountered, there is every reason to acknowledge his readiness to support Christianity in every way he could. He generously endowed Christian shrines, especially those in the Holy Land, and in 321 he made Sunday an official holiday. He called the Council of Nicaea, which met in 325. Byzantium had had a Christian community from at least the 2nd c., so that it was not unduly difficult to transform it into the new capital of the Empire. Predictably, however, jealousy developed between Rome and Constantinople (the "New Rome"), such as politically helped very much to create the breach and foster the schism that eventually occurred in 1054 between the Church in the East and the Church in the West.

Constantinople. This city (now named Istanbul), was founded by and named for Constantine I at ancient Byzantium in 330 as the new capital of the Roman Empire and became the largest city in medieval Europe. In its heyday, it must have been indeed an impressive city. Built upon seven hills and situated on the Bosphorus, with a great fortress enclosing magnificent palaces and gilded domes and towers, it had c. a million inhabitants in the 10th c. It was the site of Hagia Sophia, the focus of all Christendom and one of the grandest buildings in the world, and of the Imperial Palace. Its literary and artistic treasures eclipsed the holdings of any other center in the Empire. Eventually, in 1453, it fell to the Turks. See **Hagia Sophia.**

Constantinople, The Three General Councils of. Three of the early General Councils of the Church were held at Constantinople. (1) The first (which was the second General Council of the Church, the first having been held at Nicaea in 325) was convened by the Emperor Theodosius. It was held in 381 to unite the Church after the long Arian controversy. Some 186 bishops participated, 150 of them on the "orthodox" and 36 on the "heterodox" side, presided over by the Bishop of Antioch, Melitus, who died during the Council. The council ratified what the Council of Nicaea had determined concerning the doctrine of Christ, and by condemning Apollinarianism it asserted the full humanity of Christ. Traditionally it has

been regarded as having completed the Nicene Creed as it has come down to us, but whether it was actually involved in the work of that completion is not entirely clear. Although no bishops from the West were present, its work seems to have satisfied both West and East and was and is universally accepted as the second of the General Councils of the Christian Church. (2) In 553 the Second Council of Constantinople, which was the fifth General Council of the Church, was held, convened by the Emperor Justinian, to decide upon a variety of theological questions. Held a century after the Council of Chalcedon, its purposes included a review of the implications of what that council had determined. The Monophysites, who had fared ill at Chalcedon, wanted to diminish its authority if possible. They also wished that certain theologians such as Theodore of Mopsuestia should be condemned as exemplifying Nestorian attitudes that Chalcedon had condemned. The Three Chapters (see **Three Chapters, The**) were condemned, after much Monophysite pressure, so, by implication condemning Pope Vigilius; an act that was adduced at the First Vatican Council (1869–70) by the opponents of the doctrine of Papal Infallibility as evidence for their position. (See **Vigilius.**) The Council was convened under the presidency of Eutychius. The 165 bishops who signed the various acts of this council were almost all Eastern ones, so that once again the West was not adequately represented. Vigilius had declined to attend and drew up a protest, but in the long run he accepted the decisions of the Council. The anathemas issued by this council were mostly directed against Theodore of Mopsuestia. (3) The Third Council of Constantinople, which is recognized as the sixth General Council of the Church, was held in 680. It was held principally to decide upon the Monothelite controversy. (See **Monothelitism.**) This council reaffirmed the doctrinal assertions of the Council of Chalcedon and, against the Monothelites, declared that as there are two natures in Christ so there are also two wills, the human and the divine. Macarius, Patriarch of Antioch, and Pope Honorius were among those anathematized as Monothelites.

Constantinopolitan Creed, The Niceno-. See **Nicene Creed, The.**

Constitutional Church, The. On July 12, 1790, during the French Revolution, a schismatic Church representing a sort of caricature of the Gallicanism that had been so influential in French thought was established under this name and organized the following year under the protection of the National Assembly. When this Church began to depart dramatically from traditional discipline and practice (e.g., divorce was to be permissible and priests and bishops began to marry), the faithful for the most part turned their backs on the "new" Church. When the Concordat of 1801 had been made between Napoleon and Pius VII, the Constitutional Church was abolished.

Consubstantiality. In the Nicene Creed, Jesus Christ, as the "only begotten Son of God," is declared to be "consubstantial", i.e., being of one substance or essence with the Father. (See **Homoousios.**) This affirmation was directed against the Arians. According to orthodox Christian teaching, the three Persons of the Trinity are One, having the same essence (*ousia*).

Consubstantiation. Against the Eucharistic doctrine of transubstantiation, which by the 12th c. had become widely accepted and then made *de fide* as the official doctrine of the Church by the Lateran Council in 1215, Luther offered an alternative formula. According to the transubstantiation theory, the substance of the bread and the wine is changed during the Mass when the priest consecrates them. (See **Accident** and **Transubstantiation.**) Luther offered instead the theory of consubstantiation, according to which, after the consecration, the

substances of the bread and the wine, on the one hand, and, on the other, of the Body and Blood of Christ, co-exist. He used the analogy of iron put into the fire: they are united, yet each remains unchanged. Both doctrines depend on and perpetuate the categories of an Aristotelian philosophy which, despite its brilliant ingenuity at the time it was formulated in the 4th c. BCE, is generally regarded as outmoded in respect of this part of its vocabulary: nevertheless, both transubstantiation and consubstantiation were serious attempts to state the Catholic doctrine that Christ is really present (see **Real Presence, The**) in the consecrated bread and wine, not only symbolically as a wedding ring is a symbolic token of a marriage although by no means necessary to the reality or validity of the marriage.

Contakion. In the liturgical usage of the Eastern Church, a type of hymn that was very popular and still is used although now in a modified arrangement.

Contarini, Gasparo (1483–1542). Cardinal. Of a great Venetian family and educated at Padua, where he imbibed renaissance humanism, he was ambassador from Venice to the court of Charles V. Although a layman, he became noted as a theologian and was made a cardinal in 1535. He sought unsuccessfully to reconcile the Lutherans with the Roman Catholic Church.

Contemplation. (1) In traditional Catholic treatment of the spiritual or interior life, contemplation and meditation are contrasted. The latter is discursive and represents a more elementary stage in the life of prayer. (The Spiritual Exercises of Ignatius Loyola is an example of meditation, so understood.) Contemplation, which is non-discursive, is a higher form, more difficult to attain. Mystical writers recognize, moreover, various forms of contemplative prayer. (2) Religious Orders are classified as "contemplative" and "active" according to their respective emphases. Those that devote most of their time and energy to prayer (e.g., Carthusians) are said to be contemplative; those who engage in teaching, preaching, nursing, or other such kinds of work are called active Orders (e.g., Ursulines and Salesians).

Contextualism. According to the American philosopher Stephen C. Pepper (1891–1972), all philosophical systems are developed out of root metaphors that control the way in which the fundamental categories of the system are to be understood. He recognized four such root metaphors: (1) the root metaphor of form as used by Aristotle; (2) the root metaphor of mechanism as used by Hobbes; (3) the root metaphor of organism as Whitehead uses it; and (4) the root metaphor of contextualism that lies at the heart of the outlook of the pragmatists. See **Pragmatism.**

Continence. In a general sense this term is used to express the moral state of the individual who keeps his or her irrational desires in check by reason: a state that plainly entails self-control. In the narrower sense in which the term is widely used in Christian moral theology it refers to abstention, temporary or permanent, from all intentional sexual expression. Continence is expected of all persons not within the married state. The vow of chastity taken by members of religious orders, congregations, and societies, like the vow of celibacy taken by Roman Catholic priests in the Latin rite, implies total continence as a lifelong state. See also **Chastity.**

Contingency. A philosophical concept of the utmost importance in Christian theology. The "contingent" must be considered in contrast to the "necessary". According to Aristotle, a being is contingent if it might not have existed. For example, if one's parents had not met each other, one would not have existed. There is no necessity in nature why any entity such as a particular human being *must* exist. Its existence is contingent upon certain circumstances and events. By contrast, according to Aristotle and the medieval schoolmen

and others who followed him on this point, God exists of necessity. He is Necessary Being. Other thinkers such as Leibniz and Whitehead have treated the necessity-contingency contrast somewhat differently. The distinction in some form or other is vital to the concept of the Otherness of God that is central to the Judaeo-Christian understanding of the nature of the relation between God and his creation. Whatever God is, he is qualitatively different from his creation. Even though creation be taken to be in some way a reflection of God's nature, he stands over and against it; he may involve himself in it (Christian faith recognizes that he does), but he remains nevertheless independent of it, as the eternal is independent of the temporal and the infinite of the finite.

Contraception. Contraception consists of any method by which the occurrence of conception as a natural consequence of sexual intercourse may be prevented. Christians today are severely divided on the moral legitimacy of contraceptive methods. Contraception is certainly not new. Contraceptive methods have been used in one form or another for centuries, probably from time immemorial. Modern technology has merely rendered them more efficient, and modern communications has made them more widely known. Although it is true that in ancient times most of the great religions of the world at some stage or other encouraged fertility to insure the survival of the society, its sustenance from the tilling of the land, and its defense from marauding enemy neighbors, they also (at least in some circumstances) sought ways to prevent conceptions or abort births, sometimes even to countenance infanticide. Women were sometimes supportive of such procedures when, in view of their inferior social status, no other way was available to secure for them their own survival and that of their existing children. Infant mortality was so great in the past, however, that it took care of much of the problem. As recently as last century it was still common for a majority of children in a family to die in the first year of life. Medical advances have been so great within the past hundred years or so as to make infant mortality comparatively negligible, so that without some form of contraception the population of our planet would soon explode intolerably. The question of the contraceptive methods, if any, that might legitimately be used by married Christians emerged, therefore, with urgency, sometimes no doubt from selfish motives but often through recognition of Christian responsibility to plan the size of a family. In general, Anglicans and other heirs to the Reformation have been open to the use by married couples of mechanical devices, such as condoms, diaphragms, and intra-uterine devices, or chemical agents. The Eastern Orthodox hierarchy, although traditionally encouraging fertility, has taken no official stance against contraception, so that couples feel free to seek medical counsel and to follow it. In most of the non-Christian religions, acceptance of contraceptive methods has grown notably in recent years. Hindu, Buddhist, and Muslim leaders have generally felt able to justify within their respective traditions the use of contraceptive methods such as are now widely used in the rest of the civilized world. Unfortunately, such acceptance is not commonly linked to programs for economic betterment, so that populations continue to explode. The official Roman Catholic position, which is deviant from that of virtually the rest of Christian thought and practice on the subject and from that of the major non-Christian religions too, is that the procreation of children is one of the fundamental purposes of marriage, so that any procedure that interferes with that purpose is immoral and sinful. On this view, only one method is available to Roman Catholic couples, apart from total abstention from intercourse: the so-called "rhythm" method, which consists of avoiding intercourse during the fertile period of the woman's menstrual cycle: a method that is for various reasons inefficient as well as emotionally disturbing. (See **Humanae Vitae**.) Resistance to this view has been very widespread among some Roman Catholics. Various attempts have been made by Roman Catholic theologians to interpret papal pronouncements on this subject in such a way as to sanction the use of contraceptives, at least in certain circumstances. Throughout all branches of the Christian Church the traditional ideal of total abstinence from sexual intercourse outside marriage persists even in permissive societies and since contraceptives are so widely available, another and different question arises: ought they to be made available, for example, to adolescents as a means of avoiding pregnancy or disease? No Christian would wish to encourage sexual promiscuity, but in a society in which it is common among young people, is not education in the use of contraceptive devices and their ready availability a lesser evil than the spread of venereal disease, especially in view of the alarming and terrifying incidence of AIDS throughout the world? Many Christians who most loudly deplore sexual promiscuity and premarital intercourse recognize that, in view of the strength of the sexual urge in healthy human beings, it is better to permit the availability of efficient contraceptive devices while trying to train young people in the mastery of their passions than to expose society to the terrible risks involved if ignorance about or unavailability of such devices were to prevail.

Contra-Remonstrantie. The document drawn up by the strict Calvinists in response to the Arminian Remonstrance. Prepared for a conference held at the Hague in 1611, it asserted: (a) that some persons are absolutely predestined to damnation; (b) that the elect include children as well as adults; (c) that election is by God's arbitrary choice having no relation either to good works or right belief; (d) that Christ died for the elect only (see **Campbell, John McLeod**); (e) that the Holy Spirit of God speaks through the Bible to the elect only; (f) that true belief can never be lost to anyone who is elected; and (g) that this assurance, far from leading to smugness or sloth, as the profane might expect, is a spur to a virtuous life and an active zeal for the coming of God's Kingdom.

Contrition. In Catholic theology, contrition as a disposition is distinguished from attrition. (1) The latter is a penitence for one's sins that arises from a fear of God and of the punishment that one knows to be justly due. It is an adequate disposition even for death bed repentance, yet it leaves in the soul a residue of guilt that must be cleansed in purgatory. (2) Contrition is perfect repentance, because it springs from the pure love of God and from grief at having done what alienates the soul from him as the fountain of life and love. It carries with it an authentic resolution not merely to try to amend one's manner of life but to love God so much that one will be eventually incapable of being separated from him.

Convent. Strictly, in traditional ecclesiastical usage, a convent is a community or the building that houses a community of monks, friars, nuns, or any other body of people living under the customary vows. In popular parlance it refers only to nunneries.

Conventionalism. In the philosophy of science the view that those theories or hypotheses about the universe that are popularly called "the laws of physics" are only convenient ways of expressing, organizing, and explaining human experience relative to the framework of human knowledge at any given time. They do not exhibit reality as it is in itself, and so they may be replaced and are likely to be replaced as human knowledge expands. Such views are plainly of special interest to Christians and others with religious concerns.

Conventuals. That branch of the Franciscan Order that followed a mitigated form of the Franciscan rule, contradistinguished from the Observants, who sought to uphold it more strictly and who, in the spirit of Francis, renounced even the indirect ownership of property of any kind.

Conversi. Lay brothers, who follow the rule of the Order to which they belong and share in its life but whose function is to serve in some capacity such as cooking for the community or attending to the maintenance of buildings and other such functions. They are not trained for the singing of the Office in choir or for priestly or teaching functions. Their tasks, although often menial ones, may involve administrative and organizational skills. (See **Cellarer**.) In a well-conducted conventual establishment their contribution can be immense. See also **Choir Monks and Nuns**.

Convocations of Canterbury and York, The. The two ancient assemblies of the Church of England clergy. Church assemblies in England date from the 7th c., but not till 733 did the two assemblies of Canterbury and York come into being as separate, each with its own provincial authority, as has been the case ever since. Although exclusively clerical, there has also been in each of the two provinces since 1855 a house of lay representatives selected by the various dioceses. In 1919 the Convocations established the National Assembly of the Church of England (Church Assembly) to consider all matters concerning the English Church as a whole. This body was superseded in 1970 by the General Synod. The Convocations still meet separately, however, for the transaction of certain formal business.

Convulsionaries. Certain extremists among the Jansenists who opposed the papal bull *Unigenitus* (1713) were so called because of their habit of going into a sort of convulsion, said to be accompanied by miraculous cures and other phenomena, first observed at the church of Saint-Médard, Paris in 1731.

Coornheert, Dirck Volckertszoon (1522–1590). Dutch theologian. At a time when a rigid Calvinism was strong in Holland, he took a stance against the prevailing outlook by advocating toleration and opposing the death penalty for heretics. He was inclined to distrust the concept of a visible Church of any kind and to rely, rather, on personal piety nourished by the Bible. His views may have played some part in the subsequent development of Pietism and kindred movements. Calvin personally wrote a polemic response to him in 1562. Coornheert's Works were published posthumously in three volumes at Amsterdam in 1630.

Cope. A vestment, often richly woven and ornamented for use in liturgical services, especially on festive occasions. Its form is derived from that of the old Roman *paenula,* a cloak that was worn like an overcoat to protect against cold and rain. There is ample evidence from early Christian representations that the *cappa* was regarded as a characteristically clerical costume at least as early as the 6th c., being a garment of similar shape that was widely used in the Middle ages and has remained in use by monks in some monasteries, both as a ceremonial choir garb and also, made out of heavy wool, as a protection against cold in ill-heated or non-heated monastic churches in Europe and elsewhere. The *cappa,* for similar practical reasons, was designed with a hood: an appurtenance sometimes conserved at least symbolically, in the design of the liturgical cope. The cope is widely used by cantors, by bishops, and by priests, on festive occasions. Although the chasuble is the vestment proper to the celebrant at Mass, the cope has been used in the past, having been prescribed, for instance, at various times in the Church of England for use by the celebrant.

Copernicus, Nicolas (1473–1543). Polish astronomer. Born at Torun, he was educated at Cracow, Bologna, Padua, and Ferrara. A pioneer in astronomy, he introduced the heliocentric theory of the solar system, i.e., the theory, then revolutionary, that the planets orbit the sun. Because he assumed the orbits to be circular, he had to conserve some elements in the ancient theory that Ptolemy had developed in the 2nd c. CE, in order to make his own theory work. His own theory was perfected later by Tycho Brahe and the latter's assistant and successor Johannes Kepler, notably by their making the planetary orbits into ellipses. Copernicus's work, *De revolutionibus orbium coelestium* (1543) was placed on the Index of Forbidden Books in 1616 and remained there till 1757.

Coptic Church, The. (See **Coptic Language, The.**) The Church in Egypt existed from early Christian times and suffered grievously in the Diocletian persecution. There is even a tradition, recorded by Eusebius, that it was founded by Mark himself. The great Christian school of Alexandria fostered an intellectual tradition of unique importance in the history of Christianity. Unfortunately, bitter controversies between the Church there and in Constantinople issued in the repudiation by the Copts of the decrees of Chalcedon and their commitment to a Monophysitism that has isolated them. The Coptic Church suffered intermittently from Muslim persecution and its numbers declined gradually through the centuries. The Ethiopic Church is a daughter of the Coptic Church and has a similar theological heritage.

Coptic Language, The. The Coptic language was spoken in Egypt from about the 3rd c. to the 10th c., when it was gradually superseded by Arabic. It is still used in the liturgy of the Coptic Church. The Coptic alphabet had kinship with that of Greek and included a good many Greek words. It is of importance to biblical and patristic scholars, not least because the New Testament was translated into all four of the Coptic dialects (Sahidic, Bohairic, Fayumic, and Akhminic) and much Gnostic and early Christian literature is in Coptic.

Corbie. A monastery near Amiens, founded *c.* 660 as an offshoot of the Abbey of Luxeuil toward the end of the 6th c. by Columbanus. Corbie had an exceptionally good library and played a great part in the transmission of ancient texts, both classical and patristic, some of which are in the Bibliothèque Nationale, Paris.

Cordeliers. The Franciscan Observantines were sometimes so called in France, in allusion to the cord they wore as a cincture for their habits.

Corinthians, Third Epistle to the. An apocryphal letter dating from probably late in the 2nd c.

Cornelius. A 3rd c. pope, elected 251. Some of his correspondence with Cyprian survives. He died in exile in what is now Civitavecchia but was buried in Rome in the crypt of Lucina in the Catacombs of Callistus. His inscription bears the designation "martyr", according to a tradition about his death.

Cornill, Carl (1854–1920). Biblical scholar. Professor of Old Testament successively at Königsberg, Breslau, and Halle, he followed Wellhausen's methods.

Corporal. A square white linen cloth, usually about 12x12 inches, used in the West on the altar to receive the bread that is to be consecrated. It has been in use in much its present form since the 9th c., except that formerly it was large enough to cover the chalice. (The Carthusians continue this usage.) In modern usage the chalice is covered by the pall. See **Pall** and **Burse.**)

Corporal Works of Mercy See **Works of Mercy, Corporal and Spiritual.**

Corpus Christi, The Feast of. This feast in the Christian calendar commemorates the institution of the Eucharist and was first authorized by Pope Urban IV in 1264, becoming universal

in the West the following century. The practice is said to have been inspired by Juliana, a 13th c. nun in Liège.

Corpus Juris Canonici. Until 1917, the general collection of all provisions of canon law had come to be so entitled. It was based on Gratian's *Decretum*, compiled in the 12th c. and had been added to so extensively that it had become intolerably cumbersome. Much condensed and simplified, it was superseded in 1917 by a work issued as the *Codex Juris Canonici.*

Correspondence Theory of Truth. On the philosophical question of the meaning and nature of truth, two theories may be taken as the most basic: the correspondence theory and the coherence theory. According to the former, truth consists in correspondence to reality. According to a coherence theory, it consists in a coherent arrangement of ideas. Both of these theories may be found in Plato. The question is, however, both extremely complex and of fundamental importance in philosophical and in theological discussions. For a brief account of the development of philosophical opinion on the subject, see **Truth.**

Cosmas and Damian. Two saints who are both mentioned in the canon of the Roman Mass, and are traditionally regarded as the patrons of the medical profession. Their origin is so obscure as to make their historicity doubtful, yet so strong and so early is the tradition about them that they may well have existed. They were already being venerated in the East by at least the 5th c. and at Rome by at least the 6th c. They are supposed to have been twin brothers who practiced medicine and charged no fee.

Cosmas of Jerusalem. An 8th c. monk, also known as Cosmas Melodus, he wrote many liturgical hymns, called *kanones*, of which some are used in the Eastern Orthodox liturgies, and other poetical works. They are also know as Cosmas Melodus.

Cosmetic Surgery. Ethical objections to such surgery are sometimes raised either on the ground that it is unnatural to tamper with the body merely for its beautification or that it is morally wrong for the rich so to try to improve their appearance while the poor sometimes cannot get the surgery they need for their health. Distinctions must be made. For example, few would object to straightening the eyes of a cross-eyed child, although such a mild condition of that kind might not seriously affect one's health, only one's looks. If correctives for irregular teeth are approved, why not surgery for a child with an ugly nose? Is the reconstruction of the face after a skin cancer cosmetic? It is not uncommon for people to accept cosmetic surgery in the case of children but not in that of adults, but why should it be condemned for an adult brought up in conditions too poor for the question to have arisen, yet accepted for children of affluent parents? Is surgery for a hare lip cosmetic, when it may be plainly necessary for the mental health at least of the patient? It would seem, then, that the only cosmetic surgery that can be unequivocally condemned is that which is performed for mere whim, such as to make a person's face whose appearance is acceptable in terms of his or her age, look artificially younger. Even that might be ethically justified when the patient's livelihood depended upon a youthful appearance.

Cosmogony and Cosmology. Both terms come from the Greek. "Cosmogony" means literally the coming into being of an orderly universe. It may be applied therefore to any speculative hypothesis about the origin of the universe, from the most primitive to the most recent scientific proposal. The Genesis account, for example, represents an ancient cosmogony. The "Big Bang" theory of a single, unique event that brought the universe into existence represents a modern astronomical cosmogony. The term "cosmology" literally means a discussion about the nature of the universe. The use of this term as a philosophical discipline apart from ontology and theology was introduced by Christian Wolff in the 18th c. (See **Wolff, Christian.**) It both encompasses a much wider range of problems and questions and is a more radical philosophical discipline. It has as its function not merely the discussion of speculative questions about the origin of the universe, but the analysis of the presuppositions that underlie the formulation of cosmogonies. It is concerned, moreover, with whether the universe is to be considered the result of a single, unique event or as an ongoing, everlasting evolutionary process. The structure of the universe and the nature of space, time, and causality are also cosmological concerns. For example, the view that the universe had a beginning as a specific, unique event presents enormous difficulties both theologically and scientifically. On the latter side it raises the question why the "Big Bang" or the cloud of dust that was, *ex hypothesi*, the origin of the universe, occurred when it did and why it did not do so before. On the theological side, it presents peculiar difficulties, such as why, since God is eternal and self-sufficient, he would create anything at all, having no need of anything. The traditional answer that he did so because of the love in his nature leaves us with an image of God as eternally "in heaven" and totally happy, then (if there could be a "then") suddenly deciding to create a universe. If his nature is to love, why did he not do so before, if indeed there could be a "before". Such types of problems are of great importance in modern thought, since they raise questions that involve both theological and scientific reflection and analysis.

Cosmological Argument for the Existence of God. This, one of the traditional arguments for the existence of God (see **God**) and one of the five proposed by Thomas Aquinas (see **Quinque Viae**), goes back to Aristotle and is based on the concept of causality. It proceeds from observed facts about the universe; it notes that every event has a cause; and it concludes from an analysis of these facts there must be a first cause. Since everything in the universe is in process and everything that exists exists contingently on the existence of something else, there must be some entity or principle, the first cause, who is not in process but is the prime mover (he who moves but is himself unmoved) and, in contrast to all contingent beings, necessarily exists. The cosmological argument, whether in Aristotle's or any other form, emphasizes the notion that this principle or being who necessarily exists does not depend on the universe yet the universe depends on him. He is likewise changeless while all else is in process of change. Against this view is the objection that it need not be so. The causal series leading into the past need have no beginning. The causal chain may regress infinitely. Hume, attacking the principle of causation as traditionally understood, rejected the Cosmological Argument. Kant rejected it on the ground that the principle, while it applies to the world of phenomena, cannot be known to apply to the real world, i.e., the reality that lies behind the world as we see it. Although the objection is by no means without weight, this form of the argument for the existence of God remains a very powerful one. We must note, however, that one might accept the Cosmological Argument as valid yet not accept the existence of God exactly as he is portrayed in the Bible and in traditional Christian theology. That is, even though it proves that a principle or entity exists as the prime mover, necessary being, and first cause, it does not prove that that principle or entity has the attributes that are traditionally assigned by Christians and others to God, e.g., the first cause or prime mover need not care for the fall of a sparrow or exercise a providential governance over the universe. Christian faith looks beyond the notion *that God is* to the question of *what God is* and arguments of this type,

valid though we may deem them, do not yield all that Christian believers traditionally assert about the nature of God. See also **Causa Sui.**

Cosmology. See **Cosmogony and Cosmology.**

Cotelier, Jean Baptiste (1627–1686). French patristic scholar. His writings include an important edition of the Apostolic Fathers (1672).

Cotta. An abbreviated form of the surplice, used in the Roman Catholic Church. Anglican practice has almost universally favored the surplice, preferably long and ample, and recent tendencies in the Roman Catholic Church have been in the direction of a return to the surplice.

Cottonian Library. A large collection of valuable manuscripts many of theological interest, from the library of Sir Robert Bruce Cotton, now housed in the British Museum. It includes the Lindisfarne Gospels (see **Lindisfarne**) and a manuscript of the Septuagint.

Council. Any formal meeting of bishops or other representatives of the Church may be called a council. Many are local and sometimes also called synods. In the Reformed tradition such meetings are often called assemblies. A General Council, because of its universality or claim to universality, has a special historical importance. Councils have also played a significant role in the history of Buddhism, especially those held between the 5th c. BCE and the 1st c. CE for the purpose of determining the canon of Buddhist Scripture and for considering matters of discipline and procedure.

Councils, Buddhist. Buddhists recognize the authority of various councils that have been held over the centuries for various purposes, such as determining the canon of Buddhist scripture, laying down rules for the practice of the monastic life, and other purposes considered of great importance in Buddhism. The number of councils is quite large (five of them date from the 15th c. CE onwards), but recognition of them as authoritative varies from country to country; e.g., Thailand recognizes ten, while Burma and Sri Lanka recognize six. All Buddhists, however, recognize as authoritative the following three early councils: (1) the council held at Rajagṛha in the monsoon season following the death of the Buddha, c. 483 BCE; (2) the council held at Vasāli about a century later; and (3) the council held at Pātaliputra (Patna) during the reign of the emperor Aśoka, in the 3rd c. BCE. All these councils were held in the lower Ganges valley at an early period in Buddhist history.

Counter-Reformation. Historians use this term to designate a movement that occurred in the Roman Catholic Church, running from c. the mid-16th c. to the mid-17th c. It has been widely considered as a reactionary response to the Reformation movement, which to a considerable extent indeed it was; nevertheless, it had certainly other dimensions, for the late medieval Church has been already much aware of grievous abuses that demanded reform, and many notable leaders were attempting to make them within the structure of the Church, e.g., Ximenes and some of the new religious Orders such as the Capuchins. (Luther himself had at first hoped to be able to do so within that structure and without schism.) For more than a century, however, before the birth of Luther, all attempts (e.g., by the conciliarist party and the humanist scholars) to achieve reformation had failed. The success of the Reformation movement was attained at the cost of schism, and (as in all schisms) both sides tended to proceed to uphold their respective cases in an exaggerated form. At any rate, the Jesuits became the spearhead of the Counter-Reformation and the Council of Trent (1545–1563), the longest General Council in the history of the Roman Catholic Church, determined the course the Roman

Catholic Church was to take, not only in zealously emphasizing attitudes openly hostile to those of the Reformers but in seeking to ignore the values that that movement had indubitably created for the enrichment of the Christian Church. By the use of the Inquisition it sought to impose a militaristic type of government on the Church and encourage such an ethos in the outlook of the faithful, alienating still further those in the Reformation heritage, many of whom had been already spiritually impoverished by that alienation.

Courage. Along with wisdom, temperance, and justice, courage is one of the four cardinal virtues. (The English word comes from the Latin cor, meaning "heart".) Plato regarded it as the virtue proper to the guardians-auxiliary in his ideal Republic. In modern thought it has been sometimes regarded (e.g., by Tillich) as one of the principal means of approaching the Ultimate Reality that we call God. It consists not merely in "physical courage" such as may be displayed in battle or natural catastrophe such as fire or earthquake but, rather, in an internal disposition toward the living of one's own life. It is therefore closely allied to the Christian concept of faith by which the Christian walks fearlessly through life.

Courayer, Pierre François Le (1681–1776). French theologian. Professor of theology at Paris and Librarian of St.-Geneviève, he wrote a treatise supporting the validity of Anglican Orders, publication of which was delayed by censorship till 1723 when it was published in France but with the name of a Brussels bookseller on the title page. He was eventually excommunicated from the Roman Catholic Church and took refuge in England.

Cournot, Antoine (1801–1877). French philosopher and mathematician. After teaching at Paris and elsewhere, he became rector of the Academy at Grenoble in 1835 and of the Academy at Dijon in 1854. In his philosophical thought he took the view that chance and discontinuity are no less real than are continuity and order; nevertheless, through philosophical analysis and inquiry we can attain at least an approximation to knowledge of reality. This involves a systematization of the categories, e.g., unity, simplicity, form, and symmetry. Biological entities do not conform to the "laws" of physics, so one must provide for more than the physical world in any system of categories that we may develop. Among his works are: *Exposition of the Theory of Chance and of Probability* (1843); *An Essay on the Foundations of our Knowledge*, 2 volumes (1851); and *Treatise on the Linkage of Fundamental Ideas in the Sciences and in History* (1881).

Cousin, Victor (1792–1867). Philosopher. Born in Paris, he became in 1840 Minister of Public Education. Intellectually, he was influenced by Locke, Condillac, Thomas Reid, Maine de Biran, Schelling, and Hegel. His philosophy was a philosophy of the spirit in which a study of the nature of humanity, especially in its creative activity and the spontaneity of the actions of ordinary men and women is seen as disclosing a step from psychology to ontology, so opening up the concept of God not only as the ultimate cause of all things but as the supremely spontaneous agent of creation. He saw the various traditional systems of thought as each representing an aspect of truth but none of them complete. The work of the authentic philosopher is to unite the insights of the past with present knowledge and so exhibit the unity of both. His extensive writings include a *Course in the History of Modern Philosophy* (5 volumes, 1841).

Coustant, Pierre (1654–1721). French Benedictine patristic scholar. Born at Compiègne and educated by the Jesuits, he entered the monastery of the Maurist congregation of the Benedictines at Reims, whence he was sent to the Abbey of Saint-Germain-des-Prés to help

with an edition of the works of Augustine. Among his many works is a very scholarly edition of the works of Hilary (1693).

Couturat, Louis (1868–1915). Philosopher. Born in Paris, he became professor at Toulouse, Caen, and the Collège de France. Indebted to Leibniz, he took the development of symbolic logic to be adequate to the entire philosophical enterprise, so adumbrating the standpoint that characterized the work of later 20th c. logicians.

Couturier, Paul (1881–1953). French priest and ecumenist. Educated at Lyons, he was ordained priest in 1906. In 1933 he introduced a three-day period of prayer for Church unity and the following year an octave from January 18–25, which led to the Church Unity Octave observed annually by a group of Anglicans and others. Eastern Orthodox and other Christians became involved in the movement. From 1939 the observance came to be known as the Week of Universal Prayer.

Covenant. The concept of a covenant between God and man is deeply rooted in the Old Testament, where it appears as an undertaking initiated by God and given to the people of Israel: an agreement under which God sets his people apart, promises fidelity to them, and requires their fidelity in return. In Christian thought the concept is sometimes seen as the background of that divinely initiated bestowal of grace that enables Christians to do what otherwise they could not achieve by themselves.

Covenanters. The policy of King Charles I toward Scotland was singularly unfortunate, not least in matters of religion, for just as the internal strife in Scotland between those who had favored a Presbyterian and those who desired an Episcopal form of government had quietened, he persisted in inflaming it, seeking total conformity to Anglican practice both in government and in liturgy. The Scottish Kirk was not only to have bishops; they were to have bishops directly controlled by the King and the Archbishop of Canterbury, William Laud. When an attempt was made to impose on the Scots the Book of Common Prayer sent up by Laud to be used at St. Giles Cathedral, Edinburgh, on Sunday, July 23, 1637, a riot ensued, the leadership of which is traditionally attributed to a vegetable seller named Jenny Geddes. Reaction to this inflammatory action came in a document called the National Covenant, pledging on oath to maintain the Presbyterian form of government and to resist all attempts to undermine Scottish religious independence. This document, which had had modest predecessors in the previous century, was signed in 1638 by many, nobles and commoners alike. Some signed in their own blood. It implied no disloyalty to the Crown, only insistence on Scotland's religious independence. After the outbreak of civil war in England, the English Parliament tried to form an alliance with the Scots by attempting, with a document entitled the Solemn League and Covenant, to win the Scots not only with an undertaking to maintain the Presbyterian Kirk but to abolish Episcopacy in England. This document was formally accepted by the General Assembly of the Kirk on August 17, 1643. Between 1661 and 1688 the Presbyterians were persecuted, but with the collapse of the Stuart dynasty in 1688 and the Settlement of 1690 that guaranteed the independence of the Presbyterian Kirk in Scotland, one might have expected an end to the strife and the beginning of a period of religious toleration. Extremist elements among the Presbyterians in Scotland remained dissatisfied and expressed their dissatisfaction in a series of violent acts such as the ejection of some two hundred Episcopalian clergy in Scotland from their livings. These acts were popularly called the "Rabbling." These extremists, who called themselves Covenanters, formed the body sometimes known as Cameronians.

Coventry. The Christian history of Coventry, England, goes back to a Benedictine foundation there, founded in 1043. In the 12th c. it became an episcopal See. The Church of St. Michael, completed in 1433, became the cathedral, and it is this cathedral that was virtually destroyed in an air raid during World War II. The shell of the old building including the charred Cross has been preserved, and the new one, designed by Sir Basil Spence, built at right angles to it, contains many features that have made it much celebrated as an outstanding example of the best in 20th c. ecclesiastical architecture. It is built of stone, with a seventy-two foot high tapestry, designed by Graham Sutherland and executed in France, hanging behind the high altar. The many other splendid features include a bronze sculpture by Jacob Epstein on the exterior of the east wall of the cathedral, showing Michael and Satan.

Coverdale, Miles (1488–1568). Bible translator. Ordained priest in 1514, he later embraced the Reformation cause. Forced to flee from England, he worked on a translation of the Bible, using William Tyndale's New Testament and Pentateuch, Luther's Bible, the Vulgate, and such other sources as he could find. It was printed in 1525, probably at Zürich. Returning to England when conditions were more favorable to the Reformation cause, he became Bishop of Exeter in 1551 but had to flee again when Mary Tudor became Queen, remaining in exile till after her death in 1558.

Cow. Reverence for the cow had steadily grown in Hinduism from the time of the *Mahābhārata*, one of the great epics of Indian literature, composed between the second c. BCE and the second c. CE. The killing of a cow is a very serious crime in Hindu law. Ghandi regarded veneration for the cow as a doctrine essential to Hinduism. All her five products (milk, curd, butter, urine, and manure) are regarded as purifiers.

Cowl. A garment for covering the head, worn by monks. It is usually attached to the monastic cloak, over the neck of which it hangs down when not in use. Some forms of it are detached.

Cowley Fathers. See **Society of St. John the Evangelist, The.**

Cowper, William (1731–1800). English poet. Educated at Westminster School, London, he was trained for the practice of law and became a barrister in 1754. He suffered, however, from such depression that he had to be periodically hospitalized for mental illness. Of a devout disposition, he worked for a time as a lay assistant in a parish, where he was encouraged to exercise his literary abilities and inclinations by the writing of hymns, some of which are among the most beloved in Christian hymnody in the English language, e.g., "O for a closer walk with God," "God moves in a mysterious way," and "Hark, my soul! It is the Lord." Even in his poems on secular subjects his religious temper shines through at many points. His sentiment for nature and the general sensitivity of the feeling he expresses in his poetry suggest an anticipation of the Romantic Movement of the 19th c.

Cox, Richard (c. **1500–1581**). English divine and Bishop of Ely. Educated at Eton and Cambridge, he soon became involved in the support of the Reformation cause in England and was responsible, when Dean of Christ Church and Chancellor of the University of Oxford, for bringing many continental divines to Oxford, including Peter Martyr. He disliked both Romanism and Puritanism and was extraordinarily zealous in his attempts to extirpate from the University all evidence of what he accounted popish influence. On the accession of Mary Tudor, he was imprisoned and then went into exile at Frankfurt, where he met John Knox. Under Elizabeth I, he returned to England, becoming Bishop of Ely in 1559, a position he held almost to the end of his life.

Cranmer, Thomas (1489–1556). English divine and Archbishop of Canterbury. Educated at Cambridge, he was ordained priest in 1523. While in the service of Henry VIII, he went on a diplomatic mission to the Emperor Charles V, and during his stay on the continent he met and was secretly married in 1532 to Margaret Osiander, the niece of Andreas Osiander, one of the Lutheran Reformers. On his return to England he was appointed Archbishop of Canterbury. No doubt Henry saw him as a convenient tool for his own political and private interests and to some extent Cranmer conformed to Henry's expectations. He was temperamentally inclined to see the Church's interests as best served through subordination to the State. (See **Erastianism.**) On the death of Henry in 1547, he became one of the chief advisers to the boy King, Edward VI. Henry's personal taste in churchmanship had been, despite his quarrel with the Pope in the matter of his marriage, distinctly conservative and Catholic, with no relish for the Reformation cause at all. Cranmer, however, under Edward VI, skillfully succeeded in moving England toward policies expressive of Reformation thought and practice, inclining it toward greater ties with those continental Churches that had espoused the Reformation stance. His greatest contribution as a churchman lies in the dignity and grace of his use of the English language in the Book of Common Prayer, which bequeathed a priceless heritage to the English-speaking world. On the accession of Mary Tudor in 1553, Cranmer was sentenced to death at Oxford and eventually was burnt at the stake on March 21, 1556, in which ordeal he exhibited great fortitude.

Crashaw, Richard (c. **1613–1649**). English poet. Educated at Charterhouse School and at Cambridge, he was elected to a fellowship at Peterhouse, Cambridge, in 1637. Three years later he was expelled for his refusal to sign the National Covenant. He went to

France, became a Roman Catholic, lived in destitution for some time, but through the kindness of a friend was rescued from it and eventually became an attendant to Cardinal Palotta. He died at Loreto. His poetry, collected in *Steps to the Temple* (1646) and *Carmen Deo Nostro* (1652) had a considerable influence on later poets such as Milton, Pope, and Coleridge.

Creatio ex Nihilo. The view that the universe is not only created by God but that it is created "out of nothing" (i.e., it is created out of nothing other than God himself), in contrast to the notion proposed in Plato's *Timaeus* that the universe is created out of existing "stuff".

Creation. The doctrine that the universe is created stands in opposition to various alternatives, e.g., emanationism, pantheism, and dualism. On an emanationist view, the universe eternally emanates from God as sunshine emanates from the sun and vapor emanates from boiling water. Pantheistic views vary in detail, but in principle they understand by "God" a universal principle running through everything, so that everything can be properly said to be in some sense identified with God; i.e., God *is* the nature of things, so that persons differ from things only in the sense and to the extent that they are aware (or more aware) of their divine nature. Dualism takes two distinct forms: (1) that good and evil are the product of two separate causes, both ultimately and equally real; and (2) that mind and matter are opposed, distinct, equally real, and not necessarily interrelated. The doctrine of creation is not at all, however, opposed to or incompatible with an evolutionary understanding of the universe. On the contrary, by recognizing as it does the Otherness (i.e., the Transcendence of God) and at the same time his Immanence in all things, it sees God as Necessary Being and all other entities as contingent and dependent on him. As soon as they become

aware of their relationship to him and their participation in his goodness, it is natural for them to adore and praise him as the source of their own being and of all that is.

Creation, Buddhist doctrine of. The notion of a personal God, creator of all things, does not exist in Buddhism. Indeed, the Hindu concept of creation by Brahma seemed to the Buddhists to be tainted with the notion of achievement and that therefore, from a Buddhist standpoint, Brahma as a creator deity is inferior to the Buddha who attains enlightenment with no sense of achievement. Generally speaking, Buddhist thinkers are agnostic on the question of how the universe came or comes into being, regarding it as unanswerable, not to say futile. Nevertheless, the Buddha is reported to have declared that the *samsāra* or chain of being is such that no beginning is discoverable. As elsewhere in the comparison of Hindu and Buddhist attitudes, while Hinduism has from an early period exhibited great interest in ontological questions, which relate to the nature of Being, Buddhism is metaphysically agnostic, functioning rather as a way of salvation. It exhibits itself as a psychological rather than as a theological concern: a therapy for the human psyche rather than an ontology or philosophical theology. This does not by any means exclude, however, its having its own metaphysical presuppositions, which it takes as its starting-point. It does exclude its taking any interest in questions such as creation, which are so fundamental in Judaism and Christianity and which have played an important part in Hindu thought.

Creationism. This term is used in a technical sense in Christian theology in opposition to Traducianism. On the Creationist view, God creates a new soul for each individual at its conception. This view was upheld by Jerome against those of his time who opposed it in favor of what has come to be called Traducianism. Thomas Aquinas clearly upheld Creationism and Calvinists have generally done so too. Lutherans, however, have generally upheld the Traducianist view that the soul is generated with the body. Any form of the doctrine of the pre-existence of the soul, such as was certainly taught by Origen, and any reincarnationist view, implies a Traducianist rather than a Creationist stance. This Creationist/Traducianist controversy is entirely separate from the teaching, fundamental to the Judaeo-Christian theological tradition, that the universe is created by God. (See **Creatio ex Nihilo** and **Creation**.) For the popular use of "Creationism" in antithesis to "Evolutionism", see **Evolution.**

Creativity. In modern philosophy creativity is associated with the problem of novelty. Whitehead, for instance, regarded creativity as the Category of the Ultimate. On his view the universe is continuously involved in creative advance. Berdyaev saw creation as self-creation. All creation, human or divine, is in his view *creatio ex nihilo*. Such philosophical stances are by way of response to the question: how, in a universe governed by inexorable "laws", can novelty emerge?

Credence. A small table, usually placed near the altar to hold the eucharistic vessels and the bread and wine that are to be consecrated at Mass.

Credo Quia Absurdum (Impossibile, Ineptum). Literally, "I believe because it is absurd (impossible, inept)." Expressions used to designate a view propounded by Tertullian. Such dicta express the notion that Christianity as delineated in the New Testament is so astonishing that no human being could have fancifully invented it or fraudulently propagated it and therefore it must be divinely revealed and so command acceptance.

Credo ut Intelligam. See **Fides Quaerens Intellectum.**

Creed. From the Latin *credo* ("I believe"). Any doctrinal formula accepted by any religious group or even adopted by a private individual may be so designated. The classic Christian creeds are the so-called Apostles' Creed and the Nicene Creed. The Eastern Church traditionally uses the Nicene Creed as a formula for the Sacrament of Baptism, and in the West the Apostles' Creed is used for that purpose. The use of the Nicene Creed at the Eucharist began in the East *c*. the 5th c. and was not included in the Roman Mass till early in the 11th c. Creeds are generally formulated as a result of theological controversy and in response to opinions that are accounted heterodox or alien. They tend, therefore, to be declarations *against* such views rather than spontaneous affirmations. For example, if belief that God is "almighty" or "creator of all things, visible and invisible," were universal, there would be no need to compose a declarative formula to that effect, for the belief would be presupposed by all. The creed is, rather, a repudiation of views such as are implicit in, say, the polytheistic society in which Christianity in the Gentile world emerged, or in an emanationist view of God. See **Apostles' Creed; Nicene Creed; Creation; Emanationism.**

Cremation. The incineration of the body of the deceased, causing it to be reduced to ashes. In the ancient world, it was virtually universal in civilized societies, except in China, in Egypt, and among the Jews and the Zoroastrians. (The last exposed their dead, as they still do, to be consumed by vultures.) For more than one reason, early Christian sentiment was against cremation, and (as can be seen from the catacombs) burial was from the first regular Christian practice. For this there was more than one reason. For example, not only was cremation associated with pagan practice, the resurrection of the body was widely interpreted as implying the reassembling of the physical particles in such a way that the dead would rise with their bodies. Through Christian influence, burial became general throughout the Roman Empire by the 5th c. and until the 19th c. was still almost universal among Christians. Because the nature of resurrection has come to be understood by educated Christians in a less literalistic way, cremation has gained favor in the eyes of many, on the ground that it merely does more quickly what burial takes very much longer to accomplish. So cremation, which was formerly forbidden by canon law in the Roman Catholic Church, is now permitted, since July 5, 1963, and a form of service for cremation is provided. Cremation is likewise recognized in modern Anglican practice, and some Anglican liturgies provide even for disposal of the ashes at sea or otherwise, although interment of the ashes in consecrated ground is advocated.

Crib. A widespread, popular custom prevails in churches in the West according to which a crib, containing a statuette of the Christ Child and usually with figures such as those of the Virgin Mother, Joseph, angels, cattle, shepherds, and the Magi, is placed within the church building on Christmas Eve and kept there for a week or so. The origin of the practice is obscure, although tradition ascribes it to Francis of Assisi.

Crisis, Theology of. The theology developed by Karl Barth and his school is sometimes so designated. The Greek word *krisis* to which the allusion is made has connotations of separateness that are apposite to the Barthian emphasis on inter alia, the sharp distinction between the divine order and the human, between time and eternity. See **Dialectical Theology.**

Crispin and Crispinian, The Brothers. No evidence exists to attest their historical existence. According to legend they were of a noble Roman family and fled to Soissons during the Diocletian persecution. Becoming shoemakers, they made no charge for their work, accepting only donations, and in the end they were martyred. They are regarded in tradition as the patrons of cobblers and shoemakers.

Critical Apparatus. In editions of biblical texts a list of "variant" readings (i.e., readings different from those of the accepted text) is provided. By this means the student using a text such as that of the Greek New Testament can conveniently ascertain alternative readings and judge their value and importance in the particular scholarly enterprise in which he or she is engaged.

Critical Idealism. The name Kant gave to his philosophical system, which is an idealism based upon a critique of the capacities of human reason.

Critical Realism. A theory of perception. A group of American thinkers, including A. O. Lovejoy, George Santayana, and R. W. Sellars, published a volume entitled *Essays in Critical Realism* (1920). (Sellars had already used the term in earlier writings.) The Critical Realists' views of what is to be understood as Critical Realism varied considerably, but their common affirmation was to the effect that the sense-datum yields a complex set of "characters" to awareness and so points to the object that is being perceived. So, although a distinction is to be recognized between the sense-datum and the object, knowledge of the former reveals the latter. Some, notably Santayana, argued that in perception we become aware of "essences" that lead us directly to a grasp of the object.

Criticism, Biblical. The term "criticism" comes from the Greek verb *kritein*, "to discern." What has been traditionally called biblical criticism consists of the textual and literary analysis and interpretation of the Bible. Far from being necessarily destructive, its purpose is essentially to attain a fuller and richer understanding of the Bible: first by trying by the best scientific methods available to discover, as far as possible, the authentic biblical text;

then to understand it in its historical context so as to ascertain what the biblical writers meant in the circumstances in which they wrote and, moreover, what it would have meant to those who read or heard their words. Without such study much of the Bible is either unintelligible or misleading, thus resulting, to say the least, in a tragic impoverishment of its power as the instrument of divine illumination and the spur to Christian action that all Christians would see to be among its great functions. See **Textual Analysis** and **Critical Apparatus.**

Criticism, Philosophical. In philosophy, the significance of the term "criticism" or "critique" is exhibited in its use by Kant, e.g., his *Critique of Pure Reason* and *Critique of Judgment.* Kant's purpose was to demonstrate the limits of human understanding and in what sense we can be said to understand what is presented to us in our consciousness.

Croce, Benedetto (1866–1952). Italian philosopher. Born in Pescasseroli, he studied law at Rome and there came under the then pervasive influence of Hegel. He was led to philosophy by his interest in art history and criticism. He never held any academic position but held important political office in the Italian government, being senator, cabinet member, and (twice) Minister of Education. During the fascist régime he retired from public life. His first work was his *Estetica* (1901), a highly original philosophy of art, which he regarded as the lowest and therefore the most fundamental, of the four modes of human experience. These modes he classified under four heads: (1) the aesthetic or intuitive mode; (2) the conceptual or logical mode, which stands upon and is dependent on the aesthetic; (3) the "economic" (individual will); and (4) the ethical (rational will), which stands to (3) as (2) stands to (1), while the pair (3) and (4) stand to the pair (1) and (2) as (2) stands to (1) and as (4) stands to (3). His aesthetic is an expressionist the-

ory: art is the expression of an impression. History and philosophy are inseparable, for both are involved in the development of the spirit. The four realms or modes of experience constitute a whole that *is* the spirit. The basic function of philosophy is to describe them. His thought, although in a Hegelian mold, differs distinctly from Hegel's. (See his *What is living and What is Dead in the Philosophy of Hegel.* English tr., 1907). In his *Breviario di Estetica* (1913), he extrapolated and modified what he had written in the *Estetica*, especially in his treatment of the Ugly. Croce's Italian style is pellucid. Most of his writings have been translated into English, sometimes, however, misleadingly. In Hegelian fashion he recognized religion as a form of the aesthetic mode of experience and therefore (in his view of the aesthetic) an aspect of the most fundamental movement of the spirit. Theology, however, he regarded as an "impure" form of the conceptual mode: impure in the sense that it represents an illicit mixture of the modes. Croce's thought was introduced to the English speaking world mainly through the work of the Oxford philosopher R. G. Collingwood. Most of Croce's life was spent in Naples.

Cromwell, Oliver (1599–1658). Born at Huntingdon and educated at Cambridge, he was elected a member of Parliament in 1640. A zealous supporter of the Puritan party in the English Church, he sympathized with the spirit of the Independents. He assembled a splendidly trained "new model" army, which he used to great effect in the Civil War that had broken out in 1642 and which he saw as a religious or "holy" war against the forces of evil in the Church, which eventually he came to see as personified in the King (Charles I), who symbolized for him the forces opposing his aims. He was ruthless both as a military and as a political leader. Because of his fear that Ireland could become a military base for foreign sympathizers with the Stuart cause he put down insurrection in Ireland with terrible ferocity; so much so that to this day his name is remembered in Ireland as a symbol of savagery. In December 16, 1653, he was installed as "Lord Protector of England", and he was beyond all doubt the one supreme instrument whose genius led to the establishment (temporary though it was) of the Commonwealth, with all its political and religious implications. He was motivated by an intense religious zeal and an unshakable sense of having been called by God to act as he did. Such motivation is usually dangerous. Evidence points to his not having the personal ambitions characteristic of most political dictators, yet despite his virtues, few could have loved such a man, even among those who admired his purposes. No one can doubt, at any rate, that he played a unique role in the development of the subsequent political and religious history of England.

Cromwell, Thomas (*c.* **1485–1540**). Having spent his early life on the continent of Europe, he returned to England, where he won the favor of Wolsey. When the latter incurred the displeasure of the King (Henry VIII). Cromwell entered the latter's service and quickly became a champion of the royal supremacy over the Church. He rose rapidly to great influence as Henry's chief adviser. He was the principal instrument in the dissolution of the monasteries between 1536 and 1539: an action that provided large revenues for the Crown. At the same time he instituted some salutary reforms, such as the requirement that every clergyman should perform specific duties, and he also provided that a Bible should be kept in every church and that a register of births, deaths, and marriages should be kept. On April 7, 1540, he was made Earl of Essex and received large landed estates from the proceeds of the dissolution of the monasteries, but his day of glory was thereafter soon ended. The marriage with Anne of Cleves that he had arranged for Henry displeased the

latter. On July 28 of the same year, Cromwell, having been sentenced to death for treason, was beheaded.

Crosier. A staff used liturgically by bishops and sometimes also by certain abbots and abbesses. Its precise origin is disputed. In the West it is usually in the form of a shepherd's crook, but there is no historical or other important reason why it should be so designed. In the Eastern Church it is surmounted by a cross between two serpents. The crosier is to be distinguished from the cross used by archbishops.

Crown of Thorns. According to the Gospel account (John 19.2), a crown of thorns was placed on the head of Jesus in mockery and to add to his sufferings before the Crucifixion. According to a tradition from at least the 5th c., it had been preserved at Jerusalem. It was later said to have been then moved to Constantinople and to have come into the possession of Louis IX of France in the 13th c., who built the Sainte-Chapelle in Paris to house it.

Crozier. See **Crosier.**

Crucifix. A cross bearing the image of Christ crucified upon it. Although traditionally associated with Catholic worship in the West, its use has not been universal. In the Eastern Churches it is of course disallowed along with all three dimensional art, but may be represented in an ikon. In the Celtic Church in Scotland, is was unknown till Queen Margaret introduced Roman usages in the 11th c. It was often used, in the form of a rood screen hanging above the chancel entrance, in churches in Western Europe, but its use as the central ornament on the altar itself was not common till the 15th c.: a practice that remained general in the Roman Catholic Church till 1969, when it began to be sometimes replaced by a crucifix or cross on the wall. Except in the Lutheran Churches, the crucifix was generally regarded among Protestants to be "popish" and therefore was absent from their churches and private homes. Although Queen Elizabeth I had a crucifix in her private chapel, such a practice was rare in Anglican churches until the Tractarian movement in the 19th c. The cross itself, however, was widely accepted and its use common. In Protestant Churches even the use of the cross is often avoided.

Crucifixion. This terrible form of punishment by death, inflicted upon Jesus, originated in the East but was adopted by the Romans as the ultimate punishment for slaves. Neither crucifixion nor the flogging that customarily preceded it could be inflicted on a Roman citizen, but they could be inflicted in extreme cases on anyone unable to prove Roman citizenship. Crucifixion continued to be inflicted in the Roman Empire till the time of Constantine, who abolished its use. Some of the early Christian martyrs suffered it, including (according to tradition) some of the apostles. The victim was nailed through the wrists and feet and straddled upon a peg or other support to prevent the body from sagging. The cross on which Jesus suffered is generally depicted as having an upright beam above the transverse one, but there is some evidence (e.g., from the Epistle of Barnabas) that it was T-shaped. All the Gospels record his having been crucified between two malefactors.

Cruets. Vessels, usually of glass or crystal, in which the wine and water for Mass are contained and placed on the credence to be eventually brought to the altar.

Crusades. Expeditions from Western Europe to the East, often at first called pilgrimages, began to be undertaken in 1095 with a view to recovering the Holy Land from the Muslims. The motivation was partly political (to stem the tide of Islamic encirclement that posed a threat to Europe), but religious fervor of a kind was the principal stimulus among those who participated in these expeditions. Probably because of the cross conspicuously worn by them, they became known as crusaders, from the Latin, *crux*, a cross. The Church encouraged them by the grant of indulgences. If they were killed, they would have the status of martyrs. Even without such inducements from the Church, the sense of adventure no doubt sustained them, and many behaved more like soldiers marching off to battle than as pilgrims on their way to the Homeland of the Prince of Peace. The first series of expeditions ran from 1095 to 1204. Antioch was captured in the summer of 1098 and Jerusalem a year later. Baldwin, the brother of one of the leaders, Godfrey of Bouillon, was crowned King of Jerusalem on Christmas Day, 1100. The entire coastline of Syria and Palestine was captured and several regions held, if precariously, for some decades. As Islamic power grew, further contingents went out in 1147, inspired by the preaching of Bernard of Clairvaux and led by Louis VII of France. The recapture of Jerusalem and other territories by the Muslims provoked another crusade from 1189 to 1192, but it did not succeed in regaining Jerusalem for the Christians. In 1202 yet another crusade set out, but although it established a Latin Empire at Constantinople, the Christian side was weakened by divisions while Islamic influence expanded. Through the next two and a half centuries intermittent attempts were made under the Christian banner, but with the defeat by the Turks of a large expedition in 1396 at Nicopolis, the movement was irrevocably weakened and the Papacy turned its attention on less distant threats, while the Ottoman Empire grew in strength and survived till its final collapse in 1919.

Crusius, Christian August (1712–1775). German philosopher and theologian. Educated at Leipzig, where he eventually became professor, he was a vigorous opponent of Leibniz and Wolff, whom he accounted anti-Christian and whose deterministic philosophy he believed to be dangerous to morality. He followed the Pietistic tradition of Christian Thomasius and exercised considerable influence over Kant, who makes references to him in his own writings. Crusius's works include *Sketch of Necessary Rational Truths* (1745) and *The Way to Certainty and Reliability of Human Knowledge* (1747). According to Crucius, the logical principles of identity and contradiction rest on a principle of *cogitabilitas*, i.e., they are capable of being thought. What cannot be thought false is true and what cannot be thought at all is false. Most propositions fall between, yielding "moral" certitude and depending on hypotheses and inductive methods. Determinism cannot deal satisfactorily with the central problem of moral evil. He argues strongly for the principle of freedom of the will. The existence of God cannot be proved by the traditional arguments, but recognition of it is implied by the moral evidence, when this is taken seriously.

Crutched Friars. By "crutched" is meant "cross-bearing" (Latin, *cruciferi*). Their history is obscure, but several congregations of canons regular seem to have arisen in the Holy Land during the Crusades. Other congregations of this type appeared in Italy, Flanders, Poland, and Bohemia in the Middle Ages, but were suppressed at the French Revolution. A revival occurred later, and a body answering to this description now has houses in several European countries and in the United States.

Crypt. A basement underneath a church, sometimes used as a burial place or as a chapel.

Crypto-. This adjectival prefix is used by theologians in expressions such as "Crypto-Pelagian', "Crypto-Calvinist", "Crypto-Monophysite" and the like. It is used to signify what may be a secret allegiance to a stance, a latent predisposition toward it, or a tendency, conscious or otherwise, in the direction of a theological view. For example, the view that was officially accepted and taught

by the Church in the Middle Ages on the subject of grace and free will was the Augustinian one, which had triumphed over that of Pelagius. Nevertheless, it may be very plausibly argued that in popular devotions and practices encouraged by the Church, a sort of Crypto-Pelagianism, with an emphasis on "merit" and "good works," seems to have prevailed. Similarly, despite the clear insistence at Chalcedon on the belief that Christ is both fully human and fully divine, the popular image of Christ in medieval life seems to have more and more been one in which the humanity is ousted by the divinity to the point where, as in Michelangelo's famous painting he becomes more the Divine Judge in majesty rather than the loving Good Shepherd. This might be called a Crypto-Monophysitism. See also **Semi-Pelagianism.**

Cudworth, Ralph (1617–1688). Cambridge Platonist. Born in Somerset and educated at Cambridge, he became Master of Christ's College and one of the leaders of the Cambridge Platonists. His writings include *The True Intellectual System of the Universe* (1678) and *A Treatise Concerning Eternal and Immutable Morality* (1731). In ethics he held that moral distinctions are not merely created by the State, as was Hobbes's contention; they are eternal. Religious truth, he held, is embodied in three great principles: (1) the reality of the divine Intelligence and of the spiritual dimension of being created by that Intelligence; (2) the eternal reality of ethical concepts; and (3) the reality of moral freedom and responsibility.

Cujus Regio, Ejus Religio. The principle enunciated by the "Peace of Augsburg" in 1555, that each principality in Germany should follow the religion of its prince, and that if one did not like the religion one should migrate to a principality where the religion was to one's liking. This was a device to remedy the dispeace created by the controversies between Catholics and

Lutherans at the time of the Reformation in Germany. See **Augsburg Confession**.

Culdees. The name given to certain monks in the Celtic Church in the 8th c. and later. The Culdees seem to have been originally eremitical or quasi-eremitical and to have later come together in groups, apparently in groups of thirteen, modelled on the concept of Christ and the twelve apostles. With the romanization of the ancient Celtic Church they disappeared, being eventually superseded by the canons regular.

Cullmann, Oscar (1902–   ). Biblical scholar and theologian. Born at Strassburg and educated there and at Paris, he became professor at the University of Strassburg in 1930, later at Basel and also at the Faculté Protestante in Paris. The main focus of his work is in a theory of sacred history (*Heilsgeschichte*), expounded in writings such as his *Christ and Time* (English tr., 1951) and his *Salvation in History* (English tr., 1967). He contends (against existentialist interpretations such as those of Bultmann) for the objectivity of what he sees as "sacred history." His work has also encompassed an active participation in ecumenical enterprises. His essay on "Immortality of the Soul or Resurrection of the Dead" (Ingersoll Lecture for 1955), published in K. Stendahl, *Immortality and Resurrection* (New York: The Macmillan Company, 1965), is an especially notable contribution to an understanding of an important aspect of New Testament theology.

Culture. From the Latin, *colere* ("to till, to cultivate"). In a general sense this term has been used for all human endeavors and enterprises, but in a narrower sense it has been used to designate the results in human society of the cultivation of the liberal arts. The term came into use in the 18th c. Spengler distinguished between culture and civilization, regarding the latter as the final stage in a society's development. Some have seen the civilizing process as continuous and the cultural as sporadic. At all events, the terms are not to be taken as synonymous. Although the term "culture" is of comparatively recent invention, it stands for a concept that is so embedded in the history of thought and life from antiquity that for long the need to name it could hardly have arisen.

Culverwell, Nathanael (c. 1618–1651). English philosopher. Born in London and educated at Cambridge, he studied under philosophers of the Cambridge Platonist school there, but he combined such influence with a mixture of Aristotelian, Thomist, and Calvinist thought, emphasizing the absolute authority of God in both natural law and election to salvation. His writings include *Spiritual Opticks* (1651) and *An Elegant and Learned Discourse on the Light of Nature* (1652).

Cumberland, Richard (1632–1718). English philosopher and, from 1691, Bishop of Peterborough. His *De legibus naturae disquisitio philosophica* (1672) was conceived as a refutation of Hobbes and may be regarded as an adumbration of utilitarianism, if not its seminal document.

Cum Occasione. The papal bull issued in 1653 condemning Jansenism.

Cunciform. From the Latin *cuneus* ("wedge"). The script used widely throughout the Near East in antiquity, probably invented by the Sumerians and developed out of pictorial writing. Ancient Akkadian and other inscriptions are written in it. It is so called because of the wedge-shaped element in the characters.

Curate. Strictly, a curate is a cleric who has the "cure" (i.e., the charge of a parish), such as would be called in France a *curé* and in Anglican churches a rector or vicar. In popular usage, however, an assistant or associate priest serving a parish without tenure is often so designated, especially in England.

Curé d'Ars. See **Vianney, Jean-Baptiste Marie.**

Curia. This is the name given to the central administration of the government of the Roman Catholic Church, including the Pope and the various tribunals, permanent commissions, and others, as well as the cardinals and bishops at Rome in whom the highest executive authority under the Pope is vested. The term was used in the Middle Ages of any court, and nowadays it is sometimes applied to diocesan legal and other officials who advise a local bishop. A reform of the structure of the Roman Curia was undertaken under Paul VI in 1967.

Cursive. In antiquity the characters of the alphabet were written separately, but eventually, c. the 8th c. CE, a speedier form of writing began to appear, in which the rounded Greek miniscule (i.e., lowercase) alphabet was used with the characters gracefully joined together to form the words. By the 9th c. this new method, called cursive script, had become general except in certain liturgical texts in which a bolder form of writing seemed desirable. (See **Uncial.**)

Cusanus, Nicolaus. See **Nicholas of Cusa.**

Custom. Any course of action that becomes habitual. The psychological effect of custom in every society is immense, not least in all forms of organized religion. People tend to become quickly "accustomed" to the way in which things have been done in the past and that they have come to find natural and congenial. They also tend to come to believe, as Montesquieu pointed out in his satire on his own French society (see **Montesquieu, Charles de Secondat**) that their own customs are or ought to be universal. Hume drew attention to the power of custom over thought, especially in his critique of the concepts of causation in traditional philosophy. In religious thought and practice, custom provides psychological solace and may have some beneficial effects, but it can stultify thought and inhibit the development of authentic religious experience. It is notorious that people often cling more tenaciously to comparatively recent customs than to ancient ones that may have more to commend them so long as one recognizes their consuetudinary nature. Nowhere is this more patent than in organized religion. As every parish priest and pastor knows, it can be easier to persuade people to abandon a venerable liturgical practice that has proved its value throughout many centuries than to change a hymn tune.

Customaries. The customary was a book setting forth the various rites and ceremonies used in the service, together with the disciplinary rules and customs of the particular religious order, monastery or cathedral in which it was used. Known also as the *Liber Ordinarius*, it was important in the Middle Ages when local practice varied considerably and each place tended to guard jealously its traditional ways. The customaries are of importance to liturgical and other scholars.

Cuthbert. A 7th c. Bishop of Lindisfarne. A monk at Melrose, Scotland, where he became prior, he (with his abbot) moved in 664 to Lindisfarne, where they adopted the Roman usages. Two years later he withdrew to the nearby island of Farne where he remained a hermit for some eight years. Eventually, in 685, he became Bishop of Lindisfarne. Three centuries later, in 999, his body was moved to Durham Cathedral.

Cybernetics. The study of communication systems found in machines as well as in living organisms, notably the study of the self-regulatory features of artificial automata that exhibit "purposiveness" and other functions such as are traditionally assigned to the human mind. This is an area of some importance for modern Christian thought, since it is necessary to distinguish between the kind of "purposiveness" that may be predicated of computers and the like and of certain functions of the brain, on the one hand, and, on the other, the kind of "purposiveness" that Christian and other philosophical theologians see in the actions of the human spirit when exercising the freedom given to creatures by the grace of their divine Creator.

Cynewulf. A 9th c. Anglo-Saxon poet whose poetry is almost all devoted to Christian topics.

Cynicism. One of the Greek philosophical schools, founded in or about the 5th c. BCE and, revitalized in the 1st c. CE, continued till at least the 5th c., by which time some of its representatives had fused it with other philosophical schools and with Christianity as expressed in Nicene orthodoxy. (See **Maximus of Alexandria.**) The term probably comes from the name of the building in Athens in which the Cynics were first housed, the Cynosarges, although some have seen in it a derogatory allusion to *kyōn*, meaning "doglike", an epithet that may have been applied to them in derision. The Cynics led a life of simplicity and independence such as tends to enrage conventional society and did evoke such reaction both in Greek and in Roman society. They taught rigorous self-control and practiced austerity and restraint. Although traditionally they are said to have been founded by Antisthenes, a disciple of Socrates, who in turn taught Diogenes Laertius, it is more likely that Diogenes was in fact the founder and that the traditional account was the invention of later Cynics who wished to invoke the name of Socrates by way of enhancing the school's prestige. It was Crates, one of the followers of Diogenes, who originated the style of satirical parody that was developed by Bion of Borysthenes in the 3rd c. BCE into the literary form known as the diatribe. Zeno of Citium, the founder of Stoicism, was a disciple

of Crates and a Cynic who modified and adapted Cynic teachings in developing his own school which, in one of its later forms deeply influenced early Christian thought. Others, such as Sallustius in the 5th c. CE, combined Cynic views with a Neoplatonic outlook. The Cynics' ridicule of the follies of society, its deceits, and its abuse of power, made them especially feared and hated: emotions that Socrates himself had evoked.

Cyprian. Early 3rd c. Bishop of Carthage. Converted to the Christian faith *c.* 246, he quickly became well versed in the Bible and became Bishop of Carthage within two years of his conversion. He had to flee when the Decian persecution broke out in 249 but was able to return two years later. He is important among the early Fathers of the West. Although not gifted with any notable theological perceptivity, he was a practical man and his works (including his many letters) reflect his practical outlook. His work *On the Unity of the Catholic Church* (251) is much admired by those who see the Church as the indispensable instrument of divine grace. It is in that work that his much quoted saying occurs: "He cannot have God as his Father who has not the Church as his Mother." He was martyred on September 14, 258.

Cyprian. A 6th c. Bishop of Toulon. In 529 he took a prominent part in opposing Semi-Pelagianism at the Council of Orange. In one of his letters he defends himself against a charge of Theopaschitism. He also wrote a life of Caesarius of Arles.

Cyrenaicism. This school of Greek philosophy that fourished in the fourth and third centuries BCE takes its name from the city of Cyrene in Libya, where Aristippus, its founder, was born. Aristippus held that physical pleasure is to be preferred to intellectual pleasure. Intensity is the criterion of pleasure. This extreme and simplistic view was modified by some of his followers in the 3rd c., e.g., by Annikeris, who recognized the importance of the pleasures of friendship and other social relationships. The teachings of this school were too meager to support its continuance and, in contrast to the comparatively long-lived Epicurean school, Cyrenaicism lost influence, declined, and eventually vanished.

Cyril (826–69) and Methodius (*c.* 815–85). These two brothers, popularly known as "the Apostles of the Slavs," came of a senatorial family in Thessalonica. Cyril's name was originally Constantine; he adopted the name Cyril on becoming a monk in 868. After some time as librarian at Hagia Sophia in Constantinople, he went with his younger brother on a mission to what is now Moravia. Naturally they had to teach in the vernacular language and Cyril invented an alphabet that scholars call "Glagolithic", although the Cyrillic alphabet (a similar one deriving from about the same period) is attributed to him. (See **Cyrillic**.) He may be credited, therefore, not only with providing a liturgy for the Slavonic peoples in the Slavonic language but also with founding Slavonic literature. Some years later the two brothers went to Rome, where Cyril died and was buried in San Clemente. Methodius returned to Moravia.

Cyrillic. The alphabet used by the Slavonic peoples and attributed, although not with strict accuracy, to the Cyril who with his brother Methodius introduced Christianity to the Slavs in the 9th c. Cyrillic is based on Greek uncials. See **Cyril and Methodius**.

Cyril Lukar (1572–1638). Patriarch of Constantinople. Born in Crete, he studied at Venice and Padua, where he imbibed and became much interested in the thought of the West. Having attended the Synod of Bresk-Litovsk, he became disillusioned with the Roman Catholic Church and developed an interest in Calvinism. His interest in the Anglican Way impelled him to send Metrophanes Critopoulos to Oxford in 1617 to study there. Appointed Patri-

arch of Constantinople in 1620, he introduced ideas to the Eastern Church that were unacceptable to many, and he encountered much opposition from various quarters. He presented the Codex Alexandrinus, one of the most important of all biblical manuscripts, to King James in 1625, through diplomatic channels. By the time it reached England, James was dead and it was received by Charles I. (See **Codex Alexandrinus**.) A far-sighted and theologically sensitive churchman, the best the Eastern Orthodox Church had produced since the Fall of Constantinople in 1453, he became more and more the victim of political and ecclesiastical hostility and intrigue, and, accused of inciting the Cossacks against the Turks, he was cruelly executed by the Sultan Murad.

Cyril of Alexandria. Early 5th c. Patriarch of Alexandria. In accordance with the spirit of the Alexandrian school, he championed the use of the term Theotokos. He opposed and was prominent in the condemnation of Nestorius. He was a theologian of great perspicacity, incisive and precise in his thought. He is also said to have been a great preacher, although comparatively few of his sermons survive.

Cyril of Jerusalem (*c.* 315–86). Bishop of Jerusalem from *c.* 349. Banned for a time by Acacius on account of his resistance to the latter's Arian views, he was recalled in 359 by the Council of Seleucia.

Cyril of Scythopolis. A 6th c. hagiographer. A Greek monk and priest, his writings provide one of the best and most accurate sources for the lives of early Eastern saints.

D

Dachéry, Jean Luc (1609–1685). Patristic scholar. A Benedictine of the Maurist congregation, he was for many years librarian at the abbey of Saint Germain-des-Prés, Paris. He engaged in many important scholarly works including an edition of the works of Lanfranc.

Dadhikrā. A deity in Hindu literature (e.g. Ṛgveda IV, 39, 7), in the form of a heavenly horse and symbolizing the highest form of knowledge (*madhuvidyā*). He is allied with the sun and with various deities who order the universe. He also guides human beings through the journey of life.

Dadhyac. Son of the fire-priest Atharvan (Ṛgveda I, 80, 16) who kindled Agni, the fire-god. Indra taught him the highest knowledge (*madhuvidyā*) with the warning that if he divulged it he would lose his head. To outwit Indra, Dadhyac's head was removed and replaced with that of a horse and when Indra cut off the equine head it was then replaced by his own. There are variants of this legend. According to one account, Dadhyac possessed a mysterious power over the gods, which kept them in their place in heaven until he went up thither and then they spread across the earth. He embodies the concept of service for others. See **Horse.**

Daibutsu. The name given to several colossal images of the Buddha (sometimes also to those of bodhisattvas) in Japan, notably three: (1) the 53 foot seated Buddha in the Todaiji temple at Nara, erected in 754 CE as a witness to the importing of Buddhism into Japan and its assimilation with Shinto, the national religion; (2) the one at Kyoto, also a seated figure, 58½ feet high, completed early in the 17th c., destroyed by earthquake in 1662 and replaced by the present one that dates from 1801; and (3) the image, 49½ feet high, of Amida Buddha at Kamakura, erected in 1252. It was built in celebration of the "Pure Land" Buddhist sect, which venerates the Buddha under the transcendental form of Amida, who is believed to lead his devotees to "Pure Land" of light.

Daillé, Jean (1595–1670). Reformed Church theologian and controversialist.

Trained in Poitiers and Saumur, he travelled in Italy and England and from 1626 till his death was pastor at Charenton, the center of the French Protestants of Paris, where he acquired great repute as a preacher and theologian. He engaged in much literary controversy with both Roman Catholic and Anglican theologians, e.g., in *La Foi fondée sur les saintes écritures* (1634).

D'ailly, Pierre (1350–1420). Theologian and cardinal. Born at Compiègne, he studied at the College of Navarre, Paris, a stronghold of Nominalism, at that time. This influence is seen in his writings, which also reflect the strong influence of William of Occam and Roger Bacon. As a churchman he was much preoccupied with attempts to end the great schism of his time that had brought about rival claimants to the papacy. He supported the claims of Alexander V, whose successor, John XXIII, made him a cardinal. In 1414 he participated in the Council of Constance, supporting the conciliarists. He also contended that priests receive their authority directly from Christ, not through the Pope, and he specifically rejected both the infallibility of the Pope and that of the General Council. He exercised considerable influence both on Gallicanism and on the Reformation Fathers.

Dair Balaizah Fragments. Part of a papyrus codex dating from *c.* the 6th c. and discovered in 1907. Now in the Bodleian Library, Oxford, it contains various liturgical prayers that are very helpful for an understanding of the development of liturgical practice in Egypt. The text of the prayers has been variously dated from *c.* the early 3rd c. to the late 6th c.

Daityas. Giants, titans represented in the post-Vedic period of Hindu literature as demons resistant to the gods (*devas*). Sometimes they are represented as those tribes who resisted Aryan expansion, both politically and religiously.

Ḍākinis. In both Hindu and Buddhist Tantrism they are represented as powerful spirits. In Hinduism they attend Kālī, who both gives and destroys life. One of them, Pūtanā, is said to have tried to poison the child Kṛṣṇa. In Buddhist Tantrism, one of them, often found in Buddhist iconography, is the goddess Vajravāhārī, who has the power to bewitch men and women. The male counterpart of the *ḍākini* is the *ḍāka*.

Dakṣa. A son of Brahmā and one of the six (according to some accounts twelve) Ādityas. In the Vedic period existence and non-existence are represented in paradoxical ways, e.g., Dakṣa was born of Aditi, yet Aditi was the offspring of Dakṣa. The gods, having a common origin, are born of each other. In the literature come further developments, e.g., in the Brāhmaṇas, Dakṣa, who stands for universal creative energy, comes to be associated with priestly power. In the Purāṇas, as a secondary creator, he is present in each age (*manvantara*). Dakṣa also comes to be represented as coming to perceive the futility of "mental" progeny and so decided to introduce sexual intercourse. Along with this development comes an insistence on the virtues of family life. So many were the conflicting accounts about Dakṣa that the compilers of the Purāṇas came to explain the inconsistencies by the notion that in every *manvantara* or cosmic age, different situations arise, each requiring an apposite treatment.

Dakṣiṇā. The honorarium given to Hindu priests who perform a sacrifice on behalf of the donor. The priests depended on such gifts for their maintenance. The original form of the gift was a cow and the concept of such giving is identified with a goddess Dakṣiṇā, who is regarded as the Cosmic Cow or Nature.

Dalai Lama. Buddhism came to Tibet, in the 7th c. CE. The Tibetan Buddhist monks are called *lamas*, a term signify-ing "one who is superior." Of the three principal orders of monks, the largest is the Gelukpa (often called by Westerners the "Yellow Hats") and the Grand Lama of that order, whose headquarters were at Lhasa, came to be called, in the 16th c., the Dalai Lama. According to tradition, he had gone to Mongolia at the request of a Mongol ruler to revive Buddhism there and was given the title "Dalai", which means "the sea", in allusion to the depth of wisdom he displayed. Until the Chinese communists invaded Tibet in 1950, he was both the spiritual and the temporal ruler of Tibet and widely regarded as an incarnation of the Buddha. When the Tibetans rose in rebellion in 1959, they were ruthlessly quelled and the Dalai Lama and some others made their escape to India.

Dale, Robert (1829–1895). English Protestant theologian and educationist. For most of his life he was associated with Birmingham, England, in the municipal affairs of which he took a very prominent part. In *The Atonement* (1875) he upheld a traditionalist theological view against the "liberals" of his day. In 1891 he was President of the International Congregational Council.

D'alembert, Jean Le Rond (1717–1783). Philosopher and mathematician. A foundling child, he was educated by the Jansenists. He showed a remarkable mathematical aptitude, which bore fruit in important discoveries in mathematics and mechanics. A contributor to the *Encyclopédie*, he was associated with Diderot and other thinkers having "advanced" views.

Dalmatic. In the Western Church, the name of a knee-length vestment worn over the stole and alb by deacons at High Mass. Its name may be derived from its possible origin in Dalmatia. It has two colored strips, traditionally called *clavi*, that run from front to back over the shoulders. It is probably derived from a garment favored by the upper classes at Rome in the 2nd c. The *sakkos* worn by Eastern Orthodox bishops is similar in appearance.

Damascius (c. 470– c. 530). Last head of the Neoplatonic School of Athens. When Justin closed the school in 529 he went into exile. He recognized that "the One" cannot be determined either positively or negatively, because the finite and the imperfect cannot grasp the infinite and the perfect. The One, therefore, can be approached only through mystical experience.

Damascus. This extremely ancient city, mentioned by the Egyptian king Thutmoses III in the 16th c. BCE, was the capital of Syria. After it fell to the Assyrian king Tiglath Pileser in 732 BCE, it lost much of its importance and eventually Antioch became the Syrian capital. Paul was converted to the Christian Way while traveling on the road from Jerusalem to Damascus, according to Acts 9, and since the days of the apostles a Christian community has continuously lived in Damascus.

Damasus (c. 304–384). Pope from 366. Of Spanish descent, he was much involved in the suppression of Arianism, Pelagianism, and other theological movements, and in 382 he held a council, probably at Rome, in which the canon of Scripture that was to be recognized by the Christian Church was determined. He also commissioned Jerome to provide a new Latin translation of the Bible, which was to become known as the Vulgate and remained the official text of the Bible in the West throughout the Middle Ages.

Damien, Father (1840–1889). Joseph de Veuster, he took the name of Damien and became famous as a missionary to the lepers (some 600 of them) on the island of Molokai in the Pacific, who had been without spiritual ministry or medical attention. He devoted himself to this work till inevitably he became a victim to the disease but, now assisted by others, he continued his work until no longer able to do so.

Dāna. In Pali this word means literally "giving", which is one of the principal Buddhist virtues. It may take many forms, from simple hospitality to guests to bequeathing something important to a monastery or building a pagoda.

Dance of Death, The. In medieval art, the representation of Death as a skeleton leading people of all ages to the grave was a favorite subject for artists, providing a reminder of the brevity of human life. An engraving by Hans Holbein provides an example. It is also known by the French name: *Danse macabre.*

Daṇḍa. The term has two meanings in Hindu usage. (1) It is a rod or sceptre placed in the hands of the goddess Kālī, personifying her inexorable power, the power of Time; but it is also a protection against evil spirits. (2) It also represents the embodiment of the principle of universal law. By submitting to punishment one may escape the consequences in a future life of the offenses one commits in the present one.

Daniel. A partly narrative, partly apocalyptic book in the Old Testament dating from c. 165 BCE.

Daniel. A 5th c. Stylite, disciple of Simeon Stylites. After some years in various monastic houses, he went to a place four miles from Constantinople, where he took up his habitation on a pillar which he is said never to have left for more than thirty years except for one occasion when he went to the Emperor (Basiliscus) to rebuke him for supporting Monophysitism. For more on this curious development of the eremitical ideal see **Simeon Stylites.**

Dante (1265–1321). Except that he was born in Florence, the early circumstances of the life of Dante Alighieri, one of the greatest literary figures in human history and sometimes called the Father of Italian poetry, are some what obscure. In his *Vita Nuova*, written in his twenty-sixth year, he tells us that, when he was nearly ten, he first saw "the glorious lady of his mind," Beatrice. When he saw her again nine years later in the street she politely saluted him. A few years later, in 1290, she died. Beatrice became, for Dante, the symbol of human perfection. He promised in the *Vita Nuova* that he would write for her a poem such as had been written for no lady before: a promise he redeemed by making her the heroine of his *Paradiso*, the third part of the *Divina Commedia*, the greatest epic poem in the history of Christian literature. He studied philosophy at Florence, probably under the Dominicans, and wrote several poems on the Lady Philosophy and other subjects. In 1294 he engaged in politics, joining the party of the Bianchi (politically the opponents of Pope Boniface VIII), so incurring the pope's wrath, which led to Dante's exile in 1301 from his beloved Florence. He thenceforth led a wandering life. He was for some time in Paris and he died in Ravenna. His *Convivio* is a sort of philosophical counterpart to his earlier *Vita Nuova*. His *De Monarchia* argues for a universal monarch to insure liberty and peace for all humankind. Nevertheless, he acknowledged the independence of the Church and certainly recognized that this life is but a prelude to and a test for the life hereafter. What is so distinctive in Dante's outlook as exhibited in his greatest work is the importance he gives to the individual soul both in its earthly pilgrimage and in its destiny. The great human drama extends from this life to the afterlife, about which Dante provides an allegory of extraordinary power in the three parts of his masterpiece: the *Inferno*, the *Purgatorio*, and the *Paradiso*. Dante is, besides much else, the forerunner of the great Christian humanists, as is attested by his admiration for Virgil, who conducts him through hell and purgatory yet must give place to Beatrice for the journey through heaven. See **Divina Commedia.**

Darboy, Georges (1813–1871). Archbishop of Paris from 1863. He was one of the leading opponents of the doctrine of Papal Infallibility at the First Vatican Council. He was a good bishop who, when Paris was under siege in 1870–1871, devoted himself unstintingly to the care of his people, especially the destitute. When the Commune triumphed, he was callously shot and killed on May 24, 1871, and he died uttering a blessing on those who killed him.

Daridrā. In Hindu lore, the goddess of poverty, disappointment, and despair.

Dark Ages. When it was fashionable to denigrate everything medieval, this term was often applied by way of abuse to the entire millennium called the Middle Ages, which comprises much of the finest culture in Europe, many of the greatest painters, and some of the great thinkers, as well as vivacious spirituality, diligent scholarship, and remarkable technological skill. As such it was inapposite to the point of absurdity. It is nowadays sometimes applied, with more propriety, to the earlier Middle Ages (*c.* 500–*c.* 800), a period during which conditions were primitive, anarchy prevalent, and culture stagnant. Genuine thinkers were rare. The later Middle Ages, especially from the 12th c. till the Renaissance, were anything other than dark.

Darkness. As a mythological category, darkness is used throughout the Bible, from the opening of Genesis onward, as a symbol of chaos and of the primeval abyss out of which the universe is created. In this sense it is always set in opposition to light, a symbol of divinity, revelation, and truth. So in John's Prologue (John 1), the Logos comes to the world as the light coming into the darkness, but the darkness could not understand it, so the light went generally unnoticed. Darkness at noon (Amos 8.9) is represented the ultimate catastrophe. Darkness is seen as evil: Satan and other wicked agencies work out of darkness although often assuming the appearance of light in order to achieve the deception they must employ to corrupt the minds and hearts of men and women. Sinners are cast into darkness: the darkness to which their sin belongs. The term functions both mythologically and metaphorically in such ways, especially in John; nevertheless, it is sometimes used of course in a straightforward empirical sense as would anyone use it in referring to night or a room devoid of sunlight. The mythological and empirical uses are sometimes confused, e.g., in the opening verses of Genesis, in which God not only creates light, thus dispelling darkness (chaos), but at the same time gives darkness a name (night) as he gives a name to light (day).

Darpa. In Hindu usage an epithet meaning "insolence" or "pride", given to the god Kāma, who personifies pride.

Darshana. Sanskrit term meaning "vision" or "view". In Indian philosophy the goal of every system is to attain an intuitive vision of the whole of reality. Each of the various philosophical and religious systems claims to provide such a vision but can do so only in an imperfect way. In the last resort, each individual has his or her own *darshana*. The notion is expressed in the old tale of the four blind men who encountered an elephant. One, grasping its huge leg said it was like a tree trunk; another who had caught its tail declared it to be like a rope; yet another, taking hold of its trunk, pronounced the elephant to be like a snake; the last, feeling its big, flappy ear, said the elephant is like a rug. None of them was wrong; each of them was right, but each was limited in his *darshana* of the whole.

Dāruka. The name of Kṛṣṇa's charioteer in Hindu folklore.

Darwin, Charles (1809–1882). English scientist. Born in Shrewsbury and educated at Cambridge, he began, soon af-

ter graduation, a five-year voyage on the "Beagle", during which he collected an enormous amount of evidence as a naturalist that eventually served him well as he developed his theory of the evolution of life. Early in 1858 he received a paper from Alfred Wallace pointing to the same conclusions that he was reaching. This paper, along with an abstract of Darwin's own findings, was read a few months later that year at the Linnaean Society. Wallace, a self-educated naturalist, thenceforth became second only to Darwin in arguing for the theory.

Darwin published his epoch-making book, *The Origin of Species*, on November 24, 1859. The theory of evolution was not entirely new, for some writers in antiquity and the eccentric Scottish Lord Monboddo in the 18th c. had suggested such ideas, each in his own way; but Darwin and Wallace were the first to amass such a vast array of evidence. Moreover, while their influence in the biological field was enormous, great thinkers in other fields were veering toward an evolutionary understanding of the universe as a whole. Although at first Darwin's views shocked many and much Christian opinion resisted the theory he developed, by the end of the century many of the most thoughtful Christians had begun to see evolution as "God's way of doing things," and therefore could look upon not only Darwin's biological theory but the general tendency of late nineteenth-century evolutionary thought as a promise of the enrichment of Christian thought rather than the threat that so many at first had taken it to be. Although evolutionary concepts still meet with hostility in certain Christian circles, the vast majority of educated Christians and Jews accept it, many seeing it indeed as a notable example of how "science" and "religion" can be allies when each is at its best.

Dasein. This German term is used in existentialism to designate that kind of existence that applies properly to things, contradistinguished from the kind of existence that applies to individuals who are living authentically, not merely as things. Sartre represents *Dasein* by the French expression *être en soi*, which he contrasts with *être pour soi*, the existence proper to authentic exis tence in individuals. See **Existentialism**.

Davenport, James (1716–1757). Revivalistic preacher during the "Great Awakening," a movement that spread in the 18th c. from Nova Scotia to Georgia, affecting all classes. While the movement was an emotional one that tended to evoke weeping and even swooning among the hearers, its leaders generally sought to discourage excesses of this kind. Davenport, however, was an extremist who did much to bring the movement into disrepute through his encouragement of such displays. In 1741 he followed the trail blazed by Whitefield and Tennent into Connecticut. He would sing as he made his way to the place of preaching, where he indulged in indiscrimate denunciations of ministers and in incoherent utterances. He also publicly greeted the elect (whom he claimed to recognize on sight) as "brethren" while hailing the non-elect as "neighbors". Eventually, those opposed to the movement used him as an example to discredit it. See **Great Awakening, The**.

Davenport, John (1597–1670). English Puritan divine. Educated at Oxford, he was for some time vicar of an English parish, then served in the English church at Amsterdam. In 1637 he sailed with other refugees to Boston and the following year founded the colony of New Haven, which in 1665 was absorbed in Connecticut. His many works include *The Power of Congregational Churches Asserted and Vindicated* (1672).

David. The 6th c. Patron saint of Wales. The story of his life is very obscure. According to legend reported centuries after his death he belonged to a noble family, was ordained priest, lived for some time in retirement, then founded a dozen monasteries, and finally settled in Mynyw (Menevia) where he founded an abbey. He attended, *c*. 560, the Synod of Brefi.

David, King of Israel. The exact date of his reign cannot be stated with precision, but he succeeded Saul, whose reign may be estimated to have lasted 1020–1000 BCE. According to the biblical record (I Samuel 16.1–13), he was anointed king by Samuel as divinely chosen, not for any hereditary or other claim. He is represented as having been introduced to Saul (I Samuel 16.14 ff.) as a musician. Then, in an independent story we hear of his slaying of Goliath. As a result of such gifts and early accomplishments he quickly attains great popularity. Despite confusions in the account, it seems clear that (a) David was by no means an exemplar of the best that Hebrew tradition has bequeathed to us either in religion or in ethical conduct, for plainly he was an intellectually simpleminded man, ambitious and at time ruthless and violent, being also ready to see his own actions as divinely approved, and (b) he was, in terms of his time and other circumstances, a great ruler and probably a politically shrewd one. The Bible makes no attempt to cover up his failings or his misdeeds. David suffered many misfortunes, but he did well what a potentate of his time was expected to do, and he has survived in history as such. Traditionally the Book of Psalms is attributed to him and seventy-three of them bear his name. Only a very few of them, however, could possibly have been composed by him as they have come down to us in their present form.

Davidic Descent. See **Genealogies of Jesus Christ, two**.

David of Augsburg (*c*. 1200–1272). German mystic. Born at Augsburg, he joined the Franciscans at Regensburg, eventually gaining great repute as a preacher. He was the first to write spiritual works in German. He emphasized humility and obedience, taught a practical kind of spirituality but one that held before his readers the vision of a mystical union of the soul with God. His German works include *Die sieben Vorregeln der Tugend* and *Der Spiegel der Tugend*.

David of Dinant. Early 13th c. philosopher and naturalist. He probably came from Dinant on the Meuse. His writings show a good knowledge of Aristotle, whose thought was the major influence on his own. According to Albertus Magnus and Thomas Aquinas, he identified God with prime matter. In 1210 the Provincial Council of Paris forbade the teachings of Aristotle's "natural philosophy" in public or private and a few years later prohibited Aristotle's works on metaphysics and natural philosophy, along with other thinkers such as David of Dinant and (probably) Averroes. If David thought he was interpreting Aristotle rightly, he was of course much mistaken. What is historically important and interesting is that at least he was instrumental in pointing the way to the great 13th c. schoolmen's recognition that Aristotle (who represented to the 13th c. the threat of "science" to "religion") was in fact much more of an ally (an *ancilla* or handmaiden) to religion than its foe.

Davidson, Andrew Bruce (1831–1902). Scottish biblical scholar. Educated at Aberdeen and Edinburgh Universities, he became, at the latter, professor of Hebrew and Oriental languages in 1863 and was among the first in Scotland to introduce historical methods of biblical interpretation. Among his students was W. R. Smith, who carried his methods further and alarmed conservative opinion. (See **Smith, William Robertson.**) In 1874 Davidson wrote a Hebrew grammar that was widely used for generations. He also wrote several biblical commentaries.

Davidson, Randall Thomas (1848–1930). Archbishop of Canterbury (1903–1928). He was a trusted adviser to Queen Victoria and exercised a great deal of influence on both Church and State in the England of his time.

Davies, Samuel (1723–1761). American Presbyterian divine. Sent to Virginia by the Synod of New York in 1748, he spearheaded the Presbyterian cause. In 1759 he became President of the College of New Jersey, which later became Princeton University. He was an important leader in the "Great Awakening." Although he regarded Presbyterianism as the ideal form of church polity, he opposed the sectarian spirit and did much to encourage an ecumenical and tolerant outlook. See **Great Awakening, The.**

Dayā. A term used in Hindu tradition to denote "sympathy" and "compassion". It is personified as a daughter of Dakṣa and the wife of Dharma.

Day Hours. The services known as the *Opus Dei* and set forth in the Breviary traditionally included Mattins (the night office) and the rest, which constituted the "day hours" such as Lauds, Prime, Vespers, and others. These were to be found in the book called the Diurnal or Day Hours. See also **Breviary.**

Deacon. From the Greek *diakonos*, servant. According to Acts 6.1–6, seven men were appointed to assist the apostles in the service of the poor and for other such duties. Traditionally that is taken to have been the origin of the diaconate. Within New Testament times, however, deacons are already cited as a rank or class of men serving in the ministry of the Church. They are frequently mentioned by writers in the sub-apostolic age and in patristic times. They read or sang the Epistle and Gospel and assisted the priest in various ways. The deacon wears the dalmatic with the stole worn over the left shoulder and tied at the waist on the right. In the Lutheran Church, assistant clergy are called deacons and in Presbyterian churches, the name "deacon" is often applied to persons who manage the temporal affairs of the church. In Congregational and some other Protestant churches deacons have more definitely spiritual functions.

Deaconess. The concept of an office in the Church for women charged with certain duties connected with the care of the sick and the instruction of women catechumens goes back to New Testament times (Romans 16.1 and I Timothy 3.11), but the office of deaconess as so designated (*diaconissa*) with specific functions emerged later. In the Eastern Church the deaconess was invested with the stole and was authorized to distribute the chalice. Carthusian nuns, at their solemn profession, receive the maniple and stole: apparently a survival of an ancient custom in the Church. Various Protestant churches in the 19th c. developed orders of women charged with the performance of certain duties and called deaconesses. The term is mentioned in the Didascalia Apostolorum, which reduced the age of admission to the office to 50 years. The Council of Chalcedon (451) reduced it to 40.

Dead, Prayers for the. The practice of offering prayers for the dead is ancient, dating (in Christian tradition) from the 1st c. CE. The practice presupposes that the destiny of the departed may be in some way improved by such intercession, implying therefore an intermediate state of some kind. Because of the abuse of the doctrine of purgatory in the late medieval period, the Protestant Reformers, having renounced that concept, discouraged and even denounced prayers for the dead on the ground that the fate of the deceased had been sealed. With the revival of the concept of an intermediate state (e.g., by the Tractarians in the 19th c.), prayers for the dead have come to be generally accepted throughout the Christian Church except in the more extreme Protestant circles.

Dead Sea Scrolls. See **Qumran.**

Dean. This designation, from the Latin *decanus* (from *decem*, ten), was originally applied to a person in charge of ten subordinates. It is nowadays used in a variety of ways, principally ecclesiastical and academic. Example: the dean of a cathedral is head of the cathedral chapter, which takes care of the fabric and property. He is in charge of the services and in the older foundations in the Anglican communion is the highest ranking clergyman in the diocese other than the bishop, of whom he is largely independent. In the past, the dean of a great ancient diocese was often, if not generally, a notable scholar. In more recent cathedral foundations in the Anglican communion and also in Roman Catholic practice, he has much less (if any) independence. Rural deans merely assist the bishop in the administration of the diocese. The deans of certain English churches (called "peculiars") such as Westminster and Windsor are exempt from episcopal jurisdiction. The dean of the College of Cardinals is (since 1965) elected by the suburbicarian cardinals. He is always a cardinal bishop. In academic usage, a university or college has, besides the president who is in charge of the administration of the institution, a dean of academic affairs. Each school within a university usually has a dean at its head and in the larger universities there may be many other officials so designated, e.g., deans of students. The heads of theological seminaries are often designated as deans. The ecclesiastical and academic uses of the term should be kept, however, distinct, since they have little, if any, historical connection. The term is also used in a loose and general sense in allusion to a leading figure in any area of human endeavor at any particular time, e.g., the dean of American novelists or the dean of German chemists.

Death of God Theology. This label is affixed to the views of a group of theologians, mostly American, who had a certain vogue in the 1960s. The phrase "God is dead" is one that had been familiar to historians of philosophical theology in the 19th c. Philipp Mainländer (1841–1876), for instance, had proposed in *The Philosophy of Redemption* (1876) that the world begins with the death of God, since God is a principle of unity shattered in the plurality of the world. The original unity, with the joy that accompanies it, persists in the recognition that non-existence is better than existence. (His thought owed much to Schopenhauer.) Nietzsche's well-known use of the phrase "God is dead" was a literary device to express in dramatic form the concept that moral values are constantly evolving and changing and with them "the old gods" who expressed the values of past ages. The 20th c. group revived the phrase, making it sound novel to the generation of students in the 1960s, at a time when an a historical approach to philosophy and theology was especially prevalent. Members of the group varied considerably in their use of the concept. Thomas Altizer, for instance, suggested that God literally died on the cross and has remained dead ever since. Vahanian used the concept to express the vaguer view that the phrase "Death of God" aptly describes a cultural phenomenon. William Hamilton and Paul van Buren took other views. Ronald Gregor Smith, a British theologian, and Harvey Cox, an American one, both dealt with the subject in their respective attempts to perceive the meaning of Christianity in secular terms: the former in his *Secular Christianity* (1966), and the latter in his *The Secular City* (1965).

De Benneville, George (1703–1793). First proponent in America of Universalism, he was born in London of Huguenot ancestry. After preaching in Germany and Holland, he came to America in 1741 and by 1745 he was preaching Universalism at Oley, Pennsylvania. He converted Elhanan Winchester (1751–1797), a popular and eloquent Baptist preacher, who in 1781 resigned his pulpit in Philadelphia, formed a Universalist church there and

then established others elsewhere. For an account of de Benneville's spiritual pilgrimage, see E. Winchester, *Some Remarkable Passages in the Life of Dr. George de Benneville* (Germantown, Pennsylvania (1800), which is a translation from the original autobiography, written by de Benneville in French.

Deborah. Deborah, according to the biblical report in Judges 4 and 5, must have been a woman of extraordinary intelligence and power. She is described as a prophetess (Judges 4.4) to whom the children of Israel came for judgment. She lived in the hill country of Ephraim between Ramah and Bethel. She is represented as exercising impressive, not say awesome qualities of leadership, exemplified in the military victory celebrated in Judges 5: a poem traditionally called "The Song of Deborah." Whether its attribution to her is warranted is disputable, but the poem is certainly of great antiquity, possibly the most ancient literary piece in the Bible. The biblical accounts of women such as Deborah attest the very considerable influence that wise and intelligent women could exercise in ancient Hebrew society.

Decalogue. The Ten Commandments set forth in Exodus 20.2–17 (also in another form in Deuteronomy 5.6–21) are traditionally attributed to Moses but are no doubt the result of centuries of experience and reflection as well as of borrowing from other peoples who had evolved similar ethical precepts. They are useful general guideposts to conduct and have been recognized as such by both Christians and Jews. They do not cover, and could never have been intended to cover, every ethical question.

Decision Theory. A branch of modern probability theory. It is concerned with methods of making optimal decisions in the absence of complete information.

Decius. A 3rd c. Roman Emperor who reigned from 249 to 251 CE and was notorious for undertaking the first thoroughgoing, systematic persecution of the Christians. Thousands were tortured and killed. Decius was killed by the Goths in June 251.

Declaratory Acts. In the Scottish Kirk, the Westminster Confession was the traditional formula to which every candidate for the ministry had to give his assent. The Declaratory Act of 1879 passed by the United Presbyterian Church of Scotland and the Declaratory Act of 1892 passed by the Free Church of Scotland modified in various ways the rigidity of the original requirement, making possible a less literalistic subscription to the Westminster Confession.

Decreation. See **Weil, Simone.**

Decretals. Papal letters pronouncing legal judgment on questions presented to the Pope. Collections of such decretals have been made at various times in the Roman Catholic Church. See also **False Decretals, The.**

Dedication of Churches. Churches are dedicated either by solemn consecration by the bishop as a permanent structure or by a simple blessing by a priest in the case of temporary structures. Eusebius, in his *Historia Ecclesiastica* reports the earliest recorded case: the cathedral at Tyre, 314. The ceremonies connected with the solemn dedication of a church (blessing of the altar vessels, consecration of the altar, etc.) grew more and more elaborate through the centuries, but in 1961 they were much simplified in the Roman Catholic Church.

Deduction. See **Induction and Deduction.**

Deer, The Book of. A manuscript dating from the 9th or 10th c. in the Cambridge University Library, formerly belonging to the monastery at Deer, Aberdeenshire, Scotland, containing the Gospel according to John (a corrupt text), the Apostles' Creed, and some other texts.

Defender of the Faith. See **Fidei Defensor.**

Defensor. Late 7th c. monk from the region of Poitiers, France, who compiled the *Liber Scintillarum*, which was very popular during the Middle Ages as an anthology of works on the spiritual life. The extracts were drawn from the Bible and the Fathers.

De Fide. When a proposition has been officially and expressly defined and declared by the Roman Catholic Church to be true, the faithful are required to accept the definition as *de fide catholica:* a phrase normally abbreviated to *de fide.* It means that the faithful are to regard it as part of the essential teaching of the Church. See **Infallibility.**

Definition. Traditionally, the way in which a term is going to be used is called definition. The term is called the *definiendum* and the explanatory phrase is the *definiens.* Example: a sophomore may be defined as an undergraduate in his or her second year. Dictionary definitions are generally simple; for scientific or scholarly purposes a more detailed analytical definition is often required. The most primitive way of defining is to point to the object. This is called ostensive definition, as where you ask me what a giraffe is and I, not being a zoologist, take you to the zoo and show you one. The most noteworthy classical type of definition is that proposed by Aristotle, by genus and difference, i.e., when you ask me what an armchair is I might reply that it is a species of the genus chair, distinguished from other chairs by its having rests of one sort or another to lean the occupant's arms on. John Stuart Mill contended that definitions yield information only about the use of language. Poincaré held that a definition ought not to refer to the whole class in which the object being defined is a member, and he held that definitions that do not conform to this requirement should be called impredicative definitions. Definition must be seen, then, as varying from the simplest (ostensive) type to highly complex forms that may be required for certain purposes. The concept of definition is of course as important in religious as in other kinds of philosophical reflection.

In Roman Catholic usage the term "definition" has a technical sense: a theological proposition is said to be "defined" when it has been officially declared to be the Church's teaching, denial of which would be accounted heresy.

De Foucauld, Charles Eugène (1858–1916). Sometimes known as "the Hermit of the Sahara," he had begun life as a French army cavalry officer. In 1889–1890 he made a pilgrimage to the Holy Land and the following year he entered the Trappist monastery of Notre-Dame-des-Neiges. He left the Trappists in 1897, seeking a more eremitical life. He now went to the Holy Land, first to Nazareth, then to Jerusalem, as a servant of the Poor Clares. In 1901 he went back to France where he was ordained priest, then soon afterwards he moved to Algeria, leading the life of a hermit, studying the native languages but principally devoting himself to a deepening of his spiritual life. He was killed in 1916. Although he founded no order, several communities emerged after his death whose members look to him as their ideal.

De Haeretico Comburendo. In the reign of Henry IV, an Act of the English Parliament of 1401 was passed, the purpose of which was to destroy the Lollard movement. Persons holding views suspect of heresy were to be handed first to the ecclesiastical courts and, if found guilty, they were then to be handed over to the secular courts to be burned. It was expressly stated that the intent was "to strike fear to the minds of others" who might be harboring heretical notions. This Act was repealed by Henry VIII. Mary I revived it during her terrible reign, but it was finally repealed under Elizabeth I.

Deiniol. A 6th c. Welsh saint. A church was dedicated to him at Hawarden, not far from the English Border, where W. E. Gladstone founded a library in 1896 known as St. Deiniol's Library. It is a residential library where scholars may stay to pursue their work with simple accommodation and meals, in pleasant surroundings, and at very moderate cost.

Deism. From the Latin *deus*, "god". Historically, the term "deism" was generally taken as synonymous with "theism" (from the Greek *theos*, "god") in opposition to atheism and polytheism. In the 17th c., however, a tendency emerged, which came to fuller fruition in the 18th c., to repudiate all revelational religion and to seek instead a religion based upon reason alone. In the intellectual climate of that time and the mechanistic view of the universe that prevailed, the concept that developed out of that attitude was of a God who created the world but thereafter did not intervene in its operation. For if, as was commonly held, the universe is a machine, like a clock, then, if it is created by God, presumably the divine clockmaker is to be credited with making it perfectly. Any tinkering with it would imply that the divine clockmaker had done his work inefficiently. Deists, however, might recognize, as indeed many did, a moral law in the universe entailing an objective difference between right and wrong and even belief in an afterlife in which one's condition would be determined by one's conduct in the present one. The Socinians, who may be regarded as the forerunners of the modern Unitarians, represented a move in this direction. Some would regard Lord Herbert of Cherbury as the founder of deism. He set out five "pillars" of the deist position. The movement was expressed in what came to be called "natural" as opposed to "revealed" religion. Matthew Tindal, William Wollaston, John Toland, and Thomas Woolston, are among writers of the period who may be called deists.

Voltaire was notably influenced by the English deists. The movement, however, had an influence far beyond those who could properly be so designated. Deistic attitudes were widespread among the educated classes in Germany, England, and France and indeed might be said to be characteristic of a majority of the signatories of the American Declaration of Independence. Many churchmen held views, if only more or less privately, in that direction. Deism was even more explictly and widely held in France and Germany than in England. Voltaire and Rousseau were both deists, as indeed were the Encyclopaedists, and Kant may be regarded as a philosophical exponent of a system in which God was seen in characteristically deistic terms. The most vigorous critic of deism in the English 18th c. scene was Joseph Butler, whose *Analogy of Religion* (1736) was a classic refutation in its time. In the light of intellectual developments early in the 20th c. (not least in the light of modern physics), much of the deistic outlook became outmoded and irrelevant.

Deissmann, Adolf (1866–1937). New Testament scholar. Professor at Heidelberg and later at Berlin. Among important works is his *Light from the Ancient East* (1910) translated from the original *Licht vom Osten* (1908), which was very influential in the way in which it used recently discovered papyri. Deissmann was much interested in ecumenical relations and edited *Mysterium Christi* (1930) with the Anglican scholar W. K. A. Bell (1881–1958), Bishop of Chichester from 1929 to 1958 and a prominent figure in ecumenical circles.

Delehaye, Hippolyte (1859–1941). Bollandist. Born in Antwerp, he entered the Jesuit Order in 1879 and was ordained priest in 1890, then devoting himself to the work of the Bollandists and becoming their president in 1912.

Delitzch, Franz Julius (1813–1890). Biblical scholar. As professor at various German universities he wrote extensive critical commentaries and also works on rabbinics. He anticipated in some respects the concept of the unconscious that Freud was later to develop.

Delitzsch, Friedrich (1850–1922). Assyriologist. As professor at various German universities, he wrote many works on Orientalist topics, among which was his famous *Babel und Bibel* (1902–1903), in which he showed the Babylonian origin of many Old Testament passages.

Della Robbia, Luca (1399–1482). Italian sculptor whose marble sculptures for the organ gallery of Florence cathedral (now in the Museo del Duomo) are his most famous work of that kind. From about 1440, however, he began developing a technique of doing reliefs, principally in majolica and typically with white figures on a pale blue background, framed by flowers and fruits, for which he is now best known. His Madonnas in the Bargello at Florence are especially notable. His nephew Andrea della Robbia (1431–1528) continued his uncle's tradition. Among the latter's work the Madonna and Child in the National Museum at Florence is probably the best known.

Delphic Oracle. The oracle of Apollo at Delphi in Greece, who was widely famed even before the time of Socrates for her cryptic counsel on many matters on which her devotees consulted her, is of importance in Christian thought if only because of her great dictum "gnōthi seauton" ("know thyself"), which Socrates adopted and used and for her having perceived him to be the wisest man in all Greece. For Christian thought was developed in an atmosphere imbued with the religious humanism of Socrates. The need to know oneself is surely indeed a first step in every kind of religious enterprise.

De Maistre, Joseph (1753–1821). Ultramontanist who, educated by the Jesuits and much influenced by 18th c. rationalism, became, after the French

Revolution, a reactionary, seeing in the Roman Catholic Church an instrument for the conservation of the old cultural values of France and a weapon against anarchy and mob rule. He did much to promote Ultramontanism and to weaken Gallicanism.

Demetrius. Bishop of Alexandria from 189. Notorious for his persecution of Origen, he is still highly regarded by the Coptic Church.

Demetrius the Cynic. Greek philosopher of the 1st c. CE. Although his general outlook was in the Stoic direction, he held to the Cynic insistence on the indispensability of effort, without which wisdom cannot be attained. The way to wisdom is through adversity and the surmounting of obstacles.

Demiurge. From the Greek, *demiourgos*, "craftsman". The concept that the universe is created by a god who works on a "given" as a sculptor works on clay or marble, is classically expressed by Plato in his *Timaeus*, although it is very unlikely that he intended the concept to be taken otherwise than as a useful myth. The notion that besides the "good God" there is an inferior god or *demiourgos*, who is the creator of the universe, is one that occurs in various Gnostic systems. Marcion is a well-known example of a 2nd c. Christian who considered the God of the Old Testament to be an inferior deity, the *demiourgos*, who created the world.

Democracy. The term, meaning "rule by the people" comes from two Greek words, *dēmos*, the people, and *kratein*, to rule. Small societies such as clubs and village meetings may be ruled directly by the people who compose them, at least in leisured circumstances, but generally democracy is representational, i.e., the people elect bodies such as Congress or Parliament to represent their will. Democratic forms of government were known in the ancient world but were by no means approved by either Plato or Aristotle. Plato regarded

democracy as the worst of lawful forms of government and the best of unlawful ones and specifically placed it as but one step better than tyranny, toward which he held that it had a tendency to lead. Aristotle took it to be preferable to tyranny and oligarchy, yet with them a degenerate form of government. The seeds, although only the seeds, of modern democracy may be found in medieval political theory where (in the West only) the recognition of the competitive claims of Church and State led to the emergence of an awareness of the rights of the individual against both. After the Renaissance, the concept of democracy (often with a constitutional monarchy built into it) began to be seen by many at least as an ideal and eventually came to be developed in practice, although generally with caution and in limited forms. The perception of the importance of human freedom greatly fostered the development of democratic ideals. Both the American and the French Revolution were considered by their proponents to exhibit the ideals and foster the practice of democracy. They occurred, however, in circumstances very different from those that were later to develop. According to PLUS (Project Literacy United States), 23 million adult Americans are functionally illiterate (i.e., with basic skills at the fourth-grade level or below) and another 35 million have skills below the eighth-grade level. Of these adults 56% are under 50 years of age. Since according to the same body's report, the Constitution of the United States requires at least an eleventh-grade level to comprehend, the practice of representational democracy is bound to be very different indeed from what it was intended to be by the framers of that most treasured of national documents. So while democracy may be regarded as a safeguard against tyranny in its most flagrant forms and therefore as protective of human freedom, the wisdom of Plato's and Aristotle's judgments upon it must be seen to be at least as warranted today as it was to thoughtful people among the ancients. The recognition of this in no way denigrates the democratic ideal.

Demons. The notion that there are demons or evil spirits, inferior to the gods and inclined to the destruction of humans is widespread in the history of religion. In the polytheistic religions such spirits are so mixed up with the gods that it is often difficult to distinguish the "good" gods from the "bad" ones. In the monotheistic religions, however, such as Judaism, Zoroastrianism, Christianity, and Islam, not only is the distinction made abundantly clear; the demons are hierarchically arranged, some being more potent than others and all being under the rule of a chief: Satan, Lucifer, or, in Zoroastrianism, Angra Mainyu, the enemy of Ahura Mazda, the beneficent deity corresponding to the Hindu Dyaus-pitar, the Father of light. In many forms of Gnosticism emphasis on the war between the forces of good and evil is especially strong.

Demythologizing. A term used by Bultmann to designate the procedure he advocated and developed in which certain old presuppositions belonging to now discarded mythologies must be removed before biblical interpretation can be usefully undertaken. Examples are the concept of demonic possession and the notion of a three-storied universe. In the nature of the case, however, ancient writings such as the Bible are so saturated with such conceptions, now generally admitted to be irreconcilable with what we know of the way things are, that the procedure is more difficult than it appears at first sight. Moreover, when old mythological presuppositions are eliminated they are inevitably modified by what are, in fact, new presuppositions that will also have to be discarded in the future (as the presuppositions of Newtonian physics have had to be modified by those of 20th c. physics), so that, as some conservative biblical critics say, demythologizing is in fact *re*mythologizing. Nevertheless, the *rec-*

ognition of the problem must be faced by all scholars in dealing with the writers of antiquity, biblical or profane. See **Myth.**

Denifle, Heinrich Seuse (1844–1905). Born in the Tyrol, he was admitted to the Dominican Order in 1861 and ordained priest in 1866. In 1880 he was appointed associate to the General of the Order and travelled extensively in search of manuscripts to assist him in the compilation of a new edition of the works of Thomas Aquinas in which he was collaborating. His prolific writings include his great work on the history of the University of Paris, *Chartularium Universitatis Parisiensis,* in four volumes (1889–1897).

Denney, James (1856–1917). Scottish Presbyterian theologian. Although he began with a doctrinally somewhat liberal attitude, he moved to a much more conservative one, defending traditional teaching in Christology. His works include *The Death of Christ* (1902), *Jesus and the Gospel* (1908), *The Christian Doctrine of Reconciliation* (1917), and various editions of the text of New Testament books.

De Noailles, Louis Antoine (1651–1729). French churchman and controversialist. Through the influence of Madame de Maintenon he became Archbishop of Paris in 1695. Innocent XII made him a cardinal in 1700. He was an energetic advocate of clerical reform and a vigorous controversialist. Although he wrote against some Jansenist positions, he disapproved no less of certain views on moral questions such as Probabilism, which the Jesuits generally favored, and for this and other reasons he was suspect of Jansenist sympathies. He certainly upheld Gallican positions.

De Nobili, Robert (1577–1656). Jesuit missionary to India. Born in Tuscany, he was sent on a mission to India in 1604, where he developed novel procedures such as the appointment of special missionaries for each of the Indian castes. He was remarkably successful in making the Brahmins and others of the higher castes less suspicious of Christianity than had formerly been the case. He knew Sanskrit and other Indian languages fluently and wrote extensively in them.

Denotation and Connotation. These correlative terms are generally understood in philosophy as follows: the denotation of a term is the thing or set of things to which the term refers (e.g., the term "chair" denotes all chairs that exist anywhere), while its connotation refers to the qualities or characteristics essentially pertaining to it (e.g., a chair connotes the capacity to be seated upon it and perhaps also its having been constructed with this purpose in view). J. S. Mill developed this now fairly standard interpretation of the distinction. (See **Mill, John Stuart.**) Not all logicians, however, would accept such definitions, at any rate not in such simple forms. Example: William of Occam made a distinction between "absolute" terms and "connotative" terms, seeing in the latter primary and secondary modes, the primary modes being a quality and the secondary modes the subject of that quality, e.g., respectively, "clever" and a particular boy to whom that adjective would be properly applied.

We should also notice that some nouns have connotation but lack denotation, e.g., we all know the characteristics attributed to dragons, so that we could state what a dragon is supposed to be, yet we cannot point to one since dragons do not exist. Some modern logicians, perceiving the complexity of the concepts of denotation and connotation, have argued for various refinements in the use of the terms. Example: the dodo, so far as we know, no longer exists, but it did at one time. May we then say that it has denotation, unlike dragons, which have never existed except in imagination? By the same token, the superman does not exist, he may exist in the future or be even in process of coming into existence. Is he then to be said to have denotation? Such puzzles exhibit the complexity of the distinction, which, however, remains an important one in logic.

Denys. A 3rd c. Bishop of Paris and patron saint of France. According to a medieval tradition he had been sent from Rome to convert Gaul. Having become Bishop of Paris, he was martyred. His life is obscure. His reputed remains were sent to the Benedictine abbey of St.-Denis, founded in the early 7th c. some four miles north of Paris. This abbey became the burial place of the kings of France and probably the richest abbey in France. Jeanne d'Arc hung up her arms there in 1429, and Henri IV renounced Protestantism there in 1593. The buildings, sacked at the French Revolution, were restored by Napoleon III and are now a national monument.

Deo Gratias. Latin phrase meaning "thanks be to God." It is a traditional liturgical response.

Deontology. In ethics, this term has come to be applied to those systems in which rightness is determined without regard to consequences, e.g., that expressed in Kant's "Categorical Imperative," contradistinguished from teleological theories of ethics, which focus upon the result of moral action, such as "the greatest good for the greatest number" (Bentham) and the attainment of the Beatific Vision of God (e.g., Thomas Aquinas.)

Deo Optimo Maximo. This Latin phrase (meaning "To God, the Best and the Greatest" and generally abbreviated to D.O.M.) is widely used on the doors of churches and other Christian monuments. Originally addressed to Jupiter and used on temples, it is a striking example of the way in which ancient pagan usages were adapted to Christian practice.

De Profundis. Latin phrase, "Out of the depths," the opening words of Psalm 130. It is traditionally used in Burial services.

Dereliction, The Cry of. See **Deus Absconditus.**

De Rossi, Giovanni Battista (1822–1894). Italian archaeologist. A prolific writer, his methods were original and innovative. Before his time, no archaeologist had adequately recognized, as he did, the value and immense importance of knowledge of literary sources (e.g., the early Christian writers) for the development of methodology in archaeological enterprises.

Dervish. From the Persian *darvish*, "beggar". A member of a Muslim order that emerged in the 12th c. CE. Characteristic of their ritual practice are howlings and whirlings culminating in ecstasy and a trance-like state.

De Sacramentis. A treatise on the Sacraments, probably the work of the 4th c. Ambrose.

Descartes, René (1596–1650). French philosopher whose methodological originality has made him one of the epoch-making thinkers in human history. After a conventional education at the Jesuit College of La Flèche, he went to Paris in 1613 and six years later resolved to travel and to devote himself exclusively to philosophical inquiry. Eventually he settled in Holland. He believed that the key to philosophy must lie in mathematical methods and procedures, and he resolved to try to denude his mind of all traditional metaphysical presuppositions and assumptions and begin with the resolve to doubt everything, which led to the datum of self-awareness, expressed in his famous dictum: *cogito, ergo sum*, "I think, therefore I exist." He then proceeded to the view that, as in mathematics, whatever can be conceived as part of a coherent whole in experience must be taken as true, representing what he called "clear and distinct ideas." The first such idea is that God exists, which he took to be such that could not arise in the mind unless God did in fact exist. He used a form of the ontological argument as well as an argument from the principle of causation (only God could cause the idea to arise in the human mind) and a form of the cosmological argument of Aristotle. Because of his methodological starting point, he perceived a great difficulty in relating mind to matter. How can the mind, as a "thinking substance," reach out to and make its own the radically different "substance" that we call "matter"? Here he was led to formulations that gave rise to epistemological theories of "representative perception" that for long plagued the thinkers of the British Empiricist school such as Locke, Berkeley, and Hume. For in the dualistic scenario that Descartes provided, if mind can assimilate matter at all, it can be only through some sort of representational image accommodated to mind, and who can attest the veracity of the image? How indeed can we ever know what the reality is that we call "material"? I am aware of the contents of my own mind, but how can I say, on the view that Descartes takes of the separation of mind and matter, that I know anything at all of the reality outside my mind to which these mental images are presumed to correspond? Much of the importance of Descartes lies in the development of the character of doubt in philosophical inquiry. Through his drawing attention to questions of this kind, his importance in the history of philosophical thought cannot easily be exaggerated either in the philosophy of religion or in the philosophy of science.

Descent of Christ into Hell, The. This difficult concept, to which allusion seems to be made in several biblical texts (e.g., Matthew 27.52f, I Peter 3.18–20) is specially mentioned in the Apostles Creed, although not in the Nicene. Scholars generally take the concept as referring to the *limbus patrum* (see **Limbo**) or some other state intermediate between heaven and hell as these two concepts came to be understood in mainstream Christian theology.

De Smet, Pierre Jean (1801–1873). Jesuit missionary to the American Indians. It was largely through his activities that the Roman Catholic Church moved into a number of Indian tribes in the Far West, including the Pacific Northwest.

Determinism and Indeterminism. The most extreme form of determinism is that which is sometimes called fatalism, a view that is much encountered in fictional literature but is rarely held either by philosophers or by people in general. It means that the future is always immutably fixed in such a way that there is nothing anyone could ever do to alter the course of events. This is plainly a view irreconcilable with any of the great religions of the world, certainly with Christianity, in any of its forms. Determinists, however, generally prefer to say that human actions and choices are links in a causal chain. Every event is caused, but the cause may be extremely complex. Philosophers sometimes distinguish between "hard" and "soft" determinism. Hard determinists hold that our actions are caused in such a way that the notion of freewill is illusory. On such a view moral responsibility, if we may talk of it at all, is deprived of the importance with which religious people invest it. I behave in a certain way because of circumstances that are in the last resort beyond my control. Soft determinists contend that, although our actions are indeed caused, our choices are real choices within the complex causal chain. Example: I might have a genetic ancestry such as can be shown to dispose me to, say, alcoholism and this predisposition might then make the probability of my becoming an alcoholic incalculably great; nevertheless, it is still possible for me to overcome the encumbrance in me and

many heroic individuals have overcome even greater obstacles. Indeterminists, however, insist that for freedom to be real it must not be causally hampered. On what is sometimes called a libertarian view, an entity such as the "self" may be postulated as lying in some way outside the causal chain, but such a view is fraught with serious difficulties. To bring intelligibility to any view such as is implied in a Christian ethic, one must *both* recognize a world of obstacles that constitute our circumstances *and* establish a degree of freedom, however minimal and limited, enabling us to make free choices within the circumstantial framework in which one is imprisoned. Central to Christian teaching is the Gospel promise that through our knowledge of eternal truth freedom will ensue (John 8.32). This concept, moreover, is implicit in one way or another in the ethical teaching of all the great religions. See **Freedom.** See also, for a classic ancient view, Aristotle's *Nicomachean Ethics.* For classic modern discussions, see: Gilbert Ryle, *The Concept of Mind* (1949); B. Berofsky (ed.), *Free Will and Determinism* (1966); J. R. Lucas, *The Freedom of the Will* (1970). For a brilliant discussion by a Christian theologian, see Austin Farrer, *The Freedom of the Will* (1958). See BIBLIOGRAPHY under **Ethics.**

Deus Absconditus. This Latin term, meaning "the hidden God," is used in contrast to the term *deus revelatus,* "the revealed God." If the latter is taken seriously, then of course what is revealed *is* the *deus absconditus;* nevertheless behind the *deus revelatus* is a divine hiddenness. From the believer's standpoint, God may indeed be better known through the anguish of his absence than through the joy of his presence. The cry of dereliction on the Cross (*Eli, Eli, lama sabachthani*) is for Christians the classic expression of the "forsakenness" that can bring authentic knowledge of God. As sunshine is better apprehended in the darkness and water in the desert, so God may be better known when he withdraws himself than in his disclosure.

Deus ex Machina. Literally, this Latin phrase means "god from a machine." It originally referred to the device used in tragedies on the stage in which a god was brought into the action by way of solving problems in a plot. It came to refer to anything introduced in an artificial way to solve difficulties, notably in religious philosophy.

Deus sive Natura. Latin phrase meaning "God or nature." See **Spinoza, Baruch.**

Deuterocanonical. Those books contained in the Septuagint Version of the Old Testament but not in the Hebrew are so designated. They are more popularly known as apocryphal, but since that term is ambiguous, referring also to certain early Christian literature and in a pejorative sense to spurious or legendary literature, the term "deuterocanonical" is to be preferred in scholarly allusion to books such as Tobit, Wisdom, and Ecclesiasticus, which are not in the Hebrew Bible but are in the Septuagint and sometimes quoted by the New Testament writers. Usage has been further complicated, however, for example by the fact that Sixtus of Siena (1528–1569) applied the term to those books of the Bible whose place in the canon has been at some time denied or doubted.

Deutero-Isaiah. Literary analysis of the Bible has shown that the later chapters of the Book of Isaiah were written much later than the time of the prophet of that name who lived in the 8th c. BCE. Chapters 40–55 are generally ascribed to an unknown author who is designated Deutero-Isaiah, being apparently written in the later years of the Babylonian Exile, c. the middle of the 6th c. BCE.

Deva. A Sanskrit term meaning "bright heavenly being." Originally, the term was used of the polytheistic nature gods of the Vedic pantheon. In Zoroastrianism, the *devas* became evil powers, demons, who struggle against the good God. The Greek term *theos* and the Latin *deus* ("god") both have an etymological connection with *deva*, as has also *diabolus*, "devil".

Deva-Dāsīs. A class of women who in Hindu practice were dedicated to the service of the temple and were held to be married to the particular god associated with it. The term means literally "slave of the god" In early times they seem to have been expected to be models of devout propriety, but later they appear to have become temple prostitutes available to the priests of the temple and in some regions of India to any of the temple worshippers. Such temple prostitution was especially common in the south of India and survived until comparatively recent times. Girls destined for this purpose might be drawn from any caste. They were taught from childhood the traditional dances and were generally trained in other arts such as the playing of a musical instrument and in reading and writing. They had a recognized place in society, partly because of their liberal giving to deserving causes, and took a place at public and official ceremonies at which other women were not admitted.

Deva-Dūta. In Buddhist thought, there are three messengers (*deva-dūtas*) sent to man to remind him of the frailty of the human condition: (1) age, (2) disease, (3) death.

Devanāgarī. The Sanskrit script. The present script, used also for Hindī, Marāthī, and Prākrit, is a highly developed form of an early style (Brāhmī), exhibiting the very high degree of literary culture attained long ago in Indian centers of learning and representing one of the greatest civilizations the world has ever known.

Devayāna. In Hindu literature, the "path of the gods", of those who attain faith and knowledge either in this life or hereafter. The path they follow leads eventually to complete absorption in brahman. See the Chāndogya Upaniṣad, IV, 15, 5–6.

Devī. The feminine form of *deva*, used in Hindu literature of goddesses or female personifications of religious concepts. In the Ṛgveda the wives of the gods are called devīs.

Devil. From the Greek *diabolos*, the term is applied to the "fallen" or "bad" angels generally and sometimes to designate their chief, i.e., Satan. The concept of evil angels warring against the good ones is taken over by the New Testament and other Christian writers from the Old Testament and especially from later pre-Christian Jewish writings and tradition. The Roman Catholic Church has made comparatively few pronouncements on the subject, but theologians throughout the ages have engaged in much speculation about the cause of the fall of the rebellious angels, which has been generally supposed to have arisen from pride. In Christian tradition devils, like other angels, are regarded as being by nature superior to human beings. They are for that reason terrible adversaries, having great powers that no human being can hope to match except through help from Christ who is victorious over the powers of evil. In Islamic tradition, however, based upon the Qur'ān, the angels were created before man and when God then created man he called on the angels to bow down before his latest and greatest creation. Some declined to do so and so fell. The concept of evil agencies is deeply rooted in Christian literature from the New Testament onwards and the notion of possession of human beings by such evil agencies appears frequently in the Gospels.

Devil's Advocate. A popular term used for the official who, in the Roman Catholic procedure for the canonization of saints, is charged with the duty of raising objections against the candidate under consideration and of procuring evidence against him or her. See **Promotor Fidei.**

Devotio Moderna. From *c.* 1400 a new genre of literature on spirituality began to appear in which the emphasis was on the individual in his or her quest for the deepening of the interior life. It found a classic expression in *The Imitation of Christ* (*De Imitatione Christi*) attributed to Thomas à Kempis. It encouraged methods designed to produce such results. It seems to have spread from the Netherlands to other parts of Western Europe. It was called modern in contrast to the then traditional methods of "contemplation" practiced and encouraged in Benedictine spirituality.

De Wette, Wilhelm Martin Leberecht (1780–1849). German theologian. Born at Ulla, near Weimar, he was trained at Jena and then taught at Heidelberg, Berlin, and finally at Basel. In his earlier years he was extremely radical in his approach to biblical analysis. In later years he grew more temperate but seems to have displeased both the rationalists by his attempts to justify religious faith and the Pietists by his skeptical approach to the central beliefs of traditional Christian theology. His prolific writings include his *Das Leben des christlichen Glaubens* (1846).

Dewey, John (1859–1952). American philosopher. Born at Burlington, Vermont, and educated at Johns Hopkins University, he taught at various universities including Chicago and Columbia. Much influenced by William James, he developed a great interest in educational theory and practice, combining this interest with his professional work in philosophy both at Chicago and at Columbia. He saw philosophy as true to itself when it deals not so much with problems that philosophers pose as with a philosophical method that deals with human problems. He wanted to see philosophy turn away from the pursuit of absolutes and devote itself to fostering human control of our circumstances by the use of creative intelligence. Also interested in the work of Darwin he saw the need for humanity to adapt itself to its environment and perceived that doing so entails a change in our intellectual orientation. He saw ideas as instruments that lead to action and must be so understood. His philosophy is therefore commonly called "instrumentalism." Dewey also saw his thought as a form of naturalism, holding that values no less than facts can be discovered in, and receive their warrant from experience, which he presents as the ultimate forum of philosophy. He defended democracy as the best means of pursuing the goal of freedom because it is the best equipped for pursuing the method of free inquiry. His educational philosophy sees education as having its focus on the needs of individuals. It involves therefore experimental and forward-looking methods. In his religious thought the term "God" was properly defined as the relation between the actual and the real, but since he perceived that this interpretation of the term would probably confuse the reader and obfuscate the issues he wanted to clarify, he generally did not use it. His influence has been very considerable indeed, predominantly in educational philosophy.

His writings included *Psychology* (1887), *Studies in Logical Theory* (1903), *How We Think* (1910), *Reconstruction in Philosophy* (1920), *Human Nature and Conduct* (1922), *Experience and Nature* (1925), *The Quest for Certainty* (1929), *Art as Experience* (1934), *A Common Faith* (1934), *The Teacher and Society* (1937), and *Theory of Valuation* (1939).

Dhamma. The Pali form of the Sanskrit *Dharma*, much used in Buddhist literature in a variety of meanings, ranging from "the ultimate" to righteousness and true teaching. It also represents that which continues while all else is fleeting. In some respects it has similarities to the Greek *logos:* eternal idea or "word". See **Dharma.**

Dhammapada. A well-known and important book of the canon of Buddhist scripture. It consists of 423 verses, each an epigrammatic utterance putting into brief form some truth or saying about the Buddhist way of life.

Dhamma-Sangani. In Theravada Buddhism, the name of a part of the third section (Abhidhamma-Piṭaka) of the scriptural canon. It enumerates and arranges various psychic elements in human existence.

Dhanurveda. The science of archery, in which every king and nobleman was expected to excel, in Hindu tradition.

Dhanus. The archer's bow that in Hindu tradition was, along with the arrows and other equipment, the badge of the kṣatriya or warrior class.

Dhanvantari. According to Hindu tradition, the first exponent of the medical arts. According to the Viṣṇu Purāṇa, IV, 8, he was told in a previous incarnation that he would be born into a noble family and develop the eightfold medical system. Some accounts connect him with the king of Kāśī, which may have some historical foundation since Kāśī (the modern Banāras) has been a center of learning, especially medical learning, from early times down to the present day. The name is said to have been given in later times to physicians as a title as is nowadays the title "doctor".

Dharma. In Hindu tradition, ethical and religious duty, from *dhar,* "to hold": that which constitutes law or custom. It has therefore conceptual affinities with the Chinese *li.* In the earlier Hindu literature (e.g., the Vedas) the term seldom if ever has this philosophical sense, but it is developed later, e.g., in the Brāhmaṇas, where it means "duty", although generally in some sense relating to the religious sacrifices. Dharma comes to be codified, as was the Torah in Judaism, so that the term (like Torah) could mean both the principle itself (divine law) and its codification. Penalties were provided, called daṇḍa. See **Daṇḍa** and **Dhamma.**

Dharmasastra. See **Āyurveda.**

Dhātu. A term very widely used in Buddhism to designate any of the "elements", physical or psychical, in human consciousness.

Dhyāna. Sanskrit term meaning "meditation" (Pali form is *Jhāna*) and representing a notion central to the practice of Hinduism, Buddhism, and Jainism. In its penultimate stage, it leads to the final Samadhi, absorption. It is fully achieved only after passing through a series of preliminary mental states, and it is accompanied by a particular experience of the enhancement of one's inner vitality. The word itself is that from which comes the Chinese word *Ch'an*, the name of a Chinese mystical Buddhist school, and the Japanese word *Zen*.

Diaconicon. In Eastern Orthodox practice, the name given to the south part of the sanctuary of a church, where the altar vessels, vestments, and other equipment for the performance of the Liturgy are kept. It is roughly the counterpart of the sacristy in the West. The corresponding area on the north side of the sanctuary is called the prosthesis.

Diadochus. The 5th c. author of the *Capita Gnostica*, in which he treated the various ways of attaining spiritual perfection.

Dialectic. From the Greek *dialektos* (discourse or debate). In the classic form in which dialectic is used by Plato, it is the science of drawing rigorous distinctions. Aristotle preferred demonstration from first principles, but he recognized dialectic as a method of criticism. Throughout the Middle Ages dialectic was treated as in partnership with logic and listed as one of the three disciplines that constituted the trivium in the medieval educational system. (See **Liberal Arts, The Seven** and **Quadrivium.**) From the same Greek root comes the word "dialogue", which is used to describe the literary form in which Plato wrote his earlier works and which exhibits what is nowadays commonly called the Socratic method: a way of philosophizing through discussion between two or among more than two parties.

Dialectical Materialism. This phrase was used by Friedrich Engels (1820–1895) in the context of Marxism. Kant had seen dialectic as the name to be given to man's futile attempt to apply the principles that govern phenomena to the "things-in-themselves" that lie behind the phenomena. Fichte was the first to present the dialectical process as a triad: thesis, antithesis, and synthesis. Hegel had used this triadic formula to exemplify the principle that he saw working everywhere in reality. Engels then turned the Hegelian concept round in such a way that the dialectical process always occurs in a material context, insisting that qualitative changes are attained through quantitative changes. In political realities the thesis-antithesis-synthesis is then said to apply to the way in which human societies develop through class conflict.

Dialectical Theology. A name given to the genre of theology expounded by Karl Barth and his followers, which repudiated the "liberal" tradition in Protestant theology (e.g., as expressed by Schleiermacher) and adopted a method designed to restore a dogmatic theology of the Calvinist type. This type of theology seems to have been so called because, in contrast to the traditional method in dogmatic theology, which treats God as an object, and the mystical method, which uses the *via negativa*, the Barthian way purports to transcend both such ways and to keep God, the focus of faith, free from all formulation and to accept and study him as revealed in the Scriptures. The theological attraction of Barth's stance for those who came strongly under its influence seems to have lain chiefly in its emphasis on the Otherness of God, i.e., his transcendence over all else, and its resistance to all pantheistic and panentheistic tendencies. In the English-speaking world, its influence was particularly notable in the Scottish Kirk in the 1940s. See **Barth, Karl.**

Diamond Sūtra. The title of a Mahayana Buddhist treatise belonging to a particular type of literature in that tradition, the central theme of which is the doctrine of Śūnyatā: the attainment of perfect wisdom. See **Śūnyatā.**

Diamper, Synod of. In 1599, at Diamper (now Udayampērur, about 12 miles southeast of Cochin, India), a diocesan synod was held at which Nestorianism was renounced and total submission to Rome undertaken, bringing into existence the Malabar Uniate Church, in full communion with Rome. When Portuguese influence in that region had diminished in the 17th c., the Malabar Uniate Church began to crumble. See **Malabar Christians.**

Diaspora. From the Greek *diaspora,* dispersion. The term is applied in a general sense to any dispersion of a large number of a nation's people throughout the world, e.g., in modern times, the Irish and others who have emigrated in large numbers to the United States and elsewhere, creating a larger population of Irish descent than exists in the mother country. The term is traditionally used in a special sense, however, of the dispersion of the Jews, which had its beginnings in the Assyrian and Babylonian deportations in 722 and 597 BCE. This dispersion eventually spread through almost the entire Roman Empire so that by the time of Christ there were possibly a million Jews in Alexandria alone. Although these Jews of the Diaspora looked with deep affection and respect toward their Palestinian homeland, the influence of Hellenic culture upon them was very strong indeed and transformed their attitudes, separating them from the Jews of the Palestinian homeland to some extent as in modern times expatriate Greeks, Irish, and others have become

alienated from their respective homelands while retaining at the same time an awareness of their roots in the land of their fathers. In the case of the Jewish Disapora, however, the situation was exacerbated by the fact that with the rise of Christianity in Europe and, later, of Islam in the Arab world, the Diaspora Jews found themselves doubly alienated while being at the same time pulled in both directions. This resulted in an exclusiveness that estranged them from the life of the Gentile world and inevitably brought upon them the attitudes of suspicion and fear that exclusively-minded minorities generally evoke. It was in such circumstances that the Jews in the medieval ghettos of Europe were thrown more and more in upon themselves in separatist communities that generated an inward-looking mindset, which in turn fostered many distinctive features, including the emergence of an exceptionally large number of men and women of extraordinary talents and gifts in philosophy, science, mathematics, music, and other expressions of humanistic culture and individualism.

Diatesseron. About the middle of the 2nd c. Tatian compiled an edition of the four Gospels in a continuous narrative that circulated in some churches (especially the Syrian) down to the 5th c. The language in which it was originally written is unknown, although the evidence points to Greek.

Dibelius, Martin (1883–1947). German New Testament scholar. After appointments at various universities, he was professor at Heidelberg from 1915 till his death. As such he was in the forefront of the method of "form history" (*Formgeschichte*). He was a moderate exponent of that method (first used by H. Gunkel in 1901) and took a more conservative stance than most of those who adopted it. He wrote many works, including *From Tradition to Gospel* (1934), the first edition of the original German of which had appeared in 1919. He was a cousin of Otto Dibelius.

Dibelius, Otto (1880–1967). Bishop of Berlin from 1945 to 1949. He had been noted during the Nazi regime for his resistance and was held in restraint during much of that period. He was a cousin of Martin Dibelius. In 1949 he became Presiding Bishop of the Evangelical Church in Germany and in 1954 President of the World Council of Churches.

Didache, The. This is the name given to a brief, early Christian manual of great interest and value for ascertaining the practices of the Church in very early times. It is of unknown authorship, and the date is uncertain. There is considerable evidence pointing to its dating from the 1st c., but many scholars date it somewhat later. It contains 16 short chapters dealing with subjects such as fasting, prayer, the celebration of the Eucharist, and others. A manuscript exists written in 1056, which was discovered in Constantinople in 1875 and published in 1883. The practices it describes apparently relate to a Syrian Christian community.

Didascalia Apostolorum. A book of Church order probably dating from the early 3rd c., dealing with subjects such as how to conduct oneself in times of persecution, liturgical worship, how disputes among Christians are to be settled, and other topics. It was originally written in Greek, but the only extant version is a Syriac one with parts in Latin. Its contents were eventually embodied for the most part in the Apostolic Constitutions.

Diderot, Denis (1713–1784). Editor of the renowned French *Encyclopédie*. Born at Langres, he was educated at the Jesuit college, Louis-le-Grand, Paris. A follower of Locke, he was hostile to religion and metaphysics. His influence on thought, including Christian thought, was considerable. He wrote extensively on philosophy, religion, political theory, and literature. See **Encyclopedists.**

Dilthey, Wilhelm (1833–1911). Philosopher. Born in Biebrich and educated at Heidelberg and Berlin, he taught at various universities and eventually became professor of the History of Philosophy at Berlin. He is generally regarded as a neo-Kantian. His influence on the social sciences has been considerable, and his writings have relevance to certain problems in Christian thought, especially to problems in the philosophy of history.

Ding an Sich. This German phrase, meaning "thing-in-itself", was used by Kant to signify that which lies behind the phenomena that we see in the world of our experience. See **Noumenon** and **Phenomenalism.**

Diocese. A territorial area that is an administrative unit of the Church, governed by a bishop, sometimes with the assistance, in large dioceses, of other bishops and/or other ecclesiastical administrators. It is divided into parishes and sometimes also into other administrative units. Historically what is now called a diocese was in early Christian times known simply as an *ekklēsia*, i.e., a church or Christian community. Then the word *paroikia* (parish) came to be used for the territory administered by a bishop, and this usage persists in the Greek Church to this day. The word "diocese" seems to have been originally borrowed from the term used for certain administrative units in the government of the Roman Empire.

Diocletian (245–313). Roman Emperor from 284 to 305. An energetic organizer and administrator, his purpose was to consolidate and reform the Empire on absolutist lines, centering all power on himself and investing himself with divine authority, which implied the permanent subordination of the Senate to his will. Under his rule Christians were at first treated well enough, as had been the case from 260, but early in 303, under political pressure, a great and widespread persecution of Christians broke out, varying in severity from region to region but resulting in great cruelties. Books were burned and churches demolished. Clergy who resisted were imprisoned, tortured, and in some cases executed. The following year these penalties were extended to lay Christians. Only the victory of Constantine ended the persecution. So terrible was the memory of that era that it came to be known among Christians as "the Era of the Martyrs" or "the Diocletian Era." The Copts and the Abyssinians still reckon time from the date of Diocletian's accession in 284.

Diogenes Laertius. A 3rd c. CE biographer. His compilations of biographical and other material on the Platonic, Skeptic, and other great philosophical schools provides an invaluable source, more especially because most similar compilations have been lost. His principal work is translated as *Lives of Eminent Philosophers*.

Diogenes of Sinope (413–327 BCE). A Cynic and probably founder of that school. (See **Cynicism**.) He lived such an extremely simple life that, according to legend, he lodged in a tub at the temple of Cybele and possessed only one wooden bowl from which to drink. When he saw a slave boy drinking from his hands he threw away his own bowl as superfluous. He taught self-control and that pain and discomfort are aids to the attainment of virtue, but above all he despised the artificiality of social life, insisting that it is a positive obstacle to both the discovery of truth and the attainment of virtue.

Diognetus, The Epistle to. This letter, dating from the 2nd or 3rd c. CE, is by an unknown Christian writer and purports to show that Christians are "the soul" or leaven of the world. It also asserts that Christianity is the unique revelation of God.

Dionysius. A 3rd c. Bishop of Alexander and pupil of Origen. He engaged in many theological controversies and showed considerable independence of mind both in christological questions and in biblical exegesis.

Dionysius the Carthusian (1402–1471). Mystical theologian. Having entered the Charterhouse at Roermund in 1423, he wrote commentaries on the Bible and on medieval writers such as Boethius and Peter Lombard. He accompanied Nicholas of Cusa to Germany in 1451, helping him in a program of ecclesiastical reform and in a preaching crusade against the Turks.

Dionysius the Pseudo-Areopagite. (See **Areopagite**.) The name given to the unknown author who wrote mystical treatises about the year 500 CE. He was much revered during the Middle Ages, partly because he was erroneously associated with the Dionysius mentioned in Acts 17.34; but, even apart from the mistaken attribution, his writings were influential because they represented the source of a mystical tradition that was important in medieval thought and life. He wrote as a Christian deeply affected by Neoplatonic concepts. While the Bible tells us all we can know about God (since we can know nothing except through divine revelation), what it tells us is obscured by the highly metaphorical language it uses in its way of naming and talking about God. We must go beyond such terminology to better metaphors. Dionysius favors the metaphors of light and love. The divine light bathes humanity in such a way as to apprise us of our being bound to one another in love. The divine light is mediated to us through a celestial hierarchy of angelic powers. (See **Angels**.) His principal works are *On the Divine Names, The Mystical Theology, The Celestial Hierarchy,* and *The Ecclesiastical Hierarchy*. Although some of his concepts seem fanciful and his method was almost as alien to the mainstream of medieval scholasticism as it would be to that of much of modern philosophical theology, it is of great value and importance for the development of certain aspects of the history of Christian thought and especially for the various mystical traditions that have emerged in the life of the Christian community. Modern scholars also refer to him, with slightly less precision, as Pseudo-Dionysius. See BIBLIOGRAPHY under **Christian Mysticism.**

Dionysus. This Greek god takes his name from a combination of roots that together signify literally "tree god". He became primarily the god of wine and nature, a Thracian deity. He was associated with orgiastic rituals, possibly rooted in human sacrifice as practiced in primitive times. Dionysian religion as it was developed stands in contrast to the Homeric outlook. It regarded the human psyche as the higher principle in man, being exiled from a starry world and bound to an earthly embodiment from which occasionally, through ecstatic rituals and other performances it can temporarily escape its earthly prison and become united with the divine. The Greeks were much affected by the notion of the contrast between this Dionysian spirit and the rational one that was to find its supreme expression in philosophers such as Plato and Aristotle. The concept of the entrapment of the psyche in an earthly embodiment is recognized in both these elements, but in the Platonic tradition and in Stoicism liberation is not achieved by any such frenzied orgies as the Dionysian cults encouraged but, rather, through the mastery of emotion by reason. In terms of the Pythagorean tradition that Plato inherited, this liberation might well take myriads of embodiments and rebirths before its accomplishment.

Dioscurus. A 5th c. Patriarch of Alexandria. He supported the christology of Eutyches and when this was condemned at the third session of the Council of Chalcedon in 451 he was deposed, excommunicated, and sent into exile in Paphlagonia.

Dipankara. The name of a legendary Buddha supposed to have been the first

of 24 Buddhas who preceded Gotama Buddha. According to legend he lived for 100,000 years. See **Buddha.**

Dīpāvalī. The traditional name of a Hindu festival during which all the household lamps are lighted in celebration of the reappearance of the sun after the rainy season. The festival is nowadays called Divālī. It is held in the day of the new moon in the month of āsvina (mid-October through mid-November).

Dippel, Johann Konrad (1673–1734). German Pietist. Educated at Giessen, he was at first an Orthodox Lutheran but later became a Pietist and wrote in support of this cause, notably in his *Orthodoxia Orthodoxorum* (1697) and his *Papismus Protestantia Vapulans* (1698). He regarded the development of the Church as in sharp contrast with the Christian Way of the first centuries. When he was eventually forbidden by the Church authorities to write further in this vein, he turned his energies to the study of chemistry and took a degree in medicine at Leyden in 1711. He also interested himself in alchemy and other occult pursuits, which at that time invited persecution. He went to Denmark where he was sentenced to life imprisonment for his opposition to the State Church. Having been freed, he sought refuge in Sweden, where once again he met with difficulties and was eventually expelled. He returned to his native Germany where he died.

Diptychs. In early Christian times, lists of the names of Christians, living and dead, were read during the liturgy so that the faithful might keep them in their prayers. Later the names of those traditionally included were recited in the Western Church inaudibly by the celebrant of the Mass. Such lists are technically known as diptychs.

Dirge. The service known as the Office for the Dead. The name is derived from the opening words of the antiphon: *Dirige Domine Deus.*

Diriment Impediment. A term used in canon law to denote a circumstance or fact that makes a person incapable of contracting a valid marriage, e.g., impotency, consanguinity, insufficient age. A marriage by anyone in such circumstances is not merely unlawful but invalid.

Discalced. The term, which means "shoeless" is used of certain religious orders or branches of orders whose members wear no shoes, following a primitive practice among eastern monks that Francis of Assisi revived in the West. Example: some Franciscans and some Carmelites are discalced while others are calced, that is, the latter wear shoes while the former wear only sandals. The discalced usually represent a stricter observance of the spirit of the order to which they belong.

Disciples of Christ. An American group of Christians founded in 1809. The group prefers not to be considered a sect or denomination. Their polity and organization may be described as Congregational. See **Campbell, Alexander.**

Disciplina Arcani. This term relates to a theory advanced in the 17th c. to the effect that in the early Church certain theological doctrines and practices were concealed from catechumens and outsiders. It was proposed in several forms, e.g., by J. Daillé, I. Casaubon, and E. Schelstrate. The practice did exist in the early Church, being attested by Cyprian, Origen, Chrysostom, Augustine, and others; but the reasons advanced by the 17th c. writers are now generally abandoned. No doubt the early practice of withholding some aspects of Christian doctrine and practice from outsiders and catechumens was motivated by considerations such as Paul suggests (I Corinthians 3.2). All developed religions have some degree of esotericism in them. Converts cannot be expected to understand all at once, without study, their inner meaning.

Discipline. This term has several senses in ecclesiastical usage: (1) Any system of ascetic life such as is practiced by those living under monastic rule; (2) in a more general sense, the entire system of ecclesiastical law, custom, and administration; (3) in a special sense the term is used to designate the system of Church government instituted by the Calvinists and later adopted in Presbyterianism including the methods of dealing with offenders by the imposition of penalties varying from simple admonition to deposition and, in extreme cases, excommunication, through a system consisting of a hierarchy of courts; and (4) the term is applied to a whip of cords traditionally used in certain monastic and other religious communities as a penitential exercise. Its regular, moderate use for self-flagellation is still encouraged in the more austere orders of men and women.

Discipline, Buddhist. The disciplinary rules imposed on Buddhist monastic communities vary in severity. Theft, murder, and sexual misconduct are generally accounted the gravest offenses, usually entailing expulsion, but there are many gradations of recognized offenses and traditionally the complete set of rules dealing with all of them down to bad table manners and the like is recited by the entire community once a month. (No such rules are imposed on lay people, except of course the general precepts for ethical conduct.) Punishments have varied considerably from place to place. Corporal punishment has been extensively used.

Discipline, The Books of. In the Scottish Kirk, after the Reformation led by John Knox, a document was drawn up by the Scottish government at his request, providing in detail for the administration and government of the National Kirk. This document is known as "The First Book of Discipline." In 1578 a document prepared chiefly by Andrew Melville was issued by way of establishing Presbyterian government in the Kirk against the development of an episcopal system. This document came to be known as "The Second Book of Discipline."

Discus. In the Eastern Church, the counterpart of the paten used in the West as the plate for the offering and consecration of the eucharistic bread.

Dismas. The name traditionally given to the "Good Thief" (Luke 23.39–43), who was crucified with Jesus. The name Gestas is likewise traditionally assigned to the other malefactor crucified with him.

Dispensations. In ecclesiastical practice permission is sometimes granted to do acts that are normally forbidden by canon law or to free persons from the obligation of doing acts that are normally required of them. The practice is ancient. The Church claims the right to dispense from its own laws, not from laws that derive from the Bible or are regarded as pertaining to the "natural law." See **Jus Naturale.**

Disruption, The. The schism that took place in the Scottish Kirk in 1843. On May 18 of that year, out of total of 1203 ministers of the Kirk at that time, 474 walked out of the General Assembly in protest and formed "The Free Church of Scotland." The controversy leading up to this dramatic event related to the traditional practice of presenting a minister to an incumbency by a "patron" who had the right to do so by law: sometimes an individual with no or inadequate interest in the parish of which he was the patron. There were, however, as in other schisms in the Church throughout the ages, other reasons leading up to the split that eventually took place that year and was not healed till 1929. The protesting ministers were generally well supported by their people and the Free Kirk produced many scholars among its ministers.

Dissolution of the Monasteries. The virtues of industry and thrift practiced by the ancient monastic orders in the Middle Ages led to their accumulation of enormous wealth, resulting in some cases in abuses that led to popular criticism of the great monastic houses of Europe. Some attempts were made to suppress such houses in which decadence had become scandalous. In England, however, Henry VIII, acting out of motives of personal ambition and greed, completely abolished the monastic system. The dissolution was not accomplished at once because the popularity of such houses in certain cases made it politically inexpedient to do so, but eventually the suppression was total. It was conducted unscrupulously and entailed immense cultural impoverishment for the nation. The spoils passed to the Crown and the nobility. See also **Pilgrimage of Grace.**

Dittography. One of several fairly common errors made in the transcription of manuscripts. It consists in the copyist's inadvertent repetition of a word, letter, or phrase, e.g., "Consider the lilies lilies of the field". The opposite error, that of omitting what ought to have been retained, e.g., "Consider the field," is called *haplography.*

Diurnal. The traditional service book containing all the canonical "hours" (e.g., Prime, Vespers) except Mattins.

Divāli. See **Dīpāvali.**

Divina Commedia. Dante's great epic work, consisting of a trilogy (*Inferno, Purgatorio, Paradiso*), in which he travels through these regions with Virgil as his guide through the first two and Beatrice through the third. It was written in the first decade of the 14th c. Distinctive of Dante are his great originality, his allegorical style (characteristic of so much of medieval literary practice), his Christian humanism (expressed in his admiration for Virgil as representing the philosophy and literature of the ancient Graeco-Roman world), and his loyal acceptance of Catholic faith as understood in his day, while he nevertheless is highly critical of the lives and conduct of popes and other churchmen, some of whom he locates in hell. The *Commedia* quickly gained great popularity. It was read in the Duomo in Florence as a religious book. Large numbers of commentaries have been written on it. It has been widely translated. Through the English translations (e.g., Cary's and Longfellow's) it has exercised a very special influence on English literature and has been the subject of the copious illustrations by Gustav Doré. No poet, not even Shakespeare or Goethe has exercised more influence on European literature than has Dante in his *Commedia*. See also **Dante.**

Divine Light Mission. A religious movement that grew rapidly after the appearance in London in 1971 of Guru Maharajji, then thirteen years old. Many thousands of his followers have since "taken Knowledge," believed to be attained through four meditation techniques. These the aspirant learns from a *mahatma* who instructs him or her in how to engage in them. They are claimed to turn one's senses inward in such a way that one perceives divine light, divine nectar, divine harmony, and the "primordial vibration": the Sacred Name. Followers are called "premies", some of whom live celibate lives in ashrams. Most premies, however, live less ascetic lives, many of them in communities. They are expected to give *sat sang* (i.e., to give testimony to their spiritual experiences), to serve, and to meditate. Large festivals are arranged in various places throughout the world.

Divine Right of Kings. In the long medieval struggle between the rival claims of Church and State, the medieval canonists, while recognizing the prince (the authority on the "secular" side) as divinely anointed, recognized also that a prince who flagrantly abused his office and his power and was inflicting grievous injustice, could be (at least in theory) deposed by an uprising of his subjects and the uprising, in such ex-

ceptional circumstances, would not be rebellion but a just act. This was the doctrine that John Locke developed and that was the basis for the action taken by the American colonies against the British government in the 18th c. In England, however, a doctrine prevailed that, formulated by the middle of the 16th c. and developed by the Stuart kings, claimed that a monarch in the hereditary line of succession to the throne has a divine right to his kingship and to his authority in the exercise of it and that no crime can be more grave than for a citizen to rebel against him, even where he is plainly acting unjustly. Even after the acceptance of William and Mary on the British throne, the doctrine, in modified forms, lingered to some extent, but with the passing of the Stuarts it had become moribund. In modern practice, under a constitutional monarch who reigns by the will of the people and the love and respect evoked in them, the doctrine is of course entirely outmoded.

Divorce. Christian marriage is indubitably intended to be indissoluble. The Hebrew legal codes, unlike the codes of Mesopotamia, provided no clear regulations relating to divorce. Although the teaching of Jesus on the subject may seem clear (Mark 10.1–12; Luke 16.18), two passages in Matthew (Matthew 5.32 and 19.1ff.) leave room for interpretation. Scholars recognize that there were two schools in Hebrew legal tradition at the time of Jesus: that of Hillel which held that a man might divorce his wife for any reason, such as his finding any fault in her conduct, while the school of Shammai allowed divorce only for adultery. Since the legal punishment for adultery was death, the question would seem not to have had much practical significance, yet some argue that the Greek word that in English is rendered "adultery" (*porneia*) may translate the Aramaic *zenût*, which means any illicit union, e.g., concubinage. At any rate, the answer given by Jesus to the question put to him by the Pharisees here is open to more than one interpretation. In modern usage the term "divorce" is employed in two senses: (1) *a vinculo*, i.e., a total dissolution of the marriage bond, and (2) *a mensa et thoro*, i.e., legal separation. The Roman Catholic Church forbids divorce *a vinculo*, but the Pope reserves the right to dissolve by annulment a marriage that has not been consummated and in practice the Roman Catholic Church does so annul marriages on a variety of grounds (such as lack of full consent, impotence, and others). The Eastern Church allows divorce on a number of grounds. Practice elsewhere varies considerably. Wherever divorce is permitted at all, adultery of either of the spouses is generally regarded as the gravest, if not the only, justifiable ground. A clergyman, if his conscience permits him and his Church does not forbid him, may perform a marriage ceremony according to the civil law of the society to which he belongs, which marriage is of course subject to the civil legislation only. Fundamentally, however, divorce is abhorrent to the Christian concept of the sacramental nature of marriage.

Docetism. In the Mediterranean world in which early Christianity developed, a view widely prevailed in the intellectual world according to which the realm of matter (e.g., the flesh) was alien to and at war with the realm of the spirit. The concept that divine Being could be contaminated with matter by entering into humanity and especially by suffering the ignominy of crucifixion seemed to many intolerable. They tried to escape the consequences of it by proposals such as that Jesus did not actually live as a human being but only appeared to live and to be crucified and to die. They were called docetists, from the Greek verb *dokeō*, "I seem". The first to use the term (*dokētai*) seems to have been Serapion, Bishop of Antioch. The docetists were bitterly attacked by Ignatius of Antioch and others.

Docta Ignorantia. See **Nicholas of Cusa.**

Doctor. The title "doctor" means simply a learned man (Latin, *doctus*, learned). In academic practice it has been officially conferred in European universities, from the Middle Ages onward, in Divinity, in Law, and in Medicine, and in more recent times also in Letters and in Sciences. These remain, in European (including British) practice the "higher doctorates" and are given usually for original published work, while the doctorate in philosophy (Ph.D.) is treated as a lower doctorate. In the U.S., however, the Ph.D. has come to be regarded as the crowning degree that can be earned, other doctorates being honorary. The term has nevertheless a variety of ecclesiastical uses. In Anglican usage, for example, a D.D. has certain ecclesiastical precedence. (See **Chimere.**) The Calvinist system provided for a class of trained persons not pastors but doctors. The title is traditionally also given as a sort of sobriquet to various celebrated theologians, e.g., Thomas Aquinas is called *doctor angelicus*, Bernard of Clairvaux, *doctor mellifluus*, and Duns Scotus *doctor subtilis*. See also **Doctors of the Church.**

Doctors of the Church. In the Middle Ages this title (*doctores ecclesiae*) was given to four Christian theologians noted both for their learning and for their personal holiness: Gregory the Great, Ambrose, Augustine, and Jerome. In more recent times the Roman Catholic Church has awarded it to at least some twenty-five others.

Dodd, Charles Harold (1884–1973). New Testament scholar and theologian. After studies at Oxford and Berlin, he was ordained to the Congregationalist ministry and eventually, in 1935, became the Norris-Hulse Professor of Divinity at Cambridge. His works include *The Authority of the Bible* (1928), *The Bible and the Greeks* (1935), *History of the Gospel* (1938), *The Interpretation of the Fourth Gospel* (1953), and *The Historical Tradition in the Fourth Gospel* (1963). He played a leading part both in the direction and in the translation of the Bible published as *The New English Bible*, a scholarly rendering of the Bible into 20th c. colloquial English for purposes of private devotion and study. See also **Driver, Godfrey Rolles.**

Doddridge, Philip (1702–1751). English Protestant divine. The youngest child of a family of twenty children of a successful merchant in London, he declined the opportunity of a university training, preferring to train for the ministry in an independent seminary. He worked very hard throughout his life as an ordained minister to encourage and promote ecumenicity in England among all those sympathetic to the cause of the Independents. In 1736 the University of Aberdeen honored him with the degree of Doctor of Divinity. He wrote several works including *On the Rise and Progress of Religion in the Soul* (1745) and many hymns, among which are *O God of Bethel* and *Hark, the Glad Sound!* He died in Lisbon.

Dōgen (1200–1253 CE). The founder of the Sōtō branch of Zen Buddhism in Japan. He is reputed to have been a man of noble parentage, orphaned at the age of seven, very humane, irreproachable in his conduct, and deeply religious. He taught that the Buddha-nature is to be realized by the elimination of all selfish cravings and self-centeredness. He much emphasized the practice of meditation through Zazen, which entails sitting upright with legs crossed while mentally concentrating on the realization of the Buddha-nature. He disapproved of the tendency in Chinese and Japanese Buddhism to split into various sects and held Zen to be the direct way to salvation. His most important writing is the *Shōbōgenzō.* See **Zen** and **Za-Zen.**

Dogma. From the Greek *dokeō*, "I think" or "I have an opinion," hence *dokēma*, "opinion". The term was used by classical writers in antiquity to designate the distinctive views of the various philosophical schools. As developed by the Christian Fathers it came to designate the formulation of any view taken to be revealed in Scripture and taught by the Church.

Döllinger, Johann Joseph Ignaz (1799–1890). Church historian. Ordained priest in 1822, he was professor of Ecclesiastical History at Munich from 1826 till 1873. In his earlier years he took an Ultramontane outlook, but through friendship with Lord Acton and other distinguished Catholics of his time he developed a critical and independent scholarly spirit. His works include his *Reformation* (3 vols., 1845–1848), *Hippolytus und Callistus* (1853), *Christentum und Kirche* (1860). By about this time he was attacking the concept of the temporal power of the papacy and urging a more liberal form of Catholic churchmanship. As the policies of Pope Pius IX grew more and more intransigently hostile to such influences (expressly condemned in the *Syllabus of Errors* that was published in 1864), culminating in the calling of the Vatican Council (1869–1870), now known as Vatican I, with the clear intention of declaring the extremely controversial doctrine of Papal Infallibility to be part of the official faith of the Roman Catholic Church, Döllinger became prominent as a leader of scholarly opinion within that Church against the direction in which it was moving under Pius IX. Amongst others, he declined to accept the decrees of Vatican I, was excommunicated in 1871 by his archbishop (von Scherr), and became a leader of the Old Catholic Church movement. He continued to write extensively in the period of his greatest scholarly maturity. His last great work was his *Briefe und Erklärungen über die Vatikanischen Dekrete* (1890). Highly respected as a scholar, he was appointed in 1873 president of the Bavarian Royal Academy of Sciences.

Dom. A title traditionally used by monks of the Benedictine and other ancient orders and by some canons regular. It is a contraction of the Latin *Dominus*, meaning "master" or "lord". Since Vatican II, the practice has fallen into disuse. The word *Dom* is also used in German for "cathedral" (i.e., "house", the house of the People of God), corresponding to the Italian *duomo*. The cathedral foundation at Oxford (Christ Church) is likewise officially known as *Aedes Christi* ("the House of Christ") and popularly called "The House".

Dome of the Rock. The beautiful mosque built within the area of the former Jewish Temple and dating from about the year 700. The rock on which it is built is believed by Jews to be that on which Abraham prepared to sacrifice his son Isaac in obedience to God's command. In Muslim lore it is held to be the rock from which Muhammad ascended to heaven.

Domine Quo Vadis? (Latin, "Lord, whither are you going?") According to an apocryphal writing called *The Acts of Peter*, Peter was fleeing from Rome to escape torture and death. On the way he met the Risen Christ and asked him "Domine, quo vadis?" When the Lord replied that he was going to Rome to be crucified, Peter turned back and gave himself up to the Roman authorities, who then crucified him. The story is commemorated in the Quo Vadis Chapel on the Appian Way.

Dominic (1170–1221). Founder of the Order of Preachers (*Ordo Praedicatorum*). Born in Calaruega, Old Castile, Spain, Dominic joined a religious community of which he became the head, but in 1203 he left it to go on a preaching mission against the Albigensians in Languedoc. When, in 1208, Pope Innocent III began a crusade against the Albigensians, Dominic took a leading part in trying, although unsuccessfully, to bring about their submission to Rome. Some years later his plans to found a new Order began to take shape. In 1216, Honorius III formerly sanctioned

the new Order. He died in Bologna. See **Dominican Order**.

Dominica in Albis. The traditional name for the First Sunday after Easter ("Low Sunday"). Since 1969, the Roman Catholic Church has dropped this terminology.

Dominican Order (See **Dominic**.) This Order, founded in the 13th c. by Dominic, officially designated *Ordo Praedicatorum* (Order of Preachers), is an order of friars. Its members wear a white habit under a black mantle; hence their popular name in England: Blackfriars. In contrast to the ancient monastic orders, the Dominicans (like the Franciscans and other orders of friars) adopted the concept of corporate poverty, not merely the lack of private, individual possession. In contrast to the Franciscans, however, they began after a century or more to accumulate considerable wealth. Some lived in luxury. In 1475, Pope Sixtus IV gave them permission to renounce their practice of corporate poverty. Both male and female members of the Order are largely engaged in teaching. Their most illustrious representative is Thomas Aquinas. They were widely used by the Church for the preaching of crusades and were notoriously involved in the Inquisition. Representing themselves as champions of Roman Catholic orthodoxy (although they traditionally opposed the doctrine of the Immaculate Conception, which was to be defined in 1854 by Pope Pius IX as an integral part of Roman Catholic belief), they came to be popularly known (by way of a pun on their name as the Lord's watchdogs (*domini canes*). Unlike the Franciscans who began as an order of simple, unlearned men (although they very quickly took their place among the intellectual leaders of Europe), the Dominicans from the first upheld the ideal of learning within the parameters of Roman Catholic orthodoxy. Dominican nuns follow the contemplative life in the cloister under strict discipline, although they may also engage in teaching, medical, and missionary work.

Dominus Vobiscum. This Latin salutation (meaning "The Lord be with you") has extremely ancient roots, e.g., it occurs in Ruth 2.4. It was probably in use in the Christian community from the earliest times and the traditional response *Et cum spiritu tuo* has been used from a probably equally early date. (A form of it is found in II Timothy 4.22.) The recent vulgarization of the response ("And also with you"), apart from its prosiness, fails to exhibit an understanding of the meaning of the salutation and response as both have been used and understood for almost two thousand years.

Donation of Constantine. A document fabricated in the 8th or 9th c. with a view to promoting the power of the See of Rome. It purported to show that Constantine had granted the Pope precedence over the four great patriarchates of Alexandria, Antioch, Jerusalem, and Constantinople, as well as granting him dominion over all Italy and giving him other extensive executive, judicial, and administrative authority. This forged document was embodied in the False Decretals and other collections that were widely accepted during the Middle Ages in the West. Nicholas of Cusa was among those who, in the 15th c., demonstrated the forgery behind it.

Donatist Controversy. In the 4th c., a schism developed within the African Church when Caecilian, Bishop of Carthage, was not recognized by a certain group of Christians, on the ground that the bishop who had consecrated him had been a *traditor*, i.e., guilty of giving up copies of the Scriptures to the Roman authorities or some other such offense. The Donatists, who *prima facie* had a good case, since they were arguing for the moral purity of the clergy, held that sacraments administered by morally unworthy priests (as they accounted the *traditores*) are invalid. Against them, however, the Church held to a principle that it has ever since maintained: the unworthiness of the minister does not invalidate the sacrament. Otherwise one would be always in doubt of the validity of any sacrament, especially when administered by a priest unknown to the recipient. The Donatists are so called after Donatus, the bishop who had succeeded Majorinus, whom the objecting party had consecrated as a rival to Caecilian.

Donne, John (1572–1631). English poet and preacher. Born into a Roman Catholic family, his father was a London ironmonger and his mother the daughter of John Heywood who had married the niece of Thomas More. From 1598 to 1602, Donne was secretary to the Keeper of the Great Seal of England (T. Egerton). He was dismissed, having lost favor by a secret marriage with Anne More, niece of his master's wife. After travels to Cadiz, he returned to England where, in 1615, he was ordained an Anglican priest. His sermons are generally accounted among the best of the 17th c. From 1621 till his death he was Dean of St. Paul's Cathedral, London. His poetry varies from the secular vein of his youth to the religious poetry of his maturer years. (See **Metaphysical Poets, The.**) His name is pronounced "dunne" and was so spelt by some of his contemporaries.

Dormition. The Feast of the Dormition in the Eastern Church corresponds to that of the Assumption of Mary in the West. It celebrates the "Falling Asleep" (*dormitio*) of Mary. The date is August 15. See **Assumption of Mary** and **Koimēsis.**

Dorner, Isaak August (1809–1884). Lutheran theologian. Educated at Tübingen, where he studied under F. C. Baur, he became professor there in 1838. After appointments at various other German universities he became professor at Berlin in 1862. His theological aim was to reconcile the various Kantian systems with the Christian faith in its Lutheran form. Among his writings is his *Geschichte der protestantis-chen Theologie* (1867), an English translation of which was published in two vols. in 1871.

Dorothea. Early Christian lady, probably martyred in the Diocletian persecution in 313.

Dorotheus. 6th c. spiritual writer who *c.* 540 founded a monastery near Gaza. He wrote a treatise (*Didaskaliai Psychōpheleis*) on the spiritual life in which he ranked humility above all other virtues.

Dorsal. A cloth, usually embroidered, hanging at the back of the altar in place of a reredos.

Dort, Synod of (1618–1619). An important national assembly of the Dutch Reformed Church, convened at Dort to consider the Arminian controversy, it was attended by representatives from several foreign countries including England and Switzerland. It was strongly Calvinistic and the five sets of articles it passed on April 23, 1619, upheld (against the Arminians) unconditional election, a doctrine of atonement limited to the elect, the total depravity of man, irresistible grace, and the final perseverance of the elect. It also upheld the Belgic Confession and the Heidelberg Catechism.

Dorter. A monastic dormitory.

Dōshō (629–700 CE). The most important Japanese Buddhist leader of his time, he studied in China and pioneered Buddhist philosophical thought in Japan. In his later years he also promoted the building of Buddhist monasteries in Japan.

Dositheus. A 2nd c. Jewish gnostic, whose writings were known to Origen. Among the Nag Hammadi papyri is a brief work attributed to Dositheus, which may possibly be identified with this writer. His followers, though apparently small in number, survived for many centuries.

Dositheus (1641–1707). Patriarch of Jerusalem from 1669, his greatest ecclesiastical achievement was the Synod of Jerusalem (1672), the most important church assembly in the Eastern Church since the Great Schism of 1054. His writings include works dealing with Photius and Gregory Palamas. He opposed, in principle, all theological influence from the West.

Dostoievsky, Feodor Michaelovitch (1821–1881). Russian novelist. Born in Moscow, he was educated for a military career at St. Petersburg. In 1849 he was arrested for revolutionary activities, imprisoned, condemned to death, then eventually freed. His journalistic and literary activities then occupied more and more of his time. His novels, many of them now classics of world literature, include *Crime and Punishment* (1865–1866), *The Possessed* (1871), and *The Brothers Karamazov* (1880). Critical of organized religion, he was deeply religious and may be rightly accounted a Russian counterpart of Kierkegaard, his Western contemporary. His short story "The Grand Inquisitor" in *The Brothers Karamazov* is as much a religious as it is a literary classic.

Douai. A center in Flanders for the training of English Roman Catholic clergy during and after the reign of Elizabeth I, it became also the focus of the production of the Douai-Reims translation of the Bible into English for the benefit of Roman Catholics in England. The college at Douai was suppressed at the French Revolution and its work continued in England at Crook Hall (near Ushaw) and at St. Edmund's Old Hall (Ware). See also **Downside.**

Double Effect. When an action, definable as good in terms of its intended aim, may be achieved only at the risk of causing some incidental harm, many Christian moralists consider it to be ethically permissible. Example: when an ectopic pregnancy (i.e., one in which the fetus is in an unusual and dangerous position in the uterus) threatens the mother's life, the obstetrician may save her life (even though so doing entails the death of the fetus), if failure so to act would result in the death of both mother and fetus. Since the intended primary effect would not be an abortion but the incidental, secondary effect of a good and legitimate action, the obstetrician would not be causing an abortion. This principle is widely recognized by Roman Catholic moralists who would not condone abortion.

Double Feasts. The designation formerly applied to the more important festivals of the Church. Within this category were further distinguished various degrees of importance, e.g., Doubles of the First Class, etc.

Double Monasteries. A designation applied to religious houses consisting of both men and women, who were housed in separate but adjacent or contiguous buildings. Monasteries of this kind existed from antiquity in the Eastern Church, and the practice extended to the West, becoming very common in the earlier Middle Ages. (Whitby in England is an example.) After the 9th c. they tended to become much less common and eventually, despite occasional attempts to revive the practice, they disappeared.

Double Procession. The Eastern Orthodox Church has always maintained the theological doctrine that the Holy Spirit proceeds from the Father *through* the Son. In the West the view has been generally accepted that the Holy Spirit proceeds from the Father *and* the Son. (See **Filioque.**) The latter view is known as the doctrine of Double Procession. The controversy is theologically significant. Generally speaking, the Latins tended not to understand the philosophical and theological subtleties of Greek thought and when Greek terms were translated into Latin they often lost their original significance. The Greek theologians have always objected to the notion of Double Procession on very solid theological grounds,

namely, that there must be in the Trinity one Source of divine Being. The formula used in the Eastern Church (without the addition of the words "and the Son") expresses and conserves the concept of the Unity of God, apart from which the doctrine of the Trinity makes no sense. In the West, those Latin Fathers, notably Augustine, who lent some support to the doctrine of the Double Procession did so by way of expressing a private opinion. (Augustine did not know Greek.) Even as late as 800, Pope Leo III caused two silver tablets to be deposited at the Tomb of Peter with the original (Greek) form of the Niceno-Constantinopolitan Creed engraved upon them. Resistance to the Double Procession concept is acknowledged by many scholars in the West today as justified both on historical and on theological grounds.

Double Truth. The notion that what is true in religion may not be true in science or philosophy and that what is true in fields such as the latter may not be true in religion. This teaching was attributed to Averroes, but probably without justification, since he never specifically affirms it. In medieval Christian thought, however, he was widely supposed to have held such a position; hence the distrust of Averroism by the medieval Christian thinkers, who insisted that truth is one, so that nothing can be true in one field yet false in another. The medieval Christian distrust of any "double truth" theory was salutary and remains so, excluding any radical opposition between "science" and "religion".

Doubt. The word "doubt" has its etymological root in two Latin words (*duo* + *bito* = to go in two directions, i.e., to stand at the crossroads). It is therefore not, as is often supposed, antithetical to faith, being, on the contrary, an implicate of it. Faith is, rather, a descant on doubt. Descartes insisted on doubt as a *method* for discovering the starting point of authentic philosophical thought. Christian thought may be likewise said to presuppose doubt. See **Belief**; also the article "Doubt and Belief" in the *Encyclopedia of Religion* (1986).

Doukhobors. A Russian sect that appears to have arisen *c.* mid-18th c. among the peasantry of Kharkov. After being persecuted and expelled to Siberia they were assisted by Tolstoy, whose pacifist ideals had influenced them, and by the Quakers, with whose outlook theirs has affinities. Many of them emigrated to Canada, where their refusal to own land and to perform various statutory duties required of citizens (e.g., registration of births, deaths, and marriages) have made them a problem for the Canadian Government. They believe in God and in his manifestation in the soul of man and they affirm the principle of reincarnation. For further information, see: J. Elkington, *The Doukhobors* (1903); H. B. Hawthorne (ed.), *The Doukhobors of British Columbia* (1955).

Douleia. See **Latria.**

Dove. The dove is used in Christian symbolism to express peace or the promise of peace. Example: in the Flood story in Genesis 8, the dove appears as an expression of the assurance of God's reconciliation with humanity. It may also be used as a symbol of Christian love (*agapē*) and of the Holy Spirit whence that love flows among the People of God. Sometimes it expresses humility or purity, even theological insight.

Downside. The leading house of the English Benedictines. Originally a settlement of English Roman Catholics living in exile at Douai, this monastic house was founded in 1814 and attained the status of an abbey in 1899. The splendid abbey church, consecrated in 1935, is architectually renowned as a fine example of modern Gothic. The community itself is famed for its scholarly traditions. See also **Douai.**

Doxa. This Greek term means "opinion". Terms such as "orthodoxy" and "heterodoxy" mean, therefore, respectively, "right opinion" and "other opinion"; i.e., what is viewed as right by a particular group or may be regarded as the outlook of the mainstream and what is not. See **Orthodoxy.**

Doxology. A liturgical expression through which honor and glory are ascribed to the Triune God, e.g., the *Gloria Patri*, which is traditionally appended to psalms and to some hymns. See **Gloria Patri.**

Drama. The early Christians so much associated stage performances with pagan spectacles, often lewd, that to take part in any such performance was virtually to renounce the Christian faith. Even to view a gladiatorial show was considered improper for a Christian, who ought to discourage warfare of every kind, certainly not to look at it for pleasure. John Chrystostom, in the 4th c., for instance, inveighs against going to see such lewd or violent spectacles and even encourages parents to take their children to see the unhappy faces of those who have just returned from viewing such a show and compare them with those of Christians coming forth radiantly after the joy of the liturgy. Such was the decadence of the later days of the Empire that even the more thoughtful of pagans disapproved of the popular spectacles. By the 9th c., however, such shows had long ceased to play any part in social life and some attempts were made to produce dramatic performances of an edifying or instructive character. Later on in the Middle Ages, various kinds of dramatic performances were developed and for the most part were accepted as serving the Church's aims. These included the Mystery Plays (also called "Miracle Plays"), sometimes performed even in church and often in the public square in front of the church. By the late Middle Ages such performances had become largely detached from the control of the Church and were technically similar to what would be today expected of any small or amateur company of players. By the 16th c. drama had been fully emancipated from ecclesiastical connection. In spite of strong resistance (e.g., on the part of the Puritans), Christians generally have accepted drama along with music and literature of every kind, so long as such art-forms do not flagrantly offend the standards of civilized human beings. In Buddhist and other Oriental cultures very similar developments have taken place in religious drama.

Drāviḍa. The name of a people of India, the Dravidians, and also of their language, which eventually was developed into Tamil. A thousand years or more before the Aryans arrived in India the northwest was occupied by a dark-skinned people, the proto-Dravidians. It was they who traded with Western Asia and later with the Roman Empire, selling ivory, peacocks, and spices (see I Kings 10.22 and II Chronicles 9.21). They gradually moved to the south of India.

Dread. A term often used, but very misleadingly, to render the term *Angst* into English. See **Angst** and **Kierkegaard, Søren Aabye.**

Driver, Godfrey Rolles (1892–1975). Semitic philologist and biblical scholar. Educated at Winchester and Oxford, he was elected a Fellow of Magdalen College, Oxford, in 1919 and was Professor of Semitic Philology at Oxford from 1938 to 1962. He took a leading part in the making of the New English Bible. (See **Bible**) His works include *Semitic Writing* (1948), *The Judaean Scrolls* (1965), and *Canaanite Myths and Legends* (1956). He was also co-editor of editions of *Assyrian Laws* (1935) and *Babylonian Laws* (1952–55), both of which are standard texts. He was the son of S. R. Driver. See also **Dodd, Charles Harold.**

Driver, Samuel Rolles (1846–1914). Biblical scholar. Educated at Winchester and Oxford, he was elected a Fellow of New College in 1870, and from 1883 till his death he was Regius Professor of Hebrew at Oxford. He was renowned for his careful and judicious Hebrew scholarship and, of Quaker ancestry, was admired for his quiet but resolute adherence to the Christian faith. His works include his *Introduction to the Old Testament* (1897), which was for half a century a standard work in the field and (although now outmoded) is still a monument to the biblical scholarship of the period. He also produced many commentaries and other scholarly works.

Drug Dependence. Dependence on certain addictive drugs has attained epidemic proportions in society today and presents a variety of serious problems in Christian ethics. The World Health Organization has defined it as "a state, psychic, and sometimes also physical, resulting from the interaction of a living organism and a drug, characterized by behavioral and other responses that always include a compulsion to take the drug on a continuous or periodic basis in order to experience its psychic effects, and sometimes to avoid discomfort of its absence." Alcoholism, a form of drug dependence, is treated separately. (See **Alcoholism.**) The ethical problems relating to drug addiction are aggravated by the wide differences in individual response to addictive drugs. Since the alarming rise in the incidence of the deadly disease AIDS, many cases of which have been traced to the use of contaminated needles, the problems associated with drug dependence have acquired both greater complexity and a new sense of urgency. Addictive drugs vary sharply both in their potency and in their effects, e.g., some are stimulant, others sedative. Amphetamines belong to the former class and can be so addictive as to cause dependence in a few weeks. Rehabilitation is usually very difficult. Cocaine is a violent stimulant producing intense euphoria that the addict wishes to experience as often as possible. It can lead to dangerous delusions, hallucinations, and result in antisocial conduct. Sedatives include the large group of barbiturates, many of which are used legitimately in mild dosages by doctors in routine prescriptions. In heavy doses however, sedatives can produce very hazardous conditions. Sudden withdrawal can be highly dangerous. Narcotic drugs are even more addictive and dangerous. Opiate narcotics include morphine, opium, codeine, and heroine. The latter is so powerful that according to statistics an addict's lifespan can be reduced by as much as twenty years. Hallucinogens ("psychedelics") can produce weird distortions of thinking, sensation, and self-awareness. The most potent and well-known hallucinogen is LSD (lysergic acid diethylamide), the use of which can result in severe mental illness as well as physical effects. Some users report pleasant imagery; others terrifying, nightmare-like experiences. Marijuana (cannabis), also in the hallucinogen family can produce grave consequences too, although it is generally less potent. Almost any drug may be dangerous if used in conjunction with other drugs. The control of drugs by legislation has proved to be very difficult; nor can judicious medical handling of the problem, important though it certainly is, cope with the complex issues attending this wide area of societal illness. Only by education from kindergarten onwards can we hope to overcome one of the greatest social problems: one which, although it has existed from time immemorial, has attained proportions capable of destroying society. According to basic New Testament teaching, the human body is the "temple of the Holy Spirit" (I Corinthians 6.19), so that its abuse is to be regarded by a Christian as a grievous ingratitude to God that alienates him or her from the Source of Being. The path leading to drug dependence appears so innocently seductive at the outset and so quickly leads to mental and moral ruin that it is a duty of paramount and unique importance on the

part of society to educate children from a very early age and by the best educational tools available so that they know the insidious dangers of ever entering it. Christians, living in a largely pagan society infested with this problem, must face their responsibilities toward the rising generation and the first step is for them to understand the nature of the problem and the devastating consequences that attend experimentation with dangerous drugs.

Drummond, Henry (1786–1860). A leader of the Irvingites. As a member of Parliament he took an active role in politico-religious questions of the day.

Drummond, Henry (1851–1897). Scottish Protestant theologian. Educated at Edinburgh and Tübingen, he conducted missions at various universities and engaged in explorations in America and Africa. He was among those of his age who strongly advanced the concept that evolution is "God's way of doing things," and he tried to promote a sense of unity as between the science and the religion of his day: a theme expounded in his *Natural Law in the Spiritual World* (1883).

Drummond, James (1835–1918). Unitarian divine. Educated at Dublin and London, he sought throughout his life to maintain an independent stance in the theological controversies of his time and found in Unitarianism a hospitable environment in which to do so. His works include *The Jewish Messiah* (1877), *Philo-Judaeus* (2. vols., 1888), *Via, Veritas, Vita* (1894), and *Studies in Christian Doctrine* (1908).

Druze, The. The Druze are a religious body that evolved from the Ismaeli faction of the Shi'a branch of Islam. (See **Shi'ites.**) They took their origin from the action of the sixth fatimid caliph, Al-Hakim Be Amrillah, who in 1017 CE proclaimed the emergence of a new order. That new order, while perceiving in the traditional Islamic emphasis on the Unity of God (*al-Tawḥīd*) the essence of the movement, went beyond the literal and even traditional Islamic allegorical interpretations of the Qur'ān.

The name "Druze" or "Druse" comes from al-Darazi, who was one of the early missionaries. His later conduct, however, warranted his being renounced by the movement, so the community prefers to be known by the more accurate designation: the Muwahhidūn. The designation "Druze", however, has become widely used, somewhat as the term "Quaker" has been generally accepted for the Society of Friends.

A basic principle in Druze theology is that God in himself, as the Absolute (*lahout*), is beyond human comprehension. Only through divine revelation (*nasout*) can man come to have such knowledge of God as God chooses to permit man to acquire. Such a view of God and revelation is of course consonant with that of all the great monotheistic religions. What is distinctive in the Druze interpretation is that the revelation is not an instantaneous disclosure. It is appropriated by each individual over a period far longer than could be encompassed in any human lifetime and therefore requires many re-embodiments. The classic doctrine of reincarnation, understood as having this specific purpose, is vital to the Druze outlook. Moreover, in contrast to the view of many reincarnationists in other religions, they hold that rebirth occurs immediately upon death.

Druze thought was developed at a time when the Muslim intellectual world had been deeply influenced by Neo-Platonism, which served as a means of interpreting the Judeo-Christian heritage of Islam. Such, however, was the nature of the Druze use of this way of thinking that it created a backlash from traditional Islam by which it came to be regarded as heterodox. Because of persecution the movement went underground. After a certain time had elapsed for those who sought to convert to the Druze community, the Druze ceased to permit such conver-

sions, so that now a Druze is by definition one born into the faith. Today the Druze population is estimated at about a million, half of whom are found in Lebanon, Syria, Israel, and Jordan, and the other half scattered through the rest of the world. There is a minimal of ritual and no organized clerical order. A tradition of ethics and piety from the heritage of the ancient Wisdom guides the Druze in their life and conduct. The Druze were the first group in the Arab world to declare polygamy illegal. They are a highly respected element in the Middle East today. What may be regarded as the Druze Scriptures is the collection of writings known as *Al-Ḥikmat al-Sharīfa*, meaning literally "The Noble Knowledge", a form of Wisdom literature comprising 111 epistles in six volumes. For further reading see the BIBLIOGRAPHY under **Islam**.

Dryden, John (1631–1700). English poet, dramatist and satirist. His political satire is notably represented in his *Absalom and Achitophel* (1681). His *Religio laici* (1682) expresses his adherence to the Anglican way. Later, however, he renounced his previous religious allegiances and became a Roman Catholic. His *The Hind and the Panther* (1687) celebrated his new allegiance. Some of his work reflects also an interest in the outlook of the Renaissance humanists.

Dry Mass. In the late Middle Ages, the practice grew of saying a devotion which, consisting of the Mass with the omission of its most important parts (e.g., the Consecration of the Host and Chalice) was not a Mass at all. It was called *missa sicca:* dry Mass. There were several reasons for the development of this practice, e.g., in rough weather at sea and where a priest had already said Mass and the rule against bination prevented his saying another. Its use was widespread, especially in France. It provided a somewhat unfortunate model for the Reformed Churches that adapted it for their regular liturgical use.

Dualism. This term, which seems to have been introduced c. 1700 by Thomas Hyde, in reference to an element in the history of Zoroastrianism, is used in several senses. The first to apply it to the metaphysical opposition between mind and matter was Christian Wolff. In the history of religion it is applied to the strong opposition of good and evil as two rival forces in the universe, as found notably in Manichaeism but also in some forms of Gnosticism and in the classical Chinese Yin/Yang antinomy. Dualism may be metaphysical or moral. Modified forms of dualism may be found in many philosophical systems. The distinction made by Descartes between the *res cogitans* (the knower) and the *res extensa* (the known) implies a thoroughgoing dualism.

Du Cange, Charles Dufresne (1610–1688). French historian and linguist. After a legal training he obtained the position of Treasurer of France. Interested in Byzantine Greek and Late Latin, he published his *Glossarium ad scriptores mediae et infimae latinitatis* in 3 folio vols. (1678), a work that has remained the most comprehensive dictionary of Late Latin, exhibiting vast learning and critical judgment. He followed it with a similarly conceived work on Greek in two folio vols. (1688) and also wrote important works on historical matters, Byzantine and French. Among the editions of the Latin *Glossarium* that have been published, the one by Le Favre in 10 volumes (1883–7) remains standard, while a photographic reproduction of his Greek glossary was issued in 1943. These works of Du Cange are standard tools for medievalists.

Ducasse, Curt (1881–1969). French-born American philosopher, he regarded causation as a fundamental category and taught a thoroughgoing form of determinism. His critical analysis of religion is expressed more especially in his later works, such as *A Philosophical Scrutiny of Religion* (1953). His study of the question of afterlife is

relevant to certain confusions in Christian teaching on that subject, e.g., his *A Critical Examination of the Belief in a Life after Death* (1961). He recognized that certain paranormal phenomena support belief in an afterlife, although he denied that they establish it.

Duchesne, Louis (1843–1922). Ecclesiastical historian. Ordained priest in 1867, he continued his theological studies in Rome and also traveled in the Middle East. Appointed professor at the Institut Catholique, Paris, in 1877, he faced opposition because of his critical interpretation of the history of Church teaching. From 1895 till his death, he directed the French school at Rome. He was elected a member of the *Académie Française* in 1910. His many scholarly works include his *Origines du culte chrétien* (1889), which was translated into English by M. L. McLure, *Christian Worship* (1903). His *L'Histoire ancienne de l'Eglise chrétienne*, in 3 vols. (1906–1910) was placed on the Index in 1912. For further information see: F. Cabrol, OSB, "Monseigneur Louis Duchesne. Son oeuvre historique" in the *Journal of Theological Studies*, xxiv (1922–23), pp. 253–82.

Duels. The practice of duelling as a way of settling questions supposedly entailing the honor of the parties was widespread in fashionable society through the Middle Ages and much later both in England and in continental Europe, even after it had been prohibited by civil law. The Church, however, repeatedly protested against the practice and today not only participants in a duel but willing spectators are liable to excommunication and, if they die impenitent, are not given Christian burial. For further information see: J. G. Mullingen, *The History of Duelling* (2 vols., 1841). K. Mörsdorf, *Lexikon für Theologie und Kirche*, 2nd ed., xii, (1965), cols. 1426–8, with biblio.

Duff, Alexander (1806–1878). The first missionary of the Scottish Kirk to go to India as a missionary. He opened a school in Calcutta that later became a center of education in India. In his later years he was instrumental in founding the University of Calcutta. His son wrote *Memorials of Alexander Duff* (1890). See also W. Paton, *Alexander Duff* (1923).

Dugdale (1605–1686). Ecclesiastical historian and antiquarian, author of the *Monasticon Anglicanum.* See also L. Fox (ed.), *English Historical Scholarship in the Sixteenth and Seventeenth Centuries* (1956).

Dukhobors. See **Doukhobors.**

Dukka. The Pali form of the Sanskrit *Duhkha.* A term universally used in Buddhism for one of the conditioning factors in human existence. It can be and has been variously understood, encompassing as it does the various forms of malaise and suffering that are part of the human condition. See **Four Noble Truths, and the Noble Eightfold Path.**

Dulia. The Latin form of the Greek *douleia.* See **Latria.**

Du Moulin, Pierre (1568–1658). French Protestant theologian. Professor at Leyden and later at Sedan, he was prominent in the theological controversies of his day, seeking to mediate between Catholic and Calvinist protagonists: an enterprise notoriously likely to displease both sides as it generally did in his case. He also conducted much correspondence with the Anglican theologians of his time. See G. Gory, *Pierre Du Moulin* (1888); J. Massip, *Un vieux Prédicateur huguenot* (1888).

Dundubhi. A war-drum celebrated in the Ṛgveda (VI. 47, 28–31). Its sound endows the devotees of the national or tribal deity, Indra, with military zest and terrifies his enemies. The rhythm of sound was believed (as by all primitive peoples) to have magical powers, e.g., the sound of a drum treated with a potion of herbs and cow urine can cure snakebite and many other ills. In iconography thunder is represented by a

drum. According to legend the gods, having failed to destroy a demon with weapons of war, eventually succeeded by the use of drums and incantations, so proving the superiority of rhythmic sound over military arsenals.

Dunkers. A German Baptist sect that insisted on the necessity of total immersion (*tunken* in Old German meant "to dip", "to dunk"). They originated in Germany in 1708. Persecuted there, they emigrated to America in the early 18th c. In the late 19th c. they split into "Conservatives" and "Progressives". They also have an *agapē* meal in conjunction with the Sacrament of Communion and they discourage all dealings with the civil authorities. They have been known as "The Church of the Brethren" since 1908. See D. F. Durnbaugh (ed. and tr.), *European Origins of the Brethren* (1958): a source book for their early history.

Duns Scotus, John (*c.* 1265–1308). One of the three great 13th c. scholastic philosophers, along with Bonaventure and Thomas Aquinas. He was born at or near the village of Duns in the Scottish border country, became a Franciscan, studied at Oxford (later also at Paris) and was ordained priest on May 17, 1291. He lectured at Cambridge, Oxford, and Paris, eventually becoming a regent at Paris in 1305. He died at Cologne.

The fundamental difference between his system and that of Thomas Aquinas lies in the fact that while the latter emphasizes reason as primary, Scotus founds his philosophy on will and love: tendencies that came to be reflected respectively in the Dominican and Franciscan orders. Nevertheless, in many ways the two agree. Example: both use Aristotle as their principal philosophical model, although Scotus tends to use Augustine more than does Thomas. Both perceive revelation as never contradicting reason. Scotus introduced, however, a novel concept: the principle of "haecceity" (*haecceitas*) or "thisness", which he used as a principle of individuation. Not only was Scotus very highly regarded in the late Middle Ages; he is being increasingly seen by contemporary historians of thought as a precursor of Renaissance and later thinkers who discovered the fundamental importance of the concept of individuality and the individual in a way that had been unknown or at least inadequately understood in antiquity and in the earlier Middle Ages.

When, at the end of the Middle Ages, the Reformers and others sought to mock medieval ways of thought, they coined the word "dunce" to denote a stupid person and for centuries the stupidest boy in a schoolroom was made to stand in a corner wearing a conical cap known as "the dunce's cap" as a sort of punishment: surely an inapposite one. How different a sentiment from that inscription on a monument erected with pride to commemorate the birth of the Franciscan and Subtle Doctor: "His learning has shed lustre on Duns and Scotland, the town and land which gave him birth."

The thought of Scotus is exhibited in his principal work, his *Commentary on the Sentences of Peter Lombard*, his *Tractatus de Primo Principio*, and other works. 20th c. philosophers as different as Charles Peirce and Martin Heidegger have perceived, each in his own way, the philosophical acuity of Scotus. See E. Gilson, *Jean Duns Scotus* (1952); J. K. Ryan and B. M. Bonansea (eds.), *John Duns Scotus* (1965).

Duomo. From the Latin *domus*, house. The Italian for a cathedral, e.g., the Duomo di Firenze. See also **Dom.**

Dupanloup, Félix Antoine Filibert (1802–1878). Born in the Savoy and educated in Paris, he was ordained priest in 1825 and became Bishop of Orléans in 1849. He was a pioneer in educational methods in France. At Vatican I he advised those reluctant to vote according to the express wishes of Pope Pius IX for the highly controversial doctrine of Papal Infallibility to abstain from voting. In the end, however, he was among those who formally (however reluctantly) accepted it. The standard biography of Dupanloup is by F. Lagrange, 3 vols. (1883–1884); English tr. in 2 vols. (1885). See also **Vatican Council, The First.**

Durandus, William (*c.* **1230–1296**). One of the chief medieval canonists. He wrote the *Speculum judiciale* and drafted the decrees eventually issued by the Council of Lyons in 1274. His *Rationale divinorum officiorum* was a treatise on the mystical interpretation of the liturgical offices. He is not to be confused with his nephew of the same name who succeeded him as Bishop of Mende. There is an annotated English translation of Book I of his *Rationale* by J. M. Neale and B. Webb, *The Symbolism of Churches and Church Ornaments*, (1843); also of Book III by T. H. Passmore, *The Sacred Vestments* (1899).

Durandus of Saint-Pourçain (*c.* **1275– 1334**). Medieval philosopher and one of the earliest of the Nominalist school, whose teachings he espoused, although he was a Dominican, against those of Thomas Aquinas, the great luminary of that order. He strongly contrasted faith and reason and regarded as meaningless the search for a principle of individuation. (See **Duns Scotus, John.**) The chief source for his thought is his *Commentary on the Sentences*, the final recession of which dates from 1313–1327, but his works include also his *De paupertate Christi et apostolorum* (1322) and a treatise on the condition of souls after their separation from the body. Durandus held several bishoprics successively. He has an important niche in later medieval thought.

Duration and Time. These terms have been variously understood in the history of philosophy. Thomas Aquinas, contrasting the two orders, time and eternity, saw both as implying duration, but time as implying also succession, while in eternity no succession is to be found.

Spinoza saw duration as the characteristic of created things and time as the way in which that duration is measured. In Leibniz, duration is to time as extension is to space. Bergson regarded duration as the defining characteristic of time. Augustine had recognized, in his own way, the philosophical puzzles presented by the concept of duration. Newton thought he could give a satisfactory account of "absolute" time, but Einstein has provided reason for rejecting it. Philosophers make various distinctions in talking of time, e.g., between objective and subjective time, public and private time, psychological time and "clock" time. Concepts relating to time assume great importance in certain aspects of Christian theology as well as in their obvious relevance to eschatological questions. See **Aeviternity.**

Dürer, Albrecht (1471–1528). Painter and engraver. Born in Nuremberg, he began to study wood engraving in 1486. Having traveled in Italy and elsewhere he eventually returned to his birthplace, where he pursued his great career as a painter and engraver of religious subjects. His work provided a link between Italian and German art. A Catholic by upbringing, he sympathized with and was admired by Luther and was a friend of Erasmus. Among his works are the "Adoration of the Christ Child" (one of his earlier works, known as the Baumgartner altar piece), the "Virgin with the Monkey," and "Jerome in his Study."

Durgā. A goddess in Hindu literature who represents a conglomeration of deities and demonesses associated with mountains, fire, and vegetation. The assimilation of these into Durgā seems to have begun toward the end of the Vedic period. In the Purāṇas she is portrayed as a fierce female warrior. She appears in many guises, one of the best known of which is that of Kālī, which is also the name of one of the tongues of the god of fire (Agni). She is also the goddess of the Himālayas and some-

times has beneficent aspects. In popular lore among the lower classes she is simply the Mother-goddess, Kālī Mā.

Durham. After Canterbury and York, Durham ranks with London and Winchester as one of the most important dioceses in England. It is also ancient, dating from the late 10th c., when the See of Lindisfarne was moved to Durham. The cathedral stands high above the river Wear. Its architecture includes the finest Norman nave (1099–1128) in England and a massive early English eastern transept ("the Chapel of the Nine Altars"). The two front towers with the high central tower beyond them give a spectacular impression of solid dignity and grandeur. Situated not far south of the Scottish Border, Sir Walter Scott called it "half church of God, half fortress 'gainst the Scot." The medieval bishops of Durham had special civil jurisdiction, ranking as Counts Palatine: a privilege that continued, at least nominally, down to the early 19th c. The University of Durham was founded in 1832. See T. S. R. Boase, *English Art 1100–1216* (1953); R. W. Billings, *Architectural Illustrations and Description of the Cathedral Church at Durham* (1843); G. T. Lapsley, *The County Palatine of Durham* (Harvard Historical Studies, viii; 1900).

Durie, John (1596–1680). Protestant divine. In Prussia he attempted without success to obtain the reunion of Lutheran and Calvinist Churches and sought most of his life to achieve Christian unity among the heirs of the Reformation. J. M. Batten, *John Durie* (1944) includes a list of his works. See also entry in the *Dictionary of National Biography.*

Dvāra. In Hindu literature a door. From early Vedic times, doors had highly religious significance, not only as the portals of a sacrificial enclosure or temple, but even that of the ordinary house. The gods enter through doors. Much importance was attached to the position of the doors. All are good in one way or another except western or back doors, which bring misfortune. Doors should be decorated. This reverence for the door or gateway has counterparts in many religions, e.g., in Shinto. The Egyptians attributed life to temple doors. The Hebrew psalmist sings of the gates of righteousness. An old Scottish superstition dictates that on New Year's Eve (Hogmanay), the back door be opened to let the Old Year out and the front to let the New Year in.

Dyaus. In Sanskrit, the sky, from *div*, "to shine", which is also the root of *deva*, a god. Gradually, Dyaus is given the significance of "Father of light" (Dyaus-pitar or Dyu-pitar), corresponding to the Greek Zeus Pater and the Roman Jupiter.

Dykes, John Bacchus (1823–1876). English hymnodist. Educated at Cambridge, he became a minor canon at Durham in 1849. Among his hymns are "Holy, Holy, Holy!" and "The King of Love my Shepherd is." He had Tractarian sympathies. See J. T. Fowler (ed.), *Life and Letters of John Bacchus Dykes* (1897).

Dynamism. From the Greek *dynamis*, "power". The term is used in two senses: (1) Historians of religion use it to designate an early stage in the development of religion in which foci of power or energy are recognized and revered or worshipped. Such foci have *mana*. Dynamism is distinguished from another primitive form of religion, animism, the worship of spirits such as the tree-spirit and the river-spirit. Some might see a vestige of dynamism in the attitude of the woman who touched the hem of Jesus's garment (Matthew 9.20–21). (2) In philosophy the term is used to designate any world view that recognizes the existence of forces that are not reducible to matter in motion, i.e., any non-mechanistic type of philosophy. See Rudjer Boscovich, *Theory of Natural Philosophy* (1763). The development of religion in primitive cultures is treated in many standard texts such as E. Nor-

beck, *Religion in Primitive Society* (1961) and Paul Radin, *The World of Primitive Man* (1953).

Dyophysites. The Monophysites used this designation for those who held to the orthodox Christian doctrine that two natures of Christ (divine and human) coexist separately.

Dyothelites. The Monothelites used this designation for those who held to the orthodox Christian doctrine that in Christ there are two separate wills, divine and human.

Dysteleology. The belief that the universe discloses a purpose is said to be teleological, from the Greek *telos*, an end. The opposite view may be called dysteleological. The notion that there are in a generally ordered, teleological universe certain elements that appear to be irrational, purposeless, has been introduced by some 20th c. philosophers of religion, e.g., E. S. Brightman, who has called such elements "dysteleological surds." The term "dysteleology" seems to have been coined by E. Häckel (1834–1919), a German biologist.

E

Earthquake. Earthquakes in Palestine seem to be due to a rift in the Jordan valley. In biblical times they were frequent and often severe. A terrible example is reported between Tyre and Ptolemais in 140 BCE. Many have occurred since biblical times down to the 20th c. The destruction of Sodom and Gomorrah may have had its origin in a severe earthquake. Earthquakes were interpreted as a sign of God's wrath and an instrument of his punishment and also have been seen as one of the features of the Day of Judgment.

Earthquake Synod, The. The Synod held at Blackfriars, London, on May 21, 1382, during which the city was shaken by an earthquake. The Synod condemned as heretical 24 theses from the writings of Wycliffe, including articles against transubstantiation and the practices of the mendicant friars.

Easter. The most ancient and the most important feast of the Christian Church, celebrating the Resurrection of Christ. The solemnity and joy of Easter is liturgically accented by the long period of preparation throughout Lent, culminating in Holy Week, which is attended by special ceremonies. Then during Eastertide (Paschaltide) the joyful "Alleluia" is reiterated throughout the Mass and other official prayers of the Church. The Eastern Orthodox Churches continue to this day the ancient practice of an all-night vigil before Easter Day. The faithful leave the church empty and in darkness, representing the tomb of Christ; then they re-enter, each bearing a candle and singing *Christos anesti:* "Christ is risen." In the Western Church somewhat different arrangements have generally prevailed, but much in the same spirit. The Eastern Church has maintained the centrality of Easter more emphatically than has the West, where the centrality has tended to be shared with Christmas. Both of these festivals have roots in old pagan festivities that they have superseded. The various practices connected with "Easter eggs" are of great antiquity and, somewhat like Santa Claus, are survivals that the Christian Church has permitted as harmless and pleasant. The date of Easter (unlike that of Christmas) varies according to a complex reckoning calculated by the date of the full moon and ranging between March 21 and April 25. The method of dating Easter was the subject of much prolonged controversy from early Christian times, partly due to differences in the methods used in Antioch and Alexandria respectively for determining the date of the "paschal moon." In 325 the Council of Nicaea followed the Alexandrian way, but further divergences between Rome and Alexandria developed later in the 4th c. The Celtic Churches, moreover, had their own way of computing the date of Easter. Gradually, greater uniformity was attained.

Eastern Orthodox Church. See Orthodoxy.

Eastward Position, The This phrase is used to designate the practice according to which the celebrant at Mass stands facing the east. It is of considerable antiquity, dating from the 9th c. or earlier when it was introduced at Rome. It was almost universal in Anglican and Roman Catholic churches until about the 1970s when the fashion of celebrating at a "free-standing" altar with the priest facing west and therefore toward the people came widely into vogue. The many advocates of the use of the eastward position perceive it as fostering the desirable "anonymity" of the priest as the symbolic representative of Christ and as enabling the people to pursue their devotions without the sense of confronting the intervening ministers at the altar.

Ebionites. A sect of Jewish Christians who flourished in early Christian times. Theologically they had a "low" christology, i.e., they regarded Jesus as the human son of Joseph and Mary who was in some way recognized by God by the visitation upon him of the Holy Spirit at his baptism by John the Baptist. They also insisted on conformity to the Jewish law as traditionally believed to have been given by Moses. They were a poor community (hence the name which alludes to a Hebrew term signifying "the poor men") and they lived a strictly ascetic form of life. Some scholars identify them with the Nazarenes; others see the two bodies as distinct.

Ecce Homo. This phrase, meaning "Behold the Man," was used as the title of a life of Jesus by John Seeley and published anonymously in 1865. It had a great popularity among the general public but evoked criticism by the leading Christian scholars of the time.

Ecclesiastes. The title of a book of the Bible traditionally ascribed to Solomon.

It is part of what is called the "Wisdom" literature. Modern scholars have good reason to see it as a work dating comparatively late among the Writings in the Hebrew Bible. See **Ecclesiasticus.**

Ecclesiasticus. A book in the Septuagint and found in what is somewhat misleadingly called the Old Testament Apocrypha. It is to be distinguished from the Book of Ecclesiastes, which is in the canonical Hebrew literature. It was originally written, however, in Hebrew. Fragments of the Hebrew text have surfaced from time to time in various places, including Qumran. It is also known as Ben Sira and as the Book of Sirach. It bears much resemblance to the book known as Proverbs. Like the latter, it personifies Wisdom, identifying it with the Torah. Wisdom is commended as elevating men of humble birth and causing them to take their place among the socially eminent. Chapter 44 is much used at memorial services.

Ecclesiology. The term is used in two senses: (1) for theological discussions on the nature of the Church; (2) for the art or science of building and decorating churches.

Eck, Johann (1486–1543). Professor of theology at Ingolstadt from 1510, he came under humanist influence and became famous in history as an adversary of Luther, with whom at first he had been on good terms. He was largely responsible for the excommunication of Luther in 1520, and in 1530 he led an attack from the Roman Catholic side on the Augsburg Confession. His works include his *De primatu Petri adv. Ludderum libri III,* a long defense of the Roman Catholic position, published in Paris in 1521, the year of Luther's excommunication.

Eckankar. An oriental technique of "soul travel" popularized in the West by Paul Tritchell, who claimed to have found the key to worlds ordinarily invisible to the human eye and intangible to the human touch. Through mastery, under the guidance of angels/masters, of the technique of Eckankar, one can, he claims, leave the body and enter into these other realms or dimensions of existence. His book *Eckankar* (1969), which has gone into many impressions, describes the process and its aim and includes an extensive glossary of terms, mosty from Hindu, Tibetan, and other oriental sources. The notion of "soul travel" is very ancient and has appeared also in more recent literature, e.g., in the novels of the popular Victorian novelist Marie Corelli (1855–1924) who used it, notably in ner novel *Ardath* (1889).

Eckhart (c. 1260–1327). Widely known as "Meister Eckhart", he was a German Dominican friar. One of the greatest preachers of his time and a distinguished theological teacher in the mystical tradition, he was charged by the Archbishop of Cologne with heresy in 1326. He appealed to the Pope and died during the proceedings. In later centuries he was admired in a variety of Protestant and other circles among which he was misunderstood. He belongs to an ancient Christian mystical tradition. The language he used, however, for the expression of ideas within that tradition was less cautious than that of other exponents of it, so that he came to be regarded as teaching a pantheistic mysticism irreconcilable with Christian orthodoxy.

Eclecticism. This term is given to any philosophical or theological system that arbitrarily combines elements from a variety of systems without adequate structure for the combination. In antiquity the Fourth Platonic Academy and some of the schools of Stoicism might be cited as examples.

Ecstasy. The term comes from two Greek words, *ex* ("out") and *stasis* ("the posture of standing") and is applied to a mystical state in which the mystic, in the course of the rapture of the experience, may have a sense of standing out from himself. We read of it in the Old Testament, in which prophets are reported to have been seized by divine action, becoming instruments of divine power. In the various mystical schools within the Christian tradition of spirituality, it is a well-recognized feature in certain of the stages of the mystical "ascent" to God. It consists of an alienation of the senses that occurs while the mystic attains a special insight into a deep religious truth during a distinct awareness of the presence of God.

Ecumenical Movement. Although the movement that was fostered by the Edinburgh Missionary Conference in 1910 had many forerunners, what is now generally understood by the term "Ecumenical Movement" may be said to date from that event, which led to the creation in 1925 of the Universal Conference on Life and Work, and in 1927 to the first World Conference on Faith and Order at Lausanne, which concerned itself with the theological basis of the Church and in what its unity may be taken to consist. This and later meetings at Edinburgh and Oxford led to the founding of the World Council of Churches, formally inaugurated in 1948. At first the movement was solely within Protestantism. Then interest was expressed on the part of the Eastern Orthodox, and eventually, under the pontificate of Pope John XXIII, some Roman Catholic interest was introduced, not least in the invitation to theologians and others from outside the Roman Catholic Church to attend the Second Vatican Council as observers. Many church people, however, have remained suspicious of the movement, both for religious reasons and because of the sometimes conspicuously "leftist" tendencies of the World Council in political matters. No one doubts, however, that an atmosphere of much greater trust has emerged in the latter part of the 20th c., which is to be warmly welcomed. Genuine understanding of the still wide differences in the divergent traditions within Christianity is nevertheless far from being fully realized. Much work, therefore, lies ahead.

Eddington, Arthur S. (1882–1944). As a prominent English physicist and astronomer at Cambridge, he exercised considerable influence on religious thought by work in which he sought to show that the principle of indeterminacy established by Heisenberg implied freedom of the will and that reality is so structured as to imply the existence of God as the fundamental principle of the universe. His writings include *The Nature of the Physical World* (1928), *New Pathways in Science* (1935), and *The Philosophy of Physical Science* (1939).

Eden, The Garden of. The reference to this in Genesis may have arisen in the mind of the writer from an imaginary picture of a fertile oasis on a Mesopotamian plain. Some scholars in the past even attempted to identify the location of such an earthly paradise as lying about a hundred miles north of Baghdad. The concept of such a primeval paradise inhabited by Adam and Eve before their ejection from it is beyond all doubt a primitive attempt to express the widespread notion of an archetypal Golden Age.

Edhas. In Hinduism, the sacred wood used for the sacrificial fire. The term comes from the Sanskrit root *edh*, "prosper". The association of fire with prosperity may have originated in a pun between *edh* and the Sanskrit *idh*, fire.

Edmund the Martyr (c. 840–869). King of East Anglia who succeeded as such in 865. Much beloved for his just governance, his territory was invaded by the Danes in 869. As a Christian he refused the offer of the pagan Danes to share the kingdom of East Anglia with them. The Danes eventually beheaded him. Quickly he was recognized as a saint and martyr and the following century his body was removed to Bury St. Edmunds, the abbey of which soon became and has remained a notable place of Christian pilgrimage in England.

Education. The concept of education poses intricate problems both for philosophers and for theologians. In what way, for instance, does education differ from programming and indoctrination? The kinds of learning that most plainly can be taught (e.g., arithmetic and chemistry) may be basic, yet not by any reckoning the most important kinds. Their acquisition does not in itself result in one's being a truly well-educated person. Can one be taught (or teach oneself) good taste in art or music or social behavior? One may be taught the rules of logic and even very advanced and intricate logical procedures without one's knowledge having the slightest effect on the sensitivity of one's conscience. Then, can one make a clear-cut distinction between learning facts and learning how to behave well in a civilized society? If so, how can one be taught ethical discernment in such a way as to improve one's conduct in a creative way and without merely copying a role model? Moreover, can anyone be taught anything by any sufficiently competent teacher, or is there a limit to the learning capacity of every individual, beyond which he or she cannot go? Such questions in the philosophy of education are distinctly relevant to Christian theology and practice as well as to many concerns, secular and religious.

Edwards, Jonathan (1703–1758). American theologian of narrow Calvinistic opinions. Ordained to the Congregationalist ministry at Northampton, MA, in 1727, his extremism led to his removal from his church there in 1749. In 1750 he began missionary work at Stockbridge. He was associated with the religious revival in New England known as the Great Awakening, although he and his fellow-preacher George Whitfield did not approve of the emotionalism that marked that movement. Intellectually, Edwards was too philosophical to encourage revivalism of that kind. He was followed by his son (also Jonathan, 1745–1801), who continued with others to expound his father's interpretation of Calvin. Edwards' works include *Faithful Narrative of the Surprising Works of God* (1737), *Inquiry into the Modern Prevailing Notions respecting that Freedom of the Will which is Supposed to be Essential to Moral Agency* (1754), and several posthumously published works. A bibliography was published by Princeton University Library in 1940.

Edward the Confessor (1003–1066). Of noble Norman lineage, he was educated in Normandy and acclaimed King of England in 1042. Reputed for sanctity of life, he was much preoccupied with religious projects, notably the building of the great abbey of St. Peter at Westminster, consecrated in 1065. See **Westminster Abbey.** He was canonized in 1161.

Efficacious Grace. In the controversies between the Dominicans and the Jesuits in the 16th c. (especially between Bañez and Molina), the Dominicans maintained that the efficacy of the grace (which both agreed is freely accepted by the recipient in such a way as always to produce its effect) is dependent on the character of the grace itself, while the Jesuits held that the efficacy consisted in its being given in circumstances foreseen by God to be in accord with the disposition of the recipient. This very subtle distinction arose through the complications attending the relation of grace and freedom of the will. Neither party in this controversy held that human freedom is destroyed. See **Sufficient Grace.**

Egāttalā. The goddess of Madras. Mircea Eliade has suggested that since some of the ritual connected with her is performed by pariahs, not by brahmins, she is probably of non-Aryan origin.

Egbert. An 8th c. Archbishop of York, whose cathedral school was of great importance, numbering the famous Alcuin among its students. Egbert's *Pontificale* is important as an early source for the English Coronation Rite and for other liturgical developments.

Egede, Hans (1686–1758). Norwegian Lutheran missionary, known as the Apostle to the Eskimos. His son, Paul Egede (1708–89), continued his missionary work in Greenland.

Egerton Papyrus. One of the oldest (possibly the oldest) among Christian writings to have survived. It consists of writings similar to but distinct from the canonical Gospels and comes from a codex (i.e., book, not scroll) that palaeographers date in the early part of the 2nd c. and certainly earlier than 150 CE. The narratives that survive in it relate to the ministry of Jesus. It is extremely probable that the original text of this manuscript is much earlier than the copy that has survived. The manuscript was first published (with an English translation) by H. I. Bell and T. C. Skeat as *Fragments of an Unknown Gospel and other early Christian Papyri* (1935).

Egidio Romano. See **Giles of Rome.**

Egoism. As a technical term in philosophy, it signifies the doctrine that all actions are or ought to be undertaken from the standpoint of self-directed concern. Historically, the view that all actions are in fact so motivated has a classic champion in Hobbes (1588–1679). (See also **Stirner, Max**) For a 20th c. view that one's actions ought to be so directed see **Rand, Ayn.** The contrasting view (altruism) acknowledges that actions may and often ought to regard the interests of others even at the expense of one's own. One cannot doubt, however, that *some* actions must be based (at least to some extent) on one's own interests, e.g., I cannot help my weaker brother without first sufficiently strengthening myself to have the capacity to do so. Paradoxically, this capacity is often attained in the doing of acts from an altruistic motive, i.e., I am strengthened and enabled by the love I have toward my brother: a most impor-

tant concept in the thought of all the great religions of the world. Nevertheless, an *element* of self-interest may enter into even the most altruistic of motives.

Eidetic. An adjective from the Greek *eidos*, shape. Husserl, beginning from Plato's identification of the shape or form of a thing with its essence or "heavenly" archetype, proposed an "eidetic reduction" as a method of reaching the essence. The essence of the existent confronts one by "eidetic intuition" and is expressed in "eidetic judgments."

Eightfold Path, The Noble. See **Four Noble Truths and the Noble Eightfold Path.**

Eikōn Basilikē. A work published secretly before the execution of Charles I in 1649 and attributed to him. It bore the subtitle: *The Pourtraicture of His Sacred Maiestie in His Solitudes and Sufferings* (1648). Probably the work of John Gauden (1605–1662), author of the vast *Ecclesiae Anglicanae Suspiria* (1659) and other works, it was no doubt based on authentic materials and eventually read and corrected by the King. Milton responded to it in his *Eikonoklastes* (1949).

Eileton. A silk cloth spread on the altar during the Liturgy in Eastern Orthodox churches. Historically it may be said to correspond to the corporal used in the West, but in fact the function of the latter is now taken over by the antiminsion. See **Antiminsion.**

Einsiedeln. Benedictine abbey in Switzerland founded in 937 and recognized since 1350 as the National Sanctuary of the Swiss Confederation. The baroque church and the large collection of important manuscripts in the abbey library attract many scholars and pilgrims.

Einstein, Albert (1879–1955). Physicist. Born in Ulm, Germany, he was professor successively at the Universities of Zurich, Prague, and Berlin, receiving the Nobel Prize in 1921 for his work. In 1933, being ousted by the German government of the time, he was given a position at the Institute for Advanced Study at Princeton, where he spent the remainder of his life. Among his various scientific discoveries, his most famous are those concerning his special and general theories of relativity. In the former he repudiated the common assumption of an absolute space and time. Among the consequences of that repudiation is the view that simultaneity cannot be experienced by observers in systems in motion relative to the given system. The energy of any mass is the product of the mass and the square of the velocity of light (expressed in the celebrated equation $E = MC^2$). Every particle of matter contains an enormous amount of energy. The velocity of light is constant. As velocity increases, so does mass, while time slows down. Time may be considered a fourth dimension. The entire Newtonian view of the universe that had been for so long taken for granted collapses in face of this theory, which has been amply demonstrated in various ways in modern physics. From this theory was deduced certain general theories. Although these have not been demonstrated so definitively as the special one on which they depend, some of them have been confirmed by actual observation; e.g., the "bending" of light rays as they pass through a gravitational field has been observed, which would seem to support the concept popularly known as an expanding universe.

Influenced from early years by Spinoza's thought, which probably much affected his view of God, he was throughout his life both philosophically and theologically a rationalist in the sense that he believed that the universe is harmonious and orderly and therefore he accepted the concept of God, although not necessarily in the terms traditionally understood in Judaism or Christianity. He was an ardent champion of freedom of conscience, supported (with some limitations) the

pacifist ideal, and argued against the uncontrolled use of atomic energy. His many writings include *Groundwork of the General Theory of Relativity* (1916), *The Meaning of Relativity* (1921), and *On the Method of Theoretical Physics* (1933). His *Out of My Later Years* (1950) is more autobiographical and contains some of his thoughts on the nature of God.

Eisai (Zenchō Kokushi, 1141–1215 CE). The founder of Zen as an independent school of Buddhism in Japan. He visited China twice, in 1168 and in 1187, where be became deeply interested in the spirit of the Ch'an school of Buddhism. He received enlightenment in the Linchi sect and transplanted it to Japan under the name of Rinzai, building in 1191 a temple in Kyushu. He expounded more and more, however, the meditative techniques of Zen. He is associated also with the development of the Japanese tea culture.

Ekadanta. A designation applied to the elephant-headed god of wisdom (Gaṇeśa) in Hindu lore and meaning "having only one tusk."

Ekamevādvitīyam. A designation of Brahman, meaning "the One, the eternally existing entity that has no 'second'." See **Brahman** and **Vedānta**.

Ekāṣṭakā. The eighth day after the full moon, personified as the goddess Śacī (Indra's wife) in Hindu lore. She is credited with the power to give her suppliants healthy and long-lived children. According to some texts she generated Indra through the performance of great ascetic practices.

Ekoddiṣṭa. In post-Vedic funerary practice in India, when burial of the dead gave way to cremation, a complex ritual was developed to obtain union with his ancestors and was so designated. In the Vedic period the relatively simple notion that the deceased immediately joined his ancestors had generally pre vailed, but this belief was later superseded by increasingly complex views envisioning stages in which layers of the self were gradually discarded.

Elamites. The inhabitants of Elam, an ancient territory that lay to the east and northeast of the valley of the Tigris and the Euphrates and is frequently mentioned in the Bible, e.g., Genesis 10.21; Isaiah 11.11; Jeremiah 49.35. Ur, a city in Mesopotamia from which Abraham's father (Terah) migrated to Haran (Genesis 11.28, 31; 15.7), was destroyed by the Elamites in the 19th c. BCE, which may be the reason for Abraham's move to Haran.

Élan Vital. A term coined by Henri Bergson to express that which is at work in the evolutionary process.

Elder. In the Presbyterian from of government, elders are of two kinds: (1) teaching elders, i.e., duly trained ministers, and (2) ruling elders, who are laymen ordained to assist the minister of a parish in its administration. The term "ruling" is used in the sense of "measuring out" as a tailor "rules out" his cloth.

Eleatic School. A group of Greek philosophers who, in the 6th and 5th c. BCE, developed a philosophical view that exhibited remarkable philosophical acuity. Believing in the unity and eternity of Being, somewhat in the manner of an occidental counterpart to Vedantist thought in India, they raised questions about permanence and change: an antithesis that was to play a central role in subsequent Greek thought. Parmenides, one of the leading figures in this monistic school of philosophy, argued that since reality must fill all available space, there is nowhere left for anything to go; therefore what appears to be change and development must be illusory. One might think of the situation as a chessboard on which every square has been eternally occupied, so that there is no way for any piece or pawn to move anywhere, and therefore what we take to be movement must be imaginary; it could not belong to the real universe. This puzzle presented by the Eleatic thinkers was the catalyst that evoked one of the most important philosophical advances made by Plato about a century later.

The teaching of Parmenides had been in opposition to that of Heraclitus. The latter had held that everything is in flux; the former seemed to show that everything is one and unchanging. Parmenides was a monist, i.e., he showed, or seemed to be able to show, that nothing really changes, appearances notwithstanding. Plato indicates in his own dialogue the *Theatetus* that Parmenides had been both reverenced and feared, because nobody seemed able to refute him. Plato may be said to have broken through the impasse by his development of the concept of Being and Becoming. The situation is not as Parmenides had depicted it, with Being and Nothing as the only categories. There is the category of Becoming, or, as we would more readily say today, of process. There are, in effect, degrees of Being, and Plato's way of saying this is that in the world as we commonly perceive it (the world of change and development and decay) things may be said to *participate* in Being. Plato, in his own way, was already seeing the evolutionary character of the universe. This world of change that we see is not unreal; yet it has not fully grasped reality. It is on its way. Plato opened the way to Aristotle's schema of potency and act, i.e., of potential or developing Being and fully realized Being (God) toward which everything is inexorably moving as nails to a magnet.

Election. See **Predestination/Election.**

Elephantine Papyri, The. A collection of documents dating from the 5th c. BCE written in Aramaic, which were found in an ancient Jewish colony at Elephantine in the south of Upper Egypt early in the 20th c. They are important for several reasons, including the light they shed on the nature of the syncretistic forms of Judaism among Jews of the Diaspora, very different from traditional Jewish orthodoxy.

Eleusinian Mysteries. The oldest and most restrained of the ancient Greek mystery religions. Demeter and her daughter, the Korē, were the central figures. Hades (Pluto) had abducted the Korē and carried her to the underworld so that she might be his bride. Her mother Demeter, during long mourning, had refused to cause the corn to grow. Zeus eventually instructed Hades to return the girl to earth, but Hades responded by giving her a pomegranate seed, which she unwarily ate. This story was told many times, mostly by women, but at some point (when precisely cannot be determined), Dionysus was introduced to the story as the companion or associate of Demeter. (He was the god of vegetation and the vine.) Although the story underlying the cult was esoteric and supposedly to be withheld from the general public, anyone in Athens could see the devotees parading to the sea and, along with the procession, the image of the young Dionysus (Iacchos). The aim of the devotees was to achieve immortality but not (as in many religious systems) by way of reward for moral virtue or nobility of character but by participation in the resurrective powers inherent in the central figures of the Eleusinian myth. The Eleusinian mysteries stand in dignified contrast to the Dionysian cult, which entailed frenzied emotion, wine drinking, wild excitement, the eating of the flesh and drinking the blood of an animal, torn apart violently in a rite called omophagia. See **Dionysus.**

Elevation, The. In the Mass, the act of the celebrant in lifting up first the Host, then the Chalice, immediately after consecrating them. The practice of elevating the Host seems to have originated in France in the early 13th c. That of elevating the Chalice was added later.

Elijah. Generally acclaimed as the greatest of the Hebrew prophets, he lived in the 9th c. BCE. Against those who continued to worship according to the Canaanite and Phoenician rites, he upheld the worship of Yahweh and the moral rectitude and social justice that were implied in such worship (I Kings 18 and 21). It was believed that he would return to earth, and we read in the Gospels that some thought (Mark 6.15; Matthew 16.4) that Jesus was Elijah in a new embodiment. The Greek form of the name, Elias, is used in the New Testament.

Eliot, Thomas Stearns (1888–1965). American poet. Born in St. Louis, he was brought up in the Unitarian tradition, educated at Harvard, the Sorbonne, and Merton College, Oxford. Having passed through a period of religious skepticism, expressed in his poems, *The Waste Land* (1922) and *The Hollow Men* (1925), he became an ardent Anglo-Catholic, which commitment he expressed in *Ash Wednesday* (1930) and *Murder in the Cathedral* (1935). He used, in his poems and other writings, a novel literary technique, involving allusion, compression, and contrast. He reflects the deeply Christian influences of Dante, the Spanish mystics, and the 17th c. English metaphysical poets. He was also an eminent literary critic whose works include many essays in criticism. *The Cocktail Party* (1950) is among his dramatic works, and his thoughts on the subject of religion are specifically reflected in works such as *The Idea of a Christian Society* (1939). In 1948 he received the very prestigious British Order of Merit and also the Nobel Prize for Literature. There is a bibliography by D. Gallup (1952).

Elkesaites. A Jewish Christian sect that came into being in the land to the east of Jordan *c.* 100 CE. They resembled the Ebionites in many of their beliefs, rejected some of the New Testament writings (including all of Paul's), and revered a document called the Book of Elkesai, which purported to contain an account of a revelation by an angel ninety-six miles in height.

Elohim. This Hebrew plural noun means literally "the gods" but is frequently used to denote Yahweh, the God of Israel, although sometimes also used in reference to the gods of other peoples. It is the term used for God in Genesis I.

Emanationism. The view that the universe flows from God as the sun's rays may be said to flow from the sun. It is characteristic of much Indian thought about religion. In the West it has been held both by Neoplatonists and Gnostics. Since Christianity was at an early period much affected by Neoplatonic ways of thinking (in the West through Augustine, whose thought was in a Neoplatonic mold), early medieval Christian thought, lacking much by way of alternative thought patterns, tended to develop along Neoplatonic lines. John Scotus Erigena is a notable exemplar of this tendency and his interesting system is plainly emanationist. Generally speaking, however, Christian orthodoxy has rejected emanationism on biblical grounds, seeing the creative process as an act of the divine will, rather than viewing the universe as exuding from God. This alternative view is called creationism.

Ember Days. The Wednesday, Friday, and Saturday following each of the four following dates: December 13, Ash Wednesday, Whitsunday, and September 14. Ember Days are traditionally days of fasting and abstinence in the West. Their early history is obscure, but they are certainly of great antiquity, being well established at Rome by the 5th c. and in some form dating much earlier than that.

Emergent Evolution. The notion that genuine novelty occurs in the course of the evolutionary process. The theory runs into certain difficulties, e.g., that

the emergence of life and mind must be explained without any postulate of their having some prior embryonic or germinal form. Where, as with Samuel Alexander, the most convinced and thoroughgoing emergentist, deity is always a step ahead of where the universe is at and evolution is continuous and never-ending, not only is God's emergence as inexplicable as all others; one cannot know what he is to be like one step ahead of the present, nor can we predict that deity will be of superior quality at the next stage or even of as good a quality as he is at present. Existence in the space-time continuum is always transcending itself but not necessarily improving in quality. See **Alexander, Samuel.**

Emerson, Ralph Waldo (1803–1882). American philosopher and divine. Educated at the Boston Latin School and Harvard, he trained for the Unitarian ministry and, being duly accepted for it, he preached for some twenty years before retiring to devote himself entirely to lecturing and writing on his philosophy. He was a close friend of Carlyle, Coleridge, and Wordsworth. His views are generally supposed to represent a form of Transcendentalism, i.e., the view that the highest revelation of God to man lies within man himself. He taught views expressive of the concept of the karmic principle and its implicate of spiritual evolution through re-embodiments. He had no place in his thought for democratic notions and only with hesitation supported, in 1856, the abolition of slavery. His writings attained wide popularity among the educated classes. His thoughts and style certainly were fresh and distinctly original. His writings include *Nature* (1838), *Essays* (1841 and 1844), *Representative Man* (1850), *English Traits* (1856), *Conduct of Life* (1860), and *Society and Solitude* (1870). A bibliography by G. W. Cooke (1908) was reprinted in 1968.

Eminence. Title given to Cardinals of the Roman Catholic Church since 1630.

Empiricism. The term is derived from the Greek *empeiros*, meaning "experienced in" from which comes the Latin *experientia*, "experience". This is the criterion invoked by philosophers in the empiricist school, which insists that the source of all knowledge is to be found in experience. This view is traditionally contrasted with rationalism, which stresses the importance of reason in the attainment of knowledge. Few philosophers, if any, could properly be said to be either pure rationalists or pure empiricists. Plato may be said to be more of a rationalist than Aristotle, yet the latter is certainly not an empiricist in the sense in which, say, Hume is.

That experience is a principal source in the attainment of knowledge is obvious: nevertheless, to classify a philosopher as empiricist demands more than reliance on experience. Locke, for example, is usually classed as one of the British Empiricists, along with Berkeley and Hume, but although he did insist against Descartes that there are no ideas innate in the mind and that we all begin with a clean slate, a *tabula rasa* on which is gradually imprinted the experiences we receive from the senses, there was a considerable rationalist element in his thought. It is nevertheless true that to be an empiricist one must make experience and observation the key elements in one's account of the emergence of knowledge in the mind. In medieval thought, for instance, the realists and conceptualists would generally be classifiable with rationalism, while the nominalists would represent the empiricist direction in the thought of that time. Nominalism, notably in the thought of William of Occam (see **Occam**), provided one of the channels through which modern empiricism was developed.

The British Empiricists (Locke, Berkeley, Hume) might be said to constitute the classical stage in the development of modern empiricism. It influenced some of the continental philosophers of the 18th c. Then came a reaction in the form of a newer type of rationalism that had Hegel as its leading champion. Nevertheless, empiricism continued to be expounded in various ways, e.g., by the American pragmatists, notably William James, who called his thought "radical empiricism."

The interest in meaning as well as truth that the pragmatist school helped to engender was at least an element in the catalyst that led to the formation of the Vienna Circle, which concerned itself especially with meaning, stressing the notion that one cannot go about discovering whether a proposition is true or false until one has first established precisely what its terms mean. Using the old Kantian distinction between synthetic and analytic propositions, the members of this school (some of whom called themselves "logical empiricists") distinguished between analytical propositions (e.g., $2 + 2 = 4$), which are really tautologies, useful and indeed indispensable as they are, and synthetic propositions (e.g., "there is a rabbit in my backyard"). The former do not give new knowledge, though they may indirectly assist in its acquisition. The latter, however, give new knowledge. Such new knowledge must be grounded in observation that is both verifiable and falsifiable. In terms of modern physics and other "hard" sciences generally, however, the criteria of verifiability and falsifiability are not so easily attainable as some of the earlier exponents of logical positivism apparently took them to be. We are left with being forced to recognize that, simplistic as both a "pure" rationalism and a "pure" empiricism must be, elements of both belong to all authentic philosophical inquiry, as both critical and speculative elements are indispensable for all philosophical progress. See **Experience.**

Enarxis. In the Eastern Church, the section of the liturgy between the Prothesis and the Little Entrance. It consists of three litanies, each followed by an antiphon. Its use probably dates from the 9th c.

Encolpion. The oval medallion (also called a panagia) worn by bishops in the Eastern Church, suspended from the neck by a chain and usually depicting Jesus Christ or Mary.

Encyclical. Historically, a letter sent out by a bishop for circulation in his diocese. In more recent Roman Catholic practice the term has been restricted to letters so issued by the Pope to the Church.

Encyclopedists. Contributors to the *Encyclopédie*, a 35-volume 18th c. work intended to bring all human knowledge into its compass. It was edited by Denis Diderot, who contributed most of the articles on religion. D'Holbach, Voltaire, Rousseau, and Toussaint were also among the contributors. The skepticism of many of the contributors roused the opposition of Church and King, delaying publication, which began, however, in 1772.

Energeia. The Greek term from which is derived the word "energy". It was used by Aristotle in a technical sense to signify a state of realized potentiality and the activity through which that realization takes place. It is opposed to *dynamis*, which in the same philosophical usage means unrealized potentiality. See also **Entelechy.**

Engels, Friedrich (1820–1895). Cofounder of the Marxist movement. (See **Marx, Karl.**) He was born in Germany, the son of an industrialist who had business interests in England. When still in his twenties, he met Marx and was immediately captivated by the latter's teaching, devoting his life thereafter to collaborating with him and assisting him in the publication of his work. He contributed certain ideas now generally associated with Marxism, e.g., dialectical materialism. He saw the process so designated as ever-moving toward the elimination of class interest in human society. His writings include *Socialism: Utopian and Scientific* (1883), *Ludwig Feuerbach and the Outcome of German Classical Philosophy* (1888), *Principles of Communism* (1919), and *Dialectics of Nature* (1925).

English Ladies. A name popularly given to an order of women (the Institute of the Blessed Virgin Mary) founded in 1609 and perhaps the only order of the Roman Catholic Church specifically intended to be a female counterpart to the Jesuits. It received formal approval from the Pope, after some initial difficulties, in 1703.

Enlightenment. After the religious wars, turmoils, and controversies of the 17th c., educated people in Europe tended to be disenchanted with religion as they knew it, especially what they saw as its "supernatural" aspects and its propensity for divisiveness. In Germany a movement expressive of this general rationalistic mood was developed and was called the *Aufklärung:* a term later anglicized as *Enlightenment* and used of the 18th c. attitude prevalent in France, England, Germany, and elsewhere. Among its ideals was that of religious toleration, represented in Lessing's *Nathan der Weise* and expressed in the political policies of Frederick the Great. This mood was predictably the one that inspired the outlook of the Founding Fathers of the United States of America. It was not an anti-religious mood in the sense of being hostile to all religious sentiment, but it was one that purported to exalt and to rely upon reason as the category in terms of which "true" religion is to be judged. Bitter hostility to both "Catholic" and "Protestant" forms of dogmatism was general among the educated classes and ridicule of the Middle Ages as full of superstition, stupidity, and general "darkness" was fashionable. This mood persisted through the end of the century, along with a belief in the fundamental goodness of human nature: a view that was especially championed by Jean-Jacques Rousseau but was a very widespread attitude in the period of the Enlightenment. The attitude of the

Enlightenment did not exclude poetic and artistic fancy, for reason was not the only idol of the period; nature, especially in the second half of the century, was another and it inevitably spawned a more romantic spirit. For example, when in 1739 the poet Thomas Gray visited the Grande Chartreuse (the mother house of the Carthusians, near Grenoble, France, he waxed ecstatic in these terms: "Not a precipice," he wrote in a letter, "not a torrent, not a cliff, but is pregnant with religion and poetry." Not, however, till early in the 19th c. did the Romantic Mood begin to supplant the mood so typical of the 18th-c. Enlightenment and to affect not only poetry, drama, and the visual arts, but also religion and philosophy, where it produced fruit of the most diverse kinds, e.g., in Kierkegaard's vitriolic satire against Hegel's rationalism, in the appreciation of patristic and medieval Christian values among the English Tractarians and others, and in the emphasis on religious feeling in the work of Schleiermacher and Chateaubriand.

On the whole, however, the distrust prevalent in the age of the Enlightenment for authority and tradition in religion and everything else left a permanent mark on European and American thinking, although duly modified by the correctives of 19th-c. thought. Goethe, for instance, is an outstanding example of an intellectual genius who combined in his thought and work the values of both the Enlightenment and the subsequent Romantic Movement. The Enlightenment should not be seen, however, as an entirely new development in the 18th c. Its concern for "reason" and its respect for scientific investigation and discovery were of course foreshadowed in the work of the "old" rationalists (Descartes, Leibniz, and Spinoza, for example) and the rise of modern science in the 17th c.

Enlil. In Mesopotamian religion, the god of the air, who rules at Nippur.

Ens. From the Latin verb *esse*, to be, it is used by the medieval schoolmen to signify any mode of being; e.g., *ens reale*, that which exists independently of the perceiving mind; *ens in potentia*, that which exists potentially (in process); *ens in actu*, realized being; and *ens rationis*, that which exists rationally within the mind. The plural is *entia*.

Entelechy. From the Greek *entelecheia* (*telos*, an end, purpose, goal), used by Aristotle to signify the full realization of essence or *energeia*. (See **Energeia**.) Leibniz also used the term in reference to the monads in his system.

Enthymeme. In traditional logic, a syllogism lacking one of the premises or the conclusion. An inference may be drawn from it, provided that the missing premise or conclusion is taken as implicit.

Epagoge. A term used in Greek philosophy for induction. The adjectival form is "epagogic" as in "epagogic demonstration"; demonstration by an inductive method.

Epanokamelavchion. The veil on top of the usually black kamelavchion and worn by bishops and monks.

Ephesians. The letter so designated in the New Testament is traditionally attributed to Paul, but for excellent reasons most modern scholars question its authorship and many attribute it to a disciple writing before 90 CE but long after Paul's death. It does reflect Pauline teaching, however, and the reasons for the widespread rejection of its ascription to Paul are complex.

Ephesus. One of the largest cities in the Roman empire and in New Testament still a great commercial center and port, it was far-famed for its great temple to Diana (Artemia), which was accounted one of the "Seven Wonders of the World." Paul spent much time and labor on his missionary work here. Traditionally regarded as the location of the disciple John in his old age, it was here that the Third General Council of the Church was held in 431 CE.

Ephod. A Jewish vestment of linen and beaten gold worn by the high priest. It is described in Exodus 28.6–12 and 39.2–5. Other persons might use a similar vestment made of linen only.

Ephpheta. The word of healing used by Jesus in the cure of a deaf-mute (Mark 7.34). It is one of the few cases in the New Testament of the use of an Aramaic word (albeit in this case in a Greek transcription of one), coming from the Aramaic for "open". The few other examples include "abba", a vocative form of the Aramaic word 'ab, father, used by Jesus and by early Christians including Paul (e.g., Romans 8.15).

Epiclesis. The Greek term (epíklēsis) originally meant "invocation". The word is now used to designate the eucharistic prayer to God to send the Holy Spirit down upon the bread and wine and make them the Body and Blood of Christ. Immense and complex controversy has been focussed on the nature and significance of the epiclesis and of its place in the liturgy. Reference to the "illapse" of the Holy Spirit upon the elements of the Eucharist occurs in the early third century and by the 4th c. the epiclesis had become almost universal as part of the process of consecration of the eucharistic elements.

Epictetus (60–138 CE). Greek philosopher, member of the Stoic school. Born in Hierapolis, he began teaching as a slave in Rome. (Roman households often employed educated Greeks as tutors or teachers.) Expelled from Rome, along with other philosophers, by Domitian in 90 CE, he went to live in southern France. Among his characteristic teachings is his view that no philosophical inquiry is worth undertaking unless it relates to the conduct of human life, which consists primarily in learning how to distinguish what is within and what is not within our capacity. What is within our capacity is our will. We need submit to nothing unless we will to do so. Our rationality is the god within us. Through reason we learn to depend only on ourselves, not on any external aid. Each individual has a given role in life and an important part of wisdom is to recognize how this role limits us and how it frees us, i.e., how much "rope" one has in the exercise of the freedom of one's will.

Epicureanism. A school of philosophy founded at Athens by Epicurus (341–270 BCE) in 306 BCE. It became, with Stoicism, one of two very important Greek philosophical schools, whose influence spread throughout the Roman world. Popularly, they have tended to be far too sharply contrasted. They are both philosophies of detachment but with different methodologies.

Epicureanism aims at achieving detachment through contentment, while Stoicism may be said to attain it through self-respect. Epicureans recognize the fact that human beings are in one way or another bent on obtaining pleasure in life, without which life would seem vacuous. They recognize, however, that any undiscriminating pursuit of pleasure is self-defeating, since it leads to excess and consequent pain or distress. Above all, the more avidly one seeks pleasure the more discontented one becomes and therefore the less pleasant is one's life. The wise man or woman recognizes his or her place in human life and perceives that the absence of pain and anxiety is indeed pleasure. Such attitudes engender contentment, which is the richest of pleasures and the most enduring. Ambition, notably political ambition, leads inevitably to discontent, for even if one conquers the world one's conquest leads only to regret that there is nothing else to conquer. By contrast, genuine friendship grounded in common intellectual interests and pursuits, yields deep and lasting pleasure. Since fear is detrimental to the attainment of any kind of pleasure and defeats any pleasure we may have, it must be overcome, so that we learn to accept with equanimity what we know we cannot change and face the future accordingly. The wise man is he who is mentally perceptive and reflective enough to learn how to enjoy life, which is a difficult art and certainly not one to be attained by sensuality or thoughtless pleasure-seeking.

The Epicureans had no belief in an afterlife of any kind, so the wise man, recognizing this, makes the most that he can of this life. The popular understanding of Epicurean philosophy as one encouraging licentiousness is therefore very wide indeed of the mark. Epicurean philosophy is quite antithetical to such a way of life. Generally speaking, the Epicureans were optimistic about humanity in the sense that, in the manner of the Confucian sages of China, they believed that man can be educated to see the limits of his potentiality, accept them, and make the most of his freedom. While they could hardly be said to have adopted a missionary attitude toward their fellow men, they had sufficient confidence in them and enough sympathy to hope for their enlightenment and assist in producing it when called upon to do so. They did not disbelieve in the gods of the popular religion of their day, recognizing them as very real forces in the world (love and war, for instance, are certainly such), but they regarded them as having no interest in the affairs of men and women. They should be regarded, rather, as the forces of nature. Perhaps they have their own struggles and achievements and goals, but if so, their lives are on a plane so different from ours that they are not interested in us; therefore we have nothing either to fear or to hope from them.

The school that Epicurus founded in Athens was co-educational, led a very simple mode of life, and is said to have attracted vast throngs of students. His principal work is *On Nature*, which contained 37 books, fragments of 9 of which are extant. Several hundred other works are attributed to him. Epicureanism even influenced early Christian thought, although to a much less extent or at least much less directly than did Stoicism. In its goal of contentment it does show an affinity with Christian ethical thought, but the absence of any concept of afterlife limits the quality of the contentment it seeks to achieve, and this not only from a Christian standpoint but from that of most of the great religions of the world. See **Stoics**.

Epicurus. See **Epicureanism**.

Epiphanius (*c.* **315–403**). Bishop of Salamis. Born in Palestine, he became a perfervid supporter of the monastic way of life and also a champion of Nicene orthodoxy. As such he was a lively antagonist of heresy and is known for his work *Panarion*, in which he attempts to refute every heresy known in the Church of his time. By no means an acute theological mind, he bordered on fanaticism in his attitudes and writings. With Jerome he attacked what he took to be the teachings of Origen. See **Origen**.

Epiphany. The Greek term *epiphaneia* means "manifestation". Originally, the feast of the Epiphany, which is observed in the Christian Church on January 6, was celebrated in honor of the Baptism of Christ and was in use in the Eastern Church as early as the 3rd c. In the 4th c. it spread to the West but lost its original significance, becoming associated with the manifestation of Christ to the Gentiles.

Epiphenomenalism. The philosophical doctrine that mental phenomena are entirely caused by physical phenomena in the brain and do not themselves have any effects, either physical or mental. In its crudest form it is the view that the brain secretes thought as the liver secretes bile. In so far as the computer-like functions of the brain are concerned, there may be little to be said against such a view, but philosophers who recognized mental functions far beyond and much more important than such computer-like functions see a very great deal wrong with it.

Epistemology. A very important department of philosophical inquiry, sometimes called "theory of knowledge." The term comes from the Greek word *epistēmē,* knowledge (especially what would be called in modern times scientific knowledge). It is concerned with questions about the possibility of knowledge and the nature and basis of such knowledge as we claim to possess, as well as of belief and experience.

If we can know anything, how do we know it and what is the difference between knowledge and belief? The way in which and the extent to which knowledge differs from belief is controversial, but by any reckoning an important difference lies between them. Can I know without knowing that I know, or does knowledge involve knowledge of my knowing? Can my dog be said to know, and if so in what sense is his knowledge different from mine? Can a computer be said to know except in a derivative sense such as that which I might employ in saying that my skin itches because it "knows" that bacteria are attacking it? When I say that I know New York, I may mean one of several things, e.g., (1) although I have never been there I know where it is on the map and can distinguish it from Boston and Philadelphia, or (2) I have lived there all my life and know at least as much about it as the average New Yorker does, or (3) I have made a lifelong study of New York and am a leading expert on its history, the form of its government, its customs, its social problems, and much else, or again (4) I know only that it is a large city as are Tokyo and Calcutta. An important distinction in contemporary philosophy, emphasized by Gilbert Ryle, is that between knowing *how* and knowing *that,* e.g., I may know that Long Island is within fairly easy reach of Manhattan but I may have no idea how to get there. I may know that French table manners are different from English ones but not know how to behave well at table in either country.

Historically, the origin of knowledge has been the subject of a long-standing debate between rationalists and empiricists. Rationalists (e.g., Descartes, Spinoza, Leibniz) insist that the mind in one way or another originates its basic furnishings (e.g., "innate ideas" such as space and time), while empiricists (e.g., Berkeley and Hume) contend that the mind is, in Locke's phrase, a *tabula rasa* (a blank page) on which is gradually impressed, through the senses, such knowledge as we may have. Rationalism and empiricism may be conjoined, however, and the rigidity of the distinction between them breaks down, e.g., both Aristotle and Locke, each in his own way, would subscribe to both rationalist and empiricist theses. Both, for instance, would subscribe to the general principle that there is nothing in the intellect that is not first in the senses, but they would apply it in different ways. Many philosophers would question the value of talking, as does Kant of categories of knowledge. A. D. Woozley, *Theory of Knowledge* (1949) provides an elementary introduction to the subject and D. W. Hamlyn, *Theory of Knowledge* (1970) a more advanced one. A. Phillips Griffiths (ed.), *Knowledge and Belief* (1967) contains both a variety of views in the field and a bibliography.

Epistolae Obscurorum Virorum. A satirical pamphlet published in two parts in 1515 and 1517 respectively, parodying the conventional style of thought and debased latinity of the late Middle Ages and the methods of the decadent forms of the schoolmen of the time. It was mainly the work of Rubianus and Ulrich von Hutten and consisted of imaginary letters written in an exaggerated form of that style. The parody was influential in discrediting the methods of the late medieval schoolmen.

Epitrachelion. The form of the stole used in the Eastern Church and consisting of a long strip of silk, fastened in front. It is used by priests. Deacons wear the Orarion. See **Orarion.**

Equality. The notion that men are "created equal" is susceptible to a variety of interpretations. It is abundantly plain that human beings are not born with equal endowments. Goethe and Mozart cannot be said to have the same endowments as a moron, nor is every man equally handsome or every woman equally beautiful. It is quite a different proposition to claim that all have equal rights, e.g., to liberty and the pursuit of happiness. Jefferson's claim that all men are "created equal" must surely be interpreted in this way. These rights, moreover, must entail corresponding duties. Humanity plainly embraces an enormous spectrum of development. Although much can be accomplished through education for the development of individual capacities, it can do nothing to bridge many natural inequalities.

Equiprobabilism. See **Probabilism** and **Alphonsus Liguori.**

Equivocity. Medieval philosophers, in their language theory, distinguished three ways in which names can be used: (1) univocally, when in their various uses they have the same meaning; (2) equivocally, when they carry different meanings; and (3) analogically, when the name carries a meaning in some respects the same and in other respects different. Certain qualities, such as goodness, can be attributed to both men and God, but the term "goodness" is not the same when predicated of God as it is when predicated of man; yet it is not *entirely* different, i.e., it is used neither equivocally nor univocally but analogically. See **Analogy.**

Erasmus, Desiderius (1467–1536). Christian humanist, born in Holland, studied in Paris, Oxford, Louvain, and Turin. He played an important role in the movement within the Roman Catholic Church to reform it from within by learning and discipline rather than by the methods used by the Reformers. He represented the Renaissance spirit in the northern form that it took as it spread from Italy to Germany and elsewhere. He appealed to the learned and cultivated of his time and exhibited immense erudition as well as literary skill

and judgment. He published the Greek text of the New Testament in 1516 and also a series of the early Christian Fathers, Greek, and Latin. Besides his scholarly achievements he also showed skill in pillorying the ignorance of the clergy of his time and the need for intellectual as well as moral reform. He stood in a great ancient tradition of Christian learning, despising preoccupation with the narrow and trivializing theological concerns he saw both in the Roman Catholic Church and among the Reformers. Although theologically his perceptions were limited, from the standpoint of the long tradition of Christian thought, he was unique in his age as a defender and proponent of an understanding of Christian faith in terms of the tradition of the *umanisti* that had its roots in Socrates and had been developed in the great School of Christian Platonism at Alexandria in the third c. CE. Erasmus vigorously defended the freedom of human will against Luther's opposition to it. His writings include *The Contempt of the World* (1490), *In Praise of Folly* (1509), *Discussion on Free Will* (1524), and *The Epicurean* (1533). Erasmus was above all a defender of the role of reverent agnosticism in religion: an insistence on the intellectual modesty that acknowledges the limitations of human knowledge and therefore the role of doubt in authentic Christian faith. See **Doubt.**

Erastianism. That form of Church-State relationship in which the State tends to dominate the Church. It is so called after Thomas Erastus (1524–1583), a Swiss medical professor at Heidelberg who wrote against the Calvinists, holding that the State has the right and the duty to exercise jurisdiction over both civil and ecclesiastical affairs. Erastus was envisioning a very homogeneous society, not the heterogeneous society that is typical of American conditions today. The term is now used perjoratively of what is deemed to be excessive interference by the State in religious matters.

Eremitical. The adjective form of "hermit".

Erigena, John Scotus (*c.* 810– *c.* 877) Philosopher. Born in Ireland, he was educated in a monastery there, went to France, and taught at the Palatine school. He translated the works of the Pseudo-Dionysius from the Greek and wrote commentaries on the text. His writings include *On the Divisions of Nature*, in which he divides nature into four parts: (1) that which creates and is not created, (2) that which is created and creates, (3) that which is created and does not create, and (4) that which neither creates nor is created. He seems to regard God as in both categories (1) and (4), so that he sees God as both within nature and beyond it. Part 2 includes what Plato would have called the eternal forms or ideas. Part 3 consists of the created universe. Man is a microcosm of the universe. Erigena's thought owes much to that of the Pseudo-Dionysius. He perceived that what is attributed to God must be attributed in a very special way. So we can say that God is good or compassionate or intelligent; yet he is not any of these in the way they would be attributed to a human being. God is to be understood, however, as the essence of all things. So God is beyond space, time, quality, and quantity, yet he is related to all of them. The universe therefore is within God: a notion that in modern terms would make him classifiable as a panentheist. (See **Panentheism.**) Erigena was one of the few thinkers of the earlier Middle Ages and exercised considerable influence on later writers in the Golden Age of medieval thought.

Erōs. For the use of this term for "love" or "desire" in Greek, see **Agapē.**

Eroticism in Religion. In the history of religion can be found many instances of erotic cultic practices. In Mesopatamia, for example, as in other parts of the ancient world, erotic rituals occurred in which priests and priestesses emulated the marriage of deities. Temple prostitution was common. In Hindu tradition, *Kāma* is the name of the god of love corresponding to the Greek *Erōs*. Both, however, function also as common nouns with a wide range of meaning, sometimes relating to artistic enjoyment, sometimes more specifically sexual. The *Kāma Sūtra* of Vatsyayana is frankly a guide to sexual conduct perceived as a good and celebrated in erotic painting and sculpture. Examples may be seen at Khajuraho and at Konarak. This tradition in Hinduism is in sharp contrast to the central Hindu outlook, which emphasizes the view that not only sexual but all pleasure can be a hindrance to emancipation from the transitory flesh-and-blood world. The coexistence of such extremely opposed outlooks is characteristic of Hinduism. In both Hindu and Buddhist forms of Tantrism, certain practices are overtly or otherwise sexual. Each god has been considered to have a source of power recognized as female in character and often identified with the god's wife or consort. Shakti, this power or goddess, has had many devotees who see her as justifying the notion that an effective way of attaining emancipation from carnal desire is to indulge it to the point of exhaustion, perhaps somewhat on the principle that has been used in the West to discourage children from smoking tobacco by giving them each a large cigar to nauseate them. In Tantrism, this aspect of such an outlook developed into a ritual performed under the direction of a guru as a sort of sacrament involving not only sexual intercourse but the eating of certain forbidden foods and the consumption of prohibited drinks. Shaktism as a cult of female energy and power, has taken several forms, some more orgiastic and openly self-indulgent than others, but all designed to have a cathartic effect while at the same time celebrating the worship of Shiva and Shakti.

Erskine, Ebenezer. (1680–1754). Founder of the original Secession Church in

Scotland. He led a movement in which he argued for the right of the laity to elect their pastors but, being unsuccessful in doing this within the framework of the Presbyterian Church of the time, he led a secession to form an "associate presbytery." He was formally deposed from the Established Presbyterian Church in 1740 and then founded the Secession Church, which, however, was almost immediately plagued by schisms. Erskine was "deposed from the ministry" by one of the opposing splinter groups but continued to pursue his ministry at Stirling till his death. Churches following his views have continued to exist down to the present time, although adherents are few.

Erskine, Thomas (1788–1870). Scottish divine. Born at Linlathen, Angus, he studied at the University of Edinburgh and was admitted to the Scottish Bar in 1810. On inheriting estates, he devoted himself entirely to the study of theology, travelled, and made contacts with distinguished philosophers and theologians of his day, including F. D. Maurice and John McLeod Campbell, whom he supported during the latter's deposition by the Scottish Kirk. Erskine himself never formally separated himself from the Kirk, but clearly exhibited Anglican sympathies. His writings include his *Essay on Faith* (1822), *The Unconditional Freeness of the Gospel* (1828), and *The Brazen Serpent* (1831). His writings, including his letters, exhibit a strikingly mystical quality, in some ways adumbrating, for instance, the motif of Martin Buber's *Ich und Du*. See **Buber, Martin.**

Eschatology. The use of the term "eschatology" to designate doctrine about "last things" (final judgment and the afterlife) is a comparatively recent fashion, first coming into vogue in the English-speaking world not very much more than a hundred years ago. A standard biblical dictionary for scholars, edited by Sir William Smith and published in London in 1893, calls it

"the name that has of late become common for doctrine concerning both the future state of the individual . . . and the end of the world with its accompanying events." The term is derived from New Testament phrases such as "in the last day, *en tē eschatē hēmera*" (John 6:39), and "the last state", *ta eschata* (Matt. 12:45). Since all such notions of this kind to be found in the New Testament have deep roots in ancient Hebrew prophecy, messianic expectation, and apocalyptic literature, we must turn first to that literature before attempting to assess the significance of them as they appear in New Testament and other early Christian writings.

The idea of a final day of reckoning, the "Day of the Lord," seems to have had currency even in pre-exilic Israelite religion, for Amos (Amos. 5:18–20) takes it for granted as part of the conceptual scenario of those whom he is addressing. He assures them that it will not be the day of brightness and light that they commonly expect but, on the contrary, a day of blackness. In this way he uses a popular expectation and hopes to dramatize his own prediction of the fall of Israel. As the day on which the Lord would manifest himself fully at last, it would seem indeed a day of bright light; but the prophets warn that it will be, on the contrary, a black day, a day of wrath and destruction, with cosmic convulsions, bringing disaster and desolation. Amos predicts that the sun will set at noon, and the face of the earth will grow dark (Amos 8:9); Isaiah promises that on that day Yahweh will bring low all that is now high. Zephaniah tells of crimes being punished and cries being heard all over Jerusalem. Joel and other prophets repeat and develop such language. The Day of the Lord is to be a day of reckoning, when all injustice will come to light and be punished by the avenging hand of God. Without such punishment of injustice, how should justice be victorious as popular hope expected it to be when God would come at last and make his righteousness prevail? How should the right be enthroned unless the wrong be dethroned?

The New Testament writers take over the customary Hebrew imagery almost unchanged, except that to Jesus Christ is assigned the role of divine Judge. The day of God is one on which the heavens are to be destroyed and a new heaven and earth are to appear (II Pet. 3:12). The writer of the Apocalypse sees a battle pitched between the armies of evil and the angels of God (Rev. 16:14). This great and terrible day comes unannounced, "like a thief" (I Thess. 5:2, 4). All followers of the Christian Way must be prepared for it, and they can count on God's strengthening them for the fray (I Cor. 1:8). The coming of the Lord is also aptly called the *parousia*, the ceremonial visit of a king to a city within his domain. The synoptists talk of signs and wonders that are to precede the event: the very stars in heaven are to behave erratically (Matt. 24:29; Mark 13:24, Luke 21:25, 27) and the coming itself is to be like a flash of lightning (Matt. 24:27; Luke 17:24). Yet no one, not even the Son of Man, knows the hour; hence the need to be ever alert, as for a thief in the night. Various parables attributed to Jesus exhibit this motif: the parable of the talents, for instance. Yet texts abound that show the general expectation among first-century Christians that the Second Coming was imminent (e.g, Matt. 10:23; Luke 21:32, I Peter 4:7). This does not mean that Jesus taught, or was believed to have taught, that the Day of Judgment would come within a specified period, such as ten or a hundred years; it does mean that one went to sleep at night in the knowledge that tomorrow *might* be "The Day" when the sky would darken and the Lord would appear, this time no longer in the guise of a poor man from an obscure region but enthroned, trailing clouds of glory, and manifesting the terrible power of God. The symbolism of kingship is apposite in terms of the Hebrew mold of thought in which it is conceived, for the characteristic function of the Hebrew

king was judgment (I Sam. 8:5; II Sam. 8:15). The king was the Supreme Court. In Solomon's palace, one of the rooms was the Hall of Judgment where the king appeared to exercise this function (I Kings 7:7). So kingship is the right quality to attribute to God who is to come to judge everyone according to his or her deeds and who will have the power to execute the judgment, separating the sheep from the goats and sending the latter off to eternal fire while gathering the former to enjoy eternal bliss.

Not all New Testament reference to judgment, however, is directed toward the eschaton. Judgment is such a basic concept in Hebrew thought that it has an ongoing role. We all stand all our lives under the divine judgment. The Christian judges himself daily. "Judgment" implied not only a formal pronouncement by a judicial authority but a kind of moral awareness such as we might have in mind in talking of having something on our conscience. Nevertheless, the implementation of the righteous judgment is to take place in one swoop, and with it is to come the end of the age and the heralding of a new one. So, the old triumphs associated in Jewish tradition with the coming of the Messiah are transferred to the Day of the Lord as Christians conceived it: the Second Coming of Christ. According to Christian belief, the Messiah of Hebrew prophecy has indeed come and gone unnoticed by many; but he will come again and in this Second Coming fulfill the triumphal aspect of the traditional messianic prophecy.

Esoteric. This term is from the Greek *esōteros,* meaning "inner" and is used, especially in contexts relating to Gnosticism, to designate a secret or hidden teaching that lies behind what is taught openly. The distinction between such esoteric teaching and its opposite (exoteric) has been made from antiquity in many, if not all the great religions. It is certainly to be found in much Indian thought. In some schools of Buddhism, too, there are stories of the Buddha's having taken apart certain disciples and conveyed to them a secret, hidden meaning behind his general teaching. Paul (I Corinthians 2.6ff. and 3.1f.) specifically alludes to a hidden wisdom that only the spiritually perceptive can be expected to understand, not "carnal" people. The concept may be applied to Pythagoras and to the teachings of many of the great schools of Greek philosophy. In religion there is often a marked distinction between the way in which it is understood by the vast majority of the people and that in which the learned and spiritually-minded perceive and practice it. Taoism provides a striking example of the gulf between its popular and often very superstitious forms and the teaching of its reputed founder, Lao Tzu, which provides a deeply spiritual philosophy. Traditional Christianity also exhibits a marked distinction between what is formulated for the masses and what lies behind such teaching. (The Abbé Dimnet once defined the old papal index of books, the reading of which was prohibited to the people at large, as "a convenient device for enabling the learned to write without fear of offending pious ears.") The concept of esoteric teaching in religion is virtually universal.

Essence. From the Latin essentia (*esse* = to be), corresponding to the Greek *ousia*. Essence is distinguished traditionally from existence and refers to what is deemed to be the permanent aspect of a thing or other entity, contradistinguished from what is in process or in flux. For Plato, the essence or *ousia* of existents is to be found in their eternal archetypes. Aristotle identifies essence with *eidos* or form but repudiates the Platonic archetypal ideals. In the Middle Ages, both the Islamic and the Latin Christian philosophers distinguished between God in whom essence and existence coincide and all other beings in which they are distinct. That is to say that while all entities other than God are in process, not having fully realized their potentialities, God, as the source of all beings other than himself, is the reality in which there is no process. In modern times Husserl's philosophy is very largely concerned with the exploring of essences, and Santayana views all experience as steeped in essences. See **Existence**.

Essenes. From at least as early as the second c. BCE, a Jewish group emerged in Palestine, bearing this name. Unlike other special groups such as the Zealots and the Herodians, both deeply involved in politics, the Essenes dissociated themselves from such concerns and maintained a celibate community with strictly ascetic practices, esoteric teaching, and various ritual observances such as ceremonial ablutions. They supported themselves by farming, handicrafts, and other labors, and practiced principles of non-violence. They chose barren and isolated regions such as that near the Dead Sea so as to avoid contact with the world and pursue their ideals in peace, very much in the spirit of the monastic orders that were to arise in Christianity and play such an important role in its development. They held property in common, prayed, ate, and studied together and especially devoted themselves to the copying of scrolls for the library that they assembled, so that their resemblance to the later forms of monasticism that were to flourish in Christian life is in many ways remarkably striking. They called for repentance for sin and practiced a form of ritual cleansing through baptism. Their language, with its references to their being "of the Way" and "the sons of light" and the like, both reflects Zoroastrian-influenced Jewish Gnosticism and adumbrates the temper and ethos of the early Christian communities. With the fall of Jerusalem in 70 CE and the dispersion of the Jews with all its attendant tragedies, the history of Judaism followed different lines. See **John the Baptist** and **Qumran**.

Etása. In Hindu lore, one of the horses that draw the sun's chariot. The name is also given, however, to an Indian sage traditionally believed to have cursed his children because they annoyed him during the performance of a sacred ritual.

Eternal Recurrence. The view that time is cyclical is of great antiquity and very familiar in the thought of Hindu philosophers such as Shankara and Ramanuja, but it is also to be found in the West, in the ancient world, in the early Middle Ages (see **Erigena, John Scotus**), and it has a notable exemplar in the thought of Nietzsche.

Eternity. As a philosophical concept, eternity is set in opposition to time. Time belongs to the realm of change, development, and evolution, while eternity excludes all these. The Greeks, notably Plato, recognized the difference as fundamental. Plato perceived time as nevertheless reflecting eternity. Neoplatonism, which through Augustine indelibly affected Christian thought, perpetuated this structure of thought. It is echoed in 20th c. Christian writers, e.g., Baron von Hügel, who see the spiritual life as the sprouting of a participation in the eternal life of God and the afterlife as a development of that participation. So understood, the concept of eternity has nothing to do with infinite time or endlessness, since in eternity there can be neither beginning nor end, neither future nor present, nor past. Thomas Aquinas made an important distinction between *aeternitas* (eternity) and *aeviternitas* (an infinite time series), perceiving a radical distinction between them. What is forecast in the ancient Christian creeds is not eternal life but unending, age-long life (*aiōnios*): "life everlasting" or "the life of the world to come." The New Testament often emphasizes the notion with a Hebraistic expression "the ages of ages" (*aiōnes aiōniōn*) as in Galatians 1.5. This does not exclude the separate concept of participation in the eternal Being of God, but the distinction is of the greatest importance. In Hindu and Buddhist thought likewise the Sanskrit *kalpa* (Pali

kappa) signifies an immensely long period of time. Such *kappas*, although unimaginably long, are nevertheless in process. In Christian terms one would have to say that they are not to be confused with the eternity of God, as process is not to be confused with a reality underlying it.

Ethical Culture, Society for. The movement called Ethical Culture has its roots in an association founded in New York City by Felix Adler (1851–1933) in 1876. It conducts services in many of the larger cities. These usually consist of readings, music, meditation, and a morally edifying address. Adler at first professed the Jewish faith, but the movement soon broke with both Judaism and Christianity. A similar movement was begun in England in 1887 that included in its membership some notable names in British philosophy of the time (e.g., Bosanquet, Alexander, and Muirhead), but it received much less support than did its American counterpart.

Ethics. The term "ethics" is derived from the Greek *ēthos*, which means "custom" or "usage". It has basic affinities, therefore, with similar notions in non-Western cultures, such as China, where the Confucian term *li*, meaning "propriety" or "courtesy" or "decorum" has the same fundamental significance. The Greeks, e.g., Plato, used the term *dikē*, meaning also "custom" or "usage" to designate the right way of behaving, very much as Confucius used the term *li* in Chinese. All these terms reflect, of course, a very conservative attitude toward ethical questions. Good conduct is what Victorian English schoolboys called "good form", i.e., conforming to the traditions and customs of the society in which one lives. Confucius saw *li* as reflecting a cosmic *li*, a right way such as follows or corresponds to the way the entire universe is run.

The adjectives "ethical" and "moral" are synonymous and philosophers who concern themselves with ethical problems have been sometimes known as "moral philosophers" as contrasted with logicians, metaphysicians, and other specialists. Moral philosophers may either build systems for guidance in reaching ethical decisions, i.e., decisions about what course of action is good or bad. They also analyze what is to be meant by "good" and "bad", "right" or "wrong". Modern ethics tends more in the latter than in the former direction, but both functions are necessary in the pursuit of ethical questions. Ethics as a whole belongs to value theory, which includes aesthetics and other branches. Some moralists (e.g., Kant and H. A. Pritchard; who may be called "deontologists") hold that duty is prior to value and that certain duties, e.g., the duty to keep a promise, are independent of values. Teleologists, such as utilitarians, contend that our only duties are those that refer to ends or consequences.

The most fundamental term of all in ethical discussions is the term "good", but this term abounds in ambiguities even greater than Socrates long ago noted and made central to some of his expositions as Plato recounts them. The term is logically attributive, i.e., it is applied to a particular object or situation, e.g., the qualities that make a good shoe are very different from those that make a good razor. So on hearing the term "good" we naturally ask, "good for what"? Birds are good for cats, but cats are bad for birds. Those goods that are traditionally called *intrinsic* goods are good for their own sakes or as ends; those that are called *extrinsic* are good as means to ends. Others are good only through their contribution to a complex whole, e.g., a patch in a patchwork quilt, and may be called *contributory* goods. Kant held that nothing can be called good without qualification except a good will. C. I. Lewis held that only experiences can be intrinsically good.

In religious thought a distinction arises (exemplified in the Bible) showing two radically different understandings of what goodness means: (1) goodness may be represented as bestowed by God, so that our task is to try so far as we can to preserve it, as one may be said to try to keep a white shirt clean and white to the end of the day. (2) goodness can be conceived, rather, as an attainment through toil and tribulation. The latter is plainly implied in the vision in the Apocalypse (Revelation) of the 144,000 redeemed who have passed through great tribulation and, having washed their clothes in the Blood of the Lamb, stand before the throne of God with the palms of victory in their hands. The former, by contrast, is implied in the account in Genesis of the fall of Adam and Eve from the state of innocence in which God had created them: a radically different concept.

Again, what is called Ethical Objectivism is the view that the good and the right stand for an objective factor in things, while Ethical Subjectivism is the view that they are subjectively posited. Ethical Naturalists hold that the good and the right can be known as natural objects can be known, so that empirical verification and falsification can be provided in ethics as in empirical inquiries. Ethical Intuitionists deny that and contend that the good and the right are known intuitively and cannot be demonstrated by such means. A fundamental distinction must be noted between those who regard the basic moral category as duty and those who see it hedonistically as the aim to achieve a goal such as happiness. Jeremy Bentham, for instance, took the aim of ethics to consist in the pursuit of that which achieves the greatest good for the greatest number. Many see all ethical inquiries as relativistic to culture, e.g., suicide may be accounted a virtue in one society while another society condemns it as a vice. Adam Smith saw sympathy as the foundation underlying all ethical judgments.

Virtually all religions express in one form or another the notion ("Golden Rule") that one ought to do to others as one would wish others to do to oneself, but such injunctions demand clarification. A mother very rightly sings a lullaby to help her child to go to sleep; she does not act as she would expect the child to act towards her. So, to the Golden Rule we must add some phrase such as "in identical circumstances." But are circumstances ever strictly identical? Again, Jesus tells us how to tell a good tree from a bad one: the good tree bears good fruit. But are we always able to know good fruit from bad? Satan is said to be skillful at disguising himself as an angel of light. Hence the ancient Christian collect in which one prays for those things "which for our unworthiness we dare not and for our blindness we cannot ask." Kant, agnostic though he was in respect to knowledge of the thing-in-itself, since we see only phenomena, was more confident about the *moral* knowledge we can have and which he expressed in the principle of the Categorical Imperative. It may be, however, that in the long run we need as much agnosticism in moral as in epistemological inquiries.

Ethiopian Church. Christianity was introduced to Ethiopia (Abyssinia) in the 4th c. It declined with the spread of Islam in the region and seems to have suffered persecution in the early 10th c. under a Jewish ruler, but a new Christian dynasty was established *c.* 960 and lasted for at least 300 years. In 1268 the Ethiopian Church began to regain its strength and despite persecutions and other trials survives to this day. Historically it has been at times Monophysite and at other times Chalcedonian in its christology. It uses Ge-ez as the language for the liturgy, as it has done for centuries, and has some distinctive features. The worshippers are provided with long crutches on which they may rest their necks while standing during the very long service. The clergy, who may be secular and married or regular and quasi-monastic are generally lacking in formal education, general and theological, but a class of laymen (*dabt-*

aras), who look after Christian education and the singing of the liturgy, have some training for their work. The Church plays an important role in Christian history.

Etiology. From the Greek *aitia*, cause. An inquiry into causes. Its use is popularized in medical practice (e.g., the etiology of a specific disease such as cancer, influenza, or diabetes), but it may be applied to phenomena in any field of human inquiry, such as history, linguistics, or geology.

Eucharist. The term comes from the Greek *eucharistia*, thanksgiving, which is an aspect of the central act of Christian worship known as the Eucharist or Mass and sometimes, in Protestant circles, as Holy Communion or the Lord's Supper. There is no doubt that it was at a very early date a regular part of Christian worship. It is generally taken by scholars to have roots in the Jewish Passover and Kiddush. As it has developed in Christian worship it has acquired a multiple significance: not only is it a commemoration of the Last Supper as recounted in the Gospels and performed in obedience to the recorded command of Jesus to his disciples on that occasion; it is a thanksgiving to God for the gift of Christ and for all his other mercies, the central means of mystical communion between God and his Church, and (for those faithful to Catholic tradition, whether Eastern Orthodox, Roman Catholic, or Anglican) a sacrifice to God of his Son Jesus Christ, under the guise of the Bread and Wine. (See **Mass** and **Real Presence, The.**)

Controversy on the nature of this central act of Christian worship only gradually developed as attempts were made to formulate its meaning in theological terms, especially from the 9th c. onwards, but the view that eventually prevailed in the Middle Ages was what is called transubstantiation, i.e., that while the "accidents" of the bread and wine remain after the priest has consecrated them, their "substance" is changed into the Body and Blood of Christ. This way of expressing the reality of the presence of Christ in the Eucharist made much sense in terms of the intellectual thought of the Middle Ages, from the 12th c. (when Aristotle was "discovered" in the Latin West), for it was cast in the mold of Aristotelian philosophy. Like the doctrine of the Trinity itself, it was a stroke of genius in the way in which it expressed the mysteries of the Christian faith in terms of the intellectual climate of the day. It is not likely to be the best way of expressing them in other times and intellectual circumstances, such as our own. At the Reformation, violent controversies developed on the subject and several theories were advanced on the nature of the Eucharist and the way in which Christ may be said to be "really" present in it, varying from the traditional transubstantiation view to that of Zwingli, the Swiss theologian and Reformer who regarded the Eucharist as merely a memorial in the way in which a wedding ring is a memorial and symbol of the marriage vows that the parties to a marriage have taken: a view antithetical to a very wide spectrum of Christian tradition and practice.

Since the Reformation much attention has been given to eucharistology as a most important aspect of Christian theology and much useful work has been done on it in the 20th c., especially by Anglican and Roman Catholic theologians. The Second Vatican Council, while affirming the reality of the presence of Christ in the Eucharist, has avoided precise formulation of how it occurs, which is in the spirit traditionally upheld in Anglican theology, which not only accommodates a wide variety of theological opinions but is in marked sympathy to the lines attributed to Queen Elizabeth I (T. Fuller, *The Holy State* [1642], p. 315):

'Twas God the word that spake it,
He took the bread and brake it;

And what that word did make it,
That I believe and take it.

Euchelaion. The term used in the Greek Church to designate the sacrament known in the West as Holy Unction.

Eudaemonism. From the Greek term *eúdaimonia* (happiness). It is applied to ethical views that take happiness as the chief end of every human being. Aristotle's *Ethics* provides a classic example of such a view. Happiness, as Aristotle well recognized, is by no means identifiable with pleasure, although pleasure is included within it. The Christian theological tradition, viewing man's chief end as the attainment of a state of beatitude with God plainly belongs to this class, as do other religious philosophies. See **Ethics**.

Euhemerism. The term given to the view that the gods venerated in antiquity had their origin in popular heroes. It received its name from the 3rd c. BCE Greek philosopher Euhemerus, who propounded the view, which became widespread among thoughtful people in the ancient world. Christians appealed to it in support of their contention that the gods of the Graeco-Roman world were human inventions, not ontological realities. Euhemerus belonged to the Cyrenaic school of philosophy, which flourished in the 4th and 3rd centuries BCE, having taken its name from the birthplace of its founder, Aristippus, a disciple of Socrates, born in Cyrene, Libya. The Cyrenaics taught that pleasure is the aim of human life. Members of the school, who included the wife of Aristippus (Arete) and Aristippus the younger (a grandson), varied in their interpretation of the pleasure principle. The school eventually decayed, failing to compete with the more soundly founded Epicurean school. (See **Epicureanism** and **Cyrenaicism**.) The name Euhemerism continued to be used in the 18th c. by those who, according to the fashion of that age, sought to discredit all concepts of the supernatural.

Eunuchs. In oriental courts the practice prevailed of keeping eunuchs, i.e., male slaves who had been castrated for the purpose, as attendants in the women's quarters of the palace. (The Greek term *eunouchos* means literally "keeper of the bed".) The Code of Hammurabi mentions eunuchs, and in Mesopotamia they are known to have formed part of the cult of Ishtar and other religious worship. The castration of males for such purposes was not practiced, however, in Egypt, Greece, or Rome, except perhaps occasionally through oriental influence. The references to eunuchs in the Old Testament demand scrutiny, for sometimes they refer to eunuchs in the sense of such bedchamber attendants and the like, while elsewhere they probably do not. In Deuteronomy 23.2 we read that eunuchs are not permitted to become members of the Israelite community, while in later times (e.g., Isaiah 56.3ff.) both eunuchs and aliens are accepted as full members of it. (See also Wisdom of Solomon 3.14.) Jesus (Matthew 19.12) makes a distinction among three classes: those who are eunuchs by birth, those who are been castrated, and those who "make themselves eunuchs for the kingdom of heaven." By the last category is to be understood, of course, those who for religious reasons commit themselves (as did the Essenes and as do Christian monks and others) to abstinence from sexual intercourse. Some Christians in early times (Origen is the most famous example) voluntarily castrated themselves, interpreting the text in Matthew literally, but happily these cases were aberrant and rare. The Italian practice of castrating boys to train them as adult sopranos in the service of the Church ended with the accession of Pope Leo XIII in 1878.

Euphrates. The largest river in West Asia, 1700 miles long from its source in Armenia to the Persian Gulf. Many of the greatest cities in Mesopotamia lay on its banks. It was to Mesopotamia what the Nile was to Egypt: that which made the development of the civilization possible.

Euthanasia. The term (from the Greek *eu*, good, and *thanatos*, death) means literally a good death, but as used in modern ethical and theological discussion it signifies "mercy killing," e.g., through the deliberate administration of a drug specifically intended to accelerate death and so diminish and terminate suffering when no hope of recovery from a painful disease is within the bounds of reasonable possibility. Much may be argued both for and against the practice.

First we must distinguish voluntary from compulsory euthanasia. By "voluntary" is meant euthanasia requested by the sufferer, which some would call assisted suicide or homicide by request and which others would regard as an act to be encouraged by all humane members of a civilized society. Compulsory euthanasia implies a decision made by an individual (e.g., a doctor, relative, or friend of the sufferer) to end the life of a terminally ill patient who is suffering great pain yet who (e.g., because of mental incompetence or physical disability) cannot express a wish for such an action. Compulsory euthanasia is patently open to the possibility of abuse, e.g., if medical or other bureaucracies were to be granted the right to make such decisions, the effect could be even to lead to a form of genocide. Yet the alternative implies the grief and distress of a parent or spouse or close friend obliged to watch his or her most dearly beloved condemned to prolonged suffering with no outcome but death. The question is a very lively one today on which not only the general public but the Churches themselves are sharply divided. It is also one on which even those most favorable to it would recognize legislation to be extremely difficult. Among modern societies, Holland is probably the one that has taken the most lenient attitude toward the subject, yet even there legislation permitting it proved difficult to obtain.

Although a burning question today, the problems it raises were well known in antiquity. In classical India, for example, where the brahmanical outlook strongly encouraged the individual to live as long as possible and suicide in the sense of self-killing for the sake of pride or in rage or through fear was deemed one of the worst of sins, to be punished by many thousands of years in hell, certain forms of self-willed death were accepted, e.g., when one is suffering from an illness from which one cannot recover or when one is too old and feeble to have the capacity to perform even the minimum ritual requirements imposed by Hindu society. In such circumstances the voluntary termination of life was not only blameless but to be preferred. (See Pandurang V. Kane, *History of Dharmassatra* [1974], Vol. 2, Part 2, pp. 924–6.) The brahmanical writers were plainly aware of the difficulties that are so widely recognized in modern controversies on the subject, such as we have noted, yet they could justify euthanasia even in the face of the principle of *ahimsā* (non-violence to any living being). They did so, however, by way of exception from an immensely strong rule against and distaste for suicide, and they permitted the exception by way of philosophical argument rather than by specific legislation, which they seem to have recognized, as we do in a modern Western context, to be hazardous to society since likely to open the way to abuse.

The case against euthanasia in modern times is based on the principle of the "right to live" as defined, for instance, by the European Convention of Human Rights (1953), section 1, article 1. National medical associations throughout the civilized world have affirmed voluntary euthanasia to be unethical and legislatures, have been generally reluctant to provide any legal support for the practice. The case for euthanasia depends on whether the individual, in case of extreme suffering, has the "right to die", affording his doctors and friends the right or even

the duty to provide him with assistance to do so if necessary. A very large body of literature exists on the subject, many attempts have been made in many countries to obtain official legal recognition of the legitimacy of the practice, and various societies actively engage in trying to secure such recognition; but the problems have proved generally intractable. Meanwhile, such euthanasia has been quietly practiced by many humane doctors and others, some of whom have had their licenses revoked or have even been sent to prison, although often with lenient or nominal sentences.

Eutyches (*c.* 378–454). Generally accounted the founder of the Monophysite school of christology, which held that in Christ there was only one nature, the divine, against the Nestorians who taught that in the incarnate Christ there were two separate Persons, one divine and one human. Eutyches, who was an ecclesiastical dignitary at Constantinople, with much influence at court, vehemently opposed Nestorius and in effect denied the humanity of Christ by contending that his humanity was not "consubstantial" with ours: a view that made impossible the redemptive work of Christ as generally understood in the Church. He was condemned at the Council of Chalcedon in 451, which maintained that in Christ there were two natures, one fully human, the other fully divine, in one Person. See **Monophysitism.**

Evagrius Ponticus (346–399). A native of Pontus, he became a noted preacher at Constantinople, but in 382 he left for the Nitrian desert where he spent the remainder of his life, devoting himself to the cultivation of spirituality. He was much influenced by and deeply sympathic to Origen's teachings and is regarded by modern scholars as in more than one way a pioneer in Christian spirituality. He wrote copiously and influenced many of the great early writers on that subject such as Cassian and Dionysius the Pseudo-Areopagite, passing on to them much of the spirit and outlook that had motivated the Alexandrian school of which Origen had been the greatest exemplar.

Evangelical. This adjective means literally "pertaining to or expressive of the Gospel", but it has come to be used in much more specific senses, being adopted since the Reformation by many Protestant churches as designating their claim to follow the teachings of the Gospel more directly or more specifically than the way in which they see the Gospel used in traditional Catholic thought and practice. The term is used, for example, in the name adopted by a group of Protestant churches in Germany (*die Evangelische Kirche*). In both Germany and Switzerland the term is generally applied to Lutherans contradistinguished from Calvinists. In the English-speaking world the term generally signifies an outlook that claims to go to the "heart" of the Gospel and in its extreme forms to emphasize the importance of a specific decision to accept Christ as one's personal Savior by answering his call. In the Anglican Communion the term is traditionally applied to those who, within the comprehensiveness that traditionally characterizes Anglicanism, tend in such directions and to suspect the Catholic attitudes and usages that many Anglicans treasure as vital to the life of the Church.

Evensong. The term used in the English-speaking world for the office of Vespers.

Evolution. The concept of evolution, popularly associated with the work of Charles Darwin that culminated in the appearance of his influential book, *The Origin of Species* (1849), has roots in the philosophies of antiquity in both East and West. Darwin's work was distinguished by the immensity of the evidence he and his colleague A. R. Wallace amassed in the field of biological evolution, but in the latter part of the 19th c. scientists were perceiving more and more that the same principle was operating in every aspect of the universe

(e.g., astronomy), and philosophers (e.g., Nietzsche) were developing philosophical outlooks that reflected the same basic change in the climate of thought.

The change was in fact, however, a recovery and restatement of ideas that had been characteristic of ancient thought. From very early times in India, for instance, thinkers in the Hindu tradition were preoccupied with trying to understand the relation between Brahman and the development of the cosmos. They thought in terms of evolution, spiritual and material. Some systems portrayed it more spiritually, others (e.g., Sankya) more materialistically. Evolution is implicit in Greek philosophy, most strikingly in the quests of the predecessors of Socrates such as Anaximander, who saw in his own way a progression in biological entities, and Empedocles, who developed the principle of adaptation that long antedated the work of Darwin and Huxley in the 19th c. Aristotle's basic distinction between that which is in process and that which is beyond process implies an evolutionary understanding of the universe with God holding all together. The view that the universe is never-ending and cyclical, which is found in the Stoics and other schools in the West as well as in Indian thought, is an expression of the same general understanding of the way things are and always must be. It is associated, moreover, with the fundamental presupposition that underlay Greek thought generally: the antithesis between permanence and change. Parmenides and the Eleatic school generally had presented a puzzle to which Plato and Aristotle, each in his own fashion, had provided ingenious solutions, all presupposing, however, some form of evolutionary principle at work in the universe, for change and growth imply some form of evolutionary process. The Neoplatonists, whose outlook was so peculiarly influential in the way in which Christian theology came to be represented, also thought in terms that echoed this evolutionary tradition, although they dealt with it differently.

Throughout the later Middle Ages, when Aristotle had confronted the scholastic thinkers with the challenge of a mold of thought that seemed superficially at odds with the traditional Christian thought of their time, evolutionary principles once again challenged the grooves into which popular attitudes had tended to fall. True, Aristotle thought in terms of fixed species (he had difficulty with hybrids such as mules), but his entire outlook implied an evolutionary principle at work everywhere. After the Quattrocento and the Renaissance of learning that followed throughout Western Europe, evolutionary ideas kept appearing in the most diverse forms, some that could be classified as deeply religious, others the reverse. The dynamic character of the monads in the system produced by Leibniz has behind it the decision of God, but it is nonetheless evolutionary. For Hegel, existence *is* process. Herder and Comte thought in terms of cultural evolution.

After Darwin, a vast spectrum of thought from a remarkable variety of thinkers had plainly evolutionary implicates. Herbert Spencer perceived evolution as a basic natural law of the universe and Samuel Alexander constructed a system of thought entirely dependent on the principle of evolution. Henri Bergson very explicitly exhibits evolution as the ground of the creative process by which novelty emerges. Dewey and Smuts, Whitehead and Teilhard de Chardin, all very different in their interests and in their aims, reflect the immense influence of Darwin, each using evolutionary principles as fundamental to the inquiry in which each engaged. Teilhard, a Jesuit and a geophysicist by academic profession, saw life as dependent on the inorganic ground out of which it develops, mind as developing out of the "biosphere" or life-realm, and all moving toward God. A school of Protestant theologians, mostly American, about the turn of the century (e.g., John Fiske, Henry Drummond, James McCosh, and Ly-

man Abbott) thought in terms of the felicitous phrase of Fiske that evolution is "God's way of doing things."

Excardination. See **Incardination.**

Ex Cathedra. The word "cathedra" is used to designate the bishop's chair (hence "cathedral", the church where he has his chair). The phrase *ex cathedra* is used in the Roman Catholic Church to designate pronouncements made by the Pope in a solemn and official manner on questions of faith or morals. Such utterances are held by Roman Catholics to be infallible. Since there is no specific formula to indicate precisely when a papal pronoucement is intended to carry this weight, the entire concept of papal infallibility is fraught with difficulty. The Syllabus of Errors (1864) was widely accepted at the time as *ex cathedra*. Few Roman Catholic theologians today, if any, would so regard it.

Excommunication. Among the forms of censure traditionally imposed by the Christian Church for grave offenses, the most solemn and severe is excommunication, i.e., the denial of the sacraments to the offender and (in the case of clerics) from the right to adminster them. In graver forms the excommunication may even prohibit the offender's attending church services. Excommunicated clerics are automatically deprived of all offices, dignities or stipends to which they would otherwise be entitled. (Lesser ecclesiastical censures are interdict and suspension.) Anglican usage also envisions the possibility of excommunication, although it is sparingly imposed. All Christian bodies protect themselves in one way or another against grave public offenses such as persistent attempts to disturb the peace of the church during divine worship or to do bodily harm to clergy or people. After due repentance, the sentence of excommunication may be lifted. In no case does it purport to separate the offender from God; nevertheless, among those who account the sacraments the supreme channels of his grace, as in Catholic tradition, and for whom the Church is the dearest institution on earth, excommunication entails an incomparably poignant sadness, most of all when it is felt to be undeserved. It should be noted that in the primitive Christian Church discipline was much more severe than it has ever been since and certain sins (e.g., murder, adultery) committed after baptism were deemed so incompatible with the Church's expectation that the offender was excommunicated with virtually no hope of ever being received back into the fold. In Buddhism, moreover, a form of excommunication consisting of permanent expulsion is practiced in the case of monks guilty of certain offenses specified in the *Patimokkha,* an ancient text dealing with disciplinary matters: theft, murder, sexual misconduct, and boasting of supernatural powers. Other offenses, considered less grave, may be punished by temporary expulsion, approximately the counterpart, in Christian tradition, of suspension. The four offenses punishable by permanent expulsion are called *pārājikā,* i.e., "entailing defeat": both the moral defeat of the individual monk and the threat to the repute and the vitality of the monastic community to which he has belonged.

Exegesis. The term, from the Greek, means "explanation," and it is used of the process of explaining and interpreting in a scholarly way any literary text. Exegesis of the Bible is an important part of the training of both Jewish and Christian scholars and has been practiced from antiquity. Modern methods of literary exegesis have immensely enhanced understanding of the Bible. See **Hermeneutics.**

Existence. Traditionally the term "existence" is contrasted with the term "essence". (See **Essence.**) It is derived from the Latin *ex* (out of) and *sistere* (to emerge, to step forth). Plato regarded everything in what we would call the empirical world (e.g., horses and dogs,

stars and planets, tables and chairs, courageous acts and cowardly deeds) as having each behind it an essential "form" or archetype beyond the world we normally take to be the "real" world. They are phenomena, not the reality behind the phenomena, without which the phenomena could not occur. That is not to say they are illusory. On the contrary, these entities we commonly perceive all around us participate in the reality that lies behind them all, yet they are to be distinguished from that reality. The world we see is a shadow-world. In the Allegory of the Cave, Plato imagines people in a cave, looking at the wall and seeing the shadow play reflected on the wall from what is going on outside. Chained to their places they can see only these reflections (such as we might call black-and-white films on a screen), which, being all they know, they take to be realities. They are not entirely wrong, since what they see are indeed reflections of reality. One of the "film-watchers", however, breaks away from his chains and walks out to the mouth of the cave. He (the authentic philosopher) is temporarily blinded by the intensity of the light to which he is unaccustomed, but as his eyes become adapted to it he begins to see the brightness of the colors, the three-dimensional character of the people and objects passing by, and the general vitality of the scene. He calls to his companions to tell them about his vision, but they have no idea what he is talking about, being content with the forms of existence under which they see the reflection of reality. Plato's model, although modified in innumerable ways through the ages, became determinative of the entire course of traditional Western thought, from Plato to Hegel. It is echoed, moreover, in those evolutionary views that provide process-and-reality models. (See **Evolution.**) Resistance to this existence-essence antithesis developed, however, in various quarters, having its most remarkable 19th c. exemplar in Kierkegaard and, in the

20th c., a strikingly different one in Jean-Paul Sartre, the former profoundly religious and the latter a nihilist. See **Existentialism**.

Existentialism. (See **Existence**.) Although modern existentialism as a fashionable philosophy on the continent of Europe had its heyday about the middle of the 20th c., its roots go much further back, not least in the French philosophical tradition in which it is adumbrated in various ways before. Jean-Paul Sartre, now its best-known modern exponent, popularized it. Existentialism is not necessarily either sympathetic or hostile to religion. Nevertheless, when it takes a religious form it is critical of certain aspects of religious thought and, when it takes a nihilistic, antireligious form, it is no less critical of certain traditionalist types of philosophy. Most noteworthy among Christian existentialists is Kierkegaard (1813–55), one of the most penetrating religious thinkers in human history, who took his starting point in a critique of Hegel, whose influence in his time and for long afterwards was paramount in Western philosophical thought, not only in Germany but in France, England, and America too, despite the traditionally empiricist tendencies of British and American philosophy. Kierkegaard sought to introduce, against the widely accepted Hegelian presuppositions of the academic world of his day, which emphasized rationality, objectivity, and essentialism, the importance of concepts such as subjectivity. God, he contended, in the face of a view that Hegel had made fashionable, is "pure subjectivity." By this he meant, *inter alia*, that God is totally unknown until confronted in what Buber was later to call an I-Thou relationship. Pascal, a mathematician and also one of the greatest religious geniuses in history, had long before, in his 17th c. French intellectual *ambiance*, presented insights into the nature of spirituality that show much affinity with Kierkegaard's. Kierkegaard put *Angst* at the heart of human experience as the most central of all human emotions and the basis of all others. By *Angst* he meant not ordinary fear or dread or anxiety such as we feel from time to time about this or that concern (e.g., our health, our financial future, and the like) but a radical anguish underlying all life's other concerns. The English translators have usually rendered *Angst* as "the sense of dread" while in French it is usually *angoisse* (anguish) and in Spanish *agonia* (agony), all expressing an irreducible and fundamental malaise at the root of human existence. Kierkegaard, through religious satire, in which he was a master, ridiculed the traditional, especially Hegelian, modes of thought as involving an outrageous arrogance: an attitude in which the philosopher is, as we might say, not only playing God but identifying himself with God. By contrast, Kierkegaard contended, authentic Christianity requires an attitude of faith, a trust in the One who reveals himself in personal relationship and in so doing discloses both the immensity of the gulf between God and man and the awesome and surprising intimacy that God's initiative makes possible, when man takes the "leap of faith" that opens up his awareness of both the distance and the proximity of God. Kierkegaard, neglected for some seventy years after his death, was a catalyst in the emergence of the existentialist types of philosophy that emerged in Germany after World War I. Later in the twenties such influences entered the French intellectual scene, issuing in an enormous resuscitation of themes implicit in much French thought. Sartre, in his novels and plays, gave these expression and was followed by others in the same nihilist vein, while no less affected were many of the great Protestant thinkers of the earlier part of the 20th c., including Tillich, Bultmann, and (in his earlier thought, at least) Barth. In more philosophical circles, Unamuno expressed in his Spanish idiom many such themes, such as "the tragic sense of life" and the importance of the individual. Probably the most important among modern existentialists and one who immensely influenced Sartre is Heidegger, who emphasized the great existentialist themes: freedom, authenticity, and others. Bultmann was, among Christian theologians, especially influenced by Heidegger. Some French philosophers who were really in the Neo-idealist tradition were sometimes classified as *demi-existentialistes*, but that was largely because existentialist attitudes and themes had so affected all European thought by that time that no one could entirely escape their influence. Perhaps the most important element to note in viewing modern existentialism is that it has provided a vocabulary and an outlook by means of which both the protagonists and the antagonists of traditional religion can discuss the nature of their differences. Resistance to existentialism came from many diverse quarters, e.g., from idealists, from the earlier logical positivists, from Marxists, and from various highly traditionalist religious groups, Catholic and Protestant. It has indubitably altered, however, the course of both "secular" and "religious" thought.

Ex Nihilo Nihil Fit. This ancient principle, "out of nothing, nothing comes," expresses the notion that existence must have some antecedent cause.

Exodus. The term is a Greek one, *exodus*, meaning "departure" and is used to designate the events recorded in the biblical book so named (Exodus 1–15). The Israelites, oppressed under the Egyptian yoke, find a leader in Moses, who secures their escape across what is called in Hebrew *yam sûp*. Although traditionally identified with the Red Sea, biblical scholars today agree that the phrase, which means literally "the sea of reeds," must be taken to be a body of water in the Isthmus of Suez, probably near the city of Ramses. Several theories have been proposed, but all see the departure route as across the isthmus. The date of the Exodus is still controversial, but the biblical passage (I Kings 6.1) that places it 480 years before the building of the Temple by Solomon, i.e., *c.* 1440 BCE, is most unlikely, since it does not fit several known historical facts. Modern scholars generally date the exodus within the period 1290–1260 BCE. They also reckon the settlement of the Israelites (after the "wilderness" period) as between 1250–1200 BCE.

Ex Opere Operato. Since early in the 13th c. this phrase has been used by theologians to express the concept that the sacraments work independently of both the minister and the recipient; i.e., they are not to be understood as depending, for example on the sanctity of the minister or the merit of the person receiving them. This is not to say that they work mechanically, irrespective of the disposition of the recipient. The grace they confer is not forced upon the individual who, on the contrary, must receive them humbly and lovingly if they are to be effective. What the phrase expresses is that the grace the sacraments provide is made available to such a well-disposed recipient irrespective of the worthiness of anyone involved in their administration.

Exorcism. In both the pagan and the Jewish world in the time of Jesus the practice of ritually expelling evil spirits was widely recognized. It was part of the general custom of the time and Jesus himself recognized it as the way in which people understood the concept of the healing of mental or spiritual illness. Not only did it become part of the baptismal ceremonies of the Christian Church; the second of the traditional "minor orders" was that of the exorcist, whose special function was to engage in such expulsion of evil spirits. This function was exercised and understood somewhat in the way in which "spiritual healing" is understood today in many Christian churches. The office of exorcist was abolished in 1972 in the Roman Catholic Church, where it had for long fallen almost into desuetude.

Experience. Although the meaning of this term (from the Latin, *experientia*) may seem at first sight easily ascertainable and definable, it is in fact much more difficult to deal with than may appear. The observations I make through my senses (sight, hearing, smell, taste, touch) do provide much of what I may be said to experience, but my range of experience goes far beyond them. Through my imagination, for instance, I can experience a vast spectrum of mental images. I can experience heavens and hells, demons and angels. For Dewey, both observation and reasoning enter into human experience and constitute it, so that part of what we call experience is not observational. That knowledge arises only through experience may indeed be called a truism. The question is, rather, what are the forms that experience takes and what are their respective roles in the discernment of meaning and the attainment of knowledge?

Explanation. The term is derived from the Latin *ex* (out of) and *planare* (to make level) and alludes to the concept of clarification through one of various means, e.g., the demonstration that the idea under discussion can be deduced from certain simpler premises, or the division of the idea into simpler elements, or by some combination of such procedures. Explanation can be on varying levels, e.g., if a child asks why the streets are wet we may "explain" the fact by saying that the clouds are pouring rain on them, but that kind of explanation, adequate though it might be for the circumstances, would not satisfy a student of physics or metereology. Modern philosophers have in various ways provided accounts of the nature of the procedure of explanation, but all conform to the general pattern here described. That which calls for explanation is technically called the *explanandum*, while that which provides the explanation is called the *explanans*.

Exposition of the Blessed Sacrament. A devotion practiced in the Roman Catholic Church and in some Anglican parishes. It consists of the placing of the Host in a monstrance or pyx for public adoration. Its use dates from at least the 14th c. Lights and flowers adorn the sanctuary and hymns and prayers are offered during the service. Public exposition is generally confined to the Feast of Corpus Christi but may be permitted by the diocesan bishop at other times.

Ex-Sistenz. A term used by Heidegger to express a particular aspect of his existentialist thought: the "standing-forthness" of "authentic" existence.

One might compare, although with caution, the notion proposed by James Joyce, which he called "epiphany". Joyce describes how one may walk down a certain street every day for many years, each day casually noticing a street clock but paying no attention to it. Then one day, suddenly, the clock that the observer has seen so habitually (without attending to it unless perhaps occasionally to notice the time) "jumps right out at him," so to speak, causing him to see it as if for the first time. Hitherto he has merely noticed it as one notices the color of a girl's dress in a television commercial that one keeps seeing over and over again and is trying to dim out rather than to watch; then suddenly it confronts one in such a way as to command attention, being seen in a special way. Joyce's notion refers to the aesthetic level of experience; Heidegger's to the ethical or moral level.

Extinction. Western writers have generally associated extinction of being with the concept of *nirvāna*, the afterlife corresponding to the Christian goal of heaven expressed in the Beatific Vision. This is incorrect and due to a misunderstanding. What characterizes the nirvanic concept is the notion of the extinguishing of desire, of the world of *maya* (illusion) with all the passions of anger and avarice that attend it and that contain the roots of all evil and suffering. Existence as encumbered by such impediments may be said to be extinguished, but the extinction consists in the purification of the essential nature of the self from the encumbrances that seem to the ordinary person to be inseparable from it. These encumbrances are what flow like muddy streams into an ocean of forgetfulness. So much are they associated with life in the mind of the common man that they are taken to be life itself and, since they are annihilated, life is erroneously perceived as being annihilated, but that is not as the enlightened person sees nirvanic bliss.

Extreme Unction. See **Unction.**

Exurge, Domine. The name of the papal bull issued by Leo X on June 15, 1520, in which he excommunicated Luther. Luther eventually responded by publicly burning the bull on December 10 of the same year, at Wittenberg.

Ezekiel. The third and last of the greater Old Testament prophets, after Isaiah and Jeremiah. The book named Ezekiel is traditionally supposed to have been written in captivity in Babylon, in the 6th c. BCE, but questions about the circumstances and even the authorship of the book have given rise to controversy among scholars.

Ezra. In the 5th or 4th c. BCE, certain radical reforms in Judaism were achieved largely through the work of a priest or scribe so designated, whose activities are recorded in the biblical books of Ezra and Nehemiah. He championed the view that the Jews must take an exclusive attitude toward the Gentile world, in order to preserve the purity of the Jewish people and so that they might develop according to the principles laid down by Ezekiel. He promulgated a code of laws (Nehemiah 8.1–12). Such a program implied no disparagement of the Gentile world, only the recognition of the historic claim of the people of Israel to be uniquely chosen by and convenanted with God, and the need to maintain this

society as a people apart, charged with a special divine mission.

Eye. The word "eye" is much used in the Bible to designate not only the organ of vision but the entire human being as spiritually functioning. It is the organ of judgment and decision. Hence God's eye judges the deeds of men (e.g., II Samuel 11.27).

F

Faber, Frederick William (1814–1863). Oratorian priest. Influenced by Newman, he followed him in 1845 as a convert to the Roman Catholic Church. He wrote many hymns. His writings on spirituality include *Growth in Holiness* (1855) and *Bethlehem* (1860).

Faber, Jacobus (*c.* 1455–1536). French humanist. A priest, he became much interested in classical literature and the ancient Greek philosophers. Although in sympathy with the Reformation, he did not espouse Reformation teaching. Also known as Lefèvre d'Etaples and as J. Faber Stapulensis.

Faber, Johann (1478–1541). German Roman Catholic theologian. He became Bishop of Vienna in 1530. A friend of Erasmus, he was at first sympathetic to the Reformation movement, then turned against it and became an active opponent of it. His writings are mostly controversial and homiletic.

Fabian. 3rd c. Bishop of Rome, he was the first martyr in the Decian persecution. He was buried in the San Callisto catacomb in Rome. His body seems to have been removed thence to the church of San Sebastiano, where it was discovered in 1915.

Fabiola. A 4th c. Roman lady who after canonical irregularities concerning her second marriage, devoted herself to a life of great austerity, bestowing her wealth on the poor and caring for the sick and needy. She went to Bethlehem in 395 and was for some time under the spiritual direction of Jerome. Returning to Rome, she continued her life of active good works till her death in 399.

Fabri, Felix (1442–1520). A Dominican, author of an historically valuable and striking account of his pilgrimage to Jerusalem in 1483.

Fabricius, Johann Albert (1668–736). A Lutheran scholar, born in Leipzig, he was the author of a vast range of works of great importance for later historians and bibliographers. They include his 14-volume *Bibliotheca Graeca* (1705–1728), covering the period from Homer to the Fall of Constantinople to the Turks in 1453 and many other erudite works.

Facts. The concept of factuality has considerable bearing upon the study of religion. In logic and linguistic analysis the term "fact" can be shown to be much more complex than it is commonly taken to be; e.g., "factual" can be used: (1) as referring to "the real world" on contrast to "fictional"; (2) as referring to what is directly decidable by observation, in contrast to "theoretical"; (3) as referring to what is objectively and decidably in the world independent of human evaluation; (4) as referring to what concerns the world rather than human thought or outlook or discussion *about* the world; and (5) as referring to mathematical or logical statements that can be shown to be mathematically or logically true in contrast to statements that can be shown to be mathematically or logically false. What it means to say that x is a fact is related to questions about what it means to say that x is true. Some talk of "brute" facts to designate what is considered to be given independently of the way in which we see the world around us, which is different from the way in which worms and even horses and dogs see it. "I am seeing grass to be pink" might be a factual statement about an aberration in my vision, but it would

not be a "brute" fact. "In that chess game I could have checkmated you in one move" may or may not be a fact of a kind, but since it depends on the rules of the game it could not properly be called a brute fact. The importance of such distinctions for the philosophy of religion may be exhibited by the complexities arising from one's contending that the existence of God is a fact, not a fiction. What precisely is one contending in such a case? Plainly one is denying that by the existence of God one means the existence of an idea in one's mind to which the name "God" is given; one is asserting, rather, that what we are naming "God" exists independently of the human mind. What *kind* of such a fact is envisioned is, however, a separate question.

Faculty Psychology. When the soul is regarded as a substance, which is an outmoded conception, it is natural to divide it into various "parts", such as reason, sense, and will. The term "faculty psychology" is applied to the making of such a division. Yet when the ancient and medieval writers distinguished functions in the soul they did not necessarily think in such terms. Plato certainly did not do so in his tripartite arrangement of the soul. Aristotle, whose system Thomas Aquinas tended to follow, discerned "potentialities" of the soul and Thomas "powers", but such arrangements do not necessarily issue in a "faculty psychology" as the term is used by modern writers.

Fa Hsien. Chinese scholar and pilgrim-monk, born in Shansi and trained at Ch'ang-an in the west of China, which he left in 399 CE to visit India and elsewhere in search of the complete canon of Buddhist scripture. After extensive travels he returned home in 414 and began a translation of the Buddhist Scriptures. His works include an account of his travels, translated into English by various persons including a translation by H. A. Giles, *The Travels of Fa Hsien* (1923).

Fairbairn, Andrew Martin (1838–1912). Scottish Congregationalist divine. Trained at the University of Edinburgh, he held various charges in Scotland before becoming Principal of Mansfield College, Oxford. Noted for his open-mindedness and probity, his eloquence and his learning, he was much respected. His writings include *Studies in the Philosophy of Religion and History* (1876) and *The Philosophy of the Christian Religion* (1902).

Faith. Faith (the Greek term used in the New Testament is *pistis*) is one of the most central concepts in Christian thought and practice. It has been understood in several ways. Two should be specially noted. (1) The English word "faith" is derived from the Latin *fidere*, to trust. Traditionally, the Latin word *fides* as used by the medieval theologians signified assent to the body of Christian truth to be found in the Scriptures and the Church Fathers, and expressed propositionally in the Creeds, the traditions handed down through the General Councils, and the teachings of the great doctors of the Church. (2) As used in the Bible, however, it has a moral rather than an intellectual meaning. The classic passage for Christians is Hebrews 11. Paul sets it alongside hope and love as one of the three great aspects of the Christian life. Although it has an intellectual content, it requires an act of the will. It is partly founded upon experience, the assurance that comes with having seen God's workings in one's life, but it entails a trust that God who has so blessed one in the past will continue to do so in the future. The Reformers stressed the importance for the Christian of living *by* faith, which alone makes a person righteous. The Lutheran theologians distinguished three components in faith: *notitia* (knowledge), *assensus* (assent), and *fiducia* (trust), but they saw trust as supreme among them. In one sense, as Kant perceived, one must set aside knowledge to make room for faith. In Kierkegaard's terms, one must make a "leap of faith." Modern Roman Catholic theologians are now recognizing the unique importance of faith so understood. Tertullian saw an important aspect of faith in his assertion, *credo quia ineptum* (I believe because it is absurd), i.e., no one could have invented such a paradox as that which the Christian faith presents. Augustine's *credo ut intelligam* (I believe in order that I may understand) shows faith as an inductive method of arriving at knowledge. Thomas Aquinas saw faith and reason as complementary; yet without faith reason is in certain matters impotent. Calvin, despite his strong emphasis on the distinctive character of faith, recognized that it is a *kind* of knowledge. It is not intellectually blind, not totally ignorant, not totally devoid of doubt. Yet it goes beyond the kind of evidence that reason demands. In the course of living the life of faith one gradually perceives more and more clearly the hand of God in one's history. Faith has a key role in the thought of many philosophers, e.g., Pascal, Kierkegaard, Unamuno, Buber, Tillich, Tennant, and William James. In Reformation teaching its function as the response to revelation is stressed.

Falda. A white vestment worn only by the Pope and only on solemn occasions. It is worn over the cassock.

Faldstool. A folding stool used by prelates in the sanctuary when they are not occupying the episcopal throne.

Fall. In the history of Christian thought, the concept of the Fall has been most commonly understood in literalistic terms as an historical event. Adam and Eve were persuaded by Satan (under the guise of a serpent) to disobey God, as a result of which not only were they expelled from the paradise of the Garden of Eden and Adam condemned to tilling the ground by the sweat of his brow and Eve to the pains of childbirth, but the entire human race, being tainted by inheritance of their sin, are conceived and born in sin. (See **Original Sin.**) This concept of the inheritance of sin was minimized, however, by the Greek Fathers (notably Theodore of Mopsuestia), while Augustine, on the contrary, emphasized it. Since his authority was much recognized both in medieval Catholic theology and by the Reformation Fathers, his outlook on this subject has prevailed in the West until comparatively recent times. In the light of modern evolutionary understanding of creation, which Christians can see as "God's way of doing things," the mythological character of the Adam-and-Eve story is seen as excluding the notion of the Fall as an historical event. Nevertheless, rejection of the historicity of Adam and Eve does not exclude belief that human beings, having the power to choose freely how they act, have often acted wrongly in the past and that this has created certain tendencies to do the wrong rather than the right. Such a belief excludes, of course, the notion that human beings are by nature inclined to act ethically till they are led astray by environmental causes. It also fits the traditional Christian view of Redemption, according to which Christ's redemptive work is necessary for all human beings, since all are "fallen" in the sense of belonging to a race that is so situated that it cannot progress morally or spiritually without such divine intervention. The doctrine of the Fall, interpreted in some such way, is by no means at odds with a modern evolutionary understanding of the universe or with the state of affairs that we perceive in human society.

Fallacy. In order to reason validly one must discover what invalid reasoning is. The word "fallacy" is from the Latin *fallacia,* meaning "fraud" or "deceit"; but fallacies may be perpetrated unintentionally as well as intentionally, i.e., by sloppy thinking as well as by intent to deceive in order to achieve some political or other aim. Plainly, fallacies are as varied and as numerous as are failures to think clearly. Nevertheless, some have been traditionally well recognized and should be known to all stu-

dents in every scholarly and scientific discipline. Among these are the following: (1) *Argumentum ad populum,* i.e., the use of highly emotive language calculated to coerce the readers or hearers into accepting a view without any evidence but merely by acting upon their feeling, e.g., "No civilized person would ever seek to cause unnecessary suffering to a fellow human being and much of the language we hear by those advocating stiffer penalties for violent criminals shows that they do not understand this, but I know that you will elect me to represent you in Congress because I, like you, want to uphold the principles of compassion and humanity that have made this nation great." (2) *Argumentum ad baculum,* i.e., the use of threat such as "If you persist in teaching that view you will find everyone against you and then it will be too late for you to change your views." (3) *Argumentum ad hominem,* i.e., the attempt to discredit the reasoning because of the character of the person who is using it. (4) *Post hoc ergo propter hoc,* i.e., arguing that because event B followed event A, A must be the cause of B, e.g., "The incidence of crime in the West is greater than it was when Christianity came to prevail in the West, therefore Christianity generates crime." (5) *The Double Question,* i.e., "Have you stopped lying?" (6) *Petitio principii,* or "begging the question"; i.e., arguing in such a way as to assume what you are required to prove. These are among the commonest fallacies; others exist that are too numerous to list; but these well-known ones illustrate the importance of being on the lookout for fallacious reasoning, not least in religious contexts.

Fallibilism. The doctrine expounded by Charles Peirce, according to which absolute certainty, universality, and exactness cannot be attained in any area of human inquiry; nevertheless human inquiry is capable of moving toward such goals.

False Decretals, The. A collection of documents attributed to Isidore of

Seville but in fact composed in France some two centuries later, i.e., *c.* 850. It contains a mixture of spurious and authentic documents. Widely used to defend the claims of the Papacy, they were generally assumed in the Middle Ages to be all genuine. That they are predominantly spurious was shown by Flacius and the other authors of the *History of the Christian Church* published in the mid-16th c. Scholars today unanimously recognize the spuriousness of most of the documents and the falsity of their attribution to the 7th c. Isidore.

Falsifiability. That propositions and hypotheses must be verifiable is a recognized principle in modern science and philosophy. A hypothesis that is incapable of being verified is barren and useless because meaningless. (Some critics of religious and metaphysical propositions object to them on the ground of their unverifiability.) Karl Popper has suggested, however, that falsifiability is a better criterion. A falsifiable proposition is one that can be disproved by negative instances. If no negative instances can be found, we can remain at least open to the meaningfulness and the truth of the propositions.

Family of Love. A sect (also called Familists) founded by H. Nicholas. They were seemingly pantheistic and antinomian in tendency. Despite persecution under Elizabeth I, they survived till about the end of the 17th c.

Fanone. A collar-like garment worn by the Pope over his amice when he celebrates a solemn pontifical Mass.

Farabi, al. Early 10th c. Muslim philosopher. He was in the tradition of the Islamic school at Baghdad, whose aim was the reconciliation of Platonic and Aristotelian concepts. He taught that God is the One in whom essence and existence coincide. He followed Aristotle in his demonstrations for the existence of God. He saw logic as the foundation of philosophical studies and

theological inquiry. His writings include *Commentary on Aristotle; Philosophy of Plato and Aristotle; and Short Commentary on Aristotle's Prior Analytics.*

Farel, Guillaume (1489–1565). French Swiss Reformer. He came under the influence of Jacobus Faber (Stapulensis) in Paris as a student. In 1530 he introduced Reformation teachings and practice at Neuchatel and in 1535 in Geneva, which led eventually to his close association with Calvin.

Farrar, Frederick William (1831–1903). Anglican divine. Influenced by F. D. Maurice, he held several teaching and ecclesiastical appointments before being appointed Dean of Canterbury in 1895. His writings, notably his *Life of Christ* (1874), had a very wide reception and made him one of the most popular ecclesiastical figures in the England of his day.

Farrer, Austin Marsden (1904–1969). Anglican theologian. Educated at St. Paul's School, London, and at Balliol College, Oxford, he was for many years Fellow and Chaplain of Trinity College, Oxford, and latterly Warden of Keble College. From his undergraduate days he was a convinced Anglo-Catholic. He was made an Honorary Fellow of Trinity in 1963 and a Fellow of the British Academy in 1968. His many writings include *Finite and Infinite* (1943), *The Glass of Vision* (1948), *A Rebirth of Images* (1949), *A Study in St. Mark* (1951), *The Freedom of the Will* (1958), *Love Almighty, Ills Unlimited* (1961), and several posthumously published works. See also Philip Curtis, *A Hawk Among Sparrows: A Biography of Austin Farrer* (1985), Geddes MacGregor, *Apostles Extraordinary*, Chapter 4, "Austin Farrer" (1986), and I. Crombie's article in *Dictionary of National Biography*. Farrer was an exceptionally gifted mind and a highly original and incisive thinker. Although primarily a philosophical theologian, he made incursions into New Testament studies in which his originality and independence of mind were no less manifest.

Fasting. Fasting has a long history in Judaism in which it was practiced sometimes with great severity. John the Baptist followed this Jewish tradition. Jesus both practiced it and recommended it. The Didache mentions Wednesday and Friday fasts. The Lenten fast, originally brief, was by the 4th c. extended to forty days in many places. The Eastern Church observes three periods of fasting other than Lent and still imposes fasting with some of the primitive rigor associated with the practice.

Fasting in the Roman Catholic Church usually consists of eating one full meal at about midday and then a small meal ("collation") in the morning and evening. The only two fast days retained in the Roman Catholic Church are Ash Wednesday and Good Friday. In some of the religious orders, however, such as the Carthusians and the Cistercians, rigorous fasts are still observed. Fasting is recognized in the Anglican Communion as a salutary practice, especially under the influence of the Tractarian movement, although otherwise for the most part left to the individual conscience. The purpose of fasting is generally taken to be the strengthening of the spiritual life by the minimizing of the pleasures of the table. It has also been traditionally believed to diminish the urges of the flesh. It is to be distinguished from abstinence, which consists of abstaining from particular kinds of food, e.g., red meat, all meat, or all non-vegetable food, and which is traditionally practiced with rigor in some of the ancient religious orders and in a modified form on certain days by the faithful in general. See **Abstinence.**

In Buddhist tradition, fasting plays an important role. The basic regulation for monastic communities forbids eating between noon and the following morning, although water may be drunk during that period. The general principle underlying such regulations and appli-cable to all, whether in the monastic state or otherwise, is one that enjoins restraint at all times in eating rather than engaging in notably long total fasts. Three of the thirteen practices enjoined as means for cultivating spirituality relate to food: (1) eating one meal a day, (2) eating only from an alms bowl, and (3) refusing second helpings. Buddhist teachers emphasize, however, that such practices have little value in themselves; their value lies in the internal attitude of restraint that they externally express. They are recommended because they minister to the attainment of serenity and peace.

Within Hinduism we find, predictably, a variety of views on fasting, but it is widely recognized as important in spiritual development. The Jains emphasize it in addition to their severe and extreme form of vegetarianism. In Islam, the fast during the holy season of Ramadan is obligatory on all other than those who are too sick to engage in it without danger to health. It is a fast to be strictly observed from that time in the morning at which it is possible to distinguish a white from a black thread till that time in the evening at which it is no longer possible to do so. The practice is one of the "Five Pillars" of Islam. The prohibition extends also to all sexual activity during the hours of fasting. Islam is, however, not a religion that encourages asceticism in principle; Ramadan is important, rather, as a commemoration of an event in the life of Muhammad. The fasting is succeeded at sundown by much festivity and merrymaking. The role of fasting and attitudes toward it vary considerably, even radically, among the religions of the world.

Fatalism. The notion that all things happen because of inexorable destiny, entirely governed by a principle of necessity beyond human control. The concept is very ancient. In Greek and Roman mythology fate takes the form of three goddesses (Greek, the *moirai;* Latin, the *fata*), one of whom spins the thread of life, the second twists it, and the third snips the thread, so that together they totally govern human destiny. There are echoes of the concept in later philosophical and religious systems, such as (1) the predestinarianism found in Islam (*kismet,* the will of Allah) and some Christian theologies and (2) the determinism in certain philosophical systems. Contrary to a common popular misunderstanding, *karma* is not at all a fatalistic doctrine. It is, on the contrary, one that emphasizes individual freewill, the exercise of which is the cause of one's individual circumstances. (See **Karma** and **Reincarnation**.) No freedom of choice, of course, can operate except within a "given" of some kind within which certain choices are freely exercised; freedom implies acting within a set framework. See **Freedom** and **Determinism and Indeterminism.**

Father. A mode of address widely applied to priests in both Eastern and Western usage. In continental Europe, however, it is not usually applied to the secular clergy. In France, for instance, a parish priest is addressed as "Monsieur le Curé" in Italy as "Don". In the English-speaking world it is widely used of all Roman Catholic priests and may be applied with propriety even to priests who bear some ecclesiastical title or rank. Benedictine and other monks were traditionally "Dom" (*Dominus*). The Pope is popularly known as "the Holy Father." Anglican practice varies. Some Anglican priests prefer to be called "Mr." or "Dr." as the case may be, but the use of "Father" as a mode of address is widespread, especially in the United States. "Reverend" is not a mode of address; it is a title used similarly to the way in which "Honorable" is used of certain civic officials, so is used only in writing and then with the Christian name, e.g., "The Reverend John Smith" or "The Reverend Father John Smith." "Padre", commonly used of military chaplains, is of course simply the Italian form of "Father".

Fathers of the Church. From about the end of the 5th c., when the great Christian writers of the earlier centuries were increasingly carrying authority in the Church, the term "Fathers" had come to be common usage for those writers who commanded special respect. Those so designated were acclaimed not only for their learning but usually also for the Church's general acceptance of their teachings and for their holiness of life. The period known as "patristic" is a vague one, but the extreme limit must be placed at about the end of the 8th c. (See **Patristics.**) Since the 17th c., those Fathers who came immediately after the New Testament period have been called the Apostolic Fathers. Although for complex historical reasons Origen, who was both the most original theologian and the most learned biblical scholar of his age, might seem not to qualify, not having the Church's universal acceptance, he certainly would be included by modern scholars as among the Fathers. The designation is in any case not one bestowed by any ecclesiastical authority but rather by acclamation or common consent, as was largely the case with the recognition of saints in the early Church before the formal process of canonization was developed. See **Canonization.**

Fatima. A Portuguese town famed as a place of pilgrimage since 1917 when, on May 13, three illiterate children aged 10 to 13, saw a lady who reappeared to them on five later occasions claiming, on the last of these, to be "Our Lady of the Rosary." She enjoined them to say the rosary daily and asked that a chapel be erected in her name. Only one of the three survived childhood. She became a Carmelite nun and wrote two accounts of the visions she and the others had seen as children. The place is now marked by a basilica and shrine. A "secret" is believed to have been imparted, which was not to be revealed till 1960. Its publication, however, has been indefinitely postponed. The illiteracy of the recipients of the vision is considered apposite, since the rosary devotion was originally intended primarily for those who could not read.

Faustus. Late 4th c. Manichaean, native of Milevis, under whom Augustine studied while he was a Manichaean.

Faustus. (*c.* **408–*c.* 490**). Abbot of Lérins and later Bishop of Rhegium (Riez) in Provence. His Semi-Pelagian teachings were condemned at the Second Council of Orange in 529.

Fawkes, Guy. (**1570–1606**). The best known member of the conspiracy known as the Gunpowder Plot. A Yorkshireman, he became a Roman Catholic and joined the Spanish army. He was arrested on November 5, 1605, while keeping watch on the cellar where the gunpowder intended to blow up King and Parliament had been hidden. Under torture he revealed the conspiracy and was executed (with the other participants in the conspiracy) on January 31, 1606.

Fayumic. A dialect of Coptic used in Middle Egypt in early Christian times. The New Testament was translated into it and some fragments of the version are extant.

Feasts of the Church. Traditionally, a feast (Latin, *festum*) is a day on which the Church celebrates an important event in Christian history, commemorates a saint, or otherwise engages in a specific act of Christian rejoicing. It is opposed to a feria which is a day on which either nothing particular is celebrated or commemorated or else (as on Good Friday) a day of mourning is observed. Feast days may be (1) movable or (2) immovable. The dates of the former vary according to a scheme used for the Calendar; the dates of the latter are invariable. Among movable feasts Easter and Pentecost are the most notable examples, while Christmas is the best known example of an immovable feast. Notice is taken of festal days both in the Eucharist and in the Office for

the day by a proper, i.e., a special form of prayers and other liturgical acts. Every Sunday is technically a festal day, commemorative of the Resurrection and observed from very early Christian times. In 321 Constantine proclaimed it a holiday as it has been ever since in all Christian countries and in countries in which Christianity is the predominating religious faith. Since 1969 the Roman Catholic Church has recognized three levels of importance in the special days of the Christian Year; (1) Solemnities (*solemnitates*), the most important; (2) Feasts (*festa*), next in importance; and (3) memorials (*memoriae*), of less importance than (1) or (2). Traditionally, the Roman Catholic Church recognizes "feasts of obligation," being those on which the faithful are required to attend Mass and to abstain as far as practicable from manual labor, more especially gainful employment. All Sundays are feasts of obligation. The list of others varies to some extent from place to place.

Febronianism. An 18th c. movement in Germany that may be considered the counterpart of Gallicanism in France. It was directed chiefly against the more extravagant claims of the papacy, particularly those in the temporal realm. It sought to confine the papacy to the general administration of the Roman Catholic Church and to keep ecclesiastical affairs as far as possible in local hands. A work under the pseudonym of "Justinus Febronius" (J. N. von Hontheim) was published in 1763 to set forth the views of those who argued for the movement. The following year it was put on the Index of Forbidden Books. The movement received considerable support, but by the end of the 18th c. it had largely faded.

Fechner, Gustav Theodor (**1801–1887**). Psychologist and philosopher. Educated at Leipzig, he became professor of physics there in 1834. His thought grew towards panpsychism and panentheism. He saw human freedom as compatible with God's dominance in this way: God is constantly involved in the process of surpassing himself; he suffers in the struggles of humanity, yet as supreme being he is in no sense the source of evil, which is the work of creatures exercising their limited autonomy within the all-inclusive Being of God. In God is a polarity principle; he is both unchanging essence and a changing and developing existence. Among Fechner's works are *The Little Book of Life After Death* (1836), *On Physical and Philosophical Atomic Theory* (1853), and *The Three Motives and Grounds of Faith* (1863).

Feeling. The terms "feeling" and "to feel" are used in a large variety of ways and often very vaguely, not least in religious discourse, in which their use can be confusing or worse. I can be said to feel a velvety sensation in my hand or a pain in my colon; I can feel angry or sick or bored or insulted or unable to move or that something strange is going to happen or that you hate me or even that there is a ghost in the room. Is "I feel angry" distinguishable from "I am angry"? Philosophic discussions on the subject of feeling focus principally on how feelings can be identified and described and distinguished from one another. Is our knowledge of the world attained through feelings and if so to what extent? I feel what I call a toothache and it is painful to my consciousness, but does the feeling correspond to a state of affairs independently of my awareness? If we say it does, how are we to account for hypochondriac reports as when I claim that I feel a toothache only when I see my mother-in-law? Only I can feel my "own" pain; how then can I rely on your word that you have a pain, let alone sympathize with you in having it? You may feign both pain and pleasure with dramatic skill. Moreover, the fact that one feels pain or pleasure is not in itself any warranty for anything beyond the fact that one feels it. When one relates, however honestly, that one felt delicious shivers down one's back at

a religious meeting, one's hearers cannot be justified in deducing any more than that account says. If the reporter deduces more, then some reason or circumstance other than feeling is necessary to warrant any such further claim. To use feeling as the calculus of the religious value or importance of an experience is as misguided as basing the validity of an argument on the pleasure one may derive from listening to its being propounded. Historically, both "feeling" and "passion" have been understood in a variety of ways, depending on the philosophical system underlying their use. For example, Descartes, as a rationalist, sees the passions as modes of the "thinking substance" while Condillac, as an empiricist, seeks to derive everything in human experience from sensation.

In Buddhist thought, feeling (*vedanā*) is one of five primary groups of aggregates (*skandhas*) into which human personality is divided. In this sort of literature, feeling is subdivided in various ways, e.g., the physically agreeable/disagreeable and the mentally agreeable/disagreeable.

Feet, Washing of the. This ceremony, commemorating the action of Jesus (John 13), called in Latin *pedilavium*, has been performed on Maundy Thursday from at least early in the Middle Ages, being mentioned in the 17th Synod of Toledo in 694. At first restricted to great cathedral and abbey churches, it has come to be much more generally observed. During the singing of antiphons, twelve men are brought into the sanctuary and the celebrant of the Mass washes and dries the feet of each one in turn.

Felicity. 2nd c. Roman martyr. According to an early tradition she was martyred with her seven sons.

Felicity. Late 2nd c. African martyr. She was martyred in 203 along with Perpetua.

Felix. Early 7th c. missionary. Born in Burgundy, he went to England where he preached in East Anglia. According to Bede he was Bishop of Dunwich (a place in Suffolk, now virtually submerged) for 17 years. His relics are preserved in Ramsey Abbey. The Suffolk town of Felixtowe takes its name from him.

Felix. 9th c. Bishop of Urgel, Spain, he was one of the leaders of the Adoptianist movement. Charged many times with heresy, he appeared to recant more than once but seems never to have inwardly renounced his views.

Fénelon, François de Salignac de la Mothe (1651–1715). Writer and ecclesiastic. Educated at Saint-Sulpice, Paris, his distinguished early career included the tutorship of the grandson of Louis XIV, the Duke of Burgundy, to which he was appointed in 1689. For his pupil he wrote his famous *Télémaque* in 1693, a novel with a political purpose in which he taught that kings exist for their subjects, not subjects for their kings. In the French court, dominated by Madame de Maintenant, he had undertaken, at the suggestion of Bossuet, to refute certain philosophical views of Malebranche. Having become Archbishop of Cambrai in 1695, he began developing mystical ideas he had encountered through his friendship with Madame Guyon into a sort of Christian Neoplatonism adapted to the spirit of his age. He set forth his ideas in his *Maxims of the Saints* (1697). Bossuet attacked his views as incompatible with Christian orthodoxy. Under Bossuet's influence, Louis XIV banished him from the court and in 1699 Pope Innocent XII condemned his book. In the Jansenist controversy that was rekindled soon afterwards, Fénelon issued several pastorals against the Jansenist teaching on grace. According to contemporary testimony he was a man of immensely impressive bearing, a combination of earnestness and courtly elegance, of learning and nobility, gravity and wit. Not a profound thinker, he was a man of deep spiritual perception and apparently unforgettable personality.

Ferdinand, V. (1452–1516). Son of John II of Aragon, he married his cousin Isabella of Castile, so uniting the two kingdoms when he succeeded his father in 1479. He was shamelessly unscrupulous in his political actions and insatiably ambitious. The designation "Ferdinand the Catholic" was accorded him chiefly because of his leadership in the notorious Spanish Inquisition.

Ferguson, Adam (1723–1816). Scottish philosopher. One of the members of the Scottish "Common Sense" school, he was professor of "pneumatics" and moral philosophy at Edinburgh, 1764–1785. Like most of the Scottish thinkers of his time he had many contacts with France. He visited Voltaire, and was much admired by Victor Cousin, who rated him a moralist above all his predecessors. His chief writings are his *Institutes of Moral Philosophy* (1769) and his *Principles of Moral and Political Science* (1792).

Feria. In ecclesiastical usage a feria is a day in the Church Calendar on which there is no feast. See **Feast.**

Fermentum. In 5th c. Rome fragments of the eucharistic bread from the Mass celebrated by the Bishop of Rome were sent on Sundays to the various parish churches in Rome, symbolizing the unity of the People of God. The practice continued in a modified form for several centuries.

Ferrar, Nicholas (1592–1637). See **Little Gidding.**

Ferrar Group, The. A group of New Testament manuscripts dating from the 11th to the 15th c., probably of Calabrian provenance, having a text that exhibits certain affinities with the Caesarean textual family. The story of the woman taken in adultery (John 7:53–8:11), known to modern scholars not to belong to John's Gospel, is placed in these manuscripts after Luke 21:38.

Feuardent, François (1539–1610). Patristic scholar. Born in Coutance, he studied at Bayeux and Paris, became a Franciscan priest, and wrote extensively against Calvinist teachings. His editions of the Fathers are of historical importance.

Feuerbach, Ludwig (1804-1872). Philosopher. Born in Landshut and educated at Heidelberg and other German universities, he studied at Berlin under Hegel. In his writings he contended that religion consists essentially in the projection of human qualities and aspirations into an object that is worshipped and called by some name such as God. By recognizing this, one finds that if anything is to be worshipped it is humanity. This does not at all mean that humanity is perfect; it does mean that it has infinite potentialities as can be shown from history. Belief in personal immortality is as much wishful thinking as is belief in God. His works include *On Philosophy and Christianity* (1839), *The Essence of Christianity* (1841), and *The Essence of Religion* (1845). In their interpretation of the nature of religion, both Marx and Freud echo, each in his own way, a similar view of its essence.

Feuillants. In the 16th c., the Cistercians of Le Feuillant, a monastic house near Toulouse, had grown very lax. The Abbot de la Barrière introduced a reform even stricter than the original Cistercian practice. Those following it were formed into a new order called Feuillants and recognized as independent in 1589, about which time a similar order for women was organized, members of which were called Feuillantines. The Italian branch of the Feuillants were called Bernardines. The order ceased to exist about the beginning of the 19th c.

Fichte, Johann Gottlieb (1762-1814). Idealist philosopher. After his theological studies at Jena, he was introduced to Kant's thought and travelled to Königsberg to meet him. In 1792 he wrote a book, *Critique of Revelation*, from whose title page his name was inadvertently omitted, resulting in its being widely assumed to be by Kant. The lat-

ter, in reviewing the book favorably, corrected the omission. Fichte was professor at Jena from 1794 till 1799, when he was dismissed on the grounds of alleged atheism. A champion of freedom of thought, he is generally regarded as the father of German idealism. He gave "practical reason" priority over "pure reason" (using Kant's terms), making idealism spring from the moral will. The primacy of moral awareness demands a world in which we can act morally and fulfill our duties, which entail, Fichte argued, a spiritual world. Indeed, the empirical world is merely one that we postulate in order to surmount the obstacles we find in our way and that call for surmounting. The function of government in a society is to preserve the freedom and the rights of every member. God is not a supreme Being, set over and against the world as Source, Creator, and Cause, but, rather, the essence of all that is. His earliest work is his *Attempt at a Critique of all Revelation* (1792). Others include *The Foundation of Natural Rights* (1796), *A System of Ethics* (1798), and *Way to a Blessed Life* (1805), his principal work on the philosophy of religion.

Ficino, Marsiglio (1433-1499). Christian humanist. Born at Figline near Florence, his natural talents were noticed by Cosimo de'Medici who, under the influence of Gemistus Plethon, had conceived the project of founding an academy in the Platonic tradition. Ficino eventually did a new translation of Plato's works, published in 1483-1484. It remained for at least a hundred years the standard Latin translation. In 1473 he had sought priestly ordination (somewhat hesitantly, it would seem), for his vision was of a Platonic form of Christianity in the Alexandrian tradition: a synthesis of the biblical teachings with the noblest in Platonic and Neoplatonic thought. He published a work expounding his ideal, *De Religione Christiana* (1477). He was appointed a canon of Florence in 1484 and did extensive translations of Neoplatonic and other writers. Christian humanists from many parts of Europe consulted him, including Reuchlin in Germany and Colet in England. His greatest philosophical work, based largely on Plato's *Phaedo*, is on the immortality of the human soul: *Theologica Platonica de Immortalitate Animorum*, which was published in 1487.

Fictionalism. The name sometimes given to a philosophical method proposed by Hans Vaihinger, which he called Idealistic Positivism, although it is also aptly known as "the philosophy of 'As If'." Developing a Kantian theme about the nature of ideas, he held that our most important ideas are mental constructs adapted to our human minds but not necessarily conforming to the facts. They are mental conveniences enabling us to deal with problems that confront our inquisitive minds in our quest for orderliness. We hold the concepts however, only "as if" they were realities. Such are the concepts that we form in all disciplines: in physics and economics, in mathematics and law, in philosophy and religion. Only by recognizing the fictional nature of our concepts in all fields of human inquiry can we hope to come nearer to the realities we pretend to grasp.

Fidei Defensor. This title, meaning "Defender of the Faith," was conferred by Pope Leo X on King Henry VIII in 1521 in recognition of a treatise by the latter (composed with the help of John Fisher) defending the doctrine of seven sacraments against that of Martin Luther. The English Parliament recognized the title in 1544, and it has been an official title of all British sovereigns from then to the present day, corresponding to designations such as "Catholicus" formerly borne by Spanish monarchs.

Fideism. A term used by Auguste Sabatier and other Protestant theologians to designate their theological outlook in which the intellect was held totally incapable of attaining knowledge of God.

The term came to be used in a pejorative sense by their opponents, especially on the Roman Catholic side.

Fides Quaerens Intellectum. (Latin, "faith seeking understanding.") A phrase expressing the view of Augustine, which Anselm followed, on the nature of faith and its relation to knowledge. *Credo ut intelligam* ("I believe in order that I may understand") also expresses that approach.

Field, Frederick (1801–1885). A Cambridge man, he was one of the most eminent biblical and patristic scholars of the 19th c. He was a member of the Old Testament company for the Revised Version of the English Bible. Among his works is a learned edition of Origen's *Hexapla* (1875).

Field, John (1545–1588). Leader of an extreme Puritan group in the Church in Elizabethan England, for which he suffered imprisonment and other penalties.

Field, Richard (1561–1616). English divine, Dean of Gloucester, and learned author of an influential treatise, *Of the Church* (1606, 1610), in which he argued for the Anglican case against Rome. He was closely associated with other great Anglican divines of his day, such as Hooker and Savile.

Fifth Monarchy Men. An extremist sect whose members, in the time of Oliver Cromwell, sought to bring in the millennium, in which Christ would reign with his saints for a thousand years. (The "Fifth Monarch" was an allusion to Daniel 2:44). The leaders were eventually beheaded and the sect disappeared.

Figgis, John Neville (1866–1919). Anglican divine, much influenced by Lord Acton and one of the earliest of Christian thinkers to perceive the dangers to society, not least to Christian society, of the totalitarian state. In 1907 he entered the Community of the Resurrection at Mirfield. He lectured extensively and his writings include his *Civilization at* the *Crossroads* (1912), *Some Defects in English Religion* (1917), and his posthumously published *The Political Aspects of St. Augustine's "City of God"* (1921).

Filioque. Although the Great Schism in 1054 between Eastern and Western Christendom was unquestionably due to differences of long standing at that time, the phrase *filioque* ("and the Son") that the Latins added to the Nicene Creed (the Holy Spirit . . . proceedeth from the Father *and the Son*), has been traditionally viewed as that which brought about the schism. The phrase is not a part of the original form of the Creed and is not to be found anywhere till very late in the 6th c. and then only in very limited circles in the West. Not till the 9th c. did it come to be generally used in the Mass by monks in the Frankish Empire. About the middle of that century some of these monks used it in their house in Jerusalem, shocking Eastern monks in Palestine. The matter was put to the Pope (Leo III), who, although he did not formally repudiate the doctrine implied in the addition of the phrase, not only tried to discourage its use but had the Creed in its original form engraved on two silver tablets placed at St. Peter's Tomb. Nevertheless, the *filioque* continued to be used liturgically, and by the beginning of the 11th c. its use had been introduced at Rome itself. The basic objection to it on the part of Eastern Orthodox theologians has always been that in the Godhead there is a single fount or source of all that is divine. The Holy Spirit, therefore, issues from the Father, who is the Ground or Source of all Being. The doctrine implied in the *filioque* addition is technically called the Double Procession. Although it is associated with the West, whose theologians have followed the lead of Augustine, who expressed an opinion favoring it, it has had supporters and opponents on both sides. Cyril of Alexandria, for instance, upheld it. The Greeks, however were theologically subtler in their handling of such questions than were the

Latins, and the question is more complex than it tends to appear. Certainly it ought never to have been the focus of a controversy dividing the Church. Anglican theologians have traditionally argued for the *filioque*, but here again opinions on the subject vary. See **Double Procession** and **Florence, Council of.**

Fire Baptized Holiness Church. A Christian group organized in Atlanta, Georgia, in 1898 and claiming several thousand members.

Firmilian. A 3rd c. Bishop of Caesarea in Cappodocia, he journeyed to Caesarea in Palestine, to study under Origen, whom he greatly revered.

Fish. See **Ichthys.**

Fisher, John (1469–1535). Bishop of Rochester and Chancellor of the University of Cambridge, he opposed Henry VIII's proposal to seek divorce. Henry eventually had him beheaded on June 22, 1535. A learned divine, he was much esteemed by the theologians of his day.

Five Pillars of Islam. In Muslim practice, contradistinguished from doctrine, five fundamental duties are recognized. These are called the "Five Pillars" and are as follows: (1) The obligation of all Muslims to confess their faith and witness to it publicly. This is done primarily in the recitation of the *shahada: la ilaha illa'llah muhammadun rasulu'llah:* "There is no god but Allah and Muhammad is his Apostle/Prophet." These are the words enunciated by the muezzin atop the minaret of the mosque. (In some places today it is done by electronic means.) Strict orthodox Islamic teachers insist that the words must be repeated aloud, understood perfectly, believed fully in the heart, professed till death, accurately recited, and recited without hesitation or other defect. (2) Daily prayer at dawn, noon, mid-afternoon, evening, and night. Muslims are encouraged to use a prayer rug and they must face Mecca as they kneel and prostrate themselves in saying the prescribed prayers. On Friday (which approximately corresponds to the Jewish Sabbath and the Christian Sunday), public prayer is held at the mosque under the leadership of the *imam*. The faithful remove their shoes, perform the prescribed ablutions, and sit quietly while the *qari*, a reader, reads passages from the Qur'ān. Mosques have a marker to indicate the direction of Mecca, toward which the faithful turn. These are minimal prayer duties for Muslims. Additional ones are expected. (3) Fasting during the month of Ramadan is required of every Muslim. (See **Fasting**.) (4) *Zakat* (almsgiving) is a sacred obligation, corresponding approximately to the tithes imposed on Jews and Christians by biblical authority. It consists of giving a fixed portion of one's income to the relief of the poor and other worthy causes, usually one fortieth. This duty is a basic expression of the general Muslim requirement of social responsibility. (5) *Hajj* (pilgrimage) is an obligation on all whose circumstances permit the journey to Mecca. The performance of this pilgrimage is extremely valuable in welding together the Islamic world. The Muslim who has gone to Mecca to perform this duty receives the title of *hajji* and is treated with much respect. Students of the religions of the world easily perceive in the spirit and structure of these fundamental duties of the faithful Muslim profound influence from the Bible and Jewish tradition. Some Muslims (e.g., the Kharijites, an extremist sect) add a sixth pillar: *jihad*, holy war. Most Muslims treat *jihad* as a duty to propagate the faith energetically rather than by the sword, but the latter interpretation can find its defenders. Islam rigorously imposes a total ban on the consumption of alcohol and pork. Gambling is no less strictly prohibited. Polygamy is permitted. The maximum number of wives is specified as four. Women are not only prohibited from being heard in the mosque; they are not permitted to be seen: a place is reserved for them where they are hidden from view. Muhammad was, however, a staunch defender of the rights of women as he perceived them, and of all persons considered to be defenseless in society.

Flacius, Matthias (1520–1575). Lutheran theologian. He held views on the depravity of human nature that were widely perceived as exaggerated, and in his later years he moved about a great deal, finding little support in the mainstream of Lutheranism for his teachings. He was the principal author of a history of the Church (*Historia Ecclesiae Christi*) published at Basel (1559–74) that presented Christianity as having degenerated from its early purity to the corruptions that were the result of papal power-mania. He was an important figure in the Reformation.

Flagellation and the Flagellants. Whipping was such a universal form of punishment in the ancient world, being used as a standard means of correction for schoolboys and for the punishment of criminals and other public offenders, that it was taken over in monastic houses and other Christian institutions as a matter of course. The Rule of Saint Benedict, for instance, prescribes (c. 28) that a monk who repeatedly disobeys the rule is to receive "the punishment of the rod." Whipping was indeed a standard punishment for both monks and nuns and the full power to order it was vested in the superiors of religious houses. The rod was in regular use in medieval schools as it had been for centuries in the ancient Roman ones and was often administered with great severity. See **Discipline**.

The practice of self-flagellation grew during the Middle Ages and was widely admired, especially among the unlearned, as a manifestation of a contrite heart and penitential spirit. From there the transition to the use of the rod as a penance ordered by a confessor to his penitent was a natural one, so that whipping in one form or another came to be associated in the public mind with repentance and making amends for sin. Although by no means the only form of penance it was, to say the least, one of the standard ones. The emergence, therefore, of groups of men in Italy in the middle of the 13th c. who paraded themselves in procession, whipping their bare backs as they recited one or more of the seven penitential psalms, was not an unexpected development. The declared purpose was not only to win spiritual merit for themselves but to offer the pain as a sacrifice in propitiation for the sins of the world. Such processions of the flagellants, as they came to be called, were condemned by the ecclesiastical authorities, presumably on the ground of their seeming fanatical and exhibitionist. In 1348, however, with the widespread terror of the plague that was spreading through Europe, bands of flagellants reappeared, this time all over Europe. In Germany they became a distinctive sect or appeared to be one, seeming to be disseminating heretical opinions to the effect that their practice was more effectual than the Church's sacraments. Such practices have since reappeared on a much smaller scale from time to time in Roman Catholic countries and instances of them occur in some Spanish-speaking cultures even today.

Flavian. Early 5th c. Patriarch of Constantinople, who in 448 excommunicated Eutyches for his extreme form of monophysitism. The following year, however, through pressure from the Emperor, the excommunication was lifted at the Latrocinium at Ephesus, where Flavian died a few days later.

Fléchier, Esprit (1632–1710). French preacher, who won favor at the court of Louis XIV and in 1673 was elected a member of the *Académie Française*. In later life he became successively Bishop of Lavaur and Bishop of Nîmes.

Fleury, Claude (1640–1723). Ecclesiastical historian, author of the first grand scale history of the Church, his *Histoire*

ecclésiastique (1691–1720), a twenty-volume work that not only commanded deservedly great admiration in his own day but is still an important source. It was placed on the Index of Prohibited Books, because of the Gallican views it expressed, along with other works of Fleury. A gifted man of much influence in the France of his day, he held various important positions and in his last years was appointed confessor to the young Louis XV.

Fleury. An ancient Benedictine foundation in France, whither, according to legend, the bones of Benedict and Scholastica were brought from Monte Cassino after the Lombard invasion of Italy. It became a celebrated center of study, especially after coming under the control of Cluny early in the 10th c. It is also known today as Saint-Benoît-sur-Loire.

Flood, The Biblical Account of the. Stories closely paralleling what is in Genesis have been for long well known to scholars, notably the one in the Gilgamesh epic. That the biblical account may well have a basis in historical fact is suggested by excavations at Ur and Kish that have provided evidence that the Tigris-Euphrates region was subject to extensive flooding.

Florence, Council of. This important General Council, held at Ferrara, Florence, and Rome in 1438–1445, had as its principal aim the union of the Greeks with the Latins. Agreement was very difficult, especially on the filioque clause in the Creed. The Greek Church was especially eager to achieve union in order to get support against the Turks, who were already endangering Constantinople when the Council was convened. At last, on July 5, 1439, a Decree of Union (*Laetentur Caeli*) was signed and solemnly promulgated the following day. Only one bishop (Mark of Ephesus) declined to sign. After the Greeks had left, however, the Council continued to work while the Greeks had to face popular opposition to the union among their own people in Constantinople. As a result, many of the older Greek bishops repudiated the union. When Constantinople fell to the Turks in 1453, the union that had seemed such an ecumenical triumph collapsed. Not all, however, was lost, for at least the Council established an important principle: that unity does not depend on liturgical uniformity and that a variety of liturgical usages can exist (as they do now) within a common ecclesiastical structure.

Fogazzaro, Antonio (1842–1911). Italian writer whose religious views were accounted too "liberal" by the Roman Catholic Church, which put his principal work, *Il Santo* (1905), a novel, on the Index of Prohibited Books. He was among those who sought to show evolution as the way in which divine creation is accomplished.

Font. A bowl, usually of stone, for the water used for baptism. Where baptism by affusion is practiced, as is general in the West, it is often fairly small, but in the Eastern Church, where infants are immersed, it has to be large enough to receive a child's body. The font usually stands near the narthex, symbolizing the admission to the Church that baptism provides, and may be in an enclosure of some kind or even (especially in Mediterranean countries) in a separate building. See **Baptistery.**

Fools, The Feast of. In the Middle Ages, especially in France, on January 1, the people gathered for festivities that parodied the liturgy of the Church and because of their appearance of mockery of sacred rites were frowned upon by the Church authorities, who from time to time sought to suppress them. The practice disappeared about the middle of the 16th c.

Forbes, Alexander Penrose (1817–1875). After serving in the East India Company he entered Oxford in 1840 and, under the influence of Pusey, he decided to seek ordination as an Anglican priest. Pusey nominated him for a parish in Leeds and shortly afterwards he was elected Bishop of Brechin in the Scottish Episcopal Church. During the rest of his life he worked so indefatigably to bring Tractarian principles into the life of that Church that he came to be called "the Scottish Pusey." His chief writings were practical books for clergy and people. In accordance with the expectation of his age and circumstance, he was a scholarly bishop, although not of the scholarly caliber of his brother George Hay Forbes.

Forbes, George Hay (1821–75). Brother of Alexander Penrose Forbes, he was the victim of a crippling paralysis. Ordained priest in 1849, he became the faithful pastor of a parish while working at his patristic and liturgical studies, which soon bore impressive fruit in scholarly publications from the printing press he set up as a parish priest. They ranged from work on Gregory of Nyssa to studies in ancient liturgies of the Gallican Church that he did with J. M. Neale, a distinguished contemporary Tractarian.

Forged Decretals. See **False Decretals, The.**

Form. This term, of paramount importance in the history of Western philosophy, translates the Greek term *eidos*. (The ancient Greeks greatly admired that which has or gives shape.) For Plato, the individual thing takes its being from the interaction of receptacle and form, imitating the eternal form in which it participates. These imitations of the eternal form, participating as they do in it, reflect its reality, yet are no more than a reflection of it. Aristotle repudiated the Platonic view that forms exist independently of the receptacle with which they react, except in the unique case of God. For Aristotle form is still identified with reality, but since it is not separable from the substance that contains it, its role is different from that which it has in Plato. Some of the earlier medieval thinkers were more

Platonic or Neoplatonic than Aristotelian in their treatment of this question, but Thomas Aquinas followed Aristotle so closely on this as on many other points that the Thomist treatment of it hardly differs in any fundamental way from that of Aristotle. Duns Scotus, on the other hand, laying emphasis on the "thisness" (*haecceitas*) of each individual existent, departs notably from the Aristotelian-Thomist stance. William of Occam went further, regarding form as merely the structure of the material parts of the individual existent. Kant also saw form as structure, but for him matter is identified with sensation, and form is identified with the concepts that order sensation. Kant saw space and time as the pure forms of sensibility and saw the categories (quantity, quality, relation, modality, and their subdivisions) as the pure forms of the understanding.

Formgeschichte. A term used by a German school of biblical analysts, meaning literally "form history" and often rendered in English as "form criticism" or "form analysis". It consists of the attempt to find the origin and trace the history of a particular passage of the Bible through an analysis of its structure. The most notable pioneer in the use of this method was Hermann Gunkel, who at the beginning of the twentieth century applied it to his study of Genesis. He then extended his use of the method to the Psalms, leading him to perceive these expressions of Hebrew poetry as having a long history, having taken shape in oral tradition and fully developed before the Exile (586 BCE). The same method continued to be used by other scholars, who extended it to the entire Bible, but most particularly to the Gospels. Johann Weiss, Martin Dibelius, and others of this school analyzed the Gospels into various literary forms (e.g., preaching, teaching, narrative) and saw the brief homily as central and the most ancient of these forms. A little later still Rudolf Bultmann and other scholars significantly developed the same methodology in a more detailed way, enabling them to classify the Gospel stories as (1) models for preachers, (2) miracle stories, (3) sayings of Jesus, and (4) various narratives. By the use of such methods one can see the Sermon on the Mount, for instance, as a collection of sayings attributed to Jesus rather than as the actual text of a particular homily addressed to a particular audience at a particular time. The use of the principle behind the method, although (like other methods) susceptible to exaggeration, is now widely recognized by biblical scholars as a standard way of understanding the Bible. Its proponents stress the fact that the interests and needs of the Christian community at the time when the New Testament writings were composed in approximately their present form inevitably color the way in which the stories are presented. They are at the very least as much the product of the life of the Christian community as they are its inheritance.

Formula Missae et Communionis. Luther and his associates were liturgically conservative. The document under this name that Luther put out in December 1523 (prepared for him by N. Hausmann, Pastor of Zwickau) left the traditional Latin Mass in some respects almost unchanged. The general form was such that superficially it looked much like that traditional service. Nevertheless, important changes were made in the canon of the Mass and elsewhere to accommodate theological differences, especially the denial of the hitherto much emphasized concept of the Mass as the sacrifice of Christ on the altar. The *Formula* was, moreover, not obligatory but for guidance only. It was the basis of Luther's German Mass (1526) and later Lutheran liturgies.

Forsyth, Peter Taylor (1848–1921). English Congregationalist divine. His writings include *The Person and Place of Jesus Christ* (1909), in which he makes use of the kenotic theories of his day and develops them in a striking way; *The Work of Christ* (1910), which considers the doctrine of the Atonement as entailing the travail of God as well as man's reconciliation with him; and *The Justification of God* (1916). His ideas have been influential among generations of theological students.

Fortescue, Adrian (1874–1923). Roman Catholic liturgist. Ordained priest in 1898, he eventually built a church at Letchworth, England, that became a noted center of liturgical life. Among his writings are *The Orthodox Eastern Church* (1907) and *The Mass* (1912). His *The Ceremonies of the Roman Rite*, first published in 1918, became a very widely used guide to the liturgical details of ceremonies connected with the celebration of the Mass. Although now outdated by liturgical changes in the wake of the Second Vatican Council, it is still much consulted by Anglo-Catholics and others for practical guidance as well as by historians of liturgy.

Forty Hours. See **Quarant'Ore.**

Fossor. A Latin word, meaning "gravedigger". In early Christian practice the *fossor* was an important official in the Christian community, regarded as having at least a quasi-clerical status in the Church. The *fossores*, before the fall of Rome in 410, had organized themselves into corporations that handled the sale of places in the catacombs and the adornment of tombs.

Foucauld, Charles Eugène de (1858–1916). French explorer and priest. After service in the army he became fascinated by Africa and engaged in expeditions to North Africa, the nature of which is recounted in his *Reconnaissance au Maroc* (1888). Having undergone a spiritual transformation, he made a pilgrimage to the Holy Land in 1888–1889 and in 1890 entered the Trappist monastery of Notre-Dame-des-Neige. Seeking a more eremitical life than the Trappists provided, he lived for some years as a servant of the Poor Clares in the Holy Land, was ordained priest in France in 1901, and shortly thereafter went to Algeria where he lived the life of a hermit. He was greatly revered there by both Muslims and Christians for the sanctity and spiritual power of his life, and his example has remained a strong influence on those inclined to his way of life.

Foucher, Simon (1644–1696). Born in Dijon and educated at the Sorbonne, he was an opponent of Malebranche. He turned the skeptical tradition in Western philosophy against philosophy itself, in the interest of exhibiting the basic doctrines of the Church as self-evident. Among his writings are *On the Wisdom of the Ancients* (1682) and *Essays in the Search for the Truth* (1693).

"Foundations." In 1912 a theological symposium by nine Oxford scholars (with an Introduction by B. H. Streeter) was published under this title as a "statement of Christian belief in terms of modern thought." Its influence was powerful at the time, but conservative reaction in the Church inevitably ensued. The Roman Catholic scholar R. A. Knox, noted for his wit, responded characteristically with a book bearing the satirical title *Some Loose Stones* (1913).

Fountains Abbey. This English Cistercian foundation near Ripon, Yorkshire, emerged in 1132 as an offshoot of York and increased rapidly in numbers. At the Dissolution of the Monasteries at the Reformation, it was the richest of all the Cistercian houses. Today its remains provide an unequaled example of the architectural glories of the Perpendicular style as well as much else besides.

Four Noble Truths and the Noble Eightfold Path. In Buddhism there are four basic principles, the first two of which show how to diagnose what is amiss in one's human condition and the remaining two serve to show what is to be done about the situation. (1) All human existence is *dukkha*, a state of misery; (2) the root of this misery is *trishna*, that endless craving for this or that, the gratification of which merely begets more and more of the craving and so perpetuates the misery. (3) The way to abolish the misery is to abolish the craving, which is accomplished by (4) following the Noble Eightfold Path. The latter consists of (1) right understanding, (2) rightmindedness, (3) right speech, (4) right action, (5) right livelihood, (6) right effort, (7) right meditation, and (8) right emancipation. The aim is to make a final break from the fetters of *karma-saṁsāra*, the cycle of rebirths, which Buddhists regard as a weary round that binds one to the misery of imprisonment in the travail of human life as it is lived by the vast majority of people. Salvation is attained only by emancipation from the psychological constraints that bind us to the karmic chain. Buddhism is fundamentally a method of enabling the psyche to break free from the conditions that enslave it. It has in many respects the character of an analytical psychology. The specified aim is the attainment of *nirvana*, which means literally a "snuffing out", i.e., a snuffing out of the cravings and other impediments that circumscribe us and inhibit our emancipation.

Fox, George (1624–1691). Founder of the Society of Friends, called Quakers. During the civil and religious unrest in 17th c. England, many spiritually minded people felt uneasy with, if not disillusioned by, the Church. Fox, the son of a Leicestershire weaver and apprenticed to a shoemaker, gave up his apprenticeship in 1643 because he believed he had received a call to break with all earthly relationships, even of those closest and dearest to him, so that he might go on a quest for spiritual enlightenment. While many of his generation, finding in the Church no satisfaction for their hunger, had turned instead to the Bible, Fox found that even the Scriptures, helpful though they were in his quest, did not provide what he needed. Three years after his quest had begun he felt he had found it in a total reliance on what he came to call the Inner Light, the interior presence of the living Christ in his soul. He ceased to attend the services of the Church and instead went about preaching that if men and women will look into their souls they will find there the eternal truth they seek. In 1649, he was imprisoned at Nottingham, and he and his many followers suffered much persecution in the ensuing years. Fox, however, had not only unusual patience and perseverance but considerable talent for organization. From Swarthmore Hall, which he had made his home in 1652, he developed his Society into an organized, clearly identifiable, and growing movement. His personal charisma attracted many wherever he went and eventually he journeyed to other countries, first to Ireland in 1669, then to America and the West Indies, and in 1677 and 1685 to the Netherlands. His *Journal*, from which we get a great deal of our understanding of his spiritual struggle and outlook, was first published posthumously in 1694. His pilgrimage and the resolution of his struggle are reminiscent of the sages of India, notably that of Gautama Buddha; yet Fox's religious outlook was not only christocentric but in many respects hospitable to traditional orthodox teaching on the Person and Work of Christ. Among Fox's disciples was William Penn, founder of Pennsylvania.

Foxe, John (1516–1587). Martyrologist. An Oxford man and Fellow of Magdalen College (1539–1545), he was sympathetic to the Reformation cause. Having fled to the continent of Europe on the accession of Mary Tudor, he met other refugees and in 1554 wrote a history of the persecution of Protestants, which was later expanded into his *Acts and Monuments of Matters Happening in the Church*. This work, which came to be widely known and extremely popular as "Foxe's Book of Martyrs," had as its chief purpose an account of the sufferings of Protestant martyrs under Mary's reign and their remarkable fortitude under persecution.

Despite some exaggerations such as are common in works of this kind, it presented a substantially true account of the outrageous persecution of upholders of the Reformation cause under that ignorant and willful queen, and it was written in a readable style that much helped its appeal to readers in those Protestant households in which it had for centuries a place along with the Bible and Bunyan's *Pilgrim's Progress*.

Fraction. The term used by liturgists for the liturgical ceremony of the breaking of the bread at the Eucharist. In some rites it is a more elaborate ceremony than in others, but it is an integral part of the Eucharist, having its scriptural authority in the words of Jesus at the institution (e.g., Matthew 26:26), which indeed made the Eucharist known from the earliest Christian times as "the breaking of the bread." The traditional observance takes place after the Lord's Prayer, when the priest breaks the Host into three pieces, including a very small one, which is dropped into the chalice. Since 1969, practice within the Roman Catholic Church has slightly changed the place of the Fraction in the Mass.

Franciscan Order. The order of mendicant friars founded by Francis of Assisi in 1209 is one of several orders of friars founded in the Middle Ages and distinguished from the older orders of monks (e.g., the Benedictines) by their much greater mobility and their lack of detachment to the land, which in time made them more internationally minded. Like all religious orders, they took vows of poverty, chastity, and obedience, but (especially at first) they insisted on an extreme literalism in their interpretation of the vow of poverty. In contrast to other orders who understood it merely as depriving the individual member of the order of any right to the

personal possession of anything (which in the case of the members of very rich ancient abbatial foundations could leave them with access to much grandeur, even opulence), Francis wished his entire organization to be poor so that its members might be true mendicants, literally begging their bread. He took this to be the essence of the spiritual life. A story is told that when a novice asked whether he might own at least a little prayer book, Francis replied "no" on the ground that to own even a prayer book would make him capable of sitting on his chair like a great prelate and telling his brother to fetch him his prayer book. Many disputes arose over the interpretation of "poverty". In 1317–1318 two papal bulls allowed corporate ownership by the order, which was a decision against the smaller and stricter party (called "Spirituals"), many of whom fled, calling themselves "fraticelli". Further disputes, however, arose, e.g., between the Observants (a stricter party) and the Conventualists (a laxer one). In the 16th c., another reform movement occurred, resulting in the establishment of the Capuchins in 1529 as a separate order emphasizing the original ideals of Francis. Not the least remarkable feature in the history of the Franciscans is that, established early in the 13th c. as a company of poor men making not the slightest claim to even the most elementary kind of learning, they had become before the close of that same century prominent among the intellectual leaders of Europe.

Francis of Assisi. (1181(?)–1226). Founder of the Franciscan Order, he is probably the most generally popular of the saints of the Roman Catholic Church, commanding admiration as much outside it as within it. The son of a rich cloth merchant in Assisi, he led the conventional life of a young man in his station, but eventually he was drawn to prayer and the service of the poor. On a pilgrimage to Rome he found beggars with one of whom he exchanged clothes and tried to experience for a day or two what it meant to be utterly penniless and helpless. In 1208 at the church of the Portiuncula near Assisi, he heard read the words of Christ enjoining his followers to leave all and follow him in poverty. Discarding his customary clothes he donned a simple garment girded with a cord and set out to obey Christ's command literally. He drew up a simple rule for those who wished to follow his example and eventually, on a visit to Rome, obtained papal approved of it. In 1212 Clare, a neighboring noblewoman, founded a similar organization for women. After the order had been fully organized, with provinces and administrators, in 1217, Francis withdrew from the leadership, so as to devote himself more and more to a life of personal devotion. He is said to have received the Stigmata in September 1224 and he died two years later in the chapel of the Portiuncula. The love and admiration he has evoked by his simple piety and his compassion for all living creatures has surpassed even the veneration he has received among those able to appreciate the quality of his personal spirituality. See **Franciscan Order.**

Francis of Sales (1567–1622). Born in the castle of Sales in the Savoy, France, he was ordained priest in 1593. In 1602 he became Bishop of Geneva. The following year he met and became the spiritual director of Jane Frances de Chantal, with whom, in 1610, he founded the Visitandines. His *Introduction to the Devout Life* (1609), intended for people living in the world and seeking to lead a deeply spiritual life, is a great classic of Catholic spirituality. Traditionally, the attainment of the highest form of spiritual life had seemed confined, with rare exceptions, to men and women living in the cloister, and Francis did much to foster the notion that the ideal could be fulfilled by those living in the world.

Francis Xavier (1506–1552). The son of a noble Spanish-Basque family, he was born in Navarre and, having met Ignatius Loyola while at the University of Paris, he became with him one of the seven "founding members" of the Jesuits, who were ordained together at Venice in 1537. He eventually became perhaps the most famous of all missionaries in the history of the Church, being known as "the Apostle of the Indies" and "the Apostle of Japan." Although he studied many of the languages of the peoples of India and Japan, vast numbers among whom he converted to the Roman Catholic Church, he seems to have had little or no appreciation for the spirituality of the religions out of which he took his converts. Judged by the number of his converts, however, his missionary success was spectacular.

Franzelin, Johann Baptist (1816–1886). Jesuit and cardinal. An Austrian, he took a very prominent part in preparing the First Vatican Council. Among his many works is his *De Divina Traditione et Scriptura* (1870).

Fraser, Alexander Campbell (1819–1914). A student of Sir William Hamilton at the University of Edinburgh, he eventually succeeded him in 1856. He was an assiduous student of the works of Berkeley. Among his works are his Gifford Lectures, *The Philosophy of Theism* (1895–1896).

Fraticelli. A name adopted by and applied to those Franciscans who left the mainstream and who were also called "spirituals". See **Franciscan Order.**

Frederick I (Barbarossa) (c. 1122–1190). Holy Roman Emperor. Seeing himself in the tradition of Charlemagne, Barbarossa tried at first to secure peace between the Empire and the Papacy, for he was in his own way a conservative churchman. He was also, however, a soldier and a ruler who saw domination and conquest as a ruler's duty. During his lifelong conflict with the Church, in the course of which he became an extremely powerful figure, he ended by asserting the rights of the Empire against the claims of the Papacy.

Frederick III (1463–1525). Elector of Saxony and, because of his reputation for probity and justice, known as "the Wise." From his youth he had become interested in the humanist movement and saw the urgency of the need for the reform of the Church. It was he who, having founded the University of Wittenberg, invited Luther and Melanchthon to teach in it. He greatly helped Luther in various ways in the course of the latter's persecution by the Roman Catholic authorities, providing him with powerful protection.

Frederick III (1515–1576). Elector Palatine of the Rhone, he was commonly called "the Pious." Having been from his youth inclined to the Calvinist form of the Reformation, he had the Heidelberg Catechism drawn up in 1563, which he imposed on all his subjects, Lutheran and Catholic. As a staunch advocate of the Reformation, he sent military and financial aid to the Protestants in France and the Netherlands.

Free Church of Scotland. At the Disruption in 1843, about a third of the ministers and people of the established Kirk separated from it to become an independent Presbyterian body. In 1900, this group joined with the United Presbyterian Church to form the United Free Church, which in turn, in 1929, was reunited with the ancient Kirk. The reunited Kirk retained the official designation: Church of Scotland. See **Disruption, The, Sabbatarianism,** and **Wee Frees.**

Freedom. The concept of freedom is one of the most important in the history of philosophy. It looms large not only in religious philosophy but also in, for example, modern nihilistic existentialism. Freedom is the quality of being unconstrained by necessity or fate in making one's decisions and doing one's deeds. The English word means "the state of being free." John Barbour, a 14th c.

Scottish poet wrote: "Freedom all solace to man gives:/He lives at ease that freely lives." But what precisely is freedom and to what is it opposed? In both Plato and Aristotle, the freedom of human beings is assumed in the sense that we are not entirely circumscribed by an ineluctable and predetermined destiny. We can, within limits, make our own destiny. This is also very clearly the teaching of the ancient writers of India in the upanishadic tradition: the law of karma, far from determining our destiny or our fate insures that by an external law of balances we shall reap what we sow and *are* reaping what we have sown in the unimaginably long history of our existence through a long chain of embodiments. The classic Christian theologians in the West inherited the assumptions of philosophers in the Platonic-Aristotelian tradition in respect of freedom of choice. Augustine distinguished, in his *De libero arbitrio*, between *liberum arbitrium*, the ability to make a choice, be it evil or good, and *libertas*, which is the right use of that choice. For in Christian thought one is not truly free till one is doing the will of God and doing it gladly and willingly. The medieval theologians had a problem in reconciling human freedom with the foreknowledge of God: if God knows all things he must know that John will do good deeds and Peter evil ones, so in creating us he must will that this is how things will turn out. Then can we be said to be free? Calvin stressed the notion of predestination in the divine economy, and Thomas Aquinas recognized it hardly less than did Calvin; yet both held that human freedom is real in the temporal order in which we live. Luther tended to depreciate the role of human freedom, while Erasmus upheld its importance. The Renaissance humanists, e.g., Pico della Mirandola, held that it is human freedom that distinguishes humankind from all other finite entities in the universe, giving man a unique position in it. In modern philosophy various refinements have been introduced into the concept of freedom, e.g., in Peirce, in Whitehead, and in Bergson. Modern existentialists, both deeply religious ones such as Kierkegaard and nihilistic, atheistic ones such as Sartre, emphasize freedom in such a way as to make it one of the pivotal points of this type of philosophy. In opposition to the strong tradition of indeterminism in Western thought is a determinist outlook. (See **Determinism and Indeterminism**.) On a strictly determinist view nothing in the universe that ever happens could have happened in any way other than the way it has happened. Democritus for instance held that the physical universe is entirely so determined that everything that occurs has a casual necessity behind it. Epicurus, although adhering in general to that view, allowed for certain exceptions. Hobbes and others followed this general deterministic outlook. The concept of freedom of the will is often misunderstood. All freedom, including human freedom, must be limited by circumstance. A bird is free to fly; a horse is not. Neither horses nor birds are free to enjoy the freedom that is inherent in the human mind; yet human freedom is also patently limited. I might jump six feet or even seven if a good athlete, but no human being could jump seventy. My mind is no less restricted. There are limits to what even a mathematical or linguistic genius can do. All freedom, then, is limited by circumstance and only within these circumscribed limits is any freedom possible. Yet it is precisely that freedom that is important in assessing the quality of life. Christianity is by no means the only religion in the world that recognizes freedom as of infinite importance in understanding the nature of man and his possibilities, but it would be unintelligible apart from some concept of freedom of choice. See **Predestination/Election**.

Freemasonry. An international brotherhood whose ritual represents certain esoteric teachings. The language typically used about a Supreme Being who is the "Great Architect of the Universe" reflects 18th c. modes of thought, but freemasonry is of greater antiquity, derived from the craft organizations of the British free-stone masons. It is probable that in the Middle Ages a "qualified" mason seeking work at a new location and having no diploma or trade union ticket to establish his authenticity, as such a craftsman might have today, would use certain gestures, handshakes, and the like, recognized within the craft and kept secret among them. In the late 17th c. some declining lodges of masons accepted antiquarians interested in architectural history with a status such as today we might call "honorary" members. Such men would in many cases contribute speculative ideas culled from ancient sources and containing mystical and esoteric ideas going far back into antiquity and relating to topics such as the building of Solomon's Temple.

Practice and outlook vary to some extent. Generally speaking, in the English-speaking world freemasonry usually conserves a distinctly religious character, although reflecting both the Deism fashionable in the 18th c. and an esoteric tradition that tends to look upon all religions with favor yet as mere outward expressions of a common inward truth that is conserved in the "craft" of masonry. Many presidents of the United States have been masons. Men of high office or standing in Great Britain have usually been chosen for the leading roles in masonry in that country. Many leading Anglican and other churchmen have also been and are freemasons.

In continental Europe, however, the situation has been considerably different. There freemasonry has generally functioned in open rivalry with the Roman Catholic Church and in such a way as to make membership of the one incompatible with membership of the other. From the other end of the spectrum, the Communist Party has also looked on freemasonry with suspicion.

The basic rituals deal with the three basic stages leading to the degree of master mason (the two lower ones being respectively "apprentice" and "fellow craft") and symbolically represent the progress of the candidate from darkness into light. Beyond the level of "master mason," however, are numerous other levels or ranks, some with distinctively Christian motifs, at least in the terminology that they employ. Freemasonry is noted for its charitable work and the sense of brotherhood that the practice of its ideals produces among those who live according to them.

Free Presbyterian Church of Scotland.
The Free Presbyterian Church of Scotland consists of those members of the Free Kirk of Scotland, who left it in 1892. It claims more than six thousand members in Scotland and has congregations also in England and overseas, and it is bound by doctrines established in 1643, which include the doctrine that the Pope is Antichrist ("that man of sin and son of perdition") and that the Mass is an abominable corruption. They also observe Sunday with extreme rigor, refusing to perform any commercial transaction, such as selling gasoline or mailing a letter. If there is to be a pick-up on Sunday they will not mail a letter on Saturday, since to do so would implicate them in the Sabbath-breaking of those who will pick it up on Sunday. In 1988, the Lord Chancellor (Lord Mackay of Clashfern) whose office in the British legal system is so exalted that he has official precedence over even the Prime Minister, happened to be an elder of that Presbyterian body and was disciplined by it for the offense of having attended a Requiem Mass on two occasions, which he averred he did out of respect for two deceased colleagues. Proceedings were taken against him by the Synod of the denomination. Lord Mackay, widely admired for his judicial temper and exceptional clarity of mind, elected to plead his own case before the church tribunal. He lost. The Synod demanded his repentance, which the Lord Chancellor saw no reason to offer. He was suspended for six months. At some point in the course of the proceedings he was further accused of having sent a Christmas card: a practice disapproved by this body which accounts the observance of Christmas profane. At a later stage he resigned his membership. The judgment of the Synod was in line with recent decisions: only a year or so earlier a young business man was banned from receiving communion because he had been shown to be a member of a golf club that permitted golf on Sunday although the man in question never played on that day. A prominent minister had been suspended for three months for having asked a fellow cleric, a Roman Catholic, to declare open an educational conference they were attending, which constituted an offense since no Free Presbyterian is permitted to have even a casual friendship with a Roman Catholic, clerical or lay. See also **Wee Frees**, a slightly later denomination.

Frere, Walter Howard (1863–1938). A distinguished Anglican liturgical scholar, he sought to encourage English rather than Roman use. He was Superior of the Community of the Resurrection (Mirfield) from 1902 to 1913 and from 1916 to 1922 and Bishop of Truro from 1923 till 1935 when he retired to spend his remaining years at Mirfield.

Freud, Sigmund (1856–1940). Austrian founder of psychoanalysis. There is no doubt of his enormous influence on modern thought, including Christian thought, despite the fact that he was radically hostile to religion in general and Christianity in particular, as can be seen in, e.g., his *The Future of an Illusion* (1927). His primary interest was in psychotherapy. In the course of his clinical medical work with neurotic and psychotic patients, he developed a hypothesis that in man's psychological structure three "regions" may be distinguished: the ego, the id, and the superego. The ego is the center of what we may call rational awareness. The superego arises from the pressures of society, with all the moral prescriptions, directives, and inhibitions that all societies impose. From the id comes the libidinal flow into the psyche. This libidinal energy is, in Freud's view, predominantly sexual. The ego, therefore, is caught between the id and the superego and so tries (usually with limited or no success) to come to terms with both. When the pressure is too great from both the id and the superego, the ego represses the id's demands by relegating them to the unconscious. The unconscious, although much emphasized by Freud, was already a well recognized phenomenon before its birth. As Freud sees this religion of the psyche, it functions as a sort of lumber room, a dark and generally neglected place containing what was originally in the consciousness but, because of the pressure from the superego, has been stored in the unconscious in the vain hope of its being forgotten. Far from this occurring, that which has been relegated to the unconscious region of the psyche continues to affect consciousness in innumerable ways, all hidden from our awareness. Some of the energy repressed in the unconscious may be sublimated in creative work of one kind or another, but often this fails to work, resulting in neurosis, which only skilled psychoanalytical therapy can cure. The cure is effected by bringing the stored energy back into consciousness, so eliminating its poisoning effect. According to Freud, one of the most basic among the repressed desires that are pushed into the unconscious is the Oedipus/Electra complex: the desire of the son for his mother and of the daughter for her father, which of course the superego will not tolerate. Religion provides a solution of sorts by projecting the father/mother with all the love and moral demands involved on to a vast, cosmic scale. By this means, however, the individual is kept through life in a kind of imitation childhood, avoiding neurosis only by clinging to a mass fantasy that is itself neurotic in character. Freud sees religion, therefore, as false therapy. It may save the individual

from being precipitated into psychic disaster, but the cost is enormous: it is the cost of remaining, in effect, forever a child. On Freud's view, sexual fulfillment is the permanent remedy. Much of Freud's theory was developed not only in a very patriarchal society but in one of a particular type (that of the 19th c. German Jewry that was his background), so that his theories do not necessarily work in other kinds of social structure. Nevertheless, much of what he contended for is now widely recognized, even by those who may find his contentions highly exaggerated, especially as represented among his followers. Neither Christianity nor any of the other great religions of the world has ever underestimated the enormous power of the sexual drive in men and women; they have viewed it, however, as one of the circumstances of human life that provide the opportunity for sublimation, making spiritual evolution possible although by no means automatic or inevitable. On the Christian view, a genuine sublimation of the sexual and other basic drives is a coming to terms with reality and an achieving of adulthood and personal maturity of spirit. This by no means implies that the sublimation is always successful, and so Freud's portrayals of religion as a neurotic escape does represent the situation in many cases that are all too familiar to experienced pastors in all branches of the Church and indeed to all spiritually mature and perceptive observers. See **Psychology of Religion.**

Friars Minor, Order of. See **Observants.**

Frideswide. Early 8th c. saint, patroness of both the university and the city of Oxford. Although she seems to have been associated with Oxford before the foundation of the University, little is known with historical certainty of her life.

Friedrich, Johannes (1836–1917). Eminent Church historian. At the First Vatican Council he joined von Döllinger in resisting the definition of Papal Infallibility and left Rome as did many others. He continued to reject the decrees of the Council on Papal Infallibility and was excommunicated in April 1871.

Friends, Society of. See **Quakers** and **Fox, George.**

Friends of God. The name given to a 14th c. group of mystics among whom were Henry Suso and John Tauler.

Froebel, Friedrich Wilhelm August (1782–1852). Philosopher of education. He held education to be a natural development, as it had been in his own case, for he was self-educated, and that the function of the teacher is to evoke that natural desire of the human spirit to learn.

Frontal. The panel, usually of embroidered cloth, in front of the altar, the color of which is changed according to the season of the Christian Year.

Fructuosis. Early 3rd c. Bishop of Tarragona, burned at the stake in the amphitheatre, in the reign of Valerian.

Fruits of the Holy Spirit. In Catholic tradition (following Galatians 5:22f.) they are: love, joy, peace, longsuffering, gentleness, goodness, faith, meekness, temperance, modesty, continence, chastity. The last three are additions in the Vulgate, making the number twelve.

Frumentius. A 4th c. missionary to the Abyssinians. He was a staunch opponent of Arianism. Athanasius made him a bishop.

Fry, Elizabeth (1780–1845). Early Quaker and prison reformer. Born at Norwich, England, she married Joseph Fry, a Quaker, and had a large family, becoming at the same time a recognized Quaker minister. She became interested in the plight of convicts and the condition of prisons and did much to foster prison reform. She also worked hard to help the homeless and other needy people.

Fulbert (*c.* 960–1028). Born near Rome, he became Bishop of Chartres in 1007. He made the cathedral school of Chartres the greatest and most distinctive of all the great schools in Europe before the foundation of the universities.

Fulda. The Benedictine abbey of Fulda was founded in 744 and became a very important pilgrimage center and, under Rabanus Maurus, one of the greatest Christian centers in Europe. In 1802 it was secularized. Fulda became an episcopal see in 1829.

Fulke, Williams (1538–1589). Puritan divine. A Cambridge man, he became involved in the Vestiarian controversy, in which he encouraged the disuse of the surplice. He wrote treatises in defense of Puritan principles.

Fuller, Andrew (1754–1815). Baptist divine and an important force in the founding of the Baptist Missionary Society in 1792. He wrote against Deism and Socinianism and also against exaggerated forms of Calvinism, while defending Calvinist principles.

Fuller, Margaret (1810–1850). American Transcendentalist. Born at Cambridge, Mass., she was educated by her father and showed signs of intellectual precocity, reading Latin at six and many European languages when in her teens. In 1840, with the help of Emerson and others, she founded *The Dial* as an organ of the New England Transcendentalists. While in Boston she also conducted philosophical classes for women, through which she helped to advance recognition of the intellectual capacities and needs of women. Among her works are *Woman in the Nineteenth Century* (1844). In 1846 she traveled in Europe and eventually took up residence in Italy where she married the Marquis Giovanni Angelo Ossoli, a follower of Mazzini. In the siege of Rome (1848–1849) she took charge of one of the two hospitals while her husband fought on the walls. In 1850 they both embarked for the United States, but the ship was wrecked on the beach at Fire Island and both perished. A manuscript she much valued on the subject of Italy's struggle for freedom perished with them. She was indubitably a woman of extraordinary intelligence and ability who, despite the early and tragic fore-shortening of her life, was a pioneer, far in advance of her time, in the cause of the political recognition of women. She was also endowed with a spirituality in advance of her age and circumstances.

Fuller, Thomas (1608–1661). Anglican historian. A Cambridge man, he became Rector of Broadwindsor, Dorset, England and later Rector of Cranford. Among his works are his *Church History of Great Britain* (1655) and his posthumously published *Worthies of England* (1662).

Function. This term, now much used in symbolic logic, was already employed by Descartes in his analytical geometry in 1637. It was much used by Leibniz, who introduced it into mathematics in 1694. In 1734 Euler employed the now standard notation $f(x)$ for the function of the variable x. The concept of function introduces a number of factors such as variables, values or arguments of the variables, and the rules for assigning values to the variables. Derived from the Latin *fungi* (to perform or execute) it is used in modern logic to designate an expression involving one or more variable terms the meaning or truth of which is determined when the values of the variables are specified. In the philosophy of religion the term is used accordingly, e.g., one may talk of the function of aesthetic experience in religion or the function of ritual in the Eastern Orthodox Church contradistinguished from its function in Zen Buddhism.

Fundamentalism. This term is generally used by and applied to the followers of a movement within American Protestantism that arose toward the end of the 19th c. in reaction against scientific

progress, notably an evolutionary understanding not only of life but of the universe itself. Fundamentalists adopted "five points": (1) the verbal inerrancy of the Bible; (2) the divinity of Jesus Christ; (3) the Virgin Birth; (4) the substitutionary theory of the Atonement (i.e., that Jesus Christ died for us as a sacrifice for the sins of the world); and (5) the physical resurrection of Christ and his bodily return to earth on the Last Day. While the values that fundamentalists seek to conserve refer to doctrines traditionally taught in the mainstream of Christianity, those adhering to the principles as enunciated in such ways may injure rather than promote their vision by the methods they employ in pursuing it and by their simplistic understanding of the problems entailed in the beliefs. Unfortunately, the term has come to be widely applied to a literalistic approach to the Bible that is lacking not only in literary understanding but in religious depth.

Fylgia. In early Icelandic literature, a shape that accompanies a man through his life, resembling in many cases an animal and capable of leaving the body for temporary wanderings from it. It is a sort of astral body. Clairvoyants claim to be able to see it, and it also sometimes appears in dreams. The term is also used, however, for a female guardian spirit pertaining to a family. Valkyries (see **Valkyries**) sometimes function in this way, and in this role they may be seen as the counterparts of the Matres (divine Mothers) in Celtic lore and of the Vanir in Scandinavian mythology. See **Matres** and **Vanir**.

G

Galatia. This term is used in two distinct senses: (1) A region of central Anatolia lying between Pontus, Bithynia, and Lycaonia. In this case the name is derived from that of the Gauls who in the late 3rd c. BCE invaded Greece, Macedonia, and Asia Minor, finally settling at Anatolia; (2) A Roman province of the Empire that was established in 24 BCE that included the region of Galatia and also those of Pamphilia, Posidia, and part of Lycaonia. Prior to 24 BCE the name Galatia would have been understood in the first of these two senses; thereafter it would normally have been understood in the second sense. Because of the two senses of the term, New Testament scholars dispute to which Galatian community Paul's letter is addressed.

Galen, Claudius. (130–200 CE). Greek physician and philosopher, born at Pergamon in Mysia. In his youth he traveled extensively and studied the writings of the leading philosophers of his day. In later life he went to Rome where he was physician to the imperial household of Marcus Aurelius. His writings include *Institutio logica* and *Corpus medicorum graecorum*.

Galilee. A region occupying about 50 miles north to south and about 30 miles east to west, with the Jordan river and the sea of Galilee on the east, the Mediterranean on the west, the plain of Esdraelon on the south and Nahr el Qasimiyeh on the north. Its situation had made it a crossroads region from antiquity (Isaiah 8:23), and by the time of Christ it had a notably mixed population. It was a place of comparatively little importance for many centuries down to the time of Christ, and although it was the scene of most of the public ministry of Jesus, it is never mentioned in the New Testament except in the Gospels and in Acts 9:31. After 70 CE, however, it became a center of Jewish learning.

Galileo Galilei (1564–1642). Astronomer, born in Pisa and educated at the monastery of Vallombrosa near Florence and at the University of Pisa. After lecturing on philosophy and mathematics, he was censured in 1616 by the Holy Office (the Roman Congregation established in connection with the Inquisition) and admonished not to teach the "new" (see **Copernicus**) astronomy. (The Church authorities wished to uphold a geocentric view of the universe.) In 1632, however, after his dialogue on the alternative systems known in his day, he was summoned to Rome by the Inquisition to be examined on his teaching. Having arrived there in February 1633, he was examined on June 21, and the Inquisition held that his teaching as published contravened what had been decreed in 1616. The following day, June 22, Galileo read a recantation to the Inquisitors and was sentenced to imprisonment at the pleasure of the court but was eventually permitted to return to his home in Florence in what was virtually a form of house arrest. He was also required by the court to recite the seven penitential psalms once a week for three years as a penance. The popular legend that, having risen from his knees after making his recantation, he stamped the ground and murmured *"Eppur si muove"* ("And still it moves") is entirely without evidence, although of course it is likely to have been what he was silently saying to himself. His immense productivity continued till his death from a fever on January 8, 1642. Even apart from his numerous and highly important scientific discoveries, he had many natural talents; e.g., with his musical abilities and his gift for painting he must have had a Leonardesque versatility. It was in scientific discovery, however, that he made his mark. As early as 1581, as a teenager watching a lamp swinging in the Duomo of Pisa, he noticed that, whatever the range of its oscillations, they were always accomplished in equal times. His verification of this led to the discovery of the isochronism of the pendulum. He also discovered the principles of dynamics and he greatly improved the telescope, enabling him to make immense strides in an understanding of the principles of astronomy and a vast extension of knowledge of the Milky Way and the scope of the universe. His writings include *The Assayer* (1623), *Dialogue Concerning the Two*

Chief World Systems (1632), and *Dialogues Concerning Two New Sciences* (1636). For the last few years of his life he was blind; nevertheless he continued, so far as he could, his scientific inquiries. The Church's interference with his work, often regarded as a classic case of ecclesiastical obscurantism, must be understood in the context of his time; nevertheless, it remains a warning against hindering human inquiry merely because it looks as though it might upset currently held but unwarranted presuppositions.

Gallandi, Andrea (1709–1779). Patristic scholar. An Oratorian priest, he is the author of a major collection of the writings of the Christian Fathers of the first seven centuries, including many of the least well-known. His work, *Bibliotheca veterum patrum antiquorumque scriptorum ecclesiasticorum graecorum* (14 vols, 1765–1781) is of great value to patristic scholars.

Gallen, Abbey of St. One of the most famous of the Benedictine abbeys of Europe, it is about 9 miles SW of Rorschach and 53 miles E of Zürich. It owes its origin to Saint Gall, an Irish Hermit who in 614 built his cell in the forest there and remained till his death in 640. The monastery was developed and became a regular monastic foundation about the middle of the 8th c., becoming during the next three centuries one of the principal seats of learning in Europe. It still houses a library of great importance and one that has served scholars continuously for more than a thousand years.

Gallican Confession. The National Synod of Protestants at Paris adopted this, the *Confessio Gallicana,* in 1559. Written in French, it was based upon a draft by Calvin and contained a summary of his major teachings. It has sometimes been appended to French Protestant bibles.

Gallicanism. The name applied to the view, widely upheld in France and extending thence elsewhere, that the Roman Catholic Church is free of papal authority. Early proponents of this view, which had been taught at the Sorbonne from its inception, included Jean Gerson (1363–1429) and Cardinal Pierre d'Ailly (1350–1420). The French Church (*l'Eglise gallicane*) claimed special freedom from papal authority and the influence of Gallican principles remained strong in France down to the time of Napoleon. Even after the Restoration, when the ultramontanist view began, especially under Jesuit influence, to prevail, Gallican principles lingered and were still vigorously expressed (e.g., by Bishop Dupanloup at the First Vatican Council (1869–1870). Nor is its influence by any means extinct today, being represented not only in bodies such as the Old Catholic Church, but indirectly wherever resistance to the extreme centralization of authority in Rome has manifested itself within the Roman Catholic Church. It is closely linked to the conciliarist view, widely represented among medieval canonists, that a General Council of the Church has higher authority than the Pope.

Gallican Rite. Before the adoption of the Roman rite, in the time of Charlemagne, liturgical forms were used in Gaul that differ notably from Roman usage, being generally less crisp and exhibiting many signal differences in structure from the Roman sacramentaries. Because of the conflation of the Gallican with the Roman rite as early as the 8th c., the latter exhibits many Gallican features so that a study of the Gallican rite remains of great practical importance to liturgical scholars. The term "Gallican rite" is also used in a looser sense for all the non-Roman rites of the early Western Church and also for the "neo-Gallican" usages adopted in the 17th and 18th centuries.

Gamaliel. Grandson of Hillel and rabbinical teacher of Paul before the latter's conversion to the Christian Way. See Acts 5.34–40 and 22.3.

Gandhabbas. A Pali term (Sanskrit, *gandharvas*) for a class of celestial beings who form part of ancient Indian lore and were taken over in the early Buddhist scriptures. They are represented as the lowest class of *devas*. They are musicians of the celestial realm and attend the higher *devas*.

Gandhi, Mohandas Karamchand (1869–1948). Born in Porbandar, India, he was called to the English Bar and through his persistence in the practice of political resistance without violence (see **Ahiṁsā**) he eventually, in 1947, succeeded, at least in principle, in his aim of securing self-government for India. He was immensely revered by the masses, who saw in him a model of both ascetic holiness and moral virtue. He became known as Mahatma: a title signifying spiritual magnanimity. His adamant opposition to the use of force and his abhorrence of war-like measures of any kind, balanced with his immense diplomatic perceptivity and skill, made him a formidable and often incomprehensible figure to the British establishment of the time. He is by any reckoning to be numbered among the greatest world figures of the 20th c. He was assassinated in 1948.

Gaṇeśa. (Anglicized as "Ganesh" or "Ganesha".) The elephant-headed son of Shiva in Hindu lore. He has the elephant's ability to remove obstacles, so in popular Hinduism one seeks his help before embarking upon any difficult task. He is very learned in the Hindu scriptures and may be considered the god of wisdom. He is also good-natured, as is attested by his potbelly, suggesting a relish for food. Although he achieved a high status in medieval India, he was originally an animistic figure, possibly a sort of demon in popular primitive religion in India. Despite such lowly origin, however, he survived and prospered as an important deity, probably through his association with an ancient elephant cult.

Garden Tomb. Traditionally, the Holy Sepulchre in Jerusalem marks the site of the Crucifixion of Christ. In 1849, O. Thenius proposed another site lying outside the Damascus Gate, on the north wall of Jerusalem. It is often known as Gordon's Calvary, from the name of one of the strongest proponents of this opinion which, however, remains controversial among archaeologists. Nearby is a tomb, known to adherents of the theory as the Garden Tomb and taken by them to be the tomb in which Jesus was buried.

Gāthās. Versus of four lines, a collection of which constitutes one of the twelve divisions of the Mahāyāna Buddhist canon.

Gaudete. The third Sunday in Advent, so called from the opening word of the Introit. It is analogous with Laetare Sunday in mid-Lent, on both of which days rose-colored vestments may be worn.

Gaunilo. Name of an 11th c. French Benedictine monk whose critique of Anselm's form of the Ontological Argument is well-known. Anselm's response to it, however, is unfortunately sometimes overlooked. See **Anselm** and **Ontological Argument.**

Gautama. See **Buddha.**

Gay, John (1699–1745). Cambridge philosopher, forerunner of Utilitarianism. His writings include *Dissertation Concerning the Fundamental Principles of Virtue or Morality* (1731).

Gāya. One of the four holy places of Buddhist pilgrimage. It is a town in Bihar, North India, a few miles from the place where the Buddha received enlightenment under the bodhi-tree. The Buddha appears to have visited it several times during his ministry.

Geddes, Jenny. When on Sunday, July 23, 1637, the new Prayer Book designed for Scotland had been sent thither for use in Scottish churches, a tumult arose in St. Giles' Cathedral, Edinburgh, Scotland's premier church. According to a tradition that has been probably much embellished by legend, a woman called Jenny Geddes, who sold vegetables near the precincts, picked up her folding stool and threw it at the bishop's head during service by way of expressing popular indignation.

Gedo Zen. This term is given by Zen Buddhists to meditation practices outside the Buddhist framework, e.g., the Hindu Raja yoga, the "quiet sitting" of Confucius, and various practices in Christian mysticism.

Gehenna. The name (Aramaic *gehinnam*, representing the Hebrew *gehinnōm*) was originally geographical: that which divided ancient Jerusalem (Zion) from the hills to the south and west, i.e., the modern Wadi el Rababi. This valley had a bad reputation as the locus of a cultic shrine where human sacrifice was offered (II Kings 23.10). Jeremiah cursed it, predicting that it was to become the place where the corpses of Yahweh's enemies, those who rebelled against him, would lie. So in later Jewish writings, it became a symbol for a place where the wicked would go after death for punishment. In Esdras 7.36, it is represented as a burning furnace, lying within sight of paradise. In rabbinical literature it is more often regarded as a place of a purifying punishment rather than one of everlasting torture. Gehenna is mentioned several times in the New Testament as a pit or other place into which the wicked are to be cast and burned. This imagery was the basis for the doctrine of hell as traditionally developed in Christian theology. The imagery occurs frequently in the New Testament without mention of the name Gehenna but plainly derived from that association.

Geisteswissenschaften. This German term means "spiritual sciences" (e.g., ethics, aesthetics, value theory) contradistinguished from the *Naturwissenschaften* (physics, chemistry, etc.) and

seems to date from 1863, when it was used by von Schiel in a German translation of J. S. Mill's *Logic*.

Gelasian Sacramentary, The. This term is applied specifically to a very important mid-8th c. Vatican liturgical manuscript in which, for the first time, the feasts are arranged methodically according to the ecclesiastical calendar. The term is also applied, however, in a general sense to other manuscripts containing features similar to those that distinguish that Vatican manuscript. Contrary to a formerly held presupposition, such texts are not attributable directly or otherwise to Gelasius who was in the papal chair 492–496.

Gemara. A body of Jewish literature designed to amplify the Mishnah. See **Torah** and **Talmud**.

Gematria. A certain numerical value was assigned traditionally to each letter of the Hebrew alphabet. Some rabbis developed a manner of interpreting the Bible by counting the value of the letters in each word and using the result in the interpretation of a passage. Vestiges of the method occur in early Christian practice. For example, in Revelation 13.18, the writer of the Apocalypse, in designating 666 as the "number of the Beast" clearly alludes to the abhorred Roman Emperor Nero, whose name in Hebrew adds up, according to that method of computation, to this number.

Gemistus Plethon, Georgius (*c.* 1355–*c.*1450). Renaissance scholar. Born in Constantinople, he traveled to Western Europe at an early age, then returned to the east, settling at Mistra in the Peloponnese. He immensely revered Plato and, as a participant at the Council of Florence, he helped to overthrow the dominance of Aristotle that had been traditional in the West.

Genealogies of Jesus Christ, Two. Both Matthew and Luke contain genealogies of Christ. Both seek to establish the connection of Jesus Christ with the House of David. The two accounts, however, as they have come down to us, do not tally. Matthew's runs from Abraham to Jesus, Luke's runs from Jesus to Adam. There are many discrepancies, e.g., from David to Joseph they have only two names in common, Shealtiel and Zerubbabel. The one gives the natural descent of Joseph; the other gives his adopted descent. In Jewish law, legal paternity conferred all rights of natural paternity. The differences cannot be said to be explicable, except to the extent that Matthew's predictably directs attention to the interests of a Christian of Jewish background, while Luke no less predictably provides an account that would conform more to those of his fellow Gentiles. For further study of this subject, see M. D. Johnson, *The Purpose of the Biblical Genealogies with special reference to the Setting of the Genealogies of Jesus* (Monograph Series, viii, Society for New Testament Studies, Cambridge 1969).

General. This title is widely applied to the head of a religious order or congregation. Such dignitaries usually reside in Rome. The head of the Dominicans is called "Master General" and that of the Franciscans "Minister General." The General is elected by a general chapter of the order or congregation, usually for a period such as three or six or more years, but in the case of the Jesuits for life. The latter is sometimes called, in popular parlance, the "Black Pope." The term has also been traditionally used in many German churches in titles such as "General Superintendent." It is also used for the head of the Salvation Army.

General Judgment, The. See **Judgment, General and Particular.**

Genesis. From the Greek *genesis*, meaning "origin", opening and corresponding to the Hebrew word, *Bereshith*, this name is given to the first book of the Bible. Like other biblical books it is the result of a long and complex editorial process of compilation. Two distinct traditions can be easily discovered: the Yahwist and the Elohist, discernible by the respective use of the terms Yahweh and Elohim for God. The former is the dominant one, containing narrative relating not only to the patriarchal and later historical periods but to the mists of pre-history about which the Elohist component has nothing to say. The Hebrew word *Bereshith* is rendered to the Septuagint by the Greek words *en archē*, which may be understood as "archetypally".

Geneva Bible. A translation of the Bible into English published in 1560 and favored by the English Puritans and the Scots. It was the first English Bible to use the verse numeration invented by Rabbi Nathan a century earlier. It was widely used and only gradually superseded by the King James Version. It is known to book collectors and others as the Breeches Bible because of the rendering (Genesis 3.7) which, instead of calling the garment God made to cover the nakedness of Adam and Eve an "apron", calls it "breeches". It was the Bible of Shakespeare and the copy of it brought on the *Mayflower* to America is preserved at Harvard.

Geneva Gown. The black, loose-fitting gown worn by ministers in the Reformed tradition (e.g., Congregationalists and Presbyterians), although nowadays often replaced by an academic gown appropriate to the wearer. It is specifically intended as attire symbolic of the preaching office.

Genevan Academy. A famous school founded in 1559 by John Calvin with the approval of the City Council and the pastors at Geneva as a college for the education of theologians. Its first Rector was Theodore Beza. In 1872 it was enlarged by medical and other schools out of which the present university has been developed.

Genevieve. (*c.* 422–*c.* 500), patroness of the City of Paris. She is reported to have felt called to the service of God when she was 7 and to have received the veil at 15, devoting herself thenceforward to a life of great asceticism. To her influence is attributed the diversion of the invading Huns under Attila II in 451 from the city and also the remission of a plague in 1129.

Geniza. This term, from the Hebrew verb "to hide", is used to designate the room attached to a synagogue where worn or damaged copies of the Scriptures were placed so as to keep them out of use and so prevent their giving rise to errors through miscopying of the text by scribes. To this practice we owe the comparative purity of the Old Testament text over that of the New Testament, whose scribes were much less careful.

Genku. A 12th c. Japanese scholar later known as Honen Shonin (meaning "saint Shonin"), who founded the Buddhist Jodo sect. He had vainly tried to find peace through the three traditional Buddhist disciplines (precepts, meditation, and wisdom), but on reading in a library the words of a Chinese Amidist commentary an injunction to keep repeating the name of Amida (or Amitabha) incessantly, he felt that he had found salvation in the fulfillment of this injunction. In old age he is said to have repeated it 60,000 times a day or more. Although he recognized the value of doing good works he perceived that only through faith in Amida could he attain salvation.

Gennesareth. In biblical times the name given to the region at the north west corner of the Sea of Galilee, reported by Josephus to have been noted for its fertility and healthy climate.

Genshin (942–1017). A prominent exponent of Amida Buddhism, who stressed the idealistic concepts of Tendai philosophy and urged the purification of Buddhism through the rejection of elements that he accounted superstitious. In his writings and paintings he portrayed transmigrations and the splendor of the paradise of Amida. He is also known in Japan as Eshin-Sōzu.

Gentile. Although the Latin term *gentilis* from which this term is derived means essentially "member of a people," it is usually taken to refer to a foreign people; hence the distinction in Roman law between the *jus civilis* (the law pertaining to the citizenry of Rome) and the *jus gentium* (the law of "the peoples", i.e., in modern terms, international law). In Hebrew there were two words for people, *am* and *goy,* but a distinction was developed: the former came to be used to designate the people of Israel and the latter foreign peoples. In Greek these terms became respectively *laos* and *ethnē.* Since xenophobia is a worldwide phenomenon there is nothing very remarkable in the fact that, as the Jews came to be exposed, after the Exile, to foreign influences, they developed a distaste for peoples other than their own; hence the disdain we encounter in the Bible, and even more strikingly in some extrabiblical literature, for the Gentiles.

Gentile, Giovanni (1875–1944). Italian neo-idealist philosopher, contemporary with Croce (see **Croce, Benedetto**) but markedly different in standpoint. Sicilian by birth, he was educated at Pisa and was later professor at Palermo, Pisa, and Rome. He was Minister of Education in 1922–1924 and regarded himself as a philosophical exponent of Italian fascism. His philosophy, called Actualism, has roots in Hegel (as does Croce's) but (as also does Croce's) departs from it in important ways. The pure act is the Absolute Spirit in its realization of itself in the world. Gentile taught that, as one makes clear the logical structure of one's own experience, one is led ineluctably to an idealist type of philosophy. One becomes aware of oneself in the act of creating oneself.

In his philosophy of history he perceives history in the last resort as a history of thought. As with Hegel, more than one interpretation of his views were developed by his disciples; e.g., one school could be described as focused on religion, another as focused on politics. Gentile was assassinated in 1944. His principal writings include *The Philosophy of Marx* (1899), *The Reform of Hegelian Dialectic* (1913), *The General Theory of the Spirit as Pure Act* (1916), *The Philosophy of Art* (1931), and *The Genesis and Structure of Society* (1946).

Genuflection. The reverential act of kneeling on the right knee momentarily and with head erect at certain points in the Mass and at any time when passing the Blessed Sacrament, the location of which is usually marked by a hanging red sanctuary lamp. (When passing the Cross on the altar the traditional form of reverence is an *inclinatio* (bow). When the Blessed Sacrament is exposed in a monstrance or pyx for the veneration of the faithful, one genuflects on both knees with a slight *inclinatio* of the head. Roman Catholics use a genuflection when being received by the Pope or other high dignitary of the Church, but in such cases the act is performed with the left knee.

Genus and Species. In Aristotle's logic, a genus in a class that is divisible into sub-classes or species; e.g., spaniel is a species of the genus dog; dog is a species of mammal. In modern logic classification principles are generally regarded as merely conventional. Classification of one kind or another is nevertheless essential to thought.

George. Patron saint of England. His historicity, although details are obscure, is generally accepted, and it is likely that he was martyred in the region of Lydda sometime before Constantine. The legend of his slaying of the dragon became popular only about the 13th c. His connection, if any, with England is highly obscure; nevertheless references to it occur as early as the 8th c., and English churches were dedicated to him before the Norman Conquest, e.g., at

Doncaster. His recognition as patron saint of England is probably contemporaneous with the founding of the Order of the Garter by Edward III, *c.* 1347.

Gerhard, Johann (1582–1637). Lutheran theologian. Professor at Jena, he helped in the composition of the *Loci communes theologici* (1610–1622), which was for long a standard exposition of orthodox Lutheran theology.

Gerhardt, Paul (*c.* 1607–1676). Lutheran ranking as one of the greatest German hymn writers. Some of his hymns show strong influence from Catholic mysticism. Many of his hymns have become favorites in English translation.

Gerizim. Important as the site of Samaritan worship in biblical times, it is a mountain *c.* 2900 feet opposite Ebel on the south side of the pass east of Nablus, known today as Jebel el Tur. (See Deuteronomy 11.29f.; 27.12). When the Samaritans seceded from the Jerusalem Jews at some time after the Exile, they built a temple on Mount Gerizim, which was destroyed in 128 BCE. At the order of Pilate, Samaritans were massacred there in 46 CE. See **Samaritans**.

Gerson, Jean le Charlier de (1363–1429). French scholar and conciliarist, sometimes called *doctor christianissimus*. Born near Rethel in the Ardennes, he studied under Pierre d'Ailly at the Collège de Navarre, Paris, whom he succeeded as Chancellor of the University and of Notre Dame de Paris. He was indefatigable in his effort to achieve reform within the Church by conciliarist methods, asserting the superiority of the authority of General Councils over the Pope. He argued insistently that doctors of theology have the same vote and voice as bishops in such councils. Philosophically he was a nominalist. He also contributed immensely to the literature of Catholic spirituality. From his conciliarist views was developed the Gallicanism associated with him. See **Gallicanism**.

Gethsemane. The garden to which Jesus retired with his disciples after the Last Supper (Matthew 26.36) lies between Jerusalem and the Mount of Olives, across the brook Cedron. The modern Gethsemane is a grove of some eight olive trees of great antiquity although certainly not (as is sometimes asserted) as old as the time of Christ. Although the modern Gethsemane cannot be identified with precision with the one referred to in the Gospels the latter must have been very close to it, so that this is one of the comparatively few sites connected with the life of Jesus that can be identified today as authentic.

Ghats. The wide steps leading down to the Ganges and other sacred rivers. Cremations take place on certain of these, known as the Burning Ghat.

Ghazzāli, al- (1058–1111). Muslim philosopher of considerable historical importance in the development of medieval thought both in Islam and in Christianity. Beginning under the influence of al-Farabi and sharing his skepticism, his thought developed along lines that eventually assisted in the establishing of the mystical tradition of the Sufis. In his later writings he attacked both al-Farabi and Avicenna, especially on their view of the eternality of the universe. In general, he opposed the rationalistic element in Islamic thought. God is to be reached through prayer and fasting and other such practice of spirituality, not through reason. His writings include *Revival of the Religious Sciences; Incoherence of the Philosophers; Deliverance from The Incoherence of the Incoherence.*

Ghetto. The quarter (sometimes street) in which the Jewish population lived. The earliest ones were in Italy, and the term may possibly be derived from the Italian word *borghetto,* a little borough or town. Such quarters existed as early as the 11th c., but it was in the later Middle Ages that they became common. Jews were usually permitted to leave the ghetto only in daytime and even then not on Christian holy days. The ghettos were usually self-governing and under rabbinical direction. Venice, Prague, and Trieste are important examples of the late medieval ghetto. The use of the term for other settlements of special groups in a large city is a modern one, based by analogy on the medieval Jewish ghetto.

Ghuluw. A term used by Muslims to denote exaggeration rather than heresy, e.g., when the partisans of 'Ali (the *Shi'a* party) developed the theory that every legitimate leader of the Alids, from 'Ali onward, was an *imam mahdi* (a spiritual leader appointed and supernaturally guided by Allah and endowed by him with supernatural insight), the mainstream of Islam designated that view *ghuluw,* i.e., short of heresy, nevertheless an exaggeration constituting a deviation from the norm.

Gideon. Son of Joash of the tribe of Manasseh, he was one of the judges of Israel. He was called by an angel of Yahweh to save Israel (Judges 6.11–16). There are several allusions in the Old Testament to Gideon's victories over the Midianites (e.g., Psalms 83.10 and Isaiah 9.3).

Gibbon, Edward (1737–1794). Historian. Born at Putney, he was educated at Westminster and at Magdalen College, Oxford. His enormous erudition, wide outlook, accuracy, and mastery of style according to the literary fashion of his day, all contributed to the enduring success of his vast work, *The Decline and Fall of the Roman Empire,* to which he devoted virtually his entire working life. Gibbon had been in his youth converted to the Roman Catholic Church, but his conversion was of short duration and his great work is marked by an attitude of calm but definite hostility toward the Christian Church, a hostility that is more effective than any direct polemical attack could have been. He was in every way a typical English representative of the spirit of the Enlightenment. His famous work is still an unsuperseded classic of historical learning, although unfortunately on too vast a scale to be widely read today and too ponderous for contemporary literary taste.

Gifford Lectures. A series of lectures given regularly at the four older Scottish universities since 1888. The lectureship was established under the terms of the will of Lord Gifford (1820–1887), who stipulated that the foundation was for the purpose of promoting the study of natural theology "in the widest sense of that term, in other words, the knowledge of God."

Gijo. One of the three preliminary requisites for satori in Zen Buddhism. It consists of a state of doubt. The other two consist respectively of faith and perseverance. See **Doubt.**

Gilbert de la Porrée (c. **1008–1154**). Scholastic thinker. Born at Poitiers, he was trained under Bernard of Chartres, Anselm of Laon, and others and taught at Poitiers, Chartres, and Paris. He is best known for his commentary on the *opuscula* of Boethius, in which he attempts to reconcile the unity of God with the Trinity through the methods of the linguistic and logical analysis of his time.

Gilbert of Sempringham (c. **1083–1189**). Founder of the Gilbertine Order, which he developed along Cistercian lines and which eventually comprised both communities of men and communities of women. The Gilbertines were unique as the only purely English order in the Middle Ages. At the Dissolution of Monasteries under Henry VIII, the Gilbertines owned twenty-five houses all of which were duly surrendered to the Crown.

Giles. Christian saint, probably 8th c., who according to a 10th-c. account was an Athenian who went to France where he became a hermit living on herbs and the milk of a hind near the mouth of the Rhône. This traditional story, although probably with some factual basis, is largely one that has been embroidered by legend. The town of St. Gilles that developed near the place of his burial became famous as a place of pilgrimage. He was a very popular saint in the Middle Ages both in France and in England. Scotland's premier Presbyterian kirk (a medieval foundation) is dedicated to him: St. Giles' Cathedral, Edinburgh.

Giles of Rome (c. **1247–1316**). Born in Rome and possibly belonging to the Colonna family, he became an Augustinian friar at Paris and from 1269 to 1271 studied under Thomas Aquinas. He became General of the Augustinians in 1292. A prolific writer, he is best known for his *De Regimine principum*, written c. 1285 for King Philip the Fair, his pupil. He also wrote treatises on original sin, on the angels, on Aristotle's *Physics*, on Peter Lombard's *Sentences*, and against the Averroists. In general he followed the teaching of Thomas Aquinas, but he departed from it in important points, maintaining, for example, the primacy of will over reason.

Gilgamesh. A Mesopotamian epic poem of great importance as recounting tales that go back to the third millennium BCE and can be identified as sources for some of the early stories in the Old Testament, e.g., the story of the Flood and of the serpent who snatches the plant of life. Numerous fragments of the Gilgamesh epic have been preserved.

Gill, Eric (**1882–1940**). English sculptor and wood engraver. Having become a Roman Catholic in 1913 and a Dominican tertiary, he acquired much fame not only as a craftsman in the service of the Church but as a social idealist and pacifist. Among his best-known works are his Stations of the Cross in Westminster Cathedral and his bas-reliefs in the League of Nations Council Hall in Geneva, which celebrate the "re-creation of Adam" and which have above them a quotation from the Jesuit poet Gerard Manley Hopkins: "Thou mastering me God." The New Museum, Jerusalem, also contains ten panels of his work. See his *Autobiography* (1940).

Gilson, Etienne Henry (1884–1978). French Thomistic thinker and historian of medieval philosophy. Educated at the Sorbonne, he came under two major influences there: Bergson and Lévy-Bruhl. After professorial chairs at Lille, Strasbourg, and the Sorbonne, he was professor at the Collège de France from 1932 till his retirement in 1951, after which he continued, as professor and director of the Pontifical Institute of Medieval Studies at Toronto, to lecture extensively there and elsewhere, but in his last years he lived principally in his native France. Gilson's erudition in medieval studies was formidable. Perhaps the best introduction to his work for English-speaking students is his *The Unity of Philosophical Experience* (1937), in which he skillfully exhibits the perennial character of philosophical problems and shows how authentic philosophical enquiry always proceeds by a critical and analytical one. Among his earlier works, *Le Thomisme* (1919, English tr. 1924) is one of the most important, and his *La Philosophie au moyen âge* (2 vols., 1922; revised ed. 1944; English tr. 1955) shows the individuality of the various systems developed in the Middle Ages. Among the later of his very prolific writings should be noted his *L'Esprit de la philosophie mediévale* (1932), translated as *The Spirit of Medieval Philosophy* (1936), his *Héloise et Abélard* (1938), and his *Jean Duns Scot* (1952). His *History of Philosophy in the Middle Ages* (1964) provides a comparatively brief yet detailed history of medieval Christian thought. In his later years he worked also on the philosophy of art (e.g., his *Painting and Reality* (1957) and his *Introduction aux arts du beau* (1963). His *D'Aristote à Darwin et retour* (1971) is among the many important works of his later years.

Girdle. See **Cincture.**

Glanvill, Joseph (1636–1680). English churchman. Educated at Oxford, he became Rector of Bath Abbey in 1666. He devoted his life to trying to show how the scientific studies and discoveries of his time, especially in physics, supported the claims of religious people. He was one of the founding members of the Royal Society.

Glasites. A Scottish sect, so called after John Glas (1695–1773), a man of considerable learning, who along with his son-in-law Robert Sandeman (1718–1771) may be regarded as the founders of the group. (They were sometimes also called Sandemanians.) He opposed state support for the Kirk and wrote *The Testimony of the King of Martyrs concerning His Kingdom* (1727) to show that the way in which the Kirk was protected and forced upon the citizenry was not consonant with the insistence of Jesus that his Kingdom was not of this world. He was suspended from his ministry in Tealing, a village near Dundee, in 1728 and two years later was deposed. Among the practices of his followers was the distinctive one of an Agapē meal consisting of Scotch broth. They also engaged in the practice of washing one another's feet in obedience to the injunction of Jesus. Always a small body, they were still holding services in private premises near St. Andrew's Kirk in downtown Dundee in the early twentieth century.

Glastonbury. Originally a Celtic monastic establishment in England probably dating from the 7th c., it became a Saxon monastery in the early 8th c., was destroyed by the Danes in the 9th c., but in the 10th c. was revived as a Benedictine foundation that acquired much fame for religion and learning. Reputed to contain the tombs of King Alfred and Saint Dunstan, it also became a famous place of pilgrimage. Its history was written *c.* 1135 by William of Malmesbury, *De Antiquitate Glastoniensis Ecclesiae*. In the 13th c., a revised version of this work was written containing the now famous legends that associate the abbey with Joseph of Arimathea and the Holy Grail. The ruins of the abbey are now in the hands of Anglican trustees. For a modern treatment of the Glastonbury legends, see R. F. Treharne, *The Glastonbury Legends* (1967).

Glebe. This term is used both in English and in Scots law to designate the land that goes with the house of the incumbent of a parish church. Traditionally, the incumbent might either cultivate the land himself or lease it to tenants. In Scotland, under an Act of 1925, all such lands have become the property of the General Trustees of the Kirk.

Gloria in Excelsis. Originally a Greek hymn composed on the model of the Psalms, it already formed part of the Orthros in Eastern Orthodox worship. According to L. Duchesne, it was introduced at Rome as early as the fifth century, but was at first used only on very special occasions such as Christmas. Even as late as the 11th c. its use seems to have been still generally restricted to bishops and for solemn occasions. Its place in both Roman and Anglican usage today is immediately after the *Kyrie eleison* and it is used on all Sundays except those of Lent and Advent.

Gloria Patri. The practice of saying or singing this traditional doxology at the end of a psalm dates from the 4th c. It was forbidden by the English Puritans on the ground that it is not found in Scripture.

Glorious Mysteries, The Five. In the most generally used form of the Rosary there are three chaplets. The first two of these consist respectively of meditations on the five joyful and the five sorrowful mysteries of the Catholic faith. The third and last chaplet consists of the five glorious mysteries, which are: (1) the Resurrection, (2) the Ascension, (3) the Descent of the Holy Spirit (Pen-

tecost), (4) the Assumption of Mary, and (5) the Coronation of Mary in heaven. See **Rosary.**

Glory. This term abounds in biblical and in later Jewish and Christian literature. Extensively used in the Old Testament, its meaning is difficult to specify with precision. The Hebrew word used is *kābôd*, literally meaning heaviness or weight, but often signifying importance or grandeur, not least in the Wisdom literature. The idea develops into that of the splendor of the light surrounding Yahweh. To give glory to Yahweh is to recognize him as the source and ruler of all things. The heavens declare his glory (Psalms 19.2). More and more, "glory" comes to mean "light" or "luminosity", and it is primarily this notion that is inherited by the New Testament writers, notably in the story of the Transfiguration of Christ (Luke 9.31 f.), but in many other places, such as the Christmas story and the vision of Paul on the Damascus road.

Glossa Ordinaria. Medieval commentaries on the Bible were generally so designated. Sometimes the term *glossa communis* is used.

Glossolalia. This term is from two Greek words: *glōssa* (tongue) and *lalia* (speaking). The New Testament frequently alludes to the practice of "speaking in tongues." A classic example is in Acts 2.4. Paul, although he did not condemn the practice, regarded it as suspect since persons who were able to perform the act were generally unable to attach a meaning to their utterances. (See I Corinthians 14.1ff.) The term in popular use today seems to date from only the 19th c.

Gnosticism. The term comes from the Greek word *gnōsis* meaning simply "knowledge". It was not a school such as was Stoicism and certainly not a religion or a church. It was, rather, an intellectual climate, an influential mode of thought that could and did in prac tice take many diverse forms, much as was modern existentialism, for instance, to take in mid-20th c. It affected early Christian thought, enriching, if indirectly, that of the great Christian school at Alexandria of which Clement and Origen were illustrious teachers. Its influence is already to be found, however, in the New Testament itself. Paul, while inveighing against what he regarded as false forms of it, reflects its influence in his own writing, for it was an influence that no educated person of his time and circumstance could easily have escaped. Characteristic of the Gnostic outlook was the notion that the "prince of this world" is eternally at war with divine Being. (See, e.g., John 8.23; 12.31; 14.30; Ephesians 6.12.) Spirit and flesh are seen as opposed. The most striking feature of Gnosticism, however, is the breadth of its outlook, which is essentially evolutionary and geared to a vast scenario of innumerable worlds and aeons. Also fundamental to its mode of thinking is the notion that human beings are at various stages of spiritual maturity. Some have been almost if not entirely untouched by the "divine spark" from the spiritual dimension, while others are comparatively advanced in spiritual development.

Among Christians strongly affected by this way of thought, Christ's function was seen as that of bringing the divine *gnōsis* into this world. At least his coming was prominently included in that function. Such a view is notably echoed if not specifically proclaimed in the prologue to the Gospel according to John (John 1). Inevitably, the impact of such concepts produced within early Christianity a variety of results, somewhat as the outlook of the deeply religious forms of humanism in *quattrocento* Italy were to produce in the post-medieval Christian mind. Some forms of it were creative and enriching; others often aberrant and weird.

The leaders of the Christian Church, by about the middle of the 2nd c., had become afraid of what such influences might do to the stability and even to the identity of the Christian Church. Their fears were expressed in the anti-Gnostic writings of men such as Irenaeus, Tertullian, and Hippolytus, who pled for a literalistic reading of the biblical record and to what the Church had openly proclaimed about Jesus Christ, his life, his mission, his death, and his resurrection. To Christian Gnostics this appeal was seen as an appeal to engage in the impoverishment of Christian teaching, but the Church's organizational needs came first in the eyes of its leaders and their view politically triumphed.

The depth of that victory, however, is questionable. As 20th c. manuscript discoveries (e.g., Qumran and the Nag Hammadi texts) have amply corroborated, Gnostic motifs profoundly affected early Christian thought. Also clearer than ever is the fact that pre-Christian Jewish sects had been already hospitable to Gnostic ideas and had developed them in such a way as to make ideas of this kind part of the heritage of those who followed the Christian Way and accepted Jesus Christ as their Savior. Gnosticism in all its diversity persisted alongside Christianity, often as an undercurrent, and was manifested in movements such as those of the Manichees, who, from the 3rd c. onwards, spread far. It appeared also in the Bogomils, and very notably in the Albigenses, who in the 12th c. became so influential in the south of France and north of Italy as virtually to capture that entire region to the point of almost replacing the Christian Church, which eventually used genocidal methods to destroy them. The Church's fear of Gnosticism has not been unfounded, for it does provide the kind of climate of thought and practice in which the Church could easily have been submerged. So vigilance was not unjustified. Yet indiscriminate antagonism to Gnostic influences can also grievously impoverish the Church, leaving it bereft of much of its deepest spirituality and producing a caricature of the mission of the Church to the world. See **Nag Hammadi Library, The.**

Gobind Singh. See **Sikhs.**

Gobineau, Arthur (1816–1882). French philosopher. A nobleman and diplomat, he maintained a theory of Aryan supremacy in culture. His principal writings include *Essay on the Inequality of the Human Races*, 4 vols. (1853–55), and *The Religions and the Philosophies in Central Asia* (1865).

God. This term is used in so many different senses in the history of religion that it must be said to take its meaning from the context. The Greek word *theos* ("god"), from which we get words such as "theism" and "theology" could be applied to any wonderful or unusual phenomenon as well as to forces such as love and war. These were all *theoi*, gods. Some were more lasting than others. Love and war, for example, seem to be always there among us, while other gods are ephemeral. In this sense "god" means something radically different from what Jews and Christians mean by the term, and from what Muslims mean by Allah. When we say that the ancient Greeks, like many other peoples, were polytheists, we do not mean merely that they believed in a large variety of gods while we believe (or disbelieve) in only one; we recognize, rather, that they meant something different when they used the term. If America were an exclusively polytheistic society such as was ancient Greece, we would call the latest rage among pop singers a god and current movie stars goddesses. We might also, on opening the garage door on a frosty morning, utter a prayer such as "O blessed goddess Chevrolet, let me hear the purr of thy pleasure and not the noise of thy wrath." In the ancient world generally the symbols or totems of the various states and nations were important gods, each obviously powerful and therefore to be feared. Nature gods likewise were to be feared when, being angry, they brought storms and earthquakes, yet loved when they brought just the right amount of sun and rain for a good harvest. To say, in such contexts, that "the world is full of gods" (a saying attributed to Thales, one of the earliest of the Greek thinkers) is to say that everything is wonderful.

Very different is the assertion that God is One, the source and at the same time the ground of all existence. The polytheistic outlook, as described in the previous paragraph, tends historically to develop into the monotheistic one that we associate with Judaism, Christianity, and Islam. Yet when it does so, it does not necessarily take exactly the same form. God as understood in Catholic Christianity, for instance, is fundamentally akin to the concept of Allah in Islam, yet there are notable differences. Again, when in Hinduism the focus turns away from the popular polytheism of antiquity to an outlook that uses the term "God" as a unifying symbol in some ways analogous to the way in which it is used in the monotheistic religions, it does not mean precisely what it would mean to a Catholic or a Jew. The Indian concept of Brahma, for example, is similar to the Christian concept of God, yet they cannot be simply identified.

In the Old Testament, Moses received a revelation (Exodus 3.2–15 and 6.2–8) from God as "He Who Is", unique and without any possible rival. This God is just and merciful. He demands absolute fidelity and total devotion and will not brook any philandering with other so-called gods. Because he is not merely the god of the Hebrew people, although they be his chosen people, they must not expect him to be always on their side. Being the righteous God that he is, he will indeed be faithful to his own people, but he will also be just and righteous to all and will therefore chastise his own people when they deserve chastisement and bless other peoples when they merit blessing. All this is brought out especially by the great early Hebrew prophets such as Hosea and Amos.

Christianity inherited to the full that understanding of the nature of God, as did also to a considerable extent later Judaism. It mixed with it the insights of the ancient wisdom, the teachings of the thinkers of antiquity, notably of the Greek philosophers, such as Plato and Aristotle, and of the Greek philosophical schools, such as the Stoics. The Christian doctrine of God was profoundly influenced and illumined by belief in the unique relationship that was seen to exist between God and him who came to be called the "only son" (*filius unicus*) of God, Jesus Christ, a relationship expressed in the doctrine of the Incarnation. As developed by the classic Christian Fathers of the Church over the first few centuries, this relationship came to be expressed in the doctrine of the Trinity. (See **Trinity**.) Nevertheless, the ancient Hebrew insight that God is One (the Unity of God) is the foundation of the trinitarian view that the Christian Church developed to express, in the intellectual terms of the fourth century CE, the distinctively Christian concept of God. So although the trinitarian formula remains the classic expression of the Christian understanding of the nature of God, it is meaningless apart from the unitary concept of God in which it is grounded.

Both oriental and occidental thinkers outside the mainstream of religious thought have postulated a vast variety of ways in which God may be understood. Both within and outside the great religions of the world the question of God's existence has often been a central one. If, however, God is understood in biblical terms at all, the question whether he exists or not is ill put. For the biblical God, as the source of all that is, is *beyond* existence, so that existence is by any reckoning too low a category for him. Traditionally, the medieval schoolmen, notably Thomas Aquinas, taught that we can know by reason *that* God is, but only by revelation can we know *what* he is. Such "knowledge", however, even if we grant it, is so abstract that it does not in the least answer the question that people have in mind when

they ask "Does God exist?" At best it can yield only a philosophical principle of one sort or another: knowledge of a characterless and featureless entity, an entity bereft of any attributes. In modern theology the tendency is to prefer to say that God can come to be known by us only through the life of faith in which the loving and merciful nature of God is gradually revealed to those of his creatures who live in loyalty to his teaching and according to his will as revealed through the living of such a life. The individual, through a lifetime of loving and serving God, gradually attains a direct knowledge of him such as no verbal formulation concerning him could ever provide and no logical argument ever demonstrate.

Gödel, Kurt (1906–1978). Mathematician and logician. Born in Czechoslovakia, he was educated in Vienna and was from 1940 till 1946 a member of the Institute for Advanced Study, Princeton. Among his many contributions to logic and mathematics his most celebrated is his demonstration that the axiomatic method of mathematics cannot exhibit the completeness or the consistency of the system axiomatized. His writings include "The Completeness of the Axioms of the Logical Functional Calculus" (1930), "The Consistency of the Axiom of Choice and the Generalized Continuous Hypothesis with the Axioms of Set Theory" (1940), and "Russell's Mathematical Logic" in *The Philosophy of Bertrand Russell* (1944).

Godet, Frédéric Louis (1812–1900). Swiss Protestant theologian and biblical scholar. Born at Neuchâtel, he was tutor to the Crown Prince Wilhelm of Prussia from 1838 to 1844, later becoming professor of New Testament Studies at Neuchâtel. Widely known beyond his native Switzerland, he published scholarly commentaries on several of the books of the Bible.

Godparents. At a Christian baptism, particularly infant baptism, it is necessary that there be present at least two sponsors, who do not merely answer the baptismal vows on behalf of the candidate but undertake responsibility for his or her Christian upbringing. They are commonly called godparents.

Goethe, Johann Wolfgang von (1749–1832). Poet and philosopher. Born at Frankfurt-am-Main, he was educated at the Universities of Leipzig and Strassburg. His thought was much influenced by Spinoza and Leibniz as was his outlook by his friend Friedrich Schiller and by Herder. Goethe's interests, however, ranged over the entire field of human knowledge. His political wisdom was sought by the Duke of Saxe-Weimar to whom he acted as adviser and as Minister of State for much of his life. In the earlier period of his life, he became the great exemplar of the spirit of German romanticism, which he expressed in writings such as *The Sorrows of Young Werther* (1774). In 1776 an extended visit to Italy led him to modify his devotion to the ideals of Romanticism and to see the need to achieve a more mature and comprehensive view in which Romanticism would be balanced with Classicism. It was through this development that his extraordinary genius was to be fully realized. His humanism was of a profoundly religious sort and the scope of his mind and spirit overwhelming. He loved nature and although his work in the natural sciences is not generally considered to be of such enduring interest as are his philosophical and literary achievements, it too exhibits the extraordinary range and power of his mind. The fruit of Goethe's achievement of a balance between Romanticism and Classicism appears most strikingly in his *Wilhelm Meister* and in the later parts of his *Faust*.

Gog and Magog. These are mentioned in the Old Testament (Ezekiel 38.2), where Gog represents a people (almost certainly the Scythians, who about 630 BCE laid waste much of Western Asia), while Magog is a conventional symbol

for a land. In apocalyptic and rabbinical literature they are both conventional symbols for the enemies of God, as, e.g., in Revelation 20.8.

Gogarten, Friedrich (1887–1967). Protestant theologian. Born at Dortmund, he served in parishes for some years before becoming Professor of Systematic Theology at Breslau from 1931 to 1935, then at Göttingen from 1935 to 1953. A Lutheran admirer of Karl Barth's work, he proposed a new interpretation of culture founded upon the ideas and aims of that theologian. His writings include his *Von Glauben und Offenbarung* (Faith and Revelation) (1923) and his many contributions to *Zwischen den Zeiten*, a periodical devoted to Barthian themes.

Go-I. A set of five rungs in a ladder of Zen Buddhist meditation. The Zen student selects a pair (called respectively *sho* and *hen*) and proceeds to try to see the *hen* in the *sho*, then the *sho* in the *hen*. He then goes on to other exercises of a similar kind, each a "rung" in the ladder of meditation.

Golden Age. The notion that there was a perfect or ideal state in the past from which humankind has deviated or fallen away occurs in various forms in many societies. In the primitive religion of Australia, for instance, there seems to have been a belief in Alcheringa, a sort of Dream Time or Dawn Period when the earth was shaped by the gods. The concept of the Noble Savage, popular in some circles in the 18th c., relies on the presupposition of a Golden Age when all was peaceful and blissful and that something then occurred to destroy that happy state and plunge humanity into the misery in which it has ever since remained. For most of us the most familiar form of such a notion is that of the Garden of Eden as described in Genesis: an earthly paradise ruined by the transgression of Adam and Eve. The persistence of the idea throws light on certain aspects of the human psyche but has no known historical warrant. The concept of the Fall, so closely connected with the Golden Age notion, has nevertheless much theological importance. See **Fall.** Hesiod, in the 8th c. BCE, provided the basis for the notion of a golden age. He thought that human history was going through a series of ages, each one a deterioration of the one before it: the first had been a golden one, the second silver, and so on. Plato was influenced by the concept.

Golden Calf. According to the story related in Exodus 32, while Moses was up on Mount Sinai the Israelites, wearying at his long absence, decided to make a golden calf as an object of worship and they contributed earrings and other golden materials to construct it. Moses, when he eventually descended from the mountain and found what they had done, was very angry and, having burned the image and ground it to powder, he threw the powder on water and forced the Israelites to drink it. The image that so angered Moses was probably (as the Hebrew word indicates) that of a young bull. In the ancient Middle East the bull was a very common symbol of power and so of divinity. Scholars have proposed that the ancient Israelites had a cult in which a bull was represented as a pedestal supporting the invisible presence of Yahweh. This would explain the background of the Golden Calf episode and the ire and indignation of Moses on his discovery of what he would have regarded as their apostasy from his teaching. See also I Kings 12.28 for a comparable incident relating to King Jeroboam I in the 10th c. BCE.

Golden Legend, The. A manual, known as the *Lombardica Historia*, composed by Jacob of Voragine between 1255 and 1266. Designed as a sort of anthology of the lives of the saints along with stories relating to the Christian festivals and seasons and other materials intended to foster devotion, it became exceedingly popular but was discouraged by the 16th c. as lacking historical foundation. It had, however, literary qualities that should not be overlooked.

Golden Mean. This ethical notion is found in various forms in the thought of various human societies. Aristotle sees the discovery of the mean between two extremes as the achievement of "practical wisdom." For example, between an extreme of gluttony and an extreme of abstemiousness lies temperance in regard to food and drink, which is the virtuous choice. Likewise the virtue of courage lies between rash foolhardiness and cowardice.

Golden Rose. On the Fourth Sunday of Lent, called Rose Sunday, the Pope blesses an ornament wrought in gold and adorned with gems, which is afterwards presented as a mark of special favor to a particular individual or group, such as a Roman Catholic princess or Roman Catholic organization. The custom is ancient, having been alluded to as ancient even in the 11th c. by Leo IX. For illustration, further information and bibliography see the article *"Rosa d'oro"* in the *Enciclopedia Cattolica*, vol. X, cols. 1344–46.

Golden Rule. The notion that all morality is rooted in the ethical principle that one ought to behave toward others as one would like others to behave toward oneself is found in many religions. Confucius stated it many centuries BCE. Hillel, out of his very different circumstances and Jewish background, expressed it in a remarkably similar way. Jesus is reported as enunciating the principle in a very direct injunction: "as ye would that men should do to you, do ye also to them likewise" (Luke 6.31). Nearer our own time Kant expressed the same principle in his Categorical Imperative. Although putting the principle into practice is attended by certain difficulties (e.g., a father would not expect his baby son to treat him as he would treat his son), the principle is probably the best and most fundamental guide to ethical conduct that can ever be formulated. While it does not provide a complete answer to all moral problems, it does furnish us with a norm by which to arrive at moral decisions.

Gomar, Francis (1563–1641). Dutch Calvinist divine. Born in Bruges, he studied at Strassbourg, Oxford, Heidelberg, and elsewhere, eventually becoming professor of theology at Leyden, where he entered into a bitter controversy with Arminius, whose views he opposed, eventually resigning his chair in 1611 to become preacher to a congregation at Middelburg. From 1618 till his death he held a chair at Groningen. His adherence to a rigid form of Calvinism was extreme. He was one of the leading opponents of Arminianism at the Synod of Dort (1618–1619).

Good. See **Ethics.**

Good Friday. The Friday, known in the Greek Church as Great Friday (*hē megalē paraskeuē*) before Easter Day, on which the Crucifixion of Jesus Christ is commemorated. It is traditionally observed by Christians as the principal day of fasting and penitence in the entire ecclesiastical year. Traditionally it is marked by various liturgical observances such as the Veneration of the Cross. A three-hour devotion, often consisting of meditations on the Last Words of Jesus, was popularized by the Jesuits and is now widely used not only in Roman and Anglican churches but in many Protestant ones too.

Goodman, Nelson (1906–). American philosopher. Born in Somerville, MA, he took his first degree from Harvard in 1928, went into industry, then returned to Harvard where he took his doctorate in 1941, later teaching at various universities and finally at Harvard. His interest lies principally in problems of structure, especially in those arising out of the construction of phenomenalistic systems. He takes a nominalist position, arguing that classes result merely from constructions. His principal writings include *The Structure of Appearance* (1951), *Fact, Fiction and Forecast* (1954),

Languages of Art (1968), and *Problems and Projects* (1972).

Good Samaritan. The significance of this parable (Luke 10.30–37) lies in the fact that while the priest and the levite (highly respected figures in Jewish society) ignored the victim of a robbery on the roadside between Jerusalem and Jericho, a Samaritan (a man ritually and culturally separated from the Jews) went to the aid of the victim, showering care upon him. Neighborliness, the parable teaches, consists not in mere belonging to the same religion or society or group or class or club but in the behavior of one individual to another as to another soul on the same spiritual pilgrimage.

Good Shepherd, The. This symbol of Jesus Christ, found in the Gospels (e.g., Matthew 18.12–14, Luke 15.3–7, and John 10.7–18), was a very common theme in early Christian art and remained so for many centuries. Jesus is often represented as a shepherd bearing a lamb on his shoulders.

Gordon Riots. In 1778 an act of the British Parliament was passed, one of several called "the Catholic Relief Acts" that were passed mitigating the penalties against Roman Catholics and culminating in the Catholic Emancipation Act (1829), which removed all but a very few restrictions. On June 2, 1780, however, in a fanatical protest against the passing of the act in 1778, which abolished life imprisonment for keeping a Roman Catholic school and permitted Roman Catholics in future to hold landed property, a London mob, led by Lord George Gordon, marched to Parliament with a petition for the repeal of the act of 1778. "No Popery" banners were carried, Roman Catholics' homes were pillaged, and eventually the riot reached such proportions that the King (George III) personally ordered military forces to disperse the mob. More than 200 persons were killed and another seventy-five died of wounds later. Lord George was charged with high treason but acquitted, professed conversion to Judaism, and in 1793, having become mentally ill, died in Newgate Prison. For a reproduction of the shorthand reports by S. Gurney of the proceedings at the trial, see T. R. Howell (ed.), *A Complete Collection of State Trials and Proceedings for High Treason and Other Misdemeanours*, xxi (1814), cols. 485–652.

Gore, Charles (1853–1932). Anglo-Catholic leader and Bishop of Oxford. Educated at Harrow and Balliol, he was elected a Fellow of Trinity College, Oxford in 1875. In 1884, he was elected Principal of Pusey House, Oxford. He also was the leading force in the foundation of the Community of the Resurrection, an important force in the development of Anglo-Catholic life. He went farther than the more conservative Anglican theologians of his day whose churchmanship was of a Catholic temper. Disappointed and isolated, he resigned his bishopric of Oxford in 1919, remaining a perfervid exponent of the Catholic principles that so many in the Church upheld. Among his prolific writings are his *Body of Christ* (1901), *The Reconstruction of Belief* (1922–24), and his *Jesus of Nazareth* (1929). *Lux Mundi* (1889), which he edited with a paper of his own in it on the Holy Spirit, was highly influential and stirred much controversy. A standard account of his life is by G. L. Prestige, *The Life of Charles Gore: A Great Englishman* (1935), but there are others. He was indubitably a great soul and a good mind, although sometimes lacking both the caution and the openness that might have better served his aims.

Gorgias (483–380 bce). Greek philosopher. Born in Sicily, eventually he went to Athens to which he introduced the study of rhetoric. He defined it as the art of persuasion and taught it in the manner of the Sophists. See Plato's dialogue, *Gorgias*.

Gortonites. An American religious sect consisting of the followers of Samuel Gorton (*c.* 1592–1677), who sailed from England to Boston *c.* 1636 in search of religious freedom. Heterodox in his opinions (e.g., he denied the Trinity and argued for a doctrine of conditional immortality), he encountered difficulties with the Massachusetts government. The sect survived till well into the 18th c.

Goshen. That part of Egypt in which Joseph settled the Israelites, probably north east of the Delta, which was assigned to them, no doubt, because of their experience as shepherds.

Gospel. English word comes from the Old English *godspel* (good news), a translation of the Greek word *euaggelion*. The latter, used by Jesus himself in the sense of "the good news" (Mark 1.14 f.) is probably derived from the Old Testament, but it was used also in pagan contexts to denote simply good news. Each of the written accounts treating of the life and teaching of Jesus came to be called the Gospel "according to" the particular author to whom it was attributed. By the middle of the 2nd c., the four now set forth in the New Testament had come to be fully recognized and remained unrivalled by various apocryphal accounts that later appeared. Scholars distinguish between the Gospel according to John and the other three, the authors of which are known as the Synoptists because of a certain literary connectedness that is seen among them.

In the liturgy, the Gospel at Mass is read or sung by the deacon and much ancient and beautiful ceremony attends the reading of it. The deacon, accompanied by a thurifer and by acolytes bearing lighted candles, receives the celebrant's blessing and proceeds to the appointed place (usually but not necessarily on the north side of the church, symbolizing the movement of the Gospel from Jerusalem in the south to Asia Minor and elsewhere to the north) where, after signing the book and himself with the sign of the cross, he censes the book and, using a distinctive tone, sings the appointed passage. The people stand for the Gospel as a token of special reverence and joy. The use of lights for the ceremony is attested by Jerome as early as the 4th c.

Gotama. See **Buddha**.

Gourd. This term, which occurs in the Old Testament only in Jonah 4.6–10 is the name of a plant that cannot now be identified with any certainty, although many have supposed it to be the castor bean, which has large leaves such as would fit the story.

Grace. The English word "grace" translates the Latin *gratia*, which in turn (but very unsatisfactorily) translates the Greek words *charis* and *charisma* that are used in the New Testament. In Christian theology grace is a concept of paramount significance, representing the action that God initiates in a human being in such a way as to make possible his or her sanctification. Grace is given irrespective of the merit of the recipient and indeed is notably bestowed upon the seemingly least deserving. It is a divine response to faith (Romans 4.13–16), certainly not a reward for good conduct. The nature of grace was strikingly clarified for the Western Church through the work of Augustine in his opposition to Pelagius. Much controversy has developed over the relation of grace to free will, for the latter must be conserved in any theological system that fits the basic premises of the biblical view of man. By grace God provides the *conditions* for salvation, but only by the exercise of free will can they be appropriated to make that salvation effective. The relation of grace to the sacraments of the Church has also given rise to various theological controversies. Three kinds of grace have been traditionally recognized: (1) *Sanctifying* grace: the divine gift of God to the soul, enabling the individual to act righteously; (2) *Actual* grace: a particular bestowal by God of what is needed for the individual to perform a certain good action; and (3) *Prevenient* grace: the free gift of God bestowed on the individual independently of the sacraments and of all "normal" channels of God's favor.

Grace at Meals. The practice of making some form of thanksgiving before meals is of great antiquity, being observed in the pagan world as well as among Jews and Christians. Plato remarks on "beginning with Hestia" (the Roman Vesta) guardian of the hearth and home, who was always invoked at all offerings and festivals. Virgil, Horace, and Livy all allude to the practice of invoking one of the gods before eating a meal. The rabbinical writers laid down detailed instructions on invoking a blessing on food and drink. Jesus is reported in the Gospels as offering thanks at meals. In schools and colleges that date from the Middle Ages as do some of the Oxford and Cambridge foundations, the ancient grace before meals is still recited. The practice of saying grace before (sometimes also after) meals is very general even in households of only slightly religious disposition.

Gracián, Baltasar (1601–1658). Spanish Jesuit. Author of several unusual and influential books written in a humanist vein, notably a satire on European society, *The Critic* (1651–57). One of the most remarkable of his writings is a little work *Oraculo Manual y Arte de Prudencia*, which has been much translated into several languages including English. The first English translation was entitled *The Courtiers Manual Oracle, or The Art of Prudence*, attributed to an anonymous author and published in London (1685). Many English translations have been published since then, including one by Martin Fischer of the University of Cincinnati: *A Truthtelling Manual and the Art of Worldly Wisdom* (Springfield, Illinois, 1934). It might be regarded as a 17th c. approach to the art of winning friends and influencing people.

Graham, William Franklin (1918–). American evangelist, widely known as "Billy" Graham. Born in North Carolina, he had an experience of conversion at the age of sixteen and forthwith began to preach. Later he became a Southern Baptist minister and had a prominent part in the "Youth for Christ" movement. In 1949 he began, at Los Angeles, his first great evangelistic campaign, then conducted campaigns on similar lines in many countries of the world. Long and skillfully organized preparation has been an important factor in the success of his missionary work for which also he has made abundant use of modern means of communication. His style of preaching follows the Southern Baptist tradition of which he is a very notable exemplar.

Grail, The Holy. The legend of the Holy Grail, a vessel deemed to have special mystical qualities and powers, is reported in the late 12th-c. *Perceval* of Chrestien de Troyes and about the same time also in Robert de Baron's *Estoire dou Graal*. Soon thereafter the legend appears in the *Parzifal* of W. von Eschenbach, where it is joined with tales of King Arthur and the Round Table. The Grail is commonly identified with the cup used by Jesus Christ at the Last Supper and sometimes with stories about Joseph of Arimathea. The legend, which has never been officially recognized by ecclesiastical authorities, has an important place in European literature and in mystical tradition. The bibliography is extensive. See R. S. Loomis, *Arthurian Literature in the Middle Ages,* pp. 274–94 (1959).

Grande Chartreuse, La. The mother house of the Carthusian order, it is built on the site of a primitive monastic establishment built by the founder in 1084 about 15 miles north of Grenoble in the French Alps. The present monastery dates from 1676. Till the French Revolution it owned most of an important manuscript collection and library in Grenoble. The Carthusians follow

the Benedictine Rule but are strictly enclosed and lead a semi-eremitical life. The claim of the order is that it has never had to be reformed because never deformed. The name "Chartreuse", popularly associated with the famous liqueur manufactured by the order, is rendered in English as "Charterhouse". See **Carthusian Order.**

Granth. The Sikh Scriptures. As the religion of the Sikhs has developed, the Granth has become the supreme authority, the ultimate spiritual guide. See **Sikhs.**

Gratian. Author of the very important 12th c. *Concordantia Discordantium Canonum,* a work that was virtually the source of medieval canon law. Little is known of him except that he belonged to the Camaldolese order and taught at Bologna. His work consists of a collection of *c.* 4000 texts from the Church Fathers and from conciliar and papal decrees. His work was instrumental in making Bologna the first great school of canon law in Europe, and it was soon thereafter used at Paris, Oxford, and elsewhere. Upon it was founded the theory and practice of canon law in the Middle Ages and, in the Roman Catholic Church, down to the present day. See **Corpus Juris Canonici.**

Gratry, Auguste Joseph Alphonse (1805–1872). French churchman. Ordained priest in 1832, he taught at Strassburg and later in Paris, being elected in 1867 to the Académie Française. He was notably active in movements to restore the life of the Church in France, and he was among those who, at the First Vatican Council, opposed the promulgation of the decree on Papal Infallibility, although, like many others, he obediently submitted to it in the end. Among his many writings are *La Logique* (1855) and *Lettres sur la religion* (1869).

Gray, George Buchanan (1865–1922). Biblical scholar. Ordained to the Congregationalist ministry in 1893, he was professor of Hebrew and Old Testament exegesis at Mansfield College, Oxford, from 1900 till his death. Among his writings are his contributions to works such as the *International Critical Commentaries*, the most scholarly series of biblical commentaries in English in his time, and his posthumous *Sacrifice in the Old Testament* (1925). He was much esteemed in his time for his erudition, his critical judgment, and his originality.

Gray, John Henry (1866–1934). Priest and poet. Born in humble circumstances in London, he became, in his youth, associated with the literary circles of Oscar Wilde, Pierre Louÿs, and Richard Le Gallienne. Converted to the Roman Catholic Church, he entered the Scots College, Rome, in 1898 and was ordained priest on December 21, 1901, by Cardinal Respighi in the Lateran Basilica. In 1902 he was a curate in the slum parish of St. Patrick's, Edinburgh, where he worked diligently at his parochial duties, but a few years later, with the help of his friend André Raffalovitch, the scion of a rich Russian Jewish banking family in Paris, he built a charming church in Morningside, Edinburgh, where he ministered faithfully till his death. Among his writings, which are in a distinctive and often somewhat precious style, are his *Silverpoints* (1893), *Spiritual Poems* (1896), contributions to the *Oxford Book of Mystical Verse*, and *Park: A Fantastic Story* (1932). For a life of Gray, see Brocard Sewell, O. Carm., *In the Dorian Mode* (1983). See also a vignette on him in Geddes MacGregor, *Apostles Extraordinary* (1985) and Allan W. Campbell (ed.), *A Friendship of the Nineties* (1984). G. A. Cevasco, *John Gray* (1983) contains a selected bibliography.

Great Awakening, The. The name given to a religious revival that shook the American colonies beginning in the Dutch Reformed Churches of New Jersey *c*. 1726, spreading to the Presbyterians and Congregationalists, and reaching its peak in New England in the forties. Jonathan Edwards and George Whitfield were prominent in it, although both discouraged the excessive emotionalism that it sometimes engendered. In the fifties it spread to Virginia and beyond. About the end of the 18th c., a similar movement occurred, sometimes called the "Second Great Awakening," which began among the Congregationalists of New England and spread among the other mainstream denominations throughout the United States. There was even a further movement sometimes called the "Third Great Awakening", which ran its course from *c*. 1875 to 1914. See D. R. Rutman (ed.), *The Great Awakening* (1970).

Great Bible, The. In 1539 the first edition of a new version of the English Bible, the work of Miles Coverdale, which had been ordered by Thomas Cromwell to be set up in every parish church in England, was issued. A splendid achievement, handsomely produced and printed on paper 11 by 16½ inches, it bore a frontispiece depicting a somewhat idealized Henry VIII handing a Bible to Cranmer on one side and Thomas Cromwell on the other. In the clouds immediately above Henry's head God may be discerned, although less boldly outlined than Henry. This frontispiece, with this and other inconspicuously satirical features, is generally attributed to Holbein. The Great Bible was sometimes known as "Cromwell's Bible" and more popularly as the "Treacle Bible" because of its use of "treacle" where the King James Version has "balm" in Jeremiah 8.22. Cromwell's personal copy is preserved at St. John's College, Cambridge. The Great Bible was highly important in the dissemination of knowledge of the Bible in England. Its version of the Psalms was the one that continued to be used for centuries in the Book of Common Prayer.

Greater Entrance. In the Greek Church, the solemn procession immediately before the Offertory, at which the bread and wine for the Eucharist are carried from the prothesis to the altar, is so called, in contradistinction to the Lesser Entrance, which consists in the procession with the Book of the Gospels.

Great Learning, The. Chinese classic that much and for long influenced the Neo-Confucian revival, especially after Chu Hsi in the 12th c. included it among the four great classics, along with *The Analects, The Book of Mencius,* and *The Doctrine of the Mean.* All four formed the basis of the famous civil service examinations in China that were used from the early 14th c. till 1915. *The Great Learning* teaches that the basis for all good political order is to be found in the cultivation of personal morality. It celebrates the concept of respect for elders and service to the state and inculcates a disposition of love for all people, however humble. It insists upon the pursuit of knowledge as essential to moral development and so to political stability and the peace of the world.

Great Mother, The. The central figure of a religious cult that moved from Phrygia into Thrace by the 6th c. and Attica by the 4th c. BCE. Already well established in the Roman Republic, it became one of the three great religious cults in the Roman Empire, where the Great Mother was known as *Mater Deum Magna.* (The cult of Isis and that of Mithras were its only notable rivals.) The Great Mother was known by many other names in the Graeco-Roman world, e.g., Cybele, Ammas, Rhea, Demeter, and Ceres. She was the parent of all, the nurse of all, and could be identified with Mother Earth. Although the very symbol of parturition, she was also venerated as perfectly chaste. Her worship was attended by orgiastic rites and took place in caves and mountains. Her cult did not entirely disappear till near the end of the 4th c. CE.

Great Schism, The. This term is used in two distinct senses. (1) The formal schism between the Eastern and Western Christian Church in 1054 is so called. The Latin Christian use of the *filioque* in the Creed (see **Filioque**) was one of the points on which the Greeks objected, but there had been divergence and misunderstanding between East and West for centuries before the formal schism, for which the principal catalyst was the insistence of Pope Leo IX that the Greeks recognize the supreme authority of the Roman papacy, which the Greeks refused to acknowledge. (2) Between 1378 and 1417 the Christian Church in the West was divided by rival claimants to the papacy, one at Avignon and the other at Rome. The latter are now generally called "antipopes". This division is also called the Great Schism. It was finally ended by the election of Pope Martin V in 1417.

Greek. The Greek used in the Septuagint and the New Testament is the *koinē* or "common" Greek, the Hellenistic Greek used all over the Mediterranean world and beyond in consequence of the military conquest of Alexander the Great in the early 4th c. BCE. It is distinguished from Attic (classical) Greek by various simplifications and loss of literary niceties that had enriched Attic Greek, e.g., the use of the optative mood, the dual number, and the distinction between the aorist and the perfect tenses. Hellenistic Greek became then an easier language for international communication and for long served as such in commerce and diplomacy, much as a form of English is used today throughout the world. Some of the Christian Fathers, however (e.g., Chrysostom) showed a tendency to revive some of the elegance of classical Greek.

Green, Thomas Hill (1836–1882). Philosopher, educated at Balliol College, Oxford, where he became an influential tutor, being later elected to an Oxford chair of moral philosophy. He did much to interpret the thought of Kant and Hegel to the English-speaking world.

He insisted on the spiritual nature of reality, the spiritual significance of the evolutionary process, and the immortality of the individual in that process. He wrote critically against Hume. His other writings include his *Prolegomena to Ethics* (ed. A. C. Bradley, 1883) and his *Lectures on the Principle of Political Obligation* (ed. B. Bosanquet, 1895).

Green Thursday. A name sometimes given, especially in Germany, to Maundy Thursday.

Gregorian, The. The name popularly given to the Jesuit university in Rome (Pontifica Università Gregoriana), founded in 1551 by Ignatius Loyola as the *Collegium Romanum*.

Gregorian Calendar. Because the Julian Calendar (so called because devised by Julius Caesar in 44 BCE) had shown itself to have become inaccurate, accumulating an error of ten days, Pope Gregory XIII, in 1582 devised a remedy. (Hence the name of the calendar as revised.) This remedy consisted of reckoning October 4 of that year as October 15 and arranging that the century years would in future be leap years only when divisible into whole numbers by 400. The Gregorian Calendar is now recognized throughout most of the Christian world. The error in the Julian Calendar had arisen through lack of precision in its relation to the orbit of the earth. See also **Calendar, The Christian.**

Gregorian Chant. A less historically accurate designation for plainsong. See **Plainsong.**

Gregorian Sacramentary, The. The name customarily given to a group of sacramentaries traditionally ascribed to Gregory the Great (590–604). Toward the end of the 8th c., Pope Hadrian I sent Charlemagne a sacramentary described therein as the work of Gregory. A copy made from this book and dating from c. 811 is preserved at Cambrai, France. The work cannot be entirely

Gregory's but contains much that is properly attributed to him. From a combination of this sacramentary with another (see **Gelasian Sacramentary**), the later Roman Missal as reformed in 1570 by Pope Pius V (which remained standard till 1970) was constructed.

Gregorian Water. Generally, "holy water" used in Catholic tradition is water blessed by a priest who usually adds salt to it, separately blessed. What is called Gregorian water is holy water to which also ashes and wine are added. This water is used by the bishop in the consecration of churches and altars. The usage dates from at least the 9th c.

Gregory I, Pope (c. 540–604). Commonly known as "Gregory the Great," he became Pope in 590. The son of a Roman senator, he became prefect of Rome in 573. He founded several monasteries, including one in Rome, which he entered as a monk and of which, after some diplomatic missions, he became abbot c. 585. As pope he conducted widespread reforms in the administration of the Church's patrimony in Italy and promoted the spread of the Christian faith and the strengthening of the Church in other lands. It was he who sent Augustine, later of Canterbury, to England with about forty missionaries from his own monastery at Rome, to found the English Church. Characteristically Roman in the mold of his thought and outlook, his genius lay in practical administration rather than original thought. He wrote copiously, however, and his writings reflect the mind of a man of deep personal piety. He developed several of the doctrines (e.g., purgatory) that were to become so prominent in the thought and life of the medieval Church. He also encouraged the development of a liturgy reflecting the dignity and *gravitas* characteristic of the best in the Roman spirit. The nobility and simplicity of his character was expressed in his use of the title (now traditional as one of the titles of the papacy: *servus servorum Dei*, "the servant of the servants of God." Having also a mystical element in his outlook, he wrote on the nature of contemplation, helping to lay the foundations of that sober, quiet form of mystical tradition that was to become a feature of the spiritual life of the Benedictine Order. On this aspect of Gregory's contribution to posterity see Dom Cuthbert Butler, *Western Mysticism* (1922), a classical exposition of the distinctive nature of this school of Christian mysticism. The second edition (1927) contains valuable additions to the original work.

Gregory VII (*c.* 1021–1085). Known as Hildebrand, he was Pope from 1073. A Tuscan of humble birth, he came to Rome early in life and was appointed chaplain to Pope Gregory VI. As pope he made many important reforms in the Church, especially in matters involving corruption and moral laxity among the clergy. His most lasting achievement, however, sprang from his insistence on the independence of the Church from secular interference. Inevitably he met with enormous opposition, but through his work he laid the foundation for eventually securing the freedom of the Church from such interference, thus avoiding in the West in the later Middle Ages that monolithic fusion of Church and State that has so much characterized Byzantine practice in the East.

Gregory of Nazianzus (329–389). One of three great leaders of Christian philosophical and theological thought in the 4th c. (The other two are Basil the Great and Gregory of Nyssa.) Since they all happened to be Cappadocians by birth, they are known as the Cappadocian Fathers. Educated at Athens, he was a contemporary there of Basil the Great, the elder brother of Gregory of Nyssa. He was highly influential in developing the theological principles that had been enunciated at the Council of Nicaea in 325 in such a way as to secure the form in which they later appeared in the Niceno-Constantinopolitan for-

mula in 381. During the Council in 381 he was appointed Bishop of Constantinople, but before the close of that year he resigned and returned to Nazianus, then later to his own estate. His influential writings include the *Philocalia* (a compilation of writings from Origen), many poems, and his "Five Theological Orations."

Gregory of Nyssa (*c.* 330–*c.* 395). One of the three great 4th c. Christian philosophers and theologians commonly known as the Cappadocian Fathers, since they were all Cappadocians by birth, Gregory of Nyssa was the younger brother of Basil. A firm champion of the Nicene interpretation of the Christian faith, he was made Bishop of Nyssa *c.* 371. At the great Council of Constantinople in 381 he strongly supported the formulation of the Nicene Creed that has become the norm of Christian orthodoxy ever since. (But see **Filioque.**) Even more than the other Cappadocians, he was a notably original thinker and a philosophical theologian of great acumen, bringing, moreover, a wide understanding both of the Bible and of Plato to his work and a knowledge of the Neoplatonism of his time that was to become a strong influence in the development of the philosophical underpinnings of Christian theological reflection. He was much influenced by Origen, not least in his evolutionary understanding of the salvific process and the universalism that Origen's interpretation entails. Among his chief writings is his important *Catechetical Orations*, in which he sets forth a theological presentation of the meaning of the major doctrines of the Christian faith; e.g., the Trinity, the Incarnation, and the Sacraments. He also wrote much work on the exegesis of the Bible and on ascetical theology and the nature of Christian perfection. Trained in his youth in the art of rhetoric, he was noted for his eloquence.

Gregory of Rimini. A 14th c. medieval thinker. An Augustinian friar, he stud ied at Paris and taught at Bologna and elsewhere before returning to lecture at Paris in 1341. A doctor of the Sorbonne, he was elected General of the Augustinians in 1347. His thought followed the Nominalist position of William of Occam but carried it even further. Theologically he was emphatically Augustinian, teaching that without grace man can do nothing good at all.

Gregory Palamas (c. **1296–1359**). Greek theologian and the principal exponent of the Greek Orthodox mystical tradition known as Hesychasm. Born probably at Constantinople, he made a pilgrimage in 1318 with his two brothers to Mount Athos where he had an opportunity to study the Hesychast form of mystical prayer. Ordained priest at Thessalonica in 1326, he returned in 1331 to Mount Athos where in 1337 he became involved in controversy with a Greek monk from Calabria, called Barlaam, who was stating in an extreme form the doctrine of the unknowability of God. Barlaam attacked the Hesychasts, evoking Gregory's reply in the form of a treatise *Triads in Defense of Holy Hesychasts*. Gregory's fellow monks approved his Hesychast views and composed a statement supporting them, called "The Hagioritic Tome." A council held at Constantinople in 1341 also supported Gregory, who was nevertheless convicted of heresy and excommunicated in 1344. Later, however, he was exonerated and consecrated Archbishop of Thessalonica. The Hesychasts claimed to be able to see the Divine Light by their physical eyes. In their mystical forms of prayer they used both words and physical actions. Gregory, in defending the Hesychasts, made an important theological distinction between the essence (*ousia*) of God and his energy (*energeia*). God's essence is indeed unknowable. His uncreated energies, however, pour forth from God and permeate all things. These, through the mystical training and exercises provided in the Hesychast tradition, we human beings can learn to discern and experience so as eventually to perceive the Divine Light.

Gregory Thaumatourgos (c. **213–c. 270**). Greek Church Father. Of a noble family in Pontus, he studied law and went c. 233 to Caesarea, Palestine, where Origen was at that time and there he became a Christian, through Origen's influence. Consecrated bishop he was so successful in his missionary enterprises that he was nicknamed *thaumatourgos*, the wonder-worker. By no means an original thinker of the caliber of Origen, his teacher, he remained devoted to his master's teachings. His gifts, however, were more practical than philosophical.

Gremial. In the Western Church, a cloth (nowadays of linen) spread on the bishop's lap while he is seated at certain points in the liturgy, so as not to soil his vestments by his hands. The bishop is often required to use the holy oils for anointing, so that the gremial has more practical utility than might be supposed.

Greyfriars. When this term is used of medieval houses or sites in Europe, it refers to their historical connection with the Franciscan Order. The reason is that the Franciscans, who nowadays wear brown, wore at one time gray, so the connection is not self-evident even to those familiar with the Franciscan habit today. Other old names such as "Whitefriars" for Carmelites (the outer part of whose habit is white) and "Blackfriars" for Dominicans (who wear a black mantilla over their white habit) are more easily understood.

Griesbach, Johann Jakob (**1745–1812**). Biblical scholar. Professor of New Testament studies at Jena from 1775 till 1812, he was the first scholar to make systematic use of literary analysis in the study of the Gospels. His critical edition of the text of the New Testament (1775–1777) provided the textual basis for all later studies of the New Testament.

Groote, Geert de (1340–1384). Founder of the Brethren of the Common Life. Born at Deventer, he experienced a religious conversion in 1374 that changed his life from one of pleasure-seeking to one of simplicity and devotion. He became a missionary preacher in the diocese of Utrecht, where he inveighed against the ecclesiastical abuses of his time. The group of friends and disciples who gathered round him formed the beginning of the semi-monastic community known as the Brethren of the Common Life. The classic account of his life is by Thomas à Kempis, of which there is an English translation, J. P. Arthur, *The Founders of the New Devotion* (pp. 1–78, 1905).

Grosseteste, Robert (c. 1175–1253). Born of a humble Suffolk family in England, he studied at Oxford (perhaps also at Paris) and became probably the most celebrated Oxford teacher of his day. The Franciscans, who had been founded as an order of mendicant friars, simple, unlearned men, so developed during the century of their founding as to lead them to a high place in the intellectual life of Europe, and from 1224 to 1235, Grosseteste taught at their newly founded house of studies at Oxford, where he established a friendship with Adam Marsh, a pioneer in promoting the intellectual life of the Franciscans. Elected Bishop of Lincoln in 1235, he conducted rigorous reforms, and in 1250, during a visit to Rome, he made an important speech against the practice of sending Italians incapable of understanding or speaking English to serve in English parishes. Grosseteste was indubitably a man of immense and versatile abilities, which ranged over both the sciences (e.g., mathematics and astronomy) and the humanities, including philosophy and theology, in which his works include his *De anima*, his *De Veritate*, his *De potentia et actu*, and his *De libero arbitrio*, as well as various works on subjects such as Purgatory and the Eucharist. His most notable and original work, however, was in the realm of the natural sciences, his experiments in which influenced Roger Bacon. He was certainly one of the great geniuses of his time, which lay at the dawn of the "golden age" of medieval thought.

Grotius, Hugo (1583–1645). Dutch jurist and theologian. An unusually gifted boy, he went to study at Leyden at the age of twelve and by the age of eighteen was appointed Historian of the States General. He showed a keen interest in theological as well as in socio-political questions and is the author of a treatise *De Veritate religionis christianae* (1622) that was much acclaimed both in Roman Catholic and in Reformed church circles. His irenic temper had been already exhibited in his *Ordinum pietas* (1613) and in a draft in 1614 of his *Resolution for Peace in the Church*. It was precisely this irenic disposition, however, that provoked the anger of his Calvinist compatriots. In 1618 he was sentenced to life imprisonment. Implementation of this sentence was avoided by the action of his wife, who arranged for his escape from Holland in a box of books. Having settled in Paris, he was granted a pension by Louis XIII. His *De Jure belli ac pacis* (1625) is one of the greatest works on jurisprudence in the history of that field in Europe. Apart from the great theological defense of the Christian religion, already cited, he also engaged in biblical studies. In his *Annotationes in vetus et novum testamentum* (1642), he pioneered in textual criticism, upholding also the importance of ecclesiastical tradition for an understanding of the Bible. Open to all intellectually liberalizing ideas and yet, in lawyer-like fashion, an authentic conservative, Grotius is one of the greatest figures in the history of European thought.

Grottaferrata. Near Rome, on the slopes of the Alban hills, a Basilian monastery was founded in 1004. Traditionally a center of Greek learning and culture, it has been associated with many notable scholars such as the great Cardinal Bessarion and the future Pope Julius II. The monastery has an important library of Greek manuscripts.

Grundtvig, Nikolai Fredrik Severin (1783–1872). Danish churchman. Having undergone deep religious experiences, he began, in 1824, an attempt to reform the national Church of Denmark, so as to wean it from the State domination that Kierkegaard also was to inveigh so eloquently against, and to restore the Danish Church a greater focus on the ancient credal standards and a more Eucharist-centered church life. From 1839 till his death he was preacher at the Vartov Hospital, Copenhagen. He was eventually accorded the titular rank of bishop.

Guarantees, The Law of. The relations between the Vatican and the Italian state were governed by this law from its passing on May 31, 1871, within a year after the close of the First Vatican Council until the agreement reached under the Lateran Treaty, signed on February 11, 1929, under Mussolini's government. The Law of Guarantees provided for the protection of the person of the Pope, for an annual tax-free sum from the Italian government, and secured for him the Vatican, the Lateran Palace, and the summer residence of the popes, Castelgandolfo. See **Lateran Treaty.**

Guardian Angels. See **Angel.**

Guelphs. Those who in Italy in the 13th and 14th c. favored the spiritual authority (the papacy), while the opposing party, the Ghibellines, favored the temporal power (the emperor). Much focus on the controversy is to be found in Dante's writings.

Guhyaka. Literally meaning "secret, hidden", the Sanskrit term is applied in Hinduism specifically to members of a class of spirits or minor deities who exercise their powers from hidden places such as caves and crannies. The guhyakas are sometimes described as half-horse, sometimes as half-bird beings.

Gunkel, Hermann (1862–1932). Old Testament scholar and theologian. After various teaching appointments in Germany, he became professor of Old Testament theology at Halle in 1920. A pioneer in Form Criticism and prominent in the History of Religions School (*Religionsgeschichtlicheschule*), he was influential in the development of the methodology used in biblical exegesis.

Gunpowder Plot, The. In 1605 a plot that had been devised the previous year was carried out to blow up the British Houses of Parliament while in session, with a view to killing the King as well as both Houses of Parliament. The purpose was to attempt the restoration of a Roman Catholic monarchy and government. All but one of the conspirators were Roman Catholics of good family. R. Catesby headed the enterprise and arranged for barrels of gunpowder to be placed in a cellar under the place where the King and Parliament would be sitting, storing them there in March, 1605, to await a suitable opportunity. Guy Fawkes was to have carried out the terrible deed. The plot, however, was made known to some members of Parliament and revealed by them. Not only were the conspirators rounded up and executed and their plans foiled; news of the plot so shocked England that distaste for ''popery'' grew into a hatred so bitter and a distrust so profound that for centuries Roman Catholics in England lost all hope of influence. Penal acts against them were for long enforced with increased severity and they did not fully attain even basic civil rights till the 19th c. Even in the 20th c., when much of the hostility had waned, November the 5th was still being popularly commemorated as "Guy Fawkes Day." See **Roman Catholic Relief Acts.**

Gupta. A period in the history of India (c. 200–700 CE) during which Indian culture entered a golden age, especially under the Gupta emperors (320–570

CE), in which popular teachers arose who met the religious needs of the masses for rituals and imagery.

Guru. Literally "one who dispels darkness," this term is applied by Hindus to a religious guide or teacher whose function is to initiate his pupil (*dikṣā*) into the Hindu way of life and to give the pupil spiritual guidance, having therefore somewhat the role of a spiritual director in Christian tradition, but standing in such a special relationship to his pupil that the latter may not, for instance, marry the guru's daughter, since she is spiritually the pupil's sister. (Compare the prohibition, in Christian practice, against godparents marrying one another, since they acquire in virtue of their relationship a "spiritual affinity.") A guru is distinguished from a priest, who merely presides over the religious rites. Nor is the guru merely a teacher; he is, rather, more a "moral tutor" who projects his spirituality into the very heart of his pupil. He is distinguished from other holy men such as *sannyasis, yogis,* and *sadhus.* Traditionally, sannyasis are those who have attained the fourth stage of the ideal human life; nowadays they are usually ash-smeared followers of Śiva. Sadhus are acknowledged "holy men" who have attained whatever they regard as their spiritual goal. Yogis hope that their practice of yoga will gradually give them the kind of spiritual perception that is attributed to sannyasis and sadhus.

In the Sikh religion, nine gurus who succeeded Nanak, its founder, were successively recognized as official heads of the religion.

Gutenberg, Johann (*c.* **1396–1468**). Although a form of printing had been in use in the Orient centuries earlier, the invention of printing by movable type is attributed to Gutenberg, a native of Mainz, Germany, who invented a typecasting machine and, with financial help, produced *c.* 1455 the Bible that is commonly called the Gutenberg Bible, sometimes the 42-line Bible or the Maz-

arin Bible, from its having been drawn to the attention of experts in the library of Jules Mazarin, which is now incorporated in the Bibliothèque Nationale, Paris. The text was that of the Vulgate and the craftsmanship very fine. About forty copies of this edition are extant, but many of these are defective, so that good copies are extremely rare items. The Library of Congress and the Henry E. Huntington Library, San Marino, California, both have fine copies of it.

The importance of printing by movable type lay not merely in the obvious advantage of avoiding the laborious copying out of individual copies by hand that had been the former practice but in the speed of communication of ideas that the new method was able to foster. Formerly a scholar might be fortunate to find a book less than fifty years old in even a good library. Now a scholar in Germany or England could hope to read the work of an Italian or Spanish scholar soon after it fell from the printing press. The result was an immense acceleration in the "New Learning" of the Renaissance.

Guthrie, Thomas (1803–1873). Scottish divine. Trained at Edinburgh for the ministry of the Kirk, he was prominent among those who participated in the Disruption in 1843. See **Disruption, The.**

Guyard, Marie (1599–1672). First Superior of the Ursulines at Quebec. Born in Tours, she married and had a son, but in 1631 she entered the Ursuline convent in her native city and became novice-mistress there two years later. In 1639 she undertook the formation of a convent in Quebec. Her works include her *Retraites* (!682) and her *L'Ecole sainte,* in which she sets forth her mystical experiences. During her lifetime, however, she was best known for her courageous leadership and her success in the educational work in which she engaged in Quebec.

Guyon, Madame (Jeanne Marie Bouvier de la Mothe) (1648–1717). French mystic. After the death of her husband in 1676, the mystical inclination that she had evinced earlier in life increased. Along with F. Lacombe, a friar, she conducted a lengthy tour of France trying to foster interest in her teachings. Arrested in 1687 as suspect of heresy and sexual misconduct, they were imprisoned, but she, through the intervention of Madame de Maintenon, was released and soon became prominent in royal circles. Archbishop Fénelon, with whom she conducted a long correspondence, was the most eminent among her converts. Her teachings (see **Quietism**) continued, however, to alarm the ecclesiastical authorities and she was further persecuted. Among her principal writings is her *Moyen court et très facile de faire oraison* (1685).

H

Habakkuk. One of the twelve "minor" prophets in the Old Testament and the book bearing his name. The authorship of the biblical book is obscure, but it can be dated sometime late in the 7th c. BCE, from internal evidence. It is probably more of a liturgical than an historical book, although it treats of an oppressor whose identity, however, is a matter of scholarly dispute. Among the Qumran Scrolls (see **Qumran**) is a commentary on Habakkuk, which interprets the Chaldeans mentioned in it (Kasdim) as the Macedonians (Kittim). What seems clear is that the book deals with the philosophical question: why God allows his purposes to be worked out by wicked oppressors of the righteous. The answer lies at least partly in the observation that the wicked nations destroy one another while in the long run the righteous individual survives, delivered by God himself.

Habit. Traditional term for the dress of monks, nuns, friars, and other religious orders and congregations. It usually consists of a tunic with a cincture or belt and scapular (a piece of cloth worn over the shoulders and hanging down in front and back to near the hem of the habit). Men wear also a hood and women a veil. For choir use and for out of doors a mantle may be added. The color varies with the order. The rules on wearing the habit have been much relaxed in some communities in recent years.

Haburah. See **Chaburah.**

Häckel, Ernst (1834–1919). German biologist and philosopher. Much impressed by the work of Darwin and affected by the thought of Goethe and Spinoza, he developed a form of naturalistic pantheism. His writings include *The History of Creation* (Eng. tr. 1868), *The Evolution of Man* (Eng. tr. 1874), *Monism and the Bond Between Science and Religion* (Eng. tr. 1893), and *The Riddle of the Universe* (Eng. tr. 1899).

Hades. From the Greek, *hadēs*. The word is used in the Septuagint to translate the Hebrew word *sheol*, the abode of the dead. Originally this was conceived as a shadowy underworld; in later Judaism it acquired other connotations such as a place of reward or of waiting for the final judgment.

Hadith. A collection of stories and sayings on the life of Muhammad forming the basis of a large body of Islamic law, known as the Sharīa, from which are derived many of the customary practices of Muslims.

Hadrian IV (*c.* 1100–1159). Pope from 1154 and the only Englishman (Nicholas Breakspeare) ever to occupy the papal chair.

Haecceitas. A medieval Latin term meaning "thisness", used in the philosophy of Duns Scotus to designate the principle of individuation. See **Duns Scotus, John.**

Hagar. Abraham's wife Sarah, being childless, gave him her Egyptian slave Hagar, who gave birth to a son, Ishmael. (On the legal aspect of this arrangement, see **Hammurabi, The Code of.**) When Sarah, being past the age of child-bearing, has a son (Isaac) strife arises between the two women and Abraham sends them both into the desert. The story as related in Genesis 16 and 21 shows the marks of editorial attempts to harmonize rival accounts. Paul (Galatians 4. 21–31) uses the story allegorically to illustrate a view that those who follow the Christian Way are the children of the promise, i.e., figuratively they become, through accepting the promise, the children of Abraham, while those who reject the promise are bound to slavery with Hagar. The allegory rests on Paul's contention that mere hereditary descent is not what brings salvation, which comes not as a carnal inheritance but as a gift from God liberating the individual who accepts it.

Haggadah. A body of interpretations of Jewish law forming part of the Mishnah. See **Torah.**

Haggai. One of the twelve "minor" prophets. The Old Testament book bearing his name is dated in the second year of Darius (*c.* 520 BCE) and consists of four discourses, the first of which laments the failure to rebuild the Temple and attributes the drought to this neglect.

Hagia Sophia. ("Holy Wisdom.") The great Byzantine church at Constantinople (Istanbul) built under Justinian between 532 and 537 and consecrated in 538. It is a magnificent basilica with a huge dome and one of the most architecturally perfect and impressive churches in the world. When Constantinople fell to the Turks in 1453, it was turned into a mosque. For an account of the restoration of the mosaics after their destruction by the Turks, see T. Whittemore, *The Mosaics of St. Sophia at Istanbul*, 4 vols. (1933–1952).

Hagiographa. A Greek term used to designate that part of the Old Testament other than the Law and the Prophets. It means literally "holy writings."

Hagiography. Lives of the Christian saints. The term is sometimes used in a pejorative sense of biographical accounts that present only the good qualities of the persons treated, ignoring their faults.

Hagios Ho Theos. The opening words of the Trisagion, an ancient anthem in the Eastern Orthodox liturgies that survived in the West in the liturgy for Good Friday.

Hail Mary. See **Ave Maria.**

Hair. Although we do not know with certainty the ways in which the various ancient peoples wore their hair, Egyptian representations show cultivated men as clean-shaven and both men and women as wearing short hair or wigs. Priests, at least under the New Kingdom, shaved their heads as well as their faces. By contrast, peasants and foreigners are generally represented as long-haired and the men as bearded. Biblical sources, Old Testament and New Testament, imply that Hebrew custom was for the women to preserve their hair long and for the men to do likewise and to wear the full beard. Hair was cut only for special reasons such as mourning.

Hair Shirt. A shirt made of cloth woven from hair and worn by some Christian ascetics and others as a penitential act.

Halakha. A body of Jewish law forming part of the Midrash. See **Torah.**

Halal. A dietary term used in Islam and corresponding approximately to the term "kosher" in Judaism. Halal butchers follow traditional practices in handling and preparing meat. The animal to be killed is turned to face Mecca, and the butcher calls upon Allah before cutting its throat. All the blood must be drained from the body before it may be sold, for Muslims regard the eating of blood as unclean.

Halevi, Yehuda (c. 1070–1143). Jewish philosopher. Born at Tuleda, Spain, he was an apologist for Judaism against Christian and Islamic doctrines. He taught that direct revelation from God is conserved though tradition. He claimed that faith is superior to philosophy and argued for a limited freedom of the will. On the afterlife he insisted that the immortality of the soul is a doctrine that is indispensable to all true religion. His poetry is held in the highest esteem by hebraists.

Half-Way Covenant. In American Congregationalism in the 17th and the 18th c., a theory was evolved to express the relationship of unbelieving members of the community to the Church. They were deemed to be in a "half-way covenant" with God.

Hall, Joseph (1574–1656). English bishop known for his defense of the principle of episcopal government as set forth in his *Episcopacy by Divine Right* (1640).

Halo. The halo, a disk of light round the head (sometimes the entire body) was used in Hellenistic times in representations of the gods, including, in imperial Rome, the Emperor. It was not used in Christian art till the 3rd. c. and then only in representations of Christ. Gradually its use was extended to the Virgin Mary, the angels, and the saints. Although it generally is a symbol of holiness, it is very occasionally to be found in representations of the Devil, for it originally signified power, which is an attribute of the bad angels as well as of the good ones. In medieval portrayals, Christ often has a cross or other emblem within the halo, while Mary has stars. Also called nimbus or aureole.

Hamann, Johann Georg (1730–1788). German thinker. Born in Königsberg, he underwent a religious conversion in his late twenties, and as one of the founders of the *Sturm und Drang* movement he championed the claims of the individual, upholding Christian values and beliefs over those of the then fashionable rationalism.

Hamilton, William. See **Death of God Theology.**

Hammurabi, The Code of. An important legal code consisting of 282 laws supposedly given to King Hammurabi by a Babylonian deity, Shamash. Dating from sometime between 2100 and 1800 BCE, it is based on sources of even greater antiquity. When discovered in 1902, scholars perceived at once from its similarity to the injunctions of the Torah that it had probably influenced the latter.

Hampton Court Conference. An important conference held in January 1904 between the English Puritan leaders and the bishops, under the presidency of James I. James I ended by giving the bishops his support. The Conference resulted, however, in arrangements for the translation of the Bible now known as the King James Version.

Hand. The metaphorical use of the word "hand" and "hands" in the Bible is strikingly frequent. The symbolism pervades biblical literature, e.g., as signifying power (I Samuel 5.6f.); hands are lifted up to take an oath (as in law courts to this day); in both Jewish and Christian practice the laying on of hands is used in the rite of ordaining priests (Numbers 8.10; Acts 6.6; 13.3). The concept pervades Christian symbolism and has counterparts in other major religions. See **Hasta.**

Handel, George Frideric (1685–1759). Musical composer. Born in Saxony (his name was originally Händel), he came to England in 1710 and became a British subject in 1726. Of his many religious compositions the most famous is his *Messiah.*

Hands, Imposition of. A practice used in the Old Testament in blessings and later adopted by Christians in ordinations and other rites. See **Hand** and **Hasta.**

Hanukkah. Jewish festival, the Feast of Lights, coinciding with the winter solstice and close to Christmas. It commemorates and celebrates the cleansing of the Temple at Jerusalem at the time of the great Maccabean revolt. It is a family festival. A candelabrum called a *menorah* is placed in the window during a period of eight days. On the first night one candle is lighted, then the next night another, and so on till all are lighted. To the youngest child is usually given the privilege of lighting the candles. The season is an occasion for gift-giving and other festal activities. It has come to be regarded, especially in American Reform Judaism, as a sort of counterpart of Christmas.

Han Yu (768–824). Neo-Confucian thinker who sought to restore the values of the Confucian tradition and uphold them against the encroachments of Buddhism and Taoism in Chinese thought.

Haplography. A scribal error consisting in writing a word or letter once when it ought to be written twice. The opposite error (writing a word twice when it should be written only once) is called dittography. Both errors have been found in manuscripts of the New Testament.

Harakiri. See **Bushido.**

Hare Krishna Movement. The International Society for Krishna Consciousness was founded in 1965 by A. C. Bhaktivedanta Swami Prabhupada (died 1977), on his arrival in America. The name "Hare Krishna", popularly attached to the devotees, arises from the repetitive chanting of their principal mantra, "Hare Krishna . . . Hare Rama. . . . " The inspiration for the movement comes from the *Bhagavadgīta.* In the sixties they attracted many from the "hippie" culture of that time in America. Authentic devotees, however, are expected to lead lives within a temple community in which drugs, including alcohol, are forbidden. Apart from marriage they are required to lead strictly celibate lives. In their pilgrimages to India they were often very cordially received because of their somewhat simplistic presentation of the spirit of Bhakti (see **Bhakti**), which has an appeal in India similar to that of the "sawdust trail" appeal to a large segment of the population of the United States.

Hari-Hara. In the mythology of India, Viṣṇu (Hari) and Śiva (Hara) are sometimes conjoined so as to represent a single deity, signifying the union of the two gods, with Viṣṇu on the left side and Śiva on the right. In this way two of the most important cults in Hindu folklore are synthesized. According to the story, when the ocean was being churned, Viṣṇu took the form of Mohinī, a divine enchantress, who easily seduced Śiva. Their sexual union had an offspring, Hari-Hara, whose cult still persists.

Harless, Gottlieb Christoph Adolf von (1806–1879). Lutheran theologian. Trained at Halle, he held chairs at Erlangen and Leipzig and in 1852 became president of the supreme consistory of Bavaria, where he was a highly influential exponent of Lutheran orthodoxy.

Harnack, Adolf von (1851–1930). German theologian historian, and patristic scholar. Holding chairs at Giessen, Marburg, and Berlin, he was probably the foremost patristic scholar of his time. His immense erudition was displayed in a vast scholarly output of works that include his 7-volume *History of Dogma* (1889–1922), *The Apostles' Creed* (1892), *The Essence of Christianity* (1900), and *Marcion* (1921). His work on the New Testament exhibited much originality. A standard work on Harnack as historian and theologian is G. W. Glick, *The Reality of Christianity* (1967).

Harris, Howel (1714–1773). Founder of Welsh Calvinist Methodism. See also **Huntingdon, Selina, Countess of.**

Harris Movement. The largest of the mass movements in West Africa to Christianity. It sprang from the labors of William Wade Harris (c. 1850–1929), a catechist in Liberia whose influence caused more than 100,000 native inhabitants of the Ivory Coast and Western Ghana to abandon their old religious practices and adopt the Christian faith.

Harrowing of Hell. The phrase used in England in the Middle Ages and later for the Descent of Christ mentioned in the Apostles' Creed.

Hartmann, Eduard von (1842–1906). German philosopher. His first major work, *Philosophy of the Unconscious*, 3 vols. (1869), attracted much attention. He was the first to use the term "axiology" for the study of every kind of value-theory. A forerunner of Freud in recognizing the importance and significance of the unconscious as a powerful aspect of the development of the individual, he sought to join a recognition of the blind will that Schopenhauer had emphasized with an acceptance of Hegel's neo-rationalism. So we have on the one hand a blind, unconscious striving for fulfilment and, on the other, a conscious working out of the individual's aims and their fulfilment. His maturer thought along such lines was expounded in his *Phenomenology of the Moral Consciousness* (1879), his *Theory of the Categories* (1898), and his posthumous *System of Philosophy in Outline*, 8 vols. (1907–09).

Hartmann, Nicolai (1882–1950). German philosopher. Born in Latvia, he was trained at Marburg in the neo-Kantian tradition, and taught there and at other German universities. He used phenomenological methods, showing the importance of attending to the problem rather than fitting it into a system. Among his writings are *Outlines of a Metaphysic of Knowledge* (1921), *Foun-*

dations of Ontology (1935), *The Structure of the Real World* (1940), and *Teleological Thought* (1951).

Hartshorne, Charles (1897–). Philosopher of religion. Trained at Haverford and Harvard, he did advanced studies at Freiburg and Marburg, then taught at the University of Chicago, at Emory, and at the University of Texas. With Paul Weiss he edited the papers of C. S. Peirce in 6 vols. (1931–1935). He interpreted the world as panpsychic and organic, seeing the present as inclusive of the dimension of history. Critical of the traditional emphasis on the sovereignty and absoluteness of God, he sought a balance between that emphasis and another that represents God as growing, so that he is both eternal and temporal. He did not reject the traditional arguments for the existence of God but insisted on the need to take them together (as indeed Aquinas had intended), so that no single one of them can provide proof of God's existence. His position represents a panentheist view of God in whom all is, without resulting in an identification between God and the universe. He perceived the special role of the Ontological Argument, which can be viewed either as a truism that says nothing or as a proof of God's existence. Among his other works may be mentioned his *Philosophers Speak of God* (1953), which he edited with William L. Reese.

Hasideans. During the Maccabean period in Jewish history, a group of people who were noted for their devotion to the law were so designated. (See I Maccabees 2.42.) It seems that the Pharisees, so often mentioned in the New Testament, were developed out of this group.

Hasidism. A mystical movement within Judaism, founded by Israel ben Eliezer, Ba'al Shemtob. Its stress on the immanence of God alarmed the Orthodox, and the movement was persecuted, especially in the later part of the 18th c. It has nevertheless deeply affected Jewish life by showing true piety as a constant joy in and communion with God and it has produced some eminent adherents, including Martin Buber. The term is from a Hebrew word meaning "pious". Like the various mystical traditions within Christianity and other religions, it operates as an enlivening of the religious life of the community rather than as a specific philosophical or theological school. See also **Cabbala**.

Hasta. From antiquity the hand (see **Hand**) has had an important role in Hindu mythology. Hands signify power and protection. The symbolism may be seen in the traditional dances of India. It has counterparts in other religions. For example, compare the *mudras* of the Buddha, symbolism of the use of the hand in Christian liturgy (laying on of hands at ordination, the use of the hands in benediction and other rites), and the metaphors of the Bible: the hand of God, sitting at God's right hand, and many others.

Hastings, James (1852–1922). Scottish Presbyterian divine. Trained at Aberdeen, he founded the *Expository Times* in 1899 and edited the 5-volume *Dictionary of the Bible* (1898–1904), a famous work in its day of which a 1-volume edition was published in 1909 and a revised edition in 1963; also the 12-volume *Encyclopaedia of Religion and Ethics* (1908–1921), and other reference works of a similar kind.

Hatha Yoga. A branch of Yoga that emphasizes physical training. Some of the techniques used are of considerable antiquity. It is not to be regarded as an alternative to other yogic methods but, rather, a preliminary training for the more advanced mental yoga.

Headlam, Arthur Cayley (1862–1947). Anglican divine. Educated at Winchester and New College, Oxford, he was ordained priest in 1889. After various appointments he became the Regius professor of Divinity at Oxford and from 1923–1945 Bishop of Gloucester. A considerable New Testament scholar who disliked ecclesiastical partisanship, he sought ecumenical goals and was one of the most influential English bishops of his time.

Hearn, Thomas (1678–1735). English antiquary. An Oxford man, noted for the meticulous accuracy of his scholarship, he produced more than forty volumes, including critical editions of classical and medieval authors, and many notebooks preserved in the Bodlein Library, Oxford.

Hearse. This term, from the medieval Latin *hercia*, is popularly used for the vehicle carrying the funeral casket. Liturgically, it refers to the triangular frame on a stand to hold the fifteen candles used in the traditional Tenebrae service on Wednesday of Holy Week, at which the candles are extinguished one by one in the course of the service.

Heart. In biblical language, psychic activities and dispositions (will, emotion, reason, etc.) are associated with various bodily organs, notably the heart. This usage is reflected in common speech today, as when we talk of winning someone's heart (his or her love) and of losing heart in some enterprise (losing interest or courage to pursue it). The Hebrews used this language much as we do but they extended it, in the case of the heart, to encompass other ideas; e.g., the heart was also the seat of intelligence or mind (Mark 7.21; Acts 7.23) and of decision or will (Acts 11.23; II Corinthians 9.7). To lack heart is not necessarily to lack courage or boldness; it often means, rather, a sort of narrowmindedness or lack of wisdom (Proverbs 6.32). Moreover, stealing a person's heart does not mean, as it does in common speech today, winning someone's love; it more typically means to deceive someone (Genesis 31.20; II Samuel 15.16). The heart is, then, in the mind of the biblical writers, the inner core of a human being, the essential self. The ancients knew nothing of the physiological function of the heart in its relation to the circulation of the blood: a physiological fact discovered by William Harvey only in the early 17th c. Yet because the heart is to the biblical writers the core of the human being it could and did come to be seen as the trysting place of God in the individual: the organ of divine love.

Heaven. In biblical literature the word "heaven" is used both in an astronomical and in a figurative, theological sense. Various primitive cosmologies are represented in the Bible, but typically the heavens (*ha shamayim*) are perceived as an enormous hemispherical vault covering the earth as a metal or other bowl covers a plate. Underneath the "plate" that is the earth is a watery abyss. Such is the basic pattern, although it takes a variety of forms. From such a general concept of the physical universe arise the figurative ideas in which heaven comes to stand for the dimension of being that lies beyond the empirical or "natural" world, which in turn is "the earth". In classic Hebrew thought the underworld (*sheol*) is associated with whatever lies under the earth. The fact that šamāyim in grammatically plural ("the heavens") made the enumeration of heavens an easy development in Hebrew literature in which we read of three or seven or even ten heavens, Paul (II Corinthians 12.2), reflects this mode of thinking. Out of such allegorical developments comes the general association of "the good" with "up" and "the evil" with "down": associations that are still reflected in ordinary modern language in which we talk of a person of "high" ideals or "lofty" thoughts and of another whose motives are "base" or, more colloquially, "low-down". See also **Sheol** and **Gehenna**. Within this background, God is predictably associated with heaven, where he "sits" on his "throne". All language about spiritual reality is in the nature of the case figurative. The analogies that are used from the empirical world do not much matter; e.g., I habitually talk of "having something on my mind" or "in my mind", although of course since "mind" is a non-spatial concept, a spatial preposition cannot be taken literally in association with it. See also **Hell.**

Heber, Reginald (1783–1826). Anglican bishop and hymn writer. An Oxford man, he became Bishop of Calcutta. Among his hymns, "Holy, Holy, Holy" and "Brightest and best of the sons of the morning" are amongst the most enduringly popular.

Hebrew Language. Virtually all the Old Testament is written in Hebrew, which belongs to the Semitic group of languages, having a considerably different grammatical structure from the Indo-European languages. (Some passages in Ezra and Daniel written in Aramaic are exceptions.) Classical Hebrew appears as early as *c.* the 10th c. BCE in a calendar engraved on a stone from Gezer. The Old Testament represents almost the entire extant classical Hebrew literature. The earliest Hebrew script was similar to the ancient Phoenician. The now familiar "square" script was developed later. Hebrew is written from right to left. See **Aramaic** and **Massoretes.**

Hebrew People. The people who entered Palestine with the Patriarchs and Moses generally called themselves Israelites. "Hebrew" was the term used of them by foreigners.

Hebrews. The New Testament letter to the Hebrews, although well known to early Christians such as Clement of Rome, was not recognized in the Western Church as canonical (see **Canon**) till *c.* 350. For example, Tertullian, who flourished *c.* 200 CE, did not recognize it as pertaining to the biblical canon. Virtually no modern scholar accepts its traditional attribution to Paul. Its language and modes of conceptualizing are too strikingly different from his; a fact that had been already noted by early Christian writers such as Clement of Alexandria. It certainly reflects Alexandrian influences and Hellenistic thought-patterns, and its style is the most elegant of all the books of the New Testament as we now have it. It is impossible with our present knowledge to propose anyone as even the probable author of this letter, although the evidence points to a Hellenistic Jew with some Alexandrian training. Apollos is a likely candidate, but scholars both contemporary and in antiquity have suggested several plausible candidates, e.g., Barnabas, Jude, and Clement of Rome. Even Priscilla, the wife of Aquila, is a possibility and, or course, an especially interesting one, since she would be the only female contributor to the literature we call the New Testament. There is no way, however, of establishing the merits of even one such candidate over another. Although the date of composition cannot be established with precision, it must be before 90 CE and may be considerably earlier.

Hebron. A city (probably one of the oldest in the world) *c*. twenty-three miles to the south/southwest of Jerusalem, being known nowadays as El-Hâllil. When Abraham arrived in Palestine, it was here that he made his home (Genesis 13.18). It is frequently mentioned elsewhere in the Old Testament.

Hedonism. From the Greek *hēdonē*, pleasure, delight. In ethics, the view that enjoyment of pleasure is or ought to be the goal of human life and action. It is a view that has taken many forms and is susceptible to a wide variety of interpretations, depending upon how "pleasure" is understood. For example, any system of ethics in which the presuppositions are entirely "materialistic" or naturalistic or behavioristic might be called hedonistic. Hedonism, however, may be egoistic, teaching that each individual does or ought to act in such a way as to seek his or her own maximum pleasure. The Utilitarians such as Jeremy Bentham and John Stuart Mill would uphold, rather, the view that everyone ought to act in such a way as to

bring, in the end, the greatest pleasure to the largest number of people, which is a very different aim. Hedonism has been represented from antiquity; e.g., the Cyrenaics and the Epicureans would be so classified. Even traditional Christian theology, with its doctrine of the afterlife as the attainment of everlasting bliss in the direct knowledge of God (the Beatific Vision) could be called hedonistic, although envisioning a very different quality of joy.

Hefele, Karl Joseph (1809–1893). Church historian. Professor of Church history at Tübingen. He played a very prominent part in the First Vatican Council as a leader among the many learned opponents of the doctrine of Papal Infallibility. In the end, however, he formally acceded to its promulgation.

Hegel, Georg Wilhelm Friedrich (1770–1831). Born in Stuttgart, he was trained in theology at Tübingen. At the University of Jena (1801–1807), he and his colleague Schelling published a philosophical journal. After some years at the Nürenberg Gymnasium he held a chair at Heidelberg and then at Berlin, where he remained from 1818 till his death.

Hegel is one of the most influential as well as one of the most original thinkers in the history of European philosophy. Influenced strongly by the thought of Spinoza and Kant, and by the idealist philosophy of Schelling and Fichte, he developed a comprehensive philosophical system of his own: a neorationalist idealism. He identified the rational with the real. He saw the universe as exhibiting a polarity that is constantly in process of resolution. His thought was dialectic, recognizing everywhere a triadic process: thesis, antithesis, and their unification by synthesis. For example, admiration for classical forms in art (thesis) gives way to admiration for the romantic spirit (antithesis), but these then are assimilated in an art form that includes and harmonizes both. Politically a society may undergo a revolution from an anarchical to a totalitarian state (thesis and antithesis), which in time yields a corrective in the form of a government that incorporates elements of laissez-faire with elements of a more socially controlled type of government (synthesis). Since Hegel was in principle a religious type of thinker in the sense that he looked to the Absolute Mind or Spirit (*Geist*) as the ground and focus of everything, he could see the entire evolutionary process of history as the working out of the purpose of this Absolute *Geist*. (*Geist* is strictly untranslatable into English: "mind" is too "intellectual" and "spirit" too "spooky" to do it justice.)

Hegel's outstanding contribution to philosophy lies in his recognition of the limitations of mathematical procedures (useful and necessary though they are, they can be done by a computer or other mechanical instrument) and the immense importance of history, which reveals the world process. He saw working within it both reason and passion. By Absolute *Geist*, Hegel meant that which supersedes the dichotomy between the subjective and the objective modes of Being.

Such is the structure of Hegel's vast and elaborate system that it is designed to cover every aspect of experience and every mode of Being. It seeks to do justice to art, to religion, to philosophy. In doing so, however, it may, as its critics have complained, caricature each one of them in turn. For example, Hegel, although his thought is religious in the sense already specified, looked on all forms of religion as expressions of what might be called a "baby philosophy," a philosophy in cartoon form, containing truth but only in the pictorial form that a cartoon provides. Philosophy, by contrast, proceeding through historical development, exhibits "absolute" truth, i.e., the truth about Absolute *Geist* in itself and for the world. Kierkegaard bitterly criticized Hegel for his exaltation of the Absolute and for his emptying God of what Kierkegaard perceived

as that subjectivity that is *par excellence* in God. Pascal, who in the 17th c. had sharply distinguished "the God of Abraham and Isaac" from "the God of the philosophers" would have concurred, no doubt, in Kierkegaard's critique of Hegel at this point, had he lived, as did Kierkegaard, at a time when Hegel's influence had begun to dominate European thought. Nevertheless, the importance of Hegel cannot by any means be overlooked and it can hardly be overestimated. With the rise in the 20th c. of schools such as that of the logical empiricists, Hegel tended to be belittled and denigrated and with this inevitably came a belittling of the importance of the history of philosophy that eventually resulted in a radical impoverishment of the whole philosophical enterprise. During the 19th c., Hegel's influence had been so pervasive that it had penetrated the entire range of European and American thought. (As is well known, it inspired even Marx, albeit in parody.) Whatever be the lines philosophy is about to take and whatever its future shape, the significance of Hegel can never be permanently overlooked by thinking human beings.

Hegira. The name (*hijra*) given by Muslims to the movement of Muhammad from Mecca to Medina. (The Arabic word means "migration" or "emigration".) The traditional date is July 16, 622, with which the Muslim era begins. Because of the Muslim use of the lunar year, calculation of the calendar cannot be done simply from the Christian or Jewish one. See G. S. P. Freeman-Grenville, *The Muslim and Christian Calendars* (1963).

Hegoumenos. A title used in the Eastern Orthodox churches for the head of a monastery.

Heidegger, Martin (1884–1976). German philosopher. Trained under Husserl at the University of Freiburg, his important work, *Sein und Zeit* (Being and Time) was published in Husserl's

Jahrbuch für philosophie und phänomeno-logische Forschung, VII (1927). This work was revised many times with some interesting variations but without any very drastic changes. At that time Heidegger was still thought of as a phe-nomenologist, like his master Husserl; nor indeed did he ever dramatically re-nounce his early allegiance to that school or style of philosophizing. Even-tually, however, he was to become prominent in the existentialist move-ment that was to sweep continental Western Europe in the thirties. Human existence, indeed, had been the focus of his phenomenological outlook. He called it *Dasein*, which literally means simply "being there." Man is flung into the world; yet he does have freedom of choice. The freedom is not, of course, unlimited. He cannot change the color of his eyes, much less the date or place of his birth; but he does have and he does exercise freedom to a degree unique in the world.

Heidegger makes a special distinction between what he calls choosing to live "authentically" and choosing instead to live "inauthentically". He who lives au-thentically is capable of authentic un-derstanding of reality. He can talk in a way that reflects that understanding. Inauthentic life is lived not only at a dif-ferent and lower level; it is lived ambig-uously as well as superficially. The inauthentic man reflects that ambiguity and superficiality in his talk and in his entire outlook. One learns authenticity through facing *Angst*, a profound and peculiarly poignant kind of anguish. (See **Angst.**) Out of this confrontation is developed *Sorge*, care; i.e., care for real-ity, more especially for the fact that one is on one's way to death, with all that this entails. One is not as timeless as the universe around us; one is born, one grows up, one matures, one grows old, and one dies. To understand all this and face it is a fulfilment of our *Dasein*, which, if we are living authentically, be-comes *Ek-sistenz*: we have come to terms with our place in the world and have accepted as well as understood it.

Like Leibniz, although in a very dif-ferent context, Heidegger asked the question that on his view must surely be basic: "Why is there anything at all and not just nothing?" For him, "noth-ing" has a kind of ontological status; it has negative power. It is invested with power to cover with darkness a person living an inauthentic life. By contrast, once again, the person living authenti-cally is led to the discovery of the na-ture of existence and its finitude and perceives his total dependence on Be-ing.

Plainly, such a philosophy can be in-terpreted in more than one way, but its affinities with biblical emphases con-cerning the nature of man (e.g., Isaiah 40.6-8 and Psalm 37.2) are obvious. Some contemporary theologians find in Heidegger an intellectual expression of the biblical view. Heidegger's many works include: *What is Metaphysics?* (1929), *Hölderlin and the Essence of Po-etry* (1936); *Introduction to Metaphysics* (1953); *What is Thinking? (Was heisst Denken?)* (1954); *What is Philosophy?* (1956); and *Phenomenology and Theology* (1970).

Heidelberg Catechism. A Protestant confession of faith, predominantly Cal-vinistic but with some Lutheran modi-fications, compiled in 1562 chiefly by two Heidelberg theologians, Z. Ursinus and K. Olevian, and accepted in 1563 as the doctrinal standard for the region.

Heiler, Friedrich (1892–1967). German theologian. After studying Roman Cath-olic theology at Munich, he came under the influence of Nathan Söderblom, and in 1919 he became a Lutheran. Three years later he was appointed to a chair at Marburg. His most important work is his *Das Gebet* (1918), a classic study of prayer.

Heilsgeschichte. In the 18th c. some German theologians coined this term, signifying literally "salvation history" to express the concept that God's purpose for his people can be exhibited histori-cally.

Heim, Karl (1874–1958). Lutheran theologian. Trained at Tübingen, where he later held a chair, he developed a theology in which he emphasized the transcendence of faith over reason. He was much influenced by Ritschl and in some ways by existentialist thought.

Heisenberg, Werner (1901–1976). German physicist. Born at Würzburg, he was trained at Munich and taught later at Göttingen and elsewhere, becoming eventually director of the Max Planck Institute for Physics in Munich. He developed the view that at the microcosmic level one cannot by space-time coordinates supply a quantitative measurement such as would be expected. His discovery, popularly known as the Heisenberg principle of indeterminacy, exhibits the limitations of classical physics and is of great importance not only for cosmology but for its philosophical and theological implications. His writings include *The Physical Principles of Quantum Theory* (1930) and *Physics and Philosophy* (1959). He was awarded the Nobel prize in physics in 1932.

Helena (*c*. 255–*c*. 330). Mother of Constantine. Zealous in her support of the Christian Way, she made a visit, at an advanced age, to the Holy Land, where she established a basilica on the Mount of Olives and another at Bethlehem.

Hell. In traditional Christian theology Hell is a state, popularly conceived as a place, in which the wicked are punished everlastingly after death. It is to be radically distinguished from Purgatory, which is essentially a state of purification and spiritual cleansing on the way to everlasting bliss in Heaven. The New Testament, literally understood, may be interpreted as supporting such a concept of Hell. In the Middle Ages the learned interpreted the essential nature of Hell as a state of everlasting separation from God that entails as its chief quality the *poena damni*, understood as the infinite pain of the sense of the everlasting loss of God's presence. The medieval scholars, however, did also teach that some form of externally administered punishment (usually presented as physical fire of some kind) is included in the everlasting misery of the damned.

Modern theologians have tried to mitigate the horror of the traditional concept by presenting Hell as the inevitable self-exclusion of the unrepentant sinner from the presence of God, due to his having no more capacity to enjoy God than can a deaf person enjoy a symphony concert. The essential hopelessness of Hell (dramatized by Dante's inscription on its gates, enjoining entrants to abandon hope) makes it remain, however, too horrific a doctrine to be reconcilable to the essentially loving nature attributed to God in the Bible and in all Christian tradition, so the doctrine of Hell remains part of the notable confusion in Christianity on the teaching about the afterlife. Annihilation might be reconciled to the central doctrine that God is love, but Hell, all attempts to mitigate its horror notwithstanding, cannot be made to fit that central Christian teaching. The doctrine of Purgatory, on the other hand, is very amenable to Christian teaching, for the love of God does entail pain and sacrifice, although never hopelessness.

Hellenism. By this is meant the process by which, as a result of the conquests of Alexander the Great, Greek culture and civilization spread through the Mediterranean world and much of Western Asia. The influence affected the entire range of life. Greek became an international medium of communication (see *Koinē*) much as is English today; the features of cities and other centers of civilization took on standard Greek characteristics; even Jews often took personal Greek names; above all the modes of thought became deeply affected by the Greek intellectual heritage. So overwhelming was this cultural transformation of so much of the known world that it penetrated even remote and isolated regions, including Palestine, where its effects, especially on the upper classes, are clearly observable early in the 2nd c. BCE. Of course there was inevitable resistance to such cosmopolitan influence. The Pharisees represent a notable example of such resistance and of a consequent resolve to conserve what is distinctively Hebrew and Jewish; yet no region, no aspect of human life was untouched by the hellenizing influence. Without it, the speedy spread of Christianity would have been impossible. Moreover, in perceiving, as indeed we must, the Jewishness of the cradle of the Christian Way, we must at the same time recognize that it was a Jewishness already deeply influenced by the hellenizing process. These facts are of the utmost importance for an understanding not only of the spread of Christianity but of its origin in the thought and outlook and teaching of Jesus himself.

Henotheism. From the Greek word *henos* (meaning "one") and *theos* (god). The view that while there is one supreme god, the existence of other deities is not necessarily to be denied. It would seem to be implied in the biblical commandment (Exodus 20.3 and Deuteronomy 5.7) that the people should have no gods other than Yahweh. It has been taken by some to be a transitional stage between polytheism and monotheism: the result of an interim injunction suited to people before they can understand the full implications of monotheism. This is, however, a speculative view of the nature of the transition.

Henry of Ghent (*c.* 1217–1293). A philosopher of some influence, he taught at Paris and took part in the commission that led to the condemnation of Averroism in 1277.

Heraclitus (*c.* 540–475 BCE). Greek philosopher. Born at Ephesus, he grew to disdain popular religion and developed a critical attitude toward it. His views, the expression of which is extant only in many fragments, have as their focal point the contention that all things are in a state of flux. He recognized in this state of affairs a universal law or, rather, idea (he calls it *logos*) operating in the universe. Everything, then, is in a state of conflict but out of this conflict emerges value. His observation that "one cannot step into the same river twice" is well known among his many aphorisms. He is important in the development of Western thought.

Herbert, Edward (1583–1648). First Lord Herbert of Cherbury, he was a forerunner of English Deism. He much influenced Locke and, if indirectly, the religious outlook of the Founding Fathers. He taught that all religion has five essential features: (1) belief in the existence of God; (2) belief that he should be worshiped; (3) belief that virtue is the prime ingredient in the act of worship; (4) belief that man has a prime duty to repent of his sin; and (5) belief in an afterlife. He held that these are all innate ideas and he rejected the concept of divine revelation as therefore unnecessary.

Herbert, George (1593–1633). English divine and poet. A Cambridge man and notable classical scholar, he became Public Orator of the University of Cambridge in 1620 but later studied divinity and in 1630 was ordained priest. As rector of a rural parish near Salisbury, he was a model priest and his writings reflect a deep devotional spirit and sincere piety. Among his hymns is "The King of love my Shepherd is," a paraphrase of Ps. 23.

Herder, Johann Gottfried von (1744–1803). German philosopher. Trained under Kant and Hamann at Königsberg, he eventually became court preacher at Weimar. With Goethe he was one of the leaders of the *Sturm und Drang* movement. His greatest importance lies in his philosophy of history. He treated history as a natural science. He also saw speech as a key instrument in human culture and religion as an inevitable movement in human development. His evolutionary approach to history is regarded by many as anticipatory of Darwin.

Heresy. The Greek term (*hairesis*) from which this word is derived meant essentially "a choice". It came to be applied more particularly to the teachings of certain of the philosophical schools. By early Christian times it had come to bear, at least sometimes, a pejorative sense and soon it came to be used of the denial of a generally accepted theological doctrine. According to Roman Catholic teaching, a distinction is to be made between "formal" and "material" heresy. Formal heresy consists in wilfully and persistently adhering to what is incompatible with the Church's official doctrine. (Only a baptized person can be guilty of this.) "Material heresy" consists of accepting teachings that are incompatible with the Church's teaching but in good faith, e.g., because one has been brought up to accept teachings that are in fact incompatible with the teachings of the Roman Catholic Church. See also **Apostasy, Invincible Ignorance,** and **Schism.**

Hermas (2nd c.). Author of the book, "The Shepherd", which is included as Scripture in some of the earliest Greek manuscripts of the Bible and was very widely regarded as scriptural in the early Church in the East, although less esteemed in the West. Scholars date it *c.* mid-2nd c. He is regarded as one of the Apostolic Fathers and the text may be found in any standard collection of their works such as the Loeb edition: Kirsopp Lake, *The Apostolic Fathers,* 2 vols. (1912–1913), which gives it in Greek with English translation.

Hermeneutics. The term is from the Greek *hermeneutikos*, interpretation, and has been used in a general sense of all methods of interpreting philosophical or literary texts, including biblical ones. It has come to be distinguished, however, from exegesis (see **Exegesis**) as being more involved in the problem of how to achieve an authentic understanding of a culture and an age other than one's own. An extremely simple example of a hermeneutical problem arises from phrases used in the Bible such as "a day's journey" which, although the words are easily understood, is likely to give a modern American reader the impression of perhaps a few hundred miles or even, by plane, a few thousand, while the biblical writer would have in mind of course merely what one could do on foot or by mule. When such problems are magnified, the difficulty of understanding what precisely is being communicated is very serious. It includes the philosophical analysis of all human communication.

Hermetic Books. A collection of writing (Greek and Latin) ascribed to Hermes Trismegistus and dates from *c.* the mid-1st c. CE to *c.* 300. It is Gnostic and syncretistic, incorporating Platonic, Stoic, and various oriental elements in it. "Tresmigistus" was a designation of the Egyptian God, Thoth, regarded as the father of knowledge.

Hermits. The word "hermit" is derived from the Greek *erēmitēs*, which in turn comes from *erēmia*, desert. (The adjectival form in English is "eremitical".) It is used to designate a man or woman who retires from society to lead a secluded, solitary life. Christian hermits were found in the Egyptian desert and elsewhere as early as the 3rd c. Hermits are still to be found on Mount Athos and elsewhere in the Eastern Church. Some religious orders in the West, e.g., the Camaldoli and the Carthusians, retain much of the eremitical ideal, living as far as practicable a solitary life within a monastic framework, in contrast to the Trappists and others whose mode of life entails their being almost never alone.

Herodians. The partisans of the family of Herod who ruled during the life of Jesus (see Mark 12.13 and Matthew 22.16).

Herod the Great. The Romans appointed Herod King of the Jews in 40

BCE. He ruled from 37 to 4 BCE. He was still reigning when Jesus was born (modern scholars place the date of Jesus's birth a year or two before Herod's death) and it is to him that the massacre referred to in Matthew 2.16 relates.

Herrmann, Wilhelm (1846–1922). German theologian. Professor at Marburg, he was influenced by Kant and Ritschl. He argued for concentrating on the ethical teaching of Jesus, treating all else in the life of Jesus as of value only for its ethical content. Among his writings the most important is his *The Communion of the Christian with God* (1886).

Hesiod (*c.* **8th c.** BCE). Greek poet whose poetry presents at least rudimentary philosophical ideas such as the notion that Eros brought order out of chaos and the notion that a Golden Age (see **Golden Age**) existed in the remote past and that later ages represent successive deteriorations. His *Works and Days* and his *Theogony* are his most important works.

Hesychasts. Adherents of a system of mysticism called hesychasm (from the Greek *hēsychos*, "quiet") propagated in the Greek Orthodox Church by monks on Mount Athos in the fourteenth century. They taught that by an elaborate system of ascetic exercises, with special emphasis on perfect quiet of mind and body, man could arrive at the mystical vision of the Divine Light. These exercises later became more mechanical, yogalike breathing exercises, accompanying the ejaculatory prayer "Lord Jesus Christ, Son of God, have mercy on me." Hesychasm eventually became a focus of controversy between the Eastern and Western Churches. See **Gregory Palamas.**

Hexapla. The great edition of the text of the Old Testament compiled by Origen. It included the Hebrew text, the Hebrew text transliterated into Greek, and four versions in Greek, including a revised text of the Septuagint. Origen did this enormous work between 231 and *c.* 245.

Hicksites. In 1827–1828 a schism occurred among American Quakers, as a result of which those who followed the views of the more liberal party led by Elias Hicks (1748–1830) were called "Hicksites" by their opponents and are so called to this day. Hicks rejected even the minimum of doctrine that the more conservative Quakers had traditionally accepted (e.g., concerning the Person of Christ) and so opened the doors to virtually all comers, including persons from non-Christian religions.

Hieronymus. See **Jerome.**

High Church. The Anglican church party that historically has stressed the authority of the Church, the importance of the Sacraments, and the necessity of the Episcopate, has been traditionally called "High Church". The term is popularly but misleadingly used of all parishes that use Anglo-Catholic liturgy.

Higher Criticism. Scholarly study of the Bible is of two principal kinds: (1) textual analysis and (2) literary analysis. The latter includes a study of the meanings and of everything pertaining to the interpretation of the Bible. (See **Hermeneutics.**) To the latter was sometimes given the designation "Higher Criticism," but the phrase is now outmoded.

High Priest. In the Old Testament, the high priest was the head of the entire Levitical priesthood. See Exodus 28. After the Exile, he was the head of the Jewish state as well as religious head.

Hijra. See **Hegira.**

Hilary of Poitiers (*c.* **315–367**). Converted from Neoplatonism, he was eventually elected Bishop of Poitiers and defended, against the Arians, the position that came to be recognized as the orthodox one, much as did Athanasius in the East.

Hillel (1st c. BCE). Rabbinic scholar. He provided rules for interpreting the Bible and is much revered in Judaism. His followers constitute a school which, in opposition to that of Shammai, took a more liberal view of how the Torah should be interpreted and were more conciliatory toward non-Jews.

Hīnayāna. This Buddhist term was used in ancient India for one of several means of attaining enlightenment. (The word *yāna* means "methods.") It was regarded as having appeal to a few people, contradistinguished from Mahāyāna, a method expected to appeal to the many.

Hinduism. The name given in the West to the religious system of India. It designates both a general, traditional outlook and the seemingly almost limitlessness of its multifaceted expression.

Hindu society has been aptly called a great organism. Hindu life oscillates between two poles: *dharma* and *moksha*. Dharma (see **Dharma**) is an imprecise term, in some ways like the Chinese *li*, suggesting both cosmic order and spiritual law but much else besides, while moksha points to spiritual liberation: identification with the Absolute, the final goal of the pilgrimage of life. But the ways of expressing this basic outlook are innumerable. Moreover, characteristic of Hinduism is a toleration of all ways of expressing it. Each is a *darshana*: a particular vision, inevitably partial yet no less inevitably having a valuable function, for each represents an aspect of life, and life is as infinite as the universe itself. So Hinduism can come in garish, primitive guises, highly charged with emotion, especially sexual feeling, on the one hand, and, on the other, in highly intellectual forms, more philosophical than religious.

It has sacred scriptures: (1) the Vedas, an early literature including the Rig-Veda, a collection of hymns in praise of the Indian pantheon, for Vedas date from a polytheistic stage in the religious development of India; (2) the Brahamanas, consisting largely of materials treating of ceremonial and ritual; and the Upanishads (dating from *c.* 800 BCE), which are philosophical treatises, reflecting the thought of the learned. To these must be added, however, many other kinds of literature all related in one way or another to the enormous range of Hindu thought and life.

The well-known traditional caste system of India is an expression of the institutional side of Indian society. It is associated, however, with the concept of spiritual evolution (writ so deeply into Indian thought and outlook) and to the karmic principle and its entailments. (See **Karma.**) The traditional castes are: (1) the *Brahmana* or priestly and scholarly caste; (2) the *Kshatriya*, the warrior or soldier caste; (3) the *Vaisya*, the mercantile caste; and (4) the *Sudra*, the farming and peasant caste. Traditionally, each had its function in society and its recognized niche. Alongside of caste, nevertheless, were other forces, for the Indian outlook emphasizes, in its own way, the individual in his or her solitary quest for salvation and for God. Bhakti, for instance, is a movement, often highly emotional and personalistic, that seems to stand outside all institutional and social organization. Indeed, in Hinduism there are many roads to God, e.g., the way of devotion, the way of learning, and the way of good actions (karma). Bhakti, the way of devotion, has been manifested in an endless variety of ways.

Philosophical schools also developed, expressive of the intellectual side of Hinduism. Some of these are of great antiquity. By *c.* 200 CE, six had become well recognized. One of the most interesting is Vedanta, which is of great antiquity, with a literature partly going back to *c.* 500 BCE. Vedanta itself, however, comes in at least three well-defined forms. (See **Vedanta.**)

Hinduism may be regarded, then, in many ways. Orthodox Hinduism is a blood-and-soil religion. It is the religion of the great sub-continent called India with its enormous population. It is at the same time a clearinghouse of religious ideas into which virtually any religious idea can be hospitably received. Yet every such idea seems to be transformed as it is assimilated to the spiritual climate of India. It is as if it has been grafted on to a mighty tree, the character of which it gradually takes on. As a living tree, it sends offshoots beyond itself and has no care to hold them, for there can be no question of competition with such a gigantic living organism. Buddhism is the largest of these many offshoots and the most internationally widespread, but even in all its forms it expresses only certain important emphases within the outlook of its Hindu mother. The Sikhs, who stem from an attempt to overcome the striking difference between Hinduism and Islam, reflect, if more distantly, some of the traits of their Hindu parentage. The strength of Hinduism lies in its being far less a social or ecclesiastical organization than a living organism.

Hindu Medicine. See **Āyurveda.**

Hinnom. See **Gehenna.**

Hippolytus (*c.* 165–*c.* 236). Important theologian of the early Roman Church. He attacked the teaching of the Sabellians and wrote a treatise against heresies. This was for long lost, but part of it was discovered in a manuscript at Mount Athos and published in 1851 at Oxford. Theologically, he distinguished two states of the Logos: (1) the *logos endiathetos*, the eternal and immanent logos, and (2) the *logos prophorikos*, the temporal and exterior logos. (See **Logos.**) He also resisted the tendency of the Roman Church of his time (spurred by the growing numbers of converts) to relax the standards for readmission of wayward Christians to the Church. See **Callistus I.**

Hiram. King of Tyre. Both David and Solomon traded with him for their architectural projects. See II Samuel 5.11; I Kings 5.15 ff.

History. The importance of an historical approach to an understanding of humanity and the universe is controversial. One may indeed study not only subjects such as geometry, astronomy, biology, and physics, but also psychology and even architecture and linguistics apart from their history. One may even study historical events themselves without reflecting upon the nature and meaning (if any) of the historical process. The question arises, however, whether such an ahistorical method of study can ever enable us to understand any subject, more especially any subject directly relating to human experience. Moreover, one must ask whether it is enough merely to learn *about* historical events. Must not we make the past in some measure part of our own experience, living multidimensionally in history, as far as possible, instead of detaching ourselves from it?

The philosophy or philosophical analysis of history is concerned with the nature, scope, and significance of historical studies. Vico is generally taken to be the classic exponent of the view that nothing can be properly understood apart from its history. Dilthey, in calling attention to the way in which the historian himself is limited by the perspectives of his own age, showed the impossibility of a completely objective study of history. Croce, who was considerably influenced by Vico, saw philosophy and history as inseparable from each other. Philosophy cannot be understood apart from history. Hegel saw a definite process in history in which, through a dialectic of thesis and antithesis, a synthesis is achieved and this process is how the Absolute *Geist* realizes its nature in the universe. Many philosophers have been much concerned with the relation of history to philosophical understanding and some have come up with specific proposals about the nature of the historical process. For example, one may look upon history as revealing a cyclic pattern (in every age, empires rise and fall; political events occur in cycles as do fashions in clothes and coiffures) or one may see history as revealing an evolutionary progress: a spiral moving ever upward, although, like the Dow Jones Average, it has ups and downs on the way. Or again one may see history as exhibiting novel and unpredictable leaps. In all such cases, however, the study of history is seen as indispensable to any authentic understanding of ourselves and the universe.

In religion the significance of history varies with the kind of presuppositions entertained in the religion in question. For example, very broadly speaking, religions such as Hinduism and Buddhism are generally regarded as more independent of history than are the religions of the West. Hinduism, for instance, has no founder or central figure (e.g., as is Moses to Judaism, Jesus in Christianity, Muhammad in Islam) and so at least does not have the same *kind* of historical underpinnings as do these occidental religions. Buddhism, although, or course, historically focused on Gautama, is not dependent on that focus in the way in which Christianity is dependent on the Person and Work of Jesus Christ, apart from whom there could be no Christian Way at all, or even as Islam is dependent on Muhammad, who remains central to the entire structure of Islam. Both Troeltsch and Ritschl, however, while recognizing that Christianity emerged from history, contended that it is independent of it. Yet to the extent that one sees a religion as a living tree, as is the case with both Hinduism and Christianity and the cultures respectively attached to them, it is obvious that the old tree, with all its living branches, its offshoots, and its dead wood, cannot be understood apart from its history. So, if philosophical thought is also a living organism in its own way, the history of thought is inseparable from the thought-process itself.

Hittites. The Hittites were an Indo-European people who settled in Asia Minor sometime before 2,000 BCE. They are frequently mentioned in the Old Testament. At the time of Abraham, according to Genesis 23, they lived in Hebron. There were still Hittites living in the land under Solomon (I Kings 9.20) whose wives included Hittites (I Kings 11.1). Much is known about them from various sources including, since excavations in Turkey in 1906, their own cuneiform records. They had a monarchical form of government and an agricultural economy but had also valuable mineral resources. From a kingdom centered in Anatolia, they spread into an empire that attained great importance by *c.* 1400 BCE. Their pantheon included innumerable deities; their literature was copious; their art and their architecture, although not notably original, were also copious and evidences remain today in great abundance. They are to be associated with the Phoenicians and the Canaanites of Palestine and Syria.

Hobbes, Thomas (1588–1679). English philosopher. An Oxford man, he became tutor in the Cavendish family. In the course of a tour of Europe in 1610, he was impressed by the new developments in science and philosophy that were afoot. In 1636 he met Galileo in Florence. After some political difficulties he wrote his *Leviathan* which, published in 1651, brought him both fame and more political difficulties. It was seen as a blatantly "secular" approach to political theory: a charge that was indeed justified, for Hobbes, in his writing, was not merely attacking the Church; he was propounding views that implied the absence of freedom of the will and that looked upon man as totally in the grasp of his appetites and passions, his emotions and his fantasies. He saw, moreover, individuals in constant warfare with one another, so that, although men might here and there band together because of some common interest, the interest of each is in the last resort thoroughly selfish.

Hodge, Charles (1797–1878). American Presbyterian theologian, ordained in

1821 to the Presbyterian ministry and associated with Princeton for most of his life. He was widely esteemed in his day as a systematizer of the traditional Calvinist position to which Presbyterians at that time tenaciously held. His views were in some ways less rigid than the views of those whose general position was similar to his. Among his works are various commentaries and his *What is Darwinism?* (1874); but his fame rests principally on his *Systematic Theology*, 3 vols. (1871–73).

Holākā. A spring festival in India dedicated to Kṛṇṣa and the *gopīs*. It seems to have developed out of a more primitive kind of *saturnalia*, a fertility ritual in which people engaged in erotic dances and games. It is also called Holī.

Holī. See **Holākā.**

Holiness, The Code of. The collection of Mosaic laws set forth in Leviticus 17–26. Biblical scholars designate it by the letter H. Most scholars regard it as having been written during the Exile in Babylon, sometime *c.* the mid-sixth c. BCE. It was probably incorporated about a century later in the document that scholars call P. See P.

Holiness, Your. The title ("Holiness") was originally one applied to all bishops, but since *c.* 600 its use has been restricted to patriarchs. In the West it has been used of the Pope (one of whose titles is that of Patriarch of the West) since the 14th c.

Holy City, The. A name applied to Jerusalem.

Holy Club, The. A name given, no doubt in jest, to the group founded by the brothers Wesley, at Oxford in 1729. Its purposes included serious study of the Bible, emphasis on frequent reception of the Sacrament, and pastoral concern and care for the poor.

Holy Family, The. The group, often represented in Christian art, consisting of Mary, Joseph, and the Infant Jesus. Devotion to it includes an expression of the Church's concern for the values of Christian family life.

Holy Father, The. The title popularly used by English-speaking Roman Catholics in alluding to the Pope. It has been in use since at least the 14th c. The full title is *Beatissimus Pater.*

Holy Ghost. See **Holy Spirit.**

Holy Innocents. See **Innocents, Holy.**

Holy Island. See **Lindisfarne.**

Holy Mountain, The. A name given to Mount Athos as the spiritual center of Eastern Orthodoxy.

Holy Office, The. A Roman Congregation (a department of the Roman Curia, which deals with the central administration of the Roman Catholic Church) was established by Pope Paul III in 1542 as the final court of appeal in heresy trials. It was originally closely connected with the Inquisition. In the 20th c. it has been reformed and its name changed in 1965 by Pope Paul VI to "Congregatio pro Doctrina Fidei" so as to give it a less negative connotation. Although its functions are now more limited, it nevertheless is still in the forefront of the various departments of the Curia.

Holy Orders. The higher grades of the Christian ministry (bishop, priest, deacon) are so designated, traditionally distinguishing them from "minor" orders such as reader and acolyte. The phrase "Clerk" (cleric) "in Holy Orders" is still is use for certain purposes in England.

Holy Roman Empire. Following the coronation of Charlemagne as Emperor on Christmas Day of the year 800, a new empire, so to be called in the West, was set up, although the existing Roman Empire continued at Constantinople till the fall of the latter in 1453. Never strong, it helped to bring some semblances of order to the West, which in the earlier Middle Ages had been in a state of anarchy, and it also functioned at times, at least, as a brake to the political ambitions of the medieval papacy, providing in some measure two foci of power (Pope and Emperor) in the West in contrast to the Byzantine totalitarianism of the East. It has been said, however, if in jest, that it was neither holy, nor Roman, nor an empire.

Holy See, The. A name given to the papacy in formal contexts designating its authoritative jurisdiction and administrative and governmental functions. The name alludes to the "See" (bishopric) of the Bishop of Rome, one of the Pope's titles.

Holy Sepulchre, The. According to an ancient tradition, the rock cave in Jerusalem in which Christ was buried and in which he rose from the dead, is in a place on which the Church of the Holy Sepulchre now stands. The first church was dedicated c. 335, after Helena, the mother of the Emperor Constantine and a devout Christian, claimed to have discovered the site. The building, destroyed by the Persians in 614, was rebuilt a few years later. In the 10th c. a new church was begun to replace this one, which was by then in a decaying state. The Crusaders, c. 1130, built a larger one. This, rebuilt in 1310, was damaged by fire in 1808 and the present one, largely built a few years later, although partly retaining the 12th c. bell tower, dates therefore from only the early 19th c. It is much visited by Christian pilgrims to the Holy Land.

Holy Shroud. Since 1578, a relic has been preserved at Turin, bearing the imprint of the body of a man apparently crucified. Believed by many to have been the winding sheet of Jesus, it was for long the subject of much controversy. The ecclesiastical authorities for long withheld permission to have a piece of the fabric scientifically tested for dating, which, although it might have shown it to be contemporary with the time of Jesus or nearly so, of course could not by itself have established it as what so many of the faithful believed it to be. That medieval forgeries abound is widely known, but historical evidence did suggest that it could not be so lightly set aside as one of them. At last, however, permission to make scientific tests by radiocarbon methods was granted, and in October 1988 the results were published, showing that the fabric is medieval.

It should be noted that the Vatican had never made any official claim of the authenticity of the Shroud as that of Jesus. Officially it has been listed as a "representation" of Christ's burial cloth. The investigation arranged in October 1987 and conducted with every reasonable precaution at three independent laboratories all of which has specialized in dating with carbon-14 methods and had the greatest experience in dealing with archeological materials: Arizona, Oxford, and Zurich. The result was unambiguous. The relic could not possibly be dated from any time in or near the first century CE. This result need not preclude, of course, its veneration as what the Church has always proclaimed it to be: a representation of the burial cloth of Christ. After all, it has been the focus of centuries of the loving prayers of millions of people whose thoughts it has directed to the heart of the Christian faith, which certainly can never depend upon a piece of linen.

Holy Spirit. In Christian theology, the Third Person of the Trinity. The notion of the Spirit of God (*ruach*) plays an important role in Old Testament thought, being present at Creation, "brooding on the face of the waters" (Genesis 1.2). Throughout the Old Testament the Spirit is associated with deeds of valor, artistic accomplishment, and especially the communication of divine truth. Such Hebrew concepts of the function of the Spirit of God were further developed in the New Testament, as in the outpouring of the Spirit at Pentecost and the promise of Jesus to send "another Paraclete" (John 14.16). Gradually the role of the Holy Spirit in relation to the Church was developed, and after much theological controversy the place of the Holy Spirit in relation to God the Father and God the Son was expressed in the Trinitarian formula: a skillful and subtle theological way of treating the problem in terms of the intellectual climate of the early Church and one that is of great importance in all attempts to specify the Christian concept of the nature of God.

The term "Holy Ghost" is simply an older English usage that has tended to be replaced by the Latin form (from *Spiritus*, "Spirit") because "ghost" and "ghostly" have acquired a misleading connotation. In much the same way the phrase "ghostly father" (which now would be rendered "spiritual director") has fallen into disuse.

Holy Water. Water blessed by a priest in the name of the Church and set aside for various religious uses. Salt is usually added to it and is separately blessed. The custom dates from early Christian times: at least as early as the 5th c. in the West and even earlier in the East. One of the uses most commonly encountered by casual churchgoers is in the water stoup at the entrance to a church, into which the faithful dip one or more fingers before making the sign of the cross on themselves as they enter the church. One may, after so moistening one's own hand with the blessed water, touch that of the next person entering: a beautiful symbolizing of Christian love.

Holy Week. The week immediately preceding Easter Day, during which, from early Christian times, a series of rites is observed expressive of the special devotional spirit proper to that period, which includes Palm Sunday, Maundy Thursday, and Good Friday.

Homoeans. Controversies raged in the early Christian Church on the nature of Christ and his relationship to the Father. In the 4th c. the Arian party was contending that Christ is not eternal but a creature, although a unique creature, having been created by God the Father, out of nothing, for the creation of the world. Those in general sympathy with this interpretation preferred therefore to say that Christ is *homoiousion*, i.e., of *similar* substance with the Father, while the party whose views were expressed in the Nicene Creed and eventually came to be accepted by the Church as orthodox held that Christ is *homoousion*, i.e., of the *same* substance as the Father. Subtler distinctions, however, arose. The Homoeans, for instance, repudiated the use of the concept *ousia* as the locus of discussion, preferring to assert simply that Christ is *homoios* (like) the Father, and to keep further christological controversies within that framework. Against the Homoeans stood the Anomoeans, an extremist party who wished specifically to say that Christ is *dissimilar* (*anomoios*) from the Father.

Homoousion. From the Greek, meaning "of one (i.e., the same) substance." The term is used in the Nicene Creed specifically against the Arians. See **Arianism.**

Homosexuality. Sexual attraction between members of the same sex. (In women it is known as lesbianism, although "homosexual" is linguistically apposite, since "homo" derives from the Greek *homos*, "the same", not from the Latin *homo*, "man", as is supposed by some.) The term may be used to denote, on the one hand, an inclination or tendency among some people to be attracted to persons of the same sex; or, on the other hand, it may be used of sexual practices in which persons of the same sex engage. Such practices were widespread in the ancient world and are unequivocally condemned in the Bible, both in the Old Testament and in the New. That they are contrary to nature would seem to follow from the fact that the obvious purpose of the sexual instinct is to insure the reproduction of the species. Zoologists and others, however, have for long pointed out that homosexual activity is common among other mammals, notably among the simians, those biologically closest to man. Nevertheless, such activities, although very common in immature simians, have a tendency to be replaced, sometimes very suddenly, when adulthood is attained, by heterosexual behavior.

Extensive controversy on the subject continues to flourish among scientific investigators, so that it is difficult to find definite answers to important questions about it. For instance, is homosexuality as a "preference" to be regarded as a deviation from a heterosexual norm, induced or aggravated by physical, psychological, or other circumstances, or are there cases in which it is innate and therefore to be regarded as a difference such as is the difference between, say, brunettes and blondes? Havelock Ellis, one of the earlier among modern scientific investigators in the field of sexual behavior, claimed to have noticed certain tendencies among male homosexuals, such as aptitude for the dramatic and other artistic pursuits, love of personal adornment, and even the inability to whistle and a preference for the color green, which he thought to be common among both children and women! Yet in spite of much more advanced and careful methods of inquiry developed since his time, the answers to even the most obvious questions about homosexuality are hardly more satisfactory than they were then. There is a general tendency among legal experts and many moralists to take a permissive attitude toward all forms of sexual activity, however aberrant they may be from a traditionalist viewpoint, so long as they do not hurt other people. What precisely constitutes "hurt" is, however, by no means as simple as it may appear. The major religions of the world, including Christianity, have traditionally tended, to say the least, to condemn all sexual activity other than heterosexual intercourse.

Hōnen. See **Genku.**

Honorius I. A 7th c. Pope. Historically, his interest lies especially in his supporting a side in the Monothelite controversy that was eventually held to be heterodox, being condemned both at the Council of Constantinople in 681 and repeatedly by his own successors in the papal chair. The letter of Honorius containing support for the heretical view has been among those much used in arguments against the doctrine of Papal Infallibility that was declared by the First Vatican Council to be required of all members of the Roman Catholic Church.

Hooker, Richard (*c.* **1554–1600**). Anglican divine. An Oxford man, he has been probably the most powerful and certainly the most renowned among advocates of the Anglican Way. His principal work is his *Treatise on the Laws of Ecclesiastical Polity,* published partly in 1594 and partly in 1597.

Hopkins, Gerald Manley (1844–1889). Poet. Trained at Balliol College, Oxford, under Benjamin Jowett and Walter Pater, he came under Tractarian influence. In 1866 he became a Roman Catholic. Having entered the Jesuit novitiate two years later, he was ordained priest in 1877 and was appointed professor of Greek at the Royal University, Dublin, retaining that chair till his death. His poems, for which he was virtually unknown during his life but which were preserved by his Oxford friend Robert Bridges, later Poet Laureate, are marked by a distinctively personal quality and fine religious feeling. Important among them are *The Wreck of the Deutschland* and *The Windhover: to Christ our Lord.*

Horeb. The scene of the experience of Moses in face of the burning bush (Exodus 3.1). It seems to be identified with Mount Sinai, but its exact location is uncertain.

Horse. The horse was known in Mesopotamia as early as the 3rd millennium

BCE, although its use was comparatively rare till *c.* 1800 BCE. As a symbol of magical protective power the horse is both ancient and widespread. Wooden horse-heads carved on some house gables in England reflect this ancient belief. The bones of horses have been found in the walls of some old English houses where they have been embedded for such reasons. See **Dadhyac** and **Dadhikrā**. For further information see W. D. O'Flaherty, "The Submarine Mare in the Mythology of Śiva" in the *Journal of the Royal Asiatic Society,* 1, 1971.

Hort, Fenton John Anthony (1828–1892). New Testament scholar. Educated at Rugby under the famous Thomas Arnold, and at Trinity College, Cambridge, of which he became a Fellow, he showed sympathies with Charles Kingsley, F. D. Maurice, and their circle. His fame rests, however, on his work with Westcott on the text of the New Testament, which was a landmark in the development of that field of study in the English-speaking world and is still important in spite of immense progress made in New Testament studies since their time.

Hosanna. An invocation of Yahweh (see Psalm 118.25) used in later Jewish liturgy at the feast of Pentecost and elsewhere. It is a petition for salvation; hence its use by the people who met Jesus at his last entrance into Jerusalem signifies their recognition of his saving power.

Hosea. The writings contained in the Old Testament book of Hosea probably begin toward the end of the reign of Jeroboam II in mid-8th c. BCE. The book as we have it contains two distinct parts: (1) a biographical account of Hosea's marriage to Gomer with autobiographical reflections and interpretations and (2) a somewhat haphazard collection of oracles. Most scholars, despite some difficulties in the book, perceive the story of Hosea's marriage to Gomer

as based upon fact, not as an allegorical invention. His interpretation of his life's story, however, and the analogy he sees in it with the dealings of Yahweh toward his people spring from deep spiritual perception. It would appear that Hosea married a woman who was unfaithful. He divorced her, but he loved her so much that he forgave her infidelity, sought her, and won her back, perhaps even purchasing her out of slavery. This story Hosea uses to exhibit the ways of Yahweh toward his people.

Hospitaller, The Knights. The beginnings of this order are obscure, but with the Crusaders' success in 1099 they developed rapidly and with papal recognition. By early in the 14th c. they came to be known as the Knights of Rhodes and from 1530 as the Knights of Malta. At first their chief focus was on providing hospitality to pilgrims to the Holy Land, where they had headquarters in a hospital at Jerusalem. By the 12th c. they were concerning themselves with the care of the sick. They soon went on to become a regular army for the defense of Christian pilgrims and spread to many countries in Europe. They are now a Roman Catholic chivalric order known as the Knights of Malta. Its members wear the Maltese cross on a black cloak. For long dormant in England after the Reformation, it was revived there in 1831 and received a royal charter in 1888 as an order of chivalry.

Hossō. A Japanese school of Buddhism introduced from China to Japan by Dōshō (629–700 CE). Its philosophy was analytical and a mixture of realism and idealism. Ultimate reality is to be found in the mind or "store-consciousness" of each individual. This "store-consciousness" has an innumerable collection of "seeds" (*bīja*), manifesting themselves in innumerable existences. The school cultivated mystical contemplation and recognized ten stages in the achievement of its goal.

Host. From the Latin *hostia*, "victim". The term used for the consecrated Bread in the Mass.

Hosts, The Lord of. The "hosts" in this biblical phrase means literally "armies". Which armies are envisioned is not entirely clear. They may have been originally conceived as the armies of Israel, but as theologically developed they become the cosmic powers. The underlying motif seems to be an affirmation of the sovereignty of Yahweh, seen as controlling all the forces of the universe.

Hour. In classical Hebrew, there is no word "hour" as understood today, and this unit of time seems not to have been used. By the time of Jesus, however, the Jews had come to accept the Graeco-Roman custom of dividing the day into periods of twelve hours, beginning at sunrise and ending at sunset and so varying in length according to the length of daylight. If daylight ran from, say, 6 a.m. to 6 p.m., by our reckoning, the third hour would be our 9 a.m., the sixth our noon, and the ninth our 3 p.m. The word "hour" is also often used in the New Testament to signify a point in time or period or age, e.g., the "hour" when the Son of Man is delivered into the hands of sinners (Matthew 26.45) and the last "hour" of the world (I John 2.18), identified with "the present age." When Jesus declares that his "hour" has not yet come (John 2.4), the implication is that the appointed time for his triumph or his glorification has not yet arrived; as we might say, "the time is not yet ripe."

Hours. Traditionally, the canonical hours consisted of the daily prayers prescribed by the Church for recitation or singing at certain hours of the day. In monastic communities they were sung or said by the community in choir. Elsewhere they might be said privately. Their scriptural warrant could be invoked from Psalm 119.164: "Seven times a day do I praise thee. . . . " The traditional seven "hours" were: (1) Mat-

tins and Lauds, (2) Prime, (3) Terce, (4) Sext, (5) None, (6) Vespers, (7) Compline. (Prime, Terce, Sext, and None would be respectively at 6 a.m., 9 a.m., noon, and 3 p.m., or as nearly as possible according to the schedule for the other duties of the day. Compline comes immediately before retiring for the night.) In the Roman Catholic Church this traditional arrangement has been considerably modified in the 1971 Breviary. See **Breviary.**

Ho Yen. A 3rd c. CE Chinese neo-Taoist philosopher, who deeply revered Confucius. His chief works are his *Treatise on the Tao* and his *Treatise on the Nameless.*

Hsuan Hsueh. An intellectual movement that developed in China in the 3rd and 4th centuries CE. The term means literally "dark learning" and modern scholars sometimes allude to it as Neo-Taoism. One of its chief exponents was Wang Pi (226–249 CE) who wrote commentaries on the Tao Te Ching and the I Ching and exercised much influence not only on Neo-Taoist but on Neo-Confucian and even some Chinese Buddhist thought.

Hsuan-Tsang (596–664). Chinese philosopher. After long search for truth in his homeland he went to India in his early thirties and remained there for sixteen years, eventually returning home to set up a school for the translation of hundreds of works that he had collected in India. His own findings, expressed in his *Treatise on the Establishment of the Doctrine of Consciousness-Only,* focus on the contention that neither the self nor external objects exist, but only the inner, psychic awareness. This is not and probably cannot be fully realized except by the arhat.

Hua Yen. A Chinese school of Buddhism in which are expounded some of the highest developments in Chinese metaphysical thought. Its first Chinese master seems to have been Tu-shun (557–640 CE). According to the teaching of this school, whose philosophy was pre-eminently expounded by Fa-tsang (643–712 CE), there is a permanently immutable mind, universal in scope, which is the basis of all phenomena. This made Hua Yen more compatible with the Chinese outlook and temper than schools such as Ch'an, in which both Being and non-Being are illusory. Fa Chang's *Treatise on the Golden Lion* is a class exposition of Hua Yen.

Hügel, (Baron) Friedrich von (1852–1925). Roman Catholic theologian. Born at Florence, he settled in England in 1867, although spending much time on the continent of Europe. Much associated with the leaders of the Modernist movement in the Roman Catholic Church of his day, he saw the life of the Church as tripartite: mystical, intellectual, and institutional. Among his many writings, *The Mystical Element in Religion* (1908), a study of the subject in the thought and outlook of Saint Catherine of Genoa, has had perhaps the most enduring influence, but his *Essays and Addresses on the Philosophy of Religion* (1921 and 1926) and his *Eternal Life* (1912) are important witnesses to his unusual theological acumen and spiritual discernment. His influence was felt much more outside the Roman Catholic Church than within it.

Hugh (1024–1109). Abbot of Cluny. As advisor to nine popes, he not only was able to advance the role of Cluniac principles in the development of monasticism in the West but exercised a powerful influence in ecclesiastical affairs and official decisions on theological questions, e.g., the condemnation of Berengar in 1050. The new basilica at Cluny, when the high altar was consecrated in 1095, was, with a length of 555 feet, the largest church in Christendom. Hugh also was a leader in the arrangements for the First Crusade. He was canonized by Pope Callistus II in 1120.

Hugh (1052–1132). Bishop of Grenoble. He very actively reformed abuses and fostered a spirit of piety in his diocese, welcoming Bruno, founder of the Carthusians, to his diocese and granting them the Grande Chartreuse that is their motherhouse to this day.

Hugh of Saint-Victor. 12th c. theologian. Details of his life are obscure. He entered c. 1115 the house of Augustinian canons that had been founded by William of Champeaux. He wrote very extensively on a wide range in the fields of the learning of his time. In his biblical studies he emphasized the importance of looking at the literal text of Scripture: an attitude that characterized the Victorine school in contrast to a prevalent medieval practice of excessive allegorization.

Huguenots. Name given to the French Protestants, apparently at first as a nickname based on a medieval story. The inspiration of French Protestantism came from Calvin, and at the Synod of Paris in 1559 the Church was formally organized on Calvinist lines. Much persecution by the Catholic majority followed, ending with the notorious Massacre of Saint Bartholomew in 1572. The Huguenots, however, continued to play a considerable part in the religious life of France, repressions notwithstanding. After the Bourbon restoration in 1815, the restrictions against them disappeared and their numbers grew. Today they represent a significant element in French religious life, despite the strong dominance of Catholic tradition and outlook that pervades the French temper even among those only nominally attached to the institutional Church.

Huitzilopochtli. One of the most important among the Mesoamerican gods, he became the patron deity of the Aztec capital city. His shrine became the great temple of the Aztec empire, called by the Spanish the Templo Mayor: a vast pyramid temple. After the formation of the Aztec state in 1428 CE, the cult of Huitzilopochtli grew to include large-scale human sacrifice of captured peoples.

Hui Yüan (334–417 CE). This Chinese thinker, after much study of both Confucianism and Taoism, in his earlier years, was converted to Buddhism, whose teachings he then widely expounded. The Tung-lin monastery that he founded in Lu Shan in Central China attained great fame. His emphasis on the infinite compassion of Amitabha Buddha led him to be regarded as the founder of the Pure Land school of Buddhism.

Huizinga, Johann (1872–1945). Dutch historian of culture. He taught at Göttingen and Leyden, specializing in the culture of the later Middle Ages. He emphasized the concept of man as *homo ludens*, expressing the notion of man as "at play". His writings include *The Waning of the Middle Ages* (1919), *Erasmus* (1924–5), and *Homo Ludens* (1938).

Humanae Vitae. Encyclical issued by Pope Paul VI in 1968 reaffirming the condemnation of all methods of birth control other than the "rhythm method", despite the fact that most of the members of the papal commission that had been appointed by John XXIII in 1963 seem to have favored contraception as a licit procedure for married couples.

Humani Generis. Encyclical issued by Pope Pius XII in 1950, condemning a large array of movements and tendencies in the intellectual life of the 20th c. both within and outside the Roman Catholic Church, e.g., disdain for or distrust of Thomistic thought; existentialism; contempt for the authority of the Church; unwillingness to identify the Church that is in communion with the Holy See (Rome) with the Mystical Body of Christ (*Corpus mysticum*); and excessive academic freedom in the interpretation of the Bible.

Humanism. Because this term is ambiguous, having a wide variety of meanings, its use calls for special care. For example, historically it has been taken, as used by Protagoras (one of the early Greek philosophers who declared that "man is the measure of all things"), to specify a stance against philosophical absolutism. In comparatively recent times, William James and others have taken a position that might be called humanistic in the sense that it rejects metaphysical views such as Hegel's absolute idealism. The assertion attributed to Protagoras designates a methodology that may be used by people of a religious or of an anti-religious disposition or intent. Alexander Pope was not being religious or anti-religious when he wrote: "Know then thyself, presume not God to scan; The proper study of mankind is Man." He was calling attention, rather, to the fact the human knowledge is limited by our being human. Similarly, "the humanities" (philosophy, language, literature, etc.) may be studied and used by religious and by non-religious people.

There are, however, two traditions, both called humanistic, that are very different indeed from one another. One, sometimes called Socratic humanism because it stems from the outlook that Plato attributes to Socrates, is distinctly religious in the sense that it deals with religious concerns such as ultimate reality and the concept of afterlife even as it focuses on man. The humanism of the Renaissance, as expressed in men such as Pico della Mirandola, Marsiglio Ficino (among the Italian *umanisti*) and others such as Erasmus and Reuchlin, is often deeply religious while not at all following the traditional mainstream of the Church's theology. The other sort of humanism is more or less consciously non-religious or even anti-religious in attitude and intent. An extreme form of it was expressed by the French thinker Auguste Comte, who sought to formalize the worship of humanity as the highest value upon which one can focus. Many, however, without going as far as that, would think of their position as definitely "secular" in the sense that they wish at least to ignore religious concerns and interests if not to oppose all that has to do with them. So different is that secular humanism from the other kind that one historian of philosophy, Wilhelm Windelband, proposed to call them by different names: the "Socratic" type to be called humanism and the "secular" to be called hominism. The term "humanist" has been used in English since at least the time of Francis Bacon and generally referred to those who followed the Renaissance tradition and pursued the study of "humane learning" or "the humanities" in that spirit: the liberal arts, i.e., the arts proper to free men (*liberi*) contradistinguished from slaves. The term "humanism", however, although known in German under the name "Humanismus", was not used in English till it was coined by S. T. Coleridge in 1834, specifically to designate a person who, whether religious or otherwise, denied the theological doctrine of the divinity of Christ. The humanist label has since been accepted by a wide variety of nonreligious or anti-religious groups, such as Marxists, Freudians, nihilistic existentialists and others, further adding to the ambiguities attending the use of the term. In modern usage those who champion political individualism and applaud the values of what they call an "open society" and defend the "dignity of man" (see **Human Rights**) against the encroachments of government interference must be distinguished from those (e.g., B. F. Skinner) who repudiate such views as alien from the scientific study of humankind. The latter, in claiming the humanist label, would prefer to call their approach "scientific humanism." The confusion is aggravated by those who, unaccustomed to the traditions of humane learning and encountering it as an emancipation from either a narrow religiosity or an ignorant antipathy to religious concerns, assume the humanist label uncritically without understanding its ambiguities. The humanist label is also assumed by some merely as a cover for an atheistic slant

on life, undisciplined by scientific method and uninformed by humane learning; hence its widespread disrepute.

Human Rights. A modern phrase for what was known in the 18th c. (e.g., by the Founding Fathers of the United States) as "natural rights" or "the rights of man." They are claimed to inhere in all human beings as *ethical* rights: not rights that all human beings do enjoy but rights that ideally they ought to enjoy. The concept springs from what is traditionally known in jurisprudence as *jus naturale* or "natural law," which although much criticized by philosophers has played an important role in the history of Western culture and civilization. From the time when Stoic principles were influential in Rome, the basic rights recognized have been the right to life and the right to liberty. More recent claims have been made for the right to pursue happiness, to own property, and even such economic advantages as paid vacations, although such claims are generally admitted to belong to Utopian aspirations rather than to the realm of reality. Such claims confuse the issue by failing to distinguish between "ideals" and "ethical entitlements." Moreover, even what are generally admitted to be basic human rights (life and liberty) have not been uniformly accepted; e.g., John Locke gave priority to liberty over life, while Thomas Hobbes gave it to life over liberty. The view that life has the priority gives rise to controversial opinions both on abortion and on capital punishment, both on suicide and on euthanasia. No theory, indeed, of "human rights" can solve such ethical problems, for such a theory must always presuppose a particular context: not only a certain kind of civilization, but a philosophical and scientific presupposition on the subject of what constitutes a human being. Sir Ian Percival, speaking in the British Parliament twenty-two years after capital punishment had been abolished in the U.K., began by affirming that there is no place in a civilized society for capital punishment. After a pause he went on to ask that one first get the civilized society. A society in which innocent people are in daily danger of being shot to death by occupants of passing vehicles for the latter's amusement cannot be described as civilized; nor is it undebatable that a man who rapes little girls before burying them alive or burning or slicing them up alive qualifies as a human being. Not only is this not by any means philosophically indisputable; it is not clear even in law. This theme was developed in a profound French novel by Jean Vercors Bruller, translated into English under the title *You Shall Know Them* (Boston: Little Brown, 1953), which calls attention to the lack of precision in law on what constitutes a human being. The range of problems attending the ethical questions on human rights can be seen better when related to questions about human duties, which may be seen even more plainly to relate to specific contextual situations. All this does not mean that the question of human rights is meaningless; it means only that it is much more complex than is generally recognized in political polemic. For further discussion see M. Cranston, *What are Human Rights?* (1974) and A. I. Melden, *Human Rights* (1969).

Humble Access, The Prayer of. In Anglican liturgical tradition, the prayer at the Eucharist, before the Communion, "We do not presume to come to this thy Table, O merciful Lord, trusting in our own righteousness, but in thy manifold and great mercies. We are not worthy so much as to gather up the crumbs under thy Table. But thou art the same Lord whose property is always to have mercy. Grant us therefore, gracious Lord, so to eat the flesh of thy dear Son Jesus Christ, and to drink his blood, that we may evermore dwell in him and he in us." This prayer has very ancient roots in Greek and other early liturgies. For detailed historical references see Henry

Bailey, *Rituale Anglo-Catholicum* (London: J. W. Parker, 1847), pp. 212–214.

Hume, David (1711–1776). Scottish philosopher. Born and educated in Edinburgh, he lived in France from 1734 to 1737. His first important work was his *Treatise on Human Nature*, written during that time and published in 3 volumes (1739–1740). His other important works include his *Philosophical Essays Concerning Human Understanding* (1748), containing his celebrated "Essay upon Miracles", his *An Enquiry Concerning the Principles of Morals* (1751), and his posthumously published *Dialogues Concerning Natural Religion* (1779). His 6-volume *History of England* (1754–1762) was for long a standard work on the subject. Hume's writings are among the most influential in modern philosophy. The stance he took was a development of the empiricist thought of Locke and Berkeley, but he emphasized even more than they the role of experience, diminishing at the same time the place traditionally assigned to reason. He insisted that all ideas in the human mind are mere copies of impressions or sensations; e.g., from the impression or sensation of a hot iron I construct an idea in my mind that stands for all such sensations and which I call "heat". This diminishes the value of any claim to certainty that I may make about my knowledge of the external world. Such epistemological skepticism is strikingly exhibited in his famous treatment of causality, which is traditionally taken to be a logical procedure. Hume contended and persuasively argued that it is, on the contrary, based merely on association; a customary way of looking at things, not on a rationally demonstrable relationship. For example, I see the sun "rise" every morning and "set" every evening and so conclude that what I perceive constitutes a necessary relationship involving cause-and-effect, but all that I really know is that the phenomena I have perceived and that countless others have habitually perceived have come within the ambit of my and their experience. There may be a causal connection involved in what I perceive, but it cannot be proved. Therefore, Hume concludes, no metaphysical or theological investigation can yield any rationally demonstrable truth. Hume has exerted an enormous influence on all subsequent philosophy but more especially and directly on modern empiricism.

Humility. According to Catholic theology, the virtue of humility is the ground of all other virtues and the basis of the spiritual life itself. Christian humility is far from meaning the mere absence of exaggerated self-esteem: a negative attitude. On the contrary, it has its roots in a joyful submission of one's reason and will to God and expresses itself in a realistic view of one's condition both in its wretchedness and in its glory and in an outlook suffused with confidence and joy because of the strength received from God yet always moderated by the recognition of one's shortcomings. So Augustine could write, "the whole of the Christian religion is humility." Christian humility is often accompanied by gentleness and a sense of humor, because to see oneself even to some extent in the perspective that humility implies engenders such endearing qualities, while pride (the opposite of humility) dampens the spirit and blinds the interior eye. The great spiritual writers in all the great Christian ascetical and mystical traditions treat the subject of humility extensively. Benedict, in his famous Rule, specifies twelve degrees of Christian humility. To attain progress in this basic virtue demands a certain detachment from self that can be achieved only through intense love of God and of his creatures.

Huntingdon, Selina, Countess of (1707– 1791). On the death of her husband in 1746 she dedicated herself to social and religious work. To her influence is generally attributed the development of an interest in Methodism on the part of the upper classes in En-

gland. She founded a body of Calvinistic Methodists known as "the Countess of Huntingdon's Connexion." She supported the work of Harris Howell.

Hurrians. The people so named inhabited the mountain regions south of the Caspian Sea from *c.* 2300 BCE, then moved gradually to the south and west, contributing considerably to the Hittite empire. (See **Hittites.**) The Hittites drew much of their mythologies and legends from Hurrian sources. Kumarbi, the father of the gods, was prominent in this influence, but other Hurrian deities such as the weather god Teshub and his consort Hebat were widely venerated. Hebat was eventually identified with the sun goddess of Arinna.

Huss, John (*c.* **1372–1415**). Bohemian reformer. After study at Prague, he was ordained priest in 1400. Influenced by Wycliffe, he preached vigorously against corruption in the Church, at first with the approval of his superiors, but as his preaching increased in vehemence he elicited clerical opposition, and in 1412 he was excommunicated by the Pope. His principal work, *De Ecclesia* (1413) exhibits an enormous debt to Wycliffe. He was imprisoned and in the end burned at the stake on July 6, 1415. After his death, however, he won recognition as a martyr and a national hero.

Husserl, Edmund (**1859–1938**). German philosopher, trained in Vienna and taught later at Halle, Freiburg, and elsewhere. Having begun with a study of the foundations of mathematics, he developed a new philosophical method, which led to his founding of what came to be called *phenomenology*. At first he seems to have viewed his new method as a descriptive analysis of subjective processes. Later he began to see it more as the study of mental images out of which could be drawn "essences". At this point Husserl's phenomenology showed affinities with the preoccupations of metaphysics. The process of discovering "essences" remained central, however, and begins with what is called the "bracketing" of existence, i.e., the temporary suspension of the question of existence or non-existence and engaging instead in a series of "reductions" to free the "essence" of consciousness from its concrete manifestations. Husserl's phenomenology is of primary importance in the intellectual development of the 20th c. and has had great influence on religious thought. Rudolf Otto's description of the religious consciousness had fascinated Husserl, who had acclaimed it as masterly. Husserl's aim was to make philosophy into a descriptive science, not merely a psychological description, since it deals with essences. He calls his phenomenology an "eidetic science", i.e., it is one that produces a knowledge of universal essences. The "bracketing" process is really a discarding of all elements in experience that could distort our perception or inhibit our grasp of the "essence". It has some affinities with Descartes' method of doubt. For, having bracketed everything else, I am left with consciousness, which I cannot bracket, leaving consciousness as Absolute. Husserl's phenomenological method has been used by various philosophers interested in the philosophy of religion, notably Max Scheler and Mircea Eliade. The former, one of Husserl's disciples, was very directly influenced by Husserl and used his method in investigating the religious experience of humankind. Paul Tillich, too, perceived that some form of the phenomenological method must be used in attacking all theological problems. Among Husserl's works are his *Logical Investigations*, 2 vols. (1900); his *Formal and Transcendental Logic* (1929); and his *Experience and Judgment* (1939).

Hutten, Ulrich von (1488–1523). German humanist. A contributor to the famous satire, the *Epistolae obscurorum virorum*, he was laureated by the Emperor. Seeing the Reformation as the only way of liberating Germany from what he felt to be Rome's oppression, he supported Luther's movement for re-

form. In the end, as a result of an order for his arrest, he had to flee and obtained from the Swiss Reformer Hans Zwingli refuge on an island in the Lake of Zürich.

Hutterites. Name given to those Anabaptists who followed Jacob Hutter, who was burned in 1536. They established communities or settlements founded on the principle of common ownership of property. Especially strong in Moravia they suffered grievously during the Thirty Years' War (1618–1648). Many fled to Hungary and elsewhere. Many of their descendants are to be found today in the United States where they are known as Hutterites or Hutterian Brethren.

Huxley, Thomas Henry (1825–1895). English biologist. After medical studies he conducted important biological investigations in tropical waters, received quick recognition for his scientific work, and became an ardent advocate of scientific education as the best means of training the mind and producing a thoughtful and morally responsible citizenry. He recounted that when as an undergraduate, he was reading about the Gnostics (see **Gnosticism**) who, he felt, seemed to know everything about everything, it seemed to him that he, by contrast, would describe himself more modestly, as knowing nothing about anything, and it was out of that youthful experience that, later in life, he coined the word "agnostic" to designate the sort of intellectual disclaimer that he thought more suitable for a scientifically-trained person to make. (See **Agnosticism** and also **Doubt**.) After the publication of Darwin's *Origin of Species* (1859), he engaged in a famous colloquy with Samuel Wilberforce, then Bishop of Oxford, on the subject of biological evolution, in which the latter expressed the prejudiced view characteristic of even educated churchmen at that time. Huxley too, however, had intellectual limitations, lacking (despite his sincerity and his brilliance in his own field) the critical temper to be expected of a well trained philosopher and the judicial outlook that might have moderated his views, which became in his later years more and more stridently anti-Christian. These later views were summarized in the Romanes Lecture that he gave at Oxford in 1893. His defense of the Darwinian findings is to be found in his *Zoological Evidences as to Man's Place in Nature* (1863). For some of his other writings see his *Collected Essays*, 9 vols. (1893–1894). For the way in which this 19th-c. "science-and-religion" conflict was resolved, see **Evolution.**

Hylomorphism. The philosophical view that all physical things are composed of matter and form. Its classic exponent is Aristotle, whose formulation on this subject was accepted by Thomas Aquinas. Form constitutes (in this view) the principle of realization (actuality); matter the principle of process (potentiality).

Hylozoism. The doctrine that life inheres in all matter. With roots in early Greek thinkers (e.g., Thales and Anaximenes) and in the Stoic notion of the "world soul" it is expressed in the teaching of Renaissance thinkers such as B. Telesio (1508–1588) and Giordano Bruno (1548–1600) and by some of the Cambridge Platonists (e.g., H. More (1614–1687) and R. Cudworth (1617–1688) as well as by more recent thinkers.

Hymn. In the Bible, a hymn is a song of praise, often beginning with a summons to engage in the act. The Psalms provide classic examples in Hebrew practice, which had counterparts in other societies, e.g., Mesopotamian and Egyptian. The Hebrew form of the hymn was taken over into Christian practice. So we read (Matthew 26.30) that after the Last Supper, Jesus and his disciples sang a hymn (probably the Hallel) before going out to the Mount of Olives. Hymns were sung from the earliest times in Christian assemblies (Acts 16.25), and the various canticles used in traditional Christian worship (e.g., the Magnificat and the Benedictus) are in the style of Hebrew hymns. The earliest complete Christian hymn still surviving, "Bridle of colts untamed," is by Clement of Alexandria. Also very ancient is the *Phōs hilaron* ("Hail, gladdening light"), still preserved in the Eastern Church as part of the vesper office. At various points in Christian history, we find an emergence of the opinion that hymns should contain nothing not found in Scripture and indeed much of the traditional hymnody in Christian liturgy is scriptural or at least patently derived from Scripture. Under Reformation influence the demand for hymns grew. Luther favored the use of hymns, whether directly inspired by scriptural texts or not, while Calvin looked with disfavor on the use of any non-scriptural compositions of this kind. Eventually, however, the use of the modern hymn became widespread in most churches within the Reformation heritage. By the 19th c., English Roman Catholics began to call for popular hymns, but their use was limited till comparatively recent times. Although there are innumerable useful works on the hymnody of the English-speaking world, probably none has surpassed in importance or scope that of Louis F. Benson, *The English Hymn* (1915; reprinted 1962). Benson was the foremost American hymnologist of his time.

Hypatia (*c.* 375–415). Neoplatonist philosopher. The daughter of Theon, a mathematician and philosopher, she taught at the Neoplatonic School of Alexandria. Rumors were spread that she had caused the Prefect of Alexandria, a pagan, to set himself against the Christians, she was attacked by a Christian mob and put to death. She wrote on philosophy and mathematics and was highly regarded by other members of that great philosophical school.

Hyperdoulia. See **Latria.**

Hypostasis. Greek term (plural: hypostaseis) ambiguously used, sometimes almost synonymously with *ousia*, "essence" or "substance," but also to signify "individual reality." In the course of the Christological controversies of the fourth century that led to the formulation of the doctrine of the Trinity, the term was used to speak of what are now called the three "Persons" of the Godhead. The formula "three *hypostaseis* in one *ousia*" came to be acknowledged as the core of Christian orthodoxy on the subject. The Latin West came to call the *hypostaseis* "persons"–from the term used for the masks (*personae*) worn by Roman actors in performing their roles.

Hypostatic Union. According to this doctrine, which was formally accepted by the Christian Church at the Council of Chalcedon in 451, the divine and human natures were substantially (see **Hypostasis**) united in the One Person of Jesus Christ. This teaching had for long been held by many, and it had been elaborated by Cyril of Alexandria earlier in that century.

Hypothesis. This term, from the Greek, means literally a supposition, i.e., something that is "put under". Although it has been used in several somewhat different ways in the history of philosophy, it has always retained its basic meaning, i.e., it is a proposal to accept an assertion, either for lack of any clear evidence for or against it, or simply by way of establishing what it is that one is to try by experiment to verify or falsify. For example, the hypothesis that the earth is round rather than flat could not at first be verified or falsified by experiment (although astronomers in antiquity had calculated that it was round and had estimated its diameter to within fifty miles of what is known today), but eventually it was verified, through the circumnavigation of our planet. The making of hypotheses is an essential first step in the advancement of human knowledge by inductive methods. The criteria for verification and falsification must vary according to the subject matter and the nature of the enterprise. For example, the methods used and criteria required for proof that in a vacuum all bodies fall with equal speed will not be identical to the methods used and the criteria required to verify or falsify, say, a hypothesis that people living in a rural area are happier than those living in an urban one. One may treat articles of religious belief as hypotheses, but, if so, the methods and criteria proper to their verification or falsification will certainly be very different from those demanded in chemistry or physics.

Hyssop. A plant of the mint family, used, because of its absorptive quality, in the liturgical purifications practiced by the Hebrews, e.g., in sprinkling the blood of the passover on the doorposts of houses (Exodus 12. 22). According to John 19.29, Jesus on the cross was given wine in a sponge set on hyssop. In the beautiful rite of the *Asperges* traditionally used in the West before High Mass (although generally abandoned in the Roman Catholic Church since Vatican II), the ceremony begins with the singing of the words *Asperges me, Domine, hyssopo et mundabor* "Purify me, O Lord, with hyssop and I shall be clean" (from the *Miserere*, Psalm 51.7).

I

Iamblichus (*c.* 250–330). Chief among the Syrian Neoplatonists. He studied under Anatolius and Porphyry and became immensely influential in his own day and later. He considerably embellished the teachings of Plotinus, adding various mediating elements (e.g., between the One and the Nous) and introducing the notion of a large pantheon of deities, so making theurgy a feature of his system. The human soul is obliged to descend into the body, but once embodied it has freedom of choice. The purpose of this incarnation in a human body is to provide the human being with the capacity to return by means of virtuous action to the supersensible world. Reincarnation is thus a part of his system. His works include a treatise *On the Pythagorean Life* and another, interesting for an account of the various theological options of his time in the pagan world, *On the Egyptian Mysteries*, as well as various mathematical speculations.

Iatrogenic Disease. Disease caused by medical treatment. The dramatic advances in medical knowledge and practice since the early part of the 20th c. have put into the hands of physicians, psychiatrists, and others, extremely powerful weapons whose use may have good or evil effects: new drugs, for instance, and bio-engineering. The temptation to use them to relieve a condition, although their use may have a harmful effect on other aspects of the patient, is considerable. Ethical questions arise, therefore, that previously did not. The problem is exacerbated by the well-known fact that the reaction to drugs and other medical treatment is idiosyncratic; i.e., what may cause mere mild discomfort in patient A may have disastrous consequences in patient B. Some medical practitioners, knowing that patients will be less angry with them for having failed to do something they might have done than for doing something whose results have been unfortunate, may be overcautious, while others, more daring, will err in the opposite direction. Fine ethical judgment, involving not only moral discernment but a deep personal knowledge of and concern for the individual patient, is needed to make decisions in such circumstances.

Ibas. A 5th c. Bishop of Edessa who took a mediating position between the Nestorians and Alexandrians such as Cyril. Deposed at Ephesus in 449, then vindicated at Chalcedon in 451, he was anathematized in 553 by the Fifth General Council. Almost none of his writings has survived.

Ichthys. (Greek, "fish") The fish is very widely used in Christian iconography as a symbol for Christ. It would seem likely that the symbolism was derived from the acronym for *Iēsous Xristos Theou Yios Sōter* (Jesus Christ, Son of God, Saviour); but it is arguable that the acronym developed out of a fish symbolism already present. A well-known passage in Tertullian's treatise on Baptism compares the newly baptized to little fishes and Christ to the great Fish. This imagery may be coincidental, but traces of it can be found not only in still earlier Christian writings but in some pagan mythological art. It is nevertheless almost as distinctively Christian as the Cross itself.

Icon. (Also spelt *ikon*; from Greek *eikōn*, likeness) Icons are representations of Christ, Mary, or saints, always on a flat (i.e., two-dimensional surface, typically wood but often enamelled or repoussé) and are the only kind of art permitted in Eastern Orthodox churches, since Eastern Orthodoxy forbids the use of three-dimensional art such as statuary or bas-relief. They play a special role in Eastern Orthodox worship, both public and private, for they are traditionally regarded not merely as "aids to devotion" but as the very meeting place of God and man, of the spiritual dimension of being and the material world. They are widely believed to be vested, as the channels of divine grace, with power to convey divine blessings and to ward off evil. Some are reputed to be the occasion of miraculous occurrences. They became prominent in Eastern Christianity by the 5th c. and play a more vital role in the life of the Church in the East than do their Western counterparts.

Iconoclastic Controversy. The veneration of icons in the Eastern Church gave rise to prolonged and remarkable controversy from *c*. 725 to 842. Various forces operated against their use, including certain Manichaean tendencies to regard matter as evil and certain

Monophysite tendencies to diminish or even exclude the human side of Christ and therefore to deprecate visual representation of him. (In both Judaism and Islam there is a strong tradition that perceives any sort of representation of Deity as idolatrous.) In 726 the Emperor Leo III, apparently supposing that the use of icons was an important obstacle to the conversion of Muslims and Jews to Christianity, issued an edict ordering the destruction of all icons. Uproar ensued throughout the Empire. The monks tended to support the cause of the icons as did Leo IV and probably even more so his widow Irene when she became Empress. The Seventh General council, meeting at Nicaea in 787, defined the degree of veneration of icons to be permitted and restored them to their former place. Nevertheless, the army was iconoclastic and in 814 a second outbreak occurred. Persecution of icon users intensified. At last, with Methodius elected patriarch in 843, came an end to the persecution. On the First Sunday of Lent in that year a great feast was held to honor the icons. It has been held annually ever since as one of the most important and most popular feasts in the Eastern Church.

Iconostasis. The screen that separates the nave from the sanctuary in Eastern Orthodox churches. Since about the 14th c., it has consisted of a solid wooden or stone wall covered with icons. It has three doors, the one on the right leading to the Diaconicon, the one on the left to the Prosthesis, and the one in the middle, called the Royal Door leading to the altar. In English the third syllable is accented.

Idealism. Any metaphysical system that uses the ideas of mind as the basic clue to an understanding of reality. It has taken many forms in the history of thought. Characteristic of much Indian thought, it was accommodated by Plato to that of the West. Christian thought, partly because of the strongly Neoplatonic influence that entered into it, has

been much affected by idealist views. The work of Berkeley, an eighteenth-century philosopher and Christian bishop, provides an interesting example of a thoroughgoing idealism in the form of an immaterialist philosophy in which everything is referable to mind. Many, however, would account such a thoroughgoing idealism incompatible with the data of Christian revelation, which include Creation as well as the Incarnation and Resurrection. The thought both of Kant and of Hegel is in the idealist tradition. Those who, in the late nineteenth century and afterwards, sought to rehabilitate and re-express idealist principles are commonly called neo-idealists. Among these would be included Bradley, Bosanquet, Croce, Dilthey, and Royce.

Identity, Personal. This philosophical problem has special importance in religion and not least in Christian theology. The Christian doctrine of human destiny is a resurrection doctrine; i.e., my resurrection is possible through Christ, entailing my survival of my present body. But if at my death the cells of my brain die and with them the memory that they contain, how, if I am resurrected in another and "glorified" body, can I know of any relation to the body I now have and the experiences that have become an integral part of what I call "me"? My resurrection would then be meaningless to me. The difficulty is not insurmountable; but only by means of a special philosophical stance such as is to be found in Plato, in Kant, and others, can it be overcome. Proponents of personal resurrection, reincarnation, and immortality must recognize and deal with the philosophical problem of personal identity.

Idiorrhythmic Monasteries. Some monasteries on Mount Athos are so called, in which the monks are permitted to have private property and to enjoy considerable freedom and independence, in contrast to those other monasteries in which community life is more strictly observed.

Ignatius Loyola (1495?–1556). Founder of the Jesuits, an order of clerics regular. Of a noble family in the north of Spain, he entered military service, was wounded in 1521, and during his lengthy recuperation read lives of Christ and the saints and decided to become a soldier in Christ's service. He then went to Montserrat, where he made a general confession and placed his sword on the altar of the Virgin Mary to symbolize his new dedication of himself to the service of the Church. He now went for a year to Manresa, devoting himself to a life of great self-denial and prayer in the course of which he felt he had attained a spiritual insight that found expression in his much famed treatise, the *Spiritual Exercises*, most of which he apparently wrote during that year at Manresa. Now he went on a pilgrimage to Jerusalem, traveling (according to the Gospel precept) penniless and depending on alms like a beggar. Returning from Jerusalem he studied at various Spanish universities and then in 1528 went on to Paris (just as Calvin was leaving his studies there) and remained there for seven years. In 1534 he laid out the main plans for the foundation of his Society. In 1540 Pope Paul III gave it the Church's official recognition in a bull *Regimini militantis Ecclesiae*, with Ignatius as the first General. The Society or Company of Jesus, as it was officially called was an odd combination of militaristic organization, the medieval chivalric ideal, and a streak of the Renaissance spirit of individualism. The original aims of Ignatius were in the direction of purifying the Church and reforming it by means of education and the more frequent reception of the Sacraments, and encouraging missionary enterprise in faraway lands. Only after his death did it develop its reputation for political intrigue. See **Jesuits.**

Ignatius of Antioch (1st c.). According to Eusebius, he was the third Bishop of Antioch, following Euodias, Peter's successor; according to Origen he was the second, directly following Peter. Almost nothing is known of the details of his life, although a passage in his writings suggests that he had been before his conversion a persecutor of the Christians. He was conducted from Antioch to his martyrdom at Rome by a guard of ten soldiers and on his way was received by Polycarp and other Christians and wrote letters to various Christian communities, encouraging them and affirming his own readiness for martyrdom. That these letters were held in the highest esteem by the early Fathers is attested not only by what they say (e.g., Theodoret) but by the fact that spurious letters are known to have been put into circulation in imitation of the authentic ones. In his letters he emphasizes the reality of the birth, life, and crucifixion of Jesus against the Docetists who taught that he was merely a vision, an appearance (*dokēma*), insisting that he came "in the flesh." (He writes with irony that these Docetists say he was an appearance because they themselves are mere appearances.) He also likens the Christian community to the soul of the political society in which they live and he calls the Eucharist "the bread that is the flesh of Jesus Christ." He refers with much respect to the Church at Rome but makes no reference at all to its bishop, although he very much upholds the importance of bishops in the Church, as its best safeguard against dissension.

IHS. Although these letters, widely used as a Christian symbol, have been interpreted by many as an acronym for the Latin words *Iesus Hominum Salvator* (Jesus, Saviour of men), they were originally an abbreviation of the Greek name for Jesus: ΙΗΣΟΥΣ.

Illative Sense. This term was used by Newman in the course of his exposition of how one can have a reasonable basis for religious faith. Distinguishing between formal and informal reasoning, he presented formal reasoning as general and abstract (mathematics is the best example), while informal reasoning is individual and concrete. Formal reasoning leads to logical certitude, informal reasoning to psychological certainty. But how can informal reasoning lead to certainty? Newman argued that since reasoning is an operation of the individual mind, informal reasoning is more basic than formal reasoning. Fundamentally, all sound reasoning is done through a human faculty for drawing logical conclusions. This faculty he called the illative sense, which he regarded as the "sole and final judgment" of the validity of any piece of informal reasoning. The decision that a medical diagnostician makes and those of a military commander on the battlefield are examples of conclusions reached by such reasoning. Religious decision, the most basic of all personal decisions, is an example *par excellence*. He also distinguished between kinds of assent: (1) notional, (2) real. Notional assent is given to a proposition (e.g., that the sum of the angles in a triangle must be 180°), while real assent is given to the reality to which the proposition refers.

Illingworth, John Richardson. (1848–1915). Anglican priest and disciple of the Idealist philosopher T. H. Green. His writings include *Personality, Human, and Divine* (1894) and *Reason and Revelation* (1902). He was a prominent member of the *Lux Mundi* group.

Illuminati. This name has been applied to various groups such as the Rosicrucians but more especially to a masonic group founded by Adam Weishaupt in 1778 in Bavaria. Rejecting the claims of the Christian Church and all organized religious bodies, they claimed to be in a special way illumined by the grace of Christ. They claimed esoteric knowledge, sought to restore a patriarchal state and a classless society, and developed a highly organized society of their own. They were banished from Bavaria in 1784 but continued in France and elsewhere.

Illuminative Way. In the mystical journey toward union with God, several schools of Christian mysticism recognize a stage intermediate between the purgative and the unitive ways. In that intermediate stage the soul finds itself cleansed and purified from attachment to the things of sense and so prepared to proceed to spiritual enlightenment or illumination.

Imago Dei. (Latin, the image of God). According to traditional Christian theology (based upon Genesis 1.26f.), man was created "in the image of" God, which man lost through the Fall. Catholic theologians have generally contended, however, that the *imago* was blurred but not destroyed by the Fall. Precisely in what the image consists has been much disputed. Some, such as Gregory of Nyssa, have identified it with freedom of choice, while others see it in terms of immortality or rationality or some other quality believed to distinguish human beings from other forms of life. Protestant thought has characteristically seen the loss of the *imago* as much more significant if not as radical and complete. In this tradition humanity is so warped by the Fall that without God's grace we can accomplish nothing worthwhile; therefore both human reason and human freewill are powerless to achieve our salvation. It is not merely that through Christ, God provides us with an immensely valuable, indispensable instrument for our salvation; it is, rather, that we are fundamentally and totally "unable of ourselves to help ourselves." Our only hope, then, is God as revealed to us in Jesus Christ, for we cannot by ourselves even begin to understand the nature of God or what "we must do to be saved."

Imitation of Christ. To imitate Christ means to imitate him in his humanity, for in traditional Christian thought to pretend to imitate him in his divinity would be blasphemous. One of the most renowned treatises on the imitation of Christ is the book so entitled (*De Imitatione Christi*), which appeared anonymously in 1418 and has been traditionally assigned to Thomas à Kempis.

Immaculate Conception. This doctrine does not relate directly to Christ (as is often vulgarly supposed) but to the conception of Mary in the womb of her mother. According to the doctrine, Mary was, by the special grace of God, kept free from the stain of original sin and therefore conceived "immaculately", i.e., without sin. This doctrine was defined as the official teaching of the Roman Catholic Church by Pope Pius IX, *ex motu proprio* (i.e., on his own authority and without any supporting conciliar decision), on December 8, 1854. Although suggested by some of the early Fathers, and with a tradition favoring it from the 7th c. in the East and the 9th c. in the West, there is no evidence that the doctrine was of great antiquity, and it was certainly by no means universally held either in Eastern Orthodoxy or by Roman Catholic theologians. On the contrary, when it was introduced to France, probably in the first half of the 12th c., it was opposed by Bernard of Clairvaux. The great medieval schoolmen (except for Duns Scotus) opposed it, notably Thomas Aquinas, accounting it contrary to Scripture, which teaches that Christ died for all humanity (II Corinthians 5.15). Thomas, noting that certain churches were observing the Feast of the Immaculate Conception of Mary, argued that such practice could be tolerated as a devotional recognition of the holiness of Mary and that she was sanctified in some special way between her conception and her birth, but he insisted that it must not be taken to mean that she was immaculately conceived. So, although the Franciscans and the Jesuits tended to favor the doctrine, most Dominicans, following Thomas Aquinas, strongly opposed it. Even the Council of Trent (1549–1560), which was convened to reform the Church and combat Protestantism and which was notoriously well disposed to exalt Mary

in every way against the prevalent inclination of Protestants to depreciate her, expressly refused to declare in favor of the doctrine of her Immaculate Conception. Nevertheless, theological opinion in the Roman Catholic Church after Trent gained momentum in favor of the doctrine.

Immanence. See **Transcendence/Immanence.**

Immersion, Baptism by. Strictly speaking, that method of baptism in which only a large part of the candidate's body is submerged in water, which is then poured over the rest of the body. It is therefore to be distinguished from baptism by submersion, which is used in the Eastern Church for the baptism of infants. In the West the method of affusion (pouring) began to replace that of immersion about the 8th c., although immersion is still permitted in the Roman Catholic Church. It is used regularly by Baptists and in some other Protestant denominations that follow Baptist principles.

Immortality, Conditional. Immortality is generally taken to mean the infinite prolongation of the existence of that which I call "I". (See **Immortality of the Soul.**) Nevertheless, some Christians have plausibly argued for the view that immortality is not a state imposed upon the soul but rather one that is won by it, symbolically represented in the 144,000 who stand with palms of victory in their hands. Paul's view of human destiny seems clearly to support such a notion. He says (Romans 6.23) that the wages of sin is death, so that that is the normal human expectation, although through the gift of God we can have eternal life through Christ. In the ancient Church, Arnobius held a view that modern theologians would classify as conditional immortality, but that was a comparatively rare view in the history of Christian thought until the 19th c. Its incidence cannot have been entirely inconsiderable, however, since the Fifth Lateran Council formally condemned it in 1513. In the 19th c., however, some Christian divines (e.g., the Congregationalist, Edward White) adopted it, preferring it over the alternatives of which the traditional one entailed everlasting torment in hell for the wicked and the other (Origen's) entailed the notion that ultimately all creatures, including even Satan himself, would be saved. The view taken by these theologians, which came to be called conditional immortality, has been stated in several forms, but the general notion is that the wicked either lose their personal identity (a view, held by the Unitarian, James Martineau) or suffer annihilation or simply fail to acquire the prize of everlasting life and therefore never attain immortality. The view, which has many merits within an otherwise traditional Christian framework, is held by individuals and groups of Christians but is generally resisted by traditionalist theologians. In the early 19th c. some protagonists of this "middle" view were called Destructionists because they held that the wicked, after suffering a punishment proportionate to their crimes, are destroyed. See also **Purgatory.**

Immortality of the Soul. It may well be argued that the fundamental Christian doctrine concerning the afterlife is not immortality but resurrection, which in Paul's theology does not necessarily entail the immortality of the soul.. Nevertheless, from early times and under the influence of Plato and other Greek thinkers Christian thought tended from the first to marry the concept of immortality to that of resurrection. Christians have favored the opinions of those philosophers (e.g., Leibniz and Kant) who have upheld the immortality of the soul. The concept generally implies the infinitely prolonged existence of the center of awareness to which the term "I" refers. See **Identity, Personal** and **Immortality, Conditional.**

Immunization. The introduction of antigenic substances, living or dead, into the body in order to foster an immune response. Also called vaccination. Vaccines are now available for many diseases. Although they are generally safe, the effect on certain individuals may be very harmful. Conscientious individuals often accept immunization more as a duty to the community than as protection for themselves. Is it then ethical to make immunization mandatory? It is certainly unethical until laboratory experiment has shown the vaccine to be safe, but no vaccine can be absolutely safe for everyone to whom it may ever be administered. After preliminary testing a controlled "blind" trial may be carried out in the community by way of measuring the degree and kind of protection the new vaccine provides. There is a temptation to omit this step where the vaccine seems to have the desired protective effect and everyone is in a hurry to see it readily available. One must also consider how continuing programs of immunization will work. A large range of ethical problems arises because of inherent uncertainties attending any treatment of an individual patient, but since immunization procedures generally involve the rights and duties of an entire community these problems are much exacerbated.

Impanation. In the medieval Church the doctrine of Transubstantiation was developed as a description, in terms of Aristotelian philosophy, of how Christ can be said to be "in" the elements of Bread and Wine. (See **Transubstantiation.**) In the 11th c., however, some followers of Berengar (possibly himself) held a doctrine of the Real Presence of Christ according to which Christ is truly present but hidden in the eucharistic elements, being "impanated" in them as he was "incarnate" in human flesh. This view, which seems to be echoed in the poetry of Thomas Aquinas (e.g., his *Adoro te devote*) although not in his official theology, had advocates in the later Middle Ages both before and during the Reformation. In modern circumstances in which the Aristotelian presuppositions behind the theory of Transubstantiation are unacceptable and the Aristotelian categories recognized to be outmoded, impanation is a less offensive alternative.

Impassibility of God. In Greek "to suffer" implies "being acted upon" and since in theology it seemed plain that God, (being by definition Creator, "the one who acts,") could not suffer. The Greeks also held the permanent to be intrinsically superior to the changing; therefore God cannot change. So neither can he be acted upon from outside himself nor can he change internally, nor can he experience the sensations of pleasure or pain that we humans experience. The Bible, however, characteristically refers to God as loving his creatures and caring for even the fall of a sparrow, indeed as though God travails in, with, and through his creation. Without some such concept we are left with a Deistic view of the nature of God: a view alien to all modern thought and depending on a mechanistic understanding of the universe. Several contemporary theologians have expounded, each in his own way, the view (not without adumbrations in the 19th c., e.g., James Hinton, *The Mystery of Pain,* 1966) that God, although not in any way dependent on anything outside himself, nevertheless is in constant travail with his creation. Examples are: Kazoh Kitamori, *Theology of the Pain of God* (1st English ed., 1965); Geddes MacGregor, *He Who Lets Us Be* (1975 and 1987); Jürgen Moltmann, *The Crucified God,* 1974.

Impediment. A term used in canon law to denote an obstacle to marriage, e.g., consanguinity (too close blood-relationship).

Imprimatur. In the Roman Catholic Church, any book containing the discussion of theological or ethical questions requires certification by an official known as a censor, generally appointed by the the diocesan bishop. If the censor finds nothing in the book to warrant withholding permission to publish it, it is published with the word *Imprimatur* (Latin, "Let it be printed") and the censor's name. Religious orders such as the Dominicans and Jesuits require permission of their own authorities as well and this is additionally attested by the words *Imprimi potest* ("It may be printed"). The term was used for some time in England after the Reformation in connection with the licensing laws that arose out of the ordinances of the Star Chamber in 1586 and 1637. After the Restoration in 1660, a law was enacted forbidding the import of books containing matter judged contrary to the teaching and practice of the Church of England. All books had to be licensed by an official such as the Lord Chancellor or the Archbishop of Canterbury, and the license was called an imprimatur.

Imputation. A theological term, used especially in Lutheran theology, to designate the ascribing of the guilt or righteousness of one person to another, e.g., the ascription of the righteousness of Christ to sinful man so that he becomes (according to Lutheran teaching) righteous by imputation although having no personal righteousness of his own.

Incardination. A widespread rule in the ancient Church required that an ordinand be bound for life to the diocese in which he had been ordained. The practice of incardination was introduced to avoid the inconveniences of the ancient principle while not entirely abrogating it. It means the transfer of a cleric from one diocesan jurisdiction to another. The correlative term is "excardination," the liberation of a cleric from one diocese in order permit his incardination in another.

Incarnation. One of the central doctrines in traditional Christian theology, Orthodox, Catholic, and Protestant, according to which the Logos took human flesh from a human mother with the consequence that Christ is both fully God and fully man. Although it is not totally different from the concept of an avatar of deity such as occurs in Hinduism and its offshoots, it is to be radically distinguished in at least one important point: it is to be understood as an abiding union of deity and humanity in Christ while nevertheless maintaining the essential and inextinguishable difference between humanity and God. Such, at any rate, is the view that emerged as a result of efforts to unite the humanizing tendencies of the Antiochene school on the one hand and, on the other, the divinizing tendencies of the Alexandrian school. The compromise that the solution expressed predictably gave rise to a wide range of theological problems. For instance, had Christ, being "True God and True Man," two wills or one? (See **Monothelitism.**) Would the Incarnation have taken place had not the Fall occurred? Is the Church properly to be called an extension of the Incarnation? (This is a view much favored by some theologians but bitterly resisted by others as dangerously tending to the kind of sacerdotalism that exalts the structure of the Church to the level of God.) Did Jesus, being divine and human, have the attributes of God, such as omnipotence and omniscience when he was a baby on his mother's knee? (See **Kenosis.**) What the doctrine of the Incarnation specifically implies is that God, who transcends his creation as a cause transcends its effects is also immanent in his creation. But precisely how God is immanent is a question that has given rise to a multitude of philosophical and theological speculations without any uniform result. Nevertheless, the Incarnation, however interpreted, goes to the heart of Christian belief and remains at the core of all christological problems.

Incense. Incense has been and still is very generally used in many of the major religions of the world. It is mentioned frequently in the Bible (e.g., Exodus 30.8; Leviticus 16.13) and was used in Jewish worship in the great Temple in Jerusalem before the time of Christ. The smoke was accounted a symbol of prayer. A passage (Revelation 8.3–5) suggests, although it does not establish, that it was used in Christian worship in the 1st century. By about the year 500, however, we have clear evidence of its use in Christian worship and by the 9th c. the censing of the altar and the people is recorded. Traditionally the use of incense is more extensive in the East than in the West, although since 1969 the Roman Catholic Church, which had restricted its use to the more solemn ceremonial occasions, now permits it at any Mass. In Protestantism its use was from the first very generally abandoned. In the Church of England, its use occurred between the 16th and the 19th c. but was uncommon. Through the influence of the Tractarian movement and the revival of the use of ritual that attended it, incense came to be widely used in many churches in the Anglican Communion.

Incumbent. A term, English in origin and generally used only in Anglican practice, designates the holder of any parochial charge, whether as rector, vicar, or otherwise.

Incunabula. (Latin, *incunabula*, "swaddling clothes".) Books printed during the early stages of printing, generally taken to conclude with the year 1500.

Independents. A name widely used in England till about the end of the 18th c. for Congregationalists. It was intended to emphasize independence from the Church of England by law established, but it also carried the significance of theological freedom such as was not generally obtainable in any organized Churches at that time. The term never gained favor in the United States.

Index of Prohibited Books. The official list of books that were, till 1966, officially prohibited by the Roman Catholic Church and the reading of which, without permission, could constitute mortal sin. It was first published in 1557 by

Paul IV. In 1571 Pius V formed a special commission, the Congregation of the Index, to take care of it and to add to or subtract from the list as occasion seemed to require. From about the beginning of the present century the duty of safeguarding the faithful in this way passed more into the hands of local bishops, and the papal Index became less important being finally abolished in 1966. The Index consisted of books judged to be contrary to Christian faith or dangerous to Christian morals. Books listed in an edition of the papal Index issued in the Vatican City in 1929 included *Kant's Critique of Pure Reason*, Locke's *Essay Concerning Human Understanding*, Berkeley's *Alciphron*, and the *Meditations* and some other works of Descartes, although in the case of Descartes only *donec corrigatur*, i.e., literally, "until corrected." To the Abbey Dimnet is attributed the whimsical definition of the Index as "a convenient device for enabling the learned to write without fear of offending pious ears."

Individuality and the Individual. The ancients attached little or no importance to the concept of individuality as it is understood today. In Plato, the State is assumed to be more important than the individual citizen as the human body is more important than any of its parts. The universal is better than the particular. In Duns Scotus we can see the dawn of an appreciation of the unique value of the individual as such, and in the 16th c. Renaissance a sense of that value begins to bloom. In some 19th c. Idealism it is developed as an antidote to the concept of the Absolute and the organic nature of society, and in modern Existentialism it is one of the most fundamental emphases. In Bosanquet and in Royce, as in Kierkegaard and Sartre, far apart as their outlooks are, individuality is central. For illustration of the meaning and importance of the concept for Christian thought, see H. V. and E. H. Hong, *Søren Kierkegaard's Journals and Papers*, Vol. II (Bloomington, Indiana: Indiana University Press), pp. 389–448.

Induction. After a priest has been nominated and instituted to a vacant parish, he is inducted. His induction gives him legal control of the parish and possession of whatever temporal benefits, such as stipend and house, that go with the benefice.

Induction and Deduction. In the simplest and most general terms, induction may be defined as probable inference and deduction as necessary inference. Deduction is generally taken to have been invented by Aristotle. It moves from given premises to their implication in the form of a conclusion. It does not yield new knowledge, strictly speaking, but draws out the implications of what is already conceded or known. The study of induction began with Aristotle but was much developed by later logicians. Francis Bacon sought to show induction as the basic method of all scientific inquiry. He made considerable advances on the traditional methods, notably in showing the need for both positive and negative instances to isolate the cause of an effect. John Stuart Mill saw induction as the only logical procedure to produce new knowledge. He proposed that by correlating the positive and negative instances with the presence or absence of the phenomenon under investigation, one could isolate the causes. He set forth five methods or canons (rules) for doing that: (1) Agreement, (2) Difference, (3) Agreement and Difference, (4) Concomitant Variations, and (5) Residues. Other logicians, notably Whewell, Jevons, and Peirce, offered criticisms and refinements of Mill's proposals.

In modern logic, largely through the influence of Rudolf Carnap, induction has been fused with probability theory. He proposed five kinds of inductive inference: (1) *Direct*, as from the frequency of a property in the population of a nation to its frequency in a sample; (2) *Predictive*, from one sample to another and overlapping the first; (3) *Analogical*, from one individual to another on the basis of a known similarity between them; (4) *Inverse*, as from a sample of the population of a nation to the population as a whole; and (5) *Universal*, from a sample to a hypothesis universal in form. R. B. Braithwaite defended induction against the charge of circularity by pointing out that the movement is from mere belief to reasonable belief. Induction in mathematics is a special case. Example: if one can prove that *p*, being the property of the number *x*, is also the property of the number *x + 1* (simply by reason of the fact that *x + 1* is the numerical successor of *x*), one can conclude that the property *p* is the property of every number.

Indulgences. The theory of indulgences in the Church has a long and checkered history. From the 3rd c. confessors and those who were awaiting martyrdom were believed to have special access to the throne of God and to his mercy. The ecclesiastical authorities recognized this and permitted them to intercede for those who were under canonical penance of any kind, in such a way as to reduce the length of that penance. In course of time such canonical penance came to be considered a substitute for punishment in purgatory. Gradually the belief came to be accepted that the prayers of the saints could shorten the duration of a purgatorial stay. Later still, as penitential discipline was relaxed, the Church found it convenient to prescribe certain "works" as a substitute for the traditional penitential exercises and claimed the power to apply the merits of Christ and the saints to make up the difference. The theory was that, although sins must be expiated either on earth or in purgatory, the Church had at its disposal a "treasury of merits" (the merits of Christ and the saints) that it had the right to apply or withhold in consideration for the prayers and other works in which the faithful might engage. It was probably the most flagrant arrogation by the hierarchy of raw power over the souls of the faithful that the Church has ever successfully claimed in the entire

course of Christian history. It resulted in the practice of indulgences which by the 12th c. had already become common. Indulgences could be limited or plenary. Plenary indulgences were believed by the ignorant to remit the whole of the temporal punishment supposed to be due to a person's sins. The petitioner might choose to apply a plenary indulgence to himself, for his own benefit, or to bestow it on friends or others whom he wished to help. Plenary indulgences were customarily awarded, for instance, to those who took part in the Crusades. Limited indulgences were given for less ambitious enterprises. By the time of Luther the practice had become so flagrant that popular preachers such as Johann Tetzel (*c.* 1465–1519) who about 1490 had become a Dominican friar at Leipzig, began preaching openly that money contributed for the building of the new church of St Peter at Rome could be directly applied to the deliverance of one's own soul or that of someone of one's choosing from the terrible punishment of purgatory. Although this belief accorded with what large numbers of the faithful had been in one way or another led to believe and did believe, it profoundly shocked the more learned and less credulous among the faithful, leading them to see, however dimly, the basic conception behind the principle of indulgences, namely, that the Church had arrogated to itself the control of one's spiritual destiny even beyond death. Since Tetzel's preaching had been prohibited in Saxony, he did not preach there but in the neighboring town of Jüterbog, which lay just beyond, and it was there that Luther heard him and was so revolted as to be led to compose and on October 31, 1517, to nail on the door of the church at Wittenberg his famous Ninety-five Theses condemning various currently accepted doctrines and practices of the Church, including the practice of indulgences.

The practice of granting indulgences had continued in the Roman Catholic

Church down to the present time. Indeed, the Church has encouraged it. Supporting propaganda in favor of the practice has commonly defended it on the ground that the activities of priests such as Tetzel were abuses of a practice that was in itself salutary. The Second Vatican Council made certain suggestions to Pope Paul VI, who in the constitution *Indulgentiarum doctrina* attempted to revise the form of the traditional understanding in such a way as to cause the faithful to regard indulgences as a spur to pious acts rather than as a remission of punishment. So the traditional computation of indulgences in terms of so many days or years was abolished. The Church has now openly although belatedly acknowledged that it has no jursidiction beyond the grave: a comfort to millions of the faithful, had they not been discouraged through the centuries from entertaining such a belief.

Infallibility. The notion that the Church is safeguarded from error in its teaching of divine truth is a traditional one of many centuries standing. The question is: wherein precisely resides that safeguard? In the 5th c. Vincent of Lérins, emphasizing that in the last resort Scripture must be the final test, recognized that the difficulty lies in its interpretation. He proposed a rule for determining what is the interpretation to be followed, namely what has been believed everywhere, always, and by all (*quod ubique, quod semper, quod ab omnibus creditum est*). This, which has come to be known as the Vincentian canon, has provided a maxim to which scholars have widely appealed throughout the centuries.

The Church has also from early times recognized, however, the authority of general (ecumenical) councils representative of the entire body of Christians to settle disputes and specify what Christians ought to accept as orthodox teaching. As papal power increased within the Roman Catholic Church, the question arose: in case of a conflict between the Pope and the Council, which of the two authorities is to be regarded as superior and decisive? Throughout much of the Middle Ages the canonists were divided, some (the papalist party) holding that the Pope had the final authority, others (the conciliarist party) contending that a general council of the Church had authority over the authority of the Pope.

Such was the notoriety of the corruption within the Church during the Late Middle Ages that for at least a century and a half before the beginnings of the Reformation, scholarly clerics and others were desperately trying to bring about concord by means of conciliar reform within the structure of the Church. The breakdown of such efforts precipitated the Reformation, after which, in the Roman Catholic Church, the papalist-conciliarist debate persisted, with a very strong scholarly support for the conciliarist position while the popes and their entourage in the papal court and their supporters beyond it naturally favored the papalist party. The notion that some special authority resides in papal utterances on questions of faith and morals was recognized in the Middle Ages, but the circumstances making it infallible teaching of the Church were still very vague. Not only was the relation between Pope and Council undetermined; there was no specific verbal formula, no precise wording, that pointed to the infallibility of any papal utterance. In 1870, however, at the First Vatican Council, a decree was enacted declaring that when the Pope makes a definition of any question relating to faith or morals, when he speaks *ex cathedra* (i.e., officially in the discharge of his office as the pastor of all Christians) the definition is to be deemed the infallible teaching of the Church. This decree, reached by political maneuvers of extradordinary ingenuity and persistence on the part of the papalist party, led by the Pope (Piux IX), still leaves vague when the Roman Catholic faithful are required to recognize a papal utterance as infallible and when they are not so required. The notorious Syllabus of Errors, for instance, which Pius IX had issued in 1864, was almost universally regarded as infallible by Roman Catholic theologians in the last decades of the 19th c., while very few today if any would accord it any such status.

Infertility. Infertility is distinguished from sterility, which entails a total incapacity on the part of either the man or the woman to achieve conception. Infertility means only a present impairment and possibly curable condition impeding conception. To the extent that a society seeks to encourage its members to have children, it has an ethical obligation to assist those who are willing to achieve that end. The married couple should be assisted as far as possible to achieve it through normal sexual intercourse. The objection that such encouragement is undesirable in view of the overpopulation of our planet carries no weight, since the number of births it adds is insignificant and success is likely to result in happier home circumstances than can be expected in very large families that have no adequate means of sustenance and little hope of cultural development. However, every reasonable care should be taken to avoid injury either to the mother or to the unborn child. Ovulation induction, for example (i.e., treatment intended to stimulate the release of an ovum from the ovary) is known to carry risks that must be carefully weighed. Failing such measures, artificial insemination with the semen of the husband may be tried by those who have no religious or other scruples against it. Few couples have such scruples where the donor is an impotent but not infertile husband (AIH); many more would have scruples where, because of the husband's apparent infertility, the donor is another man (AID). Adoption is of course an obvious solution to an infertile couple's problem, but one that is becoming more and more difficult because of lack of available children to adopt. See also **In Vitro Fertilization.**

Infralapsarians and Supralapsarians. Calvin, in emphasizing the doctrine of Predestination of the elect, was careful to insist that the whole subject of Predestination (which Thomas Aquinas also taught, although with less specific reference to human salvation) is shrouded in mystery. His followers, less reticent, speculated on the nature and even the time of the divine decree that predestined the elect to salvation and the reprobate to damnation. Some, the supralapsarians, held that the decree occurred before the Fall of Adam; others, the infralapsarians, held that the decree was made after the Fall. The latter view tended in the long run to prevail, especially after the Synod of Dort (1618). Infralapsarianism is also called sublapsarianism and postlapsarianism, while supralapsarianism is sometimes called antelapsarianism.

Inge, William Ralph (1860–1954). Anglican divine. Strongly disposed to the interpretation of Christianity along Platonistic and Neoplatonistic lines, he wrote extensively in a clear and incisive style during much of his long life and was very influential in his day in the life of thoughtful people in England. Educated at Eton and King's College, Cambridge, he was for a few years a Fellow of Hertford College, Oxford, then Vicar of All Saints, Knightsbridge, London, then Lady Margaret Professor at Cambridge, and from 1911 till his retirement in 1934 Dean of St Paul's Cathedral, London, with which he was for long much identified in the mind of his generation. Among his writings are *Christian Mysticism* (1899), *The Philosophy of Plotinus* (1918), and two series of *Outspoken Essays* (1919 and 1922).

Ingersoll Lectureship. Established at Harvard University under the terms of a bequest of Caroline Haskell Ingersoll in 1894. The topic specified is "The Immortality of the Soul," which lecturers have treated from very notably diverse viewpoints. William James, Josiah Royce, George Herbert Palmer, and Kirsopp Lake, were among the earlier lecturers under this foundation.

Inhibition. When a bishop deems it desirable in the interest of a parish to suspend a cleric from the exercise of his ecclesiastical duties, he may do so either temporarily on an emergency basis or for a longer period after judicial inquiry. His order in doing so is called an inhibition.

In Hoc Signo Vinces. In the year 312, the Emperor Constantine, according to legend, saw these words written across the sun in the sky. They signify: "In this sign you shall conquer."

Inner Light. This is the principle upheld by the Society of Friends (Quakers). According to the society neither the Bible nor ecclesiastical tradition, although they may contain much truth, is the ultimate authority for the individual, who must find this authority in an inward knowledge that comes through the direct, personal infusion of the Holy Spirit into the soul, enlightening it by the light of that same Spirit.

Innocent I, Pope. Early 5th c. Bishop of Rome who made more specific claims for the primacy of the See of Rome than had been made by his predecessors. He asserted a right to have all disputes, whether in the East or in the West brought to Rome for judicial settlement. His letter to Decentius, Bishop of Eugubium, dated March 19, 416, is of great historical significance both for his mention in it of the principle of reserving confirmation to bishops and for what he says concerning the canon of the Mass. A man of ability and authoritarian temper, he set a notable pattern for authoritarian and centralized government in the Roman Catholic Church.

Innocent III (1160–1216). Of a noble family, he entered the papal service and became a cardinal in 1190; then before he was ordained priest he was elected to the papacy. One of the most influential popes in history, he was aided by the circumstances of his time to exert his will to enhance both the spiritual and the temporal power of the papacy, asserting his authority both within the Empire and beyond it, even as far north as Scandinavia and as far east as Armenia. He preached a crusade against the Albigensians, who were subjected to a virtual genocide, and he convoked the Fourth Lateran Council (1215), the most important of all the Lateran Councils and the one at which the term transubstantiation was first used. He was the first pope to use the designation "Vicar of Christ" for the holder of the papal office. He also denied that any temporal ruler reigning without devoutly serving the Vicar of Christ is reigning unlawfully. He even declared Magna Charta null and void on the pretext that the English king had consented to it under pressure. He was almost incontestably the most successful pope in history to validate the absolutist claims of the papacy to supreme power not only within Christendom but beyond it. He accounted the papal office "below God but above man."

Innocents, Holy. A feast of this name is held on December 28 to commemorate the children of two years old and under ordered by Herod the Great to be massacred, according to Matthew 2.18.

Inopportunists. The name given at the First Vatican Council by those who succeeded in promulgating the doctrine of papal infallibility to the large body of bishops who opposed it. The aim was to try to minimize the nature of the opposition by implying that it was based merely on the view that it was inexpedient to promulgate it at that particular time, although this was only one (and by no means the most weighty) of the arguments that the opposition used against the decree.

Inquisition. In the early Church those whose opinions were held to deviate fundamentally from the teaching of the Church might be excommunicated. The early Fathers tended to disapprove any form of physical punishment or even financial penalty for heresy. From as early as the 4th c., however, secular authorities tended to see heresy as an offense against the secular prince and therefore punishable in a variety of ways, even death. The Church's disapproval of the notion of inflicting physical punishment on heretics continued for many centuries and is well expressed in the maxim of Bernard of Clairvaux in the 12th c. to the effect that the Christian faith is to be promoted by persuasion, not by force. Nevertheless, so much did the Albigensian movement frighten the Church authorities that, on the pretext that it threatened the secular as well as the ecclesiastical arm, they eagerly enlisted the help of the secular authorities. The result was the establishment of what was technically called the Inquisition: a judicial system of trying heretics and others by ecclesiastical courts, who assumed wide powers, including the authority to hand the accused, if found guilty, to the secular authorities for punishment, usually burning at the stake. At first the Emperor (Frederick II) in 1232 issued an edict entrusting to state officials the hunting down of heretics. It was then that the Pope (Gregory IX), jealous of the papal power and fearing its erosion to the state, claimed the Church's right to deal with heretics and entrusted it to the Dominicans and Franciscans who as scholars under a vow of poverty could be supposed to lack the less worthy motives that might affect the judgment of bishops and other members of the hierarchy. The inquisitors combed the areas where heresy was most suspected. When they encountered it, they urged the suspect to confess. Then they gave him or her a time of grace to do so, on the expiration of which (about a month) the suspect was taken to trial, unless he or she had meanwhile voluntarily confessed to heresy in which case a fast or other penitential exercise was imposed.

Otherwise the suspect, having been summoned by the parish priest, was taken before the inquisitor, who was assisted by a group of clerics and laymen. Two witnesses were required to establish the testimony. The suspect was permitted an attorney, but even he was by no means a defense counsel as we would understand that role today. He was cast rather more in the role of an impartial observer present to see that the trial was conducted correctly according to the accepted rules. If the suspect remained obdurate he or she might be imprisoned under extremely hard conditions. In 1252 torture was for the first time allowed to extract a confession of guilt. The torture was often extremely cruel. The penalties varied from confiscation of goods to burning at the stake. In 1542 Pope Paul III established the Congregation of the Inquisition as the highest court of appeal in such trials. The Inquisition in Spain began much later (toward the end of the 15th c.) and had close connections with the state. Established in 1479 by Ferdinand and Isabella in conjunction with the Pope, and originally designed to focus on Marranos (converts from Judaism) and Moriscos (converts from Islam), it was eventually extended to include Protestants and others whose views were displeasing to the Roman Catholic Church. It was highly organized. At least 2,000 persons, possibly many more, were burnt at the stake under Torquemada, its first inquisitor. The Spanish Inquisition was not abolished till 1808. Reintroduced six years later it was finally abolished in 1814. Probably no evil in the history of the Church has had greater notoriety than the Inquisition, both in its earlier and in its later form.

Institutes, The. The principal work of John Calvin, *Christianae Religionis Institutio* is commonly so called in English. The first edition, in Latin, was published in 1536 as a theological interpretation of the Bible and a defense of Reformation principles. An enlarged edition appeared in 1539, and a French translation in 1541. The final edition appeared in Latin in 1559, and in French in 1560. The central theme is the sovereignty of God, but the emphasis on human incapacity to attain salvation without the help of God is very noteworthy. Calvin's style is notably clear and readable.

Institution. When a cleric is admitted to the care of a parish he is first instituted, which gives him spiritual charge of it. He is later inducted.

Institution, The Words of. By this phrase is meant the words Christ is reported in the Gospels to have used at the Last Supper: "This is My Body" and "This is My Blood." They are central to all Christian forms of the Liturgy and have been since earliest times.

Instruments, Delivery of the. (Latin, *Traditio* or *Porrectio Instrumentorum*) When a cleric is admitted to one of the Sacred Orders, he receives the symbols pertaining to it, e.g., a candidate for the diaconate receives the Book of the Gospels, one for the priesthood a paten and chalice. In Anglican usage deacons receive a copy of the New Testament and priests a copy of the Bible.

Insufflation. The action of breathing on a person or thing to symbolize the action of the Holy Spirit. The rite is still used in the Roman Catholic Church for the consecration of the chrism on Maundy Thursday, and in some Eastern rites the baptismal water is insufflated.

Intention. In Christian thought and practice the word is used in several distinct senses as follows: (1) In the administration of the Sacraments it is essential that the intention be present in order that the sacrament be validly administered; otherwise it would sometimes be administered by accident or, for instance, when a cleric in training was practising; (2) In ethics a good intention can make an indifferent action good, while a bad intention can make an indifferent action bad; (3) In medi-

eval epistemology, the term was sometimes used of the objects of knowledge to the extent that they are present in the cognitive awareness of the knower, i.e., in contrast to the table that is "really there" independent of me, the table that is conceptually there for me is said to have intentional existence; (4) When a priest is said to say Mass for a special intention, it means that he undertakes to pray that its fruits may be applied to a particular object, such as the restoration of someone to health or the repose of the soul of a deceased person.

Intercession. That form of petitionary prayer that is directed to the benefit of others, e.g., prayers for a sick friend or for the hungry or oppressed in distant lands. It is a form of prayer universally used in Christian worship.

Interdict. In the Roman Catholic Church, a punishment excluding the faithful from participation in the Sacraments and other spiritual benefits without their being excommunicated from the Church. It may be personal (to one individual) or local (to a parish or group of parishes) or general (to an entire region). The practice dates as early as the 6th c. In the Middle Ages, when papal influence was immense, its effect was formidable. Nowadays it is seldom imposed and then only for very special and limited purposes.

Intinction. The practice of dipping the eucharistic bread in the consecrated wine before Holy Communion. It was used in various circumstances in the early Middle Ages (e.g., for administering Communion to the sick in a more convenient way), but in the West the practice had disappeared from about the end of the twelfth century. Since 1965 it has been recognized in the Roman Catholic Church as one of the permitted ways of administering Communion. In Anglican practice it is an optional way: the person receiving Communion reverently retains the Host, and then when the priest brings the Chalice, he or she returns the Host to the priest, who dips it slightly in the Chalice and administers the intincted Host.

Introit. Traditionally, a psalm or part of a psalm sung as the celebrant is approaching or at the altar and about to say Mass. The term is also used in Protestant churches of any opening verse or other devotion used as an opening to divine service.

Invention of the Cross, The. According to an ancient legend, Helena, mother of Constantine, found the three crosses on Golgotha and miraculously identified the one on which Jesus was crucified. A large part of the wood was distributed to churches throughout the world, but the major piece was retained in the Church of the Holy Sepulchre in Jerusalem. It was for many centuries venerated by pilgrims. The word "invention" is traditional English usage, from the Latin *inventio*, meaning a "finding" or "discovery". In this primary sense the term has nothing to do with "creative imagination" or "fiction," although this has become a common but historically secondary meaning.

Investiture Controversy, The. An important dispute, dating from the late 11th and the 12th c. over the claims of the Emperor and princes to invest a bishop-elect with the ring and staff and to receive his homage before the consecration took place. Pope Nicholas condemned the practice in 1059, and in 1075 Pope Gregory VII expressly forbade it. (The practice had been closely tied to lay patronage.) The matter did not end there by any means, and the controversy raged for about sixty years. In the end a compromise was reached in which lay rulers retained a good deal of control over ecclesiastical elections although on the issue of the ceremony of lay investiture the papacy won.

Invincible Ignorance. Roman Catholic theologians have used this term to signify the state of those who, by reason of their upbringing are indisposed to accept the Church's teachings. This means that they are not culpable as they would be accounted were they in a state in which their condition was surmountable, for example, by education and training.

Invitatory. The psalm *Venite* (King James Version Ps. 95; Vulgate Ps. 94) with its antiphon is so called. It occurs in the Roman Breviary at the beginning of the Day Office and in the Anglican Book of Common Prayer it is found at the beginning of Morning Prayer, but without the antiphon.

In Vitro Fertilization. The fertilization with semen of an oöcyte in a receptacle outside the uterus. Oöcytes are withdrawn from the woman's ovary just before ovulation (not an unduly difficult procedure), semen is collected from the husband or other donor, and after a few days a few sperm are added to the oöcytes. After a few days embryos can be transferred to the woman's uterus *per vaginam*.

A related but different procedure, which has been highly successful in many cases, is the transfer of an ovum from a female donor to another woman. The embryo may be obtained from the female donor after normal sexual union. Apparently no significant increase in natal abnormalities occur in connection with this procedure, which has been used for a century or more on other mammals.

Special ethical questions arise with all such experimental procedures, e.g., when does the embryo attain human rights? When may it continue to be used experimentally by invasion or neglect? To what extent have we the right even to initiate such artificial procedures? On the one hand, it may be argued that many births accounted perfectly natural entail some medical assistance or interference and such very experimental cases are merely extensions of such assistance. On the other hand it may be objected that there is a radical difference between such highly artificial procedures and, say, surgical procedures to assist the development of the embryo or to facilitate a birth.

Iona. A little island to the west of Mull in the Inner Hebrides, Scotland. When Columba landed there in 563 it was already regarded as a sacred place. The monastic house that he founded there became the center of Celtic Christianity. Missionaries were sent thence to various places in Scotland, England, and elsewhere and it became a great place of pilgrimage for Christians everywhere. Many times robbed by the Norse it was often rebuilt, notably by Queen Margaret in the 11th c. It served for a short time before the Reformation as the cathedral of the diocese of the Western Isles. After falling into ruins the church was restored about 1900, and in 1938 George MacLeod (later Lord MacLeod) took the first steps toward rebuilding it. Although hampered by the conditions prevailing during the next seven years by reason of the outbreak of World War II, the work of building was undertaken, conjoined with what the Founder and his supporters felt to be essential to the restoration: the development of a group of persons, clerical and lay, prepared to live together in community on the island in summers and to go out during the rest of the year to work in difficult industrial parishes and express the social implications of the Gospel as they saw them. Spiritual healing is also part of the program of the Iona Community, which, after years of pleading by its founder, at last received the official recognition of the General Assembly of the Scottish Kirk in 1951. The work of the Iona Community is supported by a group of Friends from all over the world and belonging to many Christian denominations. The restored abbey in its unique setting on one of the loveliest of Scotland's 787 islands is incomparably beautiful.

Irenaeus. 2nd c. Bishop of Lyons. Little is known about his early life or by what means he met his death, but a good deal of what lies between. It is likely that he was born in Smyrna and he is known to have studied in Rome. Gnosticism was a prevailing climate of thought in his day and the Christian Church saw it as a danger because of extravagant forms of it and because the Christian message seemed to be in danger of being lost in it. Scholars of the Alexandrian school (e.g., Clement and Origen) sought to counter this danger by establishing in effect a form of Christianity that included Gnostic insights and motifs, but Irenaeus, by contrast, made a direct attack on the Gnostics. Much of the text of Irenaeus's work survives, part of it in the original Greek, all of his principal work *Against All Heresies* in Latin translation. Another work of his has been discovered in modern times in an Armenian translation: *The Demonstration of the Apostolic Preaching.* He emphasized what he took to be the biblical tradition as interpreted by the earliest Christian Fathers and stressed the organizational elements in the growing Church, especially the episcopate.

Irish Articles, The. In 1615 the Church of Ireland (Anglican) adopted 104 articles of faith on the lines of the 39 articles adopted by the Church of England in 1562 but much more specifically Calvinistic. They insist on a strict predestinarianism and affirm that the Pope is the Antichrist. They were largely if not wholly the work of James Ussher, then professor of divinity at Dublin and afterwards Archbishop of Armagh.

Irving, Edward (1792–1834). Born in Annan, Dumfriesshire, Scotland, and educated at the University of Edinburgh, he was licensed by the Kirk of Scotland in 1815. In 1822 he went as Minister of the Caledonian Chapel in Hatton Place, London. After some time he developed both a taste for Catholic ritual and an interest in what would nowadays be called Pentecostalism, but he was especially drawn to eschatological speculations and the Second Coming of Christ. His tendencies in these varied directions alarmed his congregation and after much controversy he was deposed in 1833 by his presbytery from the ministry of the Scottish Kirk. His followers, often popularly called "Irvingites", constituted themselves "The Catholic Apostolic Church" and professed belief in the Second Coming. They developed a considerable organization with "apostles" and "angels" among their ministry and they had many fine churches, in which they used a liturgy derived from Eastern and other rites, with the use of incense and other liturgical practices, spreading themselves not only through England and Scotland but to the European continent and the United States. It was expected that the Second Coming would occur before the death of the last of the "apostles", and when this one died in 1901 the Church inevitably declined but has nevertheless continued to survive in Britain, Germany, and the United States, often (at least in England) in the form of a group offering itself to a local Anglican parish and worshipping publicly with the regular parishioners but having private gatherings of their own as well. Irving, was a member of a group of interesting men who included, e.g., Henry Drummond and Thomas Carlyle.

Isaac. The son of Abraham and Sarah after a long childless marriage. According to Genesis 22, God tried Abraham's faith by asking him to offer the boy Isaac as a human sacrifice, but when he saw Abraham's dutiful obedience he accepted a ram in his place. Isaac appears often in the New Testament as a type prefiguring Christ.

Isaac. (*c.*350–440). Catholicos (patriarch) of the Armenian Church appointed in 390. Translated large parts of the Bible into Armenian, wrote many Armenian hymns, and in various ways fostered the national spirit of Armenia.

Isaac. A 7th c. Nestorian Bishop of Nineveh, known both as Isaac of Nineveh and as Isaac Syrus. He wrote in Syriac, mostly on ascetic subjects, and his writings were translated into Greek and other languages.

Isabella (1451–1504). Queen of Spain, daughter of John II, King of Castile and León, and wife of Ferdinand. The reign of Ferdinand and Isabella marked the beginning of an era of great Spanish power. Devoutly Catholic, she much assisted Ximenes in his program of reform within the Roman Catholic Church. See **Ferdinand V.**

Isaiah. Hebrew prophet of the 8th c. BCE who, like Amos and Hosea, much emphasized the ethical expectations of God, giving an ethical content to the then primitive people's concept of the divine nature. The book of the Bible ascribed to him can be his work only in part. Chapters 1–12, 16–22, and 28–32 are very probably attributable to him. His authorship of other sections of Chapters 1–35 is at best doubtful, and some of them may be definitely attributed to some other writer. Biblical scholars are satisfied, moreover, that Chapters 40–55 are the work of another author, whom they designate "Deutero-Isaiah," which section they date shortly before the liberation of the Jews by Cyrus in 537 BCE. Chapters 56–66 are the work of yet another writer (more probably other writers), and this section is called by scholars "Trito-Isaiah" and dated later than 520 BCE.

Isho'dad of Merv. A 9th c. Nestorian Bishop of Hedatta. His works, in Syriac, shed much light on the history of biblical interpretation in the ancient and early medieval Church. He wrote extensive commentaries on the Bible.

Ishtar. Babylonian and Assyrian goddess, known also as Astarte and as Ashtoreth. She was the goddess of vegetation and herds as well as of sexual love and maternity. She was identified with the planet Venus and corresponded in some fundamental respects with the Roman goddess of that name and with the Greek Aphrodite.

Isidore. Early 5th c. abbot of a monastery near Pelusium on the eastern estuary of the Nile. In his writings he opposed both Nestorius and Eutyches.

Isidore (c. 560–636). Of a noble family of Cartagena, he became Archbishop of Seville. Very erudite and with great administrative ability, he labored zealously in the fostering of Christian knowledge by founding schools and convents, and he gave money generously for charitable causes. The great esteem in which he was held in later times was due mainly, however, to his writings, which were impressive repositories of the learning of his age. His *Etymologiae*, for instance, provides a sort of encyclopaedia of the learning of his day, from mathematics and grammar to medicine and theology. His *De Ecclesiasticis Officiis* describes the functions of various clerical ranks as well as of laypeople in the Church and shows the liturgical sources of the Mozarabic liturgy. Although in accordance with the practice of his day he borrowed very liberally from his predecessors, his work is nevertheless of great historical value for the history of Christian thought. See also **False Decretals, The.**

Isis-Osiris, The Myth of. Great Egyptian goddess of nature, Isis had flourished in Egypt from at least 1,700 BCE and her cult was still strong when Christianity appeared on the scene. The Isis-Osiris myth had a solar significance, although its nature is not clear. Osiris is slain by his brother Set and enclosed in a chest, which is sent adrift in the Nile and then discovered eventually by his wife Isis, after much searching and mourning by Isis and her sister Nephthys, Set's wife. Set regains possession of the body, which he divides into fourteen parts and disperses them throughout Egypt. Isis gives birth to Horus and hides him in the Delta marshes. She eventually succeeds in recovering the parts of the body of Osiris, and he is somehow miraculously restored and becomes the god of the dead.

Horus wreaks revenge on Set for the death of Osiris, his father, but Isis pleads successfully for Set's life. Then Horus and Set appear before the great court of the Egyptian pantheon, at which the gods assign to Horus the crown of his father Osiris. Osiris is also identified with the sun, Isis with the dawn, Set with the night, and after the crowning of Horus he is likewise identified with the sun. The myth pertains to a group of "Mystery Religions" that flourished in the Hellenic world and had certain common features such as rebirth, a claim to esoteric, theosophical knowledge of the spiritual world, and various ceremonies and rites of purification, some of which have seemed to some scholars to adumbrate certain features developed in Christian ritual connected with the Sacraments. See **Mystery Religions.**

Islam. The religion founded by Muhammad (570–632). It emphasizes the sovereignty and the oneness of Allah. The word "Islam" means "submission" to the will of Allah. The teachings of Islam are set forth in the Qur'ān (Koran), to which are added the *sunna* or traditions relating to Muhammad and his successors. Muhammad drew freely from the teachings of the Bible, and from both Jewish and Christian ideas as well as Arabic sources and Gnostic concepts. A powerful leader of men, he welded the warring Arab tribes together under the banner of Israel, proclaiming the unity of God. He recognized the prophetic tradition as found in the Bible and counted Jesus among the prophets. For his followers, Muhammad is the final prophet. Muslims practice ritual prayer five times a day, recited while looking in the direction of Mecca, which is the holiest focus of the religion and the place to which every good Muslim hopes to make a pilgrimage at least once in his life. They also observe the great fast of Ramadan. Islam has spawned many sects. Notable, however, are two (1) the Sunnites, who regard themselves as having a teaching founded directly on the Qur'ān and the *sunna* and (2) the Shi'ites (strong in Iran) who hold that the prophetic authority was transmitted to Muhammad's descendants and can still be exercised by certain leaders today. The sufis represent a mystical wing of Islam. Some historians of religion have classified Islam as a heretical offshoot of Christianity, but although it does have some features that reflect Christian sources, it is clearly a distinct religion and is very generally so regarded.

Isomorphism. (Greek, meaning literally "equal form".) An important concept in various scientific fields and deriving from mathematics, it has a relevance to some discussions of the philosophy of religion. Any two groups of entities are said to be isomorphic when they have the same structure in the sense that the elements of one group can be correlated with the elements of the other by a one-to-one correspondence.

Israel. According to Genesis 32.28, the name Israel was bestowed by God on Jacob, the son of Isaac. It is then used in the Bible, because of this heritage, as the name of the twelve tribes who were named for Jacob's twelve sons, becoming eventually a synonym for the Hebrew people as a whole. Later biblical writers, however, came to restrict the designation to the ten northern tribes who on the death of Solomon *c.* 930 BCE attached themselves to Jeroboam and who in 721 BCE were taken to Assyria. So it came to be used in contrast to the Judah that by *c.* 1000 BCE had become the predominant tribe and eventually became the separate kingdom that outlived the northern tribes and is commended in some of the biblical writings for its greater fidelity. The term Israel is also used in a general sense for the Hebrew nation in its special situation as a partner to the covenant it had with God. The New Testament writers then adopted Israel as the name of the new community formed by the followers of the Christian Way, calling it the new (or true) Israel to which was being accorded the special relationship with God that had formerly pertained to the Hebrew people only by now was accessible to people irrespective of race.

Issy, The Thirty-Four Articles of. In the Quietist controversy in France in the 17th c., when the works of Madame Guyon and Archbishop Fénelon were under suspicion, an ecclesiastical commission was appointed to examine certain works, and in 1695 it condemned theses proposed by Madame Guyon and implicitly some teachings of Fénelon. The condemnation was directed at the Quietist teachings of their authors. Bossuet was the most influential opponent of Fénelon in this dispute.

Itala, The. A name sometimes given to the Old Latin versions of the Bible, i.e., those before the Vulgate. Modern scholars in the English-speaking world use the term Old Latin, but the other term was sometimes used in the past and by German biblical scholars.

Ite Missa Est. (Latin, meaning "go, you are dismissed.") The traditional words used at the conclusion of Mass. In contemporary Roman Catholic usage, it is said immediately after the blessing. The modern English-speaking usage is: "The Mass is ended, go in peace." Anglican usage is simply "Depart in peace." The word "alleluia" is added in Eastertide.

I-Thou. See **Buber, Martin.**

Itinerarium. (1) The short title of one of Bonaventure's mystical works: *Itinerarium mentis ad Deum* (The Journey of the Mind to God). (2) A short office formerly prescribed in the Roman Breviary for those about to set forth on a pilgrimage or other journey. It probably had its origin in a blessing of pilgrims about to depart on a pilgrimage to Jerusalem.

Ives. (1) According to legend, Ives was of Persian birth and came to England with some companions, perhaps in the

7th c. His bones were allegedly discovered at St Ives, Huntingdonshire, in 1001. (2) A woman after whom, according to legend, St. Ives, a Cornish town, is named.

Ivo (*c.* **1040–1115**). Bishop of Chartres, trained in Paris under Lanfranc. He was probably the most learned of the canonists of his age, and his works on the subject had considerable influence on the development of canon law in future generations. They are: *Collectio Tripartita*; *Decretum* (17 books); and *Panormia* (8 books). Letters and sermons also survive. In the Investiture controversies, he advocated moderation. For some time he was imprisoned for his courageous opposition to King Philip I.

J

Jabneel. See **Jabneh.**

Jabneh. A city about twelve miles south of Joppa, known also as Jabneel (Hebrew, "El will build") and by its Greek name (Jamnia. The modern Yebna.) In Hellenistic and Roman times it probably had a predominantly Greek population, but after the Fall of Jerusalem in 70 CE an assembly of Jewish leaders was established there. According to Talmudic tradition an important rabbinical council was held there about 100 CE that finally settled the books to be included in the Hebrew canon. The tradition that a specific council so determined the Hebrew canon is doubtful, but Jabneh does seem to have been the place where the Hebrew canon was finally fixed.

Jacob. Isaac and Rebekah had twin sons, of whom Esau was the elder and Jacob the younger. Jacob bought the rights of his elder brother for the price of a meal (Genesis 25.19–26) and obtained by a ruse the blessing of his father that had been intended for Esau. The date of these events is probably about 1750 BCE. Jacob's ancestry was probably Aramaean, as indicated in

Deuteronomy 26.5. In the Old Testament the name of Jacob is often used as a synonym for Israel itself, especially where the motif is the forgiveness of Israel: as Jacob was forgiven by God, so can Israel obtain that divine forgiveness.

Jacob Baradaeus (*c.* **500–578**). Born in Tella and educated at a monastery near Nisibis, he is considered to be the founder of the group of Syrian Monophysites called Jacobites, who rejected the christological teaching of the Council of Chalcedon. (See **Jacobites.**) With another monk, Sergius he went to Constantinople to plead the case for Monophysitism to the Empress, and there he remained for about fifteen years till he was consecrated Bishop of Edessa. He then travelled in Egypt and other countries founding Monophysite churches. To avoid his being recognized and probably arrested, he wore a beggar's clothes as a disguise, from which comes his nickname, Baradaeus (Greek *baradaios*, ragged).

Jacob of Edessa (*c.* **640–708**). Monophysite Syrian scholar, Bishop of Edessa. He has sometimes been called the Syrian Jerome, because of his great learning and his work on the revision of the Peshitta.

Jacob of Nisibis. Early 4th c. Syrian Church scholar, reported by Theodoret to have taken a leading part in the Council of Nicaea in 325. He is much revered by both Syrian and Armenian Christians.

Jacob of Voragine. The 13th c. author of the Golden Legend. Born at Varazze, near Genoa, he entered the Dominican Order in 1244 and in 1292 became Archbishop of Genoa. Among his other writings is his *Chronicon Genuense*, which is valuable for the history of the region of Genoa.

Jacobi, Friedrich Heinrich (1743–1819). Philosopher. Born in Düsseldorf, he pursued a business career till he was in his forties, then turned to philosophy. He found that dogmatic rationalism leads to a pantheistic determinism and turned to a stance based on a sense of immediate certainty. Here he thought he had found grounds for belief in God and freedom. His writings include *On the Teaching of Spinoza in Letters to Moses Mendelssohn* (1785), *Open Letters to Fichte* (1799), and *On Divine Things* (1811).

Jacobins. The first Dominican house in Paris was established in 1218 in the rue Saint-Jacques, Paris, because of which the Dominican friars were sometimes called Jacobins. The name was much later given to a political club that acquired the property at the French Revolution.

Jacobites. (1) Through the work of Jacob Baradaeus (see **Jacob Baradaeus**), the Syrian Monophysites who repudiated the doctrine of the "two natures" (human and divine) of Christ that had been decreed as orthodox by the Council of Chalcedon in 451, became the national Church of Syria. They came to be know later as Jacobites and are so designated by name in the Second Council of Nicaea in 787. (2) At a much later date and in very different circumstances the name was given to those (many although not all of them Roman Catholics) who, after the Revolution of 1688 in Great Britain, when William and Mary came to the British throne, adhered to the exiled British king James II (Jacobus Secundus) and his successors.

Jacopone Da Todi (*c.* 1230–1306). Franciscan Spiritual. After law studies, probably at Bologna, he underwent a conversion on the death of his wife in 1268 and about ten years later became a Franciscan lay brother. His many beautiful poems (*Stabat Mater* is attributed to him), his deeply mystical spirit, and his rigorous way of life made him widely venerated. Pope Boniface VIII caused him to be imprisoned for about five years and he died three years later.

Jains. The Jains follow a system of Indian philosophy developed by Mahavira (Vardhamana) who lived *c.* 540–468 BCE and taught that in all that exists, including not only humans, animals, and plants, but even rocks and dust, is sentient feeling, particles of life that are bound up with material that imprisons them in a sort of enveloping coating. The concept of karma is emphasized: through the karmic law one gets what one seeks, entailing a certain kind of embodiment, with all its limitations and its capacity for misery and pain. One then finds oneself in a predicament from which one struggles to be free, but how? Since it was action that got one into the prison of one's circumstance, the way out is through abstinence from action. Since lust has captured one in a body, the way out is by rigorous asceticism. As one starves a fevered body to rid the body of the fever, so the lusts of the flesh must be starved so that the soul can loose itself. The Jains go to extremes in trying to avoid hurt to any living thing. They are strict vegetarians and maintain hospitals and homes for the lowest and least loved forms of animal life. They build beautiful temples and encourage the cultivation of art and literature. Their extreme devotion to the ideal of *ahiṁsā* (non-violence) has influenced some of the greatest of Christians thinkers and leaders such as Schweitzer. Jainism, compared to other great religions, does not have very numerous adherents: between one and two million. There is no place for God as understood in the biblical tradition, for instance. Liberated individual souls, however, eventually achieve a status that may be called divine.

James. See **Brethren, The Lord's**.

James, Apocalypses of. Two works found among the Nag Hammadi writings, purporting to be dialogues between Jesus and James (designated as "the Lord's brother").

James, The Book of. An apocryphal Gospel, probably written about the middle of the 2nd c. It is ascribed to James, "the Lord's brother" and is by a Jewish Christian who obviously knew some of the canonical Gospels. The book was known to at least some of the early Fathers, including Origen. It contains the first known mention of the names of the Virgin Mary's parents: Anne and Joachim. It has been also known as the Protevangelium. See **Protevangelium.**

James, Epistle of. A work (to be distinguished from the canonical New Testament book of that name) found among the Nag Hammadi writings and purporting to report the last utterance of Jesus before his ascension into heaven.

James, Liturgy of. An ancient liturgy traditionally attributed to James ("the Lord's brother") but of later date, although not later than the middle of the 5th c.

James, William (1842–1910). American philosopher and psychologist. Born in New York, the son of a Swedenborgian theologian and the brother of the novelist Henry James, he was educated at Harvard, but both brothers received much of their education in Europe. William earned an M.D. at Harvard in 1869 but turned more and more to psychology and philosophy, becoming in 1885 professor of philosophy at Harvard. Although the term "pragmatism" was introduced by Peirce in 1878, it is much associated with James who popularized it. James's thought may be said to have developed out of the tension he felt between his commitment to science and his interest in religious faith. His methodology in *The Principles of Psychology* (2 vols., 1890), the first of his principal works, is pragmatistic. He saw human consciousness as a stream gathering up, as it flows, everything that has passed through it. The "specious present" (as he calls it) refers to the real duration that we grasp, which contains past and future within it. James's interest in the nature of consciousness led him to perceive emotion

as the feeling of a bodily state, which ensues upon that state; e.g., my heart does not pound because I feel excited, I feel excited because my heart pounds. Especially significant for the philosophy of religion, not least for Christians, is James's insistence that, although a wise man does not act rashly but requires evidence before acting, life is such that we are constantly faced with having to make decisions whether we have adequate evidence to support their wisdom or not. In such circumstances, as the old proverb goes, "he who hesitates is lost." As we might say today, if on a freeway we suddenly have to decide whether to exit or go with the through traffic, we had better act quickly one way or the other, irrespective of the wisdom of our choice, for otherwise we are likely to end up in disaster on a triangle. In such cases we must and ought to act beyond the evidence. He discusses and develops such notions both in *The Will to Believe* (1897) and *The Varieties of Religious Experience* (1902). With his functional psychology goes his pragmatistic method, but his special interest in religious experience attracted a large readership whom his other philosophical writings would have been unlikely to reach. James's entire philosophy, which is not in the mold traditionally used by philosophers of religion in his day, was and remains notably hospitable to certain key concerns of the religious consciousness. His other writings include *Pragmatism: A New Name for Some Old Ways of Thinking* (1907), *A Pluralistic Universe* (1909), *Some Problems of Philosophy* (1911), and *Essays in Radical Empiricism* (1912).

Jamnia. See **Jabneh.**

Jansen, Cornelius Otto (1585–1638). Theologian. Born at Accoy, Utrecht, the nephew of Cornelius Jansen the Elder (1510–1576), who was Bishop of Ghent, he studied at Louvain, then at Paris where he met Saint-Cyran, with whom he worked intensely for about five years. From 1628 he read the works of Augustine with extreme diligence over and over again. He became Bishop of Ypres two years before his death. His studies in Augustine resulted in an immensely influential treatise, *Augustinus*, published posthumously in 1640 and pronounced heretical by the Sorbonne in 1649 and by Pope Innocent X in 1653. See **Jansenism**.

Jansenism. The name given to a 17th c. theological controversy within the Roman Catholic Church, one of the most interesting in Christian history and involving some of the most brilliant minds of the day, including Pascal. It arose as a result of Jansen's treatise, *Augustinus*. (See **Jansen, Cornelius Otto**.) Those who followed the Jansenist position held that it is impossible to do good works without God's grace and that this grace is irresistible. Such a position, which has affinities with Calvinism, can certainly be supported in Augustine's works, although some would argue that it requires a special, one-sided interpretation.

The first Jansenists were all schooled in the teachings of Saint-Cyran and looked to him as their leader after the posthumous publication of *Augustinus* in 1640. After the death of Saint-Cyran, Antoine Arnauld took over the leadership. The Convent of Port-Royal was deeply affected by the movement. Characteristic of the Jansenist outlook as it developed was a very rigorist position in Christian ethics, entailing opposition to certain kinds of moral theology fashionable at the time, such as Probabilism and Probabiliorism. In 1693 Quesnel published a work supportive of a form of Jansenism, and it was condemned in the bull *Unigenitus* in 1713. The Jansenists regarded the Jesuits as their chief and most powerful adversaries. Pascal, one of the greatest geniuses in the history of religious thought as well as one of the great luminaries in the intellectual tradition of France, was deeply influenced by and sympathetic to Jansenism and bitterly satirized its opponents in his *Lettres provinciales*.

Persecution of the Jansenists in France persisted and many took refuge in the Netherlands, where the Church tolerated and sometimes even encouraged it. By the beginning of the 19th c., Jansenism was virtually ousted from the Church in France, although it continued to have some influence as an underground movement among French Catholic intellectuals.

Januarius. Traditionally the patron saint of Naples. Almost nothing is known about him except that he died somewhere in the Neapolitan region in the persecution under Diocletian in 303. According to a popular belief his blood (preserved as a relic at the cathedral) liquefies several times a year, attracting large crowds.

Janus. The pseudonym used by Döllinger. See also **Quirinus**.

Jaspers, Karl (1883–1973). Philosopher. Born in Oldenburg, he took a medical degree in 1909 and became *Privatdozent* in psychology at Heidelberg in 1913. Turning to philosophy he became professor there in 1920. During Hitler's rule he was forbidden to teach and in 1937 was deprived of his chair. He became professor at Basel in 1945. Although he disliked any label, he is generally reckoned an existentialist. Influenced by Kierkegaard and Nietzsche, he developed a Christian form of existentialism, contrasting religion and philosophy. His fundamental quest is for authenticity. Man is *Existenz*, self-aware, free and open to everything; yet he is so only when he attains authentic selfhood; he usually falls far short of the attainment or loses it. Then be becomes like other objects that are in a state of *Dasein*; that is, of merely *being there*. Jaspers contrasts *Existenz* with Reason. Without *Existenz*, Reason is empty; without Reason, *Existenz* is mere daydreaming. The goal of the quest for *Existenz* is Being, truth about which we can never hope to achieve fully; nevertheless, philosophy enables us to read the "ciphers" that lead us toward it, taking us to a horizon beyond which the transcendent Being lies hidden yet communicating Being to us. All our philosophical enterprises carry us forward, while at the same time revealing the incompleteness and finitude of our human awareness. The self is the ground of all existence. Neither science nor religion can give us more than ciphers. They may even push the horizon forward; nevertheless, the horizon still hides from us the transcendent Being. Jaspers' many writings include *Man in the Modern Age* (1931), *Philosophy* (3 vols., 1932), *Existence Philosophy* (1938), *Nietzsche and Christianity* (1946), *The Perennial Scope of Philosophy* (1948), *Truth and Science* (1960), and *Ciphers of Transcendence* (1970).

Jassy, Synod of. This synod, held in 1642 at Jassy in what is now Romania, is (except for the Synod of Jerusalem) the most important in the Eastern Orthodox Church since the Fall of Constantinople to the Turks in 1453. It condemned as Calvinistic the teachings of Cyril Lukar and ratified, in a revised form, the *Orthodox Confession* of Peter Mogila, thereby giving Eastern Orthodoxy expression in a doctrinal form that reflects considerable influence from Catholic theology in the West.

Jean-Baptiste de LaSalle. See **LaSalle, Jean-Baptiste de.**

Jeanne d'Arc (1412–1431). As a devout child, daughter of a peasant family, she claimed to have experienced, in 1425, a vision of a great blaze of light accompanied by a heavenly voice. Later she claimed to have had revelations from the Archangel Michael and others charging her with a mission to save France. Although her visions were held suspect by many, she eventually persuaded the King of France, Charles VII, of her powers. By 1429 she had so persuaded Church and State that she was allowed to lead an expedition to Orléans, clad in white armor and carrying a banner with the words Jesus and Maria and an emblem of the Trinity.

Soon afterwards she was at the King's side as he proceeded, on her advice, to his coronation at Reims on July 17, 1429. In November of the following year, however, she was arrested and handed over to the English by the Duke of Burgundy. A few months later she was on trial in Rouen before a court of the Bishop of Beauvais on charges of heresy and witchcraft. The court, supported by the University of Paris, pronounced her claims to visions false and evil. On May 30, 1431, she was burned at the stake at Rouen, paradoxically the victim of her seemingly miraculous success with those who had supported her. Twenty-five years after her death Pope Callistus III formally pronounced her innocent, and she was canonized by Pope Benedict XV on May 9, 1920. She is held in immense esteem as the embodiment of the spirit of France, of which she is accounted the patroness, second only to Denis, the first bishop of Paris and patron saint of France.

Jehoshaphat. The personal name of a king of Judah (873–849 BCE), the son of Asa, whom he succeeded (I Kings 15.24). The Valley of Jehoshaphat (Joel 4.2, 12), the scene of the apocalyptic judgment that Yahweh is to carry out, is not a geographical entity but a symbolic name: the place where Yahweh judges.

Jehovah. A form of the name of God, which traditionally the Jews accounted too sacred to be uttered. This form was devised by Christian writers through an incorrect transliteration of the Hebrew. (See **Tetragrammaton.**) Modern scholars render it Yahweh or Jahveh.

Jehovah's Witnesses. An organization founded by Charles Taze Russell (1852–1916) as "The International Bible Students" and having as its central theme a belief that the world was coming to an end and that his followers would be the sole heirs to the Messianic Kingdom. His successor, Joseph Franklin Rutherford (1869–1941), known as "Judge Rutherford", who had originally predicted that the Second Coming would occur in

1914, took up the leadership of the organization in 1917, after Russell's death, teaching that Christ had returned invisibly in the year 1914 and that Armgeddon, the final struggle between God and Satan, was now imminent. He developed an outlook vigorously opposed to both Church and State authority and expounded it in periodicals such as *The Watchtower*, which vehemently inveighed against both institutional religion (particularly the Roman Catholic Church but also the Church of England and Protestant bodies) and the political institutions representing all the great national powers of the day. Known under various names, they have a network of printing houses throughout the world, depending heavily on audiences notably untutored in scholarly study of the Bible. They engage widely in door-to-door solicitation and appeal largely to those sections of society that are alienated from existing institutions and unprepared for intellectual analysis.

Jeremiah. The date of his birth is uncertain but probably *c*. 645 BCE. He was born at Anathoth, near Jerusalem and in his youth felt that he had received a call to be a prophet. His teaching was received with much hostility, largely because of his predictions of impending disaster. The biblical book called by his name has been extensively edited: perhaps more so than any other in the Bible. He apparently loved his land deeply and was acutely distressed by what he saw happening to it. He took very seriously the prophetic calling and the duty of the prophet to speak out fearlessly.

Jericho. In the time of David a town of this name seems to have existed (II Samuel 10.5). It was a point on the frontier of Benjamin and Joseph (Joshua 6.1, 7; 18.12). It figures frequently in the New Testament, e.g., in the story of the Good Samaritan and in that of Zacchaeus. Modern Jericho lies *c*. twenty-three miles from Jerusalem by

way of a tortuous road descending from 2250 feet above sea level to 900 feet below sea level. It lies south of the spring called the "Fountain of Elisha," which waters the region making it an exceptionally rich agricultural area. In Old Testament times it was situated on the Tell-es-Sultan to the west of that spring. The Jericho of New Testament times lies under modern Jericho. Excavations of Tell-es-Sultan conducted in 1951–1957 by the British School of Archaeology have shown the existence of walled towns in the region of far greater antiquity than the time of the Israelites, some possibly dating back to almost 7000 BCE.

Jerome (*c* 342–420). The most influential biblical scholar and (apart from Origen) the greatest in the ancient Christian Church. His name, Eusebius Hieronymus, has been generally rendered "Jerome" in English. Born at Strido near Aquileia on the Adriatic coast, he studied at Rome, travelled in Gaul, and returned to Aquileia, where he devoted himself to a strictly ascetic life. Then probably in 374, he left for Palestine, stopping in Antioch, where he had a dream in which he heard an accusation against himself to the effect that he was not a Christian at all but a Ciceronian. (*Ciceronianus es, non Christianus.*) Believing this to be an allusion to his love of pagan literature and stylistic elegance, he resolved that in future he would read only the Bible: a resolve that he later renounced, perceiving that without literary prowess he could not properly study, let alone translate the Bible. During a stay of several years in the Syrian desert, at Chalcis, he learned Hebrew with the aid of a rabbinical teacher. Returning to Antioch, he was ordained priest there, then spent some time first in Constantinople, then in Rome. In 386 he settled in Bethlehem, where he governed a monastery and devoted the rest of his life to biblical study. He wrote many biblical commentaries and engaged in controversies against the Arians, the Pelagians, and the Origenists. He was noted for his severely ascetic form of life and for his acrimony in controversy. By far his greatest and most lasting achievement, however, was his translation of the Bible from Hebrew and Greek into Latin in a version that came to be called the Vulgate (*editio vulgata*), which eventually became the standard text of the Bible in the West. See **Vulgate**.

Jerome Emiliani (1481–1537). Born in Venice and ordained priest in 1518, he devoted his life to work among the poor, especially orphans, and in 1532 he founded an order of clerics regular, the Somaschi, who follow the Augustinian rule, being formally constituted by Pope Pius V in 1568. They still conduct orphanage and other work in Italy.

Jerome of Prague (c. 1370–1416). Reformer. A friend of Huss, he studied first at Prague, then at Oxford. Embracing various causes deemed tainted with heresy, he was suspect and, when he had followed Huss to the Council of Constance in 1415 and then escaped as he perceived the peril of his situation, he was captured and brought back in chains. Eventually he was burned at the stake where he displayed great courage.

Jerusalem. This city, held sacred by the three great monotheistic religions, Judaism, Christianity, and Islam, has been shown by archaeological evidence to have been in existence as early as about 3000 BCE. Allusions to it are found in the Tell-el-Amarna letters dating from the 15th and 14th centuries BCE. When it became the capital of Judah and the site of the Temple, it was recognized as the Holy City and the focus of the Hebrew people, remaining so throughout a long history of turmoil and foreign occupation. As the scene of the crucifixion of Jesus and the focus of the first Christians, it was from the first held sacred by all followers of the Christian Way. The Dome of the Rock, built about 700 CE in the area of the Temple and also known as the Mosque of Omar, is believed by Muslims to be on the site from which Muhammad ascended to heaven. According to a Jewish tradition it is that on which Abraham prepared to sacrifice his son, Isaac (Genesis 22.1–14). As the symbol of God's meeting with man, Jerusalem has a unique place in the mind of Jesus as he is represented in the Gospels. He weeps over it and expresses his longing to save the city from the judgments it has deserved for its treatment of the prophets. In Luke and Acts, Jerusalem has a peculiarly central position. The name "Jerusalem" becomes from New Testament times that of "the heavenly city," the antithesis of Babylon.

Jerusalem, Synod of. This council, held in 1672, is the most important in the Eastern Orthodox Church since the Fall of Constantinople in 1453. It repudiated the teachings of Cyril Lukar as Calvinistic and brought Eastern Orthodoxy closer to Rome and specifically to the outlook of the Council of Trent (1545–1563).

Jesuits. (See also **Ignatius Loyola**.) The name popularly given to members of the Society of Jesus, the order of clerics regular founded by Ignatius Loyola. This unique order was conceived in an age in which the Roman Catholic Church had been confronted in an unprecedented way by the cataclysmic forces of a successful Reformation movement that seemed to be threatening to destroy the traditional expressions of the Catholic spirit. It must be understood as having been originally inspired by a valiant resolve to conserve these traditional expressions and the values they represented by invigorating the Church with a new kind of zeal. This new zeal, at first medieval and chivalric in form, reflected also the spirit of the Renaissance that was stirring the best minds and most sensitive hearts in Europe. Founded by Ignatius with six companions in Paris in 1534, it was approved by Pope Paul III in 1540. The constitution, drawn up by Ignatius himself, envisioned two general aims:

(1) to achieve moral and educational reform within the existing structure of the Church and (2) to take the Christian Gospel to those distant lands that were being opened up at the time. Especially distinctive was the special relationship to the Pope in which the order was to stand. It was to be, in effect, an instrument placed directly at his disposal for whatever work he might deem most needed. Its members would decline all ecclesiastical dignities unless ordered by the Pope to do otherwise. Provision was made for a training beyond what is normally required for the priesthood. The administration of the order was to be placed in the hands of a General, elected for life; but supreme authority was to be vested in a General Congregation representative of the members of the order. At first the Jesuits undertook whatever work came their way at the behest of prelates. Soon, however, their special expertise in teaching was recognized, and more and more they became involved in education at all levels. Ignatius himself founded many educational institutions, including, in 1551, the Collegium Romanum. Toward the end of the century it was expanded into the Gregorian University, which remains one of the leading institutions of higher learning in the Roman Catholic Church. The Order spread to India, China, Japan, Brazil, and Africa, all within the founder's lifetime. By the year 1600 it comprised 23 provinces with a total of more than 8,500 members. Highly organized, they encountered much opposition and hostility even within the Roman Catholic Church. They were expelled from Portugal in 1759, from France in 1764, and thousands were deported from the Spanish Empire in 1767. Finally, in 1773, they were suppressed by Pope Clement XIV, by a brief, *Dominus ac Redemptor.* They continued their work, nevertheless, in various countries, including the United States, where the mission in Maryland had been founded in 1634, and in 1814 Pope Pius VII formally restored the order, which now numbers over 30,000

members and remains a uniquely influential organization within the Roman Catholic Church. Jesuits wear no distinctive habit, adopting whatever costume appears to be suitable and seemly in the locality. Such is their influence that the General of the Society is popularly called "the Black Pope."

Jesus. The name "Jesus" represents the Greek form (*Iēsous*) of the Hebrew "Joshua", which means literally "Jahveh saves." (See **Yahweh.**) According to the Gospels (Matthew 1.21; Luke 1.31) the name was given by divine command to him who was to be the Savior of the human race.

Jesus, Date of the Birth of. Although a conventional date has been adopted for the birth of Jesus Christ, from which is calculated the "Christian" or "Common" era, historical evidence such as we have and the New Testament witnesses themselves do not support the conventional date.

Luke tells us (Luke 2.1) that Jesus was born under the rule of Augustus, who died 14 BCE. Matthew places Jesus' birth (Matthew 2) before the death of Herod, which occurred in 4 BCE. In view of Matthew's story of a bright star that the wise men from the east followed, pointing them in the direction of the place of Jesus' birth, one naturally turns to the history of astronomy for possible help.

Halley's comet was reported by Chinese astronomers in 12 BCE, but that is for various reasons likely to be too early a date for the birth of Jesus. They also recorded, however, the appearance of another phenomenon, possibly a comet or an exploding star in the spring of 5 BCE. (A comet would move slowly across the sky night after night while orbiting the sun.) The Jewish historian Josephus reports that shortly before the death of Herod and just before Passover an eclipse of the moon occurred. Astronomers calculate that the only lunar eclipses that could have been visible from Israel at that season of the year about Herod's time occurred on March 23, 5 BCE and March 13, 4 BCE. This, together with other astronomical witnesses and other historical pointers, suggests that Jesus was born in the first half of the year 5 BCE. The exact date cannot be determined and in the absence of further evidence is unlikely to be determinable. While a more precise date would be of some interest to historians, it would be of course of no fundamental religious importance.

Jesus Prayer. This name is given to a distinctive prayer used in the Eastern Orthodox Church and especially recommended in the Hesychast tradition. The text is: "Lord Jesus Christ, Son of God, have mercy upon me, a sinner." (The words "a sinner" may be omitted and "us" may be substituted for "me" as occasion demands.) Some form of the prayer seems to have been in use in very early times, but the full form occurs in a work dating from the late sixth or early seventh century.

Jew. The term "Jew" is derived from "Judah". (See **Judah.**) The Hebrew form is *Yehudi*. The Babylonian Exile in 586 BCE changed the outlook of the Hebrews from an emphasis on liturgical practice to ethical and religious teaching. Nevertheless, Judaism, although in a sense it arose in these circumstances, has its roots in the ancient patriarchal religion.

Jewel, John (1522–1571). Bishop of Salisbury. Much influenced by Peter Martyr, he became one of the leading forces of the Reformation movement in England. Like others so influenced he had to flee England during the reign of Mary Tudor but returned on the accession of Elizabeth I and was consecrated Bishop of Salisbury in 1560. He is noteworthy for his support of the Anglican Way as a *via media* between the Puritans and the Roman Catholic Church. His *Apologiae Ecclesiae Anglicanae*, published in 1562, is generally regarded as the most effective defense of Anglican principles and claims. Richard Hooker,

whose *Ecclesiastical Polity* is no less a principal classic of the Anglican tradition, was much influenced by Jewel, by whom Hooker had been educated as a poor boy.

Jihād. This Muslim term may be understood as the duty to fight infidels. While it would be unfair to perceive the spread of Islam as mere imperial conquest, it is true that Muhammad did preach war as a sacred duty, so inculcating his followers with a sense of the rightness of any military engagement that seemed to foster or promote the cause of Islam. Muslims today may take the view that *jihād* was intended to apply only to the age and circumstances of the prophet Muhammad and indeed the texts that urge the faithful to fight for Allah plainly refer to Arabian soil; but, as in other religions, fanaticism is never bound by such scholarly interpretations and the principle of *jihād* or "holy war" could very well be invoked in circumstances favorable to its success.

Joachim. The first mention of Joachim as the father of the Virgin Mary occurs in the 2nd c. Protevangelium of James. Thenceforward he is rarely mentioned in the East till the 7th c. and in the West till later still. See also **Anne** and **Protevangelium.**

Joachim of Fiore (*c.* 1132–1202). A visionary whose ideas exercised considerable influence on the medieval mind and indubitably issued from a deep spirituality. As a young man he experienced a conversion that led him to make a pilgrimage to the Holy Land. He then became a Cistercian, was elected Abbot of Corazzo in 1177, and resigned that office a few years later to devote himself entirely to his writings. He saw the history of humankind as divided into three stages, which he designated by the name of the Persons of the Trinity: (1) the age of the Father, the age of the Law, the *ordo conjugatorum*, which ended with the arrival of the new dispensation inagurated by Jesus Christ; (2) the age of the Son, the age of grace, the *ordo clericorum*, which he believed would end about the year 1260; and (3) the age of the Spirit, the age of a new spirituality, the *ordo spiritualis*, in which spiritual contemplation would so grow as to produce a spiritualized Church. Some of his more enthusiastic followers such as the Spiritual Franciscans saw themselves as already living in the new order and even looked on his works as in some sense superseding the Bible. Some of Joachim's views were condemned by the Lateran Council in 1215. Extravagant though his prophetic vision was, it issued from a deep personal spirituality attested by Dante and other medieval witnesses. His view of an age of the Spirit and his vision of a progressive development in the spiritualization of humankind was not entirely new. It had appeared in Montanism in the latter half of the 2nd c. and Joachim, no doubt with the petrifying effect of the medieval papacy in mind, produced a new vision of it, in which an evolution of spirituality in the history of humanity is the central principle.

Joan, Pope. In the 13th c. a legend appeared in the writings of a Dominican, Jean de Mailly, to the effect that about the year 1100 a woman had disguised herself as a man, had attained much repute as a scholar, and had eventually become pope. Then, after a reign of two years she was in a procession on the way to the Lateran and in the course of it gave birth to a child, dying in childbirth. The story is entirely without historical foundation.

Joan of Arc. See **Jeanne d'Arc**

Job. The biblical book so designated is unique both as a literary document and as an exposition of the philosophical problem: "Why do the wicked prosper and the righteous suffer?" Its authorship in unknown and its date uncertain, although most scholars think it was probably composed in the 5th or 4th c. BCE. Whether Job is an historical character or an allegorical figure is likewise undetermined. It is one of the most fas-

cinating and impressive books in the Bible, yet its literary construction is odd, not to say inchoate. It is certainly not intended to present a theological or philosophical answer to the main theme it treats. It is, rather, a powerful poetic presentation of how to live with the tragic element in human life. The stark realism in the treatment of evil gives the book a vitality that marks it as having no parallel in the Old Testament writings. It seems to convey the notion that human reason is powerless, even futile, in face of the realities of human life, in face of which even wisdom itself is in the last resort ineffectual.

Jocists. An organization of factory workers in France called the *Jeunesse Ouvrière Chrétienne*, whose purpose is to keep young people of the working classes active within the life of the Roman Catholic Church. It was developed after World War I in Brussels and spread to France.

Johannine Comma. This technical phrase is used by scholars to designate an interpolation in the text of I John 5.7 f., in which the words "in heaven, the Father . . . that bear witness in earth" appear in traditional English versions and translations but not in modern ones. The interpolation is demonstrably not part of the original text and does not appear in the ancient Greek manuscripts of the Bible. It begins to appear in Latin manuscripts about 800 CE and so came to be accepted as part of the Latin text and was transmitted accordingly to English and other translations. Daniel Mace, in the 18th c., was among the first to detect the interpolation which is now universally acknowledged by scholars as not belonging to the original biblical text.

John. To the apostle of that name has been traditionally ascribed the authorship of the Fourth Gospel and the Epistles of John. For a variety of important reasons, both the identity of John and especially the authorship of the Gospel and Epistles have been the subject of much scholarly controversy. The Gospel is certainly very distinctive in message and style, and the Epistles seem to be a practical application of its teachings. Among moderate views is one according to which the author may have been a later writer called John who nevertheless had known the apostle and reflects his outlook. The spectrum of scholarly opinion on this subject is, however, very wide.

John Chrysostom. See **Chrysostom, John**

John of Antioch. Early 5th c. Bishop of Antioch, who supported his friend Nestorius in the latter's controversy with Cyril of Alexandria.

John of Ávila (1500–1569). Spanish mystic, born near Toledo, he was ordained priest in 1525 and became such a famous preacher in the south of Spain that he was known as "the Apostle of Andalusia." Teresa of Ávila looked to him for spiritual counsel and Francis Borgia looked on him as the instrument of his conversion, as did John of God.

John of Damascus. Early 8th c. Greek theologian. His early life is obscure. He served for some time, in succession to his father, as the principal representative of the Christian community to the Caliph and later entered the monastery of St. Sabas near Jerusalem, where he was ordained priest. He strongly supported the use of icons during the Iconoclastic Controversy. His most important work is *On the Orthodox Faith*, which is the third of a tripartite work entitled *The Fount of Wisdom*. He treats the entire range of Orthodoxy, including the Incarnation and the Sacraments, Angelology and Mariology, in the light of the works of the Fathers, with a strong emphasis on Gregory of Nazianzus. He also compiled a great collection of biblical and patristic texts on the nature of the moral and spiritual life. Not only has he been one of the greatest theological authorities in the

Greek Church; he has exercised considerable influence also on the West.

John of Ephesus. A 6th c. Monophysite historian. His *Ecclesiastical History*, of which only the third part is extant, covers the years 571–585. His *Lives of Eastern Saints* consists of fifty-eight short accounts of contemporary saints. He was Bishop of Ephesus.

John of God (1495–1550). Founder of the Brothers Hospitallers, an order, mostly of laymen, which began at Granada, adopted the Augustinian rule, and was formally approved by Pius V in 1572. Born in Portugal, he was converted to a deep spirituality by John of Ávila. He was pronounced by Pope Leo XIII to be the patron of hospitals and of sick people everywhere.

John Gualbert (c 990–1073). After entering the Benedictine monastery of San Miniato, near Florence, he left it to join the Camaldoli, then at a later date left them and settled at Vallombrosa, about twenty miles east of Florence, where, c. 1036, he gathered a group of monks living under a semi-eremitical adaptation of the Benedictine rule. The Vallumbrosan Order that he founded spread quickly, with more than fifty abbeys by the year 1200. See **Vallumbrosans.**

John of Jandun (c. 1286–1328). Born in Jandun he was educated at Paris where later he taught. He collaborated with Marsilius of Padua in writing the *Defensor Pacis*. He was an interpreter of Averroes, and his works in that field were used for centuries.

John of Matha. Founder of the Trinitarian Order, for the redemption of captives. He was born in Provence. Many legends were created about him, but almost nothing is known of historical value about his life. He died in 1213.

John of Mirecour. 14th c. Cistercian. His commentaries on Peter Lombard's *Sentences* were condemned by the Sorbonne. He held, with William of Occam, that God's existence cannot be proved by reason and that there are no rationally objective ethical propositions, since according to him all good and evil in the world arise from the arbitrary will of God.

John of Nepomuk. A 14th c. Bohemian cleric and Vicar-General of Prague. He resisted the efforts of King Wenceslas IV to suppress an abbey in order to create an episcopal See for a royal favorite. Drowned by the King's command, he later became widely acclaimed as a saint and was canonized in 1729. According to a tradition, he also refused to obey a royal command that would have involved his breaking the seal of a confession made by the Queen.

John of Parma (1209–1289). Franciscan friar who, after studies at Parma and later at Paris, became famed for his teaching and was elected Minister General (head) of his order in 1247. His admiration for the teachings of Joachim of Fiore roused hostility and suspicion, and he was charged with heresy. Having resigned his office, he retired to a hermitage. He was a man of deep spirituality who led an austere form of life and endeavored to bring his order back to the ideals of its founder. He also, although unsuccessfully, sought to unite the Eastern Church with the West.

John of Ragusa. Two persons are so designated: (1) Cardinal Giovanni Dominici (1356–1420), Archbishop of Ragusa, who played an important role in the Council of Constance; (2) John Stojković, a 15th c. Dominican born in Ragusa whom Pope Martin V sent to the Council of Basel as papal theologian in 1431. He was much involved in negotiations with the Greeks that were intended to achieve union between East and West and he attended the Council of Constantinople as legate in 1435 and 1437. He also collected many Greek manuscripts, which came to the Dominican house in Basel and were used by Erasmus.

John of Salisbury (c. 1115–1180). Philosopher, born in Salisbury, England,

and educated under Abelard, William of Conches, and others in France. He is one of the chief representatives of the School of Chartres, famed for its humanistic tradition. He was secretary both to Theobald, Archbishop of Canterbury, and his successor Thomas Becket. In 1176 he became Bishop of Chartres. He combined a philosophical skepticism about the limits of human knowledge with an acceptance of revealed doctrine. On the subject of the Universals he followed Abelard's position, holding that *genera* and *species* are mental constructs, but that nevertheless they are derived through abstractions from realities. His principal writings include his *Policraticus* and his *Metalogicon*.

John of the Cross (1542–1591). Founder of the Discalced Carmelites, Spanish poet, and one of the leading exponents of the Spanish mystical tradition. Along with Teresa of Ávila, he reformed the Carmelite Order. His poems are by any account among the greatest in Spanish literature, and he ranks among the most profound mystical writers in the history of the Christian Church. Among his numerous writings are *The Spiritual Canticle, The Ascent of Mount Carmel,* and *The Living Flame of Love.*

John of Wesel (c. 1400–81). German Reformer. Born at Oberwesel am Rhein, John Rucherat was educated at Erfurt and later held various offices including that of cathedral-preacher at Worms, serving as such from 1463 till he was deposed in 1477 by the Bishop of Worms on the ground of heresy. He was latter tried by the Inquisition. His doctrines reflected the teaching of Huss and anticipated in some notable respects those of Luther.

John the Baptist. The name given to a prophet contemporary with Jesus who according to the Gospels was a forerunner whose mission was to herald the coming of the latter, who accepted Baptism from him. It is probable that John had at least some connection with a group such as the Mandaeans, a Gnostic sect, and even more probably with a group such as one whose teachings and practices are recorded in the Qumran Scrolls.

John the Presbyter. It is not clear whether the individual so designated in the second and third of the Epistles of John and by Papias is the Apostle John or another person of that name. The traditional view upholds the former, but a number of modern scholars defend the latter opinion.

John XII, Pope. The son of a Roman patrician, he became pope in 955 at the age of eighteen. His youth, inexperience, and inclination to vice, together with his political ineptitude, led to great scandal and in 963 a synod at Rome, called by the Emperor Otto, caused him to be deposed from the papacy. In his place a layman was elected as Pope Leo VIII. In 964, when Otto had left Rome, John returned and called a synod depriving Leo and repealing all enactments of the previous synod. He died later and was succeeded by Benedict V. John's scandalous reign left the papacy enfeebled.

John XXII (1249–1334). Jacques Duése, born at Cahors, studied law at Paris and after holding several bishoprics was elected pope in 1316, choosing as his residence Avignon, where he remained all his life. His reign involved him in innumerable controversies, political and theological, but his administrative skills enabled him to cope well with them on the whole. When Marsilius of Padua produced his *Defensor Pacis*, upholding the emperor as having absolute supremacy over the Pope, John anathematized the book in 1327. Louis of Bavaria, whom John had declared a heretic, then seized Rome, installing himself in the Vatican, and setting up as Nicholas V, an antipope. See **Antipope** and **Avignon**.)

John XXIII. Antipope. Baldassare Cossa was born of an impoverished no-

ble Neapolitan family. After studying law at Bologna, he entered the service of the Curia and in 1410 was elected one of three claimants to the papacy. He was antipope from 1410 to 1415. He had had the largest number of supporters, but his election was held to be tainted with simony. He died in 1419.

John XXIII (1881–1963). Angelo Giuseppe Roncalli was born of poor parents and after the usual studies was ordained priest in 1904. After service in World War I, he was invited to Rome for various administrative duties and was soon engaged in diplomatic services, being Papal Nuncio to Paris after the Germans had retreated from France in World War II: a very delicate mission because of charges that many of the French bishops had collaborated with the Nazis during the German occupation. In 1953 he became Patriarch of Venice and in 1958 was elected pope. As such he quickly increased and internationalized the College of Cardinals. His most epoch-making act arose from his decision to convene a council, known as the Second Vatican Council (Vatican II). His pontificate was extremely popular both inside and outside the Roman Catholic Church, due both to his ecumenical spirit and to his deeply pastoral commitment. Such was his repute for sanctity that he is likely to be eventually a candidate for canonization. Under Pope Paul VI preliminary steps were taken in that direction.

Johnson, Samuel (1709–1784). Lexicographer and celebrated conversationalist, he was converted by reading Law's *Serious Call to a Devout and Holy Life*. He was a strong Anglican churchman. Among his many writings are his famous *Dictionary of the English Language* (2 vols., 1755) and *A Journey to the Western Islands of Scotland* (1775). His biographer, James Boswell (1740–1795) met Johnson in 1763 when the latter was fifty-three and thoroughly established in the world of letters. His *Life of Samuel Johnson* (1791) is certainly one of the greatest biographies in the history of literature, combining scholarly care with a journalist's flair for the kind of trivial detail that makes a human being come alive to the reader.

Jonah. This biblical book, belonging almost certainly to the postexilic period of Hebrew history, is of unknown authorship. For many reasons the well-known story it contains cannot be regarded as historical. It is on the contrary, an allegory in which the Assyrians, the ancient enemy of the people of Yahweh, repent and receive God's forgiveness. Jonah, however, standing as the symbol of the Israelite, is narrow, exclusivistic, and xenophobic. The message lies in the contrast between Jonah's outlook and the ways of Yahweh. The book is a deeply spiritual one set within the framework of literary fiction.

Jonas, Justus (1493–1555). German Reformer. Trained in law at Erfurt and Wittenberg, he was elected Rector of Erfurt University in 1519. An admirer of Erasmus and Luther, he brought Greek and Hebrew into the university curriculm and gradually became more and more involved in the Reformation cause. He translated works of Luther and Melanchthon from German into Latin. He preached the sermon in 1546 at Luther's funeral.

Jones, Inigo (1573–1652). An important English architect, who, although much influenced by the Palladian style, preserved a distinctive one of his own. Having studied in Italy, he was appointed architect to Queen Anne in 1605. Lincoln's Inn Chapel and St Paul's, Covent Garden, are among his works in London.

Jones, Rufus Matthew (1863–1948). Quaker writer. Educated at Haverford College, Pennsylvania, with which he had a lifelong connection, he taught philosophy there from 1904 till 1934 and was much beloved for his unique personality and deep dedication to Quaker principles. The college pre-

serves a room reconstructed as his study during his lifetime. His many works include *A Dynamic Faith* (1901), *Studies in Mystical Religion* (1909), *The Later Periods of Quakerism* (1921), *The Church's Debt to Heretics* (1925), and *The Testimony of the Soul* (1936). He was one of the most influential Quakers in American religious history. Biographies include Elizabeth G. Vining, *Friend of Life* (1958).

Jonestown. See **People's Temple.**

Jordan. The river Jordan is formed by the convergence of four streams in the upper part of Lake Huleh, eventually forming a delta at the head of the Sea of Galilee, whence it emerges and runs for about 200 miles to enter the Dead Sea. The Hebrews deeply revered it as their entrance to the Promised Land. Elijah was believed to have ascended to heaven from it and John the Baptist baptized Jesus in it. It has remained, in Christian lore, a symbol of the passage through death to the life beyond.

Josaphat. According to medieval Catholic legend he was the son of an Indian king who was converted to the Christian faith. His name may be a corrupt from of "Bodhisattva". See **Bodhisattva.**

Joseph. The husband of Mary. According to the Gospel account he was a devout Jew, humble in parentage but of Davidic descent, and a carpenter (*tektōn*) by trade. Although mentioned little in the New Testament, he figures prominently in early Christian and in medieval literature, is officially the patron saint of the Church, and is also invoked as patron of a happy death. In iconography he is often represented bearing a staff and a lily, emblem of purity.

Joseph Calasanctius (1556–1648). Founder of the Piarists. See **Piarists.**

Joseph of Arimathaea. According to the Gospels he asked and obtained from Pilate the body of Jesus, being secretly a disciple. He buried the body with lavish care. The legend that he came to England with the Holy Grail and built the first English church at Glastonbury is without any historical foundation.

Joseph of Cupertino (1601–1663). A poor Neapolitan boy, he sought unsuccessfully to enter the Franciscans. Refused on account of his ignorance, he was at last received as a stableboy and eventually was ordained priest. He then attracted much attention from miracles he was said to have performed, including levitation and other such phenomena. He was canonized in 1767.

Joseph of Volokolamsk (1439–1515). Russian monk who founded the great monastery at Volokolamsk, near Moscow. He sought to educate monks for important positions of leadership in the Church.

Josephus, Flavius (*c.* 37–*c.* 100). Jewish historian. He was born in Palestine, of priestly descent and became a Pharisee. At Rome he secured the favor of the Emperor Vespasian and his successors and devoted himself to literary work. His major work, *The Jewish War*, appeared about the year 77 C.E. A brief passage in it alludes to Jesus as "a wise man, if indeed one should call him a man" (XVIII, iii, 3). It has been of immense interest to Christians from at least the time of Eusebius in the early 4th c., but modern scholars discredit the passage as spurious, being in its traditional form the interpolation of a Christian writer in antiquity. There is no doubt, however that Josephus alludes more than once in his writings to Jesus, and his allusions are to the Jesus of history, whom Christians revere as the Savior of the world. It is the phrase "if indeed one should call him a man" that is notably suspect as a Christian interpolation. So Josephus remains one among the few witnesses, outside the Gospel narratives, to the historicity of Jesus and is at least on that account of much interest to serious students of Christianity.

Jovian (*c.* 332–364). Succeeded the Emperor Julian. In contrast to his predecessor, Julian, he supported Christian orthodoxy.

Jowett, Benjamin (1817–1893). Master of Balliol, Oxford, and translator of Plato and Aristotle. Educated at St. Paul's, London, and Balliol College, Oxford, he became Regius Professor of Greek in 1855 and Master of Balliol in 1870. His studies in the ancient classics and in Hegel made him sympathetic to theological views that were considered heterodox in his time. One of the most influential figures in Oxford life in late Victorian England, he instituted many academic reforms and his translations of Plato and Aristotle won him a lasting place among those students of literature who were untrained in the classical languages, opening up Greek philosophy to the general reading public.

Joyful Mysteries of the Rosary. See **Rosary.**

Jubilate Sunday. The 3rd Sunday after Easter, from the traditional Introit of the day, *Jubilate Deo.*

Jubilee. Every 50 years Jewish slaves (according to Leviticus 25) could be emancipated. The practice is echoed in the modern practice of the Roman Catholic Church by which a special "plenary" Indulgence is granted to pilgrims who visit Rome. The benefits are published in advance of the Jubilee year. They included powers to confessors to absolve from certain vows.

Judaea. The region which, after the Babylonian Captivity, was occupied by the Jews in 537 BCE. It was, in the time of Jesus, one of three regions, Galilee, Samaria, and Judaea. The term was sometimes used, however, to designate the whole area of Palestine.

Judah. by about 1000 BCE, Judah had become the predominant of the twelve tribes of Israel. It later formed, with

Benjamin, a separate kingdom, more conservative and considered to have been more faithful to ancient tradition.

Judaizers. Already in New Testament times a dispute arose between those Christians who, like Paul, thought the ancient Levitical laws were merely optional for Christians, and those Christians who insisted on them as mandatory. The latter group are called the Judaizers.

Judas Iscariot. The disciple who betrayed Jesus. He has become a symbol for treachery and in Christian lore has been generally represented as the supreme example of human perfidy. Dante places him in the ninth and lowest circle of hell, where he is chomped everlastingly in Satan's mouth.

Judas Maccabaeus. Leader of the Jews in their revolt against the Syrians, whose life is recounted in the Books of Maccabees. He died in 161 BCE. See **Maccabees, Books of.**

Jude. One of the twelve apostles of Christ, he has generally been supposed to be (Jude 1) the brother of James. (See **Brethren, The Lord's.**) In popular Roman Catholic devotion Jude is nowadays invoked as the patron saint of "impossible" or "lost" causes.

Jude, Epistle of. The purpose of this New Testament letter is to warn against the rise of teachings that the writer perceived as a peril to the Church and especially against the evil life of those who were propagating these doctrines. Among the calamities that Jude lists (Jude 5–7), the fall of Jerusalem in 70 CE is not mentioned, so it seems likely that the letter may be dated before that event.

Judgment. This term has been used in various ways in the history of Western philosophy. Aristotle regarded judgment as a procedure lying behind the determination of whether a proposition is true or false. Thomas Aquinas considered judgment to be the act of compos-

ing and dividing. In the Thomist view, therefore, judgment is that upon which all knowledge depends. Kant, who made judgment central to his thought, found judgment essential to the process of our construction of the phenomenal world, the world as we construct it in order to cope intelligibly with it. Kant made an important distinction between analytic judgment and synthetic judgment. In the case of the former, the predicate is already implicit in the subject, e.g., "Matter exists in time and occupies space." Such a proposition is necessarily true or necessarily false, since matter is so understood that it implies what is predicated of it. In synthetic judgments, however, the case is otherwise. When I report that elm trees are particularly susceptible to certain kinds of disease, my statement is not *necessarily* true or false, for the situation might well be otherwise and arboricultural studies might so change it as to make the statement true in America but not in Europe or true today but false tomorrow.

Judgment, General and Particular. According to Catholic theology, each soul is judged immediately on death. Immense confusion developed in connection with the concept. Some early theologians such as Tertullian and Ambrose taught that souls on death went into a deep sleep till the resurrection of the body at the General Judgment: a view suggested by early inscriptions in the Roman Catacombs, such as "he/she sleeps in peace" (*dormit in pace*) or "sleeps in Christ" (*dormit in Christo*), and this notion has persisted widely. Nevertheless, Pope Benedict XII in 1336 issued a bull declaring that at death the soul goes immediately either to heaven, hell, or purgatory, a view which, in face of the Christian doctrine of resurrection, greatly compounds the difficulties. All mainstream Christian theology envisions a resurrection of the dead accompanied or immediately followed by a general judgment in which God passes a final verdict on the individual (body and soul) and decrees accordingly his eternal destiny. For more details on confusions attending this question see **Eschatology.**

Judith. An apocryphal book originally written in Hebrew but translated into Greek and forming part of the Septuagint. It is quite unhistorical and no doubt never was intended to be represented as otherwise. Most biblical scholars have dated it within the Maccabaean period in the 2nd c. BCE.

Julian (332–363). Roman Emperor from 361 and traditionally designated "Julian the Apostate" because of his efforts to weaken Christianity, (by then a *religio licita* and so theoretically exempt from persecution) and restore pagan worship throughout the empire. He did all he could to accomplish this end without resorting to open persecution. Instruction in schools was ordered to be run on pagan lines. He published tracts against the Christian faith. He tried to create dissension among the clergy and in every way to enfeeble the spread of the faith while trying to raise pagan ideals to a high ethical level and present the result as a moral triumph of ancient beliefs and practices over the rising influence of the Christian faith. He was not ignorant of the best in pagan tradition. A decade or so before his being proclaimed Emperor in 360, he had been introduced to Neoplatonism, which was a very real and respectable rival to Christianity among the intellectuals of the time, and also to the Eleusinian mysteries at Athens, where he probably visited various philosophical schools. He had felt much impressed by what seemed to him to be the richness of pagan thought and practice and the inferiority of the Christian Way. Among his many writings is his "Adversos Christianos", written during the Persian campaign and consisting of arguments against Christianity. Cyril of Alexandria wrote a refutation of it. The bibliography of works on Julian is very extensive and much of it predictably hostile.

Julian (c. 386–454). Bishop of Eclanum, Apuleia, from c. 416. In 417, because of his Pelagianism and his refusal to subscribe to a document condemning that theological view, he was deprived of his See and banished. He traveled widely, in hope of finding a more tolerant ambience, but was repeatedly snubbed. His works, which include four books "Ad Turbantium" and eight others "Ad Florum" exhibit profound philosophical and much logical ability. He charged Augustine with error in the latter's teaching that human nature is totally depraved. Augustine's reply is not such as would convince everyone, but it prevailed.

Julian. Early 6th c. Bishop of Halicarnassus, Caria, deposed from his See in 518 for his Monophysite opinions. He then took refuge in Alexandria, where he became head of a school there. See **Aphthartodocetae.**

Julian of Norwich. This English mystic, although very little is known of her life, is one of the most interesting women in the history of the Church. She lived in the 14th–15th c., probably as an anchoress (see **Anchorite**) near the church of St. Julian, Norwich. She claimed to have received on a specific day, May 8, 1373, a series of fifteen revelations during a period of five hours and one further vision the next day. Twenty years later she wrote an account, *The Sixteen Revelations of Divine Love.* It contains a treatment of prayer, faith, and especially Divine Love, which she regarded as the key to all other mystical and theological questions. Her work suggests the influence of the *Cloud of Unknowing.* The treatment reflects the Neoplatonic outlook that was a vital element in medieval mysticism and the philosophical heritage of the schoolmen that affected their thought even after the rediscovery of Aristotle.

Jülicher, Adolf (1857–1938). New Testament scholar. Born at Falkenberg, he was professor of theology at Marburg from 1889 to 1923. Among his writings was his *Die Einleitung in das Neue Testament* (1894, translated as *Introduction to the New Testament* (1904). He was a very careful scholar, whose work included a study on the historicity of Jesus.

Julius Africanus Sextus (*c.* 160–*c.* 240). Probably born at Jerusalem, he was an early Christian writer of notable interest. His chief works are a history of the world and an encyclopedia on a wide variety of subjects. He corresponded with Origen and others, showing clarity of perception and considerable ability.

Julius I, Pope. Early 4th c. pope who, in the Arian controversy, strongly supported the anti-Arian view that triumphed in the Church, convening the Council of Sardica, which both supported Athanasius and caused the Arian position to be renounced by the Church.

Julius II, Pope (1443–1513). More statesman than churchman, he was virgorously attacked by Erasmus. The indulgence he granted in connection with the building of the new St. Peter's in Rome was the catalyst for Luther's protest and so indirectly for the success of the long awaited Reformation. He was born Giuliano della Rovere, of an impoverished noble family. When his uncle became Pope Sixtus IV in 1471, he made his nephew a cardinal and bestowed a large number of rich benefices on him. Juliano later secured the election of Pope Innocent VIII by bribery and continued under that pontificate to take a leading role in papal affairs. When the notoriously immoral Rodrigo Borgia became pope as Alexander VI, Giuliano fled to France but returned to Rome in 1503 on Alexander's death. He was elected pope later that year, as Julius II, having promised the cardinals to call a General Council of the Church within two years: a promise he did not keep and one whose fulfilment might possibly have averted the Reformation or at least modified its form. He re-

stored and extended the temporal power of the papacy by skillful diplomacy. He was, however, a patron of the arts. Among the great works he patronized are Michelangelo's statue of Moses, the paintings in the Sistine Chapel, and Raphael's frescoes in the Vatican.

Julius III (1487–1555). Giammaria Ciocchi del Monte, after studying law at Perugia and Siena, was ordained priest and became archbishop of Siponto in 1511. He held various offices in the papal service and in 1545 opened the Council of Trent as its first president and papal legate. Elected pope in 1550, he strengthened the privileges and the influence of the Jesuits. Like Julius II he much patronized the arts and especially supported Michelangelo.

Jumpers. A nickname applied to some Welsh Calvinistic Methodists, in allusion to their practice of jumping in frenzied emotion in the course of worship. The practice of jumping apparently began about 1760 and was defended by the Welsh poet William Williams in a pamphlet he wrote on the subject. Those who engaged in the practice also encouraged loud singing with repetitions of the same line or stanza as often as thirty or forty times. Itinerant preachers urged the people to cry out "Glory" and other such ejaculations. John Evans, an historian of the period when such practices were still popular among the people recounts his own visit to such as assembly in 1785 at which the preacher worked the people up to such a state of emotional excitement that nine men and seven women around him began to rock to and fro, groaning aloud and jumping "with a kind of frantic fury." Finally they knelt down in a circle, holding hands, praying, and wildly pointing up toward the sky as a reminder that they "should soon meet there, and be never again separated." Such practices, not only discouraged but disdained by the more staid elements in the Church, would seem to adumbrate those associated with modern Pentecostalist movements. See **Pentecostalism.**

Jung, Carl Gustav (1875–1961). Swiss psychologist and founder of the very influential school of analytical psychology. He worked from 1900 to 1902 at the University of Zurich, to which he later returned to teach. With Pierre Janet at the Salpêtrière in Paris, he encountered in 1907 Sigmund Freud, whose psychoanalytical school he abandoned in 1913. For Jung, the focus of investigation is the psyche, considered as a totality. The various "regions" of the psyche are not its parts but its functions. This infinite "psychic ocean" comprises both the conscious and the unconscious, but the conscious is but a small island floating on that ocean. The "collective unconscious", which may be considered the ocean floor, is the psychic heritage of all humanity. The "person" is not, strictly speaking, even a psychic reality in itself but, rather, a function of the psyche directed outward as the "soul" is a function of the psyche directed inward. The basic hereditary potentialities express themselves in "archetypes", which appear as symbolic forms such as collective myths. Jung calls one of the archetypal projections "the shadow." The shadow is a negative principle. It represents the "inferior," the "repressed" or "denied" dimension of the self, pushed into the unconscious, which under pressure may sometimes explode, e.g., where an excessive outward rigidity covers a repressed and denied sexual desire. Another and different archetypal projection is what Jung calls the anima/animus projection. The male ego has an archetypal *anima*, which it projects upon the world; the female ego has an *animus* archetype. In human love, the man takes possession of the woman's *animus* and the woman takes possession of the man's *anima*.

Archetypal elements in the unconscious also take pictorial forms such as the sun, the star, the snake, and what Jung calls the *mandala*: a symbol of the unity that the soul seeks, e.g., in the unity of the four parts of a quaternity and in the rose window of a Gothic cathedral. (Jung takes quaternity to be a symbol of wholeness.) The concept of the archetype is fundamental to Jung's thought. In contrast to Freud, who saw religion as not only illusion but even as a neurosis detrimental to one's own psychic warfare, Jung saw his analytical psychology as friendly to religion, not least to Christianity, in the sense that he saw in religion mythological descriptions of how the psyche works. He also saw religion as a means of bringing health (salvation) to the psyche. He was, however, uninterested in, not to say radically agnostic about, the underlying onotological questions that are the fundamental concern of theological inquiry and constitute the central focus of Christian thought. The methods employed by Jung have nevertheless much affected the outlook of many thoughtful Christians in the 20th c. One of his best known techniques is his word association testing procedure.

Jung Codex. One of the Nag Hammadi manuscripts, it was acquired in 1952 by the Jung Institute at Zurich. See **Nag Hammadi Library, The** and **Gnosticism.**)

Jurieu, Pierre (1637–1713). French Calvinist divine, born at Mer, a small town between Orléans and Blois, he studied at Sedan and then in England. He was an ardent Calvinist who engaged in vigorous controversy with Bossuet, Arnauld, and others.

Jus Canonicum. Canon (i.e., ecclesiastical) law. See **Canon Law** and **Justinian I.**

Jus Civile. The civil law. The phrase is used to designate the civil law of Rome (Roman law), contradistinguished from *jus canonicum* or ecclesiastical law. The term *jus civile* is familiar also, however, in modern jurisprudence, since some legal traditions (e.g., the Law of Scotland) are based upon Roman law, the principles of which are still sometimes quoted in court.

Jus Devolutum. In the Kirk of Scotland, when a congregation has failed for a period of six months to elect a minister, the presbytery has the right to elect one. The canonical provision for this is called *jus devolutum*. Generally, however, an extension of time is granted, so that this prerogative of presbytery is not often exercised.

Jus Divinum. The eternal law of God.

Jus Gentium. The law of nations, i.e., international law.

Jus Naturale. (Also *jus naturae*). The law of nature, natural law. (See **Stoicism.**) Thomas Aquinas uses the phrases *jus naturale, jus divinum, jus civile*, and *jus gentium*, as aspects of his philosophy of law.

Justice. In contrast to the Sophists who tended to see justice as the interest of the stronger, Socrates and Plato saw it as the virtue of the State, the condition in which everyone is acting in such a way as not to interfere with the interests of another. Aristotle saw it as a mean between interfering with another and subjecting oneself to another's interference. Thomas Aquinas followed Aristotle and distinguished between how things are ordered by nature and how they are ordered (e.g., in society) by reason.

Justification. A theological term of great importance in the history of Christian thought and the subject of much controversy, especially in the context of Reformation theology. The English word comes from the Latin *justificatio* (plainly *justus facere*, "to make righteous"). Many theologians, however, following Luther at this point, note that the Latin is unwarranted by the original Greek *dikaiōsis*, used much by Paul. They contend that it need not have the connotation the Latin form gives it and can signify, rather, the divine act of *attributing* righteousness to a sinner on the ground of his or her faith in Christ, so that the individual is *declared* rather than made righteous.

Justinian I (483–565). Roman Emperor from 527. A great builder, administrator, and military leader, he retrieved North Africa from the Vandals and Italy from the Goths. He built the great basilican church of Hagia Sophia in Constantinople, perhaps the most perfect Byzantine church in the world, and others in Ravenna and elsewhere. His political aim was to achieve the perfect unity of Church and State throughout the world. To do so he needed a sound legal system and the Code that he established became the basis for law in East and West throughout the Middle Ages. Published in 529, it was revised by the addition of a Digest and by further constitutions known as "Novellae" and was so issued in 534. Justinian recognized a distinction between Church and State but wished to see them as interdependent and legislated accordingly, setting forth (especially in the sixth Novella) the relationship he saw between them. The *Corpus Juris Civilis*, the final embodiment of his legislative plan, incorporated the ancient principle of Roman Law adapted to the new circumstances and taking Christianity within its jurisdiction. So influential was it among medieval jurists in both East and West that Canon Law in the West was eventually modelled after it. (See **Gratian.**) Intellectually, Justinian was much more simplistic. He closed the great philosophical schools at Athens in 529, sought to be the champion of what he deemed orthodoxy, and meddled in a variety of theological disputes he could not have understood.

Justin Martyr. Early 2nd c. Christian apologist. Born of pagan parents, he studied the various Greek philosophies available and at last, probably *c.* 130, he became a Christian and taught for some years at Ephesus, moving later to Rome where he established a school and had Tatian as one of his students. He and some of his students, betrayed and denounced as Christians, were ordered to make the customary sacrifices and on refusing to do so were flogged and beheaded. Justin is of great importance as the first Christian to attempt to reconcile Christian faith with the philosophical thought of his time. He did not at all condemn pagan thought, recognizing that it contained much truth, and he tried to show this by argument; yet he insisted that only Christianity provided the full truth. He held that only Christianity could put evil agencies to flight. He defended the Church against charges of immorality and against other attacks customarily made on it in fashionable intellectual circles. His works are: *First Apology, Second Apology,* and *Dialogue with Trypho.*

Justus. Early 7th c. Archbishop of Canterbury, to which See he succeeded on the death of Mellitus in 624.

Juvenal. Early 5th c. Bishop of Jerusalem.

Juvencus, Caius Vettius Aquilinus. An early 4th c. Latin poet, he was of noble descent and from Spain. He wrote a harmony of the Gospels in hexameter verse, *c.* 330, apparently with the aim of showing that Christianity could produce poetry comparable to that of the pagan writers and consecrated to a much more sublime theme than theirs could be.

K

Kabbala. See **Cabbala.**

Kaddish. A Jewish prayer whose opening phrases are the same as those of the Lord's Prayer (the "Our Father"). The word is an Aramaic one meaning "holy".

Kafir. An Arabic term applied by Muslims to all non-Muslims. It means "infidel," "unbeliever."

Kaftan, Julius Wilhelm Martin (1848–1926). German theologian and professor

at Berlin. He opposed traditional theories of the Atonement as "satisfaction", teaching that it should be understood in terms of personal experience and in ethical and mystical categories and that Paul's own theology was grounded in his personal, mystical experience on the Damascus road.

Kaftan, Theodore (1847–1932). German churchman, elder brother of Julius Kaftan.

Kagawa, Toyohiko (1888–1960). Japanese Christian (convert from Buddhism), pacifist, social reformer, and democratic leader in Japan. Trained at the Presbyterian Seminary at Kobe, Japan, and later at Princeton.

Kähler, Martin (1835–1912). German theologian, professor at Halle. While not ignoring the attempts of his contemporaries to reconstruct the Jesus of history, he defended the more traditional understanding of Christian theology and christology as based on the testimony of the New Testament authors.

Kaiserswerth Deaconesses. An organization of Protestant deaconesses founded in 1836 by T. Fliedner for the care of the sick and the education of poor children. They must be unmarried or widowed and are otherwise also organized somewhat on the lines of a Roman Catholic religious congregation.

Kamelavchion. The black cylindrical hat worn by monks and clergy of the Eastern Church. From the Greek *kamēlauchion* (also *kalummauchion*). The veil worn by monks and bishops hanging behind the kamelavchion is called the epanokamelavchion.

Kant, Immanuel (1724–1804). German philosopher, one of the most important thinkers (along with Plato, Aristotle, Thomas Aquinas, and Descartes) in the history of Western thought, and exercising a profound influence on Christian theology, especially within the Reformation heritage. Born in Königsberg (now Kaliningrad), East Prussia, where also he died, he never traveled beyond it, holding until his death his professorship of logic at the University of Königsberg, to which he had been appointed in 1770 (*Privatdozent* 1755–1770).

In a very general way he may be considered, in the context of his age, as having synthesized the British Empiricist and the Continental European Rationalist schools of philosophy by asking neither what we know about the universe nor what is the nature of the universe, but, rather: What is possible for the human mind to know? Although his philosophy is primarily critical in the sense that he critically examines the limits of human knowledge, he ends by showing why a certain kind of knowledge is possible and what such knowledge attains.

He starts with traditional distinctions to be found in Leibniz (in whose system Kant was trained) between analytic and synthetic propositions and between *a priori* and *a posteriori* ones. Analytic propositions do not tell us anything new; for example, "all stallions are male" tells us nothing new, for a stallion is nothing other than a male horse. Mathematical propositions are of this kind: they analyze the implicates of what is already known within a system but may need extrapolation. One does not need to look at the external world to deal with them. Synthetic propositions, by contrast, purport to add some knowledge for the ascertaining of which we have to look at the external world. Analytic propositions are *a priori* in the sense that what they assert is known to be true or false *before* experience; synthetic propositions are *a posteriori* in the sense that they cannot be said to be known except *after* experience. For example, there is no use your telling me about kangaroos till I have seen one or at least a picture of one. Kant asks, then, whether there can be any synthetic propositions that are *a priori*, that is, that do not require experience, and much of his philosophy consists in a demonstration of how this could be. There are realities to be known, but

what we can actually know is a combination of these realities with the mind that is engaged in knowing them. I know the sun as a red ball in the sky that heats my body and can burn my skin. With a knowledge of physics and astronomy I can be more precise, but still I cannot know the sun "as it is in itself" (the *Ding an Sich*). Nevertheless, I am doing much better than merely recording my sensations.

Such are the kinds of question that Kant treats in his *Critique of Pure Reason* (1781). In the *Critique of Practical Reason* (1788) he sought to show that the Ideas of Reason (God, Freedom, Immortality), although not theoretically demonstrable, are nevertheless warranted in practice. Various implicates of this view are exhibited in his *Critique of Judgment* (1790), and some theological questions are raised in his *Religion within the Limits of Reason* (1793).

Although Kant's philosophy was deeply respectful of traditional belief in God and provided a basis for justifying faith as understood within the Reformation heritage, he left no quarter for the Catholic view as expounded in the seminaries that the existence of God could be proved by rational argument. He repudiated the Ontological Argument as offered by Descartes. Thomas Aquinas had repudiated that argument in the form in which it had been presented much earlier by Anselm and had provided instead five others, which he modestly called "ways" (*viae*) pointing to the existence of God. Kant, however, rejected all of these as unwarranted, although he recognized belief in God to be warranted by the "practical reason."

While Kant's thought has played an enormous role not only in Western philosophy in general but in the development of philosophical theology within the Reformation heritage, it was for long resisted in Roman Catholic circles. The *Critique of Pure Reason* was placed on the Index of Prohibited Books by papal decree of June 11, 1827, and was still included at least till the edition of the Index published in Vatican City in 1929.

Karaites. From a Hebrew term, meaning "Reader of the Scriptures" and applied to a Jewish sect in Babylon that emerged in the 8th c. CE. Repudiating the Talmud, they looked to the Hebrew Bible as their sole authority. The movement flourished for several centuries and still exists although no longer influential.

Karma. Sanskrit term meaning "deed" or "action". The karmic principle is the basic principle of the spiritual dimension of being. It is a principle of balance. Although commonly associated with Hinduism, Buddhism, and other oriental religions, it can be seen as expressive of the Torah in Judaism, considered as the eternal principle of righteousness embodied in the written Torah and also as expressed in the Golden Rule, to be found in Confucius, in Kant's Categorical Imperative, and in the form laid down by Jesus: "Do unto others as ye would have others do unto you." Contrary to the vulgar misunderstanding of it as a fatalistic principle, it is in fact a principle that preeminently implies and is based upon freedom of choice. It is associated with the principle of Reincarnation and may be thought to imply it. Actions, good or bad, have consequences upon the karma of each individual. Each individual has a karmic inheritance, good and bad, and sooner or later must work off the bad and develop the good. See **Reincarnation.**

Katavasia. The concluding stanza of an ode in the canon in the liturgy of the Eastern Church.

Katharsis. See **Catharsis.**

Kathisma. In the Eastern Church, a term applied to each of the twenty sections into which the Psalter is divided.

Kattenbusch, Ferdinand (1851–1935). German theologian and historian of the Creeds of the Church. A student of Ritschl, he taught at Giessen, Göttingen, and Halle.

Keble, John (1792–1866). English churchman and Tractarian leader. Cooperated with Newman in issue of the *Tracts for the Times* and appealed to the clergy to take a "high" view of their duties and privileges. He defended Alexandrian theology. After Newman's defection he continued to support Pusey in the Oxford Movement. His character and personal devotion greatly impressed all who knew him. Keble College, Oxford, was founded in his memory in 1870.

Keim, Karl Theodor (1825–1878). German biblical scholar and Church historian. Studied under F. C. Baur, then taught at Tübingen, Zürich, and Giessen. Although his views were somewhat less radical than those of the Tübingen school, he rejected "supernatural" understandings of the Gospels and his influence was considerable in German theology in his day.

Keith, George (c. 1639–1716). Born in Aberdeen and educated for the ministry of the Scottish Kirk, he became a Quaker and emigrated to America where, however, his teachings were not approved among the Quakers who insisted on the "sufficiency of the light within." His views, which were too sacramental and too Christian for the Quakers, led him to establish a group known as the "Christian Quakers." In 1700 he took Anglican Orders and in 1705 became rector of a parish in Sussex. His writings include *The Deism of William Penn and his Brethren* (1699).

Kells, Book Of. A manuscript of the Gospels written at the monastery of Kells Ireland, in County Meath, and dating from *c.* 800, although legend attributes it to the possession of Columba more than two centuries earlier. It is the finest example of Irish calligraphy in the world and is one of the treasures of Trinity College, Dublin.

Kempe, Margery (*c.* 1373-*c* 1433). English mystic. Married John Kempe by whom she had fourteen children. Claiming to have received visions, she went on pilgrimages including the Holy Land and Compostella. In her book, known as *The Book of Margery Kempe*, she describes her mystical experiences.

Kempis, Thomas à. See **Thomas à Kempis**

Kennett, Robert Hatch (1864–1932). English biblical scholar, Regius Professor of Hebrew at Cambridge from 1903 till his death. He assigned a Maccabaean date for the Psalms and other writings and an unconventionally late date for Deuteronomy.

Kennicott, Benjamin (1718–1783). English biblical scholar, Canon of Christ Church from 1770 till his death. In advance of his time he showed, what is now well known, that the variants in Hebrew manuscripts of the Bible are too insignificant to be of importance. This has been corroborated in 20th c. finds such as the scroll of Isaiah found at Qumran in 1947, which, dating from possibly the 1st c. BCE, shows few variants from the received text and these insignificant ones.

Kenosis. The term comes from the Greek verb *kenoō*, "I empty," as in Philippians 2.7. Traditional Christian teaching has always recognized a self-emptying God in the acceptance of union with a physically limited humanity in Jesus. Questions, however, arose, e.g., If God was fully in Christ, was Jesus onmiscient and omnipotent when he was apparently a helpless baby on his mother's knee?" Some Lutheran theologians in the 19th c. proposed that such divine attributes were abandoned for God to become man. English theologians of the period, such as Charles Gore (1853–1932) inclined to the view that God emptied himself only to the extent of permitting the existence in Jesus of the limitations of a human self-consciousness. The solutions to the puzzles that kenotic theory purported to answer did not work adequately in the context of 19th c. theology. The kenotic concept, however, has become very relevant to contemporary Christian theological concerns, e.g., where the concept of God as creative love is taken with theological seriousness and not as a mere pious utterance. See Geddes MacGregor, *He Who Lets Us Be* (1975, 1987).

Kensit, John (1853–1902). English Protestant extremist. As secretary of the Protestant Truth Society he became a fanatical opponent of what he considerd to be the "romanizing" tendencies of the Church of England and caused disturbances, often violent.

Kentigern (died 603). A 6th c. missionary to the Britons of Strathclyde. Also known as Mungo, he is the patron of Glasgow and is believed to be buried in Glasgow Cathedral.

Kepler, Johann (1571–1630). German astronomer who was led by Pythagorean and Neoplatonic teachings to the three laws of planetary motion on which his fame chiefly rests: (1) that the planets move in ellipses with the sun at one focus; (2) that the planets sweep out equal distances at equal times, and (3) that the squares of the periods of any two planets are proportional to the cubes of their mean distance from the sun, the period being the time needed for a complete orbit round the sun. In 1594 he went to Graz as professor of mathematics, then in 1600 to Prague as assistant to Tycho Brahe, whom he succeeded the following year as court astronomer. He held the order of nature to be an expression of God.

His discoveries, which were an advance on those of Copernicus, who had supposed that the orbits were circular, were to be an indispensable part of Newton's system. Although his theological views seemed heterodox, he acknowledged the authority of the Bible as traditionally understood. In 1604–1605 the appearance of a new star caused him to propose in 1606 and later a theory about the star the Magi were reported to have seen, which he sought to interpret in terms of an unusual conjunction of Mars, Saturn, and Jupiter in the sign of Taurus, which he calculated for the year 6 BCE. See **Jesus, Date of the Birth of**. His principal works are: *Mysterium cosmographicum* (1597); *A New Astronomy* (1609); and *The Harmony of the World*, (1618). He was the first astronomer to defend openly the Copernican cosmology.

Kerygma. An important term in modern biblical studies and theology used to designate the element of proclamation in the life of the early Church contradistinguished from *didachē* (instruction): a distinction that is very important in the life of the Church today.

Keswick Convention. A gathering held every year since 1875 at Keswick, England, for the purpose of prayer and biblical study, which attracts participants from all over the British Isles and abroad.

Kethubim. The Hebrew name for what Christian scholars generally call the Hagiographa or Writings: the last of the three parts into which the Old Testament is divided, (1) Torah, (2) Prophets, and (3) Writings. This last includes a wide variety of books such as Psalms, Proverbs, Job, Ezra-Nehemiah, Esther, and two books of Chronicles. By a century or more before the birth of Jesus the Writings had acquired much standing, although not officially included in the Hebrew canon till probably *c.* 100 CE.

Keynes, John Maynard (1883–1946). British economist and logician. Fellow of King's College, Cambridge. His work in economics is well known to general readers. His work on probability (*A Treatise on Probability*) (1921), being a theory in logic, is less widely known and has even less widely noticed theological implications. He sees probability as a relation between a series of propositions. Given one series one can go on to speak of the degree of probability in another. The maximum probability is certainty; the minimum, impossibility. Probability is the degree of rationality to be found in believing one series of propositions on the basis of the other, given series.

Keyserling, Hermann (1880–1946). Philosopher, born in Estonia; wrote in both German and French. He opposed the category of "wisdom" to that of scientific inquiry and that of life to mechanism.

Kharijites. During the early centuries of Islam, bitter conflicts troubled the faithful. The first important one was a disagreement between the Kharijites and the Murjites. The former were strict separationists who adhered to an extreme literalism in their understanding of the Qur'ān and of the nature of Islam. They held that those who departed from their position should be killed on sight. Some even held that the families of such individuals should also be exterminated. They taught, moreover, that the Caliph should be elected by the entire Muslim community throughout the world. Those who have adopted such fanatical opinions and tried to promulgate them have often found themselves on the fringes of Islam and isolated accordingly.

Out of the disputes between the Kharijites and the Murjites emerged the Mutazilites, who sought a middle position, which they developed along much more intellectual lines, seeking to do justice to the claims of reason and of Islamic faith. The Murjites had been content to let such controversial problems remain unsolved until the Day of Judgment; the Mutazilites felt a duty to use their minds in understanding the problems raised by the Qur'ān and its teaching. They sought, for example, to divest Islam of anthropomorphic concepts of Allah as having a human face and they interpreted the Qur'ān allegorically in ways that aroused the hostility of many Muslims. See **Mutazilites**.

Khomiakoff, Alexis Stepanovitch (1804 –1860). Russian philosophical theologian. One of the founders, with Ivan Kireevsky, of the Slavophil movement. In philosophy he attacked both Aristotelianism (including medieval scholasticism) and Hegelianism, which was then influential in Russia as well as in Western Europe. In the Orthodox Church he saw freedom and unity and he especially emphasized both the concept of Sobornost and the notion that those who participate in the personal inner holiness of the Orthodox Church can be saved even though not in external communion with it.

Kiddush. (Hebrew word meaning "sanctification.") The Jewish rite for the sanctifying of any holy day such as the Sabbath. The Christian Eucharist, central to Christian worship from the beginning, takes its origin in the Kiddush: a devotion preparatory to the Sabbath and performed weekly (not annually like the Passover) by groups of pious male Jews, especially in Messianic circles. It consisted of a simple meal of bread and wine, the latter mixed with water according to custom. A rabbi would generally preside. As Christians developed their worship out of the synagogual worship to which most of the first Christians were accustomed, they invested the Kiddush with elements celebrating their central religious experience: the Resurrection of Christ and his presence among them in his Risen Glory.

Kidron. The ravine lying east of Jerusalem, between it and Mount Scopus and the Mount of Olives. David, in his flight from Jerusalem, crossed it (II Samuel 23.15). Josiah burned the cultic furnishings of the shrines of Baal there (II Kings, 23.4, 6). It is mentioned only once in the New Testament (John 18.1) as along the way that Jesus passed on going to the Garden of Gethsemani.

Kierkegaard, Søren Aabye (1813– 1855). Danish thinker. Widely accounted the father of modern existentialism (although this is debatable), he wrote prolifically during his short life, incisively arguing for an intensely personal religion and showing an increasing disaffection from the State-established Lutheran Church of Denmark. Bringing a penetrating philosophical mind to his critique of conventional Christian thought and practice, he was one of the most profound exponents of the Christian Way since New Testament times, not least when (as in his last years) he was most bitterly attacking its institutional forms. Rebelling against the system of Hegel that was in vogue in his student days at the University of Copenhagen, he repudiated the entire notion that truth could be ascertained within a system of ideas. At best such systems can capture only approximations, while truth, being never objective, always subjective, eludes them.

He developed the view that there are three levels or modes of existence: (1) the aesthetic or pleasure-seeking, (2) the ethical, and (c) the religious, the life of faith. The person who has entered into the ethical mode of life assumes duties and responsibilities as a man does, for example, in marrying and raising a family instead of promiscuously philandering in search of sensual pleasure. He does so by an exercise of freedom. (Kierkegaard, like all existentialists, emphasizes the concept of freedom of choice.) Yet the person who walks the life of faith rises even higher, being committed to an intimately personal relationship to God such as transcends even the best of lives lived on the ethical plane. Through a moral life one learns self-determination; through the life of faith one learns the cost of commitment to God and the inexpressible joy of service to him. Kierkegaard saw God as "pure subjectivity"; therefore the highest values are subjective ones. That is why Christ is to be preferred to Socrates.

We are inclined to avoid facing ourselves because in doing so we are confronted with the moral demand of making choices. When we do face ourselves we are filled with a special kind of anguish (*Angst*), a sense of standing on the edge of an abyss. Only by doing this, however, can the individual find God.

Kierkegaard's most important works include the following: *The Concept of Irony* (1841); *Either-Or* (1843); *Fear and Trembling* (1843); *The Concept of Dread* (1844); *Stages on Life's Way* (1845); *Concluding Unscientific Postscript* (1846); *Works of Love* (1848); *Christian Discourses* (1848); *Sickness Unto Death* (1849); *Training in Christianity* (1850); *The Instant* (a series of ten articles in which Kierkegaard launched his final attack on the clergy and the institutional Church) (1854–1855), published in English translation with some other papers under the title, *Attack Upon "Christendom"*.

Kilham, Alexander (1762–1798). A Methodist preacher, he became leader of the radical wing of the movement and was expelled in 1796 from the Methodist Conference. Shortly before his death he founded the Methodist New Connexion.

Kilwardby, Robert (*c.* 1200–1279). Trained at Paris, he returned to England, entered the Dominican Order, taught at Oxford, became Prior of the English province in 1261 and Archbishop of Canterbury in 1273. In 1277 he visited Oxford where he condemned various propositions, notably certain ones expressing the views of Thomas Aquinas concerning the question of unity of form, which he deemed irreconcilable with Christian orthodoxy. His writings include *On the Origin of Science*; *On the Imaginative Spirit*; *On Time*; and *On Conscience*. Created a cardinal in 1278, he died the following year at Viterbo, Italy.

Kilian. A 7th c. saint and missionary to the Franks. He is the patron saint of Würzburg, in the cathedral of which city his remains were placed in 752.

Kindi, al- (*c.* 813–873). The first among the Arabian philosophers to follow Aristotle. He wrote on metaphysics, astronomy, mathematics, music, physics, medicine, and psychology. He followed Aristotle, for example, in distinguishing between the "active intellect" and the "passive intellect" and went on to specify two other kinds of intellect: discursive reasoning and demonstration. He postulated five categories of being: matter, motion, form, place, and time.

King, Edward (1829–1910). English Tractarian, friend of E. B. Pusey; Bishop of Lincoln; Regius Professor of Pastoral Theology, Oxford.

King, Martin Luther (1929–1968). Black American civil rights leader; Nobel Peace Laureate, 1964; assassinated in 1968.

Kingdom Of God. The concept is rooted in the Hebrew symbolization of God as king of the universe. His "kingdom" is therefore the universe, and earthly kingdoms are usurpations of the kingship that belongs only to God and are to be swept away on the Day of Judgment. Jesus taught accordingly but also and importantly emphasized the presence of the Kingdom here and now to those who are spiritually ready to participate in it. So the Kingdom is "at hand" (*ēggiken*) and is even "in your midst" (*entos hymōn*); it is "now upon you and within you." The significance of this aspect of Christ's teaching seems to have been lost as the Kingdom was more and more identified with the Church. In the New Testament and the Early Church no such identification seems to have been normally made.

King James Version. The designation given to the version of the English Bible that was done with the support of King James I by forty-seven translators and published in 1611. In England it is traditionally called the Authorised Version, although it was never formally authorized by anyone. Its excellence, however, enabled it to win general acceptance over all other English versions and translations of the Bible then available, even the Geneva Bible, which had been favored by the Puritans and the Scots.

Kings. In the Bible, the two books (originally one) so entitled recount the history of the Hebrew monarchy from the accession of Solomon (*c.* 970 BCE) to the Fall of Jerusalem (586 BCE).

Kingsley, Charles (1819–1875). Anglican divine, novelist, and vigorous opponent of the Tractarian movement. Under the influence of F. D. Maurice and Thomas Carlyle, he became associated with the movement known as "Christian Socialism." His novels include *Westward Ho!* (1885) and *The Water Babies* (1863), a popular children's book.

Kirk. The Church of Scotland, Presbyterian in government, is traditionally called "The Kirk," although the term was dropped in the 17th c. as an official designation, except for the lowest ecclesiastical court, the Kirk-Session which consists of the minister and elders of a local parish.

Kiss Of Peace. The greeting (traditionally an embrace) given mutually by clergy and people at the Eucharist. It is very ancient, being mentioned by Justin Martyr in the 2nd c. and probably dating from apostolic times. In the Eastern Church and in some Western rites it is traditionally given before the offering of the Oblations, but generally in Roman and Anglican usage it occurs soon before Communion. Since Vatican II a handshake is often substituted.

Klosterneuberg. An important monastic foundation of Augustinian canons regular near Vienna, acquired by the Augustinian canons in 1133. It is famous for its great art treasures and its library and in recent times for its participation in the modern liturgical movement. Its present buildings represent the best in Austrian Baroque.

Knights. See **Hospitallers, The Knights** and **Templar, The Knights**.

Knowledge. In Plato knowledge (*epistēmē*) is contrasted with opinion (*doxa*). The highest form of knowledge is wisdom (*sophia*). Aristotle regarded knowledge of the first principles as the highest form of knowledge. In the history of European philosophy, two schools are distinguished: (1) the Continental Rationalists (e.g., Descartes, Spinoza, Leibniz) who recognized in one way or another that the mind has innate ideas that provide the basis for knowledge, and (2) the British Empiricists (e.g., Locke, Berkeley, Hume) who see all knowledge as rooted in the senses. The distinction between knowledge and belief is of great importance in philosophical theology.

Knox, Alexander (1757–1831). Anglican divine, descendant of John Knox, and friend of John Wesley, he anticipated the churchmanship of the Tractarians.

Knox, John (*c.* 1513–1572). Leader of the Scottish Reformation. Much influenced by George Wishart and later by John Calvin. For some years chaplain to Edward VI, exercising considerable influence on the English Reformation. In 1555 he returned to Scotland and in 1556 went to Geneva to the charge of the English congregation there, returning finally to Scotland in 1559 where, after the death of Mary of Guise in 1560, he drew up the Scots Confession and secured legislation abolishing the jurisdiction of the Pope and making the celebration of Mass or attendance thereat a capital offense. On the advent of the young, widowed Mary Stuart as Queen of Scots, who had been nurtured from childhood in France to be devoted to the Roman Catholic faith, he was soon embroiled in bitter confrontations that were to become famous in the annals of the Scottish Reformation. Knox was politically astute. The nobles, who in Scotland were strong while the monarchy was relatively weak, were divided on the question of a difficult choice: (1) to continue to accept the powerful protection of France against England as the common enemy, a course that entailed supporting the Roman Church in Scotland, where it was especially corrupt, and (2) to foster the Reformation cause, which meant some sort of alliance with England, traditionally Scotland's bitter enemy. Knox chose the latter course, so separating Scotland from both France and the Pope and embracing the Reformation cause in a much more radical way than the temper of England was generally disposed to encourage. The influence of Knox on subsequent Scottish history, religious, educational, and secular, was enormous. Although quarrelsome, theologically narrow, and opinionated, he had the courage and vigor that make for leadership. As the Earl of Morton, then Regent of Scotland, said at his funeral, he "neither flattered nor feared any flesh."

Knox, Ronald Arbuthnott (1888–1957). Educated at Eton and Balliol College, Oxford, he became involved in the more extreme wing of the Anglo-Catholic movement. Received into the Roman Catholic Church in 1917, he was ordained Roman Catholic priest in 1919. He translated the Vulgate Bible from Latin into English (a felicitous rendering) and was a noted apologist and witty and gifted writer.

Knutzen, Martin (1713–1751). German philosopher, follower of Christian Wolff and chiefly known as Kant's teacher at Königsberg.

Koan. An important concept in Zen Buddhism. It is an exercise of the mind, held to be beyond thought and seeming to violate reason. The Zen master, being skilled in the techniques of Zen, prescribes a koan for the disciple to meditate upon and to answer. A well-known example is, "What is the sound of one hand clapping?" Many of the "standard" koans have been collected and are regularly used. Answers that show that the disciple has "caught on" have been collected and classified. The good disciple does not give up; he perseveres until he finds an answer. The term *koan* comes from a Chinese word *kung-an,* which originally referred to a document and signified approximately "topic on the agenda." The koan in Zen practice is a question on the meditation agenda.

Koimēsis. The term used in the Greek Church for the "falling asleep" of Mary, who is generally believed to have escaped death. See **Dormition** and **Assumption of Mary**.

Kolyva. A cake made of wheat or rice and sugar coated, which in the Eastern Church is blessed during memorial services for the dead and distributed to the mourners.

Komvoschinion. A knotted cord, usually woollen, used while reciting the Jesus Prayer. It is to some extent the Eastern counterpart of the Rosary.

Koran. See **Qur'ān**.

Koridethi Codex. An uncial, probably 9th c., manuscript of the Gospels that belonged to the monastery of Koridethi near the Caspian Sea but is now at Tiflis. Its text of Mark differs considerably from that of the great uncial manuscripts.

Kornthal. A Pietist settlement near Stuttgart, Germany, founded in 1819 as a center of Pietist life and reflecting Moravian influence. Members, although accepting the Augsburg Confession, renounced what they took to be a spirit of rationalism in the Lutheran Church. They emphasized the imminent approach of the Millennium. Like the Quakers in England they have been traditionally exempted from military service and from taking oaths. They have done much work for the education of neglected children.

Kraus, Franz Xaver (1840–1901). German ecclesiastical historian, noted for his great erudition, and Roman Catholic priest. His political views, which upheld the rights of the State against Church interference, were unacceptable to the hierarchy.

Krause, Karl Christian Friedrich (1781–1832). German philosopher who studied at Jena under Hegel and Fichte. Held the universe to be a divine organism. God includes in his being both nature and humanity, yet transcends both: a view he named Panentheism and which, in various modifications, has been accepted by many modern theologians as more satisfactory than either Theism or Pantheism. His writings include *Sketch of the Philosophical System* (1804) and *Lectures on the System of Philosophy* (1828). See also **Panentheism.**

Krishna. An ancient and still very popular deity in Hinduism. Along with Rama, one of the two last incarnations of Vishnu.

Kshatriya. In traditional, institutional Hinduism, the warrior caste, second to the Brahmin.

Kuenen, Abraham (1828–1891). Dutch biblical scholar, professor at Leyden, whose views were in advance of conservative opinion in his time.

Kulturkampf. A political movement in Germany in the 1870s, largely inspired by Bismarck, against the Roman Catholic Church, which he feared would endanger the unity of the German Empire. The Jesuits were expelled, all education was placed under State control, and in 1873 the "May Laws" were passed, drastically limiting Roman Catholic Church power. These evoked strong opposition. Bismarck eventually agreed to seek a concordat and by 1887 most of the legislation against Roman Catholics was repealed.

Kuyper, Abraham (1837–1920). Dutch Calvinist theologian. Founded a Calvinistic university at Amsterdam. Politically active, he was Minister of the Interior from 1901 to 1905.

Kyriale. Liturgical book used for the Ordinary of the Mass, separated for convenience from the Gradual.

Kyrie Eleison. A brief prayer ("Lord, have mercy") used from early times in Christian worship, having had also an ancestry in pagan worship. The "ninefold" Kyrie, at the beginning of the Mass (the thrice repeated "Lord, have mercy" followed by the thrice repeated "Christ, have mercy" followed by another thrice repeated "Lord, have mercy") is to be found in the Ordo Romanus IV (8th.–9th c.) and became traditional for the Latin Mass. The *Kyrie* has been modified in Roman Catholic practice since Vatican II, but it is still sung at Solemn High Mass in Anglo-Catholic churches.

L

Laberthonnière, Lucien (1860–1932). Roman Catholic theologian. Ordained priest as an Oratorian, he taught at Juilly and at Paris, becoming in 1900 Rector of the Collège at Juilly. In his writings he developed a pragmatic view of the nature of religious truth and, working during the period when so-called Modernism was being condemned by the Roman Catholic Church, he found himself out of favor and his books listed in the papal Index of Prohibited Books. In 1913 he was forbidden to publish anything. He influenced George Tyrrell.

Lacey, Thomas Alexander (1853–1931). Anglican divine. Trained at Oxford (Balliol), he was ordained priest in 1876, becoming a Canon of Worcester in 1918. A devoted Anglo-Catholic of notable learning and originality, he was active in attempts to bring about a reunion of the Roman Catholic and Anglican Churches. His writings include *Nature, Miracle, and Sin* (1916) and *Unity and Schism* (1918).

Lachish. A city of Judah, the site of which is to be identified with the modern Tell el Duweir, 25 miles SW of Jerusalem. Frequently mentioned in the Bible, it is also mentioned in the Amarna Letters and was excavated in the 1930s by J. L. Starkey, uncovering a city that had been about eighteen acres (somewhat larger than had been Jerusalem during the early monarchy) within its walls. Among the many and exciting finds, the Lachish letters written to the commander of the garrison during the last years of Zedekiah just before the fall of the kingdom to the Babylonians are of special interest.

Lachmann, Karl (1793–1851). Textual scholar and philologist. Professor of classical and German philology at Berlin, he was the first scholar to produce an edition of the Greek New Testament in which the received text (*textus receptus*) was set aside in favor of that of the oldest Greek manuscripts available. His work considerably influenced later textual scholars.

Lady Chapel. A chapel dedicated to the Virgin Mary and forming part of a larger church. It is often found at the side of the High Altar and sometimes (when constructed as an addition to the church) behind it.

Lady Day. The Feast of the Annunciation (March 25).

Laetare Sunday. The fourth Sunday of Lent (in France *Mi-carême*) is so named from the opening word of the Introit (Isaiah 66.10). Instead of the violet used as the liturgical color for Lent, rose pink may be used on Laetare Sunday.

LaGrange, Marie Joseph (1855–1958). Roman Catholic biblical scholar. Having entered the Dominican Order in 1879, he founded a school of biblical studies at Jerusalem in 1890 and the *Revue Biblique*. His views went as far in the direction of modern biblical scholarship as was compatible with the Roman Catholic position in his time.

Lailat-ul-bara'h. In Islam, the "Night of Forgiveness," which falls two weeks

before the beginning of Ramadan. It is a time for seeking forgiveness and reconciliation.

Lailat-ul Qadar. In Islam, the "Night of Power," which falls at the end of Ramadan. It commemorates the giving of the Qur'ān to Muhammad.

Lake, Kirsopp (1872–1946). Anglo-American biblical scholar. Trained at Oxford (Lincoln College), he was ordained priest in 1895 and was professor of the New Testament at Leyden from 1904 until 1914, later holding chairs at Harvard. His works, some of which were highly critical of traditional Christian beliefs, showed great textual and palaeographical skills. His *Historical Evidence for the Resurrection of Jesus Christ* (1907) challenged the historicity of the Empty Tomb. *The Earlier Epistles of Paul* (1911) depicted the primitive Church as much affected by the mystery religions of the Graeco-Roman world. His first book, *The Text of the New Testament*, which went into many editions, was a small and extremely useful account of the work of New Testament criticism in his time. He co-edited *The Beginnings of Christianity*, 5 vols. (1920–1923). There is a biographical account of him by F. C. Grant in the *Dictionary of National Biography*, 1941–1950.

Lakṣmī. In the Rig Veda, a mark, sign, or token. Originally it did not in itself signify any positive or negative quality. This was signified by a good or bad qualifier. A good sign indicated prosperity, wealth, success, good fortune. Later the term in itself became the personification of the goddess of prosperity, the wife of Viṣṇu. She is sometimes known as the lotus-goddess.

Lamaism. In the middle of the 15th c. CE, the Emperor of China included Tibet within his domains. He named two Buddhist monks to be the spiritual and the temporal rulers respectively of Tibet: the Dalai Lama (spiritual) and the Pantshen Lama (temporal). Both are regarded as incarnations of divine beings. See also **Dalai Lama**.

Lamb. The lamb is frequently mentioned in the Old Testament as a symbol of innocence and helplessness and especially in the Pentateuch as a sacrificial victim. Hence its importation into the New Testament where it is applied to John the Baptist (John 1.29), although at least one biblical scholar (J. Jeremias) has questioned whether this may have arisen through a mistranslation from the Aramaic word and ought to read "Servant of God." It is copiously used in the Book of Revelation (Apocalypse) in reference to Jesus as the sacrificial victim who is offered up for the redemption of the world: an application unique to the Apocalypse.

Lambeth. Lambeth has been the London residence of the Archbishops of Canterbury since *c*. 1190. The chapel dates from 1245. When, *c*. 1658, the palace at Canterbury had fallen into decay, the title "palace" was transferred to Lambeth, which has therefore since been known as Lambeth Palace. The Water Tower, a massive keep, was erected in 1434 and the South Gateway and two towers toward the end of the 15th c. In modern times the Archbishops of Canterbury have occupied a part of the palace, which was badly damaged in 1940 in an air raid but was restored after the war. Assemblies of the bishops of the Anglican Communion have been held there about once in ten years since 1867. Doctrinal and other questions are discussed and resolutions passed on them, expressive of the opinions of the Anglican episcopate but not binding. In this way, in characteristically Anglican fashion, guidelines are provided for the Church without forcing consciences.

Lamentabili. The decree of the Holy Office at Rome, issued on July 3, 1907, condemning sixty-five propositions taken to represent the teaching of those who were participating in a movement called Modernism. See **Modernism**.

Lamentation. This literary form is found in the Old Testament in a variety of specific kinds, e.g., a dirge and a wailing for the downfall of an individual or a people.

Lamps. Since the earliest Christian services were generally held at night, lamps were used for practical reasons. Although no evidence exists to show their ceremonial use before the time of Constantine, from that time onwards in the East they were used in large candelabra during the Liturgy, while in the West lamps or candles were burned before relics and shrines from at least the 6th c. The use of the Sanctuary Lamp perpetually lighted before the reserved Sacrament became general in the West in the 13th c., and by the 16th c. it was obligatory.

Lance. In the Eastern Church a small lance-like knife is used to cut the eucharistic bread.

Lance, The Holy. A relic said to be the lance used to pierce the side of Jesus on the Cross (John 19.34). Its existence in Jerusalem is mentioned in the 6th c. When Jerusalem was captured by the Persians in 615 it fell into alien hands, but its point was saved and brought to Hagia Sophia in Constantinople where it was placed in an icon. In 1241 it was presented to the saintly Louis IX of France and preserved, along with the Crown of Thorns, in the Sainte-Chapelle in Paris, where it vanished during the French Revolution.

Lanfranc (*c*. **1010–1089**). Schoolman and Archbishop of Canterbury. Of a family in Pavia, he was educated there and elsewhere in Italy. He became Archbishop of Canterbury in 1070. His most famous theological work dates from about that time: *De corpore et sanguine Domini*, a criticism of the eucharistic teaching of Berengar of Tours, in which Lanfranc came close to the transubstantiation view that eventually prevailed in the Western Church. He was also a vigorous and capable administrator.

Langar. The communal kitchen attached to a Sikh *gurdwara* (temple), in which, irrespective of caste or other consideration, people may share meals and those in need of food may come to eat.

Lange, Johann Peter (1802–1884). Protestant theologian. Trained at Bonn, he published an attack on D. F. Strauss' then influential *Leben Jesu*. He was appointed to a chair at Zürich in 1841 and at Bonn in 1854. His writings include a 3-vol. work on Christian Dogmatics (1849-1852). Lange was one of the leaders of the *Vermittlungstheologie*, which was much under the influence of Schleiermacher. See **Vermittlungstheologie**.

Lao Tzu (traditionally dated 6th c. BCE). According to tradition he was a contemporary of Confucius who visited him for instruction and was treated haughtily. Confucius is said to have described him as a dragon and therefore beyond his understanding. Lao Tzu seems to have regarded Confucius as a virtuous gentleman but limited in his vision and perhaps worldly and ambitious. In his own teaching Lao Tzu emphasized self-effacement. He is the author of the *Tao-Te Ching*, an exposition of his teachings.

Lapps, Religion of the. The traditional religion of the Lapps has affinities with that of the Eskimos and other very northern peoples. The gods represent environmental powers such as the sun. The *noaide* corresponds to the shaman. Drums are prominent in worship. Like other Arctic and near-Arctic peoples, they reverenced the bear.

La Salle, Jean-Baptiste de (1651–1719). Founder of the Institute of the Brothers of Christian Schools. Born at Reims, he was ordained priest in 1678 and soon thereafter began opening schools, where he pioneered new educational practices that make him important not only for his spirituality but for the history of the development of modern educational methods.

Last Gospel. In the Middle Ages, it was the custom for the priest, when he had celebrated Mass and returned to the sacristy, to recite the prologue to the Gospel according to John (John 1.1–14), as a private devotion. Later it became customary for the priest to say it aloud at the altar at the end of the Mass. At the words *Et Verbum caro factum est* ("And the Word was made flesh"), priest and people genuflected in reverence for the Incarnation. The Roman Catholic Church abandoned this beautiful practice on September 26, 1964, as part of the liturgical changes made during the Second Vatican Council. It is still observed in many Anglo-Catholic parishes.

Last Supper. The meal taken by Christ and his disciples on the eve of the Crucifixion. Traditionally the Last Supper has been taken to be the Passover, which is what Matthew, Mark, and Luke indicate. John, however, refers to the Crucifixion as taking place on the preparation for the Passover, i.e., some hours before the latter, in which case the Last Supper must be regarded as a kiddush or a preparation for the Passover, not the Passover itself. Some have suggested, from documents found at Qumran, a somewhat complex explanation relating to a calendar used by the Qumran community, but most scholars do not find such an explanation sufficiently plausible. See **Kiddush**.

Lateran Councils. Many councils have been held at the Lateran Palace. Five of them are recognized as ecumenical councils of the Roman Catholic Church: the First (1123) confirmed the Concordat of Worms, effectively ending the Investiture controversy; the Second (1139) ended the schism that had taken place at the election of Innocent II, by whom it was convoked; the Third (1179) restricted the right of electing a pope to the College of Cardinals by a two-thirds majority, and various other reforms; the

Fourth (1215) defined the doctrine of the Eucharist in terms of transubstantiation (the first official reference to this doctrine by that name), made other doctrinal definitions, and some far-reaching reforms in the organization and administration of the Roman Catholic Church; the Fifth (1512–1517), was convoked for the purpose of reforming the Roman Catholic Church of major abuses, although in fact it achieved only some minor reforms. The Fourth Lateran Council is recognized by Church historians as by far the most important of the five.

Lateran Palace and Basilica, The. The Lateran Palace in Rome is so called because in antiquity it belonged to the Laterani family. It was presented to the Church by the wife of the Emperor Constantine and was the official residence of the popes from the 4th c. till the papacy was moved to Avignon in 1309. About that time it had been destroyed by fire, was rebuilt in the 16th c., but the new building was given over to other uses. The basilica, founded by Pope Sixtus III in the 5th c. and still the cathedral church of Rome, was originally dedicated to the Redeemer but after destruction by an earthquake in 896 and rebuilding in the early 10th c., it was dedicated to John the Baptist. (It is still known as San Giovanni in Laterano.) It was burned down twice and restored. The present building and facade date from a rebuilding in the 16th to the early 18th c. It is one of four major basilicas at Rome; the others are St Peter's, St Paul's outside the Walls (*fuori le muri*), and Santa Maria Maggiore. See **Basilica.**

Lateran Treaty. In 1871 the Vatican, the Lateran, and the papal villa at Castelgandolfo had been granted extraterritorial privileges. By the Lateran Treaty (Feb. 11, 1929), after conversations between Cardinal Gasparri and Mussolini, the Vatican City was recognized as a sovereign state. For a brief account see B. Williamson, *The Treaty of the Lateran*. London: Burns Oates, 1929.

Latimer, Hugh (*c.* 1485–1555). A Cambridge man, he was elected Fellow of Clare Hall in 1510. A popular preacher, he showed sympathies with Reformation teachings and was suspect by the ecclesiastical authorities, but after Cranmer had become Archbishop of Canterbury, Latimer was appointed Bishop of Worcester in 1535. He continued to favor Reformation teachings and eventually was confined to the Tower in 1546 but released on the accession of Edward VI. Under Mary he was arrested and again sent to the Tower in 1553. After he had refused to accept transubstantiation and some other doctrines, he and Nicholas Ridley, Bishop of London, were burned in 1555.

Latin. In Hellenistic and New Testament times Greek was the language of the Roman Empire and was used more commonly than Latin even in Rome itself. In the later centuries of the Empire, however, Latin came to be widely spoken in the West, eventually becoming the parent of what we now call the Romance languages, e.g., Italian, Spanish, French, and Portuguese.

Latitudinarianism. A group of Anglican divines in the 17th c. were thought to attach too little importance to dogmatic and liturgical matters and church organization. They were called latitudinarian by their opponents in the Church of England.

La Trappe. The Abbey of Notre-Dame de la Trappe, near Soligny in Normandy, France, is the mother house of the Trappist reform of the Cistercian Order. It is commonly known as the Grande Trappe. Most famous among its abbots was the Abbot de Rancé, who instituted severe austerities through which the life of the abbey was reformed in the 17th c. Thereafter the abbey prospered but the community was expelled during the French Revolution. The monks returned, however, in 1817.

Latria. In Roman Catholic theology, three kinds of worship are recognized, all designated by Greek terms. *Doulia* is the kind proper to saints and other creatures whose sanctity merits admiration and devotion. To Mary, as preeminent among all creatures, is given *hyperdoulia*—an outstanding degree of *doulia*. *Latria*, however, being the worship proper to the Creator, must be reserved for God alone.

Latrocinium. A council held at Ephesus in August, 449, and so called by Pope Leo I in a letter to the Empress Pulcheria, in which he described it as *non judicium sed latrocinium*: a "robber council." It was held because of the condemnation of Eutyches, whom it acquitted of heresy and reinstated in his monastery. The papal legates were insulted. Bishops were deposed. Eventually, at the great Council of Chalcedon in 451, the enactments of the "Robber Council" were nullified. Leo's epithet was directed to the partisan nature of this assembly, which was dominated by a strong upholder of the Monophysite position identified with the name of Eutyches.

Latter-Day Saints. See **Mormons.**

Laud, William (1573–1645). Archbishop of Canterbury from 1633. An Oxford man (St. John's College), he was ordained in 1601. Having become a Fellow of his college in 1593, he was elected its president in 1611. He opposed the Calvinist element in the Church of England of his day and sought to uphold Catholic doctrine and practice. He argued for the Anglican position that the Roman Church and the English Church are branches of the same Catholic Church. His attempts to enforce liturgical uniformity met with opposition from the Puritans and his efforts to saddle such uniformity on the Scots in 1637 resulted in rebellion. In 1641 he was imprisoned in the Tower and executed on January 10, 1645.

Lausanne. The first conference of the "Faith and Order" ecumenical movement, which met at Lausanne in 1927.

Many Christian bodies were represented, but the Roman Catholic Church, the Russian Orthodox, and some Baptist bodies, remained aloof from it.

Lavelle, Louis (1883–1951). Philosopher. Leader of the movement "Philosophie de l'Esprit." Through discipline of our instincts by reason we gradually achieve freedom and so relate ourselves more and more to Being, i.e., God, who is the Absolute freedom. Lavelle's thought represents a form of neo-Idealism. His principal writings include: *The Total Presence* (1934), *Evil and Suffering* (1940), *French Philosophy Between the Two Wars* (1942), and *Treatise on Values*, 2 vols. (1951 and 1955).

Lavra. A group of anchorites living separately in huts or the like but together forming a colony subject to one abbot. The practice dates from early in the 4th c.. The Great Lavra on Mount Athos is probably the best known today.

Law, Biblical. Various collections of law are to be found in the Old Testament. Central is the Decalogue or Ten Commandments, set forth in two formulae: (1) Exodus 20.2–17 and (2) Deuteronomy 5.6–21. The so-called "Code of the Covenant" is found in Exodus and deals with provisions concerning property, slaves, theft, and various ritual matters. Another collection (Exodus 34.17–27) deals with cultic and ritual matters. In the Book of Deuteronomy is to be found what scholars call the Deuteronomic Code, which besides emphasizing the rejection of the old Canaanite customs and practices, transforms the spirit of Israelite law and perceives the Law as not merely an obligation but a divine gift to Israel. Yet another set of laws, the Holiness Code, found in Leviticus, deals with a wide variety of matters relating to ritual purity and sets forth various prohibitions in detail. It probably dates from the 6th c. BCE. Finally there is the Priestly Code, which is apparently for priests, not the general population, and is to be found scattered through the Pentateuch. Besides the word *tôrāh*, which is the most general Hebrew term for law, other terms are used to designate various aspects of law. The Septuagint translates *tôrāh* by the Greek term *nomos*, which is then taken over by the New Testament writers. Several extrabiblical sources (e.g., the Code of Hammurabi) contain parallels that antedate the biblical codes.

Law, William (1686–1761). A Cambridge man (Emmanuel College), he became a Fellow of his college in 1711 but was deprived of his fellowship when he refused to take the Oath of Allegiance under George I. Thereafter, living simply, he devoted himself to writing. His spirituality was profound. He pleaded for deeper individual exercise in meditation rather than corporate worship and for the cultivation of virtues such as modesty, humility, simplicity of life, and the turning of the soul to God. His best known work, *A Serious Call to a Devout and Holy Life* (1728), reflects emphases made by medieval ascetical and mystical writers such as Tauler and Ruysbroeck. It soon became a very popular classic of English spirituality.

Lawrence, Brother (c. 1605–1691). A Carmelite lay brother, Nicolas Herman, who, given charge of the kitchen of a monastery in Paris in 1649, was noted for his prayerful life. His writings, edited and posthumously published, teach a very simple and personal life of prayer consisting in the practice of constantly thinking of or imagining the presence of God. Modern selections of his writings are entitled *The Practice of the Presence of God*.

Lay Brothers. In traditional Catholic practice, religious communities typically include two classes of members: (1) choir brothers (or sisters) and (2) lay brothers (or sisters). The former have teaching, nursing, or (in the case of men) priestly duties, or other such commitments, and in many orders and congregations an obligation to recite the long choir office (the official daily prayers of the Church), while the latter serve the community in other ways, such as cooking or tailoring. The dress (habit) of the two classes is usually different; e.g., Trappist monks wear white and lay brothers brown; choir sisters might have a black veil and the lay sisters a white one. The lay brothers and sisters attend the daily Mass as the others but have much simpler and shorter devotions. Service as a lay brother or sister provides a means for a person who may not have the inclination or education for a teaching or other professional kind of vocation to participate in the life of a religious community in ways suited to his or her outlook or experience.

Lay Reader. A lay person authorized to assist the pastor of a church by reading certain parts of the service (in some cases even preaching), and otherwise helping in the work of the church without formal training for the ministry. The first lay reader in the Church of England was appointed in 1866. In the Anglican communion readers are normally licensed by the Bishop either for a particular parish or for the diocese at large.

Lazarists. A popular name given to a French congregation of secular priests living under rule and with the traditional three vows and officially known as the Congregation of the Mission. They were founded in 1625 by St Vincent de Paul, whose headquarters were the priory at Saint-Lazare, Paris. They spread first all over France, engaging in mission work, then through the French-speaking colonies, and now throughout the entire world. In many countries, including the U.S., they are known today as Vincentians.

Learned Ignorance. See **Nicholas of Cusa**.

Leclercq, Henri (1869–1945). Notable Benedictine scholar. Born in Tournai, Belgium, he became a naturalized French citizen. Ordained priest in 1896, he lived from 1914 till his death in London. He wrote learnedly and copiously on historical, liturgical and other subjects and was co-editor with F. Cabrol of the multivolume *Dictionnaire d'archéologie chrétienne et de liturgie* (1903–53). Critics have noted considerable lack of accuracy in his work, at least partly due to its immense profusion; nevertheless, it is important and his style often vivacious.

Lectern. A stand, usually heavy and of metal or wood, and often in the form of an eagle seeming to carry the book on its wings. It is for reading the Bible or other books used in the services of the Church. It normally stands on the south side of the church, opposite the pulpit, the proper place for which in parish churches is the north side.

Legate, Papal. A personal representative of the Pope. Historically there have been three kinds. In the Middle Ages, the holders of certain ecclesiastical offices were *ex officiis* legates. Such a legate was styled *legatus natus*. Nowadays his functions would be exercised by a nuncio, also known as a *legatus missus*, whose authority and functions are similar to those of an ambassador. Finally there is the *legatus a latere*, who is a cardinal appointed to execute a specific mission on behalf of the papacy. The term "papal legate" is generally applied to this last kind.

Leibniz, Gottfried Wilhelm (1646–1716). Philosopher. Born in Leipzig, the son of a professor of philosophy, he was largely self-taught. Having received a doctorate in law in 1666, he entered the service of the Elector of Mainz, which brought him into contact with many of the greatest minds of Europe, including Spinoza, Malebranche, and Huygens. He published his first paper on differential calculus in 1684 and on integral calculus in 1686. He anticipated the modern distinction between analytical and synthetic truths by his distinction between "truths of reason" and "truths of fact." Discarding many of the views of Descartes, particularly his dualism, he perceived the soul as a monad of higher grade in control of a colony of monads of lower grade, thus avoiding the sharp metaphysical dualism of Descartes. Leibniz is one of the greatest thinkers in human history and his elaborate system, although vulnerable to various forms of criticism, is not only a great edifice in itself but of special interest to thinkers with religious concerns.

Leipzig, Disputation of. A disputation held June 27 through July 16, 1519 at the order of the Duke of Saxony. Beginning with a discussion about grace and free will, it developed in such a way as to widen the gap between Luther and the medieval Church, precipitating his break with Rome in 1520.

Lent. The penitential season of forty days before Easter. The length of the season and the severity of the fasts and other austerities associated with it have varied from age to age and from place to place. In the first centuries it was usually only three days, but the fast was severe: usually only one meal a day toward evening and abstinence from meat, fish, and eggs was required. Today more emphasis is generally placed, in the West, on prayer, study, meditation, and other spiritual exercises than on fasting. See also **Holy Week.**

Leo I (Leo the Great). Pope from 444 till his death in 461. Energetic and a good administrator, he immensely enhanced the power and influence of Rome as the central focus of the Church that he wished to make it. He seems to have been politically astute, persuading the Huns to withdraw beyond the Danube and, when the Vandals took Rome in 452, obtaining concessions from them. Although not a man of notable scholarship, he wrote in a forceful and lucid style. He is probably the author of some of the prayers in the so-called Leonine Sacramentary and many of his sermons and other writings have survived.

Leo X (1475–1521). Pope from 1513, he was the second son of Lorenzo de'-Medici. A pleasure-loving man who had been created a cardinal at the age of 24, he had no idea of the issues at stake when, in 1521, he excommunicated Luther.

Leonine Sacramentary. The Sacramentary was the liturgical book used in the Western Church down to the 13th c. for the celebration of Mass. The Leonine Sacramentary is the earliest surviving book for this purpose. Strictly speaking it is not a sacramentary but, rather, a collection of the booklets (*libelli*) containing the formularies for a mass or masses for a particular church.

Le Roy, Edouard (1870–1954). Philosopher. Born in Paris, he taught at the Collège de France. His thought was a combination of Blondel's and Bergson's. Because of the pragmatic character of his philosophy, some of his writings were placed on the papal Index of Prohibited Books. His works include *Dogma and Criticism* (1907), *The Idealist Requirement and the Fact of Evolution* (1927), *Introduction to the Study of the Religious Problem* (1943).

Le Senne, René (1883–1954). Philosopher. For many years professor of moral philosophy at the Sorbonne, Paris, he worked with Louis Lavelle in editing a collection of books in the tradition of what they called "Philosophie de l' Esprit:" a philosophy of spirituality. He upheld the freedom of the will and saw human values as emerging in the overcoming of obstacles. Among French philosophers he especially venerated Pascal and among American thinkers he much esteemed Royce. His writings include his *Obstacle and Value* (1934), *Treatise on General Morality* (1942), and *Personal Destiny* (1955). In later life he developed an interest in characterology.

Lesser Entrance. In the Eastern Church, the procession with the Book of the Gospels. See **Greater Entrance.**

Lessing, Gotthold Ephraim (1729–1781). Dramatist and essayist. Born in Saxony and educated at Leipzig, he was a pioneer in the movement that resulted in the *Aufklärung*. Very influential in 18th c. German thought, he argued in his *Nathan the Wise* for complete toleration in religion, since, he tried to show, moral rectitude is to be found in all religions. He was much influenced by Spinoza. In his *Laocoön* he argued that each art has its own particular function, and each is governed by its own set of principles. Each must therefore be self-consistent and must operate within its own rules. He saw art as a sort of theodicy, in contrast to the late 19th c. philosophers of art and art critics who, perceiving art as independent of ethics and logic, hoisted the banner of "Art for art's sake."

Levellers. A politico-religious party in 17th c. England. They were anti-monarchical and sought an extension of democratic principles and total religious freedom. Their leader, J. Lilburne, was distrusted by Oliver Cromwell who had him imprisoned. They virtually disappeared by the end of the Commonwealth period in 1660.

Levirate Marriage. The Old Testament law obliging a brother to marry the widow of his deceased brother, if the brother had died without male issue.

Lévy-Bruhl, Lucien (1857–1939). Philosopher. From 1899 professor at the Sorbonne, he studied primitive societies, perceiving their mentality to be pre-rational, unencumbered by the logical distinctions that guide the outlook of civilized minds. The latter's principle of non-contradiction (A cannot be B and not-B), for example, does not enter into the thinking of primitive peoples, so that they can accept both of what civilized peoples would account incompatible assertions. His works include *The Mental Functions in Inferior Societies* (1910), *Primitive Mentality* (1922), *The Primitive Mythology* (1935), and *Mystical*

Experience and Symbols among the Primitives (1938).

Lewis, Clarence Irving (1883–1964). American philosopher. Born in Massachusetts, he was trained at Harvard where he also taught. Royce was among his teachers. He was also influenced by C. S. Peirce. Lewis, who described himself as a "conceptualistic pragmatist," held that philosophy is a reflective examination of experience. What is given in experience is to some extent beyond analysis; nevertheless philosophy can inspect certain aspects of it, e.g., ethics examines the principles of human conduct, metaphysics the problem of the real. He made important contributions to the development of modern logic. His writings incude *A Survey of Symbolic Logic* (1918), *The Pragmatic Elements in Knowledge* (1926), *Mind and the World Order* (1929), and *An Analysis of Knowledge and Valuation* (1946).

Lewis, Clive Staples (1898–1963). Born in Belfast, where his father was a lawyer, he was educated at Oxford where he had a distinguished undergraduate career before becoming a Fellow of Magdalen College. During his years at Magdalen (1925–1954) he wrote many of the books that have so endeared him to many readers all over the English-speaking world. In the last chapter of his short autobiography, *Surprised by Joy* (1955), he describes the final stage of his conversion from atheism to Christian faith. In 1954 he went to a Cambridge chair in English. Among the numerous books in which, carrying his learning lightly and writing in a deceptively simple style, he described in a uniquely original vein and with compelling sincerity untainted by emotionalism his discovery of the meaning of Christian faith. Among these are: *The Problem of Pain* (1940); *The Screwtape Letters* (1942), in which in a skillful fantasy he portrays the Devil's cunning and delight in leading men and women into temptation and securing their destruc-

tion; *Christian Behaviour* (1943); *The Great Divorce* (1945); *George MacDonald: An Anthology* (1945); *Miracles* (1947); and *Mere Christianity* (1952). Both as a Christian voice in mid-20th-c. Oxford and to his much wider circle of readers beyond, his influence on the spiritual lives of many has been immense. Among his contemporaries at Oxford were his friends J. R. R. Tolkien and Charles Williams.

Lex Talionis. The Latin name given to the ancient biblical principle of "an eye for an eye."

Lha-Dre. In indigenous Tibetan religion, the *lha* are the gods and the *dre* the demons. The Tibetan Buddhists classify them as "the gods of this world," somewhat as Christians at first regarded the deities of the Mediterranean civilizations.

Lhasa. The capital city of Tibet, which is the traditional center of Tibetan Buddhism. See **Lamaism.**

Li. A Chinese term, not strictly translatable, it signifies good manners as perceived in Confucian teaching. It represents the duty that each one has in society. Some of the Neo-Confucians developed it into a principle of the universe manifesting reason as opposed to the materialistic principle.

Libation. In polytheistic religions, the pouring out of wine or other drink, usually on the ground and sometimes in front of a statue or other image of one of the gods, as a token of honor or recognition.

Liberal Arts, The Seven. The early medieval educational program was based on a long tradition going back to pagan Roman times but more specifically owing its arrangement to Martianus Capella in the early 5th c. The subjects were listed in two categories, (1) the Trivium (grammar, rhetoric, and dialectic or logic) and (2) the Quadrivium (music, arithmetic, geometry, and astronomy). The Trivium roughly corresponded, therefore, to what would nowadays be called the humanities and the Quadrivium to what would nowadays be called the sciences. The subjects of study so listed were not treated in any strictly narrow way and in practice the seven could be made to relate to the entire corpus of human knowledge in those times and circumstances. They were originally called "liberal" as being studies proper to a *liber* (i.e., a free man as opposed to a slave) and, as we might say today, not vocational training leading to a trade such as carpentry. A training in the liberal arts was a prerequisite for proceeding to the study of theology.

Liberal Catholic Church, The. This Church derived its orders from the mother-see of the Old Catholic movement, the ancient archiepiscopal see of Utrecht, Holland. Under the authority of the See of Utrecht, Archbishop Arnold Harris Matthew had brought the Old Catholic Church to England in 1903. (See **Old Catholics.**) Although the Old Catholics made no great inroads into Church life in England, they attracted the attention of a group of theosophists (see **Theosophy**), among them James Ingal Wedgwood of the well-known family of china manufacturers. On the understanding that the theosophists would be free to keep their own philosophical views, Archbishop Matthew ordained some of them to the priesthood. Later, however, he demanded that they renounce their theosophical stance and they refused to do so. He then dissolved the movement. On February 13, 1916, James Wedgwood became the first Presiding Bishop of the now renamed Liberal Catholic Church, which in course of time spread to more than thirty-five countries with a total membership of some ten thousand persons. In the United States there are some twenty-five parishes with approximately four thousand members. The Church has no formal relation with the Theosophical Society, but there is considerable influence from each side to

the other. The Liberal Catholic Church sees itself as reintroducing to Christianity esoteric elements that it believes have been lost, to the impoverishment of the Christian Church, and it emphasizes its mission to teach these lost doctrines, which include, for instance, the karmic principle and its working out in a series of re-embodiments.

Liberalism. Both "liberalism" and "conservatism" have been so ambiguously used as to have lost all clear meaning. Liberalism can mean simply an outlook favorable to all that fosters freedom of the human spirit, which no intelligent person could well disapprove. It has also been used for a wide variety of departures from an equally wide variety of theological stances. In religion as in politics such terms have almost ceased to have any intelligible significance except in cases where the context may provide one.

Liberation Theology. A term used since the 1960s to designate a tendency among those movemens that focus politico-religious attention on areas that they perceive as foci of social oppression, notably these four: (1) exploitation of underdeveloped peoples, (2) denigration of women, (3) racism, and (4) political tyranny in general. The name "liberation" points to the fact that such movements generally interpret the theological concept of redemption as liberation from social conditions that they perceive as evil. Their analyses of social and political situations generally reflect strongly Marxist influence.

Lietzmann, Hans (1875–1942). Ecclesiastical historian. Trained at Jena and Bonn, he became a professor at Bonn in 1905, then succeeded Adolf Harnack at Berlin. Among his works is a *History of the Ancient Church*, 4 vols. (1932–1944; English trans. 1937–1951). He also contributed much in his time to New Testament studies.

Limbo. In Roman Catholic theology, the state of souls who for one reason or another cannot attain the Beatific Vision of God in heaven but are eternally in a state of more limited happiness. Limbo is understood as taking two forms: (1) the *limbus patrum* (limbo of the Fathers), in which the saints before the redemption of the world by Christ stayed till he freed them for heaven; (2) the *limbus infantium*, infants who die before baptism.

Lindisfarne. An island in the North Sea, two miles from the coast of Northumberland and often called "Holy Island," a name that has been given to it from as early as the 11th c. Saint Aidan came to it from Iona in 635 and it became a missionary center and an episcopal see. Saints Chad and Wilfrid are among those educated there. In 664 the Synod of Whitby determined to uphold the Roman Church discipline at Lindisfarne, with the result that some of the monks migrated to Iona. In the eighth and ninth centuries, pillaging of Lindisfarne by the Danes caused much havoc and dispersion of the monks; nevertheless, from the 11th c. to the Dissolution of the Monasteries in England in the 16th c. a continuous monastic life prospered on the island, the fame of which was enhanced by its association with Saint Cuthbert, to whom the abbey church, a small-scale copy of Durham Cathedral, was dedicated. The famous manuscript known as the Lindisfarne Gospels (see **Cottonian Library**) is now in the British Museum.

Linga. This Sanskrit term means simply a sign or mark or symbol, but it came to be used to symbolize the power of the sexual organs. Symbolic representations of the male and female generative organs are widely found in Hindu temples, e.g., "the hall of a thousand *lingas*" in the temple at Tanjore. It is probably the most extensively used symbol in Hindu temples. Amulets showing formalized symbols of this kind were worn by some women as protection against infertility and were also given by bridegrooms to their brides as wedding presents. Such practices, however, do not necessarily imply phallic worship. They are, rather, part of a general nature-worship in which fertility is a prominent focus.

Litany. A form of prayer consisting of petitions, said or sung by a priest or deacon or cantor to which the people make specified responses such as "Grant us thy peace, O Lord." The litaneutical form of prayer seems to date from at least as early as the 4th c. in Antioch. The Eastern Churches make abundant use of the litany in regular liturgical services. In the West, apart from the *Kyrie eleison*, litanies have tended to be used more for special occasions and for private devotion. One of the most ancient is the Litany of the Saints.

Little Flowers of Saint Francis. A collection of legends about Francis of Assisi and his companions.

Little Gidding. One of the poems in T. S. Eliot's *Four Quartets* (1944) is so entitled. Little Gidding was the name of an English manor house in Huntingdonshire, no longer standing, where Nicholas Ferrar and members of his family lived and followed for over twenty years a schedule of prayer and work, also engaging in visiting the poor and the sick. The community was raided by Oliver Cromwell's soldiers in 1646 and its members dispersed. A mostly accurate picture of life in this remarkable little community is provided in the novel *John Ingelsant* (1881) by J. H. Shorthouse. The church of Little Gidding still stands. See also **Agapē and Reconciliation, Order of.**

Liturgy. From the Greek, *laos* ("people") and *ergon* ("work"), *leitourgia*, "the work of the people." In the ancient world the term was used of any public duty, but before the time of Christ it had become well established as a term applied to the services of the Temple at Jerusalem. In Christianity it is traditionally used, especially in the Eastern

Churches, as the title of the Eucharist. In English it is also used in a broader sense to include, for instance, the canonical hours of prayer such as matins and vespers.

Locke, John (1632–1704). English philosopher. Trained at Oxford (Christ Church), he became secretary to the Earl of Shaftesbury in 1667, was elected to the Royal Society, and served on its Council. Having passed through many vicissitudes, he eventually published in 1690 his *Essay Concerning Human Understanding*: an important classic in British philosophy. Against Descartes he held that there are no innate ideas in the mind; each of us begins, as he puts it, with a *tabula rasa*, a clean slate. Ideas originate in experience, which comes in two forms: first, simple ideas enter the mind from without and are made up of sensations; then the mind sorts out these ideas by reflection, so developing the vast and complex furniture of the mind. Locke also distinguished between primary qualities such as solidity, extension in space, figure, motion, rest, number, and secondary qualities such as color and taste. Primary qualities, he thought, inhere in the objects we perceive but secondary qualities do not. He also recognized three types of complex ideas: modes, substances, and relations.

Besides his epistemological interests, Locke also concerned himself with and wrote on education, political philosophy, and religion. His work on religion, although theologically somewhat simplistic, was focused on reasonableness, for although he is the first of the great school of British Empiricism, he was also a forerunner of 18th-c. rationalism. His plea for religious toleration was novel in his day and is now generally accepted as beyond cavil. His educational philosophy emphasizes development of character and intelligence. The influence of Locke's political thought on the Founding Fathers of the United States is well known. It turns very much on his firm belief in God, which governs all Locke's thinking. His chief works include: *The Letter on Toleration* (1689), *Two Treatises on Government* (1689), *An Essay Concerning Human Understanding* (1690), *Thoughts on Education* (1693), *The Reasonableness of Christianity* (1695), and *Miracles* (1716).

Logia. This term, meaning literally "sayings" is used by Papias (*c.* **60–130**), Bishop of Hierapolis, in a work that survives in quotations in works by Irenaeus and Eusebius. He states that Mark, having become Peter's interpreter, set down everything he could remember of the sayings and actions of Jesus. Many regard the statement as an allusion to the hypothetical document Q. (See **Q**.) Fragments have been found of aphorisms and other sayings of Jesus, for example at Oxyrhynchus in 1897 and 1904, that are also called *ta logia*, some of which are not in the Gospels as we have them.

Logical Positivism. Also known as logical empiricism, this school of philosophy took its beginnings in the Vienna Circle, a movement purporting to reform philosophy and having its center, in the 1920s and later, in the University of Vienna. The aim of the proponents of this school was to purify philosophy by fading out all metaphysical elements and, while making logic the central tool of philosophy, restricting philosophers to the discussion of what can be verified or falsified by certain criteria determined by a restricted understanding of empirical evidence. See **Vienna Circle**.

Logos. Although this Greek term has several meanings, including "word," "speech," and "principle," philosophical discussion of it has generally focused upon it as meaning "reason". It appeared in the pre-Socratic thinkers with this meaning, being later replaced by *nous* ("mind" or "reason"), as we find, for instance, in Plato and Aristotle. Then it emerged again in Stoic philosophy where it is seen both as reason and as speech; hence the Stoic Latin pun, *Gloria hominis ratio et oratio*: "the glory of man is reason and speech." In the great School of Alexandria both the Jewish thinker Philo and many of the Christian Fathers used the concept of the *logos* to express the creative power of God. The prologue to the Fourth Gospel opens with the words: "In the beginning (*en archē*, i.e., archetypally) was the *logos*, and the *logos* was with God and the *logos* was God." John identifies Jesus Christ with the *logos* "made flesh" and pitching his tent among us.

Lohan. One who is regarded as among the personal disciples or associates of the Buddha. This Chinese term goes back to the early forms in which Buddhism entered China. From the 10th c., eighteen have been recognized and have been widely regarded as the guardians of Buddhism.

Loisy, Alfred (1857–1940). French biblical scholar. Writing during the so-called Modernist controversy in the Roman Catholic Church, Loisy, whose writings emphasized personal religious experience, was condemned by Rome. His writings were put on the Index of Prohibited Books in 1903, and eventually he was excommunicated. His biblical work was, generally speaking, in line with the best scholarship of his day.

Loka. In Hinduism, a sphere of a divinity or division of the universe, e.g., (as elsewhere) heaven, earth, and the underworld. The concept of spheres of divine influence goes back to early Vedic times when the gods were considered to be operating collectively rather than individually.

Lokāyata. In Hindu philosophy, a term denoting approximately what in the West has been traditionally called "materialism". It signifies the study of nature independently of any of the views taught by the brahmins. It is not, however, so much a specific philosophical view as a preoccupation with nature such as in the West would be accounted the proper focus of a "naturalist," i.e., anyone engaged in the pursuit of any of

the natural sciences (e.g., physics, chemistry, biology). Indeed learned brahmins might engage in *lokāyata* much as a philosopher or theologian might pursue, say, biological studies or astronomy as an avocation enriching his or her primary calling.

Lollards. The followers of John Wyclif in 14th c. England were so designated. Lollardy was a movement representative of an early stage in the Reformation, but it was also associated with a general social uprising. The term was first used pejoratively in 1382, then officially in 1387. It probably came from the Middle Dutch *lollen* or *lullen* ("to sing, hum;" compare English "lullaby"), although some have argued for a derivation from *lolium* (Latin, "tares"), which the ancients believed to be bad for eyesight.

Longinus. The name traditionally assigned to the Roman soldier who pierced the side of Jesus with his spear. It is sometimes also given to the centurion who at the Cross acknowledged Jesus as the Son of God.

Lord's Prayer. This formula, attributed to Jesus and given in two similar forms (Matthew 6.9–15 and Luke 11.2–4), is regarded by Christians as the model of all prayer. The literary style of the prayer is modeled on the Psalms. The form as set forth in Matthew was used liturgically by Christians as early as the first century.

Loreto. According to the legend of "the Holy House of Loreto," the house that the Virgin Mary lived in at the time of the Annunciation was transported by angels from Nazareth to Tersatz, Dalmatia, in 1291, whence it was likewise miraculously transported to Loreto, near Ancona, Italy, in 1295. Scholars universally deny the historicity of the legend. The word is sometimes spelled in English "Loretto."

Lossky, Nikolai (1870–1965). Russian philosopher. Trained at St. Petersburg, where he was a professor of philosophy until 1921, he later lived in exile in Western Europe and in America for much of his long life. Much influenced by Leibniz and by Bergson, he insisted on the reality of human freedom and perceived all things as moving toward God. He firmly believed in the Absolute, which he interpreted as the living God. Among his writings are *The Intuitive Basis of Knowledge* (1906), *The World as an Organic Whole* (1917), *Freedom of the Will* (1927), and *History of Russian Philosophy* (1951).

Lossky, Vladimir (1903–1958) Russian theologian, son of Nicolai Lossky. After study at St. Petersburg University, he was expelled by the Soviet government in 1922 and pursued his studies at Prague and at Paris, where he became a leading exponent of Eastern Orthodox theology to western scholars. Like many other Russian Orthodox theologians in modern times he remained a layman throughout his life, the later part of which he spent in Paris and in the United States.

Lotu. In the 19th c., Christian converts in the islands of the Pacific used this Tongan word to designate church services and mission teaching in general.

Lotus. The lotus flower, a water lily, is a very important symbol in Buddhism. It signifies spiritual unfolding, development, and growth. It can have other derivative meanings, however, e.g., it can symbolize meditation, enlightenment, or even buddhahood.

Lotus Position. One of the yoga postures, it is a standard position for meditation as practiced by Hindus and Buddhists. It consists of sitting with back erect and legs so crossed that each foot is resting on the thigh of the other leg.

Lotus Sūtra. One of the most important and probably best-known Sanskrit texts in Mahayana Buddhism. It contains teaching attributed to the Buddha presented as a god above all other gods.

In some ways perhaps reminiscent of Aristotle's Unmoved Mover, Buddha does not travel from one place to another in missionary campaigns but sits on a mountain surrounded by vast throngs of bodhisattvas and other subordinate deities. The teaching of the Lotus Sūtra represents a stage intermediate between that of Hīnayāna and Mahāyāna Buddhism. It has some affinities with the Bhagavad-Gītā in Hinduism. It dates principally from the 1st c. CE, although containing elements from various periods. It was known to and is quoted by Nagarjuna.

Lotze, Rudolf Hermann (1817–1881). German philosopher. Educated at Leipzig, he taught at Göttingen and Berlin. According to his teaching, the realms of fact, law, and value are separated only in our minds. The idea of God is essential to Lotze's thought. The human mind is a microcosmic replica of the divine macrocosm. His writings include *Metaphysics* (1841), *Microcosmus*, 3 vols (1856–58), and *System of Philosophy*, 2 vols. (1874 and 1879).

Lou, Tseng-Tsiang (1871–1949). Chinese statesman and Benedictine abbot. The son of a Protestant catechist, he was born at Shanghai and educated there and at Peking, eventually attaining high office in the Chinese government, including two terms as Prime Minister. In 1911 he became a Roman Catholic. After the death of his wife in 1926, he entered the Benedictine Abbey of Saint-André, near Bruges, the following year and in 1946 was appointed Titular Abbot of St-Pierre-de-Gand by Pius XII. Perceiving many parallels between Christianity, on the one hand, and, on the other, Confucianism and Taoism, he saw Christianity as the completion of the Confucian tradition. His *Souvenirs et pensées* (1945) is translated into English under the title, *Ways of Confucius and of Christ* (1948).

Louis IX. (1214–1270). King of France, noted for his embodiment of the medieval ideal of kingly sanctity. He took a prominent part in the Crusades. At home he built the Sainte-Chapelle in Paris, supported the theological work of the Sorbonne, and endowed various religious houses in France.

Lourdes. As a consequence of visions of the Virgin Mary by a young peasant girl, Bernadette Soubirous in the grotto of a rock at Lourdes, in the Hautes-Pyrénées, France, in 1858, a spring appeared at the place and miraculous healings were reported. Pilgrimages ensued, and in 1862 Lourdes was recognized by the Roman Catholic Church. According to Bernadette's testimony, the Virgin Mary had announced herself as "the Immaculate Conception": an allusion to a doctrine which had been controversial in the Middle Ages and down to 1854, when Pius IX, *ex motu proprio*, had declared it to be the official teaching of the Roman Catholic Church. Lourdes has been for long uniquely famous as a place of pilgrimage visited by millions of people. A permanent medical bureau that includes unbelievers on its panel investigates and adjudicates on the authenticity of reported cures.

Lovejoy, Arthur O. (1873–1962). American philosopher. Born in Germany and trained at Berkeley and at Harvard, he taught at Johns Hopkins University from 1910 to 1938. Arguing for a dualistic epistemology, he insisted that there must be a duality between the world and that which we sense when we perceive objects. He was also an historian of ideas and founded the *Journal of the History of Ideas*. His works include *The Revolt Against Dualism* (1930), *The Great Chain of Being* (1936), and *The Reason, the Understanding, and Time* (1961).

Ludi. The Roman games (e.g., racing, fighting, drama) were presented in a religious context, preceded by rituals and processions and dedicated to a deity. They grew in frequency and extravagance as the Roman Empire grew in grandeur and power.

Lugo, John de (1583–1660). Spanish Jesuit. After pursuing the study of law at Salamanca he entered the Jesuit Society in 1603 and taught theology at Valladolid from 1603 till 1621, when he was called to Rome. He was made a cardinal in 1643. In his theological works he showed considerable independence, perhaps especially in his understanding of the nature of the Eucharist. His openness (e.g., his teaching that everyone can find, shining through the defective systems of theology, the eternal light of divine truth) was remarkable in his day.

Lukar, Cyril. See **Cyril Lukar**.

Luke. The author of the Gospel that bears his name and of the Book of Acts, which was apparently designed as a sequel to the Gospel. Both seem to have been intended to persuade the authorities in the Gentile world of the respectability of the Christian Way and to convince them of its international appeal. According to evidence within the New Testament documents (e.g., Colossians 4.11 and 16) he would seem to have been a Gentile and a physician. His style is distinctive in being free of the Hebraisms and Aramaisms that mark the other evangelists' Greek.

Lull, Raymond (*c.* 1233 - *c.* 1315). A native of Majorca, he married and had two children. At the age of 30, having had a vision of the crucified Christ, he resolved to devote himself entirely to the Christian cause, making the conversion of Islam his primary concern. He was an exponent of a type of Christian mysticism that seems to prefigure that of the great Spanish mystical school as exemplified in Teresa of Ávila and John of the Cross. For an excellent presentation of Lull's art of memory, see Frances A. Yates, *The Art of Memory* (1966), Chapter VIII, pp. 173–198.

Lumbini. As the traditional site of the Buddha's birth, one of the four principal places of Buddhist pilgrimage. It is usually described as a park located in Sakyan tribal territory between Kapilavastu and Devadaha. The Emperor Ashoka is known to have made a pilgrimage there in *c.* 249 BCE.

Luther, Martin (1483–1546). German Reformer. Born in humble circumstances and educated at Erfurt University, he entered the Augustinian Order of friars in 1505 and was ordained priest in 1507. At first he seemed to develop along the conventional lines expected of a promising young member of such an order, but at some point, possibly *c.* 1515, he underwent an experience that has sometimes been called the *Turmerlebnis*, which so convinced him of the fundamental importance of Augustine's emphasis on theocentricity, the consequent nothingness of man alongside of God, and the sense of certainty of personal salvation that God grants to individual souls, that he began to manifest his hitherto only interior rejection of the necessity of the Church for salvation. Herein consisted the essential break between Luther and the medieval Church. He did not deny the role of the Church as an instrument of God; what he denied was the widely-held medieval belief that salvation was impossible outside of it. He saw the medieval emphasis on penitential exercises and other "good works" as unhealthy and even useless for one who could see himself as a sinner "justified" (i.e., made righteous) by God himself. On October 31, 1517, he affixed to the door of the Schlosskirche at Wittenberg a set of 95 theses assertive of his position on such matters, with more particular reference to the doctrine of Indulgences as it was being presented by Tetzel in the latter's preaching in Germany. News of the posting of the 95 theses spread like wildfire throughout Germany, being welcomed by many who by this time were in despair at the failure of all attempts to reform the medieval Church from within: attempts that by then had been made time after time for more than a century and had repeatedly failed.

Three of his writings in 1520 openly asserted views unacceptable to the Roman hierarchy. In June of that year Pope Leo X, by a bull, *Exurge Domine*, condemned forty-one of Luther's theses as heretical, to which Luther responded by burning the bull. The Pope then issued another bull, *Decem Romanum Pontificem* in January 1521, excommunicating Luther. His break with Rome was now complete.

Luther's ideas found ready response in the Germany of his day and much throughout other northern lands in Western Europe. Both in ecclesiastical circles and in the minds of the Renaissance humanists of his time the ground had been already prepared for the swift dissemination of his views. He was anything other than a rabble rouser; indeed he was in many ways temperamentally conservative both as a churchman and in his political inclinations. Before the end of the 16th c., Lutheranism had been accepted by two-thirds of the German population. It became the official religion of the Scandinavian lands. It spread eventually to large areas of the United States and Canada. Lutherans have always favored a learned ministry, and much of the best Reformation theology has emerged in the countries most influenced by Lutheran principles. Its weaknesses are well known. It has tended to leave the externals of religion to be dictated and controlled by the State. While encouraging and nurturing learning in the Church it has generally tended to create a gulf between the learned and the unlearned.

Lü Tsung. An important school of Chinese Buddhism founded by Tao Hsüan in the 7th c. CE. It is traditionally much concerned with monastic reform and its teachings emphasize ethics and a life of discipline rather than doctrinal questions.

LXX. An abbreviation used by biblical scholars to designate the Septuagint. See **Septuagint.**

Lyceum. The school founded by Aristotle in Athens *c.* 339 BCE. In accordance with the founder's interests, it emphasized biology and other natural sciences, and its philosophical investigations were conducted in relation to such scientific pursuits and investigations. The Lyceum continued to prosper after Aristotle's death in 322 BCE, but was declining by the end of the 3rd c. BCE. Both Strato of Lampsacus and Lycon of Laodicea served as head of the Lyceum.

M

Macarius of Alexandria. A 4th c. Egyptian hermit who retired to the desert at about the age of forty and apparently lived not far from the much famed hermit Antony. He is not to be confused, as too often he is, with Macarius of Egypt.

Macarius of Egypt (*c*.300–*c*.390). Born in Upper Egypt, he founded a colony of monks in the desert of Scetis (Wadi-el-Natrum), which developed into one of the most famous of Egyptian monastic settlements. Ordained priest *c*.340, he appears to have been influenced by the great Egyptian hermit, Antony. Sometimes called Macarius the Great, he is not to be confused with Macarius of Alexandria, his contemporary.

Macaulay, Zachary (1768–1838). Anglican abolitionist. When only sixteen he went to Jamaica and became manager of an estate. Outraged at the condition of the slaves on the estate, he resolved to work for the abolition of slavery as an institution. His role in the abolition movement is recorded in C. Z. Booth, *Zachary Macaulay* (1934). Among the founders of the University of London, he was also the father of the eminent British historian, Thomas Babington Macaulay.

Maccabees, Books of. These two biblical books are regarded in Catholic tradition as deutero–canonical, the name given to those books whose place in the canon of the Bible has been at some time denied or questioned. Protestants accept them only as part of the Old Testament Apocrypha, and Jews do not accept them as canonical biblical writings. The two books, First and Second Maccabees have a common subject but seem to be otherwise unrelated.

The prologue to I Maccabees gives an account of the rise of the Hellenistic party in Judaea, the profanation of the Temple, and the efforts of Antiochus to suppress Judaism and completely Hellenize the Jews. The book goes on to recount the success of the struggle of the Jews to maintain their identity and to survive. The book was written in Hebrew although it has been preserved only in Greek. (Jerome attests that he actually saw a copy in Hebrew.) It would appear from I Macc. 16.24 that the book is to be dated after 104 BCE, but some scholars have argued for an earlier date such as 135 BCE. The theme is the nature of the opposition between the people of Israel and the Gentile world at large. It is a sophisticated book in the sense that its heroes are not the Jewish martyrs but those who by diplomatic skill make such martyrdom unneeded. Nevertheless, its stance has no place for compromise with the Hellenistic forces that its author sees as not merely corrupting but destroying Judaism.

II Maccabees was written in Greek and although its author, like that of I Maccabees, is unknown, he was in all probability an Alexandrian Jew. The date of II Maccabees is uncertain. It could be as early as 120 BCE or as late as 50 CE; probably nearer the former than the latter date. The literary form of the book is that of an interpretation of historical events. It sees as central to its theme the struggle between the people of God, the Jews, with their devotion to the law of the One True God, and the civilization around them that would absorb and destroy them. The difference between I and II Maccabees is that while the former seems to identify Jewish religion and Jewish patriotism, the latter, being by a diaspora Jew, seems to de-emphasize the patriotic aspect of Judaism and to focus on the religious aspect as what defines a Jew. The term "Judaism" first appears in II Maccabees.

MacDonald, George (1824–1905). Scottish novelist and Congregationalist minister. Trained at Aberdeen University and in London, he found the ministry too restrictive and left it to engage exclusively in writing. His novels and other writings reflect both a vigorous ethical sense and a deep and unusual genre of mystical spirituality. They include *Phantastes* (1858), *David Elginbrod* (1862), *Robert Falconer* (1868), *The Marquis of Lossie* (1877), and many poems and sermons. C. S. Lewis is among those who have drawn attention to his genius. See C. S. Lewis (ed.), *George MacDonald. An Anthology* (1946). For bibliography see J. M. Bulloch, *Aberdeen University Library Bulletin*, v(1925), pp. 679–747.

Macedonia. In antiquity Macedonia, a region to the north of Greece, was regarded by the Greeks as barbarian. In New Testament times it was a province of the Roman Empire and visited by Paul on his first journey, then revisited on his third. He founded churches at Thessalonica and at Philippi.

Machiavelli, Niccolò (1469–1527). Italian political thinker. Born in Florence, he held high office in the Republic, but when his government fell he was imprisoned. Using his time to write, he published *Il Principe* (1513), translated into English as *The Prince*. This classic discusses how to gain political power and keep it. He regards man as totally given over to self-interest and inflamed by selfish desires. The prince, as ruler, will maintain power while, in one way or another, keeping his people, so far as possible, too contented to rebel. When it is not possible he must ruthlessly employ every instrument he has at his disposal and will try to have as many such instruments as possible. He will be honest with his people whenever it is expedient but will not hesitate to be dishonest with them if need be. He will

use the people's religion, whatever it is, as a means of subjugating them. Only by such means, he teaches, can law and order be preserved. His outlook is such as to have spawned the adjective "Machiavellian" to designate an attitude of political ruthlessness all too easily recognizable in the conduct of human affairs.

Mackintosh, Hugh Ross (1870–1936). Scottish Presbyterian theologian. Trained at Edinburgh, he was ordained to the ministry in 1897 and was appointed to a chair at Edinburgh in 1904, where he exercised much influence, especially in his christology, in which he maintained a modified interpretation of kenotic theory. His works include *The Doctrine of the Person of Christ* (1912) and *Types of Modern Theology* (1937).

MacLeod, Norman (1783–1862). Scottish Presbyterian divine. Ordained as a minister of the Kirk in 1806, he became Moderator of the General Assembly in 1836 and Chaplain-in-Ordinary to Queen Victoria in 1841. He was the author of religious works in Gaelic and English.

MacLeod, Norman (1812–72). Scottish Presbyterian divine. Trained at Edinburgh, he was ordained in 1838 and was much admired by Queen Victoria, one of whose chaplains he was from 1857 till his death. He was one of the most respected parish ministers in Scotland in the 19th c., being minister of the historic Barony Church, Glasgow, for many years. He was the son of Norman MacLeod (1783–1862) and the author of several books including his well-known *Reminiscences of a Highland Parish* (1867). For further information see T. Hamilton in the *Dictionary of National Biography* (1893).

Macrina (c. 327–379). Elder sister of Basil the Great and Gregory of Nyssa. She exercised a very strong influence on her brothers and established a flourishing Christian community on the family estate in Pontus. Her brother, Gregory of Nyssa attests her ability as a theologian and has also left a vivid portrait of her life in his *Vita Macrinae junioris.*

Madhi. According to a tradition widely accepted among the Shi'ite Muslims, the twelfth imam in the succession to the caliphate after Muhammad's death, Muhammad Al-Muntazar, who died in 878, "withdrew" or "vanished" into the cave of the great mosque at Samarra up the river from Baghdad, left no issue, and was never seen again. The sect of Shi'ite Muslims who accept this tradition claim that Muhammad prophesied that in the "last days" one of his descendants would return as the Mahdi, the divinely guided one, who will usher in the period of peace and justice before the Last Judgment and the end of the world. They believe that Muhammad Al-Muntazar will come out of his "concealment" and assume the role that they believe was appointed him according to the Prophet's promise.

Madhva (1197-1276). Vedanta philosopher ranking in importance with Shankara and Ramanuja among commentators on Vedanta thought. In contrast to Shankara, who was a monist, Madhva was a pluralist in his interpretation of Vedanta. He identified God with Vishnu.

Madhyamika. Founded by Nagarjuna, this Buddhist school of thought is one of the four principal philosophical schools of Buddhism. Existence that is produced by causes, this school teaches, is empty or vacuous. It has no reality at all. Neither can one be wise till one understands this basic truth, nor can nirvana be reached until everything that brings about such vacuous existence is extinguished.

Madonna. A designation for the Virgin Mary, especially used for pictorial representations. The Italian word means "my Lady."

Magdalenes. In the Middle Ages, prostitutes who felt impelled to abandon their life and express penitence for it sometimes formed themselves into religious communities. These communities were widespread in most countries in Western Europe, many of them following the Augustinian rule, and some such communities continued down to comparatively recent times although are now virtually extinct. The name "Magdalenes" by which they were called alluded to Mary Magdalene, a follower of Christ who stood by the Cross at his crucifixion (Mark 15.40).

Magi. Among the ancient Medes the magi were a priestly tribe who became the official priesthood of western Iran. Throughout the history of western Zoroastrianism they appear on the official state records as priests of that religion. They were learned men who often worked as judges or scribes as well as at their religious duties. In Greek the term *magos* is used in four senses: (1) a member of the priestly caste in Iran as here described; (2) anyone possessing or seeming to possess hidden wisdom or psychic powers; (3) a professional magician; (4) a charlatan. The *magi* in Matthew's account of the birth of Christ are presented as "wise men," astrologers, from "the East," which probably identifies them as belonging to the second of the foregoing categories. Allusions in the Old Testament (e.g., Micah 5.1-3; Psalms 72-10f., 15; Isaiah 49.23) suggest that this aspect of Matthew's account has theological reflection on such Old Testament passages as its basis rather than historical narrative.

Magic. The term, nowadays generally associated with sleight of hand and suggesting claims to perform feats beyond the "laws" of nature, is used in several senses in the history of religions. The Babylonians and Egyptians, for example, both representing high forms of civilization in their time, greatly revered magic, which the literature tends to represent as secret knowledge available to a professional class who understand how to handle the forces of nature. Such professionals were hired not only to cure illnesses, physical and mental, but to provide aphrodisiacs to enhance potency or arouse passion in the object of one's desire. The Bible, while it never affirms that magicians are necessarily fraudulent and indeed seems to recognize some efficacy in magical practices, views it as having nothing like the power of Yahweh and being therefore unnecessary for those who believe in the latter. Express prohibitions of magical practices are to be found in various places in the Old Testament, e.g., Exodus 22.17; Leviticus 19.31; Deuteronomy 18.10.

Magnificat. The name given to the canticle sung at Vespers and attributed to Mary when she heard the angel Gabriel announce that she was to be uniquely favored among women. The words are given in Luke 1.46–55. It is likely that Luke (or the source from which he drew) took the song from a Jewish psalm that had been adapted for Christian use.

Mahabharata. This, the great epic of the Bharatas, which contains 90,000 stanzas, is a Hindu compilation dating from the 2nd c. BCE to about the end of the 1st c. CE. It was probably a martial ballad, handed down by the Brahman caste and exhibiting the religious outlook and moral values of traditional Hindu society. The best known element in it is the Bhagavadgīta, delivered by Krishna to Arjuna, in which Krishna appears as the avatar or incarnation of Vishnu, the supreme god.

Mahavira. The title given to the Indian religious leader Vardhamana whose teachings are followed by the Jains. Jain tradition assigns to him the dates 540–468 BCE. He and the Buddha shared a common heritage and regional origin in northeast India and also many similarities in their outlook and personal histories. Mahavira left home for the wandering life of the Indian ascetic when he was about thirty. He is said to have become fully enlightened and

eventually to have died of voluntary starvation at Pava in Bihar. See **Jains.**

Mahāyāna. Primitive Buddhism was cradled in India and emerged as the result of the teachings of Gautama in the 6th c. BCE. About the 1st c. CE, however, a development within Buddhism began to take place emphasizing the supernatural quality of the Buddha, rejecting or "voiding" the relativistic and pluralistic elements in the teaching of the earlier schools of Buddhist thought, and exalting the bodhisattva ideal. The new school, which came to be called Mahayana ("Great Vehicle"), reinterpreted the traditional Buddhist monastic discipline in such a way as to encourage the monks to engage in missionary enterprise, settling in other lands such as China, Japan, Korea, and Tibet. The name Mahayana was assumed in contrast to Hinayana, meaning "Lower Vehicle", used by the new school of the various earlier schools (some eighteen of them), which the Mahayanists accounted too narrow and rigid. The name Hinayana, being used pejoratively, should not be applied to those Buddhist schools that continue outside of Mahayana Buddhism. For them the term Theravada is to be preferred.

Maimonides, Moses (1135–1204). The foremost among medieval Jewish thinkers, he is sometimes called "the second Moses." Born in Córdoba, he was forced to flee from a fanatical Muslim sect. As a young man he lived in North Africa where he attended a Muslim center of learning at Fes. His two greatest works are *The Guide for the Perplexed*, written in Arabic and translated into Hebrew in the 12th c. and into Latin in the 13th., and *Mishneh Torah*, a codification of rabbinical law and ritual. The purpose of the *Guide* was to show that religion and philosophy (in modern terms religion and science) are not incompatible. He took Aristotle (as Thomas Aquinas was to do in the following century) as the exponent *par excellence* of philosophy (science). His last years were spent in Egypt where he was a court physician to the sultan.

Maine de Biran (1766–1824). French philosopher. Born at Bergerac, he began by following the sensationist philosophy of Condillac but developed a view of his own. Positing the self as an active power that is developed by experience, he arrived at an explanation of the distinction we make between sensation and perception, which he found to yield, on the one hand, the notion of causality, and, on the other, that of freedom of choice. His thought has some affinities with that of Kant but very much in the French tradition of *humanisme spirituel*.

Maitreya. (In Pali, *Metteyya*, "the kind one" or "the friendly one.") According to Buddhist tradition, a Buddha appears periodically to revive knowledge among human beings such as can make available to them the path of enlightenment. Maitreya is the next such Buddha to appear.

Malabar Christians. A group of Christians living in Kerala in Southwest India and claiming that they were founded by the apostle Thomas who, according to their claim, visited India and was martyred near Madras. Historically conceivable though their claim is, most historians reject it as lacking evidence and point to a much later date (possibly the 4th c.) for the first impact of Christianity on India. India had considerable trade with East Syria and it is likely that the first Christians in India came thence. The Malabar Christians have had a very complex history, with schisms and internal dissensions. The Syrian Orthodox Church in India is now, however, active in missionary work in many parts of Asia and also in Africa. It has its own Catholicos. Others who submitted to Rome in 1662 still constitute the largest body of Malabar Christians.

Malebranche, Nicolas (1638–1715). French philosopher. Born in Paris, he entered the Congregation of the Oratory in 1660. In some ways in the tradition of both Augustine and Descartes, he developed a very original system of philosophy, denying that matter could ever have any action upon mind. He held that sensation is the result of a special creative act in the mental order to correspond with the state of affairs in the empirical world. To this system the name "Occasionalism" was given. He taught that God is the immediate cause of all human knowledge and that our first and simplest idea is that of the infinite. God, he claimed, always uses the simplest possible way to achieve his purposes. His most important works are *Recherche de la Vérité* (1674) and *Traité de la nature et de la grâce* (1680). See also **Occasionalism**.

Maltese Cross. The cross, black with eight points on a white ground, used by the Knights of Malta.

Mammon. The Greek word *mamōnas* translates the Aramaic *mamôna'*. Although it does not occur in the Old Testament, it does appear often in the Talmud, the targums, and elsewhere in Jewish literature, and in two places in the Gospels (Matthew 6.24 and Luke 16.9, 11, 13). It is often used as a term personifying the worship of what would nowadays be called "worldly possessions," i.e. all forms of property. The person who in today's society focuses all his or her attention on possessions such as real estate, stocks, and bonds, may be said to worship Mammon and such an attitude is, according to the teaching of the Sermon on the Mount, incompatible with the development of the spiritual life. Ownership of wealth is not in itself disapproved; what is condemned is the kind of attachment to possessions that becomes a fatal obstacle to the life of the spirit: one cannot "serve God and Mammon."

Mana. In primitive forms of religion, mana is a field of spiritual energy. Like electricity in the physical world, it can be harnessed for the welfare of humankind, yet it is dangerous to those who do not know how to handle it. In Melanesia success in warfare, in fertility, and other areas, gives one mana. In Polynesia it seems to be regarded as springing from a special kinship with the gods and with famous ancestors. Objects or physical areas may be changed with mana.

Mandaeans. A Gnostic sect originating as a small community near the Jordan in the 1st or 2nd c. Their teachings included characteristically Gnostic motifs such as the concept of the soul as imprisoned in a body from which it must be redeemed. Some scholars have argued that the sect has an ancestry that is connected with John the Baptist, who is indeed prominent in Mandaean writing.

Maṇḍala. In Hinduism, the maṇḍala is a circle separating a particular area from that which surrounds it. The area constituting the maṇḍala is ritually consecrated. The circle setting it apart protects from evil. Maṇḍalas are often very complex in design but fundamentally they consist of a circle enclosing a square divided into four triangles. A deity is in one way or another represented in each of the triangles. The Hindu temple itself is a maṇḍala in stone, but maṇḍalas may be painted on paper, wood, or other material. The most famous stone maṇḍala is the one in Borobudur, Java, which the worshipper circumambulates in sunwise direction, ascending the various terraces, which represent ascending psychic levels. Quaternity is an essential feature of the maṇḍala. Hindus and others see the concept of the maṇḍala in other religions, e.g., in some forms of the rose window in Christian architecture. For Carl Jung's special interest in the concept of the maṇḍala, see **Jung, Carl Gustav.**

Mani (216–277 CE). A religious teacher and prophet educated in a Gnostic sect in Babylonia. Having had a vision at the age of twelve, he later claimed to have brought about the fulfillment of Zoroastrian, Buddhist, and Christian beliefs. He received recognition by the Iranian king Shabur, and his teaching was accepted widely in the Iranian empire, but a later ruler imprisoned and executed him. His teaching had spread to the Mediterranean world. Augustine was a follower of his teaching for some nine years before his conversion to the Christian Way. Manichaeism is fundamentally a mind-matter dualism. In practice it exalts all forms of asceticism and advocates celibacy, requiring it of all followers other than mere adherents.

Maniple. A strip, usually of silk, worn over the left wrist by the ministers at Mass and of the color of the season. It was originally a hand towel. In Roman Catholic custom its use is now optional.

Manna. The food that the Israelites are reported as having eaten during their stay in the desert (Exodus 16.12–35) seems likely to have been a resinous substance exuded by certain desert shrubs and trees such as one now classified as *tamarix mannifera*. In Hebrew literature it acquired a legendary significance, no doubt because the gratitude that the Israelites had felt had transmogrified it in retrospect into a heavenly food. According to John (John 6.30–34 and 49–51), Jesus is asked whether he is going to give his followers manna such as the Israelites had received in the desert and he tells them that that was not the authentic "bread of life" that he is to provide, which is represented as the Eucharist.

Mannheim, Karl (1893–1947). Sociologist. Born in Budapest, he taught at Heidelberg and London. Generally taken to belong, in one way or another, to the Neo-Kantian school of philosophy, he distinguished between "substantial rationality" and "functional rationality." His writings include *Man and Society in an Age of Reconstruction* (1935) and *Diagnosis of Our Time* (1943).

Manning, Henry Edward (1808–1892). Educated at Harrow and at Balliol College, Oxford, he was elected to a fellowship at Merton College, Oxford, in 1832. He married, became Archdeacon of Chichester, and some years later was widowed. Gradually he veered to the Tractarian side in English Church life and in 1851 was received into the Roman Catholic Church. At the First Vatican Council he was one of the most vigorous proponents of the doctrine of papal infallibility. In 1865 he became Archbishop of Westminster and was created a cardinal ten years later.

Mantra. In Hindu practice, a formula of utterances believed to possess magical or divine power. It may consist of a syllable or a group of words or a single word. The practice of reciting mantras goes back to the Rig Veda in which the gods were invoked to produce a wide variety of beneficial effects. In post-Vedic times the mantras tended to be seen as effective for their psychological, subjective power rather than for any meaning with which the utterances might be invested. Mantras may also be used for evil purposes, e.g., to kill or to maim.

Māra. The word, from a Sanskrit root, means "death", and in Buddhism Māra is portrayed as the Destroyer, the Evil One who through negativity brings destruction upon any good enterprise. In a story that has some affinity with the story of the Temptation of Christ, Māra attempted to dissuade the Buddha from undertaking his supremely noble work by showing him a vision of immense temporal power.

Maranatha. This Aramaic phrase used in the New Testament (I Corinthians 16.22) is no doubt a liturgical one similar to *hosanna* and *alleluia*. It may be rendered "Come, our Lord," in allusion to the coming of Christ both in the Eucharist and in the Parousia.

Marburg Colloquy. The meeting convoked by Philip of Hesse with the object of achieving unity between the Swiss and the Saxon Reformers, which was held on October 1–3, 1529, at the castle at Marburg-on-the-Lahn. Zwingli, Oecolampadius, and Bucer were present to represent the Swiss, while Luther and Melanchthon represented the Saxons. Fourteen of the fifteen articles proposed were agreed upon by both sides, but the Swiss refused to accept the Lutheran doctrine of consubstantiation in the other article. The colloquy therefore failed in its purpose. Luther, however, later revised the articles and in the revised form they became the Articles of Schwabach, which led to the Augsburg Confession of 1530. See **Augsburg Confession.**

Marcel, Gabriel (1889–1973). French philosopher. Born in Paris and trained at the Sorbonne, he engaged in literary and dramatic criticism while developing his philosophy. He contrasts two ways in which one may look at life: as a problem and as a mystery. He makes a similar distinction, developed in his *Being and Having* (1935), between two kinds of having: on the one hand simply possessing, owning, and on the other, participating. If one thinks in terms of life as mystery and of having as participating, one can begin to see being as unfolding itself: a religious concept. Through such an enriched attitude to life man, as pilgrim, can find his way home: a concept developed in his *Homo viator* (1944). His Gifford Lectures at the University of Aberdeen, *The Mystery of Being*, 2 vols. (1950–51) constitute one of his major works.

Marcion (*c.*85–*c.*160). Born in Sinope, Pontus, he is, although accounted notably heretical, one of the most interesting figures in the early history of the Christian Church. A rich shipowner, he settled in Rome and, finding his views rejected by the ecclesiastical authorities, he began organizing his followers as an association intended to rival the Church. In 144 he was formally excommunicated, and thereafter he organized, with remarkable success, communities of his followers throughout almost the entire Empire, e.g., at Corinth, at Lyons, at Antioch, and at Edessa. Bitterly opposed everywhere by representatives of the Church, they persisted, and although by the end of the 3rd c. they declined as an organized society, their influence continued for long afterwards.

Marcion, who frequently undertook visits to his followers thus scattered in far-off places, somewhat in the manner of Paul whom he admired above all other apostles, has been often linked with Gnosticism. True, his strong emphasis on the opposition of spirit and flesh reflects some aspects of Gnosticism, but Gnosticism was an extremely variegated movement and it would be misleading so to label Marcion.

The main theme in Marcion's teaching is that the Christian Gospel, being nothing if not a gospel of Love, is diametrically opposed to all legalism. This theme, which he expounds in his *Antitheses*, seemed to him to entail the rejection of the entire Old Testament, which he (very mistakenly of course) held to be about a 'God of Law' who is fundamentally incompatible with the God of the Gospels and of the apostolic kerygma. Marcion identified the God of the Old Testament with the Demiurge. Only Paul, among all the apostles, had properly understood the opposition between Gospel and Law. Man, Marcion taught, was the creation of the Demiurge, who placed humankind under the law, which they could not keep and so incurred the curse of the Demiurge. The God of Love, taking pity on humanity, sent his Son who suddenly appeared, according to Marcion, preaching in the synagogues. (Marcion's christology was docetic.) The Demiurge, out of ignorance and spite, caused Christ to be crucified. The risen Christ, however, being able to show that he had indeed fulfilled the Law, triumphed over the Demiurge. Marcion, accounting himself in the succession of Paul, who alone among the apostles had understood the situation, took up the challenge that he thought necessary for the radical reform of the teaching of the Christian Church. His reform entailed a relentless struggle to overcome the flesh. Since the flesh is essentially evil, in his view, sexual intercourse, having the procreation of children as its natural outcome, is inherently sinful, as is every form of sexual expression. He taught that marriage must be renounced, and men and women must seek to overcome their sexual urges totally and live in complete continence. Predictably, he did not believe in the resurrection of the body. The body eventually dies but the soul survives, liberated from its carnal enemy.

Marcion's writings have all been lost. They can be to some extent reconstructed from the writings of Tertullian and others, but anyone attempting such an undertaking must be wary at every point, since such was the hostility of his opponents that almost all testimony concerning him is likely to have been prejudiced against him to an extent sufficient to preclude fair reporting.

Marcus Aurelius (121–180). Roman emperor. Even as a boy he had been introduced to Stoicism, reflection on which affected his outlook and the conduct of his entire life thereafter. His rule was marked by thoughtfulness, patience, and serenity: all Stoic virtues. A firm upholder of the Roman State religion, he looked unfavorably on Christianity, but he generously supported the work of the principal philosophical schools at Athens. His widely-read work, *The Meditations of Marcus Aurelius*, written in moments set aside by him during his busy life, present a most attractive picture of life lived according to Stoic principles, which he sees as life lived in accordance with nature illumined by reason. Reason in man springs from the divine reason, which informs man's conscience and guides him to lead a responsible, ethical life.

Mardi Gras. A festival held on Shrove Tuesday in French-speaking and some other regions. Literally meaning "fat Tuesday", it is so called from the fat ox that is led in procession in the streets. It may be considered the last opportunity for merrymaking and jollification before Lent, which begins the following day, Ash Wednesday. See **Shrove Tuesday.**

Marduk. Mentioned only once by name in the Bible (Jeremiah 50.2), Marduk was the god of Babylon. Because Babylon became the center of the great Mesopotamian culture, its god acquired the headship of the Babylonian pantheon.

Maredsous, Abbey of. A Benedictine house founded in 1872, noted for its scholarship. It has published the *Revue Bénédictine* for more than a century.

Marga. A Sanskrit term meaning "the path." (The Pali equivalent is *Magga.*) The term is used in Hinduism but more especially in Buddhism to designate the way of life that the devotee ought to follow, pre-eminently the Noble Eightfold Path (*atthangika magga*) that represents the Buddhist ideal. See **Four Noble Truths and the Noble Eightfold Path.**

Margaret Mary Alacoque (1647–1690). French Visitandine nun. Having entered the convent at Paray-le-Monial in 1671, she claimed to have received visions of the Sacred Heart of Jesus, beginning on December 1673 and the final one in 1675. Her claims were at first treated by her superiors as hallucinations, but gradually were looked upon with sympathy, and eventually they were officially recognized some seventy-five years after her death. Devotion to the Sacred Heart of Jesus had been known in the Middle Ages and fostered by the Carthusians, but it was limited to a few mystics. Through the influence of Margaret Mary it was popularized, despite considerable reluctance and caution on the part of the Roman Catholic hierarchy. Behind the devotion lies the concept that at the heart of the universe lies the love of God eternally outpouring to his creation. See **Sacred Heart.** Despite the not always felicitous iconography associated with the devotion, it expresses a profoundly important Christian theological concept.

Margaret of Scotland (c.1045–1093). The granddaughter of the English King Edmund Ironside, she with her mother and sister sought refuge, after the battle of Hastings in 1067, at the court of the Scottish King Malcolm III, whom she married in 1070. Of a deeply religious temper she found the ways of the Celtic Church strange to her, accustomed as she was by her upbringing to Roman usage. (The crucifix, for example, had been unknown, although Celtic crosses abounded, and the date of Easter did not follow Roman reckoning.) Margaret caused synods to be held to regulate ecclesiastical usages and to encourage devotion in the spirit of which she had been accustomed in her youth. Of the many monuments to her reforming piety, none is more beautiful than the tiny chapel dedicated to her and dating from *c.* 1090, on the great Edinburgh Castle Rock of which it is the oldest surviving structure. Her benefactions include the Church of the Holy Trinity at Dunfermline. On the chapel in Edinburgh Castle, see W. M. Bryce, "Saint Margaret of Scotland and her Chapel in the Castle of Edinburgh" in *The Book of the Old Edinburgh Club*, v (Edinburgh, 1912), pp. 1–66. She is regarded by many as the patroness of Scotland, along with its recognized patron, Saint Andrew.

Maria Laach. Benedictine abbey near Coblenz, Germany, founded in 1093 and celebrated for its work in liturgical studies and its encouragement of good liturgical practice. Its Romanesque church with dome and five towers was completed in 1156.

Maritain, Jacques (1882–1973). French philosopher. Born in Paris and trained at the Sorbonne, he was converted to Roman Catholicism in 1906. From 1914 he taught at the *Institut Catholique* in Paris. He served as French Ambassador to the Holy See from 1948 to 1956. A Neo-Thomist, he sought to solve contemporary problems in Neo-Thomist terms. One of his earliest and best-known works, *Art and Scholasticism* (1920) reflects both his acceptance of Thomistic stances and his interest in aesthetics. He was a prolific writer whose works include *The Degrees of Knowledge* (1932), which some account his best work, *The Dream of Descartes* (1932), *Man and the State* (1951), *The Responsibility of the Artist*, (1960) and *Moral Philosophy* (1960). He was Professor of Philosophy at Princeton from 1948 to 1956.

Marketplace. In biblical times, both Old Testament and New Testament, the marketplace had a vital role, combining several functions. In early Greek times the *agora* had been simply the assembly of the people; later it was the name given to the large open space that became the center of commerical life and of much else besides, such as philosophical debate. In the Old Testament, however, the marketplace was an open area, no doubt usually small and congested, within the city walls, which served as a public place for any and every purpose. The marketplace in Palestine in the time of Jesus had probably preserved much of that traditional character.

Maronites. A Christian community mainly associated with Lebanon, but found also in Syria, Alexandria, and elsewhere, including the United States. Syrian in origin they claim to have been founded by disciples of Maro, a friend of Chrysostom, in the early 5th c., although historians find no evidence for their existence earlier than the 7th c. They have been united with Rome since late in the 12th c. and retain their own Antiochene liturgy in Syriac, with some Latin modifications.

Marprelate Tracts, The. A series of brilliant satirical tracts written under the pseudonym "Martin Marprelate," attacking Episcopacy. Their tone, however, was so fiercely scurrilous that they tended to injure rather than promote the interests of the Puritan party that they represented.

Marriage. Because marriage in ancient Israel was regarded as a private contract rather than a public concern or religious matter, Hebrew law had comparatively little to say about it, and indeed there was no single word signifying it. As in many if not all societies in the ancient world, marriages were in one way or another arranged by the families, not entered into by private agreement between the bride and groom. We have almost no information, for example, on the nature of the marriage ceremony itself. When the financial arrangements had been made between the families, the wife was introduced to the husband's family and much festivity attended the event, but we do not know even the permitted age for marriage, although as in most such societies the girl would probably be married soon after puberty. Polygamy and concubinage were encouraged at certain periods of Hebrew history in the interest of maximizing the family size. The ideal of monogamy was extolled in later Hebrew literature and is obviously expected in the New Testament of Christians. For example (Titus 1.6), a bishop is to be a man who has not been married more than once. Jesus has little specific teaching on marriage except concerning its indissolubility and its divinely instituted character. See also **Divorce and Matrimony, Holy.**

Marrow of Modern Divinity, The. A book, strongly Calvinistic, written in 1645 and reprinted in 1719, when it was officially condemned the following year by the General Assembly of the Scottish Kirk, being accounted Antinomian. (See **Antinomianism.**) It created a lengthy controversy in the Kirk.

Marsilius of Padua. (*c.*1275–1342). Italian political thinker. Born in Italy, where he was educated (probably at Padua), he eventually became, in 1311, Rector of the University of Paris. Along with John of Jandun he wrote the celebrated *Defensor Pacis* (1324), which held that the empire has a higher authority than the Papacy. Marsilus recognized the Church as having a higher goal, but the State has the duty and therefore ought to have the right to govern human society so as to preserve the law and order without which no civilization can function. The ecclesiastical authorities ought to restrict their interests to the spiritual concerns that are their proper sphere of activity, including preaching and the administration of the sacraments. The State should derive its power from the people, and the Pope should be elected by the people (i.e., by all Christians) and ought to be subject in the last resort to elected general councils of the Church. See **Conciliarism.**

Martineau, James (1805–1900). English Unitarian thinker. Born in Norwich, he received his training at Manchester and held pastoral charges in Dublin and Liverpool, later returning to an academic career in Manchester, then in London. His writings include *A Study of Spinoza* (1882), *A Study of Religion*, 2 vols. (1888), and *The Seat of Authority in Religion* (1890). The last is perhaps the most interesting of his works, treating as it does an important subject from his specific viewpoint.

Martin of Tours. A 4th-c. Bishop of Tours and a patron saint of France. Born into a pagan family, he was attracted to Christianity early in life. Serving in the army, he met a beggar at Amiens whose plight moved him to give the wretch half of his cloak. He then received a vision of Christ who enjoined him to be baptized and to devote himself to the religious life. After becoming Bishop of Tours *c.* 372, he encouraged the development of monasticism in Gaul.

Martyr. The term, from the Greek *martys*, means literally "witness" and was originally used of the apostles. It was gradually restricted to designate those who, during the persecutions, remained faithful through torture and other sufferings. Finally it came to be restricted to those who suffered death for the Christian faith. Since *c.* 200, the anniversary of the martyr's death was regarded as his "birthday in heaven" and was liturgically celebrated accordingly as his or her feast day. Martyrs take liturgical precedence over all other saints. The liturgical color for the feast of a martyr is red. Traditionally, every consecrated altar had to contain relics of a martyr, but in Roman Catholic usage this practice was abandoned at the Second Vatican Council.

Marx, Karl (1818–1883). German thinker. Born in Trèves, in Rhenish Prussia, he came of a Jewish family that had left the Jewish faith and become formally Lutheran. He studied at Bonn, Berlin, and Jena. His doctorate from Jena was on Epicurus. In 1844 he began his long association with Friedrich Engels. In 1847 he wrote his now famous *Communist Manifesto*. In the 1848 revolution he went to France but soon returned to Cologne, rejoining Engels there and co-editing a paper with strong revolutionary policies. Arrested for treason he was acquitted but expelled from Prussia in 1849. Eventually he settled in London, remaining there till his death. It was there, in the British Museum that he did much of his work, including *Das Kapital*. He was a prolific writer. He did not assemble his work, however, into a system such as nowadays goes under the head of Marxism. He never used the phrase "dialectical materialism," for example (Engels coined it), but he did say that the way to do philosophy is to stand Hegel on his head. The main theme of *Das Kapital* is that the huge capital acquired by owners of industry depended on the exploitation of the workers. He did not develop a materialist philosophy. That too was the work of Engels. What has popularly come to be called Marxism is not of course entirely without roots in Marx, but it has developed into a sort of socialist religion nourished by the work of Marx, Engels, Lenin, and others. Under the umbrella of this "Marxism" have sheltered a variety of views, economic, political, and religious. With the recognition of the ambiguities it has contained, the term has become increasingly unfashionable.

Mary, The Virgin. As the mother of Christ, she has, in Catholic tradition, a unique role among creatures and is accorded a pre-eminent place of honor among angels and saints. In accordance with the biblical record she is acclaimed as both virgin and mother. (See, however, **Virgin Birth.**) That she was *aeiparthenos* (*i.e.*, that she remained *for ever* a virgin) was held by some in the early Church but contested by others. From the 5th c., however, it was generally accepted as orthodox Christian teaching. In 431 the Council of Ephesus proclaimed her *theotokos* (literally, "the God-bearer"), a title that had been accorded to her by Christians in the Alexandrian tradition from the 3rd c. and had been widespread in the 4th c. The popular Latin translation *mater Dei*, used for example in the *Ave Maria* is infelicitous, since according to the doctrine of the Virgin Birth Christ had no human father and therefore Mary was not a mother in the biological sense of "female parent"; otherwise it would have been right to call Mary's mother the grandmother of God and there has been indeed a popular devotion that did precisely that, although without ecclesiastical authority.

During the Middle Ages, despite the insistence at the important Council of Chalcedon in 451 that Jesus Christ was both fully human and fully divine, the popular tendency grew of emphasizing his divinity and attenuating his humanity till he no longer seemed to fit the role of Mediator that had been historically assigned to him as the world's Redeemer. Mary therefore became more and more set in that role, as Mediatrix between human sinners and her divine Son. In the 16th c., the Protestant Reformers moved so much in the other di-

rection that Mary was almost ignored by Protestants and devotion to her actively discouraged when not altogether forbidden. In 1950, Pius XII declared her to have been corporeally assumed into heaven: a doctrine at variance with both Eastern Orthodox and Anglican tradition. See also **Immaculate Conception.**

Mary, Gospel of. An apocryphal Gospel, Gnostic in character, of which two pages of the original Greek text survive (part of the Oxyrhynchus Papyri), now in the John Rylands Library, Manchester, England. The text describes a vision of seven stages of spiritual advancement corresponding to the seven planetary spheres. See **Oxyrhynchus Papyri.**

Mary of the Incarnation. See **Guyard, Marie.**

Mass. The central liturgical act of the Christian Church, also known as the Eucharist. The term "mass" has been used in the West in this sense since at least the 4th c. What is called High Mass (*missa solemnis*) is the traditional norm although, in the West, by no means the most usual form of the mass. By "High" Mass is meant a sung mass at which the celebrant is assisted at the altar by deacon and subdeacon, with lights, incense, Gospel procession, and other ceremonies. Even apart from its profound religious significance for Christians in the Catholic tradition, it is one of the great art forms of Europe. Low Mass is a mass said by a priest assisted by a server, often a boy, with a minimum of ceremonial observances, and only two lights on the altar. A mass without deacon and subdeacon but with music was formerly called a *missa cantata*, but the term is now obsolete. (See **Missa Cantata.**) In the Eastern Orthodox Churches the term "Liturgy" is used to designate the eucharistic service.

Massanetta Springs. Christian conference center in the Shenandoah Valley,

Virginia. The site was used for an annual camp meeting by the Methodist Church for many years from 1816 onwards. After various vicissitudes it was opened on July 18, 1922, under Presbyterian auspices, as a conference center. By 1945 many conferences, including those held by Lutherans, Baptists, and Salvationists, were being held annually. Conferences on Evangelism, Bible Study, and other Christian concerns are held annually from March through October with national and international panels of speakers. It is owned and partially supported by the Synod of the Virginias, Presbyterian Church, USA.

Massoretes. From about the 6th to the 10th c. CE, Jewish grammarians worked on the text of the Hebrew Scriptures in an attempt to obtain a text free from accretions and adulterations. To this end they provided marginal notes with instructions for the copyists and some commentary on the text to guide students. This apparatus came to be printed at the end of rabbinic Bibles. One of the best known and felicitous contributions of the Massoretes was their provision of "pointing" to guide the reader in the pronunciation of Hebrew. The biblical text as so developed by the Massoretes is known among scholars as the Massoretic text.

Mather Family, The. The Mathers were an exceptionally influential family of Congregational ministers who flourished for several generations in New England in the 17th and 18th centuries. They were: (1) Richard Mather (1596–1669), who came from England to Boston in 1635; (2) his son Increase Mather (1639–1723), who was minister of the North Church, Boston, from 1662 till his death and was acting President of Harvard College in 1681–1682; and the latter's son Cotton Mather (1663–1728), who assisted at his father's church till the latter's death, finally succeeding him there, and later actively helping in the establishment of Yale. He was elected to the Royal Society of London in 1713.

Matres. The "divine Mothers" in ancient Celtic cultures, functioning as fertility goddesses and usually accompanied by fertility symbols such as children, fruit, loaves, and sometimes, in Gaul, birds, dogs, trees. In Britain and Gaul they are often represented in groups of three. Maternal and other female deities and symbols played a prominent part in both Celtic and Scandinavian cultures. See **Fylgia**, **Valkyries**, and **Vanir**.

Matrimony, Holy. In Christian tradition and practice, Holy Matrimony differs fundamentally from marriage contracts as conceived in secular usage and also from Jewish and other religious forms of marriage. It presupposes the equality of the partners to the marriage and clearly asserts that the marriage is dissoluble only by the death of one of the partners. Because of the unique character of the undertaking by both parties and the duties imposed upon each of them, it has been regarded by Catholic theologians from the 13th c. at least, if not much earlier, as a sacrament in which a special grace is conferred to enable the parties to keep the vows that they each solemnly make before they are pronounced man and wife. Divorce has been tolerated though deplored in the Eastern Orthodox Church since early times, and in the Anglican tradition it is likewise deplored although exceptions, within limits, are reluctantly made. (E.g., multiple divorces would be almost universally not tolerated in this tradition and only for grave reason should a priest consent to the remarriage of a person divorced even once.) The Roman Catholic Church does not recognize divorce as such but does recognize circumstances in which a marriage may be declared null, leaving both parties free to marry again. Among other (e.g., Protestant) Churches rules and attitudes vary, but no Christian body fails to recognize the indissolubility of marriage as at least the ideal. See **Marriage** and **Divorce**.

Matthew of Aquasparta (*c.* 1240–1302). Franciscan philosopher and cardinal. Italian-born, he followed Bonaventure's thought, taught in Paris, Bologna, and Rome, and was named cardinal in 1287. He sought to combine Aristotelian and Augustinian concepts. The soul, he taught, needs divine illumination in order to have knowledge; nevertheless, the work of attaining knowledge is accomplished by the active intellect.

Matthias. Because of the apostasy of Judas, the number of the original company of the disciples was reduced from twelve to eleven. According to Acts 1.15–26, they decided to elect by the drawing of lots another to fill the missing place among them. The lot fell to Matthias. Nothing is known for certain about him, although it is to be presumed that throughout the ministry of Jesus he had been for long associated with the Master.

Maundy Thursday. The name traditionally given in English to the Thursday of Holy Week on which is commemorated the washing of the disciples' feet by Jesus as his lesson to them in humility. The name comes from the first antiphon used in the ceremony: *Mandatum novum* ("A new commandment," from John 13.34). At the Mass on Holy Thursday the bells are all rung continuously through the *Gloria in Excelsis*: the last time they will be heard till the Paschal Vigil, nowadays observed on the evening of Holy Saturday (Easter Eve). Hosts in the Tabernacle are removed to a separate place and the tabernacle door thrown open. Hosts needed for the Good Friday Mass of the Presanctified are carried in solemn procession after the Maundy Thursday Mass to the Altar of Repose. The principal altar is stripped bare and the church is left looking austerely deserted throughout Good Friday. Even the holy water stoups are emptied as part of this deeply impressive symbolism.

Maurice, Frederick Denison (1805–1872). Anglican divine. The son of a Unitarian minister, he was trained at Cambridge with a view to a career in law, then at Exeter College, Oxford. Ordained priest in 1834, he held various curacies and chaplaincies while writing books that included, at this early period, his *The Kingdom of Christ* (1838): perhaps the most influential of his many writings. In 1840 he was elected to a chair of English literature in London and then, in 1846, to a theological chair there. About this time he became active in what was then called Christian Socialism, in which Charles Kingsley and others were involved. Throughout his life he vigorously defended the philosophical examination of theologies, which made him suspect in many quarters in the Church of England of his day. In 1866 he became Knightsbridge Professor of Moral Philosophy at Cambridge.

Maurists. Benedictines of the Congregation of St.-Maur, founded in 1621, who later in that century devoted themselves almost entirely to literary and historical studies, eventually attaining great fame for their scholarship, notably in patristics. They were suppressed at the French Revolution.

Maximus of Alexandria (4th c.). Consecrated Bishop of Constantinople in 380, he failed to secure the recognition of the Emperor Theodosius and the following year the Council of Constantinople disowned him. He claimed to combine Cynicism with Christianity and substituted Christ for Hercules as the ideal man. He may be called a Christian Cynic. Like all who followed Cynic teaching and expressed themselves in the Cynics' fashion, he evoked hostility in conventional circles. See **Cynicism.**

Max Müller, Friedrich (1823–1900). Orientalist and historian of religion. Born at Dessau and trained at Leipzig, he came, after some time in Paris, to England in 1846, settling in Oxford where in 1858 he became a Fellow of All Souls College and from 1868 till his death professor of comparative philology. He was immensely learned and much honored by British and other governments. In 1875 he undertook an enormous work, *The Sacred Books of the East*, a series of translations of the classics of oriental religions, which ran into more than fifty volumes, more than thirty of which were devoted to the religions of India. He also wrote much on the history and philosophy of religion, including his Gifford Lectures, *Natural Religion* (1889), which were of great importance in his day. Although his methods are now largely outmoded, his work was immensely influential among scholars of his time and is still of great significance in the history of oriental studies in the West.

Māyā. The Sanskrit term means "illusion" and originally it was conceived in Hindu thought to be the magical power of creating illusion, but in Advaita Vedanta it came to refer to the illusoriness of the empirical world: a highly developed concept that has a counterpart in Plato's thought. The world is not a mere hallucination; it is, rather, reality seen in a distorted fashion so as to hide the divine unity behind all phenomena.

Mazarin, Jules (1602–1661). French statesman and cardinal. Born in Piscina in the Abruzzi, he was educated by the Jesuits and graduated in law at Rome. Urban VIII, impressed by his gifts in diplomacy, entrusted various delicate missions to him. In 1639 he became a naturalized French citizen and entered the service of Louis XIII the following year. Created cardinal in 1641 (although he was never ordained priest) he succeeded Richelieu the following year as Prime Minister of France, in which capacity he virtually ruled France for the rest of his life. Because his very valuable library (now in the Bibliothèque Nationale) contained a fine copy of the Gutenberg Bible, the attention of ex-

perts was drawn to it there, and it is sometimes called the Mazarin Bible.

Mazzoth, The Feast of. A feast commemorating the deliverance of Israel from Egyptian bondage. "Mazzoth" is from a Hebrew word meaning "unleavened cakes" (Greek *azyma*). During a week, beginning with the day of Passover, only unleavened bread was eaten. The feast is mentioned in the New Testament in connection with the narratives of the Passion of Christ.

McCosh, James (1811–1894). Scottish philosopher. Born in Ayrshire, he was trained at Glasgow and Edinburgh for the ministry of the Scottish Kirk and was appointed in 1852 to a chair of philosophy at Belfast. In 1868 he went to Princeton as professor of philosophy and was president till 1888, continuing his teaching till his death. He interpreted Darwin's concept of biological evolution in a deeply religious way, seeing the struggle for survival as God's providential way of guiding creation to its goal. In short, for the chance variations that Darwin had detected in the evolutionary process McCosh saw the hand of a creative divine providence. In his general philosophical outlook McCosh followed his compatriot Thomas Reid, founder of the Scottish school of philosophy. His writings include *The Method of the Divine Government* (1850), *The Supernatural in Relation to the Natural* (1862), *Christianity and Positivism* (1871), and *First and Fundamental Truths* (1889).

McKeon, Richard Peter (1900–1985). American philosopher. Born at Union Hill, New Jersey, and trained at the University of Paris, the École des Hautes Études, and Columbia University, he eventually became professor of Greek and Philosophy at the University of Chicago. His writings include, besides texts and other works on Aristotle and the medieval philosophers, *Freedom and History* (1952) and *Thought, Action, and Passion* (1954). He held a cyclic view of the history of philosophy. First is a stage in which systems of metaphysical speculation proliferate. Philosophers then must find a means of preferring one over the other, resulting in a period of epistemological inquiry. This in turn demands criteria for preferring one epistemology over another, which drives philosophers to a period of study of the philosophy of language. As this too exhausts itself, philosophers turn once again to the basic metaphysical and ontological questions and the cycle begins all over again.

McTaggart, John Ellis (1866–1925). British philosopher. Born in London, he was trained at Cambridge where he became in 1891 a Fellow of Trinity. Enthusiastically Hegelian in his philosophical outlook, he developed original interpretations of Hegel, which he expounds in his *Studies in the Hegelian Dialectic* (1896), *A Commentary on Hegel's Logic* (1910) and especially in *The Nature of Existence*, 2 vols. (1921 and 1927).

Mead, George Herbert (1863–1931). American philosopher. Born in Massachusetts, he was trained at Oberlin, Harvard, and elsewhere and eventually came to the University of Chicago in 1892 where he became prominent in the Chicago school of pragmatism. He was much influenced by William James.

Meaning and Truth. Both of these terms present difficulties for philosophers and philosophical theologians. Questions about the truth of propositions cannot be intelligibly discussed until the meaning of the terms can be ascertained. It may seem at first sight that since a simple term such as "box" has obvious referents in the empirical world, it must be easy for two persons A and B to understand and to agree on the meaning of the word by A's taking B to an empty chocolate box, for example, and saying: "There now, you can see what I mean." (Much good foreign language teaching is indeed accomplished by such methods.) This procedure is of course good enough for many

purposes, but it is fraught with immense difficulties and can be the occasion of much misunderstanding. Not only are there many kinds of boxes (e.g., a box at the theater and a box in an application blank) that do not at all mean anything like a chocolate box; there are many commonly used terms in language that do not have ostensive referents at all; e.g., although I can point to a chocolate box to show you what I mean by the word "box" in a particular context, how can I point to a referent for words such as "by" or "intricately"? Language abounds in ambiguities. When A tells B that C is liberal or aggressive or modest, B may receive a distinctly different impression from that which A has intended, so that when B accepts or challenges the truth of A's statement he is not in fact either agreeing or disagreeing with A, since each means something quite different from the other.

Such confusion is likely to be even more pervasive in, say, ethical and theological discussion in which, in the nature of the case, abstract terms such as "happiness" and "grace" figure largely in the discussion. The members of the Logical Positivist school that had its beginnings in the Vienna Circle devised a criterion for the meaningfulness of a sentence or proposition, namely, its verifiability. If it could not be verified empirically it must be treated as meaningless. Popper later suggested falsifiability as a better criterion. While the use of such criteria is workable and may be satisfactory at certain levels of discussion, it does not work in discussions that theologians and moralists, for instance, would account the most interesting and meaningful ones. Nevertheless, it remains true that agreement on meaning must be present before any discussion of truth-claims can be usefully entertained.

Mechthild of Magdeburg (c.1210–c. 1280). German spiritual writer. Having become a Béguine (See **Beguines**) she had a vision which, under the direction of her spiritual director, she wrote down under the title *Das fliessende Licht der Gottheit*. Her visions included one relating to the Sacred Heart: a devotion that had some currency in the Middle Ages although not popularized till much later. See **Margaret Mary Alacoque**.

Meditation. The term may be used in a variety of ways ranging from loose and vague connotations (e.g., any sort of silent reflection on ideas that spring into the stream of consciousness when one tries to focus on notions relating to the interior life or to spirituality in general) to specific, disciplined forms of mental prayer. In Christian traditions of spirituality meditation usually consists of an elementary form of mental prayer, e.g., discursive reflection on a devotional theme. One of its most familiar forms in Catholic tradition is found in the popular devotion of the Rosary in which one tries to focus on one of the great events or "mysteries" attending the life of Mary as the instrument of human redemption by her divine Son Jesus Christ. The *Spiritual Exercises* of Ignatius Loyola, designed originally for Jesuit novices, provides another example of meditation so understood. By contrast, contemplation is accounted a higher kind of mental prayer, nondiscursive, more difficult to achieve and of several degrees or forms. See **Contemplation**.

Meekness. Christianity and Buddhism are among the religions that specially commend the virtue of meekness. According to one of the Christian Beatitudes, the meek "inherit the earth" and Buddhists teach that the humble reap advantage while the haughty meet misfortune. The turning of the other cheek to which allusion is made in the Sermon on the Mount is one of the most widely known of the injunctions of Jesus. The theme runs through the Magnificat: God casts down the mighty and exalts the humble. It echoes the prayer of Hannah (I Samuel 2.1–10) and is indeed a recurring motif in the Hebrew Bible.

Megilloth. From the Hebrew meaning "rolls," this term is used to designate five books of the Bible read by Jews on specific feast days: Song of Solomon (Passover), Ruth (Feast of Weeks), Lamentations (Anniversary of the Chaldean destruction of Jerusalem), Ecclesiastes (Feast of the Tabernacles), and Esther (Purim). All these books belong to that part of the Hebrew Bible not included in either the Law or the Prophets.

Melanchthon, Philipp (1497–1560). Lutheran Reformer. After study at Heidelberg and Tubingen, he became professor of Greek at Wittenberg, exercised much influence by his teaching in the spirit of the humanistic Renaissance, then was captivated by Luther's zeal to reform the Church. In 1521 he was a leader of the Lutheran Reformation in which he played an important part as perhaps the most scholarly of its exponents. He was by natural inclination a scholar. His theological thought is expressed in his *Loci Communes* (1521) which he revised several times.

Melchites. Those Syrian and Egyptian Christians who would not subscribe to Monophysitism, accepting instead the decisions of the Council of Chalcedon. The term is applied today, however, to Christians of the Byzantine rite, whether Orthodox or Uniate, belonging to the patriarchates of Alexandria, Antioch, or Jerusalem.

Meliorism. (Latin *melior*, better.) The doctrine that although human beings cannot attain perfection, they are capable of indefinite improvement. The notion seems to have been taken by some as a corollary of the evolutionary nature of humanity and the universe.

Melville, Andrew (1545–1622). Scottish Presbyterian divine. Born at Baldovie, near Montrose, Scotland, and trained at St. Andrews. After some work in continental Europe he returned to Scotland where he became principal of the Uni versity of Glasgow. Bitter and narrow in controversy, it was he much more than Knox who was responsible for investing the Reformed Kirk in Scotland with its Presbyterian form of government. He drew up to the Second Book of Discipline in which vestiges of episcopal forms were discarded.

Mencius (*c.* 371–*c.* 289 BCE). Born in Shantung Province, he taught in the Confucian tradition, and his life was in many ways like that of the great Chinese sage, but he developed the latter's teachings in special directions, drawing from them, for instance, an even more radical affirmation of the innate goodness of man. Since human beings are innately good, they must have innate knowledge of the good and consequently the ability to act rightly. Since they are so endowed, everyone has the capacity to attain the highest wisdom, which needs only to be drawn out by education. Moreover, since the State has the duty to uphold, to inculcate, and to exemplify these fundamental principles, people confronted with a State that flagrantly fails to do so are justified in rising in rebellion against its injustice.

Mendelssohn, Moses (1729–1786). Jewish philosopher of such importance that he has sometimes been called "the third Moses." Born at Dessau, Germany, he found in Moses Maimonides (sometimes called "the second Moses"), a catalyst for his own thought. He did not build any philosophical system but argued for the existence of God and the immortality of the soul. He upheld freedom of conscience and opposed State interference with the rights of the individual. He advocated complete freedom of religion. His writings include: *Philosophical Conversations* (1755), *On Evidence in the Science of Metaphysics* (1763), and *Morning Hours or Lectures on the Existence of God* (1785). He was personally convinced that a Jew ought to be ceremonially observant but have complete freedom of opinion in the exercise of his or her faith.

Mendicant Orders. Until the beginning of the 13th c., those men and women dedicated to the religious life with the traditional three vows of poverty, chastity, and obedience, were normally attached to a monastery or convent that remained their home for life. Although their vow of poverty prohibited them from owning anything individually, they participated in the ownership of the property, real and movable, of the monastic establishment to which they belonged for life, which, often through centuries of cultivation and skilled husbandry, had made their monastic home very rich. The mendicant orders, beginning with the Franciscans and the Dominicans, were conceived on different lines. Their vow of poverty committed their members to owning nothing either individually or communally. They were to rely on the charity of the faithful for their daily bread. Moreover, unlike the older orders, they were mobile, being organized more like an army, ready to be sent anywhere at a moment's notice by their superiors who were elected for a fixed number of years, unlike the abbots and abbesses of the older orders who were normally elected for life. They had considerable privileges, including exemption from episcopal jurisdiction, and although beginning (especially in the Franciscans' case) as simple friars and sisters begging their bread, they were within a short time prominent among the intellectual leaders of Europe. The Carmelites and the Augustinian friars were mendicants as were also, some centuries later, the Servites and some other orders of men and of women. Because of their mobility they tended to become more internationally-minded and to support the papacy over national and other territorial rulers, while the ancient orders, being attached to the land, had vested interests in the local establishment, which affected their attitudes accordingly. The mendicant orders became therefore a most useful instrument in the unification of the Church under the papacy in Western Europe.

Mennonites. This Protestant religious body takes its name from that of Menno Simons (1496–1561), a priest who renounced the Roman Catholic Church and joined the Anabaptists, organizing a large body of his followers in Holland and neighboring regions. Their views were similar to those of the Separatists in England. Each congregation is a separate and independent unit. No doctrinal conformity is required and opinion varies considerably among the members, although infant baptism is commonly repudiated. They generally refuse participation in secular politics and decline, like the Quakers, to take oaths. There are now probably about half a million of them in Europe and America.

Mercier, Désiré Joseph (1851–1926). Belgian philosopher and cardinal. Ordained priest in 1874 after studies at Louvain, where he later became professor of philosophy, he was prominent in the revival of Thomistic studies and the founding of a school of Neo-Thomism. He wrote in defense of his position and was highly influential in its promotion among the clergy. He was a man of great pastoral concern and personal attractiveness and a very notable force in the life of the Church in his time.

Merit. In Christian theology "merit" is the term traditionally used to designate actions done for God that are rewarded by him accordingly. The concept is rooted in Scripture, both in the Old Testament and the New Testament (e.g., Deuteronomy 5.28–33 and Matthew 5.3–12) in which the just are promised rewards for their good works. Since human beings are completely dependent on their Creator, they cannot strictly speaking claim any such reward; nevertheless, they are entitled by God's gracious promise to expect it. Luther and other Protestant Reformers generally discarded the notion that human beings could acquire any merit at all since all human works are sinful, and only God can act rightly. Although such an extreme position has been widely modified in Protestant theology, a tendency to discountenance the notion of merit remains. See **Justification** and **Grace.**

Merkabah. A Jewish mystical tradition that focused on the divine chariot or throne (*merkabah*) portrayed in Ezekiel's vision (Ezekiel 1). The aim of those in this mystical tradition was to achieve this vision by means of a series of exercises through seven "halls" or stages, each guarded by an angel who demands a mystical password. In preparation for these exercises one had to be taught individually how to attain the secret knowledge required. Even so tutored, the aspirant faced a dangerous enterprise: the Talmud relates that four persons undertook such a mystical journey and only one of them achieved the goal unscathed.

Merleau-Ponty, Maurice (1908–1961). French philosopher. Born at Rochefort-sur-Mer, he taught at Lyon, the Sorbonne, and the Collège de France. Influenced by Husserl and by Gestalt psychology, he developed a phenomenology of his own. Rejecting the dualism of Descartes, he recognized a variety of levels arranged somewhat like Teilhard's "spheres": physical, biological, and mental. Since all consciousness is rooted in and arises out of a particular bodily circumstance, it always has a particular, individual perspective, being therefore highly subjective. Only to some limited extent is this subjectivity mitigated by the intersubjective character of human language. His writings include: *The Structure of Behavior* (1942), *Phenomenology of Perception* (1945), *Sense and Nonsense* (1948), and *The Primacy of Perception* (1964).

Merton, Thomas (1915–1968). Born at Prades, in the Pyrénées-Orientales, he was the son of Owen Merton, an artist from New Zealand, and Ruth Jenkins, an artist from Ohio. Taken to the United States in 1916, he was educated partly in Bermuda, partly in France, and partly in England, where, in 1933, he entered Clare College, Cambridge. Having entered Columbia University in 1935, he was graduated there in 1938 and the following year took his M.A. degree. On December 10, 1941, he entered the Cistercian abbey at Gethsemani, Kentucky, where he took his solemn vows in 1947 and was ordained priest in 1949. On December 10, 1968, he died at Bangkok, where he had been invited to attend a meeting of Asian Benedictine and Cistercian abbots, monks, and nuns. He wrote extensively. His autobiography, *The Seven Storey Mountain* (1948) was widely read and his unusual form of spirituality attracted much attention among his many admirers and friends. For a collection of tributes, see Patrick Hart (ed.), *Thomas Merton, Monk* (1974).

Mesrob (*c.* **345–440**). Armenian Church leader and historian. A man of scholarly interests and inclinations, he composed an alphabet for the Armenian language, which was adopted in 406, and sought to develop the Armenian Church on national lines, eliminating alien (e.g., Syrian) elements from it. He played a prominent role in the translation of the Bible into Armenian, contributing much of the translation himself and revising the whole work with use of the Greek text. He also developed Armenian monasticism.

Messiah. The Hebrew word, *mašîªh,* means literally "the anointed one," and denotes a person invested with special powers. In the Old Testament the term is used of the king of Israel. The Greek term *christos* (from *chriō,* I anoint) is used to translate it, whence the word "Christ" applied by Christians to Jesus.

The development in the Old Testament of the notion of expectation of the Messiah who should come to rule the world in righteousness is gradual, complex, and attended by some obscurities. Scholars have proposed several theories about the development of what may be called messianism or the messianic hope. The messianic idea goes through a series of stages. For example, one may claim to see it in some sense as early as in the blessings and promises connected with Abraham and Jacob. Eventually it can be seen, after the establishment of the monarchy, as the promise of a king in the lineage of David, who will save his people and "live for ever." In Isaiah 6–9 the Davidic motif appears in striking terms. He is to be the agent of Yahweh, inaugurating a kingdom of justice and righteousness. In the course of the centuries preceding the birth of Jesus, the messianic idea took on a variety of forms with no clearly discernible pattern. Yet the concept seems to have been well fixed in some way in the Hebrew mind and lying there behind the vast variety of its expressions. What the Messiah is to be is also unclear. He might be one of many possibilities. Often he is envisioned as a superhuman being. In later pre-Christian Judaism we find even hints of two Messiahs: one a royal Messiah, the other a priestly one. There is an allusion to this idea, for example, in the Qumran documents.

Metaphor. One of several figurative modes of utterance, metaphorical language uses innovative expressions and unexpected identifications to accent the ideas that the writer or speaker wishes to convey; e.g., "The sky frowned angrily as the mariners set sail." Some metaphorical expressions have become so banal with constant use that one hardly recognizes them as metaphors at all; e.g., "She let the cool breeze kiss her face." Metaphor is extensively used in literature. It plays an important role in the communication of religious ideas. It is closely allied to simile, also a common form of figurative speech. No sharp line can be drawn between metaphor and the literary form known as parable, which plays such a large part in the Gospel accounts of the teaching of Jesus. Allegory, also much used in religious literature, is often regarded as an extended form of metaphor; e.g.,

Dante's *Commedia* and Bunyan's *Pilgrim's Progress*.

In the philosophical tradition of the West there is a strong resistance to the use of metaphor in philosophical discourse. Aristotle and Locke are among those who seek to avoid such use, and the 20th-c. logical positivists professed abhorrence of it. Nevertheless there is also a lively tradition that sees the disciplined use of metaphor valuable, not to say inevitable, in serious philosophical inquiry. Plato lends his immense authority to such a view, using metaphor and myth (see **Myth**) extensively to try to communicate the most important philosophical concepts which, because of the poverty of human language, demand figurative forms of utterance. Thomas Aquinas, recognizing at the outset of his greatest work, the *Summa Theologiae*, that Scripture uses figurative language widely (he calls the usage *per similitudinem*), employs such devices in his own philosophy: the analogical method that he offers is akin to metaphorical language. It can indeed be argued that *all* language is metaphorical in one way or another. I. A. Richards alleges that "As philosophy grows more abstract we think increasingly by means of metaphors that we profess *not* to be relying on." The late Ian Ramsey, a philosophical theologian whose interest centered upon the philosophical analysis of religious language, remarked tellingly that "What is not verbally odd is devoid of disclosure power." For a very extensive bibliography on the subject, see Warren A. Shibles, *Metaphor: An Annotated Bibliography and History*. Whitewater, Wisconsin: The Language Press, 1971.

Metaphysical Poets, The. A group of 17th c. English poets so called, originally by Samuel Johnson in contempt but now merely because of traditional usage. Prominent among them were John Donne, George Herbert, and Thomas Traherne. They reflect a deep sense of Christian piety and, despite some stylistic peculiarities, they exhibit much literary merit.

Metaphysical Society, The. A group founded in England in 1869 by Sir James Knowles (1831–1908) to foster productive discussion between leaders in scientific and religious thought. They included many of the most distinguished men of the day, e.g., A. J. Balfour, A. C. Fraser, W. E. Gladstone, T. H. Huxley, H. E. Manning, J. Martineau, J. R. Seeley, H. Sidgwick, A. P. Stanley, Leslie Stephen, and C. Thirwall. For more details see A. W. Brown, *The Metaphysical Society* (New York, 1947). They met regularly till May 1880.

Metaphysics. Although the term has been used in somewhat different senses in the history of philosophy, it may be said to be the study of first principles, often (as in Aristotle) ontology: the study of being. The name is generally taken to have been given arbitrarily to a work by Aristotle that followed his work on Physics (*meta* is the Greek for "after"), although this is not unquestioned by historians of philosophy. Traditionally central to philosophical enterprises, it has been discarded by many in the 20th c. under the strongly empiricist influences at work, especially in the English-speaking world. The basic philosophical questions, not least those with religious implications, remain, however, metaphysical and ontological in character.

Metempsychosis. See **Reincarnation**.

Methodism. At a time when, in the Church of England, the life of the Church was impoverished, John and Charles Wesley devised a system of religious faith and practice that they promoted at Oxford in 1729, originally intending it to be a movement within the Church for its spiritual invigoration. Eventually the movement became a separate denomination, and the term "Methodist" was applied to those bodies that grew out of that inspiration. Most of these bodies were Armenian in theological doctrine, although the Calvinist Methodists of Wales, for instance, form an exception. In England John Wesley provided in 1784 for the organization of "the people called Methodists" and gradually the organization developed into one of the largest Protestant groups in the English-speaking world. By the end of the 18th c. there were already more than half as many Methodists in North America as in Britain, and there are now some twenty times as many in America as in Britain, with something like forty million throughout the world. Methodism, especially in the United States, has much emphasized organization as an instrument in the development of the denomination. In the United States the organization includes superintendents, called bishops although claiming no episcopal succession in the Catholic sense, and these superintendents exercise great power in the organization of the Church in the United States.

Metropolitan. In Catholic usage a metropolitan has jurisdiction over not merely a diocese but a group or "province" consisting of several dioceses. He generally bears a title such as archbishop or primate. The name "metropolitan" derives from the fact that the early Church modelled its organization roughly on that of the Roman Empire, in which authorities in the largest or most important city in a region had certain jurisdictional powers over the entire region. The term "metropolitan" first occurs in a Christian context in the fourth canon of the Council of Nicaea in 325.

Meyer, Heinrich (1800–1873). New Testament scholar. Born at Gotha and trained at Jena, he edited the scholarly 16-volume commentary on the New Testament of which a 20-volume English translation was published in 1873–1895. Such is its quality and importance that it has been frequently revised and updated down to the present time. He also published a text of the New Testament with German translation in two volumes in 1829.

Meynell, Alice (1847–1922). Poet. She became a Roman Catholic in 1872 and most of her poetry and other literary work has in one way or another a deeply religious motif. She was much admired by a wide variety of literary critics. In one of her poems, *Christ in the Universe,* she envisions (long, of course, before space travel was considered even a remote possibility) Christ moving from planet to planet across "the Pleiades, the Lyre, the Bear," and a time when the inhabitants of other planets would compare together their thoughts in hearing "a million alien gospels."

Mezuzah. A scroll on which is written the Shema (Deuteronomy 6.4–9 and 11.13–21). In the homes of observant Jews a mezuzah is attached to the door post, as prescribed in Deuteronomy 6.9 and 11.20). The traditional custom is to kiss the mezuzah on entering or leaving the house.

Michael, The Archangel. Although mentioned only four times in Scripture (twice in Daniel, once in Jude, and once in Revelation), he quickly came to have a unique place in Christian thought, both as the leader of the armies of the Lord against the Devil's and as the protector of Christians against all evil powers. He conducts faithful souls through the vale of death to the life beyond. He is acclaimed "Prince of the heavenly hosts." In the traditional form of the *Confiteor* he is ranked next after the Virgin Mary herself. In iconography he is generally depicted with a sword, often in combat with a dragon, symbolizing his triumph over evil. The fall term at Oxford, during which his feast day falls, is still named Michaelmas term. The famous abbey of Mont-St.-Michel in France is dedicated to him as are innumerable churches and other religious foundations. The famous cathedral at Coventry was originally dedicated in the 15th c. (as a parish church) to Michael, and the new cathedral replacing the historic one destroyed in an air raid in World War II is adorned by Jacob Einstein's bronze statue of the archangel.

Michelangelo (1475–1564). Italian painter and sculptor. After studying painting under Florentine masters, he was attracted to sculpture and studied it under Bertoldo, by whom he was introduced to the circle of Lorenzo de' Medici. He is uniquely famous for the immensity of the scale of his design as for his versatility and masterly grasp of the spirit of Renaissance splendor, combining as it does medieval Christian restraint with the richness, orderly beauty, and grandeur of classic models. Among his most famous sculptures are his *Pietà*, his *David*, and his *Moses*. Commissioned by Julius II, he executed the famous frescoes on the ceiling of the Sistine Chapel in Rome and eventually the *Last Judgment*. In his last years he was engaged in the direction of the building of the new Basilica of St. Peter in Rome.

Middle Ages. The period dating from the fall of the Roman Empire in 476 CE to the sailing of Columbus in 1492 (or more simply the millennium between 500 and 1500), it represents a great variety in the development of European civilization and culture. The earlier centuries were on the whole both intellectually barren and politically anarchical at a time when China, for instance, was notably civilized. Charlemagne, who was crowned at Rome in the Old St. Peter's on Christmas Day, 800, brought some semblance of order to Western Europe, being also a patron of the arts and an admirer of scholarship. Nevertheless, it was at least *c.* 1100 before the face of Western Europe began to change and to reflect what we are accustomed to think of as the glories of the Middle Ages: the splendidly constructed castles, fortresses, abbeys, cathedrals, and other monuments of medieval culture and civilization. The contrast between the face of Western Europe in, say, 800 and 1300 is enormous. The earlier period may be called

with much justification "the Dark Ages", but the later period is one of the liveliest, intellectually and culturally, in the history of humanity. It was an age, moreover, in which Christianity received a cultural shape that has affected all its later variegated development.

Midrash. (Plural: midrashim.) A distinctively Jewish type of writing in which the biblical text is studied in certain ways. Two principal kinds of midrash are recognized: the *halakha* (an explanation of the law so as to yield principles of conduct) and the *haggadah* (an explanation of the narrative passages of the Pentateuch). Midrash is not exegesis as biblical scholars understand it, being rather an attempt to uncover the most edifying messages and lessons that the text can yield. It is a method that has no obvious parallels in any other literature, certainly not at all in Graeco-Roman literature. The biblical writers themselves often resort to midrashim on earlier sources. Midrash has more affinity with the expository sermon of modern times than with the literary analysis of the Bible.

Migne, Jacques Paul (1800–1875). Parish priest near Orleans, France, 1824–1833, he went to Paris where he founded a printing house. There, despite considerable discouragement and hostility from his ecclesiastical superiors, he published Christian texts, notably the famous *Patrologia Latina* and *Patrologia Graeca*: the former in 221 volumes (1844–1864) and the latter in 162 volumes containing the Greek text with Latin translation (1857–1866). His work is defective in some respects (e.g., too many printers' errors); and some of the texts he used have now been superseded by better ones. The whole work will be eventually superseded by the *Corpus Scriptorum Ecclesiasticorum*, now in progress. Nevertheless, Migne remains the standard scholarly tool for its purpose and is widely cited. Because of its pioneering place it will always be of great scholarly importance. In 1868 his printing equipment, including his molds, were destroyed by fire. His accomplishment, for all its well-known shortcomings, has been of incalculable value to scholars and remains a witness to his astounding resolve, patience, and indefatigable industry.

Miko. In Shinto, the *miko* (formally called *kamiko* and *ichiko*) are dedicated to serve in the shrines. They undergo a strict training in preparation for their duties. The *kamiko* (ministers of the gods, the *kami*) are trained to assist the Shinto priests and to perform the sacred dances. Their training entails years of strict chastity. In the shrine they may be identified by their white blouses and red skirts. The *ichiko* have a more shamanistic vocation with functions similar to those of mediums in spiritistic circles.

Milan, The Edict of. The document so designated is misnamed, since it was neither an edict nor issued from Milan. The Emperors Constantine and Licinius met at Milan, however, in 313, to recognize the Christian Church as a *religio licita* (lawful religion) and to grant toleration to religions generally. They did not establish the Christian Church, although they did end the terrible persecutions that Christians had suffered under various emperors since the days of Nero. The document is to be found in Lactantius (*De Mortibus Persecutorum*, 48) and Eusebius (*Historia Ecclesiae*, x, 5). For an account and full bibliography see N. H. Baynes, *Constantine the Great and the Christian Church* (1930), pp. 69–74.

Mill, James (1773–1836). Scottish philosopher. Trained at Edinburgh, he worked for the East India Company. Influenced by Jeremy Bentham, he became a leader in the Utilitarian movement in British thought. Among his writings are *Elements of Political Economy* (1821) and *Phenomena of the Human Mind* (1829). Historically he has been overshadowed by his more famous son, John Stuart Mill.

Mill, John Stuart (1806–1873). British philosopher. Born in London, he was educated at home by his father (see **Mill, James**), from whom he is said to have learned Greek at the age of three. At fourteen he had found the work of Jeremy Bentham who much influenced his thought throughout the rest of his life. From his father he inherited an empiricist mold of thought and became the chief exponent in the 19th century of that outlook that has been so much identified with British philosophy. Mill saw that while traditional deductive logic does not yield new information but merely draws implicates from given premises, inductive procedures do yield new knowledge through the discovery of causal connections among phenomena. He devised and developed five methods of inductive inference that he showed to be in fact what scientists do commonly use in verifying or falsifying hypotheses. In ethics, although he started from Benthamite principles, he modified them in an important way by showing, for example, that it is not merely the greatest *amount* of pleasure that is to be sought but the highest quality of pleasure: a view much more reconcilable with the teaching of the great religious leaders in human history. In religious thought, however, Mill proposed a God who is limited in power. His writings include *A System of Logic*, 2 vols. (1843), *Principles of Political Economy* (1848), *On Liberty* (1859), *Utilitarianism* (1863), *The Subjection of Women* (1869), and *Three Essays on Religion* (1874).

Millenarianism. The belief in a thousand-year period of peace and righteous rule on earth, based on apocalyptic visions in the Bible, notably in Daniel and Revelation. Some writers and leaders in the early Christian Church held such beliefs, but Origen and Augustine are among those who rejected them, and millenarian beliefs are rarely to be found again till the Reformation, except among special groups. Among the German Pietists, the Anabaptists, and others it was a widespread expectation and several 19th-c. Christian groups held firmly to it, as do some today, although it is not common in the mainstream of Christian belief.

Milton, John (1608–74). English poet. Educated at St. Paul's School, London, and Christ's College, Cambridge, Milton quickly earned a reputation for his poetic genius, eventually winning a place among the greatest of the English poets. From his *Ode on the Morning of Christ's Nativity*, written when he was barely into his twenties, his poetry took a deeply religious tone. From an early age, however, he was inclined to sympathy with the Puritan outlook, although he was always too much of an individualist to belong to any party or even to be roughly classified with any. His *L'Allegro* and *Il Penseroso* belong to his youthful period and represent the complexity of his nature: his longing for pleasure, on the one hand, and, on the other, his joy in quiet meditation and serious thought. His *Areopagitica* (1644) is a vigorous defense of the freedom of the press. He married, was separated from his wife, then reconciled. He wrote many lively controversial pamphlets. In 1651 he became completely blind and the following year lost his wife. He argued for the universal disestablishment of all churches. In his great epic *Paradise Lost* (1667), which he had written over a period of seven years, he dealt on a grand scale with the philosophical problem of evil, trying "to justify the ways of God to men." In theology he was considered at best controversial and at worst heretical. He denied the doctrine of creation *ex nihilo* and veered toward an Arian christology. For a brief article on his life see Leslie Stephen's entry in the *Dictionary of National Biography*. The bibliography on Milton is enormous.

Mind-Body. Of all the problems in the history of Western philosophy, the mind-body problem is not only among the most important, the most intractable, and the most persistent, it is possibly the one most relevant to the serious study of religion. At the fountainhead of Western thought stands Plato, who treated the relationship as sharply dualistic, seeing mind (which for this purpose may be identified with soul and spirit) as pertaining to the world of permanence and body as relating to the qualitatively inferior world of change, growth, and decay. The Neoplatonic tradition, which immensely affected medieval thought, continued this outlook. The difficulty lay in showing how mind and body could relate to and interact with one another. Descartes, who regarded mind and body as of two radically different "substances", devised the notion that they interacted in the pineal gland. The Occasionalists, repudiating any such attempt at discovering a point of interaction, proposed that God directly intervenes at every mental decision and at every bodily motion. Thomas Aquinas and other medieval schoolmen, inheriting the Aristotelian understanding of "form" and "matter", had not been presented with the mind-body problem in such an acute form; nevertheless, it is still troublesome in that Aristotelian framework of thought. The Idealists of more modern times so diminished the importance of matter-body as to explain away the mind-body problem by virtually eliminating the reality of matter. (Berkeley does so with great ingenuity and skill.) Materialists likewise eliminate the mind-body problem by regarding what is called mind as merely a term used to signify the action of the brain, which is an empirically observable part of the body and which (they hold) secretes thought as liver secretes bile and as the glands of the body exude their respective secretions. Materialism comes in various guises, e.g., epiphenomenalists, while recognizing that mental actions have a higher quality than physical ones, must be classified as materialists since they attribute no independence or initiative to mind, regarding it in the same way as a product of the body.

The mind-body problem remains highly controversial and very relevant to religious thought today. For example, is the notion of a disembodied mind or spirit an intelligible concept? Ought one to say "I have a mind" or "I am a mind"? If the former, who is the "I" that can possess a mind? For a thorough examination of the problem as it presents itself in philosophy today, see John Hospers, *An Introduction to Philosophical Analysis*, 2nd ed., Englewood Cliffs, N.J.: Prentice Hall, 1973. Discussion on pp. 378–421; bibliography (books and articles) on pp. 422–424.

Minims. The order of friars founded in 1435 by St. Francis of Paola and officially designated *Ordo Fratrum Minimorum*. The name was chosen to express humility: they were to account theirs the least of the religious orders. They took a special vow committing themselves to a totally vegetarian diet, i.e., not merely an ovo-lacto vegetarianism. Inspired by the ideals of St. Francis of Assisi, they developed along independent lines. A Second Order (for nuns) was founded in 1495. They flourished in the 16th c. but declined in the 19th and today are much attenuated.

Minor Orders. For many centuries four minor orders were recognized in the West: porter, lector (reader), exorcist, and acolyte. The Roman Catholic Church in 1972 reduced their number to two: lector and acolyte. Those in minor orders are laymen, not clerics. Although in the past the minor orders were regarded as steps toward the priesthood, they may now be taken by laymen with no such vocation.

Minor Prophets, The. The twelve shorter prophetic books of the Old Testament: Hosea, Joel, Amos, Obadiah, Jonah, Micah, Nahum, Habakkuk, Zephaniah, Haggai, Zechariah, and Malachi. The other three (Isaiah, Jeremiah, Ezekiel) are classified as major prophets.

Minster. The term, like its German counterpart *Münster*, signifies a monastery. It is applied for historical reasons to certain English cathedrals, such as York, Lichfield, Lincoln, and others. Originally it meant any ecclesiastical establishment organized on monastic lines although not necessarily a monastery in the strict sense. Westminster, however, was originally a monastic establishment. It never was and still is not a cathedral and, as a "Royal Peculiar," it is exempt from episcopal jurisdiction. See **Peculiars.**

Miracle. The term is from the Latin *miraculum*, meaning simply a wonder: any extraordinary occurrence. The Greek words used in the New Testament for what has been traditionally rendered "miracle" are *sēmeion* (a sign, visible indication of secret power or divine truth) and *teras* (a wonder, an extraordinary act or happening), for example, in Acts 14.3: *sēmeia kai terata* (signs and wonders). Modern translators, seeing that "miracle" has become too "loaded" a word in English, generally prefer to use "sign." Traditionally, a miracle was interpreted as an act or event transcending the "laws" of nature. Such a possibility was denied not only by Hume (see **Hume, David**) but (for other reasons) by Spinoza and Hegel and by the 18th-c. deists whose mechanistic view of the universe caused them to see miracles as God's tinkering with the machine he had created, as though he must have botched it in the first place. Although some Christians today insist on upholding the traditional understanding of miracle as a suspension of the laws of nature, many educated Christians prefer to see the universe as portrayed by modern physicists as providing scope for accommodating the miraculous. Modern parapsychology, moreover, can interpret some events that would have been in the past accounted miraculous in ways that do not introduce a conflict between "science" and "religion." For example, hypnotism and telepathy are widely recognized phenomena. Alexis Carrel, an eminent French medical man and Nobel laureate testifies to seeing at Lourdes a cancerous sore shrivel to a scar before his eyes, in the course of prayer for healing. This sort of event need not call for belief in suspensions of the "laws" of nature. It may call, rather, for a deeper perception of the presence of spiritual dimensions within the universe that are ordinarily untapped.

Misericord. The word comes from the Latin *misericordia*, meaning "mercy." Choir stalls in monasteries and elsewhere sometimes have a projection on the underside of the hinged seat, which can be used by elderly or infirm monks or nuns or (in cathedrals) canons, for resting upon while appearing to stand with the other members of the choir. See G. L. Remnant, *A Catalogue of the Misericords in Great Britain* (1969).

Mishnah. The Hebrew term means "repetition" and refers to a method of exegesis of Scripture different from that of the midrash (see **Midrash**). The Mishnah, a redaction and collection of various materials, formed the basis of the Palestinian and the Babylonian Talmuds. Consisting of six divisions, it deals with subjects such as agricultural laws, festivals, marriage laws, civil and criminal law, ritual law, and purifications. Each division is divided into three "tractates" and each of these is further subdivided. It has had a profound influence on Judaism: along with the Talmud the Mishnah is second only to the Bible itself in importance.

Missa Cantata. The name formerly given to a mass in which the celebrant was not assisted by deacon and subdeacon, as at a Solemn High Mass, but in which he and a choir sang the mass: a sort of compromise between High Mass and Low Mass, usually because not enough clergy were available for the former. Since nowadays singing is encouraged at all masses, with more congregational participation generally, the term has fallen into desuetude.

Missal. The liturgical book used at the altar for Mass and containing the text and rubrics necessary throughout the Christian Year.

Mithraism. See **Mystery Religions**.

Mitre. The liturgical headdress of bishops and certain abbots. In the Eastern Church it is shaped like a crown and embroidered or decorated with medallions. In the Russian Church some archimandrites and archpriests have the right to wear it. In the West the mitre takes the form of a shield with two lappets hanging down at the back. It dates from the 11th c., and originally it was of white linen, unlike the richly ornamented mitres widely used today. It was also much shorter. In the judgment of most liturgists the shorter form as used in the 12th c. is a much more becoming headdress for bishops than the extravagantly tall mitre as developed from about the 17th c. and widely used today.

Mitzvah. This Hebrew term means "commandment." The plural is *mitzvot*, of which, according to rabbinical tradition there are 613 in the Pentateuch: 248 positive, 365 negative. The central group is of course the Decalogue or Ten Commandments, but all are regarded by Orthodox Jews as binding.

Mixed Chalice. The practice of mixing water with wine at meals was very general in antiquity. In all probability, therefore, Jesus would follow the custom at the Last Supper. According to the testimony of some of the earliest of the Fathers of the Church, Christians followed the custom in the Eucharist, so that (except in the Armenian Church) all the liturgies of the historic Churches prescribe or take for granted the mixing of water with wine in the chalice.

Moab. A name for the territory extending east of the Dead Sea and south of the river Arnon, the modern Wadi el Mojib. The people who inhabited the region are called Moabites. Almost nothing is known of them except what is reported in the Old Testament. The archeological work of the late Nelson Glueck disclosed, however, a flourishing urban civilization there between the 23rd c. and the 20th c. BCE. By the 13th c. BCE another type of civilization had been developed in Moab, which long endured. The inscription on the famous Moabite stone discovered in 1868 and brought to the Louvre, Paris, in 1873 has been shown to pertain to the 9th c. BCE and to be written in Hebrew characters of the 8th c. BCE. The language is close to if not almost identical with biblical Hebrew. According to Israelite tradition, the Moabites were the descendants of Lot and his daughter (Genesis 19.37).

Moderates. The name given to the party in the Scottish Kirk who, in the second half of the 18th c., took a more open and relaxed view, both in doctrine and in practice, than did the opposite party, the Evangelicals. The Disruption in 1843 was led largely by the Evangelicals and was partly an act directed against the Moderates although probably the main catalyst was hostility to the system of patronage then in use in the placement of ministers in parishes.

Moderator. In the Scottish Kirk the practice prevails, followed by Presbyterian churches generally, of appointing or electing a moderator to preside over each of the various courts of the Church. The parish minister is *ex officio* moderator of the lowest court, the Kirk Session. In Scotland the Moderator of the highest court, the General Assembly, is annually chosen by the ex-moderators and then elected by the Assembly. During his year of office the Moderator of the General Assembly is the chief representative of the Kirk.

Modernism. The name given to a movement that was active within the Roman Catholic Church in the last decade of the 19th c. and the early years of the 20th c., till it was condemned formally by Pius X in 1907. The tendencies of the movement were: (1) to move away from the rigid medieval scholastic tradition inherited by the Church and taught in the seminaries and to think in terms of more modern types of philosophy; (2) to value the historic process through which the Church was developed rather than to seek to know about origins that are probably forever hidden; (3) to accept the modern methods of scriptural analysis that were by that time being universally employed by scholars outside the Roman Catholic Church. The term itself came into use in the later years of the activities to which it refers. It was also used in a much looser and more general sense of all movements (e.g., in Protestantism) that favored attitudes that fostered the adaptation of Christian traditional thought and practice to "the modern mind;" but it was used specifically for the movement within the Roman Catholic Church. Pius X, who was later canonized as a saint in the Roman Catholic Church calendar, had such an abhorrence of the movement that virtually all clergy who had been active in it were excommunicated (e.g., A. Loisy and G. Tyrrell) while distinguished laymen such as Baron von Hügel and Maurice Blondel were uncensured. The papal condemnation took the form of a decree *Lamentabili* and an encyclical *Pascendi*.

Moffatt, James (1870–1944). Scottish Presbyterian New Testament scholar. Born in Glasgow, he was educated there and ordained to the ministry of the Kirk in 1896. He was for some years professor at Union Theological Seminary, New York. He is best remembered for his lively translation of the Bible (New Testament in 1913, Old Testament in 1924) and for the commentary on the New Testament that he edited, which reflected the best scholarship of the day while serving as a tool for preachers of expository sermons.

Mogila, Peter (1597–1646). Eastern Orthodox theologian. After study at the University of Paris he eventually became Metropolitan of Kiev in 1632. His *Confession,* a survey of the faith of the Greek Orthodox Church, was formally approved by various authorities of that Church, including, in 1672, the Synod of Jerusalem. His *Catechism* (1645) has also been much admired as an expression of the Greek Orthodox faith.

Mohammed. See Muhammad.

Mohel. A Jew trained to carry out the rite of circumcision.

Moksha. This Sanskrit term means literally "release" or "liberation." In the Upanishads, it appears as signifying the achievement of awareness of the identity of one's own inner self with God (Brahman), developing, however, to mean the liberation and autonomy of the self. Eventually, as in the *Bhagavadgītā,* it came to signify the liberation of every individual irrespective of caste or sex. This concept of *moksha* as personal deliverance from spiritual bondage to spiritual freedom is fundamental to Buddhism and Jainism, both offshoots of the common Hindu parent.

Molina, Luis de (1535–1600). Jesuit theologian. In his principal work, *Concordia liberi arbitrii cum gratiae donis* (1588), he developed the view that the efficacy of grace has its ultimate foundation not in the gift of the grace itself but in God's foreknowledge of how each individual would cooperate with the grace. Molinists claim that no other doctrine about grace and human freedom sufficiently protects the latter. Opposed by Thomists, Molinism remained an option for Roman Catholics and has been favored by Jesuits and also adopted by many others.

Monad. The Greek word *monas* from which this philosophical term is derived means simply "unit". Pythagoras used it in antiquity to express the first number of a mathematical series from which are derived all the other numbers in the series. Giordano Bruno used the term to express the irreducible unit of which

everything in the universe is made. Leibniz, adopting this terminology, developed the notion in his *Monadology,* giving it a permanent place in the history of Western thought. Goethe and Lotze, for example, are among those who have used this ontological model.

Monarchianism. A theological opinion held by some in the 2nd and the 3rd centuries but eventually regarded as heretical. There were two groups: (1) the Adoptionist or Dynamic Monarchians such as Theodotus, who taught that Jesus could be called God only in the sense that the power of God flowed into him from the Father; and (2) the Modalistic Monarchians (also called Sabellians), who maintained that in the Godhead were modes or operations, not distinct *personae.* A corollary was that God suffers, which was held to be a heretical view (later called "patripassianism") because to suffer is "to be acted upon" and God acts on everything else but cannot be acted upon by anything else.

Monism. The metaphysical view that all reality is fundamentally of one "substance" or character. The term was introduced into philosophical discussion by Christian Wolff in the 18th c. The view, however, is of long standing in the history of philosophy. In antiquity Parmenides and in the 17th c. Spinoza were clearly monists. Many others, however, have held views that may be called monistic, even if their monism is modified in one way or another. Alternative theories are dualism and pluralism. In India, Vedanta may take a monistic or a dualistic form.

Monophysitism. The term is derived from two Greek words, *monos* and *physis,* meaning respectively "one" and "nature". It designates a view, historically important, contrary to that which was decreed at the Council of Chalcedon (451) that Christ is both fully human and fully divine, "True God and True Man." The Monophysites affirmed instead that Christ's nature is wholly divine. Several forms of Mono-physitism developed. By the 6th c. the Coptic, the Ethiopic (Abyssinian), the Syrian Jacobite, and the Armenian Churches all subscribed to the Mono-physite doctrine and continue to do so to this day. Chalcedonian doctrine offi-cially prevailed, however, throughout Christendom generally; yet even there a tendency grew in popular piety to downplay the human nature of Christ and to see him as, rather, the divine Judge depicted in Michelangelo's fa-mous painting. See **Mary, The Virgin.**

Monotheism. Belief in the existence of one God who alone is to be worshipped. From at least the 6th c. BCE this was the religious stance of the people of Israel, but before then the situation is com-plex. Despite the urging of the prophets to abandon the older polytheisms, they long persisted. Monotheism was not the result of any intellectual movement. It was, rather, the outcome of a general at-titude that slowly developed, encom-passing a way of life, an awareness of being a people favored and set apart by this One God who is indeed unique, having, for example (unlike other great gods known to the people from sur-rounding civilizations) no female con-sort, no offspring, no relation of dependence of any kind on anything be-yond himself. He is totally alone. Since the Hebrews had no word for nature, what we call natural events such as storms and earthquakes are attributed to his mighty power; nevertheless he is not at all like any of the nature deities. Some think that the ideas of the un-usual pharaoh who adopted the name of Ikhnaton and lived in Egypt a century or so before Moses may have influenced the Hebrews in the direction of mono-theism; but not enough is known about the religion of this interesting pharaoh to permit of any definite conclusion of that kind, plausible though such a the-ory may be. What is certain is that the Hebrew people did develop a very strong monotheism and bequeathed a no less emphatically monotheistic out-look to Christianity and, if more indi-rectly, to Islam. See also **Henotheism.**

Monotheletism. From two Greek words, *monos* and *thelein*, meaning re-spectively "one" and "to will". The Council of Constantinople in 680 finally approved as orthodox the view that in Christ there were two wills, one hu-man, the other divine, thus condemning the monothelites who had held that in Christ there was only one will. The controversy that had raged on this ques-tion had begun as an attempt to enlist the Monophysites (see **Monophysitism**) to the side of the majority who upheld the Chalcedonian doctrine, the purpose of which attempt was no doubt largely to unite the Empire against the Persian invaders and also, later, against the growing power of Islam. The alternative spelling, "monothelitism", is common but etymologically less correct.

Monstrance. The vessel used for show-ing the Eucharistic Host to the people for veneration. It usually takes an or-nate form consisting of a frame contain-ing a glass through which the Host may be seen. See also **Pyx.**

Montanism. In Phrygia, in the second half of the 2nd c. CE, Montanus led an apocalyptic movement, proclaiming that the Heavenly Jerusalem would soon de-scend at a place near Pepuza, Phrygia. The Montanists, adherents of this movement, lived in expectation of the speedy outpouring of the Holy Spirit and exhibited the characteristic mood of opponents of institutionalism. They soon developed, especially in Roman Africa, extremely ascetic tendencies, with rigorous fasts and special disci-plines, and regarded as carnal those who observed only the standard Roman discipline. Their most distinguished representative was Tertullian (c. 160–c. 220), who, besides being the first Christian theologian to write in Latin, by his legally trained mind greatly af-fected the thought of the Latin Church.

Monte Cassino. The chief house of the Benedictine Order. It was founded by

Benedict himself *c.* 529, after he had left Subiaco. It lies between Naples and Rome. The buildings were destroyed in World War II but rebuilt and then reconsecrated by Pope Paul VI in 1964.

Montesquieu, Charles de Secondat (1689–1775). French thinker and satirist. Born at La Brède, near Bordeaux, he was president of the Bordeaux Parliament for several years. In *The Persian Letters* (1721) he satirized French society through a series of imaginary letters by Persian visitors to France. In *The Spirit of the Laws* (1748), he developed his thought more systematically, reflecting the influence of John Locke and showing some affinities with Rousseau. He advocated, for practical reasons, a constitutional monarchy. He believed in God, that he governs the universe benevolently, and that he bestows on human beings the power of freedom of choice.

Montserrat. A mountain near Barcelona reputed to be the site of the Castle of the Holy Grail. A Benedictine monastery containing the celebrated image of Our Lady of Montserrat was founded early in the 11th c., became an abbey in 1409, and soon a popular focus for pilgrims. These included Ignatius Loyola himself, who, after his conversion, hung his sword there in demonstration of his dedication to the Virgin Mary. The monks are famed for their studies in Scripture, Church history, and other fields of learning and culture, including a special interest in Catalonian studies. The monastery contains an important library.

Mont-St.-Michel. Early in the 8th c. Saint Aubert, Bishop of Avranche, is said to have had a vision in which the Archangel Michael commanded him to set up an oratory on an island rock just off the northern coast of France in the Gulf of St. Malo and to the south of the Channel Islands. In 966 a Benedictine monastery was established on the rock and became in time the greatest and most famous of all the sanctuaries dedicated to Michael. A fortress was added later, making the complex one of the most impressive sights as well as one of the most revered shrines in Western Europe. The buildings, surmounted by a Gothic spire on which stands a statue of the Archangel, remain, now secularized, one of the great cultural monuments of France, visited daily by throngs of tourists.

Moody, Dwight Lyman (1837–1899). American Protestant evangelist. Born in humble circumstances in Massachusetts, he joined the Congregational Church and went into business in Chicago in 1856. In 1860 he turned to evangelistic work which prospered rapidly. In 1870 he was joined in his preaching missions by Ira David Sankey and the two names "Moody and Sankey" became inseparable in popular usage. He was immensely successful in his revivalistic missions in America and also conducted missions in Great Britain, where he was widely welcomed by the clergy and people of many denominations. He was a gifted organizer and an indefatigable missioner.

Moore, G. E. (1873–1958). English philosopher. Trained at Cambridge, he taught there for most of the rest of his life before his retirement in 1939. In 1951 he was awarded the rare British distinction of the Order of Merit. Beginning his academic career at a time when Idealism was highly influential in British philosophy, he was prominent in the movement to discredit it and to establish a position called New Realism. In his epistemology he separated the sense-datum from its object. In ethics he was an intuitionist, holding that "good" cannot be identified with any natural quality such as redness or pleasure. Generally speaking, he carried on the tradition of the older "Common Sense" school of realism but developed various refinements in upholding it.

Morality. Some writers, e.g., George Santayana, have made a distinction between morality and ethics, regarding the latter as a study of rational bases for human conduct and the former as a study of how people do develop their customary modes of behavior. In popular usage, moreover, there is a noticeable tendency to treat "moral" and "morality" as terms pertaining more specifically to questions relating to sexual behavior and to regard "ethical" and "ethics" as more general and comprehensive terms. Such distinctions seem, however, to have neither logical justification nor practical utility. It is best to treat "moral" and "ethical" as synonymous. One who specializes in the subject is a "moralist" or a "moral philosopher," contradistinguished from, say, a logician or an epistemologist.

Moral Rearmament. A name given to the group founded by Frank Buchman in 1938, widely known as "the Oxford Group." (This name is misleading because the movement had only a minimal and accidental association with Oxford in its beginnings, largely due to the interest of B. H. Streeter, Provost of The Queen's College, Oxford, at the time the movement was launched.) It was an attempt to unite all Christians in a struggle to restore traditional moral values and was geared especially to the middle classes and college-educated people. It exercised remarkable influence from its inception. Its stated basis is a commitment to search for and follow the will of God, living in the light of his absolute standards, recognized under four categories: absolute honesty, absolute purity, absolute unselfishness, and absolute love. It seeks actively to change the outlook of individuals, families, politics, and international life. It established its headquarters at Caux, Switzerland, in 1946, where people of all creeds and nationalities congregate for courses, conferences, and dialogue. It has offices and branches in Washington, London, and other international centers. See also **Buchman, Frank.**

Moral Theology. The study of the rules of conduct as traditionally under-

stood in the Catholic tradition of Christian teaching. It derives from Aristotle and other pre-Christian sources but includes, of course, biblical and patristic ones. Augustine may be regarded as having given initial shape to the system of moral theology as it has developed through the centuries. In the 17th c. controversies developed among moral theologians, notably between Jesuits and Dominicans, over various interpretations of Christian ethics such as those teaching Probabilism, Probabiliorism, and Equiprobabilism, which treated questions that would nowadays be more widely regarded as problems in Situationist ethics. The *Theologia Moralis* (1753–1775) of Alphonsus Liguori, founder of the Redemptorists, had a decisive influence within the Roman Catholic Church in establishing Probabilism and Equiprobabilism (both milder interpretations of ethical duties) over the harsher Probabiliorism. Moral Theology as traditionally understood has been regarded as a basic study for priests in their function of hearing confessions and giving counsel to penitents. In the Anglican tradition moral theology has certainly a place, but most Anglicans find the traditional Roman Catholic treatment too stylized and too out of touch with the important philosophical discussions on ethical questions. Protestant Christians generally stand outside the concept of any traditional system of moral theology and discuss questions in Christian ethics more on an *ad hoc* basis with the Bible as a general reference point. By any reckoning many questions that arise in the context of the relation between Christian faith and Christian conduct, important as they certainly must be regarded, are often too complex to be fitted into any traditional system.

Moravians. The name generally used for the Church that originated in the Bohemian Brethren. After Zinzendorf had revived and re-organized the latter in 1722, it manifested a decidedly Pietistic ingredient in its outlook yet at the same time sought to be included within the Lutheran Church, developing Zinzendorf's interesting idea of "a little church within a church" (*ecclesiola in ecclesia*). While acknowledging the Augsburg Confession as a doctrinal standard in a very loose and general way, Moravians tend to distrust all doctrinal formulae and to encourage a devotional life detached from the mainstream of Christian tradition. They are nowadays represented almost equally in Europe and North America.

More, Thomas (1478–1535). Lord Chancellor of England. Having studied classics and (at his father's behest) law, he entered Parliament in 1504. He was a man of deep commitment to a strict form of Christian life and, having married in 1505, his house in Chelsea became a center in which often foregathered Erasmus, Colet, and others of that intellectual caliber and concern for the reform of the Church from within. While an envoy to Flanders he published his most celebrated work, *Utopia* (1516), partly a presentation of an ideal community living in obedience to the natural law, partly a satire against abuses in the Church. After a rapid rise to prominence in high office, he succeeded Cardinal Wolsey in 1529 as Lord Chancellor of England. He had by this time written against Luther and treated in his writings subjects such as devotion to the saints and the use of images. Opposing King Henry VIII on the latter's desire for divorce, he resigned his office in 1532. He was imprisoned in the Tower of London for more than a year and in 1535 was accused of high treason and beheaded. He was beatified in 1886 by Leo XIII and canonized in 1935 by Pius XI.

Morgan, C. Lloyd (1852–1936). English philosopher-scientist. Born in London, he was trained under T. H. Huxley and taught in South Africa and later at Bristol, England. He held that biological evolution occurs by a process of emergence, i.e., not slowly and continuously but by sudden emergence. He saw his thought as in some ways consistent with Spinozism. God is to be seen as expressing his divine purpose in the evolutionary process. He was the originator of the phrase "method of trial and error." His writings include *Emergent Evolution* (1923); *Life, Mind, and Spirit* (1926); *Mind at the Crossways* (1929); *The Emergence of Novelty* (1933).

Mormons. The name popularly given to the body officially designated "The Church of Jesus Christ of Latter-Day Saints," founded by Joseph Smith in 1830 at Manchester, New York State. Smith claimed to have discovered the text of the Book of Mormon, which came to be regarded by his followers as authoritative scripture. In the early days of the movement polygamy was taught and practiced but eventually brought the Mormons into conflict with the Federal Government. The Church decided in 1890 to conform to the law, and in 1896 Utah was admitted to the Union.

Polygamy, however, although formally repudiated, is still promised to Mormons in the future life. For there are two ways in which marriages may be entered into: (1) for time and eternity and (2) till death do part. In Morman practice a man or woman may marry consecutively as often as he or she pleases "till death do part"; but while a man may do so as often as he pleases "for time and eternity" a woman may enter into this kind of marriage only once. Moreover, when a woman reaches an age when she is not expected to marry, she may be "spiritually" married to a deceased man, so that the Mormon heaven is still envisioned on polygamous lines. Many features of a 19th c. literalistic understanding of the Bible are incorporated into Mormon teaching and practice. Smith was killed by a mob in 1844, being succeeded by Brigham Young who removed the headquarters of the Mormon Church to Salt Lake City in 1847. He was a gifted leader and organizer and saw the followers through many hardships in the course of their development as one of the most remarkable religious movements in modern times. While the claims and the theological beliefs of its followers seem (not only to outsiders but to many born within the fold) to be too fantastic to be taken seriously, the ethical standards and lifestyle of the Mormon community and the dependability of individual Mormons are widely recognized as singularly admirable.

Mortal Sin. In traditional Roman Catholic teaching, a distinction is made between venial and mortal sin. The former, although by no means to be lightly regarded, does not result in the turning away of the soul from God in such a way as to thwart God's purpose and to put the soul outside the sanctifying grace of God that is essential to salvation. Mortal sin, which has this most grievous result (it is so called because it is said to "kill" the soul), is held to entail damnation unless confessed to and absolved by a priest acting in the name of God and by the authority of the Church. (In the absence of a priest an act of contrition is held, however, to be sufficient in an emergency such as the approach of death.) No sin is accounted mortal unless intrinsically serious (e.g., murder, adultery, embezzlement, rape) and committed with full understanding of its gravity and with full consent of the will.

Mortification. The term used in Catholic tradition for a variety of practices intended to deaden (hence the term, from *mors*, "death") the desires of the flesh, including gluttony and all sensual appetites but especially sexual desire. All ascetic practices such as fasting and abstinence from meats are traditionally accounted conducive to this aim, which has counterparts in many religions. In the medieval outlook, which much favored mortification and survives even to this day in some monastic and conventual establishments, it went beyond mere "passive" practices such as ab-

stention from pleasurable foods and drinks. In face of intense sexual urge, for example, the person would resort to more "active" methods of mortification of the flesh, such as the wearing of a hair shirt or other uncomfortable clothing or encumbrance or to flagellation with the "discipline" (usually a whip of knotted cords) either self-inflicted or administered by a spiritual director. The aim in all cases was to subdue the unruly flesh and so encourage the development of a more spiritually oriented disposition and manner of life.

Moses. For such information as we have on the life of Moses we are dependent on the biblical sources, since no extrabiblical information is available. Oral traditions behind the biblical accounts of his birth and early years are found by literary critics to take several forms. So while the evidence points to the existence of a powerful leader, Moses cannot be deemed an historical figure in the sense in which David or Solomon may be so recognized. The picturesque account in Exodus 2 tells of the baby Moses having been saved from death and adopted by an Egyptian princess who brought him up to be a scribe. The story of the finding of the baby Moses in a basket resembles so closely legends current at the time that one cannot be sure whether it is a genuine narrative or a story compiled to provide a semblance of historicity or else an ornamentation of slender historical facts at the disposal of the writer. Still, it is conceivable, however unlikely, that it could have happened as related. Even the story of the Burning Bush seems to represent various tangled traditions, and the stories attending the sojourn in Sinai likewise reflect conflated source materials. One result of all this is that Moses does not emerge in the Bible as a vivid character. He is both shy and bold, both impulsive and persevering, both judicious and a rebel, both an angry guerrilla warrior and a wise legislator. The more carefully one reads the biblical stories about Moses, the dim-mer the picture one gets. Moreover, his role as lawgiver seems to have developed slowly in the minds of generations of Israelites. Only through a very gradual process did Moses acquire the immense prestige that he had attained by the time of Christ and has ever since enjoyed as the very cornerstone of Judaism. Yet when all that has been said, there seems no reason to deny that an historical figure of great perseverance and decisiveness lies behind the complex network of stylistic ornamentation of his character.

Motu Proprio. This Latin phrase is used specifically of a decree or act of the Pope on his personal initiative and authority, without consultation with and unsupported by any other authority such as an ecclesiastical council. It may be used, however, of any such action by anyone such as the president of a society acting on his or her own initiative without reference to the customary channels of authority such as a board of trustees or directors.

Movable Feasts. By this term are designated those feasts in the Christian Year which, like Easter, do not fall, as does Christmas, for example, annually on the same day.

Mowinckel, Sigmund (1884–1965). Old Testament scholar. Norwegian-born, he was educated at the University of Oslo where, after further studies in Denmark and Germany, he spent all his academic life from 1917 to 1954. He made a special study of the Psalms, which led him to important new lines of understanding of the character and structure of other Old Testament books. *The Psalms in Israel's Worship*, 2 vols. (1962) and his *He That Cometh* (1956) are among those of his works that have been translated into English.

Mozarabic Rite. This term is in general use for those liturgical forms that were used throughout the entire Iberian peninsula from early times to the 11th c. Strictly speaking, it would apply only to the part of Spain that came under Moorish rule in 711, but the other meaning is the one that has prevailed. The Mozarabic rite has affinities with the Gallican. Some liturgists see it as derived from the latter possibly with influences from North Africa. Some Byzantine features (e.g., the Procession of the Oblations) may have been introduced as early as the 6th c. Some features, such as the fraction of the Host into seven pieces representing the mysteries of the life of Christ resemble liturgical practices observed in the Celtic Church. The music of the Mozarabic rite is preserved in manuscripts originally dating in some cases as far back as the 9th c. and may have been originally less austere than Gregorian forms. With the reconquest of Spain from the Moors, various attempts were made to replace Mozarabic forms with Roman ones, but it has been preserved in modern times largely through the influence of Cardinal Ximenes in the late 15th c. and is now one of the recognized rites in the Roman Catholic Church.

Mozetta. A short cape worn by the Pope and various other dignitaries in the Roman Catholic Church. It is of late medieval origin and varies in color according to the dignity of the ecclesiastic wearing it.

Muggletonians. A remarkable Christian sect founded in England by Ludowicke Muggleton and his cousin John Reeve about the middle of the 17th c. They claimed to be the witnesses mentioned in Revelation 11.3–6. Denying the doctrine of the Trinity they taught that while God was incarnate in the Person of Jesus Christ, the universe was temporarily under the governance of Elijah. They taught the eternality of matter and that reason was created by Satan. Never more than a small sect, it seems to have persisted into the third quarter of the 19th c. A bibliography may be found in *Hastings Encyclopaedia of Religion and Ethics*, vol 8 (1915), p. 871, by W. T. Whitley.

Muhammad (*c.* 571–632). Born, according to Muslim tradition, on April 20, 571, Muhammad was by any reckoning a man of immense vitality and endowed with extraordinary powers of leadership that were to enable him eventually to weld together many warring Arab tribes and unite them under the banner of Islam and with allegiance to Allah, the One True God. Intelligent and articulate, he had been distressed by their incessant religious and family quarrels, their idolatry, their drinking, gambling, and licentiousness at commercial fairs and other occasions. How he learned of the Jewish and Christian Scriptures that are obviously strong influences in the development of his religious thought is obscure, but there is no doubt that they did influence him and provide the groundwork of his theological ideas.

According to Muslim tradition, his father was a Quraysh, member of a tribe of the Hashimite clan, who died before Muhammad was born. Muhammad's mother died when he was six and he became a ward first of his grandfather, then of his uncle. The Qur'ān indicates (Sura 93, v. 6f.) that Muhammad was brought up in poverty. On his uncle's advice, he went to work for a rich woman, a widow named Khadijah, who needed someone to manage caravans. Muhammad was so industrious and faithful in his duties that he pleased her. By this time he was about twenty-five and she about forty. He married her: apparently a happy marriage. She bore him three sons and four daughters, but only one of the children, Fatima, survived. So much did he love Khadijah that even after her death, when he married other wives, his constant praise of Khadijah incited jealousy in them.

During the years of his marriage to Khadijah he had time to reflect on the religious matters that were troubling his soul, and she seems to have encouraged him in his concern for them. At any rate, an interior fire seemed to burn within Muhammad. He brooded over the thought of the Day of Judgment and wandered off frequently alone to the hills near Mecca for contemplation on the eternal verities. At last came what Muslims call "the night of power and excellence," which he experienced during one of his visits to a cave near the foot of Mount Hira, a few miles to the north of Mecca. An angel appeared to him crying the words recorded in Sura 96 of the Qur'ān. He returned home in great excitement and fear, not yet being sure of the authenticity of his vision, and told the story to Khadija, confiding in her the doubts he was feeling about his sanity. She, however, assured him that Allah was revealing himself to him and that he must heed Allah's command.

Muslim traditions vary concerning the details of these events, but at any rate Muhammad was soon appearing in the courtyard of the Ka'ba in Mecca and in the streets reciting the revelations he claimed to have received. He was greeted with ridicule, later with hostility. Then came the Hijra (migration) to Yathrib (later renamed Medina, "the City of the Prophet," in his honor), where eventually he established himself as a prophet and wielded remarkable authority over the city. He built a mosque, held weekly Friday services, introduced the now familiar prostrations for prayer, and a call to prayer from the roof of the mosque. Before his death ten years later he had unified the Arab tribes and established a sort of theocracy. A tradition tells that soon before his death he proclaimed the brotherhood of all Muslims. Abu Bakr, to whom Muhammad had often delegated the duty of leading the prayers, was chosen as his successor or caliph and the movement Muhammad had led continued to prosper. See also **Islam**.

Muirgen. In Celtic mythology, a female sea deity who casts spells on people and in her less benign moods lures sailors and their ships to destruction. "Muir" is from one of the Celtic words for the sea (compare Latin *mare* and Greek *genesis*, "creation, birth").

Munificentissimus Deus. The name of the document (the Apostolic Constitution) issued by Pius XII in November 1, 1950, defining as divinely revealed and therefore *de fide* the doctrine of the corporeal Assumption of the Virgin Mary into heaven. This papal action, alien to both Eastern Orthodox and Anglican tradition was regarded in both these Communions as much to be regretted.

Münzer, Thomas (*c.* 1490–1525). German Anabaptist leader. Born at Stolberg, he was trained at Leipzig and Frankfurt. Having probably met Luther at Leipzig he claimed direct inspiration by the Holy Spirit and tried to form a community of followers but was unsuccessful and tried then to do something similar among the Hussites in Bohemia, again without success. By 1523 we find him bitterly attacking Luther and denouncing Infant Baptism and other practices. Taking a leading role in the Peasants' Revolt, which Luther detested, he was eventually executed.

Muratori, Ludovico Antonio (1672–1750). Italian historian and litugical scholar. Born at Vignola, near Modena, he was trained by the Jesuits there. Ordained priest in 1695, he was attached for about five years to the Ambrosiana at Milan. He conducted massive researches in Italian history and in liturgics. His many theological works, some of them under a pseudonym, drew charges of heresy. The Spanish Inquisition began proceedings against him two years before his death. See **Muratorian Canon.**

Muratorian Canon. The name given to the oldest list of New Testament writings that is now extant. It takes its name from Ludovico Muratori who discovered it in the Ambrosiana. (See **Muratori, Ludovico Antonio.**) The manuscript itself is an 8th-c. one but the list appears, from internal evidence, to date from the later part of the 2nd c. All the New Testament books are listed except Hebrews, James, and I and II Peter. It has been attributed to Hippolytus.

Murjites. See **Kharijites** and **Mutazilites.**

Mutakallimūn. In the history of Islamic thought the two principal and most powerful schools were the Mutakallim and the Mutazilites. The former represented the more orthodox outlook.

Mutazilites. In the history of Islamic thought, the name (meaning literally "seceders") given to members of a rationalistic school who accepted a free will doctrine (as did the Qadarites) in opposition to the Chaborites who held a strongly deterministic view. The two most influential of such Islamic schools of thought were the Mutazilites and the Mutakallimūn. The latter represent the more orthodox Muslim outlook. See **Mutakallimūn.**

Muwahhidūn, The. The name by which the Druze are more correctly designated. See **Druze, The.**

Mystery Religions. The cults that we call "mystery religions" became extremely popular in Hellenistic and Roman society. They were esoteric, i.e., they purported to teach secret doctrine, and those who were initiated were under oath never to reveal the nature of the rites. That is why our knowledge of the details of such rites is limited. Nevertheless, scholars have reconstructed them to a considerable extent. The mystery cults of the ancient Graeco-Roman world may be classified under seven heads: (1) *Orphism.* According to the myth of Orpheus, he rescued his dead wife Euridice from the underworld by his music, then lost her again because of his glancing back at her before they had fully emerged. Orphism taught that the soul is immortal and that it is re-embodied over and over again. It is extremely ancient, probably prehistoric in origin. (2) *The Great Mother Cult.* The rites of this cult included in some cases the self-castration of the initiates in imitation of Attis who, in remorse for his infidelity to the Great Mother, Cybele, so deprived himself. (3) *The Eleusinian Cult.* This very famous cult took its name from the place of its origin: Eleusis, near Athens. It dated from classical times. Behind it was a myth that Pluto, the god of the underworld, raped Prosperpine, the daughter of Demeter, the goddess of the earth, who however recovered Prosperpine for half of the year. The motifs celebrated included the vegetation cycle and the annual renewal of life, by participating in symbolic representations that assured one of continuing fertility. (4) *The Dionysian Cult.* This cult took various forms, all, however, having as their central theme the resurrection of the god. The rites, probably originating in Thrace, were generally orgiastic. (5) *The Adonis Cult.* Adonis, a vegetation god, also died and was resurrected. His mysteries had their origin in Byblos and he functioned similarly to Baal of the Canaanites. (6) *The Isis and Osiris Cult.* The mysteries associated with these Egyptian deities were also believed by their devotees to bring them closer to the cycle of life and so invest them with immortality. (7) *Mithraism.* The rites associated with Mithra were of Iranian origin. Mithra was a sun god. The participants in these mysteries slayed a bull to release the life-force. This form of mystery religion seems to have been popular among the Roman soldiers.

Some scholars early in the 20th c., seeing some resemblances between these mystery cults and Christianity, thought that the latter had been a development of the former and dependent upon them. This view has now been generally abandoned and most scholars today tend to see Christianity as, rather, a specific rejection of the religious path taken by the mystery religions, offering instead a way of salvation to a new quality of life: a way that takes the Christian into another dimension of being. The most basic roots of Christian life are to be sought in its Jewish ancestor, al-

though one must bear in mind that Judaism itself by the time of Christ had been already much hellenized. Paul specifically alludes to the wisdom of God, a mystery unkown to the world and its rulers and contrasted to the wisdom of that world (I Corinthians 2.7). The New Testament contains many allusions similarly distinguishing the mysteries of the Christian Way from the mysteries admired and celebrated by the world.

Mystical Theology. As a branch of Christian theology, mystical theology is traditionally contrasted to ascetical theology. Both deal with the spiritual or interior life, but while ascetical theology treats of this in terms of human efforts toward spirituality, mystical theology is concerned with spirituality as it develops under divine initiative. Differences of opinion are expressed by Christian writers on spirituality concerning the relation of these two kinds of theology, but the notion that one should seek to obtain mystical experience is generally disapproved in Christian teaching on the spiritual life. Mystical ecstasy, if one is so fortunate as to attain it, comes through the grace of God as a special gift. Christian mysticism takes many distinctive forms, e.g., Benedictine contemplation has a very different spirit from that of, say, the Spanish mystics. Generally speaking, however, all the schools that produce the extraordinarily rich texture of Christian mysticism regard authentic mystical experience as an immediate, direct knowledge of God discovered in a state of prayer. Proof of the authenticity of such an extraordinary attainment is to be found in the beautiful spiritual fruits it produces, such as a deep and special kind of humility and sacrificial love.

While mysticism is a phenomenon common to many of the great religions of the world, the Christian mystic reports a dimension of mystical experience that differs sharply from what is presupposed in Hindu, Buddhist, and other religions, which see in mystical experience the recognition of the identity of the individual soul with God. This runs counter to the reports of Christian mystics who typically find the ultimate reality that is discovered and known through this extraordinary experience as the Wholly Other, transcending both the individual and the entire universe. The analogy most commonly used by Christian mystics, when pressed to provide one, is that of human love, in which relationship one's own individuality and that of the beloved are discovered and accented by the character of the love. So there is never a complete "melting." The Spanish mystics, some of whom talk at times as if there were a complete fusion in a mystical "marriage" between the soul and God, guard against such a misunderstanding by speaking of an *hilo de amor*, a cord of love which, although it binds together God and the individual soul, nevertheless attests by its presence the fundamental separation and distinctness of Creator and creature. Some Christian theologians (especially in the Reformation heritage) regard mysticism with suspicion, but it permeates Christian life so deeply and extensively that it is an inescapable ingredient in the life of the Church. It occurs within the Reformation heritage very strikingly although no doubt usually in a different "key" from that characteristic of Catholic and Eastern Orthodox mystical traditions. It is found unmistakably in many of the biblical writers, notably Paul. That does not mean, of course, that every kind of mysticism can claim biblical warrant.

Mysticism. See **Mystical Theology.**

Myth. This term, from the Greek *mythos*, is popularly taken to signify a fictitious story involving supernatural agencies or phenomena such as are characteristic of legends and "fairy tales." Scholars recognize in myth, however, a much more important literary form and one that plays a vital part in the transmission of both philosophical and religious ideas. The great classic myths of all religions and cultures present perceptions of reality in the form of stories, usually imaginative and picturesque. On this view, myth, far from signifying the fictitious, is a means of conveying truths about reality too profound to be expressed in philosophical abstractions or theological propositions. Myth, so understood, is a channel of the deepest perception of reality: a perception that, although no form of human discourse can adequately express it, can be conveyed by a story in mythic form. In the words of Paul, we can see such truth "through a glass, darkly" (I Corinthians 13.12). A great vision of reality seen even through opaque glass is worth much more than a trivial one seen with all the clarity of logical discourse.

N

Nabataeans. This Arabian tribe is mentioned in I Maccabees 5.25 and 9.35. Beginning as a nomadic desert people, they emerged near the end of the 4th c. BCE and settled in a region comprising the former territories of Edom and Moab and beyond to the south. This position was strategic because the caravan routes between Syria and Arabia passed through this region and were therefore under the control of the Nabataeans. Petra was their most famous city. They developed a remarkably advanced type of civilization, both urban and agricultural, with technologically skillful systems of water conservation and control, for example, including cisterns, dams, and canals. They displayed also skill in diplomatic relations with other peoples. Their religion seems to have included a syncretistic mix of Semitic and Hellenistic gods. Somewhat surprisingly, they seem to have left no literature. What we know of them is due largely to the explorations of archaeologists such as Nelson Glueck.

Nabi. In Islamic usage, this term is used of all prophets, of whom, according to Muslim tradition, there were tens of thousands, all forerunners of Muhammad, to whom, however, is accorded the title as the final prophet, the prophet *par excellence*, the messenger of Allah. Although the term *rasul* is sometimes considered a higher title than that of *nabi*, both are commonly used interchangeably. See also **Rasul**.

Nāgārjuna. 2nd c. Buddhist teacher, regarded as the founder of the Madhyamika school. The method used by Nāyārjuna and others of the same class of teacher is that of reasoned discussion of ideas of the Buddha found in his own words in the *Sutras*. See **Sūtra**.

Nag Hammadi Library, The. A collection of thirteen papyrus codices found in 1945 preserved in a jar near Chenoboskion some sixty miles below Luxor, Egypt. All are now housed in the Coptic Museum in Cairo except for one, whch is in the Jung Institute, Zürich. The text is predominantly in the Sahidic dialect of Coptic and constitutes the most important modern contribution to an understanding of Gnosticism. For an English translation with introductory notes, see James M. Robinson (ed.), *The Nag Hammadi Library* (1977).

Naive Realism. Western philosophers have sometimes used this term to denote a form of realism so simplistic that probably no one with any reflective capacities at all has ever seriously entertained it, namely, that the qualities we sense in objects in the external world (e.g., the sweetness of honey, the smell of cigar smoke, the sound of B flat in a violin) actually exist as realities in precisely the way that we experience them. See **Realism**.

Nam Simaran. A meditation technique used by the Sikhs. According to the teaching of Nanak, the Sikh founder, *Nam simaran* means regular, disciplined meditation on the divine name, through repetition and remembrance. By engaging in such meditation one passes beyond the present dimension of being into ineffable bliss. A particular *mantra* or scriptural verse may be used for this kind of meditation, and a form of rosary may be employed for the purpose, as a mechanical aid.

Narsai. A 5th c. Nestorian theologian. Having become head of the important school at Edessa, he had to flee because of increasing hostility to Nestorius and his followers. He settled in Nisiblis, where he wrote commentaries, homilies, and hymns.

Narthex. The vestibule or antechamber to the nave of a church. It was originally for catechumens and others who were not permitted to enter the church but could assemble outside it in this vestibule area. When it so functioned, it was distinguished from the porch leading out to the street, which, in Byzantine churches, was called the exonarthex. In common usage in the West today the narthex is simply the vestibule area between the west door and the nave of a church.

Nash Papyrus, The. A fragment of papyrus in the Cambridge University Library containing a form of the Decalogue with some other materials. If, as some experts maintain, it is to be dated as early as the 2nd c. BCE, it is the oldest known fragment of any part of the Hebrew Bible, the Qumran scroll of Isaiah not excepted. It was acquired in 1902 by W. L. Nash.

Natalitia. This Latin term, meaning "birthday", was used in the early Church to designate the day on which a Christian died, especially a martyr or other person noted for his or her sanctity. It referred to the celebration of the person's birth into everlasting life. In the present custom adopted by the Salvation Army, in which the phrase "promoted to glory" is used in obituary notices, may perhaps be found an echo of the notion behind this early Christian practice.

National Covenant, The. See **Covenanters**.

Natural Philosophy. The term "philosophy" (literally "the love of wisdom") formerly included all knowledge (*scientia*) that could be attained through the use of human reason. What is now called psychology, for instance, was till comparatively recent times included as one of the philosophical disciplines, along with ethics and logic. Physics, chemistry, and other such sciences were called "natural" philosophy—that is, the philosophy of Nature contradistinguished from the philosophy of Being or Mind or God.

Native American Church. A religious movement with pre-Columbian antecedents that emerged among Amerindian tribes in the 19th c. Adherents used a hallucinogen, mescal, obtained from the peyote cactus and originally used for medical purposes. The movement spread quickly, especially among those who perceived themselves as disadvantaged. It led to the formation of the Native American Church, a syncretistic movement using drums, songs, visions, and the calumet (a sacred pipe) alongside elements from Christian liturgical practice. Some fifty tribes are said to be represented by the adherents of this Native American Church, who perceive themselves as Indian Christians.

Natural Theology. Medieval theologians held that though some truths about God—for example, the Incarnation and the Trinity—could be known only through divine revelation, other truths—such as the existence of God—were accessible to and could be worked out exclusively by human reason (cf. Rom. 1:18 ff.). The body of knowledge about God that could be attained through the latter means alone came to be called "natural theology" (contradistinguished from "*revealed* theology"). Natural theology may be regarded, therefore, as a philosophical rather than as a theological discipline and so as an antecedent of what is now called the philosophy of religion. Though the Reformers generally rejected the concept of natural theology, the use of the term was revived—especially by those who, like the English deists (see **Deism**), stressed the role of reason in religion.

Naturalism. The view that the universe is self-existent, self-explanatory, and self-directing. Naturalists generally see the world process deterministically (see **Determinism and Indeterminism**) and man as only its incidental product.

Natura Naturans, Natura Naturata. These phrases, as used by Spinoza, signify respectively the eternal and infinite essence and the temporal existents that follow of necessity from that eternal principle. Although their use in Spinoza is the most generally known, they had been already used by others, e.g., by the Dominican encyclopedist Vicente de Beauvais in the early 13th c., who had used them in designating the traditional Christian distinction between the creative act of God and the creatures that are the effect of that act. Giordano Bruno also used them to distinguish the transcendence and the immanence of God. Averroes (1126–1198) had used the term *natura naturata* to designate the creatures that result from the creative principle that is God.

Nature. From *natura*, the Latin counterpart of the Greek word *physis* from which we derive terms such as "physics." The early Greeks thought of nature as that aspect of reality in which change could be observed. Physics was the study of it. Plato inherited this general outlook. Aristotle saw in nature five characteristics: (1) it exists without its having been constructed as is a temple or a pair of shoes; (2) it is not eternal; (3) it contains matter or potency; (4) it has a principle of movement within it; and (5) it has essence. In Aristotle's perception, nature is one aspect of reality among others. The Stoics, by contrast, saw nature as consisting of all there is, to which, therefore, everything must be said to belong. In the 17th c. Spinoza followed the Stoic model in this respect, seeing nature as inclusive of God and man.

Naujote. The term used by Parsees for the rite of initiation into Zoroastrianism, corresponding to what Iranian Zoroastrians call sedre-pushan. Traditionally it was performed at puberty but nowadays more generally at nine or eleven. It consists of receiving and wearing for the first time the *sudreh*, a sacred shirt, and the *custi* or cord. The former is of white cotton and the latter of plaited lamb's wool.

Nave. That part of a church (in parish churches usually the largest) between the chancel or apse at the east end and the narthex or entrance at the west end of the building. Traditionally the term is taken to come from the Latin word *navis*, "ship", and this derivation suggests beautiful connotations, e.g., the "Bark of Peter," symbol of the Church itself, which affords protection as Noah found protection in the ark, being tossed on the waves of the world yet never submerged. Some suggest, however, that the term "nave" may be derived from the Greek word *naos*, "temple." The nave is separated from the chancel or apse by altar rails or, where possible, a screen carved in wood or stone.

Nayler, James (*c.* **1618–1660**). Quaker. Born near Wakefield, Yorkshire, he served in the Parliamentary army where he was known for his preaching. Having become convinced of George Fox's teaching on the Inner Light, he took a leading part in the Quaker movement. His life subsequently was stormy. He suffered much persecution, some of it no doubt justified by the extravagance of his opinions and claims, and he quarrelled with Fox with whom, however, he was reconciled before his death. See **Fox, George**.

Nazirites. This group of Israelites (commonly but less correctly spelt "Nazarites" in English) took religious vows to abstain from wine, to leave their hair uncut and their beards unshaven, and to avoid contact with dead bodies. (See Numbers 6; also Acts 21.23–6.) Samson, who probably flourished in the 11th c. BCE, was among those who had taken the Nazirite vow.

Neander, Johann August Wilhelm (**1789–1850**). Church historian. Jewish by birth, his original name was David Mendel. After his conversion and Christian baptism he assumed the name by which he is commonly known. He taught Church history at Berlin from 1813 till his death. His major work on Church history, in 6 vols. (1826–1852) was for long much used. He was a devout man who admired spirituality and had little interest in ecclesiastical institutions as such.

Neo-Kantianism. So immensely influential was Kant that after his death in 1804 and the rise of Hegel and the idealist kinds of philosophy that Hegelianism fostered, a movement developed in the 1860s that came to be called "Neo-Kantian" and that persisted till after World War I. In 1865 Otto Liebmann issued a slogan "Back to Kant," which became a sort of rallying cry of the movement, which had received its impetus from a growing impatience with the sometimes extravagant claims of the 19th c. idealists. Some Neo-Kantians saw the movement as a way back to the epistemological concerns that they perceived as the most important task of philosophers. Others saw it as a catalyst for the development of modern science. The Marburg school of Neo-Kantianism saw philosophy as a critical analysis of the sciences. The views of individual members of this school varied considerably, however, for they included men as varied as Hermann Cohen, Paul Natorp, Friedrich Lange, Ernst Cassirer, and Rudolf Stammler. Neo-Kantianism, although primarily a German movement, had representation in other countries too.

Neoplatonism. The name given to the philosophical system originated by Plotinus and developed by those who followed his mode of thought. It is so called because it was indeed inspired by the thought of Plato, whose teachings the Neoplatonists developed along very special lines and with a distinctively religious bent. Alexandria may be said to have cradled the movement, but the movement spread quickly throughout the Empire. In the 3rd c. Porphyry and in the 5th c. Proclus were among the many distinguished representatives of the school. To what extent if any Plotinus had been personally influenced by the tradition of Christian Platonism at Alexandria or by Jewish scholars in the Platonic tradition, such as Philo, is by no means clear. His intellectual heritage seems to lie, rather, in the mainstream of Greek philosophical tradition. That he gave a religious mold to his thought is plain enough, but Neoplatonism was a rival to Christianity rather than an offshoot or companion.

Neoplatonism was certainly a powerful rival to Christianity, and it may not be too much to say that its eventual failure to compete with the latter lay in its being too much of an intellectual movement to appeal to so wide an audience as that which the Christian Way eventually attracted. Its purpose was indeed to provide a philosophy that would do justice to ethical and religious values. The realms of reality and thought were united in the One who could be known to the human mind only by a method of abstract thought. One must divest the mind of all attributes and all categories in which it is accustomed to think and proceed in a negative way to find the residue, which is the One. (This procedure has obvious affinities with the one suggested in Indian philosophy in the Sanskrit phrase *neti neti*, "not this, not this," used by Upanishadic and other Indian thinkers in allusion to the way in which God is to be discovered.) This One, Plotinus taught, has its center everywhere and its circumference nowhere. This One, the principle of unity, is related to the world by a series of intermediaries derived from the One by a process of emanations. Thus is intended to be preserved both the transcendence of God and his immanence.

Tendencies toward the movement that has its focus in Plotinus may be seen in his teacher, the 3rd c. Ammonius Saccas, about whom, however, very little is known, and in Origen. The latter, however, although indubitably a Christian Platonist, is too definitely committed to the biblical tradition to be classed with the Neoplatonists. Both Platonism and Neoplatonism have influenced the mold of Christian thought to an incalculably great extent, particularly but by no means exclusively in the development of the various forms of Christian mystical theology, from the 4th c. down to the present. Till the rediscovery of Aristotle in the West in the 12th c., Latin Christian thinkers had really no other intellectual mold in which to formulate their thought, and indeed it pervaded the thought of the schoolmen in many ways even after Aristotle had challenged such traditional ways of thinking.

Nestorianism. The Nestorians took their name from Nestorius, a 5th c. monk at Antioch who had been much influenced by the teachings of the Antiochene school and who in general championed orthodox Christian teaching but opposed the use of the term *Theotokos* of the Virgin Mary. The Nestorians came to teach that in the Incarnate Christ there had been two *separate* Persons, one human, one divine. To what extent Nestorius had really departed from accepted orthodoxy is not entirely clear, but he was so emphatic in his insistence on the two natures in Christ and the impossibility of their being physically united in Christ's Person, that he fostered a schism in which the orthodox position as defined in the Council of Chalcedon in 451 CE was resisted by Monophysites, on the one hand, and, on the other, by the Nestorians. The latter eventually formed themselves into a Nestorian Church, which grew extensively, engaging in successful missionary endeavors in regions as far away as Arabia and India. See **Monophysitism** and **Theotokos**.

Neutral Monism. A philosophical attempt to resolve the long-standing opposition of those who have taken reality to be essentially mental and those who have taken it to be material. According to the neutral monists it is neither but, rather, a stuff which, when organized in one way yields what we call material and when organized in another way yields what we call mental or spiritual. Bertrand Russell, in expounding this view, used the analogy of the warp and woof of a woven cloth. See **Monism**.

Neutral Text. In modern literary analysis of the New Testament, the type of text represented by Codex Vaticanus and Codex Sinaiticus was held by F. J. A. Hort to be more reliable than other textual "families." See **Western Text**.

New Church. Name given to the "Church of the New Jerusalem" consisting of a group of followers of the great Swedish scientist Emanuel Swedenborg (1688–1772), who turned to the study of spiritual realities and held converse with angels. Awareness of the correspondence between the empirical world and the spiritual dimension of reality beyond it *is* the Second Coming of Jesus Christ. See **Swedenborg, Emanuel**.

Newman, John Henry (1801–1890). Tractarian and eventually convert to the Roman Catholic Church. In the Church of England in his childhood, the influence of 18th c. Deism had hardly abated. He found the typical sermon moralistic rather than about repentance and grace, revelation and faith. He entered Trinity College, Oxford, in 1817 and became a Fellow of Oriel College in 1822. By the early 1830s he was associated with the movement at Oxford that was bent on return to the great ancient themes of churchmanship, with an em-

phasis on both Scripture and tradition, on the great early Church Fathers and the Catholic spirit that they believed the Church of England had inherited but was in danger of losing. Newman's deep spirituality and the quiet, incisive character of his sermons found response not only at Oxford, where he was becoming a leading spirit, but to some extent through the entire English Church. His writings, such as *Parochial and Plain Sermons* (1834–1842) and *The Arians of the Fourth Century* (1833) awakened many to the spiritual torpor into which England had fallen and the need for a deeper appreciation of the Anglican heritage. At this time Newman was far from "romanizing" tendencies in his churchmanship. On the contrary, his *Tracts for the Times* (1833–1841) defended the traditional claim of the Anglican position as the *via media*, the middle way between the meretriciousness of Rome, with her incomprehension of the spiritual importance of the Reformation, on the one hand, and, on the other, the excesses, ignorance, and insensitivity of so much of Protestantism. Newman pleaded for a return to the great sources of the Christian Church. Nevertheless, as the years passed he became more and more insistent on the recovery of Catholic tradition.

To understand the situation one must bear in mind tht he was living in the age in which Romanticism was affecting almost every aspect of European life and culture. Interest in the greatness of the Middle Ages, which had been an absurdly neglected and depreciated millennium in history, was slowly being recognized. At last, in 1841, Tract 90 appeared, in which Newman openly advocated the interpretation of the Thirty-Nine Articles of the Church of England in a way that many saw as romanization. It caused a bitter controversy. By this time Newman was the undoubted leader of a movement that had very profoundly affected Oxford and, through Oxford, the entire churchmanship of England. Meanwhile, however, Newman was beginning to have misgivings about the position he had so patiently, competently, and persistently defended with immense sincerity. For some years between 1841 and 1845 he lived in Littlemore, near Oxford, in a sort of retirement and eventually was received on October 9, 1845, into the Roman Catholic Church, leaving E. B. Pusey, a learned and influential Oxford biblical scholar, as leader of the movement that was in time to become known as the Tractarian movement. (See **Tractarianism**.) Ordained priest at Rome, he established a house of the Oratorians at Birmingham, England, in 1849. In 1864, largely as a result of a literary feud with Charles Kingsley, who represented a very different party in the English Church, he wrote his *Apologia pro vita sua*, a most impressively open and sincere account of his spiritual struggles. In this book he mentioned that he had come across a Latin exercise book of his dated when he was ten years old at the top of which he had mysteriously drawn a necklace of heads with a little cross at the end of it. He recalled also that as a boy he constantly crossed himself. In the very "Protestant" ambience in which he was brought up in the English Church of his boyhood days, how could he have known of the rosary or of the sign of the cross? Much of his more mature thought is to be found in *The Grammar of Assent* (1870). His well-known estrangement from Cardinal Manning apparently delayed for long his recognition by Rome, but at last, in 1879, Pope Leo XIII made him a cardinal. His influence on Catholic spirituality both in the Anglican and in the Roman tradition is indubitably immense. He was by any reckoning one of the greatest religious figures of the 19th century.

Newton, Isaac (1642–1727). English physicist. Born at Woolsthorpe, he was trained at Cambridge where he held a chair from 1675 till 1701. Elected a Fellow of the Royal Society in 1672, he was elected its president in 1703 and re-elected regularly till his death. He received a knighthood in 1705. Indubitably one of the greatest scientists of his day in Europe, he was known to the most prominent scholars and scientists throughout the western world and was a close friend of some of them, e.g., John Locke. Voltaire admired and made known his work in France, being apparently the first to tell the now famous story of Newton's discovery of the law of gravitation through reflection on a falling apple that he had noticed at his birthplace in 1666. Newton and Leibniz independently discovered the differential calculus. In Newton's greatest work the *Principia Mathematica*, he expounded the mechanics of motion in a way that put physics and astronomy permanently in his debt. His work on gravitation was likewise extremely influential, although of course many developments have taken place since his time, and both quantum physics and Einstein's theory of relativity have changed the way that physicists today think about the universe and altered the cosmologies that scientists today can entertain. His mechanistic understanding of the universe was in line with the thought of his day as was his outlook on religion. He recognized the existence of God, seeing him as necessary to explain both why there is anything at all and why the law of gravitation permits the stars to stay apart instead of pulling them together. His chief works are his *Mathematical Principles of Natural Philosophy (Philosophiae Naturalis Principia Mathematica)* (1687) and his *Opticks* (1704).

Nibbāna. See **Nirvāṇa**.

Nibbati. See **Nirvāṇa**.

Nibbuta. See **Nirvāṇa**.

Nicaea, Council of. The first Ecumenical Council of the Christian Church was held at Nicaea in 325, with the main purpose of dealing with the Arian controversy. (See **Arianism**.) It was summoned by the Emperor Constantine, no doubt principally to achieve unity within the Church. The Council issued a short creed defending the generally accepted christology against that of the Arians and ending in the words "And in the Holy Spirit." This creed is known to scholars as "the Nicene Creed," but it is not what is generally understood and presented in liturgical documents as "the Nicene Creed." The latter is known to scholars by the more precise designation, "The Niceno-Constantinopolitan Creed," which deals more extensively with the doctrine of the Person of Christ, has a fuller section on the nature, function, and work of the Holy Spirit, and adds at the end affirmations about Baptism, Resurrection, and the Life of the World to come. It has been generally regarded (although indisputably based on the work of the Council of Nicaea of 325) as the work of the Council of Constantinople of 381. Its connection with this later council is not entirely clear, however, although it certainly contains important elements not formulated at the Council of Nicaea of 325.

Another council was held at Nicaea in 787, known as the Second Council of Nicaea and recognized as the Seventh Ecumenical Council of the Christian Church. This council had been summoned to end the controversy about the use of images. (See **Iconoclastic Controversy**.) Besides dealing with various abuses, it definitely decreed in favor of the use of images and against the iconoclasts. The restoration of the icons in devotional practice was celebrated in 842 and is commemorated annually in the Greek Church to this day. See **Orthodoxy, The Feast of**.

Nicene Creed. See **Nicaea, Council of**.

Nichiren. Name of a Japanese sect called after its founder, a 13th c. teacher, whom his followers call an incarnation of Bosatsu Jogyo, an early disciple of the Buddha.

Nicholas of Cusa (1401–1464). German philosopher and cardinal. Born at Cues on the Moselle River, he was trained at Heidelberg, Padua, and Cologne. Ordained priest in 1430, he wrote the *De Concordantia Catholica* (1433), in which important work he drew up a proposal for the reform of the Church. At first a strong supporter of the Conciliarist movement, he seems to have lost heart in the pursuit of this cause, apparently finding it unproductive of the results it had been intended to achieve. His more philosophical work is of the highest importance. His general outlook was in a Neoplatonic mold and he had been much influenced by Augustine, Proclus, Dionysius the Pseudo-Areopagite, and Bonaventure, but his thought was directed, rather, to the Quattrocento Renaissance and contained highly original elements. In his chief work, *De Docta Ignorantia* (On Learned Ignorance) (1440), he defended two central principles: (1) Since Truth, which he held to be absolute and simple, is beyond human ken, the highest intellectual stance available to humanity is "learned ignorance" by which he meant that human knowledge, in the nature of the case, is at best only an approximation to it and may often be more like a parody on it. (2) We can nevertheless discover God through an intuitive apprehension of the *coincidentia oppositorum*, the perception that God lies where all contradictions meet: the maximum and the minimal, the infinite and the infinitesimal, the center and the circumference, the farthest and the nearest, everywhere and nowhere. He wrote many other works including a defense against the charge of pantheism: *Apologia doctae ignorantiae*.

Nicolaitans. In Revelation 2.6 and 2.14f., reference is made to a group of persons so designated, who may possibly have been a Gnostic sect of that name, although it seems fairly probable that the name was merely a figurative invention on the basis of an association of the name Nicholas with that of the Hebrew Balaam of which it is the Greek counterpart. Those designated Nicolaitans, whoever they were, are represented as urging a return to pagan culture, customs, and worship.

Nicole, Pierre (1625–1695). French theologian. Born at Chartres, he was trained in Paris and went to teach at Port-Royal, where he formed a close and lasting association with Antoine Arnauld. He wrote in defense of traditional Catholic doctrines such as Transubstantiation and the Real Presence and against Calvinism, but his main thrust was in defense of Jansenism, although he wrote upon it more moderately than most Jansenist opponents of the view that eventually prevailed in the Roman Catholic Church. He also opposed mysticism in general and Quietism in particular. His major work is his *Essai de morale*, 4 vols. (1671–1678), in which he applied Christian teaching to the details of everyday life. His principal work in defense of Jansenism is his *Dix Lettres sur l'hérésie imaginaire* (1664–1665). In his posthumous *Traité de la grâce générale*, 2 vols. (1715), he renounced Jansenist teaching.

Niebuhr, Reinhold (1892–1971). American theologian and political writer. Born in Wright City, Missouri, and trained at Elmhurst College, Eden Seminary, and Yale, he was ordained to the ministry of the Evangelical and Reformed Church in 1915. For most of his academic life he was Professor of Applied Christianity at Union Theological Seminary, New York, to which chair he had been appointed in 1928. Influenced by Karl Barth and Emil Brunner, he departed very definitely from Barth in his insistence that the Christian Way must be expressed in a Christian culture. His Gifford Lectures, *The Nature and Destiny of Man*, 2 vols. (1941–1943), exercised much influence on American opinion, more especially among those inclined to "liberalism" in political and social questions.

A powerful personality, he was indefatigable as a speaker and a prolific writer whose works also include *Moral Man and Immoral Society* (1932), *Beyond Tragedy* (1938), *Christian Realism and Political Problems* (1954), and *Man's Nature and his Communities* (1965).

Niemöller, (Friedrich Gustav Emil) Martin (1892–1984). German Lutheran pastor. Born at Lippstadt, Westphalia, he was educated at the Gymnasium at Elberfeld, served in the German Navy from 1910 till 1919 (when he retired with the rank of *Kapitänleutnant*), then did his theological studies at Münster, becoming a pastor in 1924. Arrested in 1937 for his opposition to the National Socialist government, which at first he had welcomed, he was in concentration camps at Sachsenhausen and Dachau till 1945, refusing offers of release under certain conditions that he found unacceptable. He became a prominent, indeed perhaps the leading symbolic figure of heroic Christian resistance to National Socialism during the height of its power. He was President of the World Council of Churches from 1961 to 1968. Having taken a leading part, after World War II, in the "Declaration of Guilt" at Stuttgart. He was the author of many books and more than a hundred articles on theological and socio-political subjects.

Nietzsche, Friedrich Wilhelm (1944–1900). German philosopher. Born in Röcken, Prussia, he had an outstanding student career at Leipzig and was appointed to a teaching position at Basel in 1869, becoming full professor at that university the following year. In 1897 he resigned because of poor health and for ten years lived a solitary type of life in Switzerland and Italy. During the last decade of his life he was mentally ill. Cosmopolitan in outlook, and holding "the Good European" as his ideal, he broke the friendship he had had with Richard Wagner because of his distaste for the latter's enthusiasm for the new German Empire. Nietzsche is one of the greatest thinkers in the history of Western philosophy. He found in Greek tragedy the mingling of two elements, equally important: Dionysian passion and ecstasy and Apollonian serenity and calm. So he found a means of uniting the classical and romantic elements in European thought and culture. In ethics he found both a "master" morality and a "slave" morality, the former conservative of the established rules of society and of an ethic of self-affirmation, the latter an ethic grounded in hatred and revenge. Both are necessary, but the former is closer to Nietzsche's ideal, which he saw expressed in the notion of "will to power." In "slave" morality he saw the sickness that was holding Europe in its grip, condemning it to mediocrity by its exaltation of the morality of the herd over that of the individual. He found this sickness both in democracy and in Christianity as commonly interpreted. Morality had become stultified, moribund, if not dead. So he makes a madman scream "God is dead," signifying that the traditional concepts of religion and ethics had petrified. He called for a "transvaluation of values," to express the need he saw to conceive of new understandings that would lead man to a stage beyond, that of the *Übermensch*, the "overman." Man must be seen no longer as a species but, rather, as a stage in the evolutionary process, the next stage of which he expressed in the concept of the "overman." The "overman" is creative, noble, magnanimous, open, compassionate toward those at less advanced levels of evolutionary development, but above all resolute in the development and promotion of the new way of thinking that Nietzsche wished to foster, with all its ideals. By no means did he see the "superman" as about to emerge all over the world in the next generation or the next century. On the contrary, he saw the "overman" as having already emerged in noble individuals. He wished, rather, to foster conditions more favorable to the encouragement of more such development. He saw the universe as cyclic, expressing his views on this in terms of what he called "eternal recurrence," which he found to be thoroughly compatible with contemporary scientific thought.

His writings include his *Menschliches, Allzumenschliches* (*Human, All Too Human*) (1878), *Also sprach Zarathustra* (*Thus Spake Zarathustra*) (1883–91), *Jenseits von Gut und Böse* (*Beyond Good and Evil*) (1886), and his posthumous *Der Wille zur Macht* (The Will to Power) (1901).

Night. As the day was divided in antiquity into hours, the night was divided into watches. In Greek and Roman usage there were four such watches; in Jewish usage three. Most peoples in antiquity regarded the night with some degree of superstitious fear. Therefore it comes to symbolize the reign of evil spirits, the time when order and industry give way to anarchy and idleness, for one cannot control actions in the dark as one may hope to control them in daylight hours, and since artificial lighting was by today's standards meager and inefficient little work could be done.

Nihilianism. The doctrine, propounded by Peter of Poitiers and some other 12th c. Christian theologians, that Christ, in respect of his human nature, was *nihil* ("nothing"), since his essence was in his Godhead only. This teaching was condemned in 1170. See also **Monophysitism.**

Nihilism. The term comes from the Latin word *nihil*, "nothing," It was apparently first coined by Turgeniev in his novel *Fathers and Children* (1862) to apply to a movement in 19th c. Russia which, in desperation for social reform, engaged in anarchist activities (e.g., the assassination of Tsar Alexander II and various Government officials) without any political or social theory to support or justify such actions but rather on the view that such negativity and destructionism has a positive value in itself, needing no theory to justify it. The *concept* of nihilism, however, has been expressed in a variety of forms from antiquity down to the present day. For example, Pyrrhonism, an extreme form of skepticism that taught that no knowledge is possible, may be called an epistemological nihilism. Nihilism can also take ethical and theological forms.

Nikon (1605–1681). Patriarch of Moscow. As a Russian monk, he went on a journey to Moscow in 1646, where the Tsar Alexis appointed him archimandrite of the Novospaski monastery there. He rose quickly in the Russian hierarchy, becoming, in 1652, Patriarch of Moscow. Nikon made important reforms, notably in the liturgy, and for several years had immense influence with the Tsar, but then lost favor and resigned. After various vicissitudes, including many years of imprisonment, he was restored to imperial favor by Feodor II (Alexis's successor) and is now regarded by many as the greatest bishop in the history of Russia.

Nimbus. A special form of halo. See **Halo.**

Nimrod. According to the biblical account (Genesis 10.8–10), Nimrod was the first of the "heroes." In Babylonian lore he has a parallel in Gilgamesh.

Ninian (*c.* 360–*c.* 432). Scottish missionary. The son of a Cumbrian chieftain who had been converted to Christianity, Ninian went to Rome where he was consecrated bishop in 394 and returned to Scotland in hope of converting his people. He founded a church at Whithorn, Wigtownshire, in the extreme southwest, dedicating it to Martin of Tours, whom he had met on his way back from Rome. He called it *Candida Casa* (white house). It became an important center that Ninian's monks used as a base for their missionary endeavors among the neighboring Britons and southern Picts. It gained much repute for its learning.

Nirvāna. A Sanskrit term meaning "blown out," "extinguished." (The Pali form of the word is *Nibbāna.*) The term appears to have its origin in the Vedantic scriptures. It is found in the Vedas

and in the *Bhagavad-Gītā,* but it is most prominent in Buddhism. It is an extremely difficult concept and has been subject to a variety of interpretations. No doubt the Buddha himself perceived its susceptibility to misunderstanding and misinterpretation, for he stated that whatever may be said of it will be in error. It can be interpreted as annihilation, and in Hinayana Buddhism one may get that impression of its meaning. Mahayanists, however, often talk of it as indescribable bliss. In Pali it was connected with the verb *nibbati,* "to cool by blowing." In early forms of Buddhism the ideal man, the *nibbuta,* is the one who is "cooled," i.e., cooled from the psychological fever of greed, hatred, and carnal desire. To be cooled in this sense means therefore to be in a state of psychic well-being or health. To the extent that one has attained enlightenment on earth, one may be considered as having been so "cooled," but one may hope that after death *nibbāna* will be completed and that one may attain a state of complete tranquility. Westerners tend to interpret the extinction as an extinction of life (i.e., annihilation) when, Buddhist scholars point out, it is not life but the desires and passions that are extinguished, leaving an existence that has been purified from the dross with which such desires and passions stifle life.

Nisan. By the time of the Exile, the Jews used this probably Babylonian word to designate the month during which the Passover was held.

Nisus. Term used by Samuel Alexander to express his view that in the evolutionary process is a tendency to move to higher stages.

Noah. Modern scholars generally conclude that Noah, the hero of the story of the Flood in Genesis, is a composite figure into whom are merged two or more figures of popular tradition. He functions much the same as did Up-napishtim in Mesopotamia. He is also a culture hero who may well belong to the same group as the men referred to in Genesis 4.20–22, being a pioneer in viniculture (Genesis 9.20f.).

Noble Guard. A papal bodyguard, disbanded as was also the Palatine Guard, in 1970. They consisted of seventy-seven men of noble rank, headed by a commander who was always a Roman prince. They received their final constitution in 1815. See **Palatine Guard** and **Swiss Guard**.

Noesis. Greek term traditionally used in opposition to *aesthesis*, the former to express the notions of "intelligence" and "thought," the latter the notion of "sense." In 20th c. philosophy, Husserl has used *noesis* to designate the element of thought within the act of perception.

Nominalism. In the problem of the Universals, which played a particularly important part in medieval philosophical discussions although also a perennial problem, the three main positions in the Middle Ages were: Realism, Conceptualism, and Nominalism. Realists (e.g., William of Champeaux), although they varied in the extent to which they adhered to the realist position, generally held that universal concepts or terms (e.g., courage, warmth, brightness) have an objective foundation in extramental reality. (Those who adhered to a more extreme form of realism held that to the universal specific concept in the mind is a corresponding extramentally existing universal specific essence or substance.) At the other end of the spectrum, the Nominalists (e.g., Roscelin and Occam) tended to regard the universals as mere names, mere noises uttered having no reality either in the mind or in the external world, being nothing more than labels attached to groups of individual entities for convenience in classifying them. Between these two extreme positions was that of the Conceptualists, who acknowledged that the universals have a real existence in the mind but not as independent entities in an extramental order of exist-

ence. Probably most Realists and most Nominalists eventually moderated their position in the direction of the Conceptualists', but at least Realism and Nominalism may be viewed as extreme points in the spectrum of this type of discussion as it was conducted by the medieval schoolmen. See **Universals** and **Conceptualism**.

Nonconformists. Those who in the 17th c. refused to conform to the discipline and practice of the Church of England were so designated. The term is still used in England in a much wider sense for all Protestants who dissent from the Church of England, such as Congregationalists, Methodists, Baptists, Presbyterians, and Quakers.

Nonjurors. Members of the Church of England who after 1688 were unwilling to take the required oaths of allegiance to William and Mary, since to have done so would have been to have broken the oaths they had taken to James II and his successors in the Stuart succession. Some 400 priests, 9 bishops, and many laymen found themselves in this position. The clergy were deprived by Act of Parliament of their livings. The sees of the deprived bishops were filled, but the nonjuring clergy refused to accept the new bishops, insisting that their allegiance must be to the nonjuring bishops, who had included W. Sancroft, Archbishop of Canterbury. The latter, in order to insure the nonjuring succession, delegated his archiepiscopal functions to W. Lloyd, nonjuring Bishop of Norwich. The schism continued through much of the 18th c. The nonjurors were men of high principle with a deep sense of the independence of the Church from State interference and with a spirituality that in some ways might warrant their being classed as forerunners of the Tractarians of the next century. William Law was among the many notable nonjurors.

Norbert (*c.* 1080–1134). Archbishop of Magdeburg and founder of the Premonstratensian Order of canons regular. See

Premonstratensians. He was canonized by Gregory XIII in 1582.

Norris, John (1657–1711). English philosopher. Educated at Winchester and Oxford, where he was elected to a Fellowship at All Souls College, he was Rector of Bemerton, near Salisbury, from 1691 till his death. Influenced by Malebranche (he was sometimes called "the English Malebranche"), he may be regarded as the last of the Cambridge Platonists. He was the first to produce a sustained argument against Locke's epistemology. Against John Toland he held that the human mind cannot measure truth, since only divine reason can do that; nevertheless, human reason partakes of the divine reason. Among his many writings may be mentioned his *Reason and Religion*, (1689), *Reflections on the Conduct of Human Life* (1690), *Practical Discourses*, 3 vols., containing his critique of Locke (1690–1698), *An Essay Towards the Theory of the Ideal or Intelligible World*, 2 vols. (1701 and 1704), and *A Philosophical Discourse concerning the Natural Immortality of the Soul* (1708).

North. The geographically northern direction not infrequently carries with it in the Old Testament a curiously numinous quality, sometimes with even quasi-magical echoes. In Psalm 48.3, Zion is identified with the recesses of the north. In the old Canaanite religion the seat of divinity was associated with the "mountain of the north." The mysteriousness of the north seems to have continued in popular imagination long afterwards. Northward lay the land of exile, the land whence Yahweh would one day gather his people (Isaiah 43.6; Jeremiah 3.18). It could also be a focus of fear, for invaders tended to come from the north, through Syria. It may not be entirely fanciful even to suppose that the early Christian missionaries inherited, if unconsciously, this ancient, even pre-biblical, sense of mystery in the north. Their movement was typically a movement from Jerusalem northward.

North India, The Church of. On November 29, 1970, this Christian body was inaugurated by the union of six Christian denominations. It marked the culmination of negotiations that had begun at Tranquebar in 1919. The day following, seven new bishops were consecrated by bishops from the Mar Thoma Syrian Church, the Church of South India, and a former Anglican bishop from the Church of North India. The Church of North India now has sixteen dioceses, each with its own bishop. An officer with the title of Moderator presides over the Synod. See **South India, The Church of**.

Nothing. The puzzle of "Being and Nothing" was much discussed in Western philosophy, both in antiquity and in the Middle Ages, and there are counterpart discussions in some oriental thought, e.g., in Nāgārjuna. In Greek there are two terms for "nothing": (1) *mē on*, that which is not but has the potentiality to be, and (2) *ouk on*, nothing, non-being. The puzzle appeared in forms such as this: How can one predicate anything of non-being (nothing), e.g., in saying "nothing lacks existence" or "nothing is that which does not exist?" Yet it seemed that one could talk intelligibly about "nothing" as though it were meaningful, as when we say "I see nothing there" or "It is better to do nothing than to do wrong." Mystics and idealists have used the concepts "nothing" and "nothingness" in special ways of their own. Henri Bergson referred to "nothing" as a pseudo-idea, an artificial concept: one that we invent out of disappointment with "being." Heidegger, however, granted ontological status of some kind to "nothing." Beginning with the existentialist concept of *Angst* (see **Angst**), he sees "nothing" as the basis for negation, presenting us with the paradoxical phrase: *Das Nichts nichtet*, "the Nothing nots." Sartre in this as in much else follows Heidegger.

Notker. The name of several learned monks of the celebrated Benedictine foundation of St. Gall, including Notker Balbulus (*c.* 840–912), so called because of his stutter, and Notker Labeo (*c.* 950–1022), who translated many of the Latin classics of antiquity into his native German.

Notre-Dame De Paris. The cathedral church of Paris, it is famous both on its own account and as the model for several later French cathedrals. It was begun in 1163 on the Ile de la Cité in the heart of Paris and constructed in the early French Gothic style. Except for the western front that was added in the first two decades of the 13th c., it was completed and consecrated in 1182, almost a generation after the death of Peter Lombard, one of the most famous teachers in Paris in the 12th c. (See **Peter Lombard** and **Paris.**) Desecrated at the French Revolution, it was for some time turned into a "Temple of Reason" but was reopened for Christian worship in 1795. Romantic interest in it was fostered by Victor Hugo's novel so entitled and published in 1831 with Quasimodo as its endearing hero. It has been the focus of much French history.

Noumenon. A Greek term originally meaning either "what is known" or "the thing perceived." Plato used the term in the sense of "the intelligible." In the history of Western philosophy its best known use is that of Kant, who sets it in opposition to the term "phenomenon:" the latter is what appears to sense; the former is what is perceived through a rational apprehension, although some interpreters of Kant virtually identify the noumenon with the *Ding-an-Sich*, the "thing-in-itself."

Nous. Greek term, usually translated "mind." Anaxagoras (c. 500–428 BC) used it in contradistinction to matter to designate what he took to be the rational principle that provides matter with order. Plato and Aristotle used the term in their respective systems, and in Plotinus it appears as the first of the emanations from "the One" and therefore the emanation most nearly resem-

bling "the One." As thought or universal intelligence, it signifies the rationality which, according to Plotinus, undergirds the world. In some of the Gnostic systems (see **Gnosticism**) *nous* took on a function analogous to that of the Holy Spirit in Christian thought and life.

Novatian Schism. A schism arising out of the Decian persecution in the mid-3rd c. Orthodox in doctrine, Novatian insisted upon a rigorist attitude toward any form of compromise on the part of the Christian Church with the heritage of the Graeco-Roman outlook and culture. Broadly speaking, Antioch approved of his stance while Alexandria disapproved of it. The Novatianists, despite their doctrinal orthodoxy, were excommunicated, being or seeming to be a threat to Christian unity. Novatian was martyred under Valerian *c.* 257., but a Novatianist Church persisted at least as late as the 5th century.

Novena. In Catholic tradition, a form of devotion in which prayers for a special intention or grace are asked on nine consecutive days. A novena may be private or public. The practice dates from the 17th c., although it may have a much older basis.

Novitiate. In Catholic practice, when a person applies for admission to a religious community, he or she usually spends a period first as a postulant (e.g., a few months) during which he or she usually wears ordinary secular clothes. The candidate then may proceed to the novitiate, always at least one full year and in some orders two, during which time he or she wears the habit of the community, usually with some distinguishing feature such as a leather belt instead of a cloth cincture. During the novitiate the novice is not canonically obligated to the community nor the community to the novice, so that he or she may leave or be dismissed at any point without any formalities.

Numbers, The Book of. This, the fourth book of the Pentateuch, has

Moses as its principal focus and contains large passages dealing with various laws and ceremonies. The beautiful blessing, "The Lord bless thee and keep thee . . . and give thee peace," is found in Numbers 6.24–26.

Numerology. The attachment of symbolic meaning to particular numbers seems to be almost universal at certain stages of the history of religion. The Bible (e.g., the Apocalypse) abounds in such numerology. In Judaism the Cabbalists employed it copiously. In Hinduism and Buddhism as well as in Babylonian and Egyptian religion it can be extensively found. Pythagoras developed a cosmology based upon such numerological methods. Echoes of such notions are to be found in popular superstition that connect certain numbers with "good luck" and others with bad.

Numinous. A term coined by Rudolf Otto (1869–1937) to denote what he took to be the essential element, amoral and nonrational, in religious experience that includes the sense of awe and self-abasement in face of a fascinating mystery. It is unanalyzable (*unentwickelbar*). Its object is the holy (*das Heilige*).

Nunc Dimittis. The canticle of Simeon (Luke 2.29–32), drawn from the Book of Isaiah (e.g., 40.5; 42.6; 49.6, and 52.10), was very probably a liturgical song adapted by the early Christians to express, through the mouth of Simeon, the joy experienced at the coming of the Messiah.

Nuns. Although in popular usage the term is applied to all women living in any kind of Christian religious community under the canonical vows of poverty, chastity, and obedience, it is technically restricted to women living under solemn (perpetual) vows, such as Benedictines, Carmelites and Cistercians. Teaching and nursing sisters, for instance, are technically not nuns but *sorores* (sisters).

Nuptial Mass. In Catholic practice, the marriage service may take the form of a Mass within which the marriage vows are taken and other features of the marriage ceremony included, e.g., the nuptial blessing. Such a Mass is called a Nuptial Mass.

Nuremberg Declaration, The. The name given to a document of much historical importance, signed by 33 German Roman Catholic professors and others who met at Nuremberg a few weeks after the decrees promulgated at Rome on August 25–26, 1870, by the First Vatican Council asserting the infallibililty of the Pope when speaking *ex cathedra* on matters of faith or morals. The document denied that the Vatican Council had been an authentic General Council of the Roman Catholic Church. The signatories, under the leadership of J. J. I. von Döllinger of Munich, formed the nucleus of what became the Old Catholic Church, who subscribed to all that had been taught and recognized by all the General Councils of the Church from earliest times but repudiated the Vatican Council on various grounds. They represented the conciliarist tradition within the Roman Catholic Church. See **Conciliarism**.

Nyāya. One of the six philosophical schools whose founding is traditionally ascribed to the Buddha himself. It is aligned with another school, Vaiśeṣika, because of the similarities to be found in their methods, which purport to be logical and analytical. Both schools seems to have been influenced by Greek sources, but they developed their ideas in typically Indian ways, offering *moksha* (liberation) from the *saṁsāra*, the chain of re-embodiments, inherent in human existence.

O

Oakeley, Frederick (1802–1880). Tractarian divine. An Oxford man, influenced by W. G. Ward. In the dispute within the Tractarian movement between those inclined toward Rome and those opposed to it, Oakeley was among the former and quickly followed Newman into the Roman Catholic Church. His writings include *Historical Notes on the Tractarian Movement* (1865).

O-Antiphons. So called from their openings (e.g., *O Sapientia*, *O Adonai*), sung before the Magnificat at Vespers on the seven days before Christmas Eve, in Roman use. (They occur also in Sarum use in a slightly different arrangement.) They are very ancient, having been already in use by at least the 8th century.

Oaths. The taking of oaths is a practice generally recognized and approved in mainstream Christian teaching, where the need for a solemn asseveration seems warranted. Solemnities such as the touching of the Bible, or the Book of the Gospels, or the Crucifix, may accompany the ceremony. Several Christian bodies, however (e.g., the Quakers and the Mennonites), refuse to take oaths on grounds such as the obvious one that a Christian's yes or no should be as inviolable as any oath. The point of the objection may be stated thus: if a Christian's regular affirmation cannot be trusted, why should one put any more reliance in his or her oath?

Obedience. Christians universally recognize that obedience to God is not only an obligation on all Christians but should be their greatest joy. In the Roman Catholic Church the notion that a canonical superior stands "in the place of God" gives rise to various ecclesiastical usages in canon law; e.g., obedience (along with poverty and chastity) is one of the three vows taken by all monks, nuns, and other persons living under a religious rule and is generally accounted the most fundamental. It is required "in all that is not sin," e.g., it might require an undertaking not to use one's intellect in a certain situation but to offer one's intellect in sacrifice, according to the will of one's ecclesiastical superior.

In a novel (based, however, upon a true story) by Kathryn Hulme, *The Nun's Story* (1956), with a film version that starred Audrey Hepburn as the nun, numerous examples are given showing how the vow of obedience may demand the sacrifice of the intellect. Among them is the occasion on which the heroine, Sister Luke, who is depicted as an exceptionally gifted nurse and the daughter of a renowned Belgian surgeon, is asked by her superior to fail her examination in tropical medicine so as to show that humility is the paramount requirement of the religious life.

Oberammergau. In 1633 the inhabitants of this Upper Bavarian village, in gratitude for the end of the plague, took a vow to enact the Passion and Death of Christ every ten years. The play takes six hours and is performed by some 700 villagers. Occasionally an extra performance is added (e.g., in 1984, for the 350th anniversary, but it occurs normally in the decimal years.

Oberlin, Jean Frédéric (1740–1825). Lutheran educationist. Born at Strassburg, he labored in the parish ministry throughout his life, including in his ministry Catholics and Reformed as well as his own flock, promoting various schemes to encourage education, thrift, and agricultural advances. He was affected by the principles of the Enlightenment and was interested in the work of Swedenborg and other mystics. His educational methods were eventually recognized and are honored, for example in the foundation of Oberlin College, Ohio.

Oblate. This term has a variety of meanings in Christian usage. (1) In the early Middle Ages parents sometimes took their children to a monastery to be, in effect, adopted and educated. These were called oblates. (2) It is also a designation of those who, unable or unwilling to enter the full life of a religious community (e.g., the Benedictines), enter into association with it, taking on some of the prayer life of the community, for example, and living according to the rule so far as that is practicable outside the cloister. (3) Some religious communities in the Roman Catholic Church use the term as a canonical designation, e.g., the Oblates of Mary Immaculate.

Oblations. Primarily, in Christian usage, the term is applied to the bread and wine to be used in the Eucharist. It may be used also, however, for any other gifts, (e.g., food) offered to the clergy for their discretionary use, for instance, in the care of the poor.

Obscurantism. A derogatory term applied to the outlook of those who are believed to oppose the use of thought. It is very probably derived from the title of a famous 16th c. satire on the medieval methods of conducting disputes: the *Epistolae Obscurorum Virorum*. Obscurantism is usually taken to signify an unwillingness, supposedly on religious grounds, to open one's mind to available enlightenment. While it ought to be antithetical to the Christian Way, it cannot be said to be a disposition unknown within its fold or indeed within that of any other religious faith.

Observants. Those members of the Franciscan Order who in 1368 began a protest against what they saw as a departure from the original spirit of Francis of Assisi and who claimed to observe the Franciscan rule in its pristine purity. They finally separated themselves into an order in 1517. Later they split into several groups but were reunited in 1897 as the Order of Friars Minor. See **Franciscan Order.**

Occam, William of (*c.* 1285–1347). Nicknamed *Venerabilis Inceptor*, he was one of the most important philosophers of the later Middle Ages. Born in Occam (also written "Ockham"), Surrey, England, he became a Franciscan and studied at Oxford. His views were regarded with suspicion by conservative theologians and it was probably on that account that he never attained the academic rank of regent master, thus giving rise to his nickname. (An *inceptor* in the medieval scene was roughly like one who today takes his bachelor's degree but no doctorate.) His writings include commentaries on parts of Aristotle's *Organon*, a *Commentary on the Sentences*, and seven "Quodlibets." In 1331, having been excommunicated in 1328, he was expelled from the Franciscan Order for charging the Pope, John XXII, with heresy. A highly independent scholar, he is probably most famous for the principle he enunciated, now known as "Occam's razor." This principle, often misquoted, is to be found in his *Summa totius logicae* and reads: *Frustra fit per plura quod potest per pauciora*: "It is futile to do with more elements what can be done with fewer." Eliminating the concept of universals, he came to be accounted an extreme exponent of nominalism. Whether (as some modern historians of philosophy would argue) he was a conceptualist rather than a nominalist, he certainly may be said to have developed a new way (*via moderna*) in contrast to the *via antiqua* of the great 13th-c. schoolmen. Not only did he prepare the way for the development of modern scientific thought; by his political theories he provided the foundation for a strong support of the Conciliarist cause that was to be of such great importance in the thought of the canonists of the later Middle Ages and, within the Roman Catholic Church, down to the Vatican Councils of much more recent times.

Occam's Razor. See **Occam, William of**

Occasionalism. The extreme mind-body dualism of Descartes gave rise in the 17th c. to various proposed solutions of the difficulties it entailed. One was the theory, called occasionalism (Latin *occasio*, event), that God acts as the intermediary between body and soul. When a change occurs in mind, God intervenes to produce a change in matter, and when it occurs in matter he produces a change in mind. Malebranche and Geulincx were among the best known exponents, but others included Johannes Clauberg and Louis de la Forge. The concept of "preestablished harmony" propounded by Leibniz effectively supplanted the occasionalist view among those who were thinking along such lines. Occasionalism, however, was briefly revived in the 19th c. by Rudolf Hermann Lotze. In Arabic thought, moreover, the idea had been presented in a general way in a theory that God, being the intermediary between any two events, replaces the concept of causality.

Ochino, Bernardino (1487–1564). Protestant Reformer. Born in Siena, he became general of the Observants. Later, having transferred to the Capuchins, he was twice their vicar-general. Influenced by Peter Martyr, he became a Lutheran and, being wanted by the Inquisition, fled to Geneva. In 1547 Cranner welcomed him to England where he received a royal pension and became a prebend of Canterbury. After Mary's accession to the English throne he had to flee again to Switzerland and after further adventures and persecution eventually died in Moravia. His writings include *The Usurped Primacy of the Bishop of Rome* (1549), originally in Latin but extant only in translation. He was accounted a preacher of extraordinary eloquence and persuasive power.

O'Connell, Daniel (1775–1847). Irish politician and patriot. He became influential as a champion of the Roman Catholic Church in Ireland and was instrumental in bringing about the Roman Catholic Emancipation Act in 1829, which repealed most of the political disabilities that Roman Catholics had suffered. Going on to work toward repeal of the Union with Britain, he was Lord Mayor of Dublin from 1841 to 1843. A powerful orator, he knew the Irish people and could and did sway crowds, although never inciting them to violence. He had an immense influence in the shaping of modern Ireland where he is much revered.

Octave. The eighth day after a feast in the Christian liturgical calendar, reckoned so that it falls on the same day of the week as the feast. The entire period is said to fall "within" the octave of the feast. The practice is very ancient, introduced by Constantine but at first confined to only the greatest feasts. During the Middle Ages the number was greatly increased. In modern times however, the Roman Catholic Church has suppressed all octaves (at any rate in the Latin rite) except Easter and Christmas.

Octoechos. The name of a liturgical book used in the Eastern Orthodox Church. It contains the variable parts of services running for an eight-week period around Pentecost and Easter. One set of eight musical tones is used for each of the eight weeks; hence the name, which means "[the book of] eight tones."

Odilo (*c.* 962–1049). Abbot of Cluny. A gifted organizer, he developed a plan for centralization of the government of the Benedictine monasteries that accepted the Cluniac reform. During his tenure of office the number of Cluniac houses doubled. He was highly esteemed in his own day for the probity of his life and the charitableness of his nature. His influence on the entire Church in the West is remarkable, e.g., it was he who introduced the Feast of All Souls (observed on November 2, the day after All Saints' Day) at Cluny, which day came to be universally observed throughout the Church in the West.

Odium Theologicum. A much used phrase, meaning literally "theological hate," it alludes to the peculiarly acrimonious character of much theological controversy. Its incidence shocks many, but religion is a love affair with God, and as in human affairs love often issues in deeds of wrath, even murder, one need not be surprised to find bitterness in religious disputation. Nevertheless, the higher the intellectual level of the controversy and the holier the character of the participants, the less likely is it so to degenerate.

Odo (879–942). Abbot of Cluny. Born at Tours, he was brought up in the family of William, Duke of Aquitaine who in 910 founded the Abbey of Cluny. He studied at Paris under Remigius of Auxerre. On the foundation of Cluny, he was put in charge of the monastery school and in 927 became abbot. He did much to guide many of the most important Benedictine houses in the direction of the Cluniac ideals.

Odo. Early 10th c. Archbishop of Canterbury. Sometimes known as "Odo the Good."

Odo. An 11th c. Bishop of Bayeux. A uterine brother of William the Conquerer, he spent most of his life in affairs of State and was for some time William's personal adviser. Nevertheless, he was a generous patron of scholarship and art and probably commissioned the famous Bayeux tapestry. He received his bishopric at about the age of twenty from William the Conqueror, with whom he was present later at the Battle of Hastings in 1066.

Oecolampadius (John Hussgen or Hausshein) (1482–1531). German Reformer. Born at Weinsberg in 1515, he showed an early disposition toward the Lutheran Reformation, although he seems to have relented for a time, for in 1520 he entered a monastery. Two years later, however, he left it and became an active exponent of Reformation views. Having apparently some leadership qualities but lacking keen theological perception, he tended to be moved by circumstance rather than by theological conviction. At the Colloquy of Marburg in 1529, for example, he defended Zwingli's view of the Eucharist against the Lutheran view.

Oecumenius. The 6th c. author of the oldest extant Greek commentary on the Book of Revelation, the manuscript of which was rediscovered in the early 20th c. and published in 1928.

Offertory. The liturgical offering of the bread and wine to be used in the Mass. In Western rites it takes place after the Gospel and the Creed. Traditionally it was performed by the celebrant, but at Milan an old practice was preserved in which representatives of the people brought the bread and wine to the altar. In recent times this has become the customary practice in Roman Catholic and many Anglican parishes. In the Eastern Church the offertory takes place at the prothesis at the beginning of the Liturgy, with an elaborate lancing and arranging of the bread. The elements are brought to the altar at the Greater Entrance in solemn procession from the prothesis to the altar.

Office, The Divine. The public prayer of the Church (*divinum officium*) recited or sung daily in monastic houses and in some cathedrals and other churches. It is a development of a pre-Christian practice among the Jews of saying certain prayers at fixed hours. By the 6th c. the seven Day Hours (Lauds, Prime, Terce, Sext, None, Vespers, and Compline) had been developed, and Benedict made the practice of chanting or reciting them a central feature of the monks' daily round of work and prayer, calling it the *opus Dei* (God's work) and adding the Night Office (called Matins). Psalms have a central place in it, the entire psalter being recited or sung in the course of a week. The practice of reading the office from the Breviary later became obligatory on all clergy. In 1971 the Roman Catholic Church ordered an extensive rearrangement of the Divine Office, which had remained substantially unchanged since the early days of the Benedictine Order, in which it had been made the primary duty of every monk.

Oikonomos, Constantine (1780–1857). Greek scholar and theologian. He was the author of a lengthy work on the

Septuagint that is of considerable value although based on an indefensible view of its being divinely inspired in Greek: a view that was part of his strongly patriotic outlook, which was resistant to Western scholarship and practices.

Oils, Holy. Oils were used among the ancient Hebrews for solemn liturgical purposes such as the consecration of priests and kings. The Christian Church took over the practice and adapted it, using oil in Baptism and Confirmation, for example, from early Christian times. Traditionally, the oil used (called chrism) is a mixture of olive oil and balsam. The early Fathers frequently allude to its use and to the symbolism of divine grace in the oil that strengthens and the balsam that sweetens. Chrism is used for the consecration of liturgical objects such as altars and chalices as well as in the ordination of priests. The holy oils are consecrated by the bishop on Maundy Thursday and kept in a small vessel called a chrismatory for use during the year.

Olaf. (995–1030). Patron saint of Norway. While fighting the Danes in England, he was converted to Christianity and returned to Norway in 1015, becoming King of Norway the following year.

Old Believers. Those members of the Russian Orthodox Church who refused to accept the liturgical reforms imposed by the 17th c. patriarch Nikon were so designated. They were excommunicated in 1667 and much persecuted as schismatics. They consisted largely of peasants and priests who resisted Western influence. Lacking bishops, they seemed to have no future in the Orthodox Church. They split into two groups, (1) the Popovtsy, who hoped to find means of continuing as a branch of Orthodoxy, and (2) the Bezpopovtsy, who were prepared to dispense with priestly ministrations. In 1846 a deposed bishop, Ambrose of Bosnia, joined the Popovtsy, who in 1881 were

at length recognized by the Russian establishment. The Bezpopovtsy, however, split into a variety of groups.

Old Catholics. At various times groups of clergy and people have separated from communion with Rome while remaining loyal to basic Catholic doctrine (e.g., the Seven Ecumenical Councils) and maintaining apostolic succession through bishops. They have formed Churches in full communion with one another and, since 1932, with the Anglican Communion. The Old Catholics include the Church of Utrecht, which, with three bishops, separated from Rome in 1724. They also include various Churches (e.g., in Germany, Austria, and Switzerland) formed by those who after the First Vatican Council 1869–1870) refused to accept the doctrine of Papal Infallibility. They also include certain other national Churches such as the National Polish Church. Old Catholics recognize the Declaration of Utrecht as an important doctrinal standard. Their priests and bishops may marry. They have had cordial relations with Anglicans since 1874, and these relations have become increasingly close since full communion with the Anglicans was established in 1932.

Oldham, Joseph Houldsworth (1874–1969). Ecumenical Movement leader. Educated at Trinity College, Oxford, and New College, Edinburgh. He was appointed organizing secretary of the World Missionary Conference, held at Edinburgh in 1910. Virtually all his working life was spent in organizing international missionary and ecumenical projects in many countries, especially in Germany and on the African continent. His work at the Utrecht Conference in 1938 helped to launch the World Council of Churches. In the course of his work he became an Anglican. He was a key figure in the development of the Ecumenical Movement in our time.

Old Latin Versions of the Bible, The. The Vulgate, largely the work of Jerome and completed about the end of the

4th c., superseded all the older Latin versions and was so good that it eventually won its way to becoming the official Bible of the Western Church throughout the Middle Ages. The Old Latin versions, however, which differ considerably from one another, are of importance to modern biblical scholars in helping to establish the "best readings" of the original Greek text of the New Testament. For where at a particular point the biblical text cannot be established with certainty from the great Greek codices (e.g., Vaticanus and Sinaiticus) or even where the text itself is lacking, the Old Latin versions may help to provide needed evidence. The early Latin Fathers quoted from them extensively. Cyprian, for instance, used a form of the Old Latin known nowadays to scholars as "African." Such patristic quotations often antedate the oldest of the Greek manuscripts now extant, so that their testimony to or against a particular text can be weighty.

Old Syriac Versions of the New Testament, The. Before the adoption, early in the 5th c., of the Peshitta as the official text of the Bible in Syriac-speaking regions, older translations in that language had been circulating. Two such manuscripts of the Gospels have been recovered: one the "Curetonian," found in Egypt in 1842 by H. Tattam and published in 1858; the other the "Sinaitic," found by two Cambridge ladies, Mrs. Lewis and Mrs. Gibson, later in that century at St. Catherine's monastery, Mount Sinai.

Old Testament. The name traditionally given by Christians to the Hebrew Scriptures, consisting of (1) the Torah or Pentateuch, (2) the Prophets, and (3) the Writings, which include such books as Proverbs, Job, and the Psalms. See also **Apocrypha.**

Olier, Jean-Jacques (1608–1657). Founder of the Sulpicians, whose seminary of Saint-Sulpice in Paris has been regarded as a model for Roman Catholic seminaries throughout the world. (See Sulpicians.) Born in Paris, he studied with the Jesuits at Lyon and at the Sorbonne. In 1630, having gone to Rome for further studies, he was stricken with blindness but recovered his sight and experienced a conversion, being thereafter filled with intense missionary zeal. Ordained priest in 1663 he came under the influence of Vincent de Paul. At this time the Church in France was in several ways going through a period of torpor, and when in 1642 he was put in charge of the parish of Saint-Sulpice in Paris he found it in a lamentable condition. By dint of persistence and much organization he developed his seminary there, hoping to bring a spirit of piety and the practice of Christian morality into the Sorbonne and the life of that region of Paris. Olier's hope was to train students who would be not only faithful priests but priests of a caliber that would fit them for becoming seminary masters. He encouraged masters and students to mingle together at Saint-Sulpice. In 1657 he sent some of his priests to Montreal, resulting eventually in a strong Sulpician influence in French Canada. The Society he founded was not technically a religious order but, rather, a society of secular priests living according to rule but not taking any vow of poverty and therefore free to keep their own property. The rule was modeled on that of the Oratorians, with whom the Sulpicians have some organizational affinities. His spirituality, however, as expressed in his many writings, was more in the mold of that of Vincent de Paul.

Olives, The Mount of. The highest point in a range of hills to the east of Jerusalem, and a place which, according to the Gospels, Jesus much frequented. The Garden of Gethsemane is nearby.

Olivetan, Pierre Robert (c. 1506–1538). Protestant Reformer. A cousin of Calvin, he studied at Orleans and at Strassburg, where he learned Hebrew and Greek. He translated the Old Testament from Hebrew into French, publishing the result of his labors in 1535.

Olivetans. A branch of the Benedictine Order founded in 1319 at Monte Oliveto, near Siena, Italy. They wear a white habit and follow Benedict's rule very strictly.

Oman, John Wood (1860–1939). Presbyterian theologian. From 1925 to 1935 he was Principal of Westminster College, Cambridge. Emphasizing the concept of sincerity in religion, he saw the religious consciousness as self-authenticating. Among his writings are *Grace and Personality* (1917) and *The Natural and the Supernatural* (1931).

Ombrellino. In Roman Catholic usage, the small white canopy carried over the Host when it is moved from one place to another, e.g., in pubic procession.

Omophorion. A liturgical garment in the Eastern Church, worn by bishops. It is worn like a stole but is ten inches wide and nowadays made of embroidered white silk or velvet. It corresponds to the pallium used by archbishops in the Roman Catholic Church.

Oneida. A community established in 1848 at Oneida, Madison County, NY, by John Noyes, who insisted on the possibility of human perfection through Christ.

Ontological Argument, The. One of the three traditional arguments for the existence of God. It has had two principal exponents: (1) Anselm in the 11th c., who argued that when we conceive of God we conceive of that than which nothing greater can be conceived (*id quo nihil majus cogitari possit*) and such a concept of God entails his existence (an argument to which Gaunilo gave the obvious objection that one can think of a perfect island which nevertheless does not exist), and (2) in the 17th c. by Descartes who developed it along somewhat different lines. Both Thomas Aquinas in the 13th c. and Kant in the 18th re-

pudiated it. Hegel defended it. Most modern philosophers have rejected it on grounds similar to Kant's, namely, that existence is not a predicate.

One can add red apples to green apples and come up with a total that makes sense, but one cannot so add imaginary apples to real apples. Nevertheless, several modern philosophers (e.g., Charles Hartshorne and Norman Malcolm) have sought to revive interest in the Ontological Argument. It should be noted that Anselm did not find Gaunilo's objection damaging. He contended that while it applies to a perfect island and indeed to any finite thing (as a "contingent", i.e., a possible kind of being), it does not apply to the one "something" that is the necessary source of all such possible beings. To that "something" we give the name of God. See **Cosmological Argument** and **Teleological Argument.**

Ontology. That branch of philosophy that is concerned with being as being. The term seems first to have appeared in the 17th c. According to Heidegger it is the analysis of existence. Exponents of ontological questions have differed, however, in their interpretation of the ontological enterprise. Many modern philosophers, under the influence of the logical positivist school, deny its possibility as a meaningful undertaking. For the discussion of problems in the philosophy of religion, however, it is of immense importance. No one can deny that religion is a social and psychological phenomenon, but if it is no more than that, then it is not what religious people say they are talking about. Christians, for example, when they say that Christ is risen or that God cares for his creatures do not mean anything such as "The psyche of certain people includes a certain feeling of exhilaration that they call the Risen Christ" or "Many people find psychological comfort in the notion that they are cared for by an imaginary being whom they call God, so that it is a truism to affirm that this imaginary being is of paramount social and psychological importance for large masses of humanity." On the contrary, the fundamental question in the minds of religious people, whenever they give any thought to their religion, is an ontological one: Is the God whom I believe to be of supreme importance in my life merely an intellectual fiction of my mind or does he exist independently not only of me but of all humanity? Would he exist even if there were no humanity at all?" Such questions are not only unanswerable but unintelligible except by the use of an ontological method of one kind or another. A classic example of an ontological question, posed by both Leibniz and Heidegger, in very different circumstances, is "Why is there anything at all and not just nothing?" To a philosopher or theologian open to the use of ontological methods, such a question is one of the most profound that can be posed. To one who repudiates the ontological enterprise it is meaningless and therefore futile.

Ophites. A group of Gnostic sects who not only regarded the serpent as an apt symbol for wisdom (as traditionally he is regarded) but as indeed a higher god who liberates humankind from what the Ophites accounted lesser gods such as the biblical one.

Opus Dei. See **Office, The Divine.**

Oral Tradition. Literacy was not widespread till comparatively recent times. Even in now highly developed countries reading and writing skills were with some notable exceptions generally confined to a class of professional scribes. The fruits of thought and creative imagination were transmitted orally, committed to memory, and passed on from one generation to another. For example, behind the Scriptures of the great religions, including the Bible, lies a body of such oral tradition. This fact is of immense importance for an understanding of the philosophical and religious texts that have come down to us in their present form, for the mind-set of even

the learned in a society generally dependent on such oral transmission of scholarship and wisdom is different from that of one in which literacy is sufficiently widespread to be accounted the norm.

Orange, Councils of. Two ecclesiastical synods held in the south of France in 441 and 529 respectively. The second of these councils is of profound significance for theological development in the Western Church, for they upheld Augustine's view on the nature of grace as against more moderate, quasi-Pelagian views that popularly prevailed during the Middle Ages, although the decrees of the Council of Orange in 529, confirmed by Boniface II in 531, supported Augustine's strongly anti-Pelagian stance.

Orarion. The stole worn by the deacon in the Eastern Orthodox Church. It is a narrow silk band worn over the left shoulder. It usually hangs straight down, but it may be first passed under the right arm, then attached again to the left shoulder, and hung down in front.

Orate Fratres. The opening words of a formula dating from the 11th c. and consisting of a sentence addressed to the people by the celebrant of the Mass, asking for their prayers that their sacrifice and his may be acceptable to God. The people respond to the effect that they join with the celebrant in the eucharistic sacrifice.

Oratorians. In 1575 a community of priests who had been gathering around Philip Neri in Rome developed into a congregation whose constitutions were approved by Pope Paul V in 1612. They spread through various countries. Newman introduced them to England in 1848, where Brompton Oratory in Kensington, London, is a large and well known church. The Oratorians are secular priests who take no monastic vows and therefore may have private property. They lay stress on preaching and

on good music. The French Oratory
was founded in 1611 in Paris by Bérulle
and received papal approval in 1613.
One of the aims of the Oratorians is the
training of priests to teach in seminaries. They have encouraged ecclesiastical
scholarship. The musical term "oratorio" is derived from the dramatic musical services of Philip Neri in Rome in
the 16th century.

Oratorio. The setting of a religious li-
bretto for chorus and soloists with
instrumental accompaniment. Well
known ones include Handel's *Saul*
(1738) and his *Messiah* (1742) and Mendelssohn's *Elijah* (1846). The term was
derived from the musical services developed in Rome by Philip Neri. See **Oratorians.**

Oratory. This name is most generally a
designation for a chapel in a private
home but may be applied to places of
worship other than parish churches. It
is also used in a special sense by the Oratorians of their churches, e.g., Brompton Oratory, London.

Ordination. The concept of a ministry
within the Christian community set
apart to guide and serve it dates from
the New Testament itself, where already
we find clear references to the laying on
of hands with prayer for those being so
set apart (e.g., Acts 6 and 13). Even
gradations within the ministry seem to
be recognized in the New Testament,
although this is less clear. Certainly deacons appear to have been seen as a different order from that of presbyters.
The difference between presbyters (*pres-
byteroi*) and bishops (*episcopoi*) is more
obscure and has been for long controversial. By the middle of the 3rd century various gradations had come to be
apparently well recognized, for at Rome
there were not only a bishop and many
presbyters, but deacons, sub-deacons,
acolytes, exorcists, readers, and porters.
Not till much later, however, did the
Roman Catholic Church come to recognize four "minor" orders, namely (in
ascending order), porter, reader, exor-

cist, and acolyte, and three "major" orders, sub-deacon, deacon, and priest.
Duns Scotus held a curious view that
would surely have few supporters today,
namely, that there are nine orders (the
seven mentioned plus the tonsure,
which all clerics receive as a preliminary ceremony to admission to the
clergy, and the episcopate, making nine
in all): a theory he defends on the
ground that it corresponds to the nine
orders of angels in heaven. Thomas
Aquinas argues with more theological
appositeness that all order to the Sacred
Ministry is ordered to the Eucharist,
from the lowliest (porter) onward, so
that there can be no order sacramentally
higher than that of the priesthood;
therefore the episcopate is merely the
plenitude of the priesthood. A further
distinction must be noted. Order in the
Sacred Ministry is from one standpoint
sacramental, i.e., it relates to the administration of the Church's sacraments, which is surely its essential
nature if the Church is what the Church
purports to be. It has also, however, administrative and jurisdictional implications. The notion that presbyters
(priests) should be organized with one
of their number superintending and
guiding them is an ancient and very defensible one, since plainly the clergy
stand as much in need of fatherly care
as do the rest of the People of God. In
Catholic tradition, at any rate, only
bishops can ordain other priests, and
they are therefore essential to the continuity of the Church's ministry. In Protestant tradition the laying on of hands is
very widely used as part of the ordination ceremony, although the function of
the Protestant ministry is differently
conceived.

Oresme, Nicolas (*c.* 1320–1382).
French philosopher and scientist. Educated at the University of Paris, he became adviser to the King and to the
Bishop of Lisieux. He was in several
ways much in advance of most of his
contemporaries. For example, his work
in economics had considerable influ-

ence on the later development of economic ideas, while in physics and astronomy he anticipated Copernicus and Galileo and in analytical geometry adumbrated the work of Descartes.

Organic Articles, The. These contained the provisions made by Napoleon in 1802 for the regulation of public worship in France and, in general, Church-State relations. They provided for state control of all papal documents entering France and in many other ways undermined Rome's jurisdiction over the Roman Catholic Church in France. The Organic Articles, after being less and less enforced, were repealed in 1905 when Church and State in France were formally separated.

Organs. Organs of some sort have been used in church worship since at least the 8th c., but they came into general use (at first only in the larger parishes) by the 13th c., and by the time of, say, Columbus, they were virtually universal. The English Puritans disliked them, and in England in 1644 legislation was passed for their destruction, which was very generally carried out. The Scots also, under Puritan influence, developed a prejudice against the use of organs as unscriptural. They were called, in derision, "a kist (i.e., a chest) of whistles." After Puritan influence waned, organs again became a normal furnishing of all churches that could afford them. In both Europe and America all large churches have organs, in some cases on a very grand scale.

Origen (*c.* 185–*c.* 254). Theologian and biblical scholar. Origen was the most original Christian thinker of his time and also probably the most learned biblical scholar. He was born in Egypt, probably at Alexandria. His father, Leonidas, was killed in 202 during a persecution of Christians. When the persecution abated, during which Clement, leader of the famous Christian school there had fled, Demetrius, Bishop of Alexandria, appointed Origen to head it. Origen approached this as-

signment with a spiritual zeal that some would account fanatical as well as with an intellectual industry that eventually made him peerless. He studied pagan literature and Neoplatonist philosophy under Ammonius Saccas and diligently studied the Bible. He also travelled to Arabia and Palestine. Invited to preach, he did so, but since he was at the time a layman, his doing so constituted technically a canonical offense and was the beginning of a quarrel with his bishop that eventually led to the latter's taking revenge upon him by sending him into exile on an ecclesiastical technicality, which Origen's foes later tried to interpret as a theological dispute. Meanwhile Origen had enhanced his immense learning and developed the powerful creativity of his thought. After the despicable treatment he had received at the hands of his bishop, Demetrius, Origen found refuge at Caesarea in 231, establishing a school and becoming as famous there as he had been in his earlier environment. He continued his writing and preaching. He was very prolific. Unfortunately, many of his works have been lost, and most of the others are extant only in fragments or in Latin translation. He wrote many commentaries on books of the Bible and compiled a great work of biblical scholarship, the Hexapla. (See **Hexapla.**) His greatest theological work is his *De Principiis* (*Peri Archōn*), the original Greek text of which is almost entirely lost, surviving only in a not very reliable Latin translation by Rufinus. Origen, who has come to have a reputation for heterodox opinions, was in fact fundamentally very orthodox, taking as his basic theological axiom the unity of God and his otherness and independence. He even adumbrates a form of the doctrine of the Trinity, although this was officially developed in the Church much later. He taught that the world is eternally in process of creation: a doctrine that is much more intelligible than the notion that has for so long prevailed. He also taught that souls pre-existed, and that they are engaged in an evolutionary process, the outcome of which will be such that even the Devil will be saved. This concept in Origen plainly implies some form of reincarnation, although because of the defects in the extant texts of his works he is made to appear ambiguous on this question. (His followers thought to serve him by expurgating passages that they feared might make him seem heterodox, so that sometimes he sounds as though he took some form of reincarnation for granted, while in other passages he states that it is "foreign to the Church.") At any rate, as Thomas Aquinas (who did not accept Origen's concept of the pre-existence of the soul) points out with his customary philosophical acumen, such a belief *entails* some form of reincarnational belief. Origen was also deeply mystical and (in the spirit of the Alexandrian school with which he was for so long associated) represents a form of Christian Gnosticism in which he sees salvation as a process involving participation in the Divine Wisdom. For centuries after his death, Origenism was a lively issue in the Church in the course of which he was much misrepresented (e.g., by association with widely disapproved heresies), and grossly misunderstood by many. He is indubitably not only one of the very greatest minds in the history of Christian thought but one of the most deeply spiritual personalities that have emerged under the Christian banner. In 250 he was arrested in the persecution under Decius, imprisoned, cruelly and repeatedly tortured, and died. See **Origenism.**

Origenism. That the opinions of the Origenists who claimed for them the authority of Origen (see **Origen**) should often much differ from the teaching of the master is not in itself particularly remarkable. Neither Thomas nor Calvin nor Freud nor Jung, for example, should be held responsible for the opinions of those who have used their respective labels or flaunted their respective banners. In the case of the Origenists, however, special circum-

stances dictate more than ordinary need for caution, partly because of the difficulties entailed by uncertainties in Origen's text and partly because the controversies attending the interpretations of Origen were going on for three centuries after his death. So the distinction between Origen and Origenism is a very special one.

Origen, like other highly original thinkers, tended to elicit extremes of hostility and loyalty. The first important Origenist controversy came to a head toward 375 CE in relation to a very tendentious account of Origen by Epiphanius. When Jerome, who had been a strong defender of Origen, met Epiphanius when the latter was visiting Jerusalem in 395, he was apparently so impressed by the representation of Origen that he heard that he tried to have Origen condemned by the bishop, John, who, being unsympathetic to the case as presented to him by Jerome, arranged with the secular authorities to have Jerome exiled. The sentence was not in fact carried out; some time later Jerome and John seem to have been reconciled. Then the controversy flared up again with the publication by Rufinus of a Latin translation of Origen's *De Principiis,* prefaced with an allusion to Jerome's original sympathy with Origenism. In 400, Theophilus, an anti-Origenist, convoked the Council of Alexandria, which condemned Origenism. By this time Origenism was such an ambiguous term that its condemnation must have been no less ambiguous. Theophilus, however, was now becoming so infatuated with his anti-Origenism that by 402 he was calling Origen "the hydra of heresies." Many-headed indeed it was, since by this time it had come to represent a considerable variety of ideas, many of which no doubt grievously misrepresented Origen's teachings.

The controversy did not by any means end there. Ardent champions of Origenism were growing up and acquiring much influence in many places, not least in Palestine, where also, however, it had vigorous detractors. Toward the middle of the 6th c. the latter obtained from the Emperor Justinian a letter naming Origen as one of the most pernicious of heretics, and they persuaded him to convoke a council at Constantinople in 543, at which an edict was issued setting forth a long list of errors attributed to Origen. The Origenists then split into two parties: (1) the Isochrists, who held that at the Apocatastasis (see **Apocatastasis**) all humanity would attain equality with Christ, and (2) the Protoctists, who accounted Christ the most excellent among creatures. Finally, the Second Council of Constantinople, meeting in 553, issued a condemnation of what were claimed to be the teachings of Origen. By this time the teachings of Origen had been so misrepresented, no doubt on both sides, that such a condemnation could have had little if any meaning in terms of what Origen had actually taught. Hence the special importance of distinguishing Origen from Origenism.

Original Sin. According to traditional Christian doctrine, humanity was created by God in a perfectly sinless condition: a state of perfect spiritual and bodily health such as made human beings physically and spiritually immortal, incapable of knowing death. They were also free from the encumbrances of sexual and other animal desires. Both physical and mental suffering would be likewise unknown to them. They were in a state of what theologians came to call sanctifying grace. The Scriptures seemed to provide ample support for such a view, e.g., Paul affirms that it was through one man (i.e., Adam) that sin entered into the world. He also indicates that it was because of Adam that all his descendants ever since have inherited his fallen condition. The concept of an original state of perfection from which humanity has fallen has counterparts in many primitive forms of religion in which an evolutionary understanding of the universe and of God's workings within it play no part.

Although the concept of a fall *in time* does not fit our knowledge of how the universe works, the notion that we are by no means naturally inclined to do things rationally and morally but are, on the contrary, at least as ready to do them irrationally and immorally is, to say the least, very plausible. That is essentially what the classic Christian doctrine of original sin affirms: by nature we are not necessarily inclined to good but are, rather, inclined to evil and so must be taught and must learn a better way. The early Fathers saw this in their own way. Methodius, for instance, saw that the effects of the Fall could be seen in human corruptibility. Didymus "the Blind" and many others perceived that this distorted inclination in human beings is a genetic inheritance; that is, humanity inherits it along with the rest of the characteristics common to our human condition. Probably Theodore of Mopsuestia was the only early Greek Father of the Church to deny that humanity has this heritage. The medieval theologians from Augustine onwards accepted the principle of original sin and argued on fine points in its interpretation. Generally they regarded it as being transmitted through the act of coitus. The Reformers emphasized the effects of original sin, teaching that it destroyed human liberty. Catholic tradition has been less extreme; nevertheless, it recognizes that human capacity for freedom is damaged by original sin, which in this tradtion is identified with the loss of sanctifying grace. Much as the doctrine stands in need of re-interpretation, it does represent a truth about the human condition.

Orosius, Paulus. Early 5th c. historian. Augustine, who befriended him, sent him to Palestine to enlist Jerome's help in opposing Pelagianism. In 417, when Orosius had returned to the West, Augustine asked him to write an answer to the common pagan claim that the calamities that befell Rome were due to her abandonment of the ancient gods. Orosius complied in a work that has, however, only limited historical value. In respect of the period just before the time of writing it is accurate enough, but in regard to remoter Roman history it is much less so.

Orphism. One of the "Mystery Religions" of the Hellenic world in which, at least in the Eleusinian form, personal rebirth became a central theme. In Orphism, Orpheus and Eurydice formed a divine pair, and because Orpheus failed to follow exact instructions, Eurydice had to return to the underworld. Orphism, which gave birth to a considerable literature, is closely related to Pythagoreanism, and both, through their influence on the development of Neoplatonism, indirectly affected some aspects of Christian thought.

Ortega Y Gasset, José (1883–1955). Spanish philosoper. Born in Madrid, he studied at Marburg under Hermann Cohen, and from 1911 till his retirement in 1952 he was Professor of Metaphysics at the Universidad Central at Madrid. Trained in the Neo-Kantian tradition, he was dissatisfied with it and became convinced that all knowledge is rooted in life. Abstract reason can create abstract systems of thought (e.g., mathematics), but only through "vital reason" can one cope with the universe and the environment in which one is placed. The foundation for living is provided by beliefs; ideas are developed only when beliefs cease to function adequately. Beliefs provide the perspective from which the individual can understand his or her situation, and all perspectives provide knowledge of some kind, however limited. The basic reality is the individual's continual self-making. To develop oneself is the goal of life, and in the measure in which one fails to do so one fails to come to terms with reality. Reality does not lie somewhere beyond but in living an authentic life that discloses reality to oneself. Art and science, philosophy and literature are all human constructions. They may help the individual to attain the authen-

ticity that is the fundamental reality, but they merely minister to that enterprise. Society is both an instrument to which the individual must adapt and also an instrument through the use of which the individual attains freedom. Ortega's thought has affinities in some respects with that of Bergson and in other respects with existentialism. His later thought might be described as vital humanism. His many writings include *The Dehumanization of Art* (1925), *The Revolt of the Masses* (1929), *Goethe from Within* (1934), *Ideas and Beliefs* (1940), *Man and People* (1957), *What is Philosophy?* (1957), and *The Idea of Principle in Leibniz* (1967). For futher study see José Ferrater Mora, *Ortega y Gasset: An Outline of His Philosophy* (1957; 2nd ed. 1963).

Orthodoxy. The term comes from the Greek *orthos* (right, correct) and *doxa* (opinion). In a general sense it is used of beliefs that conform to a given authoritative stance. "Heterodoxy" is the term given to beliefs other than those accounted orthodox. In a much more specific sense, the term "Orthodoxy" is used in Christianity to refer to that family of Churches in or for the most part originating in Eastern Europe that recognize the Patriarch of Constantinople as their common spiritual focus. Because these Churches are independent and self-governing, although in full communion with one another, and have a complex history, a full account of them would be very intricate. They include, however, the four ancient patriarchates of Constantinople, Alexandria, Antioch, and Jerusalem, along with various less ancient ones such as Russia and also the Church of Greece and various other eastern countries. Eastern Orthodoxy represents a tradition that grew out of Christianity in the Byzantine Empire with deep cultural and historical roots in Greece. Eastern Orthodox Christians recognize the seven early Ecumenical Councils. The spirit of Eastern Orthodoxy tends to avoid the rigid doctrinal formulations so characteristic of the Roman Catholic Church and to express the faith of the Church in liturgy rather than in doctrinal propositions other than those embodied in the ancient Creeds and the decisions of the aforementioned Councils. In the devotional life of the Church, icons play a very special role. Since the 10th c., the great center of spirituality has been Mount Athos. The monastic life is highly revered, and bishops are generally drawn from the monasteries. The parochial clergy may marry and usually do, but they must marry before ordination and may not in any circumstances thereafter marry a second time. Eastern Orthodoxy represents a very large part of the Christian Church, and even in the West its numbers are not inconsiderable: about three million, for example, in the United States alone.

Orthodoxy, The Feast of. After the Iconoclastic controversy, the icons were restored by popular demand and a feast-day established in 842 to celebrate the joy of their restoration. It is observed on the First Sunday of Lent. Its original purpose, however, has been extended to include rejoicing in the Church's triumph over all opinions that it accounts heterodox.

Orthros. (Greek, *orthros*, "dawn".) The morning office in the Eastern Church. See **Office, The Divine.**

Osiander, Andreas (1498–1552). Reformer and theologian. One of the signatories of the Schmakaldic Articles in 1537, he became in 1549 professor at Königsberg. His opposition to Luther's understanding of justification by faith was expressed in his *De Justificatione* (1550).

Osservatore Romano. A daily newspaper owned by the Vatican and providing the text of papal encyclicals, reports of papal activities, and official Vatican announcements. Founded in 1861, it functions as an official Vatican organ.

Ostian Way. This famous thoroughfare is the ancient road that led from Rome to Ostia at the mouth of the Tiber fourteen miles away. The Church of San Paolo fuori le Mura, one of the four great basilicas, lies on the road about two miles from the center of Rome. It was erected in its original form over the relics of Paul in 324 and then in the late 4th c. rebuilt as a basilica. According to tradition and the testimony of Gaius, Paul's remains have lain there since at least as early as the end of the 2nd c. It was destroyed by fire in 1823 but rebuilt and the new building consecrated in 1854. The basilica is by tradition served by Benedictines.

Oswald (*c.* 605–642). King of Northumbria, canonized saint and martyr, he was converted by Columba at Iona. Later he introduced Christianity into his kingdom and received missionaries from Iona, including Aidan, who became Bishop of Lindisfarne and was very successful in missionary enterprise. Oswald who was killed in battle and mutilated by pagans is widely venerated as a Christian martyr.

Oswald. A 10th c. Archbishop of York. Nephew of Odo of Canterbury. He studied under the Benedictines at Fleury. He helped to establish many monasteries in England and both reformed the life of the clergy and tried to improve their education.

Otto (1062?–1139). Of a noble family of Swabia, he entered the service of the Emperor Henry IV, who in 1102 made him Bishop of Bamberg. In the Investiture Controversy he tried to maintain a neutral position. He was successful in missionary activities in Pomerania and was canonized in 1189.

Otto, Rudolf (1869–1937). German philosopher and theologian. A member of the Göttingen school of Neo-Kantian philosophy, he developed a special interest in the philosophy of religion. In his analysis of religious phenomena he saw the "numinous" as central. The numinous is a unique feeling of awe in the mind of the worshipper. Accompanying it is the sense of the *mysterium tremendum,* the unfathomable mystery in the numinous object. Along with the apprehension of the *mysterium tremendum* comes a sense of enchantment, an inescapable fascination for the sacred object, which he calls the *mysterium fascinosum.* That which religious people call "the holy" is unanalyzable because it is unique, not (as many have suggested) composed of various elements such as the ethical, the aesthetic, and others. Otto was influenced as a student by Schleiermacher, although he departed from the latter's position in several ways. Professor of Systematic Theology at Breslau, he published many books, the most influential and popular among which was his *Das Heilige* (1917), translated into English as *The Idea of the Holy* (1923). Otto knew more than many of his theological contemporaries both about the sciences and about non-Christian religions.

Otto of Freising. A 12th c. Bishop of Freising. He studied at Paris and elsewhere under the Victorines, became a Cistercian and eventually Abbot of Morimond in Champagne. He took part in the Second Crusade and was among the first to introduce Aristotle to Germany. His historical writings are of considerable importance, especially his *Chronicon,* in which he modified Augustine's *De Civitate Dei* by envisioning "Babylon" and "Jerusalem" as already by his time united in the Church, which he perceived as the continuation of the spirit of *Romanitas,* a spiritualized form of the Roman Empire.

Ousia. (Greek, meaning being, substance, essence.) Aristotle had used this term in reference to the individual, existing thing, the primary subject of a propostion, e.g., Socrates, Athens, this piece of clay that I hold in my hand. In Neoplatonic thought God was called *hyperousios,* i.e., beyond all individual beings or substances. In the 4th c. the

term became the focus of a controversy within Christianity. The Arians held that Christ is *similar* in substance (*homoiousios*) to God the Father, against the view that eventually prevailed in the Church as orthodox, according to which he is of the *same* substance (*homoousios*) as God the Father. The concept of substance (*ousia*) is generally treated as otiose by modern philosophers.

Overall, John (1560–1619). Bishop of Norwich and one of the forty-seven translators engaged in the making of the King James Version of the Bible. Interested in the relations between Church and State, he compiled in 1606 a book on the subject, the publication of which, however, was for political reasons delayed till 1690.

Overbeck, Franz (1837–1905). Born in St. Petersburg, he taught at Jena and Basel, developing a view that the central message of the Gospel was thoroughly world-negating. He therefore regarded the history of the Church as in effect part of secular history. He was a close friend of Nietzsche.

Owen, John (1616–1683). English Puritan divine. Educated at The Queen's College, Oxford, he developed Calvinistic views but later, finding Calvinism as intolerant as any of the traditional alternatives, he embraced an Independent stance, emphasizing religious toleration. He wrote extensively and remains one of the most interesting and spiritually-minded writers of the 17th century.

Owen, Robert (1771–1858). English social reformer. Born in Wales, he entered a cotton mill, eventually becoming the owner of such mills in Manchester, New Lanark, and elsewhere. With the support of Jeremy Bentham, he formed a company asking only a five percent return on the investment. His social work in New Lanark, which included schools for children and also stores that sold at cost price, gained international attention. In 1826 he founded a community in New Harmony, Indiana, in which he hoped to exhibit his social principles, but it was unsuccessful. He then went to London where he worked for the improvement of the lot of the lower classes. His writings include *A New View of Society* (1813) and *Revolution in the Mind and Practice of the Human Race* (1849). Sometimes accounted the father of socialism in England, he was sharply opposed to Christianity as he understood it and viewed his socialist plans as destined to overthrow it and establish an international socialist federation.

"Oxford Group." See **Buchman, Frank.**

Oxford Movement, The. A movement within the Church of England whose influence was eventually immense throughout the Anglican Communion and very considerable elsewhere. The basic aim was the restoration of historic Christian faith and practice especially entailing a recovery of patristic and medieval thought but also involving a liturgical renaissance. See **Tractarianism; Newman, John Henry;** and **Pusey, Edward Bouverie.**

Oxyrhynchus Papyri. A collection of many thousand fragments of papyri, dating from the 1st c. BCE to the 7th c. CE and including much Christian literature as well as very considerable Greek and Latin literary texts of other kinds, began to be found about the end of the 19th c. at Oxyrhynchus, a few miles west of the Nile and near what is today Behnesa. The texts of specifically Christian interest include the Sayings of Jesus, various fragments of biblical books, both Old Testament and New Testament, an early Christian hymn with musical notation of the 3rd c. that is the oldest piece of Church music known to be extant today, and various other items of great interest to Christian scholars.

Ozanam, Antoine Frédéric (1813–1853). Founder of the Society of St. Vincent de Paul, an association of laymen dedicated to personal service among the poor. A brilliant student at Paris, he became, in 1844, professor at the Sorbonne. He was closely associated with many of the leading French thinkers who were engaged in attempting to revive and develop the tradition of spirituality in the Roman Catholic Church in France.

P

P. The symbol used by biblical scholars to designate an element in the Pentateuch that Julius Wellhausen (1844–1918) called "the Priestly source," distinguishing it from other elements such as the Deuteronomic (D). Biblical scholars still recognize such an element in the Pentateuch as the latest of the editorial revisions of the Pentateuch as we now know it. It dates from the Exile (586–538 BCE) to *c.* 400 BCE. That does not exclude, however, ingredients from earlier sources. P is characterized generally by more dignified language and ideas pertaining to a more advanced culture. A very simple example may be seen in comparing the two creation accounts (Genesis 1 and 2). The first is in an elevated style and exhibits relatively advanced modes of thought. The second is a much more primitive account in which God forms Adam out of the earth, then, having anaesthetized him, removes one of his ribs out of which he constructs Eve and so on. The book of Leviticus, with its elaborate ceremonial and ritual prescriptions, also clearly belongs to this later period in the construction of the Pentateuch, i.e., the period in which Genesis 1 was constructed.

Pacifism. The name given to an attitude and outlook to be found among the adherents of many religions, including Christianity, that active participation in war is absolutely forbidden and contrary to the most fundamental of religious principles. The principle of *ahiṁsā* in Hinduism is regarded by Hindus and Buddhists as the most basic cardinal virtue and the obligation to live according to it is widely recognized. It entails nonviolence to any living creature and therefore of course is antithetical to every form of warfare.

Many Christians find participation in war fundamentally against the Christian Way of life; others, while seeing war as abhorrent in the extreme, find that their belonging to a civil society that safeguards what they recognize as important values obligates them to defend it even by force if called upon to do so by the civil authority. Early Christian practice provides no decisive precedent on this question, since considerable numbers of Christians served in the Roman army, although some ecclesiastical pronouncements expressly forbade such military service. Moral theologians in the Middle Ages generally distinguished between wars in which a Christian might serve and those in which they might not. Augustine defended a Christian's participation in war when the good of society is at stake. The Crusades were generally regarded as legitimate engagements for a Christian. The concept of the "just war" came to be widely recognized. Many Christians in modern times, however, although not receiving by any means universal support from the Church, have argued insistently and persuasively against all combatant service in the armed forces as totally contrary to the profession of Christian Faith. The grounds for this outlook are various. Prominent among them is the recognition that in modern conditions the concept of a "just war" cannot be implemented, since not only is modern warfare intrinsically brutal and cruel, "conventional" wars can turn into chemical, bacteriological, nuclear, and other such holocausts that are patently crimes against humanity even apart from Christian and other religious considerations. Quakers are among those prominent in upholding a strict pacifism.

Paedobaptism. The technical name given for the baptism of infants. See **Baptism.**

Paenitemini. The name of the document dated February 17, 1966, that mitigated and otherwise revised the rules of the Roman Catholic Church relating to fasting and abstinence. Days of fasting were reduced to two: Ash Wednesday and Good Friday. For the traditional abstinence from red meat on Fridays and certain other penitential days could now be substituted more imaginative ways of observing the penitential spirit, such as performance of charitable works and engagement in devotional exercises.

Pagan. This term is etymologically derived from the Latin word *paganus*, which meant "country fellow." It came to be applied by Christians to those who continued to adhere to the outlook and practices of the Graeco-Roman world, for predictably folk in the rural areas tended to be slow to relinquish the old ways. Eventually, it became a convenient term for the general outlook of that Graeco-Roman world of antiquity contradistinguished from the Christian outlook. In this usage the term has no necessarily pejorative connotation. It has acquired, however, also a secondary and pejorative meaning, being applied to attitudes of licentiousness and greed that leave no room for spirituality or for intellectual pursuits associated with the interior life. As so used it is of course pejorative.

Pagoda. A Buddhist shrine. The term is derived from the Portuguese *pagode*, which in turn was derived from a so far undetermined oriental word, possibly the Sinhalese *dāgaba*. The pagoda, a development of the ancient Indian stupa, a dome-shaped mound of stone and earth that dates from at least the time of Aśoka (3rd c. BCE), has been a focus for popular piety.

Pahlavi Texts. Zoroastrian writings that date mainly from the 9th c. CE but whose origins go back to the 6th c. at least. Pahlavi (Middle Persian) is the language in which they are written. They contain accounts of Zoroastrian folklore.

Palatine Guard. In 1850, Pope Pius IX created a corp of militia called in Italian the *Guardia Palatina d'Onore*. Composed of two then existing bodies, the *civiti scelti* and the *capotori*, the corps wore a dark blue uniform and a peaked cap with a plume of feathers. In 1970 it was disbanded. See **Swiss Guard** and **Noble Guard.**

Paley, William (1743–1805). English philosophical theologian. Born at Peterborough and educated at Cambridge, where he taught for a decade or so before ordination to the priesthood. He eventually became Archdeacon of Carlisle. His book *The Principles of Moral and Political Philosophy* (1785) was remarkably well received, becoming the standard text in ethics at Cambridge for many years and running through fifteen editions during Paley's lifetime. He is famous for the analogy made in his later book, *Natural Theology* (1802), in which he supports the argument from design as evidence for the existence of God as an intelligent and beneficent Creator. He sees creativity, however, in characteristically 18th-c. fashion, as mechanical. If one were to find a watch lying on the seashore, then, without even knowing what a watch is, an intelligent onlooker could perceive at once that it is the creation of an intelligent mind. He also sometimes alludes to the structure of living things, notably the astonishing complexity in the structure of the human eye and the adaptation of its parts to make a whole that can perform the act of seeing. Paley's mechanistic understanding of the nature of the universe is now thoroughly outdated. His use of the teleological argument, although not without persuasiveness, tends nowadays to be persuasive only to those who for other reasons have made up their minds· in favor of what it purports to show.

(Some writers call his argument "the argument *to* design.") Paley is nevertheless of historical importance in the philosophy of religion. In ethics he taught that egoism and altruism would coincide in the long run. Among his other writings are his *Horae Paulinae* (1790), and his *Evidences of Christianity* (1794).

Pali. The language of the Theravada Buddhist scriptures. The term "pali" means literally scripture, contradistinguished from commentary or midrash.

Palimpsest. A vellum or papyrus manuscript from which the original writing has been cleaned off or otherwise erased and new writing superimposed on it. In the past chemicals were usually employed to disclose the sometimes very valuable writing below, but nowadays experts often use photographic methods as safer and in other ways preferable for that process. Among biblical manuscripts, the most famous palimpsest is Codex Ephraemi, a 5th c. manuscript in the Bibliothèque Nationale, Paris. The term may also be applied to paintings on which others have been overlaid (sometimes very inferior ones) to save canvas.

Pall. The small, square, linen cloth (now usually stiffened with cardboard or the like) used to cover the chalice at Mass. The term is also used, however, for the black or purple or white cloth covering a funeral casket.

Pallium. In Church usage, a circular band of white wool with two hanging strips marked with six purple crosses, worn by the Pope and bestowed by him on archbishops. It is made out of the wool of lambs blessed on Saint Agnes' Day in the Church of Sant' Agnese fuori le mura during the singing of the Agnus Dei. The origin of the custom is obscure, but it seems to be of very considerable antiquity. See **Agnes.**

Palm Sunday. In Christian usage, the Sunday before Easter. Palms are blessed, and there is a procession bearing palms and representing the triumphal entry of Jesus into Jerusalem before his Passion, Death, and Resurrection. The observance is known to have been practiced in Jerusalem as early as the 4th century.

Pandit. In Hinduism a man recognized for his learning and wisdom. He may be consulted and function somewhat as a rabbi in Judaism.

Panentheism. The term, meaning literally "everything in God," was coined by K. C. F. Krause (1781–1832) and is used to designate the belief that the Being of God includes and penetrates the entire universe in such a way that though all is not to be identified with him, all exists in him. See also **Pantheism**, from which this term is to be clearly distinguished.

Panj Pyares. The five original members of the Khalsa, the inner council of the brotherhood of Sikhs. Gobind Singh, the last of the Sikh gurus, decided to form this inner group totally committed to the interests of the Sikh religion. He assembled all the Sikhs at Anandpur on the day of Baisakhi, 1699 CE and asked who would give him the head of a true Sikh. The five men, the Panj Pyares eventually went into Gobind's tent. Gobind followed each one and came out each time with his sword bloodstained. This performance, however, was merely for dramatic effect. The five then stepped out alive, were initiated, and became the Khalsa or inner circle, each receiving the additional name of Singh, meaning "lion." Gobind also took the name, which is borne by Sikhs to this day.

Panpsychism. From the Greek, *pan* (all) and *psychē* (soul). The philosophical doctrine that everything is essentially psychical. Although the "soul" nature is manifested in varying degrees, it permeates everything. When Thales (640–546 BCE) said that the world is "full of gods" he was at least veering in the direction of panpsychism. When

Giordano Bruno (1548–1600 CE) saw the basic unit of reality as animated, he was perceiving the innumerable worlds contained in the universe as organic: a form of panpsychism. The view is found in various forms in many of the greatest thinkers in the Western tradition, from Bruno to Whitehead. Sometimes views of the kind may seem to hover between panpsychism and hylozoism (see **Hylozoism**), the doctrine that everything is part of the stream of life, and the distinction between the two views may fade in some cases, but at least the emphasis in each is different.

Panth. A name given to the Sikh community.

Pantheism. The term, coined by John Toland (1670–1722), means literally "everything God." It is used of those systems in which God and Nature (or God and the universe) are identified. The most remarkable and thoroughgoing of these systems is that of Baruch Spinoza (1632–1677), who speaks of *Deus sive Natura*, God or Nature. Mysticism has a generally pantheistic tendency, and though pantheism is incompatible with Christian doctrine, writers in some Christian mystical traditions have exhibited such tendencies. It is characteristic of much Indian thought and has widely affected Asia—for example, in Mahayana Buddhism. Pantheism may be either religious or irreligous; that is, it may be interpreted in one way or the other. It is opposed, however, to traditional Jewish, Christian, and Muslim teaching; and among those who particularly stress—as did Martin Buber (1878–1965)—the transcendental character of God, pantheism is accounted fundamentally irreligious.

Pantokratōr. Almighty; literally, "ruler of all things," from the Greek verb *krateō*, "I rule," and the root *pan*, "all." Used in the Septuagint (Greek version of the Bible; compiled no earlier than the third century and translated in English versions as "Lord of Hosts." It was rendered in Latin *omnipotens*—

whence our English word "omnipotent," which misleadingly suggests "able to do anything."

Papias (*c.* **60–130**). Bishop of Hierapolis, Asia Minor. Although he is of very great importance as a witness to the earliest oral traditions of the Church, almost nothing is known about his life. Irenaeus and Eusebius, however, have preserved in their works quotations from Papias that are of immense interest to and importance for students of early Christian history. In famous fragments he tells us, for instance, that Mark,—having become Peter's interpreter, set down accurately but not in orderly arrangement whatever he could remember of the words and deeds of Jesus. The fragments are easily accessible in English translation, e.g., in J. B. Lightfoot, *Apostolic Fathers* (1891). In English the name is pronounced *paypyas*, accented on the first syllable.

Papyrus. Papyrus is mentioned in the Bible in various places (e.g., Exodus 2.3 and Isaiah 35.7), but never as writing material, although it must have been used for that purpose in biblical lands as it was in the rest of the Middle East and elsewhere. The word *papyros* is Greek. The reed from which the papyrus scroll was made grew in profusion in the marshes of the delta in Egypt and, if less copiously, along the banks of the Nile above the delta. The reed is a stalk of rind and pith. It grows sometimes as tall as 15 feet above the water's surface and has a parasol-like crown of leaves on top. It was invaluable to timber-poor Egypt, being used for innumerable purposes.

As writing material it was in use in Egypt certainly earlier than 3000 BCE, possibly even 4000 BCE. The Egyptians exported it to Greece and Italy, and it was in universal use in the Greek world before Plato's time. (By the time of Aristotle it was beginning to give way to vellum, although the process was gradual.) The papyrus sheet for writing was made by stripping the rind from the reed and cutting the pith into strips, which were then laid out in vertical rows, slightly overlapped. Then a second set of strips was laid across the first set but in horizontal rows. The sheet was then beaten and pressed. The sheets were glued together to form a roll of any length up to about thirty-five feet. A typical sheet would be about a quarter the size of a modern American newspaper such as *The New York Times*. Papyrus can survive in good storage conditions in a dry country better than in a moist one. It is not surprising, therefore, that Egypt has yielded vast numbers of papyrus manuscripts.

Parable. As a literary form the parable as used in the Gospels has its roots in Hebrew literature. The Old Testament provides at least nine examples, e.g., the ewe lamb, II Samuel 12.1–14, and the forest fire, Ezekiel 21.1–5. The parable as used by Jesus is a short fictional narrative designed to drive home to his audience the truth and wisdom of a point in his teaching. He used the parable form in a distinctive way, but the form itself was very widely used: an estimated 2,000 examples might be found in rabbinical literature. In the Gospels at least thirty-five examples are to be found, perhaps twice as many if one applies the term "parable" more loosely. In the primitive Church the parabolic form was sometimes adapted to illustrate novel apprehensions of the truth of Christian teaching.

Paracelsus (*c.* **1493–1541**). The name adopted by Theophrastus Bombastus von Hohenheim, a Swiss physician who interested himself in alchemy and other esoteric and hermetic pursuits. He held that a restless creativity permeates everything. His doctrine that everything works through a polarity such as is found in the male-female opposition in nature has affinities with the yin/yang principle in Chinese thought.

Paraclete. The Greek word *paraklētos* was used in legal and other secular contexts to designate someone who is called to the side of a person who could profit from assistance, more a friendly witness than a briefed advocate or counselor. The term never occurs in the Septuagint but does occur several times in the New Testament, where it means "helper" in the sense of the spirit of truth testifying to the authenticity of Jesus's claims and to the fulfilment of his promises.

Paradigm. From the Greek *paradeigma*, model, pattern. A term used in philosophy to designate a case that can be taken to stand as exhibiting the fundamental issue that is being argued about: a paradigmatic case. In the philosophy of science basic models, paradigms, are used in building up a cosmology or other structure intended to exhibit how things are. These paradigms will change or be modified as new theories develop and new knowledge is obtained.

Paradise. The Hebrew *pardēs* and Greek *paradeisos* may be viewed as loan words from Persian, where the original word meant a well watered, well wooded park enclosed by a wall: the sort of garden-park suited to a royal palace. In the Old Testament, the Hebrew word *gan* is rendered *paradeisos* in Greek, e.g., the Garden of Eden. The New Testament writers who use the term no doubt have in mind echoes of its use in Jewish apocalyptic literature. They use it, however, in various and sometimes in rather vague ways. Paul (II Corinthians 12.4) uses it to express the mystical ecstasy he experienced in the "third heaven." In Luke 23.43 it is the place or state where Jesus on the Cross promises the Good Thief that they will be together there that very day, which some commentators have taken to be an allusion to the intermediate state that may plausibly be regarded as the most intelligible aspect of Christian eschatology, while others have found in it merely a promise of relief from their present suffering. Yet some New Testament passages do represent paradise as a synonym for "heaven,"

considered as the reward promised the righteous. By any reckoning the term as invested with religious meaning is a usually vague and sometimes ambiguous one.

Paradise Lost. The title of John Milton's epic, the greatest in the English language and written in blank verse, describing the Fall and its result for humankind. It may be regarded as the English counterpart of the *Divina Commedia* of Dante, but it is in many ways very different both in conception and in execution. See **Divina Commedia** and **Milton, John.**

Paradox. The term, from the Greek *paradoxon*, meaning "contrary to expectation" (*para*, "beside"; *dokein*, "to think"), has several meanings in common usage today; but fundamentally it is used of a statement that appears to be either self-contradictory or at least contrary to common sense—for example, "a well-known secret agent." Logical paradoxes were known to the ancients (e.g., "I am lying" is false if true and true if false), but interest in mathematical paradoxes was much stirred in modern times by the publication in 1897 by Burali-Forti of the paradox of the greatest ordinal number, followed by Russell's publication in 1903 of the paradox of the greatest cardinal number. Mathematical and logical paradoxes are generally offered as a challenge to find their solution; that is, however puzzling they may seem, they are presumed to be soluble. The immense importance that paradox has assumed in the philosophical study of religion today is due in part to its role in the thought of Pascal and Kierkegaard and its very different function in Zen, but also to the peculiar interest that religious utterances can evoke in light of the attention that contemporary philosophers pay to the analysis of language.

Paramita. (Pali, *parami*). This term, which means "perfection", refers in Mahayana Buddhism to a mental quality such as is to be expected of one who has attained the spiritual advancement of a bodhisattva. Various qualities, such as wisdom, generosity, and moral fortitude go to make up paramita and are accumulated over many lives. All are equally necessary ingredients.

Pareto, Vilfredo (1848–1923). Italian socio-political philosopher. Born in Paris, he was educated in Italy. His view was that every society is governed by one sort or another of elites. What changes is the form the elitism takes; the elitist principle remains irrespective of all societal changes. His writings include *Course in Political Economy*, 2 vols. (1896–1897); *Facts and Theories* (1920); and *The Transformation of Democracy* (1921).

Paris. The city of Paris is of great antiquity (being mentioned by Julius Caesar) as well as a center of Christianity from at least the time of Saint Denis, who became its first bishop in the 3rd c. and was martyred. During an invasion of the Huns the city was protected by Sainte Geneviève who is venerated as patroness of the city. From the 5th c. its importance as a Christian center greatly increased and in the 9th c. Notre Dame and the famous abbey of Saint-Germain-des-Prés became foci of Christian life and culture. Paris became the official capital of France in the 10th c. and has ever since been uniquely and in virtually every way the center of France and her heart. An established community of scholars was functioning there before the end of the 12th c. and was styled *Universitas magistrorum* in 1207. It received statutes from the Pope (Innocent III) in 1215, after which it quickly attained widespread fame throughout Europe, enjoying an almost unique independence from both secular and ecclesiastical jurisdiction. In the early 13th c. it had developed the college system, including the most famous of them, the Sorbonne. By this time bearers of some of the greatest names in medieval scholarship had taught or studied there, e.g., Peter Abelard, Peter

Lombard, and the Victorines. Now, in the 13th c. both the Dominicans and the Franciscans gravitated there and among its famous teachers are to be numbered Thomas Aquinas, Bonaventure, Siger of Brabant, Alexander of Hales, William of Auxerre, and Thomas's own teacher Albertus Magnus. After the end of the Middle Ages, Paris quickly became the center of the French Renaissance. During the 17th c. it witnessed religious controversy and some religious fervor. In the 18th c. it was the center of the French Enlightenment and the rationalism that was intellectually fashionable during that period as well as, of course, the French Revolutions in 1789, 1830, and 1848. Perhaps eclipsed only by Rome in the number and splendor of its churches, Paris today is not only the center of an extraordinarily vivacious intellectual and artistic "secular" life, but the guardian of many of the richest treasures in the Christian heritage.

Parker, Theodore (1810–1860). American divine. Massachusetts born and Harvard trained, he became a Unitarian minister active in the Emancipation cause. Emerson called him the "Savonarola of Transcendentalism." Among his writings is *A Discourse of Matters Pertaining to Religion* (1842). See **Transcendentalism.**

Parmenides (*c.* 515 BCE–*c.* 450 BCE). As one of the catalysts for Plato's thought, perhaps the most decisively important thinker in the development of Greek philosophy. He founded the Eleatic school of thinkers and was much affected by Pythagorean influence. He saw in sense experience mere appearance and identified thought with being. In thought is to be found the invariable, the universal. Being is eternal, for being cannot come from nonbeing. How then can change come about, since nonbeing is by definition that which does not exist? Imagine a chess board with all the spaces occupied; movement then is impossible and change inconceivable. So,

Parmenides taught, being is a single, homogeneous whole. He is the classic champion, in Western thought, of monism. His extant writings are represented by considerable fragments of his work *On Nature*. See **Monism**.

Parochet. A curtain, usually embroidered, hanging in front of or behind the doors of the ark in a synagogue. It is so named after the curtain that hung in the Temple at Jerusalem that screened the Holy of Holies from the rest of the sanctuary. The color of the parochet is changed according to the festival in the Jewish calendar.

Parousia. The term is used frequently in the New Testament to designate the Second Coming of Christ. The imagery has its roots in the Old Testament. It is an event of supreme importance and long awaited. What it signifies precisely, however, is not by any means entirely clear. Sometimes the language suggests its imminence; sometimes the "hour" is unpredictable. It is likely that references to it in the utterances of Jesus are compiled somewhat as is the Sermon on the Mount: collections of sayings assembled to make up a unified speech but representing in fact occasional allusions remembered by the Evangelists. The Greek work *parousia* means "arrival," being used often in the sense of the arrival of a king or dignitary on a ceremonial visit. This usage is reflected in the New Testament passages in which the term occurs, but here they are invested with a theological, eschatological significance: Christ is the king who is to come in the splendor and power of righteousness to bring in the long awaited reign of justice, the consummation of the divine plan for the salvation of the world. The parousia spells the end of the age. It may occur any time, but the date is a secret known only to God.

Parsis. The word means literally "Persians" and is applied to a relatively small group of Zoroastrians who left their Iranian homeland to escape Muslim persecution and who settled in Gujarat in northwest India *c.* mid-10th c. CE. After living in peace with their Hindu neighbors, they came again under the threat of Islamic persecution by reason of Muslim invasions. Under British rule they fared much better and moved toward Bombay, the great commercial center of western India. By the time of Indian independence in 1947 they had become one of the wealthiest and most literate elements in the complicated ethnic mix of India's enormous population. They number over 100,000, more than 60 percent of whom were to be found in Bombay. See **Zoroastrianism**.

Parthians. An Iranian people whose kingdom had its center to the southeast of the Caspian Sea. They successfully resisted Roman efforts to encompass them within the Empire. The Parthians mentioned with other peoples in Acts 2.9 would have been Jews belonging to that kingdom.

Participation. Plato used the term *methexis*, which is rendered in English "participation," to expound his view of the relation between the sensible (empirical) world and the intelligible "World of Forms:" the former is neither real nor illusory; its status is that it participates in the World of Forms, which alone is fully real. The concept of participation has been used by other philosophers, functioning in similar ways in their systems. It provides for levels of apprehension of reality. As we may understand the meaning of a story at different levels, from a child's to a mature adult's and then to that of a great sage, so there are different levels of the perception of reality.

Particular Baptists. Historically, those Baptists whose theology was Calvinistic rather than Arminian were so called in contrast to the latter, the General Baptists. The first Particular Baptist group was formed in England at Southwark in 1663.

Particular Judgment, The. See **Judgment, General and Particular.**

Parvati. Wife of Shiva. The term means "mountain goddess." Both she and Shiva are associated with the Himalayas. She is their personification. She is also known as Durga.

Pascal, Blaise (1623–1662). French mathematician and religious thinker. Born at Clermont-Ferrand, he was a precocious mathematical genius who reconstructed much of Euclid's geometry at the age of eleven and had an original mathematical essay on conic sections published while still in his mid-teens. He made important discoveries in mathematics and physics, including some that led to the invention of the barometer. Brought up in a highly educated and cultured environment, he encountered the Jansenists (see **Jansenism**) in 1646. The following year he obtained the condemnation of a former monk who had maintained that the mysteries of religious faith could be understood by reason: a thesis antithetical to the deeply religious instincts of Pascal. Although not yet ready to commit himself to the Jansenists' theological program in its entirety, he studied what they were saying while at the same time pursuing his mathematical and scientific work and participating in the life of cultured society in Paris.

Then on the night of November 23, 1654, between the hours of 10:30 and 12:30, he experienced a mystical encounter so vividly memorable that he carried a record of it in his clothing for the remainder of his life. In the theological controversies in which he was subsequently involved he attacked doctrines much associated with the Jesuits of his time, e.g., the Molinist view of grace (see **Molina, Luis de**) and the doctrine of Probabilism in moral theology (see **Probabilism**), using satire to exhibit what he regarded as expressions of moral laxity, which he saw in deplorable contrast to the strictness of the Jansenist outlook. His celebrated work on

this subject, the *Lettres écrites à un provincial* (1656–1657), was put on the Index (see **Index of Prohibited Books**). It exerted an extraordinary influence on religious thought in France. Probably from the time of his mystical encounter in 1654, he formed the habit of writing notes expressive of his Christian outlook and religious experience and of collecting them without classifying them or putting them into formal sequence. He wrote out of his own experience of Christ as his personal Savior in the tragic situation that he saw human life to be: a state of greatness and wretchedness in which men and women, being half-angels, half-beasts, with one foot stuck fast in the earth and the other leaping forward toward heaven, are inevitably trapped. Only through divine intervention can they make the needed decision through which alone they can rescue themselves. Their rescue can come only through an act of faith that is an act of will, a moral decision, entailing an element of risk. Taking this risk is inseparable from the act of faith, but the risk is worthwhile and indeed calculable. For if one bets on God one will obtain either everlasting bliss or, at worst, no afterlife at all, while if one bets against God and the bet turns out to have been wrong, one will be cut off forever from that everlasting bliss and condemned to persist separated from him who is the fountain of joy and the source of life and love.

Pascal saw that in all this there is nothing rational in the sense in which one perceives reason in mathematics, but as an experimental scientist he saw the procedure as conformable to the experimental methods of the natural sciences in the sense that one can make no progress without hypotheses. As he somewhat quaintly puts it, "the heart has its reasons that reason knows not." In several ways Pascal may be regarded as a forerunner of the 19th c. Kierkegaard and the religious existentialists of the 20th century. After his death while still in his thirties (his health had never been robust), his notes were collected and published in what has come to be known to educated people all over the world as his *Pensées*: one of the most profound religious classics of all time. He is unquestionably one of the greatest religious geniuses who have ever lived: so much so that his very remarkable mathematical and scientific achievements seem almost incidental.

Paschal Candle. See **Candles.**

Passion. The term refers primarily to the sufferings endured by Christ before his death on the Cross. The importance for the early Church of the Gospel narratives relating to the suffering and death of Jesus Christ would be difficult to overestimate. It is very probable indeed that these narratives, found in all four Gospels, were constructed into a coherent account before the rest of the Gospel stories were put together, and that they were the basis of the first proclamation of the Good News by the apostles. The central motif in these narratives is that it is through the Passion that the divine plan is fulfilled. Paul uses the Passion narrative as the core of the proclamation he has to make. No more is needed to demonstrate the role of Jesus in that providential plan. If all else were forgotten, the Passion narrative would be sufficient to show how all prophecy had been fulfilled in that unique event. Such is the place of the Passion in the first preaching of the Good News as the apostles saw it. Scholarly opinion varies slightly on the date of the Passion, but it may be confidently placed as falling no earlier than 29 CE and no later than 33 CE. Most scholars uphold the traditional date of 30 CE. The dating of the event is extremely difficult, entailing very complex problems and, although an interesting scholarly exercise, the result is not of vital importance either for belief or for unbelief.

Passionists. A Roman Catholic congregation of clerics regular founded by Paul of the Cross. The rule, a severe one, was drawn up in 1720. The Pas-

sionists try to combine the contemplative aspect of the religious life with the active one that is entailed in their principal work, which consists of giving missions and retreats. Passionist nuns are strictly enclosed and devoted to the contemplative life. The official designation of the Passionist congregation is: "The Congregation of Discalced Clerics of the Most Holy Cross and Passion of our Lord Jesus Christ."

Passover. The Passover ritual is described in Exodus 12.1–28. It consists of a meal in which a yearling lamb, roasted in its entirety, is eaten standing. Those partaking of the Passover meal must be circumcised and dressed as for a journey or pilgrimage. The origin of Passover is no doubt complex, but evidence certainly suggests a connection with the Exodus, which is relived in the ritual. The Hebrew word *pesach* does not help to elucidate the meaning of the Passover, for its etymology is obscure. For Christians to have seen a connection between the Eucharist and the Passover is very understandable, but difficulties attend attempts to establish grounds for such a connection.

As observed today in Judaism, it is centered in the Seder, strictly speaking a family meal, although in America it is often turned into a synagogue ritual. Observant Jews prepare for it by cleaning house and buying new clothes. Families tend to return for it to the ancestral home. After the ritual observances have been completed, the festal meal is served with singing and rejoicing.

Pastophorion. In the Eastern Orthodox Church, the sacristy adjacent to the apse. From at least as early as the end of the 4th c., it has been used for the reservation of the Sacrament. See **Reservation.**

Pastor, Ludwig (1854–1928). Church historian. Educated at Louvain and Vienna, he became professor at Innsbruck in 1887. He is famous for his great *History of the Popes (Geschichte der Papste* *seit dem Ausgang des Mittelalters,* 16 volumes (1886–1933). At the age of nineteen he had conceived the ambition of undertaking his work, and the result was a serious attempt to provide a scholarly and balanced account. It has been translated into several languages.

Patañjali. A 2nd.-c. BCE Indian philosopher. Author of Books I—III of the Yoga-sūtras, the earliest systematic treatise on yoga. He did not claim to be the inventor of the yogic techniques but merely to have collected and systematized the early doctrinal traditions and practices of the mystics and ascetics of India.

Patareni. Name given in the late 12th c. in Italy to heretics, more particularly to the Albigenses in the north of Italy and to the Bogomils in Eastern Europe. It is mentioned in 1179 in the proceedings of the Third Lateran Council, canon 27. Originally the term seems to have been applied in the preceding century to a somewhat extremist movement for the reform of the clergy, more especially for enforcing celibacy and abolishing simony (the sale of holy things, such as sacraments). The term appears to have been derived from the name of the rag pickers' quarter at Milan. These *patareni,* favored by the papacy, whose cause they upheld against the secular powers, played a considerable part in Milanese politics. The term is usually englished "patarenes."

Patmos. According to the testimony of Irenaeus, Eusebius, and other early Christian writers, John, the writer of the Apocalypse, was exiled to Patmos under the Emperor Domitian where he saw his vision and composed the book called Revelation or Apocalypse, as mentioned in Revelation 1.9. A monastery was founded *c.* 1100 on a mountain on the island and has survived to this day, containing a valuable manuscript collection.

Patriarch. This term is applied in the Bible to Abraham and others among the great men of Hebrew antiquity. As an ecclesiastical title it has been in use since the 6th c. CE for the bishops of the five principal Christian sees, namely, Rome, Alexandria, Antioch, Constantinople, and Jerusalem. One of the Pope's titles is "Patriarch of the West." More recently, the heads of some other Churches in the East have assumed the title of patriarch.

Patrick (*c.*390–*c.*460). Apostle to the Irish. Born in Britain, he lived there till he was sixteen when he was captured by Irish pirates and served for six years as a shepherd in the northerly part of what is now County Mayo. During this period he underwent a religious experience in which he felt that God was calling him to make his escape, which, after many adventures, he did, returning to his kinsfolk. He underwent some sort of training for the ministry, although apparently not a very advanced one even for those times for in later life he seems to have much regretted the meagerness of his learning. He was sent to evangelize Ireland and remained there for the rest of his life. Near the end of his life he wrote a personal account of his spiritual pilgrimage. Unfortunately history and legend have been so mingled that it is difficult to establish details of his life with certainty.

Patripassianism. A view held by some, notably Sabellius, in the 2nd and 3rd centuries, according to which, since God is One and the Persons of the Trinity are modes of his Being, what Christ suffered God the Father must have suffered too. The view was condemned by the Christian Church as heretical and has been traditionally regarded as such. The reason was at least connected to the traditional view that God the Father cannot be acted upon since he is Pure Act; to suffer is to be acted upon; therefore God the Father cannot be said to suffer.

Patristics. In Christian theology, the study of the early Fathers—that is, the important Christian teachers who wrote between the beginning of the second and the end of the eighth century CE. "The patristic age" is generally taken to comprise approximately that period, more especially the earlier part of it.

Paul. After Jesus himself, no character in the New Testament is more important for Christians than Paul. Without him or someone like him, the spread of the Good News and the establishment of the Christian Way throughout the Mediterranean world could not have been begun. Virtually all we know of him is what we are told in the New Testament. Originally called Saul, he was a Jew from Tarsus who changed his name to Paul. Such an adoption of a Roman name by a Diaspora Jew was not unusual. The important episodes in his life can be dated fairly well with the help of reference to external events. He would have arrived in Jerusalem in 30 CE when he was between about fifteen and twenty-five. His conversion would have occurred about five years later, say between 34 and 36 CE. After three years in Damascus and Arabia, he would have returned to Jerusalem and then after some more years at Tarsus he would have arrived in Antioch in 43 or 44 CE and would have made his first great missionary journey between 45 and 49 CE, returning to Jerusalem in 49 CE and making his second missionary journey in 49–52 CE and his third between 53 and 58. Back in Jerusalem in 58, he would have made his voyage to Rome in 60–61 and he would have been martyred there in 67 or 68 CE.

Paul was proud of his Jewish heritage. He could trace his ancestry back to the tribe of Benjamin. He was also proud of his Roman citizenship. The story of his conversion to the Christian Way after having been a noted informer against the Christians and having participated in the stoning of Stephen is dramatically recounted in Acts 9. In accordance with rabbinic practice, he learned a trade, in his case that of tentmaking, to support himself without demanding teaching fees. Whatever such obligations he imposed on himself, however, he insisted on freedom from the requirements of the Jewish law. A person of Jewish ancestry who chose the Christian Way might feel obliged or might wish to follow the ritual practices and obey the requirements of the law to which he or she had been brought up, but there could be no enforcement of such obligations, certainly not for Gentiles to whom such practices would have been alien. So a Christian man could be, for example, either circumcised or uncircumcised.

Paul encountered much resistance to his attitude in such matters on the part of Jewish converts to the Christian Way, but he was either by temperament or through experience (probably both) notably cosmopolitan in outlook. Nothing about him comes through more vividly than his adaptability to and understanding of peoples he met wherever he went. He was plainly an extrovert, the sort of man who could enter into conversation immediately with strangers, engage their interest, and often enlist their support. By the same token, of course, he could invite ridicule and even antagonism, for to be outgoing one must put oneself at risk, and that means accepting such unpleasant consequences when they occur. A man of this temper is predictably loyal to his friends and associates and Paul clearly demonstrates this most admirable quality. He seems to have veered naturally to cities rather than to rural areas: a man who gravitated to the market place, the heart of urban life, where people of all sorts abound. His confidence in the Gospel and in his calling to preach it is overwhelming. Along with all these endearing traits and in the eyes of some at variance with them is the fact that he obviously had a strongly mystical strain in him. His language frequently attests an interiority of spirit that some might find unexpected in such an outgoing type of personality.

From his own impressive testimony in II Corinthians 10.10, he was not at all a man of commanding appearance or an orator skilled in the elegant forms of discourse that the Greek world so much admired. On the contrary, he seems to have been somewhat unprepossessing in appearance and style. He interprets his shortcomings on that score as God-given: he is a weak vessel expressly made so in order that the glorious message he has to proclaim may be seen clearly without any possible confusion with the instrument through which it is conveyed. Whatever value is left in him must come only from the Risen Christ, for it is that Christ who now lives in him. The immense success of his preaching must surely have owed much to the transformation that his audience saw in the glow of his face and heard in the tone of his voice as he spoke with the intoxication of one who had been totally seized by a spiritual power far beyond his probably mediocre presence.

Paulianists. Followers of Paul of Samosata. See **Paulicians,** from whom they are to be distinguished.

Paulicians. A Christian sect in the Byzantine Empire from *c.* the 5th c. Of obscure origin, they may have derived their name from Paul of Samosata or even from Paul the Apostle. They professed a dualism similar to that of the Manichees and having affinities with various Gnostic groups. They had also some affinities with the Bogomils and the Albigensians of later times, and like them they were bitterly persecuted by the Church. They taught that Jesus became the Christ through merit. They are to be distinguished from the Paulianists, who were the followers of Paul of Samosata, who repudiated the doctrine of the Trinity.

Paul of Samosata. A 3rd-c. Bishop of Antioch, who was deposed for teaching a form of Dynamic Monarchianism in which the Godhead is accounted a Trinity of Father, Wisdom, and Logos. He maintained that Jesus Christ differed from the prophets only in degree. Having been born human, he became,

through the merit of his Passion, the Savior of the world.

Paul of the Cross (1694–1775). Founder of the Passionists. See **Passionists.**

Pax Brede. A small metal, ivory, or wood plate with a handle and bearing a religious image (often the Crucifixion) used in former times to convey the Kiss of Peace at Mass. The celebrant kissed it first and it was then passed to the others in turn. It came into general use in the Middle Ages. The Kiss of Peace, traditionally exchanged by the clergy in the form of a slight embrace, is nowadays exchanged also by the people and either in that manner or by handshake.

Peace. The Hebrew word "shalom" (šālôm) is immensely rich in meaning, so that although it is translatable as "peace" and usually is so rendered in English versions and translations of the Bible, it means much more. It was the everyday greeting in biblical times, as it is still today among many Jews. It was invested, however, with theological significance: Yahweh is the source of all peace and *shalom* is therefore a divine gift, and to wish it upon anyone is to wish for the bestowal of that gift. Authentic peace is much more than mere lack of war; it is more than even contentment and a sense of well-being. It is easy to talk of peace, but authentic peace cannot be attained without righteousness. Only where righteousness reigns can there be real peace. *Shalom* entails communion with God, a being at peace with him. In the Christian Way all this is inherited. Jesus, in the Gospels, uses the customary greeting, which in the New Testament is normally rendered in Greek by *eirēnē*, but again thereby losing some of the force of the Hebrew. Nevertheless, when the New Testament writers allude to the peace of the Lord Jesus Christ the theological echoes from the Old Testament usage reverberate in the word. Indeed, the peace of God in the New Testament is seen as attained through Christ and therefore may be seen as the achievement of salvation.

Peasants' Revolt. In the late 15th c., a generation or so before the beginnings of the Lutheran Reformation, movements among the economically distressed German peasantry, such as the *Bundschuh* on the Upper Rhineland had begun to prepare the way for open revolt throughout large areas of Germany. Some of the extremist wing of the German Reformers, such as Thomas Münzer, further inflamed the peasantry toward rebellion, sentiments for which spread to townsfolk and others. Their grievances were set forth in the Twelve Articles drawn up at Memminger in March 1525, demanding the abolition of serfdom and other political changes. Lacking cautious leadership, the rebels began a rampage of violence. They burned down monasteries and other symbols of the existing order and showed clear intent of reducing to shambles everything that seemed to impede their revolt. Luther, far from supporting the rebels (although at first he had tried to mediate between them and the establishment) recommended, in a document published in 1525 that was to become famous, the extermination of "the murderous and thieving rabble" (*Wider die mördischen und räubischen Rotten der Bauern*). The armies of the *Schwäbischer Bund*, a union of the Lutheran princes, seeing the revolt as an embarrassment to the Reformation movement as well as a mortal danger to political stability, put down the revolt with merciless force. The conditions of the few rebels who survived grew even worse. They had gained nothing by their rebellion which merely enhanced the power of the Lutheran princes and the image of political respectability projected by the Lutheran movement, which now could be seen more and more as on the side of law and order.

Pectoral Cross. A cross, traditionally of precious metal and often jeweled although it may be of the simplest material, such as wood, worn hanging from a chain around the neck. It is part of the insignia of a bishop. In the Roman Catholic Church it is also worn by abbots and some others and in the Eastern Churches by archimandrites and archpriests. In some countries, however, priests having no ecclesiastical rank or dignity wear it, e.g., many Russian priests wear it as do some Anglican priests in the United States. See also **Encolpion.**

Peculiars. In England certain churches and other places are so designated, being exempt from episcopal jurisdiction as are certain abbeys and other religious foundations in the Roman Catholic Church. For example, Westminster Abbey and St. George's Chapel, Windsor, are Royal Peculiars, exempt from all ecclesiastical jurisdiction and subject only and directly to the Sovereign.

Pedilavium. See **Feet, Washing of the.**

Péguy, Charles Pierre (1873–1914). French writer. Educated at the Sorbonne and the École Normale Supérieure in Paris, he gave up his academic studies to manage a bookstore in the rue de la Sorbonne, which became a center of intellectual activity. With a deep love for France and for medieval Catholic culture and a personal devotion to the Eucharist and Christian mysticism coupled with a definite anticlericalism and some social sympathies, he estranged himself from the Church and almost all contemporary party politics in one way or another. Later generations of French Catholics have learned, however, to appreciate his work, which was influenced by the thought of Henri Bergson. Among his early writings is his *Jeanne d'Arc* (1897), pseudonymously published as by Pierre Baudouin. Later writings include *Le Mystère des Saints Innocents* (1912) and *L'Argent* (1913). He was killed in the Battle of the Marne in 1914.

Peirce, Charles Sanders (1839–1914). American philosopher, son of the Harvard mathematician, Benjamin Peirce. His principal writings are to be found in *The Collected Papers of C. S. Peirce*, edited by Charles Hartshorne and Paul Weiss (1931–1935) and further volumes edited by A. Burk (1958). Peirce invented the term "pragmatism" in 1878 to designate a theory of meaning founded on the principle that in order to ascertain the meaning of any intellectual conception one must consider what practical consequences might conceivably result by necessity from the truth of that conception. The sum of these consequences will constitute the entire meaning of the conception. He also developed three categories to be used in any philosophical analysis: (1) Firstness (quality), Secondness (reaction), and Thirdness (generality). The greatness of a system can be seen in its use of all three categories. He recognized the importance of the concept of novelty as an ultimate aspect of everything in the universe. In the universe are to be found events that have no causal antecedent; nevertheless, through a principle that he called "synechism," the universe tends to develop what might be called "habits;" hence the growth of regularities and order. In Peirce's view the idea of God is a *possible* hypothesis, but by "God" Peirce has in mind a conception that changes and grows with the universe and is therefore radically at variance with the traditional Judaeo-Christian concept. See **Pragmatism.**

Pelagianism. Both historically and theologically, both for Christianity and concerning a principle that arises in religious thought and practice in other major religions, the Pelagian controversy that raged in the late 4th and early 5th c. is of the greatest importance. The Pelagian movement associated with Pelagius (see **Pelagius**), who provided its theological vindication, was to some extent independent of him in the sense that it seems to have emerged as a lay movement, elitist in outlook and aristocratic in membership. Those who

were attracted to it generally had a high respect for the ascetic tradition in Christianity and held Jerome in special esteem. By emphasizing the freedom of the will they could point to the divinely-given power in man to choose righteousness and reject evil. In their emphasis on this principle they saw unlimited opportunities for preaching in such a way as to change men and women fundamentally and at the deepest level of their being. Their concern arose, at least in great part, from their disgust at the moral laxity, even depravity, that they were seeing in the conduct of many Christians, especially in Rome, which they perceived as issuing at least in great measure from the teaching of those who were inculcating the notion that human beings have "no power of themselves to help themselves," resulting in a sort of moral impotence among those who were imbibing such a view of the nature of man.

In opposition to the views of Pelagius and his followers was the great Western Father of the Church, Augustine, who, out of his own deep personal experience, had felt himself saved by grace not only *inter pontem et fontem* (between the bridge and the river) but by the humanly inexplicable choice of God: a view implying a form of predestinarian teaching. Augustine, feeling himself to have been not only undeserving but conspicuously unworthy to be the recipient of such grace, insisted, somewhat in the manner of the apostle Paul, that what a man or woman does by way of meritorious action must therefore be irrelevant to God's choice; otherwise God would have chosen people with a far better moral track record than Augustine felt he could show. From such misgivings about his own worthiness as the recipient of the priceless grace he had received, Augustine had gone on to see humankind as a "mass of perdition:" a notion implied in the doctrine of Original Sin that he found in Scripture and that he had not found elsewhere, e.g., neither in the Manichees whom he had followed for some nine years nor in the

Neoplatonic philosophy that he had then embraced before his conversion to Christianity. Men and women are bogged down in a morass of evil. They are so deeply entrenched in it that they can no more expect to save themselves or even contribute to the salvific process than could a man unable to swim hope to do anything to save himself alone and shipwrecked in an Atlantic storm.

Augustine began to preach against Pelagianism soon after Pelagius, with his supporter Celestius, had left Rome for Africa and thence to Palestine *c.* 410. Condemned by a Council at Carthage in 411, Pelagius found himself being gradually perceived more and more as a heretic. For various reasons Pelagianism, although it still had its supporters (e.g., Julian of Eclanum, who conducted a bitter controversy with Augustine till the latter's death), was opposed on all sides. The issues it had raised were nevertheless by no means obliterated. The controversy as such abated, but Pelagianism, in various forms, including one traditionally although perhaps a little misleadingly called "semi-Pelagianism," persisted as a mood, an inclination, and a popular tendency in the life of the medieval Church. It flared up as an issue at the Reformation and is still a live issue in Christianity today, for it has never been fully resolved, and it has counterparts in other religions too. Many today feel disgust at the consequences so often brought about by an uncritical acceptance (not to say vulgar misunderstanding) of the Pauline and Augustinian emphasis on grace, not least when it is distorted into an antinomian attitude (see **Antinomianism**). So we can understand the disgust that Pelagius felt at the conduct of many Christians at Rome and at the moral depravity implied in attitudes nowadays caricatured as "the-devil-made-me-do-it." Yet both in Augustinianism and in Pelagianism are vital theological truths, notably susceptible as they both are to popular misunderstanding that can have grievous

ethical and social as well as theological consequences.

Pelagius (*c.*360–*c.*420). British theologian. Although generally associated with a denial of the traditional Christian doctrine of Original Sin, he does not seem to have interested himself in the subject very much. What distressed him, as a layman, was the moral laxness of Rome to which he came in middle life and which he felt had its roots in the lack of moral responsibility that had been engendered by the notion that man is so corrupt by nature that he cannot be held morally responsible because to have such responsibility one must have freedom of the will. See **Pelagianism**.

Pelican. The pelican, a bird that vulns herself with her beak to feed her young with her own blood, is a symbol of very long standing in Christian art. It exhibits the redemption of humankind through the saving Blood of Christ. It symbolizes especially the Sacrament of the Altar, as in the much loved hymn attributed to Thomas Aquinas, *Adoro te devote*, in which Christ is addressed as "Pie Pelicane." On the column in the quadrangle of Corpus Christi College, Oxford, is the figure of a pelican: an apt choice for a college so named.

Penance. The word "penance" is from the Latin *poena*, meaning "punishment" or "pain." By the 3rd c. a system was already established in the Christian Church whereby an individual guilty of a grave sin was excluded from the life of the Church, enrolled in the list of official penitents, and required to perform certain public acts, usually including prayers and fasts, long and very severe by modern standards, after which he or she was publicly reconciled to the Church. So gravely did the Church look on the transgressions that qualified one for such public penance that the opportunity of so making amends for them was granted only once in a lifetime. Moreover, even when reconciled to the Church such a former penitent was further required to abstain from all sexual activity for the rest of his or her life. So harsh were the requirements under this system that by the early Middle Ages a new system was developed, still very severe by modern standards but less extreme than the practice of the primitive Church.

Out of this development gradually grew the system of formal confession to a priest, followed by the punishment imposed and absolution in the name of God and the Church. In the course of many centuries the punishment became nominal, such as the recitation of a few prayers or a decade or more of the Rosary and always of course the utterance of a statement of deep sorrow for one's sins, called an "act of contrition;" but the typical medieval pattern usually demanded, at least for sins accounted serious, arduous and painful punishments such as pilgrimages (sometimes barefoot), lengthy and severe fasts, sexual continence for a considerable period, imprisonment, or whippings often of considerable severity, or a combination of all of these. Out of this system Penance was developed as one of the Sacraments of the Church.

The Reformation by no means entirely abolished the practice of penitential exercises required as a condition of reconciliation to the Church. For example, in Scotland in the 17th c. and later, anyone guilty of a sin deemed to be a public scandal was sentenced by the Minister and the Kirk Session to stand outside the main door of the parish kirk, often with his or her neck secured in an iron collar and sometimes barefoot and bareheaded, in all sorts of weather, and to beg the forgiveness of each member of the congregation entering the kirk for the Sunday morning service. This punishment was usually to be undergone for a stated number of Sundays (e.g., three) and was followed by the penitent's being admitted to the service and subjected to the further humiliation of standing in the penitents' box and being lectured on his or her transgression before being publicly for-

given and received back into the fold. Fornication was one of the commonest of qualifying sins. Such was the humiliation entailed in the punishment that some fled the country rather than endure it.

Penn, William (1644–1718). Founder of Pennsylvania. The eldest son of Admiral Sir William Penn, he was an undergraduate at Christ Church, Oxford, whence he was sent down for his refusal to conform to Church of England doctrine and practice. Moved by a sermon he heard in Cork, preached by an Oxford tradesman, he became a Quaker and in 1688 wrote a defense of his repudiation of traditional orthodoxy, for which he was sentenced to imprisonment in the Tower of London. During his imprisonment he wrote a work entitled *No Cross, No Crown* (1669), which became a recognized Quaker classic. Having developed the ambition of founding a new colony in America to which Quakers could go without fear of persecution, he obtained land grants and drew up a constitution for the colony, providing for liberty of conscience for all forms of monotheistic religious belief. Having sailed to America and established the colony, he returned in 1684 to England where he briefly enjoyed the protection of James II, but after the Settlement in 1688 he was subjected to persecution again. He visited America again in 1699, but most of the rest of his life was spent in England, where he wrote copiously and engaged in itinerant preaching. His writings include *The Fruits of Solitude* (1692) and *Primitive Christianity* (1696).

Pentateuch. From the Greek *pente* (five) and *teuchos* (book). The term is used to designate the first five books of the Bible, also known in Judaism as the Torah and revered as the Law, which for Jews is the most important and sacred part of the Bible.

Pentecost. One of the three festivals listed in Exodus 23.14–17. The word signifies "the fiftieth day." The feast was originally an agricultural feast, celebrating the gathering of the first fruits of the harvest. Later it was given a fixed date: fifty days after the Passover. In Judaism, much later still and perhaps not till after the beginning of the Christian era, it came to be invested with an historical association: the giving of the Law by Moses. In Christian thought and practice it acquired immense importance from what is recounted in Acts 2. It came to be regarded by some as "the birthday of the Church" and is so often treated today. At the same time it is the occasion on which, in a special manner, the Holy Spirit manifested himself to the followers of the Christian Way, empowering them to witness to their faith even to the ends of the earth: an empowerment symbolized in the account by Luke in which people representing a multitude of different tongues heard the proclamation of the Gospel, each in his or her own language.

Pentecostalism. A movement, said to have had its beginnings in Los Angeles at the beginning of the 20th c., has spread throughout large areas of the world under the pentecostalist label. Both spiritual healing and *glossolalia* (a form of "speaking in tongues") generally characterize it. The *glossolalia* may take the form of unintelligible utterance or it may seem to echo to some extent existing languages. The movement is represented extensively in Black churches. The Assemblies of God constitute one of the best known denominations in which pentecostalist attitudes and practices are standard. Movements with pentecostalist characteristics have arisen in various Christian traditions, Protestant, Anglican, and Roman Catholic.

Pentecostarion. (Greek, *pentēcostarion*). A liturgical book used in the Eastern Orthodox Church, containing the variable lessons and prayers for the liturgical season from Easter through the Sunday after Pentecost. The term is also used in the Eastern Church to designate that part of the Christian Year. See **Year, The Christian.**

People's Temple. A movement founded in 1953 by a minister of the Disciples of Christ Church, Jim Jones. The group, predominantly Black, was noted for its radical political views and aims. It spread to California and to other countries. Responding to suspicions about its practices, a United States Congressman, Leo Ryan, conducted an investigation of the movement in Guyana, where he was murdered in November 1978. Following the murder, more than 900 members of the movement committed mass suicide in Jonestown, Guyana. This appalling tragedy had the unfortunate consequence of stimulating suspicion, mistrust, and fear on the part of many people about all novel religious movements.

Pepper, Stephen (1891–1972). American philosopher. Born in Newark and trained at Harvard, he taught mainly at the University of California at Berkeley. Behind his philosophical work, principally in aesthetics, lies his view that every system in philosophy is developed from a root metaphor. He notes four that have governed basic metaphysical systems: formism, mechanism, organicism, and contextualism, represented respectively by Aristotle, Hobbes, Whitehead, and those pragmatistic thinkers who find their key concept in context as a principle of interpretation. Pepper favored the contextual view but eventually modified it in the direction of perspectivism. (See **Perspectivism.**) His writings include *Aesthetic Quality* (1938); *The Work of Art* (1955), and *Ethics* (1960).

Perception. This term is of great importance in philosophy, more especially in epistemology but also in other branches of philosophy such as the philosophy of religion. The early Greek thinkers were interested in it even before the time of Socrates and Plato. Both Leucippus and Democritus held an "image" view of perception, according to which, bombarded by the images perceived by the senses, we arrive at awareness of "the way things are." Plato distinguished between what one can do through sensory perception and what one can do through the use of the mind: in the former case one can grasp the "sensible" world, which participates in the apprehension of reality, while in the latter case one sees the "intelligible" world, the World of Forms, wherein lies reality in its plenitude.

Aristotle, building upon Plato's insights, developed the view that the organs of sense provide the images that the mind then uses in such a way as to arrive, by abstraction, at the forms. There is no way that the intellect can directly attain knowledge of these forms, for there is nothing in the intellect that is not first in the senses, but the senses deliver the material out of which the intellect can so arrange and classify what the senses deliver. Locke is widely associated with the theory of Representative Perception, which had been adumbrated by some of the ancient Greeks (e.g., Democritus). On Locke's view, the mind at birth is a blank slate (*tabula rasa*) on which are gradually inscribed, through sensory perception, such ideas as we have of the world around us. The mind has nevertheless a computer-like power to arrange what it so receives, but (in modern terminology) it must be programmed before it can do anything at all. It has no built-in equipment (no "innate ideas") and so must rely entirely on sense perception to provide the pabulum it needs for its own proper work. Leibniz saw perception as an ongoing process, so providing the continuity that is presumed when one talks of being "the same person" as one was twenty years ago or even as a baby and even if one had been comatose for a year or the victim of grave long-term amnesia. What Leibniz meant by perception, however, is not entirely clear. Kant saw perception as awareness that has sensation as its concomitant.

In more recent times the term "sense datum" became fashionable, having been introduced first by George Moore and then widely used by philosophers such as Bertrand Russell and C. D. Broad, with the claim that we cannot properly be said to perceive things; we perceive only sense-data. Dogs do not perceive exactly as humans do and worms perceive in a still more different way from us. What is perceived can be only whatever is given, which may be said to resemble the thing but is not the thing. We say we see hills and valleys, but a hill is not a thing independent of its surroundings, nor is a valley, nor (it may be argued) is any entity we call a "thing." Adversaries of this type of view entailing such linguistic usage (notably Gilbert Ryle and John Austin) have argued that we do indeed perceive things and that sense-datum language is an unnecessary and confusing invention. According to Merleau-Ponty, relational forms are to be included among the elements constituting perception and they provide that bridge between sensations and ideas that has been the subject of so much philosophical controversy throughout the ages.

Perichoresis. This Greek term, *perichōrēsis*, used by John of Damascus, means literally "proceeding around," being rendered into Latin by the term *circumincessio*. It is used in theology to designate the action by which the three *hypostaseis* (*personae*) of the Trinity interpenetrate. See **Trinity.**

Pericope. A section or passage of the Bible. Before the 4th c. it seems both in the East and in the West that the passages to be read at the Eucharist were selected by the clergy apart from any systematic plan. From about that time the practice of systematizing the readings began to be developed, leading eventually to the development of the lectionary, prescribing passages suited to the liturgical season or other circumstances.

Pericope Adulterae. The technical designation of the passage (John 7.53–8.11) narrating the beautiful story of the way in which Jesus treated the woman who had been taken in the act of adultery. Biblical scholars are in no doubt that this passage does not belong to the text of John's Gospel. It is not found in any of the ancient manuscripts, excepting only Bezae (see **Codex Bezae Cantabridgiensis**). The story, however, not only has many marks of genuineness and fits into the mold of all that is known of the compassionate outlook of Jesus but is attested in a 3rd-c. extra-biblical text, the *Didascalia Apostolorum*, and other historical sources. Some evidence exists for attributing it to Luke and placing it after Luke 21.38, and some scholars have argued in favor of that proposal.

Peripatetics. The members of Aristotle's school were so called in antiquity either because he walked up and down as he taught (Greek *peripatein*, to walk about) or from the covered walkway (*peripatos*) of the Lyceum. The latter is the more likely.

Perpetua. A 2nd-c. African Christian martyr, executed at Carthage 203 CE. The previous year Septimius Severus had forbidden conversions to the Christian Way, and she was among other African catechumens who were imprisoned and eventually executed. The story of her sufferings is narrated in a contemporary account, possibly edited by Tertullian.

Perrone, Giovanni (1794–1876). Italian Jesuit theologian. His 9-volume work, *Praelectiones Theologicae* (1835–1842) was extensively used in the 19th c. as a standard treatise on Roman Catholic dogmatic theology.

Perry, Ralph Barton (1876–1957). American philosopher. Born in Vermont, he was trained at Harvard, where he taught during the rest of his career. He expounded a view called the New Realism, which was critical of Idealism in general. He defined value as inhering in any object of any interest. Harmonizing interests becomes in Perry's thought the supreme aim, leading to an all-inclusive system of values. His works include a symposium, *The New Realism* (1912); *The Thought and Character of William James*, 2 vols. (1935); and *Realms of Value* (1954).

Persecution of Christians in the Early Church. Followers of the Christian Way were at first tolerated by the Roman authorities along with Jews and adherents of other religious minorities. The policy of the Roman authorities was in fact notable for its tolerance of all religions that seemed to pose no political threat to the Empire or to foster sedition. Even when Christians refused to perform the customary recognition of the divinity of the Emperor (which they might have done by the mere pouring out of a libation of wine or the burning of a pinch of incense before the statue of the deified Emperor), official action was rarely taken at first, although popular sentiment was roused against them, resulting in local boycotting, ostracism, and the like. How active and official persecution was developed is unclear. Even Nero's ferocious and notorious measures against the Christians was not officially on the ground of their being Christians; the charge was arson. (Nero had made Christians the scapegoat for the fire that had swept through Rome in 64 CE.) There is no evidence of any official persecution of Christians outside Rome at that time. The effect, however, was to foster such popular suspicion and distrust of Christians as to cause many to class them as criminals. What came to be known in garbled accounts of their practices led to rumors of cannibalism (e.g., talk of eating flesh and blood) and other gross misunderstandings. According to the writer of the Apocalypse, severe persecution of Christians existed in his time, probably c. 95. Persecution grew but was local and intermittent. Local magistrates exercised summary jurisdiction, no doubt according to local sentiments of hostility toward Christians.

In 250, however, the Emperor Decius ordered that all his subjects should make the prescribed sacrifice to the gods of the State. This enactment was probably at least in part a thinly veiled attack on Christians, many of whom suffered cruelly and were executed. Valerian also persecuted Christians severely, ordering the execution of all clerics who would not apostatize. In 303 Diocletian ordered all churches destroyed and all copies of Scriptures to be burned. Measures against the Christians, although intermittently taken, grew in intensity and ferocity till the Edict of Milan early in 313, which recognized the Christian Churches as having legal personality. No doubt persecution occurred sporadically here and there after then, but it substantially ceased and Christianity, although in no way established, steadily made its way as a *religio licita* (legally recognized religion) and the Church actively engaged in missionary enterprise.

Persona. See **Hypostasis.**

Personalism. A philosophical view in which the concept of "person" is taken as ultimate. It took its beginnings in the thought of Schleiermacher and in those who stressed the importance of the claim that God is personal, so that "person" becomes the fundamental category distinguishing theism from materialism, pantheism, and other philosophical views on the nature of God. In 1868 Walt Whitman published a literary essay on Personalism. Philosophers such as Bronson Alcott, Charles Renouvier, Borden Parker Bowne, F. C. S. Schiller, William Stern, and Edgar Sheffield Brightman are among those who, while differing considerably in their views, can properly be assigned the Personalist label. In 1919 R. T. Flewelling founded a philosophical journal named *The Personalist*, the name of which was changed in 1980 to *The Pacific Philosophical Quarterly*.

Perspectivism. A term coined by Gustav Teichmüller (1832–1888) in upholding the philosophical view that every standpoint is in some sense true (compare the Hindu concept of Darśana), presenting as it does a particular, unique perspective of the universe. Other philosophers have used the term, e.g., Nietzsche, Ortega, and Russell.

Pesach. See **Passover.**

Peshitta. This Syriac text of the Bible has been the official one in Syriac-speaking Christian countries from the early 5th century.

Peter. The disciple so named originally bore the name of Simeon or Simon. *Petros* is a masculine form of the Greek word *petra*, rock: an additional name apparently conferred upon him by Jesus in the much discussed passage (Matthew 16.16–18) in which, according to Matthew, Jesus promises to build his Church upon that rock. The calling of Peter is reported by the Evangelists in somewhat different ways, but always linked with the call of James and John and especially with Peter's brother Andrew. According to John, they were already disciples of John the Baptist. Peter is represented as having a leadership role among the disciples: not a formal leadership but one which somehow or other he came to exercise, either through temperamental aptitude for leadership or by a specially close association with his Master. After the Resurrection, Peter, as reported in Acts, seems to exercise a clearly leading role; yet his later life is curiously unreported. After Acts 12 we hear nothing about him save for a mention in Acts 15.7–11. The tradition associating him with Rome is certainly attested late in the 2nd c., and there is good reason to suppose it to be much earlier than that; yet New Testament evidence is lacking. At any rate, the question is still controversial, as is also the nature of his primacy among the apostles.

Peter Damian (1007–1072). Church reformer and theologian. Born at

Ravenna of very humble parentage, he was in his youth a swineherd, but on being recognized as capable of education, he was sent to study at Faenza and Parma. In 1035 he entered the Benedictine monastery at Fonte Avella of which he became prior in 1043. He soon acquired great fame as a learned reformer of singular integrity and courage. He preached against simony and other immoral practices among the clergy and was widely esteemed. In 1828 Pope Leo XII declared him a Doctor of the Church.

Peter Lombard (*c.* 1100–1160). Born near Novara, Lombardy, he went to Reims, then to Paris where he taught at the cathedral school. Shortly before his death he was made Bishop of Paris. Among his writings (many of them scriptural commentaries) the most famous and influential was his *Sententiarum* (Sentences) in 4 books (*c.*1155–58). This great work deals with the central concepts of Christian theology: the Trinity, Creation, Sin, the Incarnation, the Virtues, the Sacraments, and the "Last Things." For some decades after his death Peter's work was attacked from several sides and some attempts were even made to have it censured at the Fourth Lateran Council (1215). The *Sentences*, having been then pronounced orthodox, quickly acquired prestige and fame and became in fact the standard theological text during much of the rest of the Middle Ages. It was very much in conformity with the medieval ideal for a work of this kind, being clear, lucid, and comprehensive, and above all judicial in tone, conveying a sense of magisterial authority.

Peter Martyr (1500–1562). (Pietro Martire Vermigli) Protestant Reformer. Born at Florence and educated at Fiesole, he joined the Augustinians, becoming in 1530 abbot of their foundation at Spoleto. His sympathies with the Reformation (especially with Bucer and Zwingli) led to his flight from his native Italy. With Bucer's help he became professor of theology at Strassburg in 1542, and at Cranmer's invitation he went to England in 1547, becoming Regius Professor of Divinity at Oxford the following year. After further vicissitudes he was reappointed professor at Strassburg and later taught at Zürich.

He is not to be confused with Peter Veronensis also known as Peter Martyr (*c.*1200–1252), the Dominican Inquisitor, who is depicted in a painting by Fra Angelico in the convent of San Marco, Florence, with wounded head and with his finger to his lips, because he was murdered on his way from Como to Milan. He was later canonized.

Peter the Hermit (*c.*1050–1115). One of the most famous and eloquent preachers at the First Crusade. He entered Jerusalem with the victorious army and on his return to Europe became prior of the Augustinian monastery of Neufmoutier, of which he was partly the founder.

Petite Église, La. Those French Roman Catholics who declined to recognize the Concordat of 1801 between Napoleon and Pope Pius VII, which led to the formal restoration of the Roman Catholic Church in France, by which the State was given much control over the clergy, including the right to nominate new bishops. The original bishops were reconciled to the Holy See in 1817 and 1818, except for the Bishop of Blois, who became in effect the head of the "Petite Église" till his death in 1829, leaving his people without a bishop. The last priest died in 1847 and the "Petite Église" eventually died out.

Petitio Principii. A Latin phrase (usually rendered "begging the question") designating one of the common fallacies listed in traditional, Aristotelian logic, in which one purports to reach a conclusion after first of all having assumed in the premises of the argument what one proposes to show in the conclusion. For example, an argument arises among six men over the distribution of seven

$1,000 bills that they have jointly stolen. One of them, Mr. Smith, reminding them that they must settle quickly so that they may quickly disperse, quotes Mark 4.25 ("he that hath, to him shall be given") and proceeds to hand each one of the others a $1,000 bill. The others roar in protest, "How come you get $2,000?" "Because I am the richest." "How come you are the richest?" "Because I have twice as much as any of you."

Pew. For many centuries seats were unknown in Christian churches, although sometimes a few stone ones were provided along the walls for the aged or infirm. In the West, as to this day in the East, the only postures in church were standing and kneeling. By the end of the 13th c., however, many English churches seem to have had at least some wooden benches installed and these were called "pews", presumably from the Latin *podium*, which means a seat raised above the floor level. The custom, familiar today outside the tradition of the Eastern Churches, of having fixed pews, often very heavy and solid, or rush chairs each attached to a prie-dieu, is a comparatively recent innovation in Christian practice.

Peyotism. See **Native American Church.**

Phanar. The name of the official residence of the Ecumenical Patriarch at Constantinople. It is situated in the Greek quarter of the city.

Pharisees. The name of a party or sect within Judaism, mentioned frequently in the Gospels. They centered their religious outlook on the observance of the law and so may be regarded as in the heritage of Ezra rather than that of the prophets. It was apparently on this account that Jesus and they came into such conflict. Josephus, almost the only source we have about them outside the New Testament (except for a few Talmudic references), reports them as originating in the 2nd c. BCE. They may be dated as of somewhat earlier origin; nevertheless, they were by no reckoning of great antiquity in the time of Jesus. They were probably not very numerous. In contrast to the Sadducees, a priestly group, the Pharisees were a lay group committed to a policy of working with Rome for practical, political reasons, rather than resisting or rebelling against it.

The language attributed to Jesus in speaking of the Pharisees often sounds too extreme to be warranted, for the Pharisees were a highly respected group. No doubt the Evangelists wished to emphasize the distaste that Jesus had for thinking of religion in the legalistic terms that the Pharisees as a group tended to evoke. No doubt, too, the Pharisees felt a natural hostility to the kind of teaching they found in Jesus, which they would be likely to see as threatening to their role and status in Jewish life. While the Sadducees denied resurrection of the dead and disbelieved in angels, the Pharisees affirmed both of these beliefs, which were obviously prominent in the thought of Jesus. Moreover, many Pharisees, including Paul himself, became converts to the Christian Way. All of this might lead one to expect them to be more receptive to the teaching of Jesus than some other groups in his time. The impression one gets, however, is that they saw themselves as in some way indefectible in the sense that they could not be improved upon as a group expressive of the best in the Jewish heritage and that therein lay their particular resentment to the movement that they saw in Jesus and his disciples. This very reliance on group dynamic is what would be alien to the spirit of Jesus and his insistence on interiority as the essence of his teaching.

Phelonion. The Eastern Church counterpart to the western chasuble, the principal vestment of the celebrant at Mass. In appearance it looks somewhat more like a cope.

Phenomenalism. The philosophical view that knowledge is limited to the phenomena, contradistinguished from whatever may be held to lie behind them as "noumenal realities." The Greek word *phenomenon*, (plural, *phenomena*) means "appearance" and is opposed to *noumenon*, which Kant used as a term to designate the unknowable reality behind the phenomenal world. See **Ding-an-Sich**.

Phenomenology. The term, though used in various senses since the mid-eighteenth century, is now most commonly understood as a designation for a philosophical outlook developed by Edmund Husserl (1859–1938) and others. While modern phenomenological schools vary considerably both in their understanding of the task confronting them and in their methods of pursuing it, the phenomenological approach is characterized by a preoccupation with the fundamental character of subjective processes. Intentionality, for instance, plays an important part in it. Phenomenologists interest themselves, therefore, in the characteristic themes of psychology, and their work has also some broad affinities with that of existentialism.

Philadelphians. A religious society that flourished toward the end of the 17th c. and whose beliefs had been much influenced by the visions and teachings of Boehme. Its members did not regard themselves as a church, being encouraged, rather, to continue whatever church allegiance they might have had. They were organized in 1670 under the name of the Philadelphian Society for the Advancement of Piety and Divine Philosophy. Their teachings were mystical, esoteric, and at least in tone pantheistic, and they aimed at spiritual illumination. John Pordage, Rector of Bradfield, England, encouraged the study of Boehme and had a group of followers among whom was Mrs. Jane Leade (1623–1704), who, herself a visionary from childhood, pioneered the society.

Philaret Drozdov (1782–1867). Russian theologian and Metropolitan (Archbishop) of Moscow. He rose quickly to high ecclesiastical office, becoming Bishop of Jaroslav in 1820 and in 1821 Archbishop of Moscow. He is reputed to have been a model bishop of the Russian Church, exerting a beneficent influence on both Church and State. Among his many theological writings his *Catechism*, providing a survey of the principal teachings of the Eastern Church, was highly influential in Russia before the Bolshevik Revolution, providing, at least in the eyes of many, a doctrinal standard.

Philip Neri (1515–1595). Born at Florence and educated by the Dominicans, he went to Rome, where he led a very devout life and engaged in charitable works. He helped to found a confraternity for the care of pilgrims in Rome. Ordained to the priesthood, he attracted both clergy and people to his teachings, and through his activities the Oratorians, a congregation of priests not taking canonical religious vows like monks or friars but living in community, was founded. The Oratorians, whom Newman after his conversion to the Roman Catholic Church introduced to England, have enjoyed a reputation for learning, gentility, and culture. The French Oratory, to which Malebranche belonged, has been especially influential, notably through its work for the education of priests. See **Oratorians**.

Philistines. A people known as "the Sea Peoples" seem to have attempted an onslaught on Egypt in the 13th c. BCE but were unsuccessful. At least one constituent of these people has been identified with the Philistines who appear in the Bible. Eventually, having been repeatedly repulsed by Egypt, they made their homeland in the coastal plains later known as Palestine. They appear to have had customs some of which reflect those of Mycenae and Crete, but the history of their early religious heritage is obscure.

Philo (30 BCE–50 CE). Hellenistic Jewish thinker. Born in Alexandria and a member of the Alexandrian School, he was a leading representative of Hellenistic Judaism. Not the least important of his teachings was his view that the wisdom of Moses had anticipated that of the Greeks. He interpreted the Scriptures, in Alexandrian fashion, figuratively. God, he held, is Being, but he so transcends all other beings that one can never say what God is; one can and ought, rather, to say what he is not. Through a form of mystical encounter, however, one may be said to know God, but only in the sense of perceiving the infinite distance between God and man. He also taught in Gnostic fashion the existence of a hierarchy of intermediaries (e.g., angels) between God and man. His teaching on the Logos is of special interest to Christians: it is through the Logos that God relates himself to the world. The Logos proceeds from God along with all ideas, existing eternally in the divine mind. The Logos created the world. Philo's writings include *That God is an Immutable Being*; *Concerning the Artisan of the World*; and *On the Eternity of the World*.

Philokalia. The title of two celebrated Christian works: (1) An anthology of the works of Origen, compiled by Basil the Great and Gregory of Nazianzus in 358–359, of importance to scholars for having preserved, at least in some form, parts of the immense corpus of Origen's writings, the Greek text of which would have been otherwise lost to posterity. (2) A work by Macarius Notaras and Nicodemus of the Holy Mount, being a collection of mystical writings from the 4th to the 15th c. including much relevant to Hesychasm, published in 1782, which has had a very powerful influence on Eastern Orthodoxy. The Greek word *philokalia* means "love of the beautiful."

Philosophia Perennis. This Latin phrase ("perennial philosophy") has been used since the 16th c. in slightly varying ways but generally in allusion to the philosophical style and concerns of the tradition that has prevailed in Western philosophy from the ancient Greeks and the medieval thinkers who inherited their outlook and adapted it to their purposes. It has been used, however, in a still broader sense to designate that kind of philosophizing the preoccupations of which are not with transitory problems that occur within an ephemeral intellectual fashion but pertain, rather, to the most recurrent problems and the most profound concerns of humankind. Such philosophizing might be compared to a great symphony dominated by certain motifs that recur time and again without final resolution yet apart from which the symphony would be lost under the weight of its own banality.

Philosophy of Religion. The concept of a philosophy of religion is historically the offspring of the 18th-c. movement known as the Enlightenment (*Aufklärung*). It appears in the last decade of the 18th c. in the titles of books such as J. C. G. Schaumann, *Philosophie der Religion* (1793) and J. Berger, *Geschichte der Religionsphilosophie* (1800). Its purpose is the investigation by philosophical methods of all phenomena generally known under terms such as "religion," "religious experience," and the like. The subject as a regular discipline was fostered by the Hegelian outlook that dominated much 19th-c. philosophy, in which all aspects of human experience were subjected to philosophical scrutiny, e.g., the Philosophy of Art or Beauty (aesthetics), the Philosophy of Conduct (ethics), etc. Behind this lay the characteristic Hegelian view that philosophy stands above and beyond all other human endeavors and has a particular kind of judicial function over them. So religion, which Hegel tended to see as a sort of "baby philosophy" using picture-imagery rather than intellectual understanding, called for philosophical inspection along with everything else and was indeed peculiarly deserving of such philosophical scrutiny since it was to be regarded as a sort of kindergarten philosophy.

Such a view stood far indeed, if not at the opposite pole, from the medieval view in which philosophy was seen as the handmaid, helper, or associate (*ancilla*) of theology, the mistress or queen (*domina*) of all the sciences. So in revolt against Hegelian presuppositions, not to say pretensions, philosophy of religion came under attack from two sides: (1) those who distrusted it for reasons similar to their reasons for distrusting a natural theology as opposed to revealed theology (e.g., many in the classical Reformation heritage, such as Karl Barth) or who wished to maintain the traditional Catholic distinction between natural and revealed theology (e.g., Neo-Thomists); and (2) those who (e.g., Logical Empiricists) saw no meaning in metaphysical and religious inquiry and therefore found nothing in religion meriting serious philosophical inspection.

Despite this somewhat infelicitous background, however, the philosophy of religion remains in the opinion of many not only a legitimate but an indispensable tool in the study of religion. In contrast to the dogmatic theologies of the various religions, it is closely allied to what is sometimes now called philosophical theology, in which one reflects on or analyzes intellectually the problems that arise in all forms of religion, e.g., problems concerning the nature of God, the meaning of religious ideas such as grace and freedom, immortality and re-embodiment. Such intellectual exercises may do nothing to deepen one's spiritual life, but they become duties to the extent that religiously minded people have been gifted with intellectual capacities. They are no more likely to make saints than is the study of aesthetics likely to make anyone into a pianist or a painter, but if one is a painter or pianist who happens to be endowed with intellectual gifts as well as artistic ones, intellectual reflection on the nature of such arts is inevitable

although it may have nothing to do with the work of an artist. Moreover, as an antidote to fanaticism, which is surely the enemy of all true religion, the value of the philosophical study of religion cannot easily be doubted. The danger lies only in confusing the philosophy of religion with its practice, which would be like confusing the grammar of music with its performance.

Phoenix. In antiquity this mythical bird, generally portrayed as very gorgeous, was the subject of various legends, prominent among which is that after a life of more than half a millennium it burns itself to ashes and emerges from the ashes regenerated. In early Christian literature we find Tertullian and Clement of Rome among those who allude to it as an image of the Resurrection. It was occasionally used later both in Christian art and in Christian literature. It is representative of the idea of re-embodiment: reincarnation or resurrection. Representations of the phoenix are to be found in several churches at Rome, e.g., Saint Cecilia, Saints Cosmas and Damian, and Saint Praxedes.

Photius (*c.* 810–895). Patriarch of Constantinople, venerated in the Greek Church as a saint. Of noble family, he at first thought of becoming a monk but gave up that intention and embarked upon a diplomatic career, in which he was eminently successful. In 858, while still a layman, he was appointed to succeed Ignatius, the Patriarch of Constantinople who had been deposed from that highest office in the Greek Church. He was duly consecrated, but Ignatius refused to abdicate and a bitter controversy developed in which the Pope was invited to intervene: an intervention that seriously aggravated the dispute, being seen by the Greeks as an assertion of papal authority. Photius, using the sentiment that had been so stirred, denounced the intrusion of Latin influence. He took the opportunity of calling attention to the

Filioque clause that had been introduced in the West and widely used there for some time. The controversy continued, becoming more and more complex and provoking more and more resentment among the Greeks, who perceived it as provoked principally by papal aggression. The quarrel continued till Ignatius died in 877 upon which Photius once again, by imperial edict, became Patriarch of Constantinople. The schism, however, grew from bad to worse and had very serious consequences for the unity of the Christian Church. Photius was a great scholar, said to have had an encyclopedic knowledge. He wrote profusely. His *Treatise on the Holy Spirit* has been a standard source for Greeks in their resistance to dogmatic innovations by the Roman Catholic Church, including the Double Procession. His most extensive work is his *Myriobiblion* or *Bibliotheca*, containing a description of several hundred books exhaustively analyzed, which has become increasingly valuable since it contains large extracts from works now lost. He also wrote on doctrinal and exegetical questions. See **Filioque** and **Double Procession**.

Phylactery. From the Greek word *phylaktērion* (amulet), which in Jewish practice is affixed to the forehead or upper left arm of men at morning prayer, complementing the mezuzah. It is a capsule containing little parchment rolls with the Hebrew texts commanding its use: Exodus 13.1–10 and Deuteronomy 6.4–9 and 11.13–21.

Piarists. An order of clerics regular (see **Clerics Regular**) founded in 1597 by Joseph Calasanctius and officially designated *Regulares pauperes Matris Dei scholarum piarum*, hence their popular designation. In the year of their founding they opened the first free elementary school for boys in Europe, which was very successful, drawing large numbers. In the 17th c. its status was raised first to a congregation, then to an order. Despite some vicissitudes it prospered, especially in Spain and Latin America.

Pico Della Mirandola, Giovanni (1463–1494). Italian philosopher and Renaissance humanist. Of noble birth, he was trained at Bologna and then wandered among the centers of learning in Italy and France, where he acquired a wide range of knowledge, including Hebrew and Arabic, cabbalistic lore, and Zoroastrianism, as well as independent learning in the Greek and Christian classics. Having developed a standpoint from which he could claim to enrich Christian tradition by infusing into it the intellectual and spiritual riches of the wisdom of the past and the insights of other religions, he announced a set of 900 theses that he proposed to defend in 1486. Seeing, however, that the Pope (Innocent III) was regarding them with hostility as heretical, Pico eventually retired from public controversy, spending the rest of his life quietly. He represented the best in the Christian humanism of the Quattrocento. On his deathbed he was clothed by Savonarola in the Dominican habit. He regarded religion as higher than philosophy although compatible with it. In the tradition of Plato, he saw a universal truth in the multitude of its expressions. Man's dignity springs from his capacity for self-determination, the freedom of his will. He saw God as "Being-in-itself" and all else as participating in the divine Being. His writings include *The 900 Theses* (1486); *Apology* (1487); *On Being and Unity* (1491); *Oration on the Dignity of Man* (1496).

Pietà. A representation of the Virgin Mother in grief, holding on her knees the dead body of Christ. The theme is of German origin. The most famous example is the *Pietà* in St. Peter's, Rome, by Michelangelo.

Pietism. A movement within the Lutheran tradition led by P. J. Spener (1635–1705) and A. H. Francke (1663–1705). In revolt against the dogmatic emphases in Lutheran theology and practice, especially perhaps in the 17th c., it emphasized instead interiority and practical concerns. The movement, which tended to engender a certain kind of narrowness in the ethical outlook of some of its adherents, issued in a widespread enlivening of the Lutheran heritage, expressed in great measure by Pietists who remained within the Lutheran fold, seeing themselves as a leaven within the Church, but also and more observably in the various breakaway bodies such as the Moravian Brethren who were founded on Pietistic principles.

Pilate, Pontius. The procurator of Judaea from 26 CE to 36 CE. The functions of a procurator in the provinces of the Roman Empire varied from time to time and from place to place. He was always an imperial officer appointed by the Emperor. Usually he was in office for only a relatively brief period pending the organization of the territory into a full province. Judaea, however, was a special case. It was governed by procurators from 63 BCE to 70 CE, except for the reigns of Herod and Agrippa. No doubt Judaea was regarded by the Roman authorities specially because of the fact that it had been from their point of view troublesome and, because of the history and temperament of the Jewish people, intrinsically a difficult assignment. The procurator was subordinate to the nearest provincial governor (in the case of Judaea he was subordinate to the Roman legate of Syria) but had considerable autonomy in the exercise of his functions. He had some auxiliary troops, for example, at his disposal; he administered the collection of taxes, and in capital cases he had exclusive jurisdiction. He even had power to nominate and to depose the high priest. His position was somewhat similar to that of a viceroy or colonial governor in the heyday of the British Empire.

It is with such considerations in mind that we must judge Pilate's role in the crucifixion of Jesus. He is mentioned many times in the Gospels, once in Paul's first letter to Timothy, and several times in Acts. He is also mentioned

in all the Christian creeds as indubitably the officer ultimately responsible for pronouncing the sentence of crucifixion on Jesus. There is no doubt of his historicity. His name appears on an inscription in stone at Caesarea, and there are references to him in Philo, Josephus, and (although perfunctorily) in pagan writers. The New Testament documents present him in a distinctly unfavorable light: at first seeing no cause for such a severe sentence, then giving in to the mob for fear of inviting political trouble for himself.

The testimony of Philo and Josephus, far from mitigating the judgment of the New Testament writers show him in an even more unfavorable light than do they. They represent him as harsh, cruel, dishonest, and very capable of condemning an accused with scarcely even the pretense of a fair trial, but, rather, to serve his own political interests. Josephus illustrates his contempt for the people under his jurisdiction by narrating that, contrary to a custom according to which, out of respect for the Jews' distaste for images, the Roman procurators abstained from bringing to Judaea the banners bearing the image of Caesar, Pilate introduced them by stealth at night. Then when the Jews came to wait upon him for five days at his palace in Caesarea, beseeching him to hear their protestations, he responded by turning soldiers on them and killing many of the delegation. He misused the Temple funds and, when a crowd assembled to protest, he sent soldiers among them well disguised who at a prearranged signal killed indiscriminately. Nor did he confine his murderous activities to the Jews under his jurisdiction; he attacked a Samaritan sacred procession in 35 CE at Gerizim, their holy mountain, killing some wantonly, imprisoning others, and scattering such as could not be easily captured or killed. Indeed, impartial historians in modern times have commented on the fact that even the Gospels do not put Pilate in such an extremely unfavorable light as do some of the Jewish historians. At any rate, even if the Jewish reports were exaggerated, for which there is no evidence, the traditional picture of Pilate as the model of those who habitually act from motives of political expediency and never from principle or in the interests of justice would stand as a fair representation of Pilate's character. Indeed, one might even be justified in speculating that the traditional Christian portrayal of Pilate is unduly restrained.

Pilgrimage. The practice of undertaking journeys for a religious reason is widespread and encouraged in almost all the major religions. Hindus, who look on rivers as sacred and the Ganges as especially so, go in large numbers to Benares to purify themselves in the Ganges river. Buddhists, although they tend to attach less importance on the whole to pilgrimages do visit and revere holy sites such as the birthplace of the Buddha and the place of his enlightenment. In Japan pilgrimages are made to shrines in Kyoto and elsewhere and especially to the Shinto shrine of Amaterasu at Ise. Jews of course make pilgrimages to Jerusalem. In Islam the making of a pilgrimage to Mecca at least once in a lifetime is espected of all faithful Muslims unless prevented by poverty or other sufficient reason.

Among Christians, journeys to holy places either to give thanks for graces received or as an act of penitence or simply out of piety and love for sites where saints have trod long ago, have been characteristic of Christian devotion from early times. In Christianity it is indeed to be expected, if only because of the centrality of the doctrine of the Incarnation of God in Jesus Christ, that pilgrimage to holy places associated with him, his Mother, or any of the great heroes of the Church, should be a beloved feature of the life of the Church as well as a source of personal joy to individual Christians. In Eastern Orthodoxy a special reason obtains, for the icon is regarded not merely (as in the West) as an aid to devotion; it is the trysting place for God and man, the place hallowed by centuries of such encounters between the human and the divine. In the Roman Catholic Church pilgrimages are much encouraged not only to historic Christian sites such as Jerusalem and Rome but to other places that have become celebrated in more recent times, such as Lourdes and Fatima. Anglicans also encourage and delight in pilgrimages to the ancient Christian sites in the Holy Land, in Europe, and of course to Canterbury, Walsingham, and others. Not only do such pilgrimages strengthen the faith of those who engage in them; they also are a way of witnessing that faith to others. For a group of worldly tourists wandering around, say, Chartres Cathedral to look at its medieval glories, the sight and sound of a group of a dozen or two French students suddenly rising to their feet and singing the Nicene Creed in Latin to the tune of the *Missa de Angelis* cannot but help even the dullest and least informed understand that the Christian faith is not merely a great cultural heritage but lives in the hearts and minds of many who will help to mold the future of our planet. So pilgrimage has multifaceted advantages. Protestants have traditionally downplayed it because of the attending abuses that were rampant in the late Middle Ages and continue unabated today. But all religion is notoriously susceptible to commercialization and the fact that this is so is no more reason for renouncing it than the fact that scientific inquiry and other great human endeavors are no less liable to be commercialized is any reason for abandoning them.

Pilgrimage of Grace. In the north of England, between the fall of 1536 and the early spring of 1537, a series of risings took place, the most alarming of which was in Yorkshire, whose participants called themselves "this pilgrimage of grace for the Commonwealth." It was a conservative demonstration against government innovations in church affairs, notably the dissolution of the monasteries. At the order of Henry VIII, 200 of the rebels were hanged to incite terror in the general populace.

Pilgrim Fathers, The. This designation is a comparatively modern one for the group of English people who sailed in September 1620 from Holland and England to Plymouth, Massachusetts, to found a colony there. It was William Bradford who in 1630 wrote of them as "pilgrims," and language of this sort gradually gained currency in New England. Only after many decades did the now commonly accepted phrase come into standard use. See C. M. Andrews, *The Colonial Period of American History*, 4 vols. (1934–1938), especially Vol. I, pp.249–78. It contains extensive notes on primary sources.

Pillars of Islam. See **Five Pillars of Islam.**

Pirqe Aboth. A collection of Jewish aphorisms similar to those found in Ecclesiasticus and in the general tradition of the Wisdom literature of the Bible. They are preserved in the Mishnah as a separate tractate. Like some in the Book of Proverbs some are merely prudential, but others reflect high spirituality. This tractate appears to date from the first century after the fall of the Temple, i.e., *c.* 70 CE to 170 CE. An English translation exists, by J. Goldin, *The Fathers according to Rabbi Nathan* (Yale, 1955).

Pisa, Council of. A schism in the Western Church had resulted in two rival claimants to the papacy, one at Rome, the other at Avignon. Each of these held rival councils. To try to end the schism, the Council of Pisa was convoked by the cardinals. This council deposed both rival popes, and elected instead Peter Philargi, a cardinal, who took the name of Alexander V, resulting in even greater confusion, with three rival claimants instead of two. While the conciliarist party (see **Conciliarism**) recognized the authority of the Council

of Pisa, the Roman Catholic Church has not done so. Despite its apparent failure, however, it did pave the way for the Council of Constance (1414–1417), which ended the schism. See **Constance, Council of.**

Pius V, Pope (1504–1572). A Dominican, he was ordained priest in 1528 and was noted for his zeal and piety. On the death of Paul IV, whose nepotism he had outspokenly condemned, he was elected to the papacy in 1566. As pope he conducted a series of liturgical and other reforms, setting an example by the piety and discipline of his own life and his insistence on similar standards for the papal household. A vigorous opponent of the Reformation cause, however, he used the Inquisition extensively and made the tactical error of excommunicating Queen Elizabeth in 1570, thereby aggravating the troubles of Roman Catholics in England. He was, however, compared to so many of the popes of his period, a model of probity. He was canonized in 1712.

Pius IX, Pope (1792–1878). Ordained priest in 1819 and created a cardinal in 1840, he was elected Pope in 1846. At first noted for his progressive outlook (in sharp contrast to that of his predecessor Gregory XVI), his election was immensely popular. He began by giving a general amnesty to all political prisoners and exiles. He introduced gas lighting in the streets of Rome and in general displayed an enlightened attitude in all his policies and actions. As he saw his temporal power rapidly disintegrate, his attitude changed and he became more and more intransigently resistant to all political reform. He turned instead to emphasizing papal claims to supreme authority in the Church, e.g., by announcing in 1854 by his own authority (*ex motu proprio*) the doctrine of the Immaculate Conception (see **Immaculate Conception**). This doctrine which had been very controversial since the Middle Ages and opposed by Thomas Aquinas and by the

Dominicans generally was now to be an article of faith incumbent on all faithful Roman Catholics. His notorious *Syllabus of Errors* and his encyclical "Quanta cura" (1864), condemning almost indiscriminately all intellectual movements in 19th-c. Europe, alienated educated opinion not only outside the Roman Catholic Church but among many of the bishops within it, especially in Germany and France. He convoked the First Vatican Council which met at Rome in 1869–1870. There, against the resistance of large numbers of the more learned members of the episcopate and in face of widespread opposition by scholars within the Church, he forced upon the Church his extremely controversial opinion on papal infallibility (see **Infallibility**) which, in the form defined at the council, showed contempt for centuries of learned conciliarist opinion and caused even those well disposed to the Roman Catholic Church to see it as now committed to a narrow, not to say obscurantist, ecclesiastical policy. He reigned longer than any other pope had ever reigned, even if Peter's legendary reign of 25 years were to be counted. When he died in 1878, in contrast to the immense acclaim with which he had been received in 1846, some in the crowd threw mud at his coffin.

Plainsong. The traditional music of the Western Church, commonly called Gregorian chant and attributed to Gregory the Great, although his role in establishing it is controversial. It certainly has parallels and antecedents. Monodic, it is characterized by its restrained and dignified austerity and simplicity, so much so that is can be sung without the aid of any instrumental accompaniment and indeed is preferably so sung. It has eight "modes" and has for long been printed on a staff of four lines rather than the five used in modern music. By the end of the 16th c. the growth of polyphonic music had tended to cause plainsong, along with other cultural activities associated with the Middle Ages, to be relegated to antiquarian status. It continued to be used, however, especially in the ancient monastic orders, and it was magnificently restored in the second half of the 19th c., especially through the work of Dom Joseph Pothier at the abbey of Solesmes. It was restored in other Benedictine centers too such as Maria-Laach when that ancient foundation had reverted to the Benedictines in 1892. (See **Solesmes.**) Plainsong, although designed for Latin, has been adapted for use with English words, often with considerable success. It remains, however, intrinsically as much married to Latin as is Gothic architecture to northern skies and Palladian to sunnier lands.

Plato (428–348 BCE). Greek philosopher. An Athenian by birth, he studied under Socrates. After the latter's death, Plato gave up his plans for the political career that he, being of an important Athenian family, had planned to pursue. He travelled but returned to Athens in 388 where he founded his Academy. This was a full-scale academic institution, being to the ancient world what a great university has traditionally been to the modern one. All the departments of knowledge then available came within the scope of its functions. He made several attempts to introduce his ideas into the minds of rulers in hope of influencing the political scene in a practical way, but none of these met with sufficient success to warrant his pursuing that course of activity, so he returned to Athens where for the rest of his life he devoted himself to his work at the Academy that he had founded. There he lectured and composed the dialogues that have so fundamentally influenced Western thought for more than two thousand years. The lasting success of his dialogues is due in no small measure to the fact that he knew how to write and did so with consummate literary skill as well as immense philosophical acumen. Indeed, such is Plato's genius, that he conceals his artistry and even more his intellectual perspicacity and wisdom under the cloak of a limpid style.

Plato, in his dialogues, uses his master Socrates (who left nothing in writing) as his central figure. To what extent this Socrates is the historic one and to what extent a mere literary device is controversial. It seems probable that the earlier dialogues such as the *Apology*, the *Crito*, and the *Euthyphro* represent the historic Socrates, his outlook and his thought, as closely as might be expected, while in his later writings Plato uses the figure of Socrates more as a literary prop. The subject, however, is one in which scholarly opinion varies considerably.

Most remarkable of all Plato's writings is his *Republic*, in which he sets forth his blueprint for the ideal State: one that reflects an ideal that has counterparts in other societies and has greatly affected social institutions in the West. In reading it one must bear in mind from the outset that the concept of individualism as it has developed in Western thought from the Renaissance onward (with adumbrations such as in Scotus's doctrine of *haecceitas*) was virtually unknown in Plato's time so that to modern eyes his vision of the ideal State is bound to seem totalitarian. In his day it seemed obvious that the State is more important than the individual who constitutes a small part of it, so we must be careful to read him in the context of his age. Society, in Plato's view, should be arranged in three classes: (1) The philosophers are the intellectuals, whose duty is to lead and to govern the society by their wisdom. But in Plato's vision these are not merely clever men and women but the noblest in character and the wisest. He calls them Guardians of the State. (2) The Guardians-Auxiliary, who may be regarded as the military class in the sense that their duty is to protect the State from attack and from internal uprising. As the virtue proper to the Guardians is wisdom, so the virtue proper to the Guardians-

Auxiliary is courage. (3) Then follow the large body of the citizens, the artisans.

Far from there being any danger of envy among the latter for the higher rank of the first two classes, that is the unlikeliest of hazards. For while the bulk of the citizenry enjoy family life, private property, the comforts of home and what most people would call a "normal" life, the Guardians live in what we might call barracks: a life of austere simplicity with community of property and a rigorous discipline calculated to serve the society toward which they have a unique responsibility. Plato believed in the equality of men and women in a way unusual for his age. So the Guardians as a matter of course would include both women and men. He also believed strongly in hereditary values and what would nowadays be called genetics. So one of the duties of the Guardians was to breed at the most propitious times and in the most propitious circumstances for producing the best quality of offspring qualified to accept the austerities required for their high hereditary calling. Yet heredity was not the basis of any guarantee. One needed to prove one's worthiness and capacity for so strenuous a calling.

The parallel between Plato's proposed system and that of the caste system in India is obvious: his Guardians are of course the Brahmins and his Guardians-Auxiliary the Kyashtriyas or warrior caste, while the large artisan class in Plato's *Republic* encompassed the Vaisya and the Sudra castes in institutional Hinduism. Slaves, like the outcastes in India, did not enter into the system or, rather, they were taken for granted.

Plato's ideal was also reflected, however unconsciously, in the medieval society in which, in theory at least, the holy and learned monks represented the Guardians (= the Brahmins) and the knights the Guardians-Auxiliary (= the Kyashtriyas), except that in medieval practice the monks were forced into celibacy and not recognized as having a duty to contribute to the genetic enhancement of the society, while the knights were killed off in war.

Plato's thought exhibits deeply theological concerns. In the *Timaeus* he portrays God as the *dēmiourgos*, the artist or craftsman who brings the world into existence, making it as an *eikōn* (image) of the eternal archetype and enabling it to participate in his perfection by endowing it with *nous* (mind). In the *Laws* he ridicules the gods of popular religion and the notion of wooing them for favors, despising likewise the common assumption of people of his time that the gods are too preoccupied with their own internecine battles and their own love affairs to have any interest in the plight of humans except to the extent that it serves their purposes. Instead he proposes a rudimentary form of the Cosmological Argument (see **Cosmological Argument**) to show that behind all the processes that we see at work in the world must lie a perfect *psychē* as their fountainhead. In the *Phaedo* he argues for the immortality of the human soul, while in the *Symposium* he treats the nature of *ēros* and of how in earthly beauty and love is an embryonic striving toward the love of wisdom (*philosophia*) that issues in a knowledge of the eternal Forms, the ultimate reality behind all things.

The influence of Plato on later thought, not least on the most reflective kinds of Christian thought such as issued from the traditions developed in the Alexandrian School, is incalculably great, both among those who champion his outlook and among those who denigrate it. So deeply is it embedded in reflective and educated minds that it can be ignored only by a return to unreflecting barbarism.

Plato's Academy. For Plato's Academy, which lasted in various forms from *c.* 385 BCE to 529 CE, see **Academy**.

Plenary Indulgences. See **Indulgences**.

Pleroma. From the Greek term *plērōma*, from *plēroō*, "I fill up to the full, I fulfil, I complete." In Ephesians 1.23, the Messiah is being fulfilled, completed, by the Church. So Mark 2.21 and Matthew 9.16. The word "pleroma" is used in a theological sense by Christians and by Gnostics in allusion to the joy of being fully in the stream of divine life, not merely capturing fleeting glimpses of divine life but enjoying it in its plenitude.

Plotinus (205–270 CE). Born in Lycopolis, Egypt, he was attracted to the ideas presented by Ammonius Saccas and, after some years of travel, he went to Rome where he founded his own school of philosophy. He attracted a body of students not only large in numbers but of distinguished background, including senators and members of the imperial household. His aim was to show how, out of the Eternal One, arises the temporal and spatial world that we find around us and to which we see ourselves as belonging. This comes about, he proposes, through a series of emanations: (1) The *nous* (intelligence, mind), which reflects the multiplicity within the Eternal Unity. This primary emanation corresponds to the World of Forms in Plato. (2) The World Soul, the second emanation, is the principle of life and exists in the contemplation of *nous*. (3) Finally, matter, which, lacking form, hovers on the edge of non-being. Plotinus in at least one respect adumbrated the insight of Pascal (see **Pascal, Blaise**), for he saw man as in a difficult, not to say cruel, predicament, being on the one hand a spiritual being, longing for the One, and, on the other hand, enmeshed in the material world with all its overwhelming and insatiable carnal desires and all its preoccupation with all that is remotest from the One. To escape from his predicament man needs long and arduous self-discipline: more than can usually be completed in a single lifetime. See **Neoplatonism**.

Pluralism. The opposite metaphysical view from that of Monism. Pluralists see the world as consisting of more than one basic kind of entity. (Those who hold that there are only two such basic entities are usually called dualists.) Anaxagoras was probably the first philosopher in Western thought to argue for an infinitely great number of qualitatively different substances, each irreducible. Empedocles believed they could be specified as only four: earth, air, fire, and water. Many philosophers in modern times might be called pluralists. The Cambridge philosopher James Ward would be an example.

Plutarch. (c. **45–125** CE). Greek philosopher. A Platonist, he studied at Plato's Academy (see **Academy**) in Athens, then set up his own school in his native Boetia. For a time he lived in Rome. He was an archon in the mystery religion of the Pythian Apollo, which included belief that the soul, purified of the dross of the body, rises to live in an eternal world. He is best remembered for his *Lives*, in which he compares the lives of famous Romans with those of famous Greeks. He also wrote the *Moralia*, a work on practical ethical questions.

Plymouth Brethren. A Protestant Christian body that had its beginnings in England through the work of a former Anglican priest, J. N. Darby (1800–1882). Their basic teaching is biblical with some Calvinistic and millenarian elements. Like the Quakers they recognize no separate ministry. In their worship, a meal representing a memorial of the Last Supper is central. They developed into two branches, the Open and the Exclusive Brethren. The latter are so strict in their observances that they virtually separate themselves from the rest of the world, renouncing even contact with members of their own family who are not of their number. At times they have been very aggressive in their attempts to enlist converts.

Pneuma. In Greek the term was used to signify "air" (hence in English "pneumatic drill" and "pneumonia"), but the Stoics used it also for the principle of animation that they saw in the universe. In Hebrew the term *ruach*, which likewise had the basic meaning of breath or air, acquired a spiritual significance. It was when God breathed on Adam that he became a living soul. Breath (*pneuma*) comes to be identified with that which gives life. So, e.g., in John 3.8, we find a sort of pun: as the *pneuma*, the metereological wind blows as it pleases, so is everyone who is born of *pneuma*, the Spirit of God. The word pneuma can signify spirit in general or the Holy Spirit (*to Hagion Pneuma*) of God. The adjective *pneumatikos* in the New Testament generally refers to what is characteristic of man as a spiritual being and the carnal, physical body we now have is contrasted with the "glorious," finer, more spiritualized body (*pneumatikos*) that the redeemed will enjoy. Yet the "spiritual" is not necessarily benign. We are warned (Ephesians 6.12) against *ta pneumatika tēs ponērias*, the spiritual armies of evil.

Pogrom. An organized persecution of a particular religious or ethnic group, more especially of Jews in Eastern Europe.

Poimandres. Of Egyptian provenance, written in Greek, and dating from possibly very early in the 2nd c., it is the first of the Hermetic Books. (See **Hermetic Books.**) It describes a vision seen under the guidance of Poimandres, represented as a quasi-divine entity. Clearly Gnostic in spirit, it deals with the creation of the universe and the union of spirit and matter consequent upon the Fall. It prescribes *gnōsis* as the means of redemption and exhibits several affinities with the thought and language of the Gospel according to John, e.g., his repeated use of the symbols of light and life and John's view, expressed at the outset of the prologue, that the Logos is the agent in divine creation. It was translated into Latin for the first time and published at Venice, probably in the middle of the Quattrocento, the 15th century.

Poincaré, Henri (1854–1912). French mathematician and philosopher. Born in Nancy, he taught at Caen and later at Paris. His thought, much of which was devoted to the philosophy of science, has considerable relevance to the philosophy of religion. One of his philosophical contentions, known as the "Conventional Thesis" relates to the important role of definition in mathematics and in the principles agreed upon in all the sciences. He also divided hypotheses into categories as follows: (1) Natural and necessary ones, i.e., those which facilitate the making of other, more specific, narrower hypotheses. (2) Those which may be represented pictorially (e.g., those relating to atomic theory), which in his judgment cannot be verified by experience. He called these "indifferent" hypotheses. (3) Those which he called "real generalizations," which can be tested by experience. Among his writings are *Science and Hypothesis* (1902); *Science and Method* (1909); and *Last Thoughts* (1912).

Polanyi, Michael (1891–1976). Budapest-born scientist and philosopher, he taught in Berlin and in Manchester. Much recognized in his professional field (chemistry), he also attracted considerable attention for his work in philosophy, much of which has important bearing on religious concerns, e.g., *Personal Knowledge* (1958), *Beyond Nihilism* (1960), *The Tacit Dimension* (1966), and *Knowing and Being* (1969). He saw metaphor as an essential element in religion and art and stressed the importance of "tacit" knowledge at all levels. He distinguished symbols from signs: in the former, certain qualities are projected into the object: in signs they are not.

Polarity. The philosophical principle of polarity has religious applications. The notion of polar opposites in the universe is found in several metaphysical systems, and some thinkers, e.g., Nicholas of Cusa, have seen the principle as primarily to be found in God. Schelling saw God as having an eternal polarity within his Being. In varying ways Whitehead, Hartshorne, and Przywara, in more recent times, have held similar views.

Polycarp. Bishop of Smyrna. His special importance for Christian history lies in his having lived long enough (according to tradition *c.* 69–155) to provide a link between the Apostolic Age and the well-known late 2nd c. Christian writers. For example Irenaeus reports that Polycarp had met with John and others who had "seen the Lord." Polycarp opposed groups such as the followers of Marcion and Valentinus and labored for the unity of the Church's faith while encouraging diversity of local custom such as the date for the observance of Easter. A letter of Ignatius to Polycarp has survived as has his own letter "to the Philippians." Little beyond such occasional glimpses is known of the details of his life, but when he was probably in his middle or late eighties he was arrested at Smyrna during a festival there and required by the authorities to recant his Christian faith which he refused to do, pointing out that the had lived by it all his long life. He was burned to death. An account of his trial and execution is given in the *Martyrium Polycarpi*, written from Smyrna at the request of the Church at Philomelium. *The Martyrdom of Polycarp* and the letters to and from him that are mentioned in the present article are all easily found in Greek with English translation by Kirsopp Lake in *The Apostolic Fathers*, Vols. I and II, in the well-known Loeb Classical Library collection.

Pomponazzi, Pietro (1464–1525). Italian Renaissance philosopher. He taught at Padua, Ferrara, and Bologna. In his *De immortalitate animae* (1516) he taught that the mortality of the human soul can be demonstrated by human reason. He maintained, however, that Christians could nevertheless argue that although that conclusion follows by human reason, the divine revelation to which Christians can appeal goes beyond human reason and may be accordingly cited in favor of belief in the soul's immortality.

Pontifex Maximus. One of the titles of the Pope. Originally used to designate the chief priest in pagan Roman religion, it was applied in satire by Tertullian to the Pope in his *De pudicitia*, 1, and it came to be assumed from the 5th c. as a regular title of the popes and sometimes other bishops assumed it too. It has been for many centuries exclusively one of the titles of the Pope. It is rendered in English: "Supreme Pontiff."

Pontifical. The liturgical book used by bishops and containing the text and rubrics pertaining to those rites and ceremonies proper to their office in the Church, e.g., the ordination of priests and deacons, the consecration of churches, and confirmation.

Poor Clares. A religious order for women on Franciscan lines and founded by Saint Francis and Clare, one of his disciples, between 1212 and 1214. It spread very rapidly, first in Italy, then through Europe. The rule designed for them was modelled on that of the friars. It was modified in various ways, but in the 15th c. it was reformed. There are two branches: the Urbanists and the Colettines. The order is contemplative, very strictly enclosed, and the members devote themselves to prayer and manual labor, observing severe fasts and other penitential austerities. They may be the strictest order in the Roman Catholic Church.

Pope. The term (Greek *papas*, Latin *papa*) means simply "father," and in the current usage of the Eastern Orthodox Churches it is employed as a title of respect in addressing any priest. In the West it was at first used somewhat similarly, but since at least the 11th c. its use has been confined to the Bishop of Rome. The Pope is addressed as "Holi-

ness" or "Holy Father" and the latter title is also often used by Roman Catholics in referring to the Pope.

Porphyry. (*c.232–c.303*). Neoplatonic philosopher. Born in Tyre, he was brought up in a pagan family and in his youth traveled to Syria, Palestine, and Alexandria. He studied at Athens under Longinus and at Rome under Plotinus, whose *Enneads* he compiled. After study of the various religions he encountered he was skeptical of all of them and peculiarly hostile to the Christians, on whom he wrote a treatise, *Kata Christianōn*, in fifteen books. This work was condemned to be burned in 448. Only fragments survive. Despite his hostility toward the Christians he seems to have admired Jesus and to have acknowledged him as a great teacher but certainly not divine. His antagonism was directed, rather, to the Church. His other writings include a life of Plotinus and his *Isagogē*, an introduction to Aristotle's *Categories*, which was a standard work throughout the Middle Ages. Porphyry wrote more clearly than Plotinus and so did much to popularize the latter's teaching. See **Plotinus** and **Neoplatonism.**

Portiuncula. The Umbrian village about two miles from Assisi, which Saint Francis used as his headquarters. It is also known as Santa Maria degli Angeli. It was in that village that Francis received his vocation in 1208; it was here also that in 1212 he clothed Clare in the religious habit; and here too Francis died in 1226.

Port-Royal. This Jansenist center was a convent of Cistercian nuns that had been founded in 1204 about eighteen miles to the southwest of Paris. It had been of no special importance until the appointment of Angélique Arnauld as abbess in 1602. Her extensive reforms attracted so many new novices that by 1625 the community had to move to a new house in Paris, in the Faubourg St. Jacques. There, no longer under the jurisdiction of Citeaux, they became an independent order. Known as the Ordre du St. Sacrement, they wore a large red cross on their white Cistercian habit. Their spirituality was at first inspired mainly by the spirit of the Oratorians. (See **Oratorians.**) Then in 1635 the influence of Saint-Cyran, a leading associate of Jansen (see **Jansen, Cornelius Otto,** and **Jansenism**) became and remained dominant at Port-Royal-de-Paris, as the convent was now known. Some of his converts came to live near the Port-Royal-de-Paris, then also at the old Port-Royal in the country, being known as "solitaires," which meant that they took no vows but looked to Port-Royal as the focus of their spirituality and devoted themselves to the interests of the nuns, engaging in literary pursuits and helping in the teaching of some of the schoolboys, one of whom was Racine. Both houses, the one in Paris and the other in the country, prospered so well that they became a single and spiritually powerful center for the defense of the Jansenist cause and the dissemination of its spirit. In 1661 the Port-Royal nuns refused to support the condemnation of Jansenist teaching. By 1664 they were being subjected to considerable persecution on that account. By 1669, however, some of the nuns had submitted while others had not, and the two houses were officially separated, with those nuns who had submitted to the condemnation of Jansenism being housed in Port-Royal-de-Paris, and the others being housed in the original Port-Royal-des-Champs. They prospered for a decade or so, but by 1679 the Jansenist controversy had again flared up. Persecution followed calculated to make the work of Port-Royal more and more difficult and finally, in 1705, Pope Clement XI issued a bull condemning those nuns who had resorted to mental reservation in signing the formula against Jansenism that had been required of them. The nuns declined to submit. In 1709 they were forced to disperse. The buildings were destroyed, and the site formally desecrated. Jansenism, however, had made

an indelible mark on French religious thought, and its spirit and outlook had deeply affected the life of the Church in other lands. Pascal, one of the greatest geniuses in the history of the Church, was closely associated with Port-Royal although never formally a "solitaire," and his sister Jacqueline was a professed nun there. (See **Pascal, Blaise.**) Although Church and State succeeded in stamping out Port-Royal as a physical entity, its vitality as a spiritual force proved indestructible.

Positivism. The phrase "positive philosophy" was coined by Auguste Comte in the 19th c. to express an anti-metaphysical and anti-theological view in which he distinguished three phases or stages in human societies: (1) a "theological" one in which everything is seen as the direct action of supernatural beings or agencies; (2) a "metaphysical" stage in which abstract forces are seen as so functioning: and (3) the final stage when the society abandons both of the more elementary attempts to understand the universe and directs attention to the empirical world. Comte's theory, now regarded as untenable as an historical analysis, and his use of the term "positivism" resulted in its use in a variety of often vague senses to designate almost any attitude purporting to rely heavily on the methods used in the natural sciences. The term was applied in a more specific sense to those who followed the tenets of the Vienna Circle, who came to be widely known as logical positivists. See **Logical Positivism** and **Vienna Circle.**

Post Hoc Ergo Propter Hoc. This important and common fallacy, traditionally so designated, consists in assuming that because A is the antecedent of B it is the cause of B.

Postulant. A candidate for admission to a religious order, before being admitted even as a novice, first spends a brief period, usually a few months, as a postulant, i.e., one who is requesting admission. As such he or she wears ordinary "secular" clothes until being admitted to the novitiate, when they are exchanged for the habit of the order.

Postulate. This term is much used in philosophy to indicate propositions that are set forth in order to indicate the starting point of a discussion enabling the discussants to proceed with useful argumentation. They do not purport to be either axioms or mere provisional assumptions. They are somewhere in between: claimed as worthy to be accepted as true without formal demonstration. They are neither demonstrable nor self-evident; yet in many kinds of argument they are primary tools for demonstration. According to Aristotle they are demonstrable but asserted without demonstration.

Praemunire. A highly important series of English statutes passed in the 14th c. and designed to protect the English people from foreign interference, especially. that of the papacy. The first of these statutes, passed in 1353, prohibited the taking of English cases to foreign tribunals. Another, passed in 1393, was specifically directed against such acts as the promotion of any papal decree (e.g., a bull or excommunication) and increased the penalties for acts of this kind. It was almost two centuries after the first of these Praemunire statutes that Henry VIII invoked them in forcing all clergy to submit to his authority over the Church in England.

Pragmatism. C. S. Peirce, the founder of pragmatism, introduced this term in 1878. He adapted it from Kant, who had distinguished the practical (related to acts of the will) from the pragmatic (related to consequences). Peirce developed the concept of the pragmatic into a theory of meaning and truth expressed in the following way: "Consider what effects, that might conceivably have practical bearings, we conceive the object of our conception to have." These effects that we conceive will constitute our entire conception of the object. Truth may be defined, on Peirce's view, as the set of beliefs that a community of believers would hold in the long run, after a long and exhaustive process of inquiry. Truth is what issues from such extensive inquiry.

William James, whose name is very much associated with the philosophy called pragmatism, expounded it in a somewhat more general way, to the effect that the meaning of any proposition can always be boiled down to the practical consequences that will issue from it in practical experience. Royce and others developed pragmatistic systems. By about the turn of the century the terms "pragmatism" and "pragmatic" had entered popular vocabulary and were being used in such general ways (e.g., "We must look at the situation pragmatically" and "We need someone with a pragmatic outlook") that Peirce in 1905 introduced the use of the term "pragmaticism" to specify the more precise, technical meaning originally intended by "pragmatism". See **Peirce, Charles Sanders.**

Edouard Le Roy, a Roman Catholic philosopher, developed an application of pragmatistic principles to religion as well as to science. His application of such principles to religion resulted in his work on those lines being placed on the Index of Prohibited Books. See **Le Roy, Edouard.**

John Dewey, beginning with pragmatistic views, developed a system he called "Instrumentalism," perceiving truth as "warranted assertability." F. C. S. Schiller's exposition of pragmatism had probably even more relativistic tendencies. Pragmatism has been very influential in molding aspects of 20th c. philosophy, more especially in inquiries into the nature of meaning and truth. It has a ready popular appeal in as much as it can be easily treated in loose terms along the following lines: instead of telling Tommy, whose behavior is deplorable, how objectionable his conduct is, one says instead, "I know we can count on you to be a good boy, because that's what you want to be." The statement, on the face of it, is by no means indisputably true, to say the least; nevertheless, to the extent that through such encouraging words Tommy's behavior is in fact at least temporarily transformed for the better, it becomes true, i.e., the consequences demonstrate its truth. But see **Truth**.

Prajñā. This Sanskrit term designates one of the three elements (the others are *sīla* and *samādhi*) of the Buddhist path (*mārga*). It means wisdom as understood in Buddhism: a direct apprehension of the truth that has been initially accepted in faith, therefore comparable in some respects to what would be called in the West *gnōsis* (knowledge) as opposed to *pistis* (faith).

Prakṛti. In Hinduism a Sanskrit term difficult to translate into English. It signifies not only primal material nature but also the notion of process, entailing the urge to produce. In the reservoir of *prakṛti* is contained ("in potency" as we might say in Aristotelian language) all subjects, objects, and effects. In mythology *prakṛti* is represented as a goddess. She is contrasted with the other principle, *puruṣa*, which is male and designates the spiritual core of man. *Prakṛti* is an important concept in Vedanta and in *Sāṁkhya*, both important and very different philosophies in Indian intellectual tradition.

Pranayama. This Sanskrit term, which means "breath control", is the fourth of the steps in yogic meditation. The yogin controls his breath in order to assume control over his energies in their entirety.

Praxeas. Early Christian teacher who came from Asia, where he had been persecuted and imprisoned for his faith, to Rome where he seems to have arrived about the end of the 2nd c. Little is known of his life, and even his teaching is known only through the treatise *Adversus Praxean* by his adversary Tertullian, who may have somewhat caricatured it. It appears, however, that Praxeas was Patripassianist and perhaps accounted himself their leader (see **Patripassianism**), who resolved christological problems by so emphasizing the unity of God as to propose that the entire Godhead was emptied into the Person of Christ during his Incarnation. This entailed the implicate that God the Father suffered: a doctrine that was considered by his contemporaries to be heretical. Opposition to the notion that God the Father may suffer is understandable in terms of the thought of that age, because in both Greek and Latin "to suffer" means or implies "to be acted upon" and God the Father, as *Actus Purus*, is perpetually acting upon his created universe and so cannot ever be the object of action.

Prayer. Some form of prayer is found even in the most primitive forms of religion. One comes to the gods or spirits bearing gifts to please them. These are presented in the form of sacrifices and accompanied with praise. Having so made one's homage, one may feel more confident in making requests for favors. So emerges embryonic forms of petitionary prayer. The places where such actions take place become sacred and in the course of centuries temples and shrines are erected on the sites. In course of time too a class of experts arises: priests who know the "correct" words to utter and the manner in which they are properly uttered. The Sanskrit term *brahman* has many meanings, but one of its implicates, at least, is prayer in the sense of knowledge of how to counter the mysterious forces of nature by the use of magical incantations whose power is even stronger.

Prayer is nevertheless not universally encouraged. Mahavira, for example, discouraged his followers, the Jains, from prayer, calling it of no avail since salvation lies within man himself. "Why do you want a friend beyond yourself?" The Buddha took a similar stance as a means of salvation. Mahayana Buddhism, by contrast, made prayer central to religion, teaching that the universe is filled with supernatural beings eager to help humans. One needs only to ask them. Confucius, although urging obedience to the moral law of the universe rather than proposing prayer as a means of salvation, engaged in the worship of ancestors according to ancient Chinese tradition. The importance of prayer was already well emphasized in Judaism by the time of Christ, and Christianity inherited and developed that Jewish attitude. Islam, as is well known, particularly emphasizes the importance of daily prayer at the call of the muezzin.

In Christianity, however, since God is seen both as transcendent, wholly Other, and yet revealed in the Bible and especially in the Incarnation of God in Jesus Christ as the full and final revelation of God on earth, prayer is highly developed. Through prayer the Christian is led through the pilgrimage of life to the vision of God that is his or her ultimate destiny. Petitionary prayer (for general or specific graces or favors) may not be the highest form of prayer, but it is a legitimate part of the life of prayer, so long as the requests are made subject to the will of God to whom they are addressed. (To insist on a favorable answer to all prayers is to pretend to a knowledge that we humans simply do not possess. In retrospect *unanswered* prayers may and often do turn out to have been the greatest blessings of all.) Praise and adoration, however, are central to all Christian prayer, because they focus on the love of God even when they do not, as they ought, spontaneously spring from it.

In Christian tradition, prayers are classified in many other ways, e.g., private and liturgical, vocal and mental, mystical and prophetic. Private prayer is done according to the injunction of Jesus himself (Matthew 6.6): "But when you pray, go to your private room and, when you have shut the door, pray to your Father who is in that secret place, and your Father, who sees all that is done in secret will reward you." The injunction may be followed literally or figuratively, for it may not always be possible to enter literally into a private room (Jesus went to mountains or gardens), but it is possible to enter into the recesses of one's heart where the inner life flourishes. Liturgical prayer is essentially different and ought to be, for there the priest or leader is not praying for himself and not even only on behalf of every man, woman, and child present, but for the absent ones and the unknown and, as the Preface of the Mass puts it, "with angels and archangels and all the company of heaven." Nor does even all that exhaust the list, for he is praying also for and with and to those in bygone ages and recent times who form what Christians ought to understand by "the Church." "Liturgy" means "the work of the people," i.e., the People of God in all ages and in all places. In Catholic usage it is attended by as much dignity and splendor as conditions will allow: lights, incense, and the ceremonies that are the greatest art form in the life of the Church. Vocal prayer is not to be belittled as mere outward performance. Even when it is little more than that it has its place in the life of the Church, for it is better to be uttering holy and loving words even mechanically than to be uttering foolish or trivial ones or no words at all, for the mind will store the good words which later on will be heard above the idle chatter of the world. Mental prayer, however, is a higher form and a more difficult one for all but the most advanced souls. It consists of turning the mind and heart, the entire interior life, of the individual to God. It can lead to the ladder of mystical union with God, which is the goal of all mystical prayer. It includes contemplation in which the soul is rapt in wonder and love at the very thought of the infinite generosity of God. It includes too a celebration of the joy of life as God's gift. Prophetic prayer, which is often both public and extempore, is much favored by Protestants as a feature of corporate worship and has its place with other forms in the spectrum of Christian prayer.

The literature on the vast variety of methods of prayer is predictably immense. A great classic is Friedrich Heiler, *Das Gebet*, of which there is an abbreviated translation by S. McComb and J. E. Park entitled *Prayer*, first published in 1932; but there are treatments at all levels of this subject, which forms a bond uniting not only Christians but thoughtful and loving people everywhere. Nor must we forget ejaculatory utterances such as the alleluias and the amens that spontaneously burst from the lips of the loving and the devout. Least of all should we forget what are technically classified as "arrow" prayers because of their brevity and their succinctness, which exceeds even the succinctness of the liturgical Latin collect. A celebrated example of the "arrow" prayer is one said to have been uttered by Sir Jacob Astley on the morning of the Battle of Edgehill in 1642: "Lord, thou knowest how busy I must be this day. If I forget thee, do not thou forget me." Such a prayer, apt for the occasion, is short enough for one to say while brushing one's teeth in the morning.

Prayer Mat. The small carpet used by Muslims for kneeling at prayer. Since they are required to kneel and prostrate only on a clean surface, many of the faithful carry the mat with them so that they may have it at hand when the muezzin calls the faithful to prayer. It is always placed so as to be directed toward Mecca. It is called a seggadeh.

Prayer Wheel. In Tibetan Buddhism, a cylinder with small thin papers attached to it, each carrying a mantra or mantras. The wheel may be many feet in diameter, carrying even as many as a million papers. Then in turning it once one would be symbolically repeating the mantra a million times. It is in fact a sort of mechanized prayer. The concept is not entirely without counterpart in Christianity. Mechanical rosaries have been advertised in American papers. These can be placed on the dash of

one's car automatically turning the beads. Such devices, however, have never received any ecclesiastical approval.

Pre-Adamites. In the 17th c. a Christian sect emerged, adhering to the belief that human beings existed before Adam and Eve. They interpreted Paul's assertion (Romans 5.12–14) that "sin was in the world" before the law to imply that there must have been human beings before Adam to commit sin. The sect drew much of its inspiration from a work *Prae-Adamitae* (1655) written by Isaac La Peyrère. The argument was that man as described in Genesis 1 must have been created before Adam, who is not mentioned till Genesis 2. The former (the pre-Adamites) were the race from which the Gentiles are descended, while Adam was the first of the Jews. The concept as so propounded makes no sense at all in terms either of modern biblical analysis or of modern biology.

Prebendary. In medieval usage a prebendary was a member of a cathedral chapter who held a certain kind of benefice called a prebend, which was intended to supply (Latin. *prebere*) the holder with emoluments. In the old English cathedrals some vestiges of the medieval practice remain, but in the 19th century legislation made the office an honorary one only. See also **Canon.**

Predestination/Election. Predestination is a traditional doctrine of Christian theology based partly on the ancient Hebrew conception of an elect or chosen people. It is affirmed by Augustine, Thomas Aquinas, Bellarmine, Luther, and Calvin. Predestination is held to occur in eternity, election in time. Though frequently caricatured as a peculiarly terrifying and enervating form of determinism, it has been developed alongside a vigorous assertion of human freedom and responsibility to exhibit the limitations of the creature and the gulf that lies between him and his Creator. Far from terrifying, the doctrine has been a source of profound consolation and assurance to those who have taken it into the ambit of their devotional and personal, contradistinguished from their intellectual, life. Far from enervating, it has made some of those who have held it in strong forms—for example, Calvinists—excessively activist. The reason for both the assurance and the stimulus to action is that those who believe themselves to be saved, as did Augustine, "between the bridge and the river" or, as William Camden (1551–1623) put it in an epitaph, "betwixt the stirrup and the ground," feel a deep surge to serve God loyally since they feel sure that he who so rescued them shall never forsake them and therefore, however unaccountably, must have chosen them for himself. Nevertheless, the question of predestination and election has been the source of long, bitter, and (in the view of many contemporary religious thinkers) exceedingly unprofitable theological controversy.

Predicable. A term used in philosophy to designate that which may be asserted of something. A classic example is Aristotle's use to designate the five kinds of relations in which a universal can stand towards its subject. For example, a man is a species of the genus mammal. In defining man one would go on to show how he differs from other mammals such as dogs and whales. Man has also certain properties that one would not mention in defining him by genus and difference, e.g., Aristotle mentions his capacity to learn grammar, which is unique to human beings. Inherent in man, however, are various qualities and states of being, such as the circulation of his blood, which cannot exist by itself but always in another entity. The color red or green, for instance, cannot exist except in something other than itself. It was on this theory and arrangement that the medieval schoolmen based the doctrine of transubstantiation, which prevailed as a way of understanding the Real Presence of Christ in the Bread and Wine after their consecration by a priest: the accidents remain, i.e., the elements (bread and wine) look and taste like bread and wine, retaining as they do the "accidents," but the substance (the essential being, the *ens per se*) has been transformed, leaving only the accidents.

Pre-Established Harmony. According to Leibniz, all the "monads" that together constitute the universe are so arranged by God that before creation God had established a harmony that not only insures that the created world is the best world that could possibly have been created but explains what in the empirical world we take to be the interaction of mind and body. See **Leibniz, Gottfried Wilhelm** and **Occasionalism**.

Preface. The liturgical introduction to the most solemn part of the Mass (the Canon), beginning with the *Sursum Corda* ("Lift up your hearts") and concluding with the *Sanctus* (Holy, holy, holy). In Western usage, part of this introduction is invariable and part varies according to the liturgical season. In the usage of the Eastern Church, the Preface does not vary.

Prelate. A term applied primarily to bishops but sometimes to certain other dignitaries of high rank in the ecclesiastical hierarchy.

Premonstratensians. An order of canons regular founded by St. Norbert (*c.* 1080–1134), Archbishop of Magdeburg. It is one of several orders of canons regular, who are distinguished from monks in that while monks are primarily monastic although they may be secondarily priests, canons regular are primarily priests and secondarily monastic. The Premonstratensians follow the Augustinian rule. They received official papal approval in 1126 and spread extensively over Europe, having also important foundations in England and Scotland. They attained great influence in central Europe, especially in Hungary. Their habit is of white wool or (in some countries in central Europe) silk with scapular, cincture, and white biretta; hence the name popularly attached to them in England "White Canons." They are also sometimes called Norbertines. They have traditionally stressed the liturgical offices as the essential expression of their form of spirituality. Many serve in parishes.

Presbyterianism. A form of ecclesiastical polity according to which the Church is governed by presbyters. In the primitive Church it would seem that at first there was no single form of government and that arrangements varied from place to place according to circumstances. None could possibly be identified with the systems we know today as Congregational, Episcopal, or Presbyterian, but one could point nevertheless to features reflecting one or other of the various polities that have grown up in the Christian Church over the centuries. Presbyterianism as such is not committed to any doctrinal position. Although historically it has been associated with the teachings of Calvin, it is essentially a polity, not a form of belief. At the Reformation in the 16th c. it became the form of Church government adopted in Scotland, and it was there that it was most thoroughly put into practice. Contrary to widespread supposition, Knox did not introduce it into Scottish Church life in the form in which it ultimately triumphed there. He had planned for a system of superintendents, in effect bishops having territorial jurisdiction but not having any special sacramental function. The system that eventually prevailed in Scotland was due much more to Andrew Melville and was not fully established till near the end of the 16th c., almost forty years after 1560, the date of the Reformation in Scotland.

Presbyterian government consists essentially of a hierarchy of courts. The lowest of these is the Kirk Session, consisting of the Minister and the elders of each parish or congregation. Above the Kirk Session is the Presbytery, consist-

ing of all the ministers and elders (or, in the case of the latter, their representatives) within a prescribed geographical area called a presbytery and corresponding to a diocese. This court exercises the jurisdictional functions of a corporate episcopate, serving as an appellate court to consider cases of dispute arising from the decisions of kirk sessions. It is also the normal tribunal for the consideration of complaints concerning the teaching or conduct of individual ministers within its jurisdiction. Above the presbytery stands the synod: a group of presbyteries corresponding approximately to an ecclesiastical province. Finally there is the General Assembly, which has supreme jurisdiction and is both an appellate court and a court of first instance. Ordination to the ministry in the Presbyterian system is by the Presbytery. Candidates, besides fulfilling the educational requirements, must be elected by the voting members of a parish or congregation, except in special cases where the ordinand is to be ordained for a special function in the Kirk, e.g., to a chair in a theological college.

The nature of the office of elder is controversial. On one view they have equal status in the Kirk, the former being "teaching" elders and the other "ruling" elders, i.e., they rule in the sense in which a tailor rules out cloth, meaning that they "distribute" the ministry. On this view the elders share fully in the ministry. On another view the elders constitute merely a council with the minister as their moderator but have strictly speaking no ministerial functions. In any case, however, elders do have an essential role in all the courts of the Kirk.

Presbyterianism is found in many countries, including the United States, most other countries in the English-speaking world, and many countries in Europe. Its adherents in the English-speaking world usually look to Scotland as their focus. In practice, the structure and ethos of Presbyterian churches varies considerably and are in many cases far removed from the ideals originally envisioned by the founding fathers of this polity.

Prevenient Grace. In traditional Christian theology, the grace which, springing from the Holy Spirit, precedes the free exercise of the human will. It is an essential condition of salvation, but the individual must appropriate it by his or her own free choice. The term (*gratia praeveniens*) is used by Augustine in his defense against the Pelagians, and it represents a generally accepted theological principle in Roman Catholic, Anglican, and many Protestant Churches. See also **Grace.**

Price, Henry Habberley (1899–1984). English philosopher. Educated at Winchester and New College, Oxford, he was Wykeham Professor of Logic, 1935–1955, Oxford, and Visiting Professor at Cambridge, at the University of California at Los Angeles, and at Princeton. He was President of the Society for Psychical Research, 1939–1940. Interested in the nature of perception, he was among those who, like Russell, took the immediate object of perception to be a sense-datum. (See **Perception.**) He repudiated, however, Russell's causal theory, stressing the notion of the serial convergence of every family of sense-data on the standard solid. All other sense data are distortions or variations, on his view, of the standard solid. His important work, *Perception* (1932), discusses these questions and their implications in detail. His other works include *Hume's Theory of the External World* (1940), *Thinking and Experience* (1953). His Gifford Lectures at the University of Aberdeen in 1959–1960 were published under the title *Belief*. He was much interested in problems in the philosophy of religion and especially in psychical research and parapsychology.

Prichard, H. A. (1871–1947). English philosopher. Trained at Oxford, he argues that attempts to formulate a systematic moral philosophy are futile, since the conception is fundamentally mistaken. In his view, one intuitively knows what one's duties are. His writings include "Does Moral Philosophy Rest on a Mistake?" (1912) and *Kant's Theory of Knowledge* (1909).

Pride. The first of the seven "capital" or "deadly" sins. It is traditionally that which caused the downfall of the evil angels. Dante places it as the first of the sins that must be extirpated in purgatory, being that which vitiates the soul in such a way that other forms of alienation from God (e.g., avarice, envy, and lust) cannot be removed until it is first obliterated, and replaced by Christian humility. It is denounced in the Bible, both in the Old Testament and the New Testament, as peculiarly odious in the sight of God, since it is in effect an expression of rebellion against his will as well as a barrier to an understanding of the love that God wishes to exist between him and his creatures.

Priest. The concept of priesthood is almost universal in the great religions of humankind and virtually always in connection with the function of sacrifice. In primitive societies the father of the family often acts as priest, then later or even contemporaneously a professional class of priests emerges. In Hebrew society it seems that until the time of Moses priestly functions were performed patriarchally. Moses was commanded (Exodus 28.1) to consecrate Aaron and his three sons to the exercise of priestly functions. Eventually the Levites were given charge of the Tabernacle services, while those (whether by legal fiction or otherwise) accounted the descendants of Aaron were given fully priestly office. As the importance of the Temple grew, so did that of the Jewish priesthood. With the destruction of the Temple, the concept of priesthood in effect disappeared, leaving the rabbinate in charge of the synagogue observances and the instruction of the congregation.

The development of the priestly office in the early Christian Church was somewhat complex. Etymologically the term "priest" is merely a shortened form of the Greek term *presbyteros* (presbyter), which means literally "elder." The Greek term *hiereus* (Latin *sacerdos*), which refers to the specifically sacerdotal or priestly function, is not used in the New Testament to designate the office of a particular individual functionary as is the term *presbyter* and (I Timothy 3.1) the term *episcopos* (bishop) and as are (Philippians I.1) the terms *diakonos* (deacon) and *episcopos*. The term *sacerdos* was not in common use until early in the 3rd c. At first it seems to have been applied to bishops, but as other presbyters exercised functions that had been regarded at first as episcopal the term *sacerdos* came to be more widely used, being applied to all who exercised sacerdotal (priestly) functions. As Christianity spread in the early Middle Ages until parishes were scattered throughout much of Europe with a parish priest becoming the regular celebrant of Mass and exercising most of the other priestly functions of bishops, the term *sacerdos* or "priest" came to be the normal one in talking of any ordained cleric who was not also a bishop. The term "priest" is now universal among Roman Catholics, Eastern Orthodox, Anglicans, and some others. Most Protestants avoid it because of their different conception of the nature of the Christian ministry.

Primate. The title accorded to the chief bishop of a nation or other large geographical entity, e.g., the Archbishop of Canterbury is Primate of All England and the Archbishop of York Primate of England.

Primus. The title of the presiding bishop in the Scottish Episcopal Church.

Pringle-Pattison, Andrew Seth (1856–1931). Scottish philosopher of religion. Educated at Edinburgh, Berlin, Jena, and Göttingen, he studied at the latter university under Lotze. After holding various teaching positions in Britain, he was Professor of Logic and Metaphysics at Edinburgh from 1891 to 1919. He espoused a Hegelian idealism but attempted to show that although the Absolute (God) in Hegel's system could not be an individual, he could be the source of individuation and so the value of personality and individualism could be preserved. His writings include *Hegelianism and Personality* (1887), *The Idea of Immortality* (1922), *Studies in the Philosophy of Religion* (1930) and his Gifford Lectures, *The Idea of God in Recent Philosophy*, 1917.

Prior. In monastic usage, the title of the monk who either acts as second in command after the abbot of a monastery or who is in charge of a smaller monastery dependent on and subordinate to a greater one. The title is also used, however, of the heads of the houses of Dominicans, Franciscans, and other orders of friars. The title "prioress" is the female counterpart whose functions are virtually identical with those of the prior, both in monastic and other usage. (See also **Abbess.**) Religious houses of any kind that are ruled by a prior or prioress are called priories. Some orders, e.g., the Carthusians, use the title "prior" where others would use "abbot."

Probabiliorism. See **Probabilism.**

Probabilism. A system of moral theology based on the general notion that where the morality of an action is doubtful, an opinion that may be accounted probably defensible may be adopted even against an opinion that may be accounted more probably defensible. Probabilist principles, having been discussed much earlier, were promoted by the Dominicans at Salamanca in the sixteenth century. Both Dominicans and Jesuits developed the doctrine. The celebrated Spanish Jesuit, Francisco de Suarez, taught that where there is doubt about a law, human freedom should be allowed to prevail. In 1656, however, a general chapter of the Dominican order opposed probabilism, promoting instead the system that came to be known as probabiliorism, according to which, in case of doubt, one may claim liberty only when it can be held to be more probably defensible than the opinion that favors the law. Probabilism was severely pilloried about the same time by Blaise Pascal, whose Jansenist sympathies made it abhorrent to him. The Jansenists favored the system called rigorism or tutiorism, according to which one must follow, in case of doubt, the "safer opinion" (*opinio tutior*)—that is, the one requiring adherence to the law—unless there could be shown to be moral certitude against it. Tutiorism was condemned by Pope Alexander VIII in 1690. Probabiliorism was much favored by many, notably in France under the influential leadership of Bossuet; but eventually probabilism prevailed, especially as modified in Alfonso Liguori's doctrine of equiprobabilism, according to which the stricter course is to be followed if the doubt is as to the cessation of the law, while the laxer course may be followed if the doubt is as to the law's having ever existed. See **Situationism.**

Procession. In Catholic liturgical tradition processions play a not inconsiderable part. They are of two kinds, festal and penitential. Festal processions have several functions, which include that of expressing the joy of worship, that of witnessing to the Christian faith, and that of marching as soldiers of the Cross of Christ; hence the cross that is carried by the crossbearer ahead of the procession and the banner or banners that are also sometimes part of the procession. Processions are an especially important part of Catholic Christian worship on days such as Easter, Christmas, and Palm Sunday, but in many parishes they are in regular use every Sunday at least. Penitential processions are made as occasion demands but would be in the spirit of Lent or any other season or occasion of penitence. The order of liturgical processions differs very slightly according to traditional local usage, but

in general the thurifer comes first, then the crossbearer. The clergy always walk last and in reverse order of precedence, i.e., those ranking lowest in function in the particular ceremony that is being performed walk first, and he whose function is highest walks last, e.g., at a celebration of Mass the celebrant always walks last.

Procession of the Holy Spirit. On this theological concept see **Double Procession** and **Filioque.** Procession is theologically the attribute that distinguishes the Holy Spirit from the Father and the Son in the One Holy and Undivided Trinity.

Process Theology The name given to a genre of theology that has emerged in the 20th c. and has followed a particular model, usually with a Christian context and directly or indirectly influenced by the metaphysical outlook of A. N. Whitehead (1861–1947). Charles Hartshorne, an American thinker, has also much influenced this type of theologizing. Although the term is used specifically of a 20th-c. theological movement, the fundamental notion involved is a perennial one and is classically expressed, for example, in the thought of Thomas Aquinas and other medieval schoolmen who had profited from the recovery of Aristotle. Modern process theology generally sees the real as being-in-process, i.e., continually responding to the environment in one way or another and that God is not an exception but the principal exemplar of this basic reality. (In this the Whiteheadian model moves radically away from the Aristotelian one.) Process theologians today generally see a temporal aspect in God, although they differ on the implications of this. They are classifiable neither as pantheists nor as theists but as panentheists.

Proclus. (1) Hellenic philosopher (410–485) who, born in Constantinople, studied Neoplatonic philosophy in the Alexandrian school and with Syrianus in Athens whom he followed as head of the school there. He sought to explain the process of emanation in the Neoplatonic system by the categories of identity, difference, and return. He developed out of this explanation a doctrine of "henods" that has some resemblance to Leibniz's monads. (2) A 5th c. Patriarch of Constantinople from 434. He was apparently an extremely popular preacher and a staunch and persuasive advocate of the theological positions accounted orthodox.

Profession. Religious profession in Catholic tradition consists of taking the vows of poverty, chastity, and obedience, which the candidate makes when he or she has completed the novitiate (at least one year and a day, sometimes two years), at which time simple vows are taken for a period of at least three years. In some congregations and other religious societies one continues to take such temporary vows, but in the ancient orders, after completing the period for which simple vows have been taken, one proceeds (if one so chooses) to take solemn vows, which are for life.

Progress. Three views of history are: (1) it is cyclic, so that nothing ever *fundamentally* changes for better or for worse; (2) from a Garden-of-Eden or a Golden-age condition in the remote past we have declined to our present state; and (3) everything is in process of evolutionary development, so that progress is to be expected in the long run. There may be many misadventures and setbacks along the way and periods of stagnation, but the process is in principle evolutionary and progressive. This last view was much canvassed by the French Encyclopedists, such as Voltaire and Condorcet. Hegel's system entails a view of this kind and the thought of the later part of the 19th c., nourished by Darwin, Nietzsche, and many others tended to be strongly evolutionary and usually inspired optimism about the future of man. Such optimism has become less fashionable because of devastating wars in the 20th c., the threat of nuclear holocaust and other

reasons, but the discoveries in the 19th c. that fostered evolutionary modes of thinking have permanently affected all modern thought.

Promotor Fidei. See **Advocatus Diaboli.**

Propaganda, The Sacred Congregation of. When, in the 16th c., new countries were discovered whose peoples knew nothing of the Christian faith, the Roman Catholic Church, perceiving the opportunities for missionary activity in such lands, formed a commission "for the propagation of the faith" (*de propaganda fide*). In 1622 Pope Gregory XV established the Congregation of Propaganda. In 1967 the same was extended to read *Sacra Congregatio pro Gentium Evangelizatione seu de Propaganda Fidei* (Sacred Congregation for the Evangelization of the Nations or of the Propagation of the Faith). The term "propaganda" has acquired a pejorative sense today that is not at all inherent in it. Fundamentally it means "dissemination," and one may disseminate good things or bad; a neutral term.

Prophet. Although cultic functionaries, wise men, and other figures in the religions of the world have some characteristics in common with the prophet in the Old Testament, the role of the Hebrew prophet is distinctive. Women could exercise prophetic functions as did Deborah, the wife of Lappidoth (Judges 4.4 and 5.31), to whom is attributed the Song of Deborah (Judges 5), recognized by scholars as one of the oldest, if not the oldest of all literary compositions in the Bible. The Hebrew prophet had therefore anything other than priestly functions, which were exclusively male. He or she may have carried remnants of the shaman-like functions of earlier stages of cultural and religious development, but the prophet who emerges in the biblical literature and plays such a decisive and unique role in the life of Israel is sharply distinguished from all seers and diviners and visionaries who merely pour forth their personal emotions and who attribute their abilities to powers within themselves.

What is distinctive about the Hebrew prophet is that, although exhibiting similarities to the sage or mystic or visionary or preacher in religious life in general, he or she is nothing if not the spokesman of Yahweh. Jeremiah, for instance, insists that what gives him the authority to speak as he does is precisely that what he is saying is Yahweh's word, not his own or that of any other man. The Hebrew prophet, then, whether his or her words are couched in emotional terms or unemotional ones, whether they are uncouth or elegantly phrased, speaks as the instrument of Yahweh. His or her voice is merely a trumpet for the Lord; it is the Lord who speaks. All other aspects that one may find in the style and flavor of an individual prophet are incidental. This may happen to please or displease the hearers. All that is as irrelevant as is the color of ink or the size of type on a printed page. The authentic prophet has been called by Yahweh to be the voice of Yahweh, speaking the mind of Yahweh as an ambassador or other envoy speaks not his own words but those of the king who sends him. It is this concept of the prophet's role that is reflected in the preaching ideal envisioned by theologians in the Reformation heritage such as Karl Barth.

The Talmud recognized that one prophet's style will differ from another so that no two prophets will prophesy in the same way any more than two musicians will play the same piece in exactly the same way. Nevertheless, authentic prophets will always be doing essentially the same action, as already here noted. Some of the rabbis observed a distinction between Moses and the other prophets, perceiving Moses as receiving the divine revelation face to face (Numbers 12.8) while the others received it only opaquely. The power of foreseeing future events, nowadays associated in the popular mind with prophesying, was indeed an aspect of the

prophet's role, but on the whole a very incidental one. Far more was the Hebrew prophet seen as a man who, accepting a commission from God to speak out against corruption and wickedness, did not flinch from his duty but spoke fearlessly, currying favor with no man. In Jewish tradition, the age of prophecy ended with post-exilic prophets such as Zechariah and Malachi, being superseded by the age of rabbinical wisdom. In the Christian Church the prophetic aspect of the ministry is recognized in the preaching office. At least preaching entails some measure of prophecy and is to be clearly distinguished from the priestly office that plays such a central role in those Churches that are in the Catholic tradition.

Proposition. In logic a proposition is a formal assertion that proposes or denies something and is capable of being judged true or false. (Arguments, by contrast, are valid or invalid.) Propositions may be and generally are presented in the form of statements, but a statement and a proposition are not to be equated. What precisely constitutes a proposition is controversial in modern logic. Boole, Frege, and Church, for instance, take different views on the question. There are three basic kinds of proposition: (1) *categorical*, e.g., "Some attorneys are blonde" and "No birds are mammals;" (2) *hypothetical*, e.g., "If it rains tomorrow, then the party will be postponed" (here the "if" clause is called the antecedent and the "then" clause the consequent); and (3) *disjunctive*, e.g., "Either the candidate is stupid or he is dishonest" (this is called a weak disjunction, since he could be both) and "Either the candidate is under 25 or else he is over 25" (a strong disjunction, since he could not be both).

Proselyte. Originally, this term applied to a convert to Judaism. It is sometimes used by analogy of anyone who has been converted to any religious faith from any religion or from none.

Proskomidē. In the Eastern Church the bread and wine for the Liturgy is prepared before the service begins. This is done at a table called the prothesis. The celebrant cuts the bread into pieces with a small liturgical knife (*logchē*) shaped like a lance. Historically this ceremony was part of the Offertory but was moved back to the beginning of the service. Sometimes the word for the table (prothesis) is used synonymously with the *proskomidē* to designate the ceremony.

Prosopic Union. A name applied to Nestorian christology. See **Nestorianism.**

Prosper of Aquitaine (*c.* 390–*c.* 463). Christian theologian who took an important part in the Semi-Pelagian controversy in the 5th c. At first wholeheartedly supporting Augustine's doctrines of predestination and grace, he moved away from them in their more extreme form, modifying them to exclude the notion of predestination to damnation. He exercised much influence on theological thought in the early Middle Ages and so indirectly on popular opinion and perhaps also on devotional practice.

Protagoras (490–*c*.410 BCE). Greek philosopher. Born in Thrace, he is perhaps the most important of the Sophists. His most famous saying is that man is "the measure of all things." Plato and Aristotle both took this to mean that knowledge is relative in the sense that what you perceive and what I perceive to be the case are both the case even although our perceptions differ. For example, I come in out of the cold and put my hand in a bowl of water which I call warm, while you come in out of an overheated room and call the same water cold. In ethics relativity similarly governs the situation: whatever a society finds right is right so long as the society deems it so to be. On the gods of popular religion he was agnostic in the sense that he could claim no way of knowing whether they exist or not.

Protestant. The term, as a designation for the heirs of the Reformation movement that came to its zenith in the 16th c., is an unfortunately negative one, springing as it does from a comparatively unimportant and incidental occasion in the early history of that movement: the Diet of Speyer in 1529, at which those who dissented from the Roman Catholic majority signed a document called a *protestatio*, inadvertently imposing on all heirs of the Reformation a label more redolent of hostility to Rome than many of them would wish to bear. The hope of the 16th-c. Reformation Fathers such as Luther, Calvin, and Zwingli had been to reform the Church so as to bring into being what might have become known as the Catholic Church Reformed or something of that sort. Their work was far from issuing in any such result. Luther especially was temperamentally conservative, both politically and theologically. Both he and Calvin, each in his own way, emphasized certain aspects of traditional theology, such as the unity and the transcendence of God, the importance of revelation and the faith that is the response to it, the preaching of the Word, the authority of the Bible that contains it, and the Sacraments that they found prescribed in the New Testament. They insisted also on high standards of ethical conduct.

All that program was already within the compass of the medieval Church's thought and life but, in the opinion of the Reformers, had been downplayed, not to say lost, in the labyrinth of medieval theology and practice and corrupted by the notorious abuses in the late medieval Church, which nobody denied and which learned and zealous churchmen had been actively seeking unsuccessfully for at least a century and a half to remedy. Although the Reformation movement had brought in its train fractious and revolutionary rabble rousers playing on the ignorance and spleen of the mob, the mind and heart of the movement was remote from such a spirit. Indeed its weakness lay rather in the other direction: the development of orthodoxies too rigid and liturgies too limited to accommodate the light that the Reformers sought to kindle and to foster the freedom that they sought to promote.

In the 18th c., the age of Enlightenment (*Aufklärung*), the age of reason, the heirs of the Reformation suffered equally with those who had held on to the medieval Catholic faith and practice. Both sides, weakened by enmity and strife, lost the intellectual respect they had once enjoyed. Both were swept aside as representing each in its own way, the superstitions of a dark and bygone age. Protestants, saddled with the negative image their name attached to them, were widely seen as part of the same climate of moral and intellectual enslavement that the Age of Enlightenment was blowing away. Not unpredictably, both sides responded, under the influence of the Romantic movement of the 19th c., by invoking the cultural and affective aspects of Christianity. On the "Protestant" side, Schleiermacher's influence was enormous, affecting church people at all levels, learned and unlearned alike, while on the "Catholic" side the arguments advanced by those who, in the manner of Chateaubriand, sought to uphold the faith by appeal to the beauty of its cultural consequences were no less persuasive and no less damaging to the vitality of Christian faith. Such subjectivism in the interpretation of religion still haunts the Church, the valiant efforts of great 20th-c. theologians (e.g., K. Barth) on both sides notwithstanding. See **Reformation, The Protestant.**

Protevangelium. The Book of James (to be distinguished from the canonical New Testament Epistle of James) is an apocryphal Infancy Gospel (see **James, The Book of**) which, from the 16th c., has come to be also known to biblical scholars as the Protevangelium. Known to Origen, it may be dated from about the middle of the 2nd c. It purports to

have been composed by James, the "brother" of Jesus.

Prothesis. See **Proskomidē.**

Protonotary Apostolic. A member of the College of Notaries in the papal court. Formerly of four grades, the number of grades was reduced in 1968 to two: *de numero* and *supra numerum.* The latter, supernumerary grade consists of members whose title is entirely honorary.

Proverbs, The Book of. This biblical book consists of a collection of "wise sayings" of widely differing kinds and from widely different periods in Hebrew history. Many of the proverbs are prudential; others represent a much deeper spirituality. The book belongs to what is called the Wisdom literature, which exalts and even personifies Wisdom (investing it with divine qualities) and denigrates folly.

Providence. Term referring to God's regulative action in the world. A traditional distinction has been made in Christian theology between general providence, which is achieved through the action of the general laws of the universe and special providence through which God provides for each individual according to his or her needs.

Providentissimus Deus. The papal encyclical of 1893 in which Pope Leo XIII cautioned the clergy against modern methods of biblical exegesis and analysis. Nevertheless, this encyclical, together with *Spiritus Paraclitus* (1920) and *Divino Afflante Spiritu* (1943) reflect a growing concern in the Roman Catholic Church for a fuller understanding of the role of the Bible and a search for ways in which modern methods of biblical study may serve the interests of the Roman Catholic Church.

Przywara, Erich (1889–1972). German philosopher of religion. Born in Kattowitz, he was Professor of Theology at the University of Munich. He took the *analogia entis* (see **Analogy**) as central to his philosophical inquiries and polarity as the basic law of reality, being moreover highly relevant to many theological questions, e.g., the transcendence and immanence of God, grace and freedom, faith and knowledge, *et al.* His writings include *A Newman Synthesis* (1931); *Analogia Entis* (1032); and *Polarity* (1933).

Psalms, The Book of. A psalm (Greek *psalmos*) is simply a song, usually accompanied by string music. The book constitutes one of the major parts of the "Writings" (i.e., those parts of the Old Testament other than the Law and the Prophets) and by the time of Jesus was well established as an important and beloved part of Hebrew literature. The psalter represents a wide variety of periods in Hebrew history. Some psalms may be of great antiquity or at least based upon ancient materials and perhaps some are even actually of Davidic authorship, but the majority are of much later provenance. Jesus is reported as quoting the Psalms. The Psalter became in Christian tradition and practice by far the most popular book in the Old Testament, no doubt partly because it had a universal appeal that made it for Gentile Christians probably the most comprehensible book in the Old Testament. In the Roman Catholic Church the Psalter was till recently read or sung in its entirety in the course of each week. In Anglican tradition it has also been much emphasized and has indeed nourished the spirituality of all Christians more than any other book in the Old Testament.

Pseudepigrapha. Writings ascribed to an author other than the real one. This practice was considered a perfectly respectable one in antiquity. It was not merely calculated to enhance the authority of the work by attaching a famous name to it; it was often a demonstration of admiration for and *pietas* toward the author whose name was attached. For example, the Book of Enoch provides a good example of this

type of Jewish literature. The practice, however, was very general and increases the difficulty that scholars today face in determining the authorship of certain New Testament books and others in later Christian literature.

Pseudo-Dionysius. See **Dionysius the Pseudo-Areopagite.**

Pseudo-Isidorian Decretals. See **False Decretals, The.**

Psychologism. This term is used to designate the view or tendency toward the view that the categories of psychology may be properly used in philosophical analysis. The notion is particularly relevant to the discussion of problems in theology and the philosophy of religion. (See **Ontology.**) If the only kind of certainty we can have is about what is occurring in our minds, then the only reality we can know and meaningfully talk about is a psychic reality. Religion then becomes a description of the psychological phenomena, since it cannot point to anything beyond them. Logical empiricists and other modern philosophers call attention to the concept of validity in mathematical and logical procedures, showing that validity is independent of all psychological questions. Husserl, having begun his work in an attempt to rescue mathematics and logic from the tendencies toward psychologism in modern thought, went on to extend his interest to a process of "seeing into" metaphysical and ontological realities. One must carefully note that the use of psychology in the study of religion is by no means necessarily psychologism. On the contrary it is a very important aspect of religious studies. Psychologism, however, like all reductionism, excludes the possibility of discussing what religion purports to be about, and any findings made under its banner must be evaluated accordingly.

Psychology. From the Greek term *psychē*, used in antiquity to designate the vital principle in man. The use of the term "psychology," however, dates

from only 1590, when Rudolf Gocle-
nius, a German philosopher who was
given to coining neologisms, used it as
the title of a book he published that
year. The term began to be used in the
17th c., generally in reference to an aspect of metaphysics. Christian Wolff, in
two books published in 1732 and 1734
respectively, distinguished between
what he called "rational" and "empirical" psychology. The "associationalism"
of Hume and J. S. Mill were similar to
what had by their time become known
as Empirical Psychology. In the 19th c.
experimental methods of studying psychology came to be developed, e.g., by
Wilhelm Wundt, who in 1879 founded
the first experimental laboratory for
psychology, by Ernest Weber, Gustav
Fechner, and others.

Up to about this period psychology
was generally classified as a special
branch of philosophy. Only gradually
did it come to be accepted as an independent field, and as it did so it splintered into a large number of schools
who interpreted it in many different
ways, e.g., the Functionalism of J. R.
Angell and others, the Structuralism of
Titchener, the Behaviorism of Watson,
the Gestalt school, Freud's Psychoanalysis, Jung's Analytical Psychology, and
others. Despite the development of psychology as an independent discipline,
its special relation to philosophy remains. Nowhere is the importance of
philosophical critique of psychology
more noteworthy than in the psychology
of religion. See **Psychologism.**

Psychology of Religion. As an academic discipline, the study of the psychology of religion dates from the late
19th c. and received its most notable
impetus from the work of William
James. (See **James, William**). Freud
was hostile to religion in the sense that
he looked upon it as a neurotic outlet
for a libido impeded from proceeding
through other channels. Freud's notion
of a "region" of the mind below the
level of consciousness was not by any
means Freud's invention. Franz Del-

itzsch, writing on theology in 1855, a
year before Freud's birth, had alluded
not only to the need for more attention
to the subconscious realms of the soul
but to the fact that, as he alleged, the
existence of such subconscious realms
was by that time widely recognized. He
observed that it had been a basic error
of most psychologists in former times to
make the psyche extend only so far as
its consciousness extends, when in fact
it embraces "as is now always acknowledged," far more than that. Two years
later an English churchman was writing
to his former teacher at Oxford that theology had been hitherto cast in too
scholastic a mold and that it was now
being forced into finding a basis in psychology.

About the time that psychology of religion was thus coming into its own, two
related disciplines were also in progress
of development: (1) the sociology of religion and (2) cultural anthropology.
Both of these were soon being associated with the study of the psychology of
religion. James used manuscript materials collected by E. D. Starbuck and
sought to discover from the data what
seemed to him to be needed for a scientific understanding of the nature of religion. Inevitably, their attention tended
to be focused on the more aberrant
manifestations of religion. In his work
he was joined by others, such as J. B.
Pratt, whose *Adventures in Philosophy
and Religion* (1931) is an example of the
sort of work that was being undertaken.
The works of J. H. Leuba, *The Belief in
God and Immortality* (1921) and *The
Psychology of Religious Mysticism* (1925),
represent a growing tendency on the
part of those hostile to religion to seek
to exhibit it as a fundamentally neurotic, not to say ludicrous aberration of
the human psyche. The reductionism in
the methods of writers such as Leuba,
which sometimes amounted to mere
caricature of Freud, was only gradually
discredited as distortion. Religious phenomena no less than other phenomena
affecting the human psyche may be
good or bad. Religion is not necessarily

good. Moreover, it is indubitably true and easily demonstrable that the human sexual impulse, when thwarted, can issue in obsessional and other aberrant behavior. Such behavior does not necessarily take a religious form, but in patients who have an interest in or a disposition toward religion, that is likely to be the form the aberrancy will take. Moreover, as Freud recognized, although the sexual and other drives can be sublimated (e.g., in artistic and intellectual enterprises), the sublimation is at best likely to be imperfect and the residue of the libido can give trouble.

Nowadays, methods used in the psychology of religion are more carefully explored in relation to age and other circumstances and with reference to pathological and other conditions. The psychology of religion has given way in great measure to the study of the phenomenology of religion. (See **Husserl, Edmund,** and **Phenomenology.**) The result is a more finely honed tool than the earlier psychologists of religion had at their disposal. Nevertheless, one must always bear in mind that it is only the phenomena that any such methods can be said to examine, and such examination is somewhat like examining a telephone conversation with no consideration of the reality or otherwise of the person at the other end of the line. That is to say, however apposite be the methods employed, such studies can yield at best only information about what they purport to yield, i.e., the phenomena; they are unrelated to the ontological reality of what religion is about and therefore they are not studies of religion at all. That is not to say that they are uninteresting. It might be quite interesting to study the antics of this or that orchestral conductor or concert pianist, but no one would call it a study of music.

Ptolemy. A 2nd-c. CE scientist and philosopher. He lived in Alexandria and is famed for his work on astronomy which (published *c.* mid-2nd c.) purported to show the earth as a globe in the center of the universe and that the rest of the celestial bodies make a diurnal revolution around an axis that passes through the earth's center. This geocentric conception, which Dante (1265–1321) for example, used in his vision of his pilgrimage through hell, purgatory, and heaven, was a generally accepted one down to the time of Copernicus (1473–1543), who developed the heliocentric theory of the solar system, which gradually prevailed. It had actually been substantially developed by Aristarchus of Samos in the 3rd c. BCE but later lost or obscured.

Publicans. Traditionally the Greek term *telōnēs* (Latin *publicanus*) has been translated into English in the New Testament as "publican." The publicans were members of one of the various organizations employed by the Roman government to collect taxes. Not least because of the corruption that inevitably infected the practice of their profession under the prevailing system of tax collection, they were so unpopular as to be virtually ostracized. Jesus, apparently unconcerned about outward "image," was charged with not only keeping company with sinners but with publicans also, e.g., by inviting himself to the home of Zacchaeus, described as an *architelōnēs* (head or chief tax collector).

Pūjā. In Hinduism, the worship of a god. Orthodox Hindus "do" pūjā thrice daily: just before dawn, at noon, and in the evening. Many homes set aside an area where pūjā may be performed to a god. Flowers and/or food offerings are made to the god. Pūjā may also be performed in public, e.g., before a statue or other representation of a god or goddess in the street or on a hillside. Buddhists also do pūjā to the Buddha and to bodhisattvas. Jains do pūjā to the Jinas.

Pulpit. In early Christian churches sermons were preached by the bishop from his chair (*cathedra*). Later, in basilican churches and the like, the ambo was used for preaching. Not till the late medieval period did the pulpit as we know it today come into general use. Pulpits vary very much in ornateness and size. Some are extremely simple; others, especially in baroque churches and some of the great cathedrals in Italy and elsewhere, are very grand and sometimes elaborately decorated.

Puñña. A Pali term meaning "merit" in the sense of that which is a necessary condition for attaining a better form of re-birth (i.e., one with greater scope for spiritual advancement) in the future. Such merit can be achieved at various levels, but each is important as providing the opportunity to proceed from kindergarten to grade school is as important and may be in the long run far more important than the opportunity to enter graduate school. Re-birth is always to be considered in terms of opportunity. It carries no guarantee of success, but its value and importance can be measured only in considering the alternative: lack of opportunity.

Purāṇas, The. In Hinduism, collections of tales of the past. They became, in post-Vedic times, an important medium for transmitting Vedic teaching to the uneducated, including not only the lower castes but women, most of whom were denied education. The Purāṇa was typically an exposition of five basic topics: (1) the creation of the world; (2) its destruction and its re-creation; (3) the genealogy of the gods and goddesses; (4) the reigns of the manus, the heroes or great men of old; and (5) the history of the royal dynasties. In practice, however, many accretions were made, so that other subjects such as anatomy, geography, and medicine were included. It was, then, not only a literature but an educational system and also a body of scripture that became more a counterpart to the Bible than ever the Upanishads could be, being accessible (as the Upanishads were not) to the unlearned as well as to the learned. An important background for the study of popular Hinduism, they embody many

picturesque legends, many probably very ancient in origin although the Purāṇas in their present form (of which there are eighteen principal ones) date only from the Gupta period, beginning *c.* 300 CE.

Purdah. The popular variation of the Persian word *pardih,* meaning a veil or curtain. It refers to the Muslim custom of Hijab, according to which women are permitted to show only their hands and faces in public: a custom that follows the teaching of the Qur'ān in respect to modesty in female attire.

Pure Land School. This Mahāyāna Buddhist school (in Chinese, Ching T'u) is probably the oldest. Its founding is attributed to Hui Yüan who in 402 CE established it with the name "White Lotus:" a name that was later changed. Its teaching is simple and popular. Life is to be perceived as full of sorrow and disillusionment. It is enchained to the endless cycle of re-birth and governed by the karmic law. Salvation is available, however, through the infinite grace of the Buddha and the bodhisattvas. Central to the sect's teaching is the doctrine of salvation by faith in Amitābha Buddha (known in Japan as Amida), who reigns over the "Pure Land," a western paradise. He is aided by two great bodhisattvas: Kuan Yin and Ta Shi Chih. Among the leading exponents of this school's teaching was Shan-tao (613–681 CE) who taught a doctrine that human beings, helpless through ignorance and clouded through carnal desire, cannot attain salvation by their own efforts. Only through faith in Amitābha can they achieve the power needed for their salvation. His grace is for the asking. One need but call upon his name and put one's trust in him. There are some resemblances between this Buddhist school and Indian Bhakti. Westerners will readily recognize similarities between such teaching and those aspects of Christian theology that are especially emphasized in classical Reformation teaching. Generally speaking, however, the teaching of the Pure Land sect has little philosophical content.

Purgative Way, The. This term is used in Christian mystical theology to designate the preparatory and often arduous process of cleansing the soul of selfish tendencies, lustful desires, and other impediments to spiritual progress, so that it may become capable of progressing toward the illumination that is the next step in the ladder leading to mystical union with God.

Purgatory. The notion of an intermediate state spanning the spiritual gulf between our earthly existence and our final destiny is of considerable antiquity in the Christian heritage (see II Maccabees 12, 39–45). It has counterparts too in other religions. The early Christian custom of prayers for the dead, for which abundant evidence is to be found in patristic writings, implies belief in such an intermediate state in which some sort of cleansing, purgation, or spiritual development can take place; for otherwise prayers for the dead would be futile.

True, the term "purgatory" does not appear in Latin theology till late in the 12th c. The concept, however, was presented long before the invention of the term *purgatorium*. It was developed in both East and West although predictably the West tended to do so more systematically.

Unfortunately, in the later Middle Ages, purgatory came to be viewed in too punitive a way and unscrupulous clergy, taking advantage of popular superstition and fear, encouraged the people so to view it for the enhancement of clerical power. Such corruption was at least an important factor in bringing about the Lutheran Reformation, resulting in a repudiation among Protestants generally of the concept of purgatory and the practice of prayers for the dead that it entails.

In the 19th c., under the influence of the Tractarians, Anglican theological opinion moved strongly in the direction of restoring the concept of purgatory, but shorn of the legalistic and penal elements that had disfigured it in the late Middle Ages. Purgatory could be now seen more in terms of development and growth than as punishment: a view that accorded with what we find in the way in which it was conceived in the early Church.

Purgatory so conceived becomes the most intelligible aspect of Christian doctrine about the afterlife, much of which is very confused: perhaps indeed the most confused branch of Christian theology. Modern Roman Catholic theologians are now also much more open to understanding purgatory in terms of development and growth.

Purim. Jewish festival commemorating the deliverance of Israel. The book of Esther is read and the festival, which comes in February or March, is a joyous one. According to the story in Esther, Haman, a wicked man, wanted to destroy the Jews and by drawing lots selected a certain day for the massacre that he had in mind. Esther, however, along with her husband, the Persian king, intervened and rescued the Jews from the fate Haman had planned for them.

Puritans. The Puritans were a party in the Church of England (never a majority) who, being dissatisfied with the mediating Elizabethan Settlement, demanded more thorough extirpation of the Catholic heritage of the English Church. They looked to Geneva as their pattern, as had the Scots under the leadership of John Knox. As a party in the Church they had considerable influence and power. The rising mercantile class was much inclined to favor them, and they had support from some families among the nobles and other landed classes as well as from the masses. They appealed to the Bible to an extent and in a way that encouraged bibliolatry among the uneducated classes. They attacked ancient usages such as the sign of the cross, vestments, and organs.

They emphasized preaching and sought to have the altar made to look more like a table and situated accordingly. They insisted on modelling Sunday on the Jewish sabbath, with much of the restrictiveness in conduct that is associated with orthodox Jewish observance. Emboldened, they sought to abolish the Episcopal form of church government and to substitute a form on Presbyterian lines. By the end of the 16th c. some were favoring a Congregationalist polity. The term "puritan," however, later came to be used in a somewhat vague sense, being applied to those Anglicans who had leanings or inclinations toward only particular aspects of the Puritan platform or who had a modest sympathy with the Puritan cause while in no way espousing it. The movement did polarize the English Church, and it may be that extremisms on both sides helped to encourage the moderation that had been fostered by many in the reign of Elizabeth I and that was to give the Anglican ethos its repute as a *via media*, a middle way between the excesses of Rome on the one side and those of Geneva on the other.

Puruṣa. In Hinduism, the original man, created by the god Brahma: the counterpart of Adam in the biblical story. From his body were created the four Hindu castes: from his head the brahmin caste, from his arms and torso the kshyatriya or warrior caste, from his thighs the vaisya or merchant caste, and from his feet the sudra caste. In rabbinic lore there are counterparts to this story to the effect that God, when he made Adam, used earth from various parts of the world, some from, say, the Euphrates region, some from Arabia, and so forth, but the head from the soil of Palestine.

Pūrva Mīmāṁsā. One of the six orthodox systems in Hindu thought. It is based upon the Mīmāṁsā Sūtra, which dates from *c*. 400 BCE. The Sanskrit term means "the early venerated thought." It stresses the importance of

Dharma (law, custom, the principle through which the cosmos works. Its aim was to take the theory expounded in the Vedas and show its practical application in human life. It emphasizes the eternality of Dharma and of the Vedic doctrines, even teaching that the Sanskrit language in which the Vedas are written is invested with eternality. This concept raised many questions in logic and language that teachers of this system discussed.

Pusey, Edward Bouverie (1800–1882). Leader of the Tractarian movement and party in the Church of England. Educated at Eton and Christ Church, Oxford, he was elected a Fellow of Oriel in 1823, then went to Germany for further studies. Both at Oxford and in the German universities he devoted himself to the study of the biblical languages and Arabic. At this early period of his life he was much disposed to see the rationalism that had been fostered in Germany and had spread to the educated classes all over Europe to have been the direct result of the spiritual bankruptcy of Protestantism: a much too simplistic view as he later perceived. Ordained deacon and priest in 1828, he was appointed in the same year Regius Professor of Hebrew at Oxford and Canon of Christ Church, in which office he spent the rest of his life.

After the death of his wife in 1839, which deeply affected him, he devoted himself even more zealously than ever to the Church and moved more and more, along with Newman, in the direction of the Oxford movement for the recovery of ancient Catholic doctrine and traditional Catholic liturgical practice. When Newman withdrew in 1841 from that movement Pusey became its leader. He especially defended the doctrine of the Real Presence in the Eucharist. He established the first Anglican sisterhood. He fostered the practice of confession and absolution. Newman in 1845 had submitted to Rome. Pusey remained more and more the leader of the Anglo-Catholic movement in the Church of

England, which not only transformed Anglican churchmanship and life but spread its influence, if in diluted forms, among other heirs of the Reformation. After his death his friends purchased his large library, which they presented to an institution in Oxford as a memorial to him and which is known as a lively focus of Anglo-Catholic life at Oxford as well as an important theological library.

Pusey's writings were prolific. A bibliography may be found in H. P. Liddon's 4-volume life of Pusey (1893–1897), Vol IV, pp. 395–446.

Pyramids. The Egyptian word for "pyramid" was *mer*, meaning apparently "place of ascent." The English term comes from the Greek *pyramis*. The pyramids were royal tombs built for most of the rulers of the Old and Middle Kingdoms (*c.* 2700 to 2200 and 1980–1786 BCE respectively). Each pyramid was part of a building complex. Associated with sun worship, it was exclusively for royal personages. Various magical texts were usually included by way of helping these royal personages to be victorious over death, for in Egyptian religion the concept of immortality was central. An enormous portion of the economic resources of Egypt was spent on the pyramids, but this sacrifice was no doubt considered to be well offset by the unifying function that these great edifices had on Egypt as a political and religious entity.

Pyrrho (*c.* 360–270 BCE). Greek philosopher. According to the testimony of his disciple Timon, Pyrrho taught that it is impossible to know the nature of anything. No assertion can be said to be preferred over any other. We must therefore in all cases suspend judgment in regard to everything. Our response consists of a silence that commits us to nothing, since we in fact know nothing. On questions involving value, one should cultivate an attitude of *ataraxia:* a serenity such as may have some affinities with that inherent in the Buddhist ideal for the enlightened man. According to Diogenes Laertius, Pyrrho went to India with Alexander and met Indian gymnosophists whose solitary lives and self-denying practices he admired and sought personally to use as models in his own life.

Pyrrhonism. Name given to those who followed the teachings of Pyrrho (see **Pyrrho**), but also loosely applied to all who profess an extreme form of skepticism. Much interest in Pyrrhonism was developed in Europe by Montaigne and others in the 16th c. and later.

Pythagoras (570–500 BCE). Greek philosopher. Born probably at Samos, he founded a philosophical school in Croton, Italy, which was in some respects almost like a religious order, with progress from a novitiate to full membership. Women and men were admitted. Community property was the rule, vows were taken, vegetarianism practiced. Salvation is obtained through the quest for truth. Philosophy plays a cardinal role in preparing men and women for a more advanced kind of life-situation. (Transmigration was a tenet of Pythagoras.) He saw musical intervals in mathematical terms and apparently related mathematics to reality: a notion that his disciples developed in sometimes fanciful ways. His school or brotherhood was influenced by Orphism. Pythagoras in turn influenced the thought of Plato.

Pyx. From the Greek *pyxis* (literally a box made of boxwood), a term traditionally used to denote any receptacle for containing the consecrated Host and still so used of the vessel containing the large Host in the Tabernacle, reserved for purposes of Exposition. Its most common use nowadays, however, is in reference to a small flat box of precious metal that the priest hangs around his neck for carrying the Host to the sick or others unable to come to receive Holy Communion in church.

Q

Q. A symbol used by New Testament scholars to designate the hypothetical source of the passages in the Synoptic Gospels of Matthew and Luke that resemble one another but correspond to nothing to be found in Mark. A theory, suggested by Harnack and others, was developed by Streeter, who held that behind the text as we know it must have been a document (not merely an oral tradition) accessible to and used by Matthew and Luke. Streeter admitted that the existence of Q could not be called certain but held that it was nevertheless extremely probable. The theory has nevertheless been questioned by some scholars, being vigorously repudiated, for example, by Austin Farrer.

The symbol is generally taken to stand for *Quelle* (German, meaning "source"), but this is disputed by some, who contend that it merely happens to be the next letter after P, a symbol for long in use in biblical criticism and therefore making Q convenient for the purpose to which it was applied.

Qadarites. An early Islamic school of thought whose adherents contended that man has power (*qadar*) to choose his own acts, so that the divine predestination that is so emphasized in Islamic orthodoxy is excluded. See **Mutazilites.**

Quadragesima. A name for Lent (forty days) and also used for the First Sunday of Lent.

Quadragesimo Anno. See **Rerum Novarum.**

Quadratus. Probably the earliest (2nd c.) of the Christian apologists. He is known to have been writing as early as 124 CE.

Quadrivium. In the medieval system of education the Seven Liberal Arts were divided into the Trivium (grammar, rhetoric, and dialectic) and the Quadrivium (arithmetic, geometry, astronomy, and music).

Quaestiones Disputatae. In medieval scholasticism, the *disputatio* was a formal procedure for settling disputed questions by public scholarly debate. A thesis was set forth along with its formal logical proof in syllogistic form; then someone else presented an objection by denying one of the premises; finally the master made a determination. The writings of the schoolmen, notably Thomas Aquinas, regularly illustrate the method of discussion.

Quaestiones Quodlibetales. See **Quaestiones Disputatae.** A form of the medieval *disputatio* in which the audience selected a question to be discussed by the participants.

Quakers. The followers of George Fox (1624–1691) were organized in 1688 as a distinctive group called simply the Friends. Much persecuted in England for their nonconformity, they represented a radical movement in Protestantism, rejecting many basic tenets of the Reformers in favor of an extreme emphasis on the doctrine of the Inner Light as authoritatively superior to both Bible and Church. The Friends also rejected the sacraments and made much of certain external observances such as the use of "plain speech" (for instance, "thou" and "thee" were used as the regular mode of address to each other instead of the "you" that by then had come to be customary in polite conversation), plain, unornamented dress, and the repudiation of all forms of art, including music, as foolishly secular. The use of the term "Quaker" dates from 1650, by Justice Bennet, whom George Fox had bidden to quake at the Word of the Lord. Some of the Friends, however, attributed its use to the experience of trembling or quaking that occurred among some of them at meetings. Their intransigent pacifism has generally brought them into conflict with the State, but their devotion to great social causes and to education has attracted widespread admiration, while their enviable reputation for strict honesty has won them almost universal respect. Under Elias Hicks (1748–1830), an American Quaker, a group severed themselves from the main body. Their followers are sometimes called Hicksites.

Quality. From the Latin *qualis* (literally, "of what kind"), which Cicero used to translate the Greek *poion*. One of Aristotle's basic categories, signifying "that by virtue of which a thing is such and such." Kant followed this traditional usage. A distinction was also made in Greek thought (e.g., by Democritus) between the qualities that things possess and the qualities that are produced in us by the things: the former (e.g., solidity, number, extension in space) being seen as *primary*; the latter (e.g., color, taste, smell) being seen as *secondary*. In the 16th c. Galileo and Mersenne employed such a distinction in the analysis of bodies and our relation to them. Robert Boyle seems to have been the first to use the terminology "primary/secondary qualities" and Locke adopted it for use in his philosophy, which was in turn criticized by Berkeley, who used the same terminology to show that all qualities, from his standpoint, are secondary.

Quanta Cura. The encyclical of Pius IX issued on December 8, 1864, to which was attached the highly reactionary Syllabus of Errors, for long taken to have the status of an infallible pronouncement but now generally regarded by Roman Catholic theologians as not falling within that category.

Quantum. (Latin *quantus*, how much) Term traditionally used in philosophy to refer to a finite and determinate quantity. In modern physics the term has been borrowed in reference to the *quanta* or packets of energy in quantum mechanics. In classical mechanics, which found its ultimate expression in Newton, not only can the exact position and momentum of any particle in the universe be determined, the future of the universe is determinable, at least theoretically, from the present positions and momenta of its particles. In quantum mechanics the case is otherwise. According to the principle of uncertainty attributed to Heisenberg, as the determination of the position of an electron is more precisely known, the determination of its momentum is less precisely known. The converse is also the case. So it is held by many, although not all, that the older concept of a universe governed by a principle of determinacy is to be abandoned. The implications are of very great importance for modern religious, not least for Christian, thought.

Quarant'Ore. A Catholic devotion having its beginnings in 16th-c. Italy. It consists of the exposition of the Blessed Sacrament in a monstrance or pyx for a period of forty (*quaranta*) hours. It is begun and closed with a Solemn High Mass and Procession of the Blessed Sacrament, and a Solemn High Mass for peace is sung on the intervening day. During this beautiful devotion the faithful take turns, as if on sentry duty, to pray before the Sacrament. When the Blessed Sacrament is "exposed" the faithful genuflect on both knees on entering and on leaving the church.

Quarr Abbey. A Benedictine foundation near Ryde, Isle of Wight, England. Built in 1912 on the site of a Cistercian abbey dating from the early 12th c. and destroyed in the 16th c. at the Dissolution of the Monasteries, it was erected by the Benedictines of Solesmes who in 1908 had been obliged to leave France. It is now an independent house of the Solesmes Congregation, sharing in the important liturgical work of Solesmes.

Quasimodo Sunday. An alternative title for Low Sunday, derived from the opening words of the Introit for that day: *Quasi modo geniti*, "In the manner of newborn children." It was from these words that Victor Hugo named the deformed bellringer, the endearing hero of his novel, *Notre Dame de Paris*.

Queen Anne's Bounty. A fund formed by Queen Anne in 1704 to supplement the incomes of the less well-endowed parishes in England.

Quentin, Henri (1872–1935). Benedictine scholar and reviser of the Vulgate.

Quesnel, Pasquier (1634–1719). French philosopher and theologian, an Oratorian much persecuted for his Jansenist opinions. He taught that grace is irresistible, that without it no one can do any good work, and that outside the Church no grace can be given or received.

Quiddity. (Latin *quidditas*, whatness) In medieval scholasticism, a term used to express distinction between the primary substance that inheres in all things and the secondary substance that makes an individual thing what it is: its essence or form.

Quietism. In a wide sense this term is applied to any system of spirituality that emphasizes "waiting on God." It also refers more specifically to a school of spirituality in the 17th c. that cultivated passivity, the total abandonment of the self to God and the total renunciation of the will. Its leading Spanish exponent was Miguel de Molinos. Among French quietists the most prominent were Madame Guyon, her disciple Archbishop Fénelon, and her director F. Lacombe. Typical of Quietist teaching is the notion that once the soul has succeeded in total abandonment of self, renouncing even the most laudable desires such as the love of virtue, it passes beyond the possibility of sinning, since it has become perfectly united with God. This school of mysticism alarmed the Roman Catholic hierarchy, presumably on the ground that it tended toward a pantheism that would eliminate the distinction between morality and immorality. Innocent XI, in 1687, specifically condemned the writings of Molinos on this subject.

Quine, Willard van Orman (1908–). American logician; Professor at Harvard; author of important works on logic.

Quiñones, Francisco de (1485–1540). 16th c. Franciscan and Spanish cardinal. On the eve of the Reformation many attempts were made within the Roman Catholic Church to achieve reforms within its structure. The Church in Spain was prominent in making such attempts and Cardinal Quiñones took a leading part in them.

Quinque Viae. The five "ways" presented by Thomas Aquinas in demonstration of the existence of God. (See **Thomas Aquinas.**) Although they have often been regarded as "arguments" or "proofs," none can purport to be a conclusive proof; otherwise there would be no point in having more than that one. So they are properly designated "ways" (*viae*) produced in evidence to show the rationality (or, some would prefer to say, the plausibility) of belief in the existence of God.

Quirinus. Pseudonym used by Döllinger for sixty-nine letters published in the Augsburger Allgemeine Zeitung on the subject of the First Vatican Council in 1869–1870. Using material provided by Lord Acton and J. Friedrich, he showed that those promoting the doctrine of Papal Infallibility at that Council were misguided by political influences and considerations and that the doctrine lacked adequate theological ground.

Qumran. The site of certain ruins at the northeast end of the Dead Sea, about eight miles south of Jericho. They were occupied from c. 150 BCE to c. 31 BCE and from c. 4 BCE to 68 CE; also later by Jewish insurgents during the Bar Cochba revolt 132–135 CE. In caves in this neighborhood, in 1947 and later, were found a highly important collection of Hebrew and Aramaic manuscripts, written in an early form of square or Assyrian script. They belonged to a Jewish community or sect (possibly the Essenes) that flourished at Qumran about the time of the birth of Jesus. For an account of them see M. Burrows (ed.), *The Dead Sea Scrolls of*

St. Mark's Monastery (2 vols. New Haven, 1950–1955). *The Dead Sea Scrolls* (New York, 1955), and *More Light on the Dead Sea Scrolls* (1958).

Quoad Omnia/Quoad Sacra. In Scotland those parishes to which the ancient teinds (tithes) belonged as the patrimony of the Church before the system of teinds was abolished by Act of Parliament in 1925 are called in Church law *quoad omnia* parishes, i.e., they were formed as parishes both from a civil and from an ecclesiastical standpoint. Parishes that were later carved out of such existing parishes (usually because of a growth in population that warranted it) were called *quoad sacra*, being parishes for ecclesiastical purposes only.

Quodlibet. See **Quaestiones quodlibetales**.

Quo Vadis? A legend, first mentioned in the *Acts of St. Peter*, recounts that Peter, fleeing from Rome, met Christ on the Appian Way and asked him, "Domine, quo vadis?" (Lord, where are you going?) to which Christ replied that he was going to be crucified again. Peter took this to mean that he, Peter, was to be crucified and he turned toward Rome, where he was eventually crucified. A church on the Appian Way, Santa Maria delle Piante commemorates the legend.

Qur'ān. The holy book of Islam, originating in 622 CE, when Muhammad, having migrated to Medina, began to dictate it as divine revelation. Allah (God) is the speaker throughout the Qur'ān, although an angel acts as his mouthpiece. See **Islam**.

R

Raamses. An Egyptian city in the construction of which the Hebrews were forced to work (Exodus 1.11). They set out thence to Canaan (Exodus 12.37). It was named after the Pharaoh, Ramses II, and its magnificence is attested in various Egyptian inscriptions. The name alludes to the Egyptian god Ra to whom its creation was attributed.

Rabanus Maurus. (776 or 784–856). Abbot of Fulda and Archbishop of Mainz. Trained at Fulda and at Tours under Alcuin, he was one of most learned scholars and theologians of his time. Ordained priest in 814, he fostered learning among the clergy, providing for them a manual to guide them in their priestly work. He wrote several commentaries on the Bible and an encyclopedic work on what a later age would have called "natural philosophy:" a treatment of the universe as seen through the eyes of an observant and thoughtful scholar of his time. It provided a religious perception of nature. Considering the limitations of his time, when Europe was slowly emerging from the Dark Age that had ensued upon the Fall of Rome, Rabanus showed remarkable judgment. He wrote much poetry. The *Veni Creator* is widely attributed to him. Because of his work in the evangelization of Germany, he came to be accorded the title, *praeceptor Germaniae*: the teacher of Germany. Never officially canonized by Rome, he has been generally recognized and venerated as one of the saints of the Western Church.

Rabbah. The royal city of Ammon, now entirely covered by the modern city Ammon. It lies *c*. sixty-five miles east of Jerusalem by road. It was besieged by Joab (II Samuel 11.1), who summoned David to lead an army to it when he perceived the time to be opportune (II Samuel 12.27ff.).

Rabbi. An Aramaic term of respect used in addressing a teacher and meaning literally "my master," being generally rendered in Greek *kyrie* ("sir" or "my lord"). *Rabban* and *rabbôni* represent an emphatic form of respect. Jesus disapproved of the insistence by the scribes on being addressed in such terms (Matthew 23.7f.), not because of any objection to respect from a student to his teacher but rather because dependence on a title means dependence on one's office rather than authentic respect, affection, and esteem for the teacher himself. The office represents the mere trapping of what should be the reality. This teaching reflects Jesus's contempt for the cleaning of the outside of the cup when the inside remains dirty or defective. In later Judaism the term "rabbi" was applied to any authority or teacher of the Torah. Up to the first few centuries CE, rabbinic ordination was believed to go back to the time of Moses and so implied a notion of spiritual succession. Today ordination to the rabbinate in Judaism does not imply such claims, nor of course is the rabbi in any sense a priest in either the Jewish or the Christian sense. He is one who has followed a course of rabbinic studies and been tested in his knowledge thereof. His functions are those of a teacher and spiritual guide.

Raca. This term of abuse, mentioned in Matthew 5.22, is widely used in Talmudic literature and elsewhere. Less contemptuous than "fool," it meant, rather, an empty-head, somewhat as in colloquial language today, a "dope."

Rachel. In the Old Testament, Jacob's wife and the younger daughter of Laban, for whom Jacob worked seven years as her purchase price. After doing so, Laban substituted Leah, and Jacob had to work another seven years (Genesis 29.6–31). Rachel, seeming to be barren, substituted Bilhah, her slave, but finally bore Joseph. The tribes of Rachel are: Ephraim, Manasseh, and Benjamin.

Racovian Catechism, The. The first formal statement of Socinian principles and therefore a document of much interest to Unitarians. Published in Polish at Racow in 1605, it was never intended as a credal formula to be imposed on the Socinians. It was to be considered, rather, a body of opinions that were recommended as pointing them in the right direction. Except for the rejection of the doctrine of the Trinity and the af-

firmation of an Adoptianist christology, it was a more traditional and orthodox statement than one might expect. A copy, in Latin, with a dedication to King James, was publicly burned in 1614.

Rad, Gerhard von (1901–1971). Old Testament scholar. Born at Nürnberg and trained at Erlangen and Tübingen, he held chairs at several German universities. His work on Deuteronomy was a milestone in Old Testament studies. He claimed to see in it the idea of a "holy war" in ancient Israel. He used the methods of form criticism (see **Formgeschichte**) and literary analysis, not least in his great work on the theology of the Old Testament. Although his findings have been modified, of course, by later Old Testament scholars, he is of permanent importance in the development of biblical studies.

Radhakrishnan, Sarvepalli (1888–1975). Indian philosopher and statesman. After studies in India and at Oxford, he served as Ambassador and eventually as President of the Republic of India. He developed a form of Idealism in which he sought to divinize not only the individual but the human race. His works included *Indian Philosophy* (2 vols., 1923), *Eastern Religions in Western Thought* (1939), and *Religion in a Changing World* (1967).

Rahab. In the English Bible this proper name signifies two different Hebrew words: *rāhāb* and *rāḥāb* respectively. The first form is a mythological entity in ancient Semitic creation myths, probably the monster of chaos whom the creative deity slew. The Hebrews sometimes applied the name to Babylon, to Egypt, and other societies as forces resistant to the creative power of Yahweh. The second term is a proper name (Joshua 2.1–21): that of a Jericho prostitute who hid Joshua's spies in her house and, when the Israelites captured the city, was spared, with all her household. The scarlet cord hanging from her window may have been a sign indicating the nature of the house. The story may be interpreted as signifying that the woman, although a Canaanite and a harlot, was saved by her faith in Yahweh.

Rahit. The code of discipline that those who, in the Sikh religion, when they enter the Khalsa order, vow to observe. Rahit was promulgated, according to the Sikh tradition, by Gobind Singh himself when he founded the Khalsa in 1699. Its obligations include the wearing of the hair uncut, the kirpan or dagger, breeches, comb, and iron bangle. The four special offenses against the Rahit are: cutting one's hair, smoking, adultery, and eating meat in the Muslim fashion. One who is guilty of any such offense may be punished by having to do a penance or pay a fine. He is called a *tanakhahlia*. One who flagrantly transgresses the code is a *patit* (apostate). Any manual recording any version of the Rahit is called a *rahit-nama*.

Rahner, Karl (1904–1984). Roman Catholic theologian. He entered the Jesuit Society in 1922 and was ordained in 1932. After further studies at Freiburg and Innsbruck he eventually accepted a chair in theology at Innsbruck in 1949 and in 1964 was appointed to a chair at Munich. Deeply influenced by Joseph Maréchal, a French Jesuit theologian, he sought so to revise Thomistic philosophy as to shield it from Kantian critique. Perhaps less felicitously, he used the language of Heidegger, making his expositions sometimes difficult, not to say obscure. When writing less technically, however, his style is incisive and clear and has contributed much to making him one of the most influential Roman Catholic theologians of the 20th c. He was indubitably a thinker of authenticity and power.

Raikes, Robert (1735–1811). Founder of Sunday School education. Born in Gloucester, England, he became distressed at the neglected condition of local children and established a Sunday School for them in a neighboring parish, then in 1780, one in his own, which he extended to provide education on weekdays too, in the Bible and in reading and writing. Despite opposition from a remarkable variety of quarters, he succeeded in his aims, which in his lifetime he saw achieved in many places throughout England. His work was taken up by Hannah Moore and others and eventually Sunday School became a regular feature of church life. Raikes is rightly credited with the founding of the Sunday School Movement, although he had precursors in conceiving the *idea*, e.g., Joseph Alleine in the 17th c., a Puritan, and John Wesley, who held Sunday School classes during his term at Savannah, Georgia, in 1737. In the 19th c. the Sunday School became a firmly established aspect of church life in the United States and has spread to every continent in the world.

Rain in the Bible. The biblical writers generally treat rain as a gift from God, even a reward. Yahweh's help is likened to rain (Hosea 6.3). This is a natural concept in the biblical lands, where rain hardy ever falls from mid-May till mid-October and where, even in the rainy season, the precipitation varies from only *c.* 11 to 30 inches. In such a climate, rain, heavy or light, can easily be perceived as heavenly dew.

Rak'as. Muslims, during the recitation of prayers either in public or in private perform certain ritual movements and utter certain ritual words, e.g., the worshipper begins by lifting his hands to his ears and repeating in Arabic the words: "God is the greatest." In Sunni practice, when the opening chapter of the Qur'ān has begun to be recited, the worshipper places his right hand over his left and covers his navel, while in Shi'ite practice he lets his arms fall by his sides. He then bows and stands upright, repeating the movement three times, then prostrates on his prayer mat, kneeling and touching the ground with his forehead. He then looks to his left and to his right, saying each time: "Peace be upon you and the mercy of Allah."

Rāma. An *avatāra* (incarnation) of the Hindu deity Vishnu. His exploits are recorded in the *Rāmāyaṇa*. He is often presented as an ideal man, a model of perfect conduct. His spouse, Sītā, is upheld as the ideal of Hindu womanhood and a goddess presiding over agriculture. Gandhi, who came from the state of Gujarat, where the cult of Rāma is strong, is said to have exclaimed, at the moment of his assassination, "Eh! Ram!"

Ramadan. One of the most important observances in Islam. It consists of a month of fasting daily from sunrise to sunset, during which period no food or drink may be taken. It is one of the "Five Pillars of Islam," and its observance is mandatory on all except the very young, the very aged, the pregnant, and those who are traveling. Observant Muslims will try to read the entire Qur'ān during this period, which commemorates Muhammad's receiving of revelations from the Archangel Gabriel. The day after Ramadan is completed is called Id-ul-Fitr, which begins a feast lasting several days. Greeting cards may be exchanged; children receive presents of money; and families are expected to give to the poor money of value equivalent to that of a meal from each of its members.

Ramakrishna. A 19th-c. CE Hindu guru and mystic who, following the *bhakti* way, taught that the highest form of religion is mystical and that mystical experience enables all persons, irrespective of their institutional affiliation, to unite in worship.

Rāmānuja (11th c. CE). The chief exponent of the Hindu philosophical school, Viśiṣṭādvaita: a modified form of monism. (See **Monism**.) He stressed the methods of Bhakti-yoga as the way of deliverance, exercising much influence on the devotional, *bhakti* cults of later ages.

Rāmāyaṇa. An epic poem in Sanskrit traditionally ascribed to Vālmīki and constituting part of the Hindu Scriptures. It consists of 24,000 *ślokas* in seven books. Scholars now find it to have been subjected to many editorial processes. It tells of the love of Rāma and Sītā, his wife, who are presented as the ideal human couple. The poem has had much influence in the *Bhakti* movement.

Ramsey, Arthur Michael (1904–1988). Archbishop of Canterbury. Trained at Magdalene College, Cambridge, of which his father had been President, he was ordained priest in 1929 and from 1940 to 1950 was Professor of Divinity at Durham University and Canon of Durham. After two years at Cambridge as Regius Professor of Divinity, he was appointed Bishop of Durham in 1952, then translated to York in 1956 and to Canterbury in 1961. He was a considerable scholar as well as an important force for the development of ecumenical relations with the Eastern Orthodox. In 1966 he paid an official visit to Pope Paul VI. His writings include *The Gospel and the Catholic Church* (1936), *An Era in Anglican Theology: From Gore to Temple* (1960), *Sacred and Secular* (1965), and *God, Christ and the World* (1969).

Ramsey, Ian Thomas (1915–1972). Born near Bolton, Lancashire, and educated locally, he won a scholarship to Christ's College, Cambridge. After obtaining first classes in both the Mathematical Tripos and the Moral Sciences Tripos, he became interested in theology and won distinction in the Theological Tripos. After a series of chaplaincies and academic appointments he was elected Nolloth Professor of the Christian Religion in the University of Oxford and a Fellow of Oriel in 1951. He was Canon Theologian of Leicester Cathedral from 1944 till his appointment as Bishop of Durham in 1966. An extraordinarily conscientious bishop, he spoke frequently in the House of Lords on moral issues and worked very hard for social justice and for a large variety of causes ranging from relief of the poor from unemployment and the moral evils it entails to conjugal rights for prisoners. On Easter Eve, 1972, he suffered a severe heart attack. On October 6, while working late in London he fell dead at the table on which he was writing, survived by his widow and two sons. His unusual combination of intellectual brilliance, charitable disposition, pastoral instinct, and sheer industry made him one of the most felicitous choices for the Church of England episcopate in the 20th c. His books include *Religious Language* (1957), *Freedom and Immortality* (1960), *Models and Mystery* (1964), *Science and Religion: Conflict and Synthesis* (1964), *Christian Discourse* (1965), and *Words about God: the Philosophy of Religion* (1971).

Rancé, Armand-Jean le Bouthillier de (1626–1700). Son of a secretary of Marie de' Medici and a godson of Richelieu, he was a distinguished student at the Sorbonne, was ordained priest in 1651, but for some time remained a worldly one, more at home in the world of fashion than in the Church. In 1657, however, he underwent a conversion that led him to retreat for some time to his country house near Tours. Having been since early youth commendatory (lay) abbot of La Trappe, he now entered the Cistercian novitiate and in 1664 became regular Abbot of that Cistercian foundation. Under his rule, which he exercised with great severity, La Trappe became a model of the Cistercian spirit as it had been envisioned at the inception of the Order. He incurred strong opposition, even hostility from many quarters: unsurprisingly, since he prohibited studies as part of the monastic life. The Abbé Henri Bremond (1865–1933), whose ideal was a Christian life that included urbanity and intellectual joys, found in him the very essence of fanaticism and wrote a lively and interesting but unsympathetic

biography entitled *L'Abbé Tempête* (1929), English translation, *The Thundering Abbot* (1930). De Rancé had Jansenist connections, although his friends defended his doctrinal orthodoxy. See **Bremond, Henri.**

Rand, Ayn (1903–1981). Philosopher. Born in Leningrad, she came to the United States under a college scholarship and remained, eventually supporting herself by her successful philosophical novels. Among her various philosophical positions, the most original and important is probably her doctrine of individualism and its ethical and political consequences. An ardent admirer of the United States Constitution, she strongly disapproved what she took to be its misapplications. For instance, while applauding its guarantees of freedom of lifestyle and peaceable assembly, she insisted that no individual should be a non-voluntary mortgage on another. The Constitution wisely, in her view, made no mention of a duty to help others in need, although doing so voluntarily might well be regarded as a laudable act on the part of the individual undertaking it. The function of government is to protect its citizens by assuring their rights to non-interference by others. It is not to impose duties except to the extent that the duties are entailments of others' rights. The whole of my duty toward you can be summed up in my duty not to infringe upon your natural rights. Her thoughts on the application of this fundamental principle are exhibited in her philosophical novels, e.g., *We the Living* (1935), *The Fountainhead* (1943), and (probably her best known) *Atlas Shrugged* (1957).

Ranters. An antinomian group that appeared in England in the 17th c. They denied the authority of the Bible, of the Creeds, and of the Church's ministry, appealing to their inward experience of Christ as their sole guide. They were sometimes confused with the Quakers, to the disadvantage of the reputation of the latter.

Raphael (Raffaele Sanzio) (1483–1520). Among the greatest of Italian painters and one of the foremost among those of the Renaissance period. He began his work under Perugino at Perugia. His *Crucifixion* (1502) is in the National Gallery, London, and his *Espousals of the Virgin* (1504) in the Brera, Milan. Having gone to Florence about this time, he made the acquaintance of some of the greatest painters of the age, e.g., Michelangelo, Leonardo, and Fra Bartolommeo. At the order of Pope Julius II he did many famous works at Rome, including the Sistine *Madonna*. His last work, now in the Vatican, was his *Transfiguration*, which pupils finished after his death, since he had not been able to complete it.

Raphael, The Archangel. One of the archangels mentioned in the Jewish Apocrypha (e.g., Tobit 12.12; Enoch 10.7). He is associated with healing.

Rashdall, Hastings (1858–1924). English moral philosopher. An Oxford man, he developed a position in ethics that he called Ideal Utilitarianism, in contradistinction from Bentham's position. The development of character has an intrinsic value, in his view, as forming part of the ideal to be achieved. His writings include *The Theory of Good and Evil* (1907), *The Problem of Evil* (1912), and *The Moral Argument for Personal Immortality* (1920).

Rashi. An 11th-c. commentator on the Hebrew Bible, whose interpretations are highly esteemed by Jewish scholars.

Rastafarianism. The religion of a Jamaican subculture, first seriously studied by outsiders between about 1940 and 1960. Popular among the poorest and least literate Jamaicans, it is emphatically one based on strongly racial prejudice. Rastas depict Christ as black and recognize Africa as the homeland of all black people. Among the many remarkable tenets that Rastas have held and expounded (although not universally) are the following: the real Jews were black and the ones familiar to the world today were impostors; Ethiopia is Zion (Haile Selassie was accounted divine by many Rastas); the Pope is the head of the Ku Klux Klan; and Queen Elizabeth II is a reincarnation of Elizabeth I. Rastas, from the beginnings of the movement, seem to have favored the use of cannabis. They held women in low esteem. Some extremists among them have held that a woman is forbidden to cook while she is menstruating. The movement spread beyond Jamaica; e.g., Britain now has a generation of children raised in Rastafarian beliefs.

Rasul. This Arabic term, meaning literally "messenger", is used in the Qur'ān to designate those prophets (e.g., Moses, Jesus, and Muhammad) to whom Allah revealed his holy law. The term *nabi* also means "messenger" or "prophet" but tends to be used in a more general sense. All prophets are regarded as forerunners of Muhammad, the culmination of the line. He is *the* Rasul of Allah. See also **Nabi**.

Rāthā. In Hindu lore, a beautiful *gopi* (female cattle herder). Kṛṣṇa is supposed to have been on intimate terms with the wives of the cowherds and particularly with Rāthā. Much of the legend comes from a 12th c. CE pastoral drama by Jayadeva, entitled *Gītajovinda*, which exhibits affinities with Hesiod's hymn to the Delian Apollo. In Tantrism Rāthā is the infinite love that is the very essence of Kṛṣṇa. Women participate in her nature as do men in that of Kṛṣṇa.

Rationalism. A general designation for those types of philosophical systems that give a primary role to reason. The term, however, has many applications and can best be understood in terms of that with which it is set in contrast. For example, in ethics a rationalist approach may be seen in opposition to an intuitionist one in which emotion or instinct has an important role. In the context of religion a rationalist approach would be seen in contrast to one in which faith and revelation have the leading roles.

In the history of Western thought, however, rationalism is traditionally seen in contrast to empiricism. Three 17th c. thinkers, Descartes, Leibniz, and Spinoza, are generally called "the European Rationalists," sometimes "the Continental Rationalists," while Locke, Berkeley, and Hume, are called "the British Empiricists." Nevertheless, there are rationalist elements in Locke. Indeed probably no philosophical system has ever been exclusively one or the other. Nevertheless, a strong emphasis on reason justifies the rationalist label, as a strong emphasis on sense-experience justifies the empiricist one.

In antiquity Parmenides might be taken as an exemplar of an extreme form of rationalism, upholding a virtual identification of the rational and the real. Plato, although critical of the extreme form of rationalism in Paramenides, is nevertheless clearly identifiable as on the rationalist side. Appearance "participates" in reality but is to be distinguished from it. Reality is knowable in the World of Forms or Ideas. Plato also sees reason as having the function of controlling emotion, being therefore superior to it. Aristotle basically follows Plato in this as in much else, but he introduces an important ingredient into his system: an ingredient that may be called empiricist.

The meaning of "rationalist" and "rationalism" changed in the hands of the men of the 18th c., the "age of Reason," because they were using the term typically in contrast, not so much to emotion or sense-experience, but to what they regarded as superstition entailing irrational behavior and obscurantist traditionalism in thought. They thought of themselves as "enlightened" and "rational" by contrast with the men of the Middle Ages whom they viewed as sunk in a morass of irrational darkness and stupidity.

The enormous influence of Hegel in the 19th c. introduced a new vision of rationalism as philosophical reflection *par excellence.* It represents what philosophy is and what philosophy does. So Kierkegaard, in his bitter antagonism to Hegel, is sometimes classified as an "irrationalist," although what he was doing was, rather, to exhibit the shortcomings and limitations of a thoroughgoing rationalist approach to the problems of human knowledge. Under the influence of Hegelianism 19th-c. philosophers tended to accept a coherence theory of truth rather than a correspondence theory, i.e., they saw in systematic coherence evidence of the truth of a proposed system. Typical of 20th c. thought has been a suspicion, strong in both the logical empiricism of the English-speaking world and in continental European existentialism, that rationalism, especially the Hegelian type so much associated with philosophical idealism, misrepresents the nature of the philosophical enterprise. Many thinkers today believe that a more balanced view than either is now coming into prospect.

Ratisbon, The Conference of(1541). A conference of three Protestant and three Roman Catholic theologians who met at Ratisbon (Regensburg) at the bidding of the Emperor Charles V, with a view to achieving reunion. The Roman Catholic side included Johann Eck, who had been largely responsible for securing Luther's excommunication, while the Protestant side included Melanchthon and Bucer. A remarkable degree of agreement was reached even on the most controversial issues, but political considerations eventually defeated the enterprise.

Ratramus. A 9th-c. monk of Corbie (see **Corbie**) who, at the order of Charles the Bald, wrote a treatise on Predestination in which he defended the doctrine of "double" predestination and the strange and very special teaching of Paschasius Radbertus on the Eucharist, in which was maintained the notion of the Real Presence in the Eucharist as the actual flesh and blood of

Jesus as it had lived on earth, born of Mary and had suffered on the Cross, now miraculously multiplied at each consecration at Mass. The doctrine of "double" predestination is that God predestines not only his elect to heaven but the reprobate to hell. Ratramus was invoked centuries later by some of the Protestant Reformers as supporting this latter doctrine, which some of them taught. Ratramus was considered heretical in his own time, and one of his treatises was placed on the Index of Prohibited Books in 1599 but removed from it in 1900.

Realism. From the Latin word *res* ("thing"). Realism has two different principal meanings in the history of philosophy. (1) In medieval discussions, perhaps the most persistently controversial topic was that of the Universals. Opinions varied from one extreme, according to which the Universal (e.g., courage, kindness, even tableness and horseness) have a reality beyond all their individual exemplars (e.g., John's courage, Tom's kindness, and so forth), to the other extreme according to which the Universal is a mere label or name that we apply to certain objects or concepts by way of classifying them together because of certain similarities that we see in them. In this context, Realism means that the Universals do have at least some kind of existence independent of the mind that perceives them. (2) In more recent philosophy, Realism represents the view, in contrast to Phenomenalism and Idealism, that the objects of knowledge exist independently of our awareness of them. Such objects of knowledge, however, may be either a thing (e.g., a desk, a computer) or a thought (e.g., an image of a sunset in my mind or a remembrance of the face of a deceased friend). Since the time of Locke, a variety of types of Realism has developed, including Representative Realism, Critical Realism, Perspective Realism, and Scientific Realism.

Real Presence, The. This phrase alludes to the Eucharist and is used to refer to those doctrines that affirm, in one way or another, that Christ is actually present in the Eucharist, contradistinguished from those doctrines according to which he is present only in the minds of the participants as they receive the Sacrament. The difference has momentous consequences for the Christian's understanding of the nature of the Sacrament. See **Eucharist** and **Reservation.**

Reason. The concept of reason has been variously understood in the history of Western thought. In Greek philosophy, three terms, *nous, logos,* and *phrōnesis* might all be translated by the term "reason." *Nous,* in Plato and Aristotle, is the highest faculty of human knowledge. Aristotle distinguished between *nous poiētikos* or "active" reason and *nous pathētikos* or "passive" reason, which complement each other. *Nous poiētikos,* which makes all things, survives the body, being immortal. *Nous pathētikos,* being the seat of individuality, does not do so. Aristotle called God *noēsis noēseōs,* i.e., thought thinking itself. The Aristotelian distinction between active *nous* and passive *nous* became very important in medieval philosophy, both Islamic and Christian.

The term *logos* was used in Greek philosophy even before the time of Socrates. Heraclitus used it to designate the objective reason or rational principle in the universe of which the soul of man is part. The term tended, however, to be replaced by *nous* until the Stoics designated their principle of purpose in the universe as *logos* or God. The Stoics also introduced the concept of *logos spermatikos,* the principle of an active reason at work in "dead" matter. In the Roman Stoics we find a sort of pun developed: *ratio* (reason), becomes *oratio* (speech) when expressed in human language; so *Gloria hominis ratio et oratio,* "the glory of man is reason and speech." Philo identified the creative "word" in the Old Testament with the *logos.* The author of the Gospel according to John, echoing such philosophical developments, identifies the *logos* with both the creative and the redemptive aspects of God. So *logos* found its way into the thought of the Christian Apologists and Fathers of the Church.

Aristotle had drawn another distinction that was to have much importance in the subsequent history of Western thought: the distinction between *theōria* and *praxis*, i.e., between reason as "contemplative" or "onlooking" and reason as "practical". By practical reason Aristotle meant the faculty with which we perceive what means are available to us in order to achieve a contemplated goal, which among these means are the most efficient, and how to make the best use of these means.

Following the lead of Plato the thinkers of antiquity generally perceived reason as the highest activity of the human spirit, keeping the passions in check, the emotions under control, and generally ennobling humanity. Christian thought, while upholding the claims of reason that the ancients had put forward, added another category, that of faith. (See **Faith**.) In medieval thought, notably that of Thomas Aquinas, reason tended to be understood in terms of deductive reasoning. Faith stood in sharp contrast to it without in any way being a denigration of reason's claims. Against reason, so understood, faith provides a means of advancing to knowledge that is otherwise unavailable and so is seen as having some sort of kinship to inductive reasoning. Faith and reason, in Saint Thomas, are complementary. This theme has been much developed in religious thought: philosophy (reason) and religion (faith) need each other and are two aspects of the same high enterprise.

The 18th century has been called "the Age of Reason," but by then ambiguities had begun to undermine the meaning of the term, which traditionally had been invested with a significance inseparable from religious concerns. Hobbes, for instance, in the 17th c. had understood reason as what we might now call a computer-like, mechanistic process. Locke, although taking a very different stance, might be said to have envisioned the reasoning process as one of combining and arranging the simple ideas of experience in such a way as to produce general or abstract ideas. Hume's thought, especially in this doctrine of the association of ideas, tended to empty still further the traditional role of reason in the human mind. He saw reason as "the slave of the passions" and therefore limited to showing us the means to ends that the passions dictate. Kant, however, took the concept of reason very seriously, distinguishing between "pure reason" and "practical reason." Pure reason functions on its own, independent of other faculties of human consciousness such as appetite and will. What Kant called "practical" reason originates knowledge about ethical conduct and reflects on the possibilities opened up to us by human freedom. Kant also distinguished reason from understanding. Understanding is that aspect of the thinking process that deals with concepts, principles, judgments, and categories. By contrast, reason is an active principle, driven by an impossible demand to transcend the limitations of human experience. Pure reason, therefore, must modestly limit itself to being the overseer of that which is and that which is not within the range of human understanding. Yet while pure reason is limited in such ways, the practical reason, according to Kant, is not, making possible for us an authentic knowledge of "the moral law within" that we do not have about the external world: "the starry heavens above," as he called it.

The term "reason" has come to be used, however, with a wide variety of meanings. For example, it can mean the capacity to reflect and to analyze, the ability to draw inferences, to think. One may be said to act "for a reason" or even "for a good (or bad) reason." Reason may be contrasted with reasoning, the process of making inferences. Reasoning may be seen as one of several kinds of states of consciousness (e.g., dreaming, imagining, recollecting) and it may be used honestly in a quest for truth or dishonestly in trying to confuse or "make the worse appear the better cause." See **Rationalism**.

Recluse. A man or woman who chooses to live alone, apart from the world, for religious reasons. Eremitical orders or orders whose members are hermit-monks or hermit-nuns, such as the Carthusians, are not recluses, although they may provide for certain members' choosing to adopt that way of life.

Reconciliation. Paul applies the term, which is the Greek legal one for the restoration of the marriage relationship, to the process of salvation. Through Christ, God and man are reconciled. Man is perceived as at enmity with God, who acts to bring about reconciliation by means of Christ. The theme has variations. For example, the author of Ephesians uses it in expressing the idea that God has actually created out of two races (Jews and Gentiles) a single new entity, a new being: the Church, the Household of Faith (Ephesians 2.14f.).

Rector. The title traditionally pertaining to a priest in whom is vested the control of a parish and who enjoys full independence in its administration, although ultimately subject of course to the authority of the bishop or other administrative superior. In Anglican usage he is distinguished from a Vicar, who has some, but not such full independence. The title is also used by the heads of Jesuit houses, of some Oxford colleges, of the administrative heads of European universities, and of some British schools. In Scotland the Rector of a university is elected by the student body and his function as their representative is largely honorific.

Recusants. (*Note*: The first syllable is accented.) In England, from about 1570, those who persisted in their refusal to recognize the Anglican Church and who adhered to Rome, came to be so designated. The recusants presented a considerable social problem because in some regions they were strong enough to pose a threat of armed rebellion. That this was averted was due in considerable measure to the erosion of the penal laws against Roman Catholics. These were at first extremely severe, so much so that judges were often unwilling to implement them. In 1778, however, the first of a series of mitigations in the laws was enacted, e.g., Roman Catholics were permitted to buy and to inherit land. Many disabilities, however, remained till 1829 when, under the Roman Catholic Relief Act, these disabilities, with a few exceptions, were removed. See **Roman Catholic Relief Acts**.

Redemption. The concept of redemption, found in many if not most of the great religions of the world, represents emancipation or deliverance from the limitations and miseries of human existence, including sin, guilt, suffering, and death. Christians claim that it has been fundamentally achieved through the Incarnation, Death, and Resurrection of Christ. In the New Testament it appears under two aspects: (1) deliverance from the power of sin; (2) restoration of man and the world to communion with God. Paul, in his letters, develops the concept under both aspects. Redemption is held to be objective, i.e., it provides the *conditions* that make possible man's restoration to his Creator. The Protestant Reformers emphasized "justification" by the "imputation" of the righteousness of God to the sinner who accepts it through faith.

Redemptorists. The popular name for the Roman Catholic "Congregation of the Most Holy Redeemer" (C.SS.R.), founded by Alphonsus di Liguori at Scala, Italy, in 1732. Its primary function is missionary, and its members have been widely known for the conduct of parochial missions calculated to stir the members of parishes to greater fervor in the practice of their faith.

Red Hat. Traditionally, a cardinal was invested by the Pope with a flat, broad-brimmed hat having two clusters of fifteen tassels each, which was not worn again after the investiture and was eventually suspended over his tomb. Cardinals now wear a red biretta, which is popularly called "the red hat."

Red Letter Day. The phrase, often used popularly of the day on which any important occasion occurs, alludes to the practice of printing in red ink the dates of important feast days in church calendars.

Red Sea, The. The Hebrew name of this sea is *yam-sûp*, which means "the sea of reeds," and so might be better rendered "the Reed Sea." There are some ambiguities in identifying the body of water to which the name is applied by the biblical writers. For example, sometimes the term means the Red Sea as we know it today (the body of water lying between Africa and Arabia and enclosed by Suez in the north and the Straits of Aden in the south; at other times it may mean (as in the Exodus crossing, e.g., Exodus 15.4) one of the lakes lying toward the Mediterranean on the north coast of the Isthmus of Suez.

Reductio ad Absurdum. A Latin phrase meaning literally "reduction to the absurd," i.e., to the extreme limit to which an argument can be stretched. The phrase is applied to a method of indirect proof in logic, in which, from the contradictory of the proposition to be proved, one deduces a contradiction, e.g., one wishes to prove X, so one supposes not-X to be true. One then deduces a contradiction from not-X, i.e., Y and not-Y. A proposition so leading to a contradiction plainly cannot be true, so not-X must be false.

Reductionism. Reductionism may take many forms, e.g., in the interpretation of religion it may take the form of reducing all religious values to an ethical core they are supposed to contain, or to psychological values that exclude the consideration of ontological questions, or to aesthetic values in which religion is recognized for its worth in producing great art forms. It is a common trap for beginners in religious studies.

Referent. In logic, the first term of a relation that has as its second term a "relatum," i.e., if X has the relation of R to Y, X is the referent and Y the relatum.

Reformation, The Protestant. The term is used by historians in a somewhat loose sense for a series of movements and tendencies in the Western Church occasioned by the universally recognized need for dealing with widespread corruption that had been rife in the Church for many generations and which efforts within the Church had failed to control. The Lollards in England, the Hussites in Bohemia, and the Waldensians in Italy may all be regarded as precursors of the main thrust of the Reformation Movement that is generally held to have had its beginning in 1517 in the act of Martin Luther's affixing to the door of the church at Wittenberg 95 theses that he proposed to defend, more specifically focusing on the theory and practice of Indulgences. The background of this catalyst was extremely complex. The papacy was the target of much of the criticism among learned and unlearned alike, but it was only one focus of discontent. The morals of the clergy were the butt of much ribaldry, not only concubinage and sexual promiscuity, but avarice leading to simoniacal practices and, in general, a worldly attitude that was, although by no means universal, too widely accepted.

The Reformation, like the Renaissance that was its concomitant, focused on restoration of values of the past, believed to have been lost. It was therefore in principle a conservative movement, although its followers often traduced it by excesses and innovations. It was in fact a failure in terms of its own central aim, which was to reform the Church, maintaining its unity, not to revolt against it and set up a rival Church. Political circumstances, however, impeded the fulfilment of the best intentions of the Reformers and in the long run the great theological issues were lost under the squabbles of the ignorant on both sides, which resulted in enormous bitterness and, for many centuries, gross misunderstanding of the issues.

In Germany and Scandinavia the Reformation, inspired by the teachings and work of Martin Luther, took a Lutheran form, depending much on the "godly princes" to whom was confided plenitude of power. In Switzerland, Hans Zwingli, with the help of the civic authorities of Zürich, carried out the Reformation there in a much more radical form.

With Zwingli's death in 1531, leadership passed from Zürich to Geneva, where, in 1541, John Calvin's blueprint for a thoroughgoing and carefully organized system, virtually a theocracy, was established. His movement, sometimes called "the Second Reformation," triumphed in many countries, becoming embroiled in complex political machinations and imposing a strict doctrinal orthodoxy of its own wherever it succeeded.

In England the Reformation took a very different form, resulting in much milder Calvinist influence along with the preservation of Catholic order and a great deal of ancient Catholic piety and practice, with a strong element of openness to Renaissance learning and culture. In Scotland where, after some influence from Lutheran and Zwinglian ideas, the Reformation under John Knox took a rigorously Calvinistic shape, it was much more radical and extreme.

One should note that what is found in Protestant thought, organization, liturgy, and practice, either in its so-called "conservative" or its so-called "liberal" wing, is usually far from what the Reformation Fathers respectively had in mind. See **Protestant**.

Reformed Churches. This term is used in two senses: (1) in a narrow and stricter sense to designate those Churches that adhere to and are specifically committed to the Calvinistic type of Reformation; (2) in a wider sense to include Protestant Churches in general. The latter usage, however, is inexact and misleading. Lutherans, although obviously much affected by the Reformation, would not generally regard themselves as in the family of Reformed Churches. Anglicans, although heirs of the Reformation, certainly would not be properly so designated.

Reform Judaism. In the atmosphere of the late 18th c., when medieval Jewish society was disintegrating, the views developing under the influence of the Enlightenment began to take hold in Judaism. The views and teachings of Moses Mendelssohn appealed to many, especially among Jews who had begun to move in cultivated European society. Synagogal services began to reflect such influences, and the liturgy underwent some modifications. In the 1840s rabbis who were sympathetic to such changes met in conferences to try to achieve a common stance. Predictably, some were more radical, others more moderate in what they wanted to see happen. For example, Abraham Geiger (1810–1874), a moderate, was willing to accept considerable changes so long as the core of Jewish tradition was upheld, while Samuel Holdheim (1806–1860) was inclined to throw out all ancient ritual and keep only a core of ethical monotheism. In the U.S., Rabbi Wise (1819–1900) was very actively instrumental in developing Reform Judaism in the middle of the 19th c., and the version of Reform Judaism, veering toward the radical side, was formulated in 1885 in the Pittsburgh Platform. Reform Judaism in the U.K. has been on the whole more conservative of Jewish tradition. The other principal divisions in American Judaism are the Conservative and the Orthodox. The latter try to uphold ancient ritual and practices, including the dietary laws, with extremely strict observance, while the Conservatives represent a middle-of-the-road position, valuing tradition more than do the Reform yet being less rigorous in interpreting it than are the Orthodox. The academic focus of Reform Judaism is Hebrew Union College, a four-campus institution of rabbinical learning with high academic standards and great openness to all forms of contemporary thought while also fostering the special kind of learning that has characterized the best in Jewish life for centuries. The four campuses are at Cincinnati, New York, Jerusalem, and Los Angeles.

Regeneration. According to traditional theology, Catholic and Reformed, the soul at Christian Baptism is spiritually regenerated (reborn) by being ingrafted into the Body of Christ, the Church.

Regensburg. See **Ratisbon, The Conference of.**

Regina Coeli. The Eastertide anthem so named after its opening words. It is ancient, probably dating from the 12th c., and addresses Mary as the Queen of Heaven, celebrating with her the joy of the Redemption resulting from her bearing of the Christ.

Regular Clergy. The designation applied to priests who belong to orders or congregations as distinguished from "secular" priests, i.e., those living in the world. They are called "regular" because they live under a specific "rule" such as that of Saint Benedict.

Reification. In philosophy, the fallacy of treating a mental (psychological) entity as though it were a thing (*res*). It is sometimes called hypostatization.

Reimarus, Hermann Samuel (1694–1768). Biblical scholar. Born in Hamburg, he was from 1727 till his death Professor of Hebrew and Oriental Languages there. He not only unequivocally rejected all concepts of the miraculous but charged the biblical writers with deliberate fraud and other offenses. He wrote two treatises defending "Natural Religion," i.e., religion shorn of its "supernatural" elements.

Reincarnation. The term means "reembodiment" or "rebirth" and is in principle synonymous with "transmigration" and "metempsychosis." Resurrection, a belief widely held, e.g., by the Pharisees and other Jewish groups and central to Christian faith, is of course a *form* of reincarnational belief. Reincarnation represents a view of the afterlife and of the nature and destiny of man that is found both in very primitive and in highly advanced forms. In primitive forms it may have little or no ethical element in it, but as developed in Hinduism, for example, it takes on deeply ethical consequences, being closely associated with the concept of *karma*, a strongly "freewill" concept. (See **Karma.**) In the Upanishads it is developed into a basic metaphysical view governing the thought, life, religion, and practice of the hundreds of millions of people in India. Typically it postulates that each individual has a self surrounded by a series of embodiments of which the physical one, the outer "shell," is the coarsest. At death this "shell" is discarded and, after more "shedding," the self is eventually reembodied, choosing its new embodiment according to the karmic law, i.e., according to the needs of the self for the process of spiritual evolution in which, like the rest of the universe, it is engaged. Its new embodiment will be determined by the *karma* it has accumulated, "good" or "bad." For example, a man who is cruel or insensitive toward women may need, in the next embodiment, a female incarnation; a lazy person may need a situation in which he or she must be forced by circumstance to be industrious; and so forth. This common way of presenting the working of the reincarnational process, governed by the karmic principle is, however, although basically correct, too much like that of a balance sheet and profit-and-loss accounting. It is in fact much more delicate and complex. For one may be helped by powerful and good agencies somewhat as grace plays an important role in the Christian life as well as do good works.

Buddhism inherits this upanishadic tradition with some modification, for since Buddhist thought does not recognize the existence of the self in such terms, the Buddhist will generally prefer to talk of the transmigration of karmic *states*, but the principle is very similar and affects the outlook and the lives of hundreds of millions of adherents of various forms of Buddhism throughout the world.

In Judaism, *gilgul* ("the turning of the wheel") was central to the Cabbalistic teaching about the destiny of the soul, which envisioned a variety of rebirths leading up to a final resurrection in a future age. In Hasidic Judaism, which has affinities with Cabbalism, reincarnation became a familiar concept appearing in much Yiddish literature and found, for instance, in the *Dybbuk*, a popular mystical legend, and in the writings of Sholem Asch.

Contrary to popular misunderstanding, reincarnation has a long history in Western thought. Pythagoras taught it, as did Plato, Plotinus, and others in antiquity. It was one of a number of beliefs about the afterlife that are to be found in the early stages of Christian thought, and although discouraged when not suppressed by the Church it prospered in various underground movements: in the crypt if not in the nave. Among the Bogomils it was an accepted teaching and among the Albigenses, who flourished so well around the 12th c. that until their eventual genocide they threatened to supplant the Church in southern France and parts of the north of Italy, reincarnation was a central doctrine. With the revival of humane learning that accompanied the Renaissance it came into great prominence, being represented in countless guises in the humanists and poets of that period of the revitalizing of European culture and thought. Since

then there are traces of it in more than half the poets and other writers as well as in the humane, Socratic tradition of philosophical thought; many of the greatest among men of letters (e.g., Emerson, Masefield, and Yeats) as well as among military leaders (e.g., Lord Dowding and General Patton) and statesmen, have been fully committed to it. See BIBLIOGRAPHY under **Afterlife**.

Relativism. The term is used in philosophy in a general sense to express the notion that no absolutes exist. One must distinguish, however, two applications: (1) As expounded from antiquity (e.g., by Protagoras) it signifies the notion that all knowledge is relative. For example, if two boys come into a moderately heated room, the one from the freezing outdoors and the other from an adjacent overheated room, and both are asked to put their hands into a bowl of water standing at room temperature, the one boy will say the water is warm and the other that it is cold. To a pedestrian, traffic passing at 40 miles an hour seems fast; to motorists riding at 70 it seems to crawl. All depends on one's stance. (2) In ethics, relativism is the doctrine that criteria for ethical judgments do not exist; therefore one cannot lay down absolute standards of "right" conduct. The rightness of an action depends upon the agent, upon the cultural milieu, upon the circumstances, and many other factors.

Relativity. The principle or theory of relativity is generally taken to be one or other of Einstein's: (1) his special theory of relativity, expressed in the celebrated formula $E = MC^2$, or (2) his general theory of relativity, which deals with space-time curvature. It should be noted that Einstein modified his theory (e.g., in a letter to Lincoln Barnett, June 19, 1948) and that of course relativity theory and quantum theory have both been modified since expounded respectively by Einstein and by Planck. But see also **Whitehead, Alfred North.**

Relics. The veneration of relics, i.e., material remains of a saint or objects connected with him such as parts of his or her clothing, is common in many religions. A highly popular Buddhist relic is in Kandy, Sri Lanka, in the Temple of the Tooth, believed to contain the tooth of the Buddha. In the Old Testament may be found several examples, e.g., the miracles wrought through the mantle of Elijah (II Kings 2.14), and in the New Testament we read of handkerchiefs that had touched Paul's body (Acts 19.12) and of their having thereby acquired healing power. By the 4th c. the Eucharist was celebrated over the tombs of the martyrs. Islam, which like early Buddhism, had no physical object of worship, developed a cult of relics. In the Middle Ages the abuse of relic-veneration became notorious. False relics were fabricated and genuine ones sold by the unscrupulous. The Church punished both of these activities by excommunication, but the evil trade persisted.

Religionsgeschichtlicheschule. "History of Religion School:" an important group of German biblical scholars toward the end of the 19th and in the early decades of the 20th c. who, in contrast to other groups such as those influenced by Albrecht Ritschl, sought to examine and use data provided by the study of all religions in interpreting the nature and meaning of Christianity. The emphasis of the school was on history and evolution. Its members taught that only through an understanding of how a religion evolved could one hope to grasp the meaning of what it says. The historical methods that this school advocated were those of historians such as Mommsen and von Ranke. Its emphasis on evolution was inspired in part by a Hegelian philosophical outlook, in part by the general trend toward evolutionary thinking that had deeply affected all aspects of European thought. Through the work of this school, many parallels to the stories recounted in the Bible were found in Egyptian, Hellenistic, and Babylonian lore.

Religious. In Catholic usage this term is used as a noun to designate anyone living under canonical vows of poverty, chastity, and obedience in a community and under a rule, whether as monks, nuns, friars, sisters, clerics regular (e.g., Jesuits), canons regular (e.g., Premonstratensians), or otherwise. Any such person is a "religious."

Remigius of Auxerre (*c*.841–*c*.908). Medieval Christian philosopher. Trained under Heiric at the monastic school of Auxerre he later taught at Reims and Paris. He wrote on Boethius and on Martianus Capella. Although not a particularly original thinker, he is important for his presentation of ancient materials in a form that was readily adaptable to the needs of his age.

Remnant. This term is used in the Bible to refer to that part of a conquered tribe which for one reason or another was spared from the destruction that the victors in war usually visited upon the vanquished. (See **War**.) Out of this commonplace usage was evolved a theological idea: the Israel that survives after conquest is God's remnant, which he has spared. The people will be largely destroyed, but a remnant remains to attest the power and love of Yahweh and his will for the eventual triumph of Israel as represented in the remnant. In Christian thought the idea is echoed in the sense that individuals experience in having been, e.g., in Augustine's phrase, saved *inter pontem et fontem* (between the bridge and the river) and in Wesley's as "snatched like a brand from the burning."

Remonstrance, The. A statement of Arminian teaching drawn up at Gouda in 1610. It is in five parts. It rejected various doctrines much associated with Calvinism, e.g., Supralapsarianism and Infralapsarianism (also known as Sublapsarianism), and the doctrine that Christ died only for the elect. The document, signed by forty-five ministers, was addressed to the States of Holland and Friesland. The Synod of Dort formally condemned the signatories in 1619. They were deprived of their livings and banished. The condemnation was withdrawn in 1630. The signatories were called "the Remonstrants."

Renaissance. Etymologically the word means simply "rebirth." It is used by historians to designate various epochs in human history in which some sort of cultural, religious, or other revival took place, e.g., the Carolingian Renaissance refers to events taking place in the wake of Charlemagne's activities in the 8th and 9th c. CE. It is most generally understood, however, to refer to the immense changes that took place in Europe from the 14th through the 16th centuries, more especially to the 15th c., which the Italians call the Quattrocento, i.e., the 1400s. The term, used with that reference, dates from just after the mid-19th c. The period of the Renaissance is taken to be that in which the medieval outlook was replaced by a new spirit entailing the revival of classical learning and culture and even a dedication to the lifestyles and outlook of Greek and Roman antiquity. The methods used by the medieval schoolmen were repudiated and, generally speaking, virtually everything medieval, including even Gothic architecture, tended to be denigrated if not despised. Platonism was revived, especially through the work of the Florentine Academy. Openness and a sense of wonder at the vastness that seemed to be presenting itself to humanity as never before were cultivated. The dignity and glory of man were among the themes celebrated. An interest in mysticism and esoteric ideas was developed. The intellectual outlook favorable to the development of modern sciences was fostered. The religious movement called the Reformation (see **Reformation, The**) was among other things a biblical Renaissance, i.e., it, too, was a reaction against the medieval reliance on "au-

thorities" and a movement that encouraged (as did the Renaissance) a going back to the sources, in this case the Bible. As the cultural Renaissance sought to return to the cultural roots of Europe, so the Reformation sought to return to the roots of Christianity: the biblical text.

Renan, Joseph Ernest (1823–1892). Orientalist and theologian. Born at Tréguier, Brittany, he was led by his study of Semitic languages and contemporary German theology to such a deep questioning of the truth of the Christian faith that he left the seminary of Saint-Sulpice, Paris. In 1852 he published a work on Averroism (*Averroës et l'averroisme*) that brought him swift recognition as a scholar. Some years later, having been sent on a mission to Palestine, he wrote there the *Vie de Jésus* which, published in 1863, brought him international acclaim. So controversial was the book, by reason of its total repudiation of the supernatural in Jesus, that his appointment as Professor of Hebrew at the Collège de France in 1862 was followed by his dismissal thence two years later. He wrote much else, mainly on biblical topics, including a 5-volume history of Israel. His autobiographical *Souvenirs d'enfance et de jeunesse* (1883) was very popular.

Renouvier, Charles (1815–1903). Philosopher. Born in Montpellier, he became the leading representative of Neo-Kantianism in France. While rejecting Kant's concept of the *Ding-an-Sich*, he accepted his phenomenalism. Among his writings are *The New Monadology* (1899) and *The Dilemmas of Pure Metaphysics* (1903). In general his view was relativistic. He strongly upheld human freedom, being opposed to all forms of determinism. In looking at history he liked to foster what he called *uchronie*, by which he meant imagining a slight change occurring at a critical point resulting in enormously different consequences. He believed in a form of human immortality.

Repentance. Deep sorrow for one's sin, accompanied by sincere purpose of amendment of life. The Greek word used in the New Testament is *metanoia*. The Latin used in the Vulgate and elsewhere is *poenitentia*, which emphasizes the element of reparation rather than the sense of sorrow that, if authentic, must issue in the desire to make reparation. See also **Contrition**.

Repose, The Altar of. In traditional Catholic usage, the altar to which, in a beautiful ceremony, dating from at least the 15th c., the Reserved Sacrament (see **Reservation**) is taken in procession after the evening Mass on Thursday of Holy Week (Maundy Thursday) and kept there while through Good Friday the tabernacle normally containing it is thrown open and the church stripped bare of its customary adornments, in token of the mourning of the faithful. Formerly the Altar of Repose was much adorned with lights and flowers and members of the faithful took turns in keeping watch over it through night and day, but in Roman Catholic usage since 1970 the extent of such elaborations has been left to the local parish priest.

Republic, Plato's See **Plato**.

Requiem. The term comes from the prayer for the dead (*Requiem aeternam dona eis, Domine*: "Rest eternal give unto them, O Lord") and is used of a Mass for the dead, which traditionally began with these words.

Rerum Novarum. An encyclical issued on May 15, 1891, by Pope Leo XIII, the purpose of which was to show how traditional Christian teaching about social relationships should be applied to the conditions prevailing at the time. While insisting on private ownership as a natural right, it approved the right of employees and employers to combine to protect their respective interests. It notably upheld the concept of a "just wage" by which was to be understood a wage sufficient to support the wage earner "in reasonable and frugal com-

fort," including his family, for the encyclical upheld the traditional view that ideally women should be at home and caring for the family. The encyclical came to be regarded as a landmark in the struggle for Christian social justice. On May 15, 1931, Pius XI marked the fortieth anniversary of Leo's encyclical by the issue of another, *Quadragesimo Anno*. This, while upholding the general principles of *Rerum Novarum*, emphasized both the evils of free competition and the evils of doctrinaire socialism. On May 14, 1971, Pope Paul VI published an Apostolic Letter on Christian social justice in which he updated both encyclicals of his predecessors by considering problems such as those presented by such evils as racial and other forms of discrimination.

Reservation. The custom of keeping the consecrated Bread of the Eucharist for later Communion dates from the earliest period in Christian history, being mentioned by the 1st c. Justin Martyr in his First Apology, chapter 65. The Fathers of the Church mention it frequently from the 2nd c. onwards. In the first centuries the faithful often kept the Sacrament on their persons and until *c.* the 13th c. hermits who lived a long distance from any church continued to do so, in order that they might receive Communion frequently. From the time of Constantine, however, the church became more and more the normal place for the Sacrament to be kept, sometimes in the sacristy, sometimes in a wall, sometimes in a pyx (see **Pyx**), sometimes in a tabernacle on the altar. By "Reservation of the Sacrament" is meant this practice.

Anyone entering a Roman Catholic or Anglican church can tell from the lamp perpetually burning in honor of the Reserved Sacrament where it is kept. It is usually convenient and liturgically preferable that it should be kept at a special altar, but this depends on local circumstances and the character of the church or chapel. In some places it is obviously best to have it in a tabernacle at the high or principal altar of the church; in other cases it may be more fitting to keep it in an aumbry or elsewhere. The practice of having the Sacrament reserved is, in any case, of singular importance to all who value Catholic tradition. It provides the faithful with focus on the Eucharist as the central reality of Christian worship. While it is customary to bow slightly before the Cross or Crucifix, as reminders or symbols of Christian salvation, one genuflects before the Reserved Sacrament as holding the Real Presence of Christ apart from which, from a Catholic standpoint, a church or chapel lacks the vitality that brings to the faithful the most joyous focus of their life in the Church.

Resurrection. The doctrine, central to Christianity and to be found in other religions, that the dead shall individually rise again in embodied form. It was already a belief taught by some in Judaism (e.g., by the Pharisees) before the time of Christ, although alien to classical Hebrew thought. Zoroastrian influences may have contributed to its appearance in later Jewish thought. It came to be prominent in Jewish apocalyptic. The nature of the embodiment according to Christian teaching is attended by considerable difficulties. In some of the Gospel accounts of the Risen Christ, he appeared in bodily form, so that Thomas could satisfy his doubts by putting his hand into Christ's side and feeling the wound in it and Christ could eat fish and honey in his risen state. Yet he is also represented as walking through closed doors and as vanishing from the disciples' sight in the beautiful story of his walking with some of them on the road to Emmaus. Paul, although accepting the Gospel accounts and attributing to the Risen Christ an embodied form, generally depicts the risen body (to be received by those who are to rise through the power of Christ) as a "glorified" one: a "spiritual" (*pneumatikos*) body, presumably of a finer and more luminous kind than the body of flesh and bones that we now have. The Muslim concept of the resurrection is one that has roots in Zoroastrian, in Jewish, and to some extent also in Christian teaching. Resurrection, as a view of the afterlife, is quite different from the notion of immortality as this is found in Plato and other philosophers; but the two concepts are not mutually exclusive. Resurrection has affinities with reincarnation in that both imply re-embodiment of one kind or another. See also **Reincarnation.**

Retreat. A period, usually of several days, spent in quiet, often but not necessarily with meditations under the direction of a "conductor." The practice, although it has antecedents, is currently much recommended in Christian devotional life having been especially advocated since about the 17th c. Under the influence of the Tractarians, the practice of annual or other retreats has been general among Anglicans. The first such retreat was held in Christ Church, Oxford, in 1856. Nowadays, in both the Roman Catholic and the Anglican Church, retreats are a well recognized part of the life of those wishing to live a life fully dedicated to Christ, who according to the Gospel records was accustomed to withdrawing periodically to a quiet place to meditate and to be alone with God. A retreat, whether accomplished on one's own or under a spiritual director or guide, is essentially such a withdrawal from the turmoil of the world to find the refreshment of at least a brief time of quiet recollection and the enjoyment of the peace of God.

Reuchlin, Johannes (1455–1522). Christian humanist. (See **Humanism.**) After studies in Greek and Latin he became a Master of Arts in 1477, studied law at Orleans and Poitiers, taking his degree in law in 1481. Some years later he began, with the help of learned Jews, to study Hebrew, which led him to an interest in Cabbalism, on which he wrote two works. His most useful work in terms of his time and circumstance was *De Rudimentis Hebraicis*, a Hebrew grammar and dictionary that for the first time stimulated the serious study of Hebrew by his Christian contemporaries. After publishing further works in Hebrew studies he became involved, along with other Christian humanists, in an acrimonious controversy with the Dominicans, whom they pilloried in the celebrated *Epistolae Obscurorum Virorum* (see entry under that title), a fiercely satirical work whose barbs were sharpened by the use of a style that ludicrously parodied the debased Latin of the churchmen of their time. The *Epistolae* became very popular among all capable of appreciating their thrust and they were instrumental in discrediting the scholastic method of disputation that was by then sadly deteriorating, not to say petrifying.

Reusch, Franz Heinrich (1825–1900). Old Catholic theologian. Closely associated for most of his life with Döllinger, his own teacher, he held a chair in Old Testament exegesis at Bonn from 1861. Having strongly opposed the decree on Papal Infallibility at the First Vatican Council (1869–1870), he was excommunicated by Rome in 1872. He took an important part with his friend Döllinger in organizing the Old Catholic Church. He was a diligent and prolific scholar and wrote extensively on post-Tridentine Roman Catholic Church history, on the Index of Prohibited Books, and on other controversial topics of the day. See **Döllinger, J.J.I.** and **Old Catholics.**

Revelation. This term, derived from the Latin *revelare* ("to unveil"), is an important theological concept, expressing a truth that is inaccessible to reason alone, although it may be consistent with reason. It is unfolded, disclosed, revealed by God, e.g., through the biblical writings that contain the truth, illumined by the action of the Spirit of God. The correlative theological term is "faith," the act of receiving and accepting the revelation. Some Christian theologians have made much of a distinction between general revelation and special revelation: God reveals himself in a more general way in the writings of noble men and women through the ages and the leaders of other religions, but in a special way in Christ as the "full and final" revelation of God. Karl Barth took the extreme position that the revelation that God gives in the Bible is such that there is not even an analogy between it and what is accessible to human reason. Emil Brunner, Barth's contemporary, held a more moderate opinion to the effect that there is a dialectical relationship between reason and revelation. All the three great monotheistic religions rely fundamentally on revelation as their cornerstone, and so the theological concept is central in all of them. The notion of revelation can be found, in various ways, in other religions too, since all imply some form of unfolding of eternal truth. In Judaism, Christianity, and Islam, however, revelation is so central and so fundamental that these religions would be meaningless apart from it.

Reverend. A title prefixed to the names of clergy. Ecclesiastical dignitaries are traditionally accorded titles such as "Very Reverend" and "Right Reverend" (*Reverendissimus*). Abbesses and other superiors in orders of women are addressed as "Reverend Mother." The title "Reverend" may be used with other titles, e.g., "The Reverend Father" and "The Reverend Doctor" or with the Christian name (e.g., "The Reverend John Smith"); but it should not be used with the surname only.

Revivalism. In the 1720s an international mass "Evangelical Revival" began that included evangelical groups such as the Moravians in Germany, and the Methodists in England. The emphasis was on a conversion accompanied by a vivid sense of experiencing a "new birth" and a moral commitment of dedication to Jesus Christ. Sociologically it was in general a "working-class" movement, but by no means exclusively. (See **Clapham Sect** and **Wilberforce, William.**) A sense of putting away a sinful life and of being "justified" by Christ saturated the experience. It was in great part a reaction against the rationalism of the 18th c. In the 19th c. a movement of this kind caught fire in America. Charles Finney (1792–1875) was among the first to develop special techniques for arranging such revivals on a large scale. Dwight L. Moody (1837–1899) and his musical associate Ira D. Sankey (1840–1908) were a successful team. Billy Sunday (1862–1935) was no less well known, and in our own time Billy Graham has been extraordinarily successful in large-scale organization of revivalistic campaigns of this kind. The Salvation Army's work was from the first conducted along such lines and was also from an early stage influential in achieving various social reforms. The approach represented by such revivalism, although never strong in Anglicanism, has been represented somewhat among Evangelicals within that Communion. Pentecostalism has to some extent replaced Revivalism as an expression of the kind of outlook represented in movements of this sort, but "hitting the sawdust trail" has remained an image deeply writ into the average person's understanding of Protestantism in America, the vast variety of other influences notwithstanding.

Revue Bénédictine. A learned periodical issued quarterly by the Benedictines of the Abbey of Maredsous, Belgium.

Revue Biblique. A learned periodical on biblical studies issued quarterly by the French Dominicans of Saint-Etienne, Jerusalem. Founded by Lagrange, it first appeared in January 1892.

Ṛgveda Saṁhitā. A collection of 1,017 hymns of praise arranged in ten books, the Ṛgveda (Rig Veda or Royal Veda) is the most venerated part of Hindu sacred literature, being regarded as the record of divine revelation. It also pro-

vides the best source of information about the social, religious, linguistic, and political development of India.

Rhetoric. The art of oratory, the aim of which is to persuade one's audience. In the West it seems to have been developed among the Sophists and so has an historic connection with philosophy, its relation to which was for long controversial although philosophers today would at best minimize any relation that might be seen between them.

Ricci, Matteo (1552–1610). Jesuit missionary in China. After studies that included special training in the natural sciences and mathematics, he was sent to Macao, where he studied Chinese language and culture. After various difficulties and misadventures he finally settled in Beijing, where he made many converts through the respect he gained both for his knowledge of European technology and for his skill in presenting Christianity to the Chinese in a form intelligible to them. Some, for one reason or another, disapproved his methods, especially his willingness to adapt the Christian message to Chinese culture, and after his death they were condemned by Pope Clement XI.

Richard of Saint-Victor. A 12th c. Victorine theologian and mystic. Among his many works, mostly on the interpretation of the Bible, his most important was that on the Trinity, *De Trinitate*, in six books. He adumbrated in some important ways the work of the 13th-c. schoolmen, insisting on reasoned argument in theological issues and deploring the common habit of relying on authorities. He carried this to the point of claiming that it is possible through reasoning to arrive at the doctrine of the Trinity.

Richelieu, Armand Jean du Plessis (1585–1642). Cardinal and statesman. One of the most powerful men in French history, he aimed at the establishment of absolutist government in France, in the pursuit of which he sought the destruction of the Hapsburgs, fought the Huguenots, opposed both the Jesuits and the Jansenists, and openly favored the independence of the French Church from Rome. By his great diplomatic skill he exercised immense influence in both Church and State. He was a generous patron of the arts and, in 1635, founded the French Academy that became one of the glories of France.

Riddle. This term is often used in the Bible to designate a wise saying, a profound aphorism. (See **Wisdom Literature, The.**) The Queen of Sheba tested Solomon by means of riddles (I Kings 10.1 and II Chronicles 9.1). The age-old problem, why the wicked prosper and the righteous suffer, is presumably behind the riddle in Psalm 49.5. Moses is noted for receiving the revelation of Yahweh in plain language, not in riddles (Numbers 12.8).

Ridley, Nicholas (*c.* **1500–1555**). Bishop of London. Having become, in 1537, chaplain to Thomas Cranmer, he succeeded Bonner in 1550 as Bishop of London. Inclined to support the Reformation cause, he fared ill under Mary Tudor, being excommunicated and eventually burned for heresy along with Latimer.

Rievaulx. One of the earliest Cistercian foundations in England, the abbey, about twenty miles north of York, is now in ruins apart from the very beautiful Early English abbey church, most of which remains. Founded in 1131, at the instigation of Bernard of Clairvaux himself, it became a great center of learning and devotion, with rich farmland and, in its heyday, a community of some 600 monks. The name means "rye vale."

Right and the Good, The. The term "right" comes from the Latin *rectus*, meaning "straight." It has affinities with the Greek words *dikē* and *dikaios*, which express the ideas of custom, that which is fitting. (Compare the Chinese *li*, which Confucius perceived as the outward expression of an inner harmony: that which pertains to propriety in conduct and good manners.) In the study of ethics, "the right" and "the good" are highly important terms. One may understand them respectively as "that which ought to exist as of its own right" and "that which one ought to do." Some ethical theories stress the one over the other, but each has an indispensable function. (See **Ethics**; also **Ross, William David.**) The plural, "rights," is used in social ethics, e.g., in the concept of "civil rights:" those rights that inhere in individuals in virtue of their citizenship. In a longstanding philosophical tradition, however, are recognized as even more fundamental those rights called "natural rights," which are traditionally held to inhere in a human being by virtue of his or her being human and irrespective of citizenship. It is to such rights that the American Declaration of Independence and other such documents refer. The concept of rights, whether natural or civil, entails correlative duties.

Ritschl, Albrecht (1822–1889). Protestant theologian. After studies at several German universities, he became Professor of Theology at Bonn and, in 1864, at Göttingen. He began as a follower of Baur and the Tübingen school, but in the maturer stage of his thought, he came to emphasize the theme that religion is irreducible to all other forms of experience. He insisted on faith as the religious category. All philosophical investigations and hypotheses are therefore irrelevant. He also insisted that the Christian revelation is to a community, not to individuals. Ritschl distrusted mysticism along with all other individual expressions of religion. His great emphasis was on the Church as the community of faith and he stressed the ethical consequences of participating in it. Many important Protestant theologians were influenced by him, e.g., Harnack, Troeltsch, Herrmann, and Kattenbusch. His main principles were enunciated in his 3-volume work, *Die christliche Lehre* (1870–1874). Among his later books, his *Theologie und Metaphysik* (1881) is especially important.

Ritual. In all religions, ritual of one sort or another plays an important role. Christian liturgists generally insist on a distinction between (1) ritual as a form of words and (2) ceremonial, a form of action. Generally, however, it is understood as a patterned form of behavior, generally communal and consisting of prescribed actions and words. Its functions include that of expression and communication. It is a special kind of language. While some forms of religion include highly elaborate ritual, others reduce the ritual element in religion to a minimum, but some ritual feature is always present, e.g., even Quakers sit when silent and stand when moved by the Spirit to speak. Sikhs, Muslims, Jews, Hindus, Buddhists, and Christians all have their respective forms of ritual, used in public worship.

Robinson, Henry Wheeler (1872–1945). Old Testament scholar and theologian. Trained for the Baptist ministry, he came to be recognized far beyond his own Church. His works include *The Christian Doctrine of Man* (1911), *The Christian Experience of the Holy Spirit* (1928) and *Inspiration and Revelation in the Old Testament* (1946).

Robinson, John (*c*. 1575–1625). Pastor to the Pilgrim Fathers. His early life is somewhat obscure but, probably after training at Cambridge, he was ordained in the Church of England. Being of Puritan sympathies, he was forced in 1608 to flee to Holland where he settled at Leyden. He assisted the Pilgrim Fathers in their preparation for their journey, although unable to join them on the *Mayflower*. His works include his *Apologia* (1619) in which he defended the principles of Congregationalism.

Roch (also Roque and, in Italian, Rocco). The 14th c. patron saint of the plague-stricken. His life is very obscure. According to one of his early biographers he was born at Montpellier, France. Having become a pilgrim, he found, on his way to Rome, some plague-stricken people at Aquapendente, many of whom he was believed to have cured by making the sign of the Cross over them. Eventually stricken, he withdrew to the woods where according to legend, his faithful dog brought him every day a loaf of bread. In iconography he is usually represented in the habit of a pilgrim, with wallet and staff, exhibiting a nodule on his thigh (the mark of the plague), and accompanied by his dog. He is often associated with Sebastian, a 3rd-c. martyr whose life is even more obscure but who according to legend was sentenced to be killed by arrows (he is so depicted in art), recovered , but was later clubbed to death. The association of Sebastian and Roch is not rationally explicable, since historically they have nothing to do with one another. Yet they are so frequently named together that one can almost map the course of the plague by the churches dedicated jointly to them. It is possible, perhaps even probable, that people likened the pain attending the plague to that caused by a spear or arrow and the nodules to the bite of a dog; hence, by a form of association in the popular mind of those times, they seemed together apt for the healing of the plague-stricken.

Rolle of Hampole, Richard (*c*.1300–1349). English mystic. Although details of his life are not entirely clear, it seems he was born in Yorkshire, did some study at Oxford, then left at the age of eighteen to become a hermit. He was a prolific writer on mystical experience and the value of a vocation to the hermit's life and also wrote biblical commentaries, poems, and letters of spiritual counsel. Many of his works were widely circulated in manuscript in the Middle Ages.

Roman Catholic Relief Acts. After the Reformation in England, and especially after the Gunpowder Plot, severe penalties and restrictions were imposed on Roman Catholics in Britain. (See **Recusants.**) These were mitigated by a series of enactments. By an act in 1778, they were permitted, on taking an oath that did not entail any repudiation of their religious beliefs, to own land. The punishment of life imprisonment, formerly imposed for keeping a Roman Catholic school, was abolished and in 1793 Roman Catholics in Ireland became eligible to vote and admissible to the universities and the learned professions. The most important of the series of such legislative acts was the Roman Catholic Relief Act of 1829 (10 Geo. IV, c.7), which removed almost all of the disabilities of Roman Catholics in Britain. The remaining ones were mostly removed in 1926. The law still excludes a Roman Catholic from the royal throne. Certain high offices of State also cannot be held by a Roman Catholic, e.g., the Lord Chancellor; nor, in the event of a regency, may the Regent be a Roman Catholic. Some other less conspicuous disabilities remain, but the vast majority of Roman Catholics are unaffected by them, so that for almost all practical purposes British Roman Catholics are as politically emancipated as is any other section of the population. See also **Gordon Riots.**

Romanes, George (1848–1904). Biologist. A Cambridge man and friend of Darwin's, he was a champion of Darwin's theory of evolution but dissented from other Darwinians whose emphasis on natural selection seemed to him narrower than was warranted and alien from Darwin's own position, since Darwin had allowed for the inheritance of acquired characteristics. His works include *Mental Evolution in Animals* (1883), *Mental Evolution in Man* (1888), and *Thoughts on Religion* (1895).

Romanticism. Towards the end of the 18th c. a movement so designated began in European arts and letters, in revolt against the neo-classicism of the 18th c.

It was expressed in many ways, e.g., in a renewed interest in human sentiments and passions. The novels of Victor Hugo and Sir Walter Scott expressed the new mood, which swept cultivated society all over Europe, where works of this kind had an enormous popularity. In painting and music, tastes similarly veered away from the classical to the romantic. In philosophy and religion an emphasis on the subjective began to be felt and was expressed in an extreme form in the work of Kierkegaard. There were elements of it in the revival of interest in medieval thought and life, which for long had been disparaged but now received much more attention, e.g., in the work of the Tractarians in England, such as J. H. Newman and E. B. Pusey. In Germany, Schleiermacher had a tremendous influence along such lines in Protestant theology and outlook, while in France, Chateaubriand drew attention to the cultural impoverishment that had attended the denigration of traditional Christianity. In Goethe is to be found a mixture of the two elements: the Classical and the Romantic, showing the importance of both for the fullness of the human spirit.

Rome, Early Christianity in. As soon as the Christian Way had spread to the Gentile world, it was inevitable that it should soon be represented in Rome, the center of the vast Roman Empire. By the time that Paul was writing his letter to the Christian community at Rome (*c.* 58 CE) a large community of Christians was already established there. The early tradition that Peter came to Rome in 42 CE is doubtful, but Paul certainly arrived there sometime between 59 and 61 CE and it seems that both he and Peter were martyred there in the general persecution of Christians under Nero in the wake of the great fire at Rome in 64 CE, which had been a pretext for the persecution of Christians whom popular superstition could blame for its occurrence. At any rate there is abundant evidence that the Church prospered at Rome, persecution not-withstanding, attracting people of all ranks, including not only patricians but members of the imperial family. The bishops who administered the affairs of this community of Christians at Rome can be reliably identified. They included Clement of Rome toward the end of the first century and Pius (c.141–154), brother of Hermas who wrote "The Shepherd," a book that is included in early Greek biblical codices although eventually not included in the New Testament canon. Until Victor (c.189), they were all Greek-speaking. None of these early bishops could be called a scholar or theologian; they were all church administrators. In these early centuries the Church at Rome acquired considerable wealth through benefactions and bequests of the rich among them, although there were confiscations of it in the Diocletian persecution, which broke out in 303. During the last century and a half of the Roman Empire (from the victory of Constantine to the fall of the Empire, from 313 to 476), the bishops of Rome asserted more and more an authoritative jurisdiction, habitually intervening in theological disputes and encouraging cases to be brought to them for decision. They were generally quite incapable of understanding the subtler points of Greek theological controversy, but they displayed a characteristically Roman sense of legal tradition and common sense. Inevitably, with the transference of the capital of the Empire from Rome to Constantinople in 330, the prestige and power of Rome diminished. Nevertheless, even this diminution in the political might of Rome made it possible for able popes (as the bishops of Rome were now being called), such as Gregory the Great, who reigned from 590 to 604, to assert a spiritual authority over the Christian Church. By the 7th c., however, relations between the Papacy in Rome and the Byzantine Emperors in Constantinople had begun to deteriorate. The Popes, now in danger of political subjection to their nominal overlords in Byzantium, began to assert a claim to what eventually became the claim to the "temporal power" of the Papacy: a controversy that remained lively down to the 20th c. See **Lateran Treaty**.

Romuald (c. 950–1027). Founder of the Camaldolese Order. A Ravenna nobleman, he became abbot of an Italian Benedictine monastery in 988, but on finding the life inadequately austere he retired to lead a hermit's life. Later he wandered round Italy, founding some thirty hermitages here and there. His foundation at Campus Maldoli became the center. Given him by a Count Maldoli, it is in Arrezzo in an Appennine valley not far from Florence and about 4,000 feet above sea level. According to tradition he was a man of a conspicuously happy countenance who made everyone around him happy. One legend tells that when he was being trained for his vocation his master used to box his right ear when he made a mistake in reciting the psalms. One day Romuald asked him if in future he might box the left one instead, because the right ear was becoming deaf with so much cuffing. This so amused his master that Romuald got no more such treatment to either ear. Be that as it may, the Order, a great but never very large one, is represented in the United States in the Hermitage of the Immaculate Heart of Mary, built on a magnificent site, the Lucia Ranch, about 50 miles south of Monterey at Big Sur, California, acquired c. 1958 and now flourishing. It is situated about five miles up a mountainside off the main road and commanding a spectacular view of the Pacific Ocean. The hermit-monks live in separate cells each equipped with a tiny living room, an altar, a workshop, a nook for study, and other facilities. See also **Camaldoli**.

Rosary. Since the 15th c. a tradition has persisted attributing the origin of this very popular Roman Catholic devotion to Saint Dominic (1170–1221) in his work against the Albigensians. The devotion, however, is of considerably greater antiquity than the age of Dominic, although he no doubt popularized it. The most general form of the Rosary devotion consists of meditation on each of fifteen mysteries connected with the Virgin Mary, five known as the Joyful, five as the Sorrowful, and five as the Glorious Mysteries. While one meditates on each of these in turn one recites the Lord's Prayer once, then the Ave Maria ten times, and finally the Gloria Patri. This constitutes what is popularly called a "decade" (ten) and normally one recites only five decades at a time, constituting together a "chaplet." The vocal recitation ought to be a mere background or accompaniment to the meditation on the mystery. In the physical object called a rosary, beads are provided to measure out the number of the prayers and so, indirectly, the length of the meditation upon each of the mysteries. Rosaries, however, may be adapted for other types of devotion, e.g., the twelve articles of the Creed. In Ireland, in penal days, when the practice of the Catholic faith was forbidden, a "thumb" rosary (*An Paidrin Beag*) was used, consisting of a simple ring for the thumb and beads for only one decade, which could be used while concealed in the hand. Replicas are now made in Connemara marble.

Roscelin (1050–1120). Medieval schoolman and Abelard's teacher. In the medieval controversy over the Universals he was one of the earliest to hold that the universal is a mere *flatus vocis*, a mere vocal sound, and it is from his enunciation of that view that the position came to be known as Nominalism, expressive of the belief that the universal is only a name, not in any sense an entity.

Rose of Lima (1586–1617). The first person from the Americas to be canonized by Rome. Her entire life was spent in Lima, Peru. She was canonized by Pope Clement X in 1671.

Rosetta Stone. In 1799 a basalt stele was discovered by a group of French soldiers near Rosetta on the west bank of the western mouth of the Nile. It provided Jean François Champollion "le Jeune," (1790–1832) with the clue to the deciphering of Egyptian hieroglyphics. (He is now generally acknowledged as the founder of Egyptology.) The decipherment dates from 1821. The Rosetta stone records, both in hieroglyphic and demotic Egyptian as well as in Greek, a decree of the priests assembled at Memphis in favor of Ptolemy V Epiphanes, who reigned 204–181 BCE. When Alexandria fell in 1801, the stone passed into the hands of the British authorities and it is now in the British Museum.

Rosicrucians. Early in the 17th c. two anonymous writings were published in Kassel, Germany, now assigned to a Lutheran pastor, J. V. Andreae (1586–1654). They recount a story of a Christian Rosenkreutz, who, it was claimed, had brought from the Orient in the 15th. c. esoteric knowledge of truths lying behind Christianity. The two books aroused such great interest that both Descartes and Leibniz sought to find out more about them. In the English-speaking world the best known representative was Robert Fludd (1574–1637), a London physician. The books called for the establishment of the Order of the Rosy Cross. A society was founded in Vienna, which spread through Germany, Poland, and Russia, accepting only freemasons and allying itself to masonic ideas and principles. It influenced many highly important people such as Friedrich Wilhelm II of Prussia. Many institutions today claim Rosicrucian ancestry, e.g., The Ancient and Mystical Order of the Rosy Cross (AMORC), which has headquarters at San José, California.

Rosmini-Serbati, Antonio (1797–1855). Italian philosopher and priest. Born at Rovereto of a noble family and trained at Padua, he was ordained priest in

1821. With papal encouragement, he undertook a renewal of Italian philosophy, including a systematic study of Thomas Aquinas. In 1828, following a suggestion of Maddalena di Canossa, who had founded a congregation called the Daughters of Charity, he established a congregation of priests called the Fathers of Charity, later sometimes known as Rosminians. In the course of his attempted reconstruction of Italian philosophy he attacked, in his *Treatise on the Moral Conscience* (1839), probabilism, so evoking the hostility of the Jesuits, who spread rumors of his being a Jansenist and a pantheist. (See **Probabilism.**) Some of his writings were temporarily placed on the papal Index of Prohibited Books. After his death his 5-volume work, *La Teosofia* (1859–1874) was examined and some forty propositions in it were censured by Leo XIII in 1887–1888. His system distinguishes degrees of being, with God as perfectly complete, and is founded on the concept that indeterminate being is innate in the human soul. He incorporated into his system various ideas from Plato, Augustine, Thomas Aquinas, Descartes, Kant, and Hegel. It is indubitably a system reflecting ideas of much interest to the theosophically minded. It had much influence in intellectual circles in Italy. The Rosminians, whom he had founded in 1828, received papal approval in 1838 and have spread to several countries, as has a women's branch, the Sisters of Providence, founded in 1831.

Ross, William David (1877–1971). British philosopher. Born in Scotland, he was associated for many years with Oxford, where he was a Fellow of Oriel College from 1902–1929 and Provost from 1929–1947. He was highly regarded for his philosophical work, especially in Aristotle and in the field of ethics. As a moral philosopher he was an intuitionist. In distinguishing the right from the good he saw the former as pertaining to acts, the latter as pertaining to motives. (See **Right and the Good, The**) He may be said to have anticipated aspects of modern Situationism in ethics by recognizing conflicts in moral duties, e.g., when telling the truth and preserving human life are in conflict, how is one to deal with the situation? Ross, borrowing from the language of jurisprudence, taught that in such a case one's *prima facie* duty would be the preservation of life. He held that man intuitively perceives, at least to a great extent, how to rate his duties when they seem to be in conflict.

Rossetti, Christina Georgina (1830–1894), English poet, the younger sister of Dante Gabriel Rossetti. The first of her poems appeared in the *Germ*, the organ of the Pre-Raphaelite Brotherhood, which her brother had helped to found. Many of her poems reflect a very deep Christian spirit and almost all of them, including those that treat of "secular" themes show immense sensitivity to language as an expression of the finest feelings of the human soul. Her religious books include *Seek and Find* (1879) and *Time Flies* (1885). "In the bleak mid-winter," one of her hymns, is still familiar to Christians throughout the English-speaking world.

Rossetti, Dante Gabriel (1828–1882). Poet and painter, he was among those who founded the pre-Raphaelite Brotherhood in 1848. In early life he was deeply influenced by Dante. "The Blessed Damozel" (1847) expresses that influence strikingly. The medieval spirit that he sought to recapture in his paintings somewhat eluded him, but they do exhibit a unique quality. Much affected by the death of his wife in 1862, his work from that point onward is injured by great melancholy pessimism.

Rota Sacra Romana. The regular tribunal for cases brought to the Holy See of the Roman Catholic Church. It dates from the 13th c. In its present form, its judges (*auditores*) must be priests who are doctors in both civil and canon law. It is nowadays best known for the matrimonial cases (e.g., nullity cases) that come before it. The name is said to be derived from the round table used by the judges in the 14th c. when the papacy was at Avignon.

Rousseau, Jean-Jacques (1712–1778). Philosopher. Born in Geneva, he adopted France as his home. Brought up privately and with little formal education, he was very much a romantic before Romanticism had become the mode. His fame came in 1750 when he published an essay that had won him a contest at the Academy of Dijon on whether letters and sciences had affected moral conduct. He was on terms of friendship with many of the greatest men of the day, both in France and abroad. Some credit him with providing some of the intellectual stimulus for the French Revolution, but Rousseau was temperamentally too ambivalent about almost everything to have any such direct influence on any concrete political event. Still, many elements in his political thought are conformable with progressive ideas in his time. His theories in *Social Contract* (1762) and other writings are based upon special and, many would contend, unwarranted assumptions such as his view of the natural goodness of man when uncorrupted by civilization. Yet many of Rousseau's ideas are highly original and not least those in the philosophy of education, expressed in his *Émile* (1762). His *Confessions* (1782) is a classic in autobiography and of immense psychological interest and importance.

Routh, Martin Joseph (1755–1854). Patristic scholar. As President of Magdalen College, Oxford, he strongly supported the traditional Catholic outlook in Anglicanism and was highly respected by the Tractarians, not least Newman. He is of special interest to Anglicans in the United States, since it was he who counseled Samuel Seabury to inaugurate an episcopal succession in the United States and to obtain it through the Scottish Episcopal Church.

His *Reliquiae Sacrae*, a collection of pre-Nicene patristic texts, was published in 4 volumes at Oxford, 1814–1818. It was thoroughly revised with the addition of a volume and the revised, 5-volume edition was published in 1846–1848.

Rowntree, Joseph (1836–1925). Quaker social reformer and philanthropist. Having entered his father's grocery business early in life he became, in 1883, head of the great cocoa and chocolate business, Rowntree and Company, in which capacity he pioneered a movement to assure workers reasonable hours, provision for unemployment and old age, fair wages, and generally humane conditions. He also promoted adult education.

Royce, Josiah (1855–1916). American philosopher. He was trained at Berkeley, California and Johns Hopkins University, where he received his doctorate in 1878. He also studied at Göttingen under Lotze. Royce was for long the principal exponent of Idealism in American thought. He sought to show a movement from the finite and fragmentary character of "ordinary" experience to the Absolute. This view he first expounded in *The Religious Aspect of Philosophy* (1885), but in his later works he honed his thought to encompass special problems attending his position. For example, in pessimism he came to see a failure to find the ideal that all men instinctively seek and expect to find. The fact, however, that they seek it and are disappointed at not finding it shows that there is an inner demand that is implicit and that can be satisfied. From the fact that we are prone to error cannot be deduced the position that the error is in the universe rather than in us. In *The Spirit of Modern Philosophy* (1892) he tried to exhibit the role of the will and how individuality and an infinite unity are reconcilable. In *The Conception of God* (1897) he sought to show that our fragmentary experience looks fragmentary because we are seeing only the fragment, not the whole of which it is a fragment. In his later works he developed a theory of humanity as "the Great Community" and his Idealism is transformed into what he began to call Absolute Pragmatism.

Rubrics. The directions in liturgical service books delineating the ceremonial actions to be performed at certain points were traditionally printed in red; hence the name, from the Latin *ruber* or *rubeus,* "red."

Rufinus, Tyrannius (*c.* **345–410**). Translator. Born near Aquileia, Italy, he went to Egypt *c.*372, where he studied under Didymus the Blind and was deeply interested in the work of Origen and his school. About this time knowledge of Greek in the West was waning. Rufus translated Origen's great work, *De Principiis,* into Latin. Unfortunately, his translation, now the only complete text of that work to survive, was a free one in which he seems to have rendered the original in such a way as to make Origen seem to conform better to the standards of doctrinal orthodoxy that were prevailing in the West at the time. Rufinus also translated other works, including some of Origen's biblical commentaries.

Ruh. The Muslim counterpart of the Jewish *ruach,* "spirit" or "breath," contrasted with *nefs,* the Muslim counterpart of the Hebrew *nephesh,* soul.

Runes. Runic symbols, each representing a sound and having a special name, were arranged in sets of eight. This set formed an alphabet called *futhark.* Runes were used by the Scandinavian and Germanic peoples from the 2nd c. CE till after the Viking age, which lasted from the 8th to the 11th c. CE. The god Odin was credited with having taught humanity runic lore, which conveyed messages, sometimes poetic, sometimes straightforward prose, but often magical. Ireland also used runic ("Oram") symbols, but these were based on the Latin alphabet.

Rūpa. In Sanskrit, literally "form" or "shape," somewhat like the Greek *eidos.* The formless *brahman* brought forth his own form spontaneously. In Hinduism the term is applied to iconographic representations of the gods, i.e., they are not natural formations such as rocks and mountains, yet neither are they the gods themselves. They embody the divine and so announce, so to speak, the divine presence beyond them. The unlearned may not be able to make the distinction, yet they understand in their own way. Only the vulgar outside spectator sees in such worship only "idolatry."

Russell, Bertrand (**1872–1970**). Born into an ancient English family (John Russell, the first Earl of Bedford was born in 1486) noted for their achievements throughout the ages and for their vehement, not to say headstrong, efforts for societal reform often far ahead of their times, as well as for their wealth and influence, Bertrand Russell had a lineage of unusual distinction in a remarkable diversity of ways. He was the third Earl Russell, whose grandfather, Lord John Russell, had been the only Prime Minister in the family and known as "Finality Jack" because of his immense belief in the Reform Bill (1831), which after great struggles he had eventually succeeded in passing through Parliament, so that early in 1833 the first "reformed Parliament" met. Bertrand, while fitting the family tradition of unpredictable individualism was unique in developing into one of the greatest philosophical and mathematical minds in the English-speaking world of the 20th century.

Having won a mathematical scholarship to Trinity College, Cambridge, with which much of the rest of his life was associated, he was the recipient of many honors. Elected to the Royal Society in 1908, he was awarded the rare distinction of the Order of Merit in 1949 and received the Nobel Prize for Literature in 1950. At least two and probably four stages may be discerned in Russell's intellectual and personal development. Beginning as a brilliantly gifted mathematician, he quickly developed his interest in mathematical logic. In 1916 he was fined for publishing a leaflet on conscientious objection at a crucial point in the war between Britain and Germany, then jailed for six months in 1918 for a further piece on the same topic. In philosophy his development was, however, complex. He began with the Idealist or neo-Idealist types of philosophy that were fashionable in his day but quickly and predictably lost interest in them and, along with G. E. Moore, he led the revolt against them in England. At the same time he was fascinated by Leibniz. In the *Principles of Mathematics* and the *Principia Mathematica* he developed a new system of logic. He proposed his famous theory of types to solve a contradiction that he had discovered in the idea of classes in which he held that a class is on a higher level than its members. He relied on a causal theory of perception although departing from it in his *Our Knowledge of the External World* (1914). In *The Analysis of Mind* (1921) he developed a form of neutral monism, according to which the world is neither "mental" as the Idealists held nor material, as had been supposed by the old-fashioned "materialists." It is, rather, composed of a neutral stuff which, when organized in one way yields physical objects and when organized in another way yields minds. Russell's views on political philosophy are expressed in many of his writings, of which one of the most incisive is his *Power* (1938). The range of his thought, however, has few parallels and few philosophers in the English-speaking world have written philosophy so elegantly. He was married four times, had several children, and lived not far short of a hundred years. His literary output is too enormous to permit one to do justice to it in the scope of an article of this kind. One of his best books, however, is his *Human Knowledge* (1948).

Russell, Charles Taze (1852–1916). See **Jehovah's Witnesses.**

Russian Christianity. In the 10th c. CE, under Byzantine influence, Christianity came to Russia, being eventually sponsored by Vladimir (956–1015). It had its headquarters in Kiev. Monasticism spread rapidly. In the 15th c. the Church became autocephalic, i.e., a fully self-governing, independent Church within the Eastern Orthodox Communion. In 1589 Kiev was replaced by Moscow as the chief center of Russian Orthodoxy.

Ruth, The Book of. This short book in the Hebrew canon of the Bible is placed in the Writings. (See **Writings.**) The date of its composition is very probably after the Exile. The story in it is simple, pleasant, and peaceful. Scholarly opinion varies on the extent to which it is to be taken as historical, but most modern scholars regard it as fiction used as a literary device for showing the heroism of two women in their trust in Yahweh. That does not exclude, of course, the use of historical elements in the story.

Rutherford, Joseph Franklin (1869–1941). See **Jehovah's Witnesses.**

Rutherford, Samuel (c. 1600–1661). Scottish Presbyterian divine. Trained at the University of Edinburgh he became professor of Humanity in 1623. ("Humanity" was the name under which the study of classical languages and literature was known in the Scottish universities at that time.) Because of his having had a love affair outside of marriage he was deprived of his position. He underwent a religious conversion and in 1627 was appointed minister of a church in Kirkcudbrightshire. A book of his on divine grace, published at Amsterdam in 1636, incited controversy at a time when the Calvinist theology to which it conformed was not universally favored. He was deposed the same year but (such was the volatility of the politico-ecclesiastical climate of that century in

Scotland) only three years later we find him a professor at St. Mary's College, Saint Andrews, of which he became principal in 1647. In 1643 he was one of the eight Scottish Commissioners at the Westminster Assembly. A staunch defender of Scottish Presbyterian Church polity, his writings in its defense include *The Divine Right of Church Government and Excommunication* (1646). His *Lex Rex* (1644) was considered treasonable at the Restoration in 1660 and he was in fact charged with high treason but died before trial. He was an acrimonious controversialist. (Acrimony was customary in 17th-c. theological and ecclesiological disputes, not least among the Scots.) Yet Rutherford had a deeply religious spirit, expressed with great beauty and sensitivity in his devotional writings in which he lamented the follies of his youth and wrote with a passionate love of Christ in whom, in good Calvinist fashion, he placed his whole trust. Robert Louis Stevenson said of him that he "went to sleep with Christ as his pillow and awoke in Christ." At his death, when reminded of his achievements, he disclaimed all credit and glory. "I disclaim all," he is reported to have said, "The port I would be in at is redemption and salvation through his Blood." He is an impressive exemplar of the spirit of his age and circumstance, both in its narrownesses and in its deep sense of spiritual assurance that (paradoxically to some) incites those who have it in its authentic form to work harder, not at all to wallow in smugness.

Ruysbroeck, Jan van (1293–1381). Flemish mystic. Ordained priest in 1317, he established late in life, with the help of a few companions, a religious community devoted to meditation and the cultivation of the inner life. In the tradition of Meister Eckhart, he is generally regarded as one of the greatest of the medieval Christian mystics. His writings include *The Seven Steps of the Ladder of Spiritual Love, Adornment of* *the Spiritual Marriage*, and *The Spiritual Espousals*.

Ryle, Gilbert (1900–1976). An Oxford man, he was a leader in the movement that saw philosophy chiefly as a means of avoiding conceptual confusion and category mistakes. He thought that traditional metaphysics was notably afflicted by a copious number of such mistakes. He saw the mind-body dualism of Descartes as spawning a multitude of such mistakes through what Ryle regarded as the myth of "the Ghost in the machine." Probably his most influential book was *The Concept of Mind* (1949).

Ryobu-Shinto. This Buddhist-Shinto syncretism in Japan was fostered, at least in part, by the spread of Buddhist temples into remote rural areas of Japan. The cult was officially forbidden in the Meiji period (1868–1912) as derogatory to Shinto, the national religion of Japan, but religious syncretism is widespread in Japanese life so that forms of Ryobu-Shinto still prosper.

S

Sabatier, Auguste (1839–1901). French Protestant theologian. Professor at Strassburg University (1867–1873) and later at the Protestant theological faculty at Paris. Bringing modern methods of literary analysis to the study of the New Testament and, following the views of Schleiermacher, he interpreted Christian doctrine as the symbolization of religious feeling. His writings include *Outlines of a Philosophy of Religion* (1897) and *The Religions of Authority and the Religion of the Spirit* (1903).

Sabatier, Paul (1858–1928). French Calvinist pastor at Strassburg and elsewhere, he became widely acclaimed for his *Life of Saint Francis* (1893), which greatly stimulated studies of Francis of Assisi. He founded societies dedicated to this end, including, in 1908, the British Society of Franciscan Studies. The Roman Catholic Church put his *Life of Saint Francis* on the Index of Prohibited Books in 1894.

Sabbatarianism. Extreme observance of Sunday as a day of rest for Christians on the lines of Jewish sabbath observance has been virtually unknown except among the English Puritans and the Scots. From early in the 17th c., Sabbatarianism was so strong in Scotland that all recreation was banned, even reading of any but the most explicitly religious books, all travel other than to church, and all manual work that could possibly be performed ahead of time. (For example, shoes had to be cleaned and clothes prepared on Saturday evening and meals cooked so as to minimize if not totally exclude work on Sunday.) Both the English Puritans and the Scots regarded even going for a country walk on Sunday afternoon as a sinful act. After a Sunday mail pickup had been introduced, some Scots would not even mail a letter on Saturday after the last pickup on that day, since doing so would implicate them in the mailman's dishonoring of "the Lord's Day." Such attitudes survive even to this day in some of the remoter islands of Scotland, as do other survivals of 17th c. attitudes. See **Free Presbyterian Church of Scotland.**

Sabbath. The seventh day of the week (Saturday) according to the Israelite calendar and strictly observed by orthodox Jews to this day. Observance of Sabbath (*šabbat*, rest) as a day of rest from labor may certainly be dated as far back as the monarchy. How much earlier than that it was observed is uncertain, but it is unlikely to date as far back as Moses. A nomadic people could not easily have observed it. Critical scholars today generally regard the attribution of sabbath observance law to Moses as retrojective, i.e., sabbath observance in the form that became generally recognized and accepted in Hebrew society could not date as far back as Moses, although some form of Sabbath recognition

might have occurred as early as that. The rigor with which the Sabbath was observed by the time of Jesus was the result of a cumulative process. The rabbis themselves disputed moot points on the subject, but lighting a fire, slapping one's thigh, and jumping are examples of what would seem to many today as picayune prohibitions yet were generally recognized as forbidden to Jews.

In modern Judaism, the Sabbath rituals include the lighting of at least two candles by the woman of the household before sundown on Friday evening (when the Sabbath begins), the *kiddush* or sanctification which is recited over wine on Friday evening and at the time of the mid-day meal on Saturday, and the *havdalah* with blessings recited over wine, spices, and a lighted candle on Saturday night, marking the end of the Sabbath.

Sabellianism. In the 2nd and 3rd c. a theological movement occurred to safeguard the concept of the Unity of God, which is essential to orthodox Christian teaching. Those who subscribed to the movement in either of the two forms that it took were commonly called Monarchians. One group held that the only differentiation in the Godhead is a succession of modes or operations. These were called Modalistic Monarchians, sometimes also Patripassians (because their teaching implied that God the Father suffered, which was accounted heretical), and sometimes Sabellians, after Sabellius, one of the leaders among the Modalistic Monarchians. See also **Patripassians.**

Sach-Khand. In Sikh tradition, one who faithfully pursues the discipline of the meditation technique known as *nam simaram*, which includes the repeated naming of the divine name (Nam), obtains *mukti* (liberation) and eventually, if only after many rebirths, will attain Sach-khand: the realm of truth in which harmony reigns. In popular belief this highly mystical concept is often understood as a place of bliss whither one *may* go immediately after death. So popularized, therefore, the concept becomes very similar to the popular Christian understanding of heaven. See **Sikhs.**

Sackcloth. In biblical usage the term refers to a fabric used for clothing proper to a variety of circumstances, e.g., mourning, penitence, national disaster, or personal grief. It was a rough sort of fabric such as is used for bags to carry grain, as jute is widely used today.

Sacrament. From the Latin *sacramentum*, "oath," a misleading rendering of the Greek *mystērion*, "mystery." A sacrament is defined by St. Thomas as "the sign of a sacred thing in so far as it sanctifies men" and in the English Book of Common Prayer as "an outward and visible sign of an inward and spiritual grace. . . . " The Eucharist is the Christian sacrament *par excellence* and constitutes the day-to-day sacramental life of the Church. Baptism, as a sacrament, has also a unique place, since it is the means of initiation into the Church as the Body of Christ. Other rites, however, including marriage and ordination, are recognized as having a sacramental character. In Catholic theology certain accessories used in the sacramental life of the Church (such as vestments, altar lights, holy water, ashes, and oil) and pious practices (such as grace at meals) are sometimes called "sacramentals." Traditionally, in both East and West, Catholic usage has recognized seven sacraments: Baptism, Confirmation, the Eucharist, Penance (Confession), Extreme Unction, Holy Orders, and Holy Matrimony.

Sacramentary. In the Western Church, the liturgical book used down to the 13th c. for the celebrant at Mass and for some other liturgical purposes was called the Sacramentary. The old sacramentaries (e.g., the Leonine, Gelasian, and Gregorian) are of great importance to liturgical scholars in tracing the history and development of usages.

Sacred Heart. Catholic devotion to the Sacred Heart of Jesus can be traced as far back as Bernard in the twelfth century; but it was for long restricted to a special circle of mystics. Later, in the sixteenth century, it was fostered by the Carthusians as a more general devotion. In France, both the Jesuits (founded in 1540 by Ignatius Loyola) and the Visitandines (an order of contemplative nuns founded in 1610 by Francis of Sales) fostered the devotion, for which Jean Eudes tried to provide a theological foundation. The visions of Margaret Mary Alacoque, a Visitandine, immensely popularized the devotion throughout the Roman Catholic Church, in which it came to be permitted by Pope Clement XIII in 1765. In 1856 in honor of it Pope Pius IX proclaimed a special feast of the whole Church.

Sacrifice. The offering of a gift to God. It occurs in the most primitive and in the highest forms of religion. Human sacrifice was practiced in many primitive societies, and there are echoes of it even in the Old Testament, where, however, animal sacrifice was a regular part of temple worship, being only temporarily suspended after the Exile in 586 BCE and briefly by Antiochus Epiphanes in 168 BCE until the destruction of the Temple in 70 CE. The chief annual sacrifice was that of the Paschal Lamb at the Passover in each household. The Old Testament prophets and the psalmists, however, remind the people that the best sacrifice is that of the heart, given in love and gratitude to God inwardly. Jesus, while accepting sacrifice as part of the customary traditional ritual of his people, also emphasized the importance of inwardness in the sacrificial act. Jesus Christ is frequently represented in the New Testament as the "perfect" and "eternal" sacrifice to God. This concept, exaggerated though it was in medieval theory and practice, is held by both Roman Catholic and (with some exceptions) Anglican churchmen to be essential to the life of the Church and is of the utmost importance in contemporary Catholic theology and practice.

Sacrilege. Although the term is popularly used in a loose sense, it can be more strictly defined in traditional usage in Catholic moral theology. It consists of the violation or contemptuous treatment of a person, thing, or place, e.g., irreverently or jestingly receiving Holy Communion, making a mock confession under pretext of engaging in the Sacrament of Penance, committing a sin (e.g., fornication) in a church or other consecrated place. Killing or seriously injuring a priest, monk, or nun, is a very grave form of sacrilege.

Sacring Bell. (Also known as the Sanctus bell.) A bell used at the Elevation of the Host and Chalice at Mass. The practice dates from the 12th century.

Sacristy. A room adjoining or near a church or chapel set aside for keeping the vestments, liturgical books, and sacred vessels and for the clergy to vest. The practice goes back to at least *c.* 400 in the Syrian Church and came to be general in the West in the Middle Ages.

Saddhā. This Pali term (Sanskrit *sraddhā*) is translated "faith" and plays an important role in the Buddhist scheme at all stages. It may take several forms, some with more intellectual, others with more emotive content, but it is taken to be an essential element in all forms of Buddhism. In some forms of Mahayana Buddhism (especially the Amida sects) a doctrine of salvation by faith has been developed in a way that seems to approximate to some understandings of the role of faith in popular Protestant Christianity.

Sadducees. A party within Judaism in the time of Jesus. Comparatively little is known about them beyond what is reported in the New Testament and in Josephus. According to Acts (23.6–8) they did not believe in the resurrection from the dead (as did the Pharisees); nor did they believe in angels. Apparently they did not recognize tradition in the way it was recognized by the mainstream of Judaism, looking, rather, directly to the Torah.

Sahidic. One of the chief dialects of the Coptic language. The Scriptures were translated into Sahidic probably as early as *c.* 200 CE. Many papyrus fragments and biblical manuscripts in Sahidic have been found and are of importance for biblical scholarship.

Saint-Cyran, Abbé de (1581–1643). One of the leading Jansenists. (See **Jansenism.**) His name was Duvergier de Hauranne, but he is almost always cited as Saint-Cyran. He worked with Jansen and was closely associated with the Arnauld family and with Port-Royal. See **Port-Royal.**

Saint-Denis, Abbaye de. See **Denys.**

Sainte-Chapelle, La. The chapel built in Paris *c.* 1245 by Saint Louis IX to house the Crown of Thorns and other relics of the Passion. Desecrated during the French Revolution, it was restored in 1837 to religious purposes. It still contains much priceless medieval glass, some of it having undergone 19th-c. restoration, and is one of the very finest examples of Gothic architecture, if not indeed the finest in the world. It was the work of Pierre de Montereau.

Saint Helena, Order of. An Anglican order for women, founded in 1945. The Mother House is in Vails Gate, New York, sixty miles north of New York City. Members take the usual vows of poverty, chastity, and obedience.

Saint Patrick's Purgatory. A place of pilgrimage in Ireland since early in the 13th c. It is on Station Island, Lough Derg, Donegal. According to an ancient tradition, Saint Patrick saw a vision there according to which a plenary indulgence would be granted to all who made the pilgrimage thither, together with a glance both at the bliss of heaven and at the torments of the damned.

Saint Paul's Cathedral, London. Ethelbert, King of Kent, built a church *c.* 607 as a cathedral for Saint Mellitus, the first Bishop of London. Toward the end of the 7th C. it was rebuilt in stone. It perished in a great fire in 1087. A new cathedral in the Norman style was begun that same year and completed in 1332, being then the largest building of any kind in England, 690 feet long with a spire almost 500 feet high and covering an area of 3 acres. Destroyed in the Great Fire of London in 1666, it was rebuilt, beginning in 1675 and completed in 1710. The design was that of Sir Christopher Wren, who watched the building process from his house on the other side of the Thames. It is in the classical style although with a traditionally Gothic ground plan. The interior (over 84,000 square feet) is in a restrained form of Baroque, enhanced by woodwork by Grinling Gibbons and ironwork by Jean Tijou. It contains both the Chapel of the Order of the British Empire and that of the Order of Saint Michael and Saint George. Both Nelson and Wellington are among those buried in the crypt, as is also Wren, his place adorned with the famous inscription: *Lector si monumentum requiris circumspice* ("Reader, if you require a monument, look around you"). The surrounding area of Saint Paul's was almost entirely destroyed by German bombs in 1940, but the Cathedral, although not unscathed, was spared.

Saint Peter's Basilica, Rome. The largest Christian church in the world, containing the remains of more than 130 popes, it was built over the traditional burial place of Peter. A basilican structure had been erected by Constantine early in the 4th c. on the site believed to have been the site of the place where Peter had been crucified. The "Old Saint Peter's" where Charlemagne had been crowned on Christmas Day, 800, fell into disrepair in the later Middle Ages. Nicholas V, in the 15th c., planned to replace it, and under Julius II the first stone was laid on April 18, 1506. The new basilica was completed in 1614 and consecrated on 18 November 1626 by Urban VIII. The baldachino over the high altar is supported by the famous spiral columns by Bernini. The area of the basilica is over 160,000 square feet, almost twice that of Saint Paul's Cathedral, London, and considerably more than twice that of Hagia Sophia, Istanbul. The dome rises 308 feet above the roof and is 630 feet in circumference.

Saint-Simon, Claude-Henri (1760–1828). French philosopher. Born in Paris, he was educated privately by d'Alembert the Encyclopedist and other tutors. Sympathetic to the American and the French Revolutions, he renounced his title of nobility and worked for a positivist and socialist philosophy, having among his disciples Auguste Comte. His writings include *The Reorganization of European Society* (1814) and *The New Christianity* (1825). Seeing the Christianity of his time as outmoded and fossilized, he sought to promote a new form of it shorn of traditional teachings and focused on the brotherhood of man.

Saint Sophia. See **Hagia Sophia**.

Saint-Sulpice. See **Sulpicians**.

Sakkos. A liturgical vestment worn by bishops of the Eastern Orthodox Churches, similar in form to the dalmatic in the Western Churches and probably dating from *c.* the 11th century.

Śakti. In Hinduism, divine power or energy personified as female, contradistinguished from the passive function attributed to the male aspect of divinity as represented in Śiva, although in a few passages of Hindu Tantric works an active function is assigned to Śiva and a passive one to Śakti.

Sākyas. The tribe into which Gotama the Buddha was born in the region now known as Nepal. Their chief town,

Kapilavatthu, is that in which Gotama spent his childhood and youth.

Salat. The name designating the sequence of utterances and actions that together make up Muslim worship. Salat is one of the "Five Pillars of Islam." It is performed five times a day. Its performance with other Muslims in a mosque is to be preferred, but it may be performed alone and anywhere. It is expected of all able-bodied believers and is of obligation on Fridays.

Salesian Method. A method of Catholic devotion, similar, to, but less formal than, that of the Jesuits. Developed in France in the seventeenth century, it owed its inspiration to the teaching of Francis of Sales (1567–1622), Bishop of Geneva. The Salesian movement was characterized by an emphasis on the notion that the mystical life is not restricted to special classes like monks and nuns, as had been commonly supposed, but is accessible to ordinary people living in the world.

Salesians. An important Roman Catholic congregation of priests and teachers founded in the region of Turin in 1859 for the education of poor boys. After the approval of the rule in 1874 by Pius IX, the congregation spread rapidly throughout much of the world. A similar congregation of teaching sisters was begun in 1872 and has also flourished.

Salisbury. The diocese of Old Sarum was founded in 1075 as the result of the union of two other dioceses in the southwest of England. A cathedral was built there but a new one was begun at New Sarum or Salisbury in 1220 and completed in 1266. It is one of the purest examples of the Early English style. The spire, built between 1334 and 1350, is the tallest in England and has been regarded by Ruskin and others as the most beautiful. Salisbury developed a special liturgical rite known as the Sarum Rite, which modified the Roman Rite and spread from Salisbury to other English dioceses. By the mid-15th c. its use had extended to almost all of England, Ireland, and Wales. Some English cathedrals and parishes have revived the use of Sarum.

Salvation. Basically, salvation signifies rescue or release from an imperfect or evil state. Those religions that prominently emphasize salvation as their fundamental aim are sometimes called "salvation religions." They claim to provide a way or path to wholeness, i.e., *salus:* health. In Christianity, the conditions for salvation are provided through the Atonement, by which Jesus Christ has reconciled God and man (at-one-ment). The individual, in order to appropriate the fruit of that Atonement, must receive grace to do so.

Salvation Army, The. Founded by William Booth in 1865, it was organized in more or less its present form three years later on its now distinctively military lines and headed by a "general." Since 1931 the General has been elected by the High Council, which consists of senior officers. The religious teaching is traditionally on Evangelical Protestant lines but with some distinctive emphases. Neither Baptism nor the Eucharist nor any other sacramental act is recognized, although a form of "dedication" is used as a sort of substitute for Baptism. Public testimony and repentance form a part of regular worship and the general temper of the meetings is emotional. Strict militaristic obedience is required of all. The social work of the Army is well known and has been very effective with an emphasis on ministry to the lowest and most neglected classes. Especially strong in England and America, it has spread through many other countries of the world.

Salve Regina. A very widely used and extremely popular prayer to the Virgin Mary, dating from at least the year 1100. It begins with the invocation: "Hail, Holy Queen, Mother of Mercy, hail, our life, our sweetness, and our hope." The traditional plainsong is very beautiful and is sung in many of the ancient Orders after Compline.

Samādhi. Intense contemplation of any object such as unites and even identifies the perceived object with the percipient. The term is used in Hinduism of any form of deep meditation involving concentrated thought. In Buddhism, *samādhi* is one of the three major elements in the "way" or *marga* through which enlightenment is attained. The other two are *sīla* and *paññā* (*prajñā*). In the Yogacarin school of Buddhism *samādhi* had also a special meaning: more trance than meditation.

Samaritans. In New Testament times the Jews regarded the Samaritans as a schismatic group. The enmity went far back into Israelite history: the Jews who had settled in Jerusalem after the edict of Cyrus in 538 BCE refused to recognize as authentic Israelites those who inhabited the region of Samaria. That is why in the Gospels we have several examples of the bitter hostility between Samaritans and Jews, e.g., the disciples were astonished that Jesus would even talk to a Samaritan woman at the well (John 4.27), and when Jesus was called a Samaritan (John 8.48) it was by way of insult. The force of the story of the Good Samaritan (Luke 10) lies in the teaching that love must extend to everyone—even Samaritans. Today some 400–500 Samaritans still exist and make their paschal sacrifice on Mount Gerizim, their holiest site, near Nablus, their foreheads daubed with sheep's blood. They have kept their identity throughout the ages, often in face of great hardships and difficulties.

Śambhu. In Hindu, Buddhist and Jaina literature, Śambhu is recognized as a beneficent aspect of Śiva in his function of presiding over new life.

Sāṁkhya. A dualistic Hindu philosophical school, attributed to the ancient sage Kapila. It is one of the six orthodox Hindu philosophical systems or "darshanas." Originally it was an atheistic school but later merged with a theistic one. It posits an eternally existing essence (*prakṛti*) from which everything except "soul" originated. Sāṁkhya teaches "discrimination," i.e., discernment of the difference between *prakṛti* (the material matrix) and *ātman* (the "real" self), as a means of attaining a realization of freedom and immortality. The liberating process requires more than intellectual study; it demands a lengthy course of spiritual training and rigorous meditation on the "real" self.

Saṁsāra. The cycle of birth and rebirth as understood in Hindu teaching. It is dictated by the karmic principle. (See **Karma**.) Saṁsāra implies bondage: only by the control of thoughts and desires can human beings overcome that bondage and be liberated in such a way as to transcend the cycle. Karma and saṁsāra imply both biological and spiritual evolution and a relation between human beings and lower forms of animal life such as imposes on the former the duty of compassion toward the latter: reverence not only for human but for all life. See **Ahiṁsā**.

Samuel. The stories in I Samuel relating to the individual bearing this name are so interwoven that it is impossible to obtain a coherent account from them as they stand. Apparently several traditions were pieced together, presumably in an attempt to conserve them all. At the same time Samuel was probably a complex character whose personality may have lent itself to the development of such a variety of traditions about him. The two books now known as I and II Samuel were originally one book. They contain not only an amalgam of narratives and historical interpretations but more than one theological interpretation, some representing the monarchy as a divine institution, others anti-monarchical. I and II Samuel are therefore a more than ordinarily complex part of the biblical literature.

Sanbenito. A yellow penitential robe with a red cross back and front, which those who had confessed heresy were required to wear by order of the Spanish Inquisition. See **Auto-Da-Fé.**

Sanchez, Francisco (1552–1623). Portuguese philosopher. Born in Braga, Portugal, he taught medicine at Montpellier and Toulouse. He sharply opposed the medieval methodologies in philosophy, especially the reliance on authorities such as Aristotle, and was highly critical of all that he found to be based on mere superstition. Epistemologically skeptical, he sought to show in perhaps his most characteristic work, *Quod nihil scitur* (1581) why, because of the notorious unreliability of the senses and the continual flux in the objects of sense experience, nothing can be known with any certainty. Scientific inquiry, however, can yield at least practically useful conclusions. His work is historically important in exhibiting the change that the Renaissance brought about in philosophical methodology.

Sancta Sophia. See **Hagia Sophia.**

Sanctuary. That part of the church containing the altar or altars. The term is also used in connection with the medieval principle of the "right of sanctuary" by which a criminal who had taken refuge in a church could not be removed from it and was permitted, after an oath taken before the coroner, to proceed to a seaport selected by the latter. He had to do so within forty days, after which he could be removed and taken for trial. Sanctuary could be either ecclesiastical or secular. Sanctuary for criminal acts was abolished in England in 1623, although it continued for another hundred years for civil processes.

Sanctus. The hymn of adoration sung or said immediately after the Preface of the Mass. It takes its name from the opening words: "Holy, Holy, Holy, Lord God of Hosts." It is of great antiquity, possibly going back to the 1st c.

Sanday, William (1834–1920). English New Testament scholar, trained at Oxford, he was influential in persuading Anglican clergy in his time to accept and use modern methods of biblical analysis. His writings include *The Gospels in the Second Century* (1876), *Inspiration* (1893), and *Christologies, Ancient and Modern* (1910).

Sandemanians. See **Glasites.**

Sanhedrin. The supreme court of justice at Jerusalem in the time of Jesus. Although its origins cannot be dated with precision, Josephus mentions it as having existed in the reign of Antiochus the Great (223–187 BCE). The word is Greek (*synedrion*) and means "council." Besides representatives of the higher dignitaries of the Jewish priesthood it also included among its seventy-one members other learned Jews. It had very extensive jurisdiction. After the destruction of the Temple in 70 CE it came to an end. Some of its functions were assumed by a group of Pharisees, first at Jamnia, later at Tiberias.

Śankara (c. 788 to 820 CE). One of the most notable of Indian religious teachers, whose exposition of Vedānta is a great Indian classic. Converted in 800 CE to the monistic doctrine of Advaita Vedānta, he was an independent thinker and of a resolute character. He took a vow of celibacy. His commentary on the Brahma-Sūtra is entitled Naiśkarmya-siddhi. Some Hindus, e.g., Rāmānuja, were so impressed by the seeming affinity of his thought with that of Buddhist philosophy that they charged him with being a sort of crypto-Buddhist.

Sānkhya. An alternative spelling of Sāṃkhya.

Sannyāsin. In Hindu tradition, one who has renounced worldly attachments and has chosen instead a strictly ascetic life either as a recluse or as an itinerant or mendicant.

San Paolo Fuori le Mura. (St. Paul's Outside the Walls). One of the four great basilican churches of Rome. See **Ostian Way**.

Sanskrit. The classic language of India (*saṁskṛta*), the name of which signifies the notion that it is perfectly constructed, being therefore the perfect literary, cultivated language. It is a language of the greatest scholarly importance and is taught in Indian and other universities throughout the world. It is written in the *devangārī* or "divine" script, developed from an earlier style (Brāhmī) and it reflects a very high degree of sophistication and subtlety of thought.

Santa Sophia. See **Hagia Sophia**.

Santayana, George (1863–1952). Philosopher. Born in Madrid of a Spanish father and an American mother, he was removed to Boston at the age of nine and eventually educated at Harvard where he later taught, having William James and Josiah Royce among his colleagues. When his father died in 1912 he found himself able to live independently and gave up teaching for a quiet, scholarly life in Rome. Not by any reckoning a systematic thinker, he combined a variety of philosophical stances in an ingenious and interesting way. He begins his philosophical inquiry in resolute skepticism and, somewhat in the spirit of Descartes, he decided that everything is susceptible to doubt, yet doubt itself must be doubted. In a sort of perverted echo of Plato he perceives the world as consisting of essences, yet he repudiates any attempt to deduce knowledge about these essences. In an aesthetic experience that is quasi-mystical in its nature, one can then see more sharply and clearly the quality of the essences, although with no knowledge of that to which, if to anything, they pertain. It is from the sheer animality of our nature that we are impelled to survive and this drive to survival carries us beyond mere luxuriating in a narcissistic enjoyment of beauty. From this one is forced to go on to see everything as generated from matter. Everything, however noble and however spiritual, has its source in matter. This standpoint, he is eager to show, does not in any way denigrate the realms of the spirit. He sees religion, however, as a sort of aesthetic activity. Temperamentally, he found great joy in the rhythm of religion. The bells, the incense, the plainsong, the entire elaborate, aesthetically coherent structure of the life of religion that he found in Rome was to him as necessary as is the sound of the waves to a sailor who, much as he may claim otherwise, cannot live for long without feeling the need for it that W. B. Yeats expresses in his famous poem *Sea Fever*. At the same time, however, he had no theological beliefs connected with such aesthetic joy in the rhythm of Catholic life and culture. In the last resort it is "animal faith" (*fe animal*) that propels man along. His prolific writings include his *Sense of Beauty* (1896), his *Life of Reason* (1905–06), and his *Realms of Being* (1927–40).

Sanusis. A Sufi order, founded by Muhammad al-Sanusi (1791–1855), which sought to foster a simple, purified form of Islam. It has had considerable influence in North Africa and the Sahara region.

Saracens. A name widely used by medieval writers of the Arabs in general and later applied pejoratively to the Muslim peoples against whom the Crusaders fought.

Sarcophagus. A stone coffin, often adorned with bas-reliefs and much used both in the pagan world and by Christians from early Christian times. Many are to be found in Ravenna and elsewhere in Italy.

Sarpa. In Hindu tradition a term applied by the Āryan settlers to the Indian indigenes. It means "creeping" or "crawling" and it was used in contempt of them as slithering along the forests like snakes.

Sartre, Jean-Paul (1905–1980). Philosopher. Born in Paris where he studied at the École Normale Supérieure, receiving his *agrégation* in 1929. After studying phenomenology and the thought of Heidegger at Berlin, he taught philosophy at various *lycées*. A prisoner of war from 1940 to 1941, he became a member of the French resistance movement during the German occupation of France. From *c.* 1945 he became the major representative of French existentialism. His outlook he expounded at first in novels and plays, e.g., *Nausea* (1938), *The Flies* (1946) and *No Exit* (1946). Among his philosophical works are his *Being and Nothingness* (1943), *Existentialism is a Humanism* (1946), and *Critique of Dialectical Reason* (1960). Foremost among the categories in his phenomenological analysis of the human situation is that of freedom. Man is free, but how shall he choose? On Sartre's view there is no distinction (such as is traditional in Western philosophy) between "essence" and "existence." When one asks who is the "father" of existence the answer must be *le néant*, "Nothingness." Man must create his own essence. He recognizes a distinction between an authentic and an inauthentic life. Since in his view there is no God and no absolute standard of ethical conduct, each person must choose what he or she is to be and live accordingly with total involvement. Borrowing heavily from Heidegger, he distinguishes between the *en-soi*, the existence of a thing, which exists in-itself, and the *pour-soi*, the existence of human beings who project themselves to values and aims. Sartre showed sympathy toward Marxism, yet the determinist element in Marxism is antithetical to the extreme insistence on human freedom that is at the root of Sartre's outlook. One should also note that he distinguishes the conscious self from the world (subject from object) in such a radical fashion as to produce a dualism that is insurmountable; hence the inevitability of the ensuing existential *angoisse* (*Angst*). Sartre remains, however, the most radical exemplar of nihilistic existentialism that the 20th c. has produced.

Sarum. See **Salisbury.**

Sāsana. The term most generally used in Buddhist countries in South Asia in referring to what westerners might call the Buddhist "religion." The term "Buddha-Sāsana" comprises both the sense of doctrine and that of conduct.

Sat. Term used in Hinduism to designate reality contradistinguished from *maya*, illusion. In the Sikh religion, God is called Sat Nam, the "true Name" or "Real Name," the One who reveals himself and his nature to those who meditate on his name.

Satanism. Historically, although there are stories of the perversion of the Mass by wicked or heretical priests and the connection of such perversities with witchcraft, Satanism as understood now dates from only the 19th c. Satanist cults do exist today, some much more malevolent and dangerous than others. The participants often consist largely of people who find pleasure or excitement in doing what they think is considered notably wicked.

Satī. An epithet applied encomiastically to a Hindu widow who, on the death of her husband, showed her devotion by throwing herself on his funeral pyre. Probably more often than not the self-immolation was performed not literally but only by mimesis, i.e., she lay down upon the pyre with him and was then led away by others before the fire was lighted. The practice seems to have gone into desuetude for some time and was then revived *c.* the 6th c. CE and continued among some primitive communities till it was formally declared illegal in 1829. The word has been anglicized as "suttee" and sometimes mistakenly applied to the act not, as it ought to be, to the widow.

Satisfaction. In traditional Catholic theology, contrition, confession, and absolution are essential elements in the process of sacramental forgiveness, but in addition satisfaction is required and is mentioned by Christian Fathers as early as the 3rd c. It may take the form of good works of any kind or of acts of self-denial. The severity varies according to the gravity of the sin. At first it was required before absolution by the priest, later the act of satisfaction prescribed could be performed after the absolution. Augustine mentions the case of David who, after Nathan had pronounced God's forgiveness, was required to make amends afterwards (II Samuel 12.13 f.). Where the sin has resulted in injury to another person, satisfaction includes the healing of that injury, so far as possible. An obvious example is that of theft: the stolen property must be restored or, if that is impossible, compensation must be paid to the injured party, directly or anonymously. It is not enough merely to perform some painful penitential exercise. Restitution is a duty.

Satori. The Japanese term for illumination as understood in Buddhism. In Zen it is the state of consciousness of the Buddha-mind. It is a state that Zen practitioners claim to be entirely indescribable and incommunicable. It liberates the unconscious forces of the psyche. The exercise called *kōan* can help one to achieve *satori*. See **Kōan.**

Savonarola, Girolamo (1452–1498). Italian Reformer. Trained at Ferrara, he entered the Dominican Order at Bologna in 1474. At Florence he acquired great fame as an outspoken and eloquent preacher against the vices of the clergy and the Florentine nobility. He prophesied the punishment of those who did not mend their ways. His strictness and rigor proved too much for some in high places, and in 1495 he was summoned by Pope Alexander VI to give an account of his preaching. Pleading ill health as preventing his journeying to Rome, he was forbidden to preach. He continued his preaching,

now directly attacking the Pope and the Curia, and in 1497 he was excommunicated. Savonarola perceived the excommunication as a sign that he was free of ecclesiastical legislation and publicly demanded the holding of a General Council of the Church to depose the Pope. By this time, however, many had turned against Savonarola. He was imprisoned and, under severe torture he confessed that he had acted from motives of personal vanity or aggrandisement: a confession that he quickly retracted after the torture. He was eventually hanged in the marketplace.

Scala Santa. A stairway near the Lateran church in Rome, consisting of twenty-eight steps of Tyrian marble. According to the legend, they are the steps that Jesus descended, which were brought from Jerusalem by Saint Helena. They are now covered with wood and are a popular place of pilgrimage. Pilgrims ascend them step by step on their knees.

Scallop Shell. See **Compostela.**

Scapular. A rectangular piece of cloth worn over the shoulders and hanging down in front and back, usually about 15–18 inches wide and reaching to near the hem of the monastic habit. Benedict required his monks to wear it for manual labor. Miniature versions of the scapular are worn by tertiaries (see **Tertiary**) and others as a symbol of their attachment to a religious order although living in the world and as a constant private reminder of their special dedication to God.

Scheler, Max (1874–1928). Philosopher. Born in Munich, he was educated at Jena and taught there. He was much influenced by Husserl and Brentano. He began his philosophical thought as a phenomenologist, but having experienced a religious conversion that brought him to Catholicism, he entered into a phase in which his phenomenological methods led him to a more religious orientation in his thought. In the last stages of his thought he became more pantheistic in his understanding of the relation between God and the world. He never founded a school in any strict sense, and despite the maturing of his thought he cannot be said to have ever abandoned his early intuitions and phenomenological methods. His works include *On the Phenomenology and Theory of Sympathy* (1913), *On the Eternal in Man* (1921), *The Place of Man in the Universe* (1928), and *Distinguishing World Views* (1929).

Schelling, Friedrich Wilhelm Joseph (1775–1854). Philosopher. Born in Leonberg (Würtemberg), he was trained at Tübingen where Hegel and Hölderlin were among his fellow students. He taught at various German universities, finally at Berlin. The philosophical spokesman for German Romanticism, he was in close sympathy with his friends Goethe, Schiller, Schlegel, and Novalis. Beginning as a subjective idealist, his interest moved to the philosophy of nature, seeing nature as self-creative, motivated by a vitalistic force. Moving on to a more transcendental form of idealism, he saw the Absolute as revealed in history. The Absolute then began to play an even more important role in his thought as he moved toward a more pantheistic outlook reflecting in some ways a sort of Spinozistic tendency. In the final phase of his thought he was more ready to recognize a basic contrast between God and the universe and to see polarities even within God. He also became more interested in the nature and value of myth. He saw God as evolving through the persons of the Trinity: a development of Fichte's triadic thesis-antithesis-synthesis, which had influenced his earlier thought. His works include *Ideas for a Philosophy of Nature* (1797), *System of Transcendental Idealism* (1800), *Philosophy of Religion* (1804), and *Of Human Freedom* (1809).

Schism. As used in ecclesiastical contexts, schism is a formal and intentional separation from the unity of the Chris-

tian Church. It is technically distinguished from heresy in that while a heretic is doctrinally separated from the Church, a schismatic is not necessarily separated in that way. Schisms often arise as a result of a longstanding quarrel between parties in the Church. See **Great Schism, The.**

Schleiermacher, Friedrich Daniel Ernst (1768–1834). German theologian. Trained at Halle, he was ordained to the ministry in 1794, after which, as a preacher at Berlin, he was much influenced by the Romantic Movement as well as by a variety of philosophers including Spinoza, Leibniz, and Kant. In 1799 he published his *Reden:* one of the most famous, influential, and controversial religious works in Christian history. Arguing that religion is by its nature founded upon intuition and feeling (*Anschauung und Gefühl*) and independent of all doctrinal questions and formulations, he sought to bring back "the cultured despisers" of religion to an appreciation of it. Later, having occupied academic positions at Halle and Berlin, he published his greatest work, *Der christliche Glaube* (The Christian Faith) in 1821–1822. Here he argued that religion consists essentially in a feeling of independence (some of his critics were to contend against him that in that case a dog is more religious than a man) and that Christianity, although the highest form of religion, has no monopoly of truth. A basic objection to his view of religion as feeling is that it makes religion subject to a calculus of emotion such that the finer or deeper the feeling the better the religion and *vice versa*. Such a view sets aside the independent ontological reality or otherwise of that which the worshipper worships, which religious thinkers have generally taken to be the most fundamental of all religious questions. Feeling is of course a concomitant of religion; but it might even be a concomitant of the work of the mathematician, although that certainly would not reduce mathematics to feeling. Nevertheless, Schleiermacher is indubitably one of the most provocative of religious thinkers.

Schlick, Moritz (1882–1936). Philosopher. Born in Berlin and trained there, he taught at various universities including Vienna, coming to be acknowledged as a leader of the Vienna Circle of logical positivism, for long a potent force in 20th-c. philosophy. He drew attention to the basic tasks that the logical positivist school had to face: (1) exhibiting the basis of scientific knowledge, i.e., the logic of the sciences—how they may be shown to establish their findings, and (2) the clarification of philosophical language, using positivistic criteria to purge traditional philosophical language from what, from a positivistic stance, are regarded as its ambiguities and obfuscations. His works include *Space and Time in Contemporary Physics* (1917), *Philosophy of Nature* (1949), and *Aphorisms* (1962).

Scholia. Explanatory, critical, or grammatical notes in the margins of ancient manuscripts. The practice of inserting such notes was standard in classical antiquity and was followed by Christian scholars from early times. The singular form of the Greek term is *scholion*.

Schoolmen. Name given to the teachers of philosophy and theology in the medieval universities or schools such as Paris and Oxford. Thomas Aquinas and John Duns Scotus are eminent examples. After the passing of the Golden Age of scholasticism (the 13th c.), the use of the methods that had served so well in their time sometimes deteriorated into trivializing, bringing the methods themselves into disrepute.

Schopenhauer, Arthur (1788–1860). Philosopher. Born in Danzig, he was trained at Göttingen and Berlin. Profoundly influenced by Plato and Kant, he was probably the first European philosopher to draw from Buddhist sources which in his time were still very imperfectly understood in the West. His phi-

losophy glorified will, which he saw as primary and over everything. Since man's ideas are a representation of his will, so the world itself is a representation of the cosmic will. As man's will is "blind," so is the cosmic will: an unconscious striving force. Yet through the contemplation of what are in effect the Platonic Ideas, one may achieve a release by separation from the domination of will, cosmic and human. Aesthetic appreciation provides further release, more especially music, but such release is temporary. To achieve permanent release from the bondage one must renounce the will to live, which must be done through compassion for others to the point of renouncing individual selfhood: a concept borrowed from Buddhism. His best known work is *The World as Will and Idea* (1819, enlarged 1844). Other works include *On the Will in Nature* (1836) and *The Two Basic Problems in Ethics* (1841).

Schweitzer, Albert (1875–1965). Born in Kaiserberg, Alsace, and educated at Strassburg, he was an extraordinarily versatile genius: a concert organist, an important authority on Bach, a philosopher, a theologian, an influential New Testament scholar, and a medical man who devoted his life to building and serving a hospital in Lambaréné in French Equatorial Africa. His many writings include *Paul and His Interpreters* (1912), *Philosophy of Culture* (1923), *Civilization and Ethics* (1923), *Christianity and the Religions of the World* (1923), *The Mysticism of Paul* (1931), and *Out of My Life and Thought* (1933). In his epoch-making book, *The Quest of the Historical Jesus (Von Reimarus zu Wrede)* (1906) he undertook a detailed review of previous attempts at interpreting and writing on the life of Christ and concluded that none of them had penetrated to the core of the problem.

His view was that Jesus had shared with his contemporaries the expectation that the world was coming to an end soon and that when this expectation was unfulfilled in his lifetime, he felt that he must suffer ignominious death so that his people might be saved from the tribulations that would attend the last days. Schweitzer applied similar principles to the writings of Paul. Such views evoked much opposition, but he greatly influenced the thought of Christian theologians in both Europe and America. Although he had an immense regard for human personality and the importance of ethical principles such as Kant's categorical imperative, he perceived that man is part of a stream of evolutionary development. Soon after his arrival in the tropics he was on a long river journey when there came to his mind a phrase that he felt encapsulated the most essential element in all his thought, which expressed a feeling that he had instinctively experienced from his earliest childhood: *reverence for life*. Deeply influenced by Indian thought, he saw all life as hanging together and he held that no ethic is adequate that is confined only to humanity. He received the Nobel Peace Prize in 1953.

Scientia Media. A term coined in the 16th c. by the famous Spanish Jesuit theologian, Luis de Molina, in an attempt to reconcile human freedom with divine foreknowledge. *Scientia media* ("mediate knowledge") is, on the view he proposed, the knowledge that God has of things that are not now but that would be if certain conditions were realized. They are intermediate between mere possibilities and actual occurrences in the future. This "mediate knowledge" is independent of the decree of God's will. The Thomists repudiated this view. See **Molina, Luis de.**

Scientism. A derogatory term used to denote the view of those who inordinately value the findings of natural sciences such as physics and chemistry as if they had a special kind of authority beyond their own fields. The term is sometimes used synonymously with "positivism."

Scientology. A form of psychotherapy propounded in 1950 by its founder, L. Ron Hubbard, in his book *Dianetics*. The movement he founded developed into one having more of a religious orientation. It came to be known as the Church of Scientology. Its aim is to liberate the true, spiritual self from harmful accretions. The movement has met with vigorous opposition from mainstream religious bodies as well as from the governments of both the U.S. and the U.K.

Scintilla. A term much used in various traditions of Christian mystical literature (especially in Eckhart's works) to designate an element in the soul that makes possible its mystical union with God. The term means "spark". See also **Synderesis.**

Scone. (Pronounced *skoon*.) An ancient Scottish religious focus near Perth and at one time the capital of the Pictish kingdom. In 908 the Scottish King Constantine held an assembly here at which he swore to protect the Church. He recognized the Bishop of St. Andrews as Primate. The Kings of Scotland, from Malcolm IV in 1153 onwards were crowned at Scone, seated upon the Stone of Destiny. This stone, on which the Keltic kings had been crowned was carried off by the English King Edward I to Westminster Abbey in 1296 as a prize of war. On Christmas morning, 1950, a group of young Scottish nationalists who had apparently entered the Abbey before closing time slipped out the following morning, presumably with a rubber-wheeled contraption or the like, noiselessly carrying off the precious slab, a block of red sandstone 26 x 16 x 10 inches. By extraordinary good luck they were able, despite expert vigilance by the authorities on every road in the nation, to convey the stone to a hiding place in Scotland. It was eventually recovered by skillful government sleuths and restored to Westminster Abbey where it is now protected by maximum security arrangements. The dramatic story is told in Ian Hamilton, *No Stone Unturned* (1952).

Scotism. The system of scholastic philosophy expounded by Duns Scotus (see **Duns Scotus**) as distinguished from Thomism, expounded by Thomas Aquinas. Thomism has been traditionally favored by the Dominican Order, Scotism by the Franciscans.

Scots Confession. (Latin, *Confessio Scotica*.) The first Confession of Faith of the Reformed Kirk of Scotland. Adopted by the Scottish Parliament in 1560, it was the sole confessional standard of the Kirk till it was superseded by the Westminster Confession in 1647. The work of John Knox and some of his associates and reflecting his Calvinistic interpretation of Reformation principles, it affirms the Calvinist doctrine of election and claims that the True Kirk is Catholic, consists of the elect, and that outside of it is no salvation. Its marks are the right administration of the sacraments and of discipline. The Confession, while condemning the medieval doctrine of Transubstantiation, maintains the Real Presence of Christ in the Sacrament of Communion. It emphasizes both the rights and the duties of civil magistrates, especially their duty to uphold the Kirk. It recognizes the Word of God as revealed in the Scriptures to be the supreme authority for Christians. A supplemental confession, sometimes called the *Confessio Negativa*, was issued and accepted in 1581, expressing opposition to the Roman Catholic Church in sometimes bitter terms.

Scotus, Duns. See **Duns Scotus, John.**

Scotus Erigena. See **Erigena, John Scotus.**

Scourge. The term is used in the Bible in both a literal and a figurative sense. In the latter it may mean any kind of misfortune or trial afflicting an individual or a people. In the literal sense a scourge was an instrument of punish-

ment by whipping. Whipping was a very general form of punishment in the ancient world and indeed persisted widely down to comparatively recent times, e.g., as a judicially ordered punishment it was commonly administered in England down to its abolition in 1948. References to the use of the scourge are comparatively rare in the Old Testament, probably because, as in other societies in antiquity, its use was taken for granted. The number of strokes was limited to forty (Deuteronomy 25.1–3): possibly a humane reform of earlier practice. The form of the instrument is not specified but it was probably a horse whip. Roman Law prohibited the scourging of Roman citizens, but it was a common punishment for slaves and could be ordered also for non-citizen provincials. Two instruments were used: (1) the *fasces*, a bundle of rods used in the lesser punishment called *verberatio*, which Paul claims (II Corinthians 11.24) to have received five times at the hands of the Jews, and (2) the *flagellum*, a terrible instrument consisting of leather thongs sometimes reinforced with metal inserts, for use in the punishment called *flagellatio:* the punishment inflicted on Jesus. This terrible form of whipping not only must have been excruciatingly painful; it was sometimes, perhaps often, fatal.

Screen. In church architecture a screen is a partition of iron, wood, or stone separating a church or chapel into two or more parts. A screen separating the chancel from the nave and surmounted by a cross is called a rood screen. ("Rood" means "cross.")

Scribe. In few if any societies in antiquity were the skills of reading and writing widespread among the general populace. For one thing, the systems used were often difficult to master. So a professional scribal class emerged. Since the scribes, being the learned class, could control the flow of information, they inevitably acquired a great deal of power. They were often also, as in Egypt and Mesopotamia, associated with the rise of the Wisdom literature. (See **Wisdom Literature, The.**) Probably David organized his administration on the Egyptian model, and so the scribe would emerge as a standard functionary at his court. The scribe, like the lawyer, could acquire a bad reputation. So we read (Jeremiah 8.8.) that "the false pen of the scribes has turned Yahweh's law into a lie." The Jewish scribe was not a member of any politico-theological party as were the Sadducees and the Pharisees. In the Gospels, scribes are reported to be frequently hostile to Jesus and his teachings and he, while ascribing to them authority such as that ascribed to Moses, reproaches them for so interpreting the law as to impose undue, not to say impossible, burdens, making the Kingdom of Heaven practically beyond reach. Yet he enjoins his disciples to exceed the scribes' righteousness if they are to hope to attain that objective. Not all scribes, however, were of such a character as to evoke Jesus' reproach, as is shown from several passages, e.g., Matthew 8.19; 12.28–34; 13.52. It is likely that some scribes were among the early Christians.

Scriptorium. Before the invention of printing by movable type in the 15th c., manuscripts had to be copied by hand. The room set aside for this purpose was called a scriptorium. A group of, say, a dozen monks could copy simultaneously from the dictation of a reader seated at a desk in front of them. A particular monastery often developed a characteristic script of its own: a great help to palaeographers in determining the provenance and the date of a manuscript.

Scruples. In Catholic moral theology the term designates the fears that trouble ultrasensitive people over picayune or imaginary sins. Experienced priests can usually recognize such dispositions in the confessional, which are to the spiritual director somewhat as hypo-

chondria is to the physician. A prudent director will deal with them patiently and compassionately but discourage discussion of them and try to get the penitent to focus on the real impediments to his or her spiritual progress.

Seal of Confession. The secrecy of what is uttered by the penitent in the confessional is absolutely inviolable. The priest is bound by the most solemn canonical obligation not to disclose directly or indirectly anything he hears in confession in any circumstances, no matter what pressure may be put on him by secular authorities or otherwise. To illustrate the care required of the priest in exercising his duties in the administration of this sacrament of the Church, the following story is told. A French countess was giving a very grand party to which a few of the guests had arrived early, including a distinguished cleric. To make conversation, the hostess remarked on the curiosity that lay people have about what a priest hears in the confessional. "But, Monseigneur," she went on. "Priests tell me that the curiosity is unwarranted since it's all rather dull and routine: the usual sins of the flesh, the little deceptions, and so forth." "Yes, Madame la Contesse," he replied, "no doubt that is in general very true. It so happens, however, that when I was a young priest thirty years ago the first confession I heard was that of a man who confessed to murder." The guests began to pour in and introductions were made. When one of them was introduced to the priest he shook hands amiably, saying to the hostess, "No need to introduce *us*, Madame la Contesse. We are old friends. In fact I was Monseigneur's first penitent." The story is told to exhibit the extreme care that a priest must exercise in safeguarding the sanctity of the confessional.

Sebastian. A Roman Christian martyr, traditionally supposed to have been put to death during the Diocletian persecution in 303. A later legend represents him as having been shot by arrows, and this is how he is depicted in iconography in which he is a favorite subject in medieval and Renaissance painting. See **Roch.**

Second Coming of Christ. See **Parousia.**

Secular Clergy. The term has been used since the 12th c. CE of priests who belong to no monastic or other religious order or society but live in the world. Not bound by religious vows, they may own property. They are, however, subject to the bishop under whose jurisdiction they exercise their priestly duties. Roman Catholic priests of the Latin rite are bound to celibacy. Secular priests are also called diocesan priests.

Seder. A Jewish ritual meal connected with the Passover. See **Passover.**

Sede Vacante. The period during which a diocese is without a bishop so that the diocese must be otherwise administered during the vacancy, e.g., in the case of a vacancy in the papacy the administration of the affairs of the Roman Catholic Church is vested in the Cardinal Camerlengo: the member of the College of Cardinals upon whom this responsibility falls during this period.

Seeley, John Robert (1834–1895). Trained at Cambridge, he published in 1865 a life of Jesus (*Ecce Homo*) in which he attempted to represent Jesus as an ethical teacher and reformer, ignoring all theological questions. The book, written in a very readable style, was immensely popular in Victorian times. He was appointed professor of modern history at Cambridge in 1869. His other works include *Natural Religion* (1882): an attempt to reconcile Christianity with natural science.

Sephardim. Jews of Spanish or Portuguese origin who toward the end of the 15th c. were expelled from the Iberian peninsula. Since they were generally cultivated and had been exposed to

Christian and Islamic cultures as well as their own, they tended the Jewish communities in which they settled in North Africa, the Near East, the Far East, and northern Europe. Jews who claim the Sephardic heritage are usually very proud of it. By contrast, the Ashkenazim, Jews from central and eastern Europe who in the early Middle Ages had been in the Franco-German Rhineland (the name "Ashkenazi" originally meant "German"), from which they spread eastward to Russia and Poland, tended to be more ingrown in their ways. While there was no important theological difference between the Sephardim and the Ashkenazim, their outlook and their traditions differed considerably. The Ashkenazim eventually developed Yiddish as a convenient means of communication. Jews today tend to be predominantly of Ashkenazi stock although Sephardic Jews abound in modern Israel.

Selah. This word occurs seventy-one times in thirty-nine of the Psalms. Its meaning is not known for certain. It is generally taken to be a musical notation. As such it is of course ignored in reading or singing.

Self-Immolation. The practice among Buddhist monks of burning oneself to death, countenanced in the Sanskrit treatise *Saddharma-Puṇḍarīka Sūtra,* which was translated into Chinese early in the 3rd c. CE, is ancient, with many famous examples between the 5th and the 10th c. CE. Generally speaking both Hinduism and Buddhism disapprove of suicide, but the authority of the Buddha himself is invoked to justify it in some very special circumstances. For example, a monk named Godhika attained a state of spiritual release called *samādhika-cetovimutti* six times successively, but each time he fell away from it. The Buddha apparently approved of his then immolating himself in order not to fall away from it again. This, however, is plainly a very extraordinary case not affecting the general disapproval of suicide in the major religions of the world. See **Suicide**.

Sellars, Roy Wood. (1880–1973). Philosopher. Born in Canada, he taught at the University of Michigan from 1905–1950. Sellars argued that all philosophical method should begin with the "plain man's Natural Realism" but should develop along the lines of the "Critical Realism" school of which he was one of the leaders. Sellars and the Critical Realist school generally contend that awareness is not an awareness of objects but of *sensa*, i.e., what is given through the senses.

Semantics. This term, widely used in a vague, popular sense, comes from the Greek *sēmantikos*, which in turn comes from the Greek *sēma*, a sign. It has been used by philosophers in several different technical senses. Philosophers have generally understood semantics to be the study of the relations between signs and the objects that they designate. Quine divided semantics into the theory of meaning and the theory of reference. Semantics has been closely allied to the study of linguistics.

Semi-Arianism. In the history of Christian thought this name is given, perhaps somewhat misleadingly, to a group of theologians who from *c.* 356 taught a christology lying between that of the Arians and that which was regarded as orthodox, although they veered much more to the latter than to the former, and their influence contributed considerably to the doctrinal decisions reached at the Council of Constantinople in 381: one of the most generally recognized determinations of orthodox Christian teaching. Among the Semi-Arians were Basil of Ancyra and Macedonius of Constantinople.

Semi-Pelagianism. In the 5th c., while the controversy between Augustine and Pelagius still raged over the question of grace and freewill, some theologians took what they claimed to be a mediating position: while grace is essential for salvation, the first step in the salvific process, antecedent to grace, consists in the resolves of individual men and women. Cassian of Marseilles was a leader in this movement, which was widely supported, especially in Gaul. Only when condemned by the Council of Orange in 529 did these teachings give way to Augustinian orthodoxy and indeed in the Middle Ages a sort of unofficial crypto-Pelagianism prospered among the masses, giving rise to the kind of emphasis on "good works" that the Reformers decried. The term "Semi-Pelagian" is of much later vintage but is now used for convenience to describe the position of those who supported this theological movement.

Seneca, Lucius Anneus (3–65 CE). The leading Roman exponent of Stoicism in imperial Rome. He was Consul under Nero. Writing in a style easily understood and appealing to reason rather than emotion, he taught a straightforward ethic entailing restraint of the passions and fairness to one's fellow human beings. Stoic ethics much influenced Christian concepts of ethical conduct.

Sense-Datum. In philosophy, that which is given directly in awareness. The term is a modern one, introduced by the highly influential English philosopher G. E. Moore early in the 20th c., and the concept was adopted with modifications into epistemological discussions.

Separatists. A term applied to the followers of Robert Browne (*c.* 1550–1633), an English Puritan, and his followers and later to the Congregationalists and others who separated themselves from the English Church.

Septuagint. The most influential of the Greek versions of the Hebrew Bible. Modern scholars generally take it to be the work of several Alexandrian Jewish translators over a lengthy period of time, being probably completed some time in the second century BCE. It includes various writings that circulated among Greek-speaking Jews and that are now designated in the English Bible as the Apocrypha—for example, books such as Wisdom and Ecclesiasticus. Commonly designated by scholars as LXX, it is of immense importance in biblical study, not least since it was the version generally accepted by the early Christian Fathers as the standard form of the Old Testament. The New Testament writers themselves quoted from it.

Sepulchre, Holy. See **Holy Sepulchre, The.**

Sergius. The 7th-c. Patriarch of Constantinople and notable exponent of Monothelitism. Two Synods at Constantinople in 638 and 639 respectively approved his teaching which was, however, condemned by the Council of Constantinople in 681. See **Monothelitism.**

Sermon on the Mount, The. What has come to be known as "the Sermon on the Mount" consists of the text as recorded in Matthew 5–7. It includes the Beatitudes and the Lord's Prayer as well as a series of ethical injunctions. A similar but shorter form recorded in Luke 6.20–49 is sometimes called "the Sermon on the Plain." Modern scholars generally take both of these to consist of collected sayings remembered by the compiler as characteristic of the teaching of Jesus: aphorisms typical of the wisdom he sought to impart, rather than an address or sermon actually delivered in the form in which it has been assembled.

Servetus, Michael (1511–1553). Born in Navarre, he was trained at Saragossa and Toulouse. As a result of his study of the Scriptures he concluded that the doctrine of the Trinity was unwarranted and he wrote a treatise in 1531 repudiating it. Such was the shock of this among his theologian friends that he went to Paris to study medicine, eventually becoming a physician to the Archbishop of Vienne, France, 1541–1553. He conducted a secret correspondence with Calvin, who also rejected his proposal to dismiss the doctrine of the Trinity. In 1553 he anonymously published his *Christianismi restitutio* in which he expounded in detail his entire theological system. Besides denying the doctrine of the Trinity, he repudiated the traditional understanding of the Divinity of Christ. A friend of Calvin's drew the attention of the Roman Catholic Inquisition to this book and its author. Servetus was imprisoned but escaped to Geneva. Calvin, however, did nothing to help him and he was burned as a heretic later in 1553.

Servites. A religious order founded in 1240 by seven rich Florentines. They followed a rule based on the Augustinian rule and wore a black habit. It was formally approved by Benedict XI in 1304. A Second Order (nuns) was founded *c.* 1285. The Servites give a special devotion to the Virgin Mary and have a special rosary of the Seven Sorrows of the Blessed Virgin, which they recite regularly.

Servus Servorum Dei. One of the titles of the Pope (meaning "servant of the servants of God"). It was used by Gregory the Great (590–604) and its use has been general since the late 11th century.

Seth. An ancient Egyptian deity represented as a pig-like animal, whom the Greeks identified with Typhon. His followers opposed those of Horus, Isis, and Osiris. In Plutarch's Myth of Osiris (*c.* 100 CE), Seth appears as the embodiment of evil. The cult of Osiris, however, generally prevailed.

Seven Liberal Arts. See **Liberal Arts, The Seven.**

Seventh-Day Adventists. A group of Protestants who expected the Second Coming of Christ to occur in 1844. They observed Saturday as the Sabbath. Although nowadays they put no date to the Second Coming they insist that it is imminent. They tend to read the Bible in a special, literalistic way. They tithe, baptize by total immersion, require total abstinence from alcohol, tobacco, and other drugs, and recommend abstinence from meat, coffee, and tea. They observe the Sabbath similarly to the way in which it is observed by Jews, from Friday at sundown. The name they adopted dates from 1861. See **Sabbath.**

Sexuality and the Christian Way. Long before Freud drew attention to the perception of religion as a special form of sublimation of the sexual drive in men and women, a connection between sexuality and religion had been amply recognized, e.g., in Plato's treatment of the Eros myth. Probably all religions perceived it in one way or another; hence the importance that is attached in virtually all the great religions of the world to controlling the sexual impulse. In Hinduism, which incorporates both very primitive and very highly developed religious ideas within its spectrum, are to be found extremes of attitudes toward sexuality, ranging from worship of the *lingam* and the *yoni* (the male and female genitalia respectively) on the one hand, to the ascetic ideal of total renunciation of sexuality, on the other. Both Jews and Christians inherit in the Bible a sharp awareness of sexuality as an aspect of human consciousness that is inseparable from religious awareness.

Behind much of the biblical and other religious heritages lies a recognition that human beings are in a divided state, i.e., men and women, although in many respects the same (e.g., there is no fundamental difference in the digestive and excretory processes of men and women), are both in some way limited by the respective forms of their sexuality. According to the ancient myth of the androgyn, time was when such dividedness had not occurred. The task, therefore, is symbolically to regain the wholeness that has been lost. The problem is how best to accomplish that goal. Much wisdom and great sophistication has gone into the various ways in which religions have sought to achieve the re-

covery of that wholeness. The ancient sages who have guided people through the various religious paths, while providing somewhat different proposals, seem to have been united in perceiving that the solution to the human sense of dividedness, which it is the function of religion both to recognize and to remedy, cannot possibly be straightforward or easy.

In the Bible the procreation and bearing of children is abundantly encouraged. To be fruitful and multiply is a primary commandment. Nevertheless, even in circumstances in which large families were plainly in the communal interest, the observance of the commandment is hedged with a mass of legislation providing for the severest of penalties for disobedience to the societal rules. Not only were practices of a homosexual character abhorred as defeating the commanded purpose, transgressions such as adultery and even simple fornication could be capital offenses. In later Judaism, e.g., by the time of Jesus, the ideal of celibacy was cultivated by certain groups. Polygamy, which had been encouraged in the patriarchal period, was by this time generally discouraged, and the virtues of monogamy extolled.

Christianity, while inheriting this biblical heritage, grew up in the midst of a decadent Roman Empire, from the sexual licentiousness of which Christians revolted as injurious to the development of the sacrificial love (*agapē*) that was at the center of the Christian Way. It was largely a disgust at this environment that led many devout Christians to eschew the haunts of such a civilization, becoming hermits or monks leading a life dedicated to the ideal of total sexual abstinence. Admiration for chastity and virginity has permeated Catholic Christian culture from earliest times and is inseparable from its structural expression at all levels. The Church itself, as the mystical Bride of Christ, is symbolized as feminine and identified in some contexts with Mary, personifying chastity, and served by an essentially male priesthood. At the same time the institution of marriage is deeply revered, and the sanctity of the family celebrated with a consequent abhorrence of divorce. Whatever disrupts this structure is antithetical to the essence of Christian tradition and therefore resisted wherever this tradition is valued.

Shaftesbury, Anthony Ashley Cooper (1801–1885). The 7th Earl of Shaftesbury, he was a social and factory reformer. Educated at Harrow School and Christ Church, Oxford, he became a Conservative Member of Parliament in 1826. At a time when factory conditions were such as to entail near-slavery for many workers and when the slums of London and other large cities in Britain were a national disgrace, he personally investigated the facts and was largely responsible for the passing of important legislation to ameliorate the odious conditions, e.g., a bill in 1847 to restrict work to ten hours a day and the passing of the Factory Act of 1874. He eloquently pleaded the case against the employment of small children in the mines and as chimney sweeps in homes. His party affiliation in the English Church was emphatically with the Evangelicals.

Shahada. The Islamic profession of faith ("There is no God but Allah, and Muhammad is his prophet"), which is one of the "Pillars of Islam," being traditionally recited five times a day by the muezzin from atop the minaret of the mosque.

Shakers. During a Quaker revival in England in 1747, a millenarian, pacifist group emerged called "The United Society of Believers in Christ's Second Appearing." One of the women leaders, Ann Lee, known as Mother Ann, was regarded as the "female principle in Christ" alongside Jesus as the male principle. In 1774 she led a few men and women to the U.S., where they settled in the woods of Watervliet near Albany, New York. They lived a disciplined communal life, abstained from alcohol, and above all the men and women were encouraged to live separately, practicing total sexual abstinence. At the height of their presence in America they numbered about 5,000. Today the movement, although not entirely extinct, has only a very few isolated representatives.

Shaman. The shaman, as an intermediary between the spirit world and the people, is an important functionary in many forms of religion. In Lapland, Siberia, and other far-northern regions, the shaman is also associated with the struggle against the harsh natural environment and is expected to mitigate its severity. Shamans may be male or female and are very often the latter. They are not priests or medicine men but distinguished, rather, for their ability to communicate directly with spirits, both dead and living.

Shammai. A prominent rabbinical teacher in the time of Jesus. The school that followed him and took his name was conservative and strict in its interpretation of the Law and contrasted with the school of Hillel, which was much more liberal, especially in its greater openness to Gentile influence. Jesus, in his replies to ethical and legalistic questions, seems to have intentionally avoided the appearance of supporting either the one side or the other.

Shankara. See Śaṅkara.

Shebuoth. A Jewish festival held fifty days after Passover, it is known to Christians as Pentecost. (See Acts 2.) Originally a barley harvest festival, it eventually came to commemorate the gift of the Torah on Mount Sinai.

Shekhinah. The term used in Judaism to designate the presence of God in the world. It is through the Shekhinah that the flow of divine energy comes down to earth. This line of thought conserves the otherness of God while finding the means of expressing his accessibility.

Shema. The name given to the Jewish confession of faith, being the first word of the set of biblical passages in which the confession consists, namely, Deuteronomy 6.4–9; 11.13–21; and Numbers 15.37–41. The Shema should be recited by all strictly observant male Jews every morning and evening.

Sheol. Sheol is the underworld, the abode of the dead, in ancient Hebrew thought, corresponding to Hades in ancient Greek mythology. The term is often used in the Old Testament as a synonym for death, whose power none can escape. It is conceived, as in the outlook of other Near Eastern peoples, as a place of darkness and dust. In Sheol there is no thought or knowledge or activity. Yet in classical Hebrew thought it is not a place of punishment for the wicked. That concept comes only into a later stage of Judaism. In the period known to scholars as "intertestamental," Sheol gradually becomes a place of punishment for the wicked, while the righteous go to Paradise. Out of this change of outlook is developed the concept of Gehenna as a place for the punishment of the wicked. The word is carried over, although with only a few references, into the New Testament, e.g., Jesus is reported as promising that the "gates" (i.e., the power) of Hades shall not overcome his Church; i.e., the Church is to be indestructible. Paul's declaration that Christ, through the power of his resurrection, has conquered death is in line with this concept. Salvation is salvation from the power of death; it is salvation from Sheol to life everlasting.

Shewbread. A term used by Tyndale and later translators of the Bible (following Luther's *Schaubrot*) for the twelve loaves used in the Jewish Temple, prepared from the finest of flour. They were arranged in two piles and placed each week beside the altar of incense. Only the priests were permitted

to consume them. The practice is mentioned in I Samuel 21.2–6. A table for the shewbread seems to have been among the furnishings of Solomon's Temple. (See I Kings 7.48.)

Shibboleth. After the defeat of the Ephraimites this word was used as a test to catch any of the Ephraimites as they fled: they could not pronounce the consonant š (sh).

Shi'ites. Islam has two principal divisions: the Sunnis, who are in the majority, and the Shi'a or Shi'ites. The latter recognize the claims of 'Ali (*c.* 598–660 CE), the fourth caliph or successor of Muhammad and also his cousin and his son-in-law, and his descendants as the true *imams* of Islam. In the 16th c., Persia was converted from Sunnism to Shi'ism, which is now dominant in Iran and Iraq and is well represented in several other Islamic lands, including Turkey, Syria, and Eastern Arabia. See **Sunnis.**

Shingon. A Japanese Buddhist sect, mystical in its outlook and also notably syncretistic. It was founded by Kōbo Daishi in 806 CE. The cosmos is represented in diagrams called *mandala,* symbolizing two elements in or aspects of the universe: (1) its fundamental essence and (2) its dynamic manifestations. The term, which is a rendering of the Chinese *Chên Yen,* means "True Word."

Shinto. Traditionally the national religion of Japan, so named from the Chinese *shin-tao,* "the way of the gods," in the 8th c. CE, to distinguish it from Buddhism which had by then been imported to Japan. Shinto celebrates Japanese national unity, its particularity, and indeed even its divinity. The ceremonies appeal to the *kami,* the gods, for protection. They consist of visits to Shinto shrines, the making of offerings, and other actions. Much stress is laid on the concept of purity. By this is understood what is conducive to life and the strength of the community and national consciousness. Shinto shrines, generally in groves of trees, are a distinctive element in the scenery of Japan.

Shofar. A ram's horn used in ancient times by the Israelites both to summon the people to religious observances and to give battle orders, somewhat as a bull horn might be used today. The shofar is still used as a liturgical call to repentance during the Jewish observances of Rosh Hashanah and Yom Kippur.

Shrine. From the Latin *scrinium,* a chest. Originally it was used in Christianity to designate a reliquary or box for the storing of relics of the saints. It is now most commonly used of holy places, more particularly those that attract pilgrims. See also **Shinto.**

Shroud of Turin. See **Holy Shroud.**

Shrove Tuesday. The day immediately preceding Lent, which begins on Ash Wednesday. It is called "shrove" from the traditional practice of "shriving" the people on that day. ("To shrive" is to give priestly absolution after sacramental confession.) See also **Mardi Gras.**

Sibylline Oracles, The. In imitation of the pagan "Sibylline Books," some Jewish and Christian authors assembled a collection of fifteen books (of which the text of twelve is extant) presenting a view of various aspects of world history as seen through Judaeo-Christian eyes. The intention of the authors seems to have been to incline pagans to biblical ways of looking at the world and the world's history. The collection is in Greek hexameters with an introduction in prose. The whole is constructed to give the impression of an example of a *genre* of literature that would be familiar to the pagan world and so would not cause a reader to be put off by a sense of his being proselytized. The Jewish parts of the collection seem to date from *c.* the mid-2nd c. BCE to *c.* the early 2nd c. CE while the Christian parts date from the late 2nd c. onwards.

Sicilian Vespers. A general massacre of the French in Sicily occurred on March 30, 1282, in which some three or four thousand were killed. It received this name because the signal for the terrible slaughter was the ringing of the bell for Vespers.

Sidgwick, Henry (1838–1900). Philosopher. Born in Skipton, Yorkshire, and trained at Cambridge, where later he taught. Predominantly interested in moral philosophy, he recognized three approaches to that field: (1) the intuitionist, which begins with ethical principles taken to be self-evident; (2) the egoistic, according to which the proper moral goal is achieved through the pursuit of individual happiness; and (3) the utilitarian, which sees the moral goal in terms of creation of the greater good. His own ethical theory was based on the last of these approaches although to some extent all are involved in it. His writings include *Methods of Ethics* (1874), *The Elements of Politics* (1891), and *Practical Ethics* (1898). He was also much interested in investigations into the paranormal and was one of the founders of the Society for Psychical Research.

Si Fallor, Sum. More than a thousand years before Descartes enunciated his famous affirmation, *cogito, ergo sum* (I think therefore I exist), it had been anticipated in Augustine's classic refutation of radical skepticism: *si fallor, sum* (if I am deceived, I exist). See also **Skepticism.**

Siger of Brabant (*c.* 1240–*c.* 1284). Medieval philosopher. He taught at the University of Paris, in which he had taken his master's degree. His most important works were studies on Aristotle, especially the *Physics,* the *De anima,* and the *Metaphysics.* An Averroist, he was criticized by Thomas Aquinas and was supposed by many theologians to teach the theory of a "double truth," i.e., that what could be true in theology might be false in philosophy and *vice versa.* Dante seems not to have shared this common opinion, for he places him among the Twelve Sages in his *Paradiso* (x, 133–137).

Sign. From the Latin *signum*, the term originally meant a verbal signal. The medieval philosopher William of Occam distinguished conventional signs, i.e., words as presented to us in speech or writing, from natural signs, i.e., those signs the meanings of which relate to the effects that objects have on us. The American philosopher Charles Peirce distinguished many kinds of signs, primarily dividing them into three main kinds: (1) icons, which carry their meaning with them; (2) indices, which call attention to their meaning; and (3) symbols, upon the meaning of which we arbitrarily agree in advance. Usage, however, varies. See also **Symbol.**

Sign of the Cross. From at least as early as the 2nd c., Christians made the sign of the cross (which in early times seems to have been made on the forehead, being later extended to the breast and shoulders) not only at Baptism but in various daily actions such as arising in the morning and retiring for sleep at night. The purpose included the sanctification of everyday life, the fortification of the spirit in moments of temptation, and the instant recognition by Christians of one another. Later it was used also not only on oneself but on other persons or objects as a means of blessing. In the Roman Catholic and Anglican Churches one normally draws the shoulder to shoulder part of the sign from left to right; in the Eastern Churches from right to left. It is used by the faithful at various points in the Mass, e.g., in the Creed at the declaration of belief in the Resurrection of the Body, at the reception of Holy Communion, at the prayers for the dead, and wherever personal devotion inclines one to use it. The celebrant of the Mass uses it more frequently. In Catholic practice it is used, as in the early Church to sanctify the every day actions of human life. At the beginning of the

Gospel at Mass, one makes the sign of the cross on the forehead, the lips, and on the heart.

Sikhs. The Sikhs are followers of the Guru Nanak (1469–1539 CE), who had been born a Hindu in an area ruled by Muslims. In Hindu society generally a guru is simply a teacher or spiritual director, but in Sikh tradition the term "guru" came to signify something more: the inner voice of God mystically apprehended and guiding the faithful along the path of *mukti.* (See **Sachkhand.**) The Sikh community, which is called the Panth, acknowledges a succession of ten gurus, including Nanak, who taught in the Punjab in the 16th and 17th c. A Sikh is defined as one who believes in Akal Purakh, the ten gurus and their teachings, the Adi Granth (the principal Sikh Scripture), and the initiation (*amrit*), as instituted by the tenth of the gurus, Gobind Singh, inaugurated at Anandpur in 1699. In this initiation rite (*amrit sanskar*) five trustworthy Sikhs administer a form of baptism with water stirred with a two-edged sword. Those who receive this baptism vow to live according to the Khalsa code, the *rahit.* Those so initiated may usually be recognized by their last name: the men add the name *Singh* to their names, the women *Kaur.* Those who account themselves Sikhs and venerate the Scriptures (the Granth) without being initiated and taking the vows required at initiation are nevertheless generally accepted as belonging to the Panth, the Sikh "way" or community. Those who retain the hair uncut, which they do up in a turban, are called *kes-dhari.* All Sikhs who have undergone the initiation rite (*amrit*) and taken the vows must be *kes-dhari.*

The Sikhs have had a remarkable history. Associated with the Punjab, they developed the military characteristics for which they were later to become famous. When the British annexed the Punjab in 1849 and the Panth seemed threatened, the Sikhs were revitalized later by various reform movements.

Many served in the British army and were generally recognized for their military valor and loyalty. Until the 19th c. they were chiefly occupied as traders in India. In the 20th c. they have spread into many other lands; e.g., East Africa, the U.S., and especially England. Nanak's intention had been not to unite Hinduism and Islam but to begin a new religious outlook and to found a new community cleansed of the corruptions of both and, while blending the insights of both, expressing itself in simple celebration of the name of the One God. He distrusted all ritual and ceremonial which, he supposed, tended to obscure rather than serve the highest purposes of true worship. A saying traditionally attributed to him is: "Why go searching for God in the forest? I have found him at home." Yet many elements from both Hinduism and Islam appear in Nanak's interpretation of religion. He accepted the traditional Hindu doctrines of karma and reincarnation and warned his followers not to prolong the chain of rebirths. At the same time he disdained the popular Hindu preoccupation with idols and pilgrimages. On the other hand, he rejected the extreme insistence on the otherness of God so traditional in Islam, preferring to see God as pervading the world and present in every human heart in which there is authentic honesty and brotherly love. Sikh teaching is, however, monotheistic.

Silence, The Argument from. When an author makes no reference to a subject or fact that seems pertinent to a context, one may argue (but on very shaky grounds) that he or she was ignorant of it. Such a deduction is called the argument from silence. It has been used both by Christians and by their opponents, usually yielding inadequate results in both cases.

Siloam, The Pool of. A pool or reservoir at Jerusalem, mentioned in the story of the blind man (John 9). It was very probably what is today known as *Birket-Silwān*, which receives its waters from an ancient underground conduit on the other side of the eastern hill of Jerusalem. It has been a place of Christian pilgrimage since at least the 4th century.

Simeon Stylites. (*c.* 390–459). The first of the Christian "pillar-hermits." (*Stylos* is Greek for "pillar.") The facts of his life would sound incredible but for their attestation by Theodoret, Bishop of Cyrrhus, who knew him personally, and the fact that Simeon had many imitators. After some time as a monk at Eusebona, between Antioch and Aleppo, he adopted a hermit's life. At about the age of thirty he built a pillar six feet high and lived on it, rapt in adoration and intercession. He periodically increased the height of the pillar until, after about ten more years, it had reached a height of sixty feet. He lived for another thirty years, never descending from the pillar, but having faithful disciples and friends who, using a ladder, brought him the necessities of life. He preached from atop his pillar and made many converts from paganism. Streams of pilgrims came to see him and many sought his counsel. He reconciled enemies and pleaded the cause of orthodoxy in the Church. Among his imitators was one of the same name who in the 6th c. took up residence on Mons Admirabilis to the west of Antioch and with whom he is sometimes confused. Much of the bibliography is in Latin or French, but see *The New Catholic Encyclopedia;* also an English translation by F. Lent of the *Acta Martyrum et Sanctorum* (a Syriac life ed. by P. Bedjan), in the *Journal of the American Oriental Society*, xxxv (1915–1917) pp.103–198. Stylites following Simeon's example were not uncommon in Syria, Mesopotamia, Egypt, and Greece, down to the 10th c. and there are instances even later.

Simon, Richard (1638–1712). French Oratorian priest and biblical scholar. A student of oriental languages, he published his *Histoire critique du Vieux Testament* in 1678 in which, even before the birth of Jean Astruc, another early Old Testament critic, he argued that Moses could not have been the author of the Pentateuch. Spinoza, his contemporary, had already denied the Mosaic authorship, but Simon laid the foundations for the development of the literary analysis and critique of the Old Testament. He was a devoted Christian to the end of his life. His publication of his critical account of the construction of the Old Testament led, however, to his immediate expulsion from the Oratorians.

Simony. The term used to designate the act of selling or purchasing spiritual things, e.g., selling ecclesiastical offices. Charging a fee for the sacrament would certainly be simoniacal and, in Catholic tradition, a very grave sin.

Sin. None of the various Hebrew words that are translated "sin" has quite the theological significance that the New Testament Greek term *hamartia* carries. The New Testament concept has its roots in the Old Testament one but adds the theological idea that God has provided man with the means of delivering himself from the bondage of sin. In the Old Testament, sin is portrayed in many guises. It can be an aggression, a failure to achieve a goal, a rebellion, a deception, a seduction, a corruption, and much else. Only comparatively late in the development of Old Testament thought is the devil seen as the cause of sin. Even then the notion that the devil seduces men and women does not in the least diminish the fundamental concept of human responsibility. In the New Testament, Paul introduces a specific idea that humanity is in the grip of sin (Romans 5–8). Paul does not represent sin, as did some later Christian writers, as a hereditary moral disease from which we suffer as the children of Adam. Rather, he notes the Old Testament view that it is because of sin that death ensues; therefore, since all men and women die, all must be under the power of sin. Therein lies the significance of the power of Christ who

through his resurrection has conquered death and so makes available to men and women the power to become victorious over sin and death. See **Original Sin.**

Sin, Original. See **Original Sin.**

Sinai. A mountain in the desert between Palestine and Egypt where, according to the account in Exodus 19, the Law was given to Moses. From antiquity it was regarded as the sacred mountain of Yahweh. In early Christian times it became the center of monasticism. Codex Sinaiticus, one of the most famous of all biblical manuscripts, is so called because it was discovered in St. Catherine's monastery on Mount Sinai. See **Codex Sinaiticus.** The Church of Sinai, ruled by the Archbishop of Mount Sinai, the abbot of the monastery of St. Catherine, is the smallest independent Church of the Eastern Orthodox Communion. Its independence was asserted in 1575.

Sins, The Seven Deadly. The seven "deadly" or "capital" sins—that is, those at the root of all evil human acts—are, based on a list found in Gregory the Great (*c.* 540–604) and traditional throughout the Middle Ages: (1) pride, (2) covetousness, (3) lust, (4) envy, (5) gluttony, (6) anger, and (7) sloth. They are used, for instance, by Dante as the scheme for his *Purgatorio* and were prominent in medieval art and literature.

Sistine Chapel. This chapel, so called because it was built in the 15th c. for Pope Sixtus IV, is the principal chapel of the Vatican Palace and celebrated for the famous frescoes by Michelangelo on the ceiling and walls. Their restoration in the late 20th c. has been controversial among art historians and other experts.

Sistine Madonna. One of the greatest of all Christian paintings, it is the work of Raphael, having been painted at Rome *c.* 1512. It is so called because of its having been placed over the high altar of the Benedictine church of San Sisto at Piacenza. It is now at Dresden.

Situationism. A view of ethics which, in its radical form, insists on an ethical decision tailor-made to the uniqueness of each individual in each particular ethical situation. Forms of situationist ethics have been expounded in the English-speaking world by Christian writers such as the American J. B. Fletcher and the English John A. T. Robinson, but the notion has its roots in continental European existentialists, e.g., Ortega, Sartre, and Jaspers, and was developed extensively by others such as Cesare Luporini, Renato Lazzarini, Antonino Poppi, O. F. M., and Angelo Parego in a literature that goes back to at least the decade preceding World War II. The notion, like that of contextualism (see **Contextualism**), was adumbrated even before World War I in some of the writings of John Dewey (1859–1952), e.g., in his *Studies in Logical Theory* (1903), and further developed in his *Logic, Theory of Inquiry* (1938). See also **Probabilism.**

Sitz im Leben. A German term meaning literally "seat (situation, place) in life," used by scholars, especially in biblical studies, to point to the circumstances in which a story was told or a saying uttered. For an appreciation of the meaning of such a story or saying, an understanding of the *Sitz im Leben* is essential. For example, it is impossible to understand the full significance of the sayings of Jesus or the writings of Paul or the nature of the Apocalypse without some appreciation of the historical circumstances, apart from which one can seldom avoid misinterpretation.

Śiva. In Hindu lore, Rudra, a storm-deity, was so fierce that it was dangerous even to utter his name. (Compare the Hebrew tradition of refraining from uttering the name of Yahweh.) So Rudra came to be addressed as Śiva by way of placating him, for *śiva* means literally "auspicious." Among the uneducated classes he came to be sometimes called Rudra-Śiva; then *c.* the 2nd c. BCE Śiva acquired a separate identity of his own, becoming an object of worship.

Six Articles, The. At the command of Henry VIII, a conservative medieval Catholic at heart, certain articles were imposed in June 1539 to prevent the spread of Reformation teachings and practices. The six articles that Henry wished to enforce were as follows: (1) Belief in transubstantiation of the Bread and Wine in the Mass; (2) Communion in one kind, i.e., its administration to the people by the Host without the Chalice; (3) the celibacy of the clergy; (4) the honoring of monastic vows; (5) the practice of private masses, i.e., masses said by a priest for a private intention and without the presence of a congregation; and (6) sacramental confession to a priest who in the name of God and by the authority of his Church grants absolution. The bill, introduced to the House of Lords, was approved by its lay members, but several of the bishops (as "spiritual peers") declined to accept it. Some even resigned their bishoprics and many other clerics simply ignored the enactment. The act intended to enforce these beliefs and practices was popularly known as "The Whip with Six Strings."

Skandha. A Buddhist term used to designate the five elements that people customarily mistake for the "I" or self, namely (1) form or embodiment, (2) feelings, (3) perceptions, (4) mental phenomena, and (5) thought. The True Self transcends all of these, which are merely its wrappings or manifestations.

Skepticism. Disbelief in the possibility of certain knowledge about anything has a long history from the Greeks onwards. (See also **Pyrrhonism.**) The term "skeptic" is more popularly applied to those who hold, for one reason or another, that there are no grounds for any purely religious belief. Thoroughgoing skeptics such as Hume perceive that even our knowledge of the empirical world, although not in precisely the same case as the truth-claims of religion, also lacks grounds to a much greater extent than is popularly supposed. A classic example is the belief, which at the time must have seemed to most people incontestable, of the geocentricity of the universe, i.e., the belief that the sun and planets move round the earth. Those astronomers who found the situation to be otherwise had much difficulty in dissuading others from persisting in that belief. Yet scientific demonstration never proves anything about the empirical world absolutely and irreformably. Deeply religious people recognize that doubt is also an element in authentic religious awareness and that faith is indeed a descant on doubt rather than its logical opposite.

Slavery. The institution of slavery, by which large classes of men, women, and children, are held as property by their owners and deprived of the rights of citizens, was virtually universal in the ancient world. The chief source of slaves was in the vanquished who, in war, survived. They formed the most valuable among the prizes of war. The Sumerian word for slave means literally "foreigner," showing how closely slavery was associated with conquest. The Assyrian records often contain exact statistics about the number of prisoners taken. Laws might protect slaves from extreme, maniacal abuse by their masters, but generally speaking the laws favored the owner, not the slave. Slavery was fully recognized in the Mosaic Law, although it may have been practiced in a somewhat more benign form than that of their neighbors. Nevertheless, slavery for debt is specifically mentioned (e.g., Leviticus 25.35 ff.), together with legislation providing for the conditions under which it could be imposed. As in other ancient societies, slaves were bred like horses and dogs to increase the holdings of their owner and their children were of course by law the property of their owner. Any female slave could be used for her master's pleasure, al-

though laws protected her against odious mistreatment. Records show that the slave population in Greece c. 300 BCE was roughly the same as that of the freemen. This was probably similar to the situation in the Roman Empire and other great societies of the ancient world.

With such a background in both Jewish and Gentile societies in the time of Jesus, the institution of slavery is taken for granted in the New Testament documents. Masters are enjoined to be kind and considerate toward their slaves, and slaves are enjoined to be obedient to their masters (e.g., Colossians 3.22–4.1; Ephesians 6.5–9; and I Timothy 6.1 f.). True, there is no distinction between freemen and slave in the sight of God, and no genuine Christian could really have regarded his slaves as chattels; nor certainly could a Christian man have used a female slave sexually against her will without a deep sense of guilt. Nevertheless, the institution itself remained inviolate at least through the 3rd c. Gradually, however, the Christian emphasis on brotherly love and the attitude of respect for all human beings that it entails made slavery on the classical model seem less and less acceptable. Under Constantine and more notably under Justinian in the 6th c. the institution of slavery was mitigated in Christian society and at least transformed into more moderate forms.

After the Renaissance only mild remnants of it persisted in Europe. By contrast, the Turks, after the Fall of Constantinople in 1453, practiced a very cruel form of slavery on large numbers of Christians. Moreover, despite papal protestations in the 16th and the 17th c. (e.g., Paul III, Pius V, and Urban VIII) and by Dominican, Jesuit, and other missionaries in the recently discovered Americas, Spanish, Portuguese, and British traders made slaves of the Indians among whom they settled and later introduced negro slaves from Africa. The slave trade was made illegal in 1808, suppressed in the British Empire in 1833, and in the United States in December 1865.

Slessor, Mary (1848–1915). Scottish Presbyterian missionary. Born in Aberdeen, she worked in the Dundee jute mills for some years, then offered herself as a missionary in Calabar, West Africa, whither she sailed in 1876. At that time Calabar practiced the most outrageous cruelties, including human sacrifice and the most brutal forms of torture. Mary Slessor, through astonishing personal bravery and resolve, gained such influence among the native population that she was able to bring many such abuses to an end. The Government eventually, in 1905, invested her with the powers of a magistrate. For more on the life of this remarkable woman see James Buchan, *The Expendable Mary Slessor* (1980).

Smith, Adam (1723–1790). Scottish moral philosopher and economist. Born at Kirkcaldy, Fife, he was trained at Glasgow University and also at Oxford. After some years of teaching and travel, during which he produced his *Theory of Moral Sentiments* (1759), he devoted ten years to work that culminated in the appearance of the book for which he is best known: *The Wealth of Nations* (1776). Adam Smith's celebrated economic theory, which favors free trade and disapproves governmental interference and protectionist policies, is grounded in his ethical theory, which is centered upon the principle of sympathy through which we enter into an understanding of the situations of other people and are propelled to work for the advantage of all, partly by reason of the benevolence that sympathy stimulates in us and partly from motives of prudence.

Smith, George Adam (1856–1942). Old Testament scholar. Born at Calcutta, he was trained at Edinburgh, Tübingen, and Leipzig. He taught Old Testament at the United Free College in Glasgow and became in 1909 Principal of the University of Aberdeen. He traveled widely in the Near East and was an important contributor to Old Testament scholarship. His works include the still valuable *Historical Geography of the Holy Land* (1894), which has gone into many editions, *Jerusalem* (1907), *The Early Poetry of Israel* (1912), *Deuteronomy* (1918), and *Jeremiah* (1923). For more on his life see Lilian Adam Smith, *George Adam Smith* (1943).

Smith, Ronald Gregor. See **Death of God Theology.**

Smith, William Robertson (1846–1894). Old Testament scholar. Trained at Aberdeen, Edinburgh, Bonn, and Göttingen, he became professor of oriental languages and Old Testament exegesis at the Free Church College, Aberdeen, in 1870, soon becoming widely recognized for his work in Old Testament scholarship. His Church, however, disapproved his work as injurious to belief in the verbal inspiration of the biblical writers, and in 1881 its General Assembly dismissed him on that ground from his professorial chair. He went to Cambridge, where a few years later he was elected a Fellow of Christ's College. He popularized the theories of Wellhausen on the structure and date of the Pentateuch and proposed theories of his own which, although now much modified by biblical scholars, played an important role in the development of critical methods of Semitic studies. His works include *The Prophets of Israel* (1882) and *The Religion of the Semites* (1889), both of which went into subsequent editions.

Smuts, Jan Christian (1870–1950). South African philosopher and statesman. Born in Cape Colony and educated at Cambridge, he participated in the founding of the League of Nations and was twice Prime Minister of South Africa. His chief philosophical work, *Holism and Evolution* (1926), sets forth the evolutionary system that he called holism, according to which there are two factors at work in the evolutionary process: a mechanical factor, which is the principal one in the less advanced stages of evolutionary development, and a mental factor, which operates more and more as evolution progresses.

Sobornost. A Russian term, difficult to render in English. It can refer to the idea expressed in the term "Catholic" and also can mean conciliarity. The word *sobor* means "council" or "assembly." In Russian theology *sobornost* generally signifies the concept that while the individual shares the corporate life of the Church, he or she retains personal freedom. Russian theologians have tended to contrast sobornost with the legalistic authoritarianism of the Roman Catholic Church on the one hand and, on the other, what they take to be the lack of cohesion in Protestant organizations.

Social Gospel. The name commonly given to a movement among certain American Protestant church leaders in the late 19th c. away from theological concerns and toward social ones. The leader of the movement, Walter Rauschenbusch, taught that the duty of the Christian Church is to develop an active concern for the practical accomplishment of bringing the Kingdom of God into the here-and-now.

Societas Fidelium. In the Middle Ages, in the Latin West, the term "Church" (*ecclesia*) became ambiguous. As controversies developed between papalist and conciliarist parties, some appealed to a theological principle implicit from earliest times—namely, that in the last resort the Christian Church consists not in bishops or councils but the whole company of Christ's faithful people, the *societas* or *congregatio fidelium*. St. Augustine had already spoken of a Christian *respublica*, borrowing a term that the Romans had used neutrally of Rome under any form of government, being applicable, for instance, to the Roman Empire at all stages.

Society of Friends. See **Quakers.**

Society of Jesus. See **Jesuits.**

Society of St. John the Evangelist. The oldest Anglican religious community for men, commonly known as the Cowley Fathers, from the place of their origin near Oxford, where they were founded in 1865. Members take the traditional three monastic vows, engage in a life of prayer, and devote themselves to study and education. Besides the mother house at Oxford, the Society has communities elsewhere in England and also in the United States, Canada, Japan, and South Africa. It includes both priests and laymen.

Socinianism. Two Italian religious teachers, Lelio Francesco Maria Sozini (1525–1562) and his nephew Fausto Paulo Sozzini (1539–1604), both natives of Siena, became famed for the Unitarian tendencies of their teaching. (Note that Fausto spelt his surname differently from that of his uncle.) Fausto, from 1579 till his death was the leader of what may be called the Unitarian party of the Reformation, whose adherents eventually became known as Socinians. (Socinus is the Latinized form of their surname.) They were continental antecedents of what in England and America later came to be recognized as the Unitarian Church. See **Unitarians.**

Socrates (470–400 BCE). Athenian philosopher. Although he was classified by his contemporaries as a member of the Sophist school (see **Sophists**), he was to say the least, a very distinctive member of the class, whose attitudes and outlook he opposed. While comparatively little is known of his life, what we do know points to a man of extreme dedication to a philosophical mission that he felt bound to fulfil. He liked to think of himself as a *narkē* (a ray fish that stings its victims) whose intellectual probing of his disciples stung them into deeper reflection. He used also another metaphor to describe his function: he regarded himself as a sort of intellectual midwife rather than as a teacher, i.e., his method (traditionally known as "the

Socratic Method") was not to foist ideas upon others but to assist them to give birth to their own as a midwife assists in the birth of another woman's child.

Plato was immensely influenced by Socrates, and in his Dialogues (see **Plato**) he makes him the central figure. Scholars regard only a few of the Platonic Dialogues as reflecting the thought of Socrates and representing him historically: the *Apology*, the *Crito*, and the *Phaedo*. They include information about the circumstances leading up to his trial, imprisonment, and death. He was charged with "atheism," i.e., with repudiating belief in the popular gods and so corrupting the youth of Athens. The account of his acceptance of death, including his belief in immortality, is one of the most moving in the literature of humankind. Controversy attends what precisely was the thrust of his own thought. No doubt he was concerned to enable people to think abstractly rather than in terms of individual cases as people in pre-literate cultures tend to do (e.g., John is called brave and Mary kind, but what are bravery and kindness in themselves?), but precisely what were the philosophical tenets of Socrates contradistinguished from those of Plato remains controversial.

Socratic Method. See Socrates.

Söderblom, Nathan (1866–1931). Ecumenist and Lutheran Archbishop of Uppsala. Born in Trönö, near Soderhamn, he was trained at Uppsala and ordained priest in 1893. The following year, having been appointed chaplain to the Swedish legation in Paris, he engaged in the study of comparative religion on which he lectured at Uppsala and Paris. In 1914 he was appointed Archbishop of Uppsala. He was a zealous ecumenist who believed that Christians could cooperate effectively without challenging the doctrinal tenets of any branch of the Church. He was theologically influenced by Ritschl, Auguste Sabatier, Loisy, von Hügel, and others in both Catholic and Protestant camps accounted "liberal" in their tendencies. He also encouraged the liturgical movement in the Swedish Church. Above all he was the principal force behind the "Life and Work" movement. Among his works available in English are *The Nature of Revelation* (1903; English trans. 1933) and *The Living God* (1933).

Sodom. A city in the neighborhood of the Dead Sea in biblical times. Others were Gomorrah, Admah, Zeboim, and Zoar. According to Genesis, Lot chose this region when he parted from Abraham. When Lot receives two guests, the men of Sodom try to assault them. It is from this episode that the vice of sodomy takes its name. The wickedness of Sodom and Gomorrah became proverbial in Israelite culture and tradition. Abraham is represented as pleading with Yahweh to spare Sodom, and Yahweh promises to do so if only a few righteous men can be found there to warrant such mercy (Genesis 18.20–33). Apparently no righteous could be found other than Lot and his family and they were therefore warned to leave the city which was then destroyed by fire. The traditional location is on the fault of the Jordan Valley and subject to earthquakes that could have resulted in extensive fires. The story, however, is attended by many elements suggestive of a mixture of history with theological allegory.

Solemn League and Covenant. An agreement between the Scots and the English Parliaments in 1643, made with the declared intention of reforming the Church of England and maintaining the Presbyterian Kirk in Scotland. It was a politico-ecclesiastical move supported by the English Parliamentarians as a means of obtaining a civil treaty against the royalists, while the Scots sought it on the ground of its vehemently antiprelatical character. The General Assembly of the Kirk formally accepted it on August 17, and the English Commons and Westminster Assembly on

September 25. For complex political reasons it soon lost practical significance in England. In Scotland, however, it was renewed in 1648 and subscribed by Charles II in 1650 and 1651. Some of the Scottish nobles who subscribed wrote their signatures in their blood.

Solesmes. This great Benedictine foundation, dedicated to Saint Peter and situated in the department of Sarthe, France, dates from 1010. Its immense fame as a leading center of the liturgical movement, however, dates from 1833, when Dom Prosper Guéranger settled there with a few other priests and, in 1837, became abbot. After difficulties with the French Government and their expulsion from France in 1901, the monks returned in 1922 to Solesmes which has remained ever since a powerful focus of liturgical studies.

Solipsism. From the Latin *solus* "alone" and *ipse* "oneself." The philosophical position that the individual self is the only one existent, so that other selves are illusory. The notion is a formal one since probably no one has ever seriously held that view. Many philosophers, however, have been methodological solipsists, holding that the self is the only real object of knowledge or else (as in much philosophy since Descartes) that it is the only profitable starting point for inquiry.

Solomon. The approximate dates of Solomon's reign over Israel are 961–922 BCE. It was a period of peace, of enormous growth in building and in economic prosperity. The temple and palace were among his greatest building projects. His wealth became proverbial. He levied heavy taxes and imposed forced labor on most of the population. He maintained close diplomatic relations with Egypt and other great powers and married foreign wives. The extent of his harem as reported in the Bible (I Kings 11.4) as 700 wives and 300 concubines must surely be much exaggerated; nevertheless it points to the grandeur and scale of his establishment.

Besides all this, he is by tradition the father of Hebrew Wisdom and his name virtually a synonym for judicial excellence. The strong kingdom that he inherited from David was maintained and developed during his reign, but its collapse after his death suggests that it was not well administered and that his grandiose and extravagant schemes did not reflect a healthy state of affairs.

Soloviev, Vladimir (1853–1900). Philosopher. Born in Moscow, he was trained there and at St. Petersburg. He was critical of both the rationalism and the empiricism in Western European thought and argued for the importance of the interior life, seeing Holy Wisdom (*hagia Sophia*) as incarnate in humanity and leading it to deification. His thought is evolutionary, panpsychic, and pantheistic. His writings include *The Crisis of Western Philosophy* (1874), *The Philosophical Principles of Integral Knowledge* (1877), *Critique of Abstract Principles* (1880), and *Stories of the Anti-Christ* (1900).

Soma. The name of a specific plant mentioned in the Vedas. Its juice, ritually filtered, was mixed with water or butter or milk and seems to have had potent qualities as an intoxicant and hallucinogen. The ceremony of drinking it seems to have had affinities with the central rite of Zoroastrian worship: *haoma*. Soma juice was essential for all sacrifices in early Vedic times and became itself an object of worship.

Somaschi. See **Jerome Emiliani.**

Song of Songs. This canonical book of the Hebrew Bible is attributed to Solomon, but biblical scholars date it from the post-exilic period, long after Solomon's time. This does not exclude, however, the possibility that it might contain elements from materials by or in the time of Solomon, for he had much fame as a lover, and the book is unique in the Bible for its plainly erotic character. So erotic is it that its acceptance into the Hebrew canon seems to have been resisted by some right up to the time of the fixing of the Hebrew canon at Jamnia *c*. 100 CE. Since then both Jews and Christians have tried to justify its presence in the sacred literature common to both of them by arguing for an underlying allegorical or mystical meaning; e.g., the love between Yahweh and his people or the relation between Christ and his Church. The language used, however, while it would not offend most modern readers in the way in which it would have offended many a hundred years ago, cannot easily be accounted suitable for the expression of such lofty mystical themes. Most critical scholars today would prefer to see in this biblical book a collection of love poems celebrating the joy of sexual love and to explain its acceptance into the canon by the recognized fact that the biblical peoples were earthier in their outlook and consequently in their standards of good taste than are people in highly cultivated societies who have more complex considerations to take into account. Nevertheless, this sort of explanation is unconvincing, since it is well known that the Bible is full of euphemisms, e.g., "feet" for the genitalia.

Son of God. This title is given to Jesus almost a hundred times in the New Testament but it does not always have the same metaphysical connotations. In Greek usage the term is quite frequently given to a demigod or superlative hero, and in some passages in the New Testament it might well mean no more than this. Some passages, however, leave no doubt that the relationship of the Son to the Father is unique, e.g., Matthew 26.63f. and Mark 12.6. The title points to the unique function of Jesus in the process of human salvation. The metaphysical implications are never clearly worked out: that remained for the early Fathers of the Church to do. There can be no doubt, however, that whatever metaphysical models should be used in expounding the nature of the status of Jesus as "Son of God," the faith of the Church as it used the term to express the uniqueness of the Resurrection of Jesus Christ was that through him had been accomplished human salvation in a way that had and could have no parallel in human history.

Son of Man. This curious term in English versions and translations of the Bible is used to render the Aramaic *bar nāšā*, meaning "a man" or "the man." The term is not used in the Epistles, and it is used in the Gospels only by Jesus of himself. Scholars take it to have a reference to a title used in Deuteronomy 7.13f. to designate "one like a man" who appears before "the Ancient of Days" and is awarded a kingdom. It may also refer to the "son of man" in Enoch 46, which probably has extrabiblical connections. Much controversy remains, however, about the precise significance of the title, but whether by adoption or otherwise it is distinctly Semitic in its background and would be foreign-sounding to Gentile hearers; hence no doubt its absence from the New Testament letters and its frequent use by Jesus to his predominantly Jewish audiences.

Sophia, Saint. See **Hagia Sophia.**

Sophists. Wandering teachers who, in the fifth century BC, came from foreign cities to Athens, where they sought to popularize learning. In showing young men how to achieve success—for example, in political life—they tended to subordinate the pursuit of truth to the use of knowledge for practical ends. Rhetoric, for instance, became more popular than the study of the cosmic panorama that had been the preoccupation of learned circles. The new concern for persuasion in argument led many to a relativism in which truth was accounted subjective (man is the measure of all things); nevertheless, that very concern raised the question whether, among the various opinions the Sophists canvassed, there might be a core of truth that was independent of the individual inquirer. Socrates, a

Sophist himself, criticized sophistic relativism but fostered the quest for the universal to which it led (e.g., the concept of bravery rather than instances of brave men or deeds) and in doing so provided the basis for a new conceptual vocabulary.

Sorbonne. Founded *c.* 1257 by Robert de Sorbon, personal confessor to Saint Louis (King Louis IX) of France, it was known at first as the *Collegium pauperum magistrorum* and, as that designation suggests, intended for advanced students. Favored by the popes, it was the recipient of many benefactions, including the King himself who gave a portion of the site. The great severity of its examinations was prominent among the factors that led to its immense repute as a center of much of the best scholarship in Europe. Toward the end of the Middle Ages it showed a tendency to support Gallican ideas (see **Gallicanism**), which it increasingly defended throughout the 17th and the 18th c. Its opposition to the educational goals of the Jesuits and its resistance to the famous papal bull *Unigenitus* in 1713 cost it much of its influence with Rome, yet its stalwart defense of Catholic principles, traditions, and practices, against the Protestant Reformers kept it a strong force in intellectual circles throughout the Catholic world. As such it was predictably suppressed in 1792. Napoleon, however, restored it in 1808 as the Theological Faculty of the University of Paris. In 1882 it finally lost its theological function. Identified thereafter with the heart of the now ever-expanding University of Paris, the Sorbonne has continued to be an irresistible focus for the intellectual life of France but also a magnet for scholars and students from all over Europe and beyond. The Cité Universitaire, a magnificently arranged residential park easily reached by *métro* from the Sorbonne *quartier* provides a unique form of student community life, with residences each representing one of a large number of the leading nations of the world together with student facilities and abundant opportunities for cosmopolitan interchange of ideas. Not only is it a most remarkable modern achievement; it reflects, although in a very modern way, the manner in which, in the Middle Ages, the various "nations" were represented in the life of the Sorbonne.

Sorley, William Ritchie (1855–1935). Philosopher. Born in Selkirk, Scotland, and trained at Cambridge where also he taught, Sorley was influenced by both Kant and Hegelian idealism. He opposed the naturalistic tendencies he found in the thought of his time. Methodologically, he used moral values as the key to metaphysics and was led to a position that may be called ethical theism with God as the source of values. His writings include *The Ethics of Naturalism* (1885) and (probably his best known work): *Moral Values and the Idea of God* (1918).

Sorrowful Mysteries, The Five. In the recitation of the Rosary are three "chaplets" each having five "decades:" the Joyful, The Sorrowful, and the Glorious Mysteries respectively. The Sorrowful Mysteries are: the Agony in the Garden of Gethsemane, the Scourging, the Crowning of Thorns, the Carrying of the Cross, and the Crucifixion. See **Rosary.**

Soteriology. That part of theology that treats of the process of human salvation. It includes doctrines such as Atonement and Grace, Resurrection, and Human Destiny.

Sōtō. One of two main streams of Japanese Zen Buddhism, Sōtō was founded in China early in the 9th c. CE by Tung-shan. Through the technique of zazen, which includes sitting cross-legged with one's breathing perfectly regulated, one achieves oneness with the Absolute. Sōtō was introduced to Japan in the 13th c. CE by Dogen.

Soto, Domingo de (1494–1560). Dominican scholastic philosopher. Born in

Segovia, Spain, he was trained at Alcalá and Paris and later taught at Alcalá and Salamanca. Generally loyal to the Thomistic tradition, he denied, however, the Thomist distinction between essence and existence. His writings include *On Nature and Grace* (1547) and *On Justice and Law* (1549). He is important in the development of international law principles. He was prominent in the Council of Trent.

Soul. The concept of a soul as representing an element in man other than that which is empirically observable occurs in one way or another in virtually all religions from the most primitive to the most developed. In primitive Semitic thought the word *nepeš* (Arabic *nafs*) is usually but misleadingly translated into English as "soul;" but "soul" as generally used today includes a variety of ideas, mostly from Greek thought and medieval extrapolation of it, that would have been alien to the Semitic way of understanding man. The *nepeš* as mentioned in Genesis 2.7 might indeed be better rendered "life" than "soul." The *nepeš* in that mode of thought is really life. Connected with the primitive notion of a fine diminutive replica of the body, which it inhabits, it escapes at death, normally through the mouth or nostrils, although possibly on the point of the sword in the case of a violent death; yet it does not escape to have a life of its own, for it *is* the man's life. It is not life in our terms, however, so that "life" would not be a satisfactory translation either. It is, rather, life in the sense of whatever man desires or loves. It is a concept that is too simple for our now more complex minds easily to grasp. The onomatopeic Hebrew word *ruaḥ*, usually translated "spirit" or "breath," also suggests an ingredient in what we understand as "soul;" yet "soul" as we understand it today, whether to affirm or deny its existence, is deeply rooted in Platonic and other Greek thought in which *psychē* might come closer to our idea of "soul." Nevertheless, both in the Old Testament

and the New Testament *psychē* is used much more often in a Hebrew than in a Greek sense.

From sources in Greek philosophy and Gnostic thought was gradually evolved the notion of a soul as in some way or other separate from the body of a human being, not merely a spiritual principle but a finer and higher dimension in men and women. Still, even then a multitude of phrases reflect the vagueness of the term, e.g., when we say of an artistically insensitive person that he or she "has no soul" we seem to be merely denying sensitivity, not making any metaphysical or ontological statement such as one might be making if one said that a stone has no soul. The term "soul" appears, then, to be by any reckoning a vague and ambiguous one, ill adapted for serious philosophical or theological use.

Souter, Alexander (1873–1949). New Testament scholar. Trained at Aberdeen and Caius College, Cambridge, he taught New Testament Greek for some years at Mansfield College, Oxford, before becoming, in 1911, Regius Professor of Humanity at the University of Aberdeen. He became noted for his exceptional knowledge of early Christian Latin. Among his works, *A Pocket Lexicon to the Greek New Testament* (1916) served several generations of students, while his posthumous *Glossary of Later Latin* (1949) is a most valuable scholarly tool.

Southcott, Joanna (1750–1814). Religious visionary. A domestic servant, she joined the Methodists in 1791 and the following year proclaimed herself the woman prophesied in Revelation 12, proceeding to "seal" the 144,000 elect for a fee in each case. One of her "sealed" was convicted of murder and hanged in 1809. She wrote copiously on her prophecies before her death of a disease of the brain.

South India, The Church of. Inaugurated on September 27, 1947, it consisted of a union of three bodies: (1)

four dioceses of the Church of India, Burma, and Ceylon (Anglican), namely, Madras, Tinnevelly, Travancore and Cochin, and Dornakal; (2) the South India Province of the Methodist Church; (3) the South India United Church, consisting of an earlier union of several Protestant bodies. The Church of South India recognizes as a doctrinal statement the Lambeth Quadrilateral (1888) and claims a membership of about a million. For further information see B. Sundkler, *Church of South India. The Movement towards Union, 1900–1947* (1954) and M. Ward, *The Pilgrim Church: An Account of the First Five Years in the Life of the Church of South India* (1953).

Space-Time. Space and time are traditionally regarded as ultimate categories. The concept of space-time appears in modern philosophical thought as the ultimate matrix out of which everything else is evolved. The German physicist and mathematician Hermann Minkowski (1864–1909) joined the three dimensions of space with time as a fourth dimension and regarded the four dimensions as coordinates. All objects and events must be seen, then, as four-dimensional and events, past and future, are present in the space-time continuum. Einstein took Minkowski's concept of space-time as the basis for his own theory. Einstein's view of space-time tends to support a Spinozistic metaphysic. See **Spinoza.**

Spalatin, Georg (1484–1545). Humanist and Reformer. Born at Spalt (from which he took the name he adopted in place of his family name, Burkhardt), near Nuremberg, he studied at Erfurt, taking his bachelor's degree there in 1499. In 1508 he was ordained priest. Soon coming to the notice of the Elector, King Frederick III ("the Wise"), he became tutor to the latter's nephew. In 1511 he was sent to Wittenberg, where he met Luther and later he influenced the Elector in the Reformation direction. He accompanied Frederick to

the Diet of Augsburg in 1518 and to the Diet of Worms in 1521. He worked closely with Luther and others in the Reformation and humanist movements and gained high repute for his scholarship.

Species. A traditional Latin term that designates a class standing between the individual and the genus, e.g., this animal is of the genus "dog" and of the species "terrier." This classification belongs to a system devised by Aristotle, which became traditional in Western philosophy. Definition is by "genus and difference;" i.e., a species (e.g., the terrier species) is defined by stating the difference between it and other species (e.g., wolfhounds and setters) within the genus "dog."

Spencer, Herbert (1820–1903). Philosopher. Born in Derby, England, he worked as an engineer. Deeply influenced by Darwin, he coined the now famous phrase "the survival of the fittest" to express what he took to be the basic principle of the working of Darwin's theory as enunciated in *The Origin of Species* (1859). He also saw Darwin's evolutionism as entailing a principle of increasing complexity: the more advanced the organism the more complex it must be expected to be. Spencer thought of himself as agnostic in respect to the existence of God, but he recognized an "Unknowable" behind all phenomena, which at least leaves room for postulating the concept of God's existence. His writings include *First Principles* (1862), *Principles of Biology*, 2 vols. (1864–67), *Principles of Sociology*, 3 vols. (1876–96), *Principles of Ethics*, 2 vols. (1879–93), and *Autobiography* (1904).

Spener, Philipp Jakob (1635–1705). Founder of German Pietism. Born in Alsace of devout Protestant parents, he studied at Strassburg and underwent a conversion that led him to a deep sense of personal religious conviction. He felt called to enhance the spiritual vitality of the Lutheran Church which at that time had become theologically scholastic and overclerical. Predictably he encountered much opposition, but toward the end of the century his movement, by then coming to be generally known as "Pietism," won increasing support, some of it in influential quarters. His influence, however, was deeper than any such manifestation of it in his lifetime. He permanently affected the life of the Lutheran Church in Germany and also, if indirectly, brought a greater interiority to Protestantism elsewhere.

Spengler, Oswald (1880–1936). Philosopher of History. Born at Blankenburg and trained at Munich, Berlin, and Halle, he was much influenced by both Nietzsche and Goethe. In human history he found a variety of cultures, each at a particular stage of development, each lasting about a thousand years, and each passing through a series of stages that may be figuratively called spring, summer, fall, and winter. As with these seasons, each has its own distinctive characteristics. His most famous work is his *The Decline of the West*, 2 vols. (1918–1922).

Speussipus (*c.* **407–339** BCE). Philosopher. A nephew of Plato, he was born at Athens and became head of the Academy there in 347, remaining in that position till his death in 339.

Speyer. In June 1526 an assembly was held at Speyer, Germany, known as the Diet of Speyer, for the purpose of consolidating the achievements of the Lutheran Reformation in Germany, which had been threatened both from the side of the Anabaptists and from that of the Roman Catholics. The Diet determined that each prince should order church affairs in his principality according to his conscience. Provision would be made for the toleration of minorities so long as order was preserved. That was as much toleration as might have been expected at that time and no doubt many must have seen it as a fair as well as a practical solution. In 1528, however, the Emperor, Charles V, under

pressure from the Pope, issued a mandate on November 30 of that year, summoning to Speyer on February 21, 1529, a carefully selected, well organized body of Roman Catholics who passed legislation ending toleration to Lutherans in Roman Catholic regions. On April 19, six princes and fourteen cities made a formal protest (*protestatio*) to the Archduke Ferdinand in which they defended minority rights. The name "Protestant" with which the signatories were labelled came to be applied to all in the Reformation heritage. See **Protestant.**

Spinoza, Baruch (1632–1677). Philosopher. Born in Amsterdam of Spanish-Portuguese Jewish descent he was expelled from the synagogue on the grounds of atheism and henceforward he devoted himself singlemindedly to philosophical studies, interesting himself especially in metaphysical problems. To eke out a livelihood he ground optical lenses. Of a singularly independent spirit, he declined a university chair at Heidelberg out of fear that the tenure of it might cramp the freedom of his thought and for a similar reason he refused a pension from Louis XIV.

Taking the Cartesian method as his starting point (see **Descartes**), he worked out its implications, concluding that there can be only one "substance," i.e., reality as a whole. God must be likewise the whole of reality, who must exist necessarily and eternally, not contingently and not temporally, in whom essence and existence coincide and who is his own cause (*causa sui*). As an infinite Being he must have an infinite number of attributes of which we know two: thought and extension. What we seek in philosophical inquiry is wisdom, which may be called the intellectual love of God. What then is that which we call Nature? It would seem to be identical with God so that we may properly use Spinoza's famous phrase: *Deus sive Natura,* "God or Nature." Nature, however, is to be understood in two ways. Spinoza calls the one *Natura* *naturata,* literally "nature natured," i.e., the reality that follows by necessity from the nature of God understood as the whole of reality, and the other *Natura naturans,* literally "Nature naturing," i.e., God as free cause, as the eternal infinite essence. *Natura naturans* is the ground, the principle of *Natura naturata.* Spinoza sees in every living entity a striving (*conatus*) which in its simplest and most obvious form consists in desire. Desire, however, can be so refined and developed till it becomes the means of intellectual salvation. Through imagination we are led to reason and eventually to an intuitive kind of knowledge (*scientia intuitiva*) through which we come to see the universal in the particular, the infinite in the finite: God in the raindrop and in the grain of sand. Eternity thus encamps itself in time.

Spinoza's system has been uniquely satisfying to many great minds. Even among those who do not relish metaphysical systems, its excellence as such is widely recognized. It lies in some ways close to the spirit of Indian theosophies, e.g., Advaita Vedanta. It may be attacked on the grounds of its ultimate determinism. For Spinoza we do have a certain kind of freedom, but in the long run this freedom has to be seen as ministering to an inevitable drive toward the kind of wisdom that culminates in perfect intellectual serenity. Freedom arises (as in God) from lack of dependence. To the extent that one achieves independence of mind one may be said to be free; yet it is not, nor can it be, ultimate freedom, i.e., man's freedom can never be freedom from God/Nature. The best starting place for the beginner in Spinoza is his *Ethics.*

Spiritual Exercises, The. A system of meditations and other devotional practices devised by Ignatius of Loyola, founder of the Jesuits. Drafted by him at Manresa, they were revised and enlarged in the course of his life and came to be known in Spanish as the *Ejercicios espirituales,* designed to extend over a month's retreat, although in abbreviated form they may be arranged for a much shorter time, such as a week or even a few days. The aim is first of all to bring men and women to the point of rooting out their carnal passions and desires in such a way as to make them long to give themselves wholly to God. This is done in the first week by engaging in meditations on the nature of sin and its terrible consequences. In the second week, one reflects upon the Kingdom of Christ; in the third on the Passion of Christ; and in the fourth week on the glory of the Risen Christ. Characteristic of the method Ignatius employed is a combination of vivid imagery and mental reflection, all copiously enriched by spiritual counsel on how to avoid pitfalls and attain one's spiritual goal. It has been probably more widely used than any other single method of spiritual vitalization and training. It includes "Rules for thinking with the Church."

Spiritual Healing. The concept of spiritual healing was well recognized in the Christian Church from its earliest times and possession of the gift of healing was regarded as among those proper to an aspirant to ordination. It should be noted that while some people have what seems to be a natural gift for healing, others who do not have that natural gift can learn to exercise a healing ministry through Christian channels including prayer, the laying on of hands, and sacramental means, notably the sacrament of Unction. Seemingly miraculous cures are attested, at Lourdes and other places of pilgrimage, by panels that include avowed skeptics as well as Christians. Spiritual healing should be understood in terms of the healing of the entire person, beginning with the spirit and reaching out to the body.

Spiritualism. In philosophy the term usually refers to a movement in 19th-c. France against the positivistic teachings of Auguste Comte. It was chiefly initiated by Victor Cousin and is associated with Maine de Biran.

The name is also given to a very different and religious movement concerned with communicating with the spirits of the departed. This latter movement had its origin in 1848, in the accidental discovery by two ladies in Hydeville, New York, the Fox sisters, that they possessed psychic powers that enabled them to expect such communication. The movement spread rapidly and was the object of much independent investigation by American and British societies for psychical research. Understandably it became even more popular in the wake of World War I. Spiritualist seances may be held in private homes or in a Spiritualist church. There is no uniform procedure, but a medium is always present to function as the intermediary and there are usually one or two hymns and prayers before the medium attempts to communicate. It has affinities with practices in societies more accustomed than the West to concepts such as spirit possession and a spirit world.

Spiritual Works of Mercy. See **Works of Mercy, Corporal and Spiritual.**

Spurgeon, Charles Haddon (1834–1892). Famous Calvinist Baptist preacher. Born in Essex, England, he was descended from a line of Independent ministers. Having become a Baptist, he soon became such a popular preacher that when, in 1854, he went to a pulpit in Southark, a new church, the Metropolitan Tabernacle, had to be built to accommodate the congregations that flocked to hear him. His unbending opposition to the literary analysis of the Bible and other views of his led to his break with the Baptist Union in 1887. Many volumes of his sermons were published. Few preachers, if any, in Victorian England matched the popularity he won through his eloquence, his interest in contemporary affairs, and not least his sense of humor.

Stabat Mater. A Latin hymn of unknown authorship but probably dating from the 13th c., it describes the sorrows of Mary at the Cross. (See **Servites** and **Sorrowful Mysteries, The Five.**) Traditionally used in the devotion of the Stations of the Cross as well as in a liturgical sequence for the two feasts of the Seven Sorrows of Mary, it is widely known in various musical settings, e.g., Palestrina and Haydn. There are many English translations, e.g., "At the Cross her station keeping/ Stood the mournful Mother weeping."

Stabilitas in Loco. The vow taken by Benedictine and other monks to remain attached for life to the monastery in which his or her religious profession was first made. This "stability" has promoted a lifelong connection with the land that has given monks and nuns a distinctive and very different outlook from that of friars and sisters (e.g., Franciscans, Dominicans, Carmelites) and clerics regular (e.g., Jesuits) who are organized on more military and mobile lines, prepared as they must be to go at short or even instantaneous notice wherever they are sent.

Stall. Cathedral and some other churches normally have fixed seats on both sides of the choir, each set aside for the use of one of the dignitaries such as the canons of the Cathedral and its dean.

Stanley, Arthur Penrhyn (1815–1881). Anglican divine. Schooled at Rugby, he reflected its spirit in his advocacy of toleration of both sides in the extremes of opinion during the early stages of the Tractarian controversy. Educated at Oxford, where he was professor of ecclesiastical history 1856–1864, he was Dean of Westminster from 1864 till his death. He was a very notable exemplar of the Broad Church movement of his time, which sought to embrace a wide variety of opinion within the Anglican Communion.

Staretz. In the Russian Church a person often, but not necessarily a monk, recognized for his personal holiness and wisdom.

Star of David. A six-pointed star, one of the most widely known symbols of Judaism.

Stations of the Cross. A popular Christian devotion dating from probably very early times and arising out of the practice by pilgrims to Jerusalem of following the route from Pilate's house to Calvary. During the Middle Ages the re-enactment of that pilgrimage took the form of visiting and praying before fourteen pictures or "stations" in turn, each representing an incident in the course of the last journey of Jesus. In the 18th–19th c. the incidents took the form now traditional, which are as follows: (1) Jesus is condemned to be crucified; (2) he receives the Cross; (3) he falls for the first time; (4) he meets his Mother; (5) Simon of Cyrene carries the Cross for him; (6) Veronica wipes the face of Jesus; (7) he falls the second time; (8) he meets the women of Jerusalem; (9) he falls the third time; (10) he is stripped; (11) he is nailed to the Cross; (12) he dies; (13) his body is taken down from the Cross; (14) his body is laid in the tomb.

Stein, Edith (1891–1942). A native of Breslau, of a Jewish family, she studied at Göttingen and Freiburg under Husserl, becoming an important figure in his phenomenological school, whose teachings, after her conversion to the Christian Way and her reception into the Roman Catholic Church in 1922, she tried to interpret along Thomistic lines. She became a Carmelite nun in 1934, taking the name of Teresa Benedicta a Cruce. She was transferred to Holland in 1938 and during the German occupation was taken to Poland where she was killed in a gas-chamber. For details of her life see Hilda C. Graef, *The Scholar and the Cross: The Life and Work of Edith Stein* (1955) and her biography by the Prioress of the Carmelite Convent at Cologne, published in 1948; English trans. 1952.

Steiner, Rudolf (1861–1925). Founder of Anthroposophy. Born in Kraljevic,

Croatia, of German ancestry he was educated in Vienna and much influenced by Goethe, whose outlook led Steiner to theosophical interests. Having served as secretary of the Theosophical Society in Germany, he broke with them in 1912 to found the *Anthroposophischer Bund,* which taught a special doctrine about the nature of man according to which human beings are composed of a series of principles in an ascending order of spirituality. The inner self, nourished by these spiritual developments in the various embodiments (etheric, astral, etc.), is eventually reincarnated. Steiner proposed educational methods to encourage a deepening of spiritual awareness and sensitivity to the realities of his situation and especially to an understanding of the spiritual nature of the universe. His writings include *Philosophy of Freedom* (1896), *Goethe's World View* (1897), and *Knowledge of the Higher Worlds* (1923).

Stephen. According to tradition he was the first deacon in the Christian Church. He was probably a Hellenistic Jew. He delivered the discourse recorded in Acts 7.2–53 to the effect that God does not depend on a temple made by human hands and that Jesus had been the prophet announced by Moses. His accusers thereupon, in the name of the Mosaic Law, stoned him for blasphemy. He died asking forgiveness for his persecutors, *c.* 35 CE. In 415 his tomb was discovered by one Lucian, a priest. The Empress Eudoxia caused a church to be built in his honor outside the Damascus Gate in 455–460. Its ruins were discovered by Dominicans in 1882 and replaced by a new church on the site.

Stephen, Leslie (1832–1904). Philosopher. Born in London and educated at Cambridge, where he was elected a Fellow of Trinity Hall, he took Anglican orders in 1859, but renounced them in 1875. From 1864 he devoted himself to a very active literary career in the course of which he directed the *Cornhill*

Magazine, a literary periodical, from 1871 to 1882, when he became director of the *Dictionary of National Biography*. Virginia Woolf was his younger daughter. After his break with the Church he identified himself more and more with the Utilitarian views of Bentham and Mill and especially with those of Darwin, whose *Origin of Species* had been published in the year of Stephen's Anglican ordination. His writings include *An Agnostic's Apology* (1893), *English Utilitarianism*, 3 vols. (1900), and *English Thought and Society in the Eighteenth Century*, 2 vols. (1904).

Stevenson, Charles Leslie (1908–1979). American philosopher. Born at Cincinnati and trained at Yale and elsewhere, he was Professor of Philosophy at the University of Michigan for most of his professional life. Believing that ethical disputes arise from differences in attitude rather than from differences of belief, he taught that ethical discussions have as their product the redirecting of attitudes, largely through "persuasive" definitions that in fact change the cognitive meanings of ethical terms. His writings include *Ethics and Language* (1944) and *Facts and Value* (1963).

Stewart, Dugald (1753–1828). Scottish philosopher. Born in Edinburgh, he studied under Thomas Reid, whose "common-sense" philosophy he generally followed, emphasizing the objectivity of ethical principles. His writings include *The Philosophy of the Active and Moral Powers of Man* (1828).

Sthanakavasi. A Jain movement that emerged in the 18th c. CE as a consequence of Islamic influence on the Jains. Its members repudiate the use of any form of images, which they regard as leading to idolatry. They hold their meetings in very simple buildings called "athanakas" and because of that they are known as "hall-dwellers."

Sticharion. A liturgical tunic worn in the Eastern Orthodox Church and functioning somewhat like an alb but usually of colored fabric.

Sticheron. A short liturgical hymn in Eastern Orthodox liturgy attached to a verse (*stichos*) of a psalm or other biblical passage.

Stigmata. The phenomenon consisting of the reproduction in a human being of the wounds of the Passion of Christ. The stigmata consist usually of wounds or blisters on the hands, feet, and side, sometimes also of wounds on the head where the Crown of Thorns was pressed down and on the back where the scourging was inflicted. The stigmata may consist either in visible appearances of such marks or in the pain suffered by the person experiencing it. The marks of the stigmata are not susceptible to medical treatment, i.e., neither do they become purulent nor can they be treated as would be any type of wounds or bruises known to physicians. They may bleed occasionally and are said to do so more often on Fridays or during Lent. The first person known to have been stigmatized is Francis of Assisi. Since then more than 300 cases have been attested, predominantly women, e.g., Catherine of Genoa and Thérèse Neumann.

While the subject is one that naturally arouses much skepticism, and the Roman Catholic Church has been characteristically cautious in making any official references to the phenomenon, at least some of the cases seem to have baffled all attempts at naturalistic explanation. Excessive, morbid preoccupation with the sufferings of Christ in his Passion could obviously bring about the phenomenon of pain in the affected areas of the body; marks that are insusceptible to regular medical treatment might be in some (even many) cases explicable as psychosomatic phenomena; but at least some cases seem to be beyond explanation in such terms. There is a considerable literature on the subject, much of it in French and German. In English, H. Thurston, S. J., *The*

Physical Phenomena of Mysticism, posthumously edited by J. H. Crehan, S. J. (1952) contains (pp. 32–129) some interesting materials. The Roman Catholic Church has not recognized stigmatization as even a contributive qualification for official recognition of sainthood. Fewer than one out of five of the persons known to have had the stigmata are on the Church's official calendar.

Stirling, James Hutchison (1820–1909). Born in Glasgow, he studied medicine, travelled in Germany and France, and returned to Scotland where he introduced the thought of Hegel and Kant. In his influential work, *The Secret of Hegel*, 2 vols. (1865), he developed a very theological interpretation of Hegel's thought. His other writings include his Gifford Lectures, *Philosophy and Theology* (1890) and *What is Thought?* (1900).

Stirner, Max (1806–1856). German philosopher. Born in Bayreuth, his original name was Johann Kasper Schmidt. He studied at Berlin, Erlangen, and Königsberg. His thought is founded on a radical individualism. Each individual is unique and should be guided by the principle of the discovery and fulfilment of his or her own will. The individual should reject all state interference with his or her freedom. His outlook might be classified as anarchism, but he claimed that his individualism, far from creating conflict among people would diminish it. By this he meant that it was not an individualism that asserted itself over the rights of others but, on the contrary, one that would encourage individuals to unite to obtain and conserve the conditions conducive to avoiding interference by others. His principal writings are: *The Ego and One's Own* (1845) and *The History of the Reaction*, 2 vols. (1852).

Stoics. Graeco-Roman philosophers whose school was founded by Zeno of Citium. They were so called from the porch (Greek, *stoa*) in which they origi-nally foregathered in Athens. In contrast to Plato they taught a monistic pantheism: God is the all-pervasive energy that creates and sustains the world. God is identified also with the principle of reason, the *Logos*. Stoic ethics had a considerable influence on the development of Christian ethics.

Stole. A liturgical vestment consisting of a long narrow strip of silk or other material, worn by priests and deacons in the Western Church as the badge of their office. Deacons (or priests functioning as deacons, e.g., at High Mass) wear it as a sash over the left shoulder and fastened under the right arm as a symbol of their service. Priests wear it around the neck and normally with the ends hanging down in front. It has been used in Rome since at least the 8th c. and has been in general use in Western Europe since the 9th. Its color varies according to the season of the Christian Year and local custom. For sacramental confession, however, it is always violet. In the Eastern Churches the priest's stole is called an epitrachelion and the deacon's an orarion which are worn over the other vestments, while in the West (except in the Ambrosian rite) the stole is worn under the chasuble or dalmatic.

Stoning. A primitive form of capital punishment frequently mentioned in the Bible. The Torah prescribes stoning as the specific form of punishment for certain crimes, e.g., adultery, fornication by an unmarried woman, blasphemy, idolatry and violation of the Sabbath are among the list. The use of this form of execution probably originated in convenience: stones abounded in Palestine. The condemned person was often taken outside the city where stones were especially plentiful. Two other considerations, however, should be noted: (1) all the community are represented and each person present participates in the execution, so that no single individual takes personal responsibility for it; and (2) because the punishment did not technically entail the shedding of blood as understood in Israelite law, blood guilt was not incurred. These were no doubt *ex post facto* arguments to justify stoning, which may very well have been originally a sort of lynching operation, as several biblical texts would suggest, then came to be invested with judicial authority and the invocation of the law. It was the duty as well as the right (e.g., see Deuteronomy 13.9) for the witnesses to throw the first stones; then the rest of the people joined in the execution.

Stoup. A bowl or basin at the entrance to a Christian church containing holy water, i.e., water blessed by a priest. On entering church one dips one's fingertips into the water, touches with them the fingertips of the next person entering, if any, and makes the sign of the Cross over oneself. The practice may have taken its origin in the fountains of the atrium of the basilicas of Christian antiquity, in which people would wash their hands and faces before entering. From the 9th c. the water stoup came into general use and is a familiar feature of Roman Catholic and many Anglican churches today. Stoups vary from tiny bowls tucked into the corner of a doorway to handsome, richly carved stone basins.

Strossmayer, Joseph Georg (1815–1905). Roman Catholic Bishop of Diakovár and one of the most prominent of the opponents of the definition of papal infallibility at the First Vatican Council (1869–1870). Born in Croatia of German descent, he became Professor of Canon Law at Vienna in 1847 and in 1850 Bishop of Diakovár. Unlike Döllinger, he eventually, although very reluctantly made formal acceptance of the decree of infallibility.

Structuralism. A philosophical view that was developed in France largely through the work of Claude Lévi-Strauss (1908–), focusing on the common structure alleged to be found in the views that all peoples take before any conscious reflection occurs. Structuralism has many aspects and applications, e.g., in linguistics, in history, and in religion. Generally speaking, the movement sets little value on and sees little importance in history and individualism. In psychology, the term "structuralism" is used to denote a structural rather than a functional approach to the problems of psychology. Structuralism represents an interdisciplinary approach to a common viewpoint that all cultures, indeed all societies, have a common structure. Freudians, Marxists, and Christians have used structuralist ideas in the interpretation of their respective stances.

Stūpa. A Sanskrit term (the Pali counterpart is *thūpa*) signifying a hemispherical mound of stone or brick and earth. Since at least the 3rd c. BCE, in the time of Aśoka, it has been the focus of much popular piety.

Stylites. See **Simeon Stylites.**

Suarez, Francisco (1548–1617). Scholastic philosopher. Born in Granada and educated at Salamanca, he entered the Jesuits. Starting from a Thomistic standpoint, he modified it considerably, rejecting, for instance, Thomas's distinction between essence and existence in finite beings and developing, on Molinist lines, a distinctive doctrine called Congruism, according to which the elect receive a special grace that leads them to accept God yet without injury to the freedom of their wills, i.e., the power of the grace is "congruent" with human freedom. Among his numerous writings the most philosophically important are his *Metaphysical Disputations*. A strong believer in the compatibility of philosophy and theology, he is generally accounted the most important scholastic philosopher of the 16th c. His work is much less dependent on Aristotle than had been that of the earlier schoolmen and he was more generally original and independent and more influential than were his scholastic contemporaries on opinion outside the Roman Catholic Church.

Subiaco. A town *c.* forty miles east of Rome. It is venerated as the cradle of Benedictine monasticism, being the site of the cave to which Benedict went *c.* 500 and from which he began his organization of the monastic order that has played an immense role in the transmission of Christian learning in Western Europe and throughout the world. There is now a monastery at Subiaco that is the mother house of the Cassinese Congregation.

Subjectivism. Any doctrine or tendency that emphasizes, in any philosophical discipline, the subjective element in human experience may be so designated, e.g., the notion that human knowledge is limited to knowledge of one's own mental states and the view that aesthetic judgment is no more than the affirming of one's own individual taste.

Submersion, Baptism by. A method of baptism in which the entire body of the candidate is submerged in the baptismal water. See **Immersion, Baptism by.**

Subordinationism. The doctrine, widespread in the early Christian Church but condemned as heretical at the Council of Constantinople in 381, according to which the Son and the Holy Spirit are subordinate to God the Father. It came to be regarded as heretical because it denied the co-equality of the Personae of the Trinity.

Subsistence. Where, in philosophy, modes of being are recognized, subsistence is generally an inferior or less complete mode than is existence. The term, however, has been invested with special meanings by some individual philosophers.

Substance. A traditional term in philosophy that from the first carried some ambiguities and is now widely discarded although of great historical importance. It comes from the Latin words *sub* and *stare* ("under" and "to stand") which together translate the Greek term *hypostasis*. The term fundamentally refers, therefore, to an underlying substratum that survives the various changes that occur in connection with it. It also is used to translate the Greek term *ousia*, "essence." Aristotle used both *ousia* and another Greek term *hypokeimenon*, which means the concrete object rather than its essence. He recognized the ambiguities, specifically pointing out that what is designated by such terms can mean a thing's essence, the universal thing, the genus, or the subject. He recognized also, however, two primary meanings: *ousia prōtē*, the subject of predication, and *ousia deutera*, general terms that function only as secondary references to the subject. Much theological controversy raged during the Middle Ages on the relation of "substance" to "accident" (see **Transubstantiation**). The term "substance" continued to be used by Descartes, Spinoza, and Leibniz, and then by the British empiricists, Locke, Berkeley, and Hume, even though Berkeley reduced all substance to mental substance and Hume denied meaning to the term as Locke had used it to denote "something I know not what." Phenomenalists dispensed with the notion entirely.

Suburbicarian Dioceses. The seven dioceses in the suburban areas of Rome, The Cardinal-bishops (see **Cardinals**) take their full episcopal titles from these dioceses, which are ancient and by modern standards extremely small in area.

Succoth. See **Tabernacles, The Feast of.**

Śūdra. In the traditional Hindu caste system, the fourth and (except for the pariahs or "outcastes") lowest of the social classes. Their occupation was generally menial and they were often aboriginal. A distinction, however, came to be recognized in reference to this caste: those who were "not excluded" from the hierarchical structure of society and those who were so close to the pariahs as to be only marginally within the social structure.

Sufficient Grace. In the controversies between the Dominicans and the Jesuits on "actual grace," two kinds were recognized: sufficient and efficacious. The Jesuits generally held with Molina that grace given by God is efficacious because it is given by God in circumstances which God foresees to be congruous with the dispositions of the recipient of the grace. The Dominicans held with Bañez that the efficacy of the grace depends on the character of the grace itself and therefore requires a further divine motion to become efficacious for salvation. Neither party, however, denied that human freedom is destroyed through the conferring of grace. See **Suarez, Francisco**.

Suffragan. In general ecclesiastical usage, a suffragan bishop is one who is appointed or elected to assist a diocesan bishop in the administration of the diocese. His duties depend largely on the will of the diocesan bishop.

Sufis. The term means "wool wearers" and refers to the clothing worn by groups of Islamic mystics who c. the 12th c. began to spread through the Islamic world. Although at first reflecting some influences from Christian ascetics and mystics, the Sufis for the most part remained within the bounds of Islamic orthodoxy, at least superficially, despite their emphasis on doctrines such as the divine nearness, which are fundamentally at odds with Muslim insistence on the otherness of God. Sufi ideas, however, long antedated such groups and those with such tendencies were often persecuted by the orthodox core of Islam. A notable example is that of al-Hallaj who in 922 was executed for the aberrancy of his views. Credit is due to a great Muslim thinker, al-Ghazali (1058–1111) who helped to make Sufism an acceptable or at least tolerated element in Islam. Sufism has exercised considerable influence on Is-

lamic literature, e.g., on the work of poets such as the 13th-c. Rumi.

Suicide. The act of deliberate self-destruction, which Albert Camus, in *The Myth of Sisyphus* (1955) called the "one truly philosophical problem," is uncompromisingly condemned in all three of the great monotheistic religions, Judaism, Christianity, and Islam, on the ground that life, being given by God, belongs to God and cannot lawfully be taken away by the recipient of the gift. Classical Hinduism also opposes suicide as contravening the general principle of *ahiṃsa*, although permitting euthanasia in some special circumstances. (See **Euthanasia**.) In some societies, however, suicide has been traditionally regarded as not only permissible but laudable and even a duty, e.g., hara-kiri, a ceremonial suicide, was obligatory in Japan for failure to perform one's duty to a feudal lord.

Although an unconscious "death wish" may cause people to engage in acts or occupations with such a high risk of death that they are sometimes accounted "suicide equivalents," suicide should be distinguished from all such behavior as a conscious and intentional act of self-destruction. Medical and social analyses of the problem of suicide generally tend to recognize a vast complex of circumstances, e.g., brain chemistry, depressive illness, and hereditary factors.

State laws for long followed the traditional ecclesiastical laws in respect of suicide. France led the way in 1790 in abolishing the anti-suicide laws. Most States have followed since then, but the extreme revulsion against suicide was not easily demolished. The bodies of suicides were often desecrated: the last burial of a suicide in England at a crossroads with a stake through the heart occurred as late as 1823. While a more compassionate view of suicide is now general and the traditional Roman Catholic refusal of public ecclesiastical burial of suicides is now much rarer than it was, the discouragement and prevention of suicide are actively pursued with the help of organizations and centers dedicated to such purposes. At least a distinction must be recognized between the case of an aged person terminally ill with an agonizing and revolting form of cancer or other disease who chooses or half-chooses to end his or her misery by a drug overdose and the case of a healthy young person, who in irreverent contempt for the gift of life wantonly engages in an act of self-destruction. What makes suicide so reprehensible from a religious standpoint is fundamentally the contempt for or at least lack of appreciation of the gift of life and no moral or legal judgment on suicidal acts should ever ignore this element in any individual case.

Sukhavati. The term means literally "happy land" and is used to signify the pure realm of being created by the ideal Amitabha in that form of Mahayana Buddhism commonly known as "Pure Land." Amitabha is credited with having created it by means of his supranormal powers. It is believed to provide a perfect environment for the acquisition of enlightenment, which is the fundamental Buddhist aim. See **Pure Land School.**

Sulpicians. A congregation of secular priests founded in 1642 by J. J. Olier. From the first this society, which took its name from the parish of Saint-Sulpice in Paris, where it originated, perceived as its aim the training of priests of an intellectual and moral caliber that would make them suited to become directors of seminaries. The spirit of the congregation had affinities with that of the Oratorians. In time it came to have a remarkably strong influence on the life of the Church in France. It has provinces in the United States and Canada.

Summa. The Latin term *summa* is used of certain forms of treatise in the Middle Ages. It means literally a compendium, and the literary form that it represents took its beginnings in the

12th c. as what were at first called Books of Sentences. The work of Abelard, for example, in the 12th c., represents a transitional stage in which the Book of Sentences was being developed into the Summa. In the 13th c. the Summa took full shape as a comprehensive collection of theological or philosophical arguments. The *Summa theologiae* of Thomas Aquinas is perhaps the best known example; others include his *Summa contra Gentiles*, the *Summa philosophiae* attributed to Grosseteste, and the *Summa logicae* of Lambert of Auxerre.

Summum Bonum. This Latin term means literally "the supreme good" or "the highest good." It is traditionally applied to that which is intrinsically good in itself and also to that which is regarded as the ultimate end of man, e.g., the enjoyment of God for ever, the maximum amount of pleasure, or whatever is held to qualify as the highest good available to a human being.

Sundar Singh (1889–c.1929). Born of a rich Sikh family, he experienced a vision on December 18, 1904, through which he was converted to the Christian Way. Wishing to preach Christianity in a way that would not seem alien to his Indian compatriots, he wore the dress of a sadhu, i.e., a Hindu holy man, and was widely known as "Sadhu Sundar Singh." In his missionary endeavors he traveled widely in Asia and later also in the West. He is presumed to have died in Tibet. For further study of his life see C. F. Andrews, *Sadhu Sundar Singh* (1934) and C. J. Davey, *The Yellow Robe* (1950).

Sunday School. The concept of the Sunday School as a function of parish work, although it may have had some earlier antecedents, is generally attributed to Robert Raikes who, in 1780, along with the incumbent of the parish, engaged four women to teach the children of Gloucester, England, basic Christian doctrine and practice. (See **Raikes, Robert.**) His example was soon followed in other English parishes and spread to continental Europe and America. Methods were gradually improved, and with the improvements in general education in the 19th c. the function of the Sunday School came to be more clearly definable. The concept has been developed in some intellectually active parishes to extend to adult classes with teaching at a more advanced level and by theologically well qualified men and women.

In Jewish circles the Hebrew school connected with the synagogue performs an important function in promoting and maintaining the high degree of literacy associated with educated Jewish life. Christian parishes exist in which a class in elementary New Testament Greek might be welcomed. Some Roman Catholics regret that more was not done to provide such instruction in elementary Church Latin, such as could have much diminished the need for abandoning its use as the regular international liturgical language in the Latin rite of the Roman Catholic Church.

Sunnis. In Islam the term *sunna* which means "custom" or "acceptable code of conduct" is applied in particular to Muhammad who, through precept embodied in the Hadith and included in the sayings attributed to the Prophet, provided Islam with a means of interpreting and applying the teachings of the Qur'ān. Those Muslims (the majority) who follow this tradition are called Sunnis or Sunnites, contradistinguished from the Shi'a or Shi'ites. See **Shi'ites.**

Śūnyatā. In Buddhist philosophy, a term used to denote the emptiness of ultimate reality. It plays an important role in the teaching of Nāgārjuna and the Mādhyamika school of Buddhist philosophy that he founded. The central doctrine of that school consists in the negation (*śūnyatā*) of all empirical concepts. Because of the strong affirmation of the śūnya principle, the Mādhyamika school is sometimes known as the Śūnyavāda.

Super-Ego. See **Freud, Sigmund.**

Supererogation. In Roman Catholic tradition, acts that are to be morally admired although not morally required. For example, a lifelong total sexual abstinence in the celibate state is regarded as much commended in Scripture, tradition, and the works of spiritual writers, yet by no means required of all the faithful as is total sexual abstinence outside the married state.

Supralapsarians. See **Infralapsarians and Supralapsarians.**

Surd. In mathematics, an irreducible radical: an irrational number whose square is an integer. The term is applied by some writers on the philosophy of religion to those elements in the universe that do not seem to be conformable to any rational or otherwise intelligible pattern.

Surplice. From the 12th c., the surplice, a loose white linen vestment with wide sleeves, came to be the normal dress of the clergy outside Mass. It originally reached to the feet like an alb but was gradually shortened till it barely covered the hips, developing into the ugly truncated version that came to be called a cotta. Under the influence of liturgical reform in the 19th c., it has now been generally restored to its more graceful length. Forms of the surplice are also used by laymen, e.g., in choir and in serving Mass.

Sursum Corda. The Latin words mean "Lift up your hearts" and are addressed to the people immediately before the Preface at Mass. The traditional response is "We lift them up unto the Lord" (*Habemus ad Dominum*). The use is extremely ancient, probably going back to at least the 2nd c. and attested by Hippolytus of Rome *c.* 215. The Greek form is: *Anō tas kardias,* with the response *Echomen pros ton kyrion.*

Suso, Henry (1295–1366). German mystic and poet. A Dominican, influenced by Eckhart, he wrote several mystical works including *The Little Book of Eternal Wisdom.*

Sūtra. In later Indian literature, the term, a Sanskrit one, which means "thread" (possibly derived from *siv*, to sew, and alluding to the stitching together of the manuscript leaves), is used of certain compositions written in an aphoritic style. The earliest examples are legal manuals. Later still emerged the *manu-smṛti*, written in a freer and more expanded style and in metre, being therefore more easily committed to memory. Almost all Indian philosophical systems adopted the terse, *sūtra* form, necessitating commentaries among which the *Brahma-sutra* is one of the best known. The Pali counterpart is *sutta*.

Sutta-Piṭaka. One of the three major divisions of the Buddhist Scriptures. It consists of discourses or dialogues. The other two divisions are the Vinaya-Piṭaka (the code of discipline governing the life of Sangha) and the Abhidhamma-Piṭaka (a systematically arranged collection of propositions considered to be of the essence of Buddhism). The Sutta-Piṭaka, full of parables and the like, are apparently intended for teaching at a popular level. (See also **Tripitaka.**)

Suttee. See **Satī.**

Svastika. In Hinduism this term, which means literally "well-being," is represented, in its righthanded form, 卐 and associated with the sun. It signifies the Vedic solar Viṣṇu and is a symbol of the evolution of the cosmos. In astronomy this form of the svastika represents the solstitial change of the sun to the Tropic of Capricorn. It is regarded as auspicious and male. The lefthanded form 卍 represents the sun during the autumn and winter seasons and is regarded as inauspicious and female. According to Hindu tradition the righthanded svastika should be painted on temple doors. It is also used as a good luck sign and for protection against evil forces, so it is

often found on the front of a house. Svastika is also the name of a mythical half-man, half-snake, called a *nāga*. Members of the Magadha and some other tribes wore svastikas when engaged in battle. The svastika was adopted by the National Socialist Party in Germany in 1919 as a good luck symbol, called the *Hakenkreuz*, and in 1935 it was incorporated in the flag of the Third Reich. As a sun symbol it is found in antiquity, however, far beyond India, e.g., in Egypt and in Aegean pottery. The word is usually but not necessarily spelt "swastika" in English.

Svetambaras. A schism divided the Jain community *c*. 80 CE into sects: the Svetambaras and the Digambaras.

Swami. An honorific title of respect given to Hindu teachers.

Swedenborg, Emanuel (1688–1772). Swedish scientist and religious thinker. Born in Stockholm and educated at Uppsala, he travelled to England where he quickly displayed his extraordinary scientific and mathematical genius. He was influenced by Locke and Newton and made important scientific discoveries in early life, anticipating many subsequently established hypotheses, e.g., nebular theory and magnetic theory, and may be regarded as the founder of crystallography. In 1716 he was appointed to a position on the Swedish Board of Mines. By his early forties his scientific studies had led him to a strong conviction that the structure of the universe has a spiritual basis, and in 1734 he published a Latin treatise in which he sought to show this by strictly scientific methods. At this stage he restricted himself to the methods of physics, but in later investigations he found that his convictions could be confirmed by biological and physiological methods too.

Ten years after the publication of his treatise he experienced a new and direct awareness of the spiritual nature of the world around him. He found himself in direct contact with the spiritual dimension of being to such an extent that it affected him both sleeping and waking. He was especially aware of and found himself in direct communication with angels. When this form of awareness had been fully established in him he became convinced that God willed him to disseminate knowledge of the spiritual world to others. To this end he organized a body called the New Church, which, however, was not to be in competition with or apart from the Swedish State Church or any other ecclesiastical body but was to serve, rather, as a society of brotherhood of spiritually minded people who could understand and profit from his teachings either inside the Churches or outside them. To this end he resigned his position in the Swedish government but strongly maintained his interest in scientific studies till the end of his life while writing copiously on his spiritual teachings. He died in London, was buried in the Swedish Church there, and in 1908 his remains were removed to Stockholm under an arrangement with the Swedish Government.

The most comprehensive of Swedenborg's presentations of his thought is the *Arcana Coelestia*, 8 vols. (1756). Among others are his *Heaven and Hell* (1758), *Divine Love and Wisdom* (1753), and *The True Christian Religion* (1771). As an introduction to his thought perhaps the best of his expositions is *The Apocalypse Revealed* (1766). The Swedenborg Foundation, Inc. publishes modern English translations of many of his works in convenient form.

Swedenborg saw reality as an organized hierarchy beginning with the mathematical point and ascending to God. Here he may show some affinity with Pascal, a mathematician and religious genius of an earlier generation who had conceived of God as a point moving at infinite speed. At any rate, Swedenborg saw mathematical points as connecting the finite with the infinite. Swedenborg saw humanity as having fallen from a higher state in which awareness of the spiritual nature of the universe would have been directly available but now may be retrieved. He distinguished three degrees of being in God: (1) the realm of ends, (2) the realm of causes, and (3) the realm of effects. This triune character of divine being is reflected in each individual man and woman as love, as wisdom, and as the living of a useful and creative life of faith and works. His system is theosophical and may be regarded as pantheistic. In spite of his desire that his doctrines should be disseminated through existing churches and in face of his aversion to "founding a new church," the "New Jerusalem Church" was founded in 1787 in Lancashire, England, by five former Methodist preachers. In America a Swedenborgian congregation was formed in Baltimore in 1792, and a General Convention met in Philadelphia in 1817. Other, smaller Swedenborgian churches also exist in America and Europe.

Swift, Jonathan (1667–1745). Anglican divine and one of the greatest satirists in English literature. Ordained priest in Ireland in 1695, he was Dean of Saint Patrick's Cathedral, Dublin, from 1713. His *Argument to Prove the Inconvenience of Abolishing Christianity* (1708) is among the wittiest of religious satires, while his *Gulliver's Travels* (1726) is an ever popular literary masterpiece.

Swiss Guard. The corps of military guardians of the Vatican Palace, instituted by Pope Julius II early in the 16th c. It consists of *c.* 100 men from all the Swiss cantons. Michelangelo designed the uniform, which consists of tunic, breeches, and stockings in cheerful red, yellow, and dark blue stripes. See **Noble Guard** and **Palatine Guard**.

Syllabus Errorum. A list of eighty propositions comprehensively condemned by Pius IX and issued along with his encyclical *Quanta Cura* on December 8, 1864. The evils it condemned ranged from Pantheism and Rationalism to Socialism and the Bible Societies. It was generally taken by Roman Catholic theologians at the time to be intended as an official pronouncement to be understood as the infallible teaching of the Church, which naturally caused great embarrassment to many educated Roman Catholics. Today few if any Roman Catholic theologians would regard it as such.

Syllogism. In traditional logic a syllogism is a form of reasoning by deductive inference; e.g., given two propositions such as "All Frenchmen understand French; this man is a Frenchman; therefore he must understand French." This is a valid argument. The conclusion is not necessarily true; its truth depends on the premises. What a syllogism shows is the validity or invalidity of the argument. The form just given is that of the categorical syllogism in which there are two premises and a conclusion, each with a subject and predicate. There are, however, other forms of deductive inference, e.g., the hypothetical syllogism. Common forms are as follows: (1) "If the car battery is dead, we cannot go to the party; the car battery is dead; therefore we cannot go to the party." (This type is called *Affirming the Antecedent*.) (2) "If I had had an aptitude for languages I could have passed this German test; I cannot pass this German test; therefore I have not a facility for languages." (This type is called *Denying the Consequent*.) Another very common syllogistic form is the disjunctive syllogism, of which there are two kinds: weak and strong. E.g., "Either the candidate is stupid or else he is wicked; he is not wicked; therefore he must be stupid." One could decline, however, to accept the second disjunct; then one could go on to conclude that the candidate is both stupid and wicked, for possession of the one quality does not exclude possession of the other. This is called a weak disjunction. If, however, one proposed a disjunctive syllogism in the following form, one could not so proceed. This is called a strong disjunction: "Either the candidate was born in Boston or he was born in Los Angeles; he was not born in Boston; therefore he was born in Los Angeles." The candidate, as we have seen, could be both wicked and stupid, but he could not have been born both in Los Angeles and in Boston.

Deductive inference in analytical, i.e., it does not yield new knowledge. What it does is to exhibit the implicates of what is already known. The examples given here are of course extremely simple ones, but the principle is the same however simple or complex the argument may be.

Symbol. In a large sense, anything that is presented to the mind as standing for something other than itself. In this sense, all thought is symbolic. Words are symbols as well as are the symbols of logic, algebra, chemistry, theology, and other fields. The symbols and signs of logic and mathematics are generally speaking arbitrary; there is no reason, for instance, other than convention, why the + should not be used for − and − for +, or why the ~ that logicians use for negation should not be replaced by, say #. Some symbols used in religion do no more than remind us of something—such as the crescent and the cross (for Islam and Christianity respectively)—while others, such as light, might possibly lead us directly to some understanding of that which they symbolize. See also **Sign**.

Synagogue. This term is a Greek one (*synagōgē*, place of assembly) applied to Jewish places of worship and instruction. When the Jerusalem Temple was destroyed in 587 BCE, resulting in the *diaspora* (dispersion) of the Jews, a temple-centered worship was no longer possible. The synagogue was an expedient devised as a substitute, probably at first consisting simply of a gathering in one of the larger private homes in the community. By New Testament times it had become a distinct building set aside for worship. Wherever there was a community of Jews, in Palestine or elsewhere, there would be a synagogue. It was administered as a lay organization, ruled by certain officers but with no priestly functions such as had been performed in the Temple. While it was indeed a mere substitute for the latter, it was sociologically the most potent factor in the survival of Judaism. It was a meeting place for Jews that preserved for them their identity as a people. From the standpoint of Christians of a later age it was much more like a Protestant church (e.g., a Congregationalist or Presbyterian one) than like a Roman Catholic or Anglican or Eastern Orthodox one. Not only was the synagogue the focus of much of the life of Jesus himself and of Paul and the other apostles (Paul began his preaching at the Damascus synagogue, as reported in Acts 9.20); it was from synagogal worship that Christian worship was gradually evolved, although with many transformations due to greater Gentile Christian acceptance of Hellenistic attitudes and culture.

Synapte. A prayer used in the Eastern Orthodox Churches constructed in litaneutical form as a series of suffrages said or sung by the deacon and each evoking from the faithful present the response *Kyrie eleison,* "Lord, have mercy." See **Litany.**

Syncretism. Originally this Greek term, introduced by Plutarch, meant simply the blending together of doctrines from various schools of philosophical or religious thought to make out of the blend a unified whole. The term is now used in a pejorative sense, signifying a mere collection of viewpoints idly put together without adequate understanding of them or of their implicates. It need not, however, always have so negative a connotation.

Synderesis (Synteresis). A Greek term apparently introduced by Jerome and used throughout the Middle Ages to signify the *scintilla* or spark of conscience that was left in man when the rest of moral and spiritual awareness

was deadened in the Fall. Because of this one remaining spark, God can gain access to fallen man and so redeem him. The concept was widely used in Christian mystical literature throughout the Middle Ages and later. See also **Scintilla.**

Synergism. Luther's colleague Philipp Melanchthon taught that the human will can be said to cooperate with the Holy Spirit and the grace of God, although the primary cause of the conversion that is accomplished is the Spirit of God, not the will of man. His teaching on this point is in the tradition of the Semi-Pelagians. See **Semi-Pelagianism.**

Synoptic Gospels. The three Gospels, Matthew, Mark and Luke, are so called. Their authors are called the Synoptists. The relation among them is a highly important and a still much debated problem in New Testament scholarship. The problem arises in several ways, but principally through the likeness among these three Gospels together with dissimilarities among them.

Syriac, Versions of the Bible in. Syriac is a branch of Aramaic spoken in Edessa and neighboring regions from just before the beginning of the Christian era. Because of the fact that there was a large Christian population in the Syriac-speaking areas as well as Jews, the Bible was translated into Syriac from an early date. The chief of the versions in Syriac is the Peshitta, which was originally made by Jews, probably early in the 2nd c. CE but used almost exclusively by the Syriac-speaking Christian community. A Syriac version of Tatian's *Diatessaron* was made, possibly as early as 200 CE. The Syriac-speaking Churches today still use the Peshitta. They include the Syrian Orthodox Church, which has been a member of the World Council of Churches since 1960 and, despite numerical losses through the centuries by reason of Turkish and other invasions, now claim *c.* one and one-half million members. There is also a body of Syrian Catholics with a patriarchate in Beirut.

Syzygy. (From the Greek *syzygia*, pair.) A Gnostic term, used by Valentinus and others to designate a pair of cosmological opposites, male and female respectively. The concept has affinities with the Chinese yin/yang.

T

Tabernacle. This term, from the Latin *tabernaculum*, a tent, is used in English to designate the sacred tent in use in ancient Israel and mentioned frequently in the Bible. The plan and its furnishings are described in Exodus 25–31. As reported there it seems to mix desert furnishings with temple structure. The historicity of the tabernacle has been disputed by Old Testament scholars, but at least both the biblical data and what is known from information outside the Bible make the existence of such a portable "holy tent" very probable. Among the nomads of the Syrian desert portable tent shrines were actually in use until recent times and are of great antiquity. The tabernacle purports to be a sort of shadow or reflection of its archetype in heaven, which, in the New Testament, is represented as the true tabernacle not made with hands (Hebrews 9.11 f.). See also Revelation 21.3.

In Christian usage, the tabernacle is the name given to the receptacle, usually ornamented, containing the Reserved Sacrament. See **Reservation.**

Tabernacles, The Feast of. The early designation given to the feast mentioned in Exodus 23.16 and 34.22, later called (as in modern Judaism) the Feast of Booths or Succoth (*sukkôt*). It commemorates God's protection of his people during their forty years of wandering through the wilderness from Egypt to the Promised Land. Deuteronomy 16.13–15 prescribes the length of its celebration as seven days. It is a harvest festival of thanksgiving for the fruits of the earth and of the vine, but at the same time a commemoration of the attainment of the Promised Land. There is a solitary allusion to it in the New Testament (John 7): Jesus, after declining to go to it publicly, secretly attends it. In Judaism today, covered booths are erected in synagogues, in gardens, on balconies, or elsewhere, and they become temporary dining and prayer rooms. They may be decorated with fruits, with pictures, and with verses from the Torah.

Taboo (or Tabu, Tapu). In Polynesian religion a term correlative to mana. (See **Mana.**) Objects that are considered to have mana, i.e., magical or mysterious power, such as the tombs of chiefs and even their household utensils, are protected by taboos, i.e., restrictive provisions forbidding people to touch or in some cases even approach such objects.

Taborites. A party of the Hussite movement in 15th-c. Bohemia who adopted an extreme, revolutionary attitude toward Church and State, not only repudiating traditional doctrine but demanding the abolition of courts of law and the other appurtenances of civilized society. They fought fanatically to resist the established powers and were for some time remarkably successful against all odds, with both the Roman Catholic Church and the more moderate wing of the Hussites joining forces against them. They were eventually defeated, however, at Lipany in 1434, after which nothing is heard of them.

Tabula Rasa. This Latin term means literally "blank tablet." The concept that the mind, having no "innate ideas," begins like a blank tablet awaiting experience to etch impressions upon it is one that John Locke enunciated in opposition to Descartes. The notion, however, was not entirely original with Locke. Duns Scotus, the last of the three great 13th-c. schoolmen, had held that the mind is a *tabula nuda* ("naked tablet") until it has experience. Bonaventure, also a 13th-c. schoolman, held this view too, although he excepted certain ideas (e.g., the idea of God) as innate.

Tahara. In Islam, before one participates in worship (see **Salat**), one must be ritually pure. The state of ritual purity is called *tahara*. Water is used normally for attaining that ritual purity, but in emergency sand may be used.

Tai Chen (1723–1777). Chinese Neo-Confucian philosopher. He developed a movement called "investigations based on evidence." For support for his movement he looked back to the Han Dynasty for an interpretation of the Confucian Classics. Among his writings is his *Commentary on the Meaning of Terms in the Book of Mencius.*

T'ai Chi. "The Great Ultimate:" a Chinese understanding of the basic principle of the universe, identical with all things. It stands in contrast to the view of those who hold that the principle engenders yin/yang.

Taizé. An ecumenical monastic order founded in 1940 by Roger Schutz, who had become convinced of a need in Protestantism to provide some form of the monastic life. He acquired a house at Taizé, near Cluny, France, in wartime and sheltered Jews and other refugees there till the Germans occupied that part of France in 1942, when he moved to Geneva and began leading a form of community life there with a few others. In 1944 they moved to Taizé. A rule was composed in 1952 on fairly traditional, although modified, monastic lines. The members of the Taizé community, who represent a variety of Protestant denominations, wear a white hooded habit in church but at other times ordinary secular clothes. They recite three offices in choir daily and run various industries such as a cooperative farm and a printing press. The fundamental purpose of Taizé, however, is to foster Christian unity.

Takht. In the religion of the Sikhs, the community is known as the Panth. Within the Panth the Takht signifies the seat of temporal authority. There are several. The Akal Takht at Amritsar has retained a certain pre-eminence among the takhts, being the place for debate and the promulgation of major decisions. The word *takht* means literally "throne."

Tallith. The four-cornered prayer shawl, usually made of white wool with black or purple stripes and, at each corner, eight-stringed fringes, worn by Jews for prayer both at home and in the synagogue. The top is decorated with an ornamental fringe of silver or gold thread, called "atarah."

Tallith Katan. A fringed undervest worn by observant Jewish men as a reminder of the commandments of God. The fringes serve as an irritant to the skin. Compare the use of the hair shirt by Christian ascetics. See **Hair Shirt.**

Talmud. The comprehensive commentary on the Mishnah that is the principal text for rabbinic Judaism. The Palestinian or Jerusalem Talmud was edited *c.* the end of the 4th c. CE; the Babylonian Talmud *c.* a century later. The latter is considered the more authoritative. See also **Mishnah.**

Tantra. Originally a Hindu sacred text, the tantra in Buddhism refers to a series of ritual texts that were delivered by the Buddha in the form of discourses. They deal with the attainment of enlightenment, with acquiring magical power, and other such matters. They are believed by many to have been transmitted secretly until *c.* the 4th c. CE and then opened up to people in general by a group of masters. Tantrism is associated with Mahayana. (See **Mahāyāna.**) In Hinduism the term is also used of certain texts dealing with certain magical practices related to the cult of Shakti, sexual and yogic in character and performed by initiates in secret.

Tantum Ergo. The opening words of a Latin hymn (consisting of the last two verses of the hymn *Pange lingua gloriosi* by Thomas Aquinas) traditionally sung at Benediction. See **Benediction.**

Taoism. As a religion, Taoism comprises a wide variety of outlooks and practices, ranging from ancient philosophical texts such as the *Tao Te Ching* to a conglomeration of ritual practices. It is highly eclectic, incorporating notions from ancient Chinese thought, such as yin-yang, with alchemy and the quest for immortality. The term *Tao Chiao*, which means literally "Teachings of the Way," is now generally used to designate those who see the Tao as the supreme reality and look for ways of access to that reality, whether by meditation, ritual, alchemy, or philosophical study. Taoism in this sense emerged *c.* the 2nd c. CE.

Tao Te Ching. The most widely known and popular of Taoist texts, it is traditionally attributed to Lao Tzu, but its authorship cannot be satisfactorily established. It seems to have been in existence, however, at least in some form, by *c.* 300 BCE.

Tao Tsang. The Taoist scriptural canon, which in 1436 CE attained its present form, enormous in length. An earlier form was even longer. Many volumes, however, were destroyed or lost when Kublai Khan ordered it to be burned in 1281 CE.

Tapas. In Sanskrit a term meaning "heat," it has great importance in Hindu thought. Heat is considered to have two forms: *kāma*, the heat of sexual desire, opposed to *tapas*, the heat generated by ascetic practices, more particularly sexual abstinence and the cultivation of chastity. *Tapas* is both the source of spiritual power and the means of attaining it. *Tapas* is greatly admired in the popular Hindu outlook. Some legends recount the dismay of the gods at the progress made by certain humans who have become advanced in the ac-

quisition of chastity, since the spiritual power it confers can make humans vie with the gods.

Targum. An Aramaic biblical translation/commentary. When the Jews had ceased to use Hebrew as a colloquial language, many found that they could not understand the public readings of the Bible in the synagogue. A translation or rather an Aramaic paraphrasing was provided, which in time was edited, becoming an official version.

Tatian. Early 2nd c. Christian Apologist. Born in Assyria, he became a Christian in Rome *c.* 150 CE, at first studying under Justin Martyr.

In a work in defense of the Christian faith he attacked Greek civilization in the most violent terms, representing it as at every point incompatible with Christian faith. More useful was his famous *Diatesseron*, an edition of the four Gospels set forth as a continuous narrative. Used in the Syriac Church till the 5th c., it still retains historical importance as a tool in helping to establish the text of the Gospels. See **Diatesseron.**

Tat Tvam Asi. This Sanskrit phrase, meaning "Thou art that," is used in Hinduism as a mantra to represent the fundamental identity between the microcosm and the macrocosm. *Tat* refers to *brahman*, the universal principle; *tvam* (thou) is the *ātman*, the individualized aspect thereof. From a Hindu standpoint the phrase points to the altruistic attitude of the ethical person, who subordinates individual self to the self of all others. The phrase occurs in the Chāndogya Upaniṣhad, 6,8,6.

Tauler, Johann (*c.* **1300–1361**). Christian mystic. Having entered the Dominican Order in 1315, he attained fame as a preacher and spiritual director. His sermons reflect the influence of Eckhart, presenting as they do a mystical teaching that stresses the indwelling of God in every human soul. He delineates the mystical way in a mode rooted in the theological orthodoxy of his age, emphasizing the bringing forth of good fruits from the mystical encounter and denigrating any luxuriating in the mere delight of the experience. During the Black Death in 1348 he was able to put into practice this aspect of his teaching, devoting himself unstintingly to the afflicted.

Tautology. In logic a proposition that is true by reason of its form only. All of its substitution instances are true. For example, $2 + 2 = 4$ is true within the system that has been pre-established, in which likewise $4 - 2 = 2$ is true. Tautologies may be useful as mathematics is immensely useful although it provides no *new* information, i.e., no new information beyond the system. Tautologies may be said to be formally true. They could not be false, while "synthetic" propositions such as "Paris is the capital of France" and "The average annual rainfall of Glasgow is 45 inches" are true but could be false.

Tawḥīd. This Arabic term, as used by the Muslim mystic al-Junayd of Baghdad, means both the assertion of the unity of God and the mystic's experience of ecstasy in mystical union. That a term meaning literally "union" should come to signify the separation of the Creator from the creature and at the same time mystical union between them is paradoxical, but one must bear in mind the extreme insistence in Islamic theology on the fundamental chasm lying between God the Creator and man the creature. To identify in any way the creature with the Creator is, in Islam, the ultimate blasphemy. Therefore Muslim mystics have had to be extremely cautious, in their descriptions of the mystical union with God, to avoid the suspicion of making any identification such as would offend orthodox believers. Junayd, eager to appear more orthodox than the orthodox, avoided the notion of a welding or absorption in the mystical union by making the term mean isolation: the separation of Allah

in his divine majesty from all his creatures. Some of the Spanish Christian mystics took similar precautions by the use of the phrase *hilo de amor*. which enabled them to talk of the binding of the soul to God in mystical union while preserving the notion that it is a binding, not an absorption.

Taylor, Jeremy (1613–1667). Anglican divine and devotional writer. Born at Cambridge and educated there, he became chaplain to King Charles I. Embroiled in the political troubles of the times, he moved to Wales in 1645, where he wrote many of the devotional works that have immortalized his name, especially *The Rule and Exercise of Holy Living* (1650) and its sequel on *Holy Dying* (1651). He pleaded for religious toleration in his *The Liberty of Prophesying* (1647). In 1660 his *Ductor Dubitantium*, a manual of moral theology, published in the year he became Bishop of Down and Connor, Ireland, provided a guide for Anglican clergy in hearing confessions.

Te Deum. Ancient Latin Christian hymn of praise to God. Although its origins are disputed by liturgical scholars, it is certainly of great antiquity, being alluded to from at least as early as *c.*500 CE. Traditionally it was attributed to Ambrose and used at Augustine's baptism, but almost no scholars today accept that attribution.

Tefillin. The two black leather boxes worn by adult male Jews. See **Phylactery,** the name by which they are known in English.

Teichmüller, Gustav (1832–1888). Philosopher. Born in Braunschweig, he taught at Göttingen. He was a proponent of "Perspectivism," a view that although each metaphysical system is partial it represents a single perspective of a reality that is more complex than any system can exhibit. His writings include *On the Immortality of the Soul* (1874), *The Real World and the Apparent World* (1882), and *Philosophy of Religion* (1886).

Teilhard de Chardin, Pierre (1881–1955). Jesuit theologian and scientist. Born near Clermont, France, he entered the Jesuit Society in 1899. From an early age much interested in the natural sciences, he pursued them along with the required studies during the long Jesuit training and was able, after service in World War I, to devote his attention to them increasingly. In the course of work in China he became a noted palaeontologist and geophysicist. Because he had been unable to obtain permission from his superiors to publish his theological writings, almost the only ones published during his lifetime were scientific papers. His philosophical and theological writings are virtually all published posthumously. They appeared from 1955 onwards, beginning with *The Phenomenon of Man* (1955; English translation 1959), still probably his best known work and certainly a good introduction to his thought which, cast in an evolutionary mold, would have been more novel and epoch-making had not he been inhibited from publishing it when it was written, for by the time of publication his evolutionary approach to the problems of theology had become familiar to educated Christians through the work of a variety of Protestant (especially American) theologians. Nevertheless, even as belatedly published, Teilhard's work was provocative to many and very influential. His concept of "spheres" of development, moving from the lowest to the highest levels of consciousness, from the realm of rocks and rivers to the "biosphere" (the realm of living organisms) to the "noösphere" (the mental realm, beginning at the point at which consciousness turns inwards), is the basis of much of his thought. The theory that he develops out of it as a presentation of the ascent of man to God, made possible through the Incarnation of God in Jesus Christ, has been much more critically received, reflecting what many find to be an unwarranted optimism. Nevertheless, his thought is a very serious attempt to bring "science" and "religion" together in a new synthesis, as of course had been the aim of Thomas Aquinas and others in the Golden Age of medieval thought.

Teinds. Historically, "teinds" were the Scottish counterpart of the "tithes" or "tenths" by which the clergy were maintained from a portion of the produce of the land. Until an Act of Parliament in 1925 abolished the system, the teinds were paid by the "heritors," i.e., those who owned heritable land in the parish. At first paid in kind, they were later paid in money. Since their value varied very much according to the value of the land and the efficiency of its cultivation, the parish ministers' financial interests were much tied to those of the landed classes.

Teleological Argument. One of the traditional arguments for the existence of God. It has its roots in Plato and Aristotle but was classically formulated in more recent times by William Paley (1743–1805), according to whom every biological species may be seen as designed to serve its own needs. From this premise he argues to an intelligent and purposeful Creator. Though it is no longer tenable in precisely that form, it is still used by those who see the survival of life in conflict and strife as evidence of a divine purpose.

Teleology. The term (from the Greek, *telos*, "end") probably originated with Christian Wolff (1679–1754) and denotes the science of final causes or ends. It refers especially to any system that interprets the universe as having purpose or design.

Tell. This Arabic word has as its Hebrew equivalent *tēl* and is used in the Old Testament to designate a mound created by long occupation of a site. A tell was often created by buildings and other debris but sometimes it was the result of the abandonment of a site because of war, famine, or other disaster. In older settlements the tell could reach a great height, e.g., Tell es-Sultan (Jericho) contained 80 feet of debris deposited from *c*. 6800 BCE to the time of the Israelite monarchy, *c*. 1000 BCE.

Temenos. In ancient Greek religion, a sanctuary dedicated to a deity or deities and serving a city or other community. The area was separated from the outside by a wall or other boundary and contained a *naos* (temple) and *bomos* (altar), usually with areas for ·dramatic performances, dining, and other purposes.

Temperance. One of the four "cardinal" virtues (see **Cardinal Virtues**) and regarded as the foundation of them all, it was much emphasized by Plato, Aristotle, and the Stoics. It is the virtue of controlling both mind and body by the dictates of reason and therefore leads to moderation in conduct and serenity of mind. It is a safeguard against licentious behavior of any kind such as sexual excess, drunkenness, and violence. It is much commended in the New Testament. In English the use of the word "temperance" was appropriated in the 19th c. by the promoters of the movement against the use of alcoholic beverages. This is a diminishment of, if not a deviation from, its classical meaning.

Templar, The Knights. (See also **Hospitaller, The Knights.**) The Knights Templar were one of the two principal military orders in Christendom in the Middle Ages. They were successively headquartered at Jerusalem, Acre, and Cyprus. In 1118 Hugh de Payens, a knight of Champagne, and eight companions bound themselves by solemn vow to undertake the protection of all pilgrims to the Holy Land from the bandits who menaced safety on the roads. They were also known as the Poor Knights of Christ and of the Temple of Solomon. They were so called because at first lodged on the site of Solomon's Temple and very poor, but with support from the Church they soon grew rich and spread extensively. By the 13th c. the Templars had become highly important and influential, with much wealth deposited in their

"temple" in London and elsewhere. The rivalry with other military orders generated strife that eventually contributed to their being suppressed in 1312 by Pope Clement V. The original Temple Church in London dated from 1185 and like their other churches was built in the round, modelled on the Church of the Holy Sepulchre at Jerusalem.

Temple, William (1881–1944). Archbishop of Canterbury. Educated at Balliol College, and for some years Fellow of The Queen's College, Oxford, he became Bishop of Manchester in 1921, was translated to York in 1929, and to Canterbury in 1942. Trained in philosophy in the Neo-Hegelian tradition, he developed an independent position of his own that won him repute in academic circles as a bridge figure between an older, 19th-c. Oxford philosophical tradition and one that was beginning to emerge by the time of his most important work in philosophical theology, *Nature, Man, and God* (1934). At Manchester and even more at York he became increasingly influential in movements for social and economic reform to which, without identifying himself with any political party, he showed great sympathy. He was also successful in promoting ecumenical relations with Roman Catholics and Protestants at a time when ecumenicity was widely viewed with suspicion and fear. His writings also include his *Mens Creatrix* (1917) and his *Christianity and the Social Order* (1942).

Temple at Jerusalem. The first temple was built by Phoenician architects on a customary Near Eastern plan under the reign of Solomon in 950 BCE. Destroyed by the Babylonians in 587 BCE, its site lay derelict; then it was rebuilt some seventy years later. Antiochus IV profaned this temple in 167 BCE, but it was reconsecrated three years later under Judas Maccabaeus. By the time of Jesus it had been greatly enhanced under Herod. It was destroyed by the Romans in 70 CE. See **Wailing Wall.**

Temptation. Some ambiguity is to be found in the biblical use of the words translated "temptation" in English. In Hebrew the concept is rooted in the verb *nāsāh*, "to test" or "to try." (The Greek translation of the noun is *peirasmos*.) A classic example of this usage is found in the story of God's tempting Abraham by commanding him to sacrifice his beloved son Isaac (Genesis 22.1–19). Likewise, God tempts (i.e., "tries out") the Israelites to see in what way they will choose to walk (Judges 2.22). This is a primary meaning of the term in the Bible, especially in the Old Testament. Man also "tries out" God, and the Devil "tries out" man, as in Genesis 3.1–19. In James 1.2 and 1.12–15, this meaning is retained: temptation is not presented as a seduction (the notion that God would in any sense seduce his creatures is totally excluded) but as a test. God does send tests and trials, however, to give them the opportunity of showing their moral fiber and developing it. This is presumably the meaning to be understood in the petition in the Lord's Prayer traditionally englished, "Lead us not into temptation." (Some modern versions render this "Do not put us to the test," i.e., "do not subject us to trial.") When Jesus rebuked Satan during the Temptation in the Wilderness, reminding him at the end of the Temptation narrative, that it is said, "Thou shalt not tempt the Lord thy God" (e.g., Luke 4.12), his rebuke implies the traditional understanding of the same biblical concept of temptation: testing or proving.

In other New Testament passages, however (e.g., I Corinthians 7.5), the concept of temptation comes closer to what is nowadays generally understood by it. Paul warns his readers against acts which, innocent though they may be, might seduce others into sin. Augustine distinguished the two ideas of temptation: one is *tentatio probationis*, testing or proving, the other *tentatio deceptionis* or *tentatio seductionis*. It is the latter that tends, because of human frailty, to lead one into sin. It is one thing to try out an athlete's quality and stamina by fair judicial tests; it is a very different thing to try him out to see whether he might be susceptible to bribery or the like.

Tenri-Kyo. A Japanese sect founded by a *miko* (a female shaman in Shinto), Nakayama Miki (1798–1887). The sect stresses diligent work and altruistic service as leading to a better state in the next incarnation. (See **Reincarnation**.)

Terah. The personal name of Abraham's father, mentioned in Genesis 11.24–32 and I Chronicles 1.26. Terah and his family left Ur to move to Canaan, but settled in Haran, where Terah died.

Teraphim. In Genesis 31.19 and 31.30–35, certain religious images are mentioned under this name. These were apparently venerated by the people in pre-exilic times, and it would seem that they were at least partly in human form (I Samuel 19.13). They were probably household gods. Their use is condemned in II Kings 23.24.

Teresa of Ávila (1515–1582). The name by which the Spanish Carmelite nun and mystic, Teresa de Jesús, is generally known. Descended from an old Spanish family, she received her education from Augustinian nuns and in 1535 entered a Carmelite convent. At first she apparently led a rather pedestrian, if not lax, life as a nun. In 1555, however, she was converted to a life of perfection. Soon after, she began to receive revelations, some in the form of interior awareness of the presence of Christ. She resolved, in face of strong opposition, to found a Carmelite house in which the rule would be very strictly observed and carried out her resolve in 1562 at Ávila, where, for her nuns, she wrote *The Way of Perfection*. (She had already finished her *Vida*, a spiritual autobiography, which she had undertaken at the order of her superiors.) From 1567, encouraged and assisted by John of the Cross, she established several such houses following the same strict rule. These houses of Discalced Carmelites were founded in face of considerable opposition from the Calced Carmelites. (See **Discalced**.) She is of paramount importance not only in the history of Spanish mysticism, one of the most important of the many Christian mystical traditions, but in the history of spirituality itself. For she developed original and carefully worked out schemes of disciplined spirituality, describing states in the mystical process between discursive prayer and meditation on the one hand and, on the other, the mystical experience of the ecstasy of quiet union with God. By no means least remarkable in Teresa is her combination of a deeply spiritual life with an extremely energetic practicality and common sense. She wrote prolifically. Among her best known works is *The Interior Castle*. She was canonized at Rome in 1622.

Teresa of Lisieux (1873–1897). She entered a Carmelite convent at Lisieux, France, at the age of fifteen, took her first vows in 1890 and became assistant novice-mistress in 1893. At the order of her superior she wrote *L'Histoire d'une âme*, a spiritual autobiography, which when eventually distributed in a revised form along with details of her death to all houses within the Order, did much to bring about her cult as a saint of a very special kind. In 1926, as a result of the miracles that were alleged to have been accomplished through her intercession, a large basilica was erected at Lisieux and quickly became a far-famed place of pilgrimage. In 1947 she was made co-patroness of France along with Joan of Arc herself. The two Teresas (Ávila and Lisieux) are compared and contrasted in a study by Victoria Sackville-West, *The Eagle and the Dove* (1943).

Tertiary. As early as the 13th c. the need was felt to provide people living in the world with an opportunity to be associated with the spirit and discipline of a religious order such as the Dominicans and Franciscans, so helping them to attain Christian perfection. Such "secular tertiaries" wear a scapular under their ordinary clothes, although they are clothed in the habit of the order, which they wear on certain prescribed occasions and in which they may be buried at death. Some of the great Christian humanists of the Renaissance, for example, were tertiaries. See also **Oblate**.

Tertium Quid. In medieval logic, after an analysis had explored two opposites, neither of which seemed to provide a satisfactory answer to the question raised, a search for a *tertium quid*, i.e., a "third something," was undertaken, to be found somewhere between the two opposing extremes.

Tertullian, Quintus Septimius Florens (*c.* 160–*c.* 225). African Church Father. A pagan by upbringing, he was well educated in the humanities and converted to the Christian Faith towards the end of the 2nd c. The chronology of his life is the subject of scholarly dispute. In the earlier years after his conversion he championed orthodoxy and was especially against Gnosticism. His rigoristic understanding of Christian doctrine led him into Montanism. (See **Montanism**.) His style is decisive and clever although sometimes very unfair to his opponents. He is regarded by some as the Father of Latin theology.

Tetragrammaton. Literally "four-lettered word." Term used by scholars for the Hebrew word JHWH (one of the proper names of God), which Jews held to be too sacred to utter. When reading the Scriptures they substituted the word "Adonai." For the reader's convenience they inserted the vowel points of "Adonai" into the unutterable word-"JHWH," so yielding in some English renderings since the sixteenth century the erroneous and mixed form "Jehovah." Modern scholars generally think that "Yahweh" represents the original pronunciation before the substitution of "Adonai."

Tetzel, Johann (*c.* 1465–1519). German Dominican friar. He acquired his notoriety in considerable measure from Luther's focus on him as a symbol of the evil trade in indulgences. (See **Indulgences.**) In 1516 an indulgence had been issued in connection with the rebuilding of Saint Peter's, Rome, and Tetzel had been made subcommissary for certain regions including Magdeburg. He was apparently a persuasive speaker. When he went so far as to defend the popular belief that one could secure the release of a loved one from Purgatory by the payment of a financial contribution to the rebuilding fund, many plain people were shocked. It was after hearing him speak at Jüterbog that Luther was moved to challenge the practice in the famous Ninety-Five Theses. The papal nuncio, C. von Miltitz, tried unsuccessfully to discourage Tetzel from his extravagant, blatant commercialization of the practice of granting indulgences. Tetzel, however, continued to defend what he had been doing.

Textual Analysis. Before the age of printing, the likelihood of errors in the transmission of any text was very great. Not many scribes were careful enough to copy a text impeccably, and by the time it had been copied over and over again errors were almost inevitable. The work of textual analysis or criticism consists in comparing and evaluating the different "readings" found in manuscripts, notably in those of the biblical books, with the object of trying as far as possible to establish the text as it had left the hands of the respective authors. The incidence of errors in New Testament manuscripts is particularly great. By methods of analysis, textual critics have made much progress toward their goal. One should not suppose, however, that the results often radically change the traditionally "received" text. On the contrary, the changes are usually

much less fundamental than is popularly imagined. If these texts were not of such singular importance to, and so beloved by, Christians, less extreme diligence might be exercised by scholars in the quest for a perfectly reconstructed text of the Bible.

Thales of Miletus (640–546 BCE). One of the earliest of the great thinkers of Greece, he was accorded the title *sophos* (wise one) and recognized as one of the Seven Sages of Greece. He was very versatile in his interests and accomplishments, e.g., he predicted the solar eclipse of 585 BCE, diverted a river to permit the passage of King Croesus and his retinue, visited Egypt where he learned the foundations of geometry, and (according to Hieronymus of Rhodes) was self-taught except for his stay in Egypt during which he associated with the priests there. Probably his prediction of the eclipse brought him most fame. It was a total eclipse, taking place during a battle between the Medes and the Lydians and causing a cessation of hostilities that led to a lasting peace between them. Although the Egyptian priests may have introduced him to the elements of plane geometry and perhaps some rudiments of solid geometry, Thales went far beyond what they could have taught him, founding the abstract geometry of lines, making possible the establishment of precise relations between the different parts of a figure: a highly original advance in human knowledge at that time. According to Aristotle, Thales found water in the origin of everything and supposed the earth to float upon a sea of water. Since we have no writings on which to rely, the precise nature of his cosmology is conjectural, but his unique greatness in the history of thought is attested by his contemporaries and successors. Like the other Greek thinkers of his time, he sought for one principle at the root of all things and thought he found it in water, possibly because it is water that sustains life. At any rate, Aristotle perceived Thales as initiating the quest for principles of explanation of all phenomena. He is credited with the aphorism: "all things are full of gods." (See **Theos.**) His approach to the philosophic quest was continued on similar lines by other members of what we now call the Milesian school, such as Anaximenes and Anaximander. Parmenides and his Eleatic School were to use a different approach. By the time we reach Socrates and Plato we have entered into a new and more developed phase of thought. In Thales, however, we have the beginnings at a time when no distinction was made between what came to be accounted different quests, each requiring a methodology of its own. To Thales, at any rate, must be given credit for initiating the process of intellectual inquiry that was eventually to foster the flowering of European thought, science, and culture.

Theism. Generally used to denote any philosophical system that accepts a transcendent and personal God who preserves and rules the world he has created. The term, probably invented by Richard Cudworth in 1678, was originally used as the antonym of atheism but later acquired a more restricted and distinctive meaning in contradistinction to pantheism, panentheism, and deism.

Theodicy. From the Greek *theos* (God) and *dikē* (Justice). Leibniz introduced this term to designate the topic of how divine government of the world can be understood in view of the presence of evil in the world. It is the term now used in philosophical theology for this aspect of the philosophy of religion.

Theodora I (*c.* 500–547). Married to Justinian I in 523, she was crowned Empress in 527, co-reigning with her husband and exercising a very extensive influence on the course of the highly complex and controversial theological issues of the time. She was inclined to the Monophysite position. (See **Monophysitism.**) She seems to have been a woman of remarkable learning and ability as well as of very strong character.

Theodore of Mopsuestia (*c.* 350–428). Theologian and biblical scholar. In 369 CE, with John Chrysostom, he entered the school of Diodore in a monastery at Antioch. In 392 he became Bishop of Antioch, as which he acquired considerable repute for his learning. He was characteristically Antiochene in his approach to his understanding of the Christian faith and of much historical importance for the development of the theological positions that were eventually to prevail in that school against the positions of the school of Alexandria.

Theodoret (*c.* 393–*c.* 466). Bishop of Cyrrhus. Born and educated at Antioch, he became a monk and was consecrated Bishop of Cyrrhus, Syria, in 423. Involved in the controversy between Nestorius and Cyril of Alexandria on the nature of Christ, he was noted as a champion of the Antiochene christology and a supporter of Nestorius, his personal friend. He was deposed and sent into exile in 449 by the Council of Ephesus, the so-called "Latrocinium." It seems that later he reluctantly anathematized Nestorius and resumed the administration of his diocese. Long after his death, however, his writings against Cyril became the subject of the "Three Chapters" controversy and were condemned in 533 by the Council of Constantinople. There is no doubt, however, of his learning and the clarity of the thought in which he expressed the ideas that the Antiochene school had tended to favor.

Theologia Germanica. A mystical treatise of unknown authorship dating from the late 14th c. and following the tradition of Eckhart and Tauler: through love one learns what it means to participate in God. It celebrates the value of personal, individual interiority. Luther admired it and later the German pietists acclaimed it. As with Eckhart's works, some thought of it as what would nowadays be called pantheistic. (See **Pantheism.**) Such fears are unwarranted.

Theological Virtues, The. Faith, hope, and love (as listed by Paul in I Corinthians 13) are traditionally so designated in contradistinction to the four "cardinal" virtues. See **Cardinal Virtues** and **Temperance.**

Theology. From the Greek *theos* and *logos,* meaning literally "God-discourse" or "God-talk," it is traditionally understood as "the science of divinely revealed truths." It may be understood and approached, however, in many different ways. For example, in the Middle Ages theology was enthroned "Queen of the Sciences," so that the rest of the medieval curriculum of learning was subordinate and preparatory to it although serving it as the *ancilla* or lady's maid serves her queenly *domina,* her mistress, being therefore indispensable. (A pale reflection of the medieval outlook is retained in the practice of the ancient universities of Europe, in many of which, as at Oxford and Cambridge, for instance, divinity takes official precedence over all other faculties, even though by ancient tradition only.) Nevertheless, the medieval schoolmen held that even without divine revelation through the Bible or otherwise one could attain *some* knowledge of God by the use of reason and the natural powers of discursive thought. They treated this kind of inquiry, however, under the head of *philosophia,* which today would be approximately represented in what is now called "Letters, Arts, and Sciences." When, in the 18th c., "reason" became the fashionable category among educated people, "Natural Theology" could be viewed as a respectable academic inquiry, since it did not rely on what many thought of as the superstitious aspect of religion, being free of traditional beliefs based on supposed revelation.

Theology has developed into several branches. The term "Natural Theology" has become unfashionable but the enterprise, in a modern form of course, had reappeared as "Philosophical Theology" or "Philosophy of Religion."

Alongside are other approaches, such as "Dogmatic Theology." The latter consists largely in considering the implicates of what is to be found in the biblical and other revelatory documents. "Historical Theology" approaches the subject as an historical investigation with a methodology such as that of the art historian, the historian of science, and other historical studies. Philosophical theology, while it should by no means ignore what the great religions of the world have to say, does not depend upon or derive its conclusions from any revelatory document.

Theopaschitism. In 519 a group of Monophysites appeared in Constantinople whose teaching included the view that God suffered: a view contrary to the orthodox belief that God is impassible, i.e., insusceptible to suffering. The Theopaschites expressed their position in the formula "One of the Trinity suffered." The Emperor Justinian could see no heresy in this, but the Patriarch of Constantinople found it (although not without some hesitation) heterodox. See **Patripassianism,** from which Theopaschitism is to be distinguished. The Theopaschites did not assert, as had the earlier Patripassians, that God the Father suffered.

Theos. The Greek word for "god." The ancient Greeks, however, being polytheists, understood *theos* as meaning the personification of any kind of wonder, e.g., the sun, the moon, an earthquake, any phenomenon that was the occasion of wonder. Some gods *(theoi)* were accounted permanent (e.g., Aphrodite, the goddess of love), while others were fleeting. They would have thought of a film star or golf champion in today's world as a god or goddess, a *theos* or *thea,* although less permanent than, say, the gods of love and war, the great fertility deities, the gods of the State, and so forth. So although *theos* is the term from which we get words such as "theology" and "theism," *theos* does not at all correspond to the term "God" as understood in the three great monotheistic religions, Judaism, Christianity, and Islam.

Theosis. In the Eastern Orthodox Church, man, through faith, virtue, prayer, and the sacraments (*mystēria*) eventually participates in the divine energies, by which he is divinized. (The term *theosis* means divinization.) This does not mean that the human being actually becomes God; it means that while remaining fully human he or she is fully united with God. See **Hesychasts** and **Gregory Palamas.**

Theosophy. The term, from the Greek, means literally "Wisdom of God" or "Divine Wisdom." It may be used in one of two ways: (1) to designate the teachings of the Theosophical Society, an international society established in the City of New York in 1875 and founded by Helena Petrovna Blavatsky and others. Its officially declared objects are (a) "To form a nucleus of the Universal Brotherhood of Humanity, without distinction of race, creed, sex, caste, or color;" (b) "To encourage the study of Comparative Religion, Philosophy, and Science;" and (c) "To investigate unexplained laws of Nature and the powers latent in man." The Society claims no monopoly on "Divine Wisdom," which cannot be limited to any group, but it sees itself as an important vehicle for the transmission of what it takes to be the Ancient Wisdom lying behind all the great religions of the world. Strains of this "hidden," esoteric Wisdom are to be found in all these religions. Although members of the Society are free to understand and to express the Ancient Wisdom each in his or her own way, all agree on a general outlook according to which all nature is immersed in the one essential life of one living, non-material, creative, homogeneous reality from which all else in the universe has sprung. The principle of evolution plays a fundamental role in theosophical teaching, but interest is focused primarily on the spiritual evolu-

tion of humanity. The karmic principle with its implicate of re-embodiment (to afford opportunity for the individual to work out his or her karma) is also a primary concern of members of the Society, whose teachings tend in the direction of pantheism. The universe is seen, not as the product of chance, but as guided from within outward. Many members of the Society are especially interested in modern science, which they see as confirming the teachings of the Ancient Wisdom and exhibiting its principles. They would see the work of Teilhard de Chardin, for instance, as in line with the ancient teaching that the entire order of nature evinces a progressive march toward a higher life.

The terms "theosophy" and "theosophical" may also be used, however, in a much more general way: (2) to designate any views or tendencies in the history of human thought, whether in the Orient or the Occident, in antiquity or today, that perceive divine purpose as being worked out in such ways. For example, Boehme, Swedenborg, and Emerson would be among the many examples in the history of religion and humane learning who may be called theosophical in their outlook and temper.

Theotokos. Greek, meaning "God-bearer." This is the much revered title of the Virgin Mary used by the Greek Fathers regularly from the early 3rd c. CE if not earlier to the present day. It was much approved by all who emphasized the divinity of Christ (e.g., Cyril of Alexandria) and was officially upheld at the Council of Ephesus in 431 and the very important Council of Chalcedon in 451. It celebrates the belief that Mary bore him who is acclaimed the divine Saviour and who is therefore the bearer of God. The Latin equivalent of the Greek term is *Deipara,* but in practice *Dei Genetrix* and *Mater Dei* (englished as "Mother of God") have been generally used, with the unfortunate consequence of creating a category confusion. For a mother is the female parent of her child as the father is the male one and she in turn has of course two parents and so on in genealogical line. If Mary were the Mother of God, then, one might argue, must not her mother (traditionally Anne) be the grandmother of God and Anne's husband God's grandfather? Such absurdities exhibit the nature of the confusion. If, as orthodox Christian teaching has generally insisted, Jesus had no human father, he stands in some way outside the genealogical line of descent. Mary is his mother in the sense that she bore him, but not in the sense of being his female parent in a genealogical series. See also **Anne** and **Genealogies of Jesus Christ, Two.**

Thérèse de Lisieux. See **Teresa of Lisieux.**

Therevada. The form of Buddhism that prevailed and is now found in Sri Lanka and Southeast Asia. It was the form upheld by one of the parties to the first great Buddhist schism, which occurred in the 4th c. BCE. The term is applied to a particular surviving branch that has claimed to preserve the authentic teachings of the Buddha and the elders of Buddhism in its original form. Theravada was widely distributed in Southeast Asia and in southern India, but its strongest center has been at Anuradhapura, Sri Lanka. The scriptural canon of Theravada Buddhism (see **Tipitaka**) was closed in the 1st c. BCE. The classic doctrines of Theravada were formulated by Buddhist scholars and commentators from the 5th to the 10th centuries CE. Theravada stands in opposition to Mahayana which, in a profuse variety of forms, is now by far the more widespread. It has spawned an endless number of Buddhist sects. Mahayana Buddhists applied the term "Hinayana" to Theravada, implying that their own form of Buddhism is in some way higher or greater and Theravada narrower or more limited. The term Theravada is to be preferred, therefore, as

lacking any such derogatory implication.

Theudas. This person is mentioned only once in the New Testament: Acts 5.36. In a speech attributed to Gamaliel he is represented as the fanatical leader of an unsuccessful insurrection. The only other ancient writer who alludes to this Theudas is Josephus (*Antiquities*, XXV, v, 1), who dates the insurrection he led as occurring *c*.45 CE. In Acts, however, he is represented as raising the rebellion (Acts 5.37) "in the time of the census" or "taxing," which is known to have been *c*. forty years earlier and during which time Jesus was born. Luke, in writing here might have obtained the information from Josephus, and inaccurately reported the date, but in that case, since Josephus's work was published *c*. 94 CE, Luke must have been writing after that date, which would be later than critical scholars place the date of the writing of Acts. It is quite possible, of course, that Luke was relying on some source earlier than Josephus and that the date of the insurrection was either inaccurately reported in that source or else inaccurately interpreted by Luke.

Third Orders. See **Tertiary.**

Thirty-Nine Articles. The doctrinal formula which, after several previous attempts, was set forth and accepted by the Church of England in 1563. It does not purport to be a Christian creed such as the so-called Apostles' Creed and the Niceno-Constantinopolitan one that are used liturgically in public worship. It consists, rather, of brief statements dealing with controversies of the time and endeavoring to strike a balance between historic Catholic teaching and Reformation emphases. The language is carefully contrived to permit a wide spectrum of interpretation, in the spirit of following the *via media* that Anglicanism has so much prized. The latitude it allows is not, however, unlimited. The clergy have traditionally undertaken not to teach anything that specifically *contradicts* the teaching of the Book of Common Prayer, including the Articles.

Thirty Years War, The. The series of politico-religious wars that took place in Central Europe between 1618 and 1648. The catalyst was the decay of the Holy Roman Empire. France gained immensely; Spain and Germany were weakened, hastening the final breakup of the Empire. The ideological effects were incalculably great. People of all classes were so weary of such prolonged religious struggles that at least the concept of religious toleration could begin to take root in some minds while in others a distaste for religion was generated, eventually finding expression in the 18th-c. worship of "nature" and "reason."

Thomas, The Gospel of. A document originally in Greek and dating from probably *c.*150 CE, a Coptic version of which was among the papyri discovered in 1945–1946 at Nag Hammadi in Upper Egypt. (See **Nag Hammadi Library, The.**) The Coptic version includes some additional material dating from *c.* 400. Unlike the New Testament Gospels, it consists of a series of sayings and discourses of Jesus not presented in historical form. It notably reflects, moreover, the Gnostic element in early Christianity.

Thomas à Kempis (*c.* **1380–1471**). Spiritual writer. Born at Kempen, near Cologne, he was educated by the Brethren of the Common Life at Deventer and in 1399 entered the house of the Canons Regular near Zwolle (a daughter house of Windesheim), where he lived for the remainder of his life. He was much sought after as a spiritual director. His book, *The Imitation of Christ*, is a classic of Christian spirituality. The traditional ascription to him of this book has been questioned and it may be that at least not all of it is his work. The Royal Library in Brussels, however, contains a copy of the work

with his signature and the grounds for doubting his authorship of it seem to be inconclusive.

Thomas Aquinas (*c.* **1225–1274**). Philosopher and theologian. Born of a noble family at Roccasecca he was sent as a child to the neighboring Benedictine abbey of Monte Cassino of which his parents hoped to see him become abbot. Despite his family's strong opposition, however, he entered the then new Dominican Order of friars in 1244. While pursuing his studies at Paris he was introduced by his master Albertus Magnus to the works of Aristotle who in that age represented the challenge of what was in effect the "secular scientific" thought of the age. This determined, at least to some extent, the aim of his greatest work, which was the resolution of what we could now regard as the conflict between "science" and "religion" as they emerged in the 13th-c. Latin world. The output of Thomas is staggering. His greatest work, the *Summa Theologiae*, consisting of about 6,000 columns in a Latin edition closely printed in octavo, represents less than a quarter of his complete works.

Thomas sharply distinguishes reason from faith. Faith is made accessible only through revelation; yet what is revealed is not contrary to reason; nor is grace contrary to nature. As the Gospel completes or perfects the law, according to Jesus's dictum about his own mission, so revelation may be said to perfect reason. Grace, Thomas explicitly affirms, does not take away nature but perfects it. In epistemology as in much else of the Aristotelian system that confronted Thomas, he is able to agree with Aristotle, e.g., that there is nothing in the intellect that is not first in the senses. A Platonist at heart and inheriting the outlook of Augustine that was deeply saturated with a Neoplatonic dye, Thomas finds in Aristotle (whom his age tended to regard with some trepidation as a challenge to faith, somewhat as in the 19th c. Darwin incited hostility and fear in the minds of many Christians) one whose thought could be not only profoundly admired but easily christened. Thomas's solution to many of the problems in medieval thought reflects his extraordinary genius. For example, he used the Aristotelian philosophy of substance and accident in working out a philosophical support, in terms of the most challenging thought of his time, for the doctrine of transubstantiation (see **Transubstantiation**), and he also perceived the episcopate to be the plenitude of the priesthood rather than a separate order, on the ground that all the orders of ministry in the Church are directed toward the Eucharist and the priesthood is focused on that central sacrament of the Church. He opposed the then controversial notion of the Immaculate Conception of Mary. (See **Immaculate Conception.**) On these last two points he was in sharp opposition to the Franciscans, who for a time forbade its members to read Thomas's writings. Thomas was indeed at first suspect of what a later age would have called "modernistic tendencies;" but soon after his death he began to be recognized more and more as the intellectual champion of the Church and by many as its most authoritative theologian. With the exception of Duns Scotus he is certainly unrivalled in the Middle Ages both for his philosophical acumen and his theological perceptivity. He is in any case one of the greatest thinkers in human history. In assessing the merit of his work, one must of course relate it to the intellectual task of his day, recognizing that if he could return today he would not be a Thomist.

In the *Summa Theologiae*, Thomas proposes five *viae* (ways) of pointing to the existence of God: (1) motion implies a First Mover. (This "way" is derived directly from Aristotle.) (2) There must be an efficient cause for the existence of the world. (3) Entities that we perceive are "contingent," i.e., they might or might not exist. Elms, for instance, exist, but they very well might not. We can also imagine certain entities that could exist, although it happens that they do not. Thomas argues that while such entities do not necessarily exist, there must be an entity that exists of necessity, a necessary Being, to which we give the name "God." (4) In the entities we perceive in the world are to be found various degrees of perfection, which points to a Being who *is* perfect. (5) There must be a Being who is the cause of the order that is in the world. Thomas did not offer these "ways" as proofs of the existence of God. If any one of them could provide a totally irrefutable proof, there would be no need for citing any of the other four "ways.") He seems to be especially interested in the first of the "ways," for he develops it more fully in the *Summa contra Gentiles;* but he does not profess to do more than provide pointers, none of which was entirely original or believed by Thomas to be original. See **Ontological Argument, Cosmological Argument,** and **Teleological Argument.**

Thomas Becket. See **Becket, Thomas.**

Thomas More. See **More, Thomas.**

Thompson, Francis (1859–1907). Poet. Born in Preston, England, he was intended for the Roman Catholic priesthood and educated at Ushaw. In 1885 he went to London, living in destitution, sometimes as a street vendor. Wilfred Meynell, then editor of a Roman Catholic magazine, discovered, rescued, and befriended him, encouraging his poetic genius, expressed in a volume of his poems published in 1893 and containing one of his greatest, *The Hound of Heaven.*

Thor. A Scandinavian sky-god, very popular as the protector of the people and analogous to the German Donar. His day was Thursday, called after him. He was depicted as red-bearded with eyes of fire and usually carrying a hammer representing lightning and driving his chariot of goats across the sky, causing thunder. He presided over the Law Assembly.

Thoreau, Henry David (1817–1862). American naturalist and philosopher. Born at Concord, MA, he was much influenced by Emerson, whose outlook he reflected in some ways, e.g., in his notable individualism and his emphasis on self-reliance. He is usually classed with the American Transcendentalists. He supported civil disobedience in cases where a large number of people perceive the government's actions to be grievously unethical. His writings include one entitled "Civil Disobedience" (1849).

Three Chapters, The. The Emperor Justinian issued an edict of 543–544 that came to be known as *ta tria kephalaia* (the three chapters) because it condemned three subjects: (1) Theodore of Mopsuestia and all his writings; (2) the writings of Theodoret against Cyril of Alexandria; and (3) the letter of Ibas of Edessa to Maris. Justinian's purpose was to conciliate the Monophysites by condemning persons and writings considered sympathetic to the Nestorians. The events that ensued show that Justinian's interference had unfortunate repercussions. At the Fifth General Council, which met at Constantinople in 533, the Three Chapters were condemned. In the long run the decree had accomplished nothing of value.

Thunderbird. A common figure in Amerindian mythology, he is generally conceived as a huge bird such as an eagle. Thunder is produced by the flapping of his wings, lightning by the opening and closing of his eyes.

Thurible. The metal vessel used in solemn liturgical Christian worship for the burning of incense. It is normally suspended on chains so that it can be swung at appropriate times during the liturgy. The person who carries it is called the thurifer.

Tiara. A papal headdress, mentioned early in the 8th c. It gradually grew in size and grandeur till, in the 15th c., it reached its present appearance. It is worn by (sometimes carried in front of) the Pope on certain official and solemn occasions. It is not worn at any liturgical acts.

Tibetan Religion. The oldest form of religion in Tibet is Bon, which seems to have been shamanistic. It still exists, but synthesized with Buddhism, which came to Tibet gradually from *c.* the 7th to the 11th c. CE., so that it now appears more as a Buddhist sect than as what originally it had been. Buddhism in Tibet, having come to it through Indian masters, may be said to be more like the Buddhism that had developed in the first millennium or so after its first appearance in India than it is like any of the Mahayana developments in China, Korea, and Japan. Nevertheless, *some* of the latter type of influence has affected Tibetan Buddhism, which is represented by four principal sects or traditions: Kagyu, Sakya, Nyingma, and Gelug.

T'ien. A Chinese term designating the absolute principle of the universe. It was worshipped by Chinese rulers from at least as early as the Chou dynasty, 11th c. BCE. The term has been used in various senses, ranging from that of "supreme being" to a fatalistic principle.

T'ien-T'ai. Founded by Chih I (538–597), this eclectic school of Chinese Buddhism is focused on the Lotus Sutra. The teaching is complex, entailing the metaphysical theory that things are both distinct from one another yet at the same time part of an organic whole . The scholastic exponents of this type of Buddhism claim that the Buddha taught at various levels, to meet the needs of beings at different levels of development. Japanese Tendai Buddhism, introduced by Saicho, a priest, in 805 CE to his monastery on Mount Hiei to the northeast of Kyoto, has the same roots as Chinese T'ien-T'ai, but has developed in various ways. Tendai Buddhism in Japan has provided the background from which Buddhist sects such as Pure Land, Zen, and Nichiren have drawn much of their inspiration. Tendai teaches that man has a Buddha-nature, which rigorous methods of meditation and strictly moral lifestyles help to draw out.

Tillich, Paul (1886–1965). Protestant theologian. Born in Starzeddel, Germany, he was trained at Berlin, Tübingen, Halle, and Breslau. An army chaplain during World War I, he taught at several German universities afterwards but was forced in 1933 to leave Germany. He came to the United States where he became successively professor at Union Theological Seminary, New York, at Harvard, and at Chicago. Tillich defined religion as the object of man's ultimate concern. He saw philosophy as relating to ontological questions (i.e., questions about Being) and theology as relating to existential questions. The two should not conflict; neither should they melt into one another. The terms used in religion are symbolic with one exception: Being, which is God himself. God is the ground of all being. Courage also plays a distinctive role in Tillich's thought, expressed in one of his books, *The Courage To Be* (1952). Tillich was a prolific writer. His most important work is his *Systematic Theology* in three volumes (1951–1964). His other writings include *The Shaking of the Foundations* (1948), *The Protestant Era* (1948), and *Morality and Beyond* (1963).

Time. In the history of philosophy the nature of time has been one of the most persistent and difficult problems. The Greeks had two words: (1) *chronos* and (2) *aiōn*. *Chronos*, which is used by Homer, and the Attic poets and from which we get words such as "chronology," is used in a variety of senses, but primarily it means a period of time: clock time, as we say. *Aiōn*, also used by Homer and the Attic poets, generally means, rather, an age, an epoch, an era. Both words occur in the New Testa-

ment, where *aiōn* is often used to contrast the present age from others that were or are to come. The adjective *aiōnios*, "age-long" has a vague sense of "going on forever," yet not in any technical sense of eternity; rather, an incalculably long period contrasted with that which is fleeting.

In much of the thought of antiquity, East and West, time was thought of in cyclic terms. For example, Heraclitus calculated that the world's time cycle is 10,000 years, i.e., in that space of time everything would go back to where it started and would start all over again. In India and China various philosophers made similar calculations, e.g., Shao-Yung, a Neo-Confucian writing in the 11th c. CE, still proposed such a calculation, providing, however, for a much longer cycle: 129,800 years.

Plato's definition of time as "the moving image of eternity" is well-known. Time embodies forms in the receptacle of space. Aristotle concluded that the world is eternal in the sense that it had no beginning. Augustine, probably more aware than anyone in the ancient world of the paradoxes attending the concept of time, confessed his puzzlement at the notion. Thomas Aquinas, although admitting that from a rational standpoint Aristotle had been right in asserting that the world has no beginning, thought that the Bible says otherwise and so he bowed to revelation as superior to reason. He recognized, moreover, a distinction between *aeternitas* (eternity) and *aeviternitas* (infinite time). Spinoza regarded time as an inadequate perception of a limited reality. If we could see the real as a whole it would be eternality. This view implies that in our perception of time we are perceiving what is in some sense illusory. Newton thought that whatever may be the relativities that we perceive in time, there is behind it all an absolute time that flows irrespective of anything else. Leibniz saw time as the order of successive existence, relative to the actualization of the monads of his system.

More recent thinkers have developed concepts of time that draw partly from advances in mathematics and the natural sciences. Henri Bergson defined time as qualitative change, having its own inner duration in an irreversible becoming. Time is better apprehended by a special form of intuition rather than by reason, which spatializes it and thereby destroys its unique significance. The German mathematician Hermann Minkowski (1864–1909) joined time to the three dimensions of space, making it a fourth dimension. All events are determinately present in the space-time continuum. His student, Albert Einstein adopted this concept of time as a fourth dimension and developed it. Time remains, nevertheless, an extremely complex, not to say baffling question and one that is of paramount relevance to religious thought. See also **History.**

Tipitaka. The Buddhist canon of scripture, called in Sanskrit *Tripitaka*, is designated *Tipitaka* in Pali, which despite the great prestige of Sanskrit became the language of Therevada Buddhism. The name means "threefold collection," referring to the three divisions: (1) the *vinaya-pitaka*, the "basket," an assemblage of material (*pitaka*) treating of Buddhism, its history, regulations, and discipline; (2) the *sutta-pitaka*, the discourses attributed to the Buddha himself, containing what is accounted the fundamental teaching of Buddhism; and (3) the *abhidhamma-pitaka*, whose content probably arose in the 4th and 3rd c. BCE and consists of metaphysical speculations although intended primarily for the practical purpose of dissolving that mental resistance, obstinacy, or rigid narrowness that can be an obstacle to authentic spiritual insight. Compare the threefold structure or arrangement of the Hebrew Bible.

Tischendorf, Constantin (1815–1874). New Testament textual scholar. Professor of theology at Leipzig from 1959, he traveled far in search of manuscripts.

He won lasting fame through his discovery of Codex Sinaiticus, one of the three most ancient and important of Greek biblical manuscripts in the world.

Tithes. The payment to the Church of a tenth of one's income or the produce of one's land is very ancient, e.g., in England it was enjoined in the 8th c. and became law in 900. In modern times the payments of tithes by individuals and families to the Church is practiced in some Christian denominations and encouraged in most throughout the world.

Tittle. The word traditionally used in the English Bible to translate the Greek *keraia*, by which is designated the little ornamental hook at the end of many letters of the Hebrew alphabet. Jesus alludes to it in Matthew 5.18 and Luke 16.17, in assuring his hearers that not the slightest element in the Torah will be lost.

Tohunga. In Polynesian religion, a functionary who serves as a medium, healer, priest, and exorcist. He officiates at all the major events in human life from birth to death. He also helps people to escape the hurtful effects of their violation of taboo. See **Taboo.**

Toland, John (1670–1722). Irish pamphleteer. Born in Londonderry, Ireland, he was educated at various universities including Glasgow and Leyden. His *Christianity not Mysterious* (1696) is generally regarded as a classic exposition of Deism. He is also credited with coining in 1705 the term "pantheism" to designate views such as Spinoza's in which God and Nature are identical or nearly so.

Toleration, Religious. The ideal of freedom to practice any form of religion that does not definitely entail breaking the law of the land is a comparatively modern one. In the ancient world the gods of the people were so identified with the people that even the concept of religious toleration as it is now understood would have seemed generally unthinkable. Although the authorities in the Roman Empire generally found it expedient to permit the numerous religious sects, parties, and movements within its bounds a great deal of freedom so long as their adherents recognized the authority of the State by at least a token recognition of the State gods, Christians were sometimes, if intermittently, persecuted cruelly until Constantine made Christianity a *religio licita*. Throughout the Middle Ages and for some time later Christendom brooked no rival. Augustine wanted corporal punishment for schismatics and heretics and the attitude throughout the Middle Ages was generally along such lines. Islam certainly had no room for those accounted infidels. Luther and Calvin had no place for religious toleration in anything like the sense in which it is now commonly understood. The 17th c. saw during the Thirty Years War a bitter and fruitless religious conflict that did nothing to advance the interests of either side. Pleas for toleration were made in some quarters, but it was not till the 18th c. that the concept of religious toleration began to take shape and then only because it was, by and large, an age of religious indifference. By the 19th c. a policy of religious toleration, such as had been proclaimed in the American Bill of Rights in 1776, had become general in most European nations, although the Roman Catholic Church was reluctant, to say the least, in conforming to such secular legislation. When, as often happens, legislation for religious toleration becomes a mere cloak for promoting religious indifference, it loses the value for which it was created.

Tolstoy, Leo (1828–1910). Russian social reformer and novelist. Of a noble family, he was much influenced by Rousseau. After a few years in the army he traveled in Western Europe for several years, studying educational methods and writing about proposals for social reform. In 1862 he married Sophia Behrs, whom he called "Sonya" and who bore him 13 children. His novels include *War and Peace* (1864–1869) and *Anna Karenina* (1873–1877), after the writing of which, feelings that had for long been deeply affecting him came to a head in a religious conversion that led him to renounce his work as a novelist and to devote himself exclusively to ethical and religious topics. His writings in this later period became more and more critical of the Russian Orthodox Church from which in 1901 he was excommunicated. From the time of his conversion he began to live a life of great simplicity, embracing vegetarianism and engaging in manual labor, while he tried to follow the Gospel injunctions literally, especially the sayings of Jesus as recorded in the "Sermon on the Mount." He emphasized the development of an entirely pacific disposition, total chastity outside marriage, total non-resistance to force, and total willingness to forgive and love one's enemies. He repudiated practically all the traditionally central theological beliefs of Christianity, such as the Incarnation and the Resurrection. Only by an increase of deep love for all humankind on the part of individuals will the Kingdom of God come. His principal writings in this later period of his life are : *A Confession* (1879–1882), *What I believe* (1882–1884), *What Then Must We Do?* (1882–1886), *The Kingdom of God is Within You* (1890–1903), *The Christian Teaching* (1894–1896), and *What is Art?* (1897–1898). He taught that the meaning of human life depends on the existence of God and that the recognition of this constitutes the core of all the great religions of the world. He opposed all forms of government as criminal conspiracy against the people and favored nonviolent resistance to government of every kind, in place of which he sought the establishment of voluntary associations by the people. His wife did not share his views, which she took to be a neurotic obsession, and she recounts in her *Diary* her intense pain at what seemed to her to be an alienation from her and their family. For a good brief account and interpretation of Tolstoy's life and thought, see "Count Leo Tolstoy" in Radoslav A. Tsanoff, *Autobiographies of Ten Religious Leaders*. San Antonio: Trinity University Press, 1968.

Tome of Leo. The name given to an historically important letter sent on June 13, 449, by Pope Leo I to Flavian, Patriarch of Constantinople, clearly stating the christology of the Western Church. The letter, which quoted Augustine and other Fathers, was directed against the heresy of Eutyches, and the doctrine it expounded received classic formulation at the Council of Chalcedon two years later as the accepted Christian doctrine of the Incarnation.

Tonsure. Traditionally, before admission to the clerical or monastic state, part of the hair was shaved. The shaven head had become customary in the East by at least the 5th c. and in the West by the 7th and was the distinctive outward sign of belonging to the clerical state. From *c.* the 16th c. it became customary to shave only a small area of the crown of the head. The tonsure as a prelude to receiving orders is nowadays only a symbolic act: the cutting of a little hair as a token of the ancient rite. It may be, however, that some monastic communities still follow the traditional practice.

Torah. In Judaism the Torah consists of the Pentateuch or first five books of the Bible. It is, however, much more. Not only is it the most sacred part of the Bible, preceding even the Prophets in importance; it is the Constitution of the entire Jewish community everywhere. It is understood in two senses: (1) the law as written out and handed down to posterity and (2) the inner, spiritual law that is the moral principle of the universe. So Torah is both the principle by which God governs and sustains the universe and the revelation to his people of his ways of governance. God has spoken and continues to speak to Israel and the world through the Torah. Yet the Torah as a document must be interpreted. The Talmud, which is a body of legal commentary on the Torah, follows the latter somewhat as English and American law follow and interpret common law by an examination of its application to individual cases. It is important as an adjunct to Torah but would be of course meaningless apart from Torah, the text of which became fixed in the 5th c. BCE. The Talmud consists of (a) the Mishnah, which sums up the oral law from the 5th c. BCE to the 2nd c. CE, and (b) the Gemara, which is a commentary on the first part of the Mishnah. Further interpretation of the Torah developed between the 4th c. CE and the 12th c. CE and consists of (a) the Halakha, comprising very detailed expositions of traditional law and precepts that are not found in the letter of the Torah but are presented as exhibiting its principles, and (b) the Haggadah, which consists of parables and other writings presenting in a more general and freer way how Torah may be interpreted. So central is the concept of Torah or Law to Jewish religion and life that the rabbinical body is both pedagogic and judicial, and every rabbi, each in his own way, is expected to act both as teacher and judge, giving not only information as one who is learned in the law but also giving judgment as one accustomed to seeing both sides of a case and forming a judicial decision on the basis of the evidence before him.

Torquemada, Tomás de (1420–1498). Grand Inquisitor. He was a nephew of the notable Spanish theologian Juan de Torquemada (1388–1468). In an age in which religious toleration as we understand it today was unknown, the papacy encouraged or at the very least permitted Spanish monarchs to set up tribunals to secure conformity with Christian practice. Torture was part of the recognized judicial procedure of that time and thousands of Jews and Muslims were subjected to it. About 2,000 were burned during Torquemada's term of office. He also expelled large numbers from Spain in 1492.

Tosefta. A collection of early Jewish traditions similar to those in the Mishnah and of approximately the same period but not included in that collection. The Hebrew word means "supplement."

Totem. Usually an animal, although it may be a plant or other natural object, regarded as somehow historically related to the origin, tradition, and welfare of a human group. It provides a sense of social cohesion to the tribe or group or family that claims it as its own. Sometimes, e.g., among some Australian tribes, a claim is made of actual genealogical descent from the totem. In more developed societies it serves as a heraldic symbol, e.g., the Lion as the symbol or totem of Venice, the Bear of California, the Eagle of the United States, the Tiger of Princeton. The totem pole is used in Amerindian and other tribal societies.

Toynbee, Arnold (1889–1975). Philosopher of history. Born in London, he was trained at Oxford and for many years directed the Royal Institute of International Affairs. Like Spengler but in a less rigid fashion, Toynbee applied an organic analysis to social groupings that he identified as operative in human history. He found twenty-one such social groupings, which he saw rising and falling as if they were living organisms being born, passing into maturity, and eventually declining and dying. While in good health such a society faces challenges to which a "creative minority" within it respond on its behalf and the society as a whole accepts and endorses that response, so conserving the basic structure of the society and maintaining it in health. A society that fails to do so declines. Among his writings are his 10-volume *A Study of History* (1934, 1939, 1954), *An Historian's Approach to Religion* (1956), and *Mankind and Mother Earth* (1976).

Tractarianism. In 19th-c. England, an important and very influential movement occurred, the aim of which was to restore to the English Church an awareness of her Catholic heritage. The aim was expounded in a series of *Tracts for the Times,* begun by John Henry Newman in 1833. When Newman defected to Rome in 1845, other Tractarians, notably Edward Bouverie Pusey and John Keble continued the movement, which gained an influential and deeply committed following. The movement was bitterly attacked by a theologically liberal wing of the English Church and widely suspect by many. It not only, however, restored and revitalized the life of the English Church; its influence was felt throughout the Anglican Communion and beyond it. It was associated with another movement of the same period, popularly called "ritualist," from which it should be carefully distinguished. The interest of this "ritualist" movement was liturgical rather than doctrinal and theological and although these interests were encompassed by those of the Tractarians, many churchmen were attracted to liturgical concerns who lacked the deeper theological and doctrinal commitments of the Tractarians.

As the Tractarian movement developed it came to be known as the Oxford Movement and fostered a profound sense of the historic continuity of Catholic tradition in its Anglican form. It greatly stimulated English theological scholarship, notably patristics. It also helped to put the Reformation into perspective, so that Anglicans, without denigrating the lasting values of the Reformation, could see themselves as heirs of historic Catholic tradition, ethos, and life. The movement had also a very considerable, although of course much less direct effect on other branches of the Christian Church.

Traditors. During the persecution of Christians by Diocletian that broke out in 303 CE, possession of the Scriptures was forbidden. Those who, under torture, revealed their whereabouts and surrendered them were stigmatized by the Church authorities as traditors.

Traducianism. A theological view that souls are inherited from parents as are bodies, in contrast to Creationism, according to which God creates a new soul at each conception. The latter is the view accepted in the mainstream of Catholic tradition and also in Reformed Church theology. Traducianism, proposed by Tertullian, has had supporters among Lutherans and others.

Transcendence/Immanence. The term transcendence comes from the Latin verb, *trans scandere*, "to climb across" or "to go beyond." In its broadest sense the term refers to anything that surpasses something else; for instance, the third dimension of solid geometry transcends the two dimensions of plane geometry. Those philosophers who admit a concept such as the Absolute (sometimes identified with God) say it transcends all other metaphysical categories. Epistemologists who postulate realities beyond the observable phenomena say these realities transcend the phenomena. Immanence, from the Latin *immanere*, "to remain in," may be accounted the opposite of transcendence. Kant treats that which is experienced as immanent in contradistinction to that which, being beyond experience, is transcendent and therefore unknowable. Pantheists take God to be entirely immanent in the universe, while Orthodox Jews and Muslims regard him as essentially transcending it. Christian orthodoxy makes much of the doctrine that God both transcends the universe and, taking human flesh in Christ, is also immanent in it.

Transcendentalism. The name given to an outlook and mode of thought that flourished in New England, having had its focus in the "Transcendental Club of Boston," which was organized in 1836. Those generally described as Transcendentalists include Emerson (probably the best-known and most eminent of the distinguished group), Thoreau, Alcott, Channing, Theodore Parker, and Margaret Fuller. Kant had used the term "transcendental" in reference to the *a priori* elements of experience: those that go beyond the empirical. The Transcendentalists, although they varied much in their opinions, generally used the term "transcendental" in a sense that took it far beyond what Kant would have approved, for they saw it as representing access to a domain beyond the temporal.

Transcendental Meditation. A technique and religious movement introduced in the West by Maharishi Mahesh Yogi in the 1950s and widely popularized by the "Beatles" toward the end of the 1960s. It claims to improve the mental state of the practitioners, each of whom at initiation is provided with a secret mantra. (See **Mantra.**) It is popularly known as TM.

Transfiguration. *Metamorphōsis*, the word used in Greek mythology to designate the change of form of which the gods were supposed to be capable, is used of the Transfiguration reported in Matthew 17.1–8 and in comparable narratives in Mark and Luke, but the episode as reported has no fundamental connection with any such primitive concept. Nor has it any parallel either in the Old Testament or the New Testament. According to all three Gospel accounts the Transfiguration occurred just after Jesus's prediction of the Passion. The change described suggests the transformation of the body of flesh and blood (*sarx*) into the "glorious" or "luminous" body that Paul affirms is to be the character of the resurrected body (I Corinthians 15.40–44). It may be taken to express also, however, a more esoteric idea that Jesus, as already fully in possession of the spiritual dimension of existence, could exhibit himself accordingly in a "body of light," shining through and standing out from the physical body.

Translation. This term is used in several different Christian ecclesiastical contexts: (1) The transference of a bishop from one diocese to another. This practice was specifically prohibited by the Council of Nicaea in 325, but soon the prohibition was ignored and the practice became and remains common. (2) When, in the Christian calendar, two observances coincide on the same day, one takes precedence over the other and the other is transferred ("translated") to another date, usually the nearest one that is free. (3) When the relics of a saint are removed from one site to another, the procedure, attended by liturgical solemnities, is called "translation" and the date celebrated accordingly.

Transmigration. See **Reincarnation.**

Transubstantiation. As classically formulated by Thomas Aquinas in the 13th c., this concept relating to the Eucharist must be understood in terms of the concepts of "substance" and "accident" as they occur in Aristotelian philosophy. The term "transubstantiation" was in widespread use as early as the later part of the 12th c., and the belief it represented about the Eucharist was defined as official Church teaching at the Lateran Council in 1215. Thomas Aquinas, using Aristotelian philosophy for his formulation, presented the doctrine as follows: at the moment at which the bread and wine for the Eucharist are consecrated they become the whole Body and Blood of Christ *substantially,* leaving only the "accidents" of bread and wine. In Aristotelian thought the "substance" *(ousia)* is the permanent underlying reality as contrasted with its visible, changing qualities, the "accidents;" i.e., by virtue of the priestly consecration of the bread and wine they become in reality so transformed, leaving only appearances such as the qualities of taste, shape, color, *et al.* of bread and wine. Thomas, with his customary genius, found a way of exhibiting, in the philosophical and scientific terms of

his time, the nature of the transmutation that was already held by the Church as taking place at the moment of consecration at Mass. The doctrine was reaffirmed by the Council of Trent in the 16th c. against the teaching of the Reformers. See **Consubstantiation** and **Virtualism.**

In the Eastern Church, teaching on the subject has been virtually the same and received formal approval at the Synod of Jerusalem in 1672. The Greek word, however, is *metousiōsis*, which has essentially the same meaning.

Trappists. The Cistercians of the Strict Observance have been popularly so called since early in the 19th c., after the name of the Abbey of La Trappe (La Grand Trappe), where the reform was introduced in the 17th c. See **Rancé, Armand Jean le Bouthillier de.**

Treacle Bible. A name popularly given by book collectors and others to the Great Bible (1539) from its use of the word "triacle" (treacle) in Jeremiah 8.22. The word used in the KJV is "balm."

Trent, Council of. (1545–1563). The Council that was called by the Roman Catholic Church to meet the very longstanding need for Church reform and to combat the spread of Protestantism. It lasted for nineteen years and issued a multitude of decisions both on matters of faith and questions of conduct and discipline. The reforms it tried to effect fell far short of the expectation of the more earnest among members of the Roman Catholic Church, but they did provide a basis for a general deepening of the Church's spiritual life and the enforcement of moral discipline throughout the Roman Catholic Church. If the Fathers had hoped to conciliate the Protestants, they failed. The Council was nevertheless a great, not to say indispensable instrument of the Counter-Reformation. (See **Counter-Reformation.**) It prudently left some controversial matters undecided, e.g., the doctrine of the Immaculate Conception and the locus of final authority in the Church, i.e., whether vested in Pope or Council or both and if the latter in precisely what way. The adjectival form of "Trent" is "Tridentine."

Trikoṇa. Sanskrit word, meaning "triangle." In Hindu iconography a vertical triangle stands for Śiva; an inverted one for the divine energy in him, his *śakti*, personified as female.

Trimūrti. This Sanskrit term designates the Hindu triad manifesting three functions of divine Being: (1) *Brahmā*, the equilibrium between the two opposing principles represented respectively by the other two members of the triad; (2) *Viṣṇu*, whose function is primarily that of preserver; and (3) *Śiva*, who represents destruction.

Trinity. The central, historic formulation of the doctrine of God in the Christian Church, which affirms that God is One God existing in three *hypostases* or *personae* and one *ousia* or *substantia:* technical terms that are traditionally rendered in English as "Three Persons and One Substance." The term "Trinity" is nowhere mentioned in the Bible, although Christian theologians generally perceive it as implicit in New Testament teaching. The doctrine was developed gradually in connection with controversies concerning difficulties arising out of questions about the nature of Christ and his relation to the Father to whom he habitually prayed yet with whom he claimed to be One (e.g., John 10.30). Moreover, although the Holy Spirit is repeatedly mentioned in the Bible and is plainly accorded a unique place in the New Testament writings, the Church came only gradually to formulating a doctrinal statement to include the Spirit with the Father and the Son as eventually was done in a simple but classic form in the Niceno-Constantinopolitan Creed in the 4th c.

In the historical circumstances and the intellectual climate of the day the doctrine of the Trinity was a master-stroke. It is acknowledged to be a mystery of faith, although not contrary to reason. The brilliant genius of it as a solution to the christological and theological problems of the early Church can be perceived only through understanding of the extremely complex issues that had been for so long so hotly debated. It is a beautiful although not necessarily the only way of formulating the solution in other ages. It has become, however, so inextricably bound up with the full expression of Christian belief about the nature of God that it is inalienable from mainstream Christian teaching. Difficulties have remained, e.g., see **Filioque.** It has always been and it remains, however, besides much else, a powerful way of expressing both what Christianity has in common with Judaism and Islam about the Unity of God (God as One) and how it differs from both of these religions in its understanding of the nature of that Unity.

Tripitaka. The Sanskrit term for the Pali *Tipitaka.* See **Tipitaka.**

Trisagion. The prayer "Holy God, Holy and mighty, Holy and immortal, have mercy upon us," is solemnly chanted or recited at various services in the Eastern Church in which it has a very distinctive place. The Greek term by which it is known means "three times holy."

Trito-Isaiah. Biblical scholars have for long established that not all of the Book of Isaiah may be properly attributed to the 8th-c. BCE prophet of that name. The internal evidence precludes attributing to him more than Chapters 1–39. The author of Chapters 40–55 is called by scholars "Deutero-Isaiah" to specify him as a "second" or "other" Isaiah. In 1892 Bernhard Duhm coined the term Trito-Isaiah to designate the author or authors of Chapters 56–66, which must have been written later still.

Trivium. See **Quadrivium.**

Troeltsch, Ernst (1865–1923). Theologian and philosopher. Born at Augsburg, he taught at Göttingen, Bonn, and Heidelberg, and from 1915 onwards at Berlin as professor of the history of philosophy and civilization. He was influenced by Ritschl, Windelband, and Wilhelm Dilthey. His most notable contribution is his analysis of the relation between history and the Christian faith. In seeking to avoid historicism on the one hand and, on the other, theodicy, he perceived a dialectic between historical studies and the life of faith. He was one of the most important among Christian thinkers of his time in Germany. His writings include *History and Metaphysics* (1888) and *The Social Teaching of the Christian Churches* (1912).

Truth. In the history of philosophy, the concept of truth has been and has remained difficult and controversial. In antiquity philosophers for the most part assumed that there is an objective truth which it is their business as philosophers to find. The Sophists, notably Protagoras, questioned this assumption, proposing that, in one way or another, truth is relative, i.e., what is true for X may not be true for Y: a Laplander might find a Frenchman dark-skinned while an Ethiopian might find him fair-skinned. Two basic theories of truth are (1) the correspondence theory and (2) the coherence theory. According to the former, that which corresponds to reality is true; according to the latter, that which coheres within a system of ideas. Other theories include the pragmatic: the true is that which "works." The meaning of truth is best perceived in examining what appears to be false. Both Plato and Aristotle, each in his own way, uphold a correspondence theory of truth. The notion of a "double truth" (e.g., that what is true in religion may be false in science and what is true in science may be false in religion) was much discussed in the Middle Ages, both in Christian and in Islamic philosophy. Thomas Aquinas and others insisted that truth must be one, so that there cannot be any such difference that is fundamental.

Leibniz made an important distinction between truths of reason and truths of fact. This became the basis for the now generally accepted distinction between the analytical and the synthetic. That there are two right angles in every triangle is an analytical truth, i.e., it follows from a mathematical system; it does not tell us anything that is not already in some sense known; i.e., it exhibits a property of all triangles and that there could not be a triangle that lacks this property any more than there could be a triangle that is not a three-sided figure. The case of synthetic propositions is radically different. There is no necessity about the statement that John's house is white; it might be yellow or pink; indeed it might have been yellow last week and now pink. The truth or falsity relates to empirical fact not to a system of thought. This distinction has been expressed in various ways, e.g., Hume distinguished between "relations of ideas" and "matters of fact." More recent philosophers have continued to discuss subtleties in the problem of the nature and meaning of truth, but the correspondence-coherence distinction, in one form or another, retains basic importance.

Truth-Claim. The claim that a proposition is sufficiently supported by evidence that warrants its acceptance as true. Though it need not be in propositional form, it should be able to be expressed in one. For a truth-claim to be meaningful certain conditions are required, for instance, that the proposition can be given a self-consistent formulation that permits the formulation of a self-consistent alternative. The logical subject of the proposition must be one that permits reference to it (not, for instance, an artificial term such as Bamwunk), and the predicate must be one that can be significantly assigned to the subject. The predicate "is pregnant" could be applied to a woman or a mare but not to a stallion or a man or a table. Nevertheless, when, precisely, the conditions are satisfied is in some cases very disputable. The concept is important in the philosophical analysis of Christian and other religious thought.

Tübingen School. A school of New Testament theologians founded by F. C. Baur (1792–1860) at Tübingen. They applied Hegel's methodology to early Christianity, perceiving the primitive Christian Church as divided into "Petrinists" (Jewish Christians) and "Paulinists" (Gentile ones): a division healed by "Catholicism" in the 2nd c. The school was highly influential in the 1840s. It declined soon afterwards and is now generally recognized as a striking example of the immense influence of Hegel over both philosophy and theology in the 19th c. but representing an outlook based on presuppositions that are unacceptable today, at least in the form in which they were presented at that time.

Tulchan Bishops. After the Scottish Reformation in 1560, the Kirk introduced titular bishops who were to be responsible to the General Assembly. They became in practice tools of the nobles who appropriated the revenues of their office. Andrew Melville, returning from Geneva in 1574, condemned all forms of episcopacy and may be said to be the effective founder of Presbyterianism in Scotland. The word "Tulchan" was applied to these bishops in derision, being a Scottish Gaelic word that designated a stuffed calfskin that was placed under a cow to induce her to give milk.

Tunicle. The vestment used in Catholic tradition by the subdeacon at Mass. It was developed out of the ordinary overcoat or *tunica* in use in the later Roman Empire, but lacking the girdle to fasten it. It became very similar in appearance to the deacon's vestment, the dalmatic.

Tunkers. See **Dunkers.**

Turin, Shroud of. See **Holy Shroud.**

Tutiorism. See **Probabilism.**

Tyāga. In Hindu thought, this Sanskrit term, which means literally "ignoring," is applied to the basic virtue of serene renunciation, implying *ahiṁsā*, nonviolence toward all living beings. It is contrasted with *tapas*, active ascetic practice. See **Tapas.**

Tyndale, William (*c.* **1494–1536**). The first translator of the New Testament from Greek into English. Born in Gloucestershire, he was trained at Magdalen Hall, Oxford, and subsequently also at Cambridge. The Bishop of London, C. Tunstall, refused to support him in his project, so Tyndale went to the continent where in 1525 the printing of his first translation was begun at Cologne. In spite of difficulties that pursued him it was published later that year at Worms. When in the following year it reached his native England it was bitterly attacked by the ecclesiastical authorities there. They not only had the book solemnly burned at St. Paul's Cross, London, but bought up so many thousands of copies that the quarto edition survives in only one solitary fragment, which is in the British Museum, while only two copies of the octavo edition survive: one at the Baptist College in Bristol and the other (an imperfect one) at St. Paul's Cathedral, London. Tyndale's style was felicitous, e.g., he uses "love," not "charity" in I Corinthians 13, and in general wrote in the free, idiomatic English of his time. His influence on the King James Version was even greater than Wyclif's. He began a translation of the Old Testament and completed the Pentateuch and some other books, but persecution prevented his finishing the work. In 1535 he was arrested and imprisoned at Vilvorde, near Brussels. In the following year he was led out from the castle prison to the stake. Knowing that Henry VIII had been the chief force behind his persecution he is said to have cried out in a loud voice, praying, "Lord, open the King of England's eyes." He was then strangled to death and his body burned to ashes.

Typology. The term is used in two distinct senses: (1) a method of interpreting any sacred literature (e.g., the Hebrew Bible) as containing characters or events that foreshadow others that occur later (e.g., Jesus as Messiah has been taken to have been prefigured in certain passages in the Old Testament; Mary has been called "the second Eve"). (2) a method of classifying religions, pioneered by Heinrich Frick (1893–1952) and others, e.g., certain religions may be classified under the head of tribal or national or "world" religions. Religions may also be classified according to whether they were founded by a charismatic figure or other individual or gradually developed out of antecedents. Again, some religions might be classified as mystical, others as prophetic, and so forth. The concept may have some practical uses but it is unsatisfactory, since at least the great religions and perhaps to some extent almost all religions have a variety of such ingredients, being at once institutional, legalistic, mystical, individualistic, community-minded, focused on one or more key figures, developing out of a long history and exhibiting gradual historical processes, deeply anchored to metaphysical and ontological concerns, emphasizing ethical results, and so on. The "amount" of any particular ingredient varies. In some cases it may be a mere "pinch," in others much more basic, but never scientifically justifying classification according to any such "type."

Tyrrell, George (1861–1909). Roman Catholic Modernist theologian. Born in Dublin, he was educated at Trinity College there, received into the Roman Catholic Church in 1879, entered the Jesuit novitiate the following year, and was ordained priest in 1891. For some years he taught moral theology at Stonyhurst, then in 1896 he was transferred to the Jesuit's principal church in Lon-

don (Farm Street) where he was much sought as a confessor and began his writings, including his *Hard Sayings* (1898) and *On External Religion* (1899). About this time he developed a friendship with Baron von Hügel, who introduced him to the writings of Bergson, Blondel, and others, and led him to be increasingly critical of the narrowness of Roman Catholic theology in his time. He went on writing in a more and more critical vein and in 1906 the Jesuits expelled him. His *Medievalism* (1908) fiercely denounced the Roman Catholic Church of his time. In his *Christianity at the Cross-Roads* (1909), published posthumously, he went so far as to propose that Christianity might be only a stepping stone on the way to a new and more comprehensive religion. Excommunicated by the Roman Catholic Church, he was refused burial in a Roman Catholic cemetery. He was buried in the Anglican churchyard at Storrington, where his friend the Abbé Bremond participated in the burial rites, being predictably suspended by his ecclesiastical superior for doing so. Tyrrell was temperamentally the antithesis of his friend Bremond, who could write critically without drawing attention to his interior rebellion and by exhibiting the deeply humane tradition in the history of Christianity that has lived for long in tandem with her more fanatical aspect, while Tyrrell could not disguise his prophetic zeal and disdain for compromise. For a bibliography of his writings, see *The Heythrop Journal*, x (1969), pp. 380–314 and xi (1970), pp. 161–9.

U

Ubertino of Casale (1259–c.1330). One of the leaders of the "Spiritual Franciscans." Having entered the Franciscan Order in 1273, he studied in Paris, then returned to his native Italy where he came under the influence of John of Parma and Peter John Olivi, who were both prominent among the "Spiritual

Franciscans." His chief work, written in 1305, is his *Arbor vitae crucifixae Jesu Christi,* a collection of his thoughts on the society of his age with special reference to the Church and bitterly critical of Popes Boniface VIII and Benedict XI. He served as chaplain to Cardinal Orsini for two years, then was called in 1310 by Pope Clement V to Avignon to defend the teaching of the movement of which he had become a leader. In 1317 he obtained permission to transfer to the Benedictine Order. Dante mentions him in the *Paradiso,* and he was much venerated by the Fraticelli but was probably suspect of heresy in his last years and nothing is known of his death.

Ubiquity. (Latin, *ubique,* everywhere.) This term is used in Luther's christology. According to his teaching, Christ is present in his human nature ubiquitously and Luther used this affirmation to uphold his teaching on the Real Presence of Christ in the Eucharist. The doctrine is called ubiquitarianism.

Uchronie. A term coined by Renouvier and much used by him in his emphasis on chance in history, to support his strongly anti-determinist stance. He asked his readers to imagine the occurrence, at critical moments in history, of a slight change that might have led to an enormous difference in what subsequently happened. The term is from Greek, meaning "out of time" or "not in time." The concept has an obvious relevance to all Christian philosophies of history.

Udall, John (*c.* 1560–1592). English Puritan scholar and writer. Educated at Cambridge, where he was entered in 1578, he was quickly convinced of the rightness of the Puritan claims, and in 1586 he was formally charged with having openly criticized the concept of Episcopacy. In 1589, having become suspect of participation in the Marprelate Tracts, he was summoned before the Privy Council for various writings and sentenced to death, although the sen-

tence was never carried out and he died in prison. A Hebrew scholar, he compiled a Hebrew dictionary and published commentaries and other works.

Udall, Nicholas (*c.* 1505–1556). English dramatist, educated at Oxford, he showed sympathies with the Reformation cause and the humanist movement. For some years Headmaster of Eton, he became in 1551 a Canon of Windsor and in 1555 Headmaster of Westminster. Among his works are translations of Erasmus's *Apophthegms* (1542) and Peter Martyr's *Treatise on the Eucharistic Sacrament* (*c.* 1550). His most popular work, a Christmas comedy, is his *Ralph Roister Doister* (1567).

Ugarit. An important ancient city near the coast of Syria, eight miles north of Latakia and on the site of the modern Ras Shamra. Its ruins were discovered in 1928 and promptly excavated by French archaeologists. The discovery included many hundreds of literary texts written in cuneiform and also in the Ugaritic script (an alphabetic one) that had been unknown to scholars before that time. These added considerably to knowledge of the political as well as the religious conditions in the Canaanite period, so illuminating our understanding of the numerous biblical references to the Canaanites as well as providing independent historical evidences of cultic and other practices that were part of the heritage of the biblical writers.

The religion of Ugarit was a nature religion, whose deities generally can be identified with natural phenomena, such as the cycle of the seasons. Fertility deities are prominent in the pantheon, whose head is El, progenitor of the gods and frequently designated "El the Bull." He is the male principle of fertility. His consort is Asherah, but Ashtar (Astarte), a younger goddess, functions as the principal fertility goddess. She appears in a dual role, as the goddess of war as well as the sex-goddess, suggesting the conjunction of sex and violence in the minds of her devotees.

Ullathorne, William Bernard (1806–1889). A direct descendant of Thomas More, Lord Chancellor of England and a Roman Catholic controversialist, Ullathorne entered the Benedictines at Downside in 1824, being ordained priest in 1831. He organized the Roman Catholic Church in Australia, where he worked among the convicts. He returned to England in 1840 where, after the restoration of the Roman Catholic hierarchy in England in 1850 he became Roman Catholic Bishop of Birmingham. His *Autobiography*, posthumously published in 1891–1892, provides an interesting view of Roman Catholic life in 19th c. England.

Ulphilas (c. 311–383). The Apostle of the Goths. He translated the Bible (or much of it) into the Gothic language. Consecrated bishop by Eusebius of Nicomedia, he was Arian in his christology and through his influence the Goths remained Arian for several hundred years. He wrote a confession of faith that has survived in part.

Ulrich (c. 890–973). Bishop of Augsburg, He supported the reforms urged by the Emperor Otto I and endeavored to impose a high standard of ethics, including sexual morality, on the clergy. He was canonized in 993 by Pope John XV: the first person on record to have been officially canonized by a pope.

Ulrich, Engelbert (1248–1278). Dominican schoolman. Having studied under Albertus Magnus, he taught at the Sorbonne. He was Provincial of the Dominican Order in Germany for five years.

Ultramontanism. With the rise of Gallicanism in the French Church in the 17th c., there arose a divergence of view in the Roman Catholic Church on the subject of ecclesiastical government. Against the Gallicans, who sought in general to uphold a very large measure of independence of the French Church from the centralized government of the Church by the papacy in Rome, those who espoused the Ultramontane position favored direct control from Rome. (The name means literally "beyond the mountains," i.e., the Alps: *ultra montes*.) The Jesuits, always close to the Roman Curia, were a potent force in securing the eventual victory of the Ultramontane view. In the 19th c. it was finally entrenched in the Roman Catholic church by the decrees of the First Vatican Council, especially by the theological claims made at that Council for the papal office.

Unam Sanctam. The name of a bull, issued by Pope Boniface VIII in 1302, which was a watermark in the claims of the papacy as the supreme head of the Church. It affirmed that apart from the Pope there is no salvation and no forgiveness of sins and that both spiritual and temporal authority are ultimately vested in him.

Unamuno, Miguel de (1864–1936). Spanish existentialist philosopher. Born in Bilbao and educated at Madrid, he taught at Salamanca. He was influenced by Kierkegaard. Characteristic of his outlook is a vigorous sense of independence in thought and action. He found in the individual "flesh-and-bone" man a longing for immortality of body and soul. For him faith means the hope that death does not annihilate existence. Since such faith lives in tension with reason, man lives in a state of agony and struggle. Such is what he calls "the tragic sense of life." He repudiates all attempts to set forth "objective truth," which is an abstraction. One should look for truth not in philosophical or religious systems but in the literary and religious expressions of individual persons. Among his many works are *The Tragic Sense of Life* (1913) and *The Agony of Christianity* (1931).

Uncial. A script used for Greek and Latin books from about the 4th to the

8th c. CE, consisting of a distinctive form of capital letters. All the three great biblical manuscripts (Codex Vaticanus, Codex Sinaiticus, and Codex Alexandrinus) are in this script.

Unconscious. The psychological doctrine that the human psyche comprises an important part or "region" whose activities operate below the level of consciousness is associated with Freud and Jung but has a long history and much relevance to religious thought. The principle is recognized and expounded in the teaching of the ancient Wisdom (notably in India) concerning the operation of the law of karma and its reincarnational implicates. In light of the karmic principle we recognize that as individuals we each have a history that goes beyond our recall, although through certain techniques some of it may be recaptured. Plato, who recognized a form of reincarnationism very similar to that of the upanishadic writers of India, taught indeed that all knowing is recollection and that although the biological processes of death and birth block that recollection, they do not entirely succeed. Knowledge consists (at least to a great extent) of a gradual drawing forth (from the storehouse of a seemingly forgotten past) that which we have already learned. In the *Meno* he reports on an intelligent slave boy who, on being given a few data is able to understand the proof of a geometrical theorem as though learning nothing new but, rather, recollecting what was in the recesses of his mind. Leibniz, nearly two thousand years later, saw the individual as receiving a continual flow of perceptions, most of them little ones so dim that we are scarcely aware of them. That too is a recognition of an unconscious level of activity in the psyche. Schelling saw artistic creativity as issuing from an unconscious level, and Schopenhauer's doctrine of "blind will" also recognizes something akin to what we now call the unconscious. Eduard von Hartmann developed a philosophy of the unconscious

out of the notion of a series of levels of awareness ranging from the unconscious to the conscious, and various modern structuralists and others have developed theories of the unconscious. Various writers before Freud anticipated the importance of the notion. Franz Delitzsch, for instance, writing in 1855, the year before Freud's birth, remarked in his book, *A System of Biblical Theology* (p. 330), that most psychologists hitherto had made the error of supposing that the soul consists only of a conscious element when it has "a far greater abundance of powers and relations than can possibly appear in its consciousness." Jung recognized a "collective" or "race" unconscious providing archetypes that pervade our experience. To the obvious question, "How can I know that which by definition I do not know?" the answer must be that I do not; I must probe for it and draw it up from the dark cellar of my psyche to the light of day; but much of what I am aware hovers at the threshold of consciousness being therefore most easily within my grasp.

Uncreated Light. See Hesychasts.

Unction. The anointing with oil used in baptism and in other rites in both the Eastern Orthodox and Roman Catholic Churches; also traditionally used in the anointing of monarchs. From at least the 4th c., following the biblical allusions in Mark 6.13 and James 5.14f., blessed oil has been used for the anointing of the sick, usually when the patient is very seriously ill (*in extremis*, hence the term "Extreme Unction") and even in danger of death. The basic purpose, however, is one of healing.

Underhill, Evelyn (1875–1941). Anglican writer on Christian spirituality and mystical experience. She was much influenced by Baron von Hügel. Her many deeply spiritual writings include her *Mysticism* (1911), a classic that ran into many editions, *The Mystic Way* (1913), and *Worship* (1936). Among her poems, *Immanence* is one of the best known.

Uniate Churches. (Also spelled Uniat.) Those Eastern Christian Churches that preserve their distinctive rites and liturgies but acknowledge as supreme the authority of the Roman papacy. They usually also retain characteristically Eastern Christian practices such as baptism by immersion, clerical marriage, and Communion under both species. The term is applied to groups such as the Maronites, Syrians, Copts, Ukrainians, and Greeks, who at various periods from the twelfth c. onward have been united with the Roman Catholic Church while retaining their distinctive usages.

Unification Church. Founded by its remarkable Korean leader, the Reverend Sun Myung Moon, in 1954, the Church has as its principal document *Divine Principle*, in which are set forth its fundamental teachings. These reflect both occidental and oriental influences: on the one hand, Christianity in the form introduced to Korea by the Presbyterian missionaries; on the other, both Taoist philosophy and Confucian ethics, including the dualism in Taoist thought, expressed in ideas such as the yin/yang principle, and the high respect for education and family that is characteristic of the Confucian tradition and contributes a highly important element in Unificationist practice. The Church is very actively engaged in interfaith conferences on a worldwide scale and in the organization of conferences for the interchange and exploration of ideas among university scholars and ecclesiastical leaders. It also publishes books, journals, and the proceedings of some of the learned conferences it sponsors and organizes on the unity of the sciences and in philosophical theology. It operates its own theological seminary at Barrytown, New York, for the training of its future leaders.

Uniformity, The Acts of. After the Reformation, there were four Acts bearing this name, followed by an Amendment Act. The first of the four was passed in 1549 and was conservative, ordaining that the service "commonly called the Mass must be said at all services in the manner prescribed in the First Prayer Book of Edward VI." In public such celebrations of the Mass were to be in English, but "for the encouragement of learning" they might be said at the universities or privately in Latin, Greek, or Hebrew. The Act of 1552 reinforced the Act of 1549 and prescribed penalties for absence from church on Sundays and Holy Days. The Act of 1559 reimposed forms of worship in use under Henry VIII and decreed stiffer punishments for disobedience. The Act of 1662 required the use of the Book of Common Prayer as revised in 1662 and as has remained on the Statute Book but modified in various ways. The Amendment Act (1872) provided for the use of various abbreviated forms of service. This Act was repealed by the Church of England (Worship and Doctrine Measure), 1974. In other parts of the Anglican Communion (e.g., in the United States, in Scotland, and in the British Commonwealth countries) liturgical usage is not regulated by these Parliamentary provisions.

Unigenitus. Two papal bulls, both famous in Church history, bear this name: (1) One issued in 1343 by Pope Clement VI, asserting that indulgences are efficacious through the papal administration of the accumulated spiritual merits that are at the disposal of the Pope as Head of the Church. This is the principle that Luther and other Reformation leaders vigorously attacked as a travesty of Christian teaching on the nature of the Church. (2) Another papal bull of the same name issued in 1713 by Pope Clement XI, which condemned 101 of the Jansenist propositions of Quenel. Many Jansenists appealed to a future General Council of the Roman Catholic Church against this papal act.

Unitarians. Unitarians, although they subscribe to no formal creed, spring historically out of a Christian background. Some today wish to be accounted Christian; others would prefer not to be specifically so designated. Unitarians reject the traditional doctrines of the Divinity of Christ and the Trinity. Unitarian teaching may be said to have roots in Monarchianism in the early Church, but it developed in a more clearly identifiable form in the teachings of some of the humanist and other scholars of the Reformation period such as Reuchlin and Servetus. Unitarian groups were organized in the 16th and 17th centuries in Poland, Hungary, and England, and were much persecuted in all these countries. Penal laws against them were enforceable till 1813 in England, where John Biddle was the earliest to propound Unitarian principles and gather groups sympathetic to the Unitarian viewpoint. Priestly wrote his *Appeal to the Serious and Candid Professors of Christianity* (1770), and in 1774 Theophilus Lindsey formally seceded from the Church of England and formed a separate denomination. During the 18th c., when Deistic views were in vogue among educated people, many in other dissenting bodies such as the English Presbyterians no doubt held Unitarian views privately. The movement, although having its roots in a biblical perspective, tended to shift to a more general stance especially under the influence, in England, of James Martineau and, in America, of Theodore Parker, both of them scholars, independent thinkers, and Unitarian leaders. The Hibbert Trust in England was founded in 1853 to promote religious thought along Unitarian lines, using its funds to organize lectures and publish the *Hibbert Journal,* which was issued regularly from 1902 through 1968. In the United States, King's Chapel, Boston, which was the oldest congregation of the Anglican Communion in New England, formally abandoned belief in the Trinity and in 1785 adopted a form of the Anglican liturgy divested of Trinitarian expressions and suited to worshippers having Uni-

tarian views. William Ellery Channing, both in his Boston pulpit and in his writings, became, after much spiritual struggle, a convinced, persuasive, and saintly exponent of views of an Arian and Socinian kind, and in 1815 he accepted the name Unitarian for the movement he was leading. Many American Congregationalists were notably sympathetic to the movement. Emerson, one of the most acute American religious thinkers of his day, was among those whose philosophical views were hospitable to Unitarian principles. As Unitarian churches prospered in the 19th c. in the United States, legal battles ensued over property disputes and the Unitarians generally succeeded in retaining possession. Harvard Divinity School, as reconstituted, supported the Unitarian cause. Although New England was a much more hospitable arena for the development of Unitarian ideas than England or continental Europe, and Unitarianism exercised an enormous influence among the educated classes in the United States, entirely disproportionate to the relatively small number of its formal adherents, the movement began to decline in the 20th c. In 1961 the American Unitarian Association and the Universalist Church of America formally combined to become the Unitarian Universalist Association. The reasons for the decline are complex. Two, however, should be noted: (1) widespread ignorance of philosophical problems and theological issues among the general populace and (2) better perceptions among the learned concerning Trinitarian belief and its function in the development of Christian thought and in the understanding of questions about the nature of God. Theologians today tend to view the doctrine of the Trinity in such a way as to make them from one standpoint more appreciative of it and from another less dogmatic, seeing it, rather, as a brilliant solution to the intellectual problems of the Greek-speaking world of the early centuries of the Christian Way, but not necessarily the only possible form of expressing the central beliefs the doctrine was designed to express when it was formulated in those ancient intellectual circumstances. The Unitarian movement, because of its seriousmindedness and independence of thought as well as its respect for openminded scholarship, has won the respect of scholarly men and women everywhere, even of those who do not subscribe to Unitarian views.

Unitas Fratrum. The Bohemian Brethren, a branch of the Hussites, are known by this name, a Latinized form of their original Czech designation, meaning "the Society of Brethren."

United Brethren in Christ. A body whose constitution dates from 1841. It is Arminian in its theology. In 1889 a division occurred concerning proposed changes in its constitution, which, however, it retained.

United Christian Church. A group that separated from the United Brethren in Christ in 1862–1870. It was organized in Campbelltown, Pennsylvania, in 1878.

United Church of Christ, a Church formed in 1957 in the United States out of a union of the Congregational Christian Churches and the Evangelical and Reformed Church. The latter had been the result of a union between the Evangelical Synod of North America and the Reformed Church of America in 1934. About fifteen percent of Congregational Churches preferred to retain independence and stayed out of the union.

United Free Church of Scotland. In 1900 the Free Church of Scotland and the United Presbyterian Church, both of which represented movements that had separated themselves from the established Kirk either by secession or disruption joined to form the United Free Church of Scotland. A small minority remained outside the Union. They were popularly known as the "Wee Frees." In 1929 the United Free

Church of Scotland was joined to the established Kirk under the name of Church of Scotland. Most ecclesiastical schisms in Scotland apart from the 17th c. struggles between Episcopal and Presbyterian government, have been within the Presbyterian framework.

United Holy Church of America. Organized in 1886 at Method, North Carolina, it practices baptism by immersion and has a quadrennial convocation.

United Methodist Church. In the 19th c. the Methodist movement had been much splintered. In 1907 various branches in England were united to form the Church so designated. In 1932 a further union was achieved. In the United States the present organization of the Methodist Church began in May, 1939, with a union of three branches of American Methodism: the Methodist Episcopal Church, the Methodist Episcopal Church South, and the Methodist Protestant Church.

United Presbyterian Church. In 1847 two seceding Presbyterian bodies, the United Secession Church and the Relief Synod, united under that name. This body was in turn united in 1900 with the Free Church of Scotland to form the United Free Church of Scotland.

United Reform Church. In England the Congregational Church of England and Wales was united with the Presbyterian Church of England in 1972 to form the body so designated.

United Secession Church. In 1820 two seceding Presbyterian bodies, the two groups into which the Burghers had been divided in the 18th c. (popularly known as the "Old Lights" and the "New Lights") were united under that name. This body was in turn united with the Relief Synod in 1847. See **United Presbyterian Church.**

United Seventh Day Brethren. In 1947, at Salina, Oklahoma, two small independent Sabbatarian bodies merged at Salina, Oklahoma, under this designation.

Unitive Way. In Catholic spirituality, three stages may be recognized: a purgative, an illuminative, and a unitive way. This last stage represents a close "walking with God" with the habitual practice of the Christian virtues and is marked by the graces of contemplative prayer. It may be seen as the culmination of the spiritual life in a mystical union with God.

Universalism. This term is used in two entirely different senses: (1) the teaching of those later Old Testament prophets who sought to wean the people from nationalism and to show that God has purposes for other races and nations too; (2) the view that hell cannot be everlasting but must be in some way educative and reformative, so that in the long run all must be saved. (See **Apocatastasis** and **Origen**.) Those who in modern times have held such a view have been called Universalists. An American group so designated joined with the Unitarians in 1961. See **Unitarians**.

Universals. The problem of the universals, raised in one way or another by the ancient Greeks, became for the medieval thinkers one of the most important for all their discussions. The Latin term *universalis* means "that which pertains to all" contradistinguished from the particular or individual. In Plato's terminology the *eidos* or "idea, form" has the function of the universal. Aristotle's term, *to katholon*, is virtually the same as *universalis*. The medieval debate took its point of departure in a passage in Porphyry's introduction to the Categories of Aristotle, which posed three questions: (1) Do the universals (e.g., courage or kindness) have an independent, substantial existence of their own, or do they exist only in the human mind? (2) If they have an independent existence, is it that of a body or that of a disembodied entity? (3) Do they exist

separated from the objects of sense or only within these objects? Boethius had specifically asked whether the universals are things *(res)* or merely names *(voces, nomina)*. Those who held that they are *res* were called Realists; those who held that they are merely *nomina* were called Nominalists; but each school had a variety of interpretations. Erigena and William of Champeaux, for instance, might be called Extreme Realists, while Roscellinus and (much later) William of Occam took, each in his own way and according to the temper of his respective generation, the opposing stance. Both Thomas Aquinas and Duns Scotus represent a critical form of realism that modern historians of thought often call "Moderate Realism." The question had important theological ramifications in Christian thought. Augustine, inspired by his Neoplatonic background of thought, which might be said to imply an absolute realism, placed Plato's "ideas" or "forms" in the mind of God, so investing them with an eternal independence of the human mind and providing them with an eternal home. After the passing of the Middle Ages the controversy took a different guise; nevertheless it has continued in one way or another, with representatives of what may be called Critical Realism and of what may be called New Realism. Bertrand Russell, for instance, would be classified among the latter and George Santayana among the former. Many 20th c. philosophers, however, such as Quine and Goodman, take a definitely Nominalist position, while Wittgenstein has substituted for universals the notion of "family resemblances."

Universe. This term comes from a Latin equivalent of the Greek term *to olon*, "the whole." It means primarily all that exists in time and space. Therefore, although one may talk of many worlds, there can be only one universe. The term may be and has been used, however, in a secondary sense to designate a particular whole, such as the totality of whatever is under discussion, e.g., the world of mammals or the totality of religious ideas.

Univocity. See **Equivocity.**

Unknowing, The Cloud of. A 14th c. English mystical treatise. No authorship is ascribed in the manuscripts, resulting in much speculation that has issued in no definite conclusion. The work is much influenced by the tradition of mysticism stemming from Dionysius the Pseudo-Areopagite. The author asserts that God cannot be known by reason but only by "a sharp dart of love" that penetrates the "cloud" lying between God and man. The treatise is addressed to those already advanced in the mystical way.

Unmoved Mover. Aristotle used this term in reference to the nature of God. Everything other than God moves and is moved by something other than itself, but God, although he moves everything, is not moved. God is not subject to change and decay as is all else.

Upādāna. In Buddhist thought, craving (*taṇhā*) is an impediment to spiritual progress and it may take any of four forms of *upādāna*, an intensified form of a specific craving: (1) clinging to sensuous desires; (2) clinging or obstinately holding on to narrow or mistaken views; (3) holding on to rituals as though they were necessary for salvation; and (4) clinging to the notion of individual personality.

Uppsala. The cathedral of Uppsala is the largest church in Sweden and dates from the late 13th c. From the middle of the 15th c. till the Reformation the archbishop had the title of Primate of Sweden and is still recognized as having a certain kind of primacy over the other Swedish bishops. The University of Uppsala is traditionally of a more· open theological temper than that of Lund, which has a more conservative tradition.

Ur. A Mesopotamian city a few miles from the mouth of the Euphrates river and that from which Abraham's father, Terah, had migrated to Haran. The site was discovered in 1853 and excavated by a joint expedition of archaeologists from the British Museum and the University of Pennsylvania, between 1922 and 1934. Besides much else, including much gold and jewelry, were the remains of a ziggurat, constructed of brick sometime between 2120 and 2015 BCE, such as is described in Genesis 11.1–9. See **Babel, Tower of.**

Urban II (*c*.1042–1099). After being prior of Cluny, he was called to Rome by Pope Gregory VII and became Cardinal Bishop of Ostia in 1080. Ten years later he succeeded Gregory as pope. He was involved in the investiture controversy and tried to reform the sexual and other morality of the clergy. In response to an appeal from the Greek Emperor, he proclaimed the First Crusade at the Council of Clermont on November 27, 1095, with the aim of obtaining free access of Christian pilgrims to Jerusalem and of relieving the Eastern Empire of the pressure of the Seljuk Turks. In his last years he tried unsuccessfully to heal the East-West Schism. See **Great Schism, The.**

Urban V (1309–1370). Pope from 1362, he was a generous benefactor to the universities, encouraging poor scholars and promoting the intellectual life of the Church. He also tried to reform the conduct of the clergy and was probably the best of the Avignon popes.

Urban VIII (1568–1644). Descended from the Barberini family, one of the oldest in Florence, he had a long career in ecclesiastical diplomacy before his election to the papacy in 1623. Historically one of the most important occupants of the papal office, he was very active in the political affairs of Europe. A gifted classical scholar he devoted his energies to the administration of the church along lines calculated to enhance its political power and streamline its organizational workings. He also interested himself very much in military defense and fortified Sant'Angelo and other strongholds. It was under him that Galileo was condemned for the second time (in 1633) and he declared the teaching of Jansen heretical.

Urbi et Orbi. A phrase used of the solemn blessing that the Pope traditionally gives from the balcony of St. Peter's. After the First Vatican Council the custom was dropped but it was revived by Pope Pius XI. The Latin phrase means "To the City and for the World."

Urgeschichte. A term used in Dialectical Theology in reference to events that are seen as having a significance beyond human history in the sense that they are taken to be acts of God used by him in revealing to humankind his purposes.

Urim and Thummim. These are mentioned in various books of the Old Testament, but we have only scanty indications of their nature. According to Exodus 28.30 and Leviticus 8.8, they were worn on the high priest's breastplate, so they were presumably objects possibly carried in a pocket-like receptacle. Since elsewhere (e.g., I Samuel 28.6) they have an oracular function, they may have been drawn at random to provide a "yes" or "no" answer to questions put to the priest to which he would respond after consulting them as to an oracle. This is suggested in Numbers 27.21. It seems that by the beginning of the period of the monarchy the oracular function had fallen into disuse, having been discarded as a survival of a primitive practice; nevertheless their use continued as an ornamental or symbolic part of the priestly vestments, somewhat as the maniple survives today in the vestments of the Catholic Mass, although having lost its original function as a hand towel.

Urmarcus. Some German scholars argued that underlying Mark was an earlier draft of that Gospel that Mark and the other Synoptists used. To this hypo-thetical document they gave the name "Urmarcus."

Ursula. The popular medieval legend of Ursula and the 11,000 virgins who were martyred comes in many forms over the centuries. That it may have had some basis in fact is suggested from ancient inscriptions, but if so the story was lavishly embellished to the point of absurdity.

Ursulines. Among the many orders and congregations of women who engage in teaching within the Roman Catholic Church, the Ursulines, founded in 1535 at Brescia by Angela Merici, is the oldest and probably the best known. At first a society of unmarried women dedicated to teaching but living in their own homes, it had developed early in the 17th c. into an order with convents following the Rule of Saint Augustine and has grown extensively.

Use. A technical term in liturgics designating a slight variation from a rite. Certain places were permitted by custom to a certain "use," e.g., the Ambrosian "use" at Milan and the Mozarabic at Toledo. Such "uses" were abolished in the Roman Catholic Church at the Council of Trent except for a few that had enjoyed long custom. Some of the ancient religious orders were also permitted to retain their slight liturgical peculiarities. In England there had been five "uses" (Hereford, York, Lincoln, Bangor, and Salisbury), but these were abolished in 1549 in the interest of a uniform liturgy.

Ussher, James (1581–1656). Irish divine. Educated at Trinity College, Dublin, he became Bishop of Meath in 1621 and Archbishop of Armagh in 1625. A learned scholar, he was admired for his tolerance. Oliver Cromwell gave him a state funeral in Westminster Abbey. His numerous writings on a wide variety of theological and biblical subjects include his *Annales Veteris et Novi Testamenti* (1650–1654) in which he proposed the year 4004 BCE as the date of creation: a hypothesis improved upon by John Lightfoot who worked out even the day and hour: Friday, October 23, at 9 a.m.

Usuard. Compiler of the most widely used martyrology in the Middle Ages, which is the basis of the Roman Martyrology today.

Usury. The lending of money for a consideration of the payment of interest. As early as the patristic age the practice of exacting interest on loans was forbidden to clerics. Various Councils from the 4th c. onward forbade it even to laymen and in 1179 the Third Lateran Council reinforced the prohibition. The Fourth Lateran Council allowed it, however, to Jews, although the exacting of interest appears to be forbidden, at least to Jewish debtors (Exodus 22.25; Deuteronomy 23.19f.). The condemnation of usury was based on Aristotle's theory of the "barrenness" of money, a theory that Thomas Aquinas supported and developed. The Reformers in varying degrees continued to support it, but with the rise of capitalism and the banking system civil legislation in Germany and England as early as the 16th c. began to tolerate moderate interest on loans. France followed, but not till the French Revolution. Nevertheless, although the entire capitalist system is founded on the principle that money, far from being "barren" is productive capital that "works for" its owner, abnormally high rates of interest are often prohibited by law as usurious, despite the arbitrariness of the line drawn between "usurious" and "fair." The Roman Catholic Church continued to condemn all payment of interest on money as unlawful as late as the 19th c.

Utica Martyrs, The. According to an early tradition attested by Augustine, a large group of African Christians were massacred at Utica, near Carthage. He puts their number at 153. According to the Roman Martyrology there were 300. The date is uncertain, probably about the middle of the 3rd c.

Utilitarianism. An early 19th c. ethical doctrine according to which the criterion in problems in ethics should be the principle of greatest utility. This principle was expressed by Francis Hutcheson (not generally regarded as himself a Utilitarian) in the phrase "the greatest happiness for the greatest number." Richard Cumberland (1631–1718), a Cambridge moralist and Bishop of Peterborough, had adumbrated the Utilitarian view by proposing a moral criterion: "the greatest good of the universe of rational beings." The term seems to have been first used by Jeremy Bentham in 1781. Utilitarian views fostered the movement in early 19th c. England that led to the passing of the great reform bills in the 1830s.

Utopia. The word means literally "not a place" (Greek, *ou*, not, and *topos*, place). It was coined by Thomas More in 1516 as the name for his ideal society. Rabelais used it a generation later as the name for an ideal island, since then it has become a name used by philosophers and social reformers for any ideal social structure. Plato's *Republic*, for instance, is a utopian expression of his political philosophy. More's *Utopia* and Samuel Butler's *Erewhon* (1872) are among classic examples of utopias.

Utraquists. The name given to those followers of John Huss who insisted that the laity should receive the Holy Communion "under both kinds" (*sub utraque specie*), i.e., both bread and wine. They were also called "Calixtines" (from *calix*, cup or chalice). Those who were satisfied to receive the bread only were called Subunites (*sub una* specie, under one kind).

V

Vaccination. See **Immunization**.

Vahanian, Gabriel. See **Death of God Theology**.

Vaihinger, Hans (1852–1933). German thinker whose writings include *Com-*

mentary on Kant's Critique of Pure Reason (2 vols., 1881, 1892) and *The Philosophy of As If* (1911). See **Fictionalism**.

Vaijayanta. The name given in Hindu lore to Indra's banner. It means "victorious."

Vaiśya. The name of the third of the four Hindu castes, whose basic occupation was cattle raising and the cultivation of land.

Valdes, Peter. See **Waldensians**.

Valentine. The traditional association of "Valentine's Day" (February 14) with a martyred 3rd c. saint is based on stories so diffused with legendary material that it is difficult to disentangle some possibly factual elements in them from the rest. The traditional association with courtship that has come down to us today in popular imagery may have originated in certain pagan customs connected with the mid-February Lupercalia at Rome. Valentine has also served in ways having nothing to do with courtship, e.g., in German-speaking countries he has sometimes been popularly regarded as the patron of epileptics: an association derived from the connection of his name with the German word *hinfallen* (*fallen hin*, "to fall down"), which is what an epileptic does during a seizure. (*Fallen hin* = Valentinus.) So although it is possible that there may have been some factual basis for a "Saint Valentine," the literature relating to him has been so embroidered as to make him popularly serviceable in almost any capacity.

Valentinus. A 2nd c. CE Gnostic teacher. Born in Alexandria, he taught there until 135 CE, when he moved to Rome, teaching there until 160. He died in Cyprus in 165. His system was characteristically Gnostic in its mind-matter dualism. It was distinctive, however, in its teaching that the Father or Abyss unites with the feminine principle, Silence, a union resulting in *nous* and *alētheia* (mind and truth). These form what he calls the first tetrad; a further union within the tetrad generates an octad, from which the fundamental forces of the universe are generated.

Valhalla. In Scandinavian lore, the place whither great men (e.g., kings and warlike heroes) were conducted after death. (See **Valkyries**.) Odin presided over a life of fighting and feasting. Only the privileged, those who had served Odin well, could hope to attain Valhalla. It was by no means a general destination such as was the Scandinavian Hel, presided over by a sinister giantess, said to be the daughter of Loki. In Valhalla the great ones, the warriors, continued to fight and to be slain and each day they were raised again to participate in the everlasting banquet with endless provisions of roast pork and mead. In Scandinavian iconography Valhalla was represented as a glorification of those who died in battle. Sometimes a woman with a drinking horn is at the gates of Valhalla to welcome and reward the slain warriors on their arrival there.

Validity. In traditional logic, validity is distinguished from truth: an argument is said to be valid or invalid; a proposition is true or false. If the premises of a syllogism are true and the argument valid, the conclusion will be necessarily true, e.g., "All men are mammals; Michelangelo is a man; therefore Michelangelo is a mammal." An argument may be valid, however, yet the conclusion false because of the falsity of one of the premises, e.g., "All men are Chinese; Michelangelo is a man; therefore Michelangelo is Chinese."

Valkyries. Originally the Valkyries in early Germanic lore were fierce battle-spirits who devoured the warriors slain in battle, somewhat as did the Celtic war-goddesses Morrigan and Badb. In Scandinavian lore, however, they appear as superwomen who both urge on the warriors in battle and receive them when they are slain. In iconography they are often represented as escorting the dead warriors to Valhalla or receiving them with draughts of mead to reward them for their military prowess. Perhaps the cheerleaders in modern football games might be seen as reflecting a similar set of functions.

Valla, Lorenzo (1405–1457). Italian humanist. Born in Rome, he taught at the University of Pavia and in 1435 became secretary to King Alfonso of Aragon, later serving as apostolic secretary in Rome under Pope Nicholas V. His work *On Pleasure* (1431) is a sort of christianized Epicureanism. In his work *On Free Will*, in which he treats human freedom in relation to divine foreknowledge, he favors a view that in some ways adumbrates the emphases of Luther and Calvin. Like other Renaissance humanists he disdained the way in which the schoolmen had used Aristotle to serve their purpose of trying to unite the realms of faith and knowledge. In *The Donation of Constantine* (1440), one of his most important works, he exhibited the spurious character of that notorious document, which had been used as a basis for the papal claims of temporal authority. Valla may be regarded as one of the most important of the Italian Renaissance humanists.

Vallumbrosans. A religious order named from the mother house at Vallumbrosa, *c.* twenty miles east of Florence, founded *c.* 1036 by John Gualbert. They followed a reform of the Benedictine rule and spread so quickly that by the end of the 12th c. there were already fifty abbeys, most of them in Italy. The Vallumbrosans were semi-eremitical and strictly contemplative. Galileo was a novice in this order. An order of Vallumbrosan nuns was also founded and has a few convents in Italy.

Value. Historically, value is a concept placed in contrast to, yet complementing the concept of fact. The concept of value depends upon a judgment of importance that constitutes the basis for a

preference. Many value theories have been proposed. For example, W. R. Sorley (1855–1935) followed Plato in the latter's classic distinction between instrumental and intrinsic values. Influenced by Kant, he saw the former as relating to things, the latter to persons. The American philosopher Ralph Barton Perry (1876–1957) proposed eight types or realms of value: ethical, aesthetic, scientific, religious, economic, political, legal, and customary. Value is the correlative of interest and the harmonizing of interests leads to greater inclusiveness, which Perry sees as the highest good. As a contributor to the movement called New Realism, he opposed Idealism. Max Scheler (1874–1928) distinguished three types of knowledge: scientific (knowledge of particulars), phenomenological (knowledge of essences), and metaphysical (knowledge of being itself). He sought to overcome the widely presumed relativity of values. Metaphysical knowledge for Scheler takes its beginning in the discovery of "person," understood as the unity of scientific and phenomenological values and leading to the concept of God, whom Scheler came to view as the totality of all things. John Dewey (1859–1952) held that values are discoverable in experience. In his system of ethical naturalism, ethical questions can be settled by evidence. That which is ethically preferable emerges in the process of inquiry. Dewey saw freedom as the ability to make intelligent choices and to act upon them from the stance of one's own situation as an individual.

Philosophers have disagreed on whether there is any value or set of values that may be regarded as ultimate in the sense that it is the goal of everyone. For example, Aristotle specified *eudaemonia* as the value sought after by everyone. His view, variously interpreted, has been followed by a great many philosophers. Stoicism took *apatheia* (serenity or mental tranquility) as the ultimate value: a view widely represented also in various forms of Buddhist thought. Confucius established a tradition of Chinese thought that saw *jen* and *li* (humanity and propriety in human relationships) as ultimate values. In Taoism, the notion of adaptability, the *wu wei* principle (symbolized in the image of the tree laden with snow, which bends its boughs that otherwise would break under the weight) may be seen as the ultimate value. In Christianity *agapē*, the special form of love that has as its source the divine love at work in the Church, the Household of Faith, is generally taken to be the supreme value in this life, leading to the vision of God in heaven (*visio beatifica*), the enjoyment of which is the ultimate goal of human beings. For Spinoza wisdom, as the means to a special kind of happiness, is the highest value. There are many other proposals among philosophers who subscribe to the view that one can point to a supreme or ultimate value. Some philosophers repudiate the notion that any such value exists.

Vanir. In Scandinavian religion the fertility deities, sometimes associated with the sea but linked with land spirits. The male fertility god was Freyr (represented as a phallic statue at Uppsala), whose sister was Freyja. The Vanir were probably connected with the female shamans who practiced divination and claimed to be able to discern the destinies of children. See **Fylgia, Matres,** and **Valkyries.**

Van Manen, Willem Christiaan. (1842–1905). Dutch biblical scholar and professor at Leyden from 1885 until his death. He was extremely radical in his methods and in his views, and he has not been influential in the development of modern biblical studies, although noteworthy in his way. In his *Paulus* (3 vols., 1890–1896) he argued that Paul's letters were in fact the work of a group of theologians who wanted to transform primitive Christianity from a Jewish movement or sect into a worldwide religion with strongly Gnostic elements. He did not contend that there was no such person as Paul but held that he had

nothing to do with the letters attributed to him. (The authorship of some of the letters, e.g., Colossians and Ephesians, is disputed by many modern scholars, but van Manen's view went far beyond that, alleging that all New Testament writings belonged to a later period).

Vārānsi. One of the seven sacred cities of India, whose earliest name was Kāśī. From the 6th c. BCE this city was a focal point in the history of northeastern India, deriving great importance from its proximity to the Ganges, a particularly sacred river. It is revered not only by Hindus but by Buddhists (a great stupa commemorates the Buddha's first exposition of his teachings there), Jains, and others.

Most Hindus hope to visit this holy city during their lifetime. At about sunrise every morning thousands of people line the banks. They bathe in its waters, wash their clothes, or simply sit on the wide stone steps (the ghats) with their hands clasped in meditation. Many are elderly people who have come to spend their last years or months here, but many young people come here too, along with goats, cows, pigeons, and other animals. Pilgrim houses are to be found all along the waterfront and visitors may stay in them for several days gratis. Along the waterfront are also the crematoria ("burning ghats") and occasionally bodies may be seen, wrapped in shrouds and lashed to bamboo stretchers. Besides the many temples in the sacred city is the eleven-hundred-acre, tree lined campus of the famous Benares Hindu University. Among the donations received by the founder, Madan Mohan Malaviya, was a loaf of bread from a beggar, which was later auctioned for 12,000 rupees and the beggar's name listed first in the list of donors.

Varuṇa. One of the earliest of the Vedic gods, somewhat similar in character to the Zoroastrian Ahura Mazda. He seems to have been originally a sky-god. His name probably comes from a Sanskrit root meaning "to cover," but gradually he came to be the all-seeing deity who has ethical functions and looks after the moral conduct of the universe: a law-and-order divinity. In time, however, his position seems to have deteriorated in such a way that he comes to be invoked by lovers to arouse passion in the object of their desires. His wife, Vāruṇāni, personifies the waters, sometimes night.

Vatican. A papal residence seems to have been erected near the court of the old basilica of St. Peter by Pope Symmachus about the beginning of the 6th c. After the return of the popes from Avignon in 1377 the Vatican became the chief papal residence. The present Vatican Palace was completed by Clement VIII *c.* the end of the 16th c., and a new wing was added by Pius VII in 1821. The Vatican is situated on the ancient Mons Vaticanus where Nero's Circus stood.

Vatican Council, The First. This Council, the first Roman Catholic council to have been held since the Council of Trent (1545–1563) was convoked by Pius IX by a bull dated June 29, 1868 and was held in Rome 1869–1870. Although it was planned to treat many matters of faith, discipline, and much else, it soon became focused on a clear difference of opinion in the Roman Catholic Church between the conciliarist and the papalist parties. Both recognized the authority of both Pope and Council, but the former (broadly speaking) held that the Council has authority over the Pope, while the latter saw the Pope as having authority over even a General Council of the Church. Some 700 bishops attended. Although the conciliarists were in the minority, their position, which had been held by many canonists during the Middle Ages and had remained widespread among the learned at Trent and thereafter, was championed by many of the bishops of the foremost historic dioceses in Europe. Those bishops more dependent on

the papacy naturally tended to favor the papalist against the conciliarist party. When the question of Papal Infallibility was raised for discussion on March 6, 1870, the division deepened. The result left much dissatisfaction on both sides, especially among extremists. What was affirmed was that the Pope is infallible when making pronouncements in his official capacity (speaking *ex cathedra*, i.e., from his official chair as Head of the Church) on matters of faith and morals, and that such papal pronouncements are "irreformable of themselves" and "not from the consent of the Church." It was the last element in the assertion that was so unacceptable to those in the conciliarist tradition because it seemed to make the papal pronouncements on these matters independent of the Church. Many of the minority party acquiesced under pressure. Many abstained. A large number simply left the Council to return to their dioceses. The Council was formally suspended on October 20, 1870. See **Infallibility**.

Vatican Council, The Second (1962–1965). Pope John XXIII conceived the idea of holding this Council as a means of invigorating the life of the Church and in hope of helping to promote Christian unity. He died in June 1963 while the Council was in progress and his successor, Paul VI announced his intention of continuing it. Among the decisions made and the reforms proposed may be mentioned: the concept of the collegiality of bishops; the restoration of the diaconate as a separate order, not merely a stepping-stone to the priesthood; a declaration on the Church's relation to religions other than Christianity; the reform of the Roman curia; a decree on ecumenism; and a decree on the apostolate of the laity. Many changes took place in the Roman Catholic Church as a result of the Second Vatican Council and in implementation of its legislation.

Vāyu. In Hinduism, the god of the wind, also known as **Vāta**.

Veda. This Sanskrit term means literally "knowledge," but it is applied to a specific kind of knowledge: the wisdom contained in the Vedic literature (the Vedas) and other Hindu scriptures. The Vedic literature for long constituted the Hindu scriptures, but Hinduism has a unique capacity for assimilating religious ideas of the most diverse kinds and representing a vast variety of stages in religious and cultural development. For example, against the primitive notion of ritual sacrifices as the sole means of liberation, *brahmins* and other learned Hindus met secretly in the forest and composed works expressing a monistic philosophy far in advance of the primitive dependence on ritual. In such ways Hinduism has been constantly revitalized without injury to the needs of those at a less advanced level of mental and spiritual development.

Vedānta. The name means literally "the end (completion) of the Veda" (see **Veda**): not an additional literature but an interpretation. It was regarded as one of the six *darsanas* of Hinduism (see **Darshana**), each of which represents a particular view of a particular school or teacher; but Vedānta was not so initiated, being directly derived from a close following of the Upanishads, so that it has a special place in the schools of Hindu thought. Vedānta itself, however, can be interpreted in more than one way and two schools of Vedānta must be distinguished: (1) *advaita*, which is purely monistic (see **Monism**) and (2) *dvaita*, which is a modified dualism. Although it was not till some time between the 3rd and the 5th c. CE that such distinctions within Vedānta were clearly exhibited, Vedānta itself is of great antiquity. Hindu scholars consider that the basic notion of the *ātman*, for instance (see **Ātman**), was already well established by the 6th c. BCE. So influential has been Vedānta in Hindu thought that from being one of the six *darśanas* it came so to permeate all Hindu thought as to establish itself as its cornerstone. The aim of Vedānta

may be summed up in its fundamental intellectual enterprise: to go beyond the limits of the world of empirical perception. Its basic motivation, therefore, may be seen as having some affinity with that of Platonism, although it would be simplistic to see the one as the mere counterpart of the other.

Vedi. In Hinduism, an elevated or excavated area serving as an altar of sacrifice. The gods were believed, in Vedic times, to descend into it, regarding it as the center of the universe.

Vegans. See **Vegetarianism.**

Vegetarianism. The practice of those who, for moral or religious or other reasons, refuse to eat meat. Some vegetarians are so strict that they exclude dairy products and may refuse to buy or wear leather or wool. These are sometimes called vegans to distinguish them from less strict vegetarians who are sometimes identified as ovo-lacto-vegetarians, i.e., they permit themselves dairy products. Jains are always vegans. Most Hindus and Buddhists either practice vegetarianism or uphold it at least as an ideal.

Veil. The wearing of the veil by women is a very ancient custom in many societies and still prevails in some. From a variety of biblical passages (e.g., Genesis 12.14f.; 24.15f.; *et al.*) the implication is that the veil was worn for a special reason and in special circumstances only. For example, the veil was apparently worn by women at the time of their marriage and in the consummation of the marriage; possibly also thereafter as a regular practice during intercourse. There are other indications that the wearing of the veil was customary during sexual intercourse whether within marriage or not. In Genesis 38.14f, Tamar's wearing of the veil seems to identify her as a prostitute. Hebrew practice appears to be at variance with that of Israel's neighbors, among whom there were many very specific rules about the wearing of the veil. It was very generally connected in one way or another, however, with sexual intercourse. For example, a temple prostitute was required to wear the veil if she were married; she was not allowed to wear it if unmarried.

The veil could also have other symbolic functions. For example, Moses, when he spoke "for" God wore a veil over his face, probably to symbolize the concept that he was not speaking for himself but as the instrument of God. In such a case the veil would become a vestment submerging the personality of the functionary and emphasizing his role as God's spokesman.

In Islam, the use of the veil seems to have originated for the protection of the wives of the Prophet, being then extended to all free women in Islam. It is adopted at puberty.

The veil was worn by Roman matrons to distinguish them from unmarried women. In Christian practice from at least the 3rd c. it was worn by consecrated women as a symbol of their spiritual marriage to Christ. It became the most distinctive part of the dress of nuns and other female members of religious orders and congregations.

Liturgical cloths used in Catholic worship such as for covering the chalice are called veils. From at least the 11th c. it was the custom to cover all statues, crucifixes, and pictures with a veil during Passiontide (the last two weeks of Lent): a practice that has now been modified in the Roman Catholic Church.

Venerable. An ecclesiastical designation used in two very different senses: (1) In the Roman Catholic Church, when a deceased person is being considered for a place on the calendar of saints and a certain stage in that process has been reached, the title of "Venerable" is bestowed. If the process does not go so far as recognizing him or her as "beatified" or "canonized," then he or she continues indefinitely to be alluded to as "The Venerable John Smith" or as the case may be. The title is also tradition-

ally given, however, to persons noted for their holiness of life although not officially recognized in the Church's list of saints. The Venerable Bede is perhaps the best-known example. (2) In Anglican usage, the title is used for the designation of an archdeacon, a cleric having a limited ecclesiastical authority assigned to him by the diocesan bishop.

Veneration of the Cross. A Good Friday ceremony in which clergy and laity kneel and kiss a crucifix at the entrance to the sanctuary. The Eastern Church has a counterpart ceremony on Holy Cross Day (September 14) and on the Third Sunday in Lent.

Venial Sin. In traditional Catholic moral theology, two classes of sins are recognized: mortal sins, which deprive the soul of sanctifying grace and are so called because they "kill" the soul, and venial sins, which, although evil (since they may incline the soul away from God), are less grave in their effect. The distinction is a medieval one, but it has roots in the writings of the early Fathers of the Church, who distinguished sins that are *levia* (light) from those that are *mortalia* (deadly). Venial sins may but need not be confessed to a priest in the Sacrament of Penance as must be mortal sins.

Veni Creator. This ancient and beautiful Christian hymn probably dates from the 9th c., having been composed in the Frankish Empire. It is usually attributed to Rabanus Maurus. It is used at Pentecost and at the ordination of priests and other ceremonies.

Verger. The church official who carries the mace or "verge" before a dignitary of the Church. The term is used, however, in a wider sense for the caretaker of a parish church.

Verifiability. The group of philosophers known as the Vienna Circle, active at the University of Vienna before World War II, developed a criterion of meaning according to which the meaning of a proposition or sentence depends upon its verifiability. For example, "God exists" and "God is benevolent" are not propositions or statements to which one can give or deny assent; nor can one be agnostic about them. They are unverifiable by the empirical criteria demanded by this school and therefore, having no meaning, cannot be discussed any more than can a proposition such as "Boofa is Tooka" or "Boofa is beautiful." K. Popper moved to a criterion of falsifiability, and W. Quine, opposing the use of the criterion, held that the basic unit of meaning cannot be found in any individual synthetic statement, even one such as "Paris is the capital of France." See **Vienna Circle** and **Falsifiability.**

Vermittlungstheologie. Members of this school of German Protestant theologians, much influenced by Schleiermacher, sought to reconcile the classic Reformation creeds with modern philosophy and science. The first issue of their principal publication, *Theologische Studien und Kritiken,* appeared in 1828. The school counted among its members F. Lücke, J. P. Lange, I. A. Dorner, J. A. W. Neander, and H. L. Martensen. They were vigorously resisted by conservative Protestants, e.g., by Ritschl and his school and by the Barthians. See **Barth, Karl.**

Veronica. A legend, probably French, began to gain currency in the 14th c. that a woman who met Jesus on his way to Calvary offered him a cloth to wipe away the blood and sweat from his face. Jesus returned it bearing the imprint of his face upon it. The name "Veronica" is said to have been derived from the words *vera* and *eikōn* ("true image"). A portrait, claimed to be the original imprint, which seems to have been at Rome since the 8th c., was greatly venerated throughout the Middle Ages. The woman was identified by some as the woman mentioned (Matthew 9.20–22) in the Gospel as having been healed by Jesus. Although the veneration of the cloth is a devotion dating from the Middle Ages, a reference to the woman in the Gospel as bearing the name Bernice (Beronice in Coptic = Veronica in Latin) occurs in the *Acts of Pilate* (chapter 7), a document of uncertain date but indubitably long antedating the 8th c. The image is now popularly known as "Veronica's veil."

Versicle. A brief sentence, very often from the Psalter, said or sung and followed by a "response," either by the people or by another section of the choir. For example, "O Lord, show thy mercy upon us," which is answered by the response, "And grant us thy salvation."

Vespers. The Evening Office in the Western Church and one of the most ancient, being accounted, along with Lauds, the most important of the Church's official public devotions. Solemn Vespers is conducted with much beautiful ceremony. The hour of Vespers has varied very much through the ages. It is always the last service of the day before Compline, which is said or sung in monastic communities immediately before retiring for the night.

Vestal Virgins. The name given to priestesses of a Roman cult that flourished in an organized form during the first half of the 1st c. CE. They were so named after Vesta, chief of the Roman household or hearth deities.

Vestments. In ecclesiastical usage, by "vestments" is understood articles of dress used for the performance of liturgical acts and other services of the Church, e.g., chasuble, dalmatic, tunicle, and alb. Vestments used in Catholic tradition originated in the secular dress of the world of antiquity. Their development took place more particularly from the 4th c. and probably represented the retention by the Church of a style of dress that was giving way by the general population to a fashion shortening and otherwise modifying the traditional style, e.g., while convenience at least partly dictated the shortening of the tunic (much as it did with women's skirts in the early part of the 20th c.), the Church retained the older and more graceful style for liturgical purposes. Vestments in the Eastern Church differ slightly from those worn in the West, and the shape and style of ecclesiastical vestments have varied through the centuries, according to the taste of the period and the region, but on the whole Catholic tradition has maintained considerable uniformity. For example, the surplice seems to have been a modification of the alb for use on more informal occasions. From time to time, as certain vestments had undergone excessive elaboration and ornamentation, reforms took place in recognition of the fact that simplicity is often unsurpassable as a principle of dignity and beauty. The dress of bishops, for example, has at times been developed so extravagantly as to detract from rather than enhance the solemnity of their function in the Church. Such abuses have elicited from liturgical scholars calls for reform.

Vestry. A room in a church where the clergy vest. Because parishioners and committees often held their meetings in it, the term came to be used of the body of parishioners principally responsible for cooperating with the clergy in the administration of the parish. In the United States the term is generally understood among Anglicans to mean the body responsible for the financial administration of the parish and consisting of the rector or vicar, two wardens, and a number of persons representing the parishioners. See also **Sacristy.**

Vetāla. In Hinduism, a class of ghouls or vampires who frequent burial grounds. Sometimes a circle of stones was placed around the area to prevent them from escaping from it. The name is also used for one of the attendants of Śiva.

Via Dolorosa. The way believed to have been followed by Jesus from Pilate's judgment hall to Mount Calvary, the place of his crucifixion. It is marked by fourteen "Stations of the Cross," representing episodes occurring on the way. Pilgrims follow the route as a special devotion and traditionally the Franciscans lead their devotions every Friday.

Via Media. Literally, "the Middle Way." The term used by the Tractarians (especially perhaps by John Henry Newman) to designate the outlook and polity of Anglicanism as a middle road, avoiding the extravagances of Rome on the one hand and, on the other, of Geneva. The vision of the Anglican Way in such terms antedates, however, its use by the Tractarians, being found in the great 17th-c. Anglican divines. It encompasses a claim to recognize both the fundamental importance of the ancient Catholic spirit and traditions and the values in the Reformation heritage, instead of ignoring or combating the latter (as was for long the policy of the Roman Catholic Church) or (as was the Puritan tendency) to fail to perceive the vital importance of Catholic tradition and life.

Via Negativa. Literally, "the Negative Way." Although God is revealed in the Bible and elsewhere through figurative language (e.g., as Father, Light, He-Who-Is, Being), we must recognize that these are no more than metaphors and at best can only point to the mystery of Divine Being. In the nature of the case, such is God that no name can denote or define him. The *via negativa* is the procedure by which one says, in effect, "God is not this, God is not that," and so forth, and by exclusion one may hope to arrive at a point at which one is forced to some form of mystical enterprise. Our confession of ignorance predisposes us to a humility through which we may be guided to intuitive knowledge of God. The metaphorical language has played a role in the early stages of our understanding, but at some point one has to recognize that the "Light" is not any other light; nor is the goodness of God to be identified with any merely human kind of goodness. The notion that one can enhance one's understanding of God by *adding* qualifiers (e.g., "God is not only a Shepherd; he is also a Friend and at the same time a Judge") pertains to a comparatively immature stage in the attainment of knowledge of God.

Vianney, Jean-Baptiste Marie (1786–1859). Patron of parish priests. Born at Dardilly, near Lyons, France, his ordination to the priesthood was delayed by several circumstances, such as lack of ability as a student, including his difficulty in learning Latin. At last he was ordained in 1815, and after a few years as an assistant at Ecully, he was appointed parish priest at Ars, a remote little village. Here he attained international fame as a confessor till in his last years, because of the enormous numbers of penitents that sought him (estimated at more than 20,000 a year), he had to spend almost all his waking hours in the confessional. He was canonized in 1925. He is widely known as "the Curé d' Ars."

Vicar Apostolic. When, in the Roman Catholic Church, there is a region that is either not ready to be established as a regular diocese or is in a political situation in which it would be impracticable or impossible to establish one, the region may be constituted as a missionary district under a vicar apostolic who administers it with much the same authority as would a bishop.

Vicar of Christ. From the 8th c. this has been one of the titles of the Pope. The older title was "Vicar of Saint Peter," which, however, was entirely superseded by the 13th century.

Vicious Circle. See **Petitio principii**, a fallacy sometimes so designated.

Vico, Giovanni Battista (1668–1744). Philosopher. Born in Naples, he taught there and in 1734 was appointed historiographer to Charles III. He was probably the foremost philosopher to develop a philosophy of history. Since man can understand only what he makes, history is and must be at the heart of his experience. He repudiated the attack that Descartes had made on the value of historical study and showed that the methods of the natural sciences must be distinguished from those of history. He also perceived that Descartes was wrong in his estimate of the role of mathematics: it does not describe the structure of reality in any way, being only the application of rules that we invent in our attempt to understand nature. He showed the fundamental importance of historical studies and of the study of the nature of such studies. His most important work was his *Principles of a New Science* (1725), which he revised and much expanded in a second edition (1730) and again revised in a third edition (1744).

Victor. Late 5th-c. Bishop of Vita, North Africa, and the author of a history of the persecution of the Church in that region. It is of importance and much interest as an historically dependable account and for the vivid picture it portrays of conditions there at that time.

Victor. Bishop of Capua from 541 till his death in 554. He is famed for his Harmony of the Gospels, made on the basis of the Vulgate. It is preserved at Fulda in the Codex Fuldensis, which contains the Gospels harmonized after the manner of Tatian's *Diatesseron*. He was also the author of many other writings, which survive only in fragments.

Victorines. The name given to the canons regular of the former abbey of St. Victor in Paris, which had been founded by William of Champeaux, Abelard's teacher and himself perhaps the greatest scholar of his day. The Victorine school, whose members included Adam of St. Victor, Hugh of St. Victor, and Walter of St. Victor, was highly respected and was responsible, *inter alia*, for guiding biblical scholarship in the Middle Ages in such a way as to discourage the tendency to excessive and fanciful allegorical interpretations. The abbey no longer exists, having been secularized in the French Revolution.

Vienna Circle. A philosophical movement having its center in the University of Vienna and dating from the 1920s. Its aim was to reform philosophy on the lines of a methodology constructed according to a positivistic understanding of the natural sciences. All propositions not reducible to its criteria of meaning were to be excluded as meaningless. Such propositions included metaphysical and religious propositions, since these were accounted empirically unverifiable and unfalsifiable and therefore devoid of meaning. As early as 1910 there had been at Vienna a group interested in the work of Ernst Mach (1836–1916), who, after professorial appointments in mathematics and physics at Graz and Prague respectively, had been Professor of the History and Theory of Inductive Science at Vienna (1895–1902). He was one of the most important influences on the development of the Vienna Circle, sometimes even regarded as its father. By 1920 the group had become interested in the work of Russell and Wittgenstein. Two years later Moritz Schlick became the holder of the Mach Chair of philosophy at Vienna. Rudolf Carnap came to the group about the same time, which had drawn to itself Philipp Frank, Otto Neurath, Hans Hahn, Kurt Gödel, Herbert Feigl, Richard von Mises, and E. Schrödinger. Some other groups, e.g., the Warsaw Circle of logicians, including Alfred Tarski and others, were in one way or another in correspondence with or related to the Vienna Circle. Several circumstances (e.g., the *Anschluss* in 1938, followed in 1939 by the outbreak of World War II), brought about the dispersal of the group, many members of which moved to the United States. Directly or indirectly, the group exercised a great deal of influence on philosophy in the English-speaking world. Among its early exponents and interpreters at Oxford was Alfred J. Ayer whose *Language, Truth, and Logic* (1936) drew much severe criticism and was followed by a second edition (1946) modifying some of the extremist positions he had championed. See **Logical Positivism.** The influence of this genre of philosophy, salutary though it has been in some respects, has been much attenuated since that time. It represents a critical element in philosophy and as Etienne Gilson has stated the case, philosophy, which has within itself both a speculative element and a critical one that emerges from time to time with intent to bury it, has a way of rising up and burying its undertakers.

Vigil. In the first centuries CE, night services (sometimes even lasting through the night) were common, possibly because of a popular belief that the Second Coming would occur at midnight. From about the 8th c., the custom of "anticipating" vigil services was developed, transferring them to the afternoon or even the morning before the feast day to which they related. In 1969 the Roman Catholic Church abolished vigils, with a very few exceptions.

Vigilius. Pope from 537 till his death in 555. Much involved in political forays and ecclesiastical controversies, he was even excommunicated at a synod in Carthage.

Vihara. A Buddhist monastery, today typically a walled compound containing gardens, huts for the monks, a bodhitree, a *stupa* (see **Stūpa**), and a large room or hall usually containing a statue of the Buddha.

Village. In biblical usage, cities were understood to be walled. Villages, although often small communities, could be as large as cities but were distinguished from them in being unfortified by walls. Probably the majority of people in Israel lived in villages in biblical times.

Vinaya-Piṭaka. The first of the three piṭakas ("baskets") that constitute the

Buddhist Scriptures. It is the "discipline-piṭaka," being principally concerned with the rules that govern monastic life. There are several versions, e.g., the version of the Theravādins, which is in Pali, and various Chinese and Tibetan versions.

Vincentian Canon. See **Vincent of Lérins** and **Infallibility.**

Vincentians. See **Lazarists.**

Vincent of Lérins. 5th-c. author of the *Commonitorium*, a very famous work, written under the pseudonym "Peregrinus" and embodying the now much celebrated "Vincentian Canon" designed to provide (II, 3) a guide to Christian orthodoxy in the form of a three fold test: what has been believed everywhere, always, and by all (*quod ubique, quod semper, quod ab omnibus creditum est*). The order of the three elements in the test is important. Vincent fully recognized and indeed emphasized the Bible as the ground of Christian teaching, but perceived also that the Bible must be interpreted, that it will be interpreted either wisely or foolishly, and that the Church may be invoked to determine the best interpretation in case of doubt. He recognized, moreover, the very important concept that in doctrinal matters the truth of Scripture is clarified in the course of the process of history. His "canon" provided a guide to the principles governing wise interpretation.

Vinegar. As used in the Bible, vinegar is not what is commonly understood by the term today. It was a sort of cheap wine, sour and not very pleasant, nevertheless thirst quenching. The soldiers who offered Jesus vinegar (Matthew 27.48) would be sharing with him what they were drinking themselves.

Vinet, Alexandre Rudolf (1797–1847). Swiss Reformed theologian. Born at Ouchy, near Lausanne, he came under the influence of W. M. L. De Wette at Basel and was ordained to the ministry in 1819. He stressed individual freedom in religion, seeing doctrine as important only as it bore fruit in ethical conduct. His collected sermons, *Discours sur quelques sujets religieux* (1831 and 1841), being scholarly and exhibiting deep spirituality, have been influential among French and Swiss Protestants. His posthumous *Études sur Blaise Pascal* (1848) shows his profound sympathy with that religious genius, at least in the latter's emphasis on the role of the "heart."

Vipassanā. A Buddhist term in Pali usually rendered "insight" or "inward vision:" one of the two chief factors in the attainment of enlightenment. The other is *samatha*, "mind-quieting." The development of both factors is closely connected with the practice of meditation. Combined as *samatha-vipassanā* they may be regarded as synonymous with *samādhi-paññā* (meditation-wisdom).

Virgin. Virginity was highly prized in antiquity, both as an ideal and as a physiological and psychological state. A virgin was more esteemed than a woman who had "known" man, being supposed to have greater fertility and therefore more to be desired. The biblical words traditionally translated "virgin" do not necessarily connote what would nowadays be understood in a medico-legal sense as *virgo intacta*. Neither the Hebrew *bᵉtûlāh* nor the Greek *hē parthenos* (which term is as old as Homer) necessarily signifies virginity in that technical sense, although no doubt a young unmarried woman would generally be virginal in that sense, because girls married, as a rule, soon after puberty. Still, like the English word "maiden," it could be used of a young girl in a general sense without specifically designating virginity. Virginity, prized though it was in Hebrew tradition, was not cherished as a state to be maintained. In the New Testament, however, virginity in both women and men is occasionally upheld as an ideal state of life. Jesus recommended it (Matthew 19.12), and Paul advocated it (I Corinthians 7.2, 9, 38f.) while recognizing that only very few would follow his recommendation; most would marry: a laudable state too. While Catholic tradition follows the classic Hebrew emphasis on and respect for marriage and family as institutions on which the entire structure of a healthy society depends, it also recognizes the precepts of both Jesus and Paul that some are called to a state of lifelong continence which, for them, is even higher.

Virgin Birth. The traditional belief among Christians is that Jesus was virgin-born, i.e., that he had no human father. The narratives of his birth as found in Matthew and Luke provide biblical support for this belief, although it is noteworthy that the New Testament is otherwise silent on the subject; even John, where one might expect it in his famous Prologue (John 1) does not allude to it. The belief, although questioned by a few sectaries in the early Church, was so strongly upheld in the mainstream of Christian theology from very early times that it came to be regarded as almost an implicate of the central doctrine of the Incarnation. It was an expression of the uniqueness of Jesus Christ. Nevertheless, in modern times the belief that Jesus was virgin-born has been much questioned, not only by those inclined to suspect all miraculous elements in the biblical narratives as unhistorical, but even by theologians whose personal beliefs generally conform in principle to Christian orthodoxy.

The most powerful argument commonly used by such theologians against the notion of the Virgin Birth is not that it contravenes all that we know about human biology (even what was known in antiquity) or even that it is suspect because stories of virgin births are found in other religions (the Buddha, for instance, was virgin-born, according to some accounts), but on the

ground that it is inconsistent with the claim, no less central to Christian orthodoxy, that Jesus Christ is fully human as well as fully divine. (See **Chalcedon, Council of.**) To be fully human, the argument runs, entails having a human father as well as a human mother. Such theologians question the traditional belief in the Virgin Birth as derogating from the humanity of Christ. They would typically interpret the belief as unhistorical although a beautiful mythopoeic expression of the uniqueness of Jesus Christ. Others, of course, would insist on the Virgin Birth as an historical event.

Virtualism. In the history of theological disputes on the nature of the Eucharist, this was the name given to that doctrine according to which no change occurs in the bread and the wine after their consecration, yet the recipient of the sacrament receives through it the *virtus* (spiritual power) of the Body and Blood of Jesus Christ. It was expounded by Calvin in opposition to the traditional medieval doctrine of transubstantiation. See **Transubstantiation.**

Visitandines. An order of contemplative nuns founded in 1610 by Francis of Sales and Jane Frances de Chantal, designed more especially for women who, although not disposed to bear the austerities of the traditional orders of contemplative monks and nuns, had an authentic vocation to the religious life. The Visitandines began as a congregation with simple vows. (See **Vows.**) The novices were strictly enclosed as part of their training for the spiritual life, but the professed sisters went out on nursing and other tasks. Later, however, the Visitandines were developed into a contemplative order on more traditional lines yet with modifications in the Salesian spirit that Francis of Sales fostered: the concept of spirituality as best expressed in humility, in gentleness, and in sisterly affection: a kind of spirituality that could be adapted even for people living in the world. Traditionally it had been widely supposed that perfection in the spiritual life cannot be attained except in the strictly enclosed type of monastic or conventual life represented in the ancient contemplative orders with all their harsh discipline and with austerities such as repelled many sensitive souls. Francis of Sales wished to have spirituality seen as attainable to men and women living in the world. His Visitandines, although following to some extent the traditional pattern of the religious life as popularly perceived, were different in spirit from the ancient orders for women. One of the most celebrated of its members is Margaret Mary Alacoque (1647–1690), much associated with the fostering of devotion to the Sacred Heart, which Francis of Sales had encouraged among the Visitandines.

Visuddimagga. One of the most important books of post-canonical literature in Theravāda Buddhism. Buddhaghosa, its author, is credited with having restored to the Pali language some of the prestige that it had yielded to Sanskrit by the 5th c. CE. It sets forth the three stages of the Buddhist life with a detailed description of each: morality, meditation, and wisdom (*sīla, samādhi,* and *Paññā*). It is an exposition of the Buddhist "Eightfold Path" to perfection.

Vitalism. A philosophy that claims that in the realm of biological phenomena a vital force or principle governs them. In the biological realm the phenomena cannot be reduced to the categories of physics and chemistry.

Vivisection. This term, although strictly applicable only to the use of surgical procedures on living animals, is widely used for medical procedures such as testing new drugs to ascertain their safety for human use. The use of any form of experiment on animals that entails their suffering is plainly objectionable on humanitarian grounds and rightly evokes protest. By no means all experiments on animals do, since in many cases the experiment may be performed under anaesthesia. The question whether a human being has the right to use animals for experiment at all is, however, a serious one for the Christian moralist. Christianity has inherited or acquired the questionable presupposition that the entire "animal kingdom," as "the lower creation" is for the use of man. Human beings have used horses, oxen, camels, and other "beasts of burden" from earliest times, as they have kept various animals (e.g., cats and dogs) as pets, all on the assumption that humans have an inalienable right to make any use they please of "the lower creation" that does not entail gross cruelty. If, however, we see all life as given by God and even the most primitive organisms as part of the same stream of life that we enjoy (albeit in greater degree), ought not a Christian to respect lower forms of life as much as the human form of it and perhaps even more, on the principle that *noblesse oblige?* Although we might justify the destruction of forms of life dangerous or lethal to us (e.g., pneumococci), how could we justify using animals as things for our pleasure, amusement, or research, when almost all moralists would concur in regarding such an attitude toward human beings as the very essence of unethical behavior? Among Jains, Hindus, and in other religious traditions having roots in ancient India (e.g., Buddhism), greater respect prevails for lower forms of life than Christians have traditionally accorded them. Many contemporary Christians have become sensitive to such considerations and therefore oppose vivisection and other such procedures not only on humanitarian grounds but for a deeper moral principle: reverence for all life. (See **Schweitzer, Albert.**) Even if, however, one does not choose to take such a principle into consideration, other ethical questions arise, e.g., people often have a revulsion against experiments on dogs or cats but none against them on, say, mice: a distinction founded on a highly subjective human preference rather than on any scientific assessment of the respective thresholds of pain. In any case, no one can pretend that his dog's is higher or lower than my cat's or the neighbor's rat's. Researchers often prefer to use animals specially bred for their purposes, but that entails recognizing an entire breed of cat or dog condemned to what can be called only by macabre euphemism a lower standard of feline or canine life than the rest. We cringe at stories of a group of human beings used for experiments whose results are calculated to improve the betterment of the lot of other human beings accounted higher in the evolutionary scale; but can we justify raising an entire breed of animals destined for nothing but such service to man? Yet few would claim that a rat's welfare is to be judged equal to that of a human being's. Christians do need, however, to rethink the entire question of the relation of human beings to other forms of life, not merely the relation of one human being to another.

Vladimir (956–1015). Of Christian ancestry, he was brought up as a pagan but later, after many territorial conquests, he was converted to Christianity and became a zealous promoter of the Faith, founding numerous monasteries and churches. His methods, however, reflected a meager understanding of the Christian spirit and exhibited too often a resolve to force Christianity upon Russia and Ruthenia, severely punishing those who declined to accept baptism.

Voltaire. Pseudonym used by François-Marie Arouet (1694–1778). Born in Paris where he was educated by the Jesuits, he soon became famous for his literary abilities and his sharp satire, which he directed particularly against the Roman Catholic Church, in which he saw only superstition and deceit. He became the most celebrated of the French *philosophes*. He defended the deistic views of his age (see **Deism**) and sought passionately to encourage reli-

gious toleration. He worked incessantly with scarcely enough time for food or sleep. He admired Locke and Newton and depicted in his *Lettres sur les Anglais* (1734) an idealized picture of England as an idyllic society where rationalism and religious toleration prevailed. This book was publicly burned in Paris, whence he was forced to flee. His mordant satire naturally won him many enemies and he suffered much persecution. Unlike many of the French *philosophes*, who were atheistic (especially those of a younger generation than he), Voltaire championed moral standards and belief in God, so long as the standards and the belief were, in his view, rational. He is indubitably one of the greatest figures in the history of Western thought. Among the more famous of his works are his *Candide* (1759) and his *Philosophical Dictionary* (1764).

Voluntarism. The philosophical doctrine that the will has primacy over the intellect. It stands in contrast to rationalism, which is intellectualist. It may be attributed to a variety of thinkers, e.g., Augustine, Scotus, Occam, Maine de Biran, William James, and Henri Bergson. The term, however, was apparently invented or at least introduced into the philosophical vocabulary in 1883 by Ferdinand Tönnies (1885–1936).

Volva. A female shaman or seer who presided over a *seid* or divination ceremony in Scandinavian and other northern religion. Accounts of her functions are to be found in some of the Icelandic sagas. She sat on an elevated platform and in the course of a trance was believed to obtain a form of hidden knowledge. The most famous account is in the saga of Eric the Red, set in Greenland.

Von Hügel, (Baron) Friedrich. See **Hügel, (Baron) Friedrich von.**

Voodoo. The folk religion of Haiti. African in origin, it acknowledges a supreme Being but emphasizes the use of rituals believed to appease or influence the *loa*, the spirits who inhabit the invisible world. These spirits or *loa* are the spirits of natural forces such as procreation and death, fire and water, and so forth, and they may take possession of individual votaries in the course of the voodoo rituals, e.g., causing them to mimic the action of fire while they do a ritual dance over a pit of flames. The rituals are apparently believed to have a cathartic power. Voodoo originally developed alongside of Roman Catholic teaching with which in Caribbean slave plantations from the 17th c. it was blended. The devotees were often baptized Roman Catholics and attended both church and the voodoo rites, which were led by an *ongan* (priest) or *mambo* (priestess).

Vows. The making of vows occurs frequently in the Old Testament and always implies the recognition of divinity in the One to whom the vow is made. Examples are: Jacob's vow to worship at Bethel (Genesis 28.20), Hannah's vow in hope of obtaining a son (I Samuel 1.11), and David's vow (Psalm 132.2) to secure a dwelling for the ark. Such vows were taken very seriously indeed, for renunciation of a vow so made was believed to be attended by drastic retribution. Vows are common in most of the great religions of the world. In Christian practice, vows, to be binding, must have been made freely, must tend to some future good, and must be made by a person in full possession of his or her mental faculties.

The vows most widely known and officially recognized in Catholic tradition are those by persons undertaking the religious life, e.g., those seeking to become monks or nuns: the triple vow of poverty, chastity, and obedience to one's canonical superior. Since the 13th c. a distinction has been made between simple vows, which are for a limited period and are revocable, and solemn vows, which are for life and are irrevocable. Vows may also be made to perform any

legitimate and salutary act, e.g., to endow a chapel, to undertake a fast, to go on a pilgrimage, or to maintain total sexual abstinence for a certain period of time. Such vows may be private, although usually one would take them under the direction and advice of one's spiritual director, or public, i.e., uttered openly and accepted by a recognized ecclesiastical authority such as a bishop or abbot. No vow made rashly, capriciously, or without due understanding of and reflection upon its consequences is binding. A vow to perform an evil act is, of course, never binding in any circumstances.

Vows are common in Buddhism and Taoism and may be taken by lay people as well as by monks and nuns, although monastic vows may be more strictly interpreted. The four basic vows taken by Buddhist monks are: (1) to seek the salvation of everyone, (2) to extirpate from oneself all evil and passion, (3) to study the law of the Buddha, and (4) to attain perfection leading to Buddhahood. In Mahāyāna a basic vow is never to rest till the salvation of all sentient beings is achieved.

Vulgate. The name *(editio vulgata)* given to the Latin version of the Bible traditionally and most widely used in the Western Church. It was so called because it was adopted in Western Europe as the "vulgar," i.e., common edition. It was fundamentally the work of Jerome, who began it at the request of Pope Damasus in 382. Its purpose was to end certain confusions that had arisen on account of the considerable textual variations in the Old Latin manuscripts that were in circulation at that time. The work occupied Jerome for almost the rest of the century. Predictably, Jerome's text was resisted from many sides, but such was its excellence that it won in the end through sheer merit. After he had done much work in translating from Greek texts, he perceived that the projected edition could not be properly achieved without translation from the Hebrew, to the study of which he turned, using the Hebrew text thereafter. During the Middle Ages textual variations proliferated in manuscripts of the Vulgate and efforts were made from time to time to determine a standardized form of the Vulgate. Careless copying exacerbated the problem. Even the efforts of great men such as Alcuin (800), Lanfranc (1089), and others of like importance and influence failed. The Paris text became, because of the supremacy of Paris in theological studies, a standard one, but it was by no means entirely reliable. This was the text followed in the first printed Bible, the famous Gutenberg Bible printed 1450–1452 at Mainz. The Council of Trent prescribed a new and corrected edition in 1546, and Sixtus V forced its completion. The result, however, was not considered good enough for publication, and after his death in 1590 the work was revised and the Clementine edition (so named after Pope Clement VIII) was published in 1592–1593 with 3000 corrections and came into general use. The Vulgate is regarded by the Roman Catholic church as a safe source for Roman Catholic teaching and to be revered because of its long use in the Western Church. The Church does not pretend to guarantee its scholarly accuracy in detail. Moreover, a series of papal encyclicals beginning with *Providentissimus Deus* (1893) have encouraged the use of modern scholarly methods in biblical studies. That of Pius XII, *Divino afflante Spiritu* (1943) is a particularly notable one.

W

Wahhabis. A reform movement in Islam led by Muhammad ibn 'Abd al-Wahhab (1703–1792) in Arabia, aimed at reviving the purity of the conservative tradition that resisted all idolatry (representational art and the like) and the worship of saints. It is well represented today in Saudi Arabia.

Wailing Wall. This remnant of the western wall of the Temple at Jerusa-

lem, which the Romans destroyed in 70 CE, is all that remains of that great focus of Judaism. Since the Middle Ages Jews have come there to pray, bewailing the dispersion of their people throughout the world. The wall passed to the control of the State of Israel after the Arab-Israeli war of 1967.

Wake, William (1657–1737). Archbishop of Canterbury from 1716. Trained at Christ Church, Oxford, he went in 1682 to Paris as chaplain to the English ambassador there and became closely acquainted with Gallicanism. From 1717 to 1720 he was in negotiation with representatives of the Gallican party in France, notably with L. E. Dupin, with a view to achieving union between the French Church and the Church of England. The plan seemed promising, but unfortunately it was halted by the death of Dupin in 1719. It is not very likely, however, that it would have succeeded even had the events taken a different course, for although there was willingness on both sides for compromise, considerable obstacles stood in the way. Wake was a man of tolerant spirit and on the whole sympathetic to dissenters and others. His most important work is *The State of the Church and Clergy of England* (1703). The definitive biography is by Norman Sykes in 2 vols. (1957), written while he held his Cambridge chair.

Waldensians. A small Christian community in Italy, especially in Piemonte, the *Chiesa Evangelica Valdese*, originating in the 12th c. in the followers of Peter Valdes who were known as "the poor men of Lyons." They are generally regarded as precursors of the Reformation movement of a much later age. The earliest representatives of this body chiefly directed their preaching against the worldliness of the clergy. At first seeking to work within the Church they found themselves forced by the Church to work outside it. Like the Quakers and others of later times they refused to take oaths or to engage in any form of killing, whether in warfare or otherwise. They spread rapidly in the south of France, in Spain, in Germany, and elsewhere and were severely persecuted, but in the less accessible areas of Piemonte and the Savoy they survived. In the 16th c. they associated themselves with the Reformation cause, of which today they are in effect the Italian representatives. They have a theological college, originally near Turin but since 1920 at Rome.

Wali. In Islam a holy person is designated by this name, which means literally "a person near to or friendly with God." Despite the protests of conservative Muslims (see **Wahhabis**), a hierarchy of saints is popularly recognized in Islam, and local saints are sought out to make intercession for the living and the dead. Many Sufi leaders are so regarded. Pilgrimage (*ziyara*) is made to the tombs of saints.

Walsingham. A place of pilgrimage in Norfolk, England. A replica of the Holy House of Nazareth is said to have been built there in the 11th c. Walsingham became one of the most important places of pilgrimage in England during the Middle Ages. The shrine was destroyed in 1538. In recent times Walsingham has been revived as a place of pilgrimage and is visited by many, both by Roman Catholics and by Anglicans.

War. War in biblical times, although waged without the hideous technological instruments available today, was cruel and barbaric. The cruelty and barbarism were accepted as being as inseparable from the conduct of warfare as is wetness inseparable from the ocean. The victor did not enter into negotiations with the vanquished. No international treaties provided for any sort of rights. If the vanquished were for any reason accounted a potential danger to the victorious army, the latter might exterminate them. Prisoners of war were not excepted. Like the rest of the population they could be enslaved if not destroyed. The spirit of battle was sustained by each side's sense or pretense that the war was the war of its god. Israel was not an exception: the battle was, at least till the time of the monarchy, the execution of Yahweh's will. The prophets to some extent denounce war as counterproductive, but no one, not even Jesus, seems to foresee war's end, although he points out (Matthew 26.52) that those who resort to it perish by it.

Ward, James (1843–1925). English philosopher and psychologist. A Cambridge man, he took a genetic approach to psychology. He distinguished three phases leading to ideas: (1) a sensory stage, in which presentations are differentiated, retained, and assimilated; (2) an integrative stage in which sensations become percepts, and (3) a derivative continuum of images forming "ideational tissue." He classified mental experience as of three kinds: cognitive, affective, and conative (mind, emotion, will). He inclined to a sort of theistic idealism.

Watch Tower Bible and Tract Society. See **Jehovah's Witnesses.**

Water. The biblical writers are all very conscious of the value of water, and it plays a very prominent part in the symbolic imagery they use. Palestine, although having a rainfall sufficient to support agriculture, is arid compared with anywhere in Europe and almost anywhere in North America. Water in biblical times was obtained from springs and wells, but archaeologists have found some ingenious hydraulic installations for channeling and storing water. The land lacked rivers and water was a precious commodity, sold on the streets as it still is in many cities in the Middle East. When the Bible speaks of "living" water it means water from springs rather than pools. Despite the scarcity of water, hospitality and compassion required that it be offered to travelers who were thirsty. Water has immense symbolic significance in the Bible. It signifies life and salvation. It is not a created element but a primordial one (Genesis 1.2). In Christian symbolism it is an essential element in the sacrament of Baptism. In the Eucharist, moreover, water is mingled with the wine to be consecrated.

Watson, John Broadus (1878–1958). American psychologist. After studies at the University of Chicago, he became professor of experimental and comparative psychology at Johns Hopkins University and was later a lecturer at the New School for Social Research. Generally regarded as the founder of Behavioral Psychology, he rejected introspective methods and sought to restrict psychological data to the results of observation and laboratory experiment. His writings include *Behavior* (1914) and *The Ways of Behaviorism* (1928).

Watts, Isaac (1674–1748). Hymn writer. Born in Southampton, England, and educated there, he became, in 1702, pastor of the congregation of Independents at Mark Lane, London. His health declined soon afterwards. He is generally acknowledged to have been very influential in spreading the habit of hymn-singing among Protestants in the English-speaking world, and his many collections of hymns include some that are still very popular, e.g., "Our God, our help in ages past," and "When I survey the wondrous Cross."

Way. (Hebrew, *derek;* Greek, *hodos*) The Bible uses this term not only in its literal sense (a road or path) but also in several figurative senses. In the Old Testament it often means simply human experience: the life a person chooses or is allotted to him. The Wisdom literature uses the term abundantly in such a figurative sense. The instructions of the wise are a way of life (Proverbs 6.23), and one must expect to reap the fruit yielded by one's way of life (Proverbs 1.31). The ways of God are his nature: his love, his fidelity, his care for his creatures. In the New Testament such usages continue. Jesus talks of the "broad" or "wide" way that leads to de-

struction and of the "narrow" way that leads to salvation and life. That kind of distinction occurs also in the Manual of Discipline, one of the Qumran documents. Jesus explicitly calls himself "The Way" (John 14.4–6). Christianity itself was designated "The Way" (e.g., Acts 9.2; 22.4), and this usage was perpetuated: wisely so, as defining Christianity as not mere acceptance of a teaching or even faith in Christ himself but as a way of life. The Christian Way implies a moral choice to follow the Way prescribed by "God the Father of the Lord Jesus Christ."

Weber, Max (1864–1920). German sociologist and economist. Born at Erfurt, he was professor at Berlin, Freiburg, and Munich. He was much interested in the relation between religion and the social and economic conditions associated with it. His works include *Capitalism and the Protestant Ethic* (1904–05) and *The Economic Ethic of the World Religions* (1915).

Wee Frees. A name popularly given to the small number of members of the Free Church of Scotland, the body that had broken from the Established Church of Scotland in 1843 (see **Disruption**) who refused to join in uniting in 1900 with the United Presbyterian Church in order to form the United Free Church. The "Wee Frees" are to be distinguished from another Presbyterian body that had broken away from the Free Kirk in 1892. See **Free Presbyterian Church of Scotland**.

Week of Universal Prayer. See **Couturier, Paul**.

Weights and Measures in the Bible. Biblical usage is complicated by the fact that it is derived partly from Babylonian, partly from Greek, partly from Roman, and partly from Mesopotamian systems. Merchants often carried weights with them along with their merchandise. Cheating in the use of weights and measures was regarded as an "abomination" to Yahweh (e.g.,

Proverbs 11.1; 16.11 and Micah 6.11). Legal standards were developed in a variety of ways, e.g., we hear of "the royal weight" even in early biblical times (II Samuel 14.26). Here are some rudimentary examples of biblical weights and measures and their relation to one another:

50 shekels = 1 mina; 60 minas = 1 talent. Archaeologists have found weights in which a shekel is approximately 11.5 grams. Measurements or surface were calculated from the human body, e.g., a cubit represents the length of a human arm from the elbow to the fingertips: approximately 18 inches. When Greek measures came into use we hear of the *stadion*, a distance of 607 feet. The Roman mile mentioned in Matthew 5.41 was 1620 yards. Measures of volume combined a Babylonian (duodecimal) system with a decimal one, e.g., one "homer" (literally a donkey and so, by derivation, the load that an average donkey can be expected to carry) = 180 "kab" and a kab = 2.3 litres. One homer also = 10 bushels and a bushel = 39.3 litres. The area that a team of oxen could plow in a day was calculated in Mesopotamia as two-thirds of an acre but according to Roman calculation it was five-eighths of an acre.

Weil, Simone (1909–1943). French philosopher and mystic. Born in Paris, she showed early signs of intellectual precocity (e.g., quoting passages from Racine at the age of six) and despite interruptions in her studies due to World War I, she received her *baccalauréat ès lettres* with distinction at the extraordinary age of fifteen. Preparing for the competitive entrance examination for the École Normale, she worked under René Le Senne and Emile Auguste Chartier ("Alain"), who recognized her philosophical genius. In the course of her teaching career she quickly became interested in the problems of the manual workers whom she encouraged with her support. In 1933, two years after receiving her qualification as a philosophy

teacher, she decided to take a year's leave so that she might fully experience a manual worker's life, which she did by taking a job in a Renault factory, living in exactly the same conditions as the other workers, despite the poor health and severe headaches to which she was subject. After the outbreak of World War II in 1939, she settled in Marseilles.

Jewish by birth, she became intensely interested in Christian and Hindu philosophy, continued her Sanskrit studies, and conducted a long and profound correspondence with a Dominican priest, Father Perrin, who in 1943 was to be arrested by the Gestapo. In 1942 she was called to serve under the French provisional government. Commissioned to make a study of certain official documents in London, she exhausted herself, insisting on restricting her diet to the rations to which her French compatriots were limited at that time. She died on August 29, 1943. During her last years she had shown clearly in her correspondence with Father Perrin her passionate attachment to the Christian Way, although she had stopped short of receiving baptism. She expounded her views on Christian Platonism to a circle who met in the crypt of the Dominican Convent in Marseilles and became increasingly mystical in her religious orientation. She found the answer to the conflict she saw in the sacred expectations of the person and its enslavement to a technological dehumanization in what she called "decreation:" the systematic relinquishing of self-centeredness in mystical experience. One of the great religious geniuses of the 20th c., her writings include: *Gravity and Grace* (1946), *The Need for Roots* (1949), *Waiting for God* (1950), *Letter to a Priest* (1951), *On Science, Necessity, and the Love of God* (1968), and three volumes of *Notebooks* (1951–1956).

Weiss, Johannes (1863–1914). New Testament scholar, the son of Bernhard Weiss, also a New Testament scholar, he was trained at Marburg and other universities and became professor at Heidelberg in 1908. He was a pioneer in Form Criticism (see *Formgeschichte*), which he expounded in his *Religion in Geschichte und Gegenwart* (1912). His views were developed by his successor at Heidelberg, Martin Dibelius, and by his student, Rudolf Bultmann.

Weiss, Paul (1901–   ). American philosopher. Born in New York City, he was educated at City College and Harvard. He taught for many years at Bryn Mawr, then at Yale, after his retirement from which he continued to teach at the Catholic University of America. He was the founder of the Metaphysical Society of America and the *Review of Metaphysics*. His original system of metaphysics is constructed on the view that reality consists of four modes of being: actuality, ideality, existence, and God. These modes of being cannot be treated hierarchically, as has been the tendency in many philosophies in the past, which have sought to subsume one mode or set of modes under another. For, according to Weiss, the modes of being are independent, so that each must be explored by itself and in relation to the others. See especially his *Modes of Being* (1958) and *The God We Seek* (1964). His other works include a six-volume edition (which he edited with Charles Hartshorne) of *The Collected Papers of Charles Peirce* (1931–1935) and a vast work, also in six volumes, entitled *Philosophy in Process* (1963–1975), consisting of philosophical thoughts, conversations, and discussions over a period from 1955 through 1971, as well as a large number of other books on a wide variety of philosophical concerns. Weiss, who in his early career was noted for his outstanding gifts as a teacher, developed into one of the most original metaphysical thinkers of his time and possibly of singular importance in the future history of Western thought. Although thoroughly trained and well versed in the analytical methods of his age, he declined to follow philosophical fashions and conducted his researches with independence of mind, extraordinary mental vivacity, and striking philosophical acumen.

Weisse, Christian (1801–1866). German philosopher. Born and trained in Leipzig, he was at first a Hegelian but became disenchanted with the abstractness of Hegel's system and especially with its identification of God with "the Absolute *Geist*." With Hermann Fichte (1796–1879) he constructed what he called "speculative theism," in which he sought to provide a role for revelation and history in philosophy, for which Hegel, they felt, made no provision. His writings include *The Idea of the Divine* (1833) and *Dogmatic Philosophy, or the Philosophy of Christianity* (3 vols., 1855–1862).

Wellhausen, Julius (1844–1918). Biblical scholar. After holding academic positions in various German universities he became professor of Semitics at Göttingen in 1802. His study of the two sources in Genesis, J and E, and his detection of editorial "layers" in the Pentateuch, culminating in the component now known as the "Priestly Code," revolutionized 19th-c. biblical studies. In his later years he turned his attention to problems in New Testament studies, applying similar methods.

Welsh Bible. The first Bible in Welsh appeared in 1567, translated by William Salesbury from the Greek. The entire Bible in Welsh was published by William Morgan, Bishop of St. Asaph, in 1588, then revised and published in 1620 in the form still in general use among Welsh-speaking people. The English Prayer Book of 1559 was translated into Welsh by Richard Davies and published also in 1567. Various revisions of the Prayer Book or parts of it have since been made. Both the Welsh Bible and the Welsh Prayer Book have greatly influenced the development of the Welsh language and helped to promote its use and preserve its beauty.

Weltanschauung. German term, meaning "world view." Used to express a panoramic view of the way things are, such as exhibits fundamental metaphysical presuppositions.

Wesley, Charles (1707–1788). Brother of John Wesley, with whom he was associated in the Methodist movement. He accompanied his brother to Georgia, and they shared many of their missionary endeavors together. Charles won lasting acclaim as the most prolific hymn writer in the English-speaking world. Among his more than 5,500 hymns, many are still highly popular, e.g., "Hark the herald angels sing," "Love divine, all loves excelling," "Jesu, lover of my soul," and "O for a thousand tongues to sing/My great Redeemer's praise." Unlike his brother, he remained within the Anglican Communion. His gifts as a hymn writer were unique, reflecting a deep understanding of the function of the hymn as a liturgical art form.

Wesley, John (1703–1791). Founder of the Methodists. Educated at Christ Church, Oxford, he was elected in 1726 to a fellowship at Lincoln College, Oxford, where he gathered a group of scholarly young men who formed a society called "the Holy Club" or "Methodists." Among them were his brother Charles and George Whitefield. He was influenced by William Law and others bent on a cultivation of the interior life. In 1735 he and his brother Charles undertook a Christian missionary journey to Georgia where his preaching met little success, alienating many by his denunciation of slavery. He returned to England in 1737 and the following year, on May 24, he experienced a conversion associated with the reading of Luther's preface to Paul's Letter to the Romans. The Church of England, the spiritual life of which was at this time lacking in vitality, would not recognize his work, so in 1739 he began to preach independently to the colliers at Kingswood, whose encouragement prompted him to organize a group of lay preachers to do follow-up work. Gradually this work

spread all over the British Isles. It is reported that he rode 8000 miles a year on horseback, preaching wherever he went and receiving much encouragement from his hearers although meeting with coldness or open hostility on the part of the clergy. In 1744 he held the first of what became an annual conference of lay preachers. The movement spread to Ireland and Scotland and from 1760 to the United States where, in 1768, a Methodist chapel was opened in New York. Wesley's personal inclination would have been to have made his movement under Anglican auspices, but its rapid success on independent lines had made that impossible. By the time of his death there were almost 300 of his preachers in England, almost 200 in America, and over 70,000 members in England and over 40,000 in America. See **Methodism** and **Whitefield, George.**

Westcott, Brooke Foss (1825–1901). New Testament scholar and Bishop of Durham. Trained at Trinity College, Cambridge, he was ordained priest in 1851 and after various appointments became Regius Professor of Divinity at Cambridge, where, with F. J. A. Hort, he published, in 1881, his highly important critical edition of the Greek New Testament, followed by three great commentaries. In 1890 he became Bishop of Durham, where he exhibited his social concerns in successful mediation in labor-management disputes in the region and in other ways. The names of Westcott and Hort were famous to generations of serious-minded biblical students in the English-speaking world. See also **Western Text.**

Western Text. The name given to a family of early texts of the Greek New Testament. They were so named by Westcott and Hort, two of the greatest New Testament scholars of the late 19th c., who found them to be of Western provenance. The Western text exhibits changes, many accidental, made as early as before the middle of the 2nd c. It has been useful in helping to establish the "best" text by comparison with other texts such as the Caesarean, the Neutral, and the Byzantine.

Western Wall. See **Wailing Wall.**

Westminster Abbey. Although legends accord the Abbey much greater antiquity, at least it had come clearly into history by the time of its restoration as a Benedictine foundation by Edward the Confessor (1003–1066). Since his successor, William the Conqueror, chose it as the place for the coronation of the Sovereign, it has been there that the kings and queens of England have been crowned, and the Dean of Westminster today retains this function. The new choir and transepts of the Abbey were dedicated in 1065, and the nave, begun c. 1100, was finished in 1163. It quickly became one of the richest monastic foundations in England and has been from very early times till the present a unique focus of the life of England. Already in the 12th c. the Abbot was mitred and exempt from the jurisdiction of the Bishop of London, an independence the Abbey retained when, in the 16th c., it became a Royal Peculiar. (See **Peculiars.**) Until 1547 the House of Commons often used the 13th-c. octagonal chapter house for its proceedings. The Jerusalem Chamber has been used throughout the centuries for many ecclesiastical assemblies. Architecturally, one of the most notable features of the Abbey is the fan vaulting in the chapel of Henry VII.

Westminster Assembly, The. On June 12, 1643, the English Parliament issued an ordinance to hold a synod with the purpose of reforming the Church of England. It resulted in the preparation of various documents, such as the two Westminster Catechisms, the Westminster Confession, and the Directory for the Public Worship of God, none of which was more than very temporarily and partially accepted by the Church of England, but all of which came to be officially recognized documents in the Scottish Kirk.

Westminster Catechisms. (See **Westminster Assembly.**) The Larger Catechism was a popular presentation of the teaching of the Westminster Confession. (See **Westminster Confession.**) The Shorter Catechism came to be a standard instrument in the Scottish Kirk for the teaching of young children, who for centuries were nurtured on its teaching and expected to know by heart the answers it sets forth. It was also used by some other Protestant bodies.

Westminster Cathedral. The building in London, begun in 1895 under Cardinal Vaughan and consecrated in 1910. It was designed by J. F. Bentley and is the cathedral of the Roman Catholic Archbishop of Westminster. It is constructed mainly in red brick.

Westminster Confession. The confessional standard set forth by the Westminster Assembly. (See **Westminster Assembly.**) It was soon adopted as the official doctrinal standard of the Scottish Kirk, and it has been influential in the teachings of other Protestant bodies.

Westphalia, The Peace of. This treaty of 1648, which helped to hasten the dissolution of the Holy Roman Empire, was made to end the series of politicoreligious conflicts fought in Central Europe and known to historians as the Thirty Years War.

Westward Position. Until about the 8th c. the customary position of the celebrant at the Eucharist was facing the people, i.e., facing the west end of the church. In monastic houses the monks' choir would be behind him so that he would be facing away from them and towards the lay congregation, as continued to be the arrangement in many monastic establishments. The usual arrangement after about the 8th c. was, in parish churches, for the celebrant to face the east, i.e., away from the people, to whom he turned round at the

"Dominus vobiscum" and other greetings and of course in homilies. The modern use of the "Westward Position," usually at a free-standing altar is highly controversial among theologically-minded liturgists, many of whom see it as de-emphasizing the "otherness" of God that is so fundamental not only in Christian thought but in that of the other two great monotheistic religions: Judaism and Islam.

Whately, Richard (1787–1863). Anglican Archbishop of Dublin. Trained at Oriel College, Oxford, of which he became a Fellow in 1811, he is important as one of the great exponents of an anti-Erastian and anti-Evangelical position and as such had a definite influence on J. H. Newman, although in later life Whately opposed the Tractarians. His *Elements of Logic* (1826) was a standard text in England for many generations.

Whiston, William (1667–1752). Mathematician and theologian. Cambridge trained, he succeeded to Newton's chair in mathematics at that university. His theological opinions were very controversial and sometimes ill-founded. He is much remembered for his translation (1737) of Josephus (see **Josephus, Flavius**), which contained useful notes and comments, went into many printings, and was much read, being a standard item on the shelves of educated lay people for many generations.

Whitaker, William (1548–1595). English Puritan divine. Educated at St. Paul's School, London, and Trinity College, Cambridge, he became, in 1580, Regius Professor of Divinity in that university. He was an extreme Calvinist, who taught that the Pope is Antichrist: a view that even many of his sympathizers took to be exaggerated.

Whitby, The Synod of. An English ecclesiastical assembly held in 664, mainly for the determination of the date of Easter. It was through this synod that the English Church severed connection with the Celtic Church in favor of Roman custom.

White, Joseph Blanco (1775–1841). Born in Seville of an Irish Roman Catholic family, he was ordained priest in 1800. Later, on account of intellectual difficulties with the Roman Catholic Church, he became an Anglican and spent some time at Oriel College, Oxford, where he was well known in Tractarian circles. Later still, influenced by J. Martineau, he became a Unitarian. His works include his *Letters from Spain* (1822) and *Practical and Internal Evidence against Catholicism* (1825).

White Fathers. A society of secular priests founded at Algiers in 1868 by Archbishop Lavigerie, committed to missionary work in Africa that includes preparation of Africans for trades, agricultural work, and other careers, as well as for the priesthood. The *Pères Blancs*, as they have been traditionally known from their white tunic and mantle, have also done much practical work for the improvement of agriculture and for the scientific exploration of the African continent.

Whitefield, George (1714–1770). Methodist associate of the Wesley brothers (see **Wesley, Charles** and **Wesley, John;** also **Methodism**). More decidedly Calvinist in his theology than others in the Methodist movement, he set up a chapel at Moorfields, Bristol, and through the patronage of Selina, the Countess of Huntingdon, he opened a tabernacle in Tottenham Court Road, London. His branch of the movement came to be known as "the Countess of Huntingdon's Connexion" or "the Calvinistic Methodists."

White Friars, The. A name popularly given to the Carmelites, from their white mantle. (See **Carmelites.**) The Cistercians are sometimes called "the White Monks" from the color of their habit. Premonstratensians, who are not monks but canons regular, wear not only a white habit but traditionally also a white biretta. They have been sometimes known as "the White Canons." Various orders of women, notably Cistercian nuns, have been called, from the color of their dress, "the White Ladies" or "the White Sisters."

Whitehead, Alfred North (1861–1947). British philosopher. Trained at Cambridge in mathematics, he was elected a Fellow of Trinity College, Cambridge, in 1880 and a Fellow of the Royal Society in 1903. While at Cambridge he collaborated with Russell on the foundations of mathematics. Professor of Applied Mathematics at the Imperial College of Science, London, from 1910 to 1924, he developed during his tenure there an interest in the philosophy of science and from 1924 to 1947 he was professor of philosophy at Harvard, where he developed his metaphysical system. He received in 1945 the very prestigious British Order of Merit. To his philosophy Whitehead brought a uniquely varied and balanced understanding of mathematics, logic, philosophy of science, and metaphysics. After his decade of collaboration with Russell, his student, they contributed, in the 3-vol. *Principia Mathematica* (1910, 1912, and 1913), an epoch-making work that both extended the scope of logic and showed its basis in mathematics. In his next period he turned more and more to the philosophy of science, which he understood as the analysis of nature, i.e., the world as it confronts us in our awareness. From this study he excluded the entire realm of mental events and the individual minds in which they occur as being outside nature. In the philosophy of science, however, events constitute the ultimate facts. Extended in space and time, they occur, then are gone. Objects, on the other hand, recur. Whitehead saw them as abstractions entering experience through intellectual recognition. He distinguished several kinds of object, e.g., perceptual objects and scientific objects (e.g., electrons, molecules). It is a mistake, on Whitehead's view, to take objects for concrete elements in nature. He calls this the fallacy of misplaced concreteness. Objects are not concrete; they are abstractions. They "ingress into" events. Events occur in the four-dimensional "extensive continuum" of space-time. Whitehead developed a theory of relativity different in many ways from Einstein's; nevertheless, despite fundamental differences, they do have some affinities. In the metaphysical and final stage of his thought, Whitehead developed a metaphysical system that provides for a process theology that is highly controversial, since, although it posits a God who is primordial and beyond challenge by any other being, God is such that all the happenings in the world become part of his nature: a notion not consonant with the central teaching of any of the three great monotheistic religions: Judaism, Christianity, and Islam. Among the writings of Whitehead pertaining to the later stages in his intellectual development may be mentioned *The Principles of Relativity* (1922), *Science and the Modern World* (1926), *Process and Reality* (1929), *Adventures of Ideas* (1933), *Nature and Life* (1934), *Modes of Thought* (1938), and *Essays in Science and Philosophy* (1947).

Whitsunday. The Christian Feast of Pentecost (see **Pentecost**) is traditionally so designated in England, presumably from the white garb worn by candidates for baptism which was closely associated with the Vigil of Pentecost as well as with that of Easter. The usual liturgical color for Whitsunday is red.

Whittier, John Greenleaf (1807–1892). American poet. A Quaker, he was prominent in the movement for the abolition of slavery. His poems reflect a deep spirituality and some of his hymns (e.g., "Dear Lord and Father of mankind") are still widely used in churches.

Whole Duty of Man, The. A devotional manual published *c.* 1658 and for long widely used, so that references to it in English literature are not uncommon. It contained seventeen discourses and was designed to be read through three times a year. It was chiefly concerned with Christian conduct, and it upheld very strict standards. Its authorship is not certain, but it is probably to be attributed to Richard Allestree (1619–1681). Henry Hammond (1605–1660), also an Anglican divine, wrote the preface to it.

Widows. In antiquity a widow could not inherit from her husband on his death and was dependent, if she was childless, on her father and otherwise on her eldest son. A widow's position was therefore economically difficult. She was also obviously a ready target for the exactions of unscrupulous creditors, dishonest judges, and others who preyed upon her. A widow such as Naomi, who lost all her male kin, was in a particularly sorry plight. Some customary provisions were made to help widows in their distress; e.g., they received a share of the sacrificial festivals and were allowed to take what was left over from the harvest (Deuteronomy 24.19–21). Jesus, following the prophets, denounced those who oppressed or neglected the widows. In the early Church a list of widows was kept and food and clothing were provided for them, but if they had relatives these were expected to care for them. No doubt many widows and orphans suffered cruel deprivation, notwithstanding the solicitude of the Church.

Wieman, Henry Nelson (1884–1975). American philosopher. Educated at Jena and at Harvard, he taught at Occidental College, at Chicago, and at Southern Illinois University. His philosophical system envisions a fourfold creative event resulting in "creative good." Sub-events consist of emerging awareness of qualitative meaning, integration of this and other meanings, and a consequent expansion of awareness and appreciation of the world. He did not merely see creation as an act of God but identified it

as God: an aspect of his system that shows some affinities with the views of the British philosopher Samuel Alexander.

Wilberforce, Robert Isaac (1802–1857). Anglican divine. The second son of William Wilberforce (see **Wilberforce, William**), he was educated at Oriel College, Oxford, where he became a Fellow in 1826, so coming into close contact with J. H. Newman and the Tractarians, among whom he was one of the most learned. (See **Tractarianism.**) He became a Roman Catholic in Paris in 1854. His writings include *The Doctrine of the Incarnation* (1848) and *The Doctrine of the Holy Eucharist* (1853).

Wilberforce, Samuel (1805–1873). Bishop of Oxford from 1845 till 1869 when he was translated to Winchester. The third son of William Wilberforce, he was educated at Oriel College, Oxford, and became well-known for his persuasive oratory, which caused hostile critics to nickname him "Soapy Sam:" an unfair sobriquet for one whose diaries show him to have had a deeply spiritual life. It was he who initiated the revision of the King James Version of the English Bible. His preaching and pastoral administration came to the notice of the Prince Consort, who in 1840 appointed him one of his chaplains. He also founded Cuddesdon, a highly respected theological college, in 1854. His attack on Darwin at a meeting of the British Association in 1860 was an unfortunate incident (sixty-five years before the even more notorious Scopes Trial), but in Wilberforce's day theologians had not had enough time to grasp fully the implications of an evolutionary understanding of the universe and to see it, as theologians were soon to see it, as "God's way of doing things."

Wilberforce, William (1759–1833). English philanthropist and opponent of the slave trade. Born in Hull, he was trained at Cambridge and in 1780 entered Parliament. His conversion to

Christianity while in his twenties was the leading motivation for the rest of his life's work. In 1789 he settled at Clapham where he became a prominent member of the "Clapham Sect," an Anglican group. (See **Clapham Sect**.) Two of his four sons became prominent Anglican divines.

William of Auvergne (*c*. **1180–1249**). Schoolman and theologian. Canon of Notre-Dame de Paris from 1223 and Bishop of Paris from 1228, he was influential at the Court of Saint Louis. An ardent seeker after ecclesiastical reform, he was a supporter of the new orders of friars and a prolific theological writer whose works include the *Magisterium Divinale* (1223–1240), a great compendium covering a large spectrum of the theological concerns of his age. He taught a moderate form of realism and was an important precursor of the great 13th-c. schoolmen.

William of Champeaux (*c*. **1070–1121**). Schoolman. Having studied under Anselm of Laon, he taught an extreme realism that in later years he seems to have modified, probably as a result of Abelard's ridicule of his earlier position on the Universals. In 1113 he became Bishop of Châlons.

William of Conches (*c*. **1080 –***c*. **1154**). Schoolman. Having studied under Bernard of Chartres, he sought, as had the latter, to encourage "profane" as well as ecclesiastical learning and cultivated a form of Christian humanism. His *Philosophia Mundi* and his *Dragmaticon* are among his writings on the natural sciences.

William of Occam. See **Occam, William of.**

Williams, Charles Walter Stansby (**1886–1945**). Poet and Christian writer. Educated at London University, he was engaged from 1908 till his death in the publishing business of the Oxford University Press, spending the last few years of his life at Oxford, where he oc-

casionally talked to groups of his admirers who crowded to hear his highly original and unusually vivacious presentation of his themes. He had a special gift for conveying, in his poems, novels, and plays, a new approach to an understanding of the way in which a Catholic culture and a sacramental outlook relate to the inner life and workings of the Church. His outlook had affinities with, although expressed in a different mode from, that of his fellow Anglican, T. S. Eliot, and his success in reaching a literary public matched that of C. S. Lewis. His earlier writings include *War in Heaven* (1930) and *Descent into Hell* (1937). Probably the best known among his theological writings is his *The Descent of the Dove* (1939), in which he helped many to see the Church directed by the action of the Holy Spirit of God in history. Most famed is probably his work on the Arthurian romance, expressed in his *Taliessen through Logres* (1938) and his *The Region of the Summer Stars* (1944).

Williams, Isaac (**1802–1865**). Anglican poet and theologian. Educated at Harrow and Trinity College, Oxford, where John Keble attracted him to the Tractarian movement. Ordained priest in 1831, he became Newman's assistant at St. Mary's, Oxford, about 1833. His autobiography, edited by Sir G. Prevost, was published in 1892.

Williams, Ralph Vaughan (**1872–1958**). English composer. Trained at the Royal College of Music, at Trinity College, Cambridge, and abroad, he composed many anthems, hymns, Masses, and other pieces, including a festal *Te Deum* for the Coronation of George VI and was music editor of *The English Hymnal*.

Williams, Roger (*c*. **1604–1683**). Pioneer in religious toleration. Trained at Pembroke College, Cambridge, he went in 1630 to Boston in search of religious liberty but, dissatisfied with what he found there, he set up a church of his own and, in 1635, having come into conflict with the authorities of Massachusetts, he was forced to leave. He took refuge with the Indians and founded a settlement called "Providence" in 1636, where in 1639 he established a church in what was to become the colony of Rhode Island. By this time he had become a doughty champion of religious toleration, which he put into practice in his administration, e.g., although he personally did not approve of Quaker teaching he gave Quakers the same toleration as he granted to all religious bodies. Among his writings against religious persecution is *The Bloudy Tenent of Persecution for the Cause of Conscience* (1644).

Will to Believe, The. A concept in the thought of William James. In simple terms it may be represented as justifying, in cases where our options are forced upon us and are of deep personal import, the act of believing beyond the strictly construed evidence. The notion has obviously important consequences in religion. See **James, William.**

Wilmart, André (1876–1941). Patristic scholar. Born in Orléans, he published (with Pierre Batiffol) *Tractatus Origenis* (1900). The following year he entered the Benedictine Order at Solesmes. He was the author of several important works on patristics and liturgics.

Wilson, Cook (1849–1915). An Oxford man, he began his philosophical development as an idealist but became the leader of the school called Oxford Realism, which was to include H. A. Prichard, H. W. Joseph, and W. D. Ross. The central teaching of this school, against the neo-idealism of F. H. Bradley and others, was that knowledge contains a simple, indefinable apprehension of reality. His chief work is his *Statement and Inference* (1926).

Wilson, Thomas (1663–1755). Anglican Church reformer and bishop. Trained at Trinity College, Dublin, for the medical profession, he turned to the Church and

eventually accepted the See of Sodor and Man, being consecrated in 1698. In this office he was assiduous in imposing his very high standards of discipline, which naturally involved him in acrimonious controversies. He was even imprisoned for a time, and on his acquittal he was offered, by way of compensation, the See of Exeter but declined it, preferring to stay in the Isle of Man in whose long history he is a memorable figure. Words in his *Maxims of Piety* exhibit his style and reflect his outlook: "You say that you believe the Gospel: you live as if you were sure not one word of it is true."

Winchester. One of the most ancient dioceses in England, officially ranking in importance after Canterbury, York, London, and Durham. Apart from legends of its having even greater antiquity, we can date its beginnings with the transference *c*. 670 of the bishopric of the large diocese of Dorchester to Winchester. As the city grew, the cathedral was enlarged. Recent excavations have disclosed extensive remains of it. In the 11th c. the cathedral was entirely rebuilt in the Norman style. Of this the transepts remain; the rest was gradually rebuilt till it reached its present form, now being the longest of all the medieval English cathedrals. Among its many famous bishops was William of Wykeham (1324–1404), who also founded Winchester College, one of the oldest and greatest of English public schools, and (in 1379) New College, Oxford. The Bishop of Winchester is *ex officio* Prelate of the Order of the Garter, England's premier chivalric order.

Windelband, Wilhelm (1848–1915). German philosopher and historian of philosophy. Born in Potsdam, he taught at various universities in Switzerland and Germany. He was the leader of the Neo-Kantian school of philosophy at Heidelberg. His writings include *A History of Philosophy* (2 vols., 1878), *History and Science* (1894), and *On Free Will* (1904).

Window. In biblical times, since there was no glass, windows of houses consisted of openings normally covered by shutters, mats, or curtains. They were apparently often large enough for a thief to pass through, although they were probably small by today's standards. They would often if not usually be also protected by bars or a grill, which could be opened, enabling a person to look out. In palaces and the like larger windows opening out on to a balcony enabled royal persons and other dignitaries to appear before the crowds at a distance, receiving their homage.

Windsor. The Royal Free Chapel of Windsor, England, was constituted by Edward III to take the shrine of the Order of the Garter which, founded *c.* 1348, received its statutes in 1352. The chapter is under the direct jurisdiction of the Sovereign. The chapel, in the perpendicular style, dates from the end of the 15th c. See also **Winchester.**

Wine. Wine has been produced in Palestine and elsewhere in the Middle East from prehistoric times. It was the customary drink with meals and was also carried by travelers as part of their baggage. Paul recommends it to his pupil Timothy (I Timothy 5.23) as medically beneficial. Jesus praises it while disapproving drunkenness. Nowhere in the Bible is the use of wine regarded unfavorably in itself. Its use is universal and taken for granted. The Nazirites and the Rechabites took a special vow of abstinence from wine, but these were groups with very special traditions and distinctive outlooks far from the biblical mainstream.

In Islam, the Qur'an condemns wine drinking, and it came to be regarded as a grave sin *(kabira)*. Legalistic disputes arose on the subject, e.g., does wine that is made from substances other than the grape fall within the condemnation? In the Sufi tradition of Islamic mysticism, wine seems to have been popular and is a common motif in Arabic, Turkish, and Persian poetry.

Wisdom in Philosophical Tradition. The Greek term *hē sophia* (wisdom) originally had a general significance, being directed to the practical arts for which today we might more readily apply the term "skill." It gradually attained a more distinctive meaning in the Greek philosophical tradition and in Western thought generally. Plato saw wisdom as "knowledge of the whole:" a knowledge the attainment of which demands both scientific training and practical experience and reflection. Aristotle made an important distinction between *theoria* and *praxis* (the speculative and the practical). This basic distinction issued in a contrast between *sophia* (wisdom as understood to be the aim of metaphysical and theological studies: understanding of first principles) and *phronesis* (practical or, as might be said today, prudential wisdom). This *phronesis* was the kind of wisdom generally pursued by Greek schools such as the Stoics, the Epicureans, and the Cyrenaics. It related to the conduct of life. The medieval schoolmen, notably Thomas Aquinas, generally followed Aristotle's distinction between *sophia* and *phronesis*, interpreting it in such a way as to present revealed theology as the highest form of *sophia*. In the medieval system of education (built upon that of Roman antiquity), the Seven Liberal Arts (i.e., the studies proper to one who is *liber,* free, as opposed to a slave) are presided over in iconography by the Lady Philosophy, plainly to be identified with *hē Sophia* (Wisdom personified as a lady). Spinoza distinguishes between *ratio* (reason understood as knowledge of scientific "laws") and *scientia intuitiva,* which he perceived as the capacity to see the universal in all the particular existents in our experience. This is to see them, in his phrase, *sub specie aeternitatis:* under the aspect of eternity. *Scientia intuitiva* is, for Spinoza, wisdom.

Whatever wisdom is, it is etymologically the goal that philosophers are presumed to seek because they love it: *philo-sophia:* love of wisdom. See also **Wisdom Literature, The.**

Wisdom in Zen. "Horizontal" wisdom, according to Zen teachers, is knowledge *about* something. One goes on learning more and more *about* the object of one's knowledge. "Vertical" teaching, by contrast, penetrates to knowledge of the object as it is in itself. It goes "upward" to a higher understanding and realization of the object, penetrating to its fundamental nature. Wisdom, the Zen masters teach, goes beyond scientific knowledge by taking life into account. The parallel with existentialism in the West is notable.

Wisdom Literature, The. What is called "the Wisdom Literature" represents a distinctive literary genre within the Bible. Its distinctiveness lies in part in the international character and cosmopolitan outlook that it reflects. It includes, for instance, maxims, epigrams, aphorisms, and other sayings such as have many counterparts in the literatures of neighboring peoples. The educated classes in Egypt, for instance, had a copious literature of this kind. Egyptian Wisdom texts often presented advice as given by a father or sage and intended to guide intelligent and thoughtful young men to take their place in society and prosper. The earliest works of this kind are of Ptah-Hotep (*c.*2400 BCE). Later texts include the maxims of Ani (dating from *c.*1550 BCE but committed to writing *c.* 900 BCE). Such texts were preserved in exercises for schoolboys. They may have seemed a wearisome task for the schoolboys who had to copy them out, but they reflected a cultivated frame of mind. They had counterparts in many ancient civilizations, to be found, for example, in Roman sources such as the *Meditations* of Marcus Aurelius and as far away as the writings of Confucius and other Chinese sages. In the Middle East, as in the Orient, schoolboys, when they learned the rudiments of reading and writing, received along with that basic training instruction in the manners of a good scribe. Some of these maxims are prudential and comparatively common-place, at the level of "A bird in the hand is worth two in the bush" and the like. Others are much more profound. Professional scribes, who kept the records and administered the affairs of temples, palaces, and other such institutions, collected them. They were often practical and they would appeal, therefore, to the Israelites, who were a practical people, but that was not the only reason, by any means, that they found their way into the Bible. They introduced into the Bible, in some cases, profound reflections on some of the greatest problems the human spirit has to face, such as the problem of evil: why do the righteous suffer and the wicked prosper? To Solomon, a cosmopolitan figure, is ascribed much of this literature. Of course as it entered the Bible it was invested with the characteristic attitudes of those who had shared in the faith in Yahweh that was the outcome of living with and seeing beyond the trials of a particular form of human experience.

Typical of this literature in the Old Testament are books such as Proverbs and Ecclesiastes. It is also well represented in so-called apocryphal or deuterocanonical books such as Ecclesiasticus and the Wisdom of Solomon. Reverence for Wisdom, however, is already well recognized by the biblical writers long before books of that kind as we know them came into the Bible. References abound in books such as Genesis, Kings, and Isaiah.

Wisdom is eventually personified as a feminine proper noun in Greek, *hē Sophia*. The concept of Wisdom is carried over into the New Testament, being found both in Paul and in the Evangelists. Paul saw the Divine Wisdom as incarnate in Christ (I Corinthians 1.24). He also connects it closely with the Holy Spirit (I Corinthians 12.8). Many of the Fathers identify Wisdom with the Logos, some with the Holy Spirit. Wisdom was a very important concept in the Gnostic systems, some of which found a specific place for Wisdom, e.g., as the spouse of the Logos. The Eastern

Orthodox Church has always tended to revere Hagia Sophia, "Holy Wisdom," in a special way. Some modern Orthodox theologians distinguished the uncreated Wisdom of God from his created Wisdom. See **Hagia Sophia** and **Wisdom in Philosophical Tradition.**

Wishart, George (c. 1513–1546). Scottish Reformer. After travels in England and on the continent of Europe, he returned to his native Scotland in 1543 and soon began preaching Reformation doctrine, assisted by John Knox. He was burned at the stake under the order of Cardinal David Beaton, Primate and Chancellor of Scotland, at Saint Andrews, where, and also under Beaton's orders, the first native Scottish martyr, Patrick Hamilton, had suffered, in 1528, the same form of execution.

Witchcraft. Three distinct usages may be noted for this term: (1) Anthropologists recognize the concept of witchcraft as it appears in African cultures, as a maleficent power believed to inhere in certain individuals who can harm others and do so unconsciously, i.e., they may be unaware even of their powers as a carrier of a disease might be unaware of his or her capacity for harm. It must be noted, however, that the fact of their being innocent of their own condition and powers does not in the least protect them from extermination. A society is no less afraid of the carrier of a plague when the carrier is unaware of being one than it is of one who is aware of it. (2) In Europe, by contrast, witchcraft came to be regarded, at least by the middle of the 14th c., as a "false religion" inspired by Satan in the sense that its practitioners, witches, had made a pact with Satan who in return gave them their evil powers. By 1700, at least 200,000 had been executed for witchcraft, mainly at the instigation of the Church (Roman, Lutheran, Anglican, and Reformed), in continental Europe, in England, in Scotland, and (e.g., at Salem, Massachusetts, in 1692) in the American colonies. A papal bull of 1484 had specifically sanctioned the extermination of witches on much the same principles as those governing the hunting down and execution of heretics. Before the 14th c., however, witchcraft had not been generally so treated. It was a "magical art" and as such it could be maleficent or beneficent in its effects. So, at that time, it had not been viewed with the same kind of horror and fear that later attended its manifestation. Although apart, of course, from the life of the Church, it had not necessarily been seen as the Church's enemy. (3) Witchcraft today has emerged as the name for a specific religious movement, having its inspiration chiefly in the theories propagated by Margaret Murray, an anthropologist who perceived European witchcraft as a survival, perhaps sometimes distorted, of a pre-Christian fertility religion.

Wittenberg. The cradle of the Reformation and since 1922 officially designated Lutherstadt Wittenberg. Luther became professor at the University of Wittenberg in 1508, six years after the founding of that institution, which since 1815 has been united with the University of Halle. It was on the door of the Schlosskirche, the Castle Church, that he affixed his famous 95 theses on October 31, 1517. Both he and Melanchthon are buried in that church. The Augustinian monastery to which Luther was attached as a friar is preserved as a museum: the "Lutherhaus."

Wittenberg, The Concord of. An agreement reached in 1536 by theologians, representing respectively the Lutheran and Zwinglian parties, on the nature of the Eucharist. The Concord eventually failed, however, through the unwillingness of the Swiss Zwinglians to accept it.

Wittgenstein, Ludwig (1889–1951). Philospher. Born in Vienna, he did engineering studies at Berlin and Manchester and through these studies he became interested in the work of mathematical logicians such as F. L. G.

Frege and Betrand Russell. At Cambridge in 1912–1913 he worked with Russell. In World War I, serving with the army of his native Austria, he underwent at the front some sort of mystical experience. His famous *Tractatus Logico-Philosophicus* was published in Germany in 1921 and in England the following year. Apparently as a consequence of his mystical experience in the battlefield he decided to give away a fortune that he had inherited and to go to work as an elementary schoolteacher in Austria. Returning to Cambridge in 1929, he was offered and accepted the chair of philosophy that G. E. Moore had held, but resigned it two years later as his health deteriorated in his last years.

According to the *Tractatus*, which was written during the war years and much of which he later rejected, the world is made up of rudimentary facts, apparently independent of one another. Language has the statement of facts as its primary purpose. It does so by picturing. Language also, however, is used to state what are really tautologies, but useful ones, because they assist the process of acquiring knowledge. These are the tautologies of mathematics, which tell us nothing new, nothing about the empirical world, but are nevertheless immensely useful. (What could we learn of astronomy, for instance, without mathematics?) Every proposition must fall into either of these two categories; otherwise it is nonsense. All metaphysical statements, for example, are nonsense. But then the *Tractatus* itself turns out to be a sort of metaphysics, so it, too, merely serves the purpose of demonstrating the nonsensical character of all such pseudo-philosophical enterprises. It becomes indeed a warning signal to talk no more philosophy. This is the mood that helped to foster the development of the logical positivist school that for some decades in the 20th c. virtually "took over" academic philosophy in the English-speaking world. For those who uncritically or at least unresistingly accepted the outlook it engendered, philosophy was emptied of all of its traditional purposes, with the exception of logic. The effect was, e.g., both to make the history of philosophy useless and to make the philosophy of history meaningless. No longer did the pursuit of philosophical studies demand the wide preparation and intellectual maturity that had been traditionally required of aspirants; it could now be undertaken by almost any mathematical "whiz-kid" with a quick mind and a flair for logical implications.

To a great extent, however, Wittgenstein later repudiated the *Tractatus*. In his later writings, including the *Philosophical Investigations*, his interest moved to linguistic analysis. Language, he now perceived, is not to be understood as having a one-to-one relationship with that which it denotes; it has many purposes and many functions. Chemistry might seem to come nearest to the one-to-one relationship that logical positivists might see as ideal (H_2O = water and $C_6 H_6$ = benzene), although even there the situation is not so simple. Wittgenstein now saw language as having many purposes, each being a "language game." For example, the picturing of facts (e.g., "this is a book;" "that is a table") is only one of the many functions of language. Other functions include requesting ("Please be seated"), greeting ("Hello! How are you?"), praise ("Alleluia"), and prayer ("May their souls rest in peace"). The variety of such "picturing" is endless. Through analysis of language the philosopher comes to recognize what surely all persons with even an elementary literary training discover, if they do not already instinctively perceive it, the difference between, e.g., so-called "literal" and figurative kinds of language. Through analysis of language, however, one can understand better the ways in which groups or "families" of language games develop and how the one stands to the other. One must know the language "game" in order to understand what is being said. If you had never heard of chess or at least knew nothing of its rules and I told you "I took John's bishop" you might well suppose that I had kidnapped an ecclesiastical functionary in my friend's Church. Private jokes may be set up in a way that is unintelligible unless one knows the "game" to which they refer, e.g., "The tiger is coming to dinner tonight" would be puzzling, if not alarming, unless one knew that the family had developed the habit, over the years, of so designating a possible future son-in-law, a Princetonian, and that the totem of Princeton University is the tiger. See also **Austin, John,** on performative utterances and other concepts in linguistic analysis that have some reference to religious concerns.

Nevertheless, the extension of the later Wittgenstein's interest to linguistic analysis does not fundamentally alter the highly restrictive stance that he and others have taken in 20th-c. philosophy. As Berkeley in the 18th c. complained of what he called the "minute" philosophers, that they "first raise a dust and then complain they cannot see," so one might say of such 20th c. philosophers that they first burn down their workshop and then complain they are unemployed. As Etienne Gilson, however, once observed, philosophy has a way of rising up and burying its own undertakers.

Wolff, Christian (1679-1754). German philosopher. Born in Breslau, he was educated at Jena and Leipzig. Personally much influenced by Leibniz, he sought to develop a philosophical system that would rigorously follow his principles. At Halle, where he taught for some time, he was bitterly attacked by the Pietists whose chief center was at Halle, and in 1723 King Frederick William expelled him from the city, causing him to move to Marburg University, where he remained till 1740, when the King's successor, Frederick the Great, recalled him to Halle. Wolff was highly respected in philosophical circles everywhere in Western Europe, counting Kant himself as one of his ad-

mirers. In 1743 he was named Chancellor of Halle University. Wolff saw philosophy as embracing all human knowledge. His classification of philosophy into divisions such as (1) Logic and Metaphysics, (2) Moral or "practical" Philosophy (ethics, economics, politics), and (3) Epistemology (theory of knowledge) had considerable influence on the way in which the study of philosophy was set up in the great universities of Europe. A great deal of Wolff's importance lies, indeed, in his classification and organization of philosophical studies. It was he, for instance, who introduced terms such as "monism," "dualism," and "teleology," and it was he who introduced the term "cosmology" to designate a specific philosophical discipline. The popularization of "ontology" was also largely due to him. His writings include *Rational Philosophy or Logic* (1728), *General Cosmology* (1731), *Natural Theology* (2 vols., 1736–1737), *Elements of Universal Mathematics* (1740–1746), *Law of Nature* (8 vols., 1740–1748), *Economics* (1750), and *Moral Philosophy or Ethics* (1750–1753).

Wolsey, Thomas (c. 1474–1530). English statesman and churchman. After becoming a Fellow of Magdalen College, Oxford, he was ordained priest in 1498. Under Henry VIII not only did he rapidly obtain ecclesiastical preferment, being appointed Archbishop of York in 1514 and the following year created a cardinal; he became also in 1515 Lord Chancellor of England, arrogantly wielding enormous power and through his great political skill retaining the royal favor and at the same time conducting international intrigue. When, in 1527, Henry wished to divorce Anne Boleyn, Wolsey, while personally opposed to the idea, used all his skill to comply with the royal wish. He even tried to persuade the Pope to give him full authority to deal with the question. He failed. Anne blamed him and he lost the royal favor. He had to cede all his property and offices to the Crown, although his archbishopric was later restored to him. His ruthless personal ambition did much to promote the absolutism in affairs of Church and State that so notoriously disfigured the reign of Henry VIII.

Woolman, John (1720–1772). American Quaker. Born in Burlington, New Jersey, he was a persistent opponent of slavery, campaigning against it from his early twenties till his death. Best known among his writings is his *Journal* (1774).

Word. In the Prologue to the Gospel according to John and in other early Christian literature, the term *Logos* is traditionally rendered "Word" in English. See **Logos.**

Wordsworth, Christopher (1807–1885). A nephew of the poet William Wordsworth, he was educated at Trinity College, Cambridge, of which he became a Fellow in 1830 and of which his father was Master. He was a conservative Anglican churchman with a deep veneration for the early Fathers. Among his patristic studies his *Saint Hippolytus and the Church of Rome* (1853) is especially significant. In 1869 he became Bishop of Lincoln.

Wordsworth, William (1770–1850). Poet. Educated at St. John's College, Cambridge, he was in his youth politically a radical and religiously an unbeliever. He formed in 1797 an enduring friendship with Samuel Taylor Coleridge and the two poets published jointly, the following year, *Lyrical Ballads.* Wordsworth settled in 1799 at Grasmere in the English Lake District. He drew great inspiration from his acute observation of nature which for some years he almost divinized, so deeply did he see it as the vehicle of spirituality. In his later period he showed a deeper appreciation of traditional Anglican churchmanship and some sympathy with the Tractarians. He was made Poet Laureate in 1843.

Works of Mercy, Corporal and Spiritual. A distinction is traditionally made between the two kinds of acts expected of a Christian: (A) Seven "corporal works of mercy": (1) to feed the hungry; (2) to give water to the thirsty; (3) to clothe those inadequately clad; (4) to lodge the stranger; (5) to visit the sick; (6) to visit those in prison; (7) to bury the dead. (B) Seven "spiritual works of mercy": (1) to turn sinners from their wayward path; (2) to instruct the ignorant; (3) to counsel the perplexed; (4) to comfort the bereaved and others in grief; (5) to bear wrongs with patience; (6) to forgive those who do us wrong; (7) to pray for both the living and the dead.

World Council of Churches, The. An association or fellowship of Christian Churches constituted at Amsterdam in 1948, emerging from a fusion of two earlier movements, (1) Life and Work and (2) Faith and Order. It now has headquarters at Geneva. Its Central Committee meets annually and it has assemblies that have met at intervals of six or seven years, e.g., at Evanston, Illinois in 1954, at New Delhi in 1961, at Uppsala in 1968, and elsewhere since. It represents an important achievement of the ecumenical movement in 20th c. Christianity. Most of the Eastern Orthodox Churches are members as well as almost all the mainline denominations in the West, where the chief exception is the Roman Catholic Church, which, however, in 1968 accepted full membership of the Faith and Order Commission and now has some other links with the Council's work, much of which is advisory. Not all individuals in the various constituent Churches are equally supportive of the work of the Council, but at least all recognize it as a means of communication among Christians of very diverse understandings of the nature of the Christian Way. Much work is undertaken by the Council for the relief of famine-stricken peoples and others in distress, and one of its commissions has consultative status with the United Nations.

World Soul. A concept of God found in ancient Greek thought in which the divine is envisioned as extended in space and including the universe. Plato represents this as a sort of subordinate divinity, being subject to movement and therefore only as divine as a changing entity can be. The Stoics' view of the soul was materialistic, yet in other respects somewhat like Plato's concept of the world soul. On the Stoic view God and mind as extending through the universe come to be seen as the same. Plotinus, and through him the Neoplatonist school generally, saw the world soul as a divine emanation from the One. This emanation is made by way of Nous, "mind," which contains the world as its body. The notion that the universe is the body of God has roots in such views which in terms of a later terminology are pantheistic or panentheistic rather than theistic.

Worm. As used in the Bible, the term very often is figurative, signifying destruction or death. The worm that "does not die" is a figure of "eternal death." When Job regards himself as consumed by worms (Job 7.5), we must understand this allusion not as signifying a specific disease arising from physical worms but, rather, as meaning that he sees himself as already dying. The worm is, in short, a figure for human mortality.

Worms, The Concordat of. In 1122 this concordat between Pope Callistus II and the Emperor Henry V ended the Investiture Controversy.

Worms, The Diet of. At this meeting, held at Worms in 1521, Luther defended his theological stance before the Emperor Charles V. It was here, on April 18, that, according to a well established tradition, he made his celebrated refusal to recant, ending with the words: "Hie stehe ich. Ich kan nicht anders. Gott helff mir. Amen." (Here I stand. I cannot do otherwise. God help me. Amen.)

Worms, The Synod of. This was a synod held in 1076, which was convened by the Emperor Henry IV during the Investiture Controversy to defend his claims. It issued a strong statement against the Pope, Gregory VII, calling upon the people of Rome to depose him for alleged crimes. The Pope responded by excommunicating Henry.

Wreath, Advent. See **Advent Candle.**

Wright, Chauncey (1830–1875). American philosopher. A New Englander, Harvard trained, he proposed an evolutionary view entailing natural selection, which Darwin learned about and supported. He was especially interested in the development of self-consciousness in the process of evolution from lower to higher forms of life. He is of considerable historical importance in the history of American philosophy, not least because of his influence on the characteristically pragmatistic element in American thought as found in the work of Charles Peirce and William James, with its obvious evolutionist implicates.

Writings. The third of the three divisions of the Hebrew Bible. The first and most revered division is the Torah, consisting of the first five books of the Bible (the Pentateuch); the second is the Prophets, the next sacred; the Writings consist of the rest of what Christians call the Old Testament, such as the Psalms, the Wisdom Literature, and other books much revered yet not belonging to "the Law and the Prophets."

Wu Hsing. In traditional Chinese thought, the five basic elements in the universe (earth, wood, metal, fire, and water) are so named. Developed by Tsou Yen (305–240 BCE) as a cosmological theory, they came to be associated with the Yin/Yang principle. See **Yin/ Yang.**

Wundt, Wilhelm (1832–1900). German philosopher. After being professor of physiology at Heidelberg, he held a chair of philosophy at Leipzig, where, in 1879, he initiated psychology as an independent discipline, establishing the first experimental psychology laboratory. He was influential in opposing 19th-c. positivism by showing that the *Geisteswissenschaften* (the sciences of the spirit) cannot be reduced to the methods proper to the *Naturwissenschaften* (the natural sciences). Psychology, however, he perceived as open to both external experience and internal experience. He saw metaphysics as extending the sciences into a coherent understanding of existence. Seeing the mental or psychic as having a primacy over the physical, he could see God as the ground of the evolution of all existence, psychical and physical. Logic is the groundwork of the methodologies of all the sciences, natural and spiritual. Wundt's writings (apart from works in physiology) include *The Influence of Philosophy on the Empirical Sciences* (1876), *Logic* (1880–1883), *Ethics* (1886), *System of Philosophy* (1889), and *The Sensible and the Supersensible World* (1914).

Wu-Nien. Zen Buddhists apply this term (meaning literally "no-thought") to meditation on one's own self-nature. Wu-nien does not imply the exclusion of mental activity except in this special kind of meditation. Only when one has achieved the realization of one's own self-nature can one know the essential nature of other minds and other bodies. Wu-nien is not a cessation of consciousness but, rather, a seeing and a knowing that exclude all attachment and so is called "thoughtlessness" (*wu-nien*). It is related to *shūnyatā* (emptiness): the self-nature cannot be what anything else is. "I am what *I* am."

Wu-Wei. The Chinese principle whereby one achieves one's goal without aggressive or meddlesome action. The Taoist sage, knowing that he is one with all things, does not resist but yields to Nature. So, in consciousness of his power, he is able to produce without

possessing, to act without pushing himself forward. As a ruler he will govern without dominating. The term also appears in Zen and some other forms of Buddhism and is associated with *salori:* when the *salori* comes, there is no action in it. An illustration of the principle frequently offered is that of the boughs of a healthy tree which, when laden with snow, bend with it and so remain lively and resilient instead of breaking, and therefore dying under the burden. The concept is implicit in the teaching of Jesus, e.g., in the collection of sayings attributed to him in what is generally known as "the Sermon on the Mount."

Wyclif or Wycliffe, John (*c.* 1330–1384). English Reformer. He was Master of Balliol College, Oxford, *c.* 1360, and lived mainly in Oxford at Queen's College from 1363. In his early life he was chiefly interested in philosophical questions, inclining toward the views of Grosseteste. He wrote a *Summa de Ente*. As he became more and more interested in theological questions he grew impatient with institutional religion and sought to distinguish the institutional Church from the invisible reality that he thought it so ill represented. In various writings such as his *De Ecclesia*, his *De Veritate Sacrae Scripturae*, and his *De Potestate Papae* he insisted that the Bible is the sole criterion of Christian life and teaching. In the *De Eucharistia* he specifically attacked the doctrine of transubstantiation. This attack on the by then accepted doctrine was officially condemned by the University in 1381. He was blamed for the Peasants' Revolt and lost much of his earlier following. His disciples, notably Nicholas of Hereford, translated the Bible from the Vulgate into English *c.* 1380–1392: a project that was no doubt much approved by him and whose result is traditionally called "Wyclif's Bible." The achievement was a remarkable one for its time and copies of the text of this Bible, circulating several generations before the age of printing and about a century and a half before the first printed English version of the New Testament by William Tyndale, were eagerly sought. Wyclif's personal contribution as a precursor of the Reformation lay more, however, in his philosophical and theological critiques. See also **Lollards.**

X

Xenocrates (396–314 BCE). Greek philosopher. On the death of Speusippus in 339 he was head of Plato's Academy till his death.

Xenophanes of Colophon (c. 570–c. 470 BCE). Greek philosopher. He held that there is no certain knowledge about anything and pointed out the anthropomorphic character of human conceptualization of the gods. He taught that God is unmoving and changeless. He is generally credited with adumbrating the principal teachings of the Eleatic school.

Xenophon (c. 430–c. 355 BCE). Greek writer and friend of Socrates. In his *Symposium* he makes Socrates praise nobility of character and contrast earthly love with its loftier counterpart. In his *Memorabilia* he defends Socrates from the charges of impiety brought against him and exhibits him as a teacher of virtue with an ennobling influence on his hearers.

Xiberta y Roqueta, Bartomeu Maria (1897–1967). Spanish Carmelite historian and theologian whose work *El Yo de Jesucristo* was published in the year of his death.

Ximénes de Cisneros, Francisco (1436–1517). Spanish churchman, reformer, and patron of learning. Cardinal Archbishop of Toledo; confessor to Queen Isabella; founded the University of Alcalá; revived the Mozarabic rite; produced the very important Complutensian Polyglot, so called from the Latin name (Complutum) for Alcalá.

Xirau, Joaquin (1895–1946). Spanish philosopher. Influenced by Ortega. Among his works are *The Meaning of Truth* (1927) and *The Philosophy of Husserl* (1941).

Y

Yad. A silver pointer used in the synagogue to guide the reader of the Torah. This serves a dual purpose: the liturgical one of so reverencing the sacred text as to avoid physical contact with it and the practical one of keeping the scroll clean.

Yasakuni. A Shinto shrine built to commemorate the souls of those Japanese who, up to the end of World War II, died in battle for their country.

Yahweh. The name most commonly used in the Old Testament to designate God. It was the personal name of the God of Israel. The name is probably derived from an older form of the verb to be (*hāwāh*) and may be part of a longer form meaning "He who brings into being whatever comes into being," thus designating his creative function. In the Greek version of the Old Testament (LXX) it is rendered *ho ōn*, traditionally englished as "He who is." So sacred was the name to the Jews that although it could be written it might not be spoken. In speech the word adonai ("Lord") was used as a substitute, to avoid utterance of the sacred name. Since the correct pronunciation of the name was thereby lost in Judaism, the name "Jehovah" was artificially constructed in English translation. Modern scholars, however, use the form "Yahweh" as nearest to the original Hebrew pronunciation. Other terms are also used in the Old Testament to designate divine Being (e.g., *El* and *Elohim*), but they have historical connections with the pantheons of antiquity, while Yahweh is the distinctive personal name of the God of Israel. We must be careful, however, not to read philosophical and theological speculation into the text in which such terms appear, for the Hebrews did not engage in the kind of philosophical speculation and analysis that delighted the minds of educated Greeks in the time of Socrates, for example. What does come out forcefully in the Old Testament is the resolute resistance of the Hebrews to all tendencies to assimilate Yahweh to any fashionable foreign or international pantheon. Yahweh, to the Hebrew mind, was the *living* God, by which no doubt they meant, although they could not have so expressed it, that he was no mere construct of the human mind but a reality ontologically independent of his creation.

Yazatas. In Zoroastrianism, entities functioning somewhat as do angels in Judaism, Christianity, and Islam. The faithful venerate them as guides and helpers and may ask them to intercede on their behalf to God, Ahura Mazda.

Year, The Christian. The two focal points in the liturgical year of the Christian Church are Easter and Christmas. Easter is a "movable" feast, determined according to the lunar calendar, and the reckoning in the Western Church differs from that in the Eastern Church. Christmas is an "immovable" feast, fixed in the 4th c. as December 25, to coincide with what was at that time the winter solstice. Traditionally, Epiphany follows on the twelfth day after Christmas, January 6. From Easter may be reckoned Ash Wednesday, the first day of Lent, the penitential period commemorating the forty-day Temptation in the Wilderness, culminating in Palm Sunday and Passion Week. Ascension Day is the Thursday forty days after Easter and is followed by Pentecost or Whitsunday. Thereafter, until Advent, the Sundays are counted as following Pentecost. Although Roman Catholic practice since Vatican II has varied this arrangement, the foregoing represents the essential rhythm of the Christian Year. In the Eastern Orthodox Church

three parts of the year are recognized: the Triodion (ten weeks before Easter), the Pentecostarion (the season of Eastertide), and the Octoechos (the remainder). See **Pentecostarion.**

Yiddish. A language still both written and spoken by many Jews. Dating from the 10th c. CE, it was composed of several German city dialects with elements of other European languages and a considerable element of Hebrew. It has an interesting literature.

Yin/Yang. From remote times two principles have been recognized in Chinese thought: *yin*, the feminine, passive principle, and *yang*, the masculine, active principle. Everything is a product of the two. The notion has been enormously influential throughout the history of Chinese thought.

Yoga. A Sanskrit word, meaning both "yoke" and "union." It represents a practical means of so training the individual self as to unite it eventually to the universal self. Although it is a concept that is rooted in Hindu and Buddhist thought and practice, it has parallels in Christianity, and many Christians today find yogic training helpful. Several forms of yoga are traditionally recognized, e.g., bhakti yoga, which stresses devotion; karma yoga, which stresses ethical conduct; and mantra yoga, which seeks self-control through the rhythmic repetition of certain sounds. The earliest description of yoga is found in the Upanishads and the technique was developed by Patañjali.

Yoke. The term is frequently used in both the Old Testament and the New Testament as a symbol of slavery and oppression, but sometimes simply of submission to the will of God or obedience to the Torah. The physical yoke in use among the Hebrews in antiquity, from which these images are derived, was not very different from what is used in the Middle East to this day. It was a heavy bar of wood laid on the shoulders of the ox or donkey and attached by thongs or pins passing under the animal's throat, with a long pin attaching the yoke to the shaft of the plow. In the New Testament, Jesus claims (Matthew 11.29 f.) that his yoke is easy to bear, i.e., although following him imposes obligations that he describes in the traditional language of a yoke, the freedom that his teaching bestows makes the yoke easy and the burden of it light: a joy compared to the heavy yoke of oppression that his people had become accustomed to suffer.

Yom Kippur. The Hebrew name for the Day of Atonement, the annual Jewish fast day. Falling generally in October, it is calculated to fall on the tenth day of the seventh month (Tishri). As the only fast ordained in the Mosaic Law it is of the utmost importance in Jewish life. Its purpose is to cleanse the people from sin and re-establish good relations between God and his people.

York. The northern province of the Church of England. From late in 1st c. to early in the 5th c., York was under Roman rule and was the military headquarters in Britain. Built on the site of previous churches, the present great church of York Minster dates from the 13th to the 15th c.

Young, Patrick (1584–1652). Biblical and patristic scholar. Royal Librarian. Among his many publications was the Codex Alexandrinus, one of the most important manuscripts of the Bible in existence, which Cyril Lukar had presented to the Royal Library in 1628.

Young Men's/Women's Christian Association. The YMCA was founded in London in 1844 by George Williams. Its purpose has always been to gather young men together in a Christian atmosphere in such a way as to develop their bodies, minds, and spirits for service to Jesus Christ. The club buildings usually provide for social activities and often for lodging. The international membership is estimated at between three and four million. The YWCA was founded in 1855 for women. The YMCA and the YWCA united in 1877. The work has been and is of incalculable value in training young men and women along Christian lines.

Yule. Probably a Scandinavian winter festival. In later usage it came to be applied to Christmas. The term is no longer commonly used but survives with a somewhat nostalgic flavor, especially in "Yuletide."

Z

Zabarella, Francesco (1360–1417). Italian canonist. He taught canon law at Florence and Padua, served in the Paduan and in the Venetian diplomatic services, and was called to Rome by Pope Boniface IX in an advisory capacity in connection with the Great Schism (1378–1417). He also participated in the Council of Pisa in 1409. His work *De schismate*, printed in 1545, was placed on the Index of Prohibited Books because it asserted the right of a General Council over papal authority. He was probably the ablest of the great conciliarists before the Council of Constance.

Zabarella, Jacopo (1533–1589). Italian philosopher. A Renaissance Aristotelian, he wrote several works including his *Logic* (1587) and his *Physics* (1601).

Zacharias. The father of John the Baptist. See **Zechariah.**

Zacharias Scholasticus. A 6th c. Monophysite; Church historian. One of the "Gaza Triad," along with Procopius and Aeneas. Engaged in controversy against the Neoplatonists and the Manichees.

Zacharius. Pope from 741 till his death in 752. A Greek by birth, he made a Greek translation of the *Dialogues* of Gregory the Great.

Zadokite Documents. Part of the manuscript discoveries at Qumran. Also called the Damascus Fragments. Similar in character to the Manual of Discipline, which sets forth rules governing the conduct of the religious community for which they are designed, they have some general resemblance to the Didachē.

Zahn, Theodor (1838–1933). New Testament and patristic scholar. He taught at Göttingen, Kiel, Erlangen, and Leipzig. He was immensely erudite and extremely thorough in his methods, doing much pioneering work on the canon of the New Testament and writing and editing many biblical and patristic studies.

Zarathustra. (Zoroaster). Founder of Zoroastrianism; also the central figure in Nietzsche's *Also sprach Zarathustra,* in which he expounds his concept of the superman.

Zawiya. A house in which Sufi sheiks live in community. The term is also used of any place where a Sufi lives apart from the world.

Za-Zen. The term used in Zen to designate meditation.

Zealots. A Jewish party of extremists who wrested Jerusalem from the more moderate party and led a fanatical resistance to the Romans that eventually resulted in the destruction of the Temple in 70 CE. It may be that Simon, one of the twelve apostles of Jesus, had belonged to this party (see Luke 6.15).

Zechariah. A very common personal name in the Old Testament, meaning "Yahweh has remembered." In Greek it is rendered Zacharias, e.g., in the name of the father of John the Baptist as it appears in the New Testament. The biblical book of the post-exilic period that is so entitled is substantially the work of the minor prophet of that name, but modern scholars generally recognize that certain passages are interpolations by later writers. The messianic theme is prominent and is treated in an apocalyptic fashion.

Zeller, Eduard (1814–1908). Neo-Kantian philosopher. Having studied at Tübingen, he taught at various universities including Marburg and Heidelberg. Influenced by both Hegel and Kant, he accounted epistemology the most fundamental of the philosophical disciplines.

Zen. A form of Buddhism. "Zen" is a Japanese rendering of the Chinese Ch'an', meaning "meditation." This school developed as a reaction to classical forms of Buddhism. Originating in India it was brought by Bodhidharma (460–534) to China. It has been especially influential in Japan and has become popular in the West. Typical among Zen teaching is the notion that since the Buddha-nature is in all men and the Buddha-mind is everywhere, *satori* (enlightenment) can be achieved at any time by anyone in any ordinary situation in human life. It is not to be achieved either by asceticism or by thought but by techniques that carry the seeker to a level below (and therefore independent of) intellectual and moral activity.

The *koan* is used as a jolt, to arrest the mind and the will, wrenching them from their customary bondage and eventually bringing about the seeker's enlightenment. A well-known and characteristic example of the *koan* is the Zen master's injunction to think of the sound made by one hand clapping. Za-zen, which includes yogic techniques, is used to help the seeker to attain the needed detachment for the "solution" of the *koan*. (See **Koan**.) Counterparts of the central notions of Zen abound in Christian mystical literature and also in some forms of Western philosophy and literature, for instance, in Croce's concept of the "purity" of the "aesthetic moment" and in the "epiphanies" of James Joyce. The notion that detachment from the habitual categories of thought is necessary for the continued vivacity of thought itself is familiar in Christian existentialism, notably in Kierkegaard, which has antecedents, if not exemplars, in Pascal and other Christian thinkers.

Zend-Avesta. See **Avesta.**

Zeno. 4th c. Bishop of Verona, an African by birth.

Zeno. 5th c. Emperor who engaged in ill-advised, not to say disastrous, attempts to reconcile the differences between the Eastern and Western Church, which resulted in further alienating them.

Zeno of Citium (c.355–264 BCE). Greek thinker, probably founder of the Stoic school. He was a disciple of Crates of Thebes, who flourished in the late 4th c. BCE and was the last of the great Cynic teachers.

Zeno of Elea (490–430 BCE). Greek philosopher, disciple of Parmenides, whose teachings he defended. He is noted for his use of paradox to show what he took to be insoluble contradictions in the world as it is ordinarily apprehended by the senses. Perhaps the best known of these is the paradox of Achilles and the tortoise.

Zephaniah. The name of one of the minor prophets and of the book of the Old Testament attributed to him by virtually all modern scholars. The book dates from the reign of Josiah (640–609 BCE) and for various reasons should be dated before 621 BCE, although in its present form it is of later compilation. Notable in the book is Zephaniah's vivid description of the "Day of the Lord:" Judgment Day, which has much affected popular imagination.

Zephyrinus. An early Bishop of Rome who succeeded Victor in 198 and was succeeded on his own death in 217 by Callistus. Hippolytus, his contemporary and the most important theologian of his time, depicts him as a simple-minded and weak man.

Zermelo, Ernst (1871–1953). German mathematician. He studied at Göttingen and taught at Zürich. He is notable for his having shown that set theory can be organized into a deductive system. His "axiomatic set theory" avoids the paradoxes that led Bertrand Russell to the theory of types.

Zetetic. A Greek term signifying the art of inquiry and applied specifically to the followers of Pyrrho.

Zeus. Chief among the gods of the Greek pantheon. See **Dyaus.**

Ziegler, Theobald (1846–1918). German thinker and philosopher of religion, who regarded feeling as the basic process in the human psyche, from which reason, will, and religious belief are derived. His writings include *Feeling* (1893), *Faith and Knowledge* (1899), and *Men and Problems* (1914).

Zillerthal Evangelicals. A body of Protestants in the Tyrol who seceded from the Roman Catholic Church, beginning in 1829. As a result of persecution instigated by the Roman Catholic clergy and people, they were forced to leave but found refuge in Erdmannsdorf in Prussia.

Zinzendorf, Nikolaus Ludwig Graf von (1700–1760). Leader of a "Christianity of the heart" movement expressed in his founding of an evangelical brotherhood, the Herrnhuten Brüdergemeine, to which from 1827 he devoted his principal energies. Persecuted by the Lutheran Church, he travelled in England and the United States. In 1737 he received Moravian episcopal consecration and founded communities in many countries of the world, including the Moravian Episcopal Church (*Unitas Fratrum*) in England. In the Pietist tradition of Spener who had established what he called "little churches within the Church" (*ecclesiolae in ecclesia*), Zinzendorf sought to unite all churches within the Reformation heritage, but circumstances forced him to develop a separate organization for his movement.

Zina. A term used in Islam to denote sexual misconduct, understood as all sexual relationships outside of marriage and concubinage. To establish guilt the testimony of four eyewitnesses is required. The punishment varies according to the legal school and the legal status of the parties but usually consists of whipping or stoning.

Zionism. The movement for the return of the Jews to their Palestinian homeland. It began in the 19th c. and achieved a landmark after World War II with the creation of the modern State of Israel.

Zita. 13th c. Italian saint and patroness of domestic servants; canonized in 1696.

Zohar. Cabbalistic work compiled by Moses de Leon in the 13th c., it provides occult interpretations of the Torah. The word means "splendor."

Zonaras, Johannes. 12th c. Byzantine canonist and historian.

Zoroastrianism. The ancient Iranians were of the same stock as the Aryans who invaded and settled in India, and their religion probably resembled that of the writers of the Vedas. The date of the founder, Zoroaster, is very controversial, but many scholars would place it as late as *c.* 600 BCE. Zoroastrianism was the national religion of Iran till the advent of Islam and the conversion of the Iranians to that religion. Zoroastrianism, despite a dualistic emphasis, is (like Judaism, Christianity, and Islam) a monotheistic religion. Its influence spread to the Middle East and the Mediterranean lands and the Manichees were an important offshoot. The Scriptures are the Avesta. The center of worship is the holy flame on the altar. Instead of burial or cremation Zoroastrians use the Tower of Silence on which the bodies of the dead are placed to be devoured by vultures. In India the religion is represented by the Parsees, an influential although relatively small body consisting of the descendants of a

group of Zoroastrians who fled to India when the Muslims conquered Iran in the 8th *c.* CE. A strong emphasis is placed on the concept of human life as a struggle between good and evil, with judgment and afterlife. After the exile of the Hebrews to Babylon, Zoroastrian influences affected later Judaism and such influences passed into Christianity, although the extent of the influence is a matter of scholarly controversy.

Zosimus. Early 5th c. Bishop of Rome. Greek by birth. Augustine led the African Church in forcing him to rescind his support of Pelagianism.

Zosimus. A later 5th c. Greek historian who in his history of the Roman Empire, written from a non-polemical but pagan view of its decline, has furnished his posterity with the means of making a more balanced historical perspective than Christian histories would have provided.

Zucchetto. A small skull-cap used since the 13th c. by Roman Catholic clergy, more especially by members of the hierarchy. Bishops wear violet, cardinals red, and the Pope white.

Zwickau Prophets. A group of Anabaptists who sought to establish a sort of theocratic community at Zwickau in Saxony. They moved to Wittenberg, where Melanchthon seemed to receive them favorably late in 1521, but a few months later, in 1522, Luther, returning to Wittenberg, vigorously opposed them.

Zwingli, Ulrich (1484–1531). Swiss Reformer educated at Berne, Vienna and Basel. An admirer of the Renaissance humanists, especially Erasmus, he perceived the crying need for Church reform. His lectures on the New Testament in 1519 mark the beginning of the Reformation in Switzerland, although his activities in the preceding years had been leading up to it. His teachings, although in line with the Reformation movement elsewhere seem to have been developed apart from any direct influence from Luther. Distinctive is his teaching on the nature of the Eucharist. In 1524–1525 he developed a view of it as a mere memorial, regarding its symbolism as somewhat like that of a wedding ring in marriage: a far cry from traditional views on both sides of the Reformation curtain: transubstantiation, consubstantiation, impanation, and virtualism.

SELECTED BIBLIOGRAPHIES

The bibliographies are classified under the following heads:

AFRICAN RELIGIONS

Awolalu, J. O., *Yoruba Beliefs and Sacrifical Rites* (1979).

Berglund, A.-L., *Zulu Thought Patterns and Symbolism* (1976).

Booth, N. W. ed., *African Religions: A Symposium* (1977).

Goody, J., *The Myth of the Bagre* (1972).

Kuper, H., *An African Aristocracy: Rank Among the Suazi of Bechuanaland* (1947, 1980).

Kyewalyānga, F., *Traditional Religion, Customs, and Christianity in Uganda* (1976).

Lienhardt, G., *Divinity and Experience: The Religion of the Dinka* (1961).

Mbiti, J. S., *Concepts of God in Africa* (1970, 1975).

Ray, B. C., *African Religions: Symbol, Ritual, and Community* (1976).

Werbner, R. P. ed., *African Ideas of God: A Symposium* (1961).

Wilson, M., *Communal Rituals of the Nyakyusa* (1959, 1970).

AFTERLIFE

Addison, J. T., *Life Beyond Death in the Beliefs of Mankind* (1932).

Armstrong, A. Hilary, *Expectations of Immortality in Late Antiquity* (1987).

Augustine, "On the Immortality of the Soul" in Vol. 1, pp. 301–316 of *Basic Writings of St. Augustine*, 2.vols. (1948). A Christian classic on the subject.

Baillie, John, *And the Life Everlasting* (1933).

Berdyaev, Nicolas, *The Destiny of Man* (1937). See especially pp.249–265.

Cranston, Sylvia, and Williams, Carey, *Reincarnation: A New Horizon in Science, Religion, and Society* (1984). A comprehensive and highly informed treatment of the concept of reincarnation.

Ducasse, C. J. A., *A Critical Examination of the Belief in a Life After Death* (1961).

El-Saleh, Soubhi, *La Vie future selon le Coran* (1971).

Farrer, Austin, *The End of Man* (1972). A collection of brilliant addresses by an Oxford scholar. The first three are especially relevant to the question of Afterlife.

Hadad, Yvonne, and Smith, Jane I., *The Islamic Understanding of Death and Resurrection.* (1981). Appendix C, "The Special Case of Women and Children in the After-life."

Head, J., and Cranston, Sylvia, *Reincarnation: The Phoenix Fire Mystery* (1977). An indispensable source book, providing expressions of belief in reincarnation from antiquity to the present time and by eminent people in all literature, science, and a vast variety of walks of life.

Hick, John, *Death and Eternal Life* (1977). An important discussion.

Hügel, Friedrich von, Baron, *Eternal Life* (1912). By a Roman Catholic layman, a theologian of great distinction in his time.

Jaspers, Karl, *Death to Life* (1968).

Kant, Immanuel, *Critique of Practical Reason*, Book II, Chapter 4: "The Immortality of the Soul as a Postulate of Pure Practical Reason." An important classic passage in Kant on the question of afterlife. Those not already familiar with Kant's thought should read also the context: at least Chapters 2–5.

Lewis, H. D., *The Self and Immortality* (1973). The author argues that an interactionist mind/body theory does better justice to human experience than do theories of mind/brain identity. Chapter VI treats the concept of reincarnation.

MacGregor, Geddes, *Reincarnation in Christianity* (1978, 1986).

———, *Reincarnation as a Christian Hope* (1982).

———, *The Christening of Karma* (1984).

———, ed., *Immortality and Human Destiny:* A Variety of Views, 1985.

Macquarrie, John, *Principles of Christian Theology* (1966, 1977). See Chapter 15, "The Last Things."

McTaggart, John Ellis, *Some Dogmas of Religion* (1930). The author affirms belief in immortality but does not affirm belief in God.

Moody, Raymond, *Life After Life* (1975).

Myers, F. W. H., *Human Personality and Its Survival of Bodily Death* (1903, 1961). A classic document in Psychical Research.

Phillips, D. Z., *Death and Immortality* (1970).

Plato, *Phaedo*. An indispensable classic for students of the concept of Immortality.

Pringle-Pattison, Andrew Seth, *The Idea of Immortality* (1922). Although outdated, an interesting approach by a Scottish thinker much influenced by Hegel.

Ramsey, Ian, *Freedom and Immortality* (1960).

Rawlings, Maurice, *Beyond Death's Door* (1978).

Stendahl, Krister, ed., *Immortality and Resurrection* (1965). A provocative series of four lectures, respectively by Oscar Cullmann, Harry A. Wolfson, Werner Jaeger, and Henry J. Cadbury, each taking a special point of view.

Stevenson, Ian, *Twenty Cases Suggestive of Reincarnation* (1974).

———, "Some Questions Related to Cases of the Reincarnation Type," in *The Journal of the American Society for Psychical Research*, Vol.68 (1974), pp.396–416. The author, who heads the Department of Psychiatry and Parapsychology, School of Medicine, University of Virginia, is well-known for his scientific investigation of cases of claimed remembrances of previous lives.

Taylor, A. E., *The Christian Hope of Immortality* (1938).

Toynbee, Arnold, *Life After Death* (1976).

Wittgenstein, Ludwig, *Tractatus Logico-Philosophicus* (1961), 6·431–6·4312.

BIBLICAL STUDIES

The basic tools needed for biblical studies are: (1) a modern critical text of the Scriptures comprising the Hebrew Bible, the Septuagint, and the New Testament in Greek; (2) at least one readable, scholarly modern English translation, e.g., the Jerusalem Bible or the New English Bible; (3) access to a practical, scholarly commentary on the Bible such as the Anchor Bible; and (4) a biblical atlas. While a profound knowledge of the biblical languages is not necessary for making a beginning in biblical studies, an elementary knowledge of them is essential to make an intelligent use of the commentaries and other helps for an understanding of the biblical literature. The following is a list of books that can help the serious student to understand the great and complex literature we call the Bible.

Albright, William F., *The Archaeology of Palestine* (1954).
Anderson, Bernhard W., *Understanding the Old Testament* (1957).
———, *The Unfolding Drama of the Bible* (1988).
Anderson, G. W., *A Critical Introduction to the Old Testament* (1959).
Baly, Denis, *The Geography of the Bible* (1957).
Bornkamm, G., *Paulus* (1971).
Bruce, F. F., *The Books and the Parchments* (1950, 1963).
———, *New Testament History* (1969).
———, *The Making of the New Testament* (1972).
Bultmann, Rudolf, *Theology of the New Testament*, 2 vols. (1951–55).
Burrows, Millar, *The Dead Sea Scrolls* (1955).
———, *More Light on the Dead Sea Scrolls* (1958).
Cross, Frank M., *The Ancient Library of Qumran* (1958).
Davies, W. D., *Paul and Rabbinic Judaism* (1948).
———, *Invitation to the New Testament* (1966).
Dibelius, Martin, *From Tradition to Gospel* (1934).
Dodd, C. H., *According to the Scriptures* (1953).

Dupont-Sommer, André, *The Jewish Sect of Qumran and the Essenes* (1956).
Ehrman, Bart D., *Didymus the Blind and the Text of the Gospels* (1987).
Epp, Eldon, and MacRae, George W., eds., *The New Testament and Its Modern Interpreters* (1988).
Finegan, Jack, *Light From the Ancient Past* (1959).
Gaster, Theodore H., *The Dead Sea Scriptures* (1956).
James, M. R., *The Apocryphal New Testament* (1924). Still a valuable collection of apocryphal New Testament literature in translation.
Keck, Leander E., *Paul and His Letters* (1988).
Knight, Douglas A. and Tucker, Gene M., eds., *The Hebrew Bible and Its Modern Interpreters* (1984).
Koch, Klaus, *The Growth of the Biblical Tradition: The Form Critical Method* (1969).
Luedemann, Gerd, *Paul, Apostle to the Gentiles* (1984).
———, *Early Christianity According to the Traditions in Acts* (1988).
McKenzie, John L., *Dictionary of the Bible* (1965). A reliable work by a distinguished Jesuit.
———, *The Power and the Wisdom: An Interpretation of the New Testament* (1965).

——, *The Two-Edged Sword* (1956).
McNeile, A. H., *Introduction to the New Testament* (1948, 1952).
Meeks, Wayne A., ed., *The Writings of St. Paul: Annotated Text Criticism* (1972).
Moule, C. F. D., *Worship in the New Testament* (1961, 1977–1978).
Nock, A. D., *St. Paul* (1938).
Oesterley, W. O. E., *Introduction to the Books of the Apocrypha* (1935).
Pfeiffer, R. H., *Introduction to the Old Testament* (1948, 1952).
Robinson, James M., ed., *The Nag Hammadi Library in English* (1977).

An indispensable work for study in this field.
Sandmel, Samuel, *The Hebrew Scriptures: An Introduction to Their Literature and Religious Ideas* (1963).
——, *The First Christian Century in Judaism and Christianity: Certainties and Uncertainties* (1969).
Stendahl, Krister, *The Bible and the Role of Women* (1966).
Vermes, G., ed., *The Dead Sea Scrolls in English* (1973, 1974).

For those undertaking serious textual study of the Bible, the following works, available at modest cost through the American Bible Society, 1865 Broadway, New York, New York 10023, are recommended:

Biblia Hebraica Stuttgartensis (1984). This is a thorough revision of the text and apparatus of the Hebrew Bible, based on manuscript B19^A in the Leningrad Public Library. 1574 pages, cloth 24 x 16.5 cm. Item 60555.
Biblia Sacra iuxta Vulgatam Versionem. Based on the Old Testament edition of St. Jerome's monastery in Rome and the New Testament edition of Wordsworth and White. Item 71686.
Konkordanz zum hebräischen Alten Testament (1958). Concordance to the Hebrew Bible. Item 60910.

Septuaginta (1979). One volume edition of the Septuagint. Item 56404.
The Greek New Testament (1983). Includes a Greek-English dictionary. Item 56492.
Synopsis of the Four Gospels (1987). The Greek text with parallel English translation (Revised Standard Version) with critical apparatus. Item 56691.
Handkonkordanz zum griechischen Neuen Testament (1989). A new, small-size edition of this standard concordance of the New Testament in Greek. Item 56852.

BIOETHICS

Amirikia, H. and Booker, J. H., "Legal and Ethical Aspects of Artificial Insemination" in Emperaire, J. C.; Audebert, A.; Hafez, E. S. E., eds., *Homologous Artificial Insemination (AIH)* (1980), 221–228.
Arnold, J. M., and Joyce, D. N., "Artificial Insemination by Donor (AID)" in *Practitioner* (July 1982), 1324–1329.
Bancroft, J., *Deviant Sexual Behaviour: Modification and Assessment* (1974).
Batchelor, Edward, ed., *Abortion: The Moral Issues* (1982). A variety of viewpoints.

Blair-St. Giles, B. A., and Hillman, H., "Dying and Death, with special reference to Brain Death: a bibliography" in *Resuscitation*, 10 (Aug. 1983), 235–251.
Brahams, Diana, "Prescribing for Unlawful Sexual Intercourse" in *Practitioner* (June 1982), 1025–1026.
——, "The Right to be Allowed to Die" in *Lancet* (Feb. 11, 1984), 351–352.
Burtchaell, James Tunstead, ed., *Abortion Policy* (1980). National Conference on Abortion, University of Notre Dame (1979) 353 pages.

Campbell, A. V., *Moral Dilemmas in Medicine* (1975).

Caronna, John J., "Diagnosing Brain Death" in *Western Journal of Medicine*, 140 (April 1984), 608–609. An editorial.

Christoph, James B., *Capital Punishment and British Politics: The British Movement to Abolish the Death Penalty, 1945–57* (1962).

Connelly, R. J., "Reform of Brain Death Legislation: a proposal" in *Proceedings of the American Catholic Philosophical Association*, 56 (1982), 154–161.

Daniel, William J., "Sexual Ethics in relation to IVF and ET: the fitting use of human reproductive power" in Walters, William A. W., and Singer, Peter, eds., *Test-Tube Babies: A Guide to Moral Questions* (1982), 71–78 and 153–154. Christian ethics on questions such as embryo transfer and in vitro fertilization.

Davis, Nancy, "Abortion and Self-Defense" in *Philosophy and Public Affairs*, 13 (Summer 1984), 175–207.

Dunstan, G. R., *The Artifice of Ethics*, (1974), Chapter 5.

——, "The Moral Status of the Human Embryo" in *Journal of Medical Ethics*, 10 (March 1984), 38–44.

Fulton, R., ed., *Death and Identity* (1965).

Häring, B. *Medical Ethics* (1972).

Hilgers, Thomas W.; Horan, Dennis J.; and Mall, David, eds., *New Perspectives on Human Abortion (1981)*.

Himes, Norman E., *Medical History of Contraception* (1963).

Hinton, J., *Dying* (1967).

Jacobson, Sol, "The Right to Life" in *Journal of the Forensic Science Society*, 19 (April 1979), 87–93.

Jellinek, E. M., *The Disease Concept of Alcoholism* (1960).

Jennett, Bryan, "Brain Death in 1983" in *Practitioner*, 227 (March 1983), 451–454. Standards for the determination of death in the United States and Great Britain.

Kremer, J.; Frijling, B. W.; and Nass, J. L. M., "Psychosocial Aspects of Parenthood by Artificial Insemination Donor" in *Lancet* (March 17, 1984) 628. A letter.

Kukin, Marrick, "Tay Sachs and the Abortion Controversy" in *Journal of Religion and Health*, 20 (Fall 1981), 224–242. Treats Jewish Ethics: Orthodox, Conservative, and Reform.

Loraine, J. A., ed., *Understanding Homosexuality: Its Biological and Psychological Bases* (1974).

MacNeil, Everett, "Cessation of Treatment-euthanasia-suicide of patients" in *Catholic Hospital*, 7 (November-December, 1979), 12–13.

Mahoney, John, et al., *Euthanasia and Clinical Practice Trends. Principles and Alternatives—Report of a Working Party* (1982).

McLean, Sheila A. M., ed., *Legal Issues in Medicine* (1981). A British study of bioethical issues, medical ethics, artificial insemination, sterilization, et al.

Mitchell, G. D. and Singer, Peter, "*In vitro* Fertilization: the Major Issues—a Comment" in *Journal of Medical Ethics*, 9 (December 1983), 196–199. Discussion of the effects on society resulting from artificial reproduction and also on the children.

Noonan, J., *Contraception* (1965).

Nortman, Dorothy, *Population and Family Planning Programs: A Factbook* (1975).

Pappworth, M. H., *Human Guinea-pigs* (1967).

Pitts, Lawrence H., "Determination of Brain Death" in *Western Journal of Medicine* 140 (April 1984), 628–631.

Quinn, Warren, "Abortion: Identity and Loss" in *Philosophy and Public Affairs*, 13 (Winter 1984), 24–54.

Roberts, Thomas D. et al., *Contraception and Holiness* (1964).

Robinson, Hillian E. et al. "Legislation and Teenage Sex" in *British Medical Journal*, 288 (January 1984), 234–235. Letters on questions such as abortion, parental notification, contraception, et al.

Storr, A., *Sexual Deviation* (1964).

Tobin, Thomas, "An Abortion Referendum in Ireland" in *Georgetown University Right to Life Journal*, 3 (Spring 1983), 3–7.

Vaux, Kenneth, "Baby Fae and Human Wholeness" in *Christian Century*, 101 (December 5, 1984), 1144–1145. Discussion of organ transplants from animals to humans and related issues.

BUDDHISM

Ch'en, K., *Buddhism in China* (1964, 1974).

———, *The Chinese Transformations of Buddhism* (1973).

Conze, Edward, *Buddhist Thought in India* (1962, 1967).

———, *Buddhist Scriptures* (1959, 1979). A convenient introduction to a variety of Buddhist Scriptures.

———, *A Short History of Buddhism* (1979).

———, *Buddhist Meditation* (1956, 1972).

Dayal, H., *The Bodhisattva Doctrine in Buddhist Sanskrit Literature* (1932, 1975).

DeSilva, Lynn A., *The Problem of the Self in Buddhism and Christianity* (1975).

Donath, Dorothy C., *Buddhism for the West* (1971). A brief introduction for beginners.

Gombritch, R. F., *Precept and Practice: Traditional Buddhism in the Rural Highlands of Ceylon* (1971).

Jayatilleke, K. N., *Early Buddhist Theory of Knowledge* (1963).

———, *The Message of the Buddha* (1975).

Jones, J. G., *Tales and Teaching of the Buddha* (1979).

Kalupahana, D. J., *Buddhist Philosophy* (1976).

King, W. L., *Theravada Meditation* (1980).

Ling, T., *Buddhism and the Mythology of Evil* (1962).

Murti, T. R. V., *The Central Philosophy of Buddhism* (1955, 1980).

Prebish, C. S., *Buddhism* (1975).

Rhys Davids, T. W., and Rhys Davids, C. A. F., *Dialogues of the Buddha* (1899–1921, 1977).

Saddhatissa, H., *Buddhist Ethics* (1971).

Spiro, M. E., *Buddhism and Society* (1971).

Stcherbatsky, TH., *The Central Conception of Buddhism* (1923, 1956). Especially useful on the meaning of key terms and concepts, e.g., rupa, dhatus, karma.

Streng, F. J., *Emptiness: A Study in Religious Meaning* (1967).

Vajirañāṇa, P., *Buddhist Meditation in Theory and Practice* (1962).

Welbon, G. R., *Buddhist Nirvana and Its Western Interpreters* (1968).

Wright, A. F., *Buddhism in Chinese History* (1959).

Zürcher, E., *The Buddhist Conquest of China*, 2 vols. (1959).

CHINESE PHILOSOPHY AND RELIGION

Baity, Philip Chesley, *Religion in a Chinese Town* (1975).

Bilsky, L. J., *The State Religion of Ancient China*, 2 vols. (1975).

Blofeld, John, *I Ching* (1968). A readable translation of this Chinese classic.

Bodde, D., *Festivals in Classical China* (1975).

Chan, W. T., *A Source Book in Chinese Philosophy* (1963, 1969).

Chang, K. C., *Shang Civilization* (1980).

Day, C. B., *Chinese Peasant Cults* (1940, 1974).

———, *Popular Religion in Pre-Communist China* (1975).

Eberhard, Wolfram, *Guilt and Sin in Traditional China* (1967). A helpful book for understanding popular concepts such as heaven and hell.

Fehl, N. E., *Li: Rites and Propriety in Literature and Life* (1971).

Fung-Yu-Lan, *A Short History of Chinese Philosophy* (1960).

Granet, M., *The Religion of the Chinese People* (1975, 1977).

Hsu, F. L. K., *Under the Ancestors' Shadow* (1967).

Hughes, E. R., *Chinese Philosophy in Classical Times* (1942, 1977).

Jordan, David K., *Gods, Ghosts, and Ancestors: The Folk Religion of a Taiwanese Village* (1972).

Maspero, H., *China In Antiquity* (1978, 1979).

Rawson, J., *Ancient China* (1980).

Thompson, Lawrence G., *Chinese Religion: An Introduction* (1969). A useful introduction for beginners in the field.

CHRISTIAN MYSTICISM

Blakney, B., *Meister Eckhart: A Modern Translation* (1941, 1957).

Butler, Cuthbert, *Western Mysticism* (1922, 1927, 1967). This book, the first edition of which was twenty years in the making, is not called *Mysticism in the West* but *Western Mysticism* because it deals specifically with one of the great Christian mystical traditions: that of Benedictine spirituality. The second edition (1927) added some 75 pages. An exceptionally important classic in its field.

The Cloud of Unknowing, by C. Wolters (1961, 1978). A modern version of this anonymous 14th c. English mystical treatise.

Eckhart, Meister, *Meister Eckhart: A Modern Translation*, translation by B. Blakney (1941, 1957).

Fedetov, G., ed., *A Treasury of Russian Spirituality* (1948, 1975).

Hügel, Friedrich von, Baron, *The Mystical Element in Religion as Studied in Saint Catherine of Genoa and Her Friends*, 2 vols. (1908, 1961). A classic study by a Roman Catholic theologian.

Inge, W. R., *Christian Mysticism* (1899). Although presented in a now somewhat old-fashioned style, this work by a great English churchman, still merits study.

John of the Cross, St., *Complete Works* (1934–35, 1963).

Johnston, W., *The Inner Eye of Love* (1978).

Jones, Rufus M., *Studies in Mystical Religion* (1909, 1970). By a well-known American Quaker scholar.

Kirk, Kenneth E., *The Vision of God* (1931).

Knowles, D., *What Is Mysticism?* (1967).

Kovalevsky, P., *St. Sergius and Russian Spirituality* (1976).

Lercaro, G., *Methods of Mental Prayer* (1957).

Lossky, V., *The Vision of God* (1963, 1973). Eastern Orthodox tradition.

Meyendorff, J., *St. Gregory Palamas and Orthodox Spirituality* (1974). A study of the Eastern Orthodox mystical tradition called Hesychasm.

Peers, E. Allison, *Studies of the Spanish Mystics*, 2 vols. (1927, 1951). An extensive work by a specialist, containing a bibliography of almost 2000 items.

Teresa of Avila, St., *Complete Works* (1946, 1978).

Underhill, Evelyn, *Mysticism* (1911, 1940). A classic work. Extensive bibliography.

CHRISTIAN THOUGHT AND HISTORY

Abbott, W. M., ed., *The Documents of Vatican II* (1966, 1974). A convenient text in English.

Augustine, *Basic Writings of Saint Augustine*, 2 vols. (1948).

Ayling, S., *John Wesley* (1979, 1981).

Bainton, R. H., *Here I Stand: A Life of Martin Luther* (1950, 1955).

Barth, Karl, *Church Dogmatics*, 12 vols. (1936–1969), first vol. reprinted 1975). English translation of Barth's *opus maximum*.

Benson, Louis F., *The English Hymn: Its Development and Use in Worship* (1915, 1962). A standard work on hymnody.

Benz, Ernst, *The Eastern Orthodox Church* (1963).

Bettenson, H. (ed.), *Documents of the Christian Church* (1963, 1977). An indispensable source book.

Booty, John, and Sykes, Stephen W., eds., *The Study of Anglicanism* (1988).

Brown, Peter, *Augustine of Hippo: A Biography* (1967). Excellent not only as a biography but for its portrayal of the age.

Bucke, E. S. ed., *The History of American Methodism*, 3 vols. (1964).

Bultmann, Rudolf, *Jesus Christ and Mythology* (1958, 1960).

Burleigh, J. H. S., *A Church History of Scotland* (1960, 1963).

Burr, Nelson R., *A Critical Bibliography of Religion in America*, 2 vols. (1961). A comprehensive bibliography of works relating to all aspects of religious life and teaching in America up to 1960, with extensive critical appraisals. It includes not only mainstream Churches and sects but oriental and other non-Christian religions represented in America.

Calvin, John, *Institutes of the Christian Religion*, 2 vols. (1960). English edition of Calvin's major work, edited by the foremost Calvin scholar of his generation, John T. McNeill.

Chadwick, W. O., ed., *Pelican History of the Church*, 6 vols. (1960–1971, 1962–1972).

Cobb, J. B., and Griffin, D. R., *Process Theology: An Introductory Exposition* (1976).

Collins, James, *The Mind of Kierkegaard* (1953). Unsurpassed as an introduction to the thought and spirit of Kierkegaard.

Cone, J. H., *Black Theology and Black Power* (1969).

Cross, F. L., and Livingstone, E. A., eds., *The Oxford Dictionary of the Christian Church* (1957, 1974).

Cuming, G. J., *A History of Anglican Liturgy* (1969, 1982).

Cunliffe-Jones, H., and Drewery, B., eds., *A History of Christian Doctrine* (1978, 1980).

Davies, H., *Worship and Theology in England*, 5 vols. (1961–1975).

Davies, R. E., *Methodism* (1968).

Duke, John A., *History of the Church of Scotland to the Reformation* (1937).

Fletcher, J. F., *Situation Ethics: The New Morality* (1966, 1974).

Flew, R. N., *The Idea of Perfection in Christian Theology* (1934, 1968).

Geanakoplos, Deno J., *Byzantine East and Latin West: Two Worlds of Christendom in Middle Ages and Renaissance* (1966).

Greenslade, S. L., *Schism in the Early Church* (1953).

Hales, E. E. Y., *Revolution and Papacy, 1769–1846* (1960).

Heiler, Friedrich, *Prayer* (1932, 1958).

Heimert, Alan, *Religion and the American Mind From the Great Awakening to the Revolution* (1966). An extensive study with biographical glossary and other scholarly apparatus.

Hopkins, C. H., *The Rise of the Social Gospel in American Protestantism, 1865–1915* (1940, 1967).

Hudson, Winthrop S., *Religion in America* (1965, 1973).

Hughes, Philip, *The Reformation in England*, 3 vols. (1950–1954).

Jones, R. T., *Congregationalism in England 1622–1962* (1962).

Kierkegaard, S. A., *Christian Discourses* (1940, 1971).

————, *Attack Upon "Christendom"* (1944, 1971). Many would argue that this satire, the last of Kierkegaard's writings, is the most profoundly Christian of them all.

Knowles, David, *Christian Monasticism* (1969). A good introduction to the subject, readable and with illustrations, by a Benedictine who was Regius Professor of Modern History at Cambridge.

Latourette, Kenneth Scott, *A History of Christianity* (1953, revised ed. in 2 vols. 1975).

Macquarrie, John, *Principles of Christian Theology* (1966, 1979). A good, comprehensive presentation of the main problems in Christian theology by a well-known Anglican theologian.

McNeill, John T., *The History and Character of Calvinism* (1954, 1967).

Moorman, J. H. R., *The Anglican Spiritual Tradition* (1983).

More, P. E., and Cross, F. L., *Anglicanism. The Thought and Practice of the Church of England illustrated from the Religious Literature of the Seventeenth Century* (1935). A standard source.

New Catholic Encyclopedia, 17 vols. (1967). Best general reference work on Roman Catholic Church in English.

Newman, John Henry, *Apologia Pro Vita Sua* (1864, 1977). With the exception of Augustine's *Confessions*, perhaps no other Christian spiritual autobiography is a greater classic than Newman's *Apologia*.

Origen, *On First Principles* (1966). English translation of this highly important early 3rd-c. treatise. Translation by G. W. Butterworth; Introduction by Henri de Lubac.

Parker, T. M., *The English Reformation to 1588* (1950, 1972). A concise account of the very complex story of the Reformation in the English Church.

Powers, J. M., *Eucharistic Theology* (1967, 1972).

Prestige, G. L., *God in Patristic Thought* (1936).

Reardon, B. M. G., ed., Roman Catholic Modernism (1970).

Ridley, Jasper, John Knox (1968). An extensive biography of the leader of the Scottish Reformation.

Runciman, Steven, Sir, *A History of the Crusades*, 3 vols. (1951–1954, 1966–1968).

Rutman, D. B., *American Puritanism: Faith and Practice* (1970, 1977).

Scharlemann, Robert P., *Reflection and Doubt in the Thought of Paul Tillich* (1969).

Shaw, Duncan, ed., *Reformation and Revolution* (1967). Essays on a variety of aspects of the Scottish Kirk in the 16th and 17th centuries.

Schweitzer, Albert, *The Quest of the Historical Jesus: A Critical Study of Its Progress from Reimarus to Wrede* (1968). Translated by W. Montgomery from the first German edition (1906), with introduction by James M. Robinson.

Smith, James Ward, and Jamison, A. Leland, eds. *The Shaping of American Religion* (1961).

————, *Religious Perspectives in American Culture* (1961).

Sperry, Willard L., *Religion in America* (1945).

Sykes, Stephen W. ed., *Authority in the Anglican Communion: Essays Presented To Bishop John Howe* (1987).

Thomas Aquinas, *Basic Writings of Saint Thomas Aquinas*, 2 vols. (1945).

Tillich, Paul, *Systematic Theology*, 3 vols. (1951–1963, 1973–1976). Tillich's major exposition of his thought.

Torbet, R. G., *A History of the Baptists* (1950, 1973).

Tyson, Joseph B., *A Study of Early Christianity* (1973).

Underhill, Evelyn, *Worship* (1936, 1979). A deservedly celebrated classic on Christian Worship in all its diversity. The author, while appreciating especially the riches of Catholic and Eastern Orthodox liturgical traditions, is not unsympathetic to Protestant, Quaker, and other ways of worship, and most of all she is sensitive to the nature of personal devotion. See also under *Christian Mysticism*.

Wakefield, W. L., and Evans, A. P., eds., *Heresies of the High Middle Ages: Selected Sources* (1969).

Ware, Timothy, *The Orthodox Church* (1963, 1980). A helpful short introduction to Eastern Orthodoxy by an English convert to it.

Watson, B., *A Hundred Years' War: The Salvation Army, 1865–1965* (1965).

Weber, H. R., and Neill, S., *The Layman in Christian History* (1963).

Welsby, P. A., *A History of the Church of England, 1945–1980* (1984).

Wendel, F., *Calvin* (1963, 1978).

Wolfson, H. A. *The Philosophy of the Church Fathers* (1956, 1970). By an eminent Jewish scholar.

Ziegler, Donald J., ed., *Great Debates of the Reformation* (1969).

CONFUCIANISM

Chang, C., *The Development of Neo-Confucian Thought* (1957, 1977).

Confucius, *The Analects*, translated by A. Waley, (1938, 1966).

———, *The Analects*, translated by D. C. Lau, (1979).

Creel, H. G., *Confucius, the Man and the Myth* (1949, 1973).

Fehl, N. E., *Li: Rites and Propriety in Literature and Life* (1971).

Legge, J., *The Chinese Classics* (1861–1872, 1935).

Richards, I. *Mencius on the Mind* (1932, 1980).

Shryock, J. K., *The Origin and Development of the State Cult of Confucius* (1932–1956).

Smith, D. H., *Confucius* (1973).

Wang Yang-Ming, *Instructions for Practical Living and Other Neo-Confucian Writings*, translated by W. T. Chan (1963).

EGYPTIAN RELIGIONS IN ANTIQUITY

Černý, Jaroslav, *Ancient Egyptian Religion* (1952).

David, A. R., *The Cult of the Sun: Myth and Magic in Ancient Egypt* (1980).

———, *The Ancient Egyptians: Religious Beliefs and Practices* (1981).

———, *A Guide to Religious Ritual at Abydos* (1981).

Edwards, I. E. S., *The Pyramids of Egypt* (1972, 1975).

Faulkner, R. O., *The Ancient Egyptian Pyramid Texts* (1969).

Frankfort, H., *Ancient Egyptian Religion* (1948, 1961).

Griffiths, J. G., *The Conflict of Horus and Seth* (1960).

———, *The Origins of Osiris and His Cult* (1980).

Mertz, Barbara, *Temples, Tombs, and Hieroglyphs* (1964). A popular work on the results of archaeological explorations.

Sauneron, S., *The Priests of Ancient Egypt* (1960, 1980).

GRAECO-ROMAN RELIGIONS

Brown, P. R. L., *The Making of Late Antiquity* (1978, 1979).

Burkert, W., *Structure and History in Greek Mythology and Ritual* (1979).

Cochrane, Charles Norris, *Christianity and Classical Culture* (1940, 1961).

Cumont, F., *Oriental Religions in Roman Paganism* (1911, 1956).

———, *Astrology and Religion among the Greeks and Romans* (1912, 1960).

Dodds, E. R., *The Greeks and the Irrational* (1951). A classic in this field.

———, *Pagan and Christian in an Age of Anxiety* (1965). A scholarly and readable account, of the relation between Christianity and the pagan world.

Dover, K. J., *Greek Popular Morality in the Time of Plato and Aristotle* (1975).

Ehrenberg, V., *The Greek State* (1969, 1979).

Ferguson, J., *The Religions of the Roman Empire* (1970).

Guthrie, W. K. C., *The Greeks and Their Gods* (1950, 1968).

Harvey, Paul, Sir, *The Oxford Companion to Classical Literature* (1937). A standard desk reference book.

Kirk, G. S., *The Nature of Greek Myths* (1974).

Liebeschütz, J. H. W. G., *Continuity and Change in Roman Religion* (1979).

Lloyd-Jones, H., *The Justice of Zeus* (1971).

Long, A. A., *Hellenistic Philosophy: Stoics, Epicureans, Sceptics* (1974).

Michels, Agnes Kirsopp, *The Calendar of the Roman Republic* (1967, 1978).

Nilsson, M. P., *The Dionysiac Mysteries of the Hellenistic and Roman Age* (1957, 1975).

Nock, A. D., *Conversion: The Old and the New in Religion from Alexander the Great to Augustine of Hippo* (1933, 1961). A perceptive and readable book by an eminent Harvard scholar.

Ogilvie, R. M., *The Romans and Their Gods* (1970).

Parke, H. W., *Greek Oracles* (1967).

Rose, H. J., *Ancient Roman Religion* (1948).

Scullard, H. H., *Festivals and Ceremonies of the Roman Republic* (1981).

Tomlinson, R. A., *Greek Sanctuaries* (1976).

HINDUISM

Acharya, Prasanna K., *A Dictionary of Hindu Architecture* (1927).

Allchin, Bridget, and Allchin, F. R., *The Birth of Indian Civilization* (1968).

Allchin, F. R., *Neolithic Cattle-Keepers of South India* (1963).

Allegro, J. M., *The Sacred Mushroom and the Cross* (1970).

Anand, Mulik Raj, *Kāma-kalā, Some Notes on the Philosophical Basis of Hindu Erotic Sculpture* (1958).

Auboyer, Jeannine, *Daily Life in Ancient India from 200 B. C. to 700 A. D.* (1965).

Barnett, Lionel D., *Bhagavad-Gītā* (1905). Contains a long and helpful introduction.

Behanan, K. T., *Yoga, a Scientific Evaluation* (1937).

Béteille, A., *Castes: Old and New* (1969).

Bhardwaj, S. M., *Hindu Places of Pilgrimage in India* (1973).

Bhattacharji, S., *The Indian Theogony: A Comparative Study of Indian Mythology from the Vedas to the Purānas* (1970, 1978).

Bougle, C., *Essays on the Caste System* (1971).

Burton, Richard, Sir, *The Kāma Sūtra of Vātsyāyana* (1963).

Campbell, Joseph, *The Masks of God.* Vol. II *Oriental Mythology* (1962).

Carman, J. B., *The Theology of Rāmānuja: An Essay in Interreligious Understanding* (1974).

Chaudhuri, Anil Kumar Ray, *The Doctrine of Māyā* (1950).

Coomaraswamy, Ananda K., *Hinduism and Buddhism* (1943).

Daniélou, Alain, *Hindu Polytheism* (1964).

———, *Yoga: the Method of Re-Integration* (1949).

Dasgupta, S. N., *A History of Indian Philosophy*, 5 vols. (1922, 1952).

Deutsch, Eliot, *The Bhagavad-Gītā* (1968).

Douglas, N., *Tantra Yoga* (1971).

Dowson, J., *A Classical Dictionary of Hindu Mythology and Religion* (1928, 1968).

Drekmeier, C., *Kingship and Community in Early India* (1962).

Dutt, Romesh, *The Early Hindu Civilization, B. C. 2000–320* (1888, 1963).

Edgerton, Franklin, *The Bhagavad Gītā*, 2 vols. (1944).

Eliade, Mircea, *Patanjali and Yoga* (1969, 1976).

——, *Birth and Rebirth* (1960).

——, *The History of Religions* (1959).

Ferreira, John V., *Totemism in India* (1965).

Fausboll, V. *Indian Mythology in Outline According to the Mahābhārata* (1903).

Foucher, Max-Pôl, *The Erotic Sculpture of India* (1959).

Garrett, J., *A Classical Dictionary of India* (1871, 1973).

Gonda, Jan, *Notes on Brahman* (1950).

——, *Aspects of Early Viṣṇuism* (1954, 1969).

Griffith, R. T. H., *The Hymns of the Ṛgveda*, 2 vols. (1963).

Hume, R. E., *The Thirteen Principal Upanishads* (1921).

Hutton, J. H., *Caste in India* (1946, 1963).

Jash, P., *History of Śaivism* (1974).

Kosambi, D. D., *Myth and Reality* (1962).

——, *The Culture and Civilization of Ancient India* (1965, 1975).

Kramrisch, Stella, *The Hindu Temple*, 2 vols. (1946).

——, *Unknown India: Ritual Art in Tribe and Village* (1968).

La Meri, R. M. H., *The Gesture Language of the Hindu Dance* (1941, 1964).

Lannoy, R., *The Speaking Tree: A Study of Indian Culture and Society* (1968, 1974).

Larson, G. J., *Classical Sāṁkhya* (1969).

Lommel, A., *Masks: Their Meaning and Function* (1972).

Macdonell, A. A., *A History of Sanskrit Literature* (1889, 1970).

——, *Vedic Mythology* (1897, 1963).

——, *A Vedic Reader for Students* (1917, 1970).

Mascaró, Juan, *The Bhagavad Gītā* (1970). Contains a succinct, useful introduction.

Mehta, J., *Sexual Life in Ancient India* (1953).

Michell, G., *The Hindu Temple: An Introduction to Its Meaning and Form* (1977, 1978).

Mishra, R. S., *The Text Book of Yoga Psychology* (1972).

Monier-Williams, Monier, Sir, *A Sanskrit-English Dictionary* (1899, 1973).

Mukhardji, N. S., *A Study of Śaṅkara* (1942).

Narahari, H. G., *Ātman in Pre-Upaniṣadic Vedic Literature* (1944).

O'Flaherty, W. D., *Asceticism and Eroticism in the Mythology of Śiva* (1973).

——, ed., *Hindu Myths: A Source Book* (1975).

O'Malley, L. S. S., *Indian Caste Customs* (1932, 1974).

Pandey, K. C., *Indian Aesthetics* (1955).

Parrinder, Geoffrey, *Avatar and Incarnation* (1970). The Wilde Lectures, University of Oxford.

Pocock, D. F., *Mind, Body and Wealth: A Study of Belief and Practice in an Indian Village* (1973).

Puligandla, R., *Fundamentals of Indian Philosophy* (1975).

Radhakrishnan, Sarvepalli, Sir, *The Bhagavadgītā* (1948). Contains a long introductory essay on the Gītā, the Sanskrit text transliterated, with English translation and notes by a former President of the Republic of India and one of the greatest Indian thinkers of the 20th c.

——, *History of Philosophy: Eastern and Western* 2 vols., (1952–1953).

——, *The Principal Upaniṣads* (1953).

Raghavendrachar, H. N., *Dvaita Philosophy and Its Place in the Vedānta* (1941).

Rele, V. G., *The Mysterious Kuṇḍalini* (1927).

Renou, L., ed., *Hinduism* (1969).

Sarkar, B. K., *The Folk Element in Hindu Culture* (1917, 1972).

Sastri, K. A. N., *Development of Religion in South India* (1963).

Shekhar, I., *Sanskrit Drama: Its Origin and Decline* (1960).

Singer, M., *Traditional India: Structure and Change* (1959, 1975).

———, ed., *Krishna: Myths, Rites and Attitudes* (1966).

Smart, Ninian, *Doctrine and Argument in Indian Philosophy* (1964, 1977).

Srinivas, M. N., *Caste in Modern India* (1962, 1979).

Stevenson, M., *The Rites of the Twice-Born* (1920, 1971).

Stutley, M., and Stutley, J., *Harper's Dictionary of Hinduism* (1977).

Thième, Paul, *Mitra and Aryaman* (1957).

Walker, B., *Hindu World*, 2 vols. (1968).

Werner, K., *Yoga and Indian Philosophy* (1977, 1979).

Zaehner, R. C., *Hinduism* (1962, 1966). A survey by an eminent Oxford scholar.

———, *Hindu Scriptures* (1966).

———, *The Bhagavad-Gītā* (1969, 1973).

———, *Hindu and Muslim Mysticism* (1960, 1972).

Zimmer, H. R., *Myths and Symbols in Indian Art and Civilization* (1946, 1971).

ISLAM

Arberry, A. J., *Sufism: An Account of the Mystics of Islam* (1950, 1979).

Christopher, John B., *The Islamic Tradition* (1972). A short introduction to the cultural aspects of Islam.

Cragg, Kenneth, *The Call of the Minaret* (1956). An introduction to Muslim theology.

———, *The House of Islam* (1969).

———, *The Mind of the Qur'ān: Chapters in Reflection* (1973).

Donaldson, D. M., *The Shi'ite Religion: A History of Islam in Persia and Irak* (1933, 1976).

———, *Studies in Muslim Ethics* (1953).

Encyclopedia of Islam, 5 vols. (1913–1918). The first edition of this work has been succeeded by a second edition which has been in progress since 1960.

Esposito, John L., *Islam: The Straight Path* (1988).

Guillaume, A., *The Traditions of Islam: An Introduction to the Study of Hadith Literature* (1924, 1980).

———, *Islam* (1924, 1969). A convenient general introduction to the many aspects of Islam with a glossary of key terms.

Lewis, B., *The World of Islam: Faith, People, Culture* (1976).

Lincoln, C. E., *The Black Muslims in America* (1973).

Mahmud, S. F., *A Short History of Islam* (1988).

Momen, Moojan, *An Introduction to Sh'i Islam* (1988).

Morgan, Kenneth, *Islam: The Straight Path* (1958).

Nicholson, R. A., *Studies in Islamic Mysticism* (1921, 1979).

Padwick, C., *Muslim Devotions* (1961).

Parkins, M., and Hainsworth, P., *Bahá'í Faith* (1980). An exposition of this offshoot of Islam.

Schimmel, A., *Islamic Calligraphy* (1970).

van Ess, Josef, *The Youthful God: Anthropomorphism in Early Islam* (1988).

Waddy, C., *Women in Muslim History* (1980).

Watt, William Montgomery, *Islamic Philosophy and Theology* (1962, 1979).

———, *Islamic Political Thought* (1968).

———, *What is Islam?* (1968, 1979). A helpful survey by a noted Islamic scholar.

Williams, J. A., *Themes of Islamic Civilization* (1971).

Zaehner, R. C., *Hindu and Muslim Mysticism* (1960, 1972).

JAINISM

Basham, A. L., *The Wonder That was India* (1954, 1971).

Jaini, J., *Outlines of Jainism* (1916).

Jaini, P. S., *The Jaini Path of Purification* (1979).

——, "Karma and the Problem of Rebirth in Jainism" in W. D. O'Fla-

herty, ed., *Karma and Rebirth in Classical Indian Tradition* (1980).

Kalghatgi, T. G., *Some Problems in Jaina Psychology* (1961).

Tatia, Nathmal, *Studies in Jaina Philosophy* (1951).

JUDAISM

Abrahams, I., *Jewish Life in the Middle Ages* (1896, 1975).

Altmann, A., *Moses Mendelssohn: A Biographical Study* (1973).

Baeck, L., *The Essence of Judaism* (1961).

Bamberger, Bernard J., *The Story of Judaism* (1970).

Blau, J. L., ed., *Reform Judaism: A Historical Perspective* (1973).

Buber, Martin, *Tales of the Hasidim* 2 vols. (1956, 1970).

Cohen, A., *Everyman's Talmud* (1949).

Epstein, I, ed., *The Babylonian Talmud*, 18 vols. (1961).

——, *Judaism* (1959, 1968).

Finkelstein, L., ed., *The Jews: Their History, Culture and Religion*, 2 vols. (1949, 1971).

Gaster, T., *Festivals of the Jewish New Year* (1961).

Grayzel, S., *A History of the Jews* (1947).

Grunfeld, I., *The Jewish Dietary Laws*, 2 vols. (1972).

Heschel, Abraham, *Between God and Man: An Interpretation of Judaism* (1965).

Husik, I., *A History of Medieval Jewish Philosophy* (1916, 1969).

Idelsohn, A. Z., *Jewish Liturgy and Its Development* (1932, 1967).

Jacobs, L., *A Jewish Theology* (1973).

Jacobovits, I., *Jewish Medical Ethics* (1967, 1975).

Kellner, M. M., *Contemporary Jewish Ethics* (1978).

Maimonides, Moses, *The Guide of the Perplexed* (1963, 1974). A translation by S. Pines of this great medieval Jewish classic.

Moore, G. F., *Judaism in the First Centuries of the Christian Era*, 3 vols. (1927, 1966).

Neusner, J., *The Life of Torah: Readings: The Jewish Religious Experience* (1974). A convenient anthology with an emphasis on understanding the Commandments.

Leslie, Donald D., *The Survival of the Chinese Jews: The Jewish Community of Kaifeng* (1972).

Scholem, G. G., *Major Trends in Jewish Mysticism* (1954, 1961). A definitive treatment on the subject, particularly the Cabbala.

Steinberg, M., *Basic Judaism* (1947).

Strack, H. L., *Introduction to the Talmud and Midrash* (1959, 1969).

Unterman, A., *Judaism* (1981).

Weiner, H., *9½ Mystics: The Kabbala Today* (1969). A fascinating account by a rabbi of his visits to centers of Jewish mysticism.

Weingreen, J., *From Bible to Mishnah* (1976).

Wouk, Herman, *This is my God* (1959). A well-known novelist portrays to a general audience the significance of Orthodox Judaism.

MESOPOTAMIAN RELIGIONS IN ANTIQUITY

Contenau, Georges, *Everyday Life in Babylon and Assyria* (1954).

Hooke, D. H., *Babylonian and Assyrian Religion* (1963). A useful brief introduction by a leading expert in the field.

Saggs, H. W. F., *The Greatness That Was Babylon* (1962).

Sanders, N. K., *The Epic of Gilgamesh* (1966). A readable translation with notes on this important document.

MODERN RELIGIOUS MOVEMENTS

Bach, Marcus, *Strange Sects and Cults* (1961).

Barker, E., ed., *New Religious Movements: A Perspective for Understanding Society* (1982).

Braden, C. S., *These Also Believe: A Study of Modern American Cults and Minority Religious Movements* (1949, 1957).

Bryant, D., and Richardson, H., *A Time for Consideration: A Scholarly Appraisal of the Unification Church* (1978).

Cox, H., *Turning East: The Promise and the Peril of the New Orientalism* (1977, 1979).

Ellwood, Robert S., *Religious and Spiritual Groups in Modern America* (1973). A guide to understanding the nature of the various groups by a scholar who has specialized in the study of them.

———, *The Eagle and the Rising Sun* (1974). A descriptive account of some new Japanese religious movements and their impact on the American scene.

Hollenweger, W. J., *The Pentecostals* (1972, 1977).

Hubbard, L. R., *Dianetics: The Modern Science of Mental Health* (1950, 1968). The basic text of the Church of Scientology.

Judah, J. S., *Hare Krishna and the Counterculture* (1974).

Krause, C. A., *Guyana Massacre: The Eyewitness Account* (1978). The tragic culmination of the development of the "Peoples Temple Sect."

Kwak, C. H., *Outline of the Principle, Level 4* (1980). A helpful presentation of the basic views and teachings of the Unification Church by the Founder's chief associate. The full text of *Divine Principle* is readily available from the Unification Church headquarters in Barrytown, New York.

Murphet, H., *Sai Baba: Man of Miracles* (1971).

Needleman, J., and Baker, G., eds., *Understanding the New Religions* (1978).

Roszak, T., *Unfinished Animal: The Aquarian Frontier and the Evolution of Consciousness* (1975, 1977).

Sarkar, P. R., *Baba's Grace: Discourses of Shrii Shrii Anandamurti* (1973).

Saunders, N., *Self-Exploration: A Guide to Groups Involved* (1975).

Sontag, F., *Sun Myung Moon and the Unification Church* (1977). A scholarly appraisal by a professor of philosophy at Pomona College, Claremont.

Tart, C., ed., *Altered States of Consciousness* (1969, 1972).

Washington, Joseph R., *Black Sects and Cults* (1972).

Wilson, B. R., *Religious Sects* (1970).

Wuthnow, R., *The Consciousness Reformation* (1976).

———, *Experimentation in American Religion: The New Mysticisms and Their Implications for the Churches* (1978).

Zaretsky, I., and Leone, M., eds., *Religious Movements in Contemporary America* (1974).

PHILOSOPHY OF RELIGION (PHILOSOPHICAL THEOLOGY)

Bettis, J. D., ed., *Phenomenology of Religion* (1969).

Christian, W. A., *Oppositions of Religious Doctrines* (1972).

——, *Meaning and Truth in Religion* (1964).

Cobb, J. B., and Griffin, D. R., *Process Theology: An Introductory Exposition* (1976).

Dhavamony, M., *Phenomenology of Religion* (1973).

Diamond, Malcolm L., *Contemporary Philosophy and Religious Thought: An Introduction to the Philosophy of Religion* (1974).

Farrer, Austin, *Love Almighty and Ills Unlimited* (1962, 1966).

——, *The Freedom of the Will* (1958).

——, *Finite and Infinite* (1943).

Frank, Erich, *Philosophical Understanding and Religious Truth* (1945).

Hick, John, *Philosophy of Religion* (1963).

——, *Faith and Knowledge* (1957, 1966).

——, *Evil and the God of Love* (1966, 1968).

James, William, *The Varieties of Religious Experience* (1902, 1971). A classic study.

Lewis, H. D., *Our Experience of God* (1959, 1970).

MacGregor, Geddes, *Philosophical Issues in Religious Thought* (1973, 1979).

Macquarrie, John, *Twentieth-Century Religious Thought: The Frontiers of Philosophy and Theology, 1900–1960* (1963).

——, *God-Talk: An Examination of the Language and Logic of Theology* (1967).

Marcel, Gabriel, *The Mystery of Being*, 2 vols. (1950–1951).

Mascall, Eric Lionel, *He Who Is* (1943, 1966).

——, *Existence and Analogy* (1949).

——, *Words and Images: A Study in Theological Discourse* (1957).

Miller, Ed. L., *God and Reason* (1972).

Otto, Rudolf, *The Idea of the Holy* (1923, 1968).

Ramsey, Ian, *Religious Language: An Empirical Placing of Theological Phrases* (1957).

——, *Models and Mystery* (1964).

——, *Christian Discourse: Some Logical Explorations* (1965).

——, ed., *Words About God: The Philosophy of Religion* (1971).

Santoni, Ronald E., ed., *Religious Language and the Problem of Religious Knowledge* (1968).

Scharlemann, Robert P., *The Being of God* (1981). A brilliant study of the central issue in philosophical theology.

Smith, Ronald Gregor, *Secular Christianity* (1966). A scholarly study of the background of the so-called Death-of-God movement that had a vogue during the third quarter of the 20th c.

Smith, Wilfred Cantwell, *The Meaning and End of Religion* (1963, 1978).

SHINTO AND OTHER RELIGIONS IN JAPAN

Bauer, H. and Carlquist, S., *Japanese Festivals* (1974).

Bloom, A., *Shinran's Gospel of Pure Grace* (1965). A view of the Pure Land Buddhist sect.

Dorson, R. M., ed., *Studies in Japanese Folklore* (1963).

Earhart, H. Byron, *Japanese Religion: Unity and Diversity* (1974).

Ellwood, R. S., *The Eagle and the Rising Sun* (1974). An account of some new Japanese religious movements in the U.S.

Herbert, J., *Shinto: At the Fountainhead of Japan* (1967).

Hori, Ichiro, *Folk Religion in Japan* (1968, 1974).

Kageyama Haruki, *The Arts of Shinto* (1973).

Kamstra, J. H., *Encounter or Syncretism: The Initial Growth of Japanese Buddhism* (1967).

Kapleau, Philip, *The Three Pillars of Zen* (1967).

Kitagawa, J. M., *Religion in Japanese History* (1966).

Ono, Sokyo, *Shinto: The Kami Way* (1967). An introduction by a prominent Shinto scholar.

Ponsonby-Fane, R. A. B., *The Vicissitudes of Shinto* (1963).

Saunders, E. D., *Buddhism in Japan* (1964).

SIKHISM

Archer, J. C., *The Sikhs* (1946).

Cole, W. O., and Sambhi, Piara Singh, *The Sikhs: Their Religious Beliefs and Practices* (1978).

Harbans Singh, *Guru Nanak and Origins of the Sikh Faith* (1969).

———, *The Heritage of the Sikhs* (1964).

Macauliffe, M. A., *The Sikh Religion*, 6 vols. (1909, 1970).

Trilochan Singh, *et al.*, *Adi Granth: Selections from the Sacred Writings of the Sikhs* (1960, 1974).

TAOISM

Creel, H. G., *What is Taoism?* (1970, 1977).

Kaltenmark, M., *Lao Tzu and Taoism* (1969).

Lao Tzu, *Tao Te Ching*, translated by D. C. Lau (1963).

———, *The Way and Its Power*, translated by A. C. Graham (1960).

Saso, M., *Taoism and the Rite of Cosmic Renewal* (1972).

Welch, H., *Taoism: The Parting of the Way* (1957, 1966).

Welch, H., and Seidel, A., eds., *Facets of Taoism* (1979).

TIBETAN RELIGIONS

Chang, G. C. C., *Teachings of Tibetan Yoga* (1963, 1974).

Dargyay, E., *The Rise of Esoteric Buddhism in Tibet* (1977).

Evans-Wentz, *Tibetan Yoga and Secret Doctrines* (1935, 1958).

Hoffmann, Helmut, *The Religions of Tibet* (1951).

Karmay, S. G., *The Treasury of Good Sayings: A Tibetan History of Bon* (1972).

Nebesky-Wojkovitz, R. De, *Oracles and Demons of Tibet* (1956).

Snellgrove, David, *Buddhist Himalaya* (1957).

Snellgrove, David, and Richardson, Hugh, *A Cultural History of Tibet* (1968). A standard work for Tibetan studies.

Tsong-Kha-Pa, *Tantra in Tibet: The Great Exposition of Secret Mantra* (1977).

Tucci, G., *The Religions of Tibet* (1980).

Wangyai, Geshe, *The Door of Liberation* (1973, 1979).

Willis, Janice Dean, *The Diamond Light of Eastern Dawn* (1972). An account of the experiences of an American woman with Tibetan forms of meditation.

ZEN

Dumoulin, H., *A History of Zen Buddhism* (1963, 1969).

Maezumi, Hakuyu Taizan, and Glassman, Bernard Tetsugen, *On Zen Practice* (1976).

Masunaga, Reihō, *A Primer of Sōtō Zen* (1971).

Sekida, K., *Two Zen Classics: Mumonkan and Hekiganroku* (1977).

Suzuki, D. T., *Zen and Japanese Culture* (1959). One of several books by this well-known interpreter of Zen.

Wood, Ernest, *Zen Dictionary* (1962).

ZOROASTRIANISM

Boyce, M., *Zoroastrians: Their Religious Beliefs and Practices* (1979).

———, *Sources for the Study of Zoroastrianism* (1984).

Cumont, Franz, *The Mysteries of Mithra* (1903, 1956). A classic work on the subject.

Duchesne-Guillemin, J., *The Hymns of Zarathustra* (1952, 1963).

Henning, W. B., *Zoroaster: Politician or Witchdoctor?* (1951).

Herrmann, G., *The Iranian Revival* (1977).

Hinnels, J. R., *Zoroastrianism and the Parsis* (1981).

Masani, Rustom, *Zoroastrianism: The Religion of the Good Life* (1968).

Modi, J. J., *Religious Ceremonies and Customs of the Parsees* (1922, 1980).

Moulton, J. H., *Early Zoroastrianism* (1913, 1980).

Pavry, J., *The Zoroastrian Doctrine of a Future Life: From Death to the Individual Judgment* (1926, 1929).

Pearson, J. D., ed., *A Bibliography of Pre-Islamic Persia* (1975).

Zaehner, R. C., *Zurvan: A Zoroastrian Dilemma* (1955, 1973).

———, *The Dawn and Twilight of Zoroastrianism* (1961, 1975).

———, *The Teachings of the Magi* (1956, 1976). A useful exposition of Zoroastrian doctrine.